Guide to the Euphonium Repertoire

Indiana Repertoire Guides

Guide to the
EUPHONIUM
Repertoire

The Euphonium Source Book

Compiled and Edited by
Lloyd E. Bone Jr. and Eric Paull under the
supervision of R. Winston Morris

Indiana University Press
Bloomington and Indianapolis

Publication of this book is made possible in part with
the assistance of a Challenge Grant from the National
Endowment for the Humanities, a federal agency that
supports research, education, and public programming
in the humanities. Any views, findings, conclusions, or
recommendations expressed in this publication do not
necessarily reflect those of the National Endowment for
the Humanities.

This book is a publication of

Indiana University Press
601 North Morton Street
Bloomington, IN 47404-3797 USA

http://iupress.indiana.edu

Telephone orders   800-842-6796
Fax orders   812-855-7931
Orders by e-mail   iuporder@indiana.edu

The paper used in this publication meets
the minimum requirements of American
National Standard for Information Sciences—
Permanence of Paper for Printed Library
Materials, ANSI Z39.48-1984.

Manufactured in the United States of America

Library of Congress Cataloging-in-Publication Data

Bone, Lloyd.
   Guide to the euphonium repertoire : the euphonium
source book / compiled and edited by Lloyd Bone and
Eric Paull under the supervision of R. Winston Morris.
      p. cm. — (Indiana repertoire guides)
   Includes bibliographical references and index.
   ISBN 0-253-34811-0 (cloth)
1. Euphonium music—Bibliography. 2. Euphonium—
History and criticism. I. Paull, Eric. II. Morris, R.
Winston. III. Title.
   ML128.B24B66 2007
   788.9'75—dc22
                                        2006018174
1 2 3 4 5 12 11 10 09 08 07

Editorial Board

CONTENTS

FOREWORD

R. Winston Morris, Advisor

The publication of this volume represents the final act in an extended process that goes back many years. As one who has been involved in the private instruction of tuba and euphonium students since 1959 (over 45 years!), it has always been a dream of mine to fully document the repertoire for both instruments. Although primarily a tubist, I have always been a very strong advocate for the euphonium, which I have regarded as one of the most, if not THE most, versatile musical instruments. As a tubist, I have always considered the euphonium a member of the "tuba" family. Of course the opposite is also true: a tuba can be considered a member of the "euphonium" family. There is an element of self-identity that the euphonium has grappled with and will probably always grapple with to some extent. Nevertheless, with the documentation of the incredible repertoire, discography, and history represented in this publication, I think the euphonium is more than ever establishing an identity that can be not only recognized by the public at large but, perhaps more importantly, by fellow musicians. We invite the reader to seriously consider the evolution of the repertoire and performance standards over the past thirty or forty years. This is exemplified in numerous recordings that are listed in the discography. The quality of the highest level repertoire is equal to any modern musical instrument and the standard of performance as represented by the top euphonium performers throughout the world is comparable to artists on any other brass/wind instrument. The major detriment in the past to the acceptance of the euphonium as a contemporary instrument of equal consideration stems from the limited use of the euphonium in the standard orchestral repertoire. The instrumentation for the "standard" symphonic orchestra, which does not include the euphonium, is not likely to change, but with the influence of "world-class" euphoniumists more and more composers will be encouraged to include the instrument in their major compositions. As a tubist, I can certainly identify as one "with an instrument in search of a composer" willing to write for that instrument.

Euphoniumists, and ONLY euphoniumists, hold their future in their hands. The tuba community, with the strong advocacy of a fairly large number of aggressive and dedicated individuals throughout the world, instigated primarily during the second half of the twentieth century a major "renaissance" of interest in creating repertoire for the tuba. With a similar dedication of purpose and cooperativeness amongst leaders of the euphonium world, the same thing can happen for the euphonium during the first half of the twenty-first century. But this will necessitate established euphonium artists willing to work together and above and beyond their own careers for this to happen. In my opinion, nothing less than the future of the euphonium is at stake.

The *Guide to the Euphonium Repertoire: The Euphonium Source Book* (*ESB*) documents the status of the euphonium from its inception to ca. July 2005. It has been a real delight working with such dedicated professionals who have unselfishly contributed their time and immense talents to this project. All the names are listed in several different formats throughout the publication. Even more encouraging is that there was a large number of other very dedicated individuals who would have willingly and enthusiastically contributed their time and efforts toward this initial documentation of the status of the euphonium. To those and others similarly minded we ask your continued support in the future as this publication needs to be updated. But let it be clearly stated here and now that the editors and contributors for the *ESB* deserve all the credit possible for their work on this project. Yes, they received much support and assistance from our international consultants and colleagues throughout the world, and their "thanks" are expressed in the introductory remarks to their chapters. The individuals directly responsible for producing the *ESB* are co-editors Lloyd Bone and Eric Paull; assistant editors Brian L. Bowman, Neal Corwell, and Adam Frey; and contributors Marc Dickman, Bryce Edwards,

Seth D. Fletcher, Carroll Gotcher, Atticus Hensley, Lisa M. Hocking, Sharon Huff, Kenneth R. Kroesche, John Mueller, Michael B. O'Connor, Joseph Skillen, Kelly Thomas, Demondrae Thurman, Matthew J. Tropman, and Mark J. Walker. And, on behalf of all these individuals, we express our profound gratitude to all our international colleagues throughout the world whose assistance was invaluable. Finally, the support of all our families and ultimately the support of everyone at Indiana University Press was critical throughout the multi-year process of creating this publication, and we are most appreciative of this support.

PREFACE

The *Guide to the Euphonium Repertoire: The Euphonium Source Book* (*ESB*) is primarily concerned with the identification and documentation of publications specifically designated and published for "euphonium" (baritone horn, tenor tuba, etc.).

Music for "tuba ensemble" that includes the euphonium is not represented in this publication, as this material is covered extensively in the *Guide to the Tuba Repertoire: The New Tuba Source Book* (*TSB*) (Indiana University Press, 2006).

The only areas of the *ESB* that include information on materials published for instruments other than specifically "euphonium" are the chapters Recommended Repertoire Written for Other Instruments and Methods and Studies and the possible inclusion of recommended non-euphonium publications in the Basic Repertoire sections and the chapter on Doubling.

Music included in the *ESB* generally falls into one or the other of the following categories:

1. PUBLISHED—includes all music that is currently available through commercial outlets (this could be anything from the largest established publisher to smaller private-based publishers).

2. OUT OF PRINT—includes music that was previously "published" (distributed) but is now listed as "out of print" or not listed at all. If the music could possibly exist in the holdings of a large music retail dealer or even be accessed through libraries (such as the International Tuba-Euphonium Association [ITEA] Resource Library or other major private, university, or municipal library), then it has been included.

3. MANUSCRIPT—includes music in manuscript form that is generally being made available by "professional" composers/arrangers. If the composer ever copyrighted and distributed music but it is currently unavailable, it would, for *ESB* purposes, be considered "published" but out of print. For the most part, manuscripts by students and relatively unknown composers/arrangers that have never generally been made available are not included.

To the extent that information is available, the following order and format has been utilized in the presentation of entries for musical literature for the euphonium.

1. COMPOSER NAME. (last name first)
2. COMPLETE TITLE. (as it appears on the music)
3. ARRANGER (Arr.)/TRANSCRIBER (Trans.)/EDITOR (Ed.). (first name first)
4. PUBLISHER/SOURCE. (see Appendix A: Composers', Publishers', and Manufacturers' Addresses for the complete address for all sources)
5. INSTRUMENTATION.
6. DATE. (copyright date for published works, date of composition for manuscript works, no information when no date is available)
7. PRICE. (publisher's recommended/suggested retail price, generally expressed in dollars, when possible, current August 2005)
8. DURATION. (SOLOS, expressed in minutes as indicated on the printed music or actually timed. COLLECTIONS/COMPILATIONS, etc., expressed in number of pages)
9. LEVEL.
    I—Beginner (up to one year)
    II—Intermediate (two to three years)
    III—High School
    IV—University
    V—Professional
    combinations: I–II. II–III. III–IV. IV–V.

These are general guidelines and recognized as quite subjective. Level indications describe attributes and requirements of the music more so than the expected skills of the player.

LEVEL I (Beginner): Limited range, approximately one octave: B♭–b♭. One year of instruction. Limited rhythmic/technical requirements. No note values greater than eighth notes, no syncopated rhythms. Music of a tonal nature.

LEVEL II (Intermediate): Two/three years of instruction. Range approximately F–f. Rhythmic/technical requirements involve simple sixteenth note patterns. Simple, limited syncopated patterns.

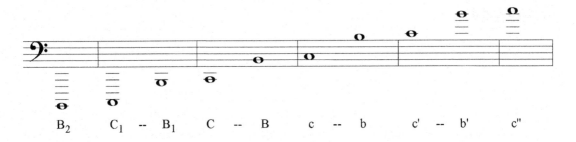

B_2 C_1 -- B_1 C -- B   c -- b   c' -- b'   c"

LEVEL III (High School, Secondary School, Pre-college): Range approximately F–b2. Moderate tessitura. More rhythmic complexity. Extended syncopations, sixteenth note patterns, triplets, and so on. Moderate amount of multiple tonguing.

LEVEL IV (University/College): Range approximately Bb–c2. Higher advanced tessitura. Increased rhythmic complexity/multimetric. Angular melodic lines. Dissonant harmonies/contemporary harmonies. Endurance factors. Introduction to avant-garde techniques (flutter tongue, multiphonics, etc.). Multiple tonguing. Dynamic control and extremes.

LEVEL V (Professional): Total range: C2–f2. Extended high tessitura. Rhythmic/technical complexity of highest order. Angular lines/large skips in melody. Advanced twentieth-century techniques. Extreme dynamic contrasts.

10. RANGE.

Every note starting with and including Bb downward may be referred to as a "pedal tone." To the extent that optional pitches (as encountered in ossia parts) impact the overall range of a composition, such pitches will be presented in parentheses.

11. MOVEMENTS. (specific names and/or numbers)

12. COMMISSION. (name of commissioning party if commissioned)

13. DEDICATION. (name of party to whom the composition is dedicated)

14. ANNOTATION. (short, concise, annotative comments concerning the general nature and style of a composition. Any outstanding technical problems or other pertinent information will be noted)

15. RECORDINGS. (when a particular composition has been recorded, reference will be made to the artist[s] responsible for the recording, and the reader should refer to the Discography chapter section Euphonium Recordings by Artist for complete information)

16. PRE-RECORDED TAPE/ELECTRONIC ACCOMPANIMENTS. (reference will be made for those few works that have taped/electronic accompaniments)

17. A final reference is made when a particular entry is included in more than one chapter of the *ESB*. For example, works for solo euphonium and orchestra almost inevitably are also available with piano reduction.

Finally, relative to the entry formatting for musical compositions, it should be noted that when there is no information available in a particular category that "field" will be simply omitted.

For the reader who cannot remember the composer/arranger for a particular composition in the Euphonium and Keyboard section, listings by title are included.

To the extent that the literature chapters are not primarily concerned with just identifying currently available materials but concerned with documenting all literature that has been generated for the euphonium, the basic repertoire chapters provide a highly selected listing of recommended literature that should be readily available to the reader. As is the case with every section of the *ESB*, the individuals responsible for identifying the basic recommended repertoire sections are preeminently qualified and present information that is thoroughly researched.

Every section of the *ESB* is without question the most extensive compilation of information ever assembled on that particular euphonium subject. The euphonium discography presented here is unprecedented in comprehensiveness and scope. The main entry for recordings will be found under Euphonium Recordings by Artist (annotated). Very important cross-references are available by consulting the listings by title and by composer.

The biographical sections of the *ESB* present information on as many professional euphoniumists and "euphonium composers" as possible that could be identified within the limited time frame of the project. Every attempt was made to contact professional euphoniumists internationally and to acquire information on their activities. Of course, some individuals who have made significant contributions to the advancement of the euphonium have been inadvertently excluded because they could not be contacted within the given time frame of the project or they failed to return requests for information. The editors hope that such individuals will receive proper recognition in future editions.

The bibliographical entries present a major documentation of past research and publications concerning the euphonium. This information represents the "starting point" for all future research efforts on the euphonium.

The equipment sections attempt to document currently available materials and services of interest to the euphoniumist.

The large majority of the *ESB* is of a reference nature intended to provide the reader with factual information on the euphonium. Some sections are provided to present the reader a historical perspective that will significantly enhance the understanding and relative comprehension of this material. These sections warrant a careful reading and understanding and include chapters on the history of the euphonium, doubling, and freelancing. These sections must be required reading for any "student" of the euphonium.

Finally, the editors, contributors, and consultants for the *ESB* take great pride in presenting this publication, which represents the most comprehensive and definitive research effort ever undertaken for the euphonium. "How sweet it is!"

ACKNOWLEDGMENTS

When I was in the middle of my studies at Tennessee Technological University (TTU) in 1993 and 1994, I remember often going to Winston Morris's home to perform cheap labor projects: remove weeds, mulch the lawn and flower beds, and so forth. When I would take breaks or have lunch, Mr. Morris would show me the immense amount of materials he was receiving for the first edition of the *Tuba Source Book*. The amount of materials he was sorting through and editing was staggering. Many days he would receive hundreds of pages of faxes of research and mind-boggling amounts of telephone calls from the many associate and contributing editors.

For over two years, I often observed Mr. Morris dedicating tireless hours to the *Tuba Source Book*. This left an unforgettable impression on my young professional life, especially when considering the other "hats" he was wearing. Mr. Morris played a major role in the TTU Department of Music and was a major influence across the campus. He was very active around the state of Tennessee in many areas of music education, he was organizing the first professional tuba and euphonium ensemble, Symphonia, and he was a major force in TUBA (Tubists Universal Brotherhood Association, later International Tuba-Euphonium Association: ITEA). If all of that wasn't enough, he was organizing tours of the internationally acclaimed Tennessee Tech Tuba Ensemble to such events as MENC (the National Association for Music Education), U.S. Army Band Tuba-Euphonium Conferences, and Carnegie Hall, as well as organizing several tuba and euphonium ensemble recording projects, which included a massive amount of new tuba and euphonium ensemble music, and organizing a host of tuba and euphonium guest artists to attend the very large annual TTU Octubafest activities and the spring Tubafest. While wearing all of these "hats," Mr. Morris's international reputation as one of the foremost tuba and euphonium instructors did not suffer, as his students continued to be successful in national and international competitions and in acquiring graduate school scholarships and teaching assistantships.

Since that time, Mr. Morris has been working on tuba and euphonium ensemble tours and recording projects, tuba and euphonium ensemble compositions, numerous tours, and several recordings with Symphonia, the creation of the Modern Jazz Tuba Project, which has now had numerous tours and is considered the world's premiere jazz tuba and euphonium ensemble. He has also been doing all of the professional activities listed in the previous paragraph, as well as being the senior editor of the second version of the *Tuba Source Book*.

As if all of the work over the past twelve years wasn't enough, Mr. Morris about three years ago approached Eric Paull and myself about helping him organize and create a book modeled after the *Tuba Source Book* for the euphonium. Needless to say Eric and I were ecstatic but a little scared as we were both well aware of the amount of time this project would demand.

So what does all of this information have to do with the *Guide to the Euphonium Repertoire: The Euphonium Source Book*? Without Winston Morris's tireless efforts and nearly unmatched dedication to the tuba and euphonium, this book would not exist. It is that energy, dedication, and selfless attitude that we all need to employ to help the euphonium world continue to grow. I, and all of the people involved with the *Guide to the Euphonium Repertoire: The Euphonium Source Book*, believe this book is a major step in the history and future of the euphonium. We play and teach one of the most beautiful, lyrical, and technically versatile instruments. We all must push forward with the drive and energy that Winston Morris has demonstrated throughout his entire career.

Many people have been invaluable in terms of support and assistance. Thanks are extended to Eric Paull, my co-editor, for his time, advice, insights, encouragement, and friendship; Adam Frey for allowing me to peruse his euphonium library; Timothy Northcut for his advice and for his assistance in mass mailing to all the many publishers and composers; the University of Cincinnati College-Conservatory of Music for their financial assistance with the mass mailing;

the many publishers and composers who were so kind as to send copies of their music for review; Glenville State College for their financial and moral support, especially my students (Scott Smith!) and my department chair, Duane Chapman; and finally, all of the world-class euphonium players and teachers involved with the *Guide to the Euphonium Repertoire: The Euphonium Source Book* for their countless hours of input and assistance. I would also like to thank all of the great euphonium players and teachers from the past and those currently still active. Without their amazing talents, hard work, and love for the euphonium, this book would not exist. I would like to especially thank my wife, Susan, my son, Casey, and all of my family members for their love and support during the many hours of research, organizing, and planning for this most wonderful undertaking.

The editors owe it to future generations of performers and composers to document their work on an ongoing basis and to make that material available. We do not know what form these updates will take, but we hope that readers will inform us about new compositions, recordings, festivals, and so forth. Please send this information to me at Glenville State College, Department of Fine Arts, Glenville, West Virginia 26351.

Lloyd E. Bone Jr.

The *Guide to the Euphonium Repertoire: The Euphonium Source Book* (*ESB*) is a culmination of years of creativity, dedication, and pride for this instrument that people from across the globe have come to know and love. The intentions for compiling a resource guide on all things related to the euphonium are as numerous as the contributions that came from so many helpful professionals interested in expanding our knowledge of the instrument.

It is not an understatement when I say that this book would not have been possible without the tireless commitment and positive encouragement from R. Winston Morris, our advisor on this project. Winston and Ed Goldstein laid the foundation for this book with their earlier contributions in the *Tuba Source Book*, and the *ESB* simply copied the format and catered its needs to relate to the euphonium.

Similarly, I am appreciative of the work that Lloyd E. Bone has done with regards to the sharing of editorial responsibilities. A great deal of thanks goes to the rest of the *ESB* editorial staff, the contributors, and all of the consultants that have been involved in the making of this book. Many people, working long hours, have put together this reference guide so that others will find the information put forth both useful and beneficial. I am especially grateful to my wife, Cindy, who has supported me with her love and gracious understanding throughout.

I also wish to thank our predecessors, who, long before we began working on this book, took the time and interest to research, compile, and publish similar contributions. These previous additions to the euphonium literature helped provide the necessary steps forward, and so it is my hope that the *Euphonium Source Book* will be a solid framework for future generations to build upon.

Eric Paull

Guide to the Euphonium Repertoire

1. A Short History of the Euphonium and Baritone Horn

Michael B. O'Connor

The history of the euphonium is inextricably linked to that of the tuba. Both instruments were created to take advantage of the new valve technology of the nineteenth century and both were welcome additions to the military bands of Europe. The tuba eventually found a secure place as the contrabass brass instrument in the large orchestras of the nineteenth century, but the euphonium remained primarily a wind band instrument. Its deep, mellow tone and facile technique were perfectly suited for the bass-baritone solo lines of these ensembles. From a modern perspective, it would seem that the euphonium failed to gain the more prestigious role earned by the tuba, but this view fails to take into account the popularity of the wind band during the nineteenth century. From about 1850 until World War I, while tubists often labored in obscurity, euphonium soloists were international celebrities. Not surprisingly, the euphonium's rapid rise in popularity and its subsequent gradual fall into relative obscurity during the twentieth century followed a similar rise and fall in the popularity of wind bands. But while many of the musical "experiments" produced by the Industrial Revolution adorn the shelves of museums, the euphonium has secured a place in the modern instrumentarium by virtue of its use in a few important orchestral works, government support for military bands, and the stability of the worldwide amateur band movement.

Definition of the Instrument

The euphonium is the bass member of the valve-bugle family, a group that includes flugelhorns, alto (tenor) horns, baritone horns, and tubas. Most modern examples are nine feet in length with a fundamental pitch of B♭, although the six-valve, French C tuba is a close relation. Like all bugles the profile of the bore is a cone that widens substantially from the mouthpiece receiver to the instrument's bell. In this sense the euphonium is the descendant of the bass ophicleide, a bassoon-shaped, keyed brass instrument popular during the first half of the nineteenth century. Most modern

euphoniums made by western European, North American, and Asian factories are constructed on a saxhorn profile, with three or four piston valves (see fig. 1), while some central and eastern European instruments are built with an oval profile, employing from three to five rotary valves (see fig. 2). Bore sizes for most euphoniums range between .563 and .654 inches (14.3–16.61 mm), with bell sizes from ten to twelve inches (25.4–30.5 cm).[1] Music for the instrument is generally written in either non-transposing bass clef or in treble clef that is written a ninth above sounding pitch. The latter is traditional in British brass bands and is commonly used to ease the transition from trumpet to euphonium in American school bands.

Figure 1. Besson Prestige Euphonium. *Photo courtesy of Besson Musical Instruments, Limited.*

Figure 2. V. F. Cerveny Model 741–5MR oval, rotary-valve Kaiser-Euphonium. *Photo courtesy of AMATI-Denak, s.r.o.*

The euphonium serves as the bass-baritone voice of the brass family, a role comparable to the violoncello of the orchestral strings. It is primarily employed in wind bands throughout the world as the solo bass instrument or as reinforcement for the tubas or trombones. Orchestral use is rare, but the euphonium, often designated "tenor tuba," is featured as a solo instrument in several important works by Richard Strauss, Béla Bartók, Dmitri Shostakovich, Gustav Holst, and Roy Harris. In chamber music, the euphonium appears in multiple tuba-euphonium ensembles, brass sextets, large brass choirs, or as a soloist with instruments outside the brass family. The instrument has no established role in jazz outside of a few "tuba-jazz" ensembles. A few soloists such as Rich Matteson (1929–1993) and Marcus

Dickman have made significant contributions to the euphonium's status as a solo jazz instrument. The euphonium rarely appears in popular music.

The term "euphonium," derived from the Greek word *euphonos,* meaning "sweet sounding," has only gained widespread application during the past quarter century. Due perhaps to the euphonium's rather recent development, the instrument has owned a variety of names over its history. Early terminology often reflected an instrument maker's attempt to immortalize his own name, but other names were more descriptive of the instrument's range and purpose. For example, the French term *saxhorn basse* proclaims the name of Adolphe Sax, the principal brass instrument innovator of the nineteenth century. The German term *Baryton,* however, is an eminently practical description of the instrument's range, and the Italian term *bombardino* draws a family connection to the tuba (*bombardone*). Similarly, American musicians and arrangers of the nineteenth century considered the large-bore euphonium as the upper member of the tuba section, simply calling it the B♭ bass. For Americans the term "baritone" was reserved for an instrument that featured a bore size midway between the B♭ bass and B♭ valved tenor horn.

Origins

The modern euphonium is a product of the flurry of brass instrument innovation that occurred during the nineteenth century.[2] Although the euphonium "descended" from the bass ophicleide, lower brass instruments equipped with valves had begun to appear within eight years of Halary's ophicleide patent. Thus, rather than its offspring, the euphonium is more properly a cousin to the ophicleide. The euphonium's development consequently followed advances in valve technology with very few instrument makers focusing on the instrument in particular. Instead, improvements to euphoniums and baritone horns during the first half of the nineteenth century were products of the overall development of valve systems and brass instrument manufacture in general.

Valve Technology

From the late fifteenth century to the eighteenth century, the slide, as applied to the trombone and slide trumpet, was the only means of providing brass instruments with a fully chromatic technique. The need for chromatic trumpets and horns became evident during the early nineteenth

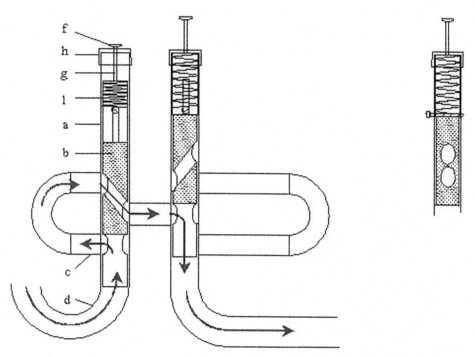

Figure 3. Stözel's early valve design showing the windway paths. *Drawings by Dr. Sabine K. Klaus, Joe and Joella Utley Curator of Brass Instruments, National Music Museum, The University of South Dakota, Vermillion, South Dakota.*

century as composers began to experiment with the sudden changes of key and chromatic melodies pioneered by Beethoven. As an alternative, some instrument makers began to experiment with the addition of keys to trumpets and bugles. The ophicleide, a bass bugle, was among the most successful products of the keyed-instrument approach. While these instruments achieved the goal of chromatic technique, a simpler method of changing pitch was desired by musicians in cavalry bands.

The earliest brass instrument valves were simple devices designed to overcome the limitations of the natural overtone series available to natural brass instruments. The first known valves were Ferdinand Kölbel's (ca. 1705–1778) 1766 push-button device attached to his *Amor-Schall,* a type of omnitonic horn, and Charles Clagget's (1740–ca. 1795) lever valve of 1788 that allowed a trumpet or horn player to alternate between two instruments, pitched a semitone apart, while playing only one mouthpiece.[3] The first successful valve design, however, was developed in 1818 by Heinrich Stölzel (1777–1844), a Prussian horn player and instrument technician. When in the upright position, his tubular valve allowed air entering the valve case to pass below the valve and

out the bottom of the case. When engaged, the valve blocked the lower opening and redirected the air through an additional loop of tubing (see fig. 3).[4]

The Vienna valve was the first competitor to Stölzel's valve. Developed by hornist Joseph Kail (1795–1871) and instrument maker Joseph Felix Riedl (ca. 1788–1837) in 1823, the Vienna valve system utilized a double-piston that, when disengaged, allowed air to pass through a straight tube. The double tubes were engaged by pushing down a metal rod. This redirected the air upward through a loop of tubing fitted over the two short pistons. Some euphoniums and tenor horns were equipped with Vienna valves during the nineteenth century (see fig. 4), but the technology has survived to the present only in the form of the Vienna horn.

The Prussian bandmaster Wilhelm Wieprecht (1802–1872) devised a new tubular valve in 1833 that avoided the many sharp windway angles inherent in the Stölzel valve. The Berlin (*Berliner-Pumpen*) valve featured windways that looped along the same side of the valve tube, creating a valve diameter that was twice the bore size of the instrument (see fig. 5). It should be noted that Stölzel had created a similar modification in

1827, but Wieprecht used his position as head of the Prussian military bands to outfit all the bands with his Berlin-valve instruments, which were constructed by Johann Gottfried Moritz (d. 1835) and his son Carl Wilhelm Moritz (1811–1855).[5]

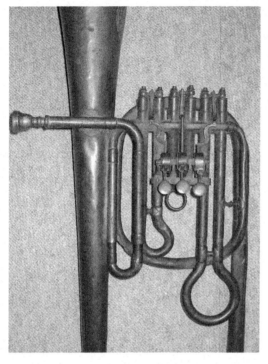

Figure 4. Vienna valve section of a nineteenth-century V. F. Cerveny tenor horn. *Photo courtesy of Frank Hosemann.*

The success of the Berlin valve prompted Adolphe Sax (1814–1894) to adopt a modified version for his first family of saxhorns in 1843.[6]

The modern piston valve is based on an 1839 design by Étienne François Périnet (fl. 1829–1855). The Périnet valve avoids sharp bends in the windway by curving the passages along both the length and width of the valve (see fig. 6). Like several of its predecessors, the disengaged Périnet valve featured a straight windway, but the innovative pathway design allowed for a much smaller valve diameter than the Berlin valve. The success of Périnet's valve was such that it has remained essentially unchanged in most modern brass instruments.

The rotary valve developed alongside piston designs. Although there is some dispute over who was the first to construct a rotary valve, enough evidence exists to credit Friedrich Blühmel (d. before 1845) with the earliest practical design. The first patent for a rotary valve, however, was granted to Kail and Riedl in 1835.[7] Their two-passage rotary valve has remained essentially unchanged today in European instruments, especially those made east of the Rhine (see fig. 7).[8] A notable variant was introduced in 1850 by American J. Lathrop Allen (1815–ca. 1905). This long, thin rotary valve featured a string linkage and turned more quickly than disk-shaped valves. It was employed on many of the lower brass instruments played during the American Civil War (see fig. 8).[9] From about 1870, however, the Périnet piston valve edged out both rotary and Berlin valves in American-made instruments.

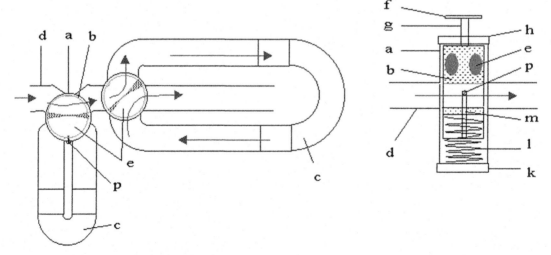

Figure 5. The Berlin valve design showing the windway paths from above. *Drawings by Dr. Sabine K. Klaus, Joe and Joella Utley Curator of Brass Instruments, National Music Museum, The University of South Dakota, Vermillion, South Dakota.*

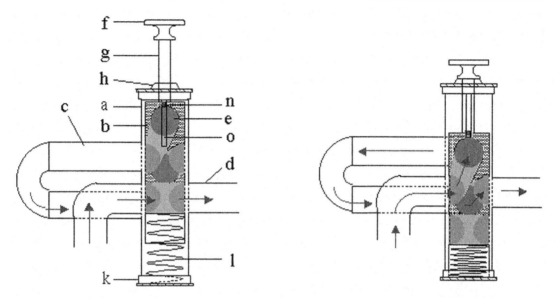

Figure 6. The bottom-sprung Périnet valve design showing the windway paths. *Drawings by Dr. Sabine K. Klaus, Joe and Joella Utley Curator of Brass Instruments, National Music Museum, The University of South Dakota, Vermillion, South Dakota.*

Figure 7. This 1885 Stowassers-Sohne euphonium features elaborately engraved rotary valves. *Photo courtesy of Phil Holcomb.*

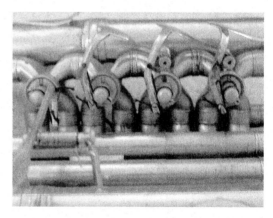

Figure 8. Allen valves on an 1858–1859 Allen & Co. over-the-shoulder style baritone. *Photo courtesy of Mark Elrod.*

While valve technology presented musicians with instruments that were more agile and uniform in tone, the three-valve system of most brass instruments created a pitch problem when the valves were used in combination. Each valve was designed to lower the pitch of the instrument by either a semitone (second), a tone (first), or a tone and half (third). When the valves were used in combination, however, the cumulative changes to the bore profile noticeably affected the pitch of the instrument. This was especially true when

the third valve was used in combination with the first or second valves. Several attempts were made to alleviate this problem during the nineteenth century. For example, some French and Belgian euphoniums that were built during the 1880s featured a third valve that lowered the instrument two full tones lower than open pitch, thus eliminating the need for the second-third combination. The unconventional fingerings that resulted may have prevented its widespread acceptance. A more popular method was the addition of a fourth valve that lowered the instrument by two-and-a-half tones, eliminating the need for the very sharp first-third valve combination. The most radical system, from a modern perspective, was the adoption of six valves, eliminating the need for combinations altogether. Sax introduced a six-valve system in 1852 that gradually *reduced* the amount of tubing, creating an ascending system rather than the conventional descending system. The system, when applied to a C/B♭ *saxhorn basse,* found some favor, but by 1892 Sax's instrument was replaced by a Courtois C tuba with a descending six-valve system. Unlike the Sax instrument, fifth and sixth valves of the Courtois instrument were used only to transpose the instrument for easier fingering of certain passages.[10]

The most satisfactory answer to the problem of valve combinations was the introduction of compensating systems. Among the early attempts to compensate for the gradual sharpening created by valve combinations was a system designed by Gustave Auguste Besson (1820–1874) in 1853. Besson fitted each valve slide with a type of rotary valve, called a *barillet,* that brought extra tubing into play when engaged. Other systems that required the player to engage extra valves and levers were introduced, but these were supplanted by the introduction of automatic compensating systems.

While Pierre Louis Gautrot's (d. 1882) *système equitonique,* a four-valve system patented in 1864, was the first documented, automatic compensating system for brass instruments, the most successful automatic system was introduced by David James Blaikley (1846–1936), the factory manager for Boosey & Co. for much of the late nineteenth century.[11] 1873 company records reveal that he fitted a euphonium in C with a valve system that, when the third valve was engaged, brought into play extra tubing fitted to the first and second valves in order to compensate for the usual sharpening of pitch.[12] In 1874 he designed a system that was triggered by the fourth valve. Blaikley was granted a patent for the system in 1878, and it remains the standard compensating system on most modern euphoniums. Competitive systems by Besson and Hawkes & Son quickly followed. Besson, perhaps as an answer to Boosey's patent on the compensating system, developed the "Enharmonic" system, which featured a mouthpipe that led directly into the third valve. When the third valve was engaged, the windway passed through the second and first valves by a reverse, alternate route that brought extra tubing into play. An extra section

Figure 9. Detail of tubing on a 1918 Besson Enharmonic Euphonium. *Photo courtesy of Charley Brighton.*

of tubing connected the third to the first valve so that, when the third valve was not in use, the air bypassed the third valve and entered the first valve in the normal manner (see fig. 9). Unlike Blaikley's system, the Besson system avoided the redirection of air through the valves. The drawback of the Enharmonic system, however, was the weight of the extra tubing, which made it impractical for smaller instruments. In the end, Blaikely's compensating system was so successful that, when his patent finally expired in the 1970s, other companies took up the original design with only a few modifications.[13]

Early Examples

The earliest tubas, euphoniums, and baritones were constructed more or less as replacements for various sizes of ophicleides. Since an instrument with two or three valves was much easier to play from horseback, the earliest valve basses were designed for cavalry bands. The divergence of tuba and baritone/euphonium was accomplished from the very beginning as well. The earliest "valve ophicleides" were constructed in F as well as B♭. The former evolved into bass tubas while the higher pitched instruments, depending on bore size, can be called the first baritones and euphoniums.

Many of the early B♭ and C bass instruments were the results of experiments by valve innovators. Stölzel, soon after introducing his tubular valve, designed a *Tenorhorn* that was constructed by Griesling & Schlott.[14] Bevan states that, as early as 1829, Wieprecht's *Trompeten-Corps* had an instrument called the *Tenorbasshorn* in B♭ as part of its inventory.[15] This instrument may have been a wider-bore version of Stölzel's instrument and its name already suggests the wide range that the modern euphonium would be expected to cover. In 1838 Carl W. Moritz constructed an instrument in B♭ with four Berlin valves (two for each hand) that closely resembled the bass tuba, patented by his father and Wilhelm Wieprecht in 1835 (see fig. 10).[16] Like the bass tuba, this early euphonium resembles the English bass horn in its rather narrow profile, very minimal bell flare, and central location of the valve section. Thus, for lack of a verifiable competitor, Moritz's instrument is generally considered to be the first euphonium. An example of his instrument survives in the Musikinstrumentensammlung (Music Instrument Collection) of the Munich Stadtmuseum.

The first instrument with the name "euphonium" was developed by Ferdinand Sommer (fl. 1840–1859), a Weimar bandmaster, in 1843.[17] This instrument, which he called the *Sommerophone*, was most likely constructed by Franz Bock of Vienna, who in turn patented the design as the *Euphonion* in 1844. Ferdinand Hell (fl. 1835–1855), who also made some improvements to Sommer's instrument, patented his own version as the *Hellhorn* only four days after Bock's patent.[18] Sommer was also the instrument's first soloist. His name appears in Louis Jullien's (1812–1860) band concerts in London (1840–1859) as Sommerophone soloist in 1849, and he received Honorable Mention for playing his instrument with organ accompaniment at the London Great Exhibition of 1851.[19] The instrumental combination, and perhaps Sommer himself, was immortalized in Strachey's biography of Queen Victoria. The Queen, upon paying a final visit to the Crystal Palace at the Exhibition's closing in October, remarked, "I could not believe it was the last time I was to see it. An organ, accompanied by a fine and powerful wind instrument called the Sommerophone, was being played, and it nearly upset me."[20] This moment is immortalized on the cover of Sommer's *Farewell to the Exhibition: Air and Variations for the Piano-Forte,* where he is shown playing his instrument to organ accompaniment for Prince Albert, the queen, and their children (see fig. 11). Sommer was not, however, as successful as his colleague Sax in fixing his own name to his invention. He made the mistake of offering two names, *Sommerophone* and

Figure 10. This early five-valve bass tuba, probably by Carl W. Moritz, ca. 1840, shares a similar bass horn profile with his 1838 euphonium. *Photo courtesy of Phil Holcomb.*

Euphonion (or "euphonic horn") at the Exhibition. The anglicized term "euphonium" was preferred by the British and has remained so to the present.[21]

The Milanese instrument maker Giuseppe Pelitti (1811–1865) produced a *bombardino* (small tuba), sometimes called the *Pelittone bombardino,* in B♭ as early as 1835.[22] Luigi Magrini provides this date in an 1845 *Gazzetta musicale di Milano* article, where he reports on the

Figure 11. Ferdinand Sommer performs on his Sommerophone with organ accompaniment at the 1851 Great Exhibition. This instrument retains the bass horn profile of Moritz's instrument, but uses rotary valves in a central location. *Photo courtesy of the Victoria and Albert Museum.*

instruments that Pelitti submitted for the Istituto Lombardo competition. He states that Pelitti invented the *bombardino baritono a quattro cilindri* as an answer to the technical deficiencies of the *bombardone* (valve ophicleide in F).[23] Magrini's claim for 1835 seems a bit early since Pelitti's bass instruments bear striking resemblances to early German examples by both Johann and Carl Moritz. While the amount of "borrowing" that occurred among instrument makers of this time prevents a definitive assessment of Pelitti's claim, the Prussian origins of the valve technology employed by all the instruments in question suggests that the Carl Moritz instrument probably preceded Pelitti's design. One can be certain, however, that Pelitti's *bombardino* was the instrument originally played in the onstage bands of Verdi's operas *Don Carlo* and *Un ballo in maschera*. Examples of the instrument survive in

the Museo Nazionale degli Strumenti Musicali in Rome and the National Music Museum in Vermillion, South Dakota, in the United States.

Pelitti's *bombardino* is a member of the Italian *flicorno* (bugle/flugelhorn) family. While Pelitti insisted on calling his instruments *Pelittone*, other nineteenth-century Italian makers were content to call their instruments *flicorni* and produced them in two sizes, the *flicorno bombardino* (with three valves) and the *flicorno basso* (with four valves). The latter instrument was considered the bass solo instrument of Italian bands, a fact underscored by the virtuosic writing in Amilcare Ponchielli's (1834–1886) 1872 *Concerto per flicorno basso*.[24] In this regard, the Italian practice follows the general European pairing of small- and large-bore B♭ instruments.

In France the most important name in brass instrument construction before 1860 was

Adolphe Sax. Although Danays had introduced a set of brass instruments that included baritone-range instruments in Db, C, and Bb, built by A. G. Guichard between 1838 and 1844, Sax's "family" of valve brasses was the most successful European design until about the 1870s.[25] Sax, a Belgian native, made a successful career, in spite of the highly political Parisian musical establishment, through tireless self-promotion, a clever manipulation of the weaknesses in patent laws, and some determined legal defenses. Yet even more important to his success was his ability to improve existing designs and to manufacture finely crafted and durable instruments.

Even as a young man working in his father's shop in Brussels, Sax had a keen ability to improve existing instruments. In 1841, he acquired several instruments, including a bass tuba with Berlin valves, from Johann Moritz in Berlin.[26] Although Sax is not counted among the pioneers of valve technology, he did improve the Berlin valve by eliminating the nine sharp angles in the windway of the valve. At some point during his time in Brussels, Sax began to think about the possibility of creating a homogenous family of valve bugles that would cover all the needed pitches.[27] He took up work on the instruments shortly after moving to Paris, and by 1844, his project had progressed sufficiently to offer a public demonstration. This first collection, patented in 1845, consisted of an Eb soprano, a Bb contralto, an Eb alto, a Bb tenor with three valves, and a Bb bass with four valves; he later added an Eb/F contrabass, and an Ab/A contralto to the family.[28] Perhaps the most enduring feature of Sax's saxhorn family is the alternation of Eb and Bb instruments, a pattern adopted by British brass bands after 1850. The Berlin valves on Sax's instruments were set as close to the mouthpiece as practical in order to keep the cylindrical tubing of the valve section as close to the narrowest diameter of the cone as possible. Sax eventually produced an entire family of tuba-shaped brass instruments with funnel-type mouthpieces that were deeper and wider than contemporaneous designs.

Although Sax's instruments were improvements on existing ideas rather than inventions, the superior craftsmanship of his products won him a virtual monopoly for production of instruments for French military bands. Rival French instrument makers were furious that Sax had taken the step of patenting pre-existing instrument types with what they viewed as minor modifications. Even more, they were insulted that the term "saxhorn," a name advanced by Sax's advocates, found favor among performers and journalists.

They attacked Sax through lawsuits and public denouncements, and although he managed to fight off the charges, the legal bills cost him most of the profits from his instruments.[29]

Two instruments of the saxhorn family are important in the development of the modern baritone horn and euphonium. The *saxhorn saryton,* or *saxhorn ténor en sí bemol,* was the prototype of the modern baritone horn and reflects Sax's understanding that an instrument of similar bore profile was needed to extend the lower range of the Eb alto. He constructed a similar instrument in A for cavalry bands.[30] The *saxhorn basse en sí bemol* had a wider bore than the *Ténor* and featured four, or even five valves. This instrument became, like its predecessors, the bass-baritone solo instrument and may be considered the earliest modern euphonium. Until the introduction of the contrabass, it also served as the lowest-pitched instrument of the family.

Sax's instruments prompted several composers to experiment with the timbral possibilities of the valve-bugle family. His first and most illustrious advocate, Hector Berlioz, extolled Sax as a man who brought brass and woodwind construction out of their respective infancies, proclaiming that all composers would benefit from the instruments once they were in widespread use. There was resistance in some quarters, however. Most of the prominent performers in Paris had connections with local instrument makers or were instrument builders themselves. Donizetti's desire to try Sax's bass clarinet and several saxhorns in a production of *Don Sebastian* was thwarted when members of the orchestra threatened to walk out.[31] Other composers were more successful. Meyerbeer wrote a coronation march for his 1849 opera *Le Prophète* that was scored for a large stage band of Sax's instruments. Charles Gounod followed this example with a similar stage band in *Faust,* and Berlioz scored eight saxhorns, including two Bb tenors and two Eb contrabasses, for his 1863 premier of *Les Troyens.* Verdi's 1847 Paris production of *Jérusalem* called for both tenor and bass saxhorns.[32]

While Sax's instruments were already known in England, it was the Distin family's enthusiasm for his designs that prompted the overwhelming success of Sax's designs in that country. After inspecting Sax's instruments during a trip to Paris in 1843, John Distin (1798–1863), along with his four sons, petitioned Sax to build a set of five instruments with some suggested modifications. In 1844 they played their new instruments, which included a Bb *ténor* serving as the bass, in Paris and London with great success, and by 1845

Henry Distin (1819–1903) became Sax's agent in London. The family's tours of England not only promoted Sax's instruments but also helped build enthusiasm for the nascent brass band movement. Their success was such that by 1850, Distin was manufacturing his own instruments.[33] These instruments were so popular that when Boosey & Co. purchased the business in 1868, they continued to stamp "Distin & Co." on his designs until 1874. With his earnings, Distin set up shop in New York and then Williamsport (Pennsylvania). There he produced finely made, and elaborately engraved, euphoniums and other brass instruments from 1877 until his retirement in 1890. In 1909, Brua C. Keefer purchased the company, gave it his own name, and continued to manufacture the Distin-designed euphonium until 1942.

The English ophicleidist Alfred Phasey (1834–1888) is often credited with creating the modern euphonium by enlarging the bore of an 1857 Courtois *saxhorn ténor* and giving the instrument the name "euphonium." This information comes from several obituaries and recollections that appeared at the time of his death.[34] The sources, however, fail to mention the name of the instrument maker who took up Phasey's suggestions or the fate of the alleged prototype. Furthermore, instruments of the proportions that Phasey desired were already available in London from Sax (through Distin) and Gustave Besson. Phasey's role in the development of the euphonium rests mostly on his promotion of the instrument in the role of soloist. This much is well documented. The story of his role as inventor, however, must be considered apocryphal.

Baritone and euphonium production in America did not lag far behind Europe during the nineteenth century. James Keat (1813–1845) began making Stölzel-valve brass instruments for the Vermont shop of Graves & Co. during the late 1830s. In New York, the Dodworth family introduced their "over-the-shoulder" (OTS) style of brass instruments at about the same time. These instruments employed top-action rotary valves (TARV) and bells that were directed over the player's shoulder. This unusual configuration allowed military troops, who traditionally followed their band in parade formations, to hear the music more clearly. According to Allen Dodworth (1822–1896), his family developed these instruments in 1838 for exactly this purpose.[35] The actual construction of the Dodworth instruments was realized by the Uhlmann shop in Vienna,[36] but popularity of the design among military bands during the American Civil War (1861–1865) prompted several American instrument makers,

notably Allen & Hall, E. G. Wright (1811–1871), J. F. Stratton (1832–1912), Graves & Co., and Isaac Fiske (1820–1894), to produce their own lines. The cross-pollination of Sax's instruments is evident in the preference for the alternation of E♭ and B♭ pitch levels for the different-sized instruments.

The American OTS instruments included tenors and basses in B♭ that were differentiated in bore size along the example set by Sax, but during the 1860s a third B♭ instrument, designated "baritone," began to appear in the musical parts. The instrument was the bass soloist in the brass band and often doubled the upper melodic part at the octave. The use of the term "baritone" was certainly a reflection of the large number of German immigrant musicians who composed music for, and served in, American military bands on both sides of the conflict (see fig. 12). Since German musicians continued to be a recognizable part of American musical life for the rest of the century, publishers and instrument makers continued to use the term "baritone" until well into the twentieth century.

Central European instrument makers were as active as their French, English, and American counterparts during the nineteenth century. In 1842, Václav Frantisek Cerveny (1819–1896) set up a factory in Königgräz, now the Czech city of Hradec Králové, and within four years introduced a four-valve *Baroxyton*.[37] Cerveny's lasting contribution was the "Kaiser" series of instruments, which featured a large, almost modern bore and a conical profile that continued through the valve section (see fig. 2). Although the instruments were available in tuba, ophicleide, and helicon

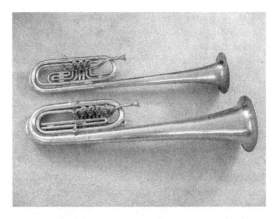

Figure 12. (From top to bottom) An 1862 D. C. Hall B♭ tenor and a rare, four-valve B♭ baritone made by Allen & Co. in 1858–1859. *Photo courtesy of Mark Elrod.*

forms, the oval *Kaiserbaryton* with rotary valves was taken up by other makers and became the standard configuration for central and eastern European euphoniums. Cerveny also made a *Phonikon*, or *Zunkoroh,* which was a type of euphonium with a bulbous bell, similar to that found on the English horn.[38]

The Scandinavian bands and small brass ensembles of the nineteenth century made good use of the new valved instruments. Swedish military bands employed Bb tenor horns and tenor tubas (euphoniums) made by Jacob V. Wahl (1801–1878) of Landskrona or, later, Ahlberg & Ohlsson or Bengt Dahlgren in Stockholm. These instruments were based on the older bass horn shapes that inspired the early Prussian models, but many came in flugelhorn configurations as well. The traditional Swedish brass sextet, or *Mässingssextett,* often used tenor horns in Bb as accompaniment instruments, but the solo low brass instrument was an instrument called the *Tenorbasun,* a type of small-bore valve trombone.[39] In Finland, military bands featured tenor horns in C, Bb, and Ab as well as euphoniums. The standard Finnish brass septet, or *torviseitsikko,* includes a Bb tenor horn and baritone (euphonium). Nineteenth-century Finnish brass players played instruments that were mostly imported from Germany, especially lower brasses from Kruspe, but some players owned domestic instruments by Alexei Apostol of Helsinki.[40]

The completion of the American Civil War released a flood of experienced brass players into civilian life. Some, such as George Ives, the father of the composer Charles Ives, tried to make a living in music by forming bands and offering lessons. Others returned to previous occupations, but their desire to continue playing band music was the impetus behind the explosion of town bands that occurred between 1870 and 1900. Town and professional bands of the late Victorian era began as replicas of military brass bands, OTS instruments and all, but by 1880, most American town bands were outfitted with inexpensive, factory-produced imports from France, England, and Austria. While some of these instruments were purchased directly by performers, many American importers purchased European instruments without trademarks and simply stamped their own brand names on the bells. Some well-known North American companies such as J. W. Pepper (Philadelphia), Lyon & Healy (Chicago), Bruno & Sons, Carl Fischer (New York), J. W. Jenkins (Kansas City), and Whaley-Royce (Toronto) imported many more instruments than they ever manufactured. The leading sources for these imported instruments were Boosey & Co.,

Hawkes & Son, and Besson in England; Courtois, Couesnon, Jaubert & Cie., Pourcelle, and Thibouville-Lamy in France; and Bohland & Fuchs in Bohemia. Imported euphoniums from this period varied in style and quality, but virtually all featured the upright-bell saxhorn shape, Périnet valves, and either silver-plate or raw-brass finish.[41] By the turn of the century, some American manufacturers began to achieve European levels of production, reducing the demand for foreign-made instruments.

The flowering of the amateur band movement in the United States provided a large market for domestically produced "American baritones." These instruments had smaller bore sizes than Bb basses, and many featured forward-facing bells that enhanced the instrument's sound during the early days of sound recording. Another American innovation was the front-action valve cluster, first produced by Charles G. Conn (1844–1931). American baritones were built in staggering numbers by mostly midwestern companies such as Conn, Buescher, York, and later Holton, King, Martin, Olds, and Reynolds. The success of American manufacturers was such that, during the period 1890–1930, American professionals played exclusively domestic instruments. Competition was fierce and prominent euphonium soloists were often recruited to help develop and promote new models.

As the professional and amateur band movements lost steam around World War II, the need for low brass instruments continued with the growth of public school wind band programs. The demand for instruments was so great that some European companies such as Boosey & Hawkes and Cousenon found it profitable enough to construct American-style, bell-front baritones for export.

Duplex Instruments

Duplex instruments offer performers the ability to rapidly change key or timbre without changing instruments or crooks. The best-known example in this category of instruments is the double horn, a staple of orchestral players worldwide. Timbral combinations such as the echo cornet and double-bell euphonium have enjoyed brief periods of popularity, but none are currently in widespread use.

Giuseppe Pelitti's *bombardino/trombone baritono,* built as early as 1847, was the first instrument to combine a euphonium and tenor trombone by means of a common valve section. It was part of an entire family of duplex brasses that included a *bombardone* (F tuba) combined with bass trombone bell. All of Pelitti's low brass duplex instruments featured two upright bells, with the alternate instrument put into play by engaging a dedicated fourth valve. The entire family was submitted to the Istituto Lombardo competition in 1851 but was not adjudicated until 1853, when it won the silver medal.[42] Pelitti was encouraged to enter his duplex instruments in the competition at the 1855 Universal Exhibition, but he made the strategic mistake of sending his instruments to Paris in advance. Adolphe Sax, a man who kept a regular eye on his competition, had the opportunity to inspect the instruments and craft his own duplex trumpet before the Exhibition. According to Magrini, Sax also used his influence to relegate Pelitti's instruments to a dark, obscure corner of the Exhibition. Pelitti arrived in Paris just in time to witness the awarding of the gold medal to Sax for his entire presentation, which included a notice of his "invention" of the duplex category of brass instruments.[43]

After Pelitti's death in 1865, his son Giuseppe Clemente (1837–1905) introduced a new series of duplex instruments for the 1878 Paris Exhibition. These instruments were constructed with one bell inside of the other, with the claim that the system increased the comfort of the player without altering the tone of either instrument.[44] Giuseppe Clemente also experimented with, but apparently never marketed, triplex instruments. The most notable of these was a variable-key *bombardone tritonio,* which played in (ascending) E♭, F, and B♭, essentially combining two tubas and a euphonium.[45]

Other European duplex euphonium/trombone combinations emerged during the late nineteenth century. Sachs mentions a model made at the Bohemian factory of Boland & Fuchs during the 1870s, although no records or examples survive.[46] Sediva of Odessa created a series of instruments called *Duettons* or *Lyrophones* in fanciful lyre configurations that included a baritone/trombone combination. Although the English flirtation with the double-bell instruments was brief, Higham, Besson, and Boosey introduced double-bell euphoniums during the 1880s (see fig. 13).[47] European interest in the instrument, however, faded by the first decade of the twentieth century.[48]

The double-bell euphonium's greatest success came in the United States. The earliest models were certainly European imports, but by the late 1880s, Conn began making double-bell euphoniums at the recently acquired Fiske factory in Worcester, Massachusetts. Conn's

Figure 13. This 1913 F. Besson Doblophone was among the few constructed by the English manufacturers. *Photo courtesy of Eric Totman.*

instrument gained an important advocate when Harry Whittier of the Gilmore Band, who had been playing an imported instrument since about 1885, took up Conn's instrument in 1888. Sousa's soloist Josef Michele Raffayalo followed suit in 1889 (see fig. 14).[49]

The double-bell euphonium was immensely popular among American euphonium players, especially during the early years of the twentieth century. Every large professional band, and virtually all of the important soloists, played double-bell euphoniums. To meet the demand, American companies such as Buescher, Conn, Distin (Keefer), Holton, King, and York produced instruments with four or five valves, in both upright and forward-facing main bells. Some European companies produced instruments for the American market that were imported by J. W. Pepper, Lyon & Healy, and Carl Fischer.

Figure 14. This 1895 gold-plated Conn double-bell euphonium was certainly made for a prominent euphonium soloist, but there is no presentation name on the bell. The instrument features a compensating fourth valve and a fifth valve to engage the smaller bell. *Photo courtesy of Phil Holcomb.*

Naturally, the highest quality models produced by American companies were named after a prominent soloist of the day. For soloists like Simone Mantia (1873–1951), the instrument offered opportunities for echo effects and alternations of timbre that worked very well with the predominantly theme and variations solos of the time. For section players, the instrument offered a chance to match timbres with the trombones on tutti sections. This golden age of the double-bell euphonium was immortalized in a line in Meredith Willson's "Seventy-Six Trombones" from his 1957 musical, *The Music Man.*

The double-bell euphonium was a fad and, like most fads, its popularity faded rather rapidly. Even during the heyday of the instrument, the dual timbres were not sufficiently exploited by composers or performers. Soloists could dream up echo passages enough, but section players soon lost interest in the instruments. Many players simply removed the bells and their added weight, replacing them only for performances.[50] By 1940,

even soloists had begun to ignore the small bell. Mallet relates a story by Arthur Lehman regarding the end of the double-bell euphonium in the U.S. military bands. In 1939, the band of a Royal Navy ship docked near Washington, D.C., was offered a new set of American-made instruments to replace their worn out British instruments. Harold Brasch (1916–1984), euphonium soloist with the United States Navy Band at that time, tried out the Boosey & Hawkes compensating euphonium that was left along with the other British instruments and found it superior in tone and intonation to the King double-bell euphonium that he and his section mates had been issued. He decided to set aside the double-bell instrument and play only the British euphonium. The British instruments became so popular with service-band players that all the double-bell euphoniums in American military bands were supplanted by British makes by the mid-1950s. This loss of market prompted all the American makers to cease production of double-bell euphoniums by the early 1960s.[51] In 1996, however, Edward Mallet completed a notable experiment that sought to create a "modern" duplex euphonium by joining a Kurath euphonium with an Edwards bass trombone bell section.[52] The result features two upright bells, recalling the duplex Pelitti instrument of the nineteenth century.

Unusual Configurations

In an attempt to carve out a market niche, instrument makers frequently produced brass instruments with innovative configurations. Sometimes these designs had acoustic or practical purposes, but often the visual aesthetic was the only motivation. Among the more practical configurations was the helicon shape, inspired by the ancient Roman *buccina* horn. The circular shape is supported by the player's shoulder with a bell that protrudes upward at a slight angle on the player's left. The design probably originated in Russia, but the earliest examples are by Ignaz Stowasser of Vienna (fl. 1830–1870) and Giuseppe Pelitti of Milan.[53] While the design is most practical for bandsmen playing contrabass instruments, shorter versions in B♭ were also made. Many central and eastern European companies produced instruments of helicon shape during the nineteenth century and many found their way to the United States and Britain.

The Metropolitan Museum of Art in New York owns an interesting figure-eight, B♭ *flicorno basso* by Ferdinando Roth (1815–1898) from around 1860. The instrument, which features

Vienna-style double valves, has an upright bell, but it is meant to be held like a cornet. Henry G. Lehnert (1838–1916) included a baritone-sized instrument among his Centennial family of brasses that were made for the 1876 American centennial celebration. The rotary-valve instruments were designed to rest on the shoulders of the player and face forward. There were also baritone and euphonium versions of Courtois's Antonio-phones. This family of instruments, which derives its name from Courtois's first name (Antoine), featured horn-style configurations with a detachable bell section that could face upward or under the arm. The Antoniophone design was licensed by other companies such as Thibouville-Lamy and Boosey & Co., which sold a set of instruments, designated "Orpheons," to the Gilmore Band between 1887 and 1889 (fig. 15).[54] The original set of Orpheons included three baritones and one euphonium, but an 1890 roster of the band shows only two still in use. The document also reveals that the Courtois terminology had created some confusion in nomenclature, with one player listed as Orpheon and the other as playing Antoniophone.[55] The Italian Bersag horn was developed for military use around 1870 and continues to be used by several Italian regiments. The tenor and baritone instruments of this family have only one valve and are in the bugle form. Bevan discusses several other experimental shapes for B♭ tenor instruments, but these generally use the funnel-shaped horn mouthpiece and should not be considered variations on the euphonium.[56]

Pitch Standards for Older Instruments

Anyone who has acquired a few old brass instruments quickly realizes that there were a number of pitch standards in use before World War II. Most British euphoniums were constructed to play at "Old Philharmonic Pitch" (A = 452.5 Hz) before 1929, after which British military bands adopted A = 439 Hz.[57] The kingdom's orchestras and bands all adopted International Pitch (A = 440 Hz) in 1939, leaving only brass bands playing at the older high pitch. To service these groups, Boosey & Hawkes instruments were stamped HP or LP until 1964, when the manufacture of high pitch instruments ceased.

A similar situation existed in the United States, although pitch standards varied even more widely than in England. Euphoniums produced for export in France and Austria, as well as American-made instruments, ranged in pitch from A = 435 Hz (Diapason Normal) to A = 462.5 Hz. The American Federation of Musicians attempted to standardize pitch to A = 440 Hz in 1917, but the transition did not begin in earnest until after 1920.[58] Due to the large number of high pitch instruments already in the country, the International Standard was called "low pitch."

Modern Instruments

The construction of all brass instruments diminished significantly during World War II as a result of the military demand for metals. Sadly, as the war progressed, many older instruments

Figure 15. A "Quintette of Antoniophones" of Patrick Gilmore's Band from *Harper's Weekly* of September 28, 1889. The set includes one B♭ tenor or baritone (second from right).

in Europe and America were converted into brass shell casings. Following the war, the major euphonium producers were joined by several new companies. The Miraphone company was formed in 1945 in Waldkreiburg, West Germany, by a group of Graslitz craftsmen that had crossed the Czech border, purportedly just in front of the advancing Soviet Army.[59] Miraphone euphoniums, which were constructed with rotary valves on Cerveny's oval *Kaiserbaryton* model, were successful in central Europe and in some areas of the United States until about the 1980s. In Graslitz, the various brass instrument makers were nationalized and collectivized between 1945 and 1948 and renamed AMATI.[60] While the traditional oval euphoniums continue to be regionally popular, AMATI, Hirsbrunner, Miraphone, Meinl-Weston, and Willson also build euphoniums on the upright bell, English/French saxhorn configuration with fourth-valve compensating systems, a style that is rapidly becoming the de facto configuration worldwide.

The consolidation of British euphonium makers began when Boosey & Co. purchased the Henry Distin factory in 1868. The company merged with Hawkes & Son in 1930, purchased Besson in 1948,[61] and then acquired the Salvationist instrument division in the 1960s. These acquisitions, accompanied by the closing of the Higham Company of Manchester in the 1950s, left Boosey & Hawkes as the dominant euphonium manufacturer in England. As the company sought to streamline production, the French Besson (Fontaine-Besson) designs were left to languish for years in favor of Boosey & Hawkes's instruments. In 1982, however, the company launched a partnership with Zig Kanstul of California to produce a modern version of the old Fontaine-Besson design, which was stamped with the traditional "F. Besson, Paris" insignia.[62] Boosey & Hawkes's history of musical instrument making ended in 2003 when the entire instrument-manufacturing branch of the company was sold to the Music Group, which marketed euphoniums under the "Besson London" brand name. In 2006, the Besson name returned to France with the purchase of Besson Musical Instruments, Ltd., by the Buffet Crampon Group. Today the only English-owned maker of euphoniums is the Sterling Musical Instrument Company.

The Yamaha Corporation of Japan has been making brass instruments since 1965. By the late 1970s, the Yamaha euphonium began to gain notice, and by the late 1980s it had become a serious alternative for professional musicians worldwide. The corporation's powerful marketing arm has also enabled Yamaha euphoniums to gain a firm foothold in many American school band programs.

In the United States, the old American baritone, along with its name, has given way to the full-size euphonium. While the old-style, bell-front instruments continue to be played and manufactured, most American college students and professionals have migrated to the euphonium. The grand old American instrument companies such as C. G. Conn and King currently offer upright bell instruments, but they are generally student-line or mid-priced models. Most American professionals prefer either European-made instruments or Yamahas.

The modern euphonium looks very much like its late nineteenth-century predecessor. Advances in design have included the introduction of larger, fully tapered bores through the valves, the expansion of bell diameters, and adjustments to Blaikley's original fourth-valve compensating system. The last quarter of the twentieth century saw the development of trigger-operated devices that allowed the player to adjust the main tuning slide in order to compensate for naturally sharp pitches in the upper range. Euphoniums, like all brass instruments, are more powerful and darker in tone than older instruments, a situation that reflects the aesthetic changes of the twentieth century. The single most important development at the turn of the twenty-first century has been the growing standardization of the upright saxhorn configuration made popular by British and French designs of the late nineteenth century. The acceptance of this configuration is due in no small part to the growing worldwide interest in British-style brass bands.

Conclusion

The euphonium is one of the few instruments that was created and developed for use in the wind band. Although performers and a few composers have worked to expand the roles of the instrument, the only secure professional positions remain among the ranks of military bands. Yet even with limited career opportunities, excellent musicians continue to take up the instrument for its beautiful tone and technical agility. The fact is that the euphonium is an excellent vehicle for developing the high-level musicality that is essential for conductors, musicologists, educators, and administrators. Although there have been painfully few advances in the use of euphoniums in orchestras, jazz bands, or popular music, there has been no discernable reduction in the amount of people playing the instrument. One encouraging trend is the growth of British-style brass bands in countries outside the commonwealth. These groups have well-established repertoires and the need for euphonium and baritone horn players of considerable skill.

Notes

1. Clifford Bevan, "Euphonium," in *The New Grove Dictionary of Music and Musicians,* 2nd ed., ed. Stanley Sadie, vol. 8 (London: Macmillan, 2000), 417.
2. For a concise discussion of brass instrument innovation during the nineteenth century, see Arnold Myers, "Design, Technology and Manufacture Since 1800," in *The Cambridge Companion to Brass Instruments* (Cambridge: Cambridge University Press, 1997), 115–130.
3. For an extensive discussion of early brass instrument valve technology see Clifford Bevan, *The Tuba Family,* 2nd ed. (Winchester, England: Piccolo Press, 2000), 181–220.
4. Myers, 121.
5. Carl Moritz's firm remained in business until 1953, and was known for exceptionally well-crafted brass instruments. Herbert Heyde, "Brass Instrument Making in Berlin from the 17th to the 20th Century: A Survey," *Historic Brass Society Journal* 3 (1993): 45.
6. Bevan, *The Tuba Family,* 189.
7. Philip Bate and Edward Tarr, "Valve (i)," Grove Music Online, ed. L. Macy, http://www.grovemusic.com (accessed September 10, 2004).
8. Myers, 123.
9. Bevan, *The Tuba Family,* 185.
10. Bevan, *The Tuba Family,* 342.
11. Arnold Myers, "Brasswind Innovation and Output of Boosey & Co. in the Blaikley Era," *Historic Brass Society Journal* 14 (2002): 403.
12. Myers, "Brasswind Innovation," 403.
13. Myers, "Brasswind Innovation," 403.
14. Bevan, *The Tuba Family,* 183. Bevan names Friedrich Belcke of the Prussian Jäger Guards as the instrument's first soloist.
15. Bevan, *The Tuba Family,* 222.
16. Bevan, *The Tuba Family,* 221.
17. Bevan, *The Tuba Family,* 221.
18. Bevan, *The Tuba Family,* 226.
19. Clifford Bevan, "Sommerophone," Grove Music Online, ed. L. Macy, http://www.grovemusic.com (accessed September 10, 2004).
20. Lytton Strachley, *Queen Victoria* (New York: Harcourt, Brace and Company, 1921), 86.
21. Bevan, "Sommerophone."
22. Renatto Meucci, "The Pelitti Firm: Makers of Brass Instruments in Nineteenth-Century Milan," *Historic Brass Society Journal* 6 (1994): 305, 307.
23. Meucci, 309.
24. See Henry Howey, "The Revival of Amile Ponchielli's *Concerto per flicorno basso,* Opus 155, Cremona, 1872," *TUBA Journal,* Vol. 23, No. 4 (Summer 1996): 42–49.
25. Wally Horwood, *Adolphe Sax, 1814–1894: His Life and Legacy* (Baldock, England: Egon, 1983), 32.
26. Horwood, 32.
27. Horwood, 32.
28. Horwood, 33.
29. Horwood, 95–96.
30. Bevan, *The Tuba Family,* 248.
31. Horwood, 48.
32. Bevan, *The Tuba Family,* 253.
33. Arnold Myers, "Instruments and Instrumentation," in *The British Brass Band: A Musical and Social History* (Oxford: Oxford University Press, 2000), 169–171.
34. *The British Bandsman* (November 1888), cited in Bevan, *The Tuba Family,* 227.
35. Allen Dodworth, *Brass Band School* (New York: H. B. Dodworth, 1853), 12.
36. Bevan, *The Tuba Family,* 427.
37. Bevan, *The Tuba Family,* 227.
38. Bevan, *The Tuba Family,* 227.
39. Ann-Marie Nilsson, "Brass Instruments in Small Swedish Wind Ensembles during the Late Nineteenth Century," *Historic Brass Society Journal* 13 (2001): 179–186.
40. Kauko Karjalainen, "The Brass Band Tradition in Finland," *Historic Brass Society Journal* 9 (1997): 83–96.
41. The best source of information regarding nineteenth-century American importers is William Waterhouse, *The New Langwill Index: A Dictionary of Musical Wind-Instrument Makers and Inventors* (London: Tony Bingham, 1993).
42. Meucci, 312.
43. Luigi Magrini, "Fabrica di strumenti in ottone di Pelitti Giuseppe, dall,' I.R. Istituto di Scienze, Lettere ed Arti premiato colla medaglia d'oro per creazione di Duplex," *Gazzetta musicale di Milano* 15/36 (1857): 283–284. Cited in Meucci, 312.
44. Pelitti catalog, cited in Meucci, 317, 331n.
45. Meucci, 320.
46. Curt Sachs, *Real-Lexicon der Musikinstrumente* (Berlin: Julius Baird, 1913), 123.
47. Bevan, *The Tuba Family,* 476.
48. Edward Keith Mallet, "The Double Bell Euphonium: Design and Literature Past and Present" (PhD diss., Michigan State University, 1996), 9.
49. Bevan, *The Tuba Family,* 476–477.
50. Mallett, 15.
51. Mallett, 18.
52. For a more complete description see Mallet's thesis as well as Charles Guy, "Exploring the *New* Double-Bell Euphonium: A Review/Commentary of Edward Mallet's Lecture/Recital," *TUBA Journal,* Vol. 23, No. 4 (Summer 1996): 64.

53. Bevan, *The Tuba Family,* 450–451.

54. Myers, "Brasswind Innovation," 404–406.

55. Roster of Gilmore's Band, 1890. American Bandmasters Association Research Center, Patrick Gilmore Collection, http://www.lib.umd.edu/PAL/SCPA/ABA/Gilmore/9.html (accessed October 6, 2004).

56. Bevan, *The Tuba Family,* 461–469.

57. Arnold Myers, "Brasswind Manufacturing at Boosey & Hawkes, 1930–59," *Historic Brass Society Journal* 15 (2003): 58.

58. Marshall Lynn Scott, "The American Piston Valved Cornets and Trumpets of the Shrine to Music Museum" (DMA diss., University of Wisconsin–Madison, 1988), 21–25.

59. Richard J. Dundas, *Twentieth Century Brass Musical Instruments in the United States* (Cincinnati, Ohio: Queen City Brass Publications, 1989), 42.

60. The company now trades under the name AMATI—Denak.

61. The Fontaine-Besson company continued as a separate firm until its purchase by Cousenon sometime before 1957. The company reverted to private ownership in 1973, but the name was retired in 1994. Edward Tarr, "Besson," Grove Music Online, ed. L. Macy, http://www.grovemusic.com (accessed 25 August 2005).

62. Dundas, 15.

2. Music for Euphonium and Keyboard

Lloyd E. Bone Jr.

The state of the euphonium and keyboard is very good. The primary purpose of this chapter, as well as the entire book, is to show the world the massive amount and variety of literature available to euphonium players. I have often had fellow musicians and teachers make disparaging remarks concerning euphonium literature. Many teachers and musicians are at best familiar with maybe ten to twenty quality solos for the euphonium. This chapter identifies a major amount of quality works for the euphonium and keyboard at all levels. It is not all inclusive, as there are a large number of collections containing just about every imaginable pop, rock, country, jazz, and folk song ever published now arranged for the euphonium.

There is also a large amount of music that has recently been made available for the euphonium on the world wide web, as smaller publishing companies are increasingly becoming more global through its use. Some publishers have many solos for euphonium and band that are available to perform with piano by using a condensed score. One such publisher is FEST-MUSIK-HAUS, Band Music from Germany in Medina, Texas (830-589-2268, www.festmusik.com). They have a very large amount of great euphonium solos with band that are playable with piano.

I attempted to list as much information as possible for each composition. However, due to a wide variety of constraints, sometimes my information concerning various compositions was limited. If you are interested in a solo that is listed but has limited information, I highly suggest utilizing the web, as more and more information is becoming available from various publishers. For example, when I began my research, many publishers only had basic information available about their compositions. By the time I ended my research, numerous publishers had made sound file examples and score examples available on their websites.

In terms of duration of the works, they were approximated. In terms of cost, I used currency calculators. Keep in mind that currency rate exchanges fluctuate, so the cost of some compositions at the time this book was printed will most likely be different (hopefully only slightly) from when the research was conducted.

The final section of this chapter is a listing of French euphonium solos. This list has been graciously given to us by Mark Thompson, author of *French Music for Low Brass Instruments: An Annotated Bibliography.*

Many thanks go out to all of the publishers (large and small) who responded to requests for information about their offerings. The large response received is truly indicative of the great professionalism and care of euphonium enthusiasts worldwide. It is my hope that through this book and with the work of all of the wonderful euphonium soloists and teachers around the world, more music educators and musicians will come to appreciate just how vast and wonderful the euphonium repertoire is, especially for an instrument as "young" as ours.

Works Listed by Composer

Adam, Adolphe. *Cantique De Noel.* Rubank, Hal Leonard Corporation. $6.95. 2:00. III. d–f′. This expressive little solo is in D♭ major, is in a slow common time, is mostly scale-wise eighth note runs, has very few accidentals, is mostly in the middle register, and is in bass clef. This would be a great lyrical solo for a middle school player.

Adams, Stephen. *The Holy City.* Rubank, Hal Leonard Corporation. $6.95. 2:30. II–III. d–f′. This solo is in E♭ major, is mostly in the middle register, has a few repeated eighth notes, has a moderate amount of accidentals, has many dynamic and style changes, is rhythmically straightforward, and is in bass clef. It is a very expressive little solo that would be most appropriate for a middle school player. See Euphonium and Keyboard Collections.

Albeniz, Issac. *Tango, Op. 165, No. 2.* Ed. R. P. Block. Philharmusica Co. $11.50. This work is a great addition to the euphonium repertoire, as very few euphonium works are in a tango style.

Albian, Franco G. *Alla Siciliana, Aria and Variations for Euphonium and Symphonic Banda.* Albian Publishing (albianjca@aol.com or

1-262-538-1477). 2004. 7:00. IV–V. F#bb'. This is a fantastic theme and variations in Bb major and common time. It begins with a beautiful lyrical theme. The first variation is a straightforward eighth note variation. The second variation is an eighth note triplet variation, while the third variation is mostly scale-wise sixteenth note runs often broken up by eighth note passages. A beautiful lyrical section follows, then a cadenza that wonderfully showcases the instrument. A very pronounced and regal section follows, which quickly moves to another cadenza. The work ends with a straightforward yet very effective vivo section. This would be a great solo for a college student.

Albian, Franco G. *Fantasia Concertante for Euphonium and Symphonic Band*. Albian Publishing (albianjca@aol.com or 1-262-538-1477). 2003. 9:00. V. F#–c". This is a fantastic showpiece for the euphonium with many beautiful melodies, soaring passages, rhapsodic lines, and expressive cadenzas. The work features a very fun fast 3/8 section with many scale-wise sixteenth note runs. The 3/8 section continues where it moves into one of the most beautiful waltz melodies ever written for the euphonium. This would make for a fantastic recital piece.

Albinoni, Tomaso. *Sonata for Violin and Bass*. Trans./arr. Ronald Dishinger. Medici Music Press. 1996. $8.50. 8:00. III–IV. G–a'. Four movements: Grave/Adagio; Allegro; Adagio; Allegro. A very musical sonata that would make a wonderful change of style for a recital. The first movement has many wonderful musical moments and is mostly sixteenth notes. The second movement is marked much slower than what you would expect for allegro. It features running sixteenth notes in a very catchy melody. The third movement is highly expressive and is mostly slow sixteenths and eighths. The last movement is a triplet feature in once again a catchy melody. The figured bass is by J. S. Bach.

Albrechtsberger, Johann Georg. *Concerto*. Arr. Daniel F. Bachelder. Tuba-Euphonium Press. 2000. $10. 5:00. V. F–c". This one movement solo is in F major, is in common time, has many challenging rhythms and technical passages, has many ornaments, has a very expressive and extended cadenza toward the end, and is in bass clef. This is a very challenging solo.

Alven, Hugo. *Herbmaiden's Dance*. Arr. Sverre Olsrud. 3:50. VI. This dance was originally composed for the violin section of an orchestra. This is the ultimate euphonium showpiece, as it is blazing fast and has a massive amount of black notes!

Anthony, Yvonne. *And It's Spring*. Spin Off Music. 2002. 4:00. V. f–b'. This is a beautiful jazzy solo with many warm and rich chords. It is in the high register often and has chord changes throughout, allowing for a high level of personal expression. If you are a comfortable jazz improviser and are

looking for a fine jazz selection for a recital, this is your piece!

Anthony, Yvonne. *Heart to Heart*. Spin Off Music. 2002. 2:00. IV–V. c#–a'. This slow and jazzy solo with optional solos with chord changes would be a fantastic change of pace on any recital. The solo part is in treble clef or bass clef.

Anthony, Yvonne. *Journey to the Centre*. Spin Off Music. 2004. 6:20. VI. D–bb'. This highly technical showpiece is a tour de force! It has challenging rhythms, many challenging technical passages, is mostly in the middle register, and comes in both bass and treble clef parts. This is a highly energetic and powerful work that keeps you on the edge of your seat. If you are looking for a different challenge that you and your audience will enjoy, this is your piece!

Anthony, Yvonne. *The Kiss of Light*. Spin Off Music. 2003. 5:00. VI. BBb–f". This work is modern and classical with dance-like sections and showy sections. This is a very cool piece! If you are looking for a great new challenge, this would be a good choice. It features many enjoyable themes! The solo part is in both bass and treble clefs.

Arban, Jean-Baptiste. *Fantaisie and Variations on Carnival of Venice*. Revised by Edwin Franko Goldman. Carl Fischer. G–g'. This is arguably the most famous theme and variations ever written for any brass instrument. This is a must study for the serious euphonium player.

Arcadelt, Jacob. *Credo*. Ed. Larry Campbell. Hal Leonard Publishing Corporation. 1977. $12.95. 2:00. II. c–c'. This work is part of a collection of solos—Master Solos, Intermediate Level—and is in cut time and marked "slow legato." It features many beautiful phrases perfect for the study of many musical concepts with a middle school player. It is well marked and easy to read. Recorded by Larry Campbell.

Arcadelt, Jacob. *Gloria*. Ed. Larry Campbell. Hal Leonard Publishing Corporation. 1977. 2:00. III. d–g'. This work is part of a collection of solos—Master Solos, Intermediate Level—and is in cut time and marked at a moderate tempo. It is mostly quarter notes with a few eighth note runs. It has many lovely phrases and would be a fine solo for a very good middle school player or high school student. Recorded by Larry Campbell. Accompaniment by Bach and H. N. Gerber. Both the solo and accompaniment are easy to read.

Armitage, Dennis. *Autumn with You*. Solid Brass Music Company. $12. IV. This is a gorgeous solo!

Armitage, Dennis. *Happy Birthday*. Solid Brass Music Company. $18. IV. A fantasy based on this most famous song.

Arne, Thomas A. *Air from "Comus."* Arr. Donald C. Little. Belwin-Mills Publishing Corp. 1978. $4.50. 1:20. II. Bb–eb'. This fun little solo has become a very popular solo and ensemble contest piece for middle school students. It is in Eb major, 3/4, is marked "moderato," has simple rhythms, stays in the middle register, has few accidentals, has an appropriate amount of rest for a young player, and has a good amount of dynamic and articulation contrast.

Artiga, Lopez. *Sonata de Abril para Bombardino y Piano.* De Haske Publications BV, Holland. Order number 991435 or ISBN: 90-431-0554-6. 1999. V. This fun character piece is showy and highly technical and is in bass clef with some tenor clef.

Aubain, Jean. *Theme et Variations pour Saxhorn-basse ou Tuba ou Trombone basse et Piano.* Amphion Editions Musicales, Paris. 1975. 8:00. V. GG–c″. This is a fresh and exciting twist to theme and variations! The solo part is in bass and tenor clef.

Bach, C. P. E. *Andante.* Trans./arr. Ronald Dishinger. Medici Music Press. 2002. $5. 4:00. III–IV. G–g′. This highly expressive solo would be a great selection on any college recital. It is in d minor, a slow 2/4, mostly in the middle register, has many sixteenth note runs, a few rhythmic challenges, many wide intervals, and loads of chromatics. This work would be an excellent style study and would be great to work on in terms of varying musical interpretations.

Bach, Jan. *Concert Variations for Euphonium and Piano.* Tuba-Euphonium Press. 1992. $20. 15:00. VI. E–d♭″. This work has become an often performed euphonium work and has been required on several international euphonium solo competitions. This theme and variations is a massive challenge, but it offers euphonium players a style of composition found in very few other works in our repertoire. It features massive amounts of rhythmic play and complexity, multiphonics, glissandos, flutter valves, multiple tonguing, flutter tonguing, and tenor clef. It is a very energetic, driving, and powerful work. The solo is well marked with lots of very specific details and instructions. The solo also comes with very detailed program notes. Recorded by Matthew Murchison.

Bach, Jan. *Concerto for Euphonium and Orchestra.* Tuba-Euphonium Press. 1994. $40. 20:00. VI. BB♭–c″. This work has become a very popular concerto and is available with a piano reduction. It is very demanding and demonstrates all possible melodic and technical capabilities of the euphonium, but it is worth the hard work. It has been required on several international euphonium solo competitions. It has three movements: Legend; Burlesca; Meditation. Legend is very rhythmically complex, has many tough technical spots, requires double tonguing, and has a good amount of tenor clef. It is a very powerful movement with many wonderful moments. The Burlesca is in 6/8 and 9/8 and is very rhythmically complex and requires a high level of technical facility. Meditation is an amazing movement! It begins in a slow 7/8 and is very sonorous and singing. It ends with a long chorale section that is amazingly beautiful! This incredible rhythmic and technical tour de force ends very peacefully. Both band and orchestra versions are available and program notes come with the solo, giving the soloist some optional alternate endings.

Bach, Johann Sebastian. *Air on a G String from Third Orchestral Suite.* Trans./arr. Ronald Dishinger. Medici Music Press. 2002. $5. 2:00. III. c–e♭′. This solo is in a slow common time, is mostly in the middle to lower register, has very few technical issues, has a few rhythmic challenges, is in bass clef, has a few chromatics, and has a few endurance issues as there are no rests. This is a beautiful solo with many expressive phrases. It would be an excellent style and lyrical study and would be a great solo for a good high school student or young college player.

Bach, Johann Sebastian. *Aria No. 1 from Cantata No. 1.* Ed. Lois Alexander. Tuba-Euphonium Press. 2002. $8. 3:00. IV–V. c–a♭′. This very regal solo is in a moderate common time, is in B♭ major, has mostly scale-wise sixteenth note and eighth note runs, and is in bass clef and treble clef. The challenge of this solo is that it often ascends into the high register and has a large amount of sixteenth note runs and some wide intervals. This solo is extremely entertaining to play. The technical issues are a worthy challenge. This would be a great recital selection.

Bach, Johann Sebastian. *Arioso, from Cantata 156.* Arr. Frank H. Siekmann. Brelmat Music. 2002. $6. 2:30. IV. G–b♭′. This work features a beautiful melody from one of Bach's most famous vocal works. It is in a very slow common time, is in F major, has a few accidentals, has many sixteenth note passages (most are scale-wise), has some wide intervals, is mostly in the middle register, is very easy to read, and is in bass clef. This is a beautiful solo with several gorgeous soaring passages and would make for a great lyrical selection for a recital.

Bach, Johann Sebastian. *Arioso from Cantata No. 156.* Carl Fischer. 3:00. IV. c–a♭′. This beautiful, lyrical aria has loads of interpretative freedoms. It is easily accessible to good high school students and college players. The solo part is in both bass and treble clefs.

Bach, Johann Sebastian. *Badinerie, from Third Orchestral Suite.* Trans./arr. Ronald Dishinger. Medici Music Press. 2002. $5. 2:00. IV. A–f′. This popular Bach tune is loads of fun to play. It is in 2/4 with a moderate tempo, key of d minor, is mostly in the middle to lower register, is mostly scale-wise sixteenth note runs with a few wide intervals, and has sporadic chromatics. It would be very appropriate for a very good high school student or young college player.

Bach, Johann Sebastian. *Bourree from Third Cello Suite.* Trans./arr. Ronald Dishinger. Medici Music Press. 1994. $5. 2:30. III–IV. A–b♭′. This is a very entertaining and fun work. It is in a quick common time, F and E♭ major, has many eighth note runs, is mostly in the middle to high register, has some chromatics, a good amount of wide intervals, basic rhythms, and is in bass clef. The challenges of this solo are endurance, as it is two pages long with lots of notes and not one single rest, and range, as it is often in the high register. This is a great solo and is worth the challenges. It would be a great solo for any type of college recital.

Bach, Johann Sebastian. *Bourree and Gigue from the Third Orchestral Suite.* Trans./arr. Ronald Dishinger. Medici Music Press. 1996. $5. 6:00. III–IV. B♭–g′. This is a very fun work that is in B♭ major. The bouree is in a lively cut time and features scale-wise runs, a few wide intervals, sporadic use of accidentals, and is mostly in the middle register. The gigue is in a fast 6/8 and poses some technical and rhythmic challenges while also often ascending into the high register often. Most of the runs are scale-wise with occasional accidentals. I highly recommend this work for a junior or senior recital as it is a great style study and loads of fun to play.

Bach, Johann Sebastian. *Canzona in D.* Trans./arr. Ronald Dishinger. Medici Music Press. 1996. $5. 4:00. III. A–a′. This expressive and lively solo has two sections: the first in a moderate common time and the second in a little quicker 3/4. The first section is lyrical in nature and features some beautiful chromatic play that is typical of Bach's harpsichord works. The second section is very lively and syncopated and has even more chromatic play. Both sections are mostly in the middle register and have few rhythmic challenges and very few difficult technical runs. The challenge is in some of the wide intervals and a few passages in the high register. This would be an excellent baroque style study and an excellent solo for a good high school student or young college student.

Bach, Johann Sebastian. *For He That Is Mighty.* Arr. Kendor Figert. Music, Inc. $6. III. This solo is based on one of Bach's most famous works. This is a great baroque study and wonderful solo for a good middle school student or high school player.

Bach, Johann Sebastian. *Fugue No. 10 from 12 Preludes and Fugues.* Trans./arr. Ronald Dishinger. Medici Music Press. 1996. $5. 5:00. III. F–f′. This fugue would be an excellent solo for a good high school student. It is in a fast common time and is mostly scale-wise eighth note runs. It remains in the middle to lower register, is in B♭ major, has very few rhythmic or technical challenges, and has several places for the soloist to rest. The only challenge of this work is the high amount of chromatics on the second page. This would be a great style study.

Bach, Johann Sebastian. *Gavotte in G Minor.* Trans./arr. Ronald Dishinger. Medici Music Press. 1996. $4.50. 3:30. III. G–g′. This work features two sections: allegro and trio. The allegro is in a moderate common time and g minor, and is mostly eighth note runs that are sometimes scale-wise. It is primarily in the middle to lower register, has a moderate use of wide intervals, and is rhythmically straightforward with some chromatic play. The trio features a lovely musette and moves into G major. It has few challenges. This is a great work that would be a wonderful baroque style study and solo for a good high school player. Highly recommend.

Bach, Johann Sebastian. *Jesu, Joy of Man's Desiring.* Arr. Kendor Conley. Music, Inc. $6. 3:30. III. This is a fine arrangement of one of Bach's most popular melodies that would be an effective solo for a good middle school or high school player.

Bach, Johann Sebastian. *Jesu, Joy of Man's Desiring from Cantata No. 147.* Trans./arr. Ronald Dishinger. Medici Music Press. 1996. $4.50. II. e♭–d♭′. This solo is in a slow 9/8, is in E♭ major, is rhythmically very simple, is in the middle to lower register, and is in bass clef. The solo never has the running eighth note theme (which is in the piano part), but has the slower dotted half note/dotted quarter note theme. This solo is most appropriate for a middle school player.

Bach, Johann Sebastian. *Menuet in G, from Anna Magdalena Bach Notebook.* Trans./arr. Ronald Dishinger. Medici Music Press. 1982. $4.50. 1:30. II. C–e♭′. This Bach melody has become a classical favorite the world over. This is the perfect solo for a middle school student performing at solo and ensemble contest for the first time.

Bach, Johann Sebastian. *Musette from Anna Magdalena Bach Notebook.* Trans./arr. Ronald Dishinger. Medici Music Press. 1986. $5. 2:20. II. e–f′. This work has several very fun and catchy tunes. It is in a good key, moderately fast, mostly eighth notes, and stays in the upper middle to high register. It has a light, staccato feel and has several repeated sections at contrasting dynamic levels. It would be a good solo for a mature middle school or young high school player.

Bach, Johann Sebastian. *Little Prelude.* Trans./arr. Ronald Dishinger. Medici Music Press. 1995. $4.50. 1:20. II–III. A–g′. This very fun little solo is in a moderate common time, is in E♭ major, is mostly scale-wise eighth note runs, has a few chromatics and wider intervals, is mostly in the middle and lower registers, is rhythmically simple, and is in bass clef. This solo would be most appropriate for a high school student.

Bach, Johann Sebastian. *Planets, Starts and Airs of Space for Euphonium and Piano.* Arr. Michael A. Fischer. Tuba-Euphonium Press. 2001. $8. 2:00. II. c–e♭′. The melody for this solo was written by Christoph Peter (1655) and harmonized by J. S. Bach. This solo is in a moderately slow 3/4, is in c minor, is mostly quarter and eighth notes with a few sixteenths, is mostly in the middle register, and is in bass and treble clef. The solo includes notes about the work and the composer. This solo would be a great second solo for a middle school student.

Bach, Johann Sebastian. *Polonaise from Third Orchestral Suite*. Trans./arr. Ronald Dishinger. Medici Music Press. 2002. $5. 3:00. III–IV. F–g'. This is a nice arrangement of a very showy and florid polonaise. It is a slow tempo and begins with a jolly theme before moving into a section with many sixteenth and 32nd note runs. It is in F major, making the runs idiomatic for the euphonium. This would make for a nice smooth and flowing small technical piece for a recital.

Bach, Johann Sebastian. *Sinfonia from Cantata No. 156*. Trans./arr. Ronald Dishinger. Medici Music Press. 2002. $5. 1:30. II–III. B♭–e♭'. This nice arrangement has many musical interpretive possibilities. It is in common time, largo, and is in a fantastic register to allow for a rich singing quality. It is primarily slow sixteenth note patterns.

Bach, Johann Sebastian. *Sleepers Awake, Wachet auf, ruft uns Stimme, from the Cantata, BMV 140*. Trans./arr. Ronald Dishinger. Medici Music Press. 1996. $5. 2:00. II–III. e♭–g'. This is a nice arrangement of this popular choral tune by J. S. Bach. It would be most appropriate for a good middle school or high school player.

Bach, Johann Sebastian. *Sonata No. 1 in B Minor, BWV1014 from Six Sonatas for Violin and Piano*. Trans./arr. Ronald Dishinger. Medici Music Press. 1998. $12. 10:00. III–IV. F–g'. Four movements: Adagio; Allegro; Andante; Allegro. This is a fantastic sonata. The first movement is very lyrical and expressive, featuring many beautiful moments. The second movement is very lively and features a wonderful main theme. The third movement is mostly expressive slow sixteenth note runs. The fourth movement is a very energetic and driving movement with many conservative yet effective sixteenth note runs. An excellent sonata that remains mostly in the middle register.

Bach, Johann Sebastian. *Sonata No. 2 in A Major, BWV 1015 from Six Sonatas for Violin and Piano*. Trans./arr. Ronald Dishinger. Medici Music Press. 1998. $12. 8:00. IV. G–b♭'. Four movements: Andante; Allegro Assai; Andante un poco; Presto. The first movement is very slow and expressive. There are countless beautiful passages and places to build tension due to the slow harmonic movement. It is mostly slurred sixteenth note runs with many embellishments. The second movement is very lively and features several great melodies. It features a section of quick runs gradually building upward, then a slower and smoother effect, ending on many beautiful quick descending runs. This movement has very few accidentals and is in the higher register often,

a technique that works well for the euphonium. The third movement is similar to the first in that it is slow and highly expressive. It remains in the lower to middle registers. The last movement is very quick and lively. It is an absolute joy to play as it features many wonderful melodies and phrases. This is a fantastic sonata that is worth taking a look at.

Bach, Johann Sebastian. *Sonata No. 3 from Six Sonatas for Violin*. Trans./arr. Ronald Dishinger. Medici Music Press. 1998. $12. 12:00. III–IV. F–f'. Four movements: Adagio; Allegro; Adagio ma non tanto; Allegro. This is a rich sounding arrangement as it rarely leaves the lower to middle registers. The first movement is very slow and expressive. There are countless beautiful passages and places to build tension due to the slow harmonic movement. It is mostly slurred 32nd note runs with many embellishments. Simply put, this is a florid and extremely beautiful movement. The second movement is very quick, in cut time and very light and playful. It has many extended eighth note runs that are idiomatic for the euphonium. It is a very fun movement to play. The third movement is similar to the first in that it is slow and highly expressive. Like the previous movements, it remains in the lower to middle registers. The last movement is dance-like in character and has many extended yet manageable sixteenth note runs. This is another fantastic sonata that would be a great recital selection.

Bach, Wilhelm Friedmann. *Grave*. Trans./arr. Ronald Dishinger. Medici Music Press. 1995. $5. 1:20. III–IV. A–b♭'. This gorgeous solo is in a slow common time, is in c minor, and is in bass clef. The solo has some rhythmic challenges, has a moderate use of chromatics, and has a fair amount of sixteenth note passages, many of which are not scale-wise. The solo ascends into the high range often, but the major challenge is endurance as it is two pages long without any rests. This is a highly expressive solo and would be most appropriate for college players and would be a most excellent recital selection.

Bachelder, D. F. *Dialogue in Abstract*. Tuba-Euphonium Press. 1998. $8. 4:30. IV–V. BB♭–d″. If you are looking for something different to perform on a recital, this is it. This work has many special effects including multiphonics, chance elements, playing into the piano strings, muted sections, and whistling airy sounds. It has a few technical and rhythmic challenges, but the major challenge comes in the one passage where it ascends very high. The solo part is in bass clef. This is a very powerful and mysterious piece and would make for a fantastic change of pace on a recital!

Balakirev, Mily. *Sad Little Song*. Trans. L. Alexander. Cimarron Music and Publications. 1998. 1:30. II–III. E–c'. This small, simple song packs a big musical message, especially when paired with Vladislav Blazhevich's *Humoresque*. It remains in the middle to lower register, creating a very rich sound throughout. It is mostly eighth notes and is very straightforward rhythmically. It would be a great solo for a middle or high school student.

Balissat, Jean. *Capriccio*. BIM Editions. 2005. 14:30. V. This is a very entertaining new work that wonderfully showcases many technical and lyrical qualities of the euphonium. Chamber orchestra accompaniment is also available.

Ball, Michael. *Euphonium Concerto*. $30. V. This concerto was composed by one of Britain's top composers and was first performed by David Childs. The work has four movements. The first is marked "If Awakening," the second is an aggressive allegro, the third is very lyrical, and the finale is a scherzo. A brass band version is available. It is available at www.euphonium.net.

Barat, J. Edouard. *Andante et Allegro*. Southern Music Company. $5.40. 4:00. III–IV. F–bb'. This work is a classic must play in the repertoire. It has two major sections, lent and allegro. It begins with a flowing triplet motive that is manipulated in many forms. There is a lovely faster section that is very open and reflective in nature before returning to the opening triplet motive. The second section is very lively and heroic in nature with many triplet passages contrasted by long eighth note runs. It is ideal for a fine high school player or young college student.

Barat, J. Edouard. *Introduction and Dance*. Arr. Glen Smith. Southern Music Company. $6. IV. This is a very popular solo that is a great selection for a young college student. It is very fun to play and is a great study for numerous musical issues.

Baratto, Paolo. *Euphonissimo for Euphonium and Klavier*. Editions BIM, Switzerland (www.editions-bim.com). 1996. $10. 4:00. V. Bb–bb'. This beautiful little character piece in treble clef would be a good challenge for college players. It is a very fun, smaller technical recital piece.

Baratto, Paolo. *Romanze in F*. Editions BIM, Switzerland (www.editions-bim.com). 1996. $10. 4:00. IV–V. e–g'. This beautiful lyrical piece in treble clef would be a good challenge for a high school player or a good small recital piece.

Barroll, Edward C. *Song of the Sun*. Rubank, Hal Leonard Corporation. $6.95. 1:00. I–II. A–c'. This little ballad is in Bb major, is a moderate tempo mostly in the lower to middle register, is rhythmically simple, has a few accidentals, and is in bass clef. It would be a good first solo. See Euphonium and Keyboard Collections.

Beal, David. *Sonata for Euphonium and Piano*. Headline Music Productions. 1997. 7:00. V. Bb–c'. This work has three movements: Allegro Moderato; Andante Moderato; Allegro Furioso. The solo part is in treble clef.

Bearcroft, Norman. *The Better World*. Arr. D. B. M. Salvation Army. 1978. 5:00. V–VI. BBb–c". This beautiful theme and variations type piece in treble clef is a challenge, especially in the high register, but is definitely worth it. It consists of "variations" on four Salvation Army songs: "There is a Better World," "There's a Crown Laid Up in Glory," "I Shall See Him Face to Face," and "The Homeward Trail." Contact Adam Frey for ordering details. A brass band version is available. Recorded by Steven Mead, Euphony.

Beethoven, Ludwig van. *Beloved from Afar, Op. 98, No. 6*. Trans./arr. Ronald Dishinger. Medici Music Press. 1989. $3.40. 2:00. II–III. Bb–f'. This beautiful and very expressive little song has two sections: andante con moto and cantabile-allegro molto e con brio. It is in 4/4 and 3/4 time, is in Eb major, is mostly quarter notes with a few eighth notes and runs, has a few chromatic passages, is in bass clef, and is mostly in the middle to lower register. It would be an excellent solo for a good middle school student or young high school player.

Beethoven, Ludwig van. *May Song, Op. 52, No. 4*. Trans./arr. Ronald Dishinger. Medici Music Press. 1990. $4.50. 2:30. II. eb–eb'. This very lively little solo features an energetic melody. It would be a great second solo for a good middle school student or young high school student for solo and ensemble contest. It remains in the middle register, is in Eb major, is a moderate tempo, has mostly eighth note scale runs, and has no accidentals.

Beethoven, Ludwig van. *Romanze in F, Opus 50*. Trans./arr. Ronald Dishinger. Medici Music Press. 2002. $8. 5:00. IV. F–a'. This work is marked "adagio cantabile" and features many sixteenth and 32nd note runs in often very chromatic passages. It is challenging yet is extremely expressive. The overall range is conservative, allowing for a consistent rich tone. There are limitless musical possibilities with the work. It would be a wonderful lyrical selection for a change of pace on any recital. Even though it has many moving notes, it is well printed and easy to read.

Beethoven, Ludwig van. *Romanze in G, Opus 40*. Trans./arr. Ronald Dishinger. Medici Music Press. 2001. $8. 4:00. IV. Bb–bb'. This is an amazingly expressive work loaded with chromaticism and slow harmonic movement, creating many areas of beautiful tension and release. It is slow but has many sixteenth note runs, triplet combinations, and 32nd note runs. It is often in the high register. This work has limitless interpretations due to the high amount of phrase, articulation, and dynamic markings.

Beethoven, Ludwig van. *Rondo from Violin Sonata in Eb Major Op. 12, No. 3*. Arr. Robert Madeson. Tuba-Euphonium Press. 1994. $12. 5:00. IV–V. G–bb'. For $12 this is a great buy for a teacher, as it comes with the euphonium part in bass, treble, and tenor clef as well as a tuba version! The solo is in an allegro 2/4, is in Eb major, has many sixteenth note runs that are mostly not scale-wise, has a large amount of chromatics, is rhythmically straightforward, and has many wide intervals. This is a very fun solo that is highly energetic and has many catchy melodies and passages. It would make for a fantastic recital selection.

Beethoven, Ludwig van. *Scherzo from Sonata Opus 30, No. 2.* trans/arr. Ronald Dishinger. Medici Music Press. 1995. $6.50. 2:50. III. F–f'. This wonderful scherzo is marked "allegro" and is very fun to play. It would be a fantastic solo for a very good middle school student or high school player. It remains in the middle register and features mostly eighth note runs.

Beethoven, Ludwig van. *Sonata for Horn and Piano.* Trans./arr. Ronald Dishinger. Medici Music Press. 1996. $14. 7:30. IV. F–f'. Three movements: Allegro Moderato; Poco Adagio/Quasi Andante; Rondo/Allegro Moderato. This is a great arrangement of a fantastic sonata. The overall range allows for a beautiful singing quality throughout. The first movement features a wonderful lively and playful theme. It consists mostly of eighth note runs with a few sixteenths. The second movement is in a minor key and is very passionate. The third movement is very lively and playful, featuring many triplet patterns and running eighth note passages. This is a very playable sonata worthy of a good look for a recital.

Beethoven, Ludwig van. *Sonata, Op. 17 for Euphonium and Piano.* Arr. D. F. Bachelder. Tuba-Euphonium Press. 1997. $15. 11:00. V. Eb–bb'. If you have natural high chops, or if you love to play high, or if you are looking for a good workout, then this is your solo! It lives in the high register! It has three movements: Allegro moderato; Poco adagio, Quasi andante; Rondo. The first movement has a very powerful opening, quickly moving to a beautiful dolce section. This movement is in Eb major, is rhythmically straightforward, has many wide intervals, has many driving and bold passages, and ends very powerfully. The second movement is short, delicate, and very expressive. It requires a high level of finesse. The final movement is loads of fun to play! It is in a moderately fast cut time, is in Eb major, has many wide, dramatic intervals, is rhythmically straightforward, and is very powerful. It you are looking for a fun and powerful solo to play, this is it. This solo would be an excellent recital selection.

Belden, George R. *Daystar.* Ed. Donald C. Little. Belwin-Mills Publishing Corp. 1978. $1.50. 2:00. II. A–f'. This is a fantastic solo for a good middle school student. It is in F major, 4/4, and a moderate allegro. It has simple rhythms and is mostly in the middle to lower register with loads of dynamic and articulation contrast, making for some very neat musical effects for a piece of this grade level. The challenge lies in all of the accidentals and endurance since there are very few breaks. This solo is very fun to play and it's entertaining as well.

Bell, A. *Sonatine in Four Movements.* Trans./arr. Ronald Dishinger. Medici Music Press. 1995. $6. 4:30. II–III. F–g'. Three movements: Allegro Moderato; Adagio; Allegro. First movement features many flowing eighth notes and beautiful smooth passages. Second movement is very expressive and lyrical, open for many musical interpretations. Third movement features a very fun and lively tune.

Bellstedt, Herman. *Napoli.* Collated by Frank Simon. Southern Music Company. 1962. $7.95. 5:00. V. F–bb'. This standard theme and variations first written for trumpet is worth all of its challenges. It is a typical theme and variations beginning with a spirited introduction and cadenza before moving to one of the most lively and most well-known themes in all of the solo brass repertoire. The work features a varied combination of sixteenths, 32nds, and triplet runs. This work is a must study for the serious player. Recorded by Steven Mead, Euphony. Recorded by Brian Bowman, American Variations.

Bigelow. *Winter Carousel.* Kendor Music, Inc. $6. I.

Bitsch, Marcel. *Intermezzo pour Tuba en Ut ou Saxhorn basse et Piano.* Alphonse Leduc, Paris. $16.70. 5:00. IV. This work has three movements: Slow; Andante; Allegro. This is a really nice French work in both bass and treble clefs.

Bizet, Georges. *Flower Song.* Arr. Darrol Barry. Kirklees Music. 2:30. III. c–g'. This is one of the most beautiful songs from Bizet's *Carmen.* It is wonderfully arranged, as it remains in the middle register, allowing for a full sonorous tone quality throughout. It has all of the musical nuances of the original thanks to very specific dynamic, tempo, style, and articulation markings. This is a wonderful selection for a recital or for a high school student to study many elements of musicianship. A brass band version is available. Recorded by Steven Mead.

Bizet, Georges. *Flower Song from "Carmen."* Arr. Snell. Rosehill Music Publishing, Rakeway Music, Hollington House, Hollington, Staffs. 1987. 3:30. III–IV. e–bb'.

Bizet, Georges. *Toreador's Song from "Carmen."* Arr. G. E. Holmes. Rubank, Chicago. 2:30. III–IV. Bb–f'. This is a great way to introduce students to quality literature while giving them a solo to work on. The solo part is in bass and treble clefs.

Blazhevich, Vladislav. *Humoresque.* Trans. Louis Alexander. Cimarron Music and Publications. 1998. $10. 3:30. III–IV. G–c''. This is a fantastically fun work! It opens with one of the most cheerful and giddy melodies in the euphonium repertoire. It is marked "moderato" and is mostly sixteenth and eighth note runs that lie well on the euphonium. It is primarily in the middle register except for the middle appassionato section, where it is in the higher tessitura with some tricky rhythms and intervals. The work ends with the cheerful melody at the beginning and a great little tag. This is a fantastic work for a good high school player or a young college student.

Boccalari, Eduardo. *Fantasia di Concerto-Sounds of the Riviera.* Carl Fischer. 1904. 11:30. VI. There is a version with band as well. See the following full description.

Boccalari, Eduardo. *Fantasia di Concerto-Sounds of the Riviera.* Tuba-Euphonium Press. $10. 11:30. VI. D–c″. This is one of the standard works for the euphonium and is one of the best works EVER written for the euphonium. It features some of the most beautiful melodies one can ever hope to play. It is highly technical and showcases the euphonium in about every possible technical medium. It has several cadenza sections, allowing for a high level of technical display and musicianship. The more difficult and elaborate cadenzas are optional as there is an easier option for each one. The highlight of the work is the fantastic bolero section, which is rarely found elsewhere in euphonium literature. The work concludes with one of the greatest technical endings in all of the repertoire. This is a must study for the serious euphonium player and teacher. This solo was recorded by Steven Mead and John Mueller.

Boccherini, Luigi. *Minuet.* Trans./arr. Ronald Dishinger. Medici Music Press. 1996. $4.50. 3:00. III. F–eb′. This work has two sections: a moderate 3/4 and a trio. The 3/4 is in C major. Both sections feature some lively syncopated sections, scale-wise eighth and sixteenth note runs, and few chromatics. They are mostly in the middle to lower register, are rhythmically straightforward, and are very energetic. The trio is in F major. This is a very fun work and would be excellent for a good high school player or young college student.

Boguslaw, Robert. *Fantasy for Euphonium and Piano.* TUBA Press. 1996. $10. 6:30. IV–V. Eb–b′. This solo has two main sections. The first section is slow, lyrical, and soaring. It soon moves to a very long building section that has tons of tension. It builds to a huge climax and segues into the second section, a vivace 3/8. The vivace is highly energetic and features some rhapsodic phrases. It also has a long section where it slow builds. It climaxes in a very powerful section with intense rips. The work ends with a mysterious muted section! This solo spans a wide range, has many chromatics, has a few rhythmic challenges, and is in bass clef. This solo is fun to play and would be an excellent recital selection as it would make for a great change of pace and style.

Borodin, Alexander. *Polovestian Dances.* Arr. Forrest Buchtel. Neil A. Kjos Music Company. 1974. $2. 2:00. II. c–eb′. This famous melody is set well for a young player. It is in Eb major, is in a moderate common time, is rhythmically simple, has some accidentals, is in the middle register, and is in bass

clef. This would be a good first or second solo for a middle school player.

Bosanko, Ivor. *Heart in Heart (Glorious Liberation).* 8:30. VI. GG–c″. This is a fantastic fantasia-like work. It is a great showy piece for a recital. The solo part is in treble clef. Contact Adam Frey for ordering information. Recorded by Steven Mead.

Bourgeois, Derek. *Euphonium Concerto, Op. 120.* Standard Diploma. 1990. $28.94. VI. This work has three movements: Allegro Vivace; Lento con Moto; Allegro molto Vivace. It features extreme tessitura and remains high for long periods of time. This is one of the most challenging works in the entire repertoire. It is a wonderful concerto with countless beautiful moments and amazing technical passages. It is not for the faint of heart! The solo is in treble clef. An orchestra version is available.

Bourgeois, Derek. *Euphoria, Op. 75.* Vanderbeek & Imrie Ltd. 1983. $30. 8:00. V–VI. Bb–c″. This is a very challenging but popular work by a fantastic composer. The solo part is in treble clef. It is an excellent showpiece for the euphonium as it is mostly fast sixteenth note runs. It opens with a gorgeous adagio section and quickly moves to a very rhapsodic slightly faster section. Next is a very fast section with many sixteenth note runs, followed by a very pronounced section that moves into a mixed meter piano section. The very fast sixteenth note runs soon return and they build to one of the most impressive endings in the entire repertoire. The work overall features a high amount of chromatics, is mostly in the middle range, and is mostly rhythmically straightforward. If you are looking for a new, fun, and fantastic challenge, this is it! There are also versions for concert band, brass band, and orchestra. Recorded by Steven Mead and Matthew Murchison.

Boutry, Roger. *Tubaroque pour Tuba Ut ou Saxhorn basse sib ou tromb base et Piano.* Alphonse Leduc, Paris. $14.90. IV–V.

Boutry, Roger. *Tubacchanale pour Tuba en Ut ou Saxhorn basse et Piano.* Alphonse Leduc, Paris. 1958. $18.80. 8:00. V. This is a fantastic French solo with many styles, expressive writing, and many wonderful technical moments. The solo part is in bass clef.

Bowen, Brian. *Euphonium Music.* Rosehill Music Publishing. 1984. $29.95. 15:45. V. E–c″. This fantastic work was first performed by Trevor Groom and has become a standard in the euphonium repertoire. It is in three movements and is very virtuosic. It is a very challenging work that has countless wonderful technical and lyrical moments. The second movement is absolutely gorgeous. This has become a very popular work and is a worthy challenge. The solo part is in both bass and treble clefs. There are versions for band and brass band. Recorded by the Childs

Brothers (Robert Childs), Steven Mead, and Robin Taylor.

Bowen, Gerard. *Theme and Variations.* United States Navy Band Library or Brian Bowman. A great work that is Out of Print.

Bradbury, William. *Two Hymn Settings for Euphonium.* Arr. Lois Alexander. Tuba-Euphonium Press. 2002. $8. IV–V. F–b♭′. This work features two classic hymns, "The Solid Rock" and "Trust in Jesus." "The Solid Rock" is set in a theme and variations and features a maestoso statement of the hymn, a double tongue variation, a lyrical variation, and a double and triple tongue ending. It has many technical challenges, ascends into the high register, and is in the keys of F and A♭ major. "Trust in Jesus" is not nearly as technically demanding. After stating the hymn it has a slow and deliberate section with scalewise sixteenth notes. This is a fun arrangement and is a worthy challenge for someone looking for something totally different for a recital. Both hymns are in both bass and treble clefs.

Brahms, Johannes. *Four Serious Songs, Op. 121.* Ed. Donald Little. Kagarice Brass Editions. 2005. $25. III. G–f′. This is a beautiful edition even before you play it! The printing is superb. It contains wonderful program notes and very easy to follow piano cues throughout. The first song features several beautiful melodies and is very sonorous, as it is mostly in the middle to lower register. It is marked "andante" and has an allegro middle section. The second song is also marked "andante" and features some wonderful use of chromatics and syncopation in places. The third song is marked "grave," is very serious in nature, and has a gorgeous ending. The last song has a wide range of emotions as it is quicker and animated in sections, then very serious and expressive. This is a fantastic edition of some wonderful Brahms songs. The essence of Brahms's vocal writing and use of harmonies is found throughout. This would be a great study of countless musical aspects for a good high school student or young college player.

Brahms, Johannes. *Gypsy Songs.* Arr. Michael A. Fischer. Tuba-Euphonium Press. 2001. $12. III–IV. d–a♭′. This is a fantastic collection of songs. There are eight songs in a wide variety of keys and styles and in bass clef. All of the songs are in 2/4 time, are rhythmically straightforward, and ascend into the high register. The piano part was edited by Dr. John Cozza and the solo part included very good program notes about the composer and the work. I highly recommend this work as it would be an excellent recital selection or would work well for a good high school student.

Brahms, Johannes. *On the Lake, Op. 59.* Trans./arr. Ronald Dishinger. Medici Music Press. 1989. $4.50. 1:45. II. d–f′. This would be a good second or third solo for a middle school player.

It is in a good register and key and is primarily quarter notes. It is a pretty little tune with some nice chromatic and dynamic contrasts. It is a moderately fast tempo and has a decent amount of accidentals.

Brahmstedt, N. K. *Stupendo.* Rubank, Hal Leonard Corporation. $6.95. 3:00. III–IV. A–a♭′. This fantastic concert polka is in B♭ and E♭ major, has some rhythmic challenges, is mostly in the middle register, has a moderate amount of scalewise sixteenth note runs, is well marked with specific style changes, dynamics, articulations, and phrasings, and is in bass clef. It features a fun opening cadenza, which moves to a beautiful andante section. The polka section is where the sixteenth note runs are introduced. This is a fantastically fun section. The work ends with a rousing trio. This is a fantastic solo for a good high school player. I highly recommend this solo. See Euphonium and Keyboard Collections.

Brooks, E. *The Message.* Arr. Forrest L. Buchtel. Neil A. Kjos Music Company. 1980. $2. 3:00. III–IV. A♭–f′. This fun solo is a great showpiece. After the slow, beautiful, lyrical opening, the rest of the work is in a quick 2/4. The solo is in A♭ and E♭ major, has many scale-wise sixteenth note runs, is rhythmically simple, has some wide intervals, is mostly in the middle to lower registers, and is in bass clef. This would be a great technical solo for a good high school player.

Brouquireres, Jean. *Au Temps De La Cour pour basse sib ou tuba ut et piano.* Editions Robert Martin, Macon Cedex, France. 1982. 1:30. II. G–c. This simple French song is best for a middle school student. The solo part is in bass clef.

Brubaker, Jerry. *Rhapsody for Euphonium.* Tuba-Euphonium Press. 1994. $12. 7:00. V–VI. GG♭–c″. This fantastic solo was written for Roger Behrend, principal euphonium of the United States Navy Band. It is a very challenging solo, but it is worth all of the effort. It begins with some very powerful statements in a freely section. It soon moves to a very lyrical section with gorgeous soaring lines. The allegro section features a very lively, bouncing theme that is repeated at various pitch levels. Toward the end the work features a long and highly technical cadenza that is an awesome showcase for the euphonium. This work is in bass clef and has many challenging rhythms, intervals, and technical passages, requires some multiple tonguing, and is in the high range often. This is very entertaining and impressive work!

Bruniau, Auguste. *Sur La Montagne.* Presser Music, Inc. $15.25.

Buchtel, Forrest. *Argonaut Waltz.* Neil A. Kjos Music Company. 1973. $1.75. 1:45. I. e♭–d′. This lovely little solo is in a slow waltz tempo, is in F and B♭ major, is rhythmically simple, has very few accidentals, has piano cues, and is in bass clef. This would be a good first solo for a middle school player.

Buchtel, Forrest. *At the Ball*. Neil A. Kjos Music Company. 1987. $1.75. 1:15. I–II. A–c′. This fun and bouncy little solo is in Bb and Eb major, is in a common time gavotte tempo, has a smooth middle section, has a few accidentals, is rhythmically simple, and is in bass clef. This would be a great first solo for a middle school player.

Buchtel, Forrest. *Beau Brummel*. Neil A. Kjos Music Company. 1964. $1.75. 2:30. I–II. Bb–bb. This solo begins in a slow common time and moves to a faster cut time. It is in Bb and Eb major, has some eighth note patterns on repeated pitches, has a few accidentals, has piano cues, is in the lower register, and is in bass clef. This would be a good first solo for a middle school player. There is a band version available.

Buchtel, Forrest. *Bolero*. Neil A. Kjos Music Company. 1972. $2.50. 3:00. III–IV. B–f′. This is a very good solo. It is in a bolero tempo and in 3/4, is in Ab and F major, has many scale-wise sixteenth note runs, has a large amount of accidentals, has piano cues, and is in bass clef. This is a fantastic solo for a good high school player and is loads of fun, especially considering it is in a style that very few solos of this grade level cover.

Buchtel, Forrest. *Bolero*. Neil A. Kjos Music Company. 1944. $5. 2:30. III. B–f′. This solo is a very fine high solo for a high school player for honor band auditions or for a solo and ensemble festival. It is marked "tempo de bolero," is primarily in the middle register with many scale-wise sixteenth note passages, is in Ab major and F major, and has a fair amount of accidentals. The challenge lies in some of the runs and the accidentals. This is a fun solo as it is full of lots of style and flair. There is also a band version.

Buchtel, Forrest. *Caissons Go Rolling Along*. Neil A. Kjos Music Company. 1973. $1.75. 1:30. I. Bb–bb. This solo based off of a popular tune is in a moderate cut time, is mostly quarter and half notes, is in bass clef, and has no accidentals. It has a few optional pitches (c) as well as piano cues. This would be a very good first solo.

Buchtel, Forrest. *Cielito Lindo*. Neil A. Kjos Music Company. 1973. $1.75. 1:30. I. c–d′. This solo is in a moderate waltz 3/4, Bb major, is mostly quarter notes, is in bass clef, and has some optional pitches (Eb′ and Bb). This would be a good first solo.

Buchtel, Forrest. *Drum Major March*. Neil A. Kjos Music Company. 1964. $1.75. 1:30. I. c–bb. This solo is in a fast common time, is mostly quarter notes, is in Bb and Eb major, and is in bass clef. This is a good first solo.

Buchtel, Forrest. *Fandango*. Neil A. Kjos Music Company. 1985. $1.75. 1:30. I–II. A–bb. This solo is in a fast 3/4, is in f minor, is mostly quarter notes, is in bass clef, and is rhythmically simple. This would be a great first solo as it has a different sound from most solos at this level.

Buchtel, Forrest. *Gladiator*. Neil A. Kjos Music Company. 1973. $1.75. 1:30. I. Bb–bb. This bass clef solo is in Bb and Eb major, is rhythmically simple, has moderato and allegretto sections, has very few accidentals, and has piano cues. This would be a good first solo.

Buchtel, Forrest. *Gobbly Gook*. Neil A. Kjos Music Company. 1978. $1.50. 2:15. III. d–eb′. This fun solo is in a moderate cut time, is in Bb and Eb major, is rhythmically straightforward, is in bass clef, and has many repeating patterns such as triplets that are marked "glissando" for trombone or are played straight on baritone. This would be a very fun solo for a good middle school student.

Buchtel, Forrest. *Happy Bugler*. Neil A. Kjos Music Company. 1975. $1.75. 1:30. I–II. Bb–bb. This fun little solo is in bass clef, is in Eb and Ab major, is in a march tempo common time, and has no accidentals. This would be a good first solo.

Buchtel, Forrest. *Harlequin*. Neil A. Kjos Music Company. 1985. $1.75. 1:30. I–II. Ab–c′. This solo is in Ab and Eb major, begins in a slow common time and moves to an allegro cut time, has simple rhythms, has piano cues, and is in bass clef. This would be a good second or third solo for a middle school player.

Buchtel, Forrest. *Hippity Hop*. Neil A. Kjos Music Company. 1978. $2. 2:00. II–III. c–c′. This fun solo is in a moderate cut time, is in Bb and F major, has some fun triplet glissando runs, has some simple syncopation, and is in bass clef. This would be a very fun second or third solo for a middle school player.

Buchtel, Forrest. *Hokus Pokus*. Neil A. Kjos Music Company. 1978. $1. 2:00. II–III. B–d′. This fun solo is in a moderate cut time, is in Bb and Eb major, has a moderate amount of accidentals, has some eighth note runs, has some simple syncopation, and is in bass clef. This would be a great solo for an advanced middle school player.

Buchtel, Forrest. *Intermezzo*. Neil A. Kjos Music Company. 1973. $1.75. 1:30. I. Bb–bb. This solo is in Bb major, is in a slow 3/4 moving later to an allegro common time, has a few accidentals, has piano cues, is rhythmically simple, and is in bass clef. This would be a good first or second solo for a middle school player.

Buchtel, Forrest. *Jiggle a Bit*. Neil A. Kjos Music Company. 1978. $1.75. 1:30. I–II. Bb–c′. This solo is in a march tempo 2/4, is in Bb and Eb major, is in bass clef, has a few accidentals, and features simple syncopation. This would be a fun second solo for a middle school player.

Buchtel, Forrest. *Jogging Along*. Neil A. Kjos Music Company. 1978. $1. 2:00. II. c–f′. This solo is in a moderate cut time, is in F major, and features simple syncopation and some scale-wise eighth note runs. This is a very fun little solo that would be great for a good middle school student.

Buchtel, Forrest. *Jovial Mood*. Neil A. Kjos Music Company. 1964. $2. 2:15. II. c–d′. This solo begins in a slow 6/8 and moves to a quicker 2/4. It is in E♭ and A♭ major, has some sixteenth notes and runs, has a few accidentals, has piano cues, and is in bass clef. This is a fun solo that would be great for an advanced middle school player or for a young high school student.

Buchtel, Forrest. *Jumpin' Jack.* Neil A. Kjos Music Company. 1978. $2.50. 2:00. II–III. c–f′. This solo is in a moderate cut time, is in F and B♭ major, has simple syncopation, some eighth note runs, and a few accidentals, and is in bass clef. This is a fun solo and would be great for an advanced middle school student.

Buchtel, Forrest. *Jumpin' Jericho.* Neil A. Kjos Music Company. 1978. $3.25. 1:30. III. A–f′. This fun solo is in a moderate cut time, is in F major, has a few accidentals, is in bass clef, is mostly in the middle and lower registers, and features loads of dotted eighth/sixteenth rhythms. This would be a good solo for an advanced middle school player or young high school student.

Buchtel, Forrest. *Jupiter.* Neil A. Kjos Music Company. 1971. $2. 2:30. II–III. e♭–f′. This entertaining solo begins in a slow 3/4 and moves to a faster, fun, and light 2/4. It is in E♭ and A♭ major, has some sixteenth note runs, is rhythmically simple, has many dynamics, and is in bass clef. This would be a great solo for an advanced middle school student.

Buchtel, Forrest. *May Moon.* Neil A. Kjos Music Company. 1973. $1.75. 1:15. I–II. B♭–e♭′. This solo begins in a slow common time and moves to a moderately fast common time. It is in E♭ and A♭ major, has simple rhythms, has a few accidentals, is mostly in the lower register, has piano cues, and is in bass clef. This would be a great second solo for a middle school player.

Buchtel, Forrest. *Meditation, from Sonatina in F.* Neil A. Kjos Music Company. 1955. $2. 1:30. II–III. e♭–f′. This solo has some lovely lines. It is in a slow common time, is in F major, has a few rhythmic challenges, has some accidentals, has a few sixteenth note runs, has piano cues, and is in bass clef. This would be a great solo for an advanced middle school student.

Buchtel, Forrest. *Minstrel Boy.* Neil A. Kjos Music Company. 1965. $2. 2:30. II–III. B♭–e♭′. This solo is in A♭ and E♭ major, begins in a slow common time and moves to a quicker 2/4, has some simple syncopation, has some scale-wise sixteenth note runs, is mostly in the lower register, has piano cues, and is in bass clef. This would be a very good solo for an advanced middle school student.

Buchtel, Forrest. *Mumbo Jumbo.* Neil A. Kjos Music Company. 1978. $2.50. 3:00. III. c–d′. This solo is in a moderate cut time, is in A♭ and E♭ major, has many scale-wise eighth note runs, has some simple syncopation, is mostly in the middle register, has a fair amount of accidentals, and is in bass clef. This is a very fun solo and would be great

for an advanced middle school player or young high school student.

Buchtel, Forrest. *Pied Piper.* Neil A. Kjos Music Company. 1985. $1.75. 1:15. I. B♭–b♭. This is a good solo for a beginner.

Buchtel, Forrest. *Razz Ma Tazz.* Neil A. Kjos Music Company. 1978. $2.50. 2:15. II–III. B♭–e♭′. This fun solo is in a moderate cut time, is in E♭ and A♭ major, has some simple syncopation, has a moderate amount of accidentals, and is in bass clef. This jazzy little solo would be great for an advanced middle school student.

Buchtel, Forrest. *Romantica.* Neil A. Kjos Music Company. 1975. $5. 4:00. III–IV. e♭–b♭′. This beautiful solo is in a slow 3/4, is in D♭ and G♭ major, is mostly scale-wise eighths, is in the higher range fairly often, and is in bass clef. This is a great lyrical solo and would be a fantastic selection and musical study for a good high school player or young college student.

Buchtel, Forrest. *Sentimental Sam.* Neil A. Kjos Music Company. 1965. $1.75. 1:50. I. B♭–c′. This solo begins in a slow 3/4 and moves to a faster common time. It is in B♭ major, is rhythmically simple, has piano cues, and is in bass clef. This would be a fun first solo for a middle school player.

Buchtel, Forrest. *Syncophobia.* Neil A. Kjos Music Company. 1978. $2. 1:30. II. c–e♭′. This fun solo is in a moderate 2/4, is in E♭ major, is mostly quarter and eighth notes, and is in bass clef. It is an excellent study in syncopation for a young player and would make for a fun second or third solo.

Buchtel, Forrest. *Waltz Medley.* Neil A. Kjos Music Company. 1959. $1.75. 1:30. I. B♭–c′. This collection includes "Tres Jolie," "Skaters' Waltz," and "Emperor's Waltz." It is in a waltz 3/4, is in B♭ major, is rhythmically simple, and is in bass clef. This would be a good first solo for a middle school student.

Buchtel, Forrest. *When the Saints Go Marching In.* Neil A. Kjos Music Company. 1966. $1.75. 1:25. I. B♭–b♭′. This solo is in a march tempo cut time, is in B♭ and E♭ major, is rhythmically simple, has piano cues, and is in bass clef. This is a fun solo and would be a great first solo for a middle school player.

Buckley, Lewis J. *The Yellow Rose of Texas Variations.* Cimarron Music and Productions. 1995. $11. 6:00. V. F–c″. Commissioned by Dan Vinson, a proud Texan, this theme and variations is a very nice addition to the euphonium repertoire. It begins with an extended introduction followed by a lyrical cowboy-like song. The theme is introduced in a light and bouncy feel quickly leading to the first variation, which is running eighth notes. The second variation adds triplets and sextuplets requiring triple tonguing. The third variation is different in that it is a polacca at a moderate tempo full of dotted sixteenth and

32nd note rhythms barred together, which eventually develop into 32nd note runs. Tempo picks up and brings back the theme in quarter notes, but very fast in cut time. The work comes to a rousing end with fast eighth notes and a glissando to high B♭. The work overall lies in the middle register and most of the runs are scalewise and idiomatic for the euphonium.

Bulla, Stephen. *Euphonium Fantasia.* DE HASKE Music Publishers Ltd., Heerenveen, Holland. 5:00. V. AA♭–b♭'. This wonderful character piece has some technical challenges, but it is a very fun, lively piece with many varying styles and places for artistic freedom. I highly recommend it! It was formerly entitled *Rhapsody for Euphonium.* The solo part is in treble clef.

Burke, Robert, Jr. *Hymn for Trombone.* Neil A. Kjos Music Company. 1987. $2. 2:20. II–III. c–e♭'. This beautiful solo is in a slow common time, is in F major, has many dotted eighth/sixteenth note rhythms, is in the middle to lower register, and is in bass clef. It is well marked and has very helpful program notes. This would be a good lyrical study for a middle school student.

Busch, Carl. *Recitative, Arioso and Poloniase.* Belwin, Inc., New York. 1940. 5:00. IV. E–c''. This is a great all-state or solo and ensemble audition piece for a good high school student, or a good work for a freshman music major. It is well written for the euphonium and was written for Leonard Falcone. The solo part is in bass clef.

Butterworth, Arthur. *Partita for Euphonium and Piano, Op. 89.* Comus Publications, Colne, Lancashire, Great Britain. 1991. $10.50. 7:30. V. F–b♭'. This work is in five short movements: Prelude; Capriccio; Sarabande; Bourree; Scherzo. It is a standard in the repertoire and is a challenging work that has something for everyone in terms of styles and musical expressions. I highly recommend this piece. The solo part was originally in treble clef but has recently been published in bass clef. Recorded by Steven Mead.

Butterworth, Arthur. *Summer Music, Op. 77(B).* 1985. This work features four movements: Allegro; Pastorale; Nocturne; Vivace. This is a challenging work that has many nice moments. It has become a popular work in the bassoon literature.

Byrd, William. *The Earle of Oxford's Marche.* Trans./ arr. Ronald Dishinger. Medici Music Press. 1989. $5. 1:30. II–III. B♭–f'. In common time with mostly eighth notes with a few sixteenths. Very easy to read with clear dynamic and articulation markings. A very playable arrangement of this classic tune.

Capuzzi, Antonio. *Andante and Rondo from Concerto for Double Bass.* Ed. Philip Catelinet. Hinrichsen Edition, Peters Edition Ltd., London. 1967. $11.95. 6:00. IV–V. F–g'. This a standard work in the repertoire from the late classical period. It is a must in anyone's library.

It is good for a good high school player and above.

Capuzzi, Antonio. *Andante and Rondo.* Arr. Philip Wilby. Winwood Music. $12.25. IV. This is a fine arrangement of this standard work. The solo part is available in both bass and treble clef.

Carastathis, Aris. *Euphemism.* Conners Publications, Canadian Music Center (416-961-6601). 3:30. V. C♯–g♯'. This work features lots of syncopation and abrupt dynamic changes and stays in the middle to low register. A neat effect piece! The solo part is in bass clef.

Cardillo. *Cattari, Cattari.* Arr. Denzil Stephens. Sarnia Music (UK) (www.sarnia-music.com). $9.20. This arrangement is of a famous ballad that has been recently recorded by numerous famous tenors.

Carissimi, Giacomo. *Vittoria! Vittoria!* Ed. Larry Campbell. Hal Leonard Publishing Corporation. 1977. $12.95. II–III. This solo is part of a collection of solos—Master Solos, Intermediate Level. This lively and stately solo is marked "allegro con brio." It is a great solo for a good middle school student or high school player, as it remains in the middle register and is mostly moderate eighth note runs. It features several style changes and is clearly marked and easy to read. Recorded by Larry Campbell.

Casey. *Remembrance of Liberati.* Arr. Forrest L. Buchtel. Neil A. Kjos Music Company. $3.25. 4:10. IV. A–a♭'. This is a fantastic little showpiece for the euphonium. It is in the keys of E♭ and A♭ major, has many style changes, is mostly in the middle register, has several optional high pitches, and is in bass clef. It is basically a small theme and variations work with a beautiful theme, a very fun, slow sixteenth note variation, a triplet variation, a great cadenza at the end, and a rousing coda. This would be an excellent work for a good high school player.

Casterede, Jacques. *Fantaisie Concertante pour Trombone basse ou Tuba Ut ou Saxhorn basse et Piano.* Alphonse Leduc, Paris. 1960. $21.95. 7:30. IV. E–a'. This is a fantastic French work, one of the standards in the repertoire. It remains in the middle register for a good portion of the work. It is challenging, but well worth it. The solo part is in bass clef. This is a great recital piece for a college student as it will challenge students rhythmically, technically, and musically, but is written so that many levels of college players can play, learn from, and enjoy this work.

Casterede, Jacques. *Sonatine pour Tuba Ut, ou Saxhorn basse, et Piano.* Alphonse Leduc, Paris. 1963. $20.85. 7:30. IV–V. This work has three movements: Defile; Serenade; Final. This fine French work deserves more attention. I highly recommend this work as a nice transitional piece or stylistic change for a recital. The solo part is in bass clef.

Catelinet, Philip. *Legend*. The Associated Board of Royal Schools of Music. 1980. $4.80. 3:00. III–IV. A–g'. Written by a tubist and a Salvation Army band and brass band arranger, this small character piece would be very appropriate for high school players. The solo part comes in both bass and treble clefs.

Censhu, Jiro. *As Wonderful Things Drift By*. Zen-On Music Company, ISBN 4-11-899635-9 C3073 P1854E. 1990. 10:00. IV–V. BB♭–c″. If you want something totally different for a recital, yet not too technically difficult, this is your piece. It has many fantastic moments and special effects. Great special effects/different sound and style work!

Censhu, Jiro. *Beyond a Distant Galaxy, Fantasia for Euphonium and Piano*. Zen-On Music Company. 1994. 8:00. IV–V. c♯–g'. If you want something totally different for a recital, yet not too technically difficult, this is your piece. It has many fantastic moments and special effects. Great special effects/different sound and style work! The solo part is in bass clef.

Chaminade, Cecile. *Rigaudon and Noveletee from Album for Children*. Trans./arr. Ronald Dishinger. Medici Music Press. 1993. $4.50. 1:30. II–III. B♭–f'. This is a great arrangement of a very lively and playful tune. It features mostly quarter and eighth note runs. It would be a wonderful solo for a good middle school or younger high school player.

Chester, Barrie. *Arabella*. Wright & Round Ltd. Gloucester. 1967. $26.30. 4:00. IV–V. c–c″. This is a wonderful little theme and variations in treble clef!

Chopin, Frederic. *Etude from 27 Etudes Op. 10, No. 3*. Trans./arr. Ronald Dishinger. Medici Music Press. 1989. $3.50. 3:00. II–III. c–f'. This beautiful solo is in a slow common time, is in F major, bass clef, is rhythmically simple, has mostly scale-wise eighth note runs, has a few accidentals, is in the middle to lower registers, and has plenty of rests. This would be a very nice solo for a good middle school player or young high school student.

Cimera, Jaroslav. *Caprice Charmante*. Neil A. Kjos Music Company. 1984. $2.50. 3:00. III. B♭–a♭'. This is a great little showpiece. It begins in a moderate common time and moves to a faster 2/4. It is in B♭, E♭, and A♭ major, has many scale-wise sixteenth note runs, a fair amount of accidentals, is mostly in the middle register, and is in bass clef. It features a great little cadenza and has some optional high pitches in the big climax sections. This is a very fun solo and would be an excellent solo for a good high school player.

Cimera, Jaroslav. *Isabella*. Neil A. Kjos Music Company. 1954. 3:30. III. B♭–g'. This is a good solo to introduce some more advanced concepts such as cadenzas, but on an easy level. The solo is in E♭ major and A♭ major, opens with a cadenza, is mostly in a 3/4 waltz tempo, has a very flexible

cadenza toward the end that allows for some technical showmanship, but is very practical for the grade level, is rhythmically simple, has a good amount of chromatic eighth note runs, is mostly in the middle register, and is in bass clef. This is a fun solo and would be a good solo for a good middle school student to study.

Cimera, Jaroslav. *Joan of Arc*. Neil A. Kjos Music Company. 1982. $2.50. 3:10. III. B♭–f'. This is a good solo to introduce some more advanced concepts such as cadenzas, but on an easy level. The solo is in F major and B♭ major, opens with a cadenza, is mostly in a 3/4 waltz tempo, has a very flexible cadenza toward the end, is rhythmically simple, is mostly in the middle register, and is in bass clef. This is a fun solo and would be a good solo for a good middle school student to study.

Cimera, Jaroslav. *Spring Caprice*. Neil A. Kjos Music Company. $2.50. 3:00. III–IV. A♭–g'. This is a great little technical solo. It begins with a cadenza and moves into a moderate common time with lyrical eighth note passages. The next section is a 3/4 allegrotto that is mostly scale-wise sixteenth note runs. There is a very practical and fun cadenza toward the end. The work comes to a rousing close with a small presto coda. The work is in B♭ and E♭ major, is mostly in the middle register, is rhythmically straightforward, has some optional higher pitches, and is in bass clef. This would be a great solo for a high school player.

Clarke, Herbert L. *The Bride of the Waves*. Arr. Arthur H. Brandenburg. Warner Bros. Inc. 1943. $6.95. 3:00. V. G–b♭'. This polka brillante is one of the most famous and popular solos in the theme and variations category. Written by the legendary trumpeter Herbert L. Clarke, it wonderfully features the capabilities of brass instruments. It features many lovely passionate themes, a very fun polka with many fast sixteenth note runs and triple tongued triplets, a trio with more sixteenth note runs, an extended cadenza with many flourishes, and a blazing ending. A concert band version and a a a band version are available. Available at Solid Brass Music Company.

Clarke, Herbert L. *Carnival of Venice*. Arr. Arthur H. Brandenburg. Alfred Publishing Company, Inc. $6.95. 4:00. V–VI. F–g'. This is the most famous theme and variations in all of the brass literature. Several versions exist, but the Clarke version remains the one most performed. It is a must study for any euphonium student. A band version is available. Recorded by Brian Bowman, American Variations.

Clarke, Herbert L. *From the Shores of the Mighty Pacific*. $5.95. V. This is a classic solo and is one of Clarke's most famous. Solo part comes in both bass and treble clef.

Clarke, Herbert L. *Maid of the Mist*. Alfred Publishing Company, Inc. $5.95. 3:00. V. One of Clarke's famous theme and variations he soloed with the John Philip Sousa Band. It is a beautiful representation of the famous boat that shuttles tourists to the bottom of Niagara Falls and the sites and sounds while on the Maid of the Mist. A band version is available. Available at Solid Brass Music Company.

Clarke, Herbert L. *Southern Cross*. Alfred Publishing Company, Inc. $5.95. V. This is a classic solo! Available at Solid Brass Music Company.

Clarke, Herbert L. *The Debutante*. Arr. Arthur H. Brandenburg. Warner Bros. Inc. 1942. $4.95 (piano $4.25). V. This is a classic brass solo! Available at Solid Brass Music Company.

Clarke, Jeremiah. *Trumpet Voluntary*. Trans./arr. Ronald Dishinger. Medici Music Press. 1995. $4.50. 3:00. II. F–d'. A fantastic and easily played arrangement of the classic wedding selection. Very easy to read with clear markings. Adheres well to the original.

Cofield, Frank. *Chartreuse*. Rubank, Inc. 1952. $7.95. 2:30. II–III. f–g'. This solo is in F and Bb major, 3/4, has basic rhythms, and is mostly in the upper middle register. This is a good advanced middle school solo for solo and ensemble contest, as it has many advanced elements such as many style and dynamic changes, several tempo changes, and a cadenza. Endurance will be an issue as it has very few rests and is often in the higher register. It is a fun solo and has some interesting chromatic play. See Euphonium and Keyboard Collections.

Cook, Vander. *Columbine*. Arr. Forrest L. Buchtel. Neil A. Kjos Music Company. 1983. $2. 2:30. II. A–bb. This solo begins in a slow 6/8 and moves to a faster 2/4. It is in the keys of Bb and Eb, is in bass clef, has a fair amount of accidentals, has a good amount of scale-wise sixteenth note runs, and has many dynamic changes. This is a fun solo that would be most appropriate for a very good middle school student or young high school player.

Cook, Vander. *Emerald*. Rubank, Hal Leonard Corporation. $6.95. 1:45. II–III. d–eb'. This fun solo is in a slow 6/8 moving to a moderate 2/4, is in Bb, Eb, and Ab major, is mostly simple eighth note patterns, is mostly in the middle register, has a few accidentals, and is in bass clef. This would be a very fun second or third solo for a middle school player as it has a good amount of style contrast. See Euphonium and Keyboard Collections.

Cook, Vander. *Hyacinthe*. Arr. Forrest L. Buchtel. Neil A. Kjos Music Company. 1980. $2. 2:00. III. A–f'. This is a great solo for a very good middle school player or for most high school players. It is in Bb and Eb major and is in bass clef. The first section is a common time andante con moto that features a beautiful simple melody. At the end of this section is a great cadenza that allows a lot of freedom. The second section is a 2/4 allegretto that has many scale-wise sixteenth note runs. The third and final section is a trio that is mostly sixteenth note runs that are arppegiated. This is a fun solo that is well marked and has piano cues.

Cook, Vander. *Lily*. Arr. Forrest L. Buchtel. Neil A. Kjos Music Company. 1980. $2. 3:00. III–IV. A–f'. This solo is in Eb and Ab major, is mostly scale-wise sixteenth note runs, is in bass clef, has a few grace notes, has a fair amount of chromatics, and is mostly in the middle register. This solo begins slowly and sweetly before moving to a slightly quicker trio section. This solo is loads of fun to play and features some very beautiful passages. This would be a great solo for a good high school student.

Cook, Vander. *Magnolia*. Arr. Forrest L. Buchtel. Neil A. Kjos Company. 1980. $2.50. 3:00. III–IV. G–ab'. This is a fantastic solo that would make for a great showpiece for a good high school player. The solo is in Eb and Ab, has four sections (moderato; allegretto; trio; brillante), has many scale-wise sixteenth note runs, a fair amount of chromatics, is rhythmically straightforward, is mostly in the middle register, has two small cadenzas, and is in bass clef. It is well marked with very specific articulations, dynamics, style changes, phrasings, and tempo changes.

Cook, Vander. *Marigold*. Arr. Forrest L. Buchtel. Neil A. Kjos Company. 1980. $2. 2:30. II–III. G–eb'. This solo has several sections: andante; allegretto; trio. It is in Bb and Eb major, has many scale-wise sixteenth note runs, is mostly in the lower register, has a few accidentals, and is in bass clef. This is a fun solo with some lovely melodies and lively passages. This would be a great showpiece for a very good middle school student or a high school player.

Copley, Evan. *Sonata for Euphonium and Piano*. Tuba-Euphonium Press. 1998. $12. 7:30. IV–V. C–g'. This is a two-movement sonata with the first movement starting slow with a fast middle section before ending with a slower section. It is in common time with mostly eighth note passages, it has a large amount of chromatics, it is rhythmically straightforward and has very wide intervals in places. It is very expressive and has many passages that are very dramatic and full of tension. The second movement is in a fast common time and is mostly eighth note passages similar to the first movement. It is also rhythmically straightforward. It features very driving and intense eighth note and sixteenth note patterns in several sections. Overall this sonata is in the middle to lower register and it is in bass clef. This solo is playable by a very good high school student and would be a nice recital selection for a college student.

Corelli, Arcangelo. *Sarabande*. Trans./arr. Ronald Dishinger. Medici Music Press. 1992. $4.50. 1:30. II–III. e–f'. This solo features a cute melody at a slow tempo with mostly quarter and eighth notes. This solo would be a very nice selection for a middle school player.

Corelli, Arcangelo. *Suite from Variations for Violin onTthemes of Tartini*. Trans./arr. Ronald Dishinger. Medici Music Press. 1991. $6.50. 3:00. II–III. d–g'. Three movements: Moderato; Andante; Allegro. The first movement is very light and playful and features several catchy melodies. It consists mostly of slow sixteenth note runs, basic rhythms, and is in the middle register. The second movement is very lyrical and features some beautifully placed chromatics. It is slow and is mostly eighth notes in the middle register. The last movement is very light and jolly and is rhythmically very simple. This work would be a good solo for a high school student to study for style contrasts.

Corwell, Neal. *Flight of the Bumble Bee*. See Music for Euphonium and Electronic Media.

Corwell, Neal. *Meditation*. See Music for Euphonium and Electronic Media.

Corwell, Neal. *Sinfonietta*. See Music for Euphonium and Orchestra.

Corwell, Neal. *Three Farewell Pieces*. Tuba-Euphonium Press. 1991. $8. 8:00. IV. G–bb'. This highly expressive work has three movements: Elegy; Intermezzo; Lullabye. The middle movement has sixteenth note passages (some tongued, some slurred) at quarter = 112, and minimal demands on range and endurance. The first and third movements are lyrical with no difficult technical demands. This work features intricate rhythmic interplay between soloist and piano in the middle movement.The *Three Farewell Pieces* for solo euphonium and piano was composed in memory of Stephanie Ann Roper, a Frostburg State University art student who was murdered in 1982. The composer attended Frostburg State (in Frostburg, Maryland) at the same time as Stephanie, and the first movement, Elegy, was written just days after hearing the news of her death. The middle movement, Intermezzo, serves as a transition between the somber mood and dissonant musical style of the Elegy and the lyrical consonant Lullabye, which brings the work to a quiet conclusion. The Lullabye was the composer's way of saying to Stephanie, "farewell, may you rest in peace." Neal Corwell premiered the Elegy during a 1983 alumni recital at Frostburg State University and the three complete movements (the Intermezzo and Lullabye were composed several years later) were premiered at a 1991 faculty recital at the same institution. The composition is brief in duration, quite modest in its technical demands, and clear in its statement of musical and emotional content.

Couperin, Francois. *Marche from Book IV for Clavier*. Trans./arr. Ronald Dishinger. Medici Music Press. 1993. $4.50. 2:00. II–III. f–f'. This very regal solo is in a moderate common time, is in F major, is mostly quarter notes with some eighth note passages, is in the middle register, has very few accidentals, is rhythmically simple, and is in bass clef. This would be a very fun solo for a good middle school player.

Couperin, Francois. *Rondeau from Clavier Book X*. Trans./arr. Ronald Dishinger. Medici Music Press. 1996. $4.50. 1:30. II. Bb–d'. This would be a good second solo for a good middle school player as it remains in the middle register, has simple rhythms, features many repeating eighth note runs, and has very few accidentals.

Couperin, Francois. *The Sailor's Song from Book III for Clavier*. Trans./arr. Ronald Dishinger. Medici Music Press. 1991. $4.50. 2:00. II. Bb–c'. This would be a good first solo for a middle school player as it remains in the middle register, consists primarily of half and quarter notes at a moderate tempo, and has no accidentals.

Crawley, Clifford. *Divertissements*. Canadian Music Center. 1991. 6:00. F–a'. This has three movements: Levet; Eclogue; Rant. It is a neat character piece that is very lively yet reflective in places. It is most appropriate for college students but could be done by a good high school student. It would be a nice piece for a change of pace on a recital. The solo part is in bass clef. Check out the Canadian Music Center website to purchase or borrow this work on loan.

Cronin, Robert P. *Sonata for Euphonium and Piano*. Tuba-Euphonium Press. 1995. $12. 13:00. V. BBb–b'. Commissioned by Atticus Hensley, this is a challenging two-movement sonata with a very wide variety of musical styles and expression. The first movement is highly expressive and very powerful with many varying sections: quazi fantasie, comodo, sostenuto, rubato, and agitato, to list a few. The second movement is fast and energetic. It has a beautiful cantabile middle section before returning to the opening section. It ends with a very powerful vivo section. The solo is in bass clef and is well marked with specific dynamics, tempos, styles, articulations, and phrasings. This solo has many rhythmic, technical, and range challenges, but it is worth it. If you are looking for a modern, powerful, and different solo for a recital, this is it!

Cummings, Barton. *Autumn Air for Euphonium/ Trombone and Piano*. Solid Brass Music Company. 2001. $8. 3:30. IV. Eb–ab'. This beautiful ballad would make a great recital piece. It is in a slow common time, is in Eb major, is rhythmically straightforward, has some optional lower and higher pitches, has some accidentals, is mostly in the middle register, and is in bass clef. This is a gorgeous solo and would be most appropriate for a college student.

Cummings, Barton. *Spring Suite for Euphonium and Piano*. TUBA Press. 1992. $10. V. F–bb'. This fun solo was written for Mary Ann Craig and has three movements: Meditation; Variation Fantasy; Finale. The Meditation is in a very slow common time, is in f minor, spans a wide range, has many scale-wise sixteenth notes, and is highly expressive. The Variation Fantasy is in c minor, begins in a slow common time, moves to an allegro 6/8, spans a wide range, and has some tricky rhythms. It is loads of fun to play, as it is very exciting. The Finale is the most technical. It is in Bb major, is in a fast common time, spans a wide range, has some challenging rhythms, has many challenging fingering and tonguing passages, and features a very showy and expressive cadenza. The Finale is very rhapsodic and impressive. The work is in bass clef and is an excellent technical showpiece while having a large amount of wonderful musical moments.

Curnow, James. *Concerto for Euphonium.* Hal Leonard Music Corp.

Curnow, James. *Rhapsody for Euphonium.* Rosehill Music Publishing Company Limited. 1990. $21.95. 6:00. IV. A–a'. Dedicated to Leonard Falcone, this work has quickly become one of the standard works in the euphonium repertoire. It opens with a chant-like quasi-cadenza version of a very lyrical and passionate theme that is established in the andante moderato section. The work gradually moves into an allegro con spirito section that introduces a lively, playful, yet confident theme. The work soon recalls the first theme while later using a driving marcato section to bring us back to the allegro con spirito tempo. The work ends with a powerful and regal maestoso section. This is a fantastic solo for a very good high school student or college player. It is a very good opening work for a recital. Both treble and bass clef versions are included and band and brass band accompaniments are available. Recorded by Roger Berhend and the Childs Brothers (Robert Childs).

Curnow, James. *Symphonic Variants.* $19.95. 19:00. VI. GG–f". This is one of the great euphonium works and has been a required piece on countless international solo competitions and auditions. It is a must study for any serious euphonium player. The work consists of a theme and five variations. The main theme is lyrical yet driving. It is rhythmically simple yet poses some range challenges. The first variation is in a rondo form and is set in a very lively and dancing 6/8. It poses some technical issues with very rapidly descending runs and extremely fast double tonguing passages. The second variation is slow and is based on the first three notes of the theme. It is highly lyrical and full of tension, which creates some of the most fantastic musical moments in all the euphonium literature. The third variation is a scherzo and features lots of double tonguing and many very technically difficult passages. It is extremely exciting and very impressive, fully demonstrating the technical capabilities of the euphonium. The fourth variation is slow and highly expressive and very reflective in nature. The last variation is a maestoso-like version of the main theme, leading to the famous range-challenging ending of the

work. There are versions for concert band, brass band, and orchestra.

Daniels, M. L. *Concertino for Euphonium and Piano.* TUBA Press. 1992. $10. 7:30. V. G–bb'. This solo is overall in a moderately fast common time with a couple of slower sections. It changes keys many times, has a large amount of scale-wise sixteenth note runs, has numerous passages in the high register, has some rhythmic challenges, and is in bass clef. This solo has many emotional sections: bold, lyrical, rhapsodic, soaring, and so forth. The initial theme is very catchy and most of the work is based off of the initial theme or slight variations of it. This is a fun piece to play and is a good showpiece for the euphonium.

Davis, Henry W. *Carnival of Venice.* Rubank, Hal Leonard Corporation. $6.95. 3:00. III–IV. Bb–f'. This solo is in Eb major, has some rhythmic challenges, is mostly in the middle to lower registers, and is in bass clef. The solo is a different take on one of the most classic of all theme and variations written for brass instruments. It begins with a moderate dolce section, moves to an elegante section, then to a gran gusto section with many scale-wise sixteenths, then to a small cadenza, before ending with a con grazia section. This would be a good solo for a high school student player to become familiar with a classic.

Davis, William Mac. *Rondo Concertante.* Tuba-Euphonium Press. 1995. $12. 9:00. V. Eb–c". This solo showcases the euphonium beautifully as it is has many regal passages, gorgeous lyrical statements, and loads of high-energy mixed meter sections. This work has many technical and rhythmic challenges and often ascends into the high register. The solo part is in bass clef. This is a fantastic work and is a worthy challenge. I highly recommend this piece. This solo was recorded by John Mueller.

De Curtis. *Return to Sorrento.* Arr. Roberts. Winwood Music. $8.75. III.

De Luca, Joseph. *Beautiful Colorado.* Carl Fischer. $8.95. 5:30. IV–V. C–c". This is one of, if not the most well-known and popular theme and variations in the entire repertoire. It is a must study for the serious euphonium player. It features some of the most beautiful melodies ever written for the euphonium. The cadenza at the beginning is fantastic, as it spans a wide variety of ranges and rhythms, thus showing off the capabilities of the euphonium at the outset! After the cadenza the gorgeous main waltz melody is introduced. This melody will return at times and will be embellished upon through the succeeding variations. Overall it remains in the middle register and is straightforward in terms of rhythms and runs that are scale-wise. The technical challenges come in the speed of the variations and some occasional tricky fingering combinations. There is also a version with band. Recorded by John Mueller and Arthur Lehman.

De Luca, Joseph. *Thoughts of Gold, Valse Caprice.* Carl Fischer. $4. 5:00. IV–V. G–bb′. This technical showpiece has become a standard work in the repertoire thanks to famous soloists such as Simone Mantia and Arthur Lehman. It features many beautiful lyrical and romantic waltz melodies as well as numerous impressive technical passages. This work is challenging but is written in a way that many levels of players can enjoy. I highly recommend this work for students who want to perform a flashy sounding solo that doesn't take a whole year to learn! The solo part is available in both bass and treble clefs. Recorded by Michael Colburn.

De la Nux, P. V. *Concert Piece.* Southern Music Company. $6.25. 3:30. IV. G–bb′. This is a standard in low brass repertoire that is often used at all-state and solo and ensemble auditions. It is a beautiful work that is a must have. It is challenging for good high school players, but well worth it. The solo part is in bass clef.

Debons, Eddy. *Divertimento for Euphonium and Piano.* Editions Marc Reift, Crans-Montana (Switzerland). 1996. $15. 4:00. IV–V. A–bb′. This is a fun, energetic, and entertaining work that features recitative and gigue sections. This would be a fine work for a recital.

Debussy, Claude. *The Girl with the Flaxen Hair.* Arr. Neal Ramsey. Medici Music Press. 2001. $5. 2:00. III–IV. G–f′. This is a very nice arrangement of the popular Debussy song. It is in F major, which places the euphonium in a comfortable range to bring out the wonderful inherent singing quality found throughout this beautiful work. This would be a fine musical challenge for a good high school player or a great lyrical selection for a recital.

Debussy, Claude. *The Girl with the Flaxen Hair.* Arr. Howard Snell. $8. III–IV. This is a fine arrangement of one of Debussy's most beloved songs. Brass band arrangements are available. Order at www.euphonium.net.

Debussy, Claude. *The Little Shepherd.* Arr. Howard Snell. $14. III–IV. This gorgeous selection is a great representation of Debussy's style and would be an excellent recital selection. Order at www.euphonium.net.

Debussy, Claude. *Prelude from Suite Bergamasque.* Trans./arr. Ronald Dishinger. Medici Music Press. 2002. $6.50. 2:30. III–IV. G–a′. This work is marked "moderato" and features many sixteenth note runs. For Debussy it is harmonically simple with very little chromatics. It is often in the middle register and the runs are idiomatic for the euphonium. This would be a good opening work for a recital.

Debussy, Claude. *Reverie.* Arr. Frank H. Siekmann. Brelmat Music. 1999. $8. 2:30. IV. Bb–bb′. This is a lovely arrangement of one of Debussy's most beautiful melodies. It would be good for both recitals and weddings. It is in the keys of Bb and

A major, is in a slow cut time, has a moderate amount of chromatics, is rhythmically straightforward, is mostly in the middle register, and is in bass clef. This is a great solo as very few works in the euphonium repertoire have this sound. This would be an excellent recital selection.

Debussy, Claude. *Reverie from Pieces for Piano.* Trans./arr. Ronald Dishinger. Medici Music Press. 1995. $2.50. 2:30. II–III. A–g′. This work features the typical harmonies found in Debussy's music. It has several key changes and tonal shifts. It is slow and primarily has quarter notes with some sections of eighth note runs. It is a lovely work and would be most appropriate for a good high school player or young college student to perform.

Dedrick, Art. *Shadows.* Kendor Music, Inc. $5. II.

Denmark, Max F. *Scene de Concert.* Ludwig Music Publishing Co. 1950. $4.95. 3:00. IV. A–bb′. This is a very nice piece with many stylistic contrasts! It is very accessible to high school and college players. The solo part is in bass clef.

Dewhurst, Robin. *Panache.* Gramercy Music. 1995. $14. 5:00. IV. This is a fantastic light jazz solo in treble clef. It is very relaxing solo and is a fantastic work not only for the performer but also for the audience. Concert band and brass band versions are available. Recorded by Steven Mead.

Dillon, Robert. *Concertpiece for Euphonium and Piano.* 6:00. IV–V. F–b′. If you are looking for a solo that features some very different musical techniques from most works in the euphonium repertoire, this is your piece. It features many sections of mixed meter and chance music. Range is mostly in the middle to middle upper register and there are a few sections with some articulated running sixteenth notes with wide intervals. There are many sections with interesting rhythmic play and chromatic tension.

Dougherty, William P. *Meditation and Celebration.* Ludwig Music Publishing Company. 1986. $7.95. 4:00. IV. Gb–bb′. This is a fun work with lots of syncopation and is very appropriate for good high school students. The solo part is in both bass and treble clefs.

Dougherty, William P. *Reflection from Sonata for Euphonium and Piano.* Heilman Music. 2:30. IV–V. F♯–bb′. Written in 1980 for Paul Droste, this is a beautiful work in ternary form with a great canon between the pianist and soloist. The solo part is in bass clef.

Dougherty, William P. *Sonata for Euphonium and Piano.* Tuba-Euphonium Press. 1993. $12. 10:00. V–VI. BBb–bb′. This solo was written for one of the great euphonium players, Paul Droste, and his wife, Anne. It has become a standard in the euphonium repertoire. It is in bass clef and has three movements: Dialogue; Reflection; Finale. The Dialogue begins in an allegro 2/4 but quickly incorporates a large amount of very driving and powerful mixed meter sections, some of which are very rhythmically challeng-ing. The movement has a small, beautiful slow section before returning to mixed meter. The Reflection is in a very slow 4/8 and has many highly expressive and dramatic passages. It slowly builds to a powerful climax before ending the movement very calmly. The Finale is in a moder-ately quick cut time and has countless powerful driving passages juxtaposed with many light and gleeful passages. This is a fantastic work that is loads of fun to play. It is challenging, but it is more than worth the effort. This is a must study for the serious euphonium player and teacher.

Doughty, George. *Grandfather's Clock*. F. Rich-ardson Limited and Wright & Round Limited. 1968. 6:00. IV–V. A–bb′. This is a wonderful theme and variations, as it is very fun and enter-taining! It has no multiple tonguing with idi-omatic scale runs. The solo part is in treble clef. Recorded by Steven Mead.

Dowland, John. *What if I Never Speed, for Eupho-nium and Piano*. Arr. Michael A. Fischer. Tuba-Euphonium Press. 2001. $8. 1:45. II. A–bb. This is based on one of Dowland's most popular songs for voice and lute. The solo is in a fast common time, is in the key of d minor, has some scale-wise eighth note runs, is rhythmically simple, has a few accidentals, is mostly in the lower register, and comes in bass and treble clef. This solo would be an excellent solo for a good middle school student.

Downie, Kenneth. *Concerto for Euphonium*. Rose-hill Music. $28. V–VI. BBb–eb″. This is a very challenging work written by a respected British brass band composer. It features many beautiful musical moments. If you are looking for a new challenge, this is worth a look. The solo part is in treble clef.

Drigo, Riccardo. *Pizzicato*. Trans./arr. Ronald Dishinger. Medici Music Press. 1995. $4.50. 2:00. III. C–a′. This is a neat one-section work that features a very lively and catchy opening theme. It has a different sound from most works of this size due to its use of key changes, rhyth-mic play, chromaticism, and thematic develop-ment. I found this work to be open to many possible interpretations and feel it would be a great small recital piece.

Druschetzky, George. *Allegro from Trio No. 3*. Trans/arr. Ronald Dishinger. Medici Music Press. 1991. $4.50. 2:00. II. Bb–eb′. This solo is in a moderate common time, is in Bb major, is mostly quarter notes and scale-wise eighth notes, is mostly in the lower register, has a few chro-matics, is rhythmically simple, and is in bass clef. This would be a good second solo for a middle school player.

Druschetzky, George. *Allegro from Trio No. 4*. Trans./arr. Ronald Dishinger. Medici Music Press. 1994. $4.50. 2:30. II–III. f–f′. This solo is in a fast common time, is in Bb major, is mostly quarter notes, is often in the higher register, has very few accidentals, is rhythmically simple, and is in bass clef. The challenge will be endurance, as it is two pages long and does not have much time for rest. It is a very nice solo that would be a good choice for a very good middle school student or younger high school player.

Druschetzky, George. *Allegro from Trio No. 9*. Trans./arr. Ronald Dishinger. Medici Music Press. 1996. $4.50. 1:30. II–III. d–eb′. This solo is in a slow 2/4, is in Eb major, has mostly scale-wise sixteenth note runs, is in the middle to lower register, has no accidentals, has a few rhythmic challenges, and is in bass clef. This solo would be most appropriate for a high school student.

Druschetzky, George. *Allegro from Trio No. 11*. Trans./arr. Ronald Dishinger. Medici Music Press. 1994. $4.50. 2:00. II–III. F–d′. This fun little solo would be a good selection for a mature middle school student. It is in F major, a moder-ate common time, has mostly scale-wise eighth notes, is mostly in the middle to lower register, is in bass clef, and has very few accidentals.

Druschetzky, George. *Allegro from Trio No. 17*. Trans./arr. Ronald Dishinger. Medici Music Press. 1995. $4.50. 1:45. II–III. Bb–ab′. This light and lovely solo that has an opera buffa feel to it would be a great selection for a good high school student to perform at solo and ensemble contest. It is in a moderate 3/4, is in Bb major, has very few rhythmic challenges, moderate use of chromaticism, and features scale-wise runs. Its challenge is a few passages where it ascends into the high register. This would be a great study of classical period style.

Druschetzky, George. *Allegro from Trio No. 18*. Trans./arr. Ronald Dishinger. Medici Music Press. 1991. $4.50. 3:00. III. F–f′. This solo is in a moderate 2/4, is in F major, is mostly in the middle register, has some rhythmic challenges, has some chromatics, has many mostly scale-wise sixteenth note runs, and is in bass clef. The challenge is in the sixteenth note runs. There are plenty of rests so endurance is not an issue. This is a fun solo to play and would be most appropriate for a good high school student or young college player.

Druschetzky, George. *Allegro from Trio No. 19*. Trans./arr. Ronald Dishinger. Medici Music Press. 1995. $4.50. 4:30. III–IV. Bb–f′. This is a very fun work that is in a moderate 2/4, is in F major, has several sixteenth note and eighth note runs that are mostly scale-wise, is rhyth-mically straightforward, has some chromatics, is mostly in the middle register, and is in bass clef. This would be an excellent solo for a very good high school student or a young college player.

Dubois, Pierre Max. *Cornemuse Tuba Ut Ou Trom-bone Basse Ou Saxhorn Basse Sib Ou Contreb. Cordes Piano*. $19.35. IV–V. This French work would be a great recital selection, as it has numerous style changes. The solo part is in bass clef.

Dubois, Pierre Max. *Piccolo Suite pour Tuba Ut ou Saxhorn basse ou Trombone basse et Piano.* Alphonse Leduc. 1957. $18.80. 6:30. V. GG–b♭'. This work has three movements (Prelude; Air; Polka). This is a challenging French work that features stylistic variety. This is a fun work that would be very appropriate as a stylistic change for a recital. The solo part is in bass clef.

Dvorak, Antonin. *Romantic Pieces, Op. 75.* Trans. Denis W. Winter. Cimarron Music and Productions. 1994. $9.50. 5:30. III–IV. F–a'. This is a fantastic transcription as it is a wonderful change of pace on a recital. Two pieces: Allegro Moderato and Allegro Maestoso. The first piece is absolutely gorgeous, as it has many small soaring lines, loads of dynamic contrast, many tension and release points, and is primarily in the middle to lower register, thus allowing for a rich singing quality throughout. There are many beautiful chromatic resolution spots. The second piece has many characters. The main theme is very regal and is alternated many times between extra loud and extra soft, creating a feeling of conversation between two people. The overall range of this piece is in the middle register and the technique is very manageable. There are several passages of running sixteenths that create a very playful feel. Both treble and bass clef versions are included. This is a very powerful piece and is very entertaining. This has become one of my favorite euphonium transcriptions.

Edelson, Edward. *Autumn Twilight.* C & E Enterprises (www.c-emusic.com). 2001. 1:30. III. A–e♭'. The solo part is in bass clef.

Edelson, Edward. *Let's Beguine.* C & E Enterprises. 1987. 1:30. III. d–e♭'. This fun little solo is very appropriate for high school students and comes in bass clef.

Elgar, Edward. *Chanson de Matin for Euphonium and Piano.* Arr. Michael A. Fischer. Tuba-Euphonium Press. 2001. $8. 3:00. IV. F–b♭'. This highly expressive solo is in a moderate 2/4, is in D♭ major, and is in bass clef. It has some rhythmic challenges, spans a wide range, has a large amount of chromatics, and has some technical challenges. This solo is well marked with very specific dynamics, articulations, phrasings, and style markings, and it has very good program notes about the composer and the work. The piano edition was written by John Cozza. This would be a fantastic recital selection as it has many fantastic musical moments and is open to many various interpretations. I highly recommend this work!

Elgar, Edward. *Chanson De Nuit, "Song of the Night," Opus 15, No. 1.* Trans./arr. Ronald Dishinger. Medici Music Press. 1996. $4.50. 1:45. III. This very expressive small song would be a great study of phrasing, breathing, dynamics, and articulation for a high school player. It would also make for a fantastic selection for solo and ensemble. It is slow and remains mostly in the middle register. It has many beautiful chromatics and is open for many forms of interpretation.

Elgar, Edward. *Chanson de nuit for Euphonium and Piano.* Arr. Michael A. Fischer. Tuba-Euphonium Press. 2001. $8. 2:30. III–IV. E♭–c″. This is a very fine lyrical solo. It is in a slow common time, is in E♭ major, and is in bass clef. It is rhythmically straightforward, has a moderate amount of accidentals, and is well marked with very specific dynamics, articulations, and style markings. The challenge of this solo is the range, as it often ascends into the higher register. This solo would be an excellent choice for a lyrical selection on a recital as it is highly expressive.

Elgar, Edward. *Gavotte from Contrasts, Opus 10, No. 3.* Trans./arr. Ronald Dishinger. Medici Music Press. 1990. $5. 3:00. III–IV. A–g'. This solo is in a fast common time and is very enjoyable to play. It features some eighth note runs that are mostly scale-wise or chromatic, is in the middle to lower register, is in bass clef, is rhythmically straightforward, and has very few technical challenges. This would be an excellent solo for a high school student.

Elgar, Edward. *Idylle, Op. 4 No. 1.* Trans. Eric Wilson. Rosehill Music Publishing. 1991. $12.25. 2:00. III–IV. F–a'. The solo comes in both bass and treble clefs.

Elgar, Edward. *Mot d' Amour, Op. 13, No. 1.* Trans. Eric Wilson. Rosehill Music Publishing. 1990. $12.25. 2:00. IV. BB♭–a'. This beautiful song comes in both bass and treble clefs.

Elgar, Edward. *Romance Op. 62.* Trans. Eric Wilson. Rosehill Music Publishing. 1988. $12.25. 3:00. V. BB♭–a'. A classic transcription of a very beautiful work! The solo part is available in both bass and treble clefs. Recorded by Steven Mead.

Elgar, Edward. *Salut d'amour for Euphonium and Piano.* Arr. Michael A. Fischer. Tuba-Euphonium Press. 2001. $8. 3:00. III–IV. A–b♭'. This solo is in a slow 2/4 and is in A♭ major. It is rhythmically straightforward, has a good amount of chromatics, is well marked with specific dynamic, tempo, and style markings, and is in bass clef. This is a beautiful work with many sweeping phrases and passionate sections. It would be an excellent solo for a very good high school player or a fantastic lyrical selection for any college recital. The piano edition is by John Cozza and the solo part includes program notes about the composer and the piece.

Ellerby, Martin. *Euphonium Concerto.* Studio Music Company. $32. VI. GG–e♭″. It has four movements (Fantasy; Cappriccio; Rhapsody for Luis; Diversions). This work has become an instant standard in the euphonium repertoire. It is extremely challenging, but worth it! It covers the gamut of emotions and musical expressions.

Very few other works in the repertoire can make this claim. This is a must study for the serious euphonium student, player, and teacher. The solo comes in both bass and treble clefs.

Endersen, R. M. *The Envoy.* Rubank, Inc. 1980. $5.95. 2:00. III. G–f′. This is a very lyrical and rich solo that has eighth and sixteenth note runs in the middle register with sporadic accidentals. It is in E♭ major, is in 4/4 time, has four sections (con spirito, con expressione, con spirito, and piu moso), many nice melodic lines, is mostly rhythmically straightforward (a few sporadic tricky rhythms), and has a dramatic ending. It has numerous cadenzas that are very playable at the same time as being showy. This is a very expressive solo for its difficulty level and would be a great solo for a very good middle school student or a high school student. See Euphonium and Keyboard Collections.

Endersen, R. M. *Forest Echo.* Rubank, Inc. 1980. $5.95. 2:00. III. B♭–e♭′. This is a very upbeat and cheerful solo that is mostly sixteenth note runs in the middle register with sporadic accidentals. It is E♭ major, has three sections (waltz, moderato, and allegro), many nice melodic lines, is mostly rhythmically straightforward (a few sporadic tricky rhythms), and has a dramatic vivo ending. This would be a good solo for a very good middle school student or a high school student. See Euphonium and Keyboard Collections.

Endersen, R. M. *Fox Hunt.* Rubank, Inc. 1980. $5.95. 2:20. III. G–f′. This is a very upbeat and cheerful solo that has eighth and sixteenth note runs in the middle register with sporadic accidentals. It is C and F major, has two sections (opening cadenza and moderato con spirito), many nice melodic lines, is mostly rhythmically straightforward (a few sporadic tricky rhythms), and has a dramatic ending with accented wide intervals. This would be a good solo for a very good middle school student or a high school student. See Euphonium and Keyboard Collections.

Endersen, R. M. *Holiday Medley.* Rubank, Inc. 1980. $5.95. 1:30. III. c–f′. This is a very fun and effective little tribute to the holidays with mostly eighth note runs in the middle register with few accidentals. It is F major, opens with a dramatic introduction, then a small cadenza followed by "Jingle Bells." It is rhythmically straightforward (a few sporadic tricky rhythms) and has a dramatic vivo ending. This would be a good solo for a good middle school student or a high school student. See Euphonium and Keyboard Collections.

Endersen, R. M. *Moonlight Serenade.* Rubank, Inc. 1980. $5.95. 2:00. III. A♭–g♭′. This is a very lyrical and rich solo that has eighth and sixteenth note runs in the middle register with sporadic accidentals. It is in D♭ major, is in 6/8 time, has four sections (andantino, animato, cadenza, and a tempo), many nice melodic lines, is mostly rhythmically straightforward (a few sporadic tricky

rhythms), and has a beautiful soft ending. This is a very expressive solo for its difficulty level and would be a great solo for a very good middle school student or a high school student. See Euphonium and Keyboard Collections.

Endersen, R. M. *Polish Dance.* Rubank, Inc. 1980. $5.95. 1:30. II–III. A–f′. This is a very energetic and pronounced solo with many dotted eighth/sixteenth note runs in the middle register with sporadic accidentals. It is in F major, is in 3/4 time, has many nice melodic lines, is mostly rhythmically straightforward, and has a dramatic ending. This is a fun solo and would be for a very good middle school student or a high school student. See Euphonium and Keyboard Collections.

Endersen, R. M. *School Musician.* Rubank, Inc. 1980. $5.95. 1:30. II–III. A–d′. This is a very energetic and pronounced march with many eighth note runs in the middle register with sporadic accidentals. It is in F major, is in 6/8 time, has many nice melodic lines, is mostly rhythmically straightforward, and has a dramatic ending. This is a fun solo and would be for a very good middle school student or a high school student. See Euphonium and Keyboard Collections.

Endersen, R. M. *Spinning Wheel.* Rubank, Inc. 1980. $5.95. 1:30. III. c–f′. This is a very fun and effective little waltz with mostly eighth note runs in the middle register with few accidentals. It is in F major and has a beautiful middle section. It is rhythmically straightforward and has a dramatic vivo ending. This would be a good solo for a good middle school student or a high school student. See Euphonium and Keyboard Collections.

Endersen, R. M. *Syncopator.* Rubank, Inc. 1980. $5.95. 1:00. II–III. c–f′. This is a very energetic and pronounced march with many quarter note runs in the middle register with sporadic accidentals. It is in F and B♭ major, is in 2/2 time, has many nice melodic lines, is mostly rhythmically straightforward, and has a dramatic ending. This is a fun solo and would be for a very good middle school student or a high school student. See Euphonium and Keyboard Collections.

Endersen, R. M. *Valse Caprice.* Rubank, Inc. 1980. $5.95. 1:30. III. B♭–f′. This is a very fun and lively little waltz with mostly eighth note runs in the middle register with few accidentals. It is in E♭ major and has a beautiful middle section. It is rhythmically straightforward and has a dramatic vivo-like ending. This would be a good solo for a good middle school student or a young high school student. See Euphonium and Keyboard Collections.

Endersen, R. M. *Whistlin' Pete.* Rubank, Inc. 1980. $5.95. 1:30. II–III. A♭–e♭′. This is a very energetic and pronounced march with many triplet note runs in the middle register with numerous accidentals. It is in A♭ major, is in 2/4 time, has many nice melodic lines, is mostly rhythmically straightforward, and has a dramatic ending. This is a fun solo and would be for a very good middle school student or a high school student. See Euphonium and Keyboard Collections.

Ewald, Victor. *Romance, Op. 2.* Trans./ed. David Reed. Edition Musicus, Inc. 1984. 2:30. III–IV. G–ab'. This is a beautiful work that is a standard in the trombone repertoire. A wonderful lyrical work to play on euphonium! Has many soaring lines and beautiful harmonies. The solo part is in bass clef.

Fahlman, Fredrik. *Horisont for Euphonium and Piano.* SVENSK MUSIK, Swedish Music Information Center. 1999. 7:00. IV. E–gb'. This Swedish composition was dedicated to Mikael Andersson. This tranquil and powerful character piece is a great addition for the euphonium as there are few works like it in the euphonium repertoire. It is mostly in 4/8 time and is in a moderate tempo. It has many chromatics, has many rhythmic challenges, a few technical challenges mostly coming due to wide intervals, is mostly in the middle to lower register, and is in bass and treble clef. This solo is highly expressive and dramatic and utilizes a very wide dynamic range. This work is most appropriate for college students and would be an excellent recital piece as it would make for a great change of pace.

Failenot, Maurice. *Introduction Et Rigaudon.* Gerard Billaudot, Paris. 1985. 2:00. III–IV. A–f'. The solo has both bass and treble clef versions.

Farben, Wogende, and James Moreau. *Couleurs En Mouvements, pour Tuba en Ut ou Saxhorn Basse Sib et Piano.* Alphonse Leduc. 1969. $17.65. 7:30. V. A challenging work with a wide use of chromatics and time signature changes. It is very technical and features several movements (Copper Yellow; Bleu Azur; Rouge Flamboyant). The solo part is in bass clef.

Fasch, Johann Friedrich. *Sonata in C Major.* Ed. Adam Frey and David M. Randolph. Athens Music Publishing. 2000. $17. IV–V. A challenging yet great baroque solo!

Faure, Gabriel. *Apres un Reve.* Arr. Steven Mead. Studio Music. $10.85. III. The solo part comes in both bass and treble clefs. This is a beautiful arrangement of this classic song and would be a great recital selection. Highly recommend.

Faure, Gabriel. *Apres un Reve (After a Dream).* Trans./arr. Ronald Dishinger. Medici Music Press. 1997. $4.50. 1:15. III. c–f'. This most beautiful song is in a slow 3/4, is in c minor, is mostly scale-wise triplets, is rhythmically straightforward, is mostly in the middle register, has a few chromatics, and is in bass clef. This would be an excellent solo for a good high school student or on a college recital.

Faure, Gabriel. *Elegie in C minor.* Ed. Adam Frey. Athens Music Publishing. 2000. IV–V.

Fernie, Alan. *Introduction and Allegro.* $15. IV. The solo part is in treble clef.

Filas, Juraj. *Concerto for Euphonium and Piano.* Edition BIM. 2002. $24. 17:00. V–VI. A fantastic new addition to our repertoire. It is also available with orchestra and concert band.

Fiocco, Joseph Hector. *Aria and Rondo.* Arr. Arthur Frackenpohl. Kendor Music, Inc. $7. IV–V.

Fiocco, Joseph Hector. *Arioso and Allegro.* Arr./ed. Robert Childs and Philip Wilby. Rosehill Music. 1997. 3:00. IV–V. F–bb'. A beautiful adagio begins the work, followed by a very fun and entertaining allegro section that ends the work. This would be a wonderful recital work! It is technical, but most runs are very idiomatic to the instrument. Both bass and treble clef parts are available.

Folse, Stuart. *Sonata for Euphonium and Piano.* Tuba-Euphonium Press. 1998. $12. 14:00. V–VI. AA–c''. This sonata has two movements that segue one into another: Moderate/Flowing and Slow/Expressive/Distant. This work is extremely challenging, as it has numerous rhythmic issues, tough technical passages, very wide intervals, loads of chromatics, a good amount of time changes and mixed meter sections, and many high register passages. The part is mainly in bass clef, but it has numerous extended tenor clef passages. This is an extremely powerful work, as it spans just about every possible musical emotion as it changes musical moods often. If you are looking for a great challenge and something that is totally different and modern, this is your piece.

Foster, Stephen Collins. *Gentle Annie.* Tuba-Euphonium Press. 1992. 2:45. III. d–bb'. This gorgeous song reflects the heavy American folk song influence in Foster's compositions. It is in Eb major, has simple rhythms, is mostly in the middle register, and is in bass clef. This is a great work for the euphonium and is highly recommended. It can be found in *The Art of Euphonium Playing*, volume 2 by Arthur Lehman. A band version is available. Recorded by Michael Colburn and Arthur Lehman.

Foster, Stephen Collins. *Stephen's Ladies of Song, for Euphonium and Piano.* Arr. Barton Cummings. Solid Brass Music Company. 2001. $10. 4:30. III. d–f'. This great collection of one of America's finest composers contains "Gentle Annie," "Oh Susanna," "Lula Is Gone," "Maggie by My Side," and "My Wife Is a Most Knowing Woman." It is rhythmically straightforward, is in the keys of Eb, G, and D major, is mostly in the middle to lower registers, has no accidentals, and is in bass clef. This would be an excellent solo for a good middle school student or high school player.

Frackenpohl, Arthur. *Air and Rondo.* Dorn Publications. 1992. $19.95. IV. AAb–bb. This work has a sweet and singing air that opens it. The rondo is very active and dance-like with many time changes. The solo part is in bass clef with some treble clef interspersed.

Frackenpohl, Arthur. *Divertimento for Euphonium or Trombone and Piano.* Tuba-Euphonium Press. 1997. $15. 12:00. V. BB♭–c″. This solo has three movements: March; Song; Gallop. The solo is mostly in tenor clef with some bass clef and features some passages with optional cadenzas. The March is in an allegro common time with some time changes into compound meters and features many wide leaps, rhythmic challenges, and tricky technical passages. It is very lively, powerful, and fun to play. The Song features many gorgeous passages that beautifully showcase the singing ability of the euphonium. It has some free passages and calls for an optional cup mute. The Gallop is very fast and highly energetic. It features typical gallop-type rhythms. It has many tricky leaps and technical passages. The movement juxtaposes a beautiful cantabile section in the middle. This is a challenging work, but it is a very rewarding challenge. It is a fantastic work and would be an excellent recital piece.

Frackenpohl, Arthur. *Sonata for Euphonium and Piano.* Dorn Publications. 1990. $12. 12:30. IV. BB♭–b♭′. This fantastic work written for Brian Bowman has become one of the standard sonatas in the euphonium repertoire. It has been a required work in several international euphonium solo competitions. This is a most enjoyable work! Three movements: Moderately Fast; Slowly; Fast. The first movement begins with a very lively and dance-like melody. It then soon introduces a lyrical section. These two contrasting sections are fragmented back and forth through the rest of the movement. The second movement is very lyrical, passionate, and makes a powerful musical statement! The last movement is very playful and rhapsodic in nature. There are some tricky fingering combinations and wide leaps in the first and third movements, but nothing that can't be handled with some practice!

Frank, Cesar. *Panis Angelicus, "O Lord Most Holy."* Trans./arr. Ronald Dishinger. Medici Music Press. 1997. $4.50. 1:45. II. B♭–c′. This is a pretty little song and would be a fine solo for a good middle school student. It is in a good key, is mostly quarters and eighths, has a few rhythmic challenges, has very few accidentals, and remains in the middle register.

Fritz, Gregory. *Concertino for Euphonium and Band.* TUBA Press. 1997. $12. 11:00. V. E–d″. This fantastic solo was commissioned by the U.S. Army Band and was composed for Robert Powers. This solo has become a standard in the euphonium repertoire. The work opens with a deliberate and regal sounding theme. It quickly moves to a gorgeous cantabile section. The work moves back and forth between very pronounced, powerful passages with soaring lyrical lines. Toward the end it features a highly expressive and showy cadenza that allows for loads of personal expression. The work comes to a rousing close with some fantastic sixteenth note runs and patterns! The work is in B♭ major mostly with some time in D major, it has many sixteenth note runs, many wide intervals, is in the high range often, is rhythmically straightforward, and is in bass clef with some tenor clef. This is a fantastic solo that every serious euphonium player and teacher should be familiar with.

Frohlich, Erich. *Solo for Posaune oder Bariton.* Blasmusikverlag Fritz Schulz. 1983. 3:00. IV–V. AA–f′. This work is in three movements (Allegro; Lento; Allegretto). The Allegro features strict sixteenth note runs, while the Lento features a beautiful lyrical melody. The Allegretto is very dance-like and tuneful. This is a very fun work and it comes with the suite (description below) on the back! The solo part is in bass clef.

Frohlich, Erich. *Suite fur Tenorhorn oder Bariton.* 2:00. IV–V. G–f′. This work is in five movements: Introduction; Sarabande; Menuetto; Aria; Giga. This would make a very good recital piece, as there are not many original works for euphonium written in this style.

Gabaye, Pierre. *Tubabillage pour Tuba Ut ou Contrebasse a Cordes ou Saxhorn basse ou Trombone basse et Piano.* Pierre Gabaye, Alphonse Leduc. 1959. 3:00. III–IV. d–f′. This would be a good solo for a high school student or a young college player. The solo part is in bass clef.

Gallaher, Christopher. *Sonata for Euphonium with Piano.* Tuba-Euphonium Press. 1991. $12. 12:00. VI. GG–g♭″. This solo was written for Dr. Earle Louder, retired principal euphonium player with the United States Navy Band. This fantastic solo has become a standard in the euphonium repertoire. It has five movements: Moderately Brisk; Slow; Allegro; Interlude; Bright. This is a very challenging solo and has some interesting special effects including metal or glass wind chimes to be played by the soloist (second movement) and taping the sides of the euphonium to a specified pattern alternating the left and right hands (last movement). The solo has no specified key signatures, has loads of sixteenth note runs, most of which are not scale-wise, has a high level of chromatics, has many rhythmic challenges, has many very challenging technical passages, spends a great deal of time in the high register, goes extremely high, has many mixed meter passages, requires some double tonguing, and is in bass clef with some use of tenor clef. With all of that said, this solo is worth all of the technical challenges, as it spans just about every possible musical feeling and emotion. There are countless syncopated and intensely driving passages, countless extremely powerful passages with intense dynamics and rips, many very exciting passages with rhythmic and meter play, dazzling technical displays, and gorgeous soaring lyrical lines. This solo has something for anyone and comes HIGHLY recommended.

Geminiani, Francesco. *Allegro from Concerto Grosso Opus 3, No. 2.* Trans./arr. Ronald Dishinger. Medici Music Press. 1992. $4. 2:30. III. G–f′. This solo is in a fast common time, is in d minor, is mostly quarter notes with a few eighth notes, is rhythmically straightforward, has sporadic use of chromatics, is in bass clef, and is mostly in the middle to lower register. This would be a good solo for an advanced middle school student.

George, Thom Ritter. *Moto Perpetuo, for Euphonium and Piano.* Tuba-Euphonium Press. 1993. $8. 3:00. V. D–a′. Written for Byron Hanson and completed in 1964, this solo is in a fast 2/4, has no key signature, is highly chromatic, has a good amount of double tonguing, is mostly in the middle to lower register, has some very wide intervals, and is in bass clef. This blazing technical showpiece is a must for those looking for a serious challenge.

George, Thom Ritter. *Sonata for Baritone Horn and Piano.* 1988. Revised version. Tuba-Euphonium Press. 1993. $12. 8:00. V. E–d″. This is one of the major standards in our repertoire and is one of the earliest. It was a challenge when it was first premiered in 1962 and it still challenges today's players. Three movements: Allegro; Andante; Presto. The first movement begins with a most memorable and bouncy theme that is reiterated and developed throughout the movement. The second movement is beautiful and features a small fast section and an incredible muted ending to the movement. The last movement is where the vast majority of the technical challenges are found. It is in tenor clef, ascends to the extreme high register often, and has very long technical runs. The last movement is very showy and energetic and is still one of the most powerful musical statements in the repertoire. Recorded by Douglas Nelson.

Gershwin, George. *Andante and Finale, from Rhapsody in Blue.* Trans. Walter Beeler. New World Music Corporation. 2:30. III. A♭–a♭′. This solo is a fantastic transcription of two of the most popular melodies from *Rhapsody in Blue*. The solo is in bass clef, is rhythmically straightforward, is highly chromatic, has some optional higher octaves, and has a wide dynamic range. This would be an excellent solo for a high school player or young college student.

Gershwin, George. *Summertime.* Arr. Howard Snell. $14. III–IV. This is one of Gershwin's most beloved songs. Solo part is written for B♭ and E♭ soloist. Brass band accompaniment is available. Order at www.euphonium.net.

Gershwin, George. *The Man I Love.* Arr. Howard Snell. $14. III–IV. This great Gershwin song was originally written for the Broadway play *Lady, Be Good*. This would be an excellent recital selection for a great change of pace and style. Order at www.euphonium.net.

Gillingham. *Vintage.* $14. This is a fantastic solo that is quickly becoming a euphonium favorite. This solo comes highly recommended.

Gluck, Christoph Willibald von. *Air from Orpheus.* Arr. Hamner. Studio Music. $7.50. III–IV. This solo features a beautiful song from Gluck's most famous work and opera. This would be a great change of pace and style on a recital. The solo is in treble clef.

Gluck, Christoph Willibald von. *Dance of the Blessed Spirits from Orpheus and Euridice.* Trans./arr. Ronald Dishinger. Medici Music Press. 1995. $4.50. 1:00. II. A–f′. This nice little lyrical solo from one of the most famous operas and beautiful early operas is in a slow 3/4, is in B♭ major, is mostly scale-wise eighth note runs, is rhythmically simple, is mostly in the middle and lower registers, and is in bass clef. This solo also comes with J. S. Bach's *Little Prelude*. This would be a good solo for an advanced middle school student.

Gluck, Christoph Willibald von. *Minuet from "Alceste."* Trans./arr. Ronald Dishinger. Medici Music Press. 1996. $4.50. 1:20. II–III. G–d′. This work features some nice melodies, is rhythmically straightforward, is in the middle to lower register, has few accidentals, and has a middle section with some very playable sixteenth note runs. This solo would be a good high school solo and ensemble selection.

Godard, Benjamin. *Berceuse from Jocelyn.* Trans./arr. Ronald Dishinger. Medici Music Press. 1993. $4.50. 4:00. III. e♭–g′. This solo has four sections: andantino; andante; andantino; andante. All of the sections are slow tempos. It is in B♭ and E♭ major and is mostly eighth note runs. It features straightforward rhythms, very few chromatics, and is mostly in the middle register. There are many beautiful lyrical passages that are well placed in terms of range to exploit the full singing quality of the euphonium. This would be a great solo for a good high school player and would be a nice selection on a college recital as well.

Goeyens, A. *All 'Antica.* Arr. Forrest L. Buchtel. Neil A. Kjos Music Company. 1975. $3.50. 4:00. IV. A–g′. This is a very energetic solo that is in a moderate common time, is in E♭ major, has many scale-wise sixteenth note runs, has some wide intervals, has some syncopation, and is in bass clef. This solo has many strong passages and is an excellent showpiece for a very good high school player or young college student.

Goldman, Franko Edwin. *Scherzo.* 4:30. IV–V. This fantastic solo was written by one of the finest cornet players of the early twentieth century and one of the finest band leaders of all time. Recorded by Brian Bowman.

Golland, John. *Euphonium Concerto.* Chester Music, London. 1984. $26.40. VI. It has three movements: Allegro; Andante Tranquillo; Allegro. This is a fantastic concerto! It is quickly becoming one of the most played euphonium concertos. It is very symphonic and highly expressive. A concert band and brass band version is available. Recorded by the Childs Brothers (Nicholas Childs).

Golland, John. *Euphonium Concerto, No. 2.* Studio Music Company. 1986. $35. VI. This fantastic solo was written for Nicholas and Robert Childs. The second movement is extremely powerful as that movement was dedicated to the memory of Nicholas and Robert's father, John Childs. The work overall is very reminiscent of Richard Strauss melodies, as it is very broad and triumphant. It has three movements: Moderato Eroico; Largo Elegaico; Allegro Energico e Scherzando. A concert band version is available. Recorded by Steven Mead.

Goodwin, Gordon. *Alborada for Euphonium and Piano.* Southern Music. 1:30. III–IV. c#–g♭'. This song is a Spanish dawn song. It is a very, very lovely melody! The solo part is in bass clef.

Gorb, Adam. *Concerto for Euphonium.* Maecenas Music. 1997. $41.95. 9:30. V. AA–b'. This fantastic concerto is in two movements. The first movement begins slow and is highly expressive. It soon moves to an allegretto section with a good amount of mixed meter. The second movement is highly energetic, is in compound meters, and has many mixed meters passages. This is a very fun solo to play and has a fantastic accompaniment. It is mostly in the middle register, has some challenging technical passages, and comes in both bass and treble clef parts. The major challenge of this work is rhythmic as it rarely features straightforward rhythms. This is a great concerto and I highly recommend this work for any recital. This solo also comes with band accompaniment.

Gordon, Stanley. *The Iceberg, King of the Northern Seas.* Adapter/arr. J. Hume. Ord, Boosey and Hawkes, Ltd. 2:00. III–IV. F–f'. This is a nice solo with many style changes and would be a very good selection for a high school student. The solo part is in both bass and treble clefs.

Gottschalk, Louis Moreau. *Caprice from Pasquinade (A Public Posting of Lampoons).* Trans./arr. Ronald Dishinger. Medici Music Press. 1991. $5. 5:30. III. c–a♭'. This lively and entertaining solo is in a fast common time and is in F and A♭ major. It is rhythmically straightforward, has very few chromatics and technical challenges, and is in bass clef. It moves into the high register a few times with some optional lower octaves. This would be a great solo and ensemble selection for a high school student.

Gounod, Charles-Francois. *Ave Maria.* Arr. Stouffer. Kendor Music, Inc. $5. 2:00. III. This arrangement of one of the most famous classical songs is a fine recital or solo and ensemble selection.

Gounod, Charles-Francois. *Hail! Ancient Walls from Faust.* Arr. Howard Snell. $14. 4:30.

III–IV. Gounod is famous for his memorable melodies. Here, one of Gounod's most famous arias from one of his most famous works. Brass band accompaniment is available. Order at www.euphonium.net. Recorded by Steven Mead.

Grady, Michael. *Concerto for Euphonium and Piano.* Tuba-Euphonium Press. 1992. $12. 12:30. V. C–b'. This very powerful concerto has three movements: Allegro furioso; Adagio sostenuto; Recitative. The first movement is very fast and furious with many powerful dynamics, big accents, and growing technical runs. The movement has a large amount of duple against triple that adds drama and energy. It also features a wide variety of style changes (pesante, dolce, marcato, slowly and freely, etc.). The second movement is gorgeous and features long, soaring lyrical lines. The third movement, like the first, features a wide variety of styles and is very powerful. It opens with a recitative section, but quickly moves to a very fast 8/8 and 10/8 section. This movement features a lot of rhythmic play and some very fun mixed meter. The work overall is in the middle register, has a large amount of chromatics, is in many keys, has a large amount of rhythmic challenges and a moderate amount of challenging technical passages, requires a wide dynamic range, and is in bass and tenor clef. I highly recommend this solo, as it is very fun to play and makes many powerful musical statements.

Grainger, Percy Aldridge. *Willow, Willow.* Arr. Carl Simpson. Masters Music Publications. 1995. III. d–a'. This is a beautiful, lyrical solo! It is well marked with specific instructions. It is a great small piece that is open to a wide range of interpretation and would be great on a recital or high school solo and ensemble contest.

Graham, Peter. *A Time for Peace, Gramercy Solo Album.* Gramercy Music. 1995. III–IV. B♭–b♭' (approximately). This solo is based on variations on a very popular church hymn, "Lily of the Valley." This solo is based on the theme from "The Essence of Time." It is playable by good high school students. The solo part is in treble clef.

Graham, Peter. *Brillante, Fantasy on Rule Britania.* Gramercy Music. $14. V. This is a fantastic showpiece made famous by Steven Mead. The solo parts comes in both treble and bass clefs and also includes a duo version. Band accompaniment is available. Recorded by Steven Mead.

Graham, Peter. *Glorious Ventures, Gramercy Solo Album.* Gramercy Music. 1995. IV. B♭–b♭' (approximately). This solo is based on variations on a very popular church hymn, "Lily of the Valley." It is most appropriate for college students. The solo part is in treble clef.

Graham, Peter. *The Holy Well,* Gramercy Music. 2000. $14. III–IV. This is a beautiful lyrical showcase for the euphonium. The solo part comes in both bass and treble clef and a brass band version is available.

Graham, Peter. *Swedish Hymn, Gramercy Solo Album.* Gramercy Music. 1995. III–IV. B♭–b♭' (approximately). This solo is most appropriate for high school students. The solo part is in treble clef.

Graham, Peter. *Whirlwind, Gramercy Solo Album.* Gramercy Music. 1995. IV. B♭–b♭' (approximately). This solo is most appropriate for college students. The solo part is in treble clef.

Grieg, Edward. *My Johann.* Arr. Corwell, Kendor Music, Inc. IV. $6.

Gruber. *Silent Night.* Arr. Fred Weber. Belwin Mills Inc. 1969. 1:00. I. A♭–d♭. A simple yet pretty arrangement of a Christmas classic. See Euphonium and Keyboard Collections.

Haak, Paul. *Amazing Grace.* Southern Music Company. $6. III. This is a fine arrangement of arguably the most popular religious song. The solo part comes in bass and treble clef.

Haak, Paul. *1812 Riff.* Southern Music Company. 1987. $3.50. 1:00. III. B♭–f'. This is a jazzy version of some 1812 licks! If you are looking for a good humorous piece for a recital, this is it! There are some optional octaves to add to the excitement. The solo part is in bass clef.

Haak, Paul. *Just a Closer Walk with Thee.* Southern Music Company. $3.50. III. This solo is a fine arrangement of one of the most popular religious songs. This would be a fun solo for a younger player to work on jazz style. The solo is in bass and treble clef.

Habbestad, Kjell. *Med Jesus vil eg fara, Op. 41.* Norwegian Music Information Center. 1994. 23:00. V. C–c''. This is a ten movements work: Meditatio; Elementum I; Elementum II; Elementum III; Canon; Variatio I; Variatio II; Variatio III; Fuga; Meditatio e Choralis. This work contains a lot of musical variety and selected movements to play could easily be chosen to accommodate various time restrictions on a recital.

Haddad, Don. *Suite for Baritone.* Shawnee Press Inc. 1966. $10. 9:00. III–IV. G–c''. Three movements: Allegro Maestoso; Andante Expressivo; Allegro con Brio. This work has become one of the standards in the euphonium repertoire. It has been asked on countless competitions and is frequently a required solo at solo and ensembles contests, state and regional honor band auditions, and for college entrance auditions. The first movement has three sections. The first section is majestic, the second section is lyrical, and the last section is an even more driving continuation of the first section. The second movement is in 6/8 and features a very sweet and lilting melody. The third movement alternates between 3/4 and 4/4 time and is mysterious in nature at the beginning. It has a middle section that is very schmaltzy, a cadenza in the middle that brings back material from the first movement, and a very powerful and driving ending. There

are range and technical challenges, but the work gives plenty of time for rest and recovery. This is a must study for a young eager euphonium student.

Halevy, Jacques. *The Cardinal's Air, from the Opera "La Juive."* Arr./ed. Frank Clark. 1:00. III. E–e'. This is a lovely little aria. The solo part is in bass clef.

Handel, George Frederic. *Allegro from Concerto Grosso Opus 3, No. 4.* Trans./arr. Ronald Dishinger. Medici Music Press. 1986. $5. 2:30. II–III. B♭–f'. This lively solo is in an allegro 3/4 and in the key of B♭ major. It is rhythmically straightforward, has very few chromatics, is in the middle to lower register, has numerous repeated sections, and is in bass clef. The only real challenge is endurance, as there are no rests. This would be a very fun solo for a good middle school student.

Handel, George Frederic. *Adagio and Allegro from Sonata in E.* Trans. Bernard R. Fitzgerald. Theodore Presser Co. 1957. $5. 3:30. III–IV. B♭–b♭'. This work is in two sections, adagio and allegro. The adagio section is very expressive and features many sixteenth runs. The allegro features a very lively and beautiful tune that ascends to the high register often. The allegro also has many sixteenth runs. This is a good piece for a young college player, especially for someone needing a range challenge. The part comes in both bass and treble clefs.

Handel, George Frederic. *Bourree.* Trans./arr. Ronald Dishinger. Medici Music Press. 1993. I$4.50. 3:00. I–III. B♭–f'. This French dance is in a moderate common time, is in E♭ major, is mostly scale-wise eighth note runs, has a few accidentals, is in bass clef, has some optional repeats, and is mostly in the lower register. This playful and fun solo would be an excellent solo for a good middle school player or younger high school student.

Handel, George Frederic. *Cantilena.* Arr. Forrest L. Buchtel. Neil A. Kjos Music Company. 1960. $2. 2:30. II–III. A–f' (optional low f in one section). This solo is in a slow common time, is in B♭ major, is mostly eighth notes, has some accidentals, has a few grace notes, has a few wide intervals, has a lot of dynamic contrast, and is in bass clef. For this level there are a good amount of musical issues to work with. This would be a good solo for an advanced middle school player.

Handel, George Frederic. *Concerto for Oboe in G Minor.* Trans./arr. Ronald Dishinger. Medici Music Press. 1997. $8. 7:30. III–IV. G–f'. This wonderful work features four movements: Grave; Allegro; Sarabande; Allegro. All of the Allegro movement's tempos are very moderate, there is sporadic use of accidentals throughout, a few rhythmic challenges, overall in the middle to lower register, and the vast majority of sixteenth note runs are scale-wise. This would be a very fine work for a junior or senior recital. It features many wonderful melodies and fun technical passages.

Handel, George Frederic. *The Harmonious Blacksmith*. Arr. K. Wilkinson. Studio Music. $7.50. III–IV. This is an air and variations from Handel's *Fifth Suite for Harpsichord*. This is one of Handel's most famous instrumental works. It is very lively, tuneful, and fun to play. The solo part is available in both bass and treble clefs.

Handel, George Frederic. *Honor and Arms from Samson*. Arr. Allen Ostrander. Edition Musicus Inc. $4.25. II–III. A very popular solo for middle school and high school players.

Handel, George Frederic. *Jubal's Lyre*. Arr. Corwell. Kendor Music, Inc. $6. IV–V. This beautiful rhapsodic work is arranged from Handel's oratorio *Joshua*.

Handel, George Frederic. *Largo and Allegro*. Ed. Larry Campbell. Hal Leonard Publishing Corporation. 1977. $12.95. 2:30. III. c–ab'. This work is part of a collection of solos–Master Solos, Intermediate Level. This solo features several different styles and many musical aspects to study. It remains in the middle register and is primarily quarter note with some long eighth note run passages. It would be a very nice solo for a high school student or very good middle school player. Recorded by Larry Campbell.

Handel, George Frederic. *Largo from Xerxes*. Trans./arr. Ronald Dishinger. Medici Music Press. 1991. $4.50. 3:00. II–III. c–f'. This beautiful solo from one of Handel's most famous operas is in a slow 3/4, is in F major, features mostly quarter notes and dotted rhythms, is mostly rhythmically straightforward, is mostly in the middle register, has few chromatics, is in bass clef, and has few technical challenges. It is a very expressive work that would be a great solo for a high school student.

Handel, George Frederic. *Menuet from Concerto Grosso, Op. 6, No. 5*. Trans./arr. Ronald Dishinger. Medici Music Press. 1993. $3.50. 2:00. II–III. F–d'. This lively little solo is in a moderate 3/4, is in F major and bass clef, has few accidentals, has many eighth note run passages, most of which are easily played, has no rhythmic challenges, and is mostly in the middle to lower register. This would be a very good second or third solo for a middle school player.

Handel, George Frederic. *O King of Kings, (Air) Alleluia*. Arr. D. F. Bachelder. Tuba-Euphonium. 2001. $10. 4:00. III–IV. G–g'. This solo is mostly in a fast 12/8 with running scale-wise eighth note passages. It is in Ab major, is in bass clef, is mostly in the middle register, is rhythmically straightforward, has a few trills, has a few accidentals, and when ascending into the high register it quickly moves lower. This solo is a nice contrast between flowing and very regal. It is a fun solo to play and would be a great solo for a good high school student or young college player.

Handel, George Frederic. *Sarabande and Menuett*. Ed. Larry Campbell. Hal Leonard Publishing Corporation. 1977. $12.95. 1:30. II. d–f'. This work is part of a collection of solos–Master Solos, Intermediate Level–and would be a fine solo for a middle school player, as it remains in the middle register, is a moderate tempo, and primarily features quarter notes with a few eighth note runs. Both the Sarabande and Menuett have sweet singing melodies. Recorded by Larry Campbell.

Handel, George Frederic. *Sarabande*. Trans./arr. Ronald Dishinger. Medici Music Press. 1991. $4.50. 2:00. II–III. d–f'. This solo would be a very appropriate solo to help a good middle school student or young high school student gain confidence in his or her high register while playing a good musical line. It ascends often, but there are plenty of sections in the middle register.

Handel, George Frederic. *Sonata in F Major, Opus No. 1, No. 12*. Trans./arr. Neal Ramsay and Ronald Dishinger. Medici Music Press. 2001. $12. 7:00. IV. F–g'. Four movements: Adagio; Allegro; Andante; Allegro. The first movement is lyrical, very expressive, slow, and has a very fluid vocal quality. It features many sixteenth note runs. The second movement is very playful in character and has many sixteenth note runs. It is an easily playable and fun technical challenge. With the third movement Handel again demonstrates his gift of writing lines that sing. The last movement is very bouncy and fun to play. It is mostly triplets and has some technical challenges that are easy to handle. This would be a fantastic solo for a good high school student or young college student to study.

Handel, George Frederic. *Sonata No. V*. Trans./arr. Ronald Dishinger. Medici Music Press. 1998. $8. 5:00. III–IV. Bb–g'. Four movements: Larghetto; Allegro; Siciliana; Giga. This is a very expressive and musically varied sonata. The first movement is slow and very lyrical and cantabile in nature. It primarily remains in the middle register and is straightforward in terms of rhythm and has few accidentals. The second movement has a driving quality throughout with many idiomatic sixteenth note runs. This movement moves into the higher register more. The third movement has a great style that is not often found in music in the euphonium repertoire. It also mainly stays in the middle register. The last movement is in 12/8 and is very lively and a lot of fun. This movement moves into the high register a little more. This is a great sonata that would make for a wonderful recital selection!

Handel, George Frederic. *Suite in Ab from Sonata No. II for Flute*. Arr. Donald C. Little. Belwin-Mills Publishing Corp. 1978. 3:00. III–IV. Bb–f'. This is a fantastic arrangement of a wonderful work. It has three sections: allegro; siciliana;

allegro. The first allegro section is marked slower than most allegros. It is 4/4, in A♭ major, and has many scale-wise sixteenth note runs and a decent amount of accidentals. It is very lively and fun to play. The siciliana is in 6/8, and is very slow, lyrical, and passionate. The last allegro section is in 12/8 and is mostly scale-wise triplet runs. This would be a great solo for a high school player. The figured bass realization is by George R. Belden.

Handel, George Frederic. *Thunder, Lightening and Whistling Wind.* Arr. Ostrander. Kendor Music, Inc. $6. IV.

Handel, George Frederic. *Water Music Suite No. 1 from Water Music Suite No. 1 and No. 3.* Trans./arr. Ronald Dishinger. Medici Music Press. 1995. $8.50. 5:00. III. F–e♭'. Includes a rigaudon, bourree, and hornpipe. All of the tempos are moderate and most of the technical demands are found in the last section, the hornpipe, where there are running eighth notes with many wide leaps. Range is moderate, staying primarily in the middle register. It has numerous repeats that could be left out to shorten the work. This solo would be a very good solo for a high school student to work on various musical styles or for a solo and ensemble contest.

Handel, George Frederic. *Water Music Suite No. 2 from Water Music Suite No. 3.* Trans./arr. Ronald Dishinger. Medici Music Press. 1995. $8. 5:00. III. A♭–g♭'. Includes three menuets and a gigue. All of the tempos are moderate and most of the technical demands are found in the last section, the gigue, where there are running eighth notes with many octave leaps. Range is moderate, staying primarily in the middle register. It has numerous repeats that could be left out to shorten the work. This solo would be a very good solo for a high school student to work on various musical styles or for a solo and ensemble contest.

Handel, George Frederic. *Where're You Walk.* trans/arr. Ronald Dishinger. Medici Music Press. 1993. $5. 1:30. II–III. c–d'. This is a good first solo for a middle school student.

Hanmer, Ronald. *Invicta,* Wright & Round LTD., Music Publishers, Gloucester, England. 5:30. V. F–c". This is a highly technical but flashy solo chock full of slurred triplet and sixteenth note runs, most of which are very idiomatic for the instrument. The solo part is in treble clef.

Harline. *When You Wish upon a Star.* Arr. Makoto Kanai. 4:00. III–IV. This is a fantastic arrangement of one of the most popular Disney themes. Recorded by Steven Mead.

Hartley, Walter. *Euphonium Concerto.* Accura Music. 1980. 11:00. V. BB♭–f". This is a great work by a great composer. It is a must study. Both bass and treble clef parts are available. The bass clef part contains some tenor clef.

Hartley, Walter. *Two Pieces.* Theodore Presser Company. 1976. 3:30. IV. AA–c". This is a lyrical

piece with a scherzino (very fun, lively, and powerful). It is a great work for a contrast in style on a recital! The solo is available in bass and treble clef.

Hartmann, John. *Robin Adair.* Wright & Round from the Liverpool Brass Band Journal, Molenaar Music. $16. 5:00. VI. E–b♭'. This highly technical theme and variations has many fantastic musical moments and some highly impressive technical lines. It is loaded with double and triple tonguing, many fun and different rhythm combinations for a theme and variations, several great cadenzas, and a bolero section!

Hauser. *Cradle Song.* Arr. Fred Weber. Belwin Mills Inc. 1969. $5. 1:20. I. A–c'. This is beautiful little lyrical song in B♭ major with simple rhythms and a few accidentals. It would be a lovely first solo and ensemble selection. See Euphonium and Keyboard Collections.

Haworth, Frank. *Nocturne.* Canadian Music Center. 1977. 3:00. III–IV. A–c". A beautiful work that would be a nice change in mood for a recital! The solo part is in bass clef.

Haydn, Franz Joseph. *Country Dance.* Arr. Stouffer, Kendor Music, Inc. $5. II. This pretty little tune would be a very good solo for a middle school student as it has simple rhythms, a modest range, and is musically effective.

Haydn, Franz Joseph. *Gypsy Rondo.* Arr. Leonard B. Smith. Belwin Mills, CPP/Belwin, Inc., 1973. $4.95. 1:30. III. c–d'. This work is in F major, 2/4, and marked "leggiero." It is primarily slurred sixteenth note runs that are sometimes scale-wise. It truly has a gypsy dance sound and feel and has some very fun dynamic changes, rhythmic changes, and chromatic alterations. This would be a very entertaining and challenging solo for a high school student. See Euphonium and Keyboard Collections.

Haydn, Franz Joseph. *Rondo from Trio in G.* Trans./arr. Ronald Dishinger. Medici Music Press. 2002. $7. 4:30. III–IV. F–e'. This lively work features many sixteenth note runs at a moderate tempo. The technique is very playable as it is all in the middle register and has few accidentals.

Haydn, Franz Joseph. *Serenade.* Trans./arr. Ronald Dishinger. Medici Music Press. 1993. $5. 3:00. III. B–a'. A beautiful work with many expressive sections. It is a moderate tempo with mostly quarter and eighth note passages with occasional sixteenth note runs. It is very vocal in quality and is mainly in the middle register, allowing for a rich singing quality throughout. Would be an excellent solo for a high school student to work on musicality.

Haydn, Franz Joseph. *Two Classical Themes.* Ed. Larry Campbell. Hal Leonard Publishing Corporation. 1977. $12.95. 1:30. III. G–a'. This work is part of a collection of solos—Master Solos, Intermediate Level—and would be a fine solo for a very good middle school player or most high school students. It is a good high register challenge, as it ascends to the high register often. Technically it features mostly quarter notes and a few eighth note runs. The first theme is very passionate while the second theme is very lively. Recorded by Larry Campbell.

Heath, Reginald. *Andante and Scherzo*. R. Smith & Company. 1969. 2:00. IV. F–a'. The solo part is in treble clef.

Henry, Jean-Claude. *Mouvement pour Tuba, Saxhorn basse Sib ou Trombone basse et Piano*. Alphonse Leduc, Paris. 5:45. V. GG–c#''. This work has many time signature changes, counting and technical issues, wide leaps, and high tessitura. If you want something TOTALLY different to play on a recital, this is it! The solo part is in bass clef.

Herbert. *Gypsy Love Song*. Arr. Forrest L. Buchtel. Neil A. Kjos Music Company. 1956. $1.75. 2:00. II. c–eb'. This beautiful little solo is in a slow 9/8 and a slow common time, is in Eb and Bb major, has a few challenging rhythms, and is in bass clef. This would be an excellent second or third solo for a young player.

Herbert, Victor. *Victor Herbert Medley*. Arr. Fred Weber. Belwin Mills Inc. 1969. $5. 1:10. I. Bb–d'. A simple arrangement marked "moderate waltz tempo" in Eb and F major of "Toyland" and "Because You're You." It has simple rhythms and a few accidentals. See Euphonium and Keyboard Collections.

Hewitt, Harry. *Six Preludes for Euphonium and Piano*. TUBA Press. 1992. $10. V. F–bb'. If you are looking for something totally different to play on a recital, this is it! Each prelude covers a wide variety of musical styles. The first prelude is slow and very animated and agitated, with several tremolo sections creating some unique sounds with the piano. Its duration is about three minutes. The second prelude is slow and extremely sustained, creating a very thick and neat wash of sound with the piano. This prelude remains in the high register for long periods of time and is about three minutes in length. The third prelude is very dance-like and features a small double tonguing passage toward the end and a section with some really neat displaced accents. It is about three minutes long. The fourth prelude is very ethereal and contains some chance music and some flutter tongue passages. This is a very neat and different little piece of music. It is about three minutes long. The fifth prelude is very energetic, is fast, requires some double tonguing, is mostly in the middle register, and is about two minutes long. It is very fun to play. The last prelude is very sustained, lyrical, is mostly in the middle to lower register, and is about four minutes in length. This work is in bass clef and can be a little challenging to read.

Hilfiger, John Jay. *Christmas Carol Suite*. Wehr's Music House. $7.50. II–III. Includes settings by Mr. Hilfiger of these popular Christmas carols: "Oh Come, Oh Come, Emmanuel," "What Child Is This?" "Joy to the World," "Good Christian Men, Rejoice," and "Away in a Manger." Solo part is in treble clef only.

Hill, William H. *Noble Hymn*. Neil A. Kjos Music Company. 1978. $1.75. 1:15. I–II. Bb–eb'. This solo is in a moderate common time, is in Bb major, has some scale-wise eighths, is rhythmically simple, is mostly in the middle register, and is in bass clef. This would be a good first or second solo for a middle school player.

Hill, William H. *The Viking*, Neil A. Kjos Music Company. 1978. $1.75. 1:15. I–II. d–eb'. This solo is in a moderate common time, is in Bb major, is mostly scale-wise eighth note runs, is mostly in the middle register, is rhythmically simple, and is in bass clef. This solo is very majestic, especially for its grade level. This would be a good solo for a middle school student.

Hirano, Mitsuru. *Euphonium Sonata*. 6:00. V. A–e''. This is a one-movement sonata that is a really neat work, but it lives in the high register!

Hogg, Merle E. *Three Studies for Euphonium and Piano*. Tuba-Euphonium Press. 2003. $12. IV–V. BBb–c''. The first study is in a moderately fast tempo and has no key signature. It features a good amount of mixed meter, mainly moving from common time to 7/8. It features very entertaining rhythmic play and is very energetic. It has a good amount of chromatics and wider intervals. This is a very fun study to play with many powerful moments. The second study is very slow and lyrical. It has a middle section with special effects including multiphonics, some chance elements, and special effects with the piano. The third study is fast and energetic, features some powerful mixed meter, and even has a middle section that is slower, in 10/8, and is in a blues style! It features a very showy and powerful ending! All three studies are in bass clef and all of them are between two to four minutes long. This is a fantastic work, as it is highly energetic, powerful, and unique in that it has so many different musical styles. It is technically demanding and has many sections in the higher register. However, it is a most worthy challenge. I highly recommend this work.

Hohne, Carl. *Slavonic Fantasy*. Editions Marc Reift. $13. IV. This flashy solo has a wide variety of melodies and would be an excellent recital selection. The solo part is in bass and treble clef.

Hopkinson, Michael E. *Concerto for Tuba (Concerto Euphonique)*. Kirklees Music. 1978. 14:00. IV–V. It has three movements: Allegro Moderato; Adagio; Allegro Giocoso. BB–bb'. This is a technical showpiece with a good deal of mixed meter. It would be a good recital piece. The solo part is in treble clef.

Hoshina, Hiroshi. *Fantasy for Euphonium and Piano*. Tuba-Euphonium Press. 1986. $10. IV–V. G–c''. This wonderful work commissioned by Toro Miura has become a standard euphonium recital piece and has been a required work on several international euphonium solo competitions. It is a tone poem-like work with a gorgeous melody that is developed throughout. It is mostly in the middle to upper register but has several places to get a high range rest. It has some rhythmic challenges and has several highly expressive cadenza-like passages. It is very passionate, emotionally powerful, and has several sections for unaccompanied euphonium. Roger Behrend described this piece best: "One can imagine a sunrise over a picturesque Japanese countryside." The work comes in bass clef and with program notes. Recorded by Steven Mead.

Horovitz, Joseph. *Euphonium Concerto.* Novello and Company Limited. 1991. $25. 16:30. VI. Bb–c″. This is a must study euphonium work as it is a very fine work and is one of our first concertos. It has been a required work on several international euphonium solo competitions. Written in 1972 and premiered by Trevor Groom, this work is classical in structure and design. The first movement begins at a moderate tempo but moves to some quicker and slower tempos later. The movement is very cheerful, animated, and bouncy and is tons of fun to play. It has many sixteenth note passages, has many powerful and dramatic moments with big articulation and dynamics, and has many tender sections. The second movement features one of the most passionate melodies written for the euphonium. It has many long lyrical phrases and has a beautiful faster middle section. This movement requires a great deal of breath control. The last movement opens with an introduction, then moves to a rondo theme that is transformed through a series of variations. This movement contains many running sixteenth triplets, many of which are very technically challenging. The overall range of the work is fairly conservative for a work of its technical difficulty. Very fine program notes accompany the solo part. Both treble and bass parts are included and there are versions for concert band, brass band, and orchestra. Recorded by Steven Mead, Robin Taylor, Robert Childs, and Thomas Rüedi.

Hutchinson, Warner. *Sonatina.* Carl Fischer. 8:00. IV. E–a′. The first movement is moderately fast and very pronounced. The second movement is slow and lyrical. The last movement is in a march style and is very fun to play! This is a wonderful work that has often been asked on all-state and solo and ensemble auditions. The solo part is in bass clef.

Hummel, Johan Nepomuk. *Fantasy.* Arr./ed. Robert Childs and Philip Wilby. Rosehill Music, 1997. $15.75. V. Eb–bb′. A challenging but fantastic work! It has many beautiful lyrical passages along with lively dance-like sections and showy technical runs. The solo part is available in both bass and treble clefs.

Iannaccone, Anthony. *Night Song for Euphonium, Trombone or Bassoon and Piano.* Tenuto Publications. 1976. $5. 2:30. II. Bb–g′. This pretty little song would be a good second solo for a middle school student. It is in Ab major, 3/4, remains in the middle register, and is marked "moderately." It is mostly quarter notes and straightforward rhythms. The challenge lies is in the large amount of accidentals. It has many sections of dynamic and articulation contrasts. Program notes accompany the piano part.

Ihlenfeld, Dave. *Clouds.* Tuba-Euphonium Press. 1997. $10. 4:00. IV–V. c–g′. This is a jazz solo with chord changes throughout. It is in a moderate 6/8, is in F major, is in bass clef, remains mostly in the middle register, and has some rhythmic challenges and a good amount of chromatics. You do not need to have improvising skills to perform this solo. However, if you do have improvising skills, then this solo allows for loads of improvisational expression. If you are looking for something totally different to perform on a recital, this is it.

Ito, Yasuhide. *Fantasy Variations.* 8:00. V. This beautiful Japanese solo was dedicated to Toro Miura. It is a very unusual variation-type solo and has variations marked "ciaccona," "rondo," and "finale" (fuga). This is a fantastic work! Recorded by Steven Mead.

Ito, Yasuhide. *Fantasy Variations for Euphonium and Band.* VI. This is a highly experimental chance music piece. If you want a big time twentieth-century piece on your recital, or something drastically different, this is your piece. The solo part is in bass clef. Contact Adam Frey for ordering details.

Jacob, Gordon. *Fantasia for Euphonium.* Boosey & Hawkes. 1973. $12:00. 12:00. V. C–d″. Written for Michael Mamminga in 1969, this is one of the first major works for the euphonium. This is a must study for any euphonium student, as it is one of our finest works by a very fine composer and today is still one of the most popular euphonium works. It has been on countless international euphonium solo competitions and college auditions. It is more challenging than it looks, but it is still one of the most enjoyable euphonium works. The work is in several sections, with the first being very slow and mysterious. The middle section is fast and has loads of style and mood changes: triumphant, playful, sneaky, surprising, powerful, and so forth. The opening material eventually returns in a beautiful muted section, leading to an extended cadenza that tests rhythm, flexibility, and range. The work comes to a rapid close with a restatement of material found at the start of the first fast section. This work beautifully demonstrates all of the range and technical possibilities of the euphonium, as it features some fast runs and double tongued passages. The range overall is moderate and there are optional pitches for the highest notes. There are versions for concert band, brass band, and orchestra. Recorded by Steven Mead and Robin Taylor.

Jacome, Saint. *Andante and March.* Arr. Roland Brom. Kendor Music Inc. 2001. $5. 1:45. II–III. e♭–f′. This work begins very stately and has a fair amount of dotted eighth rhythms and some scale-wise eighth note runs. It ends with a very fun and pronounced allegro section. The solo comes in both bass and treble clef, is in A♭ and B♭ major, is in common time, and is rhythmically straightforward. This would be a fine work for a good middle school or high school player.

Jager, Robert. *Concerto for Euphonium.* Hal Leonard Music Corp. 1996. $14.95. 12:00. V. BB♭–d♭″. Written by one of America's premiere concert band composers, this solo demonstrates all of the capabilities of the euphonium. Three movements: Slowly, Dramatically, Freely; Slowly, Reflectively; Brightly, but Not Forcefully. The first movement has many very powerful musical moments. It begins slowly and moves to a very fast section with lots of mixed meter. The full range of the euphonium is explored here, as well as many syncopated passages, technical runs, wide intervals, and flutter tonguing. In the second movement, once again the full range is explored. This movement is very passionate and has many soaring lines. It is highly chromatic, creating lots of tension, is rhythmically challenging, and has many beautiful harmonic progressions. The third movement is loads of fun, as it is highly rhythmic and features lots of mixed meter. The full range is explored, it is highly chromatic, requires some double tonguing, and has many wide intervals and some tricky technical passages. The work ends very dramatically as the tempo becomes extremely fast with some powerful and intense technical runs.

Jarrett, Jack. *Prelude and Canticle for Euphonium and Piano.* Tuba-Euphonium Press. 1994. $10. 8:30. V. F♯–d♭″. This is a great solo that was written for Bob Powers. The prelude is in a slow 3/4 and is highly expressive and lyrical. The canticle begins slow and lyrical but quickly moves to an allegro section that features some very fun mixed meter. This work spends a good amount of time in the high register, so good high chops are needed. It also has many challenging rhythms and technical passages. The solo comes in both bass and treble clef. This is a very fine work and deserves more attention. If you are looking for a fantastic new recital work, this is it.

Jenkinson, Ezra. *Elfentanz.* Winwood Music. $8.75. IV–V. This is a neat and different original work for the euphonium. The solo part is available in bass and treble clef.

Jones, Roger. *Dialogue for Euphonium and Piano.* TUBA Press. 1992. $10. 6:00. IV–V. G–b′. This work is in an allegro cut time, has no key signature, is rhythmically straightforward, has some tricky runs, has loads of accidentals, spends a

great deal of time in the high register, and is in bass clef. This is a very powerful solo with many contrasts in mood and energy. It is very driving and juxtaposes some dramatic silent and quasi-cadenza passages. Due to the high level of chromatics, there are many passages with lots of tension. This would be an excellent change of pace on most any recital.

Joplin, Scott. *The Strenuous Life.* Arr. Forrest L. Buchtel. Neil A. Kjos Music Company. 1974. $2. 2:20. II–III. B♭–f′. This is a great arrangement of a fine Scott Joplin rag. It is in a slow cut time, is in B♭ and F major, is mostly scale-wise eight note passages, has some simple syncopation, has a few accidentals, is mostly in the middle register, and is in bass clef. This would be an excellent solo for an advanced middle school student and would be a great first study in ragtime music.

Kac, Stefan. *Serenade for Euphonium and Piano.* Tuba-Euphonium Press. 2003. $12. 5:30. IV–V. E–b♭′. This highly expressive solo is overall slow, has no key signature, has several ad-lib sections, has a massive amount of chromatics, is mostly in the middle to lower register, and has some rhythmic challenges. It is well marked in terms of dynamics, tempos, articulations, style, and piano cues. This solo allows for a massive amount of artistic freedom and expression and would be an excellent recital piece.

Kaler, arranger. *Estrellita.* Al Boss, Philadelphia. 2:30. IV. c–a′. This is a nice arrangement of this beautiful song made popular by Steven Mead. The solo part is in bass clef. Contact Adam Frey for ordering information.

Kassatti, Tadeusz. *By Gaslight.* Editions BIM. 1999. $12.50. 6:00. III–IV. A–b♭′. Commissioned by Steven Mead, this is a fantastic work that features a beautiful wash of sound. Its repeating triplets over block piano chords give it a relaxing, flowing effect. The solo part is available in both bass and treble clefs. Recorded by Steven Mead.

Kassatti, Tadeusz. *Kino Concertino.* Editions BIM. $24. 16:00. IV. This is a fantastically fun work! It is extremely lively and has many gorgeous soaring lines. This would be a fantastic work to play on any recital that would be a joy for any audience! This work also comes with string orchestra accompaniment.

Keighley, Thomas. *Romance in F minor.* Boosey & Co. Ltd. 1927. 3:00. III–IV. F–b♭′. This is an absolutely beautiful lyrical solo! It is very accessible, as it doesn't stay high long and has only a few technical challenges. I highly recommend this work! The solo part is in bass clef.

King, Karl L. *A Night in June.* 3:00. III. d♭–a♭′. Most famous as a composer of fine marches, Karl King wrote many beautiful solos for various instruments in his overtures. He was a euphonium player in circus bands and here is featured one of the most beautiful and most famous euphonium solos from the circus repertoire. This is a superb recital selection! I highly recommend this work. Recorded by Steven Mead and Arthur Lehman.

Kirk-Smith, Rebecca. *Highgarth Invention*. Winwood Music. $8.75. III–IV. This is a very fun original work for the euphonium. The solo part comes in bass and treble clef versions.

Klengel, Julius. *Concertino No. 1 in B♭ Major, Op. 7, First Movement.* Arr. Leonard Falcone. TUBA Press. 1994. $10. 7:30. V. F–c″. This is a fantastic solo that was arranged by one of the greatest euphonium players. It is in an allegro common time, is in B♭ major, is mostly scale-wise sixteenth note and triplet runs, has a good amount of accidentals, has a decent amount of very wide intervals, is rhythmically straightforward, spans a wide range, and is in bass clef. This is a very showy solo, as it features the euphonium beautifully. There are countless rhapsodic passages, and it features a gorgeous opening melody that is heard again in the recapitulation. The work is in a sonata-allegro set-up and features a highly technical, impressive, and rousing ending. This would make an outstanding recital piece.

Krzywicki, Jan. *Ballade for Baritone or Tuba and Piano.* Heilman Music. 1984. 3:00. II–III. E–e′. This slow, beautifully flowing lyrical solo was first performed by Paul Krzywicki at the 1983 International Tuba-Euphonium Conference, University of Maryland, College Park. The solo part is in bass clef and is mostly in the lower register.

Krzywicki, Jan. *Pastorale for Baritone Horn and Wind Ensemble.* Tuba-Euphonium Press. 2000. $12. 9:00. IV. D–c″. This solo is based on an anonymous sixteenth-century English counterpoint exercise found in the *Fitzwilliam Virginal Book,* volume II (the counterpoint exercise is printed at the front of the solo). This is a beautiful solo with piano reduction that has many soaring lyrical lines. It is mostly in a slow 3/2 and 4/2 time, has no key signature, spans a wide range, ascends into the high range often, has some rhythmic challenges, has loads of chromatics, and is in bass clef. It is well marked, as it has very specific articulations, phrasing, dynamics, style markings, and tempo changes. If you are looking for something different in terms of a lyrical selection for a recital, this is your piece. This is a beautiful solo!

Kuhmstedt, Paul. *Humoreske fur Tuba (oder Bariton oder Posaune).* Georg Bauer, Musikverlag, Karlsruhe/Rhein, 1985. III–IV. F–c″. This work sounds just like the title suggests. It has very few technical challenges. The solo part is in bass clef.

Kummer, G. *Variations for Ophicleide.* Studio Music Co., London. 1995. $12.25. V. CC–c″. From Steven Mead's *The World of the Euphonium,* this is a classic theme and variations from the mid-nineteenth century to show off the soloist's dexterity. This work features some wonderful romantic moments as well as a great mazurka and technical flashes. The work also features program notes about the work as well as performance hints and suggestions from Steven Mead. The solo part is available in both bass and treble clefs.

Lamater, De., E. *Brilliant Polka.* Rubank, Hal Leonard Corporation. $6.50. 3:00. III. f–g′. This fun little solo would make for a great solo and ensemble selection for a good middle school student or high school player. It is in F and B♭ major, is in 2/4, has a moderate amount of scale-wise sixteenth note runs, is rhythmically straightforward, and is in bass clef. It begins with a slow polka section that accelerates, then moves to a moderato expressive section before ending with a faster polka section. See Euphonium and Keyboard Collections.

Lamater, De., E. *Congratulations.* Rubank, Hal Leonard Corporation. $6.50. 2:30. II. c–e♭′. This lovely waltz caprice is in E♭ and A♭ major, is in 3/4, has a large amount of chromatics, is rhythmically simple, is in the middle to lower register, and is in bass clef. This would be a great solo selection for a middle school player. See Euphonium and Keyboard Collections.

Lamater, De., E. *Romance.* Rubank, Hal Leonard Corporation. $6.50. 2:00. III. c–f′. This beautiful solo is in F major, is in a slow 6/8, has a few chromatics, is rhythmically straightforward, has a very small cadenza, is mostly in the middle register, and is in bass clef. This would be a great lyrical solo for a middle school player. See Euphonium and Keyboard Collections.

Lamater, De., E. *Thoughts of Home.* Rubank, Hal Leonard Corporation. $6.50. 1:30. II. c–d′. This small ballad is in B♭ major, is in 12/8, is rhythmically straightforward, has very few accidentals, is mostly in the middle to lower register, and is in bass clef. This lovely solo would be an ideal second solo for a middle school player. See Euphonium and Keyboard Collections.

Lancen, Serge. *Grave pour Tuba ut ou Baryton ou base si♭ et Piano.* Alphonse Leduc, Paris. 2:30. III–IV. A–e♭′. Slow, singing melody that features some intense syncopated swells. It has many opportunities for the soloist to work on various interpretations of many lovely melodic lines. The solo part is in bass clef.

Lane, William. *Concert Piece for Euphonium.* Tuba-Euphonium Press. 2001. $8. 3:30. IV–V. F–c″. This work is moderately fast and has numerous time signature changes. It is in F major, is in bass clef, spans a wide range, and is mostly eighth note and sixteenth note runs. Most of the runs are not scale-wise and have some tricky fingering combinations and some very wide intervals. It features a very show cadenza toward the end. This solo has a fantastic singing quality and is highly lyrical and very rhapsodic in places. This solo is worth a look to be played on a college recital.

Lantham, William P. *Eidolons.* Shawnee Press Inc. 9:30. VI. AA–b′. Written for the North Texas State University chapter of TUBA, this is a very technically and musically challenging piece, as many sections of it are chance music and feature numerous special effects, countless chromaticisms, and many double tonguing passages. It is a very powerful and impressive work. This musically challenging work would be fantastic for a big change in styles and moods for a recital. The solo part is in bass clef.

Larrick, Geary. *The Lord's Prayer, Music for Euphonium and Piano.* G and L Publishing (Stevens Point, Wisconsin). 1990. 1:30. I–II. F–b♭. This solo is in F major, slow common time, is mostly quarter notes, has a few accidentals, has simple rhythms, and is in bass clef. It is a beautiful solo that is very reflective in nature. This would be a good solo for a young player or a nice change of pace on a recital.

Lehar, F. *Merry Widow Waltz.* Arr. Fred Weber. Belwin Mills, Inc. 1969. $5. 1:00. I. B♭–d. A cute little waltz in E♭ major with simple rhythm and no accidentals. See Euphonium and Keyboard Collections.

Lehar, Frunz. *Vilia.* Arr. Daniel Bachelder. Tuba-Euphonium Press. 2000. $8. 2:30. III. d♭–b♭'. This beautiful Spanish song is in a moderately fast 2/4, is in G♭ major, is rhythmically straightforward, often ascends into the high register, and is in bass and treble clef. This is a highly expressive song that would be an excellent recital selection. I highly recommend it.

Leidzen, Erik. *The Song of the Brother.* 7:00. V–VI. This highly technically and musically demanding solo is one of the best known Salvation Army solos. Recorded by Steven Mead.

Lemare. *Andantino.* Arr. Fred Weber. Belwin Mills Inc. 1969. $5. 1:00. I. C–d. This simple little lyrical song in F major is for beginners. See Euphonium and Keyboard Collections.

Leoncavallo. *On with the Motley.* Arr. Farr. Winwood Music. $7. III. The solo part is in treble clef.

Levi, William. *A Smooth Moment.* Puna Music Company. 2001. $15.95. 3:00. II–III. d–f'. This is a nice slow lyrical solo that is in B♭ major, is mostly quarter notes with a few eighths, and is in the middle register with few accidentals. It has many nice melodic lines, is mostly rhythmically straightforward (a few sporadic tricky rhythms), and has a fun middle section with a change to a quicker tempo. This would be a good solo for a good middle school student or a young high school student. See Euphonium and Keyboard Collections.

Levi, William. *Ballad in F.* Puna Music Company. 2001. $15.95. 4:40. II–III. c–f'. This is a nice slow lyrical solo that is mostly eighth note runs in the middle register with sporadic accidentals. It has many nice melodic lines, is mostly rhythmically straightforward (a few sporadic tricky rhythms), and has a powerful ending. This would be a good solo for a very good middle school

student or a high school student. See Euphonium and Keyboard Collections.

Levi, William. *On the Move.* Puna Music Company. 2001. $15.95. 4:30. II–III. F–f'. This is a very upbeat and cheerful solo that is mostly eighth note runs in the middle register with sporadic accidentals. It has many nice melodic lines, is mostly rhythmically straightforward (a few sporadic tricky rhythms), and has a dramatic ending. This would be a good solo for a very good middle school student or a high school student. See Euphonium and Keyboard Collections.

Levy, Jules. *Carnival of Venice.* Ed. R. E. Thurston. Southern Music Company. 1991. $7.95. 5:00. V–VI. F–c''. This is a great version of one of the great classic theme and variations. It features a maestoso intrada, the theme, a fast slurred sixteenth note run first variation, a second variation with very wide intervals, a third variation that requires some double tonguing, a fourth variation that begins expressive and ends highly technical, and a coda that features loads of triple tonguing. If you are looking for a different edition of this classic, take a look at this solo. The solo part is in bass clef.

Liadov, Anatol. *Dancing Song from Eight Russian Folk Songs, Op. 58.* Trans./arr. Ronald Dishinger. Medici Music Press. 1989. $4.50. 1:20. II. e♭–e♭'. This fun little solo is in a moderate 2/4 time, is in E♭ major, is mostly scale-wise eighth note runs, is mostly in the middle register, has no accidentals, and is in bass clef. This would be a very good first or second solo for a middle school player.

Liszt, Franz. *Oh, quand je dors.* Trans. Dan Bachelder. TUBA Press. 1994. $8. 4:00. III. d–a'. This solo is in a slow common time, is in E and E♭ major, is mostly in the middle to low register, is rhythmically straightforward, and is in bass and treble clef. This beautiful little love song is very expressive and would be an excellent recital selection, especially for a young college player. The solo part includes the original text and the translation.

Little, Donald C. *Lazy Lullaby.* Belwin Mills, CPP/Belwin, Inc. 1977. $4.95. 2:00. I. c–c'. This cute solo is in F major, 4/4, is mostly quarter notes with some eighths, and features plenty of rests. It would be a good first solo for a beginner. See Euphonium and Keyboard Collections.

Little, Donald C. *Military March.* Belwin Mills, CPP/Belwin, Inc. 1977. $4.95. 1:45. I. B♭–c'. Mr. Little takes a traditional favorite military march and arranges it well for a beginner. It is in B♭ major, 2/2, is in a great range, is mostly quarter and half notes, and has plenty of rests with no accidentals. See Euphonium and Keyboard Collections.

Livingston, Jay, and Ray Evans. *Silver Bells.* Arr. Coponegro. Kendor Music, Inc. $7. 3:00. II. This melody comes from the Paramount film

The Lemon Drop Kid. This is a very fun and entertaining second solo for a middle school student.

Llewellyn, Edward. *My Regards*. Ed. Clifford P. Lillya. Remick Music Corporation. 4:00. IV. G–b♭'. This wonderful character piece features beautiful waltz and trio sections. It is a very accessible piece to introduce a college student to technical or "showy" solos since the technical passages are a modest challenge. The solo part is in bass clef.

Locatelli, Pietro. *Baroque Suite No. 2*. Trans./arr. Ronald Dishinger. Medici Music Press. 1999. $10. 5:00. IV. F–g'. This work has four movements: Allegro; Allegro; Andante; Allegro. The first movement is in a fast 2/4, is in g minor, is mostly eighth note runs, is rhythmically simple, has a moderate use of chromatics, and is mostly in the middle to upper register. It has many wide intervals and often ascends into the upper register but doesn't stay in the upper register. It is very lively, fun, and dance-like. The second movement is a fast 3/4, is in g minor, and is mostly scale-wise eighth note runs and triplet runs with a moderate use of chromatics. Range wise it is similar to the first movement with a little more time in the lower register. This movement is load of fun to play. The third movement is a slow 3/2, is in F major, and is mostly quarter and half notes. It is a very expressive movement that is mostly in the middle to lower register. The last movement is a moderate common time in F major. It is mostly sixteenth notes with many challenging wide leaps with very little chromatics. It is mostly in the lower register. This movement is very ornate and a fun challenge. The work overall is in bass clef and is a very fine work. It would be a very nice college recital piece.

Lovec, Vladmimir. *Requiem*. Ed. W. and J. Boswell. Philharmusica Co., $10.50.

Lureman, Herman. *Grootvader's klok*. Edition Molenaar, Wormerveer, Holland. 1953. IV. B♭–g'. This theme and variations remains within the middle tessitura and features typical triplet and slurred sixteenth note variations. It is a very neat solo as it has a different sound from most theme and variations I've heard. It could be due to the scale runs not being totally comprised of major scales. It is very accessible as it has no multiple tonguing and features moderate tempo markings for all of the variations. The solo part is available in both bass and treble clef.

MacDowell, Edward. *To a Wild Rose*. Arr. Merle J. Issac. Carl Fischer. 1:30. II–III. C–f'. This is a simple song that would be a good melodic study for young students. The solo part is in bass clef.

MacDowell, Edward. *To a Wild Irish Rose*. Arr. Howard Snell. $12. III. Order at www.euphonium.net.

MacMilan, Duncan J. *Gaelic Sonata*. Duncan J. MacMilan. 2002. V–VI. C–e♭". This very challenging work written for euphonium soloist Adam Frey was derived from Scottish folk songs. The sonata also tells a story. Details concerning the folk songs and story are laid out in a preface to the work. It features three movements (The Cost of Adventure; Sea Changes; Coming Home). This is a fascinating work that seems to be worth the challenge. The solo part is available in both bass and treble clefs.

Madsen, Trygve. *Sonata for Euphonium and Piano, Op. 97*. Norwegian Music Information Centre. IV–V. E♭–b♭'. It features three movements (Intrada; Intermezzo; Finale). This is a moderately challenging but very lively and powerful work with many stylistic changes. It remains in the middle tessitura and features a nice muted section. I would recommend this work, as I enjoyed studying it. The solo part is in bass clef.

Malloy, James. *A Touch of Ireland Based on a Kerry Dance*. Trans./arr. John A. Walters. Medici Music Press. 1995. $4.50. 1:30. II–III. d–g'. This solo was dedicated to Eileen and Tony Nolan of Cork, Ireland. It is a fantastically fun little solo! Marked "rollicking," this solo is in a moderate 6/8, is in F major, is rhythmically simple, has very few accidentals, is mostly in the middle register, and is in bass clef. The only challenge will be a few places in the higher register and endurance, as there are no rests. This would be an excellent solo for a high school player.

Mantia, Simone. *Auld Lang Syne*. Tuba-Euphonium Press. 1992. $8. 6:00. V–VI. F–e♭". This has become one of the standard theme and variations in the euphonium repertoire. It was written by the famous euphonium soloist of the John Philip Sousa Band. This is a classic solo and is a must study for any serious euphonium player. It has an extended and very impressive cadenza. The work is in B♭ major, is full of very rapid scale-wise runs, and requires multiple tonguing. It can be found in *The Art of Euphonium Playing* by Arthur Lehman. A band version is available. Recorded by Michael Colburn and Arthur Lehman.

Mantia, Simone. *Believe Me if All Those Endearing Young Charms*. Arr. David Werden. Cimarron Music and Publications. 1987. $12. V. CC–c". This is a fantastic arrangement of arguably the most played and popular theme and variations ever written for the euphonium. It opens with a stately and showy cadenza, followed by one of the most beautiful and lyrical tunes ever written for any instrument. It has three variations and in the first the euphonium is playing continuous running scale-wise and arpeggio sixteenth notes in 6/8, creating a very florid rhapsodic sound. The second variation is slower and more free or ad lib in nature with many extremely fast scale-wise runs. The last variation is a burner as it features extremely fast sixteenth note runs in 2/4. There is a brief very showy cadenza before the work comes to a rousing end. This work demonstrates all of the technical, melodic, and range possibilities of the euphonium. It is a must study for the serious euphonium student. Both treble and bass clef are included and there are versions for concert band, brass band, brass ensemble, brass quintet, and brass quartet. Recorded by Steven Mead and Arthur Lehman.

Mantia, Simone. *Priscilla.* 3:00. IV. A♭–c″. This beautiful waltz has a very rich sound and many soaring phrases. The only challenge to this work is the range in a few sections.

Mantia, Simone. *The Southerner.* The Dixie Music House. VI. c–d″. This fun and exciting theme and variations is good technical challenge. It has a very majestic sound in sections and requires both double and triple tonguing.

Marcello, Benedetto. *Concerto in C Minor for Oboe and Orchestra.* Trans./arr. Ronald Dishinger. Medici Music Press. 1999. $12. 7:00. IV–V. G–g. This work features three movements: Allegro; Adagio; Allegro. Both Allegro movements moderate in tempo. The first Allegro features many sixteenth note runs, most of which are not scale-wise, is mostly in the middle register, has a few rhythmic challenges, features some wide intervals and sporadic use of ornaments, and is highly chromatic. It is a very lively and fun movement to play. The Adagio is extremely slow, has many sixteenth note and 32nd note runs that are mostly scale-wise, is in the middle to lower register, has some rhythmic challenges, and is fairly chromatic. This is a very expressive movement with many gorgeous passages. The last movement is in 3/8 and is very lively and dance-like. It has many sixteenth note runs that are scale-wise with some occasional wide intervals, and for the most part it is easy to play. It is mostly in the middle register and is fairly chromatic. This work is a great substitution for the "traditional" Marcello selections. I highly recommend it for a junior or senior recital.

Marcello, Benedito. *Sonata in F Major.* Ed. Steven Mead. Studio Music Company. 1995. $10.50. IV. G–g′. This is one of the most performed and popular baroque arrangements for the euphonium. Originally written for cello, this is an excellent edition from Steven Mead's *The World of the Euphonium* as it is the most idiomatic I have played for the euphonium. It is clearly marked in terms of dynamics, stylistic markings, and ornaments. This edition helps to facilitate the proper performance of the style of this work. I highly recommend it! The solo part comes in bass clef.

Markert, Jack Russell. *Concert Waltz No. 1.* MGP. 5:00. V. G–c″. A wonderful technical display work that has numerous built-in options to allow for much interpretation and technical discretion. It remains in the middle tessitura for most of the work. I highly recommend it as it is lively, has a different sound, and is highly entertaining. The solo part is available in both bass and treble clef.

Marpurg, Friedrich. *Menuet from Three Piano Pieces.* Trans./arr. Ronald Dishinger. Medici Music Press. 1989. $4.50. 2:00. II–III. This lively little work is marked "allegretto grazioso," in 3/4, B♭ major, is mostly in the middle to lower register, has easy rhythms, is in bass clef, and is mostly quarter and eighth note runs. This would be a good second solo for a middle school player.

Mascagni, Pietro. *Intermezzo from Cavalleria Rusticana.* Trans./arr. Ronald Dishinger. Medici Music Press. 1997. $4.50. 1:00. III. c–g′. This simple yet powerful aria from a very popular opera, *The Rustic Cavalier,* is in a slow 3/4, is in E♭ major, is rhythmically straightforward, has very few accidentals, has very few technical challenges, is mostly in the middle register, and is in bass clef. The challenge is with endurance, as there are no rests and a good amount of passages that go to e♭′. This would be a great solo for a high school student or even on a college recital.

Marshall, George. *Ransomed.* 6:30. IV–V. This is a classic Salvation Army solo and a wonderful theme and variations. Recorded by Steven Mead.

Martino, Ralph. *Introspect for Solo Euphonium and Symphonic Band.* TUBA Press. 1996. $10. 8:30. V–VI. BB♭–b′. This is a very powerful solo! It is highly expressive and allows for a wide variety of personal expression in all of the slow sections. The fast sections are extremely powerful with very intense passages in the high register. The solo has many sixteenth note runs, chromatics, big dynamics, and is in bass clef. It is a fantastic showpiece all around and the ending is a rousing tour de force! This would be a fantastic opener or closer for any recital.

Meechan, Pete. *Absolute Reality.* Prima Vista Musikk. 2001. 5:30. A very powerful work inspired by the composer's reaction to the 9/11 attacks as a whole. This work reflects sadness, anger, aggression, and reflection. It was also inspired by the Allen Ginsberg poem *Howl.* The work was commissioned and first performed by euphoniumist David Thornton. This work can be ordered at www.petemeechan.com.

Meechan, Pete. *Break.* 2001. 4:30. This work can be ordered at www.petemeechan.com.

Meechan, Pete. *Still Shining.* 2004. 5:30. This work can be ordered at www.petemeechan.com.

Mendelssohn, Felix. *On Wings of Song.* Arr. Fred Weber. Belwin Mills Inc. 1969. $5. 1:20. I. B♭–c′. A beautiful simple song in E♭ major with simple rhythms and a few accidentals. See Euphonium and Keyboard Collections.

Mendelssohn, Felix. *On Wings of Song.* Arr. Forrest L. Buchtel. Neil A. Kjos Music Company. 1958. $2. 1:30. II. c–d′. This solo is in a slow 6/8, is in F major, has simple rhythms and a few accidentals, is mostly in the middle register, and is in bass clef. This is a beautiful little song that would be a good second solo for a middle school player.

Mendelssohn, Felix. *Reverie from Opus 85, No. 1.* Trans./arr. Ronald Dishinger. Medici Music Press. 1990. $5. 1:30. II. d–f′. This is a good second solo for a middle school student, as it has a few high range challenges but primarily remains in the middle register. It consists of mainly quarter and eighth notes at a moderate tempo with some occasional accidentals.

Mendelssohn, Felix. *Spinning Song, Song without Words, No. 34.* Arr. David Werden. 1989. V. BB–b′. A wonderful arrangement of one of Mendelssohn's most famous songs, as it is written in an idiomatic way for the instrument while retaining the original feel/style of the work. It is technically challenging with sustained passages of sixteenth note runs, but the tessitura primarily remains in the middle. The solo part is in treble clef.

Michel, Jean-Francois. *Scherzo for Euphonium and Piano.* Editions Marc Reift. 1996. 6:00. V. E–c″. This is a fantastic work! I thoroughly enjoyed the immense amount of energy and power in this solo. It features several cadenza sections that can be very impressive for the more developed player, or played slower without losing much of their effectiveness for less developed players. It also features great compound meter sections and a lovely lyrical section. I highly recommend this work as an opener or closer to a recital! The solo is available in both bass and treble clefs.

Miserendino, Joe. *Keystone Kapers.* Joe Miserendino. 2001. 4:30. IV–V. DD–c″. This is a great work for someone looking for a technical challenge that is fun and worth the effort. This work is very fast and is full of articulated sixteenth notes runs, many of which will have to be double tongued. Most of the work is in the middle register and features many powerful dynamic and articulated sections. The solo part is in tenor clef. There is a good amount of syncopation and rhythmic play throughout. This work can be ordered at joesmusicroom.com.

Miserendino, Joe. *Summer Celebration.* Joe Miserendino. 2003. 4:30. IV–V. G–c″. If you are looking for something different that is a worthy challenge and a lot of fun to play, you have found your piece. This work is very lively and features a wonderful main melody found in the first and last third of the work. This melody is in the middle to high register and it has many fast sixteenth note runs. The middle section melody is just as beautiful, but is slower in nature and lower in tessitura. There is a good amount of syncopation throughout and it has many powerful dynamic sections. The solo part is in tenor clef. This would be an excellent recital piece for a junior or senior in college. The work can be ordered at joesmusicroom.com.

Miserendino, Joe. *Winter Song and Summer Dances.* Joe Miserendino. 2002. 6:10. IV–V. DD–d″. This piece wonderfully represents common feelings associated with winter and summer. The winter section has a beautifully somber melody, while the summer section is very quick and cheerful. The work features a few challenging runs and the solo part is in tenor clef. It is mostly in the middle to lower registers. This work can be ordered at joesmusicroom.com.

Miura, Mari. *Romance.* Tuba-Euphonium Press. 1997. $10. 2:30. IV. F–b♭′. This beautiful little solo is loaded with many passionate phrases and Far Eastern sounds. It is in a slow common time, is very broad and lyrical, and features a small but expressive cadenza. This work is rhythmically straightforward, has a good amount of chromatics, and ascends into the high register several times. This solo would be a fantastic lyrical selection for any college recital.

Montgomery, Edward. *Mirror Lake for Euphonium and Piano.* Ludwig Music. 6:00. IV. c–b♭′. This lively work is an enjoyable melodic and technical study for good high school players and young college students. It remains in the middle tessitura and the technical challenges are mainly slurred triplet runs that are very idiomatic. It has two movements (Serenade and Festival) and the solo part comes in both bass and treble clefs.

Monti, Vittorio. *Czardas.* Arr. Marc Reift. Editions Marc Reift. 1993. V. G–c″. Features beautiful opening slow lyrical melody followed by a very showy, very fast double tongued melody. A great closer! Solo part is in tenor clef.

Monti, Vittorio. *Czardas.* Arr. Eric Wilson. Rosehill Music. 1988. V. F–b♭′. Features beautiful opening slow lyrical melody followed by a very showy, very fast double tongued melody. A great closer! This is my preferred arrangement as it has more concise markings, is easier to read, and is in a better key. The solo part is in treble clef.

Moquin, Al. *King of the Deep.* The Fillmore Bros. Co., Cincinnati, Ohio. 1948. 2:30. III–IV. F–b♭′. This is a great example of many of the early twentieth-century technical character pieces for low brass. It opens with an ad-lib cadenza followed by the main theme, then a polka section, a variation on the main theme, and a coda. It would be a great work for a talented younger player to study technical solo styles. Highly recommend for younger players. The solo part contains both bass and treble clefs.

Moquin, Al. *Sailing the Mighty Deep.* The Fillmore Bros. Co., Cincinnati, Ohio. 1948. 2:30. III–IV. F–b♭′. This is a great example of many of the early twentieth-century technical character pieces for low brass. It opens with an ad-lib cadenza followed by the main theme, then a polka section, a variation on the main theme, and a coda. It would be a great work for a talented younger player to study technical solo styles. Highly recommend for younger players. The solo part contains both bass and treble clefs.

Moquin, Al. *Sousaphonium*. The Fillmore Bros. Co., Cincinnati, Ohio. 1948. 2:30. III–IV. F–b♭′. This is a great example of many of the early twentieth-century technical character pieces for low brass. It opens with an ad-lib cadenza followed by the main theme, then a polka section, a variation on the main theme, and a coda. It would be a great work for a talented younger player to study technical solo styles. Highly recommend for younger players. The solo part contains both bass and treble clefs.

Morgan, David. *Shapes of the Morning*. David Morgan. 2004. 2:30. III–IV. E–b′. This work wonderfully represents the usual peacefulness of an early morning. It is slow and lyrical and remains in the middle tessitura for most of the solo. This work would be a nice change of mood/pace for a recital program. The solo part is in bass clef.

Mozart, Wolfgang Amadeus. *Adagio and Rondo*. Arr. Wilby/Childs. Winwood Music. $14. IV. This is a great arrangement for the euphonium, as it is full of Mozart's melodic beauty and wit. The solo comes in both bass and treble clef parts.

Mozart, Wolfgang Amadeus. *Allegretto*. Trans./arr. Ronald Dishinger. Medici Music Press. 1991. $5. 2:30. III–IV. G–d′. This delightful work is in a moderate common time, F major, mostly in the middle to lower register, and contains mostly scale-wise eighth note runs with occasional sixteenth note runs and chromatics. It has many beautiful passages and would be a fun solo and style and articulation study for a good high school student. The solo part is in bass clef.

Mozart, Wolfgang Amadeus. *Andante and Alleluja for Euphonium and Piano*. Arr. Arthur Frackenpohl. Tuba-Euphonium Press. 1993. $10. 4:45 (Andante). 2:30 (Alleluja). IV. d–a′. This solo has two sections: andante and alleluja. The andante is highly expressive and is in a very slow 3/4 and in G major. It has some scale-wise sixteenth note runs, is mostly in the middle to lower register, has some optional cuts, and has a small but showy cadenza. The alleluja is in a fast 2/4, is in E♭ major, has many scale-wise sixteenth note runs, and is mostly in the middle register. This is a fun section with many beautiful and rhapsodic moments. The solo is well marked with specific dynamics, articulations, and phrasing. It comes in both bass and treble clef and has optional high pitches. This would be a very good solo for a recital or a very good high school player.

Mozart, Wolfgang Amadeus. *Concerto in B♭ K191, Rondo*. Arr. Fote. Kendor Music, Inc. $8. IV–V. F–g′. This work was originally written for bassoon by Mozart at the age of eighteen and is in four movements. This is one of the most popular non-euphonium works and is a must study for any euphonium player. This arrangement features the third movement, the Rondo, which is sweeping in nature and a minuetto. The Rondo

has a three-note motto variant throughout and is a very exciting and fun movement to perform.

Mozart, Wolfgang Amadeus. *Concerto No. 1 in D, K. 412*. Trans./arr. Ronald Dishinger. Medici Music Press. 2000. $14.50. 7:00. IV. f–g♭′. This is a fantastic work that was originally written for horn. This is the first and second movement only, and it is Mozart at his finest with beautiful melodies and humoristic passages. The first movement is in a moderate allegro and common time while the second movement is in 6/8 but also a moderate allegro. It has a few rhythmic challenges, sporadic use of accidentals, remains in the middle register, has several well-placed longer sections of rest, and features mostly scale-wise runs. It has some technical challenges, but nothing a good college student couldn't handle. I highly recommend this work for a junior or senior recital.

Mozart, Wolfgang Amadeus. *Larghetto*. Trans./arr. Ronald Dishinger. Medici Music Press. 1993. $4.50. 1:45. III–IV. D–f′. This is a fantastic solo! It is in a moderate common time, is in B♭ major, is mostly in the middle and lower registers, and is in bass clef. The challenges are in technique, as there are many sixteenth note runs and even some 32nd note runs and many rhythmic challenges. This would be an excellent recital selection for a college player. I highly recommend this piece, as it is a very fun and worthy challenge.

Mozart, Wolfgang Amadeus. *Laudamus Te for Euphonium and Piano*. Arr. Arthur Frackenpohl. TUBA Press. 1993. $8. 4:20. IV. c–a′. This solo is taken from Mozart's famous *C Minor Mass*. This lively and fun solo is in an allegro common time and is in F major. It has a good amount of scale-wise sixteenths, some ornaments, is mostly in the middle to high register, has a few rhythmic challenges, and comes in both bass and treble clef. It is typical Mozart, as it has passages that are regal, rhapsodic, light, lyrical, and humorous. This would be a nice opening piece for a recital.

Mozart, Wolfgang Amadeus. *Menuet from Don Juan*. Trans./arr. Ronald Dishinger. Medici Music Press. 1995. $4.50. 0:45. II. d–e♭′. This lovely little solo is from a major opera. It is in a moderate 3/4, is in B♭ major, is rhythmically simple, is mostly in the middle to lower register, and is in bass clef. It would be an excellent second or third solo for a middle school player and a very fine style study. This solo also comes with J. S. Bach's *Little Prelude*.

Mozart, Wolfgang Amadeus. *Menuet from Symphony in E♭*. Trans./arr. Ronald Dishinger. Medici Music Press. 1995. $4.50. 2:00. II–III. F–d′. This most enjoyable solo is in a moderate 3/4, is in F major, is rhythmically simple, is mostly arppegiated eighth note runs, has very few accidentals, is mostly in the lower register, and is in bass clef. The only challenge is a few wide intervals, especially in the lower register. This would be a great solo for a good middle school player or a younger high school student. This is a very fun solo to play!

Mozart, Wolfgang Amadeus. *Presto from Divertimento No. 12.* Trans./arr. Ronald Dishinger. Medici Music Press. 1989. $4.50. 1:30. II–III. d–f′. This would be a good second solo for a middle school student. It is marked "presto" and has many eighth note runs. It ascends to the upper register often and would be a good endurance and range challenge. It has a very lively theme, basic rhythms, and few accidentals.

Mozart, Wolfgang Amadeus. *Rondo.* Trans./arr. Ronald Dishinger. Medici Music Press. 1991. $5. 2:00. III–IV. E–aʹ. This is a fantastic work, as it features a couple of wonderful melodies and is very light and lively throughout. It has many accidentals, is marked "allegro," and has numerous sixteenth note runs. This would be a great recital piece for a young college student, as it would be a worthy challenge.

Mozart, Wolfgang Amadeus. *Rondo from Divertimento No. 11.* Trans./arr. Ronald Dishinger. Medici Music Press. 1989. $5. 3:00. II. d–f′. This work features several lovely Mozart themes and would be a good first or second solo for a middle school player. There are very few accidentals and it consists mostly of quarter and eighth note passages in the middle register. There are several repeats that could be cut to shorten the length.

Mozart, Wolfgang Amadeus. *Sonata in B♭ Major, K292.* Arr. Marcellus. Kendor Music, Inc. $11. V. Originally written for bassoon, this work is considered to be one of the finest sonatas ever written for the bassoon. This arrangement adheres well to the original.

Mozart, Wolfgang Amadeus. *Sonatina.* Arr. Jay Ernst. Kendor Music Inc. $8. III. This wonderful arrangement is on the Kendor Music bestseller list.

Narita. *Song of the Seashore.* Arr. Makoto Kanai. 3:00. This is a famous and very beautiful Japanese song. It makes for a great recital selection. Recorded by Steven Mead (also recorded by James Galway).

Nasta, Tamezo. *Hamabeno Uto.* Arr. Makoto Kanai. 2:30. IV. b♭–d♭″. This is a beautiful small lyrical solo in treble clef with an oriental sound. Contact Adam Frey for ordering information.

Nelhybel, Vaclav. *Concerto for Euphonium.* Tuba-Euphonium Press. 1996. $20. 16:00. VI. GG–f″. Written by an internationally acclaimed composer, this concerto was written for Roger Behrend, principal euphonium of the United States Navy Band, and dedicated in the memory of his sister Charlotte C. Behrend. The work does not have separate movements but does have some very clear sections: adagio; allegretto; tranquillo; allegro. This work has a huge span of styles and emotions. It is highly technical with many rhapsodic figures, sixteenth note runs, wide intervals, challenging rhythms, massive range challenges,

and powerful dynamics. This solo is in bass clef and is well marked with very specific articulations, style changes, dynamics, tempos, and phrasings. It is very musically demanding and allows for a huge range of personal expression. This is a very challenging but a very rewarding solo. It would be a powerful musical statement for any recital.

Neukomn, Sigismond. *Andante from Andante for Horn and Piano or Organ.* Trans./arr. Ronald Dishinger. Medici Music Press. 1995. $8. 3:30. III–IV. F–g′. This very expressive solo would be a wonderful selection for a junior or senior recital. It remains in the middle register, is in B♭ major, is slow, and has many scale-wise sixteenth note runs and a moderate amount of accidentals. There are a few rhythmic and technical challenges, but nothing a good college student can't handle. This work features loads of beautiful chromaticism and tension. I highly recommend it!

Newsome, Roy. *Dublin's Fair City.* Fantasy for Euphonium, Chandos Music Ltd. 1979. 4:00. V. F–c″. This is a very nice, idiomatic technical showpiece for the euphonium. It is mostly sixteenth note runs that are scale-wise and remain in the middle tessitura. This piece comes highly recommended. The solo part is in treble clef.

Newsome, Roy. *Fantasy on Swiss Airs.* Studio Music Company. 1989. 7:00. V–VI. E–b′. This is a fantastic fantasy as it is very idiomatic for the euphonium and has numerous stylistic changes (ritmico, rumba, and several lyrical passages). It is technically challenging with many passages of sustained sixteenth note runs and some triple tonguing. However, this solo is well worth the technical challenges! The solo part is in treble clef.

Newsome, Roy. *The Mountains Mourne.* Studio Music. $7.50. 7:00. This great work has been arranged for full band and brass band. The solo part is in treble clef.

Newsome, Roy. *Southern Cross.* Studio Music Company. 1991. 4:00. V. E–b′. This is a fantastic theme and variations type work as it is very idiomatic for the euphonium and has become a standard in the repertoire. It is technically challenging, but the technical challenges are modest compared to most works in this genre. This is a great work to use for a good high school student or young college player to begin working in this genre. The solo part is in treble clef.

Newton, Rodney. *Baritone Aria.* $15. IV. This is a beautiful original solo that would make a great recital selection! Available at Solid Brass Music Company.

Niehaus, Lennie. *Appalachian Waltz.* Kendor Music, Inc, 1998. $6. 2:15. I. B♭–b♭. This is a great first solo as it has a one octave range, a fun melody, simple rhythms, a good key, a piano accompaniment appropriate and helpful for a young player, and is fun to play as it is in a very relaxed waltz tempo. The solo part comes in both bass and treble clef.

Niehaus, Lennie. *Bonaventura.* Kendor Music, Inc. 2002. $6. 2:15. II. Bb–bb. This is a great first solo as it is one octave, has simple rhythms, and has a simple accompaniment yet is an entertaining melody. The solo part comes in both bass and treble clef.

Niehaus, Lennie. *Fanflairs.* Kendor Music Inc. 1992. $5.50. 2:15. I–II. a–f'. This solo is in a moderate common time, is rhythmically simple, is mostly in the middle register, and comes in both bass and treble clef parts.

Niehaus, Lennie. *Great Scott.* Kendor Music, Inc. $5. 1:30. I. Bb–bb. This solo is a tribute to Scott Joplin and his ragtime music for beginners. It is in a lively common time, is in Bb major, is rhythmically straightforward, has very few accidentals, is mostly in the middle register, and is in bass and treble clef.

Niehaus, Lennie. *Lynn Meadows Waltz.* Kendor Music Inc. 1999. $7. 5.45. I. Bb–bb. This is a beautiful little solo in a moderate waltz 3/4, is in Bb major, is rhythmically simple, has a few accidentals, is mostly in the lower register, and is in both bass and treble clef. This would be an excellent first solo.

Niehaus, Lennie. *Timepiece.* Kendor Music Inc. $6. II.

Offenbach, Jacques. *Barcarolle, from the Tales of Hoffmann.* Arr. Steven Mead. Studio Music. $7. III. This is a great selection from Offenbach's most popular work.

Olcott. *My Wild Irish Rose.* Arr. Fred Weber. Belwin Mills Inc. 1969. $5. 1:20. I. c–c'. A very simple yet lovely waltz in Ab major with simple rhythms and a few accidentals. See Euphonium and Keyboard Collections.

Olcott. *My Wild Irish Rose.* Arr. Forrest L. Buchtel. Neil A. Kjos Music Company. 1984. $1.75. 1:30. I. d–d'. This solo is in Bb major, is in a moderate waltz 3/4, is rhythmically simple, has no accidentals, and is in bass clef. It would be a great first solo as it is a lovely melody.

Ospalec (Siebenschlafer). *Polka pre baryton, trombone nebo fagot.* Ladislav Nemec Ales Sigmund, 1993. 3:00. IV–V. F–f'. This is a classic polka. It has some technical challenges, but they are all idiomatic for the instrument and in the keys of Bb and Eb major with very little chromaticism. I highly recommend this as a fun technical challenge and as an entertaining solo for any audience. The solo part is in bass clef.

Owen, Jerry. *Variations.* Ed. David Werden. $9.50. V. A great theme and variations solo.

Pachelbel, Johann. *Canon in D.* Trans./arr. Ronald Dishinger. Medici Music Press. 2001. $5. 2:30. III–IV. Bb–ab'. This beautiful solo is in a very slow common time, Eb major, is mostly in the middle register, and contains mostly scale-wise runs. The challenge comes in the rhythms (many 32nd note and sixteenth note combinations) and some of the wide intervals. It is very lyrical

and highly ornate and would be an excellent style study and change of pace on a recital. This piece is accessible for a very good high school student.

Paganini, Niccolo. *Cantabile.* Arr. Richards. Studio Music. $13.50. 5:10. IV. This gorgeous solo makes for a perfect lyrical selection for any euphonium recital. I highly recommend this solo! The solo part is available in both bass and treble clef. Recorded by Steven Mead.

Paradies, M. *Sicilienne.* Arr. Howard Snell. $14. This work would make for a great style change on a recital. Order at www.euphonium.net.

Parry. *My Fanwy.* Arr. Denzil Stephens. Sarnia Music (UK) (www.sarnia-music.com). 1985. $7.40. 2:00. III. f–bb'. This is a small, slow, and very beautiful lyrical solo. It is a good melodic study for younger students. This solo has been performed by the Childs Brothers many times. The solo part is in treble clef.

Pascal, Claude. *Sonate en 6 minutes 30 pour Tuba, ou Trombone-Basse, ou Saxhorn en et Piano.* Durand & Cie. 1958. V. FF–b''. A two-movement work that is highly chromatic, very powerful, and energetic. It explores the lower tessitura as it is often around or below low F. It is moderately challenging with challenges coming from high use of chromatics, wide low intervals, and extreme low register. The solo part is in bass clef.

Pepusch, Johann Christopher. *Sonata in F.* Arr. Robert Madeson. Cimarron Music and Productions. 2002. 5:00. IV. Eb–f'. Four movements: Largo; Allegro; Largo; Allegro. This fantastic sonata comes from Pepusch, the composer of the music for John Gay's famous *The Beggar's Opera.* The first movement is very lyrical and passionate with many very tonal soaring lines. It allows for numerous highly expressive moments. It is very slow and is comprised mostly of sixteenth and 32nd note passages in the middle to lower register. The technique is easily played. The second movement is very pronounced and crisp. It consists of mainly scale-wise sixteenth note runs in the middle register. The third movement is very simple, mostly quarters and eighths, yet is highly expressive. It leads itself naturally to adding embellishments. The fourth movement is very dance-like and loads of fun to play. It is in 3/8 and is consists of scale-wise sixteenth note runs with brief pauses. Both bass and treble clef parts are included. This is a wonderful addition to the euphonium repertoire.

Petit, Alexandre S. *Etude De Concours.* Andrieu Freres, Paris, and Alfred Music Co., Inc., New York. 1926. 3:00. IV. Bb–f'. A fun, highly energetic one-movement work that features numerous style changes. It is very accessible, as it remains in the middle register and even though it has many sixteenth runs toward the end, they are very idiomatic. It features a wonderful polonaise section! Solo part is in bass clef.

Petit, Pierre. *Fantaisie, pour Tuba, ou Trombone-Basse, ou Saxhorn en et Piano.* Alphonse Leduc, Paris. 1953. 5:00. IV–V. GG–b″. This solo is highly chromatic, very powerful, and energetic. It explores the lower tessitura as it is often around or below low B♭. It is moderately challenging with challenges coming from high use of chromatics, wide low intervals, and extreme low register. The solo part is in bass clef with some use of tenor clef.

Phillips, L. Z. *Marines' Hymn.* Arr. Forrest L. Buchtel. Neil A. Kjos Music Company. 1973. $1.75. 1:30. I. B♭–b♭. This solo is in a moderately fast 2/4, is in B♭ major, is rhythmically simple, has very few accidentals, has piano cues, and is in bass clef. This would be a good solo for a beginner.

Piazolla, Astor. *Café 1930.* Arr. Steven Mead. 7:16. IV–V. This fantastic work was originally recorded by Yo-Yo Ma. It is a rare work in the euphonium repertoire as it is a combination of tango and classical jazz. I highly recommend this work. Recorded by Steven Mead.

Picchi, Ermanno. *Fantaisie Original.* Arr. Simone Mantia, ed. Adam Frey. Athens Music Publishing. This arrangement is similar to the original, but it is much easier to read, has clearer markings, and has easier to read optional parts.

Picchi, Ermanno. *Fantaisie Original.* Arr. Simone Mantia. 8:30. VI. BB♭–f″. Written in operatic style, this theme and variations fully demonstrates the technical capabilities of the euphonium. This work has been required on several international euphonium solo competitions. It is one of the finest and most challenging theme and variations written for the euphonium. It has long been a standard in the repertoire thanks to the great euphonium soloist Simone Mantia. A band version is available. Recorded by Steven Mead and Arthur Lehman.

Plagge, Wolfgang. *Sonata for Euphonium and Piano, Op. 64.* Norwegian Music Information Centre. 13:00. V. E–c″. A challenging work that is highly energetic and powerful. It has a very fresh sound and many stylistic variations. This work would make for a very nice change of pace on a recital. The solo part is in bass clef with some tenor and treble clef interspersed.

Pokorny, Franz Xavier. *Concerto in F Major.* Trans. Joe D. Brown. Tuba-Euphonium Press. 1991. $12. 13:00. V–VI. c–c″. This solo was originally published under the name of Luigi Boccherini. There are program notes that detail why this work was originally attributed to another composer. This is a very fine concerto originally written for flute from the late classical period. It has three movements: Allegro moderato; Adagio; Rondeau allegretto. This solo is highly technical with many very rapid runs, many very wide intervals, challenging ornamentation, and some challenging rhythms, and it spends a great deal of time in the upper register. The solo is in bass

clef and has countless rhapsodic passages and gorgeous soaring lines. If you are looking for a fun technical challenge that has loads of tonality and melody to it, this is your solo!

Ponchielli, Amilcare. *Concerto per Flicorno basso, Opus 155.* Ed. Henry Howey. Tuba-Euphonium Press. 1995. $14. 13:00. VI. F–b♭′. This is a must study for the serious euphonium student as it is a major work in our repertoire, is one of our finest works, has been a required work on several international euphonium competitions, and is the first major work written for the euphonium. This is a classic theme and variations that explores the total technical and melodic capabilities of the euphonium. After a long introduction the euphonium enters with an equally long introduction consisting of many rhapsodic runs and bold statements. After an interlude the theme is stated. It is one of the most beautiful and tender melodies ever written. The first variation is running sixteenth notes with many leaps, while the second variation is running sixteenth sextuplets with oftentimes wide intervals. The third variation is one of my favorites as it has a bolero sort of feel with 32nd note triplets in the middle of sixteenths! It is a fantastically fun variation! The work then enters a cadenza-like section that is highly passionate! There is a small moderato poco mosso area that explores a small variation of the theme before the burning fast allegro ending, which is highly impressive running sixteenths with many types of leaps. The range is fairly conservative, especially when considering its many technical difficulties. There are concert band, brass band, and orchestra versions available. Recorded by Steven Mead.

Poulton. *Aura Lee.* Arr. Fred Weber. Belwin Inc. 1969. $5. 1:00. I. B♭–a♭. A simple song in E♭ major. See Euphonium and Keyboard Collections.

Pounce, Manuel. *Estrellita.* Manuscript. A most beautiful Mexican serenade recorded by Steven Mead. There is also a brass band version. Contact Adam Frey.

Presser, William. *Rondo for Baritone Horn and Piano.* Tenuto Publications. 1967. 5:00. IV–V. GG–c″. This ternary work, even though nearly 40 years old, is still contemporary. It is a fine work with flashy technique that is idiomatic for the euphonium. It is still a good yet fun challenge for euphonium players today. The solo part is in bass clef and includes some tenor clef.

Pryor, Arthur. *Blue Bells of Scotland.* Carl Fischer. $8.95. 4:00. V. GG–c″. One of the most famous theme and variations for trombone and euphonium made famous by John Philip Sousa's solo trombonist Arthur Pryor. It begins with a fantastic introduction that features all sorts of octave leaps, fast scale patterns, pedal notes, very high notes, and arpeggios. The theme is as beautiful and lyrical as they come. The first variation is a triplet variation with mostly scale-wise movement and occasional wide leaps. The second variation is full of running sixteenth note passages with many wide leaps including numerous octave jumps. After a cadenza exploring high ascending arpeggios and sudden pedal tones, the last variation (marked "vivace") allows the performer to really showcase his or her technique through very fast arpeggios and octave leaps. This is a must study for the serious euphonium player. A band and brass band version is available. Recorded by Arthur Pryor.

Pryor, Arthur. *Blue Bells of Scotland.* Arr. Philip Sparke. Studio Music. $7.50. IV. A fine arrangement of this classic theme and variations.

Pryor, Arthur. *Love's Enchantment, Valse de Concert.* Ed. Harold Brasch. Solid Brass. $17.50. 3:30. IV–V. GG–c″. This most beautiful waltz is very Italian in nature and is written in the middle register where it really sings. This work is very accessible to many players with the exception of the cadenza in the middle, which has a few fast and high runs, and the high range toward the end.

Pryor, Arthur. *Thoughts of Love.* Carl Fischer. 1904. $17.95. 5:00. IV–V. F–c″. This popular trombone solo was made famous by the great trombone soloist of the John Philip Sousa Band, Arthur Pryor. This beautiful solo is a waltz in a quasi–theme and variations form. Like most solos from this time period, it features many fast scales and arpeggios with many wide leaps and octave jumps. Endurance is a factor as it ascends into the high range often. This is a great showpiece with less technical demand than works such as "Blue Bells of Scotland" and "All Those Endearing Young Charms." It can be ordered in a collection of solos entitled *Solos for Trombone* that contains 44 recital pieces.

Puccini, Giacomo. *Dondie Lieta.* Trans. Joseph T. Spaniola. Tuba-Euphonium Press. 1999. $8. 3:30. III–IV. d–b♭′. This beautiful aria is taken from one of Puccini's most beloved operas, *La Boheme.* It is very slow, is in D♭ and A major (briefly), is rhythmically straightforward, is often in the high register, and is in bass clef. This solo is well marked as it has very specific dynamics, tempos, styles, phrasing and articulations. I highly recommend this solo if you are looking for an extremely expressive lyrical work. This work also comes in a collection of Puccini arias (see Euphonium and Keyboard Collections).

Puccini, Giacomo. *Nessun Dorma.* Arr. Denzil Stephens. Sarnia Music (UK) (www.sarnia-music. com). $7.40. III–IV. This arrangement is based on one of the most famous and beautiful arias ever written. This would make for a wonderful recital selection.

Puccini, Giacomo. *Nessun Dorma.* Trans. Joseph T. Spaniola. Tuba-Euphonium Press. 1999. $8. 3:00. III–IV. f–b′. This solo is taken from one of the most famous of Puccini's operas, *Turandot.*

It has become one of the most beloved arias the world over. This is a fantastic arrangement! It is in a very slow common time, is in G major, is rhythmically straightforward, is in bass clef, and ascends into the high register often. This is a fantastic recital selection. I highly recommend it!

Puccini, Giacomo. *Nessun Dorma.* Arr. Howard Snell. $14. 3:00. III–IV. This fine arrangement can be ordered at www.euphonium.net.

Puccini, Giacomo. *One Fine Day, from "Madam Butterfly."* Arr. Forrest L. Buchtel. Neil A. Kjos Music Company. 1978. $1. 1:45. II–III. c–f♯′. This solo is taken from one of the most popular arias from one of Puccini's most famous operas. It is in a slow 3/4, is in F major, has a few rhythmic challenges, is mostly in the middle register, has a few accidentals, and is in bass clef. This is a great arrangement of a beautiful aria. This would be a great lyrical study for a good middle school student or young high school player.

Puccini, Giacomo. *Vissi D'Arte (from Tosca).* Arr. Steven Mead. 3:25. III–IV. This gorgeous operatic aria would be a great selection for any recital. Recorded by Steven Mead.

Puccini, Giacomo. *Vissi D'Arte.* Trans. Joseph T. Spaniola. Tuba-Euphonium Press. 1999. $8. 2:30. III–IV. e♭–b♭′. This beautiful solo is taken from one of Puccini's most famous operas, *Tosca.* It is very slow, is in E♭ major, and is in bass clef. It has a wide range of rhythms and only ascends into the high register at the very end. It is well marked with very specific dynamic, articulation, phrasing, and style markings. This would be a nice lyrical selection for any college recital.

Puccini, Giacomo. *Un Bel Di (from Madam Butterfly).* Trans. Joseph T. Spaniola. Tuba-Euphonium Press. 1999. $8. 3:30. IV. d♭–b♭′. This gorgeous solo comes from one of the most famous of all operas. It begins in a very slow 3/4, moves to a faster 2/4, moves to a slow 4/8, and ends in 3/4 and the original tempo. This is a highly expressive solo that is meticulously marked with many style and tempo markings. The main challenges are in terms of rhythm in the 4/8 section. This solo would be a marvelous choice for a lyrical selection on a recital. I highly recommend it!

Pugnani, Gaetano. *Menuetto.* Trans./arr. Ronald Dishinger. Medici Music Press. 1994. $5. 2:00. III–IV. B♭–a′. This work has several catchy tunes. It is a moderate tempo and primarily remains in the middle register with occasional sixteenth note runs. All of the technique is idiomatic and there are few accidentals. This would be a good solo for a good high school student or young college player.

Purcell, Henry. *Gavotte and Hornpipe.* Trans./arr. Ronald Dishinger. Medici Music Press. 1986. $5. 2:30. II–III. c–g′. This very fun and lively solo is in B♭ major, is in bass clef, has very few chromatics, has a few eighth note runs, and is mostly in the middle to lower register. The challenge lies in the time signature of its two sections: a slow cut time and a 3/2 section. It does get into the high register a couple of time, but it has plenty of rest. This would be a great style, rhythm, and time signature study for a very good middle school student or high school player.

Purcell, Henry. *Gavotte from Harpsichord Suite No. 5.* Trans. Anton Vedeski. Medici Music Press. 1986. $4.50. 2:00. II–III. d–f'. This little solo is allegro and in common time in B♭ major. It is in bass clef, mostly in the middle to lower register, has some scale-wise eighth note runs, and is rhythmically straightforward. This would be a great solo for a good middle school player.

Purcell, Henry. *Marche from Suite No. 5 for Clavier.* Trans./arr. Ronald Dishinger. Medici Music Press. 1989. $4.50. 2:30. II. c–d'. This solo would be a good second solo for a middle school student. It is in F major, is mostly in the lower register, is rhythmically straightforward, has very few accidentals, is in bass clef, and has very few technical challenges.

Querat, Marcel. *Allegretto Comodo pour Saxhorn-Basse et Piano.* Editions Philippo-Combre, Paris. 1971. 2:00. III. A–g'. A slow, lyrical French song that would be a good melodic study for young students, as it remains in the middle tessitura and has very few technical challenges. The solo part is in bass clef.

Rachmaninov, Sergei. *Vocalise.* Ed. Adam Frey. Athens Music Publishing. 2000. III–IV. C–g'. A fine arrangement of one of the most beautiful romantic songs.

Rachmaninov, Sergei. *Vocalise.* Ed. Steven Mead. Studio Music Co., London. 1995. $7. III–IV. C–g'. This is an extremely popular and most well-known romantic song. This arrangement is from Steven Mead's *The World of the Euphonium.* It is a fine arrangement as it is easy to read, well marked, and adheres stylistically to the original, and the key (E♭ major) is very accessible to many playing levels. It also features very fine playing hints and suggestions from Steven Mead. This is a perfect recital selection. The solo comes in both bass and treble clefs.

Rameau, Jean P. *Rigaudon from "Pieces de Clavecin, 1724."* Trans. Ronald Dishinger. Medici Music Press. 1986. $5. 1:30. II. A–e♭'. This is a good first solo for a middle school student.

Raum, Elizabeth. *Concerto del Garda.* Adapted by Larry Campbell. Tuba-Euphonium Press. 1998. $20. 15:00. V. GG–b♭'. This solo was written for Canadian tubist John Griffiths. The solo comes in a collection of parts in both bass and treble clef as well as tuba parts C and F. It has three movements: Moderato grandioso; Lento; Allegretto con anima. The first movement opens with a beautiful theme that will return later in the movement. The movement cycles through many styles and includes very bold statements, some soaring passages, and a couple of showy sections with many sixteenth note runs, most of which are not scale-wise. The second movement is very slow and highly expressive. It mostly contains sixteenth note runs and triplet passages. The third movement is very energetic and fun to play. It contains many sixteenth note passages, many of which are not scale-wise. It features an extended cadenza (one of the longer cadenzas in the euphonium repertoire) that allows for a wide range of musical and technical expression! The work ascends into the high register often, but for a work of this overall technical difficulty it is nothing excessive. This is a great concerto and would make for a wonderful recital piece.

Raum, Elizabeth. *Faustbuch, a Concerto in Three Movement for Solo Euphonium.* Tuba-Euphonium Press. 2003. $20. 13:00. VI. BB♭–c''. This solo is based off the Faust legend, specifically the version made famous by Goethe. This is a fantastic work for euphonium and orchestra, here reduced for piano. The work is in three movements: Faust and Mephistopheles; Faust and Gretchen; Walpurgis, Death and Redemption. This work is full of challenges. It has challenging rhythms, has many technical runs that are highly chromatic and often not scale-wise, has many wide intervals, spans a wide range, and is often in the high register. It has many style, meter, and time changes and it requires a player with a wide dynamic range. The solo part comes in bass, treble, and F tuba. It is well marked with very specific articulations, phrasings, dynamics, styles, and tempos. The solo part comes with excellent program notes for each movement that are very helpful in terms of interpretation. This is a fantastic solo! It is extremely powerful, highly emotional, spans a huge emotional range, has intense dramatic and driving passages, and makes a huge emotional impact. There are many challenges, but they are more than worth the effort. If you are looking for a work that will challenge you and make a huge impact upon your audience, this is it!

Raum, Elizabeth. *Pershing Concerto for Euphonium and Piano.* Elizabeth Raum. 1998. V. D–b♭'. This work is typical of Elizabeth Raum's works; it is beautiful yet energetic, very emotional and powerful. It is technically challenging, but it remains in the middle tessitura for the vast majority of the solo. I thoroughly enjoy this work and highly recommend it. The solo part is in bass clef.

Ravel, Maurice. *Pavane for an Infant Dead Princess.* Trans./arr. Ronald Dishinger. Medici Music Press. 1996. $5. 1:30. II–III. c–f'. This is a very good arrangement of one of the most beautiful and popular songs in the classical music repertoire as it is very playable for more advanced middle school students. It is in a great key, has few accidentals, remains in the middle register, and has straightforward rhythms while adhering well to the original.

Ravel, Maurice. *Piece en Forme de Habanera*. Arr. Neal Ramsay. Medici Music Press. 2001. $5. 2:30. IV. d–a′. This work is a fantastic change of pace in our repertoire. As soon as I started playing it I felt like I was in Latin America. The work is rhythmically challenging and has some tricky ensemble areas, but the overall range of the work is fine and the technique is idiomatic for the euphonium. It features many dynamic and articulation changes. The work has unlimited musical possibilities.

Redhead, Robert. *Euphony*. Copyright Robert Redhead. 1978. IV. BB♭–b♭′. This work is based on the songs of S. E. Cox ("This One Thing I Know," "He Found M," You Can Tell Out the Sweet Story," and "Deep and Wide"). It is very rhapsodic with many lively dance-like sections, triple against duple, and meter changes. This is a very entertaining work and would be a great change of pace on a recital! It also features many gorgeous melodies. This is a very popular work with Salvation Army bands. The solo part is available in both treble and bass clefs. A brass band accompaniment version is also available. Recorded by Steven Mead.

Rekhin, Igor. *Sonata for Euphonium and Piano*. Tuba-Euphonium Press. 1997. $14. 9:00. V. F–c♯″. This solo has three movements: Allegro molto; Adagio; Allegro. This solo explores many technical and musical sides of the euphonium. The first movement begins very deliberately. It moves to a very light section followed by a more lyrical section. Later it becomes even more pronounced, rhapsodic, and features glissandos, flutter tonguing, and a small cadenza. The second movement is very slow and highly expressive. It features a very ornamented cadenza section that really showcases the euphonium's technical abilities. The final movement is a technical tour de force as it features loads of sixteenth note runs and a cadenza. This solo demonstrates many of the technical and musical capabilities of the euphonium in a relatively short amount of time.

Reeman, John. *Sonata for Euphonium*. Studio Music. 1997. $16. IV–V. E♭–c″. This one-movement sonata was written for Steven Mead. It is a fantastic work that if taken to tempo is very technically challenging. Technical challenges include wide leaps, multiple tonguing, and high tessitura sections. It is extremely energetic, powerful, and passionate and is a fantastic all-around showcase for the euphonium. Steven Mead includes insightful performance hints and suggestions in the front of the solo. The solo is available in both bass and treble clefs.

Resanovic, Nikola. *Sonata for Euphonium*. 2004. $20. Ca. 7:00. IV–V. E–c″. While Mr. Resanovic was teaching theory at the University of Akron, Ohio, he wrote this new work for Travis Scott. It has three short movements: Spirals; Circles; Squares. The work is very tonal and lies mostly in the middle range. It requires both a good euphonium player and accompanist. This work comes highly recommended as a very exciting and passionate work. The third movement is especially fun as it features a good amount of mixed meter and is very lively and driving. Audio and score samples can be found at www.nikolaresanovic.com.

Rheinberger, Josef. *Prelude*. Trans./arr. Ronald Dishinger. Medici Music Press. 1996. $5. 2:30. III–IV. G–b♭′. This work was originally for violin and organ. It is very lively, fluid yet stately at times. It is marked at an andante tempo and has many sixteenth note runs and wide intervals but just briefly remains in the high register. It is an impressive sounding yet fun work to play.

Richards, Goff. *Midnight Euphonium*. Studio Music. 1993. 3:00. IV. B♭–b♭′. This one-movement character piece is a very relaxed and laid-back solo. It only has a few technical challenges and remains mostly in the middle tessitura. This would be a nice study on style for a younger player or a great mood change on a recital. The solo part comes in both bass and treble clefs, and a symphony orchestra accompaniment is available as well as brass band. Recorded by Steven Mead.

Richards, Goff. *Rangitoto*. Studio Music. 1995. 9:00. V–VI. F–b♭′. This work is very technically challenging; however, it is a wonderful character piece with an extremely high variety of stylistic changes. Solo part is available in both bass and treble clefs.

Rimmer, W. *Fantasia on Welsh Melody, "Jenny Jones."* F. Richardson Ltd., Gloucester, England. VI. F–b♭′. A famous theme and variations for trumpet that was also arranged for euphonium. It is an amazing showpiece and it is extremely challenging. Solo part is available in both bass and treble clef.

Rimmer, W. *Weber's Last Waltz, Grand Fantasia*. Ed. Steven Mead. Studio Music. 1995. V–VI. F–c″. This theme and variations edition is from Steven Mead's *The World of the Euphonium*. It was made famous by euphonium soloists such as Arthur Lehman. Its technique is very idiomatic for the euphonium and it remains mostly in the middle tessitura. It is a challenging but absolutely gorgeous work and is one of my favorite theme and variations for the euphonium. The solo part comes in both bass and treble clefs. This is a must buy for theme and variations fans.

Rimsky-Korsakov, Nikolai. *Flight of the Bumblebee*. R. P. Block, Philharmusica Co. $12.50. This is a classic technical showpiece that makes for a great end to any recital.

Roberts, Stephen. *Carrickfergus*. Tanglewind Music, Birmingham, UK. 1993. 2:30. III. A–b♭. This is a traditional Irish air. It is slow, lyrical, and beautiful. There are very few technical challenges. This would be an excellent melodic study for young students. Solo part comes in treble clef.

Rodgers, Thomas. *Sonata for Euphonium and Piano.* Tuba-Euphonium Press. 1997. $12. 13:30. V. F–c″. This work has three movements: Moderato; Song; Rondo, and is in bass clef. The first movement has many powerful passages. It is highly chromatic and has some rhythmic challenges and a fair amount of tenor clef. The second movement is a beautiful song with some very powerful and emotional climaxes. It also contains some tenor clef. The last movement is highly energetic, syncopated, and driving. It is mostly in the middle to lower register and contains a good amount of tenor clef. The work ascends into the high range often and the printing is difficult to read at times. If you are looking for something different for a recital, this would be a good piece to consider.

Rogers, Walter. *The Volunteer.* 5:20. IV–V. This fantastic solo was written in 1887 and is an excellent American patriotic showpiece. The solo includes such patriotic songs as "America," "Coming through the Rye," "Yankee Doodle," and "Annie Laurie." This would make for an excellent recital selection. Recorded by Brian Bowman.

Romberg, Sigmund. *Serenade from "The Student Prince."* Arr. David Werden. Cimarron Music Press. $15. 3:40. IV. This is one of the classic solos for euphonium. It is highly lyrical and extremely expressive. This would be a fantastic recital selection. Recorded by Brian Bowman.

Roper, Anthony. *Sonata for Euphonium.* Studio Music Company. $16. 8:30. V. BB♭–c″. A very fun and different addition to the sonata genre for euphonium! This challenging yet accessible three-movement work is very inventive with loads of dynamic contrast and specific articulation details. It covers a wide range of styles and emotions and has a muted section. Steven Mead provides fantastic detailed performance suggestions at the front of the solo. The solo part includes both bass and treble clef. This is a very exciting composition and a joy to play! Recorded by Steven Mead, *The World of the Euphonium,* volume 3.

Ross, Walter. *Bagatelles for Euphonium and Piano.* Tuba-Euphonium Press. 1992. 10:00. V. E–a♭′. This has become a standard in the euphonium repertoire. It has three movements: Spiritoso; Adagio affettuoso; Con umore. The first movement is in a fast cut time and is very jovial. It has a moderate amount of eighth note runs that are sometimes scale-wise. It is rhythmically straightforward and fun to play. The second movement is in a very slow 6/8, has a few rhythmic challenges, and is very passionate. The third movement is in a moderate 3/8, has some tricky technical passages, and has a fantastic middle section that moves to a quick 2/4 marked "burlando." This is a very fun movement! The work is in bass clef and overall it has a conservative range as it is mostly in the middle and lower registers. This is

an excellent recital piece and represents a modern style of composition that every euphonium player should be familiar with.

Ross, Walter. *Concerto for Euphonium, Symphonic Brass and Timpani.* TUBA Press. 1993. $12. V. G–a♭′. Written for the Kennesaw College Brass Ensemble, this solo with piano reduction offers a wide variety of music expression. It has three movements: Fantasia; Chorale Variations; Scherzo. The work opens with a fantastic cadenza that has some unique elements. Most of the rest of the first movement is very lively and animated and very fun to play. There is some very fun and interesting rhythmic play between the soloist and the piano (ensemble). The second movement is highly expressive and passionate with many places for the soloist to be dramatic. It is full of many gorgeous phrases. The third movement is a moderate 3/8 and is highly energetic and very dance-like. It juxtaposes a couple of beautiful cantabile sections that make the faster sections really sparkle. The solo is in bass clef and is conservative in terms of range as it is mostly in the middle and lower registers. It does have some tricky rhythms, technical passages, and intervals, but it is manageable. This is a wonderful work! If you are looking for a unique change of pace on a recital, this would be a great selection.

Ross, Walter. *Partita.* Boosey & Hawkes. 1974. $24.95. 9:00. V. This solo is a standard in the euphonium repertoire and is a fantastic work from a very popular and very good euphonium and tuba composer. This is a good piece to study, as it has been required for euphonium solo competitions.

Rossini, Gioacchino. *Aria Cuius animam, aus dem Stabat Mater.* Trans. Franz Liszt. Arr. Burghard Schloemann. TRIO Blasermusik Edition, Muhldorf/Inn. 1988. 4:00. IV. e♭–d♭″. This beautiful solo is based off of an aria from one of Rossini's more famous works. It is in bass clef, a moderate common time, A♭ major, is rhythmically straightforward, is mostly in the middle to higher register, and has many wide intervals. The challenge of this solo is endurance, as it has very few rests and ascends into the high register several times. This would be a great lyrical selection for a recital.

Roussanova-Lucas, Elena. *Fantasy for Euphonium and Piano.* Denis Wick Publishing. $27.25. IV. This is a great addition to the repertoire from a very talented Russian composer. It is basically a three-movement sonata form. The solo part is available in both bass and treble clefs.

Rubank. *Stupendo.* $4.95. 2:00. III. This fantastic concert polka comes highly recommended, as it is perfect for a high school student to perform at a solo and ensemble contest. It has a moderate range, scale-wise runs, and not too many accidentals. It has numerous style changes and wonderful melodies. It is a lot of fun to play and teach! See Euphonium and Keyboard Collections.

Rubank. *Toreador's Song.* $4.95. II. A classic selection from one of the most popular and well-known operas, Bizet's *Carmen.*

Saint-Saens, Camille. *Morceau de Concert.* Douglas A. Nelson, Shawnee Press Inc. $12. IV–V. This standard horn solo has become a popular arrangement for euphonium. It is a great solo for a young college student. Both treble and bass clefs are available as well as a band version. Recorded by Douglas Nelson.

Saint-Saens, Camille. *Romance for Euphonium and Piano, Op. 36.* Arr. Michael A. Fischer. Tuba-Euphonium Press. 2001. $8. 2:30. III. f–ab'. This is a beautiful lyrical solo. It is in a moderate 3/4, is in the key of Db major, and is in bass clef. It is rhythmically simple and has very few technical challenges. The challenge of this solo is the range, as it ascends into the high range several times, the key, and endurance, as there are few places to rest. It is well marked with very specific articulation and dynamic markings. This solo would be a fantastic lyrical selection for a recital or would be a great solo and ensemble selection for a good high school player.

Saint-Saens, Camille. *The Swan.* Ed. Larry Campbell. Hal Leonard Publishing Corporation. 1977. $12.95. 1:30. III. c–bb'. This work is part of a collection of solos–Master Solos, Intermediate Level. This is a very fine edition of one of the most well-known romantic songs. This would be a good challenge for a high school player and a fantastic study on sound, lyrical style, phrasing, musicality, and finesse in the high register. This edition would also be a nice change of pace on a college recital or for a first recital piece for a college student. Recorded by Larry Campbell.

Saint-Saens, Camille. *The Swan.* Trans./arr. Ronald Dishinger. Medici Music Press. 1996. $5. 2:00. II–III. Bb–f'. This is a very fine arrangement of this very popular romantic song. This would be an excellent study of phrasing, sound, and musicality for a good middle school student and high school player as it is arranged where it is in a very comfortable range for young players.

Saint-Saens, Camille. *The Swan.* Arr. Leonard Falcone. Southern Music Company. 1966. 2:20. III–IV. c–bb'. This is a very fine version and would be a nice challenge for a good high school student or young college player as is requires some finesse at high Bb. Being in the key of Eb this arrangement allows the player to sing through the full regular register of the euphonium. Recorded by Leonard Falcone.

Saint-Saens, Camille. *The Swan.* Arr. Steven Mead. Studio Music. 1995. 2:30. III–IV. c–bb'. This is a beautiful version of this most popular euphonium recital piece. It is arranged where it really exploits the full singing register of the euphonium. The solo part is in bass clef.

Sarasate, Pablo. *Gypsy Airs (Zigeunerweisen) for Cornet or Euphonium Solo.* Arr. Howard Snell.

Rakeway Music. 1983. $14. V–VI. F–d". This is a very flashy and highly technical work. A great piece to end a major recital.

Schmidt, Heinrich Kaspar. *Im tiefsten Walde (In the Deepest Forest).* Arr. Thomas Bacon. Southern Music. 1995. 3:30. IV. c–c". A tone poem originally written for solo winds. It has very few challenges, most being the key (E major), accidentals, and a couple of extended high tessitura sections. It is a short and beautiful work with plenty of interpretative flexibility. It works wonderfully for the euphonium. Solo part comes in both bass and treble clefs.

Schooley, John. *Vocalise for Trombone/Baritone and Piano.* Glouchester Press/Robert King Music Sales. 1981. $3. III. This gorgeous solo would be an excellent recital selection! It is similar to the Rachmaninov *Vocalise* and comes in bass and treble clef solo parts.

Schubert, Franz. *Arpreggione Sonata.* Arr. David R. Werden. 1985.

Schubert, Franz. *Fruhlingsglaube (Faith in Spring), for Euphonium and Piano.* Arr. Michael A. Fischer. Tuba-Euphonium Press. 2001. $8. 1:45. III. d–e'. This solo is in a slow 2/4, is in G major, has mostly dotted eighth rhythms and sixteenth note patterns, has some rhythm challenges, a fair amount of accidentals, is mostly in the middle register, and is in bass clef. It is well marked with very specific articulation markings, dynamics, and tempos. This is a beautiful solo. It has program notes about the work including a text translation. This would be an excellent solo for a recital if one is looking for a good lyrical selection and a relaxing change of pace. This solo would also be an excellent solo for a good high school player to study.

Schubert, Franz. *Menuetto from Violin Sonata, Op. 137, No. 2.* Trans./arr. Ronald Dishinger. Medici Music Press. 2002. $5. 2:30. III. d–a'. A short and sweet work with several stylistically different sections. It is mostly in the middle register and has many dynamic contrasts. This would be a good work for style study with a good high school player.

Schubert, Franz. *My Sweetheart's Eyes, Op. 14, No. 2.* Trans./arr. Ronald Dishinger. 1989. $4.50. 1:10. I–II. c–f'. This would be a good second solo for a middle school player. It is in a good register and key and is primarily quarter notes. It is a pretty little tune with some nice chromatic and dynamic contrasts.

Schubert, Franz. *Serenade.* Trans./arr. Ronald Dishinger. 1994. $4.50. 2:00. II–III. d–g'. This beautiful art song is wonderfully arranged for the euphonium. It remains in the middle register and has many beautiful soaring moments. It is slow and features a triplet motive throughout, many dramatic dynamic changes, and lots of beautiful chromaticism. This is a very fine arrangement for a lyrical selection on a recital or for a high school student or young college student to work on musicality.

Schultz, Patrick. *Concerto for Euphonium*. Patrick Schulz. 2000. 12:00. V. BB♭–c″. This is a very powerful and energetic concerto. The second movement features many mixed meter sections.

Schumann, Robert. *Fantasiestucke, Opus 73*. Arr. Henry Howey. TUBA Press. 1996. $8. V. E–d″. This is solo only, as a note at the beginning discusses the many good editions of the piano part that will fit with the solo part. The solo euphonium version also comes with the solo tuba version. This solo has three movements: Fast; Slow; Fast. Each movement has many rhythmic, technical, and range challenges. The solo is in bass clef but has many passages in tenor clef. This work is very challenging but has many beautiful passages. It is one of Schumann's many fine works and here it has been well edited for euphonium.

Schumann, Robert. *Five Pieces in Folk Style, Op. 102*. Arr. Paul Droste. Ludwig Music Publishing Co. Inc. 1977. $13.95. V. F♯–c″. Recorded by Paul Droste. This is a beautiful work and is one of the most popular in the euphonium repertoire. It is a fantastic study on melody and musicianship. This collection of songs is one of the standards in the euphonium repertoire. It covers a vast array of styles and emotions. They are accessible to many levels of musicians and are wonderful recital pieces. They are a must in any euphonium player's library. The solo part is in bass clef.

Schumann, Robert. *Suite Abendlied, "Evening Song."* Trans./arr. Ronald Dishinger. Medici Music Press. 1995. $5.50. 3:00. II–III. F–f′. Four movements: Prelude; Melodie; Dream Song; First Loss. The first movement is a very sweet opening to this lovely suite. The second movement is a small and simple song. The third movement lives up to its title as it is beautiful and smooth. The last movement is very gleeful in nature. Overall there are few technical challenges. The range remains mostly in the middle register and the rhythms are straightforward. The challenge lies musically, as this suite has many musical possibilities. This work would be most appropriate for a good high school student.

Schumann, Robert. *Variations on a Theme of Robert Schumann*. Arr. Williams Davis. Southern Music Company. $6.50. IV.

Schumann, Robert. *Your Ring on My Finger from Womanly Love and Life, Op. 42, No. 4*. Trans./arr. Ronald Dishinger. Medici Music Press. 1989. $4.50. 1:30. II–III. c–f′. This lovely art song would be a good early study of phrasing, shaping, and dynamic contrast for a good middle school student. It has a conservative range and has sparse use of accidentals. It mostly consists of quarter notes and isolated pairs of eighth notes.

Selmer-Collery, Jules. *Tubanova, Solo de concours*. Editions Max Eschig, Paris. 1967. 6:30. IV–V. BB♭–a′. Two-movement work that is challenging but fun to play. It has many varying moods and style changes. The solo part is in bass clef.

Senaille, John Baptiste. *Allegro Spiritoso*. Arr. Leonard Falcone. Southern Music. 1966. 3:00. IV–V. B♭–a′. This work is quick, lively, and challenging. It is a very fun work to play and features many passages of slurred sixteenth note runs, most of which are in the key of E♭ major or are idiomatic to the instrument. A very fine arrangement and the solo part is in bass clef.

Seybold, Arthur. *Dudelsack, Musette-Bagpipe, Opus 166, No. 3*. Trans./arr. Ronald Dishinger. Medici Music Press. 1993. $4. 1:45. II–III. c–e♭′. This highly entertaining and extremely fun to play solo is in a moderate 3/4, in B♭ and F major, is rhythmically straightforward, has mostly broken scale-wise eighth note runs, has very few accidentals, and is in bass clef. This would be a fantastic solo for a high school student or young college player.

Sherman, Donald M. *Concertpiece: "Sacred So" for Euphonium and Piano*. Tuba-Euphonium Press. 1994. $10. 8:00. V. D♭–c″. If you are looking for an extremely powerful and "in your face" piece, this is it! This work has many rips and glissandos over wide intervals, creating some highly intense moments. It is very rhythmic and driving as it is in fast compound meters and features very, very strong syncopated accents, big dynamics and dynamic changes, passages soaring quickly into the high register, and big hits with the piano. It also features a very deliberate cadenza. This work has many rhythmic, intervallic, and chromatic challenges. It ascends into the high range often and requires a player who can produce wide dynamic contrasts. It comes in bass and treble clef with some tenor clef. This is an intense piece, is tons of fun to play, and would definitely get your audience's attention!

Shostakovich, Dimitri. *Concerto No. 1 for Cello and Orchestra*. Trans. Nikk Pilato. Tuba-Euphonium Press. 1997. $8. 10:00. V. C–d″. This solo is mostly in cut time and 3/2, is mostly in c minor, has many wide intervals, is mostly in the middle to upper register, has a large amount of chromatics, has no separate movements but is in one large section, and is in bass clef with a large amount of tenor clef. This is a fantastic solo! It has many powerful and gorgeous lyrical moments. Like many of Shostakovich's works, it is full of many emotions and makes very big statements. If you are looking for a great transcription for a recital, take a look at this one.

Shostakovich, Dimitri. *Prelude No. 7*. Arr. Sharon Davis. Western International Music. 1983. 1:00. III. G♯–g♭′. A very short yet beautiful solo perfect for high school students. Solo part is in bass clef.

Sibelius, Jean. *Nocturne*. Carl Fischer. 1:30. III–IV. D–g♭′. Solo part is in treble clef.

Sibelius, Jean. *Valse Triste, from the music to Arvid Jarnefelt's Drama "Kuolema" (Death), Op. 44*.

Arr. A. Siniaviski. Tapiola Music Publishers. 1994. 2:30. II–III. B–a'. A slow waltz that would be a good lyrical stylistic study for young players. Solo part is in bass clef.

Sibbing, Robert. *Reverie and Frolic for Euphonium and Piano*. Tuba-Euphonium Press. 1997. $12. 6:30. V. BB♭–c''. This highly expressive and lively solo is in A♭, F, and E♭ major and is in bass clef with many sections in tenor clef. The *Reverie* begins in a slow 3/4 and moves into a slow 6/8 section before returning to the slow 3/4 section. The *Frolic* is in a fast 2/4 and has a slower middle section. This solo is full of extremely beautiful phrases and very energetic and powerful musical statements. The challenge is in terms of range, as it often spans a wide range and has many tricky technical passages. The technical challenges of this solo are worth it as it would be a great recital piece. If you are looking for a change of pace on a recital, this is your piece.

Siekmann, Frank H. *Gregarious*. Brelmat Music. 1984. $10. 4:00. III. B♭–a'. This is a lovely little work that features numerous style changes. It begins cantabile with a beautiful soaring melody, moves to a nice muted section, then to a jazz/rock section before ending with a really fun Latin melody. It is mostly in the middle register and mostly eighth notes. It has a decent amount of syncopation that is all straightforward. This solo would be perfect for a good high school player or young college student. There are also band and orchestra accompaniment versions.

Siekmann, Frank H. *Norwegian Christmas Fantasy*. Brelmat Music. $17. IV. C–b'. This collection of Norwegian Christmas melodies was commissioned by Frederick Boyd, bass trombonist of the Syracuse Symphony. It was premiered at the U.S. Army Band Tuba-Euphonium Conference in 2000. This is a nice collection of holiday melodies and an especially good work if you are looking for something different to play during the holidays. The melodies are "Precious Child," "So Sweetly Sleeping" (Norwegian folk song), "Beautiful Is the Blue Heaven" (Jacob Gerhard Meidell), and "You Green, Glittering Tree, Good Day" (C. E. F. Weyes). The first melody is in G major and E♭ major, is in a moderately slow 3/4, and features scale-wise triplets and eighth notes. It is a beautiful melody and has many highly expressive passages. The second melody is in a moderately fast common time and has many mostly scale-wise sixteenth note runs. It is a very light and lively melody and has a glistening sound and feel in the technical passages. The last melody is in a moderate 6/8, is in A major, and features some mixed meter and very rhapsodic passages. The work has some rhythmic and technical challenges, is mostly in the middle register, and is in bass clef. This is a very fun work to play and it comes highly recommended.

Siekmann, Frank H. *Norwegian Christmas Fantasy*. Tuba-Euphonium Press. 2000. $12. See above for details.

Siekmann, Frank H. *Reflections*. Brelmat Music. 1994. $8. 3:20. III. G–b♭'. Dedicated to the University of Vermont Concert Band, this is very lyrical work that beautifully demonstrates the singing quality of the euphonium. It also has some fun Latin sections. It is in c minor, is in common time, is mostly in the middle register, has a few rhythmic challenges, has some sixteenth note runs, has a moderate use of chromatics, has piano cues, and is in bass clef. The solo opens with a gorgeous tranquillo section and moves to a soaring con moto section. It features a very fun tempo di beguine section before ending with the original tranquillo feel. I highly recommend this solo as it would be a great solo for just about any type of college recital. There are also band and orchestra accompaniment versions.

Simon, Frank. *Zillertal*. Rubank, Miami. 4:00. IV. B♭–c''. A fantastic theme and variations that sounds very flashy but isn't nearly as hard as it sounds! It remains mostly in the middle tessitura. Most runs are tongued with some multiple tonguing and are in the key of B♭. I really enjoyed playing through this work! The solo part is in both bass and treble clefs.

Simons, Gardell. *Atlantic Zephyrs (Novelette)*. Carl Fischer. 4:00. IV. e♭–b♭'. This is a very accessible and light and fun theme and variations. It remains in the middle register and has numerous optional sections and pitches in most of the variations. I highly recommend this work for a young college student. Solo part is in bass clef.

Skolnik, Walter. *Lullaby for Curly for Baritone Horn and Piano*. Tenuto Publications. 1975. 3:00. III. F–e♭'. A beautiful little solo that would be a great slow lyrical study for young players. Solo part is in bass clef.

Smith, Clay. *Friends, Waltz Caprice*. Rubank, Hal Leonard Corporation. $6.95. 2:00. II–III. d–f'. This fun waltz has many beautiful phrases, is in E♭ major, is in 3/4, is rhythmically simple, has a moderate amount of accidentals, is mostly in the middle register, and is in bass clef. The work features a beautiful waltz melody that returns, a peaceful trio, and an energetic vivo closing section. This is a lovely waltz and would be most appropriate for a good middle school player or young high school student. I highly recommend this solo. See Euphonium and Keyboard Collections.

Smith, Leonard B. *Concentration*. Belwin Mills, CCP/Belwin, Inc. 1968. $4.95. 1:30. II–III. B–f'. This solo is in C major, is marked "allegretto moderato" in 3/4, and begins with a lovely quarter notes melody. It soon moves into a highly chromatic section that is very passionate. The main theme soon returns and ends dying away. This is a pretty little solo that stays in the middle register (has some optional higher notes) and would be a great second or third solo for a middle school player. Some very appropriate performance suggestions can be found below the solo. See Euphonium and Keyboard Collections.

Smith, Leonard B. *Debonair.* Belwin Mills, CCP/Belwin, Inc. 1973. $4.95. 1:30. I–II. e♭–f'. This solo is in E♭ major and is marked "spirited" in 3/4. It is mostly quarter notes with dotted quarters creating many dance-like sections due to the syncopation. This is a fun little tune that remains in the middle register and has no accidentals. It would be a very good second solo for a middle school student. See Euphonium and Keyboard Collections.

Smith, Leonard B. *Little Norway.* Belwin Mills, CCP/Belwin, Inc. 1970. $4.95. 1:10. II. d–c'. Written for Walter Beeler, this solo is in F major, 2/4, and is marked "allegretto." It features mostly off beat eighth note patterns creating a great syncopated dance feel. It has a decent amount of accidentals but remains in the middle to lower register. This would be a very fun second solo for a middle school student. Some very appropriate performance suggestions can be found below the solo. See Euphonium and Keyboard Collections.

Smith, Leonard B. *Sentinel.* Belwin Mills, CCP/Belwin, Inc. 1973. $4.95. 1:20. II–III. c–e♭'. This solo is in A♭ major, 2/4 time, and is marked "leisurely." It features mostly eighth notes and sixteenths and has a very lively dance quality. It has a good amount of accidentals but remains in the middle register. This would be a fine solo for a mature middle school player. See Euphonium and Keyboard Collections.

Smith, Leonard B. *Unicorn.* Belwin Mills, CCP/Belwin, Inc. 1970. $4.95. 1:00. II. G–d'. This solo is in E♭ major, 2/4, and is marked "allegretto giocoso." It is primarily scale-wise eighth note runs in the middle to lower register with some syncopation and a few accidentals. This would be a good second solo for a middle school player. Some very appropriate performance suggestions can be found below the solo. See Euphonium and Keyboard Collections.

Smith, Leonard B. *Venture.* Belwin Mills, CCP/Belwin, Inc. 1973. $4.95. 1:45. I. c–c'. This solo is in B♭ major, 3/4, and is marked "waltz tempo." It is primarily dotted half notes and quarters, remains in the middle to lower registers, and has straightforward rhythms and few accidentals. This cute waltz would be a good first solo for a beginner. See Euphonium and Keyboard Collections.

Snell, Howard. *Bagatelles.* $22. Solo part is in bass clef. Available at www.euphonium.net.

Snell, Howard. *Fantasy.* $22. Solo part is in treble clef. Available at www.euphonium.net.

Snell, Howard. *Oration.* $14. Solo part is in both bass and treble clefs. Available at www.euphonium.net.

Snell, Howard. *Variations on Drink to Me Only.* Rakeway Music, Kirklees Music. 1998. $16. 9:00. V. BB♭–d♭". This is a highly technical yet very diverse and entertaining work. It is a must for theme and variations fans. Solo part comes in bass and treble clef.

Sousa, John Philip. *Stars and Stripes Forever.* Arr. Fred Weber. Belwin Mills Inc. 1969. $5. 1:00. I. B♭–b♭. A simple arrangement of America's national march. See Euphonium and Keyboard Collections.

Sousa, John Philip. *Stars and Stripes Forever.* Arr. Forrest L. Buchtel. Neil A. Kjos Music Company. 1982. $1.75. 1:30. I. B♭–c'. This solo is in E♭ major, is in a march tempo common time, is mostly quarter and half notes, has a few accidentals, has piano cues, and is in bass clef. This would be a great first solo for a beginner.

Spaniola, Joseph T. *Letters from a Friend.* Tuba-Euphonium Press. 1992. $10. 8:00. IV–V. A–e'. This is a great solo! It has three movements: Sleepless Nights; The Journey; The Hope of Tomorrow. Each movement title is well represented musically. The first movement is rhythmically very restless and has many agitato sections. The second movement begins freely and slowly gathers momentum until it is pressing forward and very decisive. It has many "stops" along the way, just like a journey, where there are varying moods: light and playful, animated, sweetly, expressive, and so forth. The last movement is a combination of being reflective and full of energy. The work is very conservative in range as it is mostly in the middle to lower register. It is in bass clef and the challenges lie in its high use of chromatics and rhythm and time issues. There are many tricky rhythm combinations and many time signature changes. For example, the last movement has a great deal of mixed meter. The solo part also comes with a version for tuba. This is a marvelous solo as there are very few solos like it in the euphonium repertoire. This would be an excellent change of pace on any recital. I highly recommend this work.

Sparke, Philip. *Aubade.* Studio Music Company. 1984. $8.50. 4:30. IV. D–b♭'. This work features one of the most incredibly beautiful melodies ever written for a brass instrument. It is a slow, reflective, and beautifully lyrical work that is an absolute joy to play! This work is an excellent lyrical study. The middle section is a little quicker and lively. This is a fantastic recital piece. Also is available with brass band accompaniment. Recorded by Steven Mead, Euphony.

Sparke, Philip. *Euphonium Concerto.* Studio Music. 1995. 18:30. V–VI. D–d♭". Written by one of the finest euphonium composers and premiered by Steven Mead, this work has become one of the major standard works in the euphonium repertoire. It has three movements, the first of which has a main theme that is very expressive and is juxtaposed with numerous highly energetic passages. The second movement has two cadenzas, allowing for a high level of artistic showmanship, and has one of the most gorgeous melodies in the euphonium repertoire. The last movement is highly rhapsodic and is a wonderful technical display. This is a must have/must study for the serious euphonium player and teacher. The solo part comes in bass and treble clefs. Also available with brass band. Recorded by Steven Mead.

Sparke, Philip. *Fantasy for Euphonium and Brass Band*. R. Smith & Co. Ltd. 1978. V. Recorded by Ian Craddock, Renato Meli, and the Childs Brothers (Robert Childs). This fantastic work by one of the great euphonium composers opens with a quasi-cadenza passage before moving to a very lively allegro section. The middle section is very beautiful and reflective. The work ends with the opening material returning and finishes with a very rousing closing!

Sparke, Philip. *Pantomime*. Studio Music Company. 1988. $10. 6:00. V. D–e♭″. Written for Nicholas Childs, this work displays all of the melodic, technical, and range capabilities of the euphonium. It opens with one of the most beautiful melodies ever written for the euphonium. It also features a highly energetic mixed meter section with an unforgettable melody. If all of the previous beautiful music is not enough, the middle 5/4 slower section features a new gorgeous melody. The work concludes with one of the most impressive technical displays in all of the repertoire. This is a must study in the euphonium repertoire. There are also versions with brass band and wind ensemble accompaniments. Treble and bass clef versions available. Recorded by Steven Mead, Adam Frey, Nicholas Childs, and Michael Colburn.

Sparke, Philip. *Party Piece*. Studio Music Company. 1986. $14. 7:00. VI. This work is divided into two sections: a sweet andante, which begins with a lovely tune that is ornamented, and a very lively allegro. This is a wonderful work and is deserved of its popularity. Recorded by Steven Mead, *The World of the Euphonium*, volume 3.

Sparke, Philip. *Song for Ina*. Studio Music. 1995. 5:30. IV. c–b♭′. Here is another beautiful lyrical work for euphonium by Philip Sparke. This is a very accessible work as it is in the key of A♭ major, stays in the middle register, and has very few technical challenges. This has become a very popular recital selection. The solo part comes in both bass and treble clefs. A brass band accompaniment is available. Recorded by Steven Mead.

Spears, Jared. *Ritual and Celebration*. Southern Music Co. 1991. $6. IV–V.

Spears, Jared. *Rondo Capriccioso*. C. L. Barnhouse Co. $6.50. 5:00. IV–V. BB♭–c′. This is a very

lively and powerful work that is a very exciting solo to play. It features many flashy runs, an extended double tongue section, and a powerful cadenza. I was pleasantly surprised by this work! I highly suggest checking it out as it would be a fantastic recital work. Both bass and treble clef parts come with the solo.

Spies, Ernest. *Scherzo, Opus 66*. Trans./arr. Ronald Dishinger. Medici Music Press. 1995. $5. 3:00. III. G–f′. This cute work would be a good study in staccato articulation and typical scherzo style for a middle school or early high school student. It remains in the middle range and primarily consists of quarter and eighth notes. It begins with a lively lightly articulated melody, later moving to a nice lyrical section.

Stanford, Charles Villiers. *Caoine (Lament)*. Arr. Philip Wilby. Winwood Music. $12.25. III–IV. This is a beautiful selection from this late romantic and early twentieth-century composer.

Stephens, Denzil S. *Carnival*. Sarnia Music (UK) (www.sarnia-music.com). $9.20. IV–V. This solo is not based on *Carnival of Venice* but was originally a cornet solo.

Stephens, Denzil S. *Dizzy Fingers*. Sarnia Music (UK) (www.sarnia-music.com). $9.20. VI. If you are looking for a great new show-off piece for an encore, here it is. This work has been performed by the Childs Brothers and other famous euphonium players.

Stephens, Denzil S. *Gameplan*. Sarnia Music (UK) (www.sarnia-music.com). $9.20. IV–V. A very rhythmic solo.

Stephens, Denzil S. *Quintessence*. Sarnia Music (UK) (www.sarnia-music.com). $9.20. IV–V. In 5/4 time with many contrasting sections.

Stephens, Denzil S. *Rippling Water*. Sarnia Music (UK) (www.sarnia-music.com). $9.20. IV–V. Solo features many different styles.

Stephens, Denzil S. *Runabout*. Wright & Round Ltd. 1981, Gloucester, Enlgand, (0452) 523438. 6:00. IV–V. A–b♭′. An extremely entertaining and fun work to play! I absolutely loved this work! It is fantasia-like in that it is very active with many slurred sixteenth note runs contrasted by some beautiful melodies. The technique is very accessible and idiomatic. Bass and treble parts are available. I highly recommend this work!

Stephens, Denzil S. *Solo Rhapsody for Euphonium*. Sarnia Music (UK) (www.sarnia-music.com). 1989. $11. 6:30. V. E–b♭′. This is a fantastic solo! This is a very challenging piece with numerous key changes. However, it is mostly in the middle and upper register and is a beautiful showy piece. Most of the runs are slurred and very idiomatic. Solo part comes in treble clef and there are both concert band and brass band versions. Recorded by the Childs Brothers (Nicholas Childs).

Stephens, Denzil S. *Spring Fever*. Sarnia Music (UK) (www.sarnia-music.com). $9.20. IV–V. Mainly in 6/8 time.

Stephens, Denzil S. *Sunrise*. Sarnia Music (UK) (www.sarnia-music.com). 2005. $9.20. A beautiful solo with many varied themes.

Stevens, John. *Sonata for Euphonium or Trombone and Piano*. Edition BMI. 2002. $21.80. 16:30. V. This solo was written for Mark Fisher, trombonist in the Chicago Lyric and Santa Fe Operas, and was written by one of the finest and most prolific tuba and euphonium composers. This fantastic solo spans a huge emotional range. It has three movements: Maestoso/declamatory; Very slow and freely; Allegro energico. The first movement opens very powerfully and is pronounced. It has many style changes as it has several dolce and cantabile sections, and it has a very fast section with some changing meters, powerful accents, and driving rhythmic play. The second movement is full of gorgeous lines and passionate chromatics. It allows for a very wide range of musical expression and interpretation. It features a very moving cadenza. The final movement is very lively and features many very powerful and entertaining mixed meter sections. It also features many technically impressive passages requiring double tongued chromatic lines. This movement also features a cadenza that allows for a wide range of artistic expression. The solo overall has many rhythmic challenges, is mostly in the middle to upper register, and is in bass clef with many tenor clef passages. It is well marked with very specific dynamics, style and tempo changes, articulations, piano cues, and phrasings. This is an excellent solo and is more than worth the challenge. I highly recommend this work.

Storm, Chas. W. *Glen Eden Polka*. Rubank, Hal Leonard Corporation. $6.95. 3:00. IV. B♭–f′. This fun polka is in E♭ major, has a slow common time section, has a faster 2/4, has many scale-wise sixteenth note runs, is rhythmically straightforward, has a moderate amount of accidentals, has a few technical challenges, is mostly in the middle register, has piano cues, and is in bass clef. The solo opens with a slow and beautiful Italianet melody with some sporadic use of grace notes. After a small cadenza the polka section begins. The work features a fun trio section with many sixteenths and triplets before returning to the polka section. The work ends with a small cadenza and rousing presto section. This is a very entertaining solo and would be a great selection for a good high school player. See Euphonium and Keyboard Collections.

Stoutamire, Albert L. *Prelude and Fugue*. Ludwig Music Co. 4:00. IV. F–c′. The work remains in the middle tessitura and the few technical challenges are very accessible. It is a fine work to study fugue style with a younger student. Solo part is in bass clef.

Strauss, Franz. *Nocturne, for Euphonium and Piano, Op. 7*. Arr. Michael A. Fischer. Tuba-Euphonium Press. 2001. $8. 2:30. III–IV. A–b♭′. This is a beautiful solo that is in B♭ major, slow common time, and bass clef. It is very lyrical and has many very expressive phrases. It moves into the high register often and has a decent amount of sixteenth note runs and ornaments. This would be a perfect lyrical selection for a recital. I highly recommend this work.

Strauss, Johann. *Tales from the Vienna Woods*. Arr. William Levi. Puna Music Company. 2001. $15.95. 3:00. II–III. A–f′. This is a nice cheerful waltz that is mostly eighth note runs in the middle register with sporadic accidentals. It has many nice melodic lines, is mostly rhythmically straightforward (a few sporadic tricky rhythms), and has a powerful ending. This would be a good solo for a very good middle school student or a high school student. See Euphonium and Keyboard Collections.

Szenpali, Roland. *Pearls*. Edition BIM. 1999. $21. 13:00. V–VI. This is an awesome work that has many fresh ideas and beautifully showcases the euphonium. It has recently been a required work for major international euphonium solo competitions. I highly recommend this work. It has three movements: Ducate SPS 916; My One and Only Love; Susi. The first movement has an Italian rock feel while the second movement is beautiful and light. The last movement is a wild samba! Recorded by Steven Mead.

Szkutko, John. *Andante Brilliante*. John Szkutko (www.tubacentral.com/szkmusic). 2000. 6:00. V–VI. FF–f′. I love this work. It was written for Riki McDonnell and has tons of drive and intensity. It is challenging, yet a fun challenge. Most of the runs are scale-wise and idiomatic. The challenge lies in the high register notes here and there. I highly recommend this work! Solo part is in treble clef.

Tailor, Norman. *Four Miniatures*. $20. IV. The four selections are Grandpa's Horn, Romantic Waltz, Hunting Party, and Madavia. This would be a fantastic recital selection!

Tanner, Paul. *Las Tortillas*. Belwin Mills, CPP/Belwin, Inc. 1980. $4.94. 1:00. II. B♭–e♭′. Sitting here slaving away without any dinner this solo is making me hungry! It is in B♭ Major, 6/8, and a moderate tempo. It is mostly quarter and eighth notes with a few running eighths. It has a great little Latin sound, is in the middle to low register, is rhythmically straightforward, and has a decent amount of accidentals. This would be a fun second solo for a middle school student. See Euphonium and Keyboard Collections.

Tanner, Paul. *Weather Vane*. Belwin Mills, CPP/Belwin, Inc. 1980. $4.95. 1:00. I. B♭–d′. This solo is in F Major, 4/4, is moderately slow, is mostly quarter notes, has no accidentals, and remains in the middle to lower registers. It would be a good first solo for a beginner as it features a lovely melody.

Telemann, Georg P. *Concerto in G Major from Concerto for Viola*. Trans./arr. Ronald Dishinger. Medici Music Press. 1999. $12. 7:30. IV–V. F–g′. This is a fantastic solo with four movements: Largo; Allegro; Andante; Presto. The first movement is a slow 3/2, is in B♭ major, and is very lyrical. Its challenges are rhythm and many very wide intervals. The second movement is a moderate common time and is in B♭ major with many sixteenth note runs. Very few of the runs are scale-wise as most of them are arppegiated or have very wide intervals. This is a very technically demanding movement. The third movement is in a slow common time and is in g minor. It is highly expressive with many chromatics and sixteenth note runs. The last movement is a very fast common time in B♭ major. It has many mostly scale-wise eighth note runs with very few chromatics. Range-wise overall the work is in the middle to lower register, but it often jumps into the high register. This is a very fun work to play and is a most worthy challenge. This would be a great college recital piece.

Thingnacs, Frode. *Peace, Please*. J. Jansen B&H. 4:00. IV. A–g′. This work begins with a lovely slow lyrical theme, which is followed by an animated section, then a syncopated, jazzy section that really drives! The jazz section has chord changes above the written solo line. The technical challenges are minimal. It would be an interesting work to schedule on a recital as a change in mood! Solo part comes in treble clef.

Timokhin, Slava. *Dark Eyes*. Ed. Danny Vinson. Slava Timokhin (vtimokhin@yahoo.com). 2002. 2:30. V. F–b♭′. This is an original composition after the traditional Russian/Gypsy romance. It begins with a beautiful love song, moves into a fast double tonguing section, back to love song, and ends with a larger double tonguing section. The double tongued sections are pretty idiomatic and not as hard as they initially look. The work has a lot of beauty and drive. It was fun to work on! The solo part is in bass clef.

Timokhin, Slava. *Variations on a Theme by Arcangelo Corelli*. Ed. Danny Vinson. Slava Timokhin (vtimokhin@yahoo.com). 2002. 8:00. V. c–d♭″. This challenging theme and variations does not follow the typical "adding of notes" format as one of the variations moves into 5/8, while another one uses quintuplets, followed by a dolce lyrical variation. This is a very unique theme and variations. I found it to be a very refreshing change! I enjoyed this work and recommend it. The solo part comes in bass clef.

Toebosch, Louis. *Variatie's voor Euphonium en Piano, Op. 108b*. Molenaar's Muziekcentrale N.V., Wormerveer-Holland. 1977. 6:00. V. G–b♭′. A very unique theme and variations that is challenging but very creative, energetic, and powerful! It features numerous style changes and remains in the middle register. I highly enjoyed

this work and was pleasantly surprised. Solo parts come in both bass and treble clef.

Traditional. *All through the Night*. Arr. Fred Weber. Belwin, Inc. 1969. $5. 1:00. I. C–c′. A simple Welsh air with a little syncopation. See Euphonium and Keyboard Collections.

Traditional. *Carrickfergus*. Arr. Stephens Roberts. 3:45. Based on a traditional Irish melody, it is full of folk singer qualities and big sweeping lyrical lines. A brass band accompaniment is also available. Recorded by Steven Mead.

Traditional. *The Dove*. Arr. Denzil Stephens. Sarnia Music (UK) (www.sarnia-music.com). $9.20. Welsh ballad arranged for tenor horn and it is absolutely gorgeous!

Traditional. *Endearing Young Charms*. Arr. Denzil Stephens. Sarnia Music (UK) (www.sarnia-music.com). $9.20. A melodic solo with countermelody in the second verse.

Traditional. *Folk Song Melodies*. Arr. Fred Weber. Belwin, Inc. 1969. $5. 1:00. I. B♭–b♭′. A simple folk song collection in B♭ major: "Sweet Betsy from Pike" and "On Top of Old Smoky." See Euphonium and Keyboard Collections. •

Traditional. *French Song*. Arr. Fred Weber. Belwin, Inc. 1969. $5. 1:00. I. B♭–g. A simple folk song in E♭ major. See Euphonium and Keyboard Collections.

Traditional. *Londonderry Air*. Arr. Forrest Buchtel. Neil A. Kjos Music Company. 1978. $2. 1:30. II. A–d′. This arrangement of this classic folk song is in D♭ major, is in a slow common time, is rhythmically simple, has very few accidentals, is mostly in the middle to lower registers, and is in bass clef. This is a nice arrangement and would be most appropriate for a middle school player.

Traditional. *Londonderry Air*. Arr. Keith Mehlan. TUBA Press. 1994. $8. 2:00. III. c♯–a′. This classic folk song can be found in thousands of arrangements. This version was written for Roger Behrend, principal euphonium in the United States Navy Band. This is a great version as it adheres beautifully to all of the nuances of the original tune. It is in the key of F major and is in bass clef. This solo is accessible to many levels of player but is a strong enough arrangement to be perfect for any type of recital. I highly recommend it!

Traditional. *Military Melodies*. Arr. Fred Weber. Belwin, Inc. 1969. $5. 1:00. I. B♭–c′. A simple collection of two melodies: Marines and Army.

Traditional. *Simple Gifts*. Kendor Music, Inc. $7. 3:00. III. This most popular melody is given a little modern twist while maintaining most of the original material.

Traditional. *Three Famous Melodies*. Arr. Fred Weber. Belwin, Inc. 1969. $5. 1:10. I. B♭–a. A simple collection of three songs in E♭ Major: "Yankee Doodle," "Old MacDonald," and "The Flying Trapeze." See Euphonium and Keyboard Collections.

Traditional. *When the Saints Go Marching In.* Arr. Fred Weber. Belwin, Inc. 1969. $5. 1:00. I. e♭–c′. A simple little arrangement in E♭ major with no accidentals. See Euphonium and Keyboard Collections.

Trombey, Jack. *Nostalgia.* MOLENAAR N.V. Wormerveer, Holland. 1978. 3:15. IV. G–c″. This fine solo begins with a slow section in common time with many soaring lyrical lines. It moves to a very fast section in 5/4 with mainly eighth note runs. It is very lively and features a very catchy melody. It soon returns to the opening slow feel before ending with a very impressive cadenza with optional technical lines. The solo is mostly in the middle register, comes in bass or treble clef parts, is rhythmically straightforward, and has mostly scale-wise eighth and sixteenth note runs. This would be a great solo for a good high school student or young college player.

Tschaikovsky, Peter I. *Canzonetta from Concerto for Violin.* Trans./arr. Ronald Dishinger. Medici Music Press. 2002. $7. 6:00. IV. C♯–b. This work is the second movement and is in a slow 3/4 throughout. It is in the middle register and especially the lower register. It is a very lyrical, passionate, and beautiful solo. It has many wide leaps, chromatics, and a few rhythmic and technical challenges. This would be an excellent solo for a recital as there are many fantastic musical moments and many places open for musical interpretation. It is appropriate for college students and the solo part is in bass clef.

Tschaikowsky, Peter Ilyich. *Concerto in B♭ Minor.* Arr. Herman A. Hummel. Rubank, Hal Leonard Corporation. $6.95. 1:00. II. C–e♭′. This solo is in F major, a moderate cut time, is mostly quarter notes, is rhythmically straightforward, has a few accidentals, is in the middle register, and is in bass clef. This features one of the most prominent melodies from the concerto. This solo would be a good second solo for a middle school player.

Tschaikowsky, Peter Ilyich. *Sleeping Beauty Waltz.* Arr. Fred Weber. Belwin Mills Inc. 1969. $5. 1:00. I. B♭–c′. A very nice, simple arrangement of one of Tschaikowsky's most beautiful melodies. It is in E♭ major and has simple rhythms and a few accidentals. See Euphonium and Keyboard Collections.

Uber, David. *Autumn Afternoon.* Kendor Music Co. $5. 2:30. III.

Uber, David. *Autumn Sketches, Op. 56.* Ensemble Publications. 1965. $12. This is a beautiful work that is a fantastic recital selection, as it would be a fantastic change of pace and style. Recorded by Nobuhiro Noguchi.

Uber, David. *Ballad of the Green Mountains.* Lyceum Press. $6. $2.35. IV.

Uber, David. *Ballad of Enob Mort.* Southern Music Company. $7.95. V.

Uber, David. *The Brass Matador.* Music Express. $8. 8:00. IV. This is a fantastic solo as it is very lively and features styles not often found in the euphonium repertoire. This solo would be a great change of pace on any recital!

Uber, David. *Capriccio,* TAP Music Sales. $8. 6:20. IV.

Uber, David. *Concert Piece for Solo Trombone or Euphonium and Piano, Op. 207.* TUBA Press. 1996. $8. 5:00. IV. A–a′. This solo has two sections: it begins with a slow 2/4 section that is very calm and expressive and moves to the second section that is in a moderate 2/4 and is very light and jolly in nature. The solo is mostly in the middle to upper register, features many mostly scale-wise sixteenth note runs, has some rhythmic challenges, and is in bass clef. This is a very fun solo and would be an excellent recital piece.

Uber, David. *Concerto for Euphonium.* Tuba-Euphonium Press. 1999. $12. 11:00. V. BB♭–b♭′. This concerto was written for Roger Behrend, principal euphonium of the United States Navy Band. It has three movements: Allegro; Poco lento espressivo; Allegro con brio. The first movement is overall lively and joyful. This movement overall has many sixteenth note runs and is mostly in the middle to high register. It has a fair amount of wide intervals and chromatics and is rhythmically straightforward. It has a beautiful lyrical middle section. The second movement is very slow and expressive. It has many passionate passages and allows for a wide level of artistic freedom. The last movement is in a moderately fast 6/8 and is very dance-like. It features several small mood and style changes that help to give this movement a wide variety of emotional characters. This solo is well marked with very specific style, articulation, dynamic, and phrasing markings. It has some range, technical, and rhythmic challenges, but they are well worth the work as it is loads of fun to play.

Uber, David. *Concerto in One Movement.* Encore Music Publishers/TAP Music Sales. $16. 8:00. V.

Uber, David. *Danza Espagnola.* Virgo Music Publishers. $6.95. 4:20. IV. This is a fantastic solo as it is very lively and features styles not often found in the euphonium repertoire. This solo would be a great change of pace on any recital!

Uber, David. *Deep River.* Kendor Music, Inc. 1996. $6. 3:35. III. c–g′. This solo is based on a famous spiritual. It is slow and expressive, is in common time, is in F major, is mostly eighth notes with a few sixteenth note runs, has very few accidentals, is mostly in the middle register, is rhythmically straightforward, and comes in both bass and treble clef. This beautiful little solo by one of the premiere euphonium composers would be excellent for a good middle school student or high school player.

Uber, David. *A Delaware Rhapsody.* Kendor Music Co. $6.50. 5:45. III.

Uber, David. *Ecnamor.* Southern Music. $6.50. 5:10. IV.

Uber, David. *Elegy and Blues.* Touch of Brass Music Corp. $9.95. 7:00. V. This is a fantastic solo as it features styles not often found in the euphonium repertoire. This solo would be a great change of pace on any recital!

Uber, David. *Evensong.* Kendor Music Co. $8. 5:20. IV.

Uber, David. *Four Sketches.* Edition Musicus. $6.75. 7:00. IV.

Uber, David. *Golden Leaves.* Kendor Music Co. $6.50. 5:00. III–IV.

Uber, David. *Introduction and Allegro.* TUBA Press. 1996. $8. 5:45. IV. F–c″. The Introduction is in a maestoso, slow common time. It has many sixteenth note passages, most of which are scale-wise, but some have very wide intervals. The Allegro is in cut time, has many eighth note runs, and is in the key of E♭ major. Both sections are in the middle to upper register and both are mostly rhythmically straightforward. The work ends with a triplet section that slowly accelerates for a rousing closing. This is a very fun work to play and would be an excellent recital piece.

Uber, David. *A Jazz Rhapsody, Op. 378.* Tuba-Euphonium Press. 2002. $10. 4:00. III–IV. D–f′. This work is in one movement and is accessible to a good high school player or young college student both in terms of range and technique. This would be a great solo to begin working on numerous jazz techniques and elements. It is in bass clef and also comes with a tuba version on the back. It is in a moderate common time, is in F major, is rhythmically straightforward, has some accidentals, and is mostly in the middle register (some of the lower notes are optional). There are very few solos like this in our literature, so this one is definitely a must if you are looking for a jazz selection for a recital.

Uber, David. *Legend of Lake St. Catherine.* Kendor Music Co. $6.50. 3:40. IV.

Uber, David. *Legend of the Sleeping Bear.* Kendor Music Co. $8.50. 6:10. IV.

Uber, David. *Litany.* TAP Music Sales. $8. 8:00. V.

Uber, David. *Manhattan Blues and Ragtime.* Virgo Music Publishers. $7.95. 5:00. IV. This is a fantastic solo as it is very lively and features styles not often found in the euphonium repertoire. This solo would be a great change of pace on any recital!

Uber, David. *Mississippi Legend.* Encore Music Publishers. $9.50. 2:52. IV.

Uber, David. *Montage.* Edition Musicus. $9.50. 4:30. III–IV. This solo has become a popular selection in the euphonium repertoire. It is a very expressive solo that is fun to play and entertaining for the audience.

Uber, David. *The Neophyte.* Manduca Music Publications. $7. 4:00. III.

Uber, David. *Panorama.* Rebu Music Publications/ Encore Music Publishers. $9.50. 8:45. IV.

Uber, David. *Prelude and Scherzo.* Kendor Music Co. $6. 3:40. II–III.

Uber, David. *Rhapsody in F Minor.* Southern Music. $5.50. 6:00. V.

Uber, David. *Rhapsody in C Minor.* Kendor Music, Inc. 1998. $7. 4:00. IV. G–g′. This highly expressive and stylistic solo is yet another great addition to the euphonium repertoire by David Uber. The first page is slow and lyrical and has many soaring lines, jazzy phrases, and schmaltzy sounds. The second page is marked "scherzando" and is a moderate tempo and very lively and cheerful. The work ends with many of the moods from the beginning. It is mostly in the middle register and has many sixteenth note runs that are idiomatic for the euphonium. The solo comes in both bass and treble clef. This is a very fun work to play!

Uber, David. *Romance.* Kendor Music Inc. $7. III. This is a beautiful solo from one of the most prolific euphonium composers. This would be a great lyrical selection for a good middle school player or high school student.

Uber, David. *A Simple Song.* Manduca Music Publications. $6. 5:25. IV.

Uber, David. *Skydream for Euphonium and Piano.* TUBA Press. 1993. $8. 4:30. IV. G–a′. This solo is in a slow common time and is mostly in the middle to higher register. It is in bass clef and it features many sixteenth notes that have some tricky intervals. It is well marked with very specific dynamics, articulations, and phrasings. It includes very helpful program notes. This is a beautiful, lyrical, and dreamy solo that would make for a great recital selection.

Uber, Daivd. *Snowlight.* Rebu Music Publications. $8. 4:00. IV.

Uber, David. *Sonata Da Camera,* Manduca Music. $10. Written for Mary Ann Craig. This work is in sonata format.

Uber, David. *Sonata for Euphonium and Piano.* Edition Musicus. 1978. This solo has been required in several euphonium solo competitions and has become a standard in the euphonium repertoire. It is a must study for any serious euphonium player or teacher. It features a very light and playful first movement that is loads of fun to play. The second movement is very songful and beautifully demonstrates the lyrical abilities of the euphonium. The third movement is the most technically challenging, but it is worth it. It has many very impressive technical passages that aren't as hard as they sound. It is a very energetic and powerful movement with many great intense passages. This work comes highly recommended.

Uber, Daivd. *Sonatina.* Southern Music. $8. 8:00. IV.

Uber, David. *Sonatine No. 2.* Tuba-Euphonium Press. 1999. $10. 7:00. IV–V. F–b♭′. This is a great work as it is very fun to play. The work features a wide range of styles and musical emotions. It has several sections: a spirited allegro, a soaring and expressive andante, a powerful allargando, and a waltz. It has many sixteenth note runs, is mostly in the middle to upper register, is in bass clef, and is well marked in terms of very specific dynamic, tempo, articulation, and style markings. A solo tuba version also comes with the solo euphonium part. This would be a very fine recital selection.

Uber, David. *Soloette for Solo Euphonium and Piano.* TUBA Press. 1996. $8. 5:00. IV–V. G–c″. This work was written for Douglas Nelson and like so many of David Uber's works, it has a very energetic opening. The work is in a moderate 3/4 time, but later moves to a moderate and sweeping 6/8, is mostly sixteenth note runs, is mostly in the middle register, and is in bass clef. It has a few rhythmic challenges and ascends into the high register a few times. This is a fun solo to play and would be an excellent opening work for a recital.

Uber, David. *Summer Nocturne.* Southern Music. $6. 8:30. IV. This is a beautiful solo and would make for an excellent recital selection.

Uber, David. *Theatre Piece for Euphonium and Piano.* Encore Music Publishers. 1993. 3:00. V. d–e″. This is a fantastically fun work that showcases the euphonium well. It is full of sixteenth note runs that are often not scale-wise. The work is in B♭ major and is mostly in a moderate allegro, 2/4, and is in bass clef. It has a small middle section that is slower and in 6/8. This is a very rhapsodic work that has many challenging passages and very high sections, but the challenge is worth it. The solo part is very easy to read and is well marked with very specific markings. If you are looking for a good challenge this is the solo for you as this solo is loads of fun. I highly recommend it.

Uber, David. *The Veiled Prophet.* North Grove Music. $6.95. 4:00. III–IV.

Vasseilliere. *Air Varie for Euphonium.* 7:00. V–VI. E–d″. A very challenging theme and variations with a gorgeous theme, a beautiful andante section, and a fantastic polonaise for a finale! Solo part comes in treble clef.

Vaughn Williams, Ralph. *Six Studies in English Folk-Song, Arranged for Euphonium and Piano.* Arr. Paul Droste. ECS Publishing. 1986. $11. IV. BB♭–c″. This is one of the classic works in the euphonium repertoire and is a must study. This work was written by one of the finest twentieth-century composers and was arranged by one of the finest euphonium players. It has six movements: Adagio; Andante sostenuto; Larghetto; Lento; Andante tranquillo; Allegro vivace. Overall the work is rhythmically straightforward, is mostly in the middle range with many optional high and low notes, is in "standard" keys, has very few

accidentals, is mostly scale-wise eighth notes, and is in bass clef. The work spans a wide range of musical styles and is a fantastic lyrical study. This work is more than playable by high school students but is most appropriate for college students due to the level of musicianship needed.

Vaughn Williams, Ralph. *Winter's Willow, A Country Song.* Trans./arr. Ronald Dishinger. Medici Music Press. 1990. $5. 2:00. II–III. c–e′. This beautiful lyrical solo is in a moderate common time, is in F major, is mostly quarter notes, has no accidentals, is mostly in the lower register, and is in bass clef. This would be a great solo for a middle school student or young high school player.

Vincent, Maj. Herman. *Galaxy.* Belwin Mills, CCP/Belwin, Inc. 1971. $4.95. III–IV. B♭–f′. This solo would be a great first theme and variations for a high school student. It is in the key of B♭ major and is marked "moderato." The main theme is marked "marziale" and has a very regal feel. The first variation is primarily sixteenth note runs, some scale-wise and some with wide intervals, but with very few accidentals. The second variation is a slurred sixteenth note triplet variation and is very fluid with a decent amount of accidentals. The third variation is a tongued sixteenth note variation with some slurred sixteenth note triplet runs with chromatics and a small cadenza in the middle. The work ends with the triplet variation in a grand fashion. This is mostly in the middle to lower register. See Euphonium and Keyboard Collections.

Vivaldi, Antonio. *Concerto in A Minor Opus 3. No. 6.* Ed. Ronald Dishinger. Medici Music Press. 1997. $10. 8:30. IV. G–a′. This fantastic concerto has three movements: Allegro; Largo; Allegro. The first movement is in common time and is a very moderate tempo. It features many eighth note runs and loads of sixteenth note runs, most of which are arppegiated and with wide intervals. Rhythmically it is straightforward and has a few chromatics. There are many technical challenges in the runs and endurance is a major issue as there virtually no rests for two solid pages of lots of notes. However, this movement is very fun to play and is a most worthy challenge. The second movement is very slow, ornamented, and lyrical. With the accompaniment it is a powerful musical statement. It has many 32nd note runs that are mostly scale-wise. The last movement is highly entertaining and loads of fun to play. It has many of the same technical challenges as the first movement, especially in terms of sixteenth note runs with wide intervals. It has numerous technical challenges, but it is a most worthy challenge. Overall the work is fairly conservative in terms of range, except for the last movement where it is in the high range more often. This would be a wonderful recital piece! I highly recommend it!

Vollrath, Carl. *Sonata for Baritone Horn and Piano.* Tap Music Sales. 5008. 800–554–7628. 1992. 12:00. V. A very interesting rhythmic study, as there is a good deal of meter shifting and rhythmic displacement. This work has many energetic and powerful moments. It is a nice change from most of the sonatas in our repertoire. Solo part comes in bass clef.

Wagner, Richard. *Ride of the Valkyries.* Trans. David Uber. Kendor Music, Inc. 2002. $7. 2:35. IV. G–a♯'. This is a fine version of one of Wagner's most famous melodies by one of the foremost euphonium composers. There is some consolidation of the original score, but the vast majority of the musical elements that make "The Ride" so popular are still in place. It is in a moderate 9/8, is in the keys of D and B major, is rhythmically straightforward, has some accidentals, is often in the high register, has a few tricky fingerings, and is in both bass and treble clef. The solo contains fantastic program notes.

Wagner, Richard. *Song to the Evening Star.* Arr. Leonard B. Smith. Belwin Mills, CPP/Belwin, Inc. 1968. $4.95. 1:20. II. G–c'. This work is in E♭ major, 6/8, is marked "andante mosso," and is mostly dotted quarters and quarters. It has many dynamic changes, beautiful phrases, a decent amount of chromatics, and remains in the middle to lower registers. It is very expressive and would be a great study of melody or a fine solo contest piece for a middle school student. Some very appropriate performance suggestions can be found below the solo. See Euphonium and Keyboard Collections.

Wagner, Richard. *Walther's Prize Song.* Arr. Forrest L. Buchtel. Neil A. Kjos Music Company. 1959. $2.50. 3:20. III. c–f'. This solo is in a moderate 3/4, is in A♭ major, has many chromatics, has a few rhythmic challenges, has piano cues, and is in bass clef. It is well marked with very specific phrasings, articulations, dynamics, and style markings. It is mostly eighth note patterns in the middle register. This is an absolutely gorgeous song and would be a fantastic solo and lyrical study for a good middle school player or high school student.

Waignein, Andre. *Introduction and Dance.* Scherzando Music Publishers, Heerenveen, Holland. 3:00. III–IV. d–a'. This is a great work for good high school players and young college students as it is in a great key, stays in the middle register, has few chromatics or difficult rhythms, and is fun to play. It has great drive and energy as the dance section has a good amount of mixed meter. Solo comes in bass and treble clefs.

Waldteufel-Linke. *Waltz Themes.* Arr. Fred Weber. Belwin Inc., 1969. I. 1:00. $5. A♭–a♭. A simple collection of two songs in F major: "Chimes of Spring" and "Tres Jolie." See Euphonium and Keyboard Collections.

Walker, B. H. *The Virtuoso,* B. H. Walker, Augusta, Georgia. 1972. 2:30. IV. f–b♭'. This small, one-page theme and variations in the key of B♭ is perfect for a good high school or young college student. It begins with a cadenza, then the theme, then a moderato sixteenth note variation, and ends with a triplet variation that should be triple tongued (very basic triple tonguing) but could be slowed down and still be effective. The solo part comes in bass clef.

Walters, Harold, *Tarantelle.* Ludwig Music Publishing Company. $5.95. 2:30. III. B–f'. This work is in two sections: andante and allegro. The andante is very expressive and features a repeating triplet motive. The allegro is in 6/8 and is highly energetic and powerful. This is a wonderful work for a good high school player as it has numerous musical issues such as small cadenzas, key changes, and compound meter. It is very fun to play and is a fantastic work for the audience as well. I highly recommend this solo.

Weber, Fred. *Campus Queen.* Belwin Mills, Inc. 1969. $5. 1:30. I. c–c'. A simple solo that would be great for a beginner. It is in B♭ and E♭ major, 4/4, and has simple rhythms, a few accidentals, and two sections (larghetto and allegro). See Euphonium and Keyboard Collections.

Weber, Fred. *College March,* Belwin Mills, Inc. 1969. $5. 1:00. I. B♭–g. This is a simple and fun little march in E♭ major for a beginner with a few accidentals and simple rhythms. See Euphonium and Keyboard Collections.

Whatley, Larry. *Contrasts.* Tuba-Euphonium Press. 1993. $8. 3:00. IV. B♭–a♭'. This solo is in a slow common time, is in f minor and F major, has a large amount of chromatics, is mostly in the middle register, is rhythmically straightforward, is mostly quarter notes with a few eighths and sixteenths, and is in bass clef. This solo begins and ends with passionate andante sections. The middle is a very pronounced and powerful allegro section. This solo would be great for a college student. This is a very fun and neat solo to play and would make for a great change of pace on any recital.

White, David. *Dance and Aria.* Shawnee Press. $10. 8:00. IV–V. d–g'. This is a very energetic, powerful, and driving work with numerous mixed meter sections. The thematic material in measure ten serves as the basis for the entire composition. It remains in the middle to lower register and is clearly marked with numerous articulation and dynamic changes. The solo comes in bass clef. This is a very fun and expressive piece to play!

White, Donald. *Lyric Suite for Euphonium and Piano.* G. Schirmer, Inc. 1972. $11.95. 8:00. IV. E–b'. This work is one of the must studies of the euphonium repertoire. Four movements: Adagio Cantabile; Allegro Giusto; Andante Sostenuto; Allegro Energico. The first movement opens with a very hollow and nearly ethereal sound, slowly building to a very powerful climax in the middle, going to high b before ending as it began. The second movement features a very unique dance melody that slowly builds and develops. This movement is a ton of fun to play and features many sixteenth note runs in mostly the middle register. It has many powerful moments. The third movement is one of the my favorite musical moments in all of the euphonium repertoire. It begins very mysterious and slowly builds to a very powerful climax before ending very mysteriously. The last movement is very lively and dance-like. It has many fun and interesting syncopated sections and harmonic clashes. It has many sixteenth note passages with some of them having very tricky fingering combinations. It mainly stays in the middle register. There is a band version of this work.

Wiedrich, William W. *Reverie for Roger Behrend.* Southern Music Company. 1978. $5. 3:30. III–IV. E–g'. Written for United States Navy Band euphoniumist Roger Behrend, this is a beautiful, slow lyrical work that is accessible to many levels of player as it remains in the middle to lower register, has very few accidentals, and has very few technical challenges. I highly recommend this work as a melodic study for young musicians or for a relaxing, reflective moment for a recital. Solo part comes in bass clef.

Wiggins, Chris. *Soliloquy IX.* Studio Music. $8.50. IV–V. This is a fantastic work as there are very few solos in the euphonium repertoire like it. This work has recently been asked on euphonium solo competitions.

Wilby, Philip. *Concert Gallop.* Rosehill Music Publishing Co., Ltd. 1994. 3:00. V. FF–c''. This technical showpiece is the perfect encore to any recital or solo performance! This highly energetic and challenging work was written for Robert Childs. Except for a small cadenza toward the end, it gallops from beginning to end. It is a fun, exciting, and entertaining showpiece for the euphonium. The solo comes in treble clef. A band version is also available. Recorded by Steven Mead, *The World of the Euphonium,* volume 2.

Wilby, Philip. *Concerto for Euphonium.* Rosehill Music Publishing Co., Ltd. 1996. $28. 18:30. VI. This is one of the most beautiful yet difficult concertos in the repertoire. It is a highly emotionally charged work that has numerous energetic and powerful moments. The solo part comes in both bass and treble clefs. There is also a brass band version. This solo is highly recommended. Recorded by David Childs, Metamorphosis.

Wilby, Philip. *Flight.* Rosehill Music Publishing Co., Ltd. 1996. $17.50. 9:00. VI. EE–c''. This solo explores the many aspects of flying through the varied virtuosic demands of the music. It is a fantastic work that beautifully showcases the full capabilities of the euphonium. The solo comes

in treble clef. A brass band version is also available. Recorded by Steven Mead, *The World of the Euphonium,* volume 3.

Wilder, Alec. *Sonata for Euphonium.* Margun Music. 1968. 14:00. V. E–b'. This five-movement work is one of the standards in the euphonium repertoire and is a must study and must own. The first movement features soaring lines and many contrapuntal sections. The second movement has a very rich singing quality throughout. The third movement is very jazzy and is one of the best examples of this style in euphonium literature. The fourth movement is once again very rich and singing throughout. The last movement has big soaring lines and many contrapuntal ideas. Basically it runs the gamut from straight technical, to passionately lyrical, to jazzy, to a waltz, back to jazz, then lyrical and ending in a dance feel created from mixed meter and the displacement of phrases. It is in bass clef with some tenor clef.

Wilhelm, Rolf. *Concertino for Euphonium and Concert Band.* Trio Blasermusik Edition, Muhldorf. 1998. $20. 10:30. V. BB–d''. This fantastic solo has quickly become a standard in the euphonium repertoire. It has three movements, is available in bass and treble clefs, is extremely well marked with very specific style markings, articulations, phrasing, tempos, and dynamics, and has excellent program notes. The first movement opens with a lively and very catchy theme before quickly moving to a highly expressive tranquillo section. The movement features a great cadenza before coming to a rousing end. The second movement is slow and highly expressive, featuring many soaring lines that beautifully showcase the lyrical qualities of the euphonium. The final movement is in a lively and animated 6/8 with many soaring technical runs. It features many style changes and features a very showy cadenza. This solo has many technical challenges and ascends into the high range often, but it is more than worth the challenge. It is a very musical, expressive, lively, and powerful solo that requires a great dealt of dynamic power. I highly recommend this solo!

Wilhelm, Rolf. *Reflections for Euphonium and Piano.* Trio Musik Edition, D-84453 Muhldorf. 1999. 3:00. IV–V. Ab–ab'. This solo is very quiet and peaceful and has many beautiful moments. It has very few technical challenges, is mostly in the middle register, and is in Ab major. It is well marked with very specific style, dynamic, and articulation considerations. It comes in both bass and treble clefs and has excellent program notes. This solo would work for a good high school player and would be an excellent recital selection for a college student. I highly recommend this small yet gorgeous lyrical solo.

Williams, Adrian. *Sonate pour bassoon & piano.* Editions Max Eschig, Paris. 1997. 15:00. VI. BBb–eb''. This four-movement work was transcribed for Steven Mead and it is one of the most difficult works in the repertoire. It has numerous passages with high tessitura, many technical challenges, rhythmic issues, very few breaks, and so forth. However, this is an extremely exciting and powerful work that would be perfect for fine players looking for a new and rewarding challenge. Comes in bass clef.

Williams, Ralph Vaughan. *Six Studies in English Folk-Song*. Arr. Paul Droste. Galaxy Music Corporation. 1986. IV. B♭–b♭'. This work is one of the most studied standard works in the euphonium repertoire. It is well arranged, covers a diverse scope of styles, is accessible to many ability levels, and sounds great on euphonium. This is a must in any euphonium player's library. It comes in both bass and treble clefs and has optional octaves.

Williams, Warwick. *Air Varie*. VI. BB–c''. This theme and variations is a big technical challenge. It features an awesome bolero section and a very unique theme that has many extremely wide intervals and is marked "moderato e comodo"!

Wilson, Don. *Three Miniatures for Baritone and Piano*. Ed. Larry Campbell. Hal Leonard Publishing Corporation. 1977. $12.95. 3:30. III–IV. BB♭–b'. This work is part of a collection of solos–Master Solos, Intermediate Level. It has three movements: Moderately Fast; Slow; Fast. The first movement is very lively and syncopated and features numerous time signature changes including mixed meter and compound meters. It primarily remains in the middle register. The second movement is very passionate and lovely to play. It is somewhat of a range challenge as it ascends to the high register often. The last movement is a powerful musical statement, as it is highly energetic featuring many meter changes, mixed meter, and many powerful dynamics. This would be a great solo for a very good high school player or for a young college player. Recorded by Larry Campbell.

Woestijne, David Van De. *Muziek voor tuba-saxhorn en piano*. CeBeDeM, Brussels. 1977. 6:30. IV–V. AA–g♭'. This work is in bass clef, features some mixed meter, and is highly chromatic.

Woodforde-Finden, Amy. *Kashmiri Song*. Winwood Music. $8.75. III–IV. This is a beautiful song that is well set for the euphonium. The solo part is available in bass and treble clef.

Woodfield, Ray. *Caprice, Euphonium Solo*. Hallamshire Music, 53 Meadowhead, Sheffield, UB 0742–746825. IV–V. B♭–b♭'. This work is in treble clef and is a fantastically beautiful little technical work that features many slurred runs that are idiomatic for the euphonium, triple tonguing, and optional cadenzas.

Wurmser, Lucien. *Solo De Concours*. Editions Andrieu Freres, 72 Rue Rodier, Paris. 4:00. III–IV. A–g'. The work is in bass clef and is a good study on dealing with numerous style changes in a short period, as well as specific styles such as recitative.

Wurmser, Lucien. *Tendres Melodies, Petites Pieces De Concours*. Editions Andrieu Freres, 72 Rue Rodier, Paris. 3:00. II–IV. F–f'. The work is in bass clef and is a good study for young musicians concerning phrasing and musicality.

York, Barbara. *Arioso Gloria for Euphonium and Piano*. Tuba-Euphonium Press. 2003. $10. 4:22. III–IV. F–g'. This gorgeous solo is in a moderate 6/8 (eighth note receiving the beat), is in E♭ major, is in bass clef, and is mostly in the middle register. It has many passionate and tense passages. This solo was written for Michael Fischer. I highly recommend this solo for a good high school student and as a great change of pace on any college recital.

Yuste, Miguel. *Solo De Concurso Para Fagot Adaptado Para Saxofon Tenor O Bombardino*. Union Musical Espanola, Madrid. 1960. F–b♭'. Contains bass clef but is mainly in treble clef. An extremely technical but beautiful theme and variations–style work with numerous stylistic, dynamic, articulation, and tempo markings. Many lower passages are featured in this work. This Spanish solo has loads of Latin flavor. This would be an excellent recital selection, especially if you are looking for a great change of style, sound, and mood. Contact Adam Frey for details on ordering this work.

Zipoli, Domenico. *Larghetto*. Trans./arr. Ronald Dishinger. Medici Music Press. 1995. $4.50. 3:30. III. B♭–a♭'. This lovely work in E♭ major features a very peaceful and relaxing main melody that has a floating quality. The work is in a slow common time and has very few chromatics. The challenge comes in some of the rhythms (several sections with sextuplets) and a couple of passages in the high register. This is a beautiful work that would be a fantastic change of pace on a recital or a great study of melody and style for a very good high school student or college player.

Zobel, Edgar H. *Afterglow (Morceau Grazioso)*. Neil A. Kjos Music Company. $2. 3:30. I–II. f–g'. This solo is in a moderate common time, is in E♭ major, is rhythmically simple, has some optional high range notes, ascends into the high range several times without options, has very few accidentals, is mostly quarter notes, and is in bass clef. This is a very musical little solo with many varying styles. This would be a fun solo to play and study for a middle school student.

Works Listed by Title

A

Absolute Reality, Meechan, Pete
Adagio and Allegro from Sonata in E, Handel, George Frederic
Adagio and Rondo, Mozart, Wolfgang Amadeus
Adagio in G Minor, Albinoni, Tomaso

Afterglow, Zobel, Edgar H.

Agnus Dei II from Pope Marcellus Mass, Palestrina, Giovanni Pierluigi

Air and Rondo, Frackenpohl, Arthur

Air De Trompette in D Major, Telemann, G. P.

Air from "Comus," Arne, Thomas A.

Air on a G String from Third Orchestral Suite, Bach, Johann Sebastian

Air Varie for Euphonium, Vasseilliere

Air Varie, Williams, Warwick

Alborada for Euphonium and Piano, Goodwin, Gordon

All'Antica, Goeyens, A.

All through the Night, Traditional

Alla Siciliana, Aria and Variations for Euphonium and Symphonic Banda, Albian, Franco

Allegretto Comodo pour Saxhorn-Basse et Piano, Querat, Marcel

Allegretto, Mozart, Wolfgang Amadeus

Allegro from Concerto Grosso Opus 3, No. 2, Geminiani, Francesco

Allegro from Concerto Grosso Opus 3, No. 4, Handel, George Frederic

Allegro from Trio No. 18, Druschetzky, George

Allegro from Trio No. 11, Druschetzky, George

Allegro from Trio No. 4, Druschetzky, George

Allegro from Trio No. 9, Druschetzky, George

Allegro from Trio No. 19, Druschetzky, George

Allegro from Trio No. 17, Druschetzky, George

Allegro from Trio No. 3, Druschetzky, George

Allegro Spiritoso, Senaille, John Baptiste

Amazing Grace, Haak, Paul

And He Was Crucified for Us, Palestrina, Giovanni Pierluigi

And It's Spring, Anthony, Yvonne

Andante and Alleluja for Euphonium and Piano, Mozart, Wolfgang Amadeus

Andante and Finale, Gershwin, George

Andante and March, Jacome, Saint

Andante and Rondo from Concerto for Double Bass, Capuzzi, Antonio

Andante and Rondo, Capuzzi, Antonio, arr. Wilby, Philip

Andante and Scherzo, Heath, Reginald

Andante Brilliante, Szkutko, John

Andante et Allegro, Barat, J. Edouard

Andante et Allegro, Barraine, Elsa

Andante from Andante for Horn and Piano or Organ, Neukomn, Sigismond

Andantino, Lemare

Appalachian Waltz, Niehaus

Apres un Reve, Faure, Gabriel

Apres un Reve (After a Dream), Faure, Gabriel

Argonaut Waltz, Buchtel, Forrest L.

Arabella, Chester, Barrie

Aria and Rondo, Fiocco

Aria Cuius animam, aus dem Stabat Mater, Rossini, Gioacchino

Aria No. 1 from Cantata No. 1, Bach, Johann Sebastian

Arioso and Allegro, Fiocco, Joseph Hector

Arioso from Cantata No. 156, Bach, Johann Sebastian

Arioso Gloria for Euphonium and Piano, York, Barbara

Arioso, from Cantata 156, Bach, Johann Sebastian

Arpeggione Sonata, Schubert, Franz

As Wonderful Things Drift By, Censhu, Jiro

At the Ball, Buchtel, Forrest L.

Atlantic Zephyrs (Novelette), Simons, Gardell

Au Temps De La Cour pour basse sib ou tuba ut et piano, Brouquireres, Jean

Aubade, Sparke, Philip

Auld Lang Syne, Mantia, Simone

Aura Lee, Poulton

Autumn Afternoon, Uber, David

Autumn Air, Cummings, Barton

Autumn Sketches, Op. 56, Uber, David

Autumn Twilight, Edelson, Edward

Autumn with You, Armitage, Dennis

Ave Maria, Bach-Gounod

Ave Maria, Gounod, Charles-Francois

Ave Maria, Schubert, Franz

B

Badinerie, from Third Orchestral Suite, Bach, Johann Sebastian

Bagatelles, Ross, Walter

Bagatelles, Snell, Howard

Ballad in F, Levi, William

Ballad of Enob Mort, Uber, David

Ballad of the Green Mountains, Uber, David

Ballade for Baritone or Tuba and Piano, Krzywicki, Jan

Barcarolle, from the Tales of Hoffmann, Offenbach, Jacques

Baritone Aria, Newton, Rodney

Baroque Suite No. 2, Locatelli, Pietro

Bassutecy, Ameller, Andre

Batifol, Ameller, Andre

Beau Brummel, Buchtel, Forrest L.

Beautiful Colorado, De Luca, Joseph

Believe Me if All Those Endearing Young Charms, Mantia, Simone

Belle province: Hauterive, Ameller, Andre

Beloved from Afar, Op. 98, No. 6, Beethoven, Ludwig van

Berceuse from Jocelyn, Godard, Benjamin

Better World, Bearcroft, Norman

Beyond a Distant Galaxy, Fantasia for Euphonium and Piano, Censhu, Jiro

Blue Bells of Scotland, Pryor, Arthur

Blue Bells of Scotland, Pryor, Arthur, arr. Sparke, Philip

Bolero, Buchtel, Forrest L.

Bonaventura, Niehaus

Bourree and Gigue from The Third Orchestral Suite, Bach, Johann Sebastian

Bourree from Third Cello Suite, Bach, Johann Sebastian

Bourree, Handel, George Frederic
Brandenburg Concerto No. 2, Mvt. III, Bach,
 Johann Sebastian
Branle "Twelfth Night," Anonymous
Brass Matador, The, Uber, David
Break, Meechan, Pete
Bride of the Waves, The, Clarke, Herbert L.
Brilliant Polka, DeLamater, E.
Brillante, Fantasy on Rule Britania, Graham, Peter
By Gaslight, Kassatti, Tadeusz

C

Café 1930, Piazolla, Astor
Caissons Go Rolling Along, Buchtel, Forrest L.
Campus Queen, Weber, Fred
Canon, Pachelbel, Johann
Canon in D, Pachelbel, Johann
Cantabile, Paganini, Niccolo
Cantilena, Handel, George Frederic
Cantique De Noel, Adam, Adolphe
Canzona in D, Bach, Johann Sebastian
Canzona Per Sonare on C de. Rore, Bassano,
 Giovanni
Canzonetta from Concerto for Violin, Tschaikovsky,
 Peter I.
Caoine (Lament), Stanford, Charles
Caprice Charmante, Cimera, Jaroslav
*Caprice from Pasquinade (A Public Posting of
 Lampoons),* Gottschalk, Louis Moreau
Caprice, Euphonium Solo, Woodfield, Ray
Capriccio, Balissat, Jean
Capriccio, Uber, David
Cardinal's Air, The, from the Opera "La Juive,"
 Halevy, Jacques
Carol of the Rose, Praetorius, Michael
Carnival of Venice, Clarke, Herbert L.
Carnival of Venice, Davis, Henry W.
Carnival of Venice, Levy, Jules
Carnival, Stephens, Denzil S.
Carrickfergus, Roberts, Stephen
Cattari, Cattari, Cardillo
Cello Concerto No. 1, Opus 107, Shostakovich,
 Dmitri
Chanson de Matin for Euphonium and Piano,
 Elgar, Edward
Chanson de nuit for Euphonium and Piano, Elgar,
 Edward
*Chanson De Nuit, "Song of the Night," Opus 15,
 No. 1,* Elgar, Edward
Chartreuse, Cofield, Frank
Chiens de paille, Barraine, Elsa
Christmas Carol Suite, Hilfiger, John Jay
Christmas Concerto, Boeddecker, P. F.
Cielito Lindo, Buchtel, Forrest L.
Clouds, Ihlenfeld, Dave
College March, Weber, Fred
Columbine, Buchtel, Forrest L.
Concentration, Smith, Leonard B.
Concert Gallop, Wilby, Philip

Concert Piece for Euphonium, Lane, William
*Concert Piece for Solo Trombone or Euphonium and
 Piano, Op. 207,* Uber, David
Concert Piece, De la Nux, P. V.
Concert Variations for Euphonium and Piano,
 Bach, Jan
Concert Waltz No. 1, Markert, Jack Russell
Concertino for Euphonium and Band, Fritze,
 Gregory
Concertino for Euphonium and Concert Band,
 Wilhelm, Rolf
Concertino for Euphonium and Piano,
 Daniels, M. L.
*Concertino No. 1 in Bb Major, Op. 7, First Move-
 ment,* Klengel, Julius
Concerto del Garda, Raum, Elizabeth
Concerto for Euphonium and Orchestra, Bach, Jan
Concerto for Euphonium, Curnow, James
Concerto for Euphonium, Downie, Kenneth
Concerto for Euphonium, Gorb, Adam
Concerto for Euphonium, Jager, Robert
Concerto for Euphonium, Nelhybel, Vaclav
Concerto for Euphonium, Schultz, Patrick
Concerto for Euphonium, Wilby, Philip
Concerto for Euphonium and Piano, Fila, Juraj
Concerto for Euphonium and Piano, Grady,
 Michael
Concerto for Euphonium and Piano, Uber, David
*Concerto for Euphonium, Symphonic Brass and
 Timpani,* Ross, Walter
Concerto for Oboe in G Minor, Handel, George
 Frederic
Concerto for Tuba (Concerto Euphonique), Hop-
 kinson, Michael E.
Concerto in A Minor, Opus 3, No. 6, Vivaldi,
 Antonio
Concerto in Bb K191, Rondo, Mozart, Wolfgang
 Amadeus
Concerto in Bb Minor, Tschaikowsky, Peter I.
Concerto in C Minor for Oboe and Orchestra, Mar-
 cello, Benedetto
Concerto in F Major, Porkorny
Concerto in G Major from Concerto for Viola, Tele-
 mann, Georg P.
Concerto in One Movement, Uber, David
Concerto per Flicorno basso, Opus 155, Ponchielli,
 Amilcare
Concerto, Albrechtsberger, Johann Georg
*Concertpiece: "Scared So" for Euphonium and
 Piano,* Sherman, Donald M.
Concertpiece for Euphonium and Piano, Dillon,
 Robert
Congratulations, DeLamater, E.
Contrasts, Whatley, Larry
*Cornemuse Tuba Ut Ou Trombone Basse Ou
 Saxhorn Basse Sib Ou Contreb. Cordes, Piano,*
 Dubois, Pierre Max
Cortège, Beaucamp, Albert
*Couleurs En Mouvements, pour Tuba en Ut ou Sax-
 horn Basse Si-flat et Piano,* Farben, Wogende,
 and James Moreau

Country Dance, Haydn, Franz Joseph
Cradle Song, Hauser
Credo, Arcadelt, Jacob
Czardas, Monti, Vittorio

D

Dance and Aria, White, David
*Dance of the Blessed Spirits from Orpheus and
  Euridice,* Gluck, Christoph Willibald von
*Dancing Song from Eight Russian Folk Songs, Op.
  58,* Liadov, Anatol
Danse villageoise, Beethoven, Ludwig van
Danza Espagnola, Uber, David
Dark Eyes, Timokhin, Slava
Daystar, Belden, George R.
Debonair, Smith, Leonard B.
Debutante, The, Clarke, Herbert L.
Deep River, Uber, David
Delaware Rhapsody, A, Uber, David
Dialogue for Euphonium and Piano, Jones, Roger
Dialogue in Abstract for Euphonium and Piano,
  Bachelder, D. F.
Divertimento for Euphonium and Piano, Debons,
  Eddy
*Divertimento for Euphonium or Trombone and
  Piano,* Frackenpohl, Arthur
Divertissements, Crawley, Clifford
Dizzy Fingers, Stephens, Denzil S.
Dondie Lieta, Puccini, Giacomo
Dove, The, Traditional
Drum Major March, Buchtel, Forrest L.
Dublin's Fair City, Fantasy for Euphonium, New-
  some, Roy
Dudelsack, Musette-Bagpipe, Opus 166, No. 3,
  Seybold, Arthur

E

Earle of Oxford's Marche, The, Byrd, William
Ecnamor, Uber, David
Eidolons, Lantham, William P.
Elegie in C Minor, Faure, Gabriel
Elegy and Blues, Uber, David
Elfentanz, Jenkinson, Ezra
Emerald, Cook, Vander
Endearing Young Charms, Traditional
Envoy, The, Endersen, R. M.
Estrellita, Kaler, arranger
Estrellita, Pounce, Manuel
Etude De Concours, Petit, Alexandre S.
Etude from 27 Etudes, Op. 10, No. 3, Chopin,
  Frederic
Euphemism, Carastathis, Aris
Euphonissimo for Euphonium and Klavier, Baratto,
  Paolo
Euphonium Concerto, Ball, Michael
Euphonium Concerto, Bourgeois, Derek
Euphonium Concerto, Ellerby, Martin
Euphonium Concerto, Golland, John
Euphonium Concerto No. 2, Golland, John
Euphonium Concerto, Hartley, Walter

Euphonium Concerto, Horovitz, Joseph
Euphonium Concerto, Sparke, Philip
Euphonium Fantasia, Bulla, Stephen
Euphonium Music, Bowen, Brian
Euphonium Sonata, Hirano, Mitsuru
Euphony, Redhead, Robert
Euphoria, Op. 75, Bourgeois, Derek
Evensong, Uber, David

F

Fandango, Buchtel, Forrest L.
Fanfare "Gloria" from "Susanna," Handel, George
  Frederick
Fanflairs, Niehaus, Lennie
Fantaisie and Variations on Carnival of Venice,
  Arban, Jean-Baptiste
*Fantaisie Concertante pour Trombone basse ou
  Tuba Ut ou Saxhorn basse et Piano,* Casterede,
  Jacques
Fantaisie Original, Picchi, Ermanno
*Fantaisie, pour Tuba, ou Trombone-Basse, ou Sax-
  horn en et Piano,* Petit, Pierre
*Fantasia Concertante for Euphonium and Sym-
  phonic Band,* Albian, Franco G.
Fantasia di Concerto—Sounds of the Riviera,
  Boccalari, Eduardo
Fantasia for Euphonium, Jacob, Gordon
Fantasia on Welsh Melody, "Jenny Jones,"
  Rimmer, W.
Fantasiestucke, Opus 73, Schumann, Robert
Fantasy, Hummel, Johan Nepomuk
Fantasy, Snell, Howard
Fantasy for Euphonium and Brass Band, Sparke,
  Philip
Fantasy for Euphonium and Piano, Boguslaw,
  Robert
Fantasy for Euphonium and Piano, Hoshina,
  Hiroshi
Fantasy for Euphonium and Piano, Roussanova-
  Lucas, Elena
Fantasy on Swiss Airs, Newsome, Roy
Fantasy Variations, Ito, Yasuhide
Fantasy Variations for Euphonium and Band, Ito,
  Yasuhide
Faustbuch, a Concerto in Three Movements, Raum,
  Elizabeth
Five Pieces in Folk Style, Op. 102, Schumann, Robert
Flight, Wilby, Philip
Flight of the Bumble Bee, Corwell, Neal
Flight of the Bumblebee, Rimsky-Korsakov, Nicolai
Flower Song, Bizet, Georges
Flower Song from "Carmen," Bizet, Georges
Folk Song Melodies, Traditional
Forest Echo, Endersen, R. M.
For He That Is Mighty, Bach, Johann Sebastian
Four Miniatures, Tailor, Norman
Four Serious Songs, Brahms, Johannes
Four Sketches, Uber, David
Fox Hunt, Endersen, R. M.
French Song, Traditional

Friends, Waltz Caprice, Smith, Clay
From the Shores of the Mighty Pacific, Clarke, Herbert L.
Fruhlingsglaube for Euphonium and Piano, Schubert, Franz
Fugue No. 10 from 12 Preludes and Fugues, Bach, Johann Sebastian

G

Gaelic Sonata, MacMilan, Duncan J.
Galaxy, Vincent, Maj. Herman
Gameplan, Stephens, Denzil S.
Gavotte and Hornpipe, Purcel, Henry
Gavotte from Contrasts, Opus 10, No. 3, Elgar, Edward
Gavotte from Harpsichord Suite No. 5, Purcel, Henry
Gavotte in G Minor, Bach, Johann Sebastian
Gentle Annie, Foster, Stephen Collins
Girl with the Flaxen Hair, The, Debussy, Claude
Girl with the Flaxen Hair, The, Debussy, Claude, arr. Snell, Howard
Gladiator, Buchtel, Forrest L.
Glen Eden Polka, Storm, Chas. W.
Gloria, Arcadelt, Jacob
Glorious Ventures, Gramercy Solo Album, Graham, Peter
Gobbly Gook, Buchtel, Forrest L.
Golden Leaves, Uber, David
Grandfather's Clock, Doughty, George
Grave pour Tuba ut ou Baryton ou base si-flat et Piano, Lancen, Serge
Grave, Bach, Wilhelm Friedmann
Great Scott, Niehaus
Gregarious, Siekmann, Frank H.
Grootvader's klok, Lureman, Herman
Gymnopedie I, Satie, Eric
Gypsy Airs (Zigeunerweisen) for Cornet or Euphonium Solo, Sarasate, Pablo
Gypsy Love Song, Herbert
Gypsy Rondo, Haydn, Franz Joseph
Gypsy Songs, Brahms, Johannes

H

Hail! Ancient Walls from Faust, Gounod, Charles Francois
Hamabeno Uto, Nasta, Tamezo
Hans de Schnokeloch, Bariller, Robert
Happy Birthday, Armitage, Dennis
Happy Bugler, Buchtel, Forrest L.
Harlequin, Buchtel, Forrest L.
Harmonious Blacksmith, The, Handel, George Frederick
Heart in Heart (Glorious Liberation), Bosanko, Ivor
Heart to Heart, Anthony, Yvonne
Herbmaiden's Dance, Alven, Hugo
Herr Jesu Christ, Dich Zu Uns End, Bach, Johann Christoph
Highgarth Invention, Kirk-Smith, Rebecca

Hippity Hop, Buchtel, Forrest L.
Hokus Pokus, Buchtel, Forrest L.
Holiday Medley, Endersen, R. M.
Holy City, The, Adams, Stephen
Holy Well, The, Graham, Peter
Honor and Arms from Samson, Handel, George Frederic
Horisont, for Euphonium and Piano, Fahlman, Fredrik
Humoreske fur Tuba (oder Bariton oder Posaune), Kuhmstedt, Paul
Humoresque, Bernaud, Alain
Humoresque, Blazhevich, Vladislav
Hyacinthe, Cook, Vander
Hymn for Trombone or Baritone, Burke, Robert, Jr.

I

I Will Arise and Go to Jesus, Traditional
Iceberg, The, King of the Northern Seas, Gordon, Stanley
Idylle, Op. 4 No. 1, Elgar, Edward
If Thou Be Near, Bach, Johann Sebastian
Im tiefsten Walde (In the Deepest Forest), Schmidt, Heinrich Kaspar
Intermezzo, arr. Buchtel, Forrest L.
Intermezzo from Cavalleria Rusticana, Mascagni, Pietro
Intermezzo pour Tuba en Ut ou Saxhorn basse et Piano, Bitsch, Marcel
Introduction and Allegro, Fernie, Allan
Introduction and Allegro for Euphonium or Trombone and Piano, Uber, David
Introduction and Dance, Barat, J. Edouard
Introduction and Dance, Waignein, Andre
Introduction et Serenade, Barat, Joseph E.
Introduction Et Rigaudon, Failenot, Maurice
Introspect for Euphonium and Piano, Martino, Ralph
Invicta, Hanmer, Ronald
Irish-Cante, Ameller, Andre
Irish Tune from County Derry, Grainger, Percy
Isabella, Cimera, Jaroslav

J

Jazz Rhapsody, A, Op. 378, Uber, David
Jesu, Joy of Man's Desiring, Bach, Johann Sebastian
Jesu, Joy of Man's Desiring, Bach, Johann Sebastian, ed. Block, R. P. (organ)
Jesu, Joy of Man's Desiring from Cantata No. 147, Bach, Johann Sebastian
Jiggle a Bit, Buchtel, Forrest L.
Joan of Arc, Cimera, Jaroslav
Jogging Along, Buchtel, Forrest L.
Jovial Mood, Buchtel, Forrest L.
Jubal's Lyre, Handel, George Frederic
Jumpin' Jack, Buchtel, Forrest L.
Jumpin' Jericho, Buchtel, Forrest L.
Jupiter, Buchtel, Forrest L.

Just a Closer Walk with Thee, Haak, Paul

K

Kashmiri Song, Woodforde-Finden, Amy
Keystone Kapers, Miserendino, Joe
King of the Deep, Moquin, Al
Kino Concertino, Kassatti, Tadeusz
Kiss of Light, The, Anthony, Yvonne
Kryptos: Étude, Ameller, Andre

L

Larghetto, Mozart, Wolfgang Amadeus
Larghetto, Zipoli, Domenico
Largo and Allegro, Handel, George Frederic
Largo from Xerxes, Handel, George Frederic
Las Tortillas, Tanner, Paul
Laudamus Te for Euphonium and Piano, Mozart, Wolfgang Amadeus
Lazy Lullaby, Little, Donald C.
Legend, Catelinet, Philip
Legend of Lake St. Catherine, Uber, David
Legend of the Sleeping Bear, Uber, David
Légende, Beugniot, Jean-Pierre
L'enterrement de Saint-Jean, Bariller, Robert
Lerchen-Rondo in E-Flat, Haydn, Franz Joseph
Let's Beguine, Edelson, Edward
Letters from a Friend, Spaniola, Joseph T.
Lily, Cook, Vander
Litany, Uber, David
Little Norway, Smith, Leonard B.
Little Prelude, Bach, Johann Sebastian
Little Shepherd, The, Debussy, Claude
Logos, Ameller, Andre
Londonderry Air, arr. Buchtel, Forrest L.
Londonderry Air, Traditional
Lord Have Mercy, Christ Have Mercy, Dufay, Guillaume
Lord's Prayer, The, Music for Euphonium and Piano, Larrick, Geary
Love's Enchantment, Valse de Concert, Pryor, Arthur
Lullaby for Curly for Baritone Horn and Piano, Skolnik, Walter
Lynn Meadows Waltz, Niehaus, Lennie
Lyric Suite for Euphonium and Piano, White, Donald

M

Magnolia, Cook, Vander
Maid of the Mist, Clarke, Herbert L.
Manhattan Blues and Ragtime, Uber, David
Man I Love, The, Gershwin, George
Marche from Book IV for Clavier, Couperin, Francois
Marche from Suite No. 5 for Clavier, Purcel, Henry
Marigold, Cook, Vander
Marines' Hymn, Phillips, L. Z.
May Moon, Buchtel, Forrest L.
May Song, Op. 52, No. 4, Beethoven, Ludwig van
Med Jesus vil eg fara, Op. 41, Habbestad, Kjell

Meditation, Corwell, Neal
Meditation and Celebration, Dougherty, William P.
Meditation from "Sonatina in F," Buchtel, Forrest L.
Menuet from Concerto Grosso, Op. 6, No. 5, Handel, George Frederic
Menuet from Don Juan, Mozart, Wolfgang Amadeus
Menuet from Symphony in E-Flat, Mozart, Wolfgang Amadeus
Menuet from Three Piano Pieces, Marpurg, Friedrich
Menuet in G, from "Anna Magdalena Bach Notebook," Bach, Johann Sebastian
Menuetto, Pugnani, Gaetano
Menuetto, Schubert, Franz
Merry Widow Waltz, Lehar, F.
Message, The, Brooks, E.
Midnight Euphonium, Richards, Goff
Military March, Little, Donald C.
Military Melodies, Traditional
Minstrel Boy, Buchtel, Forrest L.
Minuet from "Alceste," Gluck, Christoph Willibald von
Minuet, Boccherini, Luigi
Mirror Lake for Euphonium and Piano, Montgomery, Edward
Mississippi Legend, Uber, David
Montage, Uber, David
Moonlight Serenade, Endersen, R. M.
Morceau de Concert, Saint-Saens, Camille
Mot d' Amour, Op. 13, No. 1, Elgar, Edward
Moto Perpetuo, for Euphonium and Piano, George, Thom Ritter
Mountains Mourne, The, Newsome, Roy
Mouvement pour Tuba, Saxhorn basse Si-flat ou Trombone basse et Piano, Henry, Jean-Claude
Mumbo Jumbo, Buchtel, Forrest L.
Musette from Anna Magdalena Bach Notebook, Bach, Johann Sebastian
Muziek voor tuba-saxhorn en piano, Woestijne, David Van De
My Fawny, Parry
My Johann, Grieg, Edward
My Regards, Llewellyn, Edward
My Sweetheart's Eyes, Op. 14, No. 2, Schubert, Franz
My Wild Irish Rose, Olcott

N

Napoli, Bellstedt, Herman
Neophyte, The, Uber, David
Nessun Dorma, Puccini, Giacomo
Nessun Dorma, Puccini, Giacomo, arr. Spaniola, Joseph
Nessun Dorma, Puccini, Giacomo, arr. Snell, Howard
Night in June, A, King, Karl L.
Night Song for Euphonium, Trombone or Bassoon and Piano, Iannaccone, Anthony

Noble Hymn, Hill William H.
Nocturne, Sibelius, Jean
Nocturne, Haworth, Frank
Nocturne, for Euphonium and Piano, Op. 7,
   Strauss, Franz
Norwegian Christmas Fantasy, Siekmann,
   Frank H.
Norwegian Christmas Fantasy for Euphonium and
   Piano, Siekmann, Frank
Nostalgia, Trombey, Jack

O

O Canada, Traditional
O Christmas Tree, Traditional
O Come, Emmanuel, Traditional, Bates Setting
Oh, quand je dors for Euphonium and Piano, Liszt,
   Franz
O King of Kings for Euphonium and Piano,
   Handel
Old Time Religion, Traditional, Bates Setting
On the Lake, Op. 59, Brahms, Johannes
On the Move, Levi, William
On Wings of Song, Mendelssohn, Felix
On with the Motley, Leoncavallo
One Fine Day from "Madam Butterfly," Puccini, G.
Oration, Snell, Howard

P

Panache, Dewhurst, Robin
Panis Angelicus, "O Lord Most Holy," Frank, Cesar
Panorama, Uber, David
Pantomime, Sparke, Philip
Partita, Ross, Walter
Partita for Euphonium and Piano, Op. 89, But-
   terworth, Arthur
Party Piece, Sparke, Philip
Pastorale for Baritone Horn and Wind Ensemble,
   Krzywicki, Jan
Pavane for an Infant Dead Princess, Ravel,
   Maurice
Peace, Please, Thingnacs, Frode
Pearls, Szenpali, Roland
Pershing Concerto for Euphonium and Piano,
   Raum, Elizabeth
Piccolo Suite pour Tuba Ut ou Saxhorn basse ou
   Trombone basse et Piano, Dubois, Pierre Max
Piece en Forme de Habanera, Ravel, Maurice
Pied Piper, Buchel, Forrest L.
Pizzicato, Drigo, Riccardo
Planets, Stars, and Airs of Space for Euphonium
   and Piano, Bach, J. S.
Polish Dance, Endersen, R. M.
Polka pre baryton, trombone nebo fagot, Ospalec
   (Siebenschlafer)
Polonaise from Third Orchestral Suite, Bach,
   Johann Sebastian
Polovetsian Dances, Borodin, Alexander
Pomp and Circumstance, Elgar, Edward
Praeludium E Toccata, Albrechtsberger, J. G.
Prelude and Canticle for Euphonium and Piano,
   Jarrett, Jack

Prelude and Fugue, Stoutamire, Albert L.
Prelude and Scherzo, Uber, David
Prélude et cadence, Barboteu, Georges
Prelude from Suite Bergamasque, Debussy, Claude
Prelude No. 7, Shostakovich, Dimitri
Prelude, Rheinberger, Josef
Presto from Divertimento No. 12, Mozart, Wolf-
   gang Amadeus
Prince of Denmark's March, The, Clarke, Jeremiah
Priscilla, Mantia, Simone

Q

Quintessence, Stephens, Denzil S.

R

Rangitoto, Richards, Goff
Ransomed, Marshall, George
Razz Ma Tazz, Buchtcl, Forrest L.
Recitative, Arioso and Poloniase, Busch, Carl
Reflection from Sonata for Euphonium and Piano,
   Dougherty, William P.
Reflections, Siekmann, Frank H.
Reflections for Euphonium and Piano, Wilhelm,
   Rolf
Remembrance of Liberati, Buchtel, Forrest L.
Réminiscences de Navarre, Barat, Joseph E.
Requiem, Lovec, Vladimir
Return to Sorrento, De Curtis
Reverie, Debussy, Claude
Reverie and Frolic for Euphonium and Piano, Sib-
   bing, Robert
Reverie for Roger Behrend, Wiedrich, William W.
Reverie from Opus 85, No.1, Mendelssohn, Felix
Reverie from Pieces for Piano, Debussy, Claude
Rhapsody for Euphonium, Brubaker, Jerry
Rhapsody for Euphonium, Curnow, James
Rhapsody in C Minor, Uber, David
Rhapsody in F Minor, Uber, David
Ride of the Valkyries, Wagner, Richard
Rigaudon and Noveletee from Album for Children,
   Chaminade, Cecile
Rigaudon from "Pieces de Clavecin, 1724,"
   Rameau, Jean P.
Rippling Water, Stephens, Denzil S.
Ritual and Celebration, Spears, Jared
Robin Adair, Hartmann, John
Rock of Ages, Bates, Jer.
Romance, DeLamater, E.
Romance, Miura, Mari
Romance, Uber, David
Romance for Euphonium and Piano, Op. 36, Saint-
   Saens, Camille
Romance in F minor, Keighley, Thomas
Romantic Pieces, Op. 75, Dvorak, Antonin
Romance, Op. 62, Elgar, Edward
Romance, Op. 2, Ewald, Victor
Romantica, Buchtel, Forrest L.
Romanze in F, Baratto, Paolo
Romanze in F, Opus 50, Beethoven, Ludwig van
Romanze in G, Opus 40, Beethoven, Ludwig van

Rondeau from Clavier Book X, Couperin, Francois
Rondo, Mozart, Wolfgang Amadeus
Rondo Concertante, Davis, William Mac
Rondo for Baritone Horn and Piano, Presser, William
Rondo from Divertimento No. 11, Mozart, Wolfgang Amadeus
Rondo from Trio in G, Haydn, Franz Joseph
Rondo from Violin Sonata in E♭ Major, Opus 12, No. 3, Beethoven
Runabout, Stephens, Denzil S.

S

Sad Little Song, Balakirev, Mily
Sailing the Mighty Deep, Moquin, Al
Sailor's Song from Book III for Clavier, The, Couperin, Francois
Salut d'amour for Euphonium and Piano, Elgar, Edward
Sanctus from Mass in E Minor, Bruckner, Anton
Sarabande and Menuett, Handel, George Frederic
Sarabande, Corelli, Arcangelo
Sarabande, Handel, George Frederic
Scene de Concert, Denmark, Max F.
Scherzo, Goldman, Franko Edwin
Scherzo for Euphonium and Piano, Michel, Jean-Francois
Scherzo from Sonata Opus 30, No. 2, Beethoven, Ludwig van
Scherzo, Opus 66, Spies, Ernest
School Musician, Endersen, R. M.
Sentimental Sam, Buchtel, Forrest L.
Sentinel, Smith, Leonard B.
Serenade Haydn, Franz Joseph
Serenade, Schubert, Franz
Serenade for Euphonium and Piano, Kac, Stefan
Serenade from "The Student Prince," Romberg, Sigmund
Shadows, Dedrick, Art
Shapes of the Morning, Morgan, David
Sicilienne, Paradies, M.
Sicilienne d'après la 1re Sonate en Sol mineur (BWV 1,001) pour Violin seul, Bach, Johann Sebastian
Silent Night, Gruber
Silver Bells, Livingston, Jay and Evans, Ray
Simple Gifts, Traditional
Simple Song, A, Uber, David
Sine Nomine, Vaughan Williams, Ralph
Sinfonia from Cantata No. 156, Bach, Johann Sebastian
Sinfonietta, Corwell, Neal
Six Preludes for Euphonium and Piano, Hewitt, Harry
Six Studies in English Folk-Song, Williams, Ralph Vaughan
Skydream for Euphonium and Piano, Uber, David
Slavonic Fantasy, Hohne, Carl
Sleepers Awake, Wachet auf, ruft uns Stimme, from the Cantata, BMV 140, Bach, Johann Sebastian

Sleeping Beauty Waltz, Tschaikowsky, Peter Ilyich
Smooth Moment, A, Levi, William
Snowlight, Uber, David
Soliloquy IX, Wiggins, Chris
Solo De Concours, Wurmser, Lucien
Solo De Concurso Para Fagot Adaptado Para Saxofon Tenor O Bombardino, Yuste, Miguel
Soloette for Solo Euphonium and Piano, Uber, David
Solo for Posaune oder Bariton, Frohlich, Erich
Solo Rhapsody for Euphonium, Stephens, Denzil S.
Sonata Da Camera, Uber, David
Sonata de Abril para Bombardino y Piano, Artiga, Lopez
Sonata for Baritone Horn and Piano, George, Thom Ritter
Sonata for Baritone Horn and Piano, Vollrath, Carl
Sonata for Euphonium, Reeman, John
Sonata for Euphonium, Resanovic, Nikola
Sonata for Euphonium, Roper, Anthony
Sonata for Euphonium, Wilder, Alec
Sonata for Euphonium and Piano, Beal, David
Sonata for Euphonium and Piano, Copley, Evan
Sonata for Euphonium and Piano, Cronin, Robert P.
Sonata for Euphonium and Piano, Dougherty, William P.
Sonata for Euphonium and Piano, Folse, Stuart
Sonata for Euphonium and Piano, Frackenpohl, Arthur
Sonata for Euphonium and Piano, Gallaher, Christopher
Sonata for Euphonium and Piano, Rekhin, Igor
Sonata for Euphonium and Piano, Rodgers, Thomas
Sonata for Euphonium and Piano, Uber, David
Sonata for Euphonium and Piano, Op. 97, Madsen, Trygve
Sonata for Euphonium and Piano, Op. 64, Plagge, Wolfgang
Sonata for Horn and Piano, Beethoven, Ludwig van
Sonata for Trombone or Euphonium and Piano, Stevens, John
Sonata for Violin and Bass, Albinoni, Tomaso
Sonata in B♭ Major, K292, Mozart, Wolfgang Amadeus
Sonata in C Major, Fasch, Johann Friedrich
Sonata in F Major, Marcello, Benedito
Sonata in F Major, Opus No. 1, No. 12, Handel, George Frederic
Sonata in F, Pepusch, Johann Christopher
Sonata No. 1 in B Minor, BWV1014 from Six Sonatas for Violin and Piano, Bach, Johann Sebastian.
Sonata No. 3 from Six Sonatas for Violin, Bach, Johann Sebastian
Sonata No. 2 in A Major, BWV 1015 from Six Sonatas for Violin and Piano, Bach, Johann Sebastian
Sonata No. V, Handel, George Frederic
Sonata, Op. 17 for Euphonium and Piano, Beethoven, Ludwig van

Sonate en 6 minutes 30 pour Tuba, ou Trombone-Basse, ou Saxhorn en et Piano, Pascal, Claude
Sonate pour bassoon & piano, Williams, Adrian
Sonatina, Hutchinson, Warner
Sonatina, Mozart, Wolfgang Amadeus
Sonatina, Uber, David
Sonatine in Four Movements, Bell, A.
Sonatine No. 2, Uber, David
Sonatine pour Tuba Ut, ou Saxhorn basse, et Piano, Casterede, Jacques
Song for Ina, Sparke, Philip
Song of the Brother, The, Leidzen, Erik
Song of the Seashore, Narita
Song of the Sun, Barroll, Edward C.
Song to the Evening Star, Wagner, Richard
Sousaphonium, Moquin, Al
Southern Cross, Clarke, Herbert L.
Southern Cross, Newsome, Roy
Southerner, The, Mantia, Simone
Spinning Song, Song without Words, No. 34, Medelssohn, Felix
Spinning Wheel, Endersen, R. M.
Spiritual Bell, Broege, Timothy
Spring, Caprice, Cimera, Jaroslav
Spring Fever, Stephens, Denzil S.
Spring Suite for Euphonium and Piano, Cummings, Barton
Stars and Stripes Forever, Sousa, John Philip
Star Spangled Banner, The, Sousa, John Philip
Stephen's Ladies of Song, Foster, Stephen Collins
Still Shining, Meechan, Pete
St. Louis Blues, Handy, W. C.
Strenuous Life, The, Joplin, Scott
Stupendo, Brahmstedt, N. K.
Suite Abendlied, "Evening Song," Schumann, Robert
Suite for Baritone, Haddad, Don
Suite from Variations for Violin on Themes of Tartini, Corelli, Arcangelo
Suite fur Tenorhorn oder Bariton, Frohlich, Erich
Suite in Ab from Sonata No. II for Flute, Handel, George Frederic
Sumer Is Icumen In, Anonymous
Summer Celebration, Miserendino, Joe
Summer Music, Op. 77(B), Butterworth, Arthur
Summer Nocturne, Uber, David
Summertime, Gershwin, George
Sunrise, Stephens, Denzil S.
Sur La Montagne, Bruniau, Auguste
Swan, The, Saint-Saens, Camille
Swedish Hymn, Gramercy Solo Album, Graham, Peter
Symphonic Variants, Curnow, James
Syncopator, Endersen, R. M.
Syncophobia, Buchtel, Forrest L.

T

Tales from the Vienna Woods, Strauss, Johann
Tango, Op. 165, No. 2, Albeniz, Isaac
Tarantelle, Walters, Harold

Tendres Melodies, Petites Pieces De Concours, Wurmser, Lucien
Theatre Piece for Euphonium and Piano, Uber, David
Theme and Variations, Bowen, Gerard
Theme et Variations pour Saxhorn-basse ou Tuba ou Trombone basse et Piano, Aubain, Jean
Thoughts of Gold, Valse Caprice, De Luca, Joseph
Thoughts of Home, DeLamater, E.
Thoughts of Love, Pryor, Arthur
Three Easter Chorales, Bach, Johann Sebastian
Three Famous Melodies, Traditional
Three Farewell Pieces, Corwell, Neal
Three Miniatures for Baritone and Piano, Wilson, Don
Three Studies for Euphonium and Piano, Hogg, Merle E.
Thunder, Lightning and Whistling Wind, Handel, George Frederic
Time for Peace, A, Gramercy Solo Album, Graham, Peter
Timepiece, Niehaus, Lennie
To a Wild Rose, MacDowell, Edward
To a Wild Irish Rose, MacDowell, Edward, arr. Snell, Howard
Toreador's Song, Rubank
Toreador's Song from "Carmen," Bizet, Georges
Touch of Ireland Based on a Kerry Dance, A, Malloy, James
Trumpet Voluntary, Clarke, Jeremiah
Tuba-abut, Ameller, Andre
Tubabillage pour Tuba Ut ou Contrebasse a Cordes ou Saxhorn basse ou Trombone basse et Piano, Gabaye, Pierre
Tubacchanale pour Tuba en Ut ou Saxhorn basse et Piano, Boutry, Roger
Tuba-concert, Ameller, Andre
Tubanova, Solo de concours, Selmer-Collery, Jules
Tubaroque pour Tuba Ut ou Saxhorn basse sib ou tromb base et Piano, Boutry, Roger
Twelve Days of Christmas, The, Traditional, Aud, Jean
Two Classical Themes, Haydn, Franz Joseph
Two Hymn Settings for Euphonium, Bradbury, William
Two Pieces, Hartley, Walter

U

Un Bel Di (from Madam Butterfly), Puccini, Giacomo
Unicorn, Smith, Leonard B.

V

Valse Caprice, Endersen, R. M.
Valse Triste, from the Music to Arvid Jarnefelt's Drama "Kuolema" (Death), Op. 44, Sibelius, Jean
Variatie's voor Euphonium en Piano, Op. 108b, Toebosch, Louis

Variations, Owen, Jerry
Variations for Ophicleide, Kummer, G.
Variations on a Theme by Arcangelo Corelli,
    Timokhin, Slava
Variations on a Theme of Robert Schumann,
    Schumann, Robert
Variations on Drink to Me Only, Snell, Howard
Veiled Prophet, The, Uber, David
Venture, Smith, Leonard B.
Victor Herbert Medley, Herbert, Victor
Viking, The, Hill, William H.
Vilia, Lehar, Frunz
Villancico: Riu, riu, chiu, Anonymous
Vintage, Gillingham
Virtuoso, The, Walker, B. H.
Vissi D'Arte, Puccini, Giacomo, arr. Mead,
    Steven
Vissi D'Arte, Puccini, Giacomo, arr. Spaniola,
    Joseph
Vittoria! Vittoria!, Carissimi, Giacomo
Vocalise, Rachmaninov, Sergei
Vocalise, Schooley, John
Volunteer, The, Rogers, Walter

W

Walther's Prize Song, Wagner
Waltz Medley (Tres Jolie, Skater's, Emperor Waltz),
    arr. Buchtel, Forrest L.
Waltz Themes, Waldteufel-Linke
*Water Music Suite No. 1 from Water Music Suite
    No. 1 and No. 3*, Handel, George Frederic
*Water Music Suite No. 2 from Water Music Suite
    No. 3*, Handel, George Frederic
Weather Vane, Tanner, Paul
Weber's Last Waltz, Grand Fantasia, Rimmer, W.
What if I Never Speed, for Euphonium and Piano,
    Dowland, John
When the Saints Go Marching In, arr. Buchtel,
    Forrest L.
When the Saints Go Marching In, Traditional
When They Ring the Golden Bells, Marbelle,
    Dion de
When You Wish upon a Star, Harline
Where're You Walk, Handel, George Frederic
Whirlwind, Gramercy Solo Album, Graham, Peter
Whistlin' Pete, Endersen, R. M.
Willow, Willow, Grainger, Percy Aldridge
Winter Carousel, Bigelow
Winter Song and Summer Dances, Miserendino,
    Joe
Winter's Willow, a Country Song, Vaughn Williams,
    Ralph

Y

Yellow Dog Blues, Handy, W. C.
Yellow Rose of Texas Variations, The, Buckley,
    Lewis J.
*Your Ring on My Finger from Womanly Love and
    Life, Op. 42, No. 4*, Schumann, Robert

Euphonium and Keyboard Collections

Many of the selections included in these collections were published separately. Acquiring them in the collections is a good way to build up a large library of euphonium solos. Many of the solos in the collections have been annotated separately previously in this chapter. There are many collections that could not be included due to time constraints and due mainly to practicality, as there are countless popular songs (rock, country, jazz, folk, etc.) that have now been arranged for euphonium.

Arban, Jean-Baptiste. *Mead Meets Arban*. Arr. Andrew Watkin. This fantastic selection includes variations on *A Favorite Theme, Do You See the Glittering Snow, Capriccio and Variations, Carnival of Venice, Brilliant Fantasy, Variations on a Tyrolese Song, Cavatina "Beatrice di Tenda,"* and *Air Varie on "The Little Swiss."* It is bass and treble clefs and comes with demo CD! It is beautifully printed with specific style and tempo markings. This is a fantastic collection of solos!

Belwin Mills. *Classic Festival Solos*. Belwin Mills Publishing Corp. 1992. $4.95 (solo book). I–III. Contains thirteen easy to intermediate solos: Concentration, Debonair, Galaxy, Gypsy Rondo, Las Tortillas, Lazy Lullaby, Little Norway, Military March, Sentinel, Song to the Evening Star, Unicorn, Venture, and Weather Vane. Many of these solos would be perfect selections for a beginner to perform at a solo and ensemble contest/festival.

Belwin Mills. *Student Instrumental Course—Level One, Baritone Soloist with Piano Accompaniment*. Belwin Mills Inc. 1969. $5. I. Contains nineteen solos, two duets, and one trio for the elementary level: French Song, Waltz Themes, Three Famous Melodies, Folk Song Melodies, Aura Lee, All through the Night, Military Melodies, Stars and Stripes Forever, Silent Night, College March, Andantino, Merry Widow Waltz, When the Saints Go Marching In, On Wings of Song, Victor Herbert Medley, Sleeping Beauty Waltz, My Wild Irish Rose, Campus Queen, Cradle Song, Skaters' Waltz (duet), The Glow Worm (trio), and Sweet and Low (duet). Piano accompaniment by Robert Girlamo.

Borton, Allen L. *Euphonium Hymns*. Tuba-Euphonium Press. 2001. $20. A♭–c″. This is a fantastic collection of classic hymns with piano accompaniment. The solo part and piano accompaniment are both very easy to read. They are rhythmically simple, in a wide variety of keys (most of them being in flat keys), mostly in bass clef, and tend to mostly be in the high register. The collection includes A Mighty Fortress Is Our God; All People That on Earth Do Dwell; Amazing Grace; Away in a Manger; Beneath the Cross of Jesus; Blessed Assurance; Break Thou the Bread of Life; Children of the Heavenly Father; Christ the Lord Is Risen Today; Come, Christians, Join to Sing; Come, Ye Thankful People, Come; Crown Him with Many Crowns; Dear Lord and Father of Mankind; Fairest Lord Jesus; For All the Saints; For the Beauty of the Earth; God of Our Fathers; Great Is Thy Faithfulness; Holy, Holy, Holy; I Love to Tell the Story; I Need Thee Every Hour; It Is Well with My Soul; Jesus Loves Me; Jesus Shall Reign; Joy to the World; Just as I Am; Lift High the Cross; May Jesus Christ Be Praised; My Faith Looks Up to Thee; O Come, All Ye Faithful; O God Our Help in Ages Past; Praise to the Lord; The Almighty; Rejoice, Ye Pure in Heart; Silent Night; The Church's One Foundation; The Old Rugged Cross; Thine Is the Glory; We Gather Together; and What a Friend We Have in Jesus.

Childs Brothers. *Childs Choice*. Winwood Music (formerly Rosehill). $21. III–V. Includes *Lucy Long*, Godfrey (arr. Eric Wilson); *Tambourin*, Gossec (arr. Eric Wilson); *Chanson de Matin*, Elgar (arr. Eric Wilson, includes optional duet version); *The Riders of Rohan*, Rodney Newton. If you are looking for something good and different to play on a recital, this is a great collection. The solo part is in treble clef.

Childs Brothers. *CZARDAS*. Winwood Music (formerly Rosehill). $21. III–IV. Includes *Czardas*, Monti (arr. Eric Wilson); *Largo al Factotum*, Rossini (arr. Childs Brothers); *Salut d'Amour*, Elgar (arr. Childs Brothers); *Calon Lân*, Hughes (arr. Eric Ball, includes optional duet version). This excellent solo collection is in treble clef.

Childs Brothers. *Softly, As I Leave You*. Winwood Music (formerly Rosehill). III–V. *Softly, As I Leave You*, de Vita (arr. Alan Catheral, includes optional duet version); *Flower Song from Carmen*, Bizet; *Silvered by the Moonlight*, Fauré (arr. Eric Wilson); *Carnival of Venice* (arr. Arthur Remmington). This is an excellent collection of several gorgeous lyrical solos. If you are looking for some great recital selections, start here. The solo part is in treble clef.

Endersen, R. M. *Indispensable Folio*. Ruband, Inc. 1980. $5.95 (solo book). III. Contains eleven intermediate solos: *The Envoy, Spinning Wheel, Fox Hunt, Moonlight Serenade, Whistlin' Pete, Holiday Medley, School Musician, Forest Echo, Polish Dance, Valse Caprice*. and *Syncopator*.

Graham, Peter. *Gramercy Lyric Album*. Gramercy Music.1995. $21. III–IV. *Rainforest—From Windows of the World* (featured soloist on the demo recording, Lesley Howie). *Celtic Dream—From Windows of the World* (featured soloist on the demo recording, David Thornton). *The Name*—recorded by Brett Baker, trombone soloist with the Black Dyke Band. *Doyle's Lament*—recorded by John Doyle, flugelhorn soloist with the Black Dyke Band. *A Little Wish*—a very

simple original melody by Peter Graham (featured soloist on the demo recording, Michelle Ibbotson). The solo part is in both bass and treble clefs.

Graham, Peter. *Gramercy Solo Album*. Gramercy Music. 1995. $21. IV. B♭–b♭'. This collection contains four solos: *Glorious Ventures* (variations on *The Lily of the Valley*), *A Time for Peace* (theme from *The Essence of Time*), *Swedish Hymn*, and *Whirlwind*. All of these solos are suitable for college students, while a couple are suitable for a good high school player. The solo part is in treble clef.

Kane, Derick. *The Derick Kane Euphonium Album*. SP&S Ltd. $44. II–VI. This is a fantastic collection of various famous Salvation Army band solos. The collection comes with piano accompaniment and a compact disc accompaniment. The solo part comes in bass and treble clef. This collection comes highly recommended! The collection includes *The Better World*, Bearcroft (9:00. V.); *Spirit of Life*, Catherwood (4:20. III.); *My Love Is Like a Red Rose*, Traditional (3:50. III.); *Travelling Along*, Mallett (4:30. V.); *Lyric Variations*, Allen (9:20. V.); *There Will Be God*, Webb (4:40. IV.); *To Live Right*, Basanko (6:30. IV.); *Welsh Fantasy*, Pearce (7:40. V–VI.); *Jesus, I Come to Thee*, Bearcroft (3:00. III.); *Ochills*, Rance (2:30. II.); *Compelled by Love*, Blythe (3:30. III.); *A New Direction*, Kane (3:30. II.); *Menuet*, Bizet (4:00. III.); and a duet. Order at www.euphonium.net.

Levi, William. *Solos for Trombone or Baritone*. Puna Music Co. 2001. $15.95 or $20 with CD. II–III. Contains four intermediate solos: *A Smooth Moment, Tales from the Vienna Woods* by Johann Strauss, *Ballad in F* and *On the Move*. There is an option for ordering the piano accompaniments on CD. The packet includes composer information and program notes.

Rubank. *Rubank Book of Trombone/Baritone B.C. Solos*. $7.95. II–III. Many of the selections are excellent for solo and ensemble contests: *Allerseelen, Berceuse, Carnival of Venice, Chartreuse, Dawn of Spring, Friends Waltz Caprice, Funeral March of the Marionette, Meditation, Red Canyons*, and *Sarabande*.

Rubank. *Sacred Solos—Trombone (Baritone B.C.) with Piano Accompaniment*. $7.95. I–III. *Adoration, Agnus Dei, Alleluia, Ave Maria, Calvary, If with All Your Hearts* (Elijah), *Meditation, Panis Angelicus, The Holy City, The Rosary, Where E'er You Walk* (Handel).

Rubank. *Sarabande, Trombone or Baritone (B.C.) Solos with Piano*. $4.95. 8 pages. I—III.

Rubank. *Soloist Folios—Trombone or Baritone B.C. and Piano*. $6.95. I—III. Many of the selections are excellent for solo and ensemble contests: *Brilliant Polka* (De Lamater), *Carnival of Venice, Congratulations, Emerald* (Vandercook), *Friends, Glen Eden* (C. W. Storm), *O Holy Night*,

Piano Concerto in B-Flat Minor, Romance (De Lamater), *Song of the Sun* (Barroll), *Stupendo* (Brahmstedt), *The Holy City, Thoughts of Home* (De Lamater).

Sparke, Philip. *Classic Hymns.* Anglo Music Press Collection. II–IV. Includes *Praise My Soul, St. Clement, O Worship the King, Crimond, Passion Chorale, Repton, Hyfrydol, New Britain, Eventide, Variations on Nicaea* (also available with wind band). The solo part is available in bass and treble clef. The collection comes with a free demo compact disk, which contains full performances as well as accompaniment-only tracks. The piano accompaniment is sold separately. This is a great collection of hymns with a wide variety of difficulty levels.

Tuba-Euphonium Press. *Four Puccini Arias.* Arr. Joseph T. Spaniola. $20. III–IV. This is a great collection of lyrical works for recitals. It includes *Vissi D'Arte, Un Bel Di, Dondie Lieta,* and *Nessun Dorma* (see individual listings for more details).

Voxman, H. *Concert and Contest Collection for B♭ Cornet, Trumpet or Baritone with Piano Accompaniment.* Rubank, Inc. $4.95 (solo part). III–IV. The collection contains numerous great solo and ensemble selections and comes in both bass and treble clefs. The collection contains the following selections: *Air Gai* (Berlioz), *Andante and Allegro* (Clerisse), *Andante from "Concerto in E♭"* (Haydn), *Calm as the Night* (Bohm), *Concertino* (Ostransky), *Dedication* (Strauss), *Elegie* (Duquesne), *L'Allegro, The Merry Man* (Koepke), *Morceau De Concours, Op. 57* (Alary), *My Regards* (Llewellyn), *Orientale* (Barat), *Petite Piece Concertante* (Balay), *Premier Solo de Concours* (Maniet), *Romance in E♭* (Ostransky), *Sarabanda and Gavotta* (Corelli), and *Serenade, Op. 22, No. 1* (Bohme).

Euphonium and Organ

Albinoni, Tomaso. *Adagio in G Minor.* Ed. R. P. Block. Philharmusica Co. $13.50. Albinoni was a fine baroque composer who unfortunately has largely been forgotten. This solo is taken from one of Albinoni's most famous and greatest works.

Albrechtsberger, J. G. *Praeludium E Toccata.* Ed. R. P. Block. Philharmusica Co. $15.50.

Anonymous. *Branle "Twelfth Night."* Ed. R. P. Block. Philharmusica Co. $10.50. This work was written ca.1570.

Anonymous. *Sumer Is Icumen In.* Ed. R. P. Block. Philharmusica Co. $10.50. Written ca. 1250, this is one of the most famous motets. This would be an excellent recital piece for a great style change.

Anonymous. *Villancico: Riu, riu, chiu.* Ed. R.P. Block. Philharmusica Co. $12.50.

Bach, Johann Christoph. *Herr Jesu Christ, Dich Zu Uns End.* Ed. R. P. Block. Philharmusica Co. $12.50. This was originally part of a set of chorale preludes. This is a beautiful work for the euphonium.

Bach, Johann Sebastian. *Brandenburg Concerto No. 2, Mvt. III.* Ed. R. P. Block. Philharmusica Co. $15.50. This is one of Bach's most famous works and is a baroque classic! This would be an excellent recital selection.

Bach, Johann Sebastian. *If Thou Be Near.* Ed. R. P. Block. Philharmusica Co. $11.50. III. This beautiful aria by Bach would be a great recital selection.

Bach, Johann Sebastian. *Jesu, Joy of Man's Desiring.* Ed. R. P. Block. Philharmusica Co. $12.50. III. This is one of the most well known of all songs and is a standard wedding selection. This is a fine edition that would serve well for a wedding or a recital.

Bach, Johann Sebastian. *Three Easter Chorales.* Ed. R. P. Block. Philharmusica Co. $12.50.

Bach, Johann Sebastian/Gounod, Charles Francois. *Ave Maria.* Ed. R. P. Block. Philharmusica Co. $14.50. III. This is one of the most popular melodies ever written. This is a fantastic edition and would make for a great recital selection.

Bassano, Giovanni. *Canzona Per Sonare on C de. Rore.* Ed. R. P. Block. Philharmusica Co. $15.50. The original work was written in 1585. Bassano was a late Renaissance and early baroque composer and director of music at St. Mark's Basilica in Venice, but he was most famous as a fine cornetist who inspired the instrumental compositions of Giovanni Gabrielli. This is would make for a fine recital selection.

Boeddecker, P. F. *Christmas Concert.,* Ed. W. and J. Boswell. Philharmusica Co. $12.50. The original was written in 1651.

Broege, Timoth. *Spiritual Bell, for Tenor Tuba or Euphonium and Harpsichord or Organ.* Allaire Music Publications. 2004. IV. D♭–f♯'. This is a fantastic work that has program notes detailing specific harpsichord considerations and specific organ considerations. The work opens slowly and freely and is very expressive. It has many dramatic pauses and phrases that make a big emotional impact. The faster section is very pronounced and powerful. The work is mostly in the middle to lower register, has some rhythmic challenges, has a few chromatics, and is in bass clef. If you are looking for something with a different sound and a big emotional impact, this is your solo. I highly recommend this solo.

Bruckner, Anton. *Sanctus from Mass in E Minor.* Ed. R. P. Block. Philharmusica Co. $12.50. This short work is considered one of Bruckner's finest and most beautiful compositions in his early career.

Campbell. *Meditation,* Southern Music Company. $4.50. IV.

Clarke, Jeremiah. *The Prince of Denmark's March.* Ed. R. P. Block. Philharmusica Co. $12.50.

Dufay, Guillaume. *Lord Have Mercy, Christ Have Mercy.* Ed. R. P. Block. Philharmusica Co. $12.50. Dufay was the most famous composer in Europe in the middle to later 1400s. This work hearkens from one of Dufay's masses for which he was most famous.

Elgar, Edward. *Pomp and Circumstance.* Ed. R. P. Block. Philharmusica Co. $10.50. This most popular commencement selection is well edited for the euphonium.

Grainger, Percy. *Irish Tune from County Derry.* Ed. R. P. Block. Philharmusica Co. $12.50. This has become one of the most arranged of all lyrical songs. This would be a great selection for any recital and is highly recommended.

Handel, George Frederick. *Fanfare "Gloria" from "Susanna."* Ed. R. P. Block. Philharmusica Co. $8.50. A great selection from one of Handel's many fantastic operas.

Handy, W. C. *St. Louis Blues.* Ed. R. P. Block. Philharmusica Co. $10.50. This solo is based on the 1914 version.

Handy, W. C. *Yellow Dog Blues.* Ed. R. P. Block. Philharmusica Co. $11.50. This solo is based on the 1914 version.

Hastings, Thomas. *Rock of Ages.* Ed. Jer. Bates. Philharmusica Co. $10.50. III. This has become a standard American hymn.

Haydn, Franz Joseph. *Lerchen-Rondo in E-Flat.* Ed. W. and J. Boswell. Philharmusica Co. $17.50. IV.

Johnsen, Hallvard. *Preludium for Euphonium and Organ, Op. 79.* Norsk Musikforlag A/S, Oslo. 1985.

Marbelle, Dion de. *Why They Ring the Golden Bells.* Ed. Jer. Bates. Philharmusica Co. $12.50. If you are looking for a great but different religious song to perform, look no further.

Pachelbel, Johann. *Canon.* Ed. R. P. Block. Philharmusica Co. $15.50. This is one of the most well-known songs and is well edited for the euphonium.

Palestrina, Giovanni Pierluigi. *Agnus Dei II from Pope Marcellus Mass.* Ed. R. P. Block. Philharmusica Co. $13.50. This is a great selection from the most well-known work from a master composer of the Renaissance.

Palestrina, Giovanni Pierluigi. *And He Was Crucified for Us.* Ed. R. P. Block. Philharmusica Co. $12.50.

Praetorius, Michael. *Carol of the Rose.* Ed. R. P. Block. Philharmusica Co. $10.50. This is a gorgeous sacred song that would make for a great recital selection.

Satie, Erik. *Gymnopedie I.* Ed. R. P. Block. Philharmusica Co. $12.50. This work is based on the first of three piano compositions that became very famous for many reasons, some more dubious than others. This is a great work and would

make for a wonderful change of style on any recital.

Schubert, Franz. *Ave Maria.* Ed. R. P. Block. Philharmusica Co. $14.50. This beautiful song has become one of the most popular classical songs ever written. Here it is based off of a version by one of the all-time great classical songwriters.

Siekmann, Frank. *Two Powerful Hymns.* Brelmat Music. $12. 4:00. III–IV. This work includes material based on "All Hail the Power of Jesus' Name" and "A Mighty Fortress Is Our God."

Sousa, John Philip. *The Star Spangled Banner.* Ed. R. P. Block. Philharmusica Co. $10.50. Here the American national anthem is edited for euphonium.

Telemann, G. P. *Air De Trompette in D Major.* Ed. R. P. Block. Philharmusica Co. $12.50.

Traditional. *I Will Arise and Go to Jesus.* Ed. R. P. Block. Philharmusica Co. $11.50. This is a very popular southern folk hymn.

Traditional. *O Canada.* Ed. R. P. Block. Philharmusica Co. $8.50.

Traditional. *O Christmas Tree.* Ed. Jer. Bates. Philharmusica Co. $10.50. This is one of the most festive of all holiday songs.

Traditional. *O Come, Emmanuel.* Ed. Jer. Bates. Philharmusica Co. $12.50. This classic American holiday selection is well arranged for the euphonium.

Traditional. *Old Time Religion.* Arr. Jer. Bates. Philharmusica Co. $12.50. This classic American song is well arranged for the euphonium.

Traditional. *The Twelve Days of Christmas.* Arr. Jean Aud. Philharmusica Co. $12.50.

Vaughan Williams, Ralph. *Sine Nomine.* Ed. R. P. Block. $11.50. This is a gorgeous selection by one of the finest English composers. I highly recommend this selection for a recital.

French Euphonium Solos with Keyboard

The information in this section is extracted with permission from the *French Music for Low Brass Instruments: An Annotated Bibliography* co-authored by J. Mark Thompson and Jeff Lemke and published in 1994 by Indiana University Press. This publication presents a complete documentation and short description of French solo and pedagogical materials generally intended for various low brass instruments. The publications listed have been specifically designated as useable by the *saxhorn basse* (euphonium).

Solos are listed alphabetically by composer, with title (and translation), editor (if any), publisher, date, range (with optional ranges shown in parentheses), difficulty, and instrumentation.

Publisher codes for this listing are found at the end of the French solos. Range is listed similar to that in the Harvard Dictionary, where c′ = middle c; c = c small; C = c great; C′ = c contra; and so forth. Difficulty is shown from 1–9, with 9 being the most difficult; this follows the French grading system. In more recent editions, the easier solos (grades 1–3) have been renamed Débutant, Préparatoire, and Élémentaire, respectively. Each new designation can also be divided into two parts; hence, a solo with the difficulty "Préparatoire level 2" is notated "P2." Instrumentation is last; abbreviations are as follows:

b = bass	orch = orchestra
bar = baritone (horn)	org = organ
bn = bassoon	pf = piano
cb = contrabass	b saxhn = basse saxhorn
ch = chamber	(euphonium)
cel = celeste	saxphn = saxophone
cor = cornet	t = tenor
db = (string)	tba = tuba
double bass	b trbn = basse
	trombone

Although it may seem arbitrary, the instrumentation is listed in the order it appears on the score. It is believed that the piece is intended for the first instrument listed, though playable on the others; however, there is no evidence to support this assertion.

Amellér, André [Charles Gabriel] (b. 1912). *Bassutecy.* Led, 1984. B♭–f′, P2–E1, tba/b saxhn, pf

Amellér, André. *Batifol.* Com. 3. (No further information available.)

Amellér, André. *Belle province: Hauterive* [*Beautiful Province: High Bank*]. Led, 1973. E♭–e♭′, 2–3, tba/b trbn/saxhn (B♭ treb clef)/b saxhn (B♭ and E♭ b clef), pf

Amellér, André. *Irish-Cante* [*Irish Song*]. Led, 1977. E♭′–g′, 7, tba/b saxhn/b trbn, pf

Amellér, André. *Kryptos: Étude* [*Hidden: Study*]. Hin, 1958. G♭′ (A♯′/B♭′)–b′(c♯″), 8, all trbns (t or b)/tba/b saxhn, pf

Amellér, André. *Logos* [*Speech*]. Led, 1982. E′–(f′)a♭′, 7, tba (C or F)/b saxhn, pf

Amellér, André. *Tuba-abut.* Esc, 1975. 5′30″. (No further information available.)

Amellér, André. *Tuba-concert, Op. 69.* Esc, 1952. D♯′/E♭′–(b′)c″, 8, tba/b saxhn, pf

Aubain, Jean [Emmanuel] (b. 1928). *Thème et variations.* Am, 1975. F′–b♭′, 8, b saxhn/tba/b trbn, pf

Bach, Johann Sebastian (1685–1750). *Sicilienne d'après la 1re Sonate en Sol mineur (BWV 1,001) pour Violin seul* [*Sicilienne After the First Sonata in g Minor for Violin Solo*]. Edited by Philippe Rougeron. Led, 1983. F–(e♭′)f′, E2.

Barat, Joseph Edouard (1882–1963). *Introduction et danse.* Led, n.d., *Introduction and Dance.* Edited by Glenn Smith. SouT, 1973. C(E)–g′, 2, b saxhn, pf (Led), bar, pf (SouT)

Barat, Joseph Edouard. *Introduction et sérénade.* Led, 1957 (reprinted, 1963). F′(F)–f′, 6, tba/b saxhn/bar saxhn, pf

Barat, Joseph Edouard. *Réminiscences de Navarre.* Led, 1950. F′–g′, 7, tba/b saxhn, pf

Barboteu, Georges (b. 1924). *Prélude et cadence.* Cho, 1977. E′–c″, 7, b saxhn/tba (C or F)/b trbn, pf

Bariller, Robert (b. 1918). *L'enterrement de Saint-Jean* [*The Funeral of Saint John*]. Led, 1960. A′(A)–f′, 1–2, tba/b trbn/b saxhn, pf

Bariller, Robert. *Hans de Schnokeloch.* Led, 1961. C♯–a′, 2, b trbn/tba/b saxhn/(t trbn), pf

Barraine, [Jacqueline] Elsa (b. 1910). *Andante et allegro.* Sal, 1958. B♭′–b♭′, 7, b saxhn, pf

Barraine, [Jacqueline] Elsa. *Chiens de paille* [*Straw Dogs*]. Job, 1966. G′(C)–b♭′, 8, tba/t or b trbn/bn/Ondes Martenot, pf

Beaucamp, Albert [Maurice] (b. 1921). *Cortège* [*Procession*]. Led, 1953. C–g′, 1–2, tba/db/b saxhn/b trbn, pf

Beethoven, Ludwig van (1770–1827). *Danse villageoise* [*Rustic Dance*]. Bill, 1989. Adapted by André Goudenhooft, piano realization by Augustin Maillard. C–c′, 2–4, b trbn/tba, pf

Bernaud, Alain. *Humoresque.* Esc, 1964. F′–b′, 9, tba/b saxhn, pf

Beugniot, Jean-Pierre (b. 1935). *Légende.* Bill, 1981. E–f′, 3, b saxhn/tba/b trbn, pf

Bigot, Eugène [Victor] (1888–1965). *Carillon et bourdon* [*Carillon and Great Bell*]. Led, 1951. E′–a♭′, 7, tba/b saxhn, pf

Bigot, Pierre. *Cortège* [*Procession*]. Com, 1983. F(B♭)–c′, D2. tba/b saxhn, pf

Bitsch, Marcel (b. 1921). *Impromptu.* Led, 1957. F′–b♭′, 7, b saxhn/tba/b trbn, pf

Bitsch, Marcel. *Intermezzo.* Led, 1968. G′–b♭′, 8–9, tba/b saxhn, pf

Boutry, Roger (b. 1932). *Pièce brève* [*Short Piece*]. Led. (No further information available.)

Boutry, Roger. *Tubacchanale* [*Tuba Revel*]. Led, 1956. E′–(a′)b′, 8, tba/b saxhn, pf

Boutry, Roger. *Tubaroque.* Led, 1955. A′–g′(a♭′), 4–5, tba/b saxhn/b trbn, pf/orch

Bozza, Eugène [Joseph] (b. 1905). *Allegro et finale.* Led, 1953. E–a′(b′), 5, db/tba/b saxhn/b trbn, pf

Bozza, Eugène [Joseph]. *Concertino.* Led, 1967. F′–a♭′/g♯′, 7, tba/b saxhn, orch/pf

Bozza, Eugène [Joseph]. *New Orleans.* Led, 1962. F′–a′, 7, b saxhn/tba/b trbn, pf

Bozza, Eugène [Joseph]. *Prélude et allegro.* Led, 1953. (A′)E–a′, 5, db/tba/b saxhn/b trbn, pf

Bozza, Eugène [Joseph]. *Thème varié* [*Theme and Variations*]. Led, 1957. G′–(f′)g′, 5, tba/b saxhn/b trbn, pf

Brouquières, Jean. *Au temps de la cour* [*At the Time of the Heart*]. Mar, 1982. F–b♭, P, b saxhn/tba, pf

Brouquières, Jean. *Tubaria*. Mar, 1983. F–f', P, tba/b saxhn, pf

Brown, Charles [Louis Georges] (b. 1898). *Récitatif, lied et final*. Led, 1961. E'(C)–(a')b♭', 8, b saxhn/tba/b trbn, pf

Carles, Marc (b. 1933). *Introduction et toccata*. Led, 1961. B'–a', 8, b trbn/tba/b saxhn, pf

Castérède, Jacques (b. 1926). *Fantaisie concertante*. Led, 1960. B'–a', 8, b trbn/tba/b saxhn, pf

Castérède, Jacques. *Sonatine*. Led, 1963. E'–a', 7, tba/b saxhn, pf

Cecconi [Botella], Monic [Gabrielle] (b. 1936). *Tuba-I*. Rid, 1971. F'–g', 7, tba, pf

Challan, Henri (b. 1910). *Intermezzo*. Led, 1970. A'–b', 7, tba/b saxhn, pf

Charpentier, Jacques (b. 1933). *Prélude et allegro*. Led, 1959. E'–(b♭')c'', 7, b saxhn/tba/db, pf

Clérisse, Robert (b. 1899). *Marine*. Com, 1962. C–g', 4, tba/b saxhn, pf

Clérisse, Robert. *Pièce lyrique*. Led, 1957. B'(F)–(f')f♯', 4, tba/db/b saxhn/b trbn, pf

Clérisse, Robert. *Voce nobile* [*Noble Voice*]. Led, 1953. C–f', 3, tba/db/b saxhn/b trbn, pf

Damase, Jean-Michel (b. 1928). *Automne* [*Autumn*]. Bill, 1987. c–c', D, b saxhn/tba, pf

Damase, Jean-Michel. *Bourrée*. Bill, 1987. E♭–e♭', 3, b saxhn/tba, pf

Damase, Jean-Michel. *Menuet éclaté* [*Split Menuet*]. Bill, 1987. G–d', P, b saxhn/tba, pf

Daucé, Edouard. *Concertino*. Com, 1961. G'–a', 5, tba, pf

Defaye, Jean-Michel (b. 1932). *Morceau de concours I*. Led, 1990. F♯–d', 4, tba, pf

Defaye, Jean-Michel. *Morceau de concours II*. Led, 1990. C–g', 5, tba, pf

Defaye, Jean-Michel. *Morceau de concours III*. Led, 1990. E♭–c'', 8, tba, pf

Defaye, Jean-Michel. *Suite marine*. Led, 1989. E♭–e♭', 6, tba, pf

Delgiudice, Michel (b. 1924). *Abuto*. Led, 1982. (D)F–d', D2–P1, tba/b saxhn, pf

Delgiudice, Michel. *Ali-Baba*. Bill, 1977. B♭–d', 1–2, b saxhn (B♭ or C)/tba/b trbn, pf

Delgiudice, Michel. *Danse l'éléphant*. Mar, 1981. E♭–c', D2, b saxhn/tba, pf

Delgiudice, Michel. *Dix [10] petits textes*. Esc, 1954. G'–g♯', 8, tba/b or cb saxhn, pf

Delgiudice, Michel. *L'antre de Polypheme* [*The Lair of Polyphemus*]. Mar, 1981. C–f, P2, b saxhn/tba, pf

Delgiudice, Michel. *Le petit baobab*. Mar, 1981. F–b♭, D1, b saxhn/tba, pf

Delgiudice, Michel. *Le petit mammouth*. Mar, 1981. G–d', P1, b saxhn/tba, pf

Depelsenaire, Jean-Marie (b. 1914). *Ce que chantait l'aède*. t trbn/b saxhn, pf

Depelsenaire, Jean-Marie. *Funambules* [*Tight-Rope Walkers*]. EdMT. (No further information available.)

Depelsenaire, Jean-Marie. *Jeux chromatiques* [*Chromatic Games*]. Bill, 1960. E–g', 6, trbn/tba, pf

Désenclos, Alfred (1912–1971). *Suite brève dans le goût classique* [*Short Suite in the Classical Style*]. Led, 1965. G'–c'', 8, tba, pf

Desportes, Yvonne [Berthe Melitta] (b. 1907). *Un souffle profond* [*A Deep Breath*]. Bill, 1981. F'–a♭', 5–6, b trbn/tba, pf

Devos, Gérard (b. 1927). *Deux [2] mouvements contrastés*. Led, 1960. D'(A')–b♭', 7, tba/b trbn/b saxhn, pf

Dondeyne, Désiré (b. 1921). *Cinc [5] études (avec accompagnement de piano)*. Bill. (No further information available.)

Dondeyne, Désiré. *Cinc [5] "pièces courtes": Pour jeune tubistes*. Bill, 1987. (G')C–c', 3, tba/b saxhn, pf

Dondeyne, Désiré. *Divertimento*. LF, 1978. (E')F'–f♯', 8, tba (C or F)/b saxhn, pf

Dondeyne, Désiré. *Tubissimo*. Bill, 1983. F'(A')–e'(g'), 7, tba/b saxhn, pf

Dubois, Pierre Max (b. 1930). *Cornemuse* [*Bagpipes*]. Led, 1961. E–a', 5, tba/b trbn/b saxhn/db, pf

Dubois, Pierre Max. *Fantaisie*. Cho, 1965. F'–c'', 7, b saxhn/tba/b trbn, pf

Dubois, Pierre Max. *Histories de tuba*. Vol. 1. *Plantez les gars!* [*Plant Them, Boys!*]. Bill, 1984. F–(d')f', 2, b saxhn/t tba/b tba, pf

Dubois, Pierre Max. *Histories de tuba*.Vol. 2. *Le petit cinéma* [*The Little Theater*]. Bill, 1984. A'–f', 4, b saxhn/t tba/b tba, pf

Dubois, Pierre Max. *Histories de tuba*. Vol. 3. *Le grand cinéma* [*The Big Theater*]. Bill, 1984. G♯/A♭'–(f♯')g', 6, b saxhn/t tba/b tba, pf

Dubois, Pierre Max. *Histories de tuba*. Vol. 4. *Concert opéra*. Bill, 1988. G'–g♯', 7, b saxhn/b tba, pf

Dubois, Pierre Max. *Piccolo suite*. Led, 1957. F'–a♯', 8, tba/b saxhn/b trbn, pf/ (orch (Mvt. 3))

Durand-Audard, Pierre [Max] (b. 1930). *Dialogue*. Led, 1970. G♯'–a', 9, b trbn/tba/b saxhn, pf

Durand [-Audard], Pierre [Max] (b. 1930). *Tournevalse* [*Turning Waltz*]. Bill, 1978. F'–(g')b♭', 7, b saxhn/tba/b trbn, pf

Faillenot, Maurice. *Introduction et rigaudon*. Bill, 1985. G–(e')g', 3, t saxphn/bar saxhn/b saxhn/tba, pf

Fayeulle, Roger. *Bravaccio*. Led, 1958. A'–(f')a', 7, tba/b saxhn/b trbn, pf

Franck, Maurice (b. 1892). *Prélude, arioso et rondo*. EdMT, 1969. A♭'–b♭', 8, (b) saxhn/b trbn/tba, pf

Gabaye, Pierre (b. 1930). *Tubabillage* [*Tuba Prattle*]. Led, 1959. C–e', 4–5, tba/db/b saxhn/b trbn, pf

Gartenlaub, Odette (b. 1922). *Essai*. Rid, 1970. F'–g♯', 6, b saxhn/tba/b trbn, pf

Gotkovsky, Ida (b. 1933). *Suite*. Sal, 1959. F'–b♭', 7, tba, pf

Henry, Jean-Claude (b. 1934). *Mouvement*. Led, 1972. F'–b', 8, tba/b saxhn/b trbn, pf

Holstein, Jean Paul. *Triade*. Cho, 1973. C–g#'/ab', 7, tba, pf

Jolas, Betsy (b. 1926). *Trois [3] duos*. Led, 1985. C'–g', 8, tba, pf

Joubert, Claude Henry. *Rudéral*. Bill, 1980. B'–c#', 3, tba (C or Bb), pf (1 or 2 hands)

Kaï, Naohiko. *Légende*. Led, 1962. F#'(B')–(ab'/g#') bb', 8, tba/b trbn/b saxhn, pf

Laburda, Jirí (b. 1931). *Sonate*. Bill, 1987. F#'–f', 6, tba, pf

Lancen, S. *Grave*. tba/bar saxhn/b saxhn, pf

Lantier, Pierre [Luis César François] (b. 1910). *Andante et allegro*. Lem, 1964. (F')A'–a', 7, tba, pf

Leclair, Jean-Marie (1697–1764). *Sarabande*. Adapted by André Goudenhooft, piano realizations by Augustin Maillard. Bill, 1989. G'–f', 7, b trbn/tba, pf

Lemaire [Sindorff], Jean (b. 1931). *Trois [3] exercises de style*. Led, 1971. E'–bb', 8, b saxhn/tba/b trbn, pf

Lesaffre, Charles. *En glissant ... [Upon Sliding ...]*. Bill, 1984. c–(d')eb', D, b saxhn/tba/trbn, pf

Lesaffre, Charles. *Petite chanson pour Marion [Little Song for Marion]*. Bill, 1988. Bb–(d')f', D, tba/trbn/bar/trpt/cor, pf

Lodéon, André. *Campagnarde [Country Woman]*. Led, 1964. c–d', 1–2, tba/b saxhn, pf

Lodéon, André. *Tuba Show*. Led, 1968. A'–(a')bb', 6, tba/b saxhn, pf

Louvier, Alain (b. 1945). *Cromagnon*. Led, 1973. C#'–c'', 6, b saxhn/tba, cel/pf

Manen, Christian (b. 1934). *Grave et scherzo, Op. 107*. Bill, 1978. F'–a', 8, b trbn/tba/b saxhn, pf

Margoni, Alain (b. 1934). *Après une lecture de Goldoni: Fantaisie dans le style du XVIIIe siècle [After a Lecture of Goldoni: Fantasy in the Style of the Eighteenth Century]*. Led, 1964. G#'/Ab'–f#', 7, b trbn/tba/b saxhn, pf

Martelli, Henri (b. 1895). *Dialogue, Op. 100*. Esc, 1966. B'–f', 8, b trbn/tba/b saxhn, pf

Martelli, Henri. *Suite, Op. 83*. Esc, 1954. G'–ab', 7, tba/b saxhn/b trbn, pf

Meunier, Gérard. *Anapausis (_____) [Repose]*. Bill, 1987. D'–(g')ab', 8, tba, pf

Meunier, Gérard. *Tubabil [Tuba Prattle]*. Lem, 1987. F–d', D', tba/b saxhn, pf

Moreau, James. *Couleurs en mouvements [Moving Colors]*. Led, 1969. A'–c'', 6, tba/b saxhn, pf

Murgier, Jacques (b. 1912). *Concertstück [Contest Piece]*. EdMT, 1961. F'–cb'', 8, tba/db, pf

Pascal, Claude (b. 1921). *Sonate en 6 Minutes 30*. Dur, 1958. E'(F')–b', 6, tba/b trbn/b saxhn, pf

Petit, Pierre (b. 1922). *Fantaisie*. Led, 1953. F'–a', 8, tba/b trbn/b saxhn, pf

Petit, Pierre. *Grave*. Led, 1952. Ab'–a', 3, tba/b trbn/db/b saxhn, pf

Petit, Pierre. *Thème varié*. Led, 1965. E'–c'', 7, b saxhn/tba, pf

Petit, Pierre. *"Wagenia."* Led, 1957. Ab'–d', 7, b trbn/tba/b saxhn, pf

Poutoire, Patrick. *Petit air*. Com. 2. (No further information available)

Quérat, Marcel. *Allegretto comodo*. Com, 1971. G–f', 4, b saxhn/tba, pf

Quérat, Marcel. *Relation*. Com, 1971. Bb–d', 3, tba/b saxhn, pf

Rougeron, Philippe. *Valse nostalgie*. Bill, 1979. C(E)–c', 2, tba/trbn, pf

Rueff, Jeanine (b. 1922). *Concertstück [Contest Piece]*. Led, 1960. Ab'–a', 8, b saxhn/tba/b trbn, pf

Séguin, Pierre. *Cortège [Procession]*. Led, 1984. D(G)–f', P1–2. tba/b saxhn, pf

Séguin, Pierre. *Tubavardage [Tuba Chatter]*. Led, 1987. C(G)–Eb', D1–2, tba/b saxhn/trbn/bn, pf

Semler-Collery, Jules. *Barcarolle et chanson bachique [Barcarolle and Drinking Song]*. Led, 1953. Bb'–gb', 5, tba/db/b saxhn/b trbn, pf

Semler-Collery, Jules. *Cantabile et divertissement*. Esc, 1963. Bb'(Eb)–gb', 9, b saxhn/tba/b trbn/cb (saxhn)/db, pf

Semler-Collery, Jules. *Deux [2] pièces brèves*. Esc, 1973. F'(Bb')–f#', 7, b trbn/tba, pf

Semler-Collery, Jules. *Saxhornia*. Led, 1959. F'–ab', 7, b saxhn/tba/b trbn, pf

Semler-Collery, Jules. *Tubanova: Solo de concours*. Esc, 1967. Ab'(Eb)–g', 8, tba/b saxhn/b trbn/cb (saxhn)/db, pf

Senallié, Jean-Baptiste (1687–1730). *Courante*. Adapted by André Goudenhooft, piano realizations by Augustin Maillard. Bill, 1989. G'–f', 7, b trbn/tba, pf

Tomasi, Henri [-Frédien] (1901–1971). *Danse sacrée [Ritual Dance]*: No. 3 des "Cinc danses profanes et sacrées." Led, 1960. G–ab', 5, tba/trbn/b saxhn, pf/ch orch

Tomasi, Henri [-Frédien]. *Être ou ne pas être!: Monologue d'Hamlet [To Be or Not to Be!: Hamlet's Monologue]*. Led, 1963. Bb'–d', 7, b trbn/tba, pf; solo b trbn/tba, 3 trbns

Toulon, Jacques. *Trois [3] caricatures*. Mar, 1989. G'–bb', E, tba/(b) saxhn

Tournier, Franz. *Récit et rondo*. Rid, 1969. F'–bb', tba/b saxhn, pf

Uga, Pierre. *Promenade*. Bill, 1978. C–e', 5, t trbn/b trbn/tba/b saxhn, pf

Villette, Pierre. *Fantaisie concertante*. Led, 1962. G'–ab', 8, b trbn/tba/t trbn/b saxhn, orch/pf

Weber, Alain (b. 1930). *Soliloque*. Led, 1969. G'–a#', 7–8, b trbn/tba/b saxhn, pf

Weber, Carl Maria von (1786–1826). *Un adagio*. Adapted by André Goudenhooft, piano realization by Augustin Maillard. Bill, 1986. G'–e, 5, b trbn/tba, pf

Werner, Jean-Jacques (b. 1935). *Libre-episode [Free Episode]*. EdMT, 1979. F'–ab', 7, b saxhn/b trbn/tba/db, pf/org

Publishers codes

Arp	International Music Diffusion Arpèges	Esc	Éditions Max Eschig
Bill	Gérard Billaudot	Hin	Hinrichsen Edition
Com	Éditions Marcel Combre (formerly	Led	Alphonse Leduc Éditions Musicales
	Éditions Philippo)	Lem	Henri Lemoine & Cie.
Dur	Éditions Durand & Cie.	LF	Lino Florenzo (Lille, France)
EdMT	Éditions Musicales Transatlantiques	Mar	Éditions Robert Martin
		Rid	Éditions Rideau Rouge

3. Music for Euphonium and Wind Band

Adam Frey

The euphonium solo with wind band accompaniment remains the standard large ensemble performance medium for euphonium solo opportunities in most countries around the world. Except for the areas with strong brass band movements, almost exclusively in Europe and commonwealth countries, the amount of repertoire, performances, recordings, and choices for euphonium and wind band are more numerous and cover a very wide variety of styles. While some solos offer avant-garde effects and others are based on jazz, most of the solos fall into two broad categories: a turn-of-the-century style dating from 1880 to 1920, often a theme and variations or character piece; or a contemporary large-scale work written after 1960. Between these two periods, few solos were composed for the instrument and this may have resulted from economic and social obstacles as well as the downturn in music education during this period. However, with the renewal and focus on education and growth of college- and university-level music programs, the expansion of wind band repertoire has also thrived. Further, the ability to communicate internationally provides a greater chance of exploring works by foreign composers, thus building a much broader music language and scope of style.

One very interesting facet of this listing involves the diverse international styles that embrace the euphonium. All these cultures have master work selections, but they differ greatly: from the American contemporary works by Bach, Curnow, Nehlybel, Jager, and Hovanhess to the oompah German and Austrian-style works, the British concerti arranged from the brass band medium by Ellerby, Golland, and Wilby, and the turn-of-the-century solos of Mantia, DeLuca, Boccolari, and Clarke. Add to that the Italian-style works of Albian and Ponchielli and the stylish works of Ito along with Scandinavian compositions, and one finds a huge variety of repertoire at one's disposal. It will be easy to find something new, something interesting, and something appropriate for many performance opportunities. One specific area that may interest those looking for duos and trios of

lighter music will be the German and Austrian-style music. A great central source is Spaeth/Schmid from Germany. There are a large number of publications that feature euphonium (tenor horn) duets and trios that are certainly audience pleasing and have very easy solo and accompaniment parts. These would be perfect for middle school and high school programs, but know that they represent a more jovial character than more "serious" music.

In regards to these annotations, an effort has been made to provide as much information as possible and subjective recommendations where appropriate, especially with lesser known repertoire. One excellent aspect of the wind band repertoire involves its availability and the great variety of work durations, skill levels, and numerous piano reductions that facilitate performances not just with large ensembles. Also, please note that in regards to the German and Austrian-style works, the instrument will often be termed a tenor horn or baritone and notated in bb treble clef. These are the Germanic equivalents to the euphonium and should not be confused with the Eb tenor horn utilized in brass bands.

Adam, Adolphe. *O Holy Night*. Arr. Chrise Donze. Ludwig Music Company. Euphonium solo and wind band. $45. III. A nice setting of this classic holiday melody. A pleasant countermelody and obligato occurs on the verse as well as a short cadenza. An excellent holiday programming choice.

Albian, Franco. *Alla Siciliana*. Albian Publishing. Euphonium solo and wind band (Italian style). 2004. 6:45. IV. E–bb'. This work hearkens back to the turn-of-the-century variation solos with catchy melodies and typical variations. The merits of this work (and Albian's other compositions) lie in its charm and character: theme—a nice Italian influenced melody; variation 1—eighth notes; variation 2—triplets; variation 3—a mix of eighths and sixteenths; a minor melodic interlude; a cadenza demonstrating great range, triple tonguing, and flexibility; a march variation; a brief final cadenza; and an arpeggiated allegro vivo that brings the work to a close. A nice short work with a much different character than most band works. A unique work with an Italian band setting that utilizes four-part saxophone choir.

Albian, Franco. *Fantasia Concertante*. Albian Publishing. Euphonium solo and wind band (Italian style). 1993. 7:15. IV. F♯–c″. Dedicated to the virtuoso Salvatore Mauro. This work alludes to the turn-of-the-century solos with singable melodies and lots of energy derived from the percussion section. The solo writing throughout both melodic and technical sections remains highly idiomatic and challenging, but not overly so. There are sections with a march-like feel and others with a wonderful waltz 3/8 atmosphere. There are cadenzas after the introduction and again before the final allegro brioso. A unique work with an Italian band setting that utilizes four-part saxophone choir.

Amano, Masamichi. *Euphonium Concerto*. Manuscript. Euphonium solo and wind band. Written for Shoichiro Hokazono.

Andresen, Morgens. *Prelude and Chaconne*. Morgens Andresen. Euphonium solo and wind band (symphony orchestra and brass band available). A very melodic piece that shows the euphonium's possibilities for playing in different styles.

Angst. *Bergland Idyll*. Spaeth/Schmid. Tenor horn duet and wind band. €53. German-style work.

Angst. *Capriccio*. Spaeth/Schmid. Tenor horn and wind band. €35. German-style work.

Angst. *Die beiden feinen Herren*. Spaeth/Schmid. €35. Tenor horn duet and wind band. German-style work.

Angst. *Der fidele Solistentreff*. Spaeth/Schmid. €58. Tenor horn duet and wind band. German-style work.

Angst. *Fernweh*. Spaeth/Schmid. Tenor horn and wind band. €35. German-style work.

Angst. *Zum Lieden Augustin*. Spaeth/Schmid. Tenor horn duet and wind band. €35. German-style work.

Baader, Klaus, and Franz Watz. *Urlaub am Bodensee*. Euphonium duet and wind band. III–IV.

Bach, Jan. *Euphonium Concerto*. Tuba-Euphonium Press. Euphonium solo and wind band (symphony orchestra and piano reduction available). 1992. $200 (Rental, $40). 25:00. IV–V. BB♭–d″. Written in three movements: Legend; Burlesca; Meditation. This mammoth work was extremely significant when it was written in that it was such a large-scale work conceived for orchestral accompaniment and composed by a well-known American composer. It also serves as a high-level competition piece. The scope of the concerto covers a diverse musical palette with its confident opening yet subdued statement from the euphonium. The major challenges (and listening enjoyments) result from the complex rhythms and how these weave through various tonalities. Bach often utilizes faster subdivisions of the beat to give a more hurried feeling (putting two, three,

and four notes on each successive beat). The interplay in the rhythms and hemiolas will challenge the ensemble and playing without a conductor with the piano reduction will need much rehearsal. There are many unusual fingering patterns and intervals and these will take time to master. Unfortunately, the same pattern may occur in another section but may be transposed up a half or whole step. Cadenza sections link all three movements into one continuous work; yet, alternate openings and endings are given to facilitate performance of the individual movements (approx. 8 minutes each). The Burlesca creates a rollicking feeling and provides a jolt of energy, especially with the percussion, to the listener and performer; however, the numerous glissandi and modulating sequences, as well as the continual driving technique, will challenge the performer. A long cadenza gradually restates the theme slower and slower until the tension relaxes to allow the beautiful Meditation to emerge. This movement captures the majesty of the euphonium and its melody, development, and breadth of quality make it a mainstay of the euphonium repertoire generated by American composers. This work will be difficult to program due to its length and somewhat contemporary nature. However, it remains a strong serious work and a standard for many graduate-level players.

Bach, Johann Sebastian. *Aria from Cantata No. 78*. Arr. David Werden. Euphonium and tuba duet and wind band. $55. IV.

Barnes, James. *Duo Concertante*. Southern Music. Euphonium and trumpet duet with wind band (piano reduction available). 1999 (written in 1991). Rental ($15). 9:00. IV. Euphonium: GG–d″ (e♭″); trumpet: B♭–c³ (e♭³). This work is one of few chamber works for the instrument and is written by a well-known composer. The overall form is ABA with the A sections being very light, fast, and technical. Barnes writes detailed articulations and mainly scalar patterns. An extended euphonium cadenza links to the slower B section. Here the soloists have a florid melody of sixteenth notes and eighth note melodies. This work looks like a fun composition for both soloist sand band.

Bassder, Klaus, and Franz Watz. *Erlaub am Bodensee*. FEST-MUSIK-HAUS. Euphonium solo and wind band. German-style work.

Bauer, Robert. *Concerto for Euphonium and Band*. Canadian Music Centre. Euphonium solo and wind band. 1971. 8:00. III–IV. A contemporary-style work.

Bayer, Jaroslav. *Barition Muck'l*. Georg Bauer. Euphonium solo and wind band. 1992. 3:30. III–IV. E–c″. A traditional polka with a theme many people will recognize. There are a number of arpeggios and runs, but the tempo for a polka must remain controlled, so they are not overly difficult. The only range issues keeping this from being a level III occur in the cadenza, so they could easily be altered. This is a superb selection from the German style of music.

Beasley, Rule. *Fantasy for Euphonium and Band*. Gore Publishing. Euphonium solo and wind band (piano reduction available). 1996 (written in 1959). IV. A♭–a′. Dedicated to Lida (Oliver) Beasley—Outstanding Euphonium Player and Wife to Rule Beasley. Written in three sections of moderato, meno mosso, and allegro. The demands are not overly difficult and the technique surmountable by many undergraduate-level students. The main challenge remains the older contemporary style and character of melody and harmony. This work does not seem to lean far enough to the contemporary style and therefore falls in the middle of genres. Thus, it does not differentiate itself enough from other works that have been written later that surpass it in regards to quality.

Bechet, Sydney. *Le Petite Fleur.* Hardy Schneiders. EMR. Euphonium solo and wind band. 1952. 110 CHF. III.

Bèlohoubek, Karel. *Polka für Drei.* FEST-MUSIK-HAUS. Trio for flugelhorn, tenor horn, tuba, and wind band. €31. 4:00. III. A nice trio with a festive theme and feel. The solo parts are not difficult and would be fun to perform for a high school group.

Benz, Albert. *Aentibucher Polka.* Spaeth/Schmid. Brass quartet (with tenor horn) and wind band. €44. German-style work.

Bethmann. *Sancho Pansa.* Spaeth/Schmid. Tenor horn and wind band. €77. German-style work.

Bimboni, G. *Carnival of Venice.* Lapini (Out of Print). Euphonium solo and wind band. A theme and variations work with very challenging variations.

Blank, Hans. *Schwabenklänge.* Spaeth/Schmid. Tenor horn trio and wind band. €41. German-style work.

Boccolari, Eduardo. *Fantasia di Concerto (Sounds of the Rivera).* Kent Akers. Carl Fischer (Euphonium.com—brass band, Tuba-Euphonium Press—piano). Euphonium solo and wind band (brass band, piano reduction available). Out of Print ($75, $14). 12:00. IV–V. (D) E–b♭′ (c″). This work represents one of the major romantic period works written for the euphonium. The melodies are very listenable and have a strong Spanish influence. The opening melodic section allows great freedom and has much interplay between soloist and band. One common technique employed by Boccolari involves having a simple phrase repeated in a section with extensive ornamentation. These phrases necessitate facile technique and agility. There are many cadenzas throughout the work and almost all of them offer *ossias* to facilitate range, time, and technique constraints. The Tempo di Bolero offers great appeal with its energy, articulation, style, and driving

accompaniment figures. The percussion parts add greatly here to bring out the true Spanish style. A brief recitative figure allows a final lyrical perspective before returning to the exuberant bolero and a coda that employs either chromatic triplets (C-D-C, B-C-B, etc.) or repeated triple tonguing. This work represents one of the best turn-of-the-century original works for the baritone/euphonium. Recorded by Brian Bowman, Shoichiro Hokazono, Steven Mead, Toru Miura, John Mueller, Takashi Yamamoto.

Bottje, Will Gay. *Duo Sonatina.* American Composers Alliance. Euphonium duet and wind band.

Bourgeois, Derek. *Concerto, Opus 114.* R. Smith (G&M Brand—orchestra). Euphonium solo and wind band (orchestra, brass band, and piano reduction available). 1988. £130 (Rental, £105, £10). 18:00. IV–V. GG–d″. Written in three movements: Allegro; Adagio; Presto. Commissioned by the British Trombone Society. Included in the *ESB* because Bourgeois states that "It is equally appropriate to perform this work on the Euphonium, in which case the title should be shown as Concerto," this work represents a significant work with performance options for all the major mediums. The work's charm and style lend itself to endearment by performers and audiences alike. The opening movement's marshal style and intensity requires confident articulation interspersed with a sweeping melody that soars to a d^2. Luckily, this occurs in the early part of the *Concerto* before the soloist could become fatigued. The Adagio features some very expressive phrases and a nicely contemplative feeling. The final bars require a mute. The final movement poses the most technical challenges with rapid triplet patterns that are occasionally syncopated. The final page captures Bourgeois's typical technical flourish that modulates rapidly. The valve combinations on these last pages will require much "wood-shedding" and it should be known that most trombone players perform the entire last page in first through third positions only (although some do not do this). This work is highly recommended and a standard of many programs. Thankfully, the composer encourages its performance on the euphonium. Recorded by Angie Hunter, Steven Mead, and many trombone soloists.

Bowen, Brian. *Euphonium Music.* Winwood Music. Euphonium solo and wind band (brass band, orchestral, and piano reduction available). 1984 (written in 1978). £50, In preparation, £20. 14:30. IV. E♭–c″. Written in three movements: Andante; Andante con espressivo, Moderato. *Euphonium Music* stands as one of the contemporary standards in the euphonium repertoire. The writing features many less common melodic intervals of sevenths in its opening motive, which reappears several times. The technical and rhythmic demands are numerous and the rising seventh appears in the fast sections as well. Many of the runs in the work are chromatic in nature and do not always follow major and minor patterns. The second movement features one of the most poignant melodies written for the euphonium and provides great scope for interpretation. The second movement segues into the technical third with many triplet flourishes and a rapid syncopated theme. There are some awkward mixed meter sections before a brief melodic interlude moves into the final technical flourish and a section demonstrating the lyrical power of the instrument. This is a highly recommended work and can be performed with any standard performance medium. Recorded by the Childs Brothers, Steven Mead, Robin Taylor.

Bowen, Gerald. *Theme and Variations.* Manuscript. Euphonium solo and wind band.

Briccialdi. Giulio. *Carnival of Venice.* Anton Coppola. Ludwig Music Company. (Flute, xylophone, trumpet) baritone solo and wind band (piano reduction available). $45. IV. A solo probably better performed on its originally intended instrument, flute. However, it provides another option with the well-known theme. Recorded by Stef Pilleart.

Brubaker, Jerry. *Rhapsody for Euphonium.* Tuba-Euphonium Press. 1994. Euphonium solo and wind band (piano reduction available). $50 ($12). 6:40. IV–V. GG♭–c″. Written for Roger Behrend. Written in two major sections, slow-fast, this work opens with a number of rising sequences with low range syncopations spanning two and half octaves. After this opening quasi cadenza, a melodic section begins with a nice lyrical line and Alfred Reed-–like harmonies. The allegro section incorporates optimistic melodic and rhythmic writing with highly articulated statements by the euphonium. A later obbligato line of sixteenth notes by the soloist will be a challenge before the cadenza, which requires triple tonguing and extended range that alludes to the opening of the work, before the D. S. returns to the optimistic allegro. This work remains a good choice for those looking for a short solo with wind band that highlights the lyrical and technical abilities of the instrument. The accompaniment would require an excellent high school group or better. Recorded by Roger Behrend.

Buchtel, F. *Meditation.* Euphonium solo and wind band.

Burger, Alfred. *Gute Fahrt.* Spaeth/Schmid. Tenor horn duet and wind band. €35. German-style work.

Burger, Alfred. *Zwei Gute Freunde.* Spaeth/Schmid. Tenor horn duet and wind band. €35. German-style work.

Burger, Alfred. *Zwei Sonny Boys.* Spaeth/Schmid. Tenor horn duet and wind band. €35. German-style work.

Camphouse, Mark. *Poeme.* U.S. Army Band. Euphonium solo and wind band.

Chopin, Fredric. *Minute Waltz.* Arr. David Werden. Cimarron Music. Euphonium solo and wind band. $26. IV. A brief work highlighting one of Chopin's more famous compositions. The solo part is very technical.

Clarke, Herbert L. *Bride of the Waves.* Arr. Arthur Brandenburg. Warner Brothers (featured in the *Best of Herbert L. Clarke* solos collection and individually). Euphonium solo and wind band (piano reduction available). 5:00. III. A–b♭′ (c′). A classic from the turn-of-the-century repertoire. Features scalar cadenzas, polka-themed melodies, and multiple tonguing, and requires good agility. Recorded by Brian Bowman, David Werden.

Clarke, Herbert L. *Debutante.* Warner Brothers (featured in the *Best of Herbert L. Clarke* solos collection and individually). Euphonium solo and wind band (piano reduction available). 5:00. III. E–b♭′ (e♭″). Another classic work that contains triple tonguing, great scope for interpretation, and a need for great agility. Recorded by John Swallow.

Clarke, Nigel. *The City in the Sea.* Maacenas Music. Euphonium solo and wind band (brass band and piano reduction available). $200 ($45, $32.95). 16:00. V. CC♯–c″. To Robert Childs and the Black Dyke Mills Band. One of the most demanding solos from a range and power standpoint, *The City in the Sea* takes its programmatic nature from a poem by Edgar Allen Poe depicting a coastal town that is taken by the sea. The work can be described as ethereal, barbaric, and intense. It opens with a low foghorn-type call from the soloist on low DD, followed by some melodic material in the pedal range before a sudden three and half octave jump to a c″ that becomes a reoccurring motive. The melodic writing creates an appropriate uneasy feeling before the three and half octave motive returns and the powerful section ensues with very rapid tonguing, range shifts, and technical runs. The haunting lyrical theme alternates with the barbaric section a number of times, each time growing in power. The soloist will spend much time working on octave jumps and the awkward fingerings and difficult rhythms. This work is not for the faint of heart. Requirements are a strong extreme low range, agility of rapid interval jumps of more than two octaves, and of course the needed dynamic power to balance a thickly textured accompaniment. Recorded by David Childs, Robert Childs.

Corwell, Neal. *Adagio and Scherzo from Sinfonietta.* Nicolai Music. Euphonium solo and wind band (symphony orchestra and piano reduction available). 1999. $75 ($80). This set of two movements from his larger work that is annotated in the Music for Euphonium and Orchestra chapter.

Corwell, Neal. *Dandy Noodles.* Tuba-Euphonium Press. Euphonium solo and wind band (piano and CD accompaniment available). 4:47. IV. FF–c″. A very fun, lighthearted solo that with the CD has a load of fun sounds that include duck calls, leg slaps, muted trumpet, and others. In the band version these are captured by various instruments. There are also some amusing quotes from well-known orchestral works and predictable swing patterns. A recommended fun piece that works for something slightly comic and entertaining.

Corwell, Neal. *Of the Water.* Tuba-Euphonium Press. 1999. Euphonium solo and wind band (chamber orchestra available). $75 ($80). 14:30. IV–V. GG–d″. Written in two movements: Into the Depths and The Water's Journey. Commissioned by the Garrett Lakes Arts Festival. The first movement features a number of muted sections and use of the low range, capturing colors that allude to its title. It is oftentimes lyrical but contains an undercurrent of rhythmic energy from the repeated figures in the accompaniment. The Water's Journey features the technical passages with a quick tempo and often utilizing 7/8 meter. There are numerous trills and some tremolos in the extreme high range. An interesting work with a nice programmatic theme.

Corwell, Neal. *Venetian Carnival of Animals.* Nicolai Music. Euphonium solo and wind band (CD accompaniment available). 7:15. IV. EEb–c″. This clever work juxtaposes two famous animal tunes: "The Carnival of Venice" (the doggy in the window) and "The Elephant" from Saint-Saens's *Carnival of Animals.* The solo requires a wide range to provide the necessary comic relief as well as the virtuosity to bring off the Arban variations of the Carnival with smooth élan. An entertaining work for which it may be difficult to keep the player from smiling during the performance!

Cosma, Vladimir. *Euphonium Concerto.* Lam Larghetto. Euphonium solo and wind band (symphony orchestra, brass band, and piano reduction available). 2000 (written in 1998). Rental (Rental, Rental, $75). 21:00. V. DDb–d″. Written for the 1998 World Tuba Euphonium Competition in Guebwiller, France. Written in three movements: Allegro assai; Andantino; Finale-Giocoso. One of the most challenging and rewarding solos in the repertoire, this concerto embodies in many ways the spirit of Paganini and Liszt for the euphonium and represents one of the most outstanding selections for euphonium and large ensemble. It features virtuoso technique, intense melody, and a need for panache and flair. The technical and range challenges are formidable, but WELL worth the practice. Of particular note are the flexibility, clarity, and tone quality needed in the low range from BBb to F, as there are numerous sections of slurred and tongued passages in these ranges. There is also a strong need for excellent

double and triple tonguing, as Cosma wrote the final few sections with the violin (his instrument) in mind versus the euphonium, so some of the passages are not as idiomatic as they could be. The Andantino creates an atmosphere mindful of Piazzolla, the famous tango writer. The melody sails with the euphonium. This piece stands at the top of the list of recommended repertoire for those capable. Taking this challenge will be extremely rewarding and the only caveat involves the cost of the large ensemble rental parts (more than $400) and the piano reduction. The publisher has chosen to make these choices and they greatly hinder the wide spread of this fantastic work. Recorded by Adam Frey, Ivan Milheit, Tennessee Tech Tuba Euphonium Ensemble (third movement only), and Steven Mead.

Cummings, Barton. *Autumn Air.* Barton Cummings. Euphonium solo and wind band. 2002. 5:00. III. (Eb) eb–ab′. For Tom Betts. Tempo rubato, moderato ballad. Opening with a quasi cadenza, this work provides a brief, accessible jazz ballad-style work for the euphonium. The accompaniment has some difficult moments of sixteenth notes that mirror those played by the soloist.

Curnow, James. *Concerto for Euphonium.* Curnow Music Press. Euphonium solo and wind band (orchestra available). 1997. $129 (Rental). 12:10. IV–V. D–c″ (eb″). Written in three movements: Adagio moderato e caloroso; Andante moderato e molto espressivo; Allegro con brio. Commissioned by DEG Music Products, Inc. and the Willson Band Instrument Company and composed for and dedicated to Roger Behrend. The overall form of this work is three segue movements linked with extended cadenzas as transitions. The work contains Curnow's tonal melodic writing coupled with his panache at showing the technical virtuosity of the euphonium. The work contains numerous *ossias* to allow the range extremes to be more easily negotiated as needed by the soloist. The composition opens lyrically and moves to a more spirited section that features some difficult sixteenth note runs. The cadenza that transitions to the second movement features extended range and some motives from earlier in the first movement. The second movement contains an angular theme with a number of variations and interplay between the soloist and principal ensemble positions. The cadenza moving to the rondo form final movement features more difficult fingering patterns, but similar range extremes from D–db″. The final movement highlights a light 6/8 tarantella-like theme that focuses on the pitch center of G with many runs to d″. The range issues will be the most common hurdles with this work. The technique remains scalar and idiomatic and should be easy to overcome. This work will provide a good opportunity to showcase the euphonium in a composition by a well-known composer.

Curnow, James. *Prayer.* Curnow Music Press. Euphonium solo and wind band. 2000. $64. 7:00. III. F–g'. Commissioned by Dr. Grady Hallman, MD. Curnow has made a fantastic arrangement of the *Prayer (O Divine Redeemer)* from Gonoud's oratorio, *La Redemption.* This setting captures the lyrical qualities of the euphonium and given Curnow's excellent experience with bands of all ages, the accompaniment parts remain accessible for younger groups. A fine lyrical solo work.

Curnow, James. *Rhapsody for Euphonium.* Tuba-Euphonium Press (Winwood Music–brass band and piano). Euphonium solo and wind band (brass band and piano reduction available). 1990. $80. 6:30. III. A–a¹. To Leonard Falcone. Written in four sections of slow-fast-slow-fast, the Curnow *Rhapsody* remains a core component of the repertoire for level III. It features an excellent balance of melodic playing and technical passages. An opening cadenza leads to a lyrical statement characteristic of Curnow's tonal writing. The lines are easy to shape and lend themselves to musical phrasing education. The allegro con spirito boasts an energetic accompaniment figure before the euphonium enters on a stately theme. Some sixteenth note sequences provide transition material to the next section, which has similar motives with some syncopated feel. There is a brief restatement of the lyrical theme before a transition section that contains a number of chromatic sequences and sixteenth note chromatic scales returns the player back to the high-energy tempo. The ending five bars feature a strong maestoso section. The *Rhapsody* represents an excellent work that high school students can use as a solo vehicle with an easier accompaniment figure. Recorded by Cédric Albiez, Tyronne Breuninger, Roger Behrend, the Childs Brothers, Phillip Franke, Andre Grainger, Steven Mead, David Welsh, Joseph Zuback.

Curnow, James. *Symphonic Variants.* Curnow Music Press (Tuba-Euphonium Press). Euphonium solo and wind band (symphony orchestra, brass band, and piano reduction available). 1984. $129 ($100, Manuscript, $24). 19:00. V. DD–c″ (f″²). Introduction; Theme and Variations: Allegro con brio; Allegro moderato con espressivo; Allegro con spirito; Lento con teneramente; Presto; Adagio con calore; Allegro maestoso; Peasante. One of the core repertoire works for the euphonium and also one of the most demanding works ever written for the instrument, *Symphonic Variants* runs the gamut of technical facility, range, endurance, and power to project and balance. The difficulties will mainly be annotated as the work should be a standard piece in an advanced player's library. This superb work opens with a flourish of technique and runs to c″ before presenting the lyrical theme. There are numerous *ossia* throughout the work that make the very high

tessitura more accessible. The opening theme has an optional d″ and e♭″. All this is less than one minute from the start of a nearly twenty-minute work! Variation 1, Allegro con brio, hosts a lively 6/8 version with a run down to GG. Variation 2, Lento con teneramente, exposes the soloist on some high-range entrances as well as some rapid range shifts over three octaves in the course of two measures (albeit at a slow tempo). A very nice rubato section brings this variation to a close. The Presto highlights the agility of euphonium with a bountiful number of sixteenth notes and double tonguing during the entire variation. There are numerous presentations of the motives that jump octaves between beats with many *ossias.* A long chromatic run to c″ with a diminuendo leads to the Adagio con calore. Curnow writes this lyrical section very well to suit the euphonium. It leads smoothly into the Allegro maestoso, a slower sixteenth note variation in a stately style that returns the opening material before a calm Peasante allows the soloist, accompaniment, and audience to wind up to the final powerful notes that feature an optional f″. The accompaniment parts are difficult and thickly textured. Great projection and balance will be needed by the soloist to balance. This is one of the most physical works in the repertoire and one of the standard works frequently performed. Recorded by Roger Behrend, Brian Bowman, Mary Ann Craig, Marik Denys, Phil Franke, Shoichiro Hokazono, Angie Hunter, Steven Mead, Robin Taylor.

Dammicco. *Soleado.* Harry Schneiders. EMR. Euphonium solo and wind band. 1974. 100 CHF. III.

Dammicco. *Tränen lügen nicht.* Harry Schneiders. EMR. Euphonium solo and wind band. 1974. 100 CHF. III.

Daniels, M. L. *Concertino for Euphonium and Band.* Tuba-Euphonium Press. Euphonium solo and wind band (piano reduction available). 1989. $40. 8:20. IV. G–d♭″. Written in a modified ABA form with the A sections serving as the faster outer movements and the B section as a slow, lyrical divider, this work opens with an energetic sixteenth pick-up motive in the solo part featuring a rising major sixth interval. This figure goes through a number of keys through the work. The bands parts look playable by a good high school–level group and the solo part is not overly demanding. There are two brief moments where the range goes above b♭' for the soloist, but these could easily be lowered to accommodate range limitations. This work is published in manuscript.

Danks, H. P. *Silberfäden.* Harry Schneiders. EMR. Euphonium solo and wind band. 2000. 100 CHF. III.

David. Ferdinand. *Concertino.* EMR. Euphonium solo and wind band (piano available). 1997. 190 CHF. IV. A fine transcription of the famous trombone solo.

Davis. *Variations on a Theme by Schumann.* Spaeth/ Schmid. Euphonium and wind band. €76.50. This is a variation on the *Happy Farmer* theme. A fun work indeed.

Davis, Albert O. *Desert Star.* Ludwig Music Company. Euphonium solo and wind band (piano reduction available).

Dedenon, Sylvain. *Concerto.* Spaeth/Schmid. Euphonium and wind band. €92.

Delago. *Tenorhorn Polka.* Seifert. Spaeth/Schmid. Tenor horn and wind band. €92.

Delago, H. *Tenorhorn Polka.* Arr. R. Seifert. FEST-MUSIK-HAUS. Euphonium solo and wind band.

Delbecq. *Consonnances.* Spaeth/Schmid. Tenor horn and wind band. €58.50.

DeLuca, Joseph. *Beautiful Colorado.* Carl Fischer. Baritone (euphonium) solo and wind band (piano reduction). 1924. Out of Print ($8.50 piano). 5:10. IV. A–b♭'. A waltz-style work typical of the Sousa Band era with an opening cadenza, ascending melody in triple meter, and ornamented technical sections. Much of the piece uses scalar and arpeggiated figures. One of the best-known stylized pieces from this period, it is a highly recommended work commonly performed on a double-belled euphonium. Recorded by Leonard Falcone, Arthur Lehman, Earle Louder, Steven Mead, John Mueller, Robert Reifsnyder.

DeLuca, Joseph. *Beautiful Colorado.* Arr. Stanley Boddington. Studio Music. Euphonium solo and wind band. 5:10. III. A waltz-style work typical of the Sousa Band era with an opening cadenza, ascending melody in triple meter, and ornamented technical sections. Commonly performed on a double-belled euphonium. Recorded by Trevor Groom, David Lean.

DeLuca, Joseph. *Sentimentale.* Jonathan Smith. Lismore Music. Euphonium solo and wind band. 4:25. IV. G–c″. "This solo contains all of the excitement and technical virtuosity that one would expect of a DeLuca solo. *Sentimentale* would be most appropriate for the college level performer or perhaps the adult community band soloist due to the stylistic demands of the piece and its range and endurance demands. Listening to solos of this era will certainly help in the preparation of this piece. This piece is of the same mold and character of *Beautiful Colorado* but definitely has more contrast, more lyricism, and more interesting cadenzas."—Lismore Music. Recorded by Leonard Falcone.

DeLuca, Joseph. *Thoughts of Gold.* Carl Fischer. Baritone (euphonium) solo and wind band (piano reduction). 1930. Out of Print ($4 piano). III. G–a'. To Edward J. Heney, Saxophone Soloist Sousa's Band. A waltz-stylee work typical of the Sousa Band era with an opening cadenza, an ornamented melody in triple meter, and rapid technical sections. A recommended work for level III.

Dietersen. *Gute Laune.* Spaeth/Schmid. Tenor horn trio and wind band. €41. German-style work.

Dinser. *Fantasy für Tenorhorn.* Spaeth/Schmid. Tenor horn and wind band. €26. German-style work.

Dörle. *Zwiegespräch im Walde.* Spaeth/Schmid. Tenor horn and wind band. €31.50. German-style work.

Edelson, Edward. *Autumn Twilight.* C & E Enterprises. Euphonium solo and wind band (piano reduction). 2001. $5.50. 3:30. I–II. c–e♭'. An easier work in G minor with very tonal harmonies and scalar melodic material appropriate for younger students.

Edelson, Edward. *Let's Beguine.* C & E Enterprises. Euphonium solo and wind band (piano reduction). 1987. $6.50. 3:30. II. Low D–e. An easier work based in G major (with a key signature for C) with very tonal harmonies and scalar melodic material appropriate for younger students. More accidentals and eighth notes than *Autumn Twilight.*

Elkos, Jonathan. *El Camino Real.* Southern Music. Euphonium solo and wind band.

Ellerby, Martin. *Euphonium Concerto.* Studio Music. Euphonium solo and wind band (symphony orchestra, brass band, and piano reduction available). 1997. Rental only (£10.50 piano). 22:00. V GG–e♭″. Four movements: Fantasy; Capriccio; Rhapsody (for Luis); Diversions. Commissioned by and dedicated to Steven Mead. One of THE most challenging works in the repertoire, the Ellerby *Euphonium Concerto* can be summed up as an exploration in the technical limits of the euphonium in regards to range, dexterity, and endurance. Attention to detail is a must in all movements as Ellerby clearly marks articulation and dynamic nuances. The Fantasy features the alternation of an energetic rising theme, sometimes slurred and sometimes tongued, with a beautiful melodic section. The Capriccio is the most demanding technically and rhythmically with inventive rhythmic figures and difficult fingering combinations. One of these great moments occurs as the 12/8 theme shifts from triplet to duple subdivisions. The writing can be described as melodic and motivic with a very wide palette of harmonic and melodic colors in an angular style. The chromatic appearance does not translate to chromatic-sounding harmony. A muted section occurs in the middle of the second movement. The Rhapsody (for Luis) hosts one of the best examples of lyrical euphonium writing. Dedicated to Luis Maldanado, this movement's buildup and climax leading to a d″ remains one of the most memorable moments in the euphonium's repertoire. The writing and interplay between soloist and ensemble make this movement a joy to perform, and the final repeated d's in the solo line pay homage to another great lyrical euphonium concerto by Horovitz. Diversions could be described as approximately five minutes of pure, intense rhythmic drive. From its opening accompaniment figure played by the band, which sets the pace, this movement places large technical demands on the soloist including rapid tonguing, optional multi-phonics, highly articulated figures in extreme ranges, traversing more than two octaves in a single bar, and ending with glissandi up to e♭″. One of the masterpieces of the euphonium repertoire, this concerto will require lots of practice and strength. The ensemble parts are also very difficult and a good conductor will be needed. Alternate fingerings will make the solo part clearer and easier. Recorded by Adam Frey, Steven Mead, Brian Meixner.

Eschoborn. *Tenorhorn Swing*. Spaeth/Schmid. Tenor horn trio and wind band. €31. German-style work.

Ewazen, Eric. *Concerto for Euphonium*. Southern Music Company. Euphonium solo and wind band (piano reduction). 20:00. IV. BB♭–b″. Commissioned by and dedicated to Robert Grechesky and the Butler University Wind Ensemble. Written in three movements: Allegro Moderato; Andante Teneremente; Allegro Vivace. This work from the esteemed Ewazen opens with a pleasant and light theme that weaves through the soloist and ensemble as it modulates, alters slightly, and transforms. The second movement contains the most lyrical writing of the concerto, but it often has the euphonium providing a more florid line. The final movement is cast in 6/8 and has a light dancing feel, with the most technical challenges of the work. The tempo could certainly be taken such as to make it quite virtuosic or quite relaxed. This work with its length and reserved character may be difficult to find many performance opportunities for because it does not have as much audience appeal as many other solos, but it represents one of few works of substantial duration that does not have an incredibly difficult solo part.

Faure, Gabriel. *Tuscan Serenade*. Grainger. Spaeth/ Schmid. Euphonium and wind band. €122.50. A well-known melody with band accompaniment.

Feliciangeli, Frode. *Preghiera for Euphonium and Band*. Manuscript.

Ferstl, Herbert. *Alpenklänge*. Georg Bauer. Tenor horn trio and wind band. 1987. 4:25. III. c–a♭′. A waltz-style trio with easy parts for both the trio and the band. Written in a lilting style throughout, the second part only ascends to an f′ and the third to a d♭′. A unique and fun choice to feature a trio.

Ferstl, Herbert. *Bergsteiger (Mountain Climbers' Polka)*. FEST-MUSIK-HAUS. Euphonium trio and wind band. III. A fun and easy trio that captures a German spirit. Great for a concert theme or lighter encore work. It could easily work with a trio of most brass instruments.

Ferstl, Herbert. *Bravour-Polka*. Georg Bauer. Tenor horn solo and wind band. 1987. €45. 4:25. III–IV.

B♭–c″. A more demanding work from the German/ Austrian repertoire. It highlights an oompah style of the polka with some exciting double tonguing and technical runs. There are some rhythmic challenges with sixteenth note passages grouped in sets of three. Otherwise, a straight-forward solo that is stylistically unique.

Ferstl, Herbert. *Ein fideles trio*. Spaeth/Schmid. Tenor horn trio and wind band. €48. A German-style work.

Ferstl, Herbert. *Rigadon and Musette*. Georg Bauer. Tenor horn solo and wind band. 1987. €38.50. 4:38. II–III. B♭–g′. Written in two movements: Rigadon and Musette. Written in cut time, the Rigadon has a light fun style that will capture a young player's attention. The writing has some tongued intervals of a fourth that might prove a challenge for younger players and has a few trace elements of J. S. Bach. The Musette is in 3/4 time and offers a good opportunity to discuss style and phrasing. This solo would benefit many young players.

Filas, Juraj. *Concerto for Euphonium*. Euphonium solo and wind band (symphony orchestra and piano reduction available). 2002. Rental (Rental, $20). 17:00. VI–V. D♭–d♭″ (d″). One movement, four major sections: grave; allegro vivo; grave; allegro. Commissioned for the Concours mondial de Tuba et d'Euphonium 2003 de Guebwiller. A challenging work that will gain great understanding when combined with the accompaniment, the Filas *Concerto for Euphonium* features numerous trill figures in the opening section including some on the low D♭. The melodic writing is idiomatic and enjoyable along with some interesting rhythmic figures that will require close attention to timing and subdivision. A neat motive that Filas utilizes involves a nice descending sextuplet figure that links sections and returns twice more. The allegro vivo hosts an ascending staccato eighth note theme that later morphs into a raising half note figure with emphatic sixteenth and dotted eighth figures. The section can be felt in two, although written in 4/4. Twice a lyrical allegro vivo theme appears and then modulates to the high tessitura reaching up as high as d″. The high modulations have an optional 8va lower ad-lib. The work closes with a revisit to the opening material in a different key. A high declamatory figure with stringendo brings the work to a finish with a syncopated two-octave leap to a′. This concerto will find merit in the euphonium repertoire and has a style and harmonic language its own as a positive feature. While all solos need the accompaniment parts to make complete sense, this work perhaps needs it more to bring out the comprehensive musical statement.

Forsstrom, Timo. *Majakkasaari*. Blosari. Euphonium solo and wind band.

Forte, Aldo Rafael. *Canzonetta for Euphonium and Band*. Ludwig Music Company. Euphonium solo and wind band. $65. III. Written for the United States Air Force Air Combat Heritage of America Band. This work features a lyrical solo line with a limited range along with rhythmic punctuation by the accompanying ensemble. Forte has written numerous superb works for the euphonium and tuba, especially ensemble works. Recorded by Barbara Taylor.

Foster, Stephen. *Gentle Annie*. Manuscript. Euphonium and cornet duet with wind band. III.

Foster, Stephen. *My Old Kentucky Home*. Yasuhide Ito. Yamaha Kyohan Co. Ltd.

Frackenpohl, Arthur. *Divertimento*. Tuba-Euphonium Press. Euphonium solo and wind band. 1995. $90. 12:00. IV. (Bb) F–c'' (db''). Written in three movements: March; Song; Gallop. Written for George Krem. This work has quite a high tessitura for the duration of the piece and will require good endurance. The solo part is written mainly in tenor clef and requires multiple tonguing. The March has a fanfare feeling to it and has some technically demanding areas. The Song has an optional muted opening and some of the scales have a slight jazz influence. The Gallop has a light feel with many runs. The writing is idiomatic and not overly difficult.

Frackenpohl, Arthur. *Song and Dance*. Tuba-Euphonium Press. Euphonium solo, tuba solo, and wind band. 1994. $85. 9:15. III–IV. d–bb' (c''), tuba GG–c'. Commissioned by Roy Holder and the Lake Braddock Symphonic Band. Written in two movements: Song (4:30) and Dance (4:45). The tuba solo opens with a melody that the euphonium restates one octave higher. The parts intertwine nicely before both parts have small cadenzas that lead back to the slower lyrical part. In the euphonium cadenza there is an *ossia* for the c''. The Dance movement has a slight "rag" feel to it. This movement relies on clever interplay and "question and answer" segments between the soloists and the band. The parts are rhythmic and require some technical dexterity. The work would be an excellent choice for high school–level groups that want to feature the euphonium and tuba.

François, Claude. *My Way*. Hardy Schneiders. EMR. Euphonium solo and wind band. 2000. 100 CHF. III. A nice arrangement of the song made famous by Frank Sinatra.

Gabriel. *Bariton Gaudi*. Seifert. FEST-MUSIK-HAUS. Euphonium solo and wind band.

Gaines, David. *Concertino*. Verda Stelo Music. Euphonium solo and wind band. 1999. 13:00. IV–V. BBb–c''. Written in four movements: A Jester's Promenade; A Shadow in the Dark Green Depths; A Song for All Seasons; A Half Dream Glowing. This work features some difficult rhythmic interaction and awkward finger patterns. The writing remains idiomatic but occasionally has wide intervals. Each movement holds a very unique character. The melodic and harmonic

styles are chromatic. The first movement features many sixteenth notes and energy. The second movement contains an atmospheric section with the euphonium providing a few moments of interjection. The third movement boasts a quick tempo and numerous meter changes involving 6/8, 5/8, and 7/8. The forth movement brings back the esoteric mood and evokes a dream-like feeling with lyrical lines with occasional wide interval leaps. The piece ends on a long sustained eb'.

Gershwin, George. *Summertime*. Hardy Schneiders. EMR. Euphonium solo and wind band. 2000. 100 CHF. III. A nice arrangement of the famous song from *Porgy and Bess*.

Gillingham, David. *Vintage*. Tuba-Euphonium Press. Euphonium solo and wind band (brass band in manuscript and piano reduction available). 1991. $75 ($12). 9:15. VI–V. D–c'' (DD–eb''). One of the staples of the euphonium and wind band repertoire, *Vintage* combines an intensely rhythmic and beautifully lyrical work with moments of intense power and majesty. From the opening chords and melodic statement by the soloist, the tonal harmonic colors swell to a climax on high c before a slightly aleatoric section featuring percussion leads to the quick and highly syncopated allegro. This section requires strong rhythmic discipline and ensemble given the independence of the solo and accompaniment lines. This section is interspersed through the rest of the piece between more lyrical interludes featuring the melodic high range of the euphonium. An extended cadenza occurs before the last few bars. It has numerous optional cuts to accommodate range issues, but does allow the adventurous a span of over four octaves before a flurry of meter changes and rising figures bring the piece to a triumphant finish. *Vintage* is a highly recommended work that requires strong endurance and experienced ensemble. Recorded by Roger Behrend, Shoichiro Hokazono, Steven Mead, Brian Meixner.

Glorieux, François. *Fantasy*. Glorious Sounds. Euphonium solo and wind band (brass band, orchestra, and piano reduction available). 2001. €100 (€90, €70, €12). 7:10. VI. Gb–c². Lento; Allegro con brio; Cadenza; Lento; Presto. This is the most demanding work by Glorieux and scored for all possible performance mediums so it remains a great choice for programmability. The composition contains Glorieux's signature listenable harmonies and melodies. The opening Lento lines set a relaxed atmosphere before the energetic and rhythmic Allegro con brio sixteenth note theme enters that poses some challenges to the soloist with its shapes and double tonguing. The extended Cadenza lasting approximately 1:40 will be the hurdle to make it interesting to the listener. A beautiful theme ensues afterward, leading to the exuberant tarantella in the Presto climaxing to the final high c to finish the work. This piece should be performed more often and remains one of Glorieux's best showpieces. Recorded by Nick Ost.

Golland, John. *Euphonium Concerto No. 1.* Chester. Euphonium solo and wind band (brass band and piano available). 1982. (Rental only brass band and wind band, £10.50 piano). 18:00. IV–V. D–e♭″. Written in three segue movements: Cadenza-Lento; Andante tranquillo; Allegro. This concerto remains one of the most rewarding and demanding concerti because of range, duration, and dynamics needed to balance ensemble. The opening cadenza covers two and half octaves (quickly). The first movement also features a large amount of technical interplay between band and soloist. There are moments of clever interjection and wonderful lyrical hemiolas. There is a significant cadenza that highlights triple tonguing, high tessitura, and rhythmic intensity before the lush 5/8 second movement begins. This movement emphasizes the rising octave and high-range control and contains some exquisite writing for the euphonium. It may certainly be one of the most heartfelt melodic moments in the entire repertoire and works well individually. The exciting Allegro features mixed meter, multiple tonguing, and a jovial nature. The shift from style to style helps hasten the work to the conclusion. A reprise of the opening cadenza with some development propels the work to the final coda. This work is highly recommended. Recorded by Robert Childs, Steven Mead. Ryuji Ushigami.

Golland, John. *Euphonium Concerto No. 2.* Studio Music. Euphonium solo and wind band (brass band and piano available). Rental (£10.50). 1992. 23:00. V. (DD) BB♭–e♭″ (b♭″). To Nicholas and Robert Childs. Written in three movements: Moderato Eroico; Largo Elegaico (In Memoriam: John Childs); Allegro energico e Scherzando. The second major work Golland has written for the euphonium, this composition is much more demanding than his *Euphonium Concerto No. 1.* There are many technical challenges in regards to fast runs, complex rhythms, leaps spanning between one and three octaves, rapid multiple tonguing, and the endurance necessary for the high tessitura that the work so aptly exploits. The work opens heroically and the first movement features many glissandos to c″ and technical passages moving sequentially. An extended cadenza features some contemporary notation, but make no mistake that the work is romantically based. The closing cadenza segues to the second movement; however, an optional ending to the first movement is included for performances that only features the first movement. The Largo Elegaico captures Golland's skills and knowledge of the euphonium as a lyrical tenor with grace, sensitivity, and passion. The recitative

sections feature sweeping runs and elegant technical passages before the introspective melody takes hold of the heart. The recitative section returns with some extended development before the main melody returns to be played tenderly in the extreme high range (c″ and d♭″). The final movement opens with a waltz feel, muted section and relies heavily on rapid triple tonguing of both repeated figures and difficult moving figures. There are also a number of high-range glissandos that reach nearly imperceptible heights from e♭″ to b♭″. Golland's *Concerto No. 1* may be more accessible to soloist and audience than the *Concerto No. 2,* but the later work provides fun challenges technically and musically that are worthwhile endeavors for performance. This work is definitely worth study but will be a challenge. Recorded by Ueli Kipfer, Steven Mead (second movement only).

Gorb, Adam. *Concerto for Euphonium.* Maceanes Music. Euphonium solo and wind band. 1997. $160. 15:30. IV. GG–b′. Written in two movements: Largo and Allegro Molto. The opening movement highlights the lyrical characteristics of the euphonium with its opening ascending line from pedal b♭. There are sections of 5/8 and 4/8. An unusual feature of the accompaniment near the end of the work requires the brass to remove mouthpieces and blow on their instruments while the woodwinds clatter their keys. The euphonium plays the last page with a mute and gradually descends quietly to GG to finish the work. This work may not be the most appropriate choice for this genre of serious music, but there are moments of enjoyment and Gorb's reputation continues to grow rapidly among wind band conductors.

Gott, Barrie. *From the Heart.* Muso's Media. Euphonium solo and wind band (brass band and piano reduction available). 2003. $85 Australian ($50 and $20 Australian). 3:00. III. A♭–b♭′. Written for Riki McDonnell. A short light work with a Latin groove and style. The accompaniment parts are rhythmic with an occasional melodic motive and the euphonium melody features an ascending octave. In the middle section, the soloist plays sixteenth note obligato patterns before returning to the main theme in the new key of A♭. This work is a welcome addition to the repertoire in the vein of lighter, short works. It would be perfect for a high school band looking for an easy accompaniment.

Gottolober. *Uber berg und tal.* Spaeth/Schmid. Tenor horn and wind band. €18. A German-style work.

Graham, Peter. *Bravura.* Gramercy Music. Euphonium solo and wind band (brass band and piano reduction). 2003. £59.95 (£24.95). 5:00. IV. G–c″ (f″). Written as a fantasia based on four traditional themes of Great Britain, *Bravura* combines a superb showpiece with traditional melodies. The solo part features numerous *ossia* that allow the soloist to ascend to the high range as desired. The technical demands will be the challenge in this work with rapid triple tongued passages, overall high tessitura, and running sixteenths in the final section. This work will be enjoyed by many audiences and hopefully by the soloist with all the needed preparation.

Graham, Peter. *Brillante.* Winwood Music. Euphonium solo (optional duet) and wind band (brass band, symphony orchestra, and piano reduction). 1987. (Piano £17.95). 6:00. IV. F–c″ (e♭″). Written as a fantasia based on the traditional melody *Rule Britannia, Brillante* highlights the technical powers of the euphonium. These demands will be the challenge in this work with rapid triple tongued passages, overall high tessitura, and running sixteenths as the final section. This work will be enjoyed by many audiences and is a great choice as a modern theme and variations. Recorded by the Childs Brothers, David Childs, Adam Frey, Robert Jose, David Thornton, Glyn Williams.

Graham, Peter. *The Name.* Gramercy. Euphonium solo and wind band. III. A lovely lyrical work.

Guilmant, Alexandre. *Morceau Symphonique.* John Mortimer. EMR. Euphonium solo and wind band. 1999. 100 CHF. III–IV. A nice arrangement of the well-known trombone solo that is a standard in both the euphonium and trombone repertoire. It features lush romantic harmonies and wonderful scalar technique coupled with great musical demands and range requirements. Recorded by Fred Dart, Leonard Falcone.

Haase-Altendorf. *Konzert.* Spaeth/Schmid. Tenor horn and wind band. €59.50. A German-style work.

Hackl. *Der Lustige Soloist.* Spaeth/Schmid. Tenor horn and wind band. €18.50. A German-style work.

Hartley, Walter. *Euphonium Concerto.* Accura Music. Euphonium solo and wind band (piano reduction available). 1984 (written in 1980). $108 ($11.50). 12:00. IV–V. (FF) D♭–d″ (f″). Commissioned by and dedicated to Glenn Call and *Euphonia* magazine. Written in three movements: Allegro; Andante; Presto. This work features contemporary harmonies and melodies with a strong slant toward a twelve-tone palette. The writing is quite rhythmic in the outer movements and many accidentals will require the performer to know the work very well to be secure on the patterns and runs. While this work does not have the most audience appeal, it still features some unique contemporary flavors and might be suitable for a performance with those goals. The writing also utilizes tenor clef regularly. This concerto provides a good piano reduction that would probably serve as the best performance medium.

Hartwig, Hans. *Der froliche Solist (The Happy Solist).* FEST-MUSIK-HAUS. Euphonium solo and wind band. 4:10. III. e♭–a♭′. A short light work that has an opening cadenza. It contains no major challenges and has a pleasant polka quality to it.

Heath, Reginald. *Andante and Scherzo.* Spaeth/Schmid. Euphonium solo and brass band. €79.50. A British brass band composition written in two parts that holds lyrical qualities and technical qualities owing to its name.

Hidas, Frigyes. *Euphoniada.* Johann Kliment. Euphonium solo and wind band (piano reduction available). 1996. €93. Hidas has written numerous low brass works that have been well received. Based on his history, this work should be a recommended composition.

Hiden. *Der lustige Schuster.* Spaeth/Schmid. Tenor horn and wind band. €79.50.

Hill, William. *Concerto for Euphonium.* Manuscript (California State University–Los Angeles). Euphonium solo and wind band. 1978. 15:00. IV. C–d″. Commissioned by and dedicated to Dennis Royall. Written in three movements. This work will be difficult to obtain, but its second movement remains noteworthy. There are no major obstacles to the soloist other than some technical dexterity issues. The final movement contains a series of modulations of similar material. This work would be appropriate for a graduate-level recital but does not provide a virtuosic showpiece with a lighter character.[1] Recorded by Loren Marsteller and Dennis Royall.

Hornez. *Qu'est-ce qu'on attend.* EMR. Euphonium solo and wind band. 100 CHF. III.

Horovitz, Joseph. *Euphonium Concerto.* Novello & Company Limited. Euphonium solo and wind band (brass band, orchestra, and piano available). 1991 (written in 1972). Rental only (orchestra rental only, £60 brass band, £10.50 piano). 16:00. IV. C–c″. Moderato; Lento; Con moto. Commissioned by the National Brass Band Championships of Great Britain. One of the first major concertos written for the euphonium, with each movement representing musical enjoyment for the head, heart, and toes, respectively. A piece of the standard repertoire, this concerto contains writing that will challenge and engage both performer and listener. The middle movement contains some of the most expressive lyrical writing in the repertoire. In the third movement, good technical facility will be needed as well as multiple tonguing for its jovial lighthearted nature. There are a number of dexterity challenges in this movement; thus, it is common to have younger players study the first two movements due to their significance even though they may not be ready to tackle the final movement. Horovitz provides extensive detail as to articulation, tempo, and dynamics. Orchestral parts are similar to a Mozart-type orchestra and provide an easy ensemble to balance. This is a highly recommended work. Recorded by Tyronne Breuninger,

Robert Childs, Trevor Groom, Eran Levy, Steven Mead, Thomas Rüedi, Robin Taylor.

Hovhaness, Alan. *Symphony No. 29, Opus 289*. Mount Tacoma Music Publishers. Euphonium solo and wind band (orchestra and piano reduction available). 1978. 18:00. III–IV. E–c″. Commissioned by Henry Charles Smith and C. G. Conn, Ltd. Written in four movements: Andante Religioso; Adagio Espressivo; Lento-Allegro-Moderate-Presto; Finale. One of the strongest musical statements written for the euphonium and wind band, the *Symphony No. 29* provides many great opportunities for the euphonium to demonstrate excellent lyrical and melodic capabilities. While the work does not contain many technical demands, the musicality, consistently high tessitura, phrasing, powerful dynamics, and sustained nature of the writing require a mature player. Knowing Hovhaness as a composer who explores the beauty of harmony and ambience, one will relish the wonderful tone colors and lovely chords that combine Western and Eastern concepts as well as some modal language. Each movement of this work could be performed individually as needed, but of course the entire work provides the fullest effect. This work should certainly be performed more regularly, but the parts can be difficult to obtain. Recorded by Christian Lindberg.

Hudec, Adam. *Golden Euphoniums*. Obrasso. Euphonium duet and wind band.

Hudec, Adam. *Tenoristenflirt*. Spaeth/Schmid. Tenor horn duet and wind band. €46.

Hultgren, Ralph. *Divertimento for Euphonium and Wind Orchestra*. Ralph Hultgren. 2004. 7:00. IV. "It is a work designed to be a series of conversations between the soloist and soloists and soli sections in the wind orchestra. It can be characterized as an amusement piece." —Ralph Hultgren.

Hydlgaard, Søren. *Bagetelle*. Dehaske Publishers. Euphonium solo and wind band. 2002. 3:00. Written for Jens Bjørn-Larsen. *Bagatelle* was written as an encore for a concert a few years ago in the Tivoli Gardens of Copenhagen. "Jens Bjørn-Larsen was the soloist that evening, and I simply could not resist this opportunity to write a simple, haunting piece that would bring out the soft and mild-mannered side of Jens' talent. Often playing in the alto register, he nearly makes the rotund tuba sing with an ethereal quality, not unlike a French horn playing *lontano*." —Søren Hydlgaard.

Israel, Brain. *Rhapsody*. Out of Print. Euphonium solo and wind band. 1983. 7:00. III–IV. E–b′. Commissioned by the Maine Endwell High School Band. Written as a tribute to a Maine Endwell High School euphonium player, Robert Gibbs, who died in a car accident. This work presents mainly musical challenges and has a strong symbolic gesture at the conclusion. After the final cadenza, the soloist leaves the stage performing a short repeated motive until the rest of the band have left the stage, and makes a final repetition of the theme to close the work. This work has great musical merit but will be difficult to obtain.[1]

Ito, Yasuhide. *Euphonium Concerto*. Studio Music. 2004. V. A live recording (music was not available but In preparation) provided a glimpse of this very challenging work with Ito's charm and wit. It will certainly occupy a place in the repertoire in future years.

Ito, Yasuhide. *Fantasy Variations*. Studio Music. Euphonium solo and wind band (piano reduction available). 1990. $275 ($25). 9:00. IV. FF–c″. Written in the form of a theme and variations, this work actually presents the variations before the theme. The variations are demanding and require no unusual techniques other than finesse and ease of playing. The first variation in 6/8 has a nice lilting mood and leads nicely to the more energetic 2/4 rondo with lots of interplay between soloist and accompaniment that still remains restrained in character but intense nonetheless. A brief cadenza incorporating double tonguing and the full extent of the range of the work finishes with the soloist holding a pedal F for eight bars as the true theme of the work emerges in the accompaniment. The soloist gets the opportunity to shape this beautiful pentatonic melody and provide a superb, soaring countermelody before a few moments of relaxing music leads to the final variation, a clever fugue in 6/8. The work concludes with a stellar coda section and a tour-de-force accompaniment that will excite performer and audience. This work is highly encouraged due to its unique melodic and harmonic character and should be performed much more often, but it can sometimes be difficult to obtain. Recorded by Roger Behrend, Adam Frey, Steven Mead.

Jacob, Gordon. *Fantasia for Euphonium and Band*. Boosey & Hawkes. Euphonium solo and wind band (brass band and piano reduction available). 1973. Rental (Rental, $20). 10:45. IV. (FF) CC♯–b♭′ (d″). Dedicated to Michael Mamminga. One of the earliest major works written for the euphonium, Jacob's *Fantasia* remains a standard work in the repertoire. Its haunting opening melody, fun and quirky allegro section, lyrical melodic writing, triple tonguing intensity, low muted section, and demanding cadenza make it a composition worthy of performance. There are numerous *ossias* to assist with range limitations and the technical demands will prove a challenge for many players, but this should certainly be a familiar piece for all serious euphonium players. Recorded by Anonymous, Bjorn Bogetvedt, Mary Ann Craig, Mark Fisher, Tormod Flaten, Shoichiro Hokazono, Steven Mead, Toru Miura, Wendy Picton, Thomas Runty, David Stowe, Robin Taylor, Ron Young.

Jager, Robert. *Concerto for Euphonium*. Marks/Hal Leonard. Euphonium solo and wind band (symphony orchestra and piano reduction available). 1995. Rental (Rental, $14). 12:00. IV–V. C–d♭″. Written in three movements: Slowly, Dramatically, Freely; Slowly, Reflectively; Brightly, but Forcefully. This challenging work features high-intensity writing that translates to complex rhythms and syncopations, flutter tonguing, lip trills, double tonguing, rapid meter changes, awkward trills, and sections in seven flats encapsulate most of the difficulties of the work. Yet its vigor and drive, especially in the third movement, can compensate the performer and listener for these challenges. The second movement has some nice recitative sections with ornamental runs. A strong addition to the more contemporary repertoire of the euphonium.

James, Woody. *Elegy*. Ludwig Music Company. Euphonium solo and wind band (piano reduction available). $35 ($6). III. A beautiful lyrical work utilizing some soft jazz harmonies.

Jirska. *Träumende Tenorhorner*. Spaeth/Schmid. Tenor horn and wind band. €18. A German-style work.

Juchelka, Watz. *Zwei böhmische Edelweiss*. Spaeth/ Schmid. Tenor horn duet and wind band. €28. A German-style work.

Kabec. *Enzian und Edelweiss*. Spaeth/Schmid. Tenor horn duet and wind band. €50.50. A German-style work.

Kabec. *Jockl' und Mochl'*. Spaeth/Schmid. Tenor horn duet and wind band. €28. A German-style work.

Kaempfert, Bert. *Strangers in the Night*. EMR. Euphonium solo and wind band. A setting of the tune made famous by Frank Sinatra.

Kaska, Kevin. *Euphonium Concertino*. Euphonium. com/ Horus Publications. Euphonium solo and wind band (piano reduction). 14:10 (cut version 6:45). V. D♭–f″. Written for Adam Frey and the Euphonium Foundation Consortium. This excellent work by the film music composer Kevin Kaska has a different sound than other euphonium works, with its strong influence of movie styles and traces of John Williams (one of Kaska's teachers). The solo part's main challenges involve the regular use of the high tessitura that gives the work a brilliant shine. However, this will challenge many players, especially since there are many smooth melodies incorporating notes about b♭′. There is liberal use of passages traversing two octaves in a single beat. The cut version captures the main body of the work and serves as a perfect length work for concerto competitions and shorter program lengths. There are also a number of *ossias* that make the work more accessible for players who want to experience the quality of this work. This work garners a high recommendation due to its unique sound and style compared with other similar works. Recorded by Adam Frey.

King, Karl. *Night in June*. Manuscript. Euphonium solo and wind band. III (V). A fine selection from the Sousa Band era. It has a split range part that allows this great melody to be accessible to high school levels as well as having the high tessitura available for the artist. Recorded by Arthur Lehman, Steven Mead. Thor-Arne Pederson, Ken Wood.

Klengel, Jules. *Concertino No.1 in B♭*. Leonard Falcone. Belwin-Mills (Tuba-Euphonium Press–piano). Euphonium solo and wind band (piano reduction). III–IV. This solo was promoted by Leonard Falcone and has made a rebirth with its use in numerous competitions. It is a recommended work and written in a romantic style. The range and technical demands are appropriate to the difficulty level of the work. Recorded by Brian Bowman, Fred Dart, Leonard Falcone, Steven Mead.

Koch. *Am Dorfbrunnen*. Spaeth/Schmid. Tenor horn duet and wind band. €25. A German-style work.

Kolasch. *Drei flotte Musikanten*. Spaeth/Schmid. Tenor horn duet and wind band. €24.50. A German-style work.

Kolditz. *Black and White*. Spaeth/Schmid. Tenor horn duet and wind band. €34. A German-style work.

Kolditz. *Boogie for Two*. Spaeth/Schmid. Tenor horn duet and wind band. €50. A German-style work.

Kolditz. *Concertino*. Spaeth/Schmid. Tenor horn and wind band. €46.50. A German-style work of duration.

Kolditz. *Lullaby*. Spaeth/Schmid. Tenor horn duet and wind band. €32. A lyrical German-style work.

Koper, Karl-Heinz. *Dulcamarata*. Manuscript. Euphonium solo and wind band. IV. One of the most challenging of the German-style works. The music can be difficult to obtain.

Krzywicki, Jan. *Ballade*. Heilman Music. Euphonium solo and wind band. 1983 (copyright in 1984). 5:00. III. E–e¹. An easy solo that was originally written for Jan's brother, Paul Krzywicki. The work demonstrates the wonderful singing style of the euphonium in the comfortable middle range. The accompaniment is also quite easy with some nice harmonic colors. A good choice for an easier solo with some contemporary melodic and harmonic language.

Kugler. *Fröhliche Polka*. Kolditz. *Black and White*. Spaeth/Schmid. Tenor horn trio and wind band. €23. A German-style work.

Lane, William. *Contrasts*. Tuba-Euphonium Press. Euphonium solo and wind band (with electric bass). 2002. $40. 3:30. III–IV. E♭–b♭¹. A brief work with both light rock and jazz influences. The accompaniment requires an electric bass or a keyboard performing the work. A nice rock ballad opens the work and leads to a syncopated

6/8 section, which leads to a swing section, before the D.S. leads back to the ballad. The coda features an extended cadenza before a final four bars of the rock ballad. This work is interesting because of its unique feel. The accompaniment may be difficult due to its jazz/rock idiom.

Lehner, Heinz. *Goffried auf Reisen (Gottfried's Travels)*. R. Seifert. FEST-MUSIK-HAUS. Euphonium solo and wind band. 4:10. III. E–b♭¹. One of the more showy selections from the German and Austrian repertoire, this solo features more technical runs than most of the solos, yet keeps the "oompah" of the genre. The accompaniment could easily be handled by a decent high school ensemble.

Lener. *Abenddömmerung*. Seifert. Spaeth/Schmid. Tenor horn and wind band. €14.50. A German-style work.

Lener. *Gute Freunde*. Seifert. Spaeth/Schmid. Tenor horn and wind band. €14.50. A German-style work.

Lortzing, Albert. *Recitativ und Arioso*. Gumbert. Spaeth/Schmid. Tenor horn and wind band. €45.50. A German-style work.

Lortzing, Albert. *Thema und Variationen*. Egner. Spaeth/Schmid. Tenor horn and wind band. €46.50. A German-style work.

Lugitsch, Alois von. *Lustige Bruschen Polka*. Euphonium solo, tenor horn solo, and wind band (piano reduction available). 5:00. III–IV. A♭–f¹. A brief work for an unusual combination. The tenor horn part could appropriately be played on French horn. The parts are not demanding in regards to range and technique. The final cadenza requires some coordinated exchanges between soloists. The accompaniment is quite easy.

Mañas, Franz von. *Alte Bekannte (Konzert Polka)*. Johann Kliment. Euphonium duet and wind band. 1970. €31.50. 3:45. III–IV. B♭–b♭¹. A challenging polka that features much writing in thirds with a nice mix of lyrical and technical works. This is one of the more virtuosic German-style polka works.

Mañas, Vaclav. *Tenorhorn parade (Polka)*. FEST-MUSIK-HAUS. Euphonium duet and wind band. €31.50. III. B♭–a♭¹. A lighthearted, polka-themed duet with a fairly technical accompaniment.

Mantia, Simone. *All Those Endearing Young Charms*. David Werden. Cimarron Music. Euphonium solo and wind band (piano reduction). 6:55. III–VI. One of the classic euphonium theme and variations solos specifically written for the euphonium. This work utilizes the key of F major and will certainly test out one's dexterity and technique. The lyrical variation requires great rubato and sense of rhythm. This is a highly recommended work with many arrangements to choose. Recorded by Roger Behrend, Harold Brasch, David Werden, Michael Colburn, Arthur Lehman, Earle Louder.

Mantia, Simone. *All Those Endearing Young Charms*. Harold Brasch. Tuba-Euphonium Press. Euphonium solo and wind band (piano reduction available). 2000. $40 ($12). 7:00. IV. BB♭–c″. A very legible version of the classic 6/8 theme and variations solo. As one expects, a brief cadenza sets the mood for the lyrical theme, followed by a light variation. The more demanding lyrical ornamented variation comes next, which provides a nice midpoint between technical sections and the typical melodic interlude. A band tutti brings us to the finale of sixteenth note runs that sprints to the finish, only to be interrupted by a brief cadenza and the final measures in F.

Mantia, Simone. *All Those Endearing Young Charms*. Stanley Boddington. Studio Music. Euphonium solo and wind band (brass band available). III–VI. One of the classic euphonium theme and variations solos specifically written for the euphonium. This work utilizes F and will certainly test out one's dexterity and technique. The lyrical variation requires great rubato and sense of rhythm. This is a highly recommended work with many arrangements to choose. Recorded by Lyndon Baglin, the Childs Brothers, Ian Keene, Burt Sullivan, Ken Wood, Joseph Zuback.

Mantia, Simone. *Auld Lang Syne*. Euphonium.com. Euphonium solo and wind band (piano reduction). IV–V. One of the lesser-known theme and variation solos, which requires great dexterity with runs and lip flexibility. This is a highly recommended work for those who are capable. Recorded by Michael Colburn, Earle Louder, Arthur Lehman.

Mantia, Simone. *Polka Fantastic*. Earle Louder. Cimarron Music. Euphonium solo and wind band. II. A simple polka solo with band accompaniment. A good choice for its level and appropriate for its difficulty.

Martino, Ralph. *Introspect*. Tuba-Euphonium Press. Euphonium solo and wind band (piano reduction available). $60 ($10). 8:30. IV. BB♭–c♭″. Written in one continuous movement, this contemporary work opens with a very angular and chromatic cadenza before the accompaniment begins with a slightly dissonant quality. A lighter dance section with fun percussion parts follows, as the piece gains excellent direction as the soloist plays numerous chromatic patterns. A very nice tonal lyrical section ensues, with some wonderful building moments before a very technical portion closes the work. The punctuations from the band add to the chromatic figures in the solo line that lead to the chromatic rips that conclude the piece. This work would be appropriate for a contemporary music concert but may not appeal to general audiences due to the harmonic language and sometimes unclear direction. There are also significant cello and double bass parts that will be needed. Recorded by Roger Behrend.

Maslanka, David. *UFO Dreams*. Carl Fischer. Euphonium solo and wind band. 1999. Rental. 21:30. IV. F–c″. Written in three movements: Fantasy Variations—The Water Is Wide; Home Planet—Where Do You Come From? Who Are You?; Variations: From the Bottom of My Heart. Written for his son, Matthew Maslanka. This work combines Maslanka's great concept of meter and rhythmic interplay with the lush sound of the euphonium. The opening movement with its familiar tune does not present many difficulties for the soloist, but many of the ensemble parts will require good rhythm, counting, and confidence. The variations do pose a few breathing problems. The second movement contains some great chords and colorful writing in the percussion and piano parts. The last movement, featuring variations based on a chorale by J. S. Bach, contains many clever moments of compositional inspiration that will bring a smile to an educated audience member. One variation featuring triplets will be the technical challenge of the work, but it will be within the grasp of many advanced college students. The final closing section incorporates some nice syncopation. Overall, this very interesting work represents a very substantial work by a very well-known composer. Its programmatic nature and the quality of the music and the recognizable themes will be a bonus to performer and listener alike. However, the band parts contain many exposed lines and intricate parts, and a good college ensemble will be the minimum. The work's length may also limit programming; however, this is a recommended work.

Mayer, Kurt. *Teddy tanzt*. Johann Kliment. Euphonium solo and wind band. 1993. €40.50. 4:00. III–IV. F–g′ (b♭′). A pleasant polka with a German/Austrian style. This work has a very easy accompaniment with a good challenging solo part that is mainly arpeggios and scalar runs. The trio features a slightly syncopated motive. An interesting work and one of the best from this genre.

McGain-Harding, Dean. *Cloud Dancing*. Studio Music. Euphonium solo and wind band.

Mendelssohn, Felix. *Spinning Song*. David Werden. Cimarron Music. Euphonium solo and wind band. $40. IV–V. A difficult technical solo that highlights the agility of the euphonium.

Micheletti, N. *Piccolo Concerton for Flicorot*. EM Eridania. Euphonium solo and wind band.

Millöcker. *Dunkerlrote Rosen bring ich schöne Frau*. Spaeth/Schmid. Tenor horn and wind band. €27. A German-style work.

Montgomery, Edward. *Mirror Lake*. Ludwig Music Company. Euphonium solo and wind band (piano reduction available). 1987. $40. 5:20. III. c–b♭′. Dedicated to Paul Droste. Written in two movements: Serenade and Festival. "This very accessible work opens with a lyrical solo and a quick-paced second movement. There are two

short cadenzas. The work is not overly demanding." —Ludwig Music Company. Recorded by Paul Droste.

Monti, Vittorio. *Czardas*. EMR. Euphonium solo and wind band (versions in c minor and d minor). 1999. 120 CHF. IV–V. A nice arrangement of the well-known violin solo that is standard in many instrumentalists' repertoire. Very challenging phrasing, range, and technical passages. Recorded by David Childs, Shoichiro Hokazono, Ivan Milhiet, Jukka Myllys, Hugo Verweij.

Morris, Albert. *Feelings*. Norman Tailor. EMR. Euphonium solo and wind band. 1989. 90 CHF. III. A nice arrangement of the well-known vocal work.

Mosheimer, Karl von. *Bimbos Traum*. Johann Kliment. Euphonium solo and wind band (piano reduction available). 1955. 6:30. A–b♭′. A solo written in one movement in the German style featuring an old-style accompaniment similar to the turn-of-the-nineteenth-century wind band writing (i.e., John Philip Sousa), albeit with some contemporary harmonies. The solo writing is not overly difficult and stays many times as chord members. There are a few short cadenzas that provide the primary area for technical showcase.

Mozart, Leopold. *Concerto*. Samuel Adler. Ludwig Music Company. Euphonium solo and wind band (piano reduction available). IV. A thinly textured version of the commonly used classical work, this piece has been expertly scored. It is offered with solo parts for trombone, French horn, and euphonium. Recorded by Nicolas Pfeifle.

Mueller, Fredrick. *Concerto for Euphonium*. Manuscript. Euphonium solo and wind band (piano reduction available). 1970. 10:00. IV. F–c″. Written for Earle Louder and the Morehead State University Symphony Band. Written in three movements. This accessible work may be difficult to obtain and there are two different editions available. Ensure the solo part matches with the conductor or piano score.[1] Recorded by Earle Louder.

Nagao, Jun. *The Other Garden*. Manuscript. Euphonium solo and wind band. 22:00. V. C–f″. Written for Shoichiro Hokazono. An incredibly challenging work that has unbelievably complex rhythms, wide intervallic jumps, and rapid tonguing patterns. Much of the work is in tenor clef and the high tessitura involves some complex technical work. A piece that would need a very narrow performance environment, as its complex nature may not be suitable for general audience concerts.

Nelson, Ron. *Nightsong (Homage Howard Hanson)*. Ludwig Music Company. Euphonium solo and wind band. 1998. $45. 5:30. III. G–a′. A lyrical work that contains some characteristic harmonies of Howard Hanson. The solo part is not technically demanding and the band parts contain good opportunities to perform a musical gem. This is a recommended work.

Nelhybel, Vaclav. *Concerto for Euphonium*. Tuba-Euphonium Press. Euphonium solo and wind band (piano reduction available). 1984. $80 ($20). 13:10. IV–V. GG–f″. Commissioned by Roger Behrend and dedicated to Charlotte C. Behrend. Written in three connected movements, this concerto features some major challenges for the soloist in regards to range, endurance, and flexibility. The first movement features an extended cadenza that will provide some hurdles, while the second movement contains some superb melodic writing. The final movement has a slight rondo feel to it and features some challenging technique. While the Nelhybel harmonic language is tonal, it does have chromatic moments. The band parts appear rather difficult, but this work would be an excellent challenge to both soloist and ensemble. Recorded by Roger Behrend.

Netzer, Earnest. *Ernst from Allgau*. Arr. A. Slowak. FEST-MUSIK-HAUS. Euphonium solo and wind band. €48.50.

Newsome, Roy. *Berenice's Minuet*. EMR. Euphonium solo and wind band. 1997. 100 CHF. III–IV.

Newsome, Roy. *Mountains of Mourne*. Keith Prowse. Euphonium solo and wind band. III–IV.

Newsome, Roy. *A Piece of Cake*. Obrasso. Euphonium duet and wind band. Recorded by the Childs Brothers. A very lighthearted duet with audience enjoyment the main objective.

Newsome, Roy. *Sounds of Switzerland*. Obrasso. Euphonium duet and wind band.

Niblock, James. *Concertino*. Blue Lake Publishing. Euphonium solo and wind band. 1988. 8:00. IV. G–c″ (c♯″). Dedicated to Leonard Falcone. Composed in an attaca fast-slow-fast form, the *Concertino* poses few major challenges for the soloist as most of the material is based on major scales and arpeggios. However, there are a number of b′ that are highlighted. The last allegro has a nice feature of sixteenth versus sextuplet groupings in the 8/8 section. This work would be a good choice for a more conservative band accompaniment with a solo part that provides virtuosity, but not in an overpowering way.

Nordhagen, Stig. *Concerto for Euphonium and Band*. NMIC. Euphonium solo and wind band. 1997. Rental only. 18:30. Recorded by Sverre Olsrud.

Offenbach. *Barcarolle*. Denzil Stephens. Sarinia Music. Euphonium duet and wind band. A version of the well-known lyrical melody.

Österreicher, Johann. *Berni's Polka*. German tenor horn solo and wind orchestra. 1993. €43.50. 7:00. III–IV. F–b♭¹. One of the new polka works, this composition utilizes more of the low range than most German and Austrian solos. There are some small technical challenges, including an extended cadenza at the opening. However, there are no unusual techniques and this would serve an Oktoberfest well.

Owen, Jerry. *Variations*. Ed. David Werden. Cimarron Music. Euphonium solo and wind band. 1995. IV–V. G♯–d″. Written for Rich Matteson. Written as a theme and variations, this composition explores a contemporary slant on the standard *air varie* solo. While the overall effect is an easy to listen to work with a clear form and pacing, the melodic and harmonic language, along with the styles of the variations, provide a refreshing listening experience. The solo part becomes quite challenging from the third variation with some agile playing needed in the high range above f¹. The fourth variation provides a jazzy rebirth of the theme and certainly provides a new take for the listener. Some of the solo lines here will require a relaxed feeling even though they reach the upper tessitura. The fifth variation in a rollicking 12/8 provides much of the high-energy technique and almost all of it utilizes scalar patterns or thirds. A final cadenza leads the soloist and band to a stellar final eight bars with c², d², and b¹ making appearances. A refreshing work with challenging band parts for an excellent high school group. Recorded by David Werden.

Pecha, Antonin. *Auf der Wanderschaft*. Spaeth/Schmid. Tenor horn and wind band. €25. A German-style work.

Picchi, Ermano. *Fantasie Originale*. Maurice Bale. Godiva Music (Euphonium.com). Euphonium solo and brass band (wind band and piano reduction available). £22 (£50, $17). 7:50. IV. (FF) F–c″ (e♭″). One of the classic turn-of-the-century theme and variations solos, *Fantasie Originale* remains unique because its theme features a jovial Tyrolean style versus the more traditional lyrical theme. The piece's numerous challenges start with the opening octave leaps and continue with some difficult technical requirements in the variations. This work contains some awkward-looking rhythms, and some involve ties. However, the rhythms are representative of the style and the sixteenth note runs scalar. One variation does feature 32nd notes, but of course their velocity will depend on the tempo. An upbeat, quirky interlude occurs before the coda. This remains another unique aspect as most similar pieces would have an introspective minor interlude preceding the finale. The coda is mostly the b♭ scale in various patterns, but the tempo will push the soloist. There are numerous *ossias* through the work that present different options for the soloist to choose higher or lower octaves, thus making it possible to perform the work with limited range. This work remains an excellent composition and a fine departure from the more traditional theme and variations, and it also happens to be an original work for the euphonium. Highly recommended. Recorded by Brian Bowman, Michael Colburn, Leonard Falcone, Adam Frey, Angie Hunter, Steven Mead, Thomas Rüedi, Matt Tropman.

Plog, Anthony. *Serenade for Euphonium and Band.* Anthony Plog. Euphonium solo and wind band.

Pryor, Arthur. *Annie Laurie.* Glenn P. Smith and Albert O. Davis. Ludwig Music Company. Euphonium solo and wind band (piano reduction available). $45 ($9). III. A famous theme and variations. Perfect to challenge a good high school player with an enjoyable work.

Ponchielli, Amilcare. *Concerto per Flicorno Basso, Opus 155.* Henry Howey. Tuba-Euphonium Press. Euphonium solo and wind band (universal edition can be adapted to any large ensemble; brass band, orchestra, and piano versions available). 1996 (written in 1872). $90 ($65, $80, $65, $14). 13:00. IV–V. F–b♭'. Written as a theme and variations, this is one of the few original works from the nineteenth century. The work has an extended introduction with both lyrical and technical lines from the soloist. While the work has tremendous technical difficulties and rapid range jumps, the technical focus is on E♭ major. Nevertheless, it will be quite a challenge. The theme sets a wonderful Italian picture before the fireworks begin as sixteenth notes in variation 1, sixteenth note triplets in variation 2, and triplet and sixteenth notes in variation 3. An interlude and obbligato section leads to the final allegro flourish of sixteenth notes. A fun work that captures the character of the nineteenth-century Italian wind band movement, this piece will be a challenge to prepare and will result in the mastery of the E♭ major scale! Recorded by Michael Colburn, Manfred Heidler, Steven Mead.

Puccini, Giacomo. *"Dondie lieta" from La Boheme.* Joseph T. Spaniola. Tuba-Euphonium Press. Euphonium solo and wind band. 1999. $24. 3:20. III–IV. d♭–b♭'. This excellent arrangement features one of Puccini's famous arias. The solo and band parts are playable by a good high school group. The flute part is quite demanding.

Puccini, Giacomo. *"Nessun Dorma" from Turandot.* Joseph T Spaniola. Tuba-Euphonium Press. Euphonium solo and wind band. 1999. $24. 3:45. III–IV. d–b♭'. This excellent arrangement features one of Puccini's famous arias. The solo and band parts are playable by a high school group.

Puccini, Giacomo. *"Un bel di" from Madam Butterfly.* Joseph T. Spaniola. Tuba-Euphonium Press. Euphonium solo and wind band. 1999. $24. 3:35. III–IV. d♭–b♭'. This excellent arrangement features one of Puccini's famous arias. The solo and band parts are playable by a good high school group. This aria will require good control of soft dynamics in the high range. Recorded by Adam Frey.

Puccini, Giacomo. *"Vissi d'arte" from Tosca.* Joseph T. Spaniola. Tuba-Euphonium Press. Euphonium solo and wind band. 1999. $24. 3:35. III–IV. e♭–b♭'. This excellent arrangement features one of Puccini's famous arias. The solo and band parts are playable by a good high school

group. The rhythms are more difficult than the *Nessun Dorma.*

Pütz, Marco. *Concertino for Euphonium and Band.* Bronsheim & Musiekuitgeverji. Euphonium solo and wind band (fanfare orchestra). 2004. 10:45. IV–V. BB♭–d''. Commissioned by and dedicated to Steven Mead. A new work by an esteemed young European composer. The work features a quick-paced and technical approach to the euphonium that creates great energy for performer and audience. The main challenges will be the chromatic runs, rapid double and triple tonguing that moves across the range of the instrument from the contra range up to d'', and the numerous important moments on b'. This work is excellent and it is hoped that a piano reduction will soon be available as well.

Raich. *Alpenklange.* Spath & Schmid. Tenor horn trio and wind band. €40.50. A German-style work.

Raum, Elizabeth. *Concerto del Garda.* Tuba-Euphonium Press. Euphonium solo and wind band (symphony orchestra and piano reduction available). 1997. $75 ($20). 13:05. IV. GG–b♭'. Written for John Griffiths. Written in three movements: Moderato Grandioso; Lento; Allegretto con Anima. Originally conceived as a tuba concerto, this work combines very listenable harmonies and melodies with a more neoclassical solo part. The writing (for euphonium) does not present any major challenges technically other than a few low areas around F. Most of the notes below BB♭ are approached with enough setup time to prepare the embouchure. It is slightly easier than the *Pershing Concerto.* Both works offer the opportunity for fast playing without many technical hurdles while at the same time presenting serious and substantial repertoire. This concerto does not have any unusual requirements. Raum's works would suit an advanced player with limited high range very well and are recommended for performances.

Raum, Elizabeth. *Pershing Concerto.* Tuba-Euphonium Press. Euphonium solo and wind band (symphony orchestra and piano reduction available). 1999. $70 ($60, $20). 14:00. IV. (GG) C–b♭'. Written in three movements: Allegro moderato; Andante; Allegro non troppo. Raum's style of neoclassical rhythmic style combined with neo-romantic harmonies provides a nice aural combination. Conceived for tuba, this concerto's range offers virtuosic material in a confined register. It is slightly more difficult than the *Concerto del Garda.* Both works offer the opportunity for fast playing without many technical hurdles while at the same time presenting serious and substantial repertoire. This concerto does not have any unusual requirements. Raum's works suit an advanced player with limited high range very well and are recommended for performances.

Reed, Alfred. *Seascapes.* Hal Leonard. Euphonium solo and wind band. 1962. $45. 6:50. III–IV. c–a′. Written for Hunter N. Wiley. This superb solo features superior lyrical writing and represents a work by one of the most prominent composers in the wind band medium. Perfectly suited to a high school or more advanced soloist, this work features three main themes and the instrumental writing makes it easily accessible to high school groups. This solo is highly recommended and deserves numerous performances. Recorded by Roger Behrend. Adam Frey, Shoichiro Hokazono, Toru Miura.

Reinstadler. *Freunde furs Leben.* Seifert. Spaeth/Schmid. Tenor horn and wind band. €14.50. A German-style work.

Reveaux, Jacques. *La maladie d'amour.* Tailor. Spaeth/Schmid. Tenor horn and wind band. €61.50.

Richards, Goff. *Flying Home.* Obrasso. Euphonium duet and wind band.

Richards, Goff. *Midnight Euphonium.* Dean Farrar. Studio Music. Euphonium solo and wind band (brass band and piano reduction available). 1993. 4:10. III. £15 (£45 wind band and £3.75 piano reduction). III. A♭–b♭′. This work provides a jazz ballad feeling through its harmonies and melodic style. There are some challenges to the soloist that include some unusual accidentals and developing the freedom and ease of the style, in addition to making the final cadenza section seem like an improvisation. Control of the high range will be beneficial as the tessitura often remains high. This is a strongly recommended work for its short duration and unique melodic and harmonic language. Recorded by Riki McDonnell, Steven Mead, Christian Squibb.

Richards, Scott. *Gloryland.* Spaeth/Schmid. Tenor horn and wind band. €67.50.

Riddle, Peter. *Song for Euphonium.* Seesaw Music. Euphonium solo and wind band.

Rimsky-Korsakov, Nicoli. *Flight of the Bumble Bee.* Arr. Albert O. Davis. Ludwig Music Company. Euphonium solo and wind band (piano reduction available). $55. III–IV. An accessible arrangement of this war horse solo.

Roost, Jan van der. *Sprit of Independence.* Spaeth/Schmid. Tenor horn and wind band. €126.90.

Ross, Walter. *Capriccio Furioso.* Boosey & Hawkes. Euphonium solo and wind band (piano reduction available). 1977. $90 ($14.50). 4:45. IV. A–b♭′. Written for Brian Bowman. Written in four sections, this solo features some dissonant harmonies and melodic writing that seeks coherence through using the same intervals. The opening section is upbeat, while a lyrical second section with an important saxophone solo leads to a portion in three that provides some technical challenges before arriving at the final section. This finale lacks some clear melodic character due to it coming from a musical period often more concerned with rhythm and intellectualism. However, it can make a nice work for performance if desired.

Runkel. Karl-Heinz. *Waldspaziergang.* Spaeth/Schmid. Tenor horn and wind band. €29.50. A German-style work.

Rüssman. *Drei Vagabunden.* Spaeth/Schmid. Tenor horn trio and wind band. €14.50. A German-style work.

Rutti, Carl. *Metamorphosis.* Manuscript. Euphonium solo and wind band (piano reduction available). 2001. 18:40. V. BBB♯–e♭″. Dedicated to David Childs. Written in two connected movements: Largo; Ground & Presto. This very challenging solo concentrates extensively on the flexibility, clarity of attacks, and tone quality in the very low range. The work also contains many complex rhythms and meter changes. The opening movement starts with a mysterious theme in the extreme pedal range and goes into a more melodic but chromatic development. The Presto features a slightly jazzy feel with the numerous meter changes and frequent octave jumps. With all of the key changes, this will be great fun for ensemble and soloist indeed. A few glissandi are notated in the solo part. Overall, this work will require a very adept ensemble and skilled conductor. It has very unique tone colors and the use of the harp with the wind band creates an excellent texture. This work is certainly one of the most remarkable works to date, but it will require significant skill to prepare and program effectively for audiences. Recorded by David Childs.

Schick, Berthold. *Allgäuger Baritonexpress.* Sschneebieql. Spaeth/Schmid. Tenor horn and wind band. €60. A German-style work.

Schlabach, Errol. *Concertino for Euphonium.* Manuscript. Euphonium solo and wind band. 1968. 8:30. IV. BB♭–b″. Written for Frank Fiol. "The writing is good and this piece deserves to be heard and performed."[1] Yet the work is difficult to obtain; however, one can find many gems in the unpublished repertoire.

Schmid, Hans. *Frühling in den Alpen (Springtime in the Alps).* Johann Kliment. Euphonium duet and wind band (piano reduction available). 1954. 4:30. III. B♭–b♭[1]. Written in four brief sections, the work opens with lyrical statements by the duet partners written mostly in thirds. A march-like area leads to a trio section that features some technical scalar passages before the march section returns and leads to a coda of lyrical statements followed by rapidly tongued final bars. The work is in 3/4 and has a traditional German feeling.

Schneider. *Romantische Variationen.* Watz. Spaeth/Schmid. Tenor horn and wind band. €38.50.

Schoonenbeek, Kees. *Twilight Serenade.* DeHaske. Euphonium solo and wind band (brass band and piano reduction). 1990. €101. 8:30. III. G–g′. An excellent work for high school students to perform with wind band. The writing is idiomatic for both soloist and band. The harmonic and melodic writing are quite listenable and the technical demands for the soloist are predominantly scalar. The work contains a nice mix of lyrical and technical sections with a controlled range. Recorded by Steven Mead.

Schrijver, Karl. *Concertino.* Trerolff-Muziekcentrale. Euphonium solo and wind band.

Schultz, Patrick. *Concerto for Euphonium.* Patrick Schultz. Euphonium solo and wind band. 2000. 14:00. IV. BB♭–c″. Written in two movements: Calmly, with Much Expression; Primitive, Driving. Written for Demondrae Thurman. The opening movement features the lyrical nature of the euphonium and there are some agitated moments of building tension. The piece is certainly written idiomatically and exploits the extremes of the instrument in regards to range and dynamics. The second movement is quite complicated rhythmically for both soloist and ensemble with the rhythms and meter changes, but it certainly typifies the movement's title of Primitive, Driving with a long run to c″.

Schumann, Franz. *Ave Maria.* Clarence Barber. Ludwig Music Company. Euphonium solo and wind band (piano reduction available). $45 ($10). II–III. A nice easy setting of this famous melody with some challenging rhythms. There is an optional octave higher on the repeat.

Schumann, William. *When Jesus Wept.* Theodore Presser. Euphonium and trumpet duet and wind band. 1958. $45. 5:00. III. A wonderful lyrical setting with contemporary overtones. This has long sweeping melodies and remains a great opportunity to highlight a euphonium and trumpet soloist. This is the middle movement of his *New England Triptych.* A wonderful selection.

Schwindhackl, Sepp von. *Allotria.* Johann Kliment. Euphonium solo and piano band (piano reduction available). 1976. 7:00. III–IV. F–b♭′. This concert polka is basically a more significant polka in regards to time and material. *Allotria* opens with a triplet arpeggio figure in the solo line, followed by sixteenth note flourishes, followed by a lyrical restatement of the opening. There are some sixteenth runs that are predominantly scalar or based on arpeggios.

Seeger, Peter. *Concerto Grosso.* B. Schott's Soehne. Two euphoniums, two trumpets, and wind band. 1958. Written in a similar style to a baroque concerto grosso, where the solo group interchanges statements with the accompanying band, this work provides a very unusual setting and opportunity.

Seifert, R. *Tenorhorn Dreams.* Arr. Schedler. FEST-MUSIK-HAUS. Euphonium trio and wind band.

Simons, G. *Atlantic Zephers.* Carl Fischer. Euphonium solo and wind band. III–IV. One of the classic gems from the turn-of-the-century

character pieces. It depicts a cool Atlantic Ocean breeze. This is a recommended work. Recorded by Leonard Falcone.

Smith, Claude T. *Concert Piece for Euphonium.* Wingert Jones. Euphonium solo and wind band. 1980. $75 (Rental). 5:15. IV. AA–c″. Written for Brian Bowman and the United States Air Force Band. Written as a showpiece for Brian Bowman, this work combines Smith's style of listenable melody and energetic rhythms to create an excellent lighter work for the soloist. The demands on the soloist involve range and valve dexterity. It is a shame that a piano reduction does not exist because this is a recommended work. Recorded by Brian Bowman, David Werden.

Smith, Claude T. *Variations for Baritone Horn.* Wingert Jones. Euphonium solo and wind band. 1971. 6:30. V. F–b♭″. Commissioned by the Getzen Corporation and written for Rich Matteson. This solo represents one of a handful of pieces with a jazz influence. While the work has extreme high tessitura, the jazz idiom and style will remain a challenge for many performers. The piece also contains a section of improvisation with chord symbols that may limit some players. However, this work would have great audience appeal given its jazz style and the showy nature of all the extreme high range. It will certainly be a challenge worth its investment if the jazz style and range can be tamed.

Smith, Robert. *Willson Suite.* Belwin-Mills. Euphonium solo and wind band. 1999. 14:00. IV (V). (D) A–b♭′ (f″). Commissioned by Mark Schafer of Willson Professional Brass and dedicated to Roger Behrend. Written in three movements: Tronada; In a Gentle Rain; Hurricane. This highly programmatic work contains the spirit of storms that so often permeates Smith's works. The accompaniment parts can be performed by a good high school band and the overall effect creates a great audience and band pleaser. In regards to the solo part, Smith composed and edited two different parts with one containing a much more limited range, A–b♭′, while the one labeled "Mr. Behrend's Solo" contains the full gamut of range and technical difficulties. Both solo parts contain some difficult dexterity moments. The first movement in 3/4 contains a few nice obligato lines for the soloist that require good agility. An extended cadenza offers many choices for demonstrating technique and range before a recap of the material from the beginning ensues. The second movement features one of the most unique works in the repertoire because it calls for the band members to snap their fingers to create an atmosphere of rain falling during the performance. The effect works extremely well and a piano will be very beneficial (although the piano part can be played on the keyboard percussion if needed). The final movement amounts to nearly four minutes of driving intensity and rising runs that is briefly interrupted by a cadenza. This work is highly recommended and should certainly be performed more often due to its programmatic nature and audience appeal. Unfortunately a piano reduction has not been made. Recorded by Roger Behrend.

Snell, Howard. *Drink to Me Only*. Rakeway Music. Euphonium solo and wind band (brass band and piano reduction available). 1998. (£18, £9.95). 8:45. IV–V. F–d♭″ (d″). Howard Snell has penned a tremendous work that encapsulates a classic showpiece in the form of a traditional theme and variations but makes use of contemporary harmonies and variations that are highly sophisticated and unlike other variation solos. This work certainly deserves more performance, but its challenges are many. The opening theme is of course a simple phrase to be shaped beautifully, but the variations have some chromatic passages that are a challenge technically, while later creations use many hemiolas and complex rhythmic patterns. The mandatory lyrical interlude sees the euphonium soar wonderfully to test the power and intensity before a finale that will take some finger practice to master with all the accidentals and unusual tonguing patterns, such as tongue two, slur two versus the more common slur two, tongue two. A brief cadenza makes use of some very unique harmonies that are surprising but pleasant before the flourish to finish on a c″. This piece is worth the challenges. Recorded by Tormod Flaten, Steven Mead.

Sorbon. *Drei Freunde*. Spaeth/Schmid. Tenor horn trio and wind band. €30.50. A German-style work.

Sorbon. *Spannenmänner*. Spaeth/Schmid. Tenor horn trio and wind band. €43. A German-style work.

Sparke, Philip. *Fantasy*. R. Smith and Company. Euphonium solo and wind band (brass band and piano reduction available). 1979. £55 (£24, £4.75). 9:45. IV. (D) F–c″. Written for Ian Craddock. One of the early serious works for euphonium and brass band, the *Fantasy* will challenge players with its triple tonguing and grace notes as well as the rapidly tongued and slurred sixteenth runs. The work alternates an atmospheric recitative opening with a driving allegro guisto. A methodical intermezzo builds to return to the opening lyrical music and then the fast material. This work is a standard of the repertoire in regards to early euphonium compositions. Recorded by Tyronne Breuninger, Brian Bowman, Robert Childs, Ian Craddock, Brian Crookes, Steven Mead, Renalto Meli, David Werden.

Sparke, Philip. *Pantomime*. Studio Music. Euphonium solo and wind band (brass band and piano reduction available). 1986. £90 (£15, £10.50). 9:45. IV. D–e♭″. One of the classic showpieces in the repertoire, *Pantomime* has been scored for most large ensemble performance mediums.

This only qualifies its stature as one of the most performed, studied, and enjoyed solos. It also remains very challenging due to the endurance requirements of the high lyrical statements based on a rising octave motive in the opening, as well as the high tessitura of the exuberant 10/8 section that blends the brass band world with a hint of rhythm made famous by *West Side Story*. A lyrical 5/4 section provides an interlude before returning to the 10/8 and a rollicking coda in 2/4 that demonstrates the technical agility of the euphonium in the key of E♭. There are some extended lip slurs and trills at the conclusion, climaxing with the summit e♭″. As a proper brass band work, it concludes with every brass player's dream: something high, fast, and loud!! Recorded by the Childs Brothers, Adam Frey, Richard Goosney, Shoichiro Hokazono, Angie Hunter, Steven Mead, Renalto Meli, Jukka Myllys, Joel Pugh, Carl Schultz.

Sparke, Philip. *Two Part Invention*. Studio Music. Euphonium duet and wind band (brass band and piano reduction). 2000 (written in the 1980s). 8:30. IV. C♭–e♭″; C–c″. Written for Bob and Nick Childs. This work captures all the trademarks of Sparke's wonderful writing: lyrical, soaring melodies; listenable harmonies; excellent rhythmic drive; virtuoso technique; and a touch of panache. The solo parts have a consistently high tessitura in the opening melodic section. The weaving of the duet lines showcases the singing quality of the euphonium. The fast section delivers great interplay between the lines as it moves through various harmonies. The coda section features alternating triplet patterns between the soloists. It is great fun to practice and perform but will certainly pose some technical challenges. There are some rapidly double tongued figures. This is one of the most challenging and enjoyable duets in the repertoire. Recorded by the Childs Brothers, Shoichiro Hokazono, Dominique Robyr.

Stanek. *Romanze*. Mestrini. Spaeth/Schmid. Tenor horn and wind band. €31.70.

Staněk, Pavel. *Nocturno for Euphonium*. Musikverlag Rundel. Euphonium solo and wind band. 2000. $75. 6:45. III–IV. BB♭–b′. Moderato. A lyrical composition with impressionistic harmonies. The band parts are lightly scored, allowing easy projection for the soloist and much room for expression. This work contains idiomatic writing and would be a good choice when looking for an easier band work to demonstrate the lyrical capabilities of the euphonium. There are a number of melodic parts above f¹, so stability and beauty of tone will be needed there. Staněk remains one of the Czech Republic's most respected band composers. A good choice to explore new repertoire.

Steinberger, N. M. *Badinage for Euphonium and Band*. Manuscript. Euphonium solo and wind band.

Szkutko, John. *Teddy Bears.* SZK Music. Euphonium solo, tuba solo, and concert band (piano reduction available). 1996. $65 ($20 piano) Australian. 6:50. V. E♭–f″ (euphonium) EE♭–f′ (tuba). This is a work of many contrasting sections with tonal harmonic and melodic writing. A 12/8 dance section is jovial for both voices and a very technical high-range section near the end for both parts. A lighthearted fun duet.

Taylor, Clifford. *Sinfonia Seria.* American Composers Alliance. Euphonium, flute, and wind band.

Taylor, Robert. *Prelude.* Robert Taylor.

Thingnaes, Frode. *Daydream.* Frost Music. Euphonium solo and wind band.

Thingnaes, Frode. *Peace Please!* Spaeth/Schmid. €130. 6:30. III–IV. A work in a light jazz style with a written-out improvisation section. Chord changes are also provided for the soloist enjoying improvisation. This is a recommended work, and it is lucky it is available from Spaeth/Schmid. Recorded by Steven Mead.

Thomas. *Kennst du d as Land.* Arr. Weingartner. Spaeth/Schmid. Tenor horn duet and wind band. €32. A German-style work.

Toft. *Waldesstile.* Arr. Weber. Spaeth/Schmid. Tenor horn duet and wind band. €38.50.

Toselli, Enrico. *Serenata.* Arr. Rüedi. Spaeth/Schmid. Tenor horn and wind band. €94.20.

Traditional. *Baritonegeflüster.* Arr. Hummel. Spaeth/Schmid. Tenor horn duet and wind band. €29.50. A German-style work.

Traditional. *Believe Me if All Those Endearing Young Charms.* Arr. J. Masten and Albert O. Davis. Ludwig Music Company. Euphonium solo and wind band. $80. III. A classical-style, lyrical solo for the euphonium (from Ludwig Catalog). See recordings under Mantia, Simone.

Traditional. *Good King Wenceslas.* Arr. Roger Thorne. Thornes Music. Euphonium solo and wind band (brass band). 2002. £48 (£20). 6:35. III. F–b♭′. This solo remains unique in its Christmas theme and its idiomatic nature. One of the few holiday musical selections cast as a theme and variations, this solo is firmly planted in B♭ major and the variations are standard single-tongued triplets, slurred running sixteenths, cadenza, and an allegro variation with ornamental notes finishing with a chromatic run to b♭′. A highly recommended holiday solo.

Tuschla, W. *Drei fidele Soloisten.* FEST-MUSIK-HAUS. Tenor horn trio and wind band. €35. III–IV. Waltz.

Tuschla, W. *Drei Tenöre.* Spaeth/Schmid. Tenor horn trio and wind band. €72.50.

Tuschla, W. *Tenorhorn Polka.* FEST-MUSIK-HAUS. Tenor horn solo and wind band.

Uber, David. *Sound Sketches.* David Uber. Euphonium solo and wind band.

Vančura, Adolf. *Canzonetta amorosa.* Johann Kliment. Euphonium (German tenor horn) solo and wind band. 1954. €43.50. 7:15. III–IV.

D–b♭′. An easier solo with a matching accompaniment. The one difficulty will be the overall high tessitura used in the work since it was conceived for a small-bore German tenor horn. Recorded by Manfried Hidler.

Vollrath, Carl. *Reminiscence.* Tuba-Euphonium Press. Euphonium solo and wind band. 1994. $40. 11:15. III–IV. F–g♭′. Written in three sections of cantabile, fast, and tempo primo, this work's opening highlights the low to middle range of the euphonium soloist. Many of the early lines provide atmosphere with simple rhythms. The section gradually builds, with each phrase reaching higher and higher notes, relatively speaking, and more ornamental notes being added. The fast portion contains numerous sixteenth runs with difficult accidentals. The opening returns in mood, but with different melodic character, before ending quietly.

Wagner, Joseph. *Concerto Grosso.* Arizona State University Band. Euphonium, three cornets, and wind band.

Waignein, André. *Introduction and Dance.* DeHaske Publications. Euphonium solo and wind band (piano reduction available). III. d–f′ (g′). This is a pleasant two-part solo and represents a good choice for high schools solos that are not commonly utilized. One of the difficulties and excellent training opportunities involves the meter changes in the Dance section. 3/4, 5/8, 2/4, and 3/2 time signatures are used, but the quarter and eighth note remain constant. Other than this rhythmic obstacle, this work will provide a good study and a fun solo for students.

Wakefield, Anthony. *Prelude and Blues.* Euphonium solo and wind band.

Walters, Harold L. *Tarantelle.* Ludwig Music Company. Euphonium solo and wind band (piano reduction available). $45. III. "A light concert work that is very approachable by the players and audience."—Ludwig Music Company.

Watz, Franz. *Alpenpanorama.* Spaeth/Schmid. Tenor horn and wind band. €35. A German-style work.

Watz, Franz. *Lustige Brüder.* Spaeth/Schmid. Tenor horn and wind band. €17. A German-style work.

Watz, Franz. *Solo Konzert Nr. 1.* FEST-MUSIK-HAUS. Euphonium solo and wind band. 1995. 8:45. IV. A♭–b♭′. Written in three movements: Andante Maestoso; Scherzo-Allegro; Allegretto-Quasi Swing. This lighter work from the German repertoire represents one of the larger scale works written in movements. It contains qualities of a more serious work intertwined with many characteristics of lighter music. The challenges to the soloist involve only a few technical moments; otherwise musicality can be the focus. The first movement contains a lightly articulated theme. The second movement features a faster syncopated theme. The final movement utilizes some swing and jazz nuances, before an extended cadenza yields to a final adagio that prepares a soft ending. Within the German and Austrian repertoire, this work remains very unique and would certainly enjoy greater exposure if a piano reduction was available. This is a recommended work from its specific genre.

Watz, Franz. *Wandergesellen*. Spaeth/Schmid. Tenor horn duet and wind band. €21.50. A German-style work.

Watz, Franz. *Zwei Fröhliche Musikkanten (Two Happy Musicians)*. FEST-MUSIK-HAUS. Euphonium duet and wind band. €43.50. III–IV. Polka.

Watz, Franz. *Zwei Lustige Vagabunden (Two Jovial Vagabonds)*. FEST-MUSIK-HAUS. Euphonium duet and wind band. €40. III–IV. Concert polka.

Weber, C. M. *Concertino, Op 45*. W. Schaefer. Denis Wick Publishing. Euphonium solo and wind band. A nice setting of this well-known composition that works well for the euphonium.

Weber, Hans von. *Abschied con der Alm*. Johann Kliment. Euphonium duet and wind band (piano reduction available). 1950. 4:00. III. A♭–f′. An easy melody and style-focused work written in a traditional German band feeling with a lilting 3/4 meter. The duet parts are featured often in thirds.

Werner, F. *Little Bear's Adventure*. Werner. Euphonium solo and wind band. IV.

Wessman, Harri. *Prelude and Toccata*. FMIC. Euphonium solo and wind band (piano reduction available). 2001. 10:00. IV–V. EE–e♭″. Dedicated to Adam Frey and commissioned by the ITEC 2001 Lahti. Written in two sections, the *Prelude and Toccata* features contemporary harmonies and a repeated note motive in the brief opening section, which utilizes a mute. The build to the Toccata crescendos greatly before the intensity of a rapid, repeated-note, double tongued figure provides a light rhythmic dance. The meter remains in 6/8 but moves cheerfully between duple and triple feels. A long arch-form melody serves as the second subject and returns later in fragments with flutter tonguing interspersed with the rapid double tongued theme. This work represents a nice addition to the contemporary repertoire and would be suitable for a new music festival or as a work that demonstrates excellent tonguing. Without understanding these features, the work may lead some to want more melodic material.

White, Donald. *Lyric Suite*. G. Schirmer. Euphonium solo and wind band (piano reduction available). 1972. Rental ($11.95). 10:15. IV. E–b′. Commissioned by Henry Charles Smith. Written in four movements: Adagio cantabile; Allegro guisto; Andante sostenuto; Allegro energico. A standard work in the contemporary repertoire, *Lyric Suite* captures the abilities of the euphonium very well. This solo with contemporary

harmonies and melodies has a strong chromatic nature but also has numerous tonal sections. The first movement presents a peaceful opening that climaxes on a powerful b′ before returning to the calm. The second movement features some difficult syncopations and unusual finger patterns but also holds great rhythmic energy. The third movement contains some wide intervals and building sequences. It ends peacefully while the final movement hosts a quirky theme that groups the music into a mixed meter feeling. The ensemble of this work will be a challenge and the wind band parts and piano will require careful attention to rhythmic accuracy. An excellent choice for a contemporary selection. Recorded by Dee Stewart.

Wilby, Philip. *Concerto for Euphonium*. Winwood Music. Euphonium solo and wind band (brass band, orchestral, and piano reductions available). 1996. £125 (£70, Rental, £15). 18:15. V. AA♭–d″ (e♭″). Written for Robert Childs. Written in two parts/four movements: Part I—Non troppo allegro; Dance Zeibékikos; Part II—Andante; Allegro vivace. One of the most challenging and demanding concerti, the Wilby *Concerto for Euphonium* combines incredible energy, driving intensity, soaring lyricism, and great listening enjoyment. However, the challenges present a substantial obstacle for many players. Firstly, there are tremendous technical demands including rapid repeated and moving double and triple tonguing through three of the four movements. The patterns are often chromatic, but with small modifications. Difficult rhythmic patterns also present challenges, as does the overall tempo of the work and the endurance needed to sustain the power and balance for the eighteen minutes. The most memorable portion of this concerto is the Dance Zeibékikos. It basically makes up three minutes of pure adrenaline through fast notes, crazy two-octave glissandos, fierce grace notes, and rapid meter changes before ending with the percussion section breaking plates!! The third movement then provides a very contemplative interlude before the final movement. The lyrical nature of the Andante explores the low range of the euphonium before ascending to a poignant statement in a slow 6/8. This writing is wonderfully lush and captures the best qualities of the euphonium before moving directly into the finale. The technical demands return and bring the work to a triumphant conclusion. This work will be very demanding but absolutely worth the investment. It is a highly recommended work. The accompaniment parts are scored a little thickly and will challenge college-level ensembles. Recorded by Robert Childs, David Childs, Steven Mead.

Wilder, Alec. *Concerto for Euphonium*. Margun Music. Euphonium solo and wind band (piano reduction available). 1981 (written in 1971).

Rental ($18.50). 15:00. IV–V. E–e♭″. Written for Barry Kilpatrick. Written in five movements (Fast; Slow; Fast; Slow; Fast), this work explores Wilder's individuality, which pervades his music and can often leave audiences slightly lost. The movements each capture the euphonium's agility and style. Of note is the pleasant and lyrical second movement, which is followed by a fun fast mixed meter movement that presents many technical challenges. The fourth movement presents an excellent melodic study for the high tessitura, before the final movement brings back an upbeat nature with some meter shifts. This work requires a mute and the ability to read tenor clef. This work shall (and should) remain a staple of the repertoire but will continue to be programmed much more often with piano due to the great availability of more tuneful works with band currently available. Recorded by Brian Bowman, Barry Kilpatrick, John Swallow.

Wilhelm, Rolf Alexander. *Concertino for Euphonium*. Trio Musik. Euphonium solo and wind band (brass band [manuscript] and piano reduction available). 1999. €89.50 (€14.50). 12:00. IV–V. BB–d″. Written in three movements: Allegro mon troppo; Andante ma non troppo, piacevole; Moderato con animo. A contemporary classic for the euphonium, the *Concertino* highlights the qualities of the euphonium very well. The opening movement features a slightly technical style with a great energy. There are no extremely awkward sections, but Wilhelm does occasionally use a bar with numerous accidentals. The second movement allows the soloist to show excellent control and features very lovely writing, especially the descending motive that reappears three times. The technique is manageable as the level dictates, but the range does occasionally create problems in the final movement. This remains the main challenge and features the most range extremes. The articulations are very detailed. The accompaniment will challenge a good high school ensemble, but this work should be performed more often. The piano reduction also works very well. Recorded by Steven Mead.

Wilhelm, Rolf Alexander. *Duett Concertino for Trumpet, Euphonium and Wind Band*. Trio Musik. Euphonium solo, trumpet solo, and wind band (piano reduction available). 2001. €115 (€17). 10:30. IV. G–b′ (trumpet b–c″). Written in three movements: Allegro con brio; Andante; Allegro moderato. This work features Wilhelm's characteristic harmonies and lighter style of writing. Quite famous for his cartoon music, the opening 6/8 movement captures a more restrained energy and features a short cadenza before a quicker

restatement of the opening theme. Wilhelm produced an excellent second movement with wonderful lyrical and melodic writing between the soloists that leads to a rhythmic and highly articulated final movement. There are double tongued intervals before a return to the 6/8 mood of the first movement; yet this time it creates much more energy at a faster tempo and provides a nice finale to the work. This work should be performed more often as one of the very few major chamber works for the euphonium. The accompaniment will challenge a good high school ensemble. The piano reduction also works very well.

Woodfield, Ray. *Caprice*. Hallamshire. Euphonium solo and wind band (brass band and piano reduction). 4:45. III–IV. B♭–b♭′ (c″). A nice lighthearted brass band solo, *Caprice* highlights agility and triple tonguing and allows a choice of two written-out cadenzas: a more technical choice and a more lyrical choice. Recorded by Richard Gosney.

Wunderer. *Der Traum in walde*. Kliment. Johann Kliment. Tenor horn and wind band. €27.50. A German-style work.

Wunderer. *Der Traum in walde*. Meinhold. Spaeth/Schmid. Tenor horn and wind band. €27.50. A German-style work.

Yon, P. A. *Gesu Bambino*. W. van der Beek. Molenaar. Euphonium solo and wind band. II.

Yuste, Miguel. *Solo de Concoroso*. Union M. Espana. Euphonium solo and wind band. IV–V. Recorded by Steven Mead.

Zdechlik, John P. *Ballade*. John Zdechlik. Euphonium solo and wind band (brass ensemble available, 3 trumpets, 3 horns, 3 trombones, 1 tuba). III–IV. B♭–b♭′. "This piece is written to exploit the sonorous sounds of the euphonium. Not technically challenging, this piece could be performed by the good high school performer. A short lyrical theme leads to an exposition section with accompaniment. The performer's musical expression is further exploited in an expressive cadenza, leading into a recapitulation of the main theme with coda."—John Zdechlik.

Zettler, Richard. *Concertino Classico*. Spaeth/Schmid. Tenor horn and wind band. €70.

Notes

1. David Miles, *An Annotated Bibliography of Selected Contemporary Euphonium Solo Literature by American Composers* (Annandale. Virginia: Tuba-Euphonium Press, 1992).

4. Music for Euphonium and Brass Ensemble

Adam Frey

The repertoire for euphonium and brass ensemble remains a fragment compared to the other large ensemble categories. There are fewer brass ensembles around the globe and the euphonium is not always an included member of brass ensemble compositions and arrangements. Therefore, it makes sense that it would not represent a popular choice to compose for this performance medium. Luckily, some composers have ventured on this path and created some unique works.

Brass Ensemble Works

Please note that accompaniment ensembles are listed as trumpet. horn. trombone. euphonium. tuba. percussion (0.0.0.0.0.0).

Corwell, Neal. *Tribes*. Tuba-Euphonium Press. Euphonium solo and brass ensemble (nonet). 10:00. This work contains some dissonant parts and contains a story line of two tribes (one depicted by the high brass, the other the low brass). The solo euphonium acts as an intermediary and eventually the two sides come together and work in harmony with the soloist.

Cummings, Barton. *Andante and Allegro*. Barton Cummings. Euphonium solo and brass ensemble (3.2.2.1.1.0). 1999. 5:30. III. e♭–a♭'. For Willard Minton and the Harmonious Brass Choir of Winsted, Connecticut. Andante and a la beguine. Written in two sections, *Andante and Allegro* opens with brass ensemble chords with the euphonium playing a melody with sixteenth note pickups. The harmonic language is slightly chromatic. The *Allegro* section hosts a lighthearted feeling featuring rhythmic accompaniment figures with a solo melody with many quarter note triplets. This work would be appropriate for a high school program looking for a work specifically scored for this performance medium.

Gallaher, Christopher. *Sonata for Euphonium, Brass, and Percussion*. Tuba-Euphonium Press. Euphonium solo and brass ensemble (4.4.4.0.1.4) with percussion (4). $40.

Telemann, Georg Philip. *Concerto in C Minor*. Arr. Christoph Müller. Euphonium.com. Euphonium solo and brass ensemble (4.1.4.0.1.0).

2002. $40. 8:30. IV. c–c". Originally composed for oboe, the *Concerto in C Minor* works very well for euphonium and brass ensemble in this arrangement. Care must be taken because the solo part remains in the upper range for most of the solo and there are few rests. The style also dictates that the solo playing should be light and soft. The solo part is written entirely in tenor clef and contains nothing terribly unusual in regards to baroque compositions. The main challenges will be style in the solo and ensemble parts, endurance, and ensuring the technical passages sound glib. This is a highly recommended work given its historical period and setting for brass ensemble.

Uber, David. *Caricatura*. David Uber. Euphonium solo and brass ensemble. This solo was originally written for solo tuba and brass ensemble.

Zdechlik, John P. *Balade*. John Zdechlik. Euphonium solo and brass ensemble (3.3.3.0.1.0) (wind band available). III–IV. B♭–b♭'. "This piece is written to exploit the sonorous sounds of the euphonium. Not technically challenging, this piece could be performed by a good high school performer. A short lyrical theme leads to an exposition section with accompaniment. The performer's musical expression is further exploited in an expressive cadenza, leading into a recapitulation of the main theme with coda."—John Zdechlik.

Euphonium and Brass Band

The combination of the euphonium with brass band has provided a huge number of high-quality pieces in a variety of styles. Some of the most famous euphonium concerti have been produced by the prolific brass band composers in the United Kingdom (Horovitz, Ellerby, Golland, Sparke, Wilby to name but a few). The composer's interest to write for this medium certainly evolved from the prominence that the principal, or solo, euphonium plays in the brass band. Many confer that the solo euphonium stands only second to the solo cornet in importance in the brass band, and this role creates high demands on players when works are written with brass band competitions in mind. As an aside for those unfamiliar with the tradition of brass band competitions, a test piece is chosen that all bands must perform for an adjudicator for a ranking on a specific date. Many times for these competitions, new works are commissioned with the intent of providing a significant high-quality musical piece with a very high degree of difficulty so that the bands can be properly tested. This creates wonderfully challenging repertoire that continually raises the standards of music making and performance abilities. Another inclusion in this text involves the baritone horn. Not to be confused with the "baritone" that many American music teachers and publishers misapply to euphoniums, the real baritone horn maintains a respected position in the brass band and has developed a pocket of unique literature. For the curious, the baritone has a smaller bore and body size than the euphonium, but most importantly it has a much lower ratio of conical tubing versus the euphonium, giving it a brighter and smaller tone. Further information on the differences can be found in chapter 1.

The one difficulty with the brass band medium involves its sometimes limited performance options outside of brass band heavy cultures mainly centered in Europe and the United Kingdom and other commonwealth countries (Australia, New Zealand, etc.). Another small obstacle is that brass band euphonium parts are always written in B♭ treble clef. While many of the newer works published in the last fifteen to twenty years contain solo parts for both bass clef and treble clef, most other works, and those published specifically by brass band–targeted companies, will not include a bass clef solo part. So, having an excellent working knowledge of treble clef will assist in delving deeply into the brass band repertoire. The plethora of choices of works in this medium can seem daunting, with styles ranging from the huge concerti mentioned earlier to the likes of traditional "warhorse" solos like *Rule Britannia* (Hartmann), *Grandfather's Clock* (Dougherty), and *Blaydon Races* (Newsome). They also run the gamut to the popish showpieces like *Panache* (Dewhurst) and *Varied Mood* (Woodfield) to wonderful lyrical works, such as *Peace* (Golland) or *Aubade* (Sparke), and opera arrangements. Yet two overriding themes almost always ring true with the repertoire composed for euphonium and brass band: the audience will enjoy listening to the performance of the music by a good player, and the performer will have fun practicing the work.

Brass Band

Aagaard-Nilsen, Torstein. *A Moment of Silence.* Just Music Scotland. Euphonium solo and brass band. £33.50.

Ackford. *Cornish Sunset.* Kirklee's Music. Euphonium solo and brass band. £17.50.

Amoosm, K. *Euphonium Concerto.* Just Music Scotland. Euphonium solo and brass band.

Andresen, Morgens. *Prelude and Chaconne.* Morgens Andresen. Euphonium solo and brass band (symphony orchestra and wind band available). A very melodic piece that shows the euphonium's possibilities for playing in different styles.

Anonymous. *The Poet and I.* David Cunningham. Just Music Scotland. Euphonium solo and brass band. £10.

Arban, Jean Baptiste. *The Amazing Mr. Arban.* Elgar Howarth. Chester Music. Euphonium solo and brass band.

Audoire, Norman. *We'll All Shout Hallelujah.* SP & S. Euphonium solo and brass band. 5:55. This is a fun and challenging theme and variations that contains very few lyrical moments. The opening cadenza spans the entire range of the work before presenting the allegro theme that audiences will recognize followed by a single tonguing triplet variation, a sixteenth note variation, and a final triplet variation with repeated note triple tonguing. The work holds some technical challenges in the way of sixteenth note triplets, tied figures, and agility. A fun solo that highlights the technical aspects of the euphonium. Recorded by Gordon Hildreth, Derick Kane.

Babb, Michael. *He Wipes the Tear.* SP & S. Euphonium solo and brass band. 1991. 3:50. II–III. B♭–f′. A nice lyrical solo. There are other solos that place more demands on the solo line, but this one is very appropriate for younger players.

Bach, A. *Meditation for Euphonium and Brass Band.* Manuscript. Euphonium solo and brass band. II.

Bach, Johann Sebastian. *Ave Maria.* Arr. John Golland. Hallamshire Music. Euphonium solo and brass band. £17.95. 3:20. III. d♭–b♭′. A nice setting of this standard melody. It is, however, in a higher key (D♭) versus many other arrangements of the same tune. It is also written in an augmented form where all the note values are doubled for easier understanding of the slow rhythms for the ensemble.

Bale, Maurice. *Adela.* Godiva Music. Euphonium solo and brass band (piano reduction available). 1999. £17 (£6.50). 7:45. IV. GG–b♭′ (e♭″). "Adela" means noble and this composition by Bale, who normally arranges, captures his unique humorous character with a desire to make extensive demands on the soloist. The opening cadenza spans three octaves! The overall scope of the work is indeed noble and utilizes a theme and variations format.

The first theme captures elegance and style. The second section hosts a diminuendo melody followed by a slightly ornamented version. A rapid triple tongued passage fulfills the need to have some virtuosity in the work before the slow interlude played by the band. An extended cadenza offers an area to demonstrate one's skills with a finish on the low G_1 before the final con brio brings the work to a finish. An excellent work and something refreshing as a solo work. If one has ever met Maurice Bale, then one will certainly catch all the subtle references and stylistic components.

Ball, Eric. *In the Army.* SP & S. Euphonium solo and brass band. III.

Ball, Eric. *Mountain Melody.* SP & S. Euphonium solo and brass band.

Ball, Michael. *Concerto for Euphonium.* Kirklee's Music. Euphonium solo and brass band (piano reduction available). £45 (£15). IV–V. Written for David Childs.

Barry, Darrol. *Dreamscapes.* Wright and Round. Euphonium solo and brass band. 2001. 3:45. III. d–f'. A nice lyrical work with Barry's slightly "movie theme" style of accompaniment writing with a nice florid countermelody in the work before a modulation occurs.

Barry, Darrol. *One Day in Your Life.* Spaeth/Schmid. Baritone and brass band.

Barry, Darrol. *The Summer Knows.* Spaeth/Schmid. Baritone and brass band.

Bearcroft, Norman. *The Better World.* SP & S. Euphonium solo and brass band. £24.95. 9:30. IV–V. D–d″. A very challenging Salvation Army solo featuring Salvation Army songs with some very florid embellishments and fanfares. This work utilizes much multiple tonguing and agility in the highest tessitura to produce a work that has a very light character. As with many Salvation Army solos, the writing reflects a strong knowledge of the technical capabilities of the instrument and presents challenges that will require a fair amount of work for the soloist. Recorded by the Childs Brothers, Derick Kane, Steven Mead.

Bearcroft, Norman. *Harbour Light.* SP & S. Euphonium solo and brass band. 1990. £24.95. 9:30. IV. F–c″ (d♭″). A challenging Salvation Army solo featuring a fantasia style with some elements of a theme and variations. The technical and range demands are the limiters, but most of the sixteenth note runs are scalar or based on major arpeggios. There are a number of octave leaps to c″ as well as the final scale that also culminates on a c″. Recorded by Derick Kane, Aaron Vanderweele.

Bearcroft, Norman. *Jesus, I Come to Thee.* SP & S. Euphonium solo and brass band. 1992. III. e–a♭′ (c″). A fine lyrical work with numerous *ossias* that allow the range to be more accessible. The slow 6/8 lends itself to quality phrasing and shape. Recorded by Derick Kane, Aaron Vanderweele.

Bearcroft, Norman. *Timepiece.* SP & S. Euphonium duet and brass band. 5:55. IV. G–c″; G–a′. A lighthearted duet with a programmatic overtone involving clocks. Much of the duet writing involves octaves and thirds with lots of parallel motion and question and answer. There are few independent moments for the two soloists and the technical demands are predominantly scalar. The piece also provides opportunities for lyrical expression together. This is a great duet choice for pairing a more mature player with a younger player. There are some allusions to *Grandfather's Clock.* Recorded by the Childs Brothers, Ern Harwood, Derick Kane, A. J. Scannell, Adam Sewell-Jones.

Bennett, Malcolm. *Rutland Water.* Spaeth/Schmid. Baritone and brass band.

Bernaerts, F. *Carnival of Venice.* Manuscript. Euphonium solo and brass band.

Bizet, Georges. *Deep Inside the Sacred Temple.* Wilkinson. Studio Music. Euphonium duet. 4:00. III. A very beautiful duet that captures the lyrical and melodic qualities of the euphonium superbly. Recorded by the Childs Brothers.

Bizet, Georges. *The Flower Song from Carmen.* Maurice Bale. Godiva Music. Baritone solo and brass band. £10. 4:00. III. f–b♭′. A nice setting by Maurice Bale of this famous opera aria. The accompaniment parts are not difficult.

Bizet, Georges. *The Toreador's Song from Carmen.* Bram Gay. Kirklee's Music. Euphonium solo and brass band. £21.50. A setting of the well-known song from *Carmen.*

Boccalari, E. *Fantasia di Concerto (Sounds of the Riviera).* Arr. Thijs Oud. Euphonium.com, Carl Fischer (wind band), Tuba-Euphonium Press (piano). Euphonium solo and brass band (wind band and piano reduction available). $75 (Out of Print, $14). 12:30. IV. (D) F–b♭′ (c″). This work is one of the major romantic works written for the euphonium. The melodies are very listenable and have a strong Spanish influence. The opening melodic section allows great freedom and has much interplay between soloist and band. One common technique employed by Boccalari involves having a simple phrase repeated in a section with extensive ornamentation. These phrases necessitate facile technique and agility. There are many cadenzas throughout the work and almost all of them offer *ossias* to facilitate range, time, and technique constraints. The *Tempo di Bolero* offers great appeal with its energy, articulation, style, and driving accompaniment figures. The percussion parts add greatly here to bring out the true Spanish style. A brief recitative figure allows a final lyrical perspective before returning to the exuberant bolero and a coda that employs either chromatic triplets with middle neighboring tones (C-D-C, B-C-B, etc.) or repeated triple tonguing. This work represents one of the best turn of the century original works for the baritone/euphonium. Recorded by Brian Bowman, Shoichiro Hokazono, Steven Mead, Toru Miura, John Mueller, Takashi Yamamoto.

Boddington, Stanley. *Long Long Ago*. Wright and Round. Euphonium solo and brass band.

Boon, Brindley J. R. *A Starry Crown*. SP & S. Euphonium and brass band. 6:10. III. A–bb'. A pleasant theme and variations solo written in the traditional format: Introduction; Theme; Variation 1 with single tongued triplets; Variation 2 with sixteenth notes; a lyrical Interlude in a minor key; and, Variation 3/Finale with tongued sixteenth notes.

Bosanko, Courtney. *Joyful Testimony*. SP & S. Euphonium and brass band. 5:25. III. F–bb'. A pleasant theme and variations solo written in the traditional format: Introduction with a cadenza; Theme; Variation 1 with single tongued triplets; Variation 2 with sixteenth notes; a lyrical Interlude in the relative minor key; and, Variation 3/Finale with rapid slurred runs of quintuplets and sextuplets.

Bosanko, Ivor. *Heart in Heart (Glorious Liberation)*. SP & S/Manuscript. Euphonium solo and brass band (piano reduction). 1969. 8:15. IV. BBb–c". Written as a fantasia based on Salvation Army songs, *Heart in Heart* typifies the Salvation Army style with incredible lyrical writing and profound, idiomatic technical passages. The flourishes of intensity along with the tenderness of melodic playing make this a stellar selection. The technical passages are demanding and the final section features multiple tonguing. A superb work that should be more widely available. Recorded by Chris Mallet, Steven Mead.

Bosanko, Ivor. *I'll Not Turn Back*. See listing under Larsson, John.

Bourgeois, Derek. *Concerto, Opus 114*. R. Smith (G&M Brand–orchestra). Euphonium solo and brass band (orchestra, wind band, and piano reduction available). 1988. £105 (Rental, £130,£10). 18:00. IV–V. GG–d". Written in three movements: Allegro; Adagio; Presto. Commissioned by the British Trombone Society. Included in the *ESB* because Bourgeois states that "It is equally appropriate to perform this work on the Euphonium, in which case the title should be shown as Concerto," this work represents a significant work with performance options for all the major mediums. The work's charm and style lend themselves to endearment by performers and audiences alike. The opening movement's marshal style and intensity requires confident articulation interspersed with a sweeping melody that soars to a d". Luckily, this occurs in the early part of the *Concerto* before the soloist may become fatigued. The Adagio features some very expressive phrases and a nicely contemplative feeling. The final bars require a mute. The final movement poses the most technical challenges with rapid triplet patterns that are occasionally syncopated. The last page captures Bourgeois's typical technical flourish that modulates rapidly. The valve combinations on these last pages will require much practice. This work is highly recommended and a standard of many programs. Thankfully, the composer encourages its performance on the euphonium. Recorded by Angie Hunter, Steven Mead.

Bourgeois, Derek. *Euphonium Concerto, Opus 120*. Brass Wind Music. Euphonium solo and brass band (chamber orchestra, piano reduction available). 1990. Rental (£16). 20:00. V. D–f". Written in three movements: Allegro vivace, Lento con moto, Allegro molto vivace. This concerto captures Bourgeois's intimate knowledge of the technical abilities of the euphonium with his special harmonic language. The writing for much of the concerto remains in the upper tessitura and is very technically based. It contains a number of range intensive areas with rapid technique, including some extended areas with chromatic writing above bb¹. The lyrical second movement features the euphonium with a more florid solo part versus one of longer note values. The final movement opens on a b' and progresses through many meter changes of time signatures based on quarter, eighth, and sixteenth notes. Overall, the runs throughout the work shift tonalities frequently and many times do not always represent traditional scalar patterns. This work will take tremendous "wood-shedding" and endurance. While the energy is deserving, there are probably other works for euphonium and band that will reward the soloist, orchestra, and audience more.

Bourgeois, Derek. *Euphoria, Opus 75*. R. Smith. Euphonium solo and brass band (piano reduction available). 1983/1988. £15.50 (£8.50). 6:50. IV–V. (Bb₁) D–c". One of the most challenging contemporary works in the brass band repertoire, *Euphoria* has immense technical demands and numerous range challenges. The opening section contains some of the most haunting melodic and harmonic colors written for the euphonium and it has some complex rhythms that serve as energetic moments between phrases. There are many wide slurs that require fluidity to remain in the style. The "carnival" section entails a rollicking jaunt through numerous meter changes of quarter and eighth note varieties. The soloist interjects with running sixteen notes that often start after the down beat and generally do not follow many patterns. There are some keys that receive some focus, but often times the underlying harmonies are shifting quickly and the solo line reflects this. The ending *Prestissimo* warrants special mention because it contains some of the most unique writing rhythmically, harmonically, and melodically over the span of twenty seconds. A most challenging work that will reward the performers. The accompaniment parts (both band and piano) require great skill, but are worth the investment of time and practice. Recorded by Steven Mead, Matthew Murchison, Ryuji Ushigami.

Bourgeois, Derek. *Fantasy Rondo, Opus 126.* Warwick Music. Euphonium duet and brass band (piano reduction available). 1990. £19.95, £9.95. 8:45. G–d♭″ (e♭″), F–d♭″. This duet is VERY challenging and incredibly fun. Both parts have very extensive range requirements and very difficult, however idiomatic technical parts. Bourgeois knows how to write to please the audience and there are numerous bits and pieces that seem to come from well known works. Yet they are cast with his undeniable quirky harmony and clever settings. The major hurdle will be making the vast technical requirements comfortable. Enjoy the practice time with a metronome. This is an excellent work if the demands can be met by the soloists that will prove an excellent choice in the duet repertoire.

Bowen, Brian. *Euphonium Music.* Winwood Music. Euphonium solo and brass band (wind band, orchestral, and piano reduction available). 1984 (written in 1978). £50 (no price, no price, £20). 14:30. IV. E♭–c″. Written in three movements: Andante; Andante con espressivo, Moderato. *Euphonium Music* stands as one of the contemporary standards in the euphonium repertoire. The writing features many less common melodic intervals of sevenths in its opening motive that reappears several times. The technical and rhythmic demands are numerous and the rising seventh appears in the fast sections as well. Most of the runs in the work are chromatic in nature and do not always follow major and minor triads. The second movement features one of the most poignant melodies written for the euphonium and provides great scope for interpretation. The second movement segues into the technical third with many triplet flourishes and a rapid syncopated theme. There are some awkward mixed meter sections before a brief melodic interlude before the final technical flourish and a section demonstrating the lyrical power of the instrument. This is a highly recommended work and can be performed with any standard performance medium. Recorded by the Childs Brothers, Steven Mead, Robin Taylor.

Bowes, Ray. *The Pathway.* SP & S. Euphonium solo and brass band. 1973. 6:50. IV. F–c″. This solo is a traditionally based euphonium solo incorporating Salvation Army songs presented in a fantasia style. There is a nice mix of slow and fast and the technical demands are not extraordinary. There are some sixteenth note triplets in chromatic patterns as well as a few wide interval upward slurs. The final (and only) c″ in the work could easily be lowered to the tonic of a♭′.

Bowes, Ray. *Song of Triumph.* SP & S. Euphonium solo and brass band. 1971. 6:30. III–IV. (BB♭)

B♭–b♭′ (c″). This solo is a traditionally based euphonium solo incorporating Salvation Army songs presented in the very popular fantasia style. There is a nice mix of slow and fast with more emphasis on the technical prowess of the instrument. There are some octave jumps throughout the piece and a fair bit of emphasis on sixteenth note triplets at tempos around 92 and 96. Recorded by William Brown, William Himes.

Bozza, Eugene. *Aria.* Klaas van der Woude. Obrasso. Euphonium solo and brass band. €75.

Bray. *Jessica Rose.* Kirklee's Music. Euphonium solo and brass band.

Bridge, Frank. *Meditation.* Arr. Thomas Rüedi. Obrasso. Euphonium solo and brass band (piano reduction available). €67 (€14). 3:45. A lovely lyrical work that combines a romantic quality with some occasional contemporary moments. The work is scored very well with lots of color added from the percussion. Recorded by Thomas Rüedi.

Bulla, Stephen. *Euphonium Fantasia (Rhapsody for Euphonium).* DeHaske Music Publishers. Euphonium solo and brass band. 6:45. IV. (AA♭) F–b♭′ (e♭″). Dedicated to Steve Kellner and the 1990 Southern Territorial Band. This is a very idiomatic, contemporary work for the euphonium and brass band. The piece opens with a rapid rising figure at a slow tempo before a stately *Allegro moderato* begins. This syncopated melody ends on a high b♭ before a more relaxed section begins and features an obligato line for the euphonium that leads to beautiful chorale in 3/4. A gradual quickening with an arpeggiated slurred solo part concludes with a cadenza with lots of technical work. The final section in 6/8 gradually accelerates and culminates with a high trill on either a♭′ or d♭″. A presto leads to final flourishes for soloist and band. Recorded by David Church, Richard Gosney, Morgan Griffiths.

Bulla, Stephen. *His Love Remains the Same.* SP & S. Euphonium solo and brass band.

Camsey, Terry. *A Joy Untold.* SP & S. Euphonium solo and brass band. 1978. £17.95. 4:15. III–IV. (F) B♭–c″ (e♭″). Written with an opening lyrical band section, which breaks into a fast section of running scalar sixteenth notes for the soloist. These contrast with a slower lyrical section of arpeggiated eighth notes that later D.S. to fast sixteenth notes, *A Joy Untold* provides a short work to showcase good technique and lyricism. One interesting component involves the various shifting accents in the opening fast section that give a slight mixed meter feel. Some optional octaves will provide some challenges if desired. Recorded by Derick Kane, Thomas Mack, Chris Mallet, Aaron Vanderweele.

Capuzzi, Guiseppe Antonio. *Andante and Rondo.* Ed. Robert Childs and Philip Wilby. Winwood Music. Euphonium solo and brass band (piano reduction available). 2004. 7:30. III–IV. F–c″.

A fine setting of this very common transcription used by many players and teachers as a representative work from the classical period. The *Andante* features exceptional lyrical possibilities and challenges involving the fluidity and ease of the rising arpeggios ascending to b♭' and c". The *Rondo* hosts a light theme that will bring joy to player and audience. The section in e♭ minor presents some technical challenges, but they can be surmounted. This solo represents one of the core transcriptions in the euphonium's repertoire. Recorded by Tyronne Breuninger, Robert Childs.

Caravelli, Romuald. *Let Me Try Again*. Arr. Alan Fernie. Obrasso. Baritone solo and brass band. €67.

Cassado, Gaspar. *Danse du Diable Vert*. Arr. Thomas Rüedi. Obrasso. Euphonium solo and brass band (piano reduction available). 2001. €67 (€14). 3:30. V. c–d♭". A turbulent and humorous encore bravura piece with a very tricky theme. Recorded by Thomas Rüedi.

Catelinet, Philip. *The Call of the Seasons*. Cinque Port Music Publishers. Euphonium solo and brass band. 1985. 8:00. IV. F–c". Dedicated to Dr. David Goldin. Written as a theme and variations that captures the moods of the four seasons of the year, this work captures the tradition of the euphonium soloist and brass band exquisitely. The style of the solo part and accompaniment typify the heritage of the brass band with excellent lyrical and technical writing that will result in listening enjoyment for the audience and performers. The melodic opening captures a somber mood before turning more optimistic with a quicker tempo and various countermelodies. Variation 1 captures a more upbeat feeling with sixteenth note, diatonic runs before variation 2 in 9/8 highlights a wonderful ascending melody. The finale, written as a vivace 6/8, contains the most technical writing with jovial melodic writing. The soloist's part remains mostly diatonic and accessible and the band parts are well written. This work will be an audience pleaser given its melodic and harmonic language and slightly programmatic nature. Recorded by Riki McDonnell, Steven Mead, Wilfred Mountain.

Catelinet, Philip. *Cheerful Volunteers*. SP & S. Euphonium cornet duet and brass band. 1983. 6:15. III–IV. G–a♭' (b♭'), cornet c'–a♭" (b♭"). The opening allegro sciolto prepares the 6/8 time signature for a lilting stroll through this duet. The theme is presented by the cornet with the euphonium providing a countermelody. There are some scalar and arpeggio techniques on sixteenth notes. There are also a few difficult syncopations later in the work, but overall the scope and style remain consistent.

Catelinet, Philip. *Duo Caprice*. Manuscript. Soprano and euphonium solo and brass band. IV.

Catelinet, Philip. *The Warrior*. SP & S. Euphonium solo and brass band (piano reduction available

in the *Salvation Army Solo Album No. 21*). 6:45. III–IV. (C) F–b♭' (c"). A traditional theme and variations solo with a unique final variation that features a fine mixture of slurred and tongued triplets intertwined with tongued sixteenths. The introduction, opening cadenza, theme, single tongued triplet first variation, and minor key interlude bear strong resemblance to many of the solos of this period. This solo can be worthwhile due to its inclusion in the *Solo Album No. 21*.

Catherwood, David. *All I Have I Am Bringing*. SP & S. Euphonium solo and brass band. 1987. 3:55. III. B♭–g'. A nice lyrical work that will allow the soloist to sing beautifully. A few small challenges may be tuning the g' that will certainly have a tendency to drift sharp, and it appears many times. Recorded by Aaron Vanderweele.

Catherwood, David. *Everybody Should Know*. SP & S. Euphonium solo and brass band. 1989. 6:15. III–IV. c–c". Written in a standard slow-fast-slow-fast form, this solo provides a few more challenges then the normal Salvation Army solo in that the fast sections have some quite difficult moments. The first section features some sextuplet figures that will test many players and the final fast section offers the performer the choice to either slur or legato tongue the section. Recorded by Derick Kane.

Chamindae. *Automne Euphonium*. Arr. Katie Bell. Wright and Round. Euphonium solo and brass band.

Chapman. *Helmsley*. Kirklee's Music. Euphonium solo and brass band. £17.50.

Chester, B. *Arabella*. Wright and Round. Euphonium solo and brass band.

Clarke, Nigel. *The City in the Sea*. Maecenas Music. Euphonium solo and brass band (wind band and piano reduction available). 1995. $45 ($200, $32.95). 16:00. V. CC♯–c". To Robert Childs and the Black Dyke Mills Band. One of the most demanding solos from a range and power standpoint, *The City in the Sea* takes its programmatic nature from a poem by Edgar Allen Poe depicting a coastal town that is taken by the sea. The work can be described as ethereal, barbaric, and intense. It opens with a low foghorn type call from the soloist on low D₁ followed by some melodic material in the pedal range before a sudden three and half octave jump to a c" that becomes a reoccurring motive. The melodic writing creates an appropriate uneasy feeling before the three and half octave motive returns and the powerful section ensues with very rapid tonguing, range shifts, and technical runs. The haunting lyrical theme alternates with the barbaric section a number of times, each time growing in power. The soloist will spend much time working on octave jumps and the awkward fingerings and difficult rhythms. This work is not for the faint of heart. Necessities are a strong extreme low range, agility of rapid interval jumps of more than two octaves, and of course the needed dynamic power to balance a thickly textured accompaniment. Recorded by David Childs, Robert Childs.

Corelli, Archangelo. *Adagio*. Philip Wilby. Kirklee's Music. Euphonium solo and brass band.

Cosma, Vladimir. *Euphonium Concerto*. Lam Larghetto. Euphonium solo and brass band (symphony orchestra, wind band, and piano reduction). 2000 (written in 1998). Rental $75. 21:00. V. DD♭–d″. Written for the 1998 World Tuba Euphonium Competition in Guebwiller, France. Written in three movements: Allegro assai; Andantino; Finale-Giocoso. One of the most challenging and rewarding solos in the repertoire, this concerto embodies in many ways the spirit of Paganini and Liszt for the euphonium and represents one of the most outstanding selections for euphonium and large ensemble. It features virtuoso technique, intense melody, and a need for panache and flair. The technical and range challenges are formidable, but WELL worth the practice. Of particular note are the flexibility, clarity, and tone quality needed in the low range from BB♭ to F, as there are numerous sections of slurred and tongued passages in these ranges. There is also a strong need for excellent double and triple tonguing as Cosma wrote the final few sections with the violin (his instrument) in mind versus the euphonium, so some of the passages are not as idiomatic as they could be. The Andantino creates an atmosphere mindful of Piazzolla, the famous tango writer. The melody sails with the euphonium. This piece stands at the top of the list of recommended repertoire for those capable. Taking this challenge will be extremely rewarding and the only caveat involves the cost of the large ensemble rental parts (at the time of writing it was more than $400) and the piano reduction. The publisher has made these choices and they greatly hinder the wide spread of this fantastic work. Recorded by Adam Frey, Ivan Milheit, Tennessee Tech Tuba Euphonium Ensemble, Steven Mead.

Curnow, James. *Lark in the Clear Air*. D. Catherwood. Curnow Music Press. Euphonium solo and brass band. III.

Curnow, James. *Rhapsody for Euphonium*. Tuba-Euphonium Press (Winwood Music–brass band and piano). Euphonium solo and brass band (wind band and piano reduction available). 1990. $80. 6:30. III. A–a′. To Leonard Falcone. Written in four sections of slow-fast-slow-fast, the Curnow *Rhapsody* remains a core component of the repertoire for level III. It features an excellent balance of melodic playing and technical passages. An opening cadenza leads to a lyrical statement characteristic of Curnow's tonal writing. The lines are easy to shape and lend themselves to musical phrasing education. The allegro con spirito boasts an energetic accompaniment figure before the euphonium enters on a stately theme. Some sixteenth note sequences provide transition material to the next section that has similar motives with some syncopated feel. There is a brief restatement of the lyrical theme before a transition section that contains a number of chromatic sequences, and sixteenth note chromatic scales return the player back to the high-energy tempo. The ending five bars feature a strong maestoso section. The *Rhapsody* represents an excellent work that high school students can use as a solo vehicle with an easier accompaniment figure. Recorded by Cédric Albiez, Tyronne Breuninger, Roger Behrend, the Childs Brothers, Phillip Franke, Andre Grainger, Steven Mead, David Welsh, Joseph Zuback.

Curnow, James. *Symphonic Variants*. Manuscript (Curnow Music Press & Tuba-Euphonium Press). Euphonium solo and brass band (symphony orchestra, wind band, and piano reduction available). Manuscript ($100, $129, $24). 1984. 19:00. V. DD–c″ (f″). Introduction; Theme and Variations: Allegro con brio, Allegro moderato con espressivo, Allegro con spirito, Lento con teneramente, Presto, Adagio con calore, Allegro maestoso, Peasante. One of the core repertoire works for the euphonium and also one of the most demanding works ever written for the instrument, *Symphonic Variants* runs the gamut of technical facility, range, endurance, and power to project and balance. The difficulties will mainly be annotated as the work should be a standard piece in an advanced player's library. This superb work opens with a flourish of technique and runs to c″ before presenting the lyrical theme. There are numerous *ossia* throughout the work that make the very high tessitura more accessible. The opening theme has an optional d″ and e♭″. All this is less than one minute from the start of a nearly twenty-minute work! Variation 1, Allegro con brio, hosts a lively 6/8 version with a run down to GG. Variation 2, Lento con teneramente, exposes the soloist on some high-range entrances as well as some rapid range shifts over three octaves in the course of two measures (albeit at a slow tempo). A very nice rubato section brings this variation to a close. The Presto highlights the agility of the euphonium with a bountiful number of sixteenth notes and double tonguing during the entire variation. There are numerous presentations of the motives that jump octaves between beats with many *ossia*. A long chromatic run to c″ with a diminuendo leads to the Adagio con calore. Curnow writes this lyrical section very well to suit the euphonium. It leads smoothly into the Allegro maestoso, a slower sixteenth note variation in a stately style that returns the opening material before a calm Peasante allows the soloist, accompaniment, and audience to wind up to the final powerful notes that feature an optional f″. The accompaniment parts are difficult and thickly textured. Great projection and balance will be needed by the soloist.

This is one of the most physical works in the repertoire and one of the standard works frequently performed. Recorded by Roger Behrend, Brian Bowman, Mary Ann Craig, Marik Denys, Phil Franke, Shoichiro Hokazono, Angie Hunter, Steven Mead, Robin Taylor.

DeCurtis, Ernesto. *Return to Sorrento*. Arr. Roy Newsome. Obrasso. Euphonium solo and brass band. €67. 4:30. III. A nice arrangement of a beautiful nostalgic melody. Recorded by Steven Mead.

DeCurtis, Ernesto. *Return to Sorrento*. Arr. Stephen Roberts. Winwood Music. Euphonium solo and brass band (piano reduction available). 4:30. III. A nice arrangement of a beautiful nostalgic melody. Recorded by Steven Mead.

DeLuca, Joseph. *Beautiful Colorado*. Arr. Stanley Boddington. Studio Music. Euphonium solo and brass band (wind band and piano reduction available–Carl Fischer). £15. 5:10. III. A waltz-style work typical of the Sousa Band era with an opening cadenza, ascending melody in triple meter, and ornamented technical sections. Commonly performed on a double-belled euphonium. Recorded by Trevor Groom, David Lean (also see Music for Euphonium and Wind Band listing for recordings of original version).

Denver, John. *Perhaps Love*. Arr. Fraser. Spaeth/ Schmid. Euphonium duet and brass band. €30.50. A well-known melody that brings a feeling of nostalgia to many audiences, this selection is an excellent choice. Recorded by the Childs Brothers.

DeVita, Alfred. *Softly, As I Leave You*. Arr. Alan Catherall. Winwood Music. Euphonium solo (duet part optional) and brass band (piano reduction available). 1987. £17.95 (£11.95). 3:15. IV. D♭–b♭′ (e♭″). A solo or duet version of this superb melody. It features the euphonium in its most sonorous range in the middle to high register. The duet version is even more enjoyable than the solo version and provides an optional e♭″ at the conclusion to finish the work off nicely. Recorded by the Childs Brothers, David Childs, Carl Schultz, Richard Wilkins.

Dewhurst, Robin. *Panache*. Gramercy. Euphonium solo and brass band (piano reduction available). 1995. £18.95 (£7.95). 4:15. III–IV. g–b♭′ (e♭″). Written in two sections, *Panache* has a very strong jazz/pop influence on melody, harmony, and rhythm. The opening lyrical section contains some nice singing moments for the solo line with syncopations being part of the norm. The tessitura does stay high regularly in the opening. In the fast section, a number of articulations are utilized to emphasis the jazz idiom and there are a few meter changes and trills. Overall, this work is a fun selection that many younger students will enjoy as the music certainly contrasts with more serious-themed music and provides something

unique for the euphonium. Recorded by Frans Burghgraef, Steven Mead, Brian Miexner.

Dockerhill. *Pleasure Complete*. SP & S (Out of Print). Euphonium solo and brass band. III.

Doughty, G. *Grandfather's Clock*. Wright and Round. Euphonium solo and brass band (piano reduction available). £14.95 (£4.95). III. a–b♭′. A classical theme and variations from the turn-of-the-century period. This one, however, has remained significantly popular due to its theme, playability, and of course the slightly cheesy clock innuendo. The variations are a single tongued triplet, slurred and tongued sixteenths, short cadenza, and rapid slurred sixteenths. This is a recommended solo for a lighthearted selection. Recorded by Lyndon Baglin, David Childs, John Clough, Stuart Cunliffe, Heather Enstwille, Ben Haemhouts, Steven Mead, Gareth Morgan, Simon Willis, Ken Wood, David Woollam.

Doughty, G. *Hermits Cave*. Wright and Round. Euphonium solo and brass band.

Doughty, G. *The Old Rustic Bridge*. Wright and Round. Euphonium solo and brass band. Recorded by Stephen Archer.

Downie, Kenneth. *Concerto for Euphonium (Eulogy)*. Winwood Music. Euphonium solo and brass band (piano reduction available). 2004. 16:00. V. B♭–e♭″. Three movements: Con moto e vigore; Andante con espressivo; Vivace festivamente. A new, large-scale composition for the euphonium, this work will challenge soloist and band. The work opens with a light 12/8 triplet theme that jumps around the range of the instrument as well as appearing as triple tonguing figures. Based in g minor, the work explores this motive before some foreshadowing of the lyrical second movement theme. There are a number of wide interval slurs in the work as well. The second movement demonstrates excellent knowledge of the euphonium and makes use of its lyricism. The climax, an allargando theme on a high b♭ and c♭, brings the main theme back again to close the movement. The finale returns to the fast tradition in brass band solos with very rapid sixteenth note runs that are slurred and double tongued. A unique figure involves an octave slur between the first two sixteenth notes in a set of runs. It will be a challenge at tempo. A quasi cadenza near the end of the work has the euphonium playing from pedal B♭ to d″ before a restatement from the first movement, at a brisker tempo, brings the work to a dramatic, powerful ending. This work will certainly receive more performances and become one of the most challenging works in the repertoire.

Elgar, Edward. *Introduction and Allegro Spiritoso*. Arr. Eric Ball. Spaeth/Schmid. Euphonium solo and brass band. €50.

Ellerby, Martin. *Euphonium Concerto*. Studio Music. 1997. Euphonium solo and brass band (symphony orchestra, wind band, and piano reduction available). Rental only (£10.50 piano). 22:00. V. GG–e♭″. Four movements: Fantasy; Capriccio; Rhapsody (for Luis); Diversions. Commissioned by and dedicated to Steven Mead. One of THE most challenging works in the repertoire, the Ellerby *Euphonium Concerto* can be summed up as an exploration in the technical limits of the euphonium in regards to range, dexterity, and endurance. Attention to detail is a must in all movements, as Ellerby clearly marks articulation and dynamic nuances. The Fantasy features the alternation of an energetic rising theme, sometimes slurred and sometimes tongued, with a beautiful melodic section. The Capriccio is the most demanding technically and rhythmically. One of the great moments of the work occurs as the 12/8 theme shifts from triplet to duple subdivisions. The writing can be described as melodic and motivic with a very wide palette of harmonic and melodic colors in an angular style. The chromatic appearance does not translate to chromatic-sounding harmony. A muted section occurs in the middle of the second movement. The Rhapsody (for Luis) hosts one of the best examples of lyrical euphonium writing. Dedicated to Luis Maldanado, this movement's buildup and climax leading to a d″ remains one of the most memorable moments in the euphonium's repertoire. The writing and interplay between soloist and ensemble make this movement a joy to perform, and the final repeated d's in the solo line pay homage to another great lyrical euphonium concerto by Horovitz. Diversions could be described as approximately five minutes of pure, intense rhythmic drive. From its opening accompaniment figure played by the band, which sets the pace, this movement places large technical demands on the soloist including rapid tonguing, optional multi-phonics, highly articulated figures in extreme ranges, traversing more than two octaves in a single bar, and ending with glissandi up to e♭″. One of the masterpieces of the euphonium repertoire, this concerto will require lots of practice and strength. The ensemble parts are very difficult and a good conductor will be needed. Alternate fingerings will make the solo part clearer and easier. Recorded by Adam Frey, Steven Mead, Brian Meixner.

Evenepohl, Johan. *Rhapsody.* DeHaske Music. 1994. Euphonium solo and brass band. IV. C₁–b♭′(e♭″). The opening allegro con fuoco sets the pace for this short work that highlights the technical abilities of the euphonium. The opening motive with either a triplet or two sixteenths as pickups pervades the entire work. The solo part contains some rapid passages of sextuplet figures that are quite brisk at the marked tempo, as well as a number of glissandi. The writing remains scalar in most passages with a few measures of intricate

articulation. A brief cadenza finishing on the low C heralds the slower section featuring a more obligato line in the euphonium, before returning to the allegro reminiscent of the opening. A light 6/8 section with numerous sixteenth note patterns ushers in a three-bar allusion to the lyrical section before the finale four bars of allegro drive the work to an energetic finish. The final solo figure has an *ossia* for the e♭″. A lesser-known work for brass band that has not been performed often. Recorded by Robert Childs.

Fernie, Alan. *Fantasy on Negro Spirituals.* Bernel Music. Euphonium duet. IV.

Fernie, Alan. *Introduction and Allegro.* Bernel Music. Euphonium solo and brass band. IV. Recorded by Morgan Griffiths.

Fiocco, Joseph Hector. *Arioso and Allegro.* Arr. Robert Childs and Philip Wilby. Winwood Music. Euphonium solo and brass band (piano reduction available). 1997. 6:20. III. F–b♭′. Written in two movements: Arioso; Allegro. A nice setting of a baroque work for euphonium and brass band, this arrangement presents a much-needed style of music that helps to diversify programs. The Arioso includes some nice melodic writing. There are a few minor challenges in the trills and ornaments, but mainly the test will be control and stylistic quality. The Allegro of course tests dexterity and agility, but the music stays scalar and in familiar territory most of the time, leaving the main concern to once again be control and style. This edition is an excellent choice and will require the band to control their dynamics as well. Recorded by Robert Childs.

Foster, Stephen. *Gentle Annie.* Arr. Roger Thorne. Thornes Music. Euphonium solo and brass band (piano reduction available). 2004. £18 (£5). 5:15. A pleasant theme and variations on this tried and true melody. The variations follow the turn-of-the-century variation pattern of slow triplets, sixteenths, and fast, triple tongued triplets. A nice take on a traditional melody.

Foster, Stephen. *Shenandoah.* Stephen Bulla. Winwood Music. Euphonium solo and brass band. A nice setting of this well-known American traditional melody.

Fraser, Bruce. *The Fantastic Fast Fingered Fandando.* Spaeth/Schmid. Euphonium duet and brass band. €20. Recorded by the Childs Brothers.

Fristrup. *Calvary's Stream Now Is Flowing so Free.* SP & S. Euphonium solo and brass band. 3:25. III. G–e♭′. A pleasant melody written in 3/4 and felt in one. It contains easy phrases and a nice controlled range. One small difficulty involves numerous grace notes in groups of two, three, and four.

Frosali, G. B. *Il Sospiro Dell'Anima.* Manuscript. Euphonium solo and brass band. IV.

Garner, Errol. *Misty.* Arr. Alan Fernie. Obrasso. Euphonium solo and brass band. €67.

Geehl. *Watching the Wheat.* Spaeth/Schmid. Euphonium solo and brass band. €25.50. A setting of a lovely traditional melody.

Gershwin, George. *Summertime.* Arr. Alan Fernie. Obrasso. Euphonium solo and brass band. €67.

Gillingham, David. *Vintage.* Manuscript. Euphonium solo and brass band (wind band and piano reduction available from Tuba-Euphonium Press). 1991. No price ($75, $12). 9:15. VI–V. D–c″ (DD–e♭″). One of the staples of the euphonium repertoire, *Vintage* combines an intensely rhythmic and beautifully lyrical work with moments of intense power and majesty. From the opening chords and melodic statement by the soloist, the tonal harmonic colors swell to a climax on high c before a slightly aleatoric section featuring percussion leads to the quick and highly syncopated allegro. This section requires strong rhythmic discipline and ensemble given the independence of the solo and accompaniment lines. This section is interspersed through the rest of the piece between more lyrical interludes featuring the melodic high range of the euphonium. An extended cadenza occurs before the last few bars. It has numerous optional cuts to accommodate range issues but does allow the adventurous a span of over four octaves before a flurry of meter changes and rising figures bring the piece to a triumphant finish. *Vintage* is a highly recommended work that requires strong endurance and experienced ensemble. Recorded by Roger Behrend, Shoichiro Hokazono, Steven Mead, Brian Meixner.

Glorieux, François. *Fantasy.* Glorious Sounds. Euphonium solo and brass band (wind band, orchestra, and piano reduction available). 2001. €90 (€100, €70, €12). 7:10. VI. G♭–c″. Lento; Allegro con brio; Cadenza; Lento; Presto. This is the most demanding work by Glorieux and scored for all possible performance mediums so it remains a great choice for programmability. The composition contains Glorieux's signature listenable harmonies and melodies. The opening Lento lines set a relaxed atmosphere before the energetic and rhythmic Allegro con brio sixteenth note theme enters, which poses some challenges to the soloist with its shapes and double tonguing. The extended Cadenza lasting approximately 1:40 will be the hurdle to make it interesting to the listener. A beautiful theme ensues afterward, leading to the exuberant tarantella in the Presto climaxing to the final high c to finish the work. This piece should be performed more often and remains one of Glorieux's best showpieces. Recorded by Nick Ost.

Golland, John. *Child's Play.* Manuscript. Euphonium duet and brass band. Recorded by the Childs Brothers.

Golland, John. *Euphonium Concerto No. 1.* Chester Music. Euphonium solo and brass band (wind band and piano available). 1982. (Rental only brass band and wind band, £10.50 piano). 18:00. IV–V. D–e♭″. Written in three segue movements: Cadenza-Lento; Andante tranquillo; Allegro. This concerto remains one of the most rewarding and demanding concerti because of range, duration, and dynamics needed to balance ensemble. The opening cadenza covers two and half octaves (quickly). The first movement also features a large amount of technical interplay between band and soloist. There are moments of clever interjection and wonderful lyrical hemiolas. There is a significant cadenza that highlights triple tonguing, high tessitura, and rhythmic intensity before the lush 5/8 second movement begins. This movement emphasizes the rising octave and high-range control and contains some exquisite writing for the euphonium. It may certainly be one of the most heartfelt melodic moments in the entire repertoire and works well individually. The exciting Allegro features mixed meter, multiple tonguing, and a jovial nature. The shift from style to style helps hasten the work to the conclusion. A reprise of the opening cadenza with some development propels the work to the final coda. This work is highly recommended. Recorded by Robert Childs, Steven Mead. Ryuji Ushigami.

Golland, John. *Euphonium Concerto No. 2.* Studio Music. Euphonium solo and brass band (wind band and piano available). 1992. Rental (£10.50). 23:00. V. (DD) BB♭–e♭″ (b♭″). To Nicholas and Robert Childs. Written in three movements: Moderato Eroico; Largo Elegaico (In Memoriam: John Childs); Allegro energico e Scherzando. The second major work Golland has written for the euphonium, this composition is much more demanding than his *Euphonium Concerto No. 1.* There are many technical challenges in regards to fast runs, complex rhythms, leaps spanning between one and three octaves, rapid multiple tonguing, and the endurance necessary for the high tessitura that the work so aptly exploits. The work opens heroically and the first movement features many glissandos to c″ and technical passages moving sequentially. An extended cadenza features some contemporary notation, but make no mistake that the work is romantically based. The closing cadenza segues to the second movement; however, an optional ending to the first movement is included for performances that just feature the first movement. The Largo Elegaico captures Golland's skills and knowledge of the euphonium as a lyrical tenor with grace, sensitivity, and passion. The recitative sections feature sweeping runs and elegant technical passages before the introspective melody takes hold of the heart. The recitative section returns with some extended development before the main melody returns to be played tenderly in the extreme high range (c″ and d♭″). The final movement opens with a waltz-like, muted section and relies heavily on rapid triple tonguing of both repeated figures and difficult moving figures. There are also a number of high-range glissandos that reach nearly imperceptible heights from e♭″ to b♭″. Golland's *Concerto No. 1* may be more accessible to soloist and audience than the *Concerto No. 2*, but the later work provides fun challenges technically and musically that are worthwhile endeavors for performance. This work is definitely worth study but will be a challenge. Recorded by Ueli Kipfer, Steven Mead (second movement only).

Golland, John. *Mieso.* Baritone and tenor horn duet and brass band. A very lovely work that deserves more performances but is unfortunately limited by its instrumentation. Recorded by John Willems.

Golland, John. *Peace.* Hallamshire Music. Euphonium solo and wind band (piano reduction available). 4:15. III. e♭–b♭′. One of the most entrancing original melodic compositions for the euphonium. Golland knows the euphonium's capabilities well and exploits its singing middle and high range excellently. This should be a standard in all players' libraries as a selection for use in churches and as a melodic interlude. Recorded by David Childs, Marcus Cutts, Tormod Flaten, Mike Fox, Adam Frey, Steven Mead, Simon Postma, Kate Williams.

Golland, John. *Rhapsody for Baritone.* Kirklee's Music. Baritone solo and brass band (piano reduction available). £20 (£12.50).

Gossec, François Joseph. *Tambourin.* Arr. Eric Wilson. Winwood Music. Euphonium solo and brass band (piano reduction available). 1991. 3:30. £15.95 (£11.95). III. (F) c–f¹. A short, lighthearted solo written in a quasi-rondo form. The technical demands are almost exclusively based in F major. There are some nice articulation nuances and the work provides numerous *ossia* to facilitate difficult sections.

Gott, Barrie. *From the Heart.* Muso's Media. Euphonium solo and brass band (wind band and piano reduction available). 2003. $50 Australian ($85 and $20 Australian). 3:00. III. A♭–b♭¹. Written for Riki McDonnell. A short light work with a Latin groove and style. The accompaniment parts are rhythmic with an occasional melodic motive and the euphonium melody features an ascending octave. In the middle section, the soloist plays sixteenth note obligato patterns before returning to the main theme in the new key of A♭. This work is a welcome addition to the repertoire in the vein of lighter, short works. It would be perfect for a high school band looking for an easy accompaniment.

Graham, Peter. *Bravura.* Gramercy Music. Euphonium solo and brass band (wind band). 2003. £24.95 (£59.95). 5:00. IV. G–c″ (f″). Written as a fantasia based on four traditional themes of Great Britain, *Bravura* combines a superb showpiece with traditional melodies. The solo part

features numerous *ossia* that allow the soloist to ascend to the high range as desired. The technical demands will be the challenge in this work with rapid triple tongued passages, overall high tessitura, and running sixteenths in the final section. An extended cadenza can be modified or changed in accordance with the soloist's wishes. This work will be enjoyed by many audiences and hopefully by the soloist with all the needed preparation. Recorded by Derrick Kane, Steven Mead.

Graham, Peter. *Brillante.* Winwood Music. Euphonium solo (optional duet) and brass band (wind band, orchestra, and piano). 1987. (Piano £17.95). 6:00. IV. F–c″ (e♭″). Written as a fantasia based on the traditional melody *Rule Britannia, Brillante* highlights the technical powers of the euphonium. These demands will be the challenge in this work with rapid triple tongued passages, overall high tessitura, and running sixteenths as the final section. This work will be enjoyed by many audiences and is a great choice as a modern theme and variations. Recorded by the Childs Brothers, David Childs, Adam Frey, Robert Jose, Steven Mead, David Thornton, Glyn Williams.

Graham, Peter. *Glorious Ventures.* Gramercy. Euphonium solo and brass band (piano reduction available). 1995. IV. B♭–b♭′ (c″). Set as variations on "The Lily of the Valley," this solo presents a fresh look at the often tired theme and variations solo. The majority of the work is accessible to younger players because the sixteenth notes are slurred in the first and final variation. A brief nostalgic melody in the minor key breaks the two and presents the only slower lyrical moment as the theme is a faster-paced one. This is a recommended solo, especially with piano accompaniment.

Graham, Peter. *The Holy Well.* Gramercy. Euphonium solo and brass band. 1999. 3:30. III–IV. c–b♭′. Taken from his brass band work *On Alderley Edge,* Peter Graham has crafted a beautiful melody that works through two keys in his version of *The Holy Well.* The work has no major difficulties other than a few wide interval slurs. It is an excellent original composition in that this melody is actually a euphonium solo in the brass band work. Recorded by Morgan Griffiths.

Graham, Peter. *The Minstrel Boy.* Just Music Scotland. Euphonium solo and brass band. £17.95.

Graugaard, Lars. *Concerto for Euphonium and Brass Band.* Euphonium solo and brass band. 1995. 15:00. IV–V. D–c″ (f″). Written in three segue movements: Powerful, Almost Violent; Calm and Flowing; Bold and Fast. Opening with a flurry of repeated note triple tonguing, the first movement captures its marking accurately. The solo part through the work remains quite demanding with rapid double and triple tonguing, with the double tonguing having repeated figures as well as moving sixteenths with accents occurring on the second, third, and fourth sixteenth. The writing utilizes accents and syncopations heavily to derive its energy, as well as repeated notes that build. There are occasional trills and mixed meter. A cadenza that reprises motives from the first movement leads to a flourish from the brass band that relaxes into the second movement. The harmonic language here has some dissonance but remains listener friendly. The accompaniment textures will be easy to balance. The final movement highlights the dexterity of the instrument with sixteenth note groups that give a mixed meter feeling while remaining in 4/4 time. The band parts punctuate the soloist's line. After a long run to a c″, the band gets its chance at the technical runs on a lengthy tutti section before a quasi cadenza leads back to the opening material in the solo line. Yet the band parts have changed slightly to punctuations with repeated notes alluding to the first movement. The ending features a high f″ figure that would work fine down an octave. This work looks quite interesting and seems like a composition that has been overlooked by many players.

Gregson, Edward. *Concerto Grosso*. Studio Music. 1973. Brass quartet and brass band. Written for the National Youth Brass Band of Scotland. This work is an excellent choice for the performance medium of a brass quartet. Gregson has written numerous works for brass band and knows the instruments' capabilities and the audiences' likes as well.

Gregson, Edward. *Symphonic Rhapsody*. SP & S. Euphonium solo and brass band. 1976. 7:15. IV. C–c″. Written while Gregson was still in his teens, the *Symphonic Rhapsody* deserves more performances. It hosts a majestic opening with very idiomatic writing and minor technical flourishes. A lyrical 5/4 section provides a wonderful melody with a slight rhythmic tilt. Following this section is a more introspective melody with many moments of ornamentation before the allegro deciso provides some faster material that leads to rapid double tonguing. The final bars feature a four-bar c″. This work represents a classic euphonium solo that does not push the soloist to the limits of the instrument but demonstrates style and agility tastefully. Recorded by the Childs Brothers, Neal Corwell, Morgan Griffiths, Steven Mead.

Hamlisch, Marvin. *The Way We Were*. Arr. Darryl Barry. Musikverlag Frank. Euphonium solo and brass band. £28.60. 3:30. III. e♭–b♭′. Darryl Barry is a well-known arranger for brass bands and his settings of television, movie, and popular melodies always ring true. This setting allows the soloist the melody in a comfortable range and then a high florid countermelody. The work is good for demonstrating style and will of course delight an audience.

Handel, G. F. *Departure from the Queen of Sheba*. Arr. Ian Jones. NJH Music. Euphonium solo and brass band. £15. 6:10. IV. A lighthearted take on Handel's very popular work, *Departure from the Queen of Sheba* features lots of rapid double tonguing and technical work. Paired with an upbeat accompaniment that gives lots of energy to the work, it feels slightly like a big band version of the tune with the solo part placed on steroids.

Hanmer, Ronald. *Flight of Fancy*. R Smith & Co. Euphonium and cornet duet and brass band.

Hartmann, John. *Le Belle Americane*. Wright and Round. Euphonium solo and brass band. 7:00. IV. An excellent theme and variations whose variations are not totally predictable. This is a recommended work but does only come with a treble clef solo part. Recommended for those who can obtain it.

Hartmann, John. *Drink to Me Only*. Arr. D. Wilby. Wright and Round. Euphonium solo and brass band. III. A turn-of-the-century classic theme and variations. Features a normal form of introduction, cadenza, theme, variations, lyrical interlude, and final. This solo utilizes multiple tonguing and will need good dexterity.

Hartmann, John. *My Pretty Jane*. Wright and Round. Euphonium solo and brass band. III. A turn-of-the-century classic theme and variations. Features a normal form of introduction, cadenza, theme, variations, lyrical interlude, and final. This solo utilizes multiple tonguing and will need good dexterity.

Hartmann, John. *Rule Britannia*. Wright and Round. Euphonium solo and brass band (piano accompaniment by Euphonium.com). III. A turn-of-the-century classic theme and variations. Features a normal form of introduction, cadenza, theme, variations, lyrical interlude, and final. This solo utilizes multiple tonguing and will need good dexterity.

Hartmann, John. *Weiderkehr*. Wright and Round. Euphonium solo and brass band. III. A turn-of-the-century classic theme and variations. Features a normal form of introduction, cadenza, theme, variations, lyrical interlude, and final. This solo utilizes multiple tonguing and will need good dexterity.

Hawkes, Fredrick G. *Honour and Arms* (Part II of *Two Solos by Handel*). SP & S. Euphonium solo and brass band. 2:55. II–III. G–e♭′. This is a nice solo with brass band accompaniment that can highlight style and articulation for young players.

Hawkes, Fredrick G. *True to Death*. SP & S. Euphonium solo and brass band. 3:55. II. B♭–d′. A melodic study that comes from the earliest Salvation Army period (No. 16 in the numbering system). It features nice easy writing with some lyrical character along with a few moments of accented parts.

Heath, Reginald. *Air and Rondo*. Midland Music Limited. Euphonium solo and brass band.

Heath, Reginald. *Andante and Scherzo*. Spaeth/ Schmid. Euphonium solo and brass band.

Heath, Reginald. *Springtime*. Midland Music Limited. Euphonium solo and brass band.

Himes, William. *Journey into Peace*. SP & S. Euphonium solo and brass band. III. Recorded by Derick Kane, Curtis Metcalf, Ken Waterworth.

Himes, William. *My Christ Is All in All*. SP & S. Euphonium solo and brass band. 3:25. III. C–bb'. A dolce melody in a slow 6/8 felt in six. There is a modulation and this new section contains a single bb¹ that could easily be lowered one octave to make this solo more accessible to younger players. Recorded by William Brown, Donald Meyer, Kelvin Richards.

Horne, Nigel. *Ascalon*. NJH. Euphonium solo and brass band. 1998. £15. 3:55. III. A nice lyrical setting of the melody *Fairest Lord Jesus*.

Horovitz, Joseph. *Euphonium Concerto*. Novello & Company Limited. Euphonium solo and brass band (wind band, orchestra, and piano available). 1991 (written in 1972). £60 (wind band and orchestra rental only, £10.50 piano). 16:00. IV. C–c″. Moderato; Lento; Con moto. Commissioned by the National Brass Band Championships of Great Britain. One of the first major concertos written for the euphonium, with each movement representing musical enjoyment for the head, heart, and toes, respectively. A piece of the standard repertoire, this concerto contains writing that will challenge and engage both performer and listener. The middle movement contains some of the most expressive lyrical writing in the repertoire. In the third movement, good technical facility will be needed as well as multiple tonguing for its jovial lighthearted nature. There are a number of dexterity challenges in this movement; thus, it is common to have younger players study the first two movements due to their significance even though they may not be ready to tackle the final movement. Horovitz provides extensive detail as to articulation, tempo, and dynamics and this makes it an excellent work for study and emphasis on these areas of performance. Orchestral parts are similar to a Mozart-type orchestra and provide an easy ensemble to balance. This is a highly recommended work. Recorded by Tyronne Breuninger, Robert Childs, Trevor Groom, Eran Levy, Steven Mead, Thomas Rüedi, Robin Taylor.

Howarth, Elgar. *Cantabile for John Fletcher*. Winwood Music. Euphonium duet and brass band. £17.95. 10:00. IV. A contemporary lyrical tribute to the acclaimed British tubist John Fletcher. It features modern harmonies and idiomatic writing. Recorded by the Childs Brothers.

Howarth, Elgar. *Paris de Soir*. Chester. Euphonium solo and brass band. III.

Howarth, Elgar. *Stories for Saroyan*. Winwood Music. Euphonium solo and brass band (piano reduction available). In preparation (£17.95). 13:00.

V. Cb–c″ (eb″). Written for Bob Childs. Written with eight stories and a coda: Now Thus; And Thus; Freddy Edmunds, No Such Thing; Still Life with Figure; The Two Philosophers; Fletcher's Roundabout; Katie Rodmel's Lullaby; In the Beginning; Hello Out There. This concerto has an interesting programmatic form and features some challenging difficulties. Knowing Howarth's other music will aid in understanding some of the sudden shifts, occasional angular melody, complex rhythms, and incredible demands placed on the soloist, as well as knowing it was written for Bob Childs. Many sections feature double and triple tonguing and less common chromatic patterns, as well as numerous glissandi and wide intervals. A mute is required and a secure low range below F will assist in preparing the work. Howarth writes some great melodic sections and the work will be well received by an audience that appreciates sophisticated contemporary music.

Hudec, Adam. *Golden Euphoniums*. Obrasso. Euphonium duet and brass band. €75. Recorded by Morgan Griffiths.

Hudec, Adam. *Slavonic Impressions*. Obrasso. Euphonium and cornet duet and brass band. €67. Recorded by Glyn Williams.

Huggens, Ted. *Air Nostalgique*. Arr. Bruce Fraser. Musikverlag Frank. Euphonium solo and brass band. 2000. 4:45. IV. Eb–c″ (eb″). A nice lyrical work that happily melds melodic playing with some elegantly ornamented solo lines that provide a nice mixture of lyrical qualities with occasions of technical flourish.

Hughes, John. *Calon Lân*. Eric Ball. Winwood Music. Euphonium duet and brass band (piano reduction available). 1988. £17.95. 3:35. III. Bb–ab' (eb″). A very nice lyrical duet with some sixteenth note flourishes at the end. A nice choice for a duet and brass band. Recorded by the Childs Brothers.

Jacob, Gordon. *Fantasia for Euphonium and Band*. Boosey & Hawkes. Euphonium solo and brass band (wind band and piano reduction available). Rental (Rental, $20). 1973. 10:45. IV. (FF) C#–bb' (d″). Dedicated to Michael Mamminga. One of the earliest major works written for the euphonium, Jacob's *Fantasia* remains a standard work in the repertoire. Its haunting opening melody, fun and quirky allegro section, lyrical melodic writing, triple tonguing intensity, low muted section, and demanding cadenza make it a composition worthy of performance. There are numerous *ossias* to assist with range limitations and the technical demands will prove a challenge for many players, but this should certainly be a familiar piece for all serious euphonium players. Recorded by Anonymous, Bjorn Bogetvedt, Mary Ann Craig, Mark Fisher, Tormod Flaten, Shoichiro Hokazono, Steven Mead, Toru Miura, Wendy Picton, Thomas Runty, David Stowe, Robin Taylor, Ron Young.

Jakeway, Albert H. *Hallelujah*. SP & S. Euphonium solo and brass band. 5:35. III–IV. G–b♭′ (c″). A challenging work from the early years of Salvation Army music, this solo features a theme and variations that opens with some brief cadenzas before the main theme gets introduced. The first variation contains some unusual trill figures but is mainly slurred sixteenth notes. A minor version of the melody precedes an ornamented version of this minor section before a final triumphant triple tongued variation concludes the work joyously.

Jakeway, Albert H. *The Happy Pilgrim*. SP & S. Euphonium solo and brass band. 1943. 6:10. III. Jakeway was known for his theme and variations solos, and this one follows the trademark characteristics with an opening cadenza highlighting numerous arpeggios before a lyrical introduction leads to a fanfare from the band and the main theme in 3/4. The variations are scalar with the first featuring slurred and tonguing sixteenth notes in a relaxed mood. The second variation hosts single tongued triplets before the traditional introspective melody in a minor key. The final variation in this solo involves double tongued sixteenths. This solo carefully challenges younger plays and the range works very well. The high range does not ascend above a g′, except in the cadenza, so that makes it a great solo for many players.

Jakeway, Albert H. *Lord of the Tempest*. SP & S. Euphonium solo and brass band. 1942. II. d–g′. A nice easy solo that features good lyrical opportunities. The only difficulty lies in its slow 6/8 counting.

Karlsen, Kjell Mark. *Concerto Grosso, Opus 98, No. 2*. Norsk Forlag A/S. Euphonium solo, cornet solo, e♭ horn solo, tuba solo, and brass band. 1991. 15:00.

Kippax. *I Love to Tell the Story*. SP & S. Euphonium solo and brass band. III. Recorded by Jack Parton.

Kitto, Gordon. *Alpine Polka*. Spaeth/Schmid. Euphonium solo and brass band. €20. A German-style work.

Kjellgren, G. *My Light and Song*. SP & S. Euphonium solo and brass band. 6:25. IV. F–b♭′. Written as a theme and variations, this solo does break some molds of the traditional *air varie* in that its introduction only contains a very brief cadenza before the theme is performed. The first variation features slurred triplets and contains a few chromatic sections. The second variation in the minor key navigates away from the traditional in that it contains a very florid andante con espressivo that has some complex rhythms and ends with a fantastic *accellarando* that leads into the final section. The last variation contains many rapid slurred sixteenth passages but occasionally includes a slurred quintuplet and sextuplet figure that is quite unusual for this period. A refreshing

theme and variations solo with some special qualities. Recorded by John Butler.

Kroll, William. *Banjo and Fiddle*. Arr. Thomas Rüedi. Obrasso. Euphonium solo and brass band (piano reduction available). 2001. €67(€14). 3:30. V. A–e♭″. The celebrated violin virtuoso composed this bravura piece for use in his own performances. The spirited and exuberant nature of the main theme stands in contrast with a sentimental cantilena. Recorded by Thomas Rüedi.

Lalo, Edouard . *Chants Russes Nr. 23*. Arr. Thomas Rüedi. Obrasso. Euphonium solo and brass band (piano reduction available). 2001. €67 (€14). 5:00. III. d–g′. This sentimental lento is taken from Lalo's *Concerto Russes* for violin and orchestra. A superb lyrical work. Recorded by Thomas Rüedi.

Langford, Gordon. *Foxtrot between Friends*. Chandos. Euphonium solo, cornet solo, and brass band. III. Recorded by Graham McEnvoy.

Larsson, John. *I'll Not Turn Back*. Arr. Ivor Bosanko. SP & S. Euphonium and cornet duet and brass band. 1992. 6:15. IV. G–c″ (cornet c′–b♭″). This solo presents the wonderful melodic character of the euphonium with well-written solo lines and countermelodies. The themes for the duet parts blend very well. There are a few complex rhythms and an overall use of the high range. A wonderful countermelody occurs near the end that finds the euphonium on soaring arpeggio lines. A highly recommended work. Recorded by the Childs Brothers, Chris Mallet.

Leidzen, Eric. *Home on the Range*. SP & S. Euphonium solo and brass band. 1979. £24.95. 7:45. IV. G–c″. One of the more substantial theme and variations solos of the Salvation Army genre, *Home on the Range* features the well-known cowboy melody in 3/4. This makes the work very programmable and unique indeed. The first variation is straightforward, but the second features a rubato 9/8 in a recitative style. The finale changes to 4/4 time and modulates and then picks up the pace vigorously with the nearly constant sixteenth note slurs. This work has great audience appeal and certainly should be programmed more often. Recorded by Robert McNalley, Ron Young.

Leidzen, Eric. *The Song of the Brother*. SP & S. Euphonium solo and brass band (piano reduction available in the *Salvation Army Solo Album No. 21*). £24.95. 7:20. III–IV. E–b♭′ (d♭″). Published in the *Salvation Army Solo Album No. 21*, this solo features the standard theme and variations format but represents one of the best of the genre. The opening and later cadenzas offer nice *ossias* and great liberty to demonstrate one's skills. The variations follow a standard form with single tongued triplets, followed by a minor key rendition of the melody with slight ornamentation, and concluding with a rollicking sixteenth note section with some very florid runs. This is an excellent selection that also offers a piano reduction. Recorded by Robert Childs, Steven Mead, Run Nygvist, Erich Schmidli, Ron Young.

Leoncavallo, Ruggero. *On with the Motley*. Arr. Ray Farr. Winwood Music. Euphonium solo and brass band (piano reduction available). 1981. £15.95 (£3.95). 4:00. III–IV. f–c″. This is one of the most famous arias from *I Pagliacci* and has been made well known with its appearance in movies. The solo part is demanding in terms of range and dynamic requirements; otherwise, the work is accessible. Recorded by Morgan Griffiths, Riki McDonnell.

Liddle, S. *Abide with Me*. Boosey & Hawkes.

Lloyd Webber, Andrew. *Variations*. See listing under Webber, Andrew Lloyd.

Lorriman, Howard. *Prelude and Scherzo*. Obrasso. Euphonium solo and brass band. €75. An original work for euphonium/baritone and brass band.

Lovatt-Cooper, Paul. *Donegal Bay*. Wright and Round. Baritone solo and brass band. 1999. £17.95. 4:15. IV. c–c″. A nice lyrical work that allows the soloist an expressive melody with a Scottish/Irish influence in a vein similar to the traditional song *Carrickfergus*. The soloist has a high countermelody that soars to b♭′ and c″ before a recapitulation that leads to a peaceful conclusion of the work. A good work to explore the lyrical nature of the brass band with a soloist.

Mack, Thomas. *Covenant*. SP & S. Euphonium solo and brass band. III. Recorded by Thomas Mack.

Mantia, Simone. *All Those Endearing Young Charms*. Arr. Stanley Boddington. Studio Music. Euphonium solo and wind band (brass band available). III–VI. One of the classic euphonium theme and variations solos specifically written for the euphonium. This work utilizes F and will certainly test out one's dexterity and technique. The lyrical variation requires great rubato and sense of rhythm. This is a highly recommended work with many arrangements to choose. Recorded by Lyndon Baglin, the Childs Brothers, Ian Keene, Burt Sullivan, Ken Wood, Joseph Zuback.

Mantia, Simone. *All Those Endearing Young Charms*. Gordon Langford. Chandos. III–IV. One of the classic euphonium theme and variations solos specifically written for the euphonium. This work utilizes F and will certainly test out one's dexterity and technique. The lyrical variation requires great rubato and sense of rhythm. This is a highly recommended work with many arrangements to choose. Recorded by Kenneth Bridge, Marcus Cutts, George Davis, Chris Mallet, Christopher Timlin.

Marcello, Benedetto. *Sonata in G Major*. Michel. Spaeth/Schmid. Euphonium solo and brass band. €64.50. A setting of one of the better-known sonatas of Marcello.

Marshall, George. *Ransomed (In Evil I Long Took Delight)*. SP & S. Euphonium solo and brass band (piano reduction available in the *Salvation Army Solo Album No. 21*). 5:25. III–IV. F–b♭′. This solo represents one of the best known Salvation Army theme and variations solos with great individuality. The solo's meter concentrates on 3/4 with only the melodic interlude before the finale in 4/4. The character of the variations in 3/4 time gives this solo great charm. It has both piano and brass band accompaniments and these characteristics make it a highly recommended solo. Recorded by Trevor Groom, Angie Hunter, Robert McNally.

Massenet, Jules. *Elegie*. Arr. Langford. Chandos/Spaeth/Schmid. Euphonium solo and brass band. €21.50.

Massenet, Jules. *Meditation from Thais*. Arr. Derek Ashmore. Hallamshire. Euphonium solo and brass band. III–IV. A nice setting of this classic melody. It will require good musicality and phrasing. Recorded by Tormod Flaten, Nicholas Pfeifle, Len Withington.

Massenet, Jules. *Meditation from Thais*. Arr. Goff Richards. Obrasso. Euphonium solo and brass band. €75. III–IV. A nice setting of this classic violin melody. It will require good musicality and phrasing. Recorded by Tormod Flaten, Nicholas Pfeifle, Len Withington.

Meechan, Peter. *Three Stories–Three Worlds*. Peter Meechan. Euphonium solo and brass band. 15:30. IV–V. Written in three movements: Hubris: The House Atreus; Discardation: Lament for Aerope; New World: Flight to Sparta. Written for David Thornton. A new very challenging work that is certainly high energy and contemporary in its nature. The rhythms drive this work and the second movement contains a sad melody properly depicting its title. The final energetic movement captures the listeners and takes them on a ride. Recorded by David Thornton.

Mendez, Rafeal. *Mexican Hat Dance*. Arr. Eric Wilson. Winwood Music. IV. A setting of this famous showpiece.

Monti, Vittorio. *Czardas*. Arr. Eric Wilson. Winwood Music. Euphonium solo and brass band (piano reduction). £17.95 (£11.95). 1988. 6:00. IV. F–b♭′. A great arrangement of the classical violin showpiece, this arrangement's key and range are beneficial to making this difficult work more accessible. It provides a great study of the lyrical and ornamented opening and its unquenchable dance that follows. Recorded by David Childs, Shoichiro Hokazono, Ivan Milhiet, Jukka Myllys, Hugo Verweji.

Moren, Bertard. *Mr. Euphonium*. Manuscript.

Mozart, Wolfgang Amadeus. *Papagenos Aria*. Arr. Alan Fernie. Obrasso. Euphonium solo and brass band. €75. A nice setting of this classic aria.

Mozart, Wolfgang Amadeus. *Papagenos Aria*. Arr. Maunder. Spaeth/Schmid. Euphonium solo, cornet solo, and brass band. €75. A nice setting of this classic aria.

Newsome, Roy. *Berenice's Menuet*. Spaeth/Schmid. Euphonium solo and brass band. €49.

Newsome, Roy. *Dublin's Fair City*. Chandos Music. Euphonium solo and brass band. 1979. 5:50. III–IV. F–b♭′ (c″). Based on an Irish tune, this work takes a simple melody and embellishes it nicely. There are three fantasies and they progressively become more difficult technically. The second fantasy will require good subdivision and rhythm given its slow tempo and use of 32nd notes. There are also a number of trills. The final fantasy, in a rumba style, features scalar runes with a tremolo and short cadenza. There is an optional run for the fifth of the final chord, a c″. A fun choice for an entertaining brass band solo. Recorded by Graham McEnvoy.

Newsome, Roy. *Fantasy on Swiss Airs*. Studio Music. Euphonium solo and brass band. 1989. 6:45. IV. BB♭–c″. Dedicated to Jean-Claude Matti. Organized as nine brief musical sections, this work provides a fun vehicle for performance. The melodic writing obviously hints of a traditional Swiss tune, while each of the other sections incorporates similar tunes. One unique aspect involves the treatment of one section as a rumba with grace notes and mordents. The final section makes use of triple tonguing in repeated figures. A fun brass band work that provides a similar listening experience as a theme and variations, but slightly more sophisticated. Recorded by Shaun Thomas.

Newsome, Roy. *A Piece of Cake*. Obrasso. Euphonium duet and brass band. €75. Recorded by Paul Walton.

Newsome, Roy. *Sounds of Switzerland*. Obrasso. Euphonium duet and brass band. €75.

Newsome, Roy. *Southern Cross*. Studio Music. Baritone solo and brass band (piano reduction available). 1991. 5:30. III. d–f′ (a′). Written in two sections highlighting the melodic nature of the baritone in an idiomatic way, the allegretto has a nice light style with very playable solo lines. The range is greatly controlled to allow focus on style and clarity. The final chord offers an optional third up to a′. A nice solo for a younger player with limited range.

Newsome, Roy. *Tête à tête*. Spaeth/Schmid. Euphonium and cornet duet and brass band. €75.

Newtown, Rodney. *Baritone Aria*. EMR. Baritone solo and brass band.

Paganini, Nicolo. *Cantabile*. Arr. Goff Richards. Studio Music. Euphonium solo and brass band.

Parfrey, Raymond. *Double Act*. Cinque Port Music. Euphonium and cornet duet and brass band.

Parry, H. *Myfanwy*. Arr. Denzil Stephens. Sarnia Music. Euphonium solo and brass band. 1985. 3:20. III. f–g¹ (b♭¹). A very nice setting of a traditional Welsh melody. Recorded by the Childs Brothers, Riki McDonnell, David Roberts.

Pattison, John, Jr. *The Gladsome Call*. SP & S. Euphonium solo and brass band. 1969. 5:55. III. B♭–a′. A traditional theme and variations with variations featuring single tonguing triplets, slow minor melodic section, and bravura slurred and tongued sixteenth note final. This solo is similar to many others. Recorded by Christopher Smith.

Pattison, John, Jr. *Soldier Fight On*. SP & S. Euphonium solo and brass band. 5:10. III. F–a′. A unique theme and variations solo that is written in 6/8 without much of an introduction. The variations are not difficult but quite special due to the time signature and its lilting feeling. The final section hosts fast slurred sixteenth note triplets in the compound meter that are scalar. This is a good choice for something that shows panache without so much driving rhythmic intensity.

Pattison, John, Jr. *Victory Sure*. SP & S. Euphonium solo and brass band. 3:55. III. A♭–a♭′. A more fast-paced theme and variations, the main theme for *Victory Sure* is an allegro versus the more standard slow melody. A slow triplet variation is followed by an andante variation that mainly qualifies as an ornamented reprise versus an independent variation and is completed with a slurred and tongued sixteenth note finale. This solo is shorter than most due to its lack of slower tempos.

Pattison, John, Jr. *What a Savior*. SP & S. Euphonium solo and brass band. 4:55. III. E–a♭′. A standard theme and variations solo with a classic introduction, allegro theme, slow triplet variation, minor key reprisal of the theme, and bravura sixteenth note slurred "moto perpetuo" to close the piece.

Pearce, Ralph. *Glory*. Ralph Pearce. Euphonium duet and brass band. IV.

Picchi, Ermano. *Fantasie Originale*. Maurice Bale. Godiva Music (piano–Euphonium.com). Euphonium solo and brass band (wind band and piano reduction available). £22 (£50, $17). 7:50. IV. (FF) F–c″ (e♭″). One of the classic turn-of-the-century theme and variations solos, *Fantasie Originale* remains unique because its theme features a jovial Tyrolean style versus the more traditional lyrical theme. The piece's numerous challenges start with the opening octave leaps and continue with some difficult technical requirements in the variations. This work contains some awkward-looking rhythms, and some involve ties. However, the rhythms are representative of the style and the sixteenth note runs scalar. One variation does feature 32nd notes, but of course their velocity will depend on the tempo. An upbeat, quirky interlude occurs before the coda. This remains another unique aspect as most similar pieces would have an introspective minor interlude. The coda is mostly the b♭ scale in various patterns, but the tempo will push the soloist.

There are numerous *ossias* through the work that present different options for the soloist to choose higher or lower octaves, thus making it possible to perform the work with limited range. This work remains an excellent composition and a fine departure from the more traditional theme and variations and it also happens to be an original work for the euphonium. Highly recommended. Recorded by Brian Bowman, Michael Colburn, Leonard Falcone, Adam Frey, Angie Hunter, Steven Mead, Thomas Rüedi, Matt Tropman.

Ponchielli, Amilcare. *Concerto per Flicorno Basso, Opus 155.* Henry Howey. Tuba-Euphonium Press. Euphonium solo and brass band (universal edition can be adapted to any large ensemble; wind band, orchestra, and piano versions available). 1996 (written in 1872). $80 ($65, $90, $65, $14). 13:00. IV–V. F–b♭′. Written as a theme and variations, this is one of the few original works from the nineteenth century. The work has an extended introduction with both lyrical and technical lines from the soloist. While the work has tremendous technical difficulties and rapid range jumps, the technical focus is on E♭ major. Nevertheless, it will be quite a challenge. The theme sets a wonderful Italian picture before the fireworks begin as sixteenth notes in variation 1, sixteenth note triplets in variation 2, and triplet and sixteenth notes in variation 3. An interlude and obligato section leads to the final allegro flourish of sixteenth notes. A fun work that captures the character of the nineteenth-century Italian wind band movement, this piece will be a challenge to prepare and will result in the mastery of the E♭ major scale! Recorded by Michael Colburn, Manfred Heidler, Steven Mead.

Powell, T. J. *Duo for Euphoniums.* Wright and Round. Euphonium duet and brass band. €14.50. III. Recorded by Harry Wilkinson.

Puccini, Giacomo. *Nessun Dorma.* Arr. Wilkinson. Spaeth/Schmid. Euphonium solo and brass band. €20. III. A setting of this very popular aria from *Turandot* made famous by Pavarotti. Recorded by Adam Frey, Riki McDonnell, Steven Mead.

Puccini, Giacomo. *Roconditia Armonia.* Arr. Woodcock. Spaeth/Schmid. Euphonium solo and brass band. €82. III. A setting of this very popular aria.

Puccini, Giacomo. *Your Tiny Hand Is Frozen (Che Gilda manina).* Arr. Maurice Bale. Godiva Music. Euphonium solo and brass band. 1998. 4:10. III–IV. f–b♭′ (c″). A fine setting of this famous aria from *La Boheme.* For those unfamiliar with this aria, it remains a standard in the tenor vocalist's repertoire. It remains consistently above b♭ and has a few rhythmic challenges. It is a highly recommended addition to the repertoire. Recorded by Adam Frey, Riki McDonnell.

Rance, Earnst. *The Reason.* SP & S. Euphonium solo and brass band. III.

Redhead, Robert. *Euphony.* SP & S. Euphonium solo and brass band (piano reduction available). 1978. 8:00. IV. GG–c″ (d″). Written for Wilfred Mountain. Written in three sections with a powerful introduction, *Euphony* is a superb Salvation Army solo that pushes the soloist to new great technical limits. While none of the writing requires any extreme techniques, the scalar and chromatic patterns matched with some intricate rhythms will prove a challenge. The middle lyrical section, based on "Deep and Wide," provides an outstanding countermelody for the soloist that soars to c″. The final section incorporates 7/8 meter with some rapid double tonguing. An option d″ leads to the final bombastic notes from the accompaniment. An excellent recommended solo that has difficult band parts that are currently in a less than neat manuscript. Recorded by Russell Davies, Mark Giles, Morgan Griffiths, Derrick Kane, Steven Mead, Curtis Metcalf, Robert O'Brien, Peter Wise.

Redhead, Robert. *Infant Holy.* SP & S. Euphonium solo and brass band. 1996. 3:15. III. B♭–g♭′. Redhead has taken the Polish carol and composed a superb solo with accompaniment. The solo part features the theme as well as a few countermelodies that modulate and then return to the home key of E♭ major. An excellent Christmas choice.

Redhead, Robert. *O Sinner Man.* SP & S. Euphonium solo and brass band. 1973. 3:05. III. d–g′. A nice lyrical work featuring Redhead's lush harmonies and pleasant countermelodies. There are a number of tied figures that will require rhythmic accuracy. Otherwise, a solo that will challenge the lyrical playing of ornamented melodic material.

Relton, Frank. *Chevailler d'Honneur.* Kirklee's Music. Euphonium solo and brass band (piano reduction available). £17.50 (£7.50). Recorded by David Moore, Erich Schmidli.

Relton, Frank. *Le Core Vole.* Kirklee's Music. Euphonium solo and brass band. £17.50.

Remmington, Emory. *Carnival of Venice.* Manuscript. Euphonium solo and brass band. A setting of one of the many versions of theme and variations of this solo by the esteemed trombonist Emory Remmington. Recorded by Morgan Griffiths, Trevor Groom, Derick Kane, Steven Mead, Glynn Parry, Brian Warrington.

Richards, Goff. *Country Scenes.* Obrasso. Euphonium and cornet duet and brass band. This work will be listed as a regular band work because the parts are not technically "solo" parts. However, the solo cornet and euphonium have significant parts that provide great scope of interpretation and lyricism. Recorded by Cédric Albiez.

Richards, Goff. *Flying Home.* Obrasso. Euphonium duet and brass band. €75.

Richards, Goff. *Midnight Euphonium.* Studio Music. Euphonium solo and brass band (wind band and piano available). 1993. £15 (£45 wind band and

£3.75 piano reduction). 4:10. III. A♭–b♭'. This work provides a jazz ballad feeling through its harmonies and melodic style. There are some challenges to the soloist that include some unusual accidentals, developing the freedom and ease of the style, and making the final cadenza section seem like an improvisation. Control of the high range will be beneficial as the tessitura remains high. This is a highly recommended work for its short duration and unique melodic and harmonic language. Recorded by Riki McDonnell, Steven Mead, Christian Squibb.

Richards, Goff. *A Night in Havana*. Obrasso. Euphonium solo and brass band.

Richards, Goff. *Pilatus (Mountain Air)*. Obrasso. Euphonium solo and brass band. 1994. €75. 8:15. IV–V. F–c" (e♭"). Written for Steven Mead and the Brass Band Bürgermusik Luzern. Composed as a tribute to the famous mountain overlooking Lake Luzern, *Pilatus* captures its mysterious nature. The solo part slowly ascends over the course of the work, ending with an optional d♭". The main difficulties lie in the extended time spent in the high tessitura without ample rests. The piece will also require fluidity with the technical figures and arpeggios that must be treated melodically. The extended cadenza in the middle of the work allows the soloist great freedom. This is a highly rewarding work that will require strong endurance and focus from the accompanying group given its atmospheric nature versus a normally fast showpiece. Recorded by Steven Mead, Erich Schmidli.

Rimmer, Walter. *The Carnival of Venice*. Wright and Round. Euphonium solo and brass band. A version of the classic theme and technical variations by the famous cornet soloist Walter Rimmer.

Rimmer, Walter. *Hailstorm*. Wright and Round. Euphonium solo and brass band (wind band manuscript). A wonderful classic turn-of-the-century work that relies heavily on multiple tonguing. Recorded by Brian Bowman, Harold Brasch, Arthur Lehman, Brian Meixner, Gareth Morgan.

Rimmer, Walter. *Jenny Jones*. Wright and Round. Euphonium solo and brass band. An Arban-esque theme and variations solo from the brass band medium. Recorded by Lyndon Baglin, John Creswell, Lindsey Lawrie, David Moore, Wendy Picton, Paul Walton, Glyn Williams.

Rimmer, Walter. *My Old Kentucky Home*. Wright and Round. Euphonium solo and brass band. Recorded by Walter Appleton, Derick Deacon, Norihisa Yamamoto.

Rimmer, Walter. *Weber's Last Waltz*. Wright and Round. Euphonium solo and brass band. An Arban-esque theme and variations solo from the brass band medium. Recorded by Steven Mead, Len Withington.

Rossini, Guiseppe. *Largo al Factorum*. Arr. Sullivan. Boosey & Hawkes. Euphonium solo and brass band. III. A setting of the humorous and very popular melody from *The Barber of Seville*. Recorded by Raymond Young.

Rossini, Guiseppe. *Prelude, Theme and Variations*. Arr. Roy Newsome. Obrasso. Euphonium solo and brass band (piano reduction available). €67 (€14). V. A setting of the famous clarinet showpiece that will require total facility in E♭ major. Great flexibility and technique will be needed, as well as the ability to transverse octaves rapidly. However, this work is highly recommended for those that can handle its challenges. Recorded by Steven Mead.

Round, H. *Scenes That Are the Brightest*. Wright and Round. Euphonium solo and brass band.

Round, H. *O Lovely Night*. Arr. M. Hopkinson. Kirklee's Music. Euphonium solo and brass band. III.

Rüedi, Thomas. *Winterdream*. Obrasso. Euphonium solo and brass band. 1995. €67. 4:00. d–f'. Dedicated to René Rüedi. A sentimental work with contrasting colors and a strong melodic line.

Saint-Saëns, Camille. *The Swan*. Arr. Ian Jones. NJH Music. Euphonium solo and brass band. £15. III–IV. A setting of this well-known melody. Recorded by Lyndon Baglin, Larry Campbell, the Childs Brothers, John Clough, E. Cod, Leonard Falcone, Adam Frey, Caspar Hardick, Angie Hunter, Derick Kane, Steven Mead, Earle Louder, Glenn Parry, Roy Robert, Erich Schmidli, David Wollom.

Saint-Saëns, Camille. *The Swan*. Arr. Michael Hopkinson. Kirklee's Music. Euphonium solo and brass band (piano reduction available). £18.50 (£5.50). III–IV. A setting of this well-known melody. Recorded by Lyndon Baglin, Larry Campbell, the Childs Brothers, John Clough, E. Cod, Leonard Falcone, Adam Frey, Caspar Hardick, Angie Hunter, Derick Kane, Steven Mead, Earle Louder, Glenn Parry, Roy Robert, Erich Schmidli, David Wollom.

Saint-Saëns, Camille. *The Swan*. Arr. Ray Steadman-Allen. SP & S. Euphonium solo and brass band. III–IV. A setting of this well-known melody. Recorded by Lyndon Baglin, Larry Campbell, the Childs Brothers, John Clough, E. Cod, Leonard Falcone, Adam Frey, Caspar Hardick, Angie Hunter, Derick Kane, Steven Mead, Earle Louder, Glenn Parry, Roy Robert, Erich Schmidli, David Wollom.

Saint-Saëns, Camille. *The Swan*. Arr. Denzil Stephens. Wright and Round. Euphonium solo and brass band. Recorded by Lyndon Baglin, Larry Campbell, the Childs Brothers, John Clough, E. Cod, Leonard Falcone, Adam Frey, Caspar Hardick, Angie Hunter, Derick Kane, Steven Mead, Earle Louder, Glenn Parry, Roy Robert, Erich Schmidli, David Wollom.

Sarasate, Pablo de. *Zigeunerweisen (Gypsy Airs)*. Arr. Thomas Rüedi. Obrasso. Euphonium solo and brass band (piano reduction available). 2001.

€67 (€14). 6:30. V. FF–d♭″. A virtuosic show-piece that seeks to explore the fiery atmosphere of this famous work. It combines many difficult runs and rapid double tonguing, as well as rapid range shifts that characterize this improvisatory violin solo. Great finesse will be needed to create the effortless and free nature of this work. Recorded by Thomas Rüedi.

Sarasate, Pablo de. *Ziguenerweisen (Gypsy Airs)*. Arr. Howard Snell. Rakeway. Euphonium solo and brass band. 6:30. V. FF–d♭″. Virtuosic showpiece that seeks to explore the fiery atmosphere of this famous work. It combines many difficult runs and rapid double tonguing, as well as rapid range shifts that characterize this improvisatory violin solo. Great finesse will be needed to create the effortless and free nature of this work. Recorded by Steven Mead.

Schoonerbeek, Kees. *Twilight Serenade*. De Haske. Euphonium solo and brass band (wind band and piano reduction). 1990. 8:30. III. G–g′. An excellent work for high school students to perform with wind band. The writing is idiomatic for both soloist and band. The harmonic and melodic writing are quite listenable and the technical demands for the soloist are predominantly scalar. The work contains a nice mix of lyrical and technical sections with a controlled range. Recorded by Steven Mead.

Sedaka. *Laughter in the Rain*. Arr. Charleson. Spaeth/Schmid. Euphonium solo and brass band. €22.50.

Senaillé, J. B. *Allegro Spiritoso*. Arr. William Hines. SP & S. Euphonium solo and brass band. 1979. 5:40. III–IV. B♭–a′. A fine arrangement of the common transcription for the euphonium and trombone. The challenges will be to play the work in the light style and to make the music sound facile. Trills and a few runs with accidentals may challenge some players. Recorded by Roger Behrend, Lyndon Baglin, Leonard Falone, Peter Finch, Barry Garmon, William Himes, Earle Louder, Chris Mallet, Ron Young.

Silfverberg, Erik. *A Song of Fight*. SP & S. Euphonium solo and brass band. 4:55. III. F–a′. A traditional theme and variations solo based on a Salvation Army song. The variations are not overly difficult and follow the standard form of solos from the turn of the century: introduction; cadenza; theme; variation; lyrical interlude; variation-finale. Some double tonguing may be required depending on the performance tempo, but otherwise this will be an enjoyable selection with a religious overtone.

Smith, Howard. *Love Lifted Me*. Arr. Ray Steadman-Allen. SP & S. Euphonium solo and brass band. 1976. 3:25. III. B♭–b♭′. A setting of this song in 6/4 featuring the theme and a pleasant countermelody. The writing is easy but does finish on b♭¹. Recorded by Trevor Clarke, Ake Hammarberg.

Snell, Howard. *Drink to Me Only*. Rakeway Music. Euphonium solo and brass band (wind band and piano reduction available). 1998. £18 (£9.95). 8:45. IV–V. F–d♭″ (d″). Howard Snell has penned a tremendous work that encapsulates a classic showpiece in the form of a traditional theme and variations, but it makes use of contemporary harmonies and variations that are highly sophisticated and unlike other variations solos. This work certainly deserves more performance, but its challenges are many. The opening theme is of course a simple phrase to be shaped beautifully, but the variations have some chromatic passages that are a challenge technically, while later creations use many hemiolas and complex rhythmic patterns. The mandatory lyrical interlude sees the euphonium soar wonderfully to test the power and intensity before a finale that will take some finger practice to master with all the accidentals and unusual tonguing patterns, such as tongue two, slur two versus the more common slur two, tongue two. A brief cadenza makes use of some very unique harmonies that are surprising but pleasant before the flourish to finish on a c″. This piece is worth the challenges. Recorded by Tormod Flaten, Steven Mead.

Snell, Howard. *Oration*. Rakeway Music. Euphonium solo and brass band. A substantial new work added to the repertoire. Snell's music holds a high place in the repertoire. Recorded by Steven Mead.

Sparke, Philip. *Aubade*. Studio Music. Euphonium solo and brass band (piano reduction). £15 (£5.50). 4:45. III–IV. d♭–b♭′. Written for Aud. A lush melodic work for the euphonium that makes use of the wonderful singing high register of the euphonium, *Aubade* captures Philip Sparke's superb listenable melodic and harmonic writing. A lilting middle section with a flowing line for the euphonium adds an excellent change of pace before the recapitulation. The difficulties lie in the endurance required to keep a beautiful sound through the work and especially on the final b♭′. Luckily there is an optional f′ that works fine. This work also allows the cornets of the brass band to rest. Recorded by Tyronne Breuninger, Steven Mead, Billy Millar, Ryuji Ushigami.

Sparke, Philip. *Euphonium Concerto*. Studio Music. Euphonium solo and brass band (piano reduction available). 1995. £55 (£10.50 piano reduction). 16:30. VI–V. E♭–d♭″. Written in three connected movements: Moderato e energico; Lento; Vivo e scherzando. A superb work with Sparke's characteristic rhythmic energy, driving intensity, beautiful melodies, and of course listenability. The technical challenges in this work are not overly taxing but will require dedicated practice on certain sections in seven flats in the opening movement and the rhythmic accuracy in mixed meter passages. The second movement contains one of the most beautiful melodies for the euphonium with an emphasis on the rising octave. It blends wonderfully with the band parts; however, it remains in the upper tessitura for most of the movement and will present an endurance challenge. The final movement is a lighthearted 6/8 tarantella that has a bit of hitch in that some of the rhythms are tied over bar lines. This will be a joy to practice and perform for all involved. Recorded by Steven Mead, Ryuji Ushigami.

Sparke, Philip. *Euphoninism*. Studio Music. Euphonium duet. III. Recorded by Riki McDonnell.

Sparke, Philip. *Fantasy*. R. Smith and Company. Euphonium solo and brass band (wind band and piano reduction available). 1979. £24 (£55, £4.75). 9:45. IV. (D) F–c″. Written for Ian Craddock. One of the early serious works for euphonium and brass band, the *Fantasy* will challenge players with its triple tonguing and grace notes as well as the rapidly tongued and slurred sixteenth runs. The work alternates an atmospheric recitative opening with a driving allegro guisto. A methodical intermezzo builds to return to the opening lyrical music and then the fast material. This work is a standard of the repertoire in regards to early euphonium compositions. Recorded by Tyronne Breuninger, Brian Bowman, Robert Childs, Ian Craddock, Brian Crookes, Steven Mead, Renalto Meli, David Werden.

Sparke, Philip. *Pantomime*. Studio Music. Euphonium solo and brass band (wind band and piano reduction available). 1986. £15 (£90, £10.50). 9:45. IV. D–eb″. One of the classic showpieces in the repertoire, *Pantomime* has been scored for most large ensemble performance mediums. This only qualifies its stature as one of the most performed, studied, and enjoyed solos. It also remains very challenging due to the endurance requirements of the high lyrical statements based on a rising octave motive in the opening, as well as the high tessitura of the exuberant 10/8 section that blends the brass band world with a hint of rhythm made famous by *West Side Story*. A lyrical 5/4 section provides an interlude before returning to the 10/8 and a rollicking coda in 2/4 that demonstrates the technical agility of the euphonium in the key of Eb. There are some extended lip slurs and trills at the conclusion, climaxing with the summit eb″. As a proper brass band work, it concludes with every brass player's dream: something high, fast, and loud!! Recorded by the Childs Brothers, Adam Frey, Richard Goosney, Shoichiro Hokazono, Angie Hunter, Steven Mead, Renalto Meli, Jukka Myllys, Joel Pugh, Carl Schultz.

Sparke, Philip. *Party Piece*. Studio Music. Euphonium solo and brass band (piano reduction available). 1996. £15 (£9.50). 8:35. IV. BBb–bb′(eb″). Written for Charles Shipp. Cast as a lighthearted showpiece with slow-fast-slow-fast sections, *Party Piece* opens with a nicely written melodic line that

undergoes some modulations. Passing tones are added to embellish the motives and a short cadenza with pedal Bb subsides to reveal the lively allegro scherzando. The fast section features a fun syncopated figure with grace notes and numerous runs. This work does not present insurmountable difficulties, but endurance will be an issue given its use of the high range for extended periods. Grace notes will also provide an area for ensuring clarity. This is a fun piece that is slightly less good than the better-known *Pantomime*, although both follow nearly identical forms. Recorded by Lyndon Cooper, Steven Mead, Joel Pugh, Ryuji Ushigami.

Sparke, Philip. *Rhapsody for Baritone*. Studio Music. Baritone solo and brass band (piano reduction available). IV. One of the strongest works originally written for baritone.

Sparke, Philip. *Song for Ina*. Studio Music. Euphonium solo and brass band (piano reduction available). 1995. £15 (£6.50). 4:30. III–IV. F♯–bb′. Commissioned by Riki McDonnell in memory of Ina Williams. A lush melodic work for the euphonium that makes use of the wonderful singing high register of the euphonium, *Song for Ina* remains one of the best short lyrical works originally composed for the euphonium. The difficulties lie in the endurance required to keep a beautiful sound through the work and especially on the final ab′. Recorded by Riki McDonnell.

Sparke, Philip. *Two Part Invention*. Studio Music. Euphonium duet and brass band (wind band and piano reduction). 2000 (written in the 1980s). 8:30. IV. Cb–eb″; C–c″. Written for Bob and Nick Childs. This work captures all the trademarks of Sparke's wonderful writing: lyrical, soaring melodies; listenable harmonies; excellent rhythmic drive; virtuoso technique; and a touch of panache. The solo parts have a consistently high tessitura in the opening melodic section. The weaving of the duet lines showcases the singing quality of the euphonium. The fast section delivers great interplay between the lines as it moves through various harmonies. The coda section features alternating triplet patterns between the soloists. It is great fun to practice and perform but will certainly pose some technical challenges. There are some rapidly double tongued figures. This is one of the most challenging and enjoyable duets in the repertoire. Recorded by the Childs Brothers, Shoichiro Hokazono, Dominique Robyr.

Steadman-Allen, Ray. *The Conqueror*. SP & S. Euphonium solo and brass band. Late 1950s. £24.95. 7:15. IV. (D) F–bb′. An early substantial solo that features numerous sections based on Salvation Army songs, *The Conqueror* represents a more challenging work than the *Ransomed Host*. It offers more low-range options and a more extended composition that contains more parts with varied material. There are no unusual challenges other than some rapid slurred triplets. A fun work from the earlier range of compositions for the euphonium. Recorded by the Childs Brothers, Derick Kane.

Steadman-Allen, Ray. *Love Lifted Me*. SP & S. Euphonium solo and brass band. III. Recorded by Trevor Clarke.

Steadman-Allen, Ray. *Lyric Variations*. SP & S. Euphonium solo and brass band. IV–V. Recorded by Derick Kane.

Steadman-Allen, Ray. *Ransomed Host*. SP & S. Euphonium solo and brass band. 1954. 6:25. III–IV. E–bb'. Written in alternating fast-slow sections, *Ransomed Host* utilizes the lyrical and technical capabilities of the euphonium well. There are some challenges with the many fast runs occurring late in the work and the flow of the recitative sections. Otherwise, this solo is one of the earlier substantial works for the euphonium. Recorded by Trevor Groom, Angie Hunter, Robert McNally.

Stephens. *Euphony*. Spaeth/Schmid. Euphonium duet and brass band. €14.50.

Stephens, Denzil. *Celeste Aida*. Wright and Round. Euphonium solo and brass band.

Stephens, Denzil. *A Country Rhapsody*. Sarnia Music. Euphonium solo and brass band.

Stephens, Denzil. *Dizzy Fingers*. Sarnia Music. Euphonium solo and brass band. IV.

Stephens, Denzil. *Gameplan*. Sarnia Music. Euphonium solo and brass band. III.

Stephens, Denzil. *Rondino*. Wright and Round. Euphonium solo and brass band.

Stephens, Denzil. *Solo Rhapsody*. Sarina Music. Euphonium solo and brass band (piano reduction available). 1989 (written in the early 1950s). £25 (£8, piano reduction). 6:40. IV. GG–c". Written in a fantasy style, the *Solo Rhapsody* was written for the composer, a euphonium player, and the Royal Air Force Central Band. It opens with a high concert bb quasi cadenza and moves to a lilting, slurred 9/8 section. Some wide intervals are slurred before moving to the allegro with energetic, rapidly tongued 9/8 figures. A very nice cantabile ensues as well as an obligato section before the final 6/8 flourish leads to thirteen bars of high bb to finish the work. This piece represents one of the older works that should be a part of the standard repertoire for the euphonium. Recorded by the Childs Brothers.

Sullivan, Arthur. *We're Called Gondolieri*. Arr. Maurice Bale. Godiva Music. Baritone duet and brass band. 1995. £18. 4:00. III. eb–f'; d–eb'. A fun cheerful duet with a show tune feel. The solo parts are simple other than a few accidentals. This would be a great piece for two talented high school students.

Sutton, Eddie. *The Brigadier*. Wright and Round. Euphonium solo and brass band.

Sutton, Eddie. *The Cavalier*. Wright and Round. Euphonium solo and brass band. Recorded by Lyndon Baglin, Colin Cranson, David Hallas, David Moore, Andrew Warton.

Sutton, Eddie. *The Connoisseur*. Wright and Round. Euphonium solo and brass band.

Szkutko, John. *Reach for the Stars*. SZK Music. Euphonium solo and brass band. 2003. $50 Australian. 5:50. V (III). A–f". Written for Riki McDonnell. With a slow rock ballad beat permeating the work, *Reach for the Stars* contains good stylistic writing in the rock genre. The solo part's range could easily be adjusted down an octave in a few locations to make the work a level III difficulty.

Tchaikovsky, Peter I. *Nocturne Op.19, Nr.4*. Arr. Thomas Rüedi. Obrasso. Euphonium solo and brass band (piano reduction available). 2001. €67 (€14). 4:30. III. Bb–bb'. A beautiful piece by the master composer. The truly lyrical quality of this work lends itself beautifully to the euphonium. Recorded by Thomas Rüedi.

Tchaikovsky, Peter I. *Variations on a Rococo Theme Op.33*. Arr. Thomas Rüedi. Obrasso. Euphonium solo and brass band. 2004. €67. 19:00. The simple theme with its attractive melodic and rhythmic movement is effectively transformed into seven virtuostic variations. This work contains some of the most demanding writing for the instrument given its key structure with a focus on D major as well as all the challenges for cello players that must be translated easily to the euphonium. Recorded by Thomas Rüedi.

Thompson, G. *Catari, Catari*. Wright and Round. Euphonium solo and brass band.

Thorne, Roger. *Andante from Concertino*. Thornes Music. Baritone solo and brass band. 2003. £18. 3:40. III. c–ab'. Written for Bob Richardson. This is the lyrical section from the larger *Concertino* annotated below. It can be heard on Thorne's website.

Thorne, Roger. *Concertino*. Thornes Music. Baritone solo and brass band. 2003. £35. 7:00. IV. c–c"(d"). Written for Bob Richardson. A nice work with a mix of a traditional turn-of-the-century brass band sound and some contemporary moments of flair for a normally underappreciated instrument. This is one of the more substantial original works for the baritone. There are some double tongued passages. It can be heard on Thorne's website.

Toselli, Enrico. *Serenata Op.6*. Arr. Thomas Rüedi. Musikverlag Frank. Euphonium solo and brass band. 2002. €67. 3:30. IV. A–bb'. The world-famous Italian song transcribed for euphonium and brass band. Recorded by John Clough, Leonard Falcone.

Traditional. *Believe Me if All Those Endearing Young Charms*. See under Mantia, Simone.

Traditional. *Carrickfergus*. Arr. Stephen Roberts. Tanglewind Music. Baritone solo and brass band (piano reduction available). 1993. £19 (£5). III–IV. A–b♭'. A beautiful lyrical work based on a traditional Irish air, *Carrickfergus* allows the soloist great liberty to shape a nice melody in the middle range. The work has a powerful middle section where the soloist plays a high countermelody that serves as the difficult area of performance due to range and dynamics. Another incantation of the melody appears near the end before the soloist finishes on an a'. This is a wonderful work with some enjoyable accompaniment parts, as well as the listening enjoyment created for the audience. Recorded by Steven Mead.

Traditional. *Danny Boy.* Arr. Ian Jones. NJH Music. Euphonium solo and brass band. £15. III. An arrangement of the well-known tune.

Traditional. *Danny Boy.* Arr. Lewis Buckley. Cimarron Music. Euphonium solo and wind band. $42. 4:30. III–IV. A pleasant setting of the classic melody audiences cherish.

Traditional. *Good King Wenceslas.* Arr. Roger Thorne. Thornes Music. Euphonium solo and brass band (wind band). 2002. £20 (£48). 6:35. III. F–b♭'. This solo remains unique in its Christmas theme and its idiomatic nature. One of the few holiday musical selections cast as a theme and variations, this solo is firmly planted in B♭ major and the variations are standard single tongued triplets, slurred running sixteenths, cadenza, and an allegro variation with ornamental notes finishing with a chromatic run to b♭'. A highly recommended holiday solo.

Traditional. *Hamabe No Uta (Song of the Seashore).* Arr. Goff Richards. Obrasso. Euphonium solo and brass band. €75. A very lovely Japanese melody that will greatly interest audiences. There is a great scope for interpretation.

Traditional. *Spread Your Wide Wings.* Arr. Baker. Kirklee's Music. Euphonium solo and brass band. £19.50.

Traditional. *Variations on a Latin Theme.* Obrasso. Euphonium solo and brass band (piano reduction available). 2001. €67 (€14).

Trenet, Charles. *I Wish You Love.* Arr. Alan Fernie. Obrasso. Euphonium duet and brass band. €67.

Verdi, Guiseppe. *Brindisi (Drinking Song).* Arr. Maurice Bale. Godiva Music. Euphonium solo and brass band.

Verdi, Guiseppe. *Celeste Aida.* Arr. John Golland. Kirklee's Music. Euphonium solo and brass band. £18.50. Recorded by Riki McDonnell.

Verdi, Guiseppe. *Fantasy on La Donna Mobile.* Arr. Roy Newsome. Obrasso. Euphonium solo and brass band. €75. A fun setting of this often programmed tune.

Vieuxtemps, Henry. *Elégie Op. 30.* Arr. Thomas Rüedi. Obrasso. Euphonium solo and brass band (piano reduction available). 2001. €67 (€14). 5:30. IV. B–b'. A passionate romantic work with extended phrasing and some technically demanding ornamentations and cadenzas. Recorded by Thomas Rüedi.

Vita. (Note: See listing under De Vita).

Vivaldi, Antonio. *Double Concerto.* Arr. Simon Kerwin. Spaeth/Schmid. Euphonium duet and brass band. €20.

Voeglein. Fritz. *Ballad.* Spaeth/Schmid. Euphonium solo and brass band. €67.50.

Voeglein. Fritz. *Caprice.* Spaeth/Schmid. Euphonium solo, cornet solo, and brass band. €67.50.

Volle, Bjarne. *Messingmesse No. 6.* Norsk Forlag. Euphonium solo, two cornet solo, alto horn solo, trombone solo, organ, and brass band. 1994.

Wagner, Richard. *The Pilgrams' Chorus from Tannhauser.* Arr. Simon Kerwin. Obrasso. Euphonium/baritone quartet and brass band. €67.

Wagner, Richard. *Walther's Prize Song.* Arr. Maurice Bale. Godiva Music. Euphonium solo and brass band. 1998. £10. 3:45. III. d–g'. A nice melody by Wagner with an easy arrangement by Maurice Bale that captures all the important components without making it overly difficult. This aria is a recommended one that should be performed more often. Recorded by Steven Mead.

Wakefield, Anthony. *Prelude and Blues.* Anthony Wakefield. Euphonium solo and brass band (wind band available). 2003.

Walton, James. *Jubiloso.* MGP. Euphonium solo and brass band. IV.

Warren. *I Know Why.* Arr. Baker. Kirklee's Music. Euphonium solo and brass band. £18.50.

Webber, Andrew Lloyd. *Variations.* Peter Graham. Winwood Music. Euphonium solo and brass band. 1993 (written in 1978). £19.95. 6:45. IV. (C) F–c" (d"). Based on the famous Paganini theme, Andrew Lloyd Webber crafts a theme and variations that are all tonally based. Originally written for Lloyd Webber's brother, an accomplished cellist, Peter Graham set the work for euphonium and brass band in a reduced format using only the theme and six variations (the original has many more). The writing is very idiomatic and requires excellent double tonguing agility. The work has many *ossias* to facilitate any range limitations. This is a fun, enjoyable solo by a famous name composer with great audience appeal. Recorded by Steven Mead.

Wiggins, Bram. *Cornucopia.* Kirkelee's Music. Euphonium solo and brass band. £17.50.

Wiggins, Bram. *The Pilgram's Song.* Kirklee's Music. Euphonium solo and brass band. £17.50.

Wiggins, Bram. *Trilogy for Euphonium.* Kirklee's Music. Euphonium solo and brass band (piano reduction available). £17.50 (£7.50).

Wilby, Philip. *Concerto for Euphonium.* Winwood Music. Euphonium solo and brass band (orchestral, wind band, and piano reductions available). 1996. £70 (Rental, £125, £15). 18:15. V. AA♭–d" (e♭"). Written for Robert Childs. Written in two parts/four movements: Part I–Non troppo allegro; Dance Zeibékikos; Part II–Andante; Allegro vivace. One of the most challenging and demanding concerti, the Wilby *Concerto for Euphonium* combines incredible energy, driving intensity, soaring lyricism, and great listening enjoyment. However, the challenges present a substantial obstacle for many players. Firstly, there are tremendous technical demands including rapid repeated and moving double and triple tonguing through three of the four movements. The patterns are often chromatic, but with small modifications. Difficult rhythmic patterns also present challenges, as does the overall tempo of the work and the endurance needed to sustain the power and balance for the eighteen minutes. The most memorable portion of this concerto is the Dance Zeibékikos. It basically makes up three minutes of pure adrenaline through fast notes, crazy two-octave glissandos, fierce grace notes, and rapid meter changes before ending with the percussion section breaking plates!! The third movement then provides a very contemplative interlude before the final movement. The lyrical nature of the Andante explores the low range of the euphonium before ascending to a poignant statement in a slow 6/8. This writing is wonderfully lush and captures the best qualities of the euphonium before moving directly into the finale. The technical demands return and bring the work to a triumphant conclusion. This work will be very demanding but absolutely worth the investment. It is a highly recommended work. The accompaniment parts are scored a little thickly and will challenge college-level ensembles. Recorded by Robert Childs, David Childs, Steven Mead.

Wilhelm, Rolf. *Concertino.* Katie Bell. Manuscript. Euphonium solo and brass band (wind band and piano reduction available from Trio Musik). 1999. €89.50 (€14.50). 12:00. IV–V. BB–d″. IV–V. Written in three movements: Allegro mon troppo; Andante ma non troppo, piacevole; Moderato con animo. A contemporary classic for the euphonium, the *Concertino* highlights the its qualities very well. The opening movement features a slightly technical style with a great energy. There are no extremely awkward sections, but Wilhelm does occasionally use a bar with numerous accidentals. The second movement allows the soloist to show excellent control and features very lovely writing, especially the descending motive that reappears three times. Overall, the technique is manageable as the level dictates, but the range does occasionally create problems in the final movement. This movement remains the main challenge and features the most range extremes. The articulations are also very detailed. The accompaniment will challenge a good high school ensemble, but this work should be performed more often. The piano reduction captures the work very well. Recorded by Steven Mead.

Woodfield, Ray. *Caprice.* Hallamshire. Euphonium solo and brass band (wind band and piano reduction). 4:45. III–IV. B♭–b♭′ (c″). A nice light-hearted brass band solo, *Caprice* highlights agility and triple tonguing and allows a choice of two written-out cadenzas: a more technical and a more lyrical choice. Recorded by Richard Gosney.

Woodfield, Ray. *Double Brass.* Obrasso. Euphonium duet and brass band. €75. Written for the Childs Brothers in the 1980s. IV. The work is a lighter concert work with popular-style harmonies. Recorded by the Childs Brothers.

Woodfield, Ray. *Euphoria.* Obrasso. Euphonium solo and brass band. €75.

Woodfield, Ray. *Varied Mood.* Obrasso. Euphonium solo and brass band. A very lighthearted solo with some very showy moments for the soloist. Enjoyable for audience and band. Recorded by the Childs Brothers, David Childs, Stephen Loyd, Steven Mead.

Zelli, Valerio, and Mauro Mengali. *Vivo per Lei.* Alan Fernie. Obrasso. Euphonium/cornet duet and brass band. €75.

5. Music for Euphonium and Orchestra

Adam Frey

The euphonium's repertoire with orchestral accompaniment remains quite limited when compared to all the choices available with wind band and brass band. However, this performance medium also embodies the briefest performance tradition for the euphonium and therefore is understandably more confined. Yet it also represents some of the most significant repertoire for the euphonium, especially in regards to duration, quality, and character. This medium also provides composers with more boundless ideals when they create works. Somehow, the stigma of a "band" can limit their thoughts; luckily all composers do not suffer from this.

A substantial addition to this genre certainly involves the numerous arrangements of wind band and brass band accompaniments for the symphony orchestra. However, as many mature musicians will agree, the compositional concept that composers utilize very often varies depending on the type of ensemble performing the work. Thus, many of the arrangements for orchestra made from other mediums continue to sound like "band" pieces being performed with strings rather than a composition inspired with the concept, beauty, and texture of the symphony orchestra as the genesis for the ideas.

One very strong aspect of this performance medium embodies the number of large-scale works originally conceived for symphony orchestra composed in the Scandinavian countries. The length of works and ability to have them programmed, as well as the support of the national music information centers, contributes greatly to their success. Of course, there are numerous new works that continue to take the instrument to the next level, as well as large-scale standard works. A short list of highlighted works originally written for euphonium and orchestra might include Aagard-Nilsen, Bach, Cosma, Feinstein, Filas, Florieux, Hovanhess, Kassati, Madsen, Linkola, Roper, and Stevens. Further, there remain a number of high-quality works that have been arranged or scored for use with symphony orchestra, and these occupy a cornerstone in the euphonium repertoire and allow a player to move comfortably around the globe with a wide variety of ensembles. This special ability, which seems to transcend other instruments in that it would certainly be unusual to perform the Mendelssohn *Violin Concerto* with a wind band or brass band, allows the euphonium to easily navigate these waters. Some may argue that the euphonium must make these concessions due to the limitations of its young repertoire. Both hold true; however, one must certainly know that the quantity of works written for the euphonium and wind band and brass band surpasses those born of the symphony orchestra, and therein lies the answer. More commissions are needed with symphony orchestra, yet the performance opportunities remain bounded. In the future, though, this will hopefully change and more people will gain respect for the instrument in the orchestral circle, as this will lead to wider recognition and more repertoire.

Aagard-Nilsen, Torstein. *Euphonium Concerto.* Norwegian Music Information Center. Euphonium solo and symphony orchestra. 20:00–24:00. V. DD–a♭″. Written in one continuous movement with numerous sections. From the first beat, one can tell this concerto will be a challenge for both soloist and ensemble. The rising sextuplet figure represents a motif that will occur many times in the work. Yet it changes key and figuration regularly. There are many very complex rhythms and multiple tongued passages that also involve a tremendous variety of shifting tonalities. The music seems to have great energy and forward motion from its complexity. There are numerous technical challenges from the extremely quick double tongued 32nd notes to the downward slurs of a seventh as recurring sixteenth notes, to the climactic a♭″!! The slow writing is haunting and wandering but comes full circle to the opening material. This work is a substantial addition to the repertoire by a well-respected figure. Yet the concerto appears to require a tremendous amount of work. This piece may also be difficult to program due to its contemporary nature, length, and lack of a piano part to provide other performance opportunities.

Ahmas, Harri. *Euphonium Concerto.* Finnish Music Information Center. Euphonium solo and chamber orchestra with percussion. 2001. Rental. 27:00. V. DD♭–d″. Dedicated to Jukka Myllys. Written in two movements. This work opens with rapid meter changes and very complex rhythms that will challenge many players. Meters include 24/16, 9/16, 15/16, 18/16, and others. Luckily, the range and technique are confined in the opening so rhythm can be the main focus. The melodic nature is certainly contemporary and chromatic. There is not always a strong cohesiveness to the listener in the writing, but the textures with orchestra may be clearer. A mute is required and there are a number of specific techniques to be utilized: vibrato as dictated by the composer, tremolo fingerings, feathered beaming, and downward glissandi. While this work is certainly a substantial piece in the chamber orchestra medium, it may be difficult to program due to its highly contemporary nature and its duration. Yet it may find its merit in a program of serious contemporary music.

Andresen, Morgens. *Prelude and Chaconne.* Morgens Andresen. Euphonium solo and symphony orchestra (wind band and brass band available). A very melodic piece that shows the euphonium's possibilities for playing in different styles.

Angell, Martin. *Concerto for Euphonium Winds.* Manuscript.

Bach, Jan. *Euphonium Concerto.* Tuba-Euphonium Press. Euphonium solo and symphony orchestra (wind band and piano reduction available). 1992. Rental ($200, $40). 25:00. IV–V. BB♭–d″. Written in three movements: Legend; Burlesca; Meditation. This mammoth work was extremely significant when it was written in that it was such a large-scale work conceived for orchestral accompaniment and composed by a well-known American composer. It also serves as a high-level competition piece. The scope of the concerto covers a diverse musical palette with its confident opening, yet subdued statement from the euphonium. The major challenges (and listening enjoyments) result from the complex rhythms and how these weave through various tonalities. Bach often utilizes faster subdivisions of the beat to give a more hurried feeling (putting two, three, and four notes on each successive beat). The interplay in the rhythms and hemiolas will challenge the ensemble, and playing without a conductor with the piano reduction will need much rehearsal. There are many unusual fingering patterns and intervals and these will take time to master. Unfortunately, the same pattern may occur in another section, but may be transposed up a half or whole step. Cadenza sections link all three movements into one continuous work, yet alternate openings and endings are given to facilitate performance of the individual movements (approx. eight minutes each). The Burlesca creates a rollicking feeling and provides a jolt of energy, especially with the percussion, to the listener and performer; however, the numerous glissandi and modulating sequences, as well as the continual driving technique, will challenge the performer. A long cadenza gradually restates the theme slower and slower until the tension relaxes to allow the beautiful Meditation to emerge. This movement captures the majesty of the euphonium and its melody, development, and breadth of quality make it a mainstay of the euphonium repertoire generated by American composers. This work will be difficult to program due to its length and somewhat contemporary nature. However, it remains a strong serious work and a standard for many graduate-level players.

Beasley, Rule. *Concerto for Euphonium.* Composer published. Euphonium solo and symphony orchestra (piano reduction available). 1967. Rental only. 15:30. IV. F to b♭′. Commissioned by Fred Dart. Written in three movements of Fast; Slow; Fast, Beasley's *Concerto for Euphonium* is difficult to obtain. 3/8 meter occurs in the first and third movements with great technical demands being made on the soloist in the third movement. This was one of the earliest substantial works written for the euphonium.

Bourgeois, Derek. *Concerto, Opus 114.* R. Smith (G&M Brand—orchestra). Euphonium solo and symphony orchestra (brass band, wind band, and piano reduction available). 1988. Rental (£105, £130, £10). 18:00. IV–V. GG–d″. Written in three movements: Allegro; Adagio; Presto. Commissioned by the British Trombone Society. Included in the *ESB* because Bourgeois states that "It is equally appropriate to perform this work on the Euphonium, in which case the title should be shown as Concerto," this work represents a significant work with performance options for all the major mediums. The work's charm and style lend themselves to endearment by performers and audiences alike. The opening movement's marshal style and intensity requires confident articulation interspersed with a sweeping melody that soars to a d^2. Luckily, this occurs in the early part of the *Concerto* before the soloist becomes fatigued. The Adagio features some very expressive phrases and a nicely contemplative feeling. The final bars require a mute. The final movement poses the most technical challenges with rapid triplet patterns that are occasionally syncopated. The final page captures Bourgeois's typical technical flourish that modulates rapidly. The valve combinations on these last pages will require much "wood-shedding" and it should be known that most trombone players perform the entire last page in first through third positions only (although some do not do this). This work is highly recommended and a standard of many programs. Thankfully, the composer encourages its performance on the euphonium. Recorded by Angie Hunter, Steven Mead, and numerous trombone soloists.

Bourgeois, Derek. *Euphonium Concerto, Opus 120.* Brass Wind Music. Euphonium solo and brass band (chamber orchestra, piano reduction available). 1990. Rental (£16). 20:00. V. D–f ″. Written in three movements: Allegro vivace; Lento con moto; Allegro molto vivace. This concerto captures Bourgeois's intimate knowledge of the technical abilities of the euphonium with his special harmonic language. The writing for much of the concerto remains in the upper tessitura and very technically based. There are a number of range-intensive areas with rapid technique, including some extended areas with chromatic writing above b♭′. The lyrical second movement features the euphonium with a more florid solo part versus one of longer note values. The final movement opens on a b′ and progresses through many meter changes of time signatures based on quarter, eighth, and sixteenth notes. Overall, the runs throughout the work shift tonalities frequently and many times do not always represent traditional scalar patterns. This work will take tremendous "wood-shedding" and endurance. While the energy is deserving, there are probably other works for euphonium and orchestra that will reward the soloist, orchestra, and audience more.

Boutry, Roger. *Tubaroque.* Leduc. Bass saxhorn and orchestra (piano reduction available). 1955. III–IV. AA–g′(a♭′).

Bowen, Brian. *Euphonium Music.* Orchestration by Eric Wilson. Winwood Music. Euphonium solo and symphony orchestra (wind band, brass band, and piano reduction available). 1984 (written in 1978). In preparation (£50, In preparation, £20). 14:30. IV. E♭–c″. Written in three movements: Andante; Andante con espressivo; Moderato. *Euphonium Music* stands as one of the contemporary standards in the euphonium repertoire. The writing features many less common melodic intervals of sevenths in its opening motive that reappears several times. The technical and rhythmic demands are numerous and the rising seventh appears in the fast sections as well. Many of the runs in the work are chromatic in nature and do not always follow major and minor patterns. The second movement features one of the most poignant melodies written for the euphonium and provides great scope for interpretation. The second movement segues into the technical third with many triplet flourishes and a rapid syncopated theme. There are some awkward mixed meter sections before a brief melodic interlude moves into the final technical flourish and a section demonstrating the lyrical power of the instrument. This is a highly recommended work and can be performed with any standard performance medium. Recorded by the Childs Brothers, Steven Mead, Robin Taylor.

Bozza, Eugène. *Concertino.* Leduc. Bass saxhorn and orchestra (piano reduction available). 1967.

IV. FF–a♭′. Well known for the tuba, this work was originally conceived for the French tuba, which is quite similar to the modern euphonium.

Bristol, Doug. *Fantasy for Euphonium and Orchestra.* Doug Bristol. Euphonium solo and orchestra (piano reduction available). 15:00. Written for Demondrae Thurman.

Butterworth, Arthur. *Summer Music, Opus 89.* Arthur Butterworth. Euphonium solo and symphony orchestra. IV–V. A challenging transcription of Butterworth's bassoon solo, *Summer Music.* The harmonic language is contemporary but accessible. Some difficult wide intervals.

Constantinidies, Dinos. *Concerto for Euphonium.* Dinos Constantinidies. Euphonium solo and symphony orchestra.

Corwell, Neal. *Meditation and Finale.* Tuba-Euphonium Press. 1999. Euphonium solo and string orchestra (piano available). $80 ($75). (EE♭) GG–c″. This solo features the *Meditation* with a setting for strings. Originally written with electronic accompaniment, this setting with strings captures the mood well. The melody and harmonies wander during the work but do resolve in the final cadence. The finale provides much energy through the numerous scalar and chromatic runs. It has a light quality to it and this gives it great audience appeal.

Corwell, Neal. *Of the Water.* Tuba-Euphonium Press. 1999. Euphonium solo and chamber orchestra (wind band available). $80 ($75). 14:30. IV–V. GG–d″. Written in two movements: Into the Depths and The Water's Journey. Commissioned by the Garrett Lakes Arts Festival. The first movement features a number of muted sections and use of the low range, capturing colors that allude to its title. It is oftentimes lyrical, but contains an undercurrent of rhythmic energy from the repeated figures in the accompaniment figures. *The Water's Journey* features the technical passages with a quick tempo and often utilizing 7/8 meter. There are numerous trills and some tremolos in the extreme high range. An interesting work with a nice programmatic theme.

Corwell, Neal. *Sinfonietta.* Nicolai Music 1999. Euphonium solo and symphony orchestra (piano reduction available). $75 ($80). IV. BB♭–d″. Written in four movements: Ostinato; Adagio, moderato; Scherzo; Finale. A large-scale work written very idiomatically for the soloist, the *Sinfonietta* boasts many different moods during its performance. The opening movement has lyrical lines set with a thirteen-note ostinato pattern that pervades the movement. The second movement features a dark opening that turns brighter in the middle before returning to the somber finish. The Scherzo features rapid double tonguing and some flutter tonguing that gives it a lighter feeling. The Finale combines the ideas of the first three movements cohesively and brings the work to an exciting conclusion. Recorded by Neal Corwell.

Cosma, Vladimir. *Euphonium Concerto*. Lam Larghetto. Euphonium solo and symphony orchestra (wind band, brass band, and piano reduction available). 2000 (written in 1998). Rental, $75. 21:00. V. DD♭–d″. Written for the 1998 World Tuba Euphonium Competition in Guebwiller, France. Written in three movements: Allegro assai; Andantino; Finale–Giocoso. One of the most challenging and rewarding solos in the repertoire, this concerto embodies in many ways the spirit of Paganini and Liszt for the euphonium and represents one of the most outstanding selections for euphonium and large ensemble. It features virtuoso technique, intense melody, and a need for panache and flair. The technical and range challenges are formidable, but WELL worth the practice. Of particular note are the flexibility, clarity, and tone quality needed in the low range from BB♭ to F, as there are numerous sections of slurred and tongued passages in these ranges. There is also a strong need for excellent double and triple tonguing as Cosma wrote the final few sections with the violin (his instrument) in mind versus the euphonium, so some of the passages are not as idiomatic as they could be. The Andantino creates an atmosphere mindful of Piazzolla, the famous tango writer. The melody sails with the euphonium. This piece stands at the top of the list of recommended repertoire for those capable. Taking this challenge will be extremely rewarding and the only caveat involves the cost of the large ensemble rental parts (more than $400) and the piano reduction. The publisher has made these choices and they greatly hinder the wide spread of this fantastic work. Recorded by Adam Frey, Ivan Milheit, Tennessee Tech Tuba Euphonium Ensemble, Steven Mead.

Croley, Randell. *Soliloquy, Opus 36*. Tritone Press (Out of Print). Euphonium solo and string orchestra. 1964. 2:30. III–IV. F–b♭′. This is a brief solo work unique for its accompaniment. It makes use of whole tone melodies and harmonies and does not have any unusual challenges other than trying to organize the accompaniment. However, it would make an excellent addition to a recital featuring euphonium and string combinations.[1]

Curnow, James. *Concerto for Euphonium*. Curnow Music Press. Euphonium solo and symphony orchestra (wind band available). 1997. Rental only ($129). 12:10. IV–V. D–c″ (e♭″). Written in three movements: Adagio moderato e caloroso; Andante moderato e molto espressivo; Allegro con brio. Commissioned by DEG Music Products, Inc., and the Willson Band Instrument Company and composed for and dedicated to Roger Behrend. The overall form of this work is three segue movements linked with extended cadenzas as transitions. The work contains Curnow's tonal melodic writing with his panache at

showing the technical virtuosity of the euphonium. The work contains numerous *ossia* to allow the range extremes to be more easily negotiated as needed by the soloist. The work opens lyrically and moves to a more spirited section that features some difficult sixteenth note runs. The cadenza that transitions to the second movement features extended range and some motives from earlier in the first movement. The second movement contains an angular theme with a number of variations and interplay between the soloist and principal ensemble positions. The cadenza moving to the rondo-form final movement features more difficult fingering patterns, but similar range extremes from D–d♭″. The final movement highlights a light 6/8 tarantella-like theme that focuses on the pitch center of G with many runs to d″. The range issues will be the most common issues with this work. The technique remains scalar and idiomatic and should be easy to overcome. This work will provide a good opportunity to showcase the euphonium in a composition by a well-known composer.

Curnow, James. *Symphonic Variants*. Curnow Music Press (Tuba-Euphonium Press). Euphonium solo and symphony orchestra (wind band, brass band, and piano reduction available). 1984. $100/Rental only ($129, manuscript, $24). 19:00. V. DD–c″ (f″). Introduction; Theme and Variations: Allegro con brio, Allegro moderato con espressivo, Allegro con spirito, Lento con teneramente, Presto, Adagio con calore, Allegro maestoso, Peasante. One of the core repertoire works for the euphonium and also one of the most demanding works ever written for the instrument, *Symphonic Variants* runs the gamut of technical facility, range, endurance, and power to project and balance. The difficulties will mainly be annotated as the work should be a standard piece in an advanced player's library. This superb work opens with a flourish of technique and runs to c″ before presenting the lyrical theme. There are numerous *ossia* throughout the work that make the very high tessitura more accessible. The opening theme has an optional d″ and e♭″. All this is less than one minute from the start of a nearly twenty-minute work! Variation 1, Allegro con brio, hosts a lively 6/8 version with a run down to GG. Variation 2, Lento con teneramente, exposes the soloist on some high-range entrances as well as some rapid range shifts over three octaves in the course of two measures (albeit at a slow tempo). A very nice rubato section brings this variation to a close. The Presto highlights the agility of the euphonium with a bountiful number of sixteenth notes and double tonguing during the entire variation. There are numerous presentations of the motives that jump octaves between beats with many *ossia*. A long chromatic run to c″ with a diminuendo leads to the Adagio con calore. Curnow writes this lyrical section very well to suit the euphonium. It leads smoothly into the Allegro maestoso, a slower sixteenth note variation in a stately style that returns the opening material before a calm Peasante allows the soloist, accompaniment, and audience to wind up to the final powerful notes that feature an optional f″. The accompaniment parts are difficult and thickly textured. Great projection and balance will be needed by the soloist. This is one of the most physical works in the repertoire and one of the standard works frequently performed. Recorded by Roger Behrend, Brian Bowman, Mary Ann Craig, Marik Denys, Phil Franke, Shoichiro Hokazono, Angie Hunter, Steven Mead, Robin Taylor.

Dubois, Pierre Max. *Piccolo suite*. Leduc. Bass saxhorn and orchestra (piano reduction available). 1957. IV. F′–a♯′. Orchestral accompaniment is only available for the third movement.

Ellerby, Martin. *Euphonium Concerto*. Studio Music. Euphonium solo and symphony orchestra (brass band, wind band, and piano reduction available). 1997. Rental only (£10.50 piano). 22:00. V GG–e♭″. Four movements: Fantasy; Capriccio; Rhapsody (for Luis); Diversions. Commissioned by and dedicated to Steven Mead. One of THE most challenging works in the repertoire, the Ellerby *Euphonium Concerto* can be summed up as an exploration in the technical limits of the euphonium in regards to range, dexterity, and endurance. Attention to detail is a must in all movements as Ellerby clearly marks articulation and dynamic nuances. The Fantasy features the alternation of an energetic rising theme, sometimes slurred and sometimes tongued, with a beautiful melodic section. The Capriccio is the most demanding technically and rhythmically with inventive rhythmic figures and difficult fingering combinations. One of these great moments occurs as the 12/8 theme shifts from triplet to duple subdivisions. The writing can be described as melodic and motivic with a very wide palette of harmonic and melodic colors in an angular style. The chromatic appearance does not translate to chromatic-sounding harmony. A muted section occurs in the middle of the second movement. The Rhapsody (for Luis) hosts one of the best examples of lyrical euphonium writing. Dedicated to Luis Maldanado, this movement's buildup and climax leading to a d″ remains one of the most memorable moments in the euphoniums repertoire. The writing and interplay between soloist and ensemble make this movement a joy to perform and the final repeated d's in the solo line pay homage to another great lyrical euphonium concerto by Horovitz. Diversions could be described as approximately five minutes of pure, intense rhythmic drive. From its opening accompaniment figure played by the band, which sets the pace, this movement places large technical demands on the soloist including rapid tonguing, optional multi-phonics, highly articulated figures in extreme ranges, traversing more than two octaves in a single bar, and ending with glissandi up to e♭″. One of the masterpieces of the euphonium repertoire, this concerto will require lots of practice and strength. The ensemble parts are also very difficult and a good conductor will be needed. Alternate fingerings will make the solo part clearer and easier. Recorded by Adam Frey, Steven Mead, Brian Meixner.

Feinstein, Allen. *Concerto for Euphonium: Swimming the Mountain*. Euphonium.com. Euphonium solo and symphony orchestra (piano reduction). 2004. Rental ($25). 20:00. V. AA♭–c″ (f″). Written in three movements: Zeus; Eclipse; Realm of Possibility. Commissioned by and dedicated to Adam Frey. This programmatic work has a unique story behind it. In the opening movement, the euphonium is Zeus. The orchestra sets a wonderful ethereal opening that brings to mind the beginning of the world. The powerful theme of Zeus enters and it includes a powerful BB♭. A stately theme ensues and develops before the major challenging section with an extended high-range obligato. The solo part has been edited throughout with numerous *ossia* to make the work more accessible, and with the reduced range requirements the work will be accessible to undergraduate students. An extended cadenza develops the Zeus theme, before the orchestra takes the theme while the euphonium provides a nice obligato. A very difficult technical section that is mostly scalar brings the work to an exciting conclusion. Of the three movements, Zeus is certainly the most difficult by far. The Eclipse requires a mute in the opening section and has a serene melody that later turns to a section that depicts the emerging stars after the eclipse. The writing is not overly challenging and phrases well. The Realm of Possibility features a lilting 6/8 that brings the euphonium into a contest with instruments of the orchestra depicting how the euphonium can be versatile: a technical test with the piccolo, a bombastic contest with the timpani, and a glissando and double stop showdown with the violin. The double stop, using multi-phonics, in the euphonium is optional and the overall writing for the euphonium features chromatic scales and arpeggios that modulate. Overall, this work is very accessible to audiences and performers and the movements work well individually. This work is one of the few originally conceived for euphonium and orchestra and this can be highlighted with the colorful scoring and orchestration. This work is highly recommended. Recorded by Adam Frey.

Filas, Juraj. *Concerto for Euphonium*. BIM. Euphonium solo and wind band (symphony orchestra and piano reduction available). 2002. Rental (Rental, $20). 17:00. VI–V. D♭′–d♭″ (d″). One movement, four major sections: Grave, allegro vivo, grave, allegro. Commissioned for the Concours mondial de Tuba et d'Euphonium 2003 de Guebwiller. A challenging work that will gain great understanding when combined with the accompaniment, the Filas *Concerto for Euphonium* features numerous trill figures in the opening section including some on the low Db_1. The melodic writing is idiomatic and enjoyable along with some interesting rhythmic figures that will require close attention to timing and subdivision. A neat motive that Filas utilizes involves a nice descending sextuplet figure that links sections and reappears twice more. The allegro vivo hosts an ascending staccato eighth note theme that later morphs into a raising half note figure with emphatic sixteenth and dotted eighth figures. The section can be felt in two, although written in 4/4. Twice a lyrical allegro vivo theme appears and then modulates to the high tessitura reaching up as high as d^2. The high modulations have an optional 8va lower ad-lib. The work closes with a revisit to the opening material in a different key. A high declamatory figure with stringendo brings the work to a finish with a syncopated two-octave leap to a'. This concerto will find merit in the euphonium repertoire and has a style and harmonic language its own as a positive feature. While all solos need the accompaniment parts to make complete sense, this work perhaps needs it more to bring out the comprehensive musical statement.

Forsberg, Charles. *Serenade, Opus 21*. Charles Forsberg. Euphonium solo and symphony orchestra. 1979. 13:30. III–IV. F–b'. Commissioned by Henry Charles Smith. Written in four movements: Slow; Slow; Fast; Fast. This work provides a fun solo that will be enjoyed by audiences and performers. The character of the work and the complete nature of each movement allows them to be used independently. This work does not present any major difficulties and would be a welcome piece for all involved.

Furlong, Greg. *Euphonium Quintet*. Greg Furlong. 2000. Euphonium solo and string quartet. See listing in the Music for Euphonium in Mixed Ensemble chapter.

Gaines, David. *Concerto*. Verda Stelo Music. 1987. Euphonium solo and symphony orchestra. 18:00. V. BBb–d". Three movements: Misterioso; Vivace; Andante con moto-Allegro energico. Written as a master's thesis at the American University. A substantial work for the euphonium, Gaines himself plays the euphonium and this shows in the logical and well-proportioned writing in the solo lines. The first movement opens softly before a highly syncopated and rhythmic figure begins in the euphonium with interplay from the orchestra. The writing sometimes spans wide intervals and utilizes trills. A cadenza with very large interval jumps spanning two and three octaves and culminating

on a d" leads to a reprise of the opening string motive before bringing the movement to an end. The Vivace features a charged 6/8 with great energy and momentum. The writing matches the euphonium's skills well. The final movement opens with a pizzicato figure in the strings before a Brazilian-inspired melody and accompaniment ensues. The entire movement has the euphonium shifting from lyrical moments to technical showcases. The Allegro con moto features a fun triple tongued figure and rhythmic energy leading to a cadenza that again explores the range and technical prowess of the euphonium spanning a few octaves. The final Allegro energico orchestra parts lead to a rapid sixteenth note pattern for the soloist that concludes with a large orchestral finish. Recorded by Jiri Vydra.

Gileadi, Michael. *Concerto*. Jerona Music Corporation. Euphonium solo and chamber orchestra (piano reduction available). 1981. 14:00. IV–V. Gb'–db". To Professor Abe Torchinsky. Written in three movements: Andante; Lento; Allegro. Composed with numerous chromatic harmonies and non-traditional melodic lines, the Gileadi *Concerto* presents some wonderful musical challenges with some technical requirements. There are numerous trills and glissando. Portions of the solo part contain tenor clef, and flutter tonguing and a mute are utilized. The work is a unique choice given its performance medium in a contemporary style.

Glorieux, François. *Contemplation*. Glorious Sounds. Euphonium solo and strings (piano reduction available). 2001. €40 (€6). 4:00. III. Bb–a¹. Meditagione: Lento. Written in 9/8 time, this work focuses on the singing sound of the euphonium and the solo part is not terribly demanding. The harmonic and melodic writing shows a slant toward impressionistic colors given that the work shares its name with a work by the Belgium impressionist artist Jacky Duyck.

Glorieux, François. *"De Kar" Waltz*. Glorious Sounds. Euphonium solo, glockenspiel, and strings (piano reduction available). 2001. €40 (€6). 4:15. III. Bb–ab'. Tempo di Waltz. A superb character piece depicting a famous restaurant, *De Kar* in Kalmthout, Belgium. The euphonium plays a wonderful theme and obligato and of course the accompaniment figure alters on each restatement with the glockenspiel adding in the color of drinking glasses being served. The final theme features a high violin line that adds sparkle to the whole work. Recorded by Nick Ost.

Glorieux, François. *Elegy*. Glorious Sounds. Euphonium solo, violin solo, and strings (piano reduction available). 2001. €45 (€10). 4:45. III. A–ab' (violin cb1–g'''). Andante. A somber quarter note pattern in the strings opens this work before the euphonium sings a sad theme that intertwines with the violin's bright colors and ornamented solo part. The writing does not tax either of the soloists and the lyrical qualities of the euphonium predominate this work. An excellent composition that features an unusual combination. Recorded by Nick Ost.

Glorieux, François. *Euphonic Moods.* Glorious Sounds. Euphonium solo and strings (piano reduction available). 2001. €90 (€16). 11:30. III–IV. F♯–b'. I. Twilight: Tranquillio; II. Promenade: Andantino; III. Romantic Waltz: Slow waltz molto rubato. The *Twilight* contains some excellent lyrical writing and was the first euphonium composition by Glorieux. Its character is romantic and pleasant. The Promenade aurally depicts a journey with a few interactions with a quasi-majestic theme opening and leading to a brief cadenza followed by a return to the walking theme. The final bars have a strong jazz influence. The Romantic Waltz provides the most charming movement of this work. In a waltz style with many rhythms that can be felt due to the jazz nature of the melodic and harmonic palette, the writing provides great expressive freedom and is a nice showcase for the instrument and a great break from showpieces. Recorded by Nick Ost.

Glorieux, François. *Fantasy.* Glorious Sounds. Euphonium solo and strings (brass band, wind band, and piano reduction available). 2001. €70 (€100, €90, €12). 7:10. VI. G♭–c″. Lento; Allegro con brio; Cadenza; Lento; Presto. This is the most demanding work by Glorieux and scored for all possible performance mediums, so it remains a great choice for programmability. The composition contains Glorieux's signature listenable harmonies and melodies. The opening Lento lines set a relaxed atmosphere before the energetic and rhythmic Allegro con brio sixteenth note theme enters, which poses some challenges to the soloist with its shapes and double tonguing. The extended cadenza lasting approximately 1:40 will be the hurdle to make it interesting to the listener. A beautiful theme ensues afterward, leading to the exuberant tarantella in the Presto climaxing to the final high c to finish the work. This piece should be performed more often and remains one of Glorieux's best showpieces. Recorded by Nick Ost.

Glorieux, François. *Regrets.* Glorious Sounds. Euphonium solo and strings (piano reduction available). 2001. €40 (€6). 4:00. III. G–g¹. Lento. A wonderfully elegant tone composition. This piece highlights the euphonium's warm tone contrasting with high string parts. A recommended work in Glorieux's prolific output. Recorded by Nick Ost.

Glorieux, François. *Revivat Scaldis Fanfare.* Glorious Sounds. Euphonium solo, strings, and percussion. 2002. €10. 1:00. III–IV. A–a¹. Maestoso. A brief fanfare featuring the euphonium with some chromatic and lush harmonic writing with occasional quasi-jazz references in the string parts. The euphonium part has some

difficult rhythmic figures and requires double tonguing. Recorded by Nick Ost.

Glorieux, François. *Sunrise on the River Scheldt.* Glorious Sounds. Euphonium solo and strings. 2001. €40. 4:00. III. A–b♭'. Andante. A nice lyrical work that features excellent listenable melodic and harmonic writing in both the euphonium and strings. All the parts are not overly difficult and might be a great lyrical work for high school or college students. The Scheldt River enters the North Sea at the port of Antwerp. Recorded by Nick Ost.

Habbestad, Karl-Heinz. *Med Jesus vil eg Fara, Opus 41.* Norwegian Music Information Center. Euphonium solo and symphony orchestra. III.

Hoddinut, Alun. *Euphonium Concerto.* Manuscript. Euphonium solo and symphony orchestra. Written for David Childs.

Hopkinson, Michael. *Concerto Euphonique.* Kirklee's Music. Euphonium solo and symphony orchestra. VI.

Horovitz, Joseph. *Euphonium Concerto.* Novello & Company Limited. Euphonium solo and chamber orchestra (brass band, wind band, and piano available). 1991 (written in 1972). Rental only (wind band rental only, £60 brass band, £10.50 piano). 16:00. IV. C–c″. Moderato; Lento; Con moto. Commissioned by the National Brass Band Championships of Great Britain. One of the first major concertos written for the euphonium, with each movement representing musical enjoyment for the head, heart, and toes, respectively. A piece of the standard repertoire, this concerto contains writing that will challenge and engage both performer and listener. The middle movement contains some of the most expressive lyrical writing in the repertoire. In the third movement, good technical facility will be needed as well as multiple tonguing for its jovial light-hearted nature. There are a number of dexterity challenges in this movement; thus, it is common to have younger players study the first two movements due to their significance even though they may not be ready to tackle the final movement. Horovitz provides extensive detail as to articulation, tempo, and dynamics. Orchestral parts are similar to a Mozart-type orchestra and provide an easy ensemble to balance. This is a highly recommended work. Recorded by Tyronne Breuninger, Robert Childs, Trevor Groom, Eran Levy, Steven Mead, Thomas Rüedi, Robin Taylor.

Hovhaness, Alan. *Concerto No. 3: Diran, the Religious Singer.* Robert King. 1962. 9:05. III–IV. F–b♭'. Written in three movements: Canzona; Aria; Gloria. An easier work that captures the harmonic language of Hovhaness in accordance with the tonal beauty of the euphonium, this piece provides a unique performance medium with accessible parts for both soloist and ensemble. The colors of the harmony far outweigh the lack of fast notes and driving rhythms. This work studies musicality, phrasing, and ambience. The solo part does remain in the upper range much of the time, but there are short durations of rest. This work does offer a nice performance opportunity and would make a nice addition to a euphonium and strings program.

Hovhaness, Alan. *Symphony No. 29, Opus 289.* Mount Tacoma Music Publishers. Euphonium solo and symphony orchestra (wind band and piano reduction available). 1978. 18:00. III–IV. E–c″. Commissioned by Henry Charles Smith and C. G. Conn, Ltd. Written in four movements: Andante Religioso; Adagio Espressivo; Lento-Allegro-Moderate-Presto; Finale. One of the strongest musical statements written for the euphonium and wind band, the *Symphony No. 29* provides many great opportunities for the euphonium to demonstrate excellent lyrical and melodic capabilities. While the work does not contain many technical demands, the musicality, consistently high tessitura, phrasing, powerful dynamics, and sustained nature of the writing require a mature player. Knowing Hovhaness as a composer who explores the beauty of harmony and ambience, one will relish the wonderful tone colors and lovely chords that combine Western and Eastern concepts as well as some modal language. Each movement of this work could be performed individually as needed, but of course the entire work provides the fullest effect. This work should certainly be performed more regularly, but the parts can be difficult to obtain. Recorded by Christian Lindberg.

Jager, Robert. *Concerto for Euphonium.* Marks/Hal Leonard. Euphonium solo and symphony orchestra (wind band and piano reduction available). Rental (Rental, $14). 1995. 12:00. IV–V. C–d♭″. Written in three movements: Slowly, Dramatically, Freely; Slowly, Reflectively; Brightly, but Forcefully. This challenging work features high-intensity writing that translates to complex rhythms and syncopations. Flutter tonguing, lip trills, double tonguing, rapid meter changes, awkward trills, and sections in seven flats encapsulate most of the difficulties of the work. Yet its vigor and drive, especially in the third movement, can compensate the performer and listener for these challenges. The second movement has some nice recitative sections with ornamental runs. A strong addition to the more contemporary repertoire of the euphonium.

Jarett, Jack. *Diversions for Euphonium.* Manuscript. Euphonium solo and symphony orchestra.

Johnson, H. *Preludium.* Norwegian Music Information Center. Euphonium solo and symphony orchestra. III.

Kassati, Tadeusz. *Kino Concertino.* Editions BIM. Euphonium solo and string orchestra (piano reduction available). 1996. $20. 16.00. IV. E♭–b′. Written in three movements: Un poco rubato ma non troppo romantico; Noncusante;

Allegro con brio. Commissioned by the SUISA Foundation for Music for the World Tuba and Euphonium Competition in Guebwiller (Alsace, France). One of the newer substantial works for euphonium and string orchestra, the *Kino Concertino* provides a wonderful contemporary vehicle for both ensemble and soloist to demonstrate agility and rhythmic precision in the highly syncopated and rhythmic first movement, which employs numerous meter shifts including 2/4, 3/4, 4/4, 2/8, 3/8, 4/8, and 7/8 with accents appearing on different notes throughout the measures. The writing is idiomatic for the soloist, but some wonderful trills and detailed articulations will provide challenges to execute convincingly. The melodic writing throughout the movements provides a somber and reflective mood and the use of a mute in the second movement provides a nice color change. The final movement is a light rondo utilizing double tongued figures that span the range of the work. This work should be performed more often and the piano reduction achieves a fine musical reproduction of the original string version.

Koper, Karl-Heinz. *Dulcamarata Variations.* Manuscript. Euphonium solo and symphony orchestra. IV.

Linkola, Jukka. *Euphonium Concerto.* Fennica Gehrman. Euphonium and symphony orchestra (piano reduction). 2004 (written in 1996). Rental ($35). 27:00. V. EE♭–f″. Written in three movements: Agitato; Quasi nocturne; Maestoso energico. This work represents one of the most difficult works currently written for the euphonium. Originally conceived for this medium, the colors and textures in the accompaniment make it one of the most superior works in this performance medium. However, its length will make it a challenge to program. The variety of character and styles makes it an enjoyable work to practice. Yet the extended range of this work and the endurance required to perform it will keep many people away from it. The opening movement contains great driving rhythms with the euphonium's lines mainly traversing wide ranges with various arpeggiated and scalar patterns. The melodic and harmonic language is defiantly contemporary but very listenable, with a hint of jazz influence. The first movement also goes through various moods: sometimes confident (loud syncopated sections), sometimes dark (very low pedal register themes), and sometimes searching (in the extended cadenza that concludes with f″). The ending of the movement leaves the listener wanting more and the Quasi nocturne brings to light a contemplative melody that is quite lovely. However, be warned that much of the theme lies above b♭ and has ascending parts and leaps to e♭″ and f″. A huge buildup with triple tonguing on repeated f's serves as the climax before the plaintive recapitulation.

The final movement boasts the most energy and technical demands. Exuberant runs and VERY angular melodies (d♭″, c♭″, d′, b♭″, b, g′) and some complex rhythms represent the major hurdles. In addition there are a number of parts that have an e″. An extended cadenza that features a lot of technique and range also incorporates the use of an open piano with pedal depressed to create some sympathetic vibrations. A restatement of the opening and powerful cadenza following a tremendous downward glissando by the orchestra brings the work to conclusion on an EE♭. This work represents a major challenge for the euphonium soloist and a work that will be enjoyable to perform if its difficulties can be mastered. Highly recommended for those brave players. Recorded by Tormod Flaten (third movement only) and Jukka Myllys.

Long, Keith B. *Concerto for Euphonium (Meditation on Reincarnation)*.Manuscript. IV.

Madsen, Trygve. *Concerto for Euphonium and Orchestra, Opus 55*. Mussik-Hussets Forlag A/S. Euphonium solo and symphony orchestra. 1985–1989. Rental only. 16:20. IV.

Martin, David. *Suite for Euphonium and Orchestra*. Canadian Music Center. Euphonium solo and symphony orchestra (piano reduction available).

Ponchielli, Amilcare. *Concerto per Flicorno Basso, Opus 155*. Henry Howey. Tuba-Euphonium Press. Euphonium solo and orchestra (universal edition can be adapted to any large ensemble; brass band, wind band, and piano versions available). 1996 (written in 1872). $65 ($65, $80, $90, $14). 13:00. IV–V. F–b♭′. Written as a theme and variations, this is one of the few original works from the nineteenth century. The work has an extended introduction with both lyrical and technical lines for the soloist. While the work has tremendous technical difficulties and rapid range jumps, the technique focuses almost exclusively on E♭ major. Nevertheless, it contains some significant challenges. The theme sets a wonderful Italian picture before the fireworks begin as sixteenth notes in variation 1, sixteenth note triplets in variation 2, and triplet and sixteenth notes in variation 3. An interlude and obligato section leads to the final allegro flourish of sixteenth notes. A fun work that captures the character of the nineteenth-century Italian wind band movement, this piece will be a challenge to prepare and will result in the mastery of the E♭ major scale! One programming difficulty can be the work's length and repetitive nature (as with many theme and variations). There are numerous possibilities to make cuts to facilitate programming. Recorded by Michael Colburn, Manfred Heidler, Steven Mead.

Pulkkis, Uljas. *Arion—A Concerto for Euphonium and Orchestra*. FMIC. Euphonium solo and symphony orchestra. 2004. 18:00. VI–V.

G♯–f″. Written for Jukka Myllys and the Lieksa Brass Week 2004. Organized as one continuous movement with five sections: adagio; allegro; moderato; allegro; adagio. This work explores extreme range and complicated rhythmic timing. The harmonic and melodic language is chromatic. The solo part plays an integral part with the orchestra adding important harmonic material and interplay. Mr. Myllys stated that the work seemed more of a tone poem featuring the euphonium versus a dedicated solo work for the euphonium.

Raum, Elizabeth. *Concerto del Garda*. Tuba-Euphonium Press. Euphonium solo and symphony orchestra (wind band and piano reduction available). 1997. $75 ($20). 13:05. IV. G–b♭″. Written for John Griffiths. Written in three movements: Moderato Grandioso; Lento; Allegretto con Anima. Originally conceived as a tuba concerto, this work combines very listenable harmonies and melodies with a more neo-classical solo part. The writing (for euphonium) does not present any major challenges technically other than a few low areas around F. Most of the notes below B♭ are approached with enough setup time to prepare the embouchure. It is slightly easier than the *Pershing Concerto*. Both works offer the opportunity for fast playing without many technical hurdles while at the same time presenting serious and substantial repertoire. This concerto does not have any unusual requirements. Raum's works would suit an advanced player with limited high range very well and are recommended for performances. Recorded by John Griffiths (tubist).

Raum, Elizabeth. *Pershing Concerto*. Tuba-Euphonium Press. Euphonium solo and symphony orchestra (wind band and piano reduction available). 1999. $70 ($60, $20). 14:00. IV. (GG) C–b♭′. Written in three movements: Allegro moderato; Andante; Allegro non troppo. Raum's neo-classical rhythmic style combined with neo-romantic harmonies provides a nice aural combination. Conceived for tuba, this concerto's range offers virtuosic material in a confined register. It is slightly more difficult than the *Concerto del Garda*. Both works offer the opportunity for fast playing without many technical hurdles while at the same time presenting serious and substantial repertoire. This concerto does not have any unusual requirements. Her works would suit an advanced player with limited high range very well and are recommended for performances.

Roper, Anthony. *Sonata for Euphonium*. Studio Music. Euphonium solo and string orchestra (piano reduction available). Rental (£9.95). 1996. 8:30. IV. BB♭–c″. Written for John Powell. Written in three movements: Quarter Note = 116; Threnody; Quarter Note = 116. An excellent contemporary work with a nice choice of either piano or string orchestra accompaniment. The writing melodically and harmonically is contemporary and contains some excellent rhythmic writing. This composition provides an ideal choice for a short, contemporary work with orchestra that has good writing, a wonderful lyrical second movement, and a showcase final movement. There is a trill on c″. A piece worthy of more performance. Recorded by Steven Mead.

Serraiocco, S. G. *Concertino for Euphonium and Chamber Ensemble*. Tuba-Euphonium Press. See the Music for Euphonium in Mixed Ensemble chapter.

Stevens, John D. *Concerto for Euphonium and Orchestra*. Editions BIM. Euphonium solo and symphony orchestra (piano reduction available). 2004. 16:00. IV–V. D–c″ (optional e♭″). Written for Brian Bowman. Commissioned by DEG Music Products, Inc., and Willson Brass Instruments. Maestoso—Allegro; Elegy; Maestoso-Vivace Energico. "The outer movements showcase mainly the technique and power of the instrument. The first movement Allegro is marked at 'half note = 138–144.' The third movement Vivace is marked at 'quarter note = 152–156' and then closes at 'quarter note = 160.' The middle movement, Elegy, features primarily the lyrical and sonorous elements of the instrument. This is a challenging work in terms of range and technical demands, but it is idiomatically written for the instrument, with no extended techniques. There are solo cadenzas in each movement."—John Stevens.

Strum, Fred. *Elysian Fields*. Fred Strum. Euphonium solo and orchestra.

Theobald, Jim. *Concerto for Euphonium, Strings, and Percussion*. Manuscript. Euphonium solo and strings and percussion. 12:00. IV. F–a′. Written in three movements: Conversations; Strange Journey; Dancing on the Edge. This work combines some exciting contemporary material for the euphonium. The opening movement features some mixed meter but mainly a rhythmic driving section with some chromatic melodic material. The second movement by far is the most intriguing of the three. The ensemble and soloist have 63 and 48 bars, respectively. The soloist picks and chooses which bars to play. So this is a creative work that will never be the same. As the ensemble comes to finish their 63 bars, the conductor signals the euphonium soloist that the end is near. The final movement features a fun 6/8 meter with nice energy. There are some contemporary and traditional moments harmonically, but it ends nicely. This work would be an excellent choice for an avant-garde work, yet the outer movements are not terrible avant-garde. The middle movement does contain some unusual techniques such as random pitches, speaking through the instrument, mouthpiece popping, multiphonics, and flutter tonguing.

Tomasi, Henri. *Danse sacrée (Ritual Dance)*. Leduc. Bass saxhorn and chamber orchestra (piano reduction available). 1960. IV. G–a♭′.

Townsend, Douglas. *Chamber Concerto No. 2, Opus 6*. Theodore Presser Company. Euphonium solo and chamber orchestra (piano reduction available). 1965. 9:20. III–IV. E–c″. Dedicated to Davis Shuman. This work was one of the first euphonium works with orchestra. Written in three movements, the piece features only a few small technical challenges. Some unique aspects include the occasional use of the euphonium as an accompanying instrument. The opening of the second movement features the euphonium just playing Fs in various octaves for more than thirty bars. There are luckily better selections with orchestra; however, this work represents a decent piece from the early period of the euphonium.

Weinstein, Michael. *Concerto for Euphonium and Chamber Orchestra*. Michel Weinstein. Euphonium solo and chamber orchestra. 1984. 15:30. V. F–e″. Written for Michael Fischer. This difficult solo features some coherent writing in three continuous movements. The language features some chromatic writing along with some very challenging technical passages. Coordinating the solo and ensemble parts will be a challenge. Given the difficulty that the work is not published, there are many other solos that would probably suit programming better.

Wilby, Philip. *Concerto for Euphonium*. Winwood Music. Euphonium solo and symphony orchestra (brass band, wind band, and piano reductions available). 1996. Rental (£70, £125, £15). 18:15. V. A♭–d″ (e♭″). Written for Robert Childs. Written in two parts/four movements: Part I—Non troppo allegro; Dance Zeibékikos; Part II—Andante; Allegro vivace. One of the most challenging and demanding concerti, the Wilby *Concerto for Euphonium* combines incredible energy, driving intensity, soaring lyricism, and great listening enjoyment. However, the challenges present a substantial obstacle for many players. Firstly, there are tremendous technical demands including rapid repeated and moving double and triple tonguing through three of the four movements. The patterns are often chromatic, but with small modifications. Difficult rhythmic patterns also present challenges, as does the overall tempo of the work and the endurance needed to sustain the power and balance for the eighteen minutes. The most memorable portion of this concerto is the Dance Zeibékikos. It basically makes up three minutes of pure adrenaline through fast notes, crazy two-octave glissandos, fierce grace notes, and rapid meter changes before ending with the percussion section breaking plates!! The third movement then provides a very contemplative interlude before the final movement. The lyrical nature of the Andante explores the low range of the euphonium before ascending to a poignant statement in a slow 6/8. This writing is wonderfully lush and captures the best qualities of the euphonium before moving directly into the finale. The technical demands return and bring the work to a triumphant conclusion. This work will be very demanding but absolutely worth the investment. It is a highly recommended work. The accompaniment parts are scored a little thickly and will challenge college-level ensembles. Recorded by Robert Childs, David Childs, Steven Mead.

Woodson, Bear. *Concerto*. Manuscript. Euphonium and symphony orchestra. 16:35. A work originally composed for horn. As described by the composer: "The First Movement is like a blend of the styles of Hindemith and Shostakovich. It ends with my signature, the first time I used the BEAR Motive, being the Notes: B♭, E, A, and R (explained in the score). The Slow Second Movement uses a 2-bar Passacaglia Theme, that modulates every 2 bars, and plays 4 times each in: Original, Inversion, Retrograde and Retrograde-Inversion. ALL of my harmony, in this concerto and in EVERY one of my compositions uses a little Quartal Harmony (chords stacked every 4th note), but is mostly Chromatic Modal Tertian Harmony (chords stacked every 3rd note). I never did like, nor use, 12-Tone, but I have to keep reminding people of that fact, and the fact that Inversion and Retrograde have been used by Modal and Tonal Composers since the Late Middle Ages! Despite the complex counterpoint, the mood is dreamy and wistful. The Third Movement is a Hunting Horn Modified Rondo (A, B, A1, C, Cadenza, A2), that is mostly in a rollicking 6/8 Meter, with the BEAR Motive (B♭, E, A, D) as the 'A' Section Theme. The mood is fun and mischievous, with comical snarls and growl in the 'C' section of the Rondo, and a comical surprise in the final 'A' Section."

Woodson, Bear. *In Memoriam for the Fallen Victims of the 9-11 Attack*. Manuscript. Euphonium and strings. 6:53. A work composed for horn and arranged for euphonium.

Notes

1. David Miles, *An Annotated Bibliography of Selected Contemporary Euphonium Solo Literature by American Composers* (Annandale, Virginia: Tuba-Euphonium Press, 1992).

6. Music for Euphonium in Mixed Ensemble

Seth D. Fletcher

As it stands today, the euphonium is one of the most unrecognized and underappreciated musical instruments. In the United States, in particular, tell someone that you play euphonium and the likely reply is, "What?!" The education of the general public, greater professional recognition, and a proliferation of literature and world-class artists are worthy goals on which the euphonium community must set its sights. So what can you do to raise euphonium awareness? Be heard!

One of the best ways to be heard is to play music that will attract a wide variety of listeners. The music listed in this chapter is just such music for two reasons. First, playing with other instruments and voices attracts audiences that know and appreciate those other instruments. For example, a college student performing a piece with flute and soprano on a recital will attract audience members from the other performers' studios and families as well as the student's own family, friends, and fans. The second way chamber music can help euphoniumists find greater audiences is in the formation of groups that play at various functions, venues, and special occasions. For example, a brass quartet can find new audiences for the euphonium in recitals; at malls, weddings, and churches; and wherever music can be played (anywhere!). Additionally, playing great chamber music is one of the most rewarding experiences a musician can have . . . it's just plain fun.

This chapter lists music scored for euphonium(s) in combination with other instruments and voices. Works written for such mixed ensembles often show the composers' creative spirit as they search for a new, innovative sonority and vehicle for expression. The works listed in this chapter are those that feature the euphonium or include the instrument as an equal member in the ensemble. For the most part, pieces calling for more than ten players have not been included, except in cases where the euphonium plays a prominent or solo role. For navigational purposes, the listings in this chapter are organized alphabetically by number of parts.

While this chapter deals solely with music written for euphonium in combination with other instruments, several pieces written for multiple tubas may have parts suitable to be played on euphonium, particularly duets and trios of easier difficulty levels. Such mixed ensembles can be especially useful for younger players. These pieces may be found listed in the *Tuba Source Book* (*TSB*) under Music for Multiple Tubas and should not be overlooked as a source of suitable repertoire. Additionally, pieces with instrumentation consisting of combinations of euphoniums and tubas with four or more parts have been excluded from this chapter as they are covered extensively under Music for Multiple Tubas in the *TSB*.

Thanks to all the publishers, composers, and international consultants who provided information and examination materials for this project. This resource would not be available without their support. Unfortunately, due to the widespread practice of illegal copying, several publishers have been unable to provide the materials necessary for review. All listings in this chapter include all verifiable information available for each piece. Legally purchasing music from publishers and composers allows for the continued development of the euphonium repertoire and prevents the loss of current literature.

I would personally like to thank R. Winston Morris, Eric Paull, Lloyd Bone, the editorial board, and authors for making the *Euphonium Source Book* a reality. My regards to Steven Mead, whose assistance, insight, and hospitality have been invaluable to this project. And a special thank you to Dr. Colin Beeson, vice principal of the Royal Northern College of Music, and Dr. Ronald Woodley for their much-appreciated support.

Two Players

Aagaard-Nilsen, Torstein. *Football!—The Great Moment.* Taan-Band Music. Euphonium and snare drum. 2001. 1:30. IV. c–b'. Dedicated to Tormod Flaten and Hogne Holmås. A fun duet for both the audience and performers.

Technically challenging for the euphoniumist. Requires brief vocalization (shouts).

Adler, Samuel. *Four Dialogues for Euphonium and Marimba.* Carl Fischer. Euphonium and marimba. V. B♭₁–e♭″. Four movements: I. Quite Slowly; II. Fast and Humorous; III. Slowly and Rather Lazily; IV. Fast with a Happy Spirit. A difficult contemporary work for a unique instrumentation that is a great recital addition. Complex rhythmic patterns, angular leaps, and fast technical passages. Includes some tenor clef. Brief flutter tongued passages. Recorded by Brian Bowman, Euphonium, Crystal Records CA393.

Anderson, Eugene. *Baroque'n Brass.* Cimarron Music. Euphonium and tuba. 1991. $10. 5:00. IV. Part I: G♯–d″, Part II: D₁–d′. Commissioned by and dedicated to David L. Aubuchon, U.S. Army Band, Ft. Dix, New Jersey. A moderate tempo fugue. Technically challenging for both players. High tessitura in the first part.

Anderson, Eugene. *Teuphm'isms I.* Cimarron Music. Euphonium and tuba. 1990. $10. 5:00. IV. Part I: G–c″, Part II: F₁–f′. Dedicated to Brian Bowman and Harvey Phillips. Technically challenging for both players. High tessitura in the first part. Extensive use of syncopated rhythms in both parts.

Anderson, Eugene. *Teuphm'isms II.* Cimarron Music. Euphonium and tuba. 1992. $10. 5:00. IV. Part I: G–c♯, Part II: E₁–f′. Dedicated to Brian Bowman and Harvey Phillips. Fanfare-like in character. Meter changes between 6/8 and 2/4. Both parts are challenging for their technical and range demands.

Armitage, Denis. *Swing for Two.* Editions Marc Reift. Trumpet and euphonium. 1994. €11.20.

Aronson, Lee. *Suite for Euphonium and Electric Guitar.* Tuba-Euphonium Press. Euphonium and electric guitar. 2001. $12. 10:00. III. F–d′. Four movements: I. Allemande; II. Courante; III. Sarabande; IV. Gigue. A collection of four dances in baroque style with traditional harmonies. Demonstrates effective use of two-part contrapuntal writing. Individual movements can stand alone or be performed in various combinations. The guitar part is written using traditional music notation.

Aronson, Lee. *Suite for Tuba and Euphonium.* Tuba-Euphonium Press. Euphonium and tuba. 2001. $12. 10:00. III. Part I: B♭–e′, Part II: A₁–e. Four movements: I. Allemande; II. Courante; III. Sarabande; IV. Gigue. A collection of four dances in baroque style with traditional harmonies. Demonstrates effective use of two-part contrapuntal writing. Individual movements can stand alone or be performed in various combinations.

Ausfahl, Jeff, arr. *Hymns.* Puna Music Company. Euphonium and guitar. 2000. $12.95. 15 pp. III. B♭–g′. Five movements: I. Count Your Blessings; II. In the Garden; III. God That Madest Earth and Heaven (All through the Night); IV. Love

Lifted Me; V. Brighten the Corner Where You Are. Dedicated to the memory of Richard Joseph Ausfahl. Great arrangements of classic hymns for a unique instrumental combination. Euphonium part not technically difficult. Guitar part requires a strong player who can read music. Comes with a pre-recorded CD of the guitar accompaniment that can be used in performance.

Bach, Johann Sebastian. *Aria—Duet from Cantata No. 78.* Arr. David Werden. Cimarron Music. One euphonium and one tuba with piano. 1995. $10. II–III. Part I: d–b♭′, Part II: A–e♭′. Effective arrangement of this highly imitative work in ternary form. Ranges and style are appropriate for young and intermediate-level performers. Second part may also be performed on euphonium. Euphonium parts also available in treble clef.

Bach, Johann Sebastian. *15 Two-Part Inventions.* Arr. Henry Howey. Cimarron Music. Euphonium and tuba. $15.

Bach, Johann Sebastian. *Five Duos.* Arr. Arthur Frackenpohl. Tuba-Euphonium Press. Euphonium and tuba. 1997. $12. 8:45. IV. Part I: F–b′, Part II: F₁–b♭. Five movements: I. Two Part Invention (No. 4); II. Sarabande (French Suite No. 1); III. Aria (Magnificat); IV. Minuet (French Suite No. 4); V. Chorale Prelude (Glory Be to God on High). These five duets would work well for a collegiate-level recital. Challenging for both parts and rewarding to play. Includes euphonium parts in treble and bass clef. The bass clef part includes some tenor clef.

Bach, Johann Sebastian. *Invention No. 8.* Arr. Mick Hesse and Connie Schultz. Brassworks 4. Cornet and euphonium. 2003. $8. IV. C–c″. A challenging arrangement of this brief invention characterized by extended sixteenth note passages with large leaps. Would work well in recital in combination with one or more of the other *Inventions* by the same arrangers. Technically difficult. Treble clef part included.

Bach, Johann Sebastian. *Invention No. 11.* Arr. Mick Hesse and Connie Schultz. Brassworks 4. Cornet and euphonium. 2003. $8. IV. C–e♭′. A good arrangement of this brief invention. Would work well in recital in combination with one or more of the other *Inventions* by the same arrangers. Technically challenging. Treble clef part included.

Bach, Johann Sebastian. *Invention No. 15.* Arr. Mick Hesse and Connie Schultz. Brassworks 4. Cornet and euphonium. 2003. $8. IV. C–e′. Excellent arrangement of this brief invention in B minor. Would work well in recital in combination with one or more of the other *Inventions* by the same arrangers. Technically challenging. Treble clef part included.

Bach, Johann Sebastian. *Invention No. 5.* Arr. Mick Hesse and Connie Schultz. Brassworks 4. Cornet and euphonium. 2003. $8. IV. E♭–f′. A great arrangement of this brief invention characterized by extended sixteenth note passages in 4/4 time. Would work well in recital in combination with one or more of the other *Inventions* by the same arrangers. Technically challenging. Treble clef part included.

Bach, Johann Sebastian. *Invention No. 4.* Arr. Mick Hesse and Connie Schultz. Brassworks 4. Cornet and euphonium. 2003. $8. IV. C–f′. Excellent arrangement of this brief invention in a moderate 3/8 meter. Would work well in recital in combination with one or more of the other *Inventions* by the same arrangers. Technically challenging. Treble clef part included.

Bach, Johann Sebastian. *Invention No. 14.* Arr. Mick Hesse and Connie Schultz. Brassworks 4. Cornet and euphonium. 2003. $8. IV. C–b♭′. A great arrangement of this challenging, brief invention. Characterized by 32nd note rhythmic patterns that sometimes rapidly shift ranges. Would work well in recital in combination with one or more of the other *Inventions* by the same arrangers. Technically difficult. Treble clef part included.

Bach, Johann Sebastian. *Invention No. 9.* Arr. Mick Hesse and Connie Schultz. Brassworks 4. Cornet and euphonium. 2003. $8. IV. C–b♭′. A great arrangement of this brief invention in 3/4 time. Would work well in recital in combination with one or more of the other *Inventions* by the same arrangers. Technically challenging. Treble clef part included.

Bach, Johann Sebastian. *Invention No. 1.* Arr. Mick Hesse and Connie Schultz. Brassworks 4. Cornet and euphonium. 2003. $8. IV. D–b♭′. A great arrangement of this brief invention. Would work well in recital in combination with one or more of the other *Inventions* by the same arrangers. Technically challenging. Treble clef part included.

Bach, Johann Sebastian. *Invention No. 7.* Arr. Mick Hesse and Connie Schultz. Brassworks 4. Cornet and euphonium. 2003. $8. IV. D–g′. A great arrangement of this brief invention in E minor. Would work well in recital in combination with one or more of the other *Inventions* by the same arrangers. Technically challenging. Treble clef part included.

Bach, Johann Sebastian. *Invention No. 6.* Arr. Mick Hesse and Connie Schultz. Brassworks 4. Cornet and euphonium. 2003. $8. IV. C–e′. Challenging arrangement of this brief invention employing extensive syncopation in a 3/8 meter. Written in the key of E major with numerous accidentals. Would work well in recital in combination with one or more of the other *Inventions* by the same arrangers. Technically challenging. Treble clef part included.

Bach, Johann Sebastian. *Invention No. 10.* Arr. Mick Hesse and Connie Schultz. Brassworks 4. Cornet and euphonium. 2003. $8. IV. D–g′. Excellent arrangement of this brief invention in 9/8 time characterized by extended passages of arpeggiated eighth notes. Would work well in recital in combination with one or more of the other

Inventions by the same arrangers. Technically challenging. Treble clef part included.

Bach, Johann Sebastian. *Invention No. 13.* Arr. Mick Hesse and Connie Schultz. Brassworks 4. Cornet and euphonium. 2003. $8. IV. D–a′. Challenging arrangement of this brief invention in A minor. Would work well in recital in combination with one or more of the other *Inventions* by the same arrangers. Technically challenging. Treble clef part included.

Bach, Johann Sebastian. *Invention No. 3.* Arr. Mick Hesse and Connie Schultz. Brassworks 4. Cornet and euphonium. 2003. $8. IV. D–b′. A great arrangement of this brief invention in a moderate 3/8 meter. Would work well in recital in combination with one or more of the other *Inventions* by the same arrangers. Technically challenging. Treble clef part included.

Bach, Johann Sebastian. *Invention No. 12.* Arr. Mick Hesse and Connie Schultz. Brassworks 4. Cornet and euphonium. 2003. $8. IV. C♯–a′. A great arrangement of this brief invention in a moderate 12/8 meter. Would work well in recital in combination with one or more of the other *Inventions* by the same arrangers. Technically challenging. Treble clef part included.

Bach, Johann Sebastian. *Invention No. 2.* Arr. Mick Hesse and Connie Schultz. Brassworks 4. Cornet and euphonium. 2003. $8. IV. C–c″. Excellent arrangement of this brief invention. Would work well in recital in combination with one or more of the other *Inventions* by the same arrangers. Technically challenging. Treble clef part included.

Bach, Johann Sebastian. *Minuet I from Partita No. 1.* Arr. Jeffrey Lazar. Lyric Brass Publishing. Euphonium and tuba. 1998. $2.50.

Bach, Johann Sebastian. *Suite in D Minor, Cello Suite No. 2.* Arr. Arthur Frackenpohl. Tuba-Euphonium Press. Euphonium and tuba. 1997. $12. III. Part I: F–g′, Part II: F₁–c′ (d′). Six movements. A good pedagogical piece useful to promote an understanding of baroque contrapuntal style. Both parts have been given ample amounts of melodic work and harmonic support. Euphonium part also available in treble clef. Reviewed in the Summer 1999 issue of the *TUBA Journal*, Vol. 26, No. 4.

Bach, Johann Sebastian. *Two-Part Inventions.* Arr. Andrew B. Spang and Jeffrey Lazar. Lyric Brass Publishing. Euphonium and tuba. 2000. $17.50. III. Part I: F–c″, Part II: C₁–c′. Fifteen movements. This is a straightforward transcription with the original ornaments. The euphonium part is scored in tenor clef in three of the movements. Reviewed in the Winter 2001 issue of the *TUBA Journal*, Vol. 28, No. 2.

Badarak, Mary Lynn. *Bass Lied and Valse to Bass.* TUBA Journal. Euphonium and tuba. 1976. $7.50. 2:30. IV. Part I: A–d′, Part II: F₁–a. Two movements: Bass Lied and Valse to Bass. The first movement is slow and lyrical, utilizing a contemporary harmonic language. The second movement employs mixed meters, including 5/8, 4/8, and 6/8. Written as part of the TUBA GEM Series and published in the *TUBA Journal*, Vol. 3, No. 3.

Barber, Clarence. *Duo for Euphonium and Percussion*. Ludwig Music Publishing. Euphonium and percussion. $9.95. IV. C–b♭'. Three movements: Movement I; Movement II; Movement III. The first movement is a playful 12/8 that employs half-valve technique. The second movement is lyrical and requires a mute. The final movement employs mixed meters at a moderate tempo. The percussion part is playable by one player.

Bartles, Alfred H. *Beersheeba Neo-Baroque Suite*. Brass Music Limited (the Brass Press). Euphonium and tuba. 1975. $5. 5:30. IV. Part I: G–g, Part II: F₁–e'. Four movements: Prelude; Gavotte; Sarabande; Gigue–Postlude. For Winston Morris. A well-written duet in the baroque style.

Beck, Jeremy. *Prelude, Dance, and Fanfare*. Tuba-Euphonium Press. Euphonium and tuba. 2001. $10. 7:00. III. Part I: B♭–f♯', Part II: G♭₁–d'. Three movements: I. Prelude; II. Dance; III. Fanfare. A complex original composition. Each part has large intervallic leaps in a pointillistic style. Reviewed in the Winter 2002 issue of the *ITEA Journal*, Vol. 29, No. 2.

Belden, George R. *Ginnungigap*. TUBA Journal. Euphonium and tuba. 1977. $7.50. 2:30. IV. Part I: F♯–b♭', Part II: F♯₁–f'. This work is a programmatic description of the creation of the world as told in Scandinavian mythology. Both parts are difficult and have challenging range demands. Utilizes a contemporary harmonic language. Written as part of the TUBA GEM Series and published in the *TUBA Journal*, Vol. 5, No. 1.

Belden, George R. *Ragnarok*. Tenuto Publications. Euphonium and tuba. 1983. $3.50. 2:20. IV. Part I: c–b♭', Part II: E₁–b♭. Originally written in 1978, this companion piece to *Ginnungigap* is a programmatic depiction of the final destruction of the world as told in Scandinavian mythology. Extensive use of syncopation in both parts.

Bell, William, arr. *Artistic Solos and Duets*. Charles Colin. Euphonium and tuba. 1975. $5.95. 15 pp. IV. Part I: B–a', Part II: F–f'. A collection of thirteen duets arranged for euphonium and tuba taken from the *Complete Tuba Method* by William Bell. Not technically difficult, but the tessitura of the second part is high. Several of the passages may be played down an octave.

Booth, Steven, arr. *Carnival Duet*. SB Music. Cornet and euphonium.

Bowder, Jerry. *Canons and Hockets*. Manduca Music Publications. Euphonium and tuba. 1995. $10. 5:45. III–IV. Part I: D–c″, Part II: (F1)B♭₁–e♭' (g♭'). A tour-de-force duet for advanced players based on a 1930s jazz motif. Both parts are

imitative and highly contrapuntal, including several passages written in parallel ninths or sevenths. Each part is in score form to assist with ensemble cohesiveness.

Brandon, Sy. *Half a Dozen or the Other*. G. Ricordi & Co. Ltd. Trumpet and euphonium.

Brown, Newel Kay. *Dialogue and Dance*. Seesaw Music Corporation Publishers. Euphonium and tuba. 1978. $12. 6:00. IV–V. Part I: G₁–b♭', Part II: A♭₁–e'. Two movements: Resolutely; Gay. Dedicated to David Kuehn and G. B. Lane. Contemporary harmonic language. Both parts technically difficult. Euphonium part contains some tenor clef. Both players read from a single score.

Burger, David E. *Five Bicinia*. Ludwig Music Publishing. Trumpet and euphonium. $5.95. II. Appropriate for younger players.

Catelinet, Philip. *The Alpha Suite*. Philip Catelinet. Out of Print. Euphonium and tuba. 7:30. IV. Part I: B♭–a♯', Part II: A₁–a♭. Three movements: Aerimony; Amiability; Affinity. All movements are polyphonic. Traditional harmonic language.

Conley, Lloyd, arr. *Christmas for Two*. Kendor Music, Inc. Euphonium and tuba. 1981. $10. 21 pp. III. Part I: A–f', Part II: A♭₁–f. Easy arrangements of ten familiar Christmas carols: O Come All Ye Faithful; We Three Kings; Deck the Halls; O Little Town; The First Noel; Hark, the Herald; It Came upon a Midnight Clear; Jingle Bells; Silent Night; and Joy to the World. Appropriate for high school concerts or church services. Last three carols are more technically challenging than the other carols.

Constantinides, Dinos. *Dedications for Baritone and Tuba*. Dinos Constantinides. Euphonium and tuba. 1989. $5. 6:20. V. Part I: E♭–d″, Part II: F₁–f'. Three movements: Pandiatonic; Polytonal; Quartal. Technically difficult. Movements are named for the harmonic language employed in that movement. Some tenor clef in the euphonium part. Technically challenging for both players. Third movement uses mixed meter. Originally written in 1978.

Corwell, Neal. *The Dream*. Tuba-Euphonium Press. Euphonium, tuba, and CD accompaniment. 1995. $20. 6:45. V. E♭1–c″(d″). An exciting duet with recorded accompaniment. Fun for audience and performer alike. Technically difficult with extreme range demands. Mixed meter and large angular leaps. Careful rehearsal needed to coordinate performance with CD accompaniment. CD includes recording with both parts as well as the accompaniment track only for performance.

Corwell, Neal. *Zeke and Zebedee*. Tuba-Euphonium Press. Euphonium (or tuba) and narrator. 1995. $10. III. C–b♭'. A fun "little ditty" about a serious subject. The narration tells the story of two men, Zeke and Zebedee. Zeke is a farmer and Zebedee a musician. There is a great deal of interaction between the two parts as the soloist paints a musical picture of the narration. Includes a number of musical quotes ranging from Bach to modern rock music.

Cummings, Barton. *Vignettes for Euphonium, Tuba and Piano.* Solid Brass Music. Euphonium, tuba, and piano. 1996. $18. 12:30. III–IV. Part I: E–c″, Part II: G₁–g′. Five movements: In Olden Style; Morning Reveries; Lazy Day; Cantilena; Random Flight. Very challenging work with large intervals and fast technical passages in both parts. Middle three movements are slow and lyrical, whereas the outer movements are fast and technical. Third movement contains jazz elements. Parts are of equal difficulty.

Deason, David. *Earthshine.* David Deason. Euphonium and vibraphone. 1982. IV. D–c″. Three movements: I. Allegro; II. Mesto; III. Allegro. An interesting contemporary work that challenges both players. Difficult rhythmic figures. Second movement calls for both players to hum or whistle. Some simple meter changes.

De Filippi, Amedeo. *Divertimento for Brass Duo.* Robert King Music Sales, Inc. Euphonium and tuba. 1968. $5.55. 9:00. III. Part I: c–g′, Part II: G₁–b♭. Five movements: March; Intermezzo I; Tempo Di Valse; Intermezzo II; Rondino. Appropriate for high school players.

DeFries, Byron. *BonMarch.* PEL Music Publications. Horn and euphonium. 1998. $8.50. 1:50. II. A–c′. A simple original duet in 2/4 time for younger players.

DeFries, Byron. *Goeppingen Gallup.* PEL Music Publications. Trumpet and euphonium. 1999. $7.50. II. A–f′. A simple original duet in 6/8 meter suitable for younger players.

De Jong, Conrad. *Music for Two Tubas.* Elkan-Vogel. Euphonium and tuba. 1964. $1.95. 5:00. III. Part I: D–c′, Part II: G₁–e♭. Three movements: Fanfare; Canon; Finale. Dedicated to Dick and Don. Appropriate for high school students.

Di Lasso, Orlando. *Two Renaissance Duets.* Arr. Andrew Spang. Lyric Brass Publishing. Euphonium and tuba. $2.50. From *O Magnum Musicum.*

Dougherty, William. *Duo.* Heilman Music. Euphonium and marimba.

Dutton, Brent. *Then and Now.* Seesaw Music Corporation Publishers. Euphonium and tuba. 1978. $12. 5:00. IV–V. Part I: G♭–b♭′, Part II: G♭₁–d′. Two movements: Then; Now. Written for Ken Henning and Mark Edwards. The second movement calls for extended performance techniques including singing and yelling through the horn, slapping the bell, and foot stomps. Very difficult.

Frackenpohl, Arthur. *Brass Duo.* Robert King Music Sales, Inc. Euphonium (horn) and tuba. 1972. $5.55. 7:00. IV. Part I: B♭–b′ (c″), Part II: F₁–b♭. Four movements: Prelude; Ballad; Scherzo; Variations. Good traditional writing. High tessitura

in the first part. Occasional irregular rhythms and shifting meters.

Frackenpohl, Arthur. *Five Bach Duos for Euphonium and Tuba.* Williams Music Publishing Company. Euphonium and tuba. 1993. $10. 8:45. IV. Part I: B♭–c″, Part II: F₁–b♭. Five movements: Two-Part Invention No. 4; Sarabande; Aria; Minuett; Chorale Prelude. Traditional arrangement of these famous Bach melodies. The first part is written in tenor clef.

Frackenpohl, Arthur. *Pop Suite No. 2.* Tuba-Euphonium Press. Euphonium and tuba. 1998. $10. 9:30. IV. Part I: c–c″, Part II: F₁–b♭. Three movements: Tango; Waltz; March. Syncopated rhythms in the Tango and March. A fun and tuneful piece.

Friedrich, Kenneth D. *Five Minute Suite.* Kenneth D. Friedrich. Euphonium and tuba. 2003. $12.

Gaines, David. *Five Miniatures for Flute and Euphonium.* Verda Stelo Music. Flute and euphonium.

Gearhart, Livingston, arr. *Bass Clef Sessions.* Shawnee Press, Inc. 1954. $7.50. 50 pp. III–IV. Part I: c–b♭′, Part II: F–g′. A collection of 62 two-, three-, and four-part arrangements for euphonium and tuba. Styles range from Renaissance to jazz.

Gillis, Lew. *Ten Duets.* Virgo Music Publishers. Euphonium and tuba. 1986. $7.95. 13 pp. IV. Part I: G–a′, Part II: D♭₁–f′. Movements vary in difficulty depending on range, key, tempo, and style. Combining two or more of the duets can make a good recital piece.

Gillis, Lew. *Ten More Duets, Book 2.* Virgo Music Publishers. Euphonium and tuba. 1986. $7.95. IV.

Glorieux, François. *6 Contrasts: Duo for Euphonium and Trombone.* Glorious Sound bvba. Euphonium and trombone. 2002. €15. 8:44. IV. F–a′. Six movements: I. Intrada; II. Andante nostalgico; III. Alla Marcia; IV. Drammatico; V. Tempo di Valse; VI. Scherzando ritmico. An exciting duet of varying musical styles. Challenging and fun to play. Good recital material. The euphonium part is in treble clef and the trombone part in bass clef. Recorded by Duotonic, *Explorations!,* Glorious Sound CD08.

Glorieux, François. *7 Travel Impressions: Duo for Euphonium and Trombone.* Glorious Sound bvba. Euphonium and trombone. 2002. €20. 14:30. IV. B♭₁–a♭′. Seven movements: I. St. Paul's Cathedral; II. Schönbrunn; III. Copacabana; IV. Maghreb; V. Pigalle; VI. New Orleans; VII. Andalusia. A clever duet of contrasting movements that depict diverse locations across the globe. Some technical challenges. Good recital material. The euphonium part is in treble clef and the trombone part in bass clef. Recorded by Duotonic, *Explorations!,* Glorious Sound CD08.

Goble, Joseph. *Five Graded Intermediate Duets.* Tuba-Euphonium Press. Euphonium and tuba.

1996. $15. 22 pp. II–III. Part 1: B♭–b♭', Part 2: F₁–a♭. Five movements: I. Bombardon Dance; II. Zéllaphon; III. Champ; IV. Abrélatas; V. Phanfare and Presto. Progressively arranged collection of duets specifically composed for intermediate-level performers. Fourth movement calls for optional percussion, including cabasa, claves, castanets, timbales, agogo bell, cowbell, vibra slap, and congas. Euphonium parts also available in treble clef. Individual movements can stand alone in concert.

Goedicke, Alexander. *Concert Suite.* Philharmusica Corporation. Euphonium and tuba. 1974. $6. 7:30. IV. Part I: B♭–a♭', Part II: B♭₁–e♭'. Six movements: I; II; III; IV; V; VI. Polyphonic writing but not technically difficult. Both parts written in a high tessitura.

Grainger, Percy. *Irish Tune from County Derry.* Arr. R. P. Block. Philharmonia Music. Euphonium and trumpet. $11.50.

Harris, Floyd O. *Two Little Stars.* Ludwig Music Publishing. Trumpet and euphonium. $5.95.

Hartley, Walter. *Bivalve Suite.* Autograph Editions. Euphonium and tuba. 1971. $8.50. 3:00. IV. Part I: F–a', Part II: E♭₁–d♭'. Three movements: Allegro moderato; Lento; Presto. For Edward Bahr and C. Rudolph Emilson. Several ensemble challenges. Recorded by Robert LeBlanc and Paul Droste, *Euphonium Favorites for Recital and Contest,* Coronet, LPS 3203.

Hartzell, Doug. *Ten Jazz Duos and Solos.* Shawnee Press, Inc. Euphonium and tuba. 1974. $6. 7:30. IV–V. Part I: B♭–a♭', Part II: F–a♭'. Six movements: Funky Monkeys; Split-Level; Swingin' in Seven; Tri-Level; Rock Pile; Short Ballad for Short Chicks. From a collection of ten jazz melodies: four solos, five duets, and one trio. Technically challenging for both parts. Chord symbols are included for rhythm section use.

Hawkins, Alan, arr. *Twenty Duets from Symphonic Masterworks.* Shawnee Press, Inc. Euphonium and tuba. 1985. $4.95. 32 pp. IV. Part I: G–c'', Part II: B♭₁–f. Twenty famous melodies from symphonies by Haydn, Mozart, Beethoven, Schubert, Brahms, and so forth. The first part is responsible for the melody in most cases.

Heussenstamm, George. *Saxophonium.* Dorn Publications. Saxophone and euphonium. $20.

Hewitt, Harry. *Six Preludes for Euphonium and Tuba, Op. 246C.* TUBA Press. Out of Print. Euphonium and tuba. 1991. 14:00. IV. Part I: A♭–g♭, Part II: B♭₁–f♭'. Six movements. Challenging pieces in a traditional harmonic language. Technically and rhythmically challenging. Several movements have ad-lib sections requiring players to watch the score and listen carefully. Originally written in 1983 and titled *Six Preludes for Baritone and Tuba.*

Hoesly, John, arr. *Christmas Collection—Duets for Brass.* Piston Reed Stick and Bow Publisher. Euphonium and tuba. 1990. $17. 19 pp. III–IV.

Part I: B♭₁–b♭', Part II: G₁–g. Fourteen movements: Jingle Bells; Good King Wenceslas; We Three Kings; Deck the Halls; God Rest Ye Merry Gentlemen; Angels We Have Heard on High; O Come All Ye Faithful; O, Christmas Tree; It Came upon a Midnight Clear; Joy to the World; We Wish You a Merry Christmas; Hark, the Herald Angels Sing; The First Noel; Silent Night. Only moderate technical problems. Ideal for good high school players. Parts and score are sold separately.

Jones, Roger. *Airs and Dances.* Tuba-Euphonium Press. Euphonium and tuba. 2000. $10. 18 pp. III. Part I: (F)G–b♭', Part II: (F₁)B♭₁–c♭'. Seven movements: Tarantella; Air No. 1; Waltz; Air No. 2; Scherzo; Air No. 3; Ritual Dance. Collection of seven contrasting duets. The three airs are slow and lyrical, while the other movements are lively and dance-like with syncopation and occasional meter changes. Individual movements can stand alone in concert.

Jones, Roger. *Four Duets.* Tuba-Euphonium Press. Euphonium and tuba. 1999. $8. 7:00. III. Part I: B♭₁–g', Part II: (G₁) A₁–b♭. Four movements: I. Moderately Fast, but Stately; II. With Speed and Intensity; III. Gently; IV. Furiously. Dedicated to Doug Baer. This collection of four contrasting duets is written in a modern, contrapuntal style. Melodic material is divided between both voices. Individual movements can stand alone in concert.

Joplin, Scott. *Euphonic Sounds.* Arr. Arthur Frackenpohl. Tuba-Euphonium Press. Euphonium and tuba. 1997. $8. 3:45. III. Part 1: G–a♭' (b♭'), Part 2: G♭₁–c'. For Mary Ann Craig. Effective arrangement of one of Joplin's more popular syncopated two-steps. Both parts are challenging with frequent arpeggiated passages and syncopated rhythms. Includes alternate passages for more advanced performers.

King, Robert. *French Suite for Trumpet and Euphonium.* Robert King Music Sales, Inc. Trumpet and euphonium. $11.20.

Knight, Steve. *Conversations.* Cimarron Music. One euphonium and one tuba. $6.50.

Lasso, Orlando di. *Fantasias.* Arr. Richard E. Powell. Southern Music Company. Out of Print. Euphonium and tuba. 1970. 4:00. IV.

Leadbetter, Martin. *Little Prelude & Fugue.* Mostyn Music. Horn and euphonium. £3.50.

LeClair, David. *Growing Up Together.* Editions Marc Reift. Euphonium and tuba. 1993. €13.30. 4:25. IV–V. Part I: G–b', Part II: A♭₁–f'. Recorded by David LeClair, Contraband, *Swingin' Low,* Marcophon CD 940-2.

Love, Randolph. *Bicinum for Euphonium and Horn.* Seesaw Music Corp. Euphonium and horn.

Mailman, Martin. *Clastics Two.* Boosey & Hawkes. Euphonium and percussion. £12.99.

Manzo, Angelo. *Three Short Duets.* Tuba-Euphonium Press. Euphonium and tuba. 2001.

$10. 3:00. II–III. Part I: G–g', Part II: C₁–c'. Three movements: Gigue; Romance; Fugue. These duets, each shorter than a minute, are all in the key of C minor. The outer movements are fast while the contrasting inner movement is slow. Reviewed in the Spring 2003 issue of the *ITEA Journal*, Vol. 30, No. 3.

McCurdy, Gary L. *Chorale and Gigue*. TMC Publications. Out of Print. Euphonium and tuba.

Meechan, Pete. *Electric Reality*. Prima Vista Musikk. Amplified euphonium and sound engineer. 2002. 6:00. V. C–c♯″. An intruiging contemporary work featuring electronic effects in real time. Difficult rhythmic figures, angular leaps, and extreme, sudden dynamic contrasts make this work a challenge. Following equipment needed for performance: microphone; delay, reverb and phase effects units or a multiple effects unit; two speakers; amplifier; four-channel mixing board with faders on all channels. Written in treble clef.

Meechan, Pete. *Last Reality*. Pete Meechan. Euphonium and drum set. 2002. 3:00. V. F₁–e″. An interesting original work in a funk style. Difficult due to complex rhythmic patterns, extreme range demands, angular leaps, and rapid sixteenth-note passages. Challenging, but fun to play. Written in treble clef.

Michel, Jean-François, arr. *Duett Album, Vol. 1: Bekannte Melodien, Spirituals & Evergreens*. Editions Marc Reift. Trumpet and euphonium. 1993. €16.80. II–III.

Michel, Jean-François, arr. *Duett Album, Vol. 2: Bekannte Melodien, Spirituals & Evergreens*. Editions Marc Reift. Trumpet and euphonium. 1994. €14. III. More advanced than Vol. 1.

Moore, S. *Prelude and Invention*. Dorn Publications. Euphonium and tuba. $15.

Mozart, Wolfgang Amadeus. *Andante & Allegro*. Arr. Thomas Wyss. Mostyn Music. Horn and euphonium. £7.60.

Mozart, Wolfgang Amadeus. *Eleven Mozart Duets for Bass Clef Instruments*. Arr. Richard E. Powell. Shawnee Press, Inc. 1972. $7. 15 pp. IV. Part I: d–c″, Part II: C₁–f'. Duets of varying style and tempo originally written by Mozart for two horns. First part should be played on euphonium and the second on tuba.

Mozart, Wolfgang Amadeus. *Twelve Easy Duets for Winds*. Arr. Henry Charles Smith. G. Schirmer Inc. Out of Print. Euphonium and tuba. 1972.

Mozart, Wolfgang Amadeus. *Two Wind Duets (K. 487)*. Arr. Randall Block. The Musical Evergreen. Euphonium and tuba. 1975. $3.50. 3:00. III–IV. Part I: B♭–c', Part II: B♭₁–g. Two movements: Allegro and Andante.

Mozart, Wolfgang Amadeus. *Two Wind Duets from K. 487*. Arr. R. P. Block. Philharmonia Music. Euphonium and tuba. $3.50.

Mueller, Frederick A. *Duet*. Frederick Mueller. Euphonium and tuba. $6.

Paasch, Antony. *Seven Miniatures (Based on Native American Themes)*. Tuba-Euphonium Press. Euphonium and tuba. 2002. $8. 7:00. III. Part I: B–f', Part II: B♭₂–g. Seven movements: Freely; With War-Like Intensity; Lively; Delicately; Chanted; Driving; Smoothly. Challenging work with shifting meter and mixed meter. Each movement is in a new key, and there is effective use of dissonance and modern harmonies. Reviewed in the Spring 2004 issue of the *ITEA Journal*, Vol. 31, No. 3.

Parker, J. *Music for Two-Six Duets*. Patterson's Publications. Trombone and euphonium. $8.95.

Patterson, Merlin E. *Two-Part Inventions*. Euphonium and tuba. 1974. $5.50. IV. Part I: A♭–b♭', Part II: G♯₁–c'. Four movements: Fughetta; Ostinato; Gigue; Allemande. Euphonium part is written in tenor clef. Movements are in mixed meters and rhythmically challenging.

Powell, Morgan. *Short Piece for Tuba and Euphonium*. TUBA Journal. 1974. $7.50. 1:30. IV. Part I: B♭–b♭', Part II: G–d'. Short duet with mixed meters and numerous tempo changes. Extended techniques include flutter tonguing and use of a mute on the last note. Written as part of the TUBA GEM Series and published in the *TUBA Journal*, Vol. 1, No. 3.

Presser, William. *Five Hag Pieces*. Theodore Presser Company. Euphonium and tuba. 1987. $5.50. 4:20. IV. Part I: E–b♭', Part II: E₁–b♭. Five movements: Gee, Dad Gaffed a Faded Hag; H.H.A. Beach Egged a Caged Hag; Abe Bach Bagged a Bead-Headed Hag; Each Fagged Hag Had a Bad Headache; A Chafed Hag Fed a Chef Chaff. Using German spellings (B = B♭ and H = B♮), the names of the movements spell out the notes in the themes. This composition is a sequel to *Two Hag Pieces*, published by the *TUBA Journal*, Vol. 11, No. 3.

Presser, William. *Two Hag Pieces for Euphonium and Tuba*. TUBA Journal. 1984. $7.50. 2:50. IV. Part I: G–b♭', Part II: G₁–a. Two movements: A Deaf, Aged, Bad Hag; A Gagged Hag Abed, Dead, Hee-Hee, Ha-Ha. Using German spellings (B = B♭ and H = B♮), the names of the movements spell out the notes in the themes. The first movement is polyphonic throughout and the second is in 6/8 with a traditional harmonic language. Written as part of the TUBA GEM Series and published in the *TUBA Journal*, Vol. 11, No. 3.

Quantz, Johann. *Twelve Duets, Op. 2 and Op. 5*. Arr. Paul Schmidt. Heavy Metal Music. Two tubas. $15. Twelve movements. Both parts may also be performed on euphonium. Euphonium parts also available in treble clef. Individual movements can stand alone in concert.

Rabushka, Aaron. *Cavatina, Op. 10*. Cimarron Music. Euphonium and tuba. $10.

Rener, Hermann. *Spielheft I*. Musikverlag Elisabeth Thomi-Berg. Euphonium and tuba. $10. 10:00.

IV. Part I: c–f', Part II: F–d'. Ten movements. Written for any two bass clef instruments and works exceptionally well for euphonium and tuba. Both parts have equal responsibility for the melody. Not technically difficult.

Roberts, Stephen, arr. *Sicilenne*. Mostyn Music. Cornet and euphonium. £5.

Scarmolin, A. Louis. *Duet Time*. Arr. Michael Boo. Ludwig Music Publishing Company. Euphonium and tuba. 1982. $5.50. 15 pp. IV. Part I: F–f', Part II: F–eb'. Twelve movements: Dialogue; Rondolette; Jumpin' Bean; Andantino; Fiesta; Drawing Room; Here and There; Swans; Spring Dance; Bambolina; Follow Me; Fughetta. Parts are of equal difficulty. Movements may be performed individually or in groups. Originally copyrighted in 1966.

Schmidt, William. *Variations on a Theme of Prokofieff*. Western International Music. Euphonium and tuba. 1990. $5. 5:00. IV. Part I: B–g', Part II: D♯–e'. High tessitura in the second part allows it also to be played on euphonium. Contemporary harmonic language.

Siekmann, Frank H., arr. *Beautiful Savior (Crusader's Hymn)*. Brelmat Music. Euphonium, tuba, and piano. 2001. $10. 4:45. III. Part I: G–g' (bb'), Part II: Bb–d'. The arrangement of this traditional hymn is scored for euphonium, tuba, and piano and works well in both a church or recital setting. Parts are of equal difficulty.

Sousa, John Philip. *The Gladiator*. Arr. R. P. Block. Philharmonia Music. Euphonium and tuba. $9.50.

Sousa, John Philip. *The Stars and Stripes Forever*. Arr. R. P. Block. Philharmonia Music. Clarinet (doubles on Bb and Eb) and euphonium. $11.50.

Sousa, John Philip. *The Stars and Stripes Forever*. Arr. R. P. Block. Philharmonia Music. Trumpet and euphonium. $9.50.

Sparke, Philip, arr. *Sweet 'n' Low, Book 5: Caribbean Cocktail*. Studio Music Company. Euphonium and tuba. 1989. $8. 8 pp. III. Part I: d–f', Part II: Bb₁–eb. Eight movements: Banana Boat Song; Mary Ann; The Mocking Bird; Mango Walk; Sloop John B; Sly Mongoose; Matilda; Jamaican Farewell. Both parts have opportunity to play melody. Suitable for young players.

Sparke, Philip, arr. *Sweet 'n' Low, Book 4: A Second Christmas Selection*. Studio Music Company. Euphonium and tuba. 1989. $8. 8 pp. II–III. Part I: c–f', Part II: Bb₁–eb. Eight movements: Infant Holy; O Come, All Ye Faithful; Silent Night; O Little Town of Bethlehem; Once in Royal David's City; We Three Kings of Orient Are; While Shepherds Watched; We Wish You a Merry Christmas. Both parts are of equal difficulty.

Sparke, Philip, arr. *Sweet 'n' Low, Book 1*. Studio Music Company. Euphonium and tuba. 1989. $8. 8 pp. III. Part I: d–f', Part II: Bb₁–eb. Eight movements: Barbara Allen; Loch Lomond; Silver

Threads among the Gold; The Ash Grove; Drink to Me Only; When the Saints; Swing Low, Sweet Chariot; Early One Morning. All five books of duets by Sparke follow the same format. Each duet appears twice, once in bass clef, once in treble clef. The same duets are available for treble clef instruments in the *Mix 'n' Match* series by the same arranger and publisher. Appropriate for high school students.

Sparke, Philip, arr. *Sweet 'n' Low, Book 3: A First Christmas Selection*. Studio Music Company. Euphonium and tuba. 1989. $8. 8 pp. III. Part I: d–f', Part II: Bb–eb. Eight movements: Away in a Manger; Ding Dong, Merrily on High; The First Noel; God Rest Ye Merry Gentlemen; Good King Wenceslas; Hark, The Herald Angels Sing; The Holly and the Ivy; Jingle Bells. Both parts have the opportunity to play the melody. Each movement lasts approximately one minute.

Sparke, Philip, arr. *Sweet 'n' Low, Book 2*. Studio Music Company. Euphonium and tuba. 1989. $8. 8 pp. III. Part I: Eb–f', Part II: Bb–eb. Eight movements: The Blue Bells of Scotland; Marching through Georgia; All through the Night; Cockles and Mussels; Santa Lucia; Müss Ich Denn?; Ye Banks and Braes; The Camptown Races.

Stevens, John. *Splinters*. TUBA Journal. Euphonium and tuba. 1982. $7.50. 1:00. IV. Part I: (Bb₁) F–f', Part II: F₁–f. A short rock duet with challenging rhythmic figures. Written as part of the TUBA GEM Series and published in the *TUBA Journal*, Vol. 9, No. 4. Recorded by John Stevens, *Power Classical*, Mark Records MRS-20699.

Stoker, Richard. *Four Dialogues*. Hinrichsen Edition Limited. Out of Print. Euphonium and tuba. 1966. 5:00. IV. Part I: A–d', Part II: C–g. Four movements: Interview; Debate; Interrogation; Argument.

Sturzenegger, Kurt, arr. *31 Easy Duets*. Editions Marc Reift. Trumpet and euphonium. 1997. €13.30. III. Suitable for high school players. Employs some simple syncopated rhythms. Both parts written in treble clef.

Swynoe, Jan. *Mirror, Mirror*. Hornblower Edition. Baritone and vibraphone. IV. G1–c''. Commissioned by Steven Booth. An interesting piece for a unique instrumentation. Moderate technical difficulty. A mute is required.

Szkutko, John. *Teddy Bears*. SZK Music. Euphonium, tuba, and piano. 1996. $20.00 Australian. 5:00. III–IV. Part I: Eb–eb'', Part II: Eb₁–f'. Challenging yet lighthearted original composition which includes the "Teddy Bear's Picnic" as its final theme. Includes complicated technical passages, large intervals, trills, and flutter tonguing.

Szkutko, John. *Teddy Bears*. SZK Music. Euphonium and tuba. This piece begins with an introduction followed by the euphonium and tuba singing a melody one at a time. Next is a "happy" dance in a compound time of 12/8. Both instruments share the honors here. The following section has the tuba playing the melody with the euphonium playing an obligato line above the melody the second time through. Next, the euphonium is the main voice with the tuba playing an underlying bass line. The piece finishes with a "Teddy Bear's Picnic" cliché.

Telemann, Georg Philip. *Air de Trompette.* Arr. R. P. Block. Philharmonia Music. Piccolo trumpet and euphonium. $11.50.

Telemann, Georg Philip. *Six Canonic Sonatas.* Arr. Michael Forbes. Tuba-Euphonium Press. Euphonium and tuba. $12.

Telemann, Georg Philip. *Three Chorale Preludes.* Arr. Arthur Frackenpohl. Horizon Press. Euphonium and tuba. 1991. $5. 6:30. IV. Part I: G–b♭', Part II: G₁–a'. Three movements: Allein gott in der Hoh Sei Ehr (All Glory Be to God on High); Vater Unser im Himmelreich (Our Father in Heaven); Christ Lag in Todesbanden (Christ Lay in Death's Bonds).

Telemann, Georg Philip. *Three Chorale Preludes.* Arr. Arthur Frackenpohl. Tuba-Euphonium Press. Euphonium and tuba. 1994. $8. 4:00. III–IV. Part I: F–b♭', Part II: G₁–b♭(a'). Three movements: I. All Glory Be to God on High; II. Our Father in Heaven; III. Christ Lay in Death's Bonds. Three short preludes that present some challenges. Playable by advanced high school students. Good recital material.

Thomas, T. Donley. *Bicinia, Op. 5.* Medici Music Press. Euphonium and tuba. 1986. $11. 10:00. IV. Part I: G♭–b', Part II: A₁–a. Five movements: Pomposo, Quasi Marcia; Allegro con Fuoco; Andante Cantabile; Scherzo; Maestoso. Written in mixed meter, the work is rhythmically challenging.

Tignor, Scott. *Boats & Ships.* Cimarron Music. One euphonium and one tuba with piano. 1997. $18.50. 10:00. III. Part I: C–g', Part II: B♭₁–c'. Three movements: Tug Boat; Sail Boat; Battleship. Written for Kelly Diamond. Lively, original duet with piano accompaniment. The outer movements are upbeat and employ mixed meter, while the inner movement features more lyrical passages. Each part is of equal difficulty. Euphonium part is also available in treble clef.

Uber, David. *Double Portraits.* Brodt Music Company. Euphonium and tuba. 1967. $4. 7:30. III–IV. Part I: B♭–g', Part II: A♭₁–b'. Four movements: The City; Times Square; Twilight; The City Awakes. Programmatic depiction of life in a big city. Excellent recital piece. Recorded by Michael Lind and Christer Torgé, BIS LP 95.

Uber, David. *Duo Concertante, Op. 97.* Kendor Music, Inc. Euphonium and tuba. 1978. $6. 5:40. III–IV. Part I: C♭–c, Part II: G₁–g. Three movements: Poco Allegretto; Andante, poco Agitato; Allegro Moderato. The first movement is rhythmic, the second lyrical, and the third a

bouncy 6/8. Appropriate for high school or college players. Moderate technical demands.

Uber, David. *Petite Duos for Trumpet and Euphonium.* David Uber. Trumpet and euphonium.

Uber, David. *Program Duets for Trumpet and Euphonium.* Editions Musicus. Trumpet and euphonium.

Uber, David. *Recital Hall Duets for Horn and Euphonium.* Kendor Music, Inc. Horn and euphonium.

Uber, David. *Silent Streets for Euphonium and Tuba.* REBU Music Publications. Euphonium and tuba. 1993. $5. 2:20.

Vaughan, Rodger, arr. *Five Carols.* Tuba-Euphonium Press. Euphonium and tuba. 1999. $8. 7:00. III. Part I: D–g', Part II: E♭₁–a(e♭'). Five movements: Good King Wenceslas; Silent Night; The Three of Us; Jingle, Jingle; We Wish You a Merry Christmas. For Marc Dickey. Humorous setting of five Christmas carols with unusual modulations, atypical cadences, and jazz elements. Tuba part calls briefly for multiphonics. Reviewed in the Fall 2000 issue of the *TUBA Journal,* Vol. 28, No. 1.

Wienhorst, R. *Two Mean Old Tubas (Intrada No. 6).* ECS Publishing. Two tubas. 1:00. II–III. Part 1: A–c', Part 2: C#–c. Brief, original composition in 6/8 time with frequent use of the tritone interval. First part may also be performed on euphonium.

Wolfe, Gordon. *Canon in the Lydian Mode.* TUBA Journal. Euphonium and tuba. 1983. $7.50. 1:30. III–IV. Part I: F#–e♭', Part II: B₁–a♭. The canon is written in treble clef. The euphonium plays the canon as a B♭ transposing instrument while the tuba plays it as an E♭ instrument (reading as if it were in bass clef and adding three flats). Not technically difficult. Written as part of the TUBA GEM Series and published in the *TUBA Journal,* Vol. 10, No. 4.

Zemp, Daniel. *Twenty Petite Duos.* Gérard Billaudot (Theodore Presser). Euphonium and tuba. 1985. $14.50. 6:00. IV. Part I: A–f', Part II: F–f'. Not technically demanding until the last movement. The movements may be grouped in any number or order. Both parts have equal responsibility for the melody. High tessitura in the tuba part.

Zettler, Richard. *Alt und Neu für Zwei (Old and New for Two).* Musikverlag Elisabeth Thomi-Berg. Euphonium and tuba. $8.50. 12.30. IV. Part I: (E♭) A–a', Part II: F–f'. Six movements: I—Andante; Minuett; Allegretto Commodo; II—Tango Sentimental; Valse Viennoise; Tarantella. Parts have equal responsibility for the melody. *Ossia* sections included in second part.

Zika, Gene. *Euphonium & Tuba Jazz Duets.* Puna Music Company. Euphonium and tuba. 2001. $9.95. 44 pp. III–IV. B♭1–a'. Thirty-nine original short duets: Gimmie My Tuba; Clark's Lark; Tuba Soup; Leadpipe Lasagna; Wind and Song; Water Key Wine; Tubop; Smokin' Tuba Blues;

Do You Take This Euphonium; Tempestuous Tubas; The Wily Euphonium; Your Inner Tuba; Tuba Tango; Baritone Nut; Mouthpiece Mousse; Jacob's Jump; Candle Light, You and My Tuba; Tuba Monster; Tuba Tonic; Embouchure Elf; Tuba Toes; Baritone Beans; Tubaville Express; Euphonium Players Have Big Horns; Glass Breakin' Blues; Tension & Release . . . Eh?; Super Tuba Strikes Again; Turbo Tubas; Tuba Talisman; Doctor Euph; Tub a Tubas; Tuba Hair Balls; How Do You Finger "A"; Tubanator Blues; Tubas Happen; Planet Euphonium; Tubariffic Blues; The Euphonium Touch; It's Not Heavy, It's My Tuba. Euphonium part stays mostly in the middle register. Includes chord changes for improvised, unwritten solos for both euphonium and tuba.

Three Players

Albian, Franco G. *Divertimento for Two Euphoniums and Piano*. Albian Publishing. Two euphoniums and piano.

Anderson, Eugene. *Fugue for Low Brass Trio*. Cimarron Music. Two euphoniums and one tuba. 1996. $7. 4:00. II–III. Part I: c–c″, Part II: G–g′, Part III: G1–b♭. This fugue in traditional style is originally for horn, trombone, and tuba. Alternate euphonium parts in both treble and bass clef are available for the top two parts.

Armitage, Denis, arr. *Christmas Joy, Vol. 1*. Editions Marc Reift. Two euphoniums and piano. 1993. €16.80. Arrangements of fourteen traditional Christmas melodies: Kling, Glöcklein, kling; In Dulci Jubilo; O Little Town of Bethlehem; Leise rieselt der Schnee; Joy to the World; Silent Night; Good King Wenceslas; Il est né le Divin Enfant; Jingle Bells; O Come, All Ye Faithful; O Come, Little Children; O Holy Night; We Wish You a Merry Christmas; Es ist ein Ros entsprungen.

Armitage, Denis, arr. *Christmas Joy, Vol. 2*. Editions Marc Reift. Two euphoniums and piano. 1993. €16.80. Arrangements of fourteen traditional Christmas melodies: O Tannenbaum; God Rest Ye Merry Gentlemen; Still, Still, Still; We Three Kings; Go Tell It on the Mountain; March of the Three Kings; Hark, the Herald Angels Sing; O du Fröhliche; The First Noel; Angels We Have Heard on High; The Holly and the Ivy; Vom Himmel Hoch, Da komm ich her; While Shepherds Watched Their Flocks; Alle Jahre weider.

Armitage, Denis. *8 Pieces*. Editions Marc Reift. Trumpet, euphonium, and piano. 1997. €17.50.

Bach, Johann Sebastian. *Adagio and Presto from Trio in G*. Arr. Robert Madeson. Cimarron Music. Trombone, euphonium, and piano. $12.

Bach, Johann Sebastian. *Adagio and Allegro from Trio Sonata, BWV 1039*. Arr. Robert Madeson. Cimarron Music. Trombone, euphonium, and piano. $14.

Bach, Johann Sebastian. *Aria*. Arr. Marc Reift. Editions Marc Reift. Euphonium, tuba, and piano or two euphoniums and piano or trumpet, euphonium, and piano. 1999. €14. Also available with CD playback accompaniment for €21. This arrangement comes in a set of five pieces: Wedding March (Mendelssohn); Trumpet Voluntary (Clarke); Aria (Bach); Trumpet Tune (Purcell); Bridal Chorus (Wagner).

Bach, Johann Sebastian. *Aria—Duet from Cantata No. 78*. Arr. David Werden. Cimarron Music. Euphonium, tuba, and piano. $10.

Bach, Johann Sebastian. *Come, Sweet Death*. Arr. Eddie Sauter. TUBA Journal. Euphonium and two tubas. 1973. 1:30. III–IV. Part I: c–g′, Part II: G–c′, Part III: G₁–c′. To the memory of William J. Bell. Arranged May 26, 1973, at the conclusion of the first International Tuba Symposium Workshop. Some of the third part may be played down an octave to make it playable for high school students. Works well with large ensembles. A traditional closer for many Octubafest concerts and ITEA conferences. Published in the first organizational newsletter, Fall 1973. There is a misprint in the original score: the third line, third measure, second beat of the first tuba part should be d♭, not d♮. Given to TUBA (now ITEA) by Eddie Sauter and may be freely duplicated and performed in the memory of William J. Bell. Recorded by the Tennessee Technological University Tuba Ensemble, Golden Crest Records, CRS 4139; Garden State Tuba Ensemble, *Karl Megules*, Recorded Publications Company, Z434471; and *Harvey Phillips/TubaChristmas*, Harvey Phillips Foundation, HPF NR1111.

Bach, Johann Sebastian. *Fugue a 3*. Arr. Paul Schmidt. Heavy Metal Music. Two euphoniums and one tuba. 1994. $7. 3:15. II–III. Part I: B♭–g′, Part II: c–a♭′, Part III: D–b♭. This three-voice fugue is an effective teaching piece for contrapuntal technique. Ranges are appropriate for intermediate-level performers. Parts may be doubled for a large ensemble. Score is not provided.

Bach, Johann Sebastian. *Fugue in C Minor*. Arr. Brian Doughty. Cimarron Music. Horn, euphonium, and tuba. $12.

Bach, Johann Sebastian. *Fugue in C Minor for Low Brass*. Arr. R. Winston Morris. Ludwig Music Publishing Company. Euphonium and two tubas. 1992. $6.95. 1:40. III–IV. Part I: d–b♭′, Part II: C–c′, Part III: G₁–d. Arranged for the Tennessee Technological University Tuba Ensemble. A transcription of a well-known Bach fugue. The euphonium part has a bass and a treble clef version. High tessitura in the euphonium part. Parts may be doubled for a large ensemble.

Bach, Johann Sebastian. *Fugue in F Major*. Arr. Paul Schmidt. Heavy Metal Music. Two euphoniums and one tuba. 1991. $7. 2:20. IV. Part I: G–f′, Part II: D–f′, Part III: (F₁) C–f. Parts may be doubled for large ensemble.

Bach, Johann Sebastian. *Sinfonia No. 6.* Arr. Mick Hesse and Connie Schultz. Brassworks 4. Cornet, trombone, and euphonium. 2002. $11. IV. B♭₁–g′. Great arrangement that works well in recital or for various occasions. Moderate technical difficulty for all parts.

Bach, Johann Sebastian. *Sinfonia No. 10.* Arr. Mick Hesse and Connie Schultz. Brassworks 4. Cornet, trombone, and euphonium. 2002. $11. IV. B♭₁–c′. An excellent arrangement that works well in recital or for various occasions. Moderate technical difficulty for all parts.

Bach, Johann Sebastian, and Charles Gounod. *Ave Maria.* Arr. Jean-François Michel. Editions Marc Reift. Two euphoniums and piano or trumpet, euphonium, and piano. 1997. €14.70. III. This arrangement comes in a set of three pieces: Halleluja (Handel); Ave Maria (Bach/Gounod); Trumpet Voluntary (Clarke).

Bachelder, Daniel. *Theatre Piece.* Tuba-Euphonium Press. Euphonium, vibraphone, and cello. 1997. $12. IV. D♭–b′. An interesting one-movement work that calls for some dramatic showmanship. The euphonium player begins offstage, playing a few lines before entering. In the middle of the piece is a free improvisatory section in which notes are given that may be played in any order and tempo. The piece ends with the euphonium exiting and playing the last few lines offstage. Finally, the vibraphonist exits in a stately fashion, leaving the cellist alone onstage. Would make for a refreshing recital addition. Includes some mixed meter.

Barber, Clarence. *Uriel: A Flourish of Joy.* Great Works Publishing. Euphonium, tuba, and percussion (vibraphone, snare drum, four tom-toms, bass drum). 1993. 5:30. III–IV. F–c″. Deceptively difficult due to the high tessitura and constantly shifting meters. Percussion part playable by a single performer.

Barnes, James. *Duo Concertante.* Southern Music Company. Trumpet, euphonium, and piano. $15.

Bassano, Giovanni. *Fantasie a tre voci, Volume I.* Arr. Michael Fischer. Tuba-Euphonium Press. Euphonium and two tubas or two euphoniums and one tuba. 2001. $20. 20 pp. II. Part I: A–g′, Part II: C–c′, Part III: F1–f. Ten fantasias. Nice collection of ten pieces in a contrapuntal style, with most of them canonic in nature. Each piece is one to two minutes in duration and is appropriate for intermediate-level performers. Individual movements can stand alone on a concert. Parts may be doubled for a large ensemble. Reviewed in the Spring 2002 issue of the *ITEA Journal,* Vol. 29, No. 3.

Bassano, Giovanni. *Fantasie a tre voci, Volume II.* Arr. Michael Fischer. Tuba-Euphonium Press. One euphonium and two tubas or two euphoniums and one tuba. 2001. $20. 20 pp. II. Part I: A–g′, Part II: C–d′, Part III: G1–g. Ten fantasias. Nice

collection of ten pieces in a contrapuntal style, with most of them canonic in nature. Each piece is one to two minutes in duration and is appropriate for intermediate-level performers. Individual movements can stand alone on a concert. Parts may be doubled for a large ensemble. Reviewed in the Spring 2002 issue of the *ITEA Journal,* Vol. 29, No. 3.

Bergenfeld, Nathan. *Chaconne.* Tempo Music Publications. Out of Print. Two euphoniums and one tuba. 1975. 4:00. III. Part I: f–f′, Part II: d–d♭′, Part III: G–a♭. A fairly easy to play composition with simple rhythms. Recommended for high school concerts or contests.

Bewley, Norlan. *Piñata.* Bewley Music Inc. Two euphoniums and one tuba or one euphonium and two tubas. 1991. $10. 1:20. III–IV. Part I: d–f′, Part II: A–b♭, Part III: G₁–d. A lot of syncopation but not technically difficult. All three parts have an opportunity to play the melody. Parts may be doubled for a large ensemble.

Bizet, George. *Deep inside the Sacred Temple.* Arr. Wilkinson. Studio Music. Two euphoniums and piano.

Blair, Dean. *The Serious Suite.* TAP Music. Two euphoniums and one tuba. $8. Four movements: I. Prelude; II. March; III. Chant; IV. Finale.

Block, R. P., arr. *Sumer Is Icumen In.* Philharmonia Music. Trumpet, euphonium, and organ. $12.50.

Boeck. *10 Stueke.* Veb Friedrich Hofmeister-Leipzig. Two horns and euphonium.

Bramson, Neil. *Two Mini-Trios.* Da Capo Music Limited. Euphonium, flute, and piano. £8.

Brown, Velvet. *Te Dago Mi.* Velvet Music Editions. Euphonium, tuba, and piano.

Bruckner, Anton. *Aequale.* Arr. Paul Schmidt. Heavy Metal Music. Euphonium and two tubas. $3. 1:20. III. Part I: f♯–f′, Part II: G–c′, Part III: G₁–g. The second part of this slow chorale may be played by euphonium or tuba. Players read from a score and parts may be doubled for a large ensemble.

Butterfield, Don, arr. *Them Baces.* DB Publishing Company. Euphonium and two tubas. 1973. 4:00. IV. Part I: F–f′, Part II: F₁–b♭, Part III: F₁–g. Dedicated to the memory of William J. Bell. A cute arrangement that paraphrases Them Basses, Under the Double Eagle, Bombasto, When Yuba Plays the Rumba . . ., and Tubby the Tuba. Written to be performed at the first Annual New York Brass Conference for Scholarships held February 3–4, 1973.

Carmody, Bill. *Disco Tuba.* TUBA Journal. Euphonium and two tubas. 1978. $7.50. 3:00. IV. Part I: B–a′, Part II: C₁–d′, Part III: A₁–e. Challenging rhythmic figures for all parts. A four-measure vamp section allows for improvised solos. Parts may be doubled for a large ensemble. Written as part of the TUBA GEM Series and published in the *TUBA Journal,* Vol. 6, No. 1.

Censhu, Jiro. *The Window Opens Toward the Ocean.* Athens Music Publishing. Two euphoniums and piano. 2000. $20. IV. Part I: D–c″, Part II: D–g′. To Ryuji Ushigami and Tamao Araki. A gorgeous lyrical duet that combines an impressionistic piano accompaniment with pentatonic melodies in the euphoniums. Great material for a recital. Not technically difficult. Recorded by Ryuji Ushigami, *Euphoria.*

Chopin, Frederick. *Valse No. 9.* Arr. Akihiko Ito. Akihiko Ito. Two euphoniums and piano. $11.

Clarke, Herbert L. *Cousins.* Arr. David LeClair. Editions Marc Reift. Euphonium, tuba, and piano or trumpet, euphonium, and piano. 1997. €13.30. IV. Part I: F–bb′, Part II: F₁–c′. Great arrangement of this classic showpiece. Technically challenging with extensive multiple tonguing required. Parts included in treble and bass clef. Recorded by David LeClair, Contraband, *Swingin' Low,* Marcophon CD 940-2.

Clarke, Jeremiah. *Trumpet Voluntary.* Arr. Dennis Armitage. Editions Marc Reift. Euphonium, tuba, and piano or two euphoniums and piano or trumpet, euphonium, and piano. 1999. €14. Also available with CD playback accompaniment for €21. This arrangement comes in a set of five pieces: Wedding March (Mendelssohn); Trumpet Voluntary (Clarke); Aria (Bach); Trumpet Tune (Purcell); Bridal Chorus (Wagner).

Clarke, Jeremiah. *Trumpet Voluntary.* Arr. Jean-François Michel. Editions Marc Reift. Two euphoniums and piano or trumpet, euphonium, and piano. 1997. €14.70. III. This arrangement comes in a set of three pieces: Halleluja (Handel); Ave Maria (Bach/Gounod); Trumpet Voluntary (Clarke).

Clarke, Rosemary. *Elegy-Suite for David, Sr.* American Music Center. Two euphoniums, tuba. 4:45.

Corelli, Arcangelo. *Sonata in G Minor.* Arr. John Glenesk Mortimer. Editions Marc Reift. Two euphoniums and piano or trumpet, euphonium, and piano. 1997. €12.60. III–IV.

Corelli, Arcangelo. *Trio Sonata, Op. 1, No. 5.* Arr. Paul Schmidt. Heavy Metal Music. Two euphoniums and one tuba. 1990. $7. 6:30. IV. Part I: c–g′, Part II: A–g′, Part III: C–g (c′). Four movements: Grave; Allegro; Adagio; Allegro. Parts one and two share the melody while the third is primarily in a continuo role. The third movement alternates between 3/2 and 4/4 meters at slow and fast tempos. No score available.

Corelli, Arcangelo. *Trio Sonata, Op. 1, No. 10.* Arr. Paul Schmidt. Heavy Metal Music. Two euphoniums and one tuba. 1990. $7. 6:45. IV. Part I: E–a′, Part II: A–f′, Part III: A–a. Four movements: Grave; Allegro; Adagio; Allegro. More challenging than other Schmidt arrangements of Corelli sonatas. No score available.

Corelli, Arcangelo. *Trio Sonata, Op. 3, No. 7.* Arr. Paul Schmidt. Heavy Metal Music. Two euphoniums and one tuba. 1990. $7. 6:30. IV.

Part I: Bb–f′, Part II: G–f′, Part III: G₁–g. Four movements: Grave; Allegro; Adagio; Allegro. The two euphonium parts are polyphonic and syncopated in nature but not technically challenging. No score available.

Corelli, Arcangelo. *Trio Sonata, Op. 3, No. 2.* Arr. Paul Schmidt. Heavy Metal Music. Two euphoniums and one tuba. 1990. $7. 7:00. IV. Part I: F–f′, Part II: G–d′, Part III: F₁–g. Four movements: Grave; Allegro; Adagio; Allegro. The top two parts present the melody polyphonically. Moderate technical demands on all parts. No score available.

Corelli, Arcangelo. *Trio Sonata, Op. 3 No. 2.* Arr. Todd Cranson. Cimarron Music. Two euphoniums and one tuba. 1997. $10. III. Part I: A–bb′, Part II: A–bb′, Part III: (Bb2)F1–d(ab). Four movements: Grave; Allegro; Adagio; Allegro. Straightforward arrangement of this baroque work originally for two violins and continuo. The two top parts present the melodic material polyphonically, while the third performs the steady continuo. Reviewed in the Winter 1999 issue of the *TUBA Journal,* Vol. 26, No. 2.

Corwell, Neal. *Twilight Dream.* Tuba-Euphonium Press. Euphonium, flute, and piano. 1995. $10. IV. D–a′. A well-written lyrical work in two sections intended to depict drifting into a fanciful dream. The first section is slow, to be played with expression and rubato. The second section is at a brisk pace but generally retains the legato and lyrical quality of the first section. Presents some technical challenges. A good recital addition.

Couperin, Francois. *Les Ondes Rondeau.* Arr. Jan Krzywicki. Theodore Presser Company. Two euphoniums and one tuba. 1984. $7.50. 2:30. IV. Part I: A–e′, Part II: F–f′, Part III: F₁–f. For Paul, Pete, and Hal. Original written by Couperin in 1713 for harpsichord. A slow, lyrical melody in 6/8 meter. No significant technical or range problems. Can also be performed by one euphonium and two tubas.

Daughtry, Russ. *The Plains of Esdraelon.* Tuba/Euphonium Music Publications. Out of Print. Euphonium and two tubas. 3:30. IV. Part I: B–d′, Part II: G₁–ab, Part III: G₁–d. Each part is featured as soloist at different times during this mixed meter trio. Technically challenging, especially for the first two parts.

Davison, John. *Fantasy for Horn, Euphonium, and Piano.* TAP Music. Horn, euphonium, and piano. 1996. $24. 10:00. IV. D–c″. Written for Barry Kilpatrick. This is a single movement work built on six motives, which are developed in a contrapuntal style. Three of the themes are traditional: Old Hundredth, Veni Creator Spiritus, and a plainchant Sanctus. An irrepressible jig fights for dominance against the liturgical melodies. Recorded by Barry Kilpatrick, *American Music for Euphonium,* Mark Records 2535-MCD.

Deason, David. *Sonata*. David Deason. Alto saxophone, euphonium, and piano.

DeFries, Byron, arr. *English Songs for Three*. PEL Music Publications. Two horns, euphonium. 2003. $9.50. 4:10. III. G–e♭'. A lyrical arrangement of traditional English folk song melodies.

De Vita, Alfred. *Softly As I Leave You*. Arr. Alan Catherall. Rosehill Music. Two euphoniums and piano. 1987. IV–V. Part I: d–b♭', Part II: d–e♭''. Excellent arrangement of this traditional melody. Written in treble clef. Recorded by the Childs Brothers with brass band accompaniment, *Child's Play,* Doyen Records CD001.

Diamond, J. Kelley, arr. *Bayerische Polka*. Tuba-Euphonium Press. Euphonium, tuba, and piano. 1996. $8. IV. Part I: E♭–a♭', Part II: E♭₁–e♭'. A fun arrangement of a classic polka tune. Extensive triple tonguing.

Di Lasso, Orlando. *Motet "Cantate Domino."* Arr. William Schmidt. Western International Music, Inc. Two euphoniums and one tuba. 1995. $5. 2:00. II. Part I: B–d', Part II: D–f, Part III: G1–A. The arrangement of this Renaissance motet is scored in A minor. Second part may also be performed on tuba. Independence of parts is the most challenging element.

Dondeyne, Desire. *Concerto Grosso*. Gérard Billaudot. Euphonium (or tuba), percussion, and piano. €40.60.

Dutton, Brent. *Choral and Folksong*. Brent Dutton. Two euphoniums, tuba, and piano. 1968. $10. 6:00. IV–V. Part I: E–b', Part II: F–g♯', Part III: B♭₂–g♭'. Two movements: Chorale and Folksong. Contemporary harmony and notation. Second movement uses special notation in all parts. Difficult piano part. Extreme range demands for the third part.

Elgar, Edward. *Chanson de Matin*. Arr. Eric Wilson. Rosehill Music. Two euphoniums and piano. 1991. IV. Part I: F–c'', Part II: G–f'. This lyrical duet is part of the *Child's Choice* collection and is also playable as a solo. Musically challenging but not technically difficult.

Fauré, Gabriel. *Two Fauré Duets*. Arr. Steven Mead. Studio Music. £7.50. Recorded by Steven Mead, *The World of the Euphonium,* volume 2, Polyphonic.

Fischer, Johann. *Marsch*. Arr. Jean-François Michel. Editions Marc Reift. Two euphoniums and piano or trumpet, euphonium, and piano. 1994. €21. III. This arrangement comes in a set including eight other arrangements of works by well-known composers: Marche Religieuse (Gluck); Air (Handel); Intrada (Pezel); Ouverture aus der Wassermusik (Handel); Pifa (Handel); Sinfonia e Gavotte (Handel); Hochzeitsmarsch (Haydn); March (Purcell).

Frackenpohl, Arthur. *Song and Dance*. Tuba-Euphonium Press. Euphonium, tuba, and piano. 1994. $12. 8:00. IV–V. Part I: F♯–c'', Part II: G₁–b. Two movements: Slowly and Moderately.

A challenging piece for both players. Melodic interest is shared between the two parts. *Ossia* passages provide alternatives to some of the difficult rhythmic and range demands. Also available with band accompaniment.

Friedrich, Kenneth D. *Arythmia*. Kenneth D. Friedrich. Two euphoniums and one tuba. 2004. $13. 6:40. V. Part I: A♭–d♭'', Part II: D♭–c'', Part III: G₁–e♭'. A difficult trio for advanced players. Difficult rhythmic figures, angular leaps, and other technical challenges for all players.

Friedrich, Kenneth D. *Canzonetta*. Kenneth D. Friedrich. Euphonium, clarinet, and piano. 2004. $14.50. 6:22. IV. C–a♭'. A sentimental lyrical work. Features a cadenza for each of the soloists. Not technically difficult.

Friedrich, Kenneth D. *Indian Point Rhapsody*. Kenneth D. Friedrich. Two euphoniums and piano.

Friedrich, Kenneth D. *Let Me Stand*. Cimarron Music. Two euphoniums and piano. 1984. $10.

Friedrich, Kenneth D. *New Dawn*. Kenneth D. Friedrich. Euphonium, tuba, and piano. 2005. $13. 5:45. III. Part I: F–b♭', Part II: F₁–b♭. Commissioned by Andy Smith. A lyrical work of moderate difficulty suitable for high school players. Extensive use of quarter note triplet figures.

Friedrich, Kenneth D. *Night Traveler*. Kenneth D. Friedrich. Euphonium, tuba, and piano. 2005. $18.

Garbáge, Pierre. *Chaser #1*. James Garrett. Out of Print. Two euphoniums and one tuba or one euphonium and two tubas. 1972. 1:20. IV. Part I: a–f', Part II: d–d', Part III: B₁–c (b). Written for R. Winston Morris and the Tennessee Technological University Tuba Ensemble. A highly syncopated melody at a "hoedown" tempo. Fun to play. Pierre Garbáge says of this composition, "Heavy in every way but one." Parts may be doubled for large ensemble. Recorded by the Tennessee Technological University Tuba Ensemble, *Pierre Garbáge Festival: A Tribute to the Music of James Allen Garrett,* Mark Records MCD-3471.

Garrett, James A., arr. *Clementine*. James Garrett. Out of Print. Euphonium and two tubas. 1971. 1:00. II–III. Part I: B♭–c', Part II: F–e♭, Part III: B♭₁–B♭. A great arrangement for junior high school students. The second part may also be played by euphonium. Parts may be doubled for a large ensemble.

Garrett, James A., arr. *Im Wald und auf der Heide*. James Garrett. Out of Print. Two euphoniums and one tuba or one euphonium and two tubas. 1974. 1:00. III. Part I: d–f', Part II: B♭–d, Part III: B♭₁–f. Suitable for young students. Parts may be doubled for a large ensemble.

Garrett, James A., arr. *I've Been Working on the Railroad*. James Garrett. Out of Print. Euphonium and two tubas. 1971. 1:00. II–III. Part I: B♭–a♭, Part II: G–g, Part III: B♭₁–B♭. Second part may also be played on euphonium. Suitable for young students. Parts may be doubled for a large ensemble.

Garrett, James A., arr. *Red River Valley.* James Garrett. Cimarron Music. Euphonium and two tubas. 1971. $10. 1:00. I–II. Part I: B♭–c′, Part II: G–e♭, Part III: B♭₁–c. A simple arrangement of the traditional American folk song. The third part plays the melody for half of the arrangement. Lack of technical or range problems makes this ideal for young students. Parts may be doubled for a large ensemble.

Geminiani, Francesco. *Concerto Grosso.* Arr. R. Winston Morris. Shawnee Press, Inc. Two euphoniums and one tuba. 1974. $12.50. 6:30. III–IV. Part I: c–a′, Part II: A–a′, Part III: G₁–e (g). Three movements: Moderato; Adagio; Allegro. Written for the Tennessee Technological University Tuba Ensemble. Includes both bass and treble clef version of each euphonium part. Easily playable by high school students, but euphonium players need a solid high range (a′). Parts may be doubled for large ensemble.

Gershenfeld, Mitchell, arr. *Two English Madrigals.* Medici Music Press. 1983. $5. 4:30. III–IV. Part I: F♯–a, Part II: E–a, Part III: G₁–c. Two movements: Weep, Oh Mine Eyes and In the Merry Month of May. Two short madrigals originally by John Wilbye and Henry Youll, respectively. Polyphonic texture. Parts may be doubled for a large ensemble.

Gershwin, George. *Gershwin by George.* Arr. Denis Armitage. Editions Marc Reift. Trumpet, euphonium, and piano. 1991. €19.60.

Gershwin, George. *Gershwin for Three.* Arr. Denis Armitage. Editions Marc Reift. Flexible trio with euphonium. 1993. €22.40.

Ghiselin, Johannes. *La Alfonsina.* Ed. Empire Brass Quintet. G. Schirmer. Horn, trombone, euphonium (tuba). 1979. $3.95. 1:20. III–IV. G–d′. A Renaissance contrapuntal work that works well for this instrumentation.

Gilfish, Trident (Gigger). *Crawfish Crawl.* Arr. James Garrett. Cimarron Music. Two euphoniums and one tuba. 1996. $10. 5:00. III. Part I: F♯–b♭′, Part II: A♭–e♭′, Part III: B♭1–f. Lighthearted original composition by James Garrett written under one of his pseudonyms. The piece is in an easy ragtime feel and the melodic material is divided among all three voices. The frequent use of accidentals may challenge young performers. Euphonium parts also available in treble clef.

Gillingham, David. *Diverse Elements.* Tuba-Euphonium Press. One euphonium, one tuba, and piano. 1996. $30. 11:15. IV. Part 1: G♯–c″, Part 2: F₁–g♭′. Five movements: Intrada; Jazz Walk; Euphony; Caccia; Fanfare-March. Commissioned by Sande MacMorran, professor of tuba and euphonium, University of Tennessee, Knoxville. Challenging original work in five contrasting movements. A fantastic addition to the repertoire. Fun to play and an audience favorite. Style

includes large intervals, syncopated rhythms, and technically challenging passages. Both parts are of equal difficulty. Recorded by David Zerkel, *American Music for Tuba,* Mark Records 5438-MCD.

Glorieux, François. *Elegy for Euphonium, Violin, and Piano.* Glorious Sound bvba. Euphonium, violin, and piano. 2001. €45. 4:41. IV. A–g′. A beautifully composed lyrical piece. Excellent recital repertoire. Recorded by Nick Ost, *Euphonic Moods,* Glorious Sound CD07.

Gluck, Cristoph Willibald Ritter von. *Marche Religieuse.* Arr. Jean-François Michel. Editions Marc Reift. Two euphoniums and piano or trumpet, euphonium, and piano. 1994. €21. III. This arrangement comes in a set including eight other arrangements of works by well-known composers: Air (Handel); Marsch (Fischer); Intrada (Pezel); Ouverture aus der Wassermusik (Handel); Pifa (Handel); Sinfonia e Gavotte (Handel); Hochzeitsmarsch (Haydn); March (Purcell).

Goble, Joseph. *Abrelatas.* Tuba-Euphonium Press. Two euphoniums with optional percussion. 1996. $10. IV. Part I: F–b♭′, Part II: F–f′. For Mark and Tim. A short, fun duet in a Latin style. The first part primarily plays the melody while the second plays a funky bass line. Extensive syncopation. Optional percussion parts include cabasa, claves, timbales, and castanets. Parts included in both treble and bass clef. See listing under Music for Multiple Euphoniums.

Graham, Peter. *Brillante—Fantasy on Rule Britannia.* Gramercy Music. Two euphoniums and piano. £7.95. Includes both treble and bass clef parts. Exciting and technically difficult.

Gyger, Elliot. *Sound Crossing.* Elliot Gyger. Trumpet, horn, and euphonium. 1999.

Hall, Percy. *From Winter to Spring.* Ludwig Music Publishing. Flexible brass trio with euphonium. $12. Two movements: I. Winter and II. Spring. Suitable for younger players.

Hall, Percy. *This Old Man Variations.* Ludwig Music Publishing. Trumpet, horn, euphonium. $8. Each variation gets faster than the last up to 1/2 note = 120 in 4/4 time. Fun variations on a familiar tune. Suitable for younger players.

Hancock, Thomas M., arr. *Tuba Carols.* Ludwig Music Publishing. Euphonium and two tubas. 1987. $6.95. 14 pp. III–IV. Part I: B♭–c′, Part II: F–b, Part III: F₁–c. A collection of twelve familiar Christmas carols. Score, but no separate parts. Second part is also playable on euphonium. Treble clef versions of the first two parts are printed at the end of the book. Parts may be doubled for a large ensemble.

Handel, George Frederic. *Air.* Arr. Jean-François Michel. Editions Marc Reift. Two euphoniums and piano or trumpet, euphonium, and piano. 1994. €21. III. This arrangement comes in a set including eight other arrangements of works by well-known composers: Marche Religieuse (Gluck); Marsch (Fischer); Intrada (Pezel); Ouverture aus der Wassermusik (Handel);

Pifa (Handel); Sinfonia e Gavotte (Handel); Hochzeitsmarsch (Haydn); March (Purcell).

Handel, George Frederic. *Halleluja*. Arr. Jean-François Michel. Editions Marc Reift. Two euphoniums and piano or trumpet, euphonium, and piano. 1997. €14.70. III. This arrangement comes in a set of three pieces: Halleluja (Handel); Ave Maria (Bach/Gounod); Trumpet Voluntary (Clarke).

Handel, George Frederic. *Ouverture aus der Wassermusik*. Arr. Jean-François Michel. Editions Marc Reift. Two euphoniums and piano or trumpet, euphonium, and piano. 1994. €21. III. This arrangement comes in a set including eight other arrangements of works by well-known composers: Marche Religieuse (Gluck); Air (Handel); Marsch (Fischer); Intrada (Pezel); Pifa (Handel); Sinfonia e Gavotte (Handel); Hochzeitsmarsch (Haydn); March (Purcell).

Handel, George Frederic. *Pifa*. Arr. Jean-François Michel. Editions Marc Reift. Two euphoniums and piano or trumpet, euphonium, and piano. 1994. €21. III. This arrangement comes in a set including eight other arrangements of works by well-known composers: Marche Religieuse (Gluck); Air (Handel); Marsch (Fischer); Intrada (Pezel); Ouverture aus der Wassermusik (Handel); Sinfonia e Gavotte (Handel); Hochzeitsmarsch (Haydn); March (Purcell).

Handel, George Frederic. *Sinfonia e Gavotte*. Arr. Jean-François Michel. Editions Marc Reift. Two euphoniums and piano or trumpet, euphonium, and piano. 1994. €21. III. This arrangement comes in a set including eight other arrangements of works by well-known composers: Marche Religieuse (Gluck); Air (Handel); Marsch (Fischer); Intrada (Pezel); Ouverture aus der Wassermusik (Handel); Pifa (Handel); Hochzeitsmarsch (Haydn); March (Purcell).

Handel, George Frederic. *Sonata No. 4*. Arr. George R. Belden and Donald C. Little. Great Works Publishing. Two euphoniums and one tuba. 1992. $8. 6:00. IV. Part I: c–b♭', Part II: c–c″, Part III: F1–c'. Four movements: Adagio; Allegro; Largo; Allegro. Euphonium parts play the melody while the tuba plays the continuo. High tessitura in the euphonium parts. Technically challenging.

Handel, George Frederic. *Sonata No. 1 in B♭ (HWV 380)*. Arr. Robert Madeson. Cimarron Music. Two euphoniums and piano. $13.

Handel, George Frederic. *Va Tácito from Giulio Césare*. Arr. Todd Cranson. Cimarron Music. Euphonium, tuba, and piano. $11.50. 4:15. III. Part I: F–f', Part II: c–d'. Effective arrangement of Handel's popular *Huntsman's Aria* originally scored for voice, horn, and orchestra. Euphonium part also available in treble clef.

Harris, Floyd O. *Flower of the Orient*. Ludwig Music Publishing. Trumpet, euphonium, and piano. $4.95. I–II. Appropriate for younger players.

Hastings, Ross. *Little Madrigal for Big Horns*. Southern Music Company. Out of Print.

Euphonium and two tubas. 1972. 2:30. III–IV. Part I: c–g', Part II: G–c', Part III: F1–d♭. Nice melodic madrigal. Frequent meter changes, but the quarter note remains constant throughout. Parts may be doubled for a large ensemble. Recorded by the University of Miami Tuba Ensemble, Miami United Tuba Ensemble Society, 14568.

Haydn, Franz Jopseph. *Hochzeitzmarsch*. Arr. Jean-François Michel. Editions Marc Reift. Two euphoniums and piano or trumpet, euphonium, and piano. 1994. €21. III. This arrangement comes in a set including eight other arrangements of works by well-known composers: Marche Religieuse (Gluck); Air (Handel); Marsch (Fischer); Intrada (Pezel); Ouverture aus der Wassermusik (Handel); Pifa (Handel); Sinfonia e Gavotte (Handel); March (Purcell).

Heger, Owe, arr. *Leichte Ragtime-Trios (Easy Ragtime Trios)*. Noetzel Edition (C. F. Peters). Two euphoniums and one tuba. 1988. $15.95. 18:00. IV. Part I: F–g', Part II: F–g', Part III: F–d'. Five movements: The Easy Winners; The Entertainer; Dickie's Rag; The Strenuous Life; The Sycamore. Dedicated to Wilhelm Ebeling. A collection of one original and four Joplin rags. Extensive use of syncopation with some challenging technical passages in each part. Movements may stand on their own or be played in groups. Fun to play.

Henderson, Kenneth, and Albert Stoutamire, arr. *Trios for All*. CPP Belwin, Inc. Two euphoniums and one tuba. 1974. $5. 21 pp. II–III. Part I: B♭–g', Part II: A–e♭, Part III: F1–e. Seventeen compositions by Purcell, Mozart, Shostakovich, Grieg, and thirteen other notable composers. Appropriate for high school students with some of the pieces appropriate for junior high students. Parts may be doubled for a large ensemble.

Hilton, John. *Ten Ayres or FaLa's for 3*. Arr. Daniel Helman. ed. Paul Schmidt. Heavy Metal Music. Two euphoniums and one tuba. 1995. $7. Part I: A–g', Part II: A–g', Part III: C–a. Ten movements, including Now Is the Summer Springing; Love Laid His Yoke upon Me; Your Lovers That Have Loved Astray; My Mistress Frowns When She Should Play. Based on *Ballets* first published in 1627. All are in ternary form, and the first two performers are asked to swap parts on the repeat of the first section. Reviewed in the Fall 1998 issue of the *TUBA Journal*, Vol. 26, No. 1.

Hounsell, Clare. *A Low-Down Trio*. PEL Music Publications. $8.50.

Hughes, John. *Calon Lan*. Arr. Eric Ball. Rosehill Music. Two euphoniums and piano. 1988. III–IV. Part I: A♭–a♭'(f″), Part II: B♭–f'(c″). A great arrangement of this traditional Welsh melody. Optional high notes for advanced players. Good recital literature. Written in treble clef. Recorded by the Childs Brothers with brass band accompaniment, *Child's Play*, Doyen Records CD001.

Isaac, Heinrich. *Four Pieces*. Trans. Kenneth Singleton. Peer International Corporation. Horn, euphonium (trombone), and tuba (bass trombone). 1976. $8. 3:45. II–III. F–g. Four Renaissance contrapuntal pieces with few technical difficulties.

Isbill, Thomas, arr. *Dona Nobis Pacem*. The Brass Press. Euphonium and two tubas. 1969. $3.50. 3:00. II–III. Part I: c–d', Part II: C–d, Part III: C–d. Written for R. Winston Morris and the Tennessee Technological University Tuba Ensemble. This lyrical piece is excellent for young students. Parts may be doubled for a large ensemble.

Isomura, Yukiko. *The Spring Suite*. Athens Music Publishing. Euphonium, violin, and piano. 2005. $30. IV. Three movements: I. Kiss!!; II. Wind through the Stars; III. Spring Has Come. A creative recital piece that hopes to depict the various moods that many people experience during that wonderful time of year when the winter chill departs, the warmth returns, and the flowers bloom. All the parts will challenge undergraduate playing levels.

Israel, Brian. *Tower Music*. Tritone Press. Two euphoniums and one tuba. 1983. $3.50. 4:17. III–IV. Part I: G–d', Part II: F#–b, Part III: G$_1$–g♭. Three movements: Praeludium; Fugua; Carol. To Jack Gallagher. Playable by good high school players. Parts may be doubled for a large ensemble.

Jager, Robert. *Variations on a Motive by Wagner*. Elkan-Vogel. Euphonium and two tubas. 1976. $15. 5:00. IV. Part I: G–b♭', Part II: D#–d', Part III: D#$_1$–f. Composed for Harvey Phillips, Earl Louder, and R. Winston Morris. A single movement with contrasting sections. The last section is particularly challenging technically, but worth the effort.

Jones, Roger. *Switched-Down Bach*. Roger Jones. Euphonium and two tubas. 1992. $5. 2:00. IV. Part I: A♭–f, Part II: A♭$_1$–a, Part III: A♭1–d♭. Written in a jazz style. All parts play the melody at one point or another. Extensive syncopation. Parts may be doubled for a large ensemble.

Jones, Roger. *Trio for Tubas*. Roger Jones. Euphonium and two tubas. 1970. $10. 4:20. IV. Part I: G–a', Part II: F–d', Part III: C–c'. Two movements: Slow but Moving; Lively. The second movement is multimetric and rhythmically challenging. Interesting to play.

Joyful Euphonium Tuba Ensemble, Book 5. Kyodo Music. Two euphoniums and one tuba. ¥2,100. 63 pp. III. Part I: G–a', Part II: G–g', Part III: C–e'. Eighteen movements: Adagio by Albinoni; Overture from *Tanhauser* by Wagner; Hallelujah Chorus by Handel; Egmont Overture by Beethoven; Prelude No. 15 by Chopin; Symphony No. 101, Second Movement by Haydn; Spring from *The Four Seasons;* Summer from *The Four Seasons;* Autumn from *The Four Seasons;* Winter from *The Four Seasons;* Aufforderung zum Tanz by Weber; Concerto for Two Violins, First Movement by J. S. Bach; Romance in F Major by Beethoven; The Moldau by Smetana;

Nocturne from *String Quartet No. 2* by Borodin; Waltz from *Serenade for Strings* by Tchaikovsky; Waltz of the Flowers from *Nutcracker* by Tchaikovsky; Hungarian Rhapsody No. 2 by Liszt. Large collection of popular arrangements. The majority is scored for trio, though four are scored for duet.

Joyful Euphonium Tuba Ensemble, Book 4. Kyodo Music. Two euphoniums and one tuba. ¥2,100. 63 pp. III. Part I: F–a', Part II: D–a', Part III: C–a. Twenty-one movements: Salut D'amor by Elgar; The Entertainer by Joplin; Andante Cantabile by Tchaikovsky; Pavane by Faure; Emperor String Quartet, Second Movement by Haydn; Waltz from *Coppelia* by Delibes; Overture from *Nutcracker* by Tchaikovsky; Clair de Lune by Debussy; Slavic March by Tchaikovsky; Minute from *L'Arlesienne* by Bizet; Hungarian Dance No. 5 by Brahms; Symphony No. 3, Third Movement by Brahms; Trumpet Voluntary by Clarke; Gymnopedie No. 1 by Satie; Als die Alle Mutter by Dvořák; Polonaise from *Orchestral Suite No. 2* by J. S. Bach; Minuet from *Orchestral Suite No. 2* by J. S. Bach; Canon by Pachebel; Concerto for Flute and Harp, Second Movement by Mozart; Piano Concerto No. 21 by Mozart; Etude No. 3 in E Major by Chopin. Large collection of popular arrangements. The majority is scored for trio, though six are scored for duet.

Joyful Euphonium Tuba Ensemble, Book 1. Kyodo Music. Two euphoniums and one tuba. ¥2,100. 63 pp. III. Part I: A–a♭', Part II: F–f', Part III: C#–a. Twenty-eight movements: Eine Kleine Nacht Musick, Second and Third Movement by Mozart; Ases Tod from *Peer Gynt* by Grieg; In the Hall of the Mountain King by Grieg; Gavotte by Gossec; Theme and Variations from *Ah, Vous dirais-je, maman* by Mozart; Csikos Post by Necke; March from *Nutcracker* by Tchaikovsky; Serenade for Strings, First Movement by Tchaikovsky; Scene from *Swan Lake* by Tchaikovsky; Serenade by Schubert; Unfinished Symphony by Schubert; Overture from the *Barber of Seville* by Rossini; Brindisi from *La Traviata* by Verdi; Cantata No. 147 by J. S. Bach; Etude No. 77 by Beyer; Etude No. 78 by Beyer; Farandole from *L'Arlesienne* by Bizet; Humoreske by Dvořák; Pomp and Circumstance No. 1 by Elgar; Scheherazade, Third Movement by Rimsky-Korsakov; Emperor Waltz by Strauss; Symphony No. 9, Fourth Movement by Dvořák; Stars and Stripes Forever by Sousa; Great Gate of Kiev from *Pictures at an Exhibition* by Mussorgsky; An der Schonen Blauen Donau by Strauss; Beautiful Dreamer by Foster; Theme from Judas Maccabeus by Handel. Large collection of popular arrangements. The majority is scored for trio, though eleven are scored for duet.

Joyful Euphonium Tuba Ensemble, Book 6. Kyodo Music. Two euphoniums and one tuba. ¥2,100. 30pp. III. Part I: A–a♭', Part II: F#–g', Part III: C–a.

Six movements: Schafe konnen Sicher Weiden from *Cantata*, BWV 208 by J. S. Bach; Dance of the Sugar Plum Fairy from *Nutcracker* by Tchaikovsky; Amaryllis, a French Folksong; Finale from *Carmen Suite No. 1* by Bizet; Waltz from *Swan Lake* by Tchaikovsky; Lacrimosa from *Requiem* by Mozart. Large collection of popular arrangements.

Joyful Euphonium Tuba Ensemble, Book 3. Kyodo Music. Two euphoniums and one tuba. ¥2,100. 62 pp. III. Part I: G–a', Part II: D–f', Part III: B₁–a. Nineteen movements: Lullaby by Mozart; Berceuse from *Jocelyn* by Godard; Blue Bells of Scotland; Song of Sorveig by Grieg; Toreador Song from *Carmen* by Bizet; Slavic Dance No. 10 by Dvořák; Turkish March by Beethoven; Carry Me Back to Old Virginny by Brand; La Paloma by Yradier; Washington Post March by Sousa; Symphony No. 6, All Four Movements by Tchaikovsky; Ich Liebe Dich by Grieg; Panis Angelicus by Frank; Sentimental Waltz by Tchaikovsky; Overture to the Light Calvary; Last Rose of Summer. Large collection of popular arrangements. The majority is scored for trio, though one is scored for duet.

Joyful Euphonium Tuba Ensemble, Book 2. Kyodo Music. Two euphoniums and one tuba. ¥2,100. 63 pp. III. Part I: A–a', Part II: G–a', Part III: E♭–b. Seventeen movements: Pavane for a Dead Infant by Ravel; Jupiter from *The Planets* by Holst; Prelude to Die Meistersinger by Wagner; Symphony No. 40, First and Third Movements by Mozart; Symphony No. 5, Four Movements by Beethoven; March Lorraine by Ganne; Night on Bald Mountain by Mussorgsky; The Fairest of the Fair March by Sousa; Overture to La Forza del Destino by Verdi; Danza dell'ore from *La Gioconda* by Ponchielli; Bolero by Ravel; Overture to Die Fledermaus by Strauss; Aragonaise from *Carmen* by Bizet. Large collection of popular arrangements.

Joplin, Scott. *Easy Winners.* Arr. David LeClair. Editions Marc Reift. Euphonium, tuba, and piano. 1979. €12.60. 2:45. IV. Part I: A–c", Part II: A♭–d♭'. A fun arrangement of this traditional ragtime piece. Euphonium part is in treble clef. Recorded by David LeClair, Contraband, *Swingin' Low*, Marcophon CD 940-2.

Kassatti, Tadeusz. *De Facto.* Editions BIM. Oboe, euphonium, and piano. 1998. $22.

Kassatti, Tadeusz. *Less Word but Soul.* Editions BIM. Euphonium, alto saxophone, and piano. 1998. $23.50.

Kerll, J. C. *Canzone.* Arr. Newell H. Long. The Brass Press. Euphonium and two tubas. 1974. $3.50. 2:00. III. Part I: A–e', Part II: A₁–f, Part III: A₁–f. A good arrangement of a work utilizing imitative counterpoint.

King, Robert, arr. *Two Medieval Motets.* Robert King Music Sales, Inc. Horn, trombone, euphonium. $5.75.

Kodály, Zoltán. *Lament.* Arr. Skip Gray. Shawnee Press, Inc. Euphonium and two tubas. 1980. $6.95. 2:30. III–IV. Part I: c♭–c", Part II: C–f, Part III: F₁–B♭. The euphonium part is written in bass clef but appears in the score in treble clef. Parts are technically easy but the euphonium part calls for extensive high-register playing. Parts may be doubled for a large ensemble.

Kohlenburg, Oliver. *Blue Gleam of Arctic Hysteria.* Finnish Music Information Centre. Euphonium, piano, and percussion. V. This virtuosic work consisting of a set of variations in sonata form is challenging and exciting for performers and audience alike. Two contrasting subjects, fast and slow, dramatic and lyrical, are developed as the piece progresses. The development of these themes is interspersed with cadenza-like passages exploring the extreme registers of the instrument. Very difficult. Recorded by Jukka Myllys, *Finnish Euphonium*, Alba Records ABCD 118.

Krush, Jay. *Two Madrigals.* Plymouth Music Company. Horn, euphonium (trombone), tuba. $5.95.

Lennon, John, and Paul McCartney. *The Beatles, Vol. 1.* Arr. John Glenesk Mortimer. Editions Marc Reift. Two euphoniums and piano or trumpet, euphonium, and piano. €14. Nice arrangements of four classic Beatles tunes: "Yesterday," "I Wanna Hold Your Hand," "Michelle," and "Yellow Submarine."

Lennon, John, and Paul McCartney. *The Beatles, Vol. 3.* Arr. John Glenesk Mortimer. Editions Marc Reift. Two euphoniums and piano or trumpet, euphonium, and piano. €14. Nice arrangements of three classic Beatles tunes: "Eleanor Rigby," "Penny Lane," and "When I'm Sixty-Four."

Lennon, John, and Paul McCartney. *The Beatles, Vol. 2.* Arr. John Glenesk Mortimer. Editions Marc Reift. Two euphoniums and piano or trumpet, euphonium, and piano. €14. Nice arrangements of three classic Beatles tunes: "Hey Jude," "It's for You," "Ob-la-di, Ob-la-da."

Liszt, Franz. *Hungarian Rhapsody No. 2.* Arr. Maurice Bale. Godiva Music. Flute, euphonium, and piano. £10. For Silk and Steel.

Marcellus, John, arr. *Trios for Brass, Volume I, Advanced.* CPP Belwin Inc. Two euphoniums and one tuba. 1986. $6.50. 15 pp. III–IV. Part I: F–b♭', Part II: A–g', Part III: A♭–f. Five melodies from the baroque and classical periods. A treble clef book is available. Tessitura of the top part is higher than in the previous books of the series and the arrangements present more technical challenges. Parts may be doubled for a large ensemble.

Marcellus, John, arr. *Trios for Brass, Volume I, Easy-Intermediate.* CPP Belwin Inc. Two euphoniums and one tuba. 1986. $6.50. 15 pp. II–III. Part I: B♭–g', Part II: B♭–f', Part III: G₁–f. Collection of eight melodies from the Renaissance, baroque, and classical periods. Appropriate for young players. A treble clef book is available. Parts may be doubled for a large ensemble.

Marcellus, John, arr. *Trios for Brass, Volume I, Intermediate.* CPP Belwin Inc. Two euphoniums and one tuba. 1986. $6.50. 15 pp. III. Part I: F–a', Part II: F–e', Part III: A₁–f. Collection of eight melodies from the baroque and classical periods. The pieces in this book are more polyphonic and slightly more challenging than the Easy-Intermediate arrangements. A treble clef book is available. Parts may be doubled for a large ensemble.

McAdams, Charles A., arr. *Swing Low, Sweet Chariot.* Encore Music Publishers. Euphonium and two tubas. 1991. $8.50. 3:00. III–IV. Part I: f–g', Part II: B♭–b♭', Part III: B♭₁–c. The tubas begin this melody in a slow, lyrical fashion, the middle section is an up-tempo swing, and the slow section returns at the end. Drum set may be added. Can work well as an introduction to teaching swing style. Parts may be doubled for a large ensemble.

McCurdy, Gary. *Chorale.* TMC Publications. Out of Print. Two euphoniums and one tuba. 1973. 2:00. III. Part I: B♭–d', Part II: A–c', Part III: C–d. A chorale in the traditional style with the melody primarily in the top part. Parts may be doubled for a large ensemble.

McGrath, F. T. *A Breezin' Cakewalk.* Arr. Paul Luhring. PEL Music Publications. Two euphoniums and piano. 1998. $8.50. III. Part I: B♭–a♭', Part II: A♭–e♭'. A fun arrangement of a cakewalk or two-step originally written in 1897. Moderate technical difficulty and syncopated rhythms.

Mealor, Paul, arr. *Nella Fantasia.* Mostyn Music. Two euphoniums and piano. £4.50.

Mendelssohn, Frederick. *Hochzeitsmarsch.* Arr. Jean-François Michel. Editions Marc Reift. Two euphoniums and piano or trumpet, euphonium, and piano. 1993. €14.70. This arrangement comes in a set of three works: Ave Verum (Mozart); Trumpet Tune (Purcell); Hochzeitsmarsch (Mendelssohn).

Mendelssohn, Frederick. *Wedding March.* Arr. Dennis Armitage. Editions Marc Reift. Euphonium, tuba, and piano or two euphoniums and piano or trumpet, euphonium, and piano. 1999. €14. Also available with CD playback accompaniment for €21. This arrangement comes in a set of five pieces: Wedding March (Mendelssohn); Trumpet Voluntary (Clarke); Aria (Bach); Trumpet Tune (Purcell); Bridal Chorus (Wagner).

Metz, Theodore A. *Hot Time in the Old Town Tonight.* Arr. R. P. Block. Philharmonia Music. Two euphoniums and piano. $10.50.

Michel, Jean-François, arr. *32 Christmas Carols.* Editions Marc Reift. Two euphoniums and one tuba or trumpet, euphonium, and piano. 1993. €27.30. A collection of carols suitable for younger players. Includes Good King Wenceslas; Alle Jahre wieder; Les Angesdans nos campagnes; Lasst uns froh und munter sein; In Dulci Jubilo; We Wish You a Merry Christmas; Süsser die Glocken nie klingen; March of the Three Kings; O Little Town of Bethlehem; Silent Night; The First Noel; Deck the Halls; Jingle Bells; Still, Still, Still; We Three Kings; O Tannenbaum; Adestes Fideles; Kommet, Ihr Hirten; While Shepherds Watched; O du Fröhliche; God Rest You; The Holly and the Ivy; O Holy Night; Hark, the Herald Angels; Joy to the World; Ihr Kinderlein kommet; Kling, Glöcklein, kling; Am Weihnachtsbaum; Es ist ein Ros entsprungen; Il est né le divin enfant; Vom Himmel hoch; Leise rieselt der Schnee.

Milford, Gene, arr. *Mountain Songs.* Great Works Publishing. Two euphoniums and one tuba. 1995. $7. 2:30. I–II. Part I: B♭–e♭', Part II: B♭–e♭', Part III: A♭₁–c. Two movements: Little Mohee and Billy Boy. An arrangement of two folk songs intended for beginning to intermediate players. Top two parts are also available in treble clef. Parts may be doubled for a large ensemble.

Morita, Kazuhiro, arr. *Euphonium and Tuba: Ensemble Works for the First Time.* Yamaha Kyohan Company Limited. Two euphoniums and one tuba. 1983. $8. 20 pp. III–IV. Part I: B♭–g', Part II: A–f', Part III: G₁–d. Seven duets for two euphoniums and seven trios for two euphoniums and one tuba. Three of the duets have an optional third part for tuba. Compositions are by Western composers, including Grieg, Mussorgsky, Brahms, Bach, Beethoven and one non-Western composer. Arrangements are short and of moderate technical difficulty.

Mortimer, John Glenesk, arr. *Happy Birthday.* Editions Marc Reift. Euphonium, tuba, and piano with optional guitar and drum parts or two euphoniums and tuba or trumpet, euphonium, and piano. 2000. €12.60. III. Various settings of this traditional classic. Styles include a march, waltz, and tango.

Mouret, J. J. *Rondeau.* Arr. Percy Hall. Ludwig Music Publishing. Trumpet, horn, euphonium. $8.

Mozart, Wolfgang Amadeus. *Allegro.* Arr. Stephen Shoop. Stephen Shoop Music Publications. One euphonium and two tubas. 1997. $5.50. 1:15. II. Part I: A–b♭, Part II: D–e♭, Part III: A♭1–c. Originally for piano, this trio consists predominantly of eighth notes performed in a detached style. Parts may be doubled for a large ensemble. The top voice may be also performed on tuba.

Mozart, Wolfgang Amadeus. *Allegro, from Divertimento No. 1, K. 229.* Arr. Paul Schmidt. Heavy Metal Music. Two euphoniums and one tuba. 1992. $5. 4:30. IV. Part I: c–f', Part II: F–e', Part III: B♭₁–f. Challenging for all parts. No score available.

Mozart, Wolfgang Amadeus. *Ave Verum.* Arr. Jean-François Michel. Editions Marc Reift. Two euphoniums and piano or trumpet, euphonium, and piano. 1993. €14.70. This arrangement comes in a set of three works: Ave Verum

(Mozart); Trumpet Tune (Purcell); Hochzeits-marsch (Mendelssohn).

Mozart, Wolfgang Amadeus. *Divertimento No. 1.* Arr. Robert King. Robert King Music Sales, Inc. Two trumpets and euphonium. $14.90.

Mueller, Frederick A. *Tuba Trio.* Frederick A. Mueller. Euphonium and two tubas. 1973. $12. 8:30. IV. Part I: E–a♭', Part II: A₁–e♭', Part III: E₁–d♭'. Five movements: Adagio; Presto-staccato; Lament; Cadenza; Perpetuum mobile. To Earl, David, and Winston, in memory of William J. Bell. Utilizes some extended techniques and a modern harmonic language. A challenging ensemble work.

Murzin, V. *Impromptu.* The Musical Evergreen. Two euphoniums and one tuba. 1975. $7.50. 1:20. III–IV. Part I: g–a', Part II: f–e, Part III: A–f. Euphonium parts written in tenor clef. Melody is primarily in the third part.

Nerijnen, J. V. *3e Suite Voor Koperblazers.* Molenaar Editions BV. Two trumpets and euphonium.

Nevin, Ethelbert, and Floyd O. Harris. *The Rosary.* Ludwig Music Publishing. Trumpet, euphonium, and piano. $4.95. I–II. Appropriate for younger players.

Nevin, Ethelbert, and Floyd O. Harris. *2e Suite Voor Koperblazers.* Molenaar Editions BV. Two trumpets and euphonium.

Olsen, Ole. *Fanitul.* Arr. L. A. Rauchut. KIWI Music Press. Out of Print. Two euphoniums and one tuba. 2:00. IV. Part I: c–a', Part II: G♯–e', Part III: A₁–c'. Some technical demands in the euphonium parts. Brief high sections in the tuba part may be played an octave lower if necessary.

Orowan, T. *Trio No. 1.* Editions Musicus. Trombone, euphonium, and tuba. 1965. $6. 10:00. IV. A technically challenging piece.

Paasch, Anthony. *Trio.* Cimarron Music. Bassoon, euphonium, tuba. $16.

Pachelbel, Johann. *Canon in D.* Arr. Frank H. Siekmann. Brelmat Music. Euphonium, tuba, and piano. 1994. $5. 4:30. III. Part I: A–f♯', Part II: C♯–a. A nice arrangement of this famous canon. Piano part is necessary for performance.

Pezel, Johann. *Intrada.* Arr. Jean-François Michel. Editions Marc Reift. Two euphoniums and piano or trumpet, euphonium, and piano. 1994. €21. III. This arrangement comes in a set including eight other arrangements of works by well-known composers: Marche Religieuse (Gluck); Air (Handel); Marsch (Fischer); Ouverture aus der Wassermusik (Handel); Pifa (Handel); Sinfonia e Gavotte (Handel); Hochzeitsmarsch (Haydn); March (Purcell).

Potter, David. *Aria and Rondo.* Southern Music Company. Two euphoniums and one tuba. 1983. $5.95. 4:30. IV. Part I: c♯–b', Part II: c♯–g', Part III: G₁–e♭'. Two movements: Aria and Rondo. For Susan Smith, Dan Satterwhite, and a friend. The Rondo is in mixed meter with alternating

technical and lyrical sections. High tessitura in the tuba part.

Purcell, Henry. *Canon on a Ground Bass.* Arr. Skip Gray. Shawnee Press, Inc. Euphonium and two tubas. 1980. $7.50. 2:20. III–IV. Part I: e–a', Part II: E–b, Part III: A₁–e. From an instrumental interlude in Purcell's opera *Dioclesian.* The tuba part plays the ground bass while the euphoniums play the melody in canon. Suitable for high school players, though the second part may present range difficulties. Parts may be doubled for a large ensemble.

Purcell, Henry. *March.* Arr. Jean-François Michel. Editions Marc Reift. Two euphoniums and piano or trumpet, euphonium, and piano. 1994. €21. III. This arrangement comes in a set including eight other arrangements of works by well-known composers: Marche Religieuse (Gluck); Air (Handel); Marsch (Fischer); Intrada (Pezel); Ouverture aus der Wassermusik (Handel); Pifa (Handel); Sinfonia e Gavotte (Handel); Hochzeitsmarsch (Haydn).

Purcell, Henry. *Trumpet Tune.* Arr. Dennis Armitage. Editions Marc Reift. Euphonium, tuba, and piano or two euphoniums and piano or trumpet, euphonium, and piano. 1999. €14. Also available with CD playback accompaniment for €21. This arrangement comes in a set of five pieces: Wedding March (Mendelssohn); Trumpet Voluntary (Clarke); Aria (Bach); Trumpet Tune (Purcell); Bridal Chorus (Wagner).

Purcell, Henry. *Trumpet Tune.* Arr. Jean-François Michel. Editions Marc Reift. Two euphoniums and piano or trumpet, euphonium, and piano. 1993. €14.70. This arrangement comes in a set of three works: Ave Verum (Mozart); Trumpet Tune (Purcell); Hochzeitsmarsch (Mendelssohn).

Raum, Elizabeth. *Duet for Flute (or Piccolo) and Euphonium.* Tuba-Euphonium Press. Flute/piccolo, euphonium, and piano. 2003. $10.

Read, Tim. *Conversations.* Euphonium, violin, and piano.

Richards, Scott. *Latin Fever.* Editions Marc Reift. Trumpet or clarinet or alto saxophone, euphonium, and piano with optional drums and percussion. €13.30.

Rimsky-Korsakov, Nicolai. *Flight of the Bumblebee.* Arr. R. P. Block. Philharmonia Music. Euphonium, tuba, and piano. $12.50.

Roberts, C. Luckeyth. *Sly and Shy.* Arr. Paul Luhring. PEL Music Publications. Two euphoniums and piano. 2001. $8.50. II. Part I: A–d', Part II: G–b♭. An easy arrangement appropriate for younger students. Some simple syncopated rhythmic patterns. Would work well for a recital or solo and ensemble contest.

Rodgers, Thomas. *Three Pieces for Low Brass Trio.* The Brass Press. Out of Print. Two euphoniums and one tuba. 1974. 7:00. IV. Part I: c♭–g', Part II: G–f, Part III: G₁–b♭. Three movements: Fanfare;

Contrapunctus; Scherzo. Written for R. Winston Morris and the Tennessee Technological University Tuba Ensemble. This is a good, challenging concert piece.

Ross, J. C. *Concertino*. Cimarron Music. Euphonium, percussion, and piano. $24.

Rossini, Gioacchino. *Duetto Buffo di Due Gatti*. Arr. Daniel Bachelder. Tuba-Euphonium Press. Euphonium, soprano, and piano. 1998. $8. IV. B–c″. A humorous duo sure to be an audience favorite. The soprano's lyrics consist of one word, "Miau." High tessitura in the euphonium part. Bass and treble clef parts included. Excellent, refreshing choice for a recital.

Rossini, Gioacchino. *Who Am I, or Dost Thou Mock Me*. Arr. Andrew Hoefle. Tuba-Euphonium Press. One euphonium and two tubas. 1997. $8. 4:45. II–III. Part I: B–b′, Part II: D–f♯′, Part III: G₁–g. Excerpted from the *Barber of Seville, Act I, No. 7*. All parts have challenging sixteenth note passages and the melodic material is divided among the voices. Parts may be doubled for a large ensemble.

Rossini, Gioacchino. *William Tell Finale*. Arr. Percy Hall. Ludwig Music Publishing. Trumpet, horn, euphonium. $10.

Rÿker, Robert. *Petite Marche, Op. 10*. Tuba-Euphonium Press. Euphonium, tuba, piano. 1995. $15. 4:00. IV. Part I: C♭–b♭′, Part II: F₁–d′. For the Tokyo Metropolitan Symphony Orchestra. A march in three short sections based on a melodic motive repeatedly imitated between two brass instruments. Parts are of equal difficulty. The euphonium part includes one measure of tenor clef.

Saint-Saëns, Camille. *The Carnival of the Animals*. Arr. Maurice Bale. Godiva Music. Flute, euphonium, and piano. 1997. £30. For Silk and Steel.

Schein, Johann Hermann. *Six Trios*. Arr. Paul Schmidt and Daniel Heiman. Heavy Metal Music. Two euphoniums and one tuba. 1997. $7. Part I: c–g′, Part II: B♭–f′, Part III: G₁–b♭. Six movements. These six short trios are transcribed from secular vocal works for two sopranos and bass from *Musica boscareccia*. Each trio contains dance-like rhythmic syncopations, and three of the movements contain a meter shift from duple to triple. An optional fourth part doubles the third part an octave lower. Individual movements can stand alone on a concert. Reviewed in the Fall 2000 issue of the *TUBA Journal*, Vol. 28, No. 1.

Schmidt, Paul, arr. *Five Trios of King Henry VIII*. Heavy Metal Music. Two euphoniums and one tuba. 1992. $5. 5:00. III–IV. Part I: F–f′, Part II: F–e♭′, Part III: B♭₁–f. Five movements: Pastime with Good Company; If Love Now Reigned; O My Hart; Fantasy; With Owt Dyscorde. Nice arrangements of famous English melodies. Younger players may need a conductor due to numerous fermatas and tempo changes. No

score available. Parts may be doubled for a large ensemble.

Schubert, Franz. *Auf dem Strom*. Arr. Daniel Bachelder. Tuba-Euphonium Press. Euphonium, mezzo-soprano, piano. 1997. $12. IV. D♭–a. A well-written arrangement of this Schubert art song. Not technically difficult for the soloists, but musically demanding. Piano part is challenging.

Schubert, Franz. *Auf dem Strom*. Arr. Akihiko Ito. Akihiko Ito. Voice, euphonium, and piano. ¥1,500 (.pdf version, ¥1,000).

Schumann, Clara. *Fugue No. 1*. Arr. Angelo Manzo. Tuba-Euphonium Press. One euphonium and two tubas. 2001. $12. 2:00. II–III. Part I: B♭–g′, Part II: E–e♭′, Part III: E♭₁–f. Brief three-voice fugue in a traditional contrapuntal style. Parts may be doubled for a large ensemble. Reviewed in the Spring 2003 issue of the *ITEA Journal*, Vol. 30, No. 3.

Seeger, Peter. *Kleine Spielmusik*. Moseler Verlag. Flugelhorn, baritone, and euphonium. 1962.

Shostakovich, Dmitri. *Waltz No.2*. Arr. Scott Richards. Editions Marc Reift. Two euphoniums and piano or trumpet, euphonium, and piano. €8.40.

Smith, Clay. *Imogene, Reverie*. C. L. Barnhouse. Two euphoniums and piano. Appropriate for younger players.

Smith, Clay, and Holmes. *Silver Threads among the Gold*. C. L. Barnhouse. Two euphoniums and piano. $12. Appropriate for younger players.

Steiger, Daniel. *Sonatina for Euphonium, Marimba, and Piano*. Tuba-Euphonium Press. Euphonium, marimba, and piano. 1992. $10. IV. B♭₁–b♭′. Two movements: I. Andante cantabile and II. Allegro Marcato. Originally written in 1985, this piece is a good college-level recital work with a unique instrumentation. The first movement is slow and lyrical featuring interplay between the three players. The second movement is fast and flashy, featuring the euphonium and marimba while the piano fulfills an accompaniment role. Moderate technical difficulty. Marimba player must be proficient with four mallets.

Stockhausen, Karlheinz. *Kinntanz (Chin Dance)*. Stockhausen Verlag. Euphonium, percussion, synthesizer. 1983. 10:00. V. Difficult contemporary work. The following sound equipment is needed for performance: one transmitter, six microphones, two loudspeakers, mixing console, and sound projector.

Sturzenegger, Kurt, arr. *11 Pieces*. Editions Marc Reift. Two euphoniums and piano. 1997. €24.50. A collection of eleven short pieces: Schütz: Choral; Praetorious: Choral; Pezel: Intrada; Pezel: Sarabande; Pezel: Bal; Reiche: Intrada; Schein: Allemande; Anonymous: Air; Susato: Pavane; Morley: Three English Madrigals; Charpentier: Entrée. Suitable for younger players.

Sturzenegger, Kurt, arr. *5 Duette alter Meister*. Editions Marc Reift. Two euphoniums and piano.

1996. €17.50. Five movements: Frank: Pavane, Allemande, Tripla; Böhm: Intrada; Telemann: Aria; Banchieri: Sonata sopra l'Aria del Gran Duca; Alcock: Voluntary.

Sturzenegger, Kurt, arr. *10 Duos*. Editions Marc Reift. Trumpet, euphonium, and piano. 1996. €17.50. Duets from the Renaissance period. Available in treble or bass clef.

Sparke, Philip. *Two-Part Invention*. Studio Music. Two euphoniums and piano. £12.50. Recorded by the Childs Brothers with brass band accompaniment, *Welsh Wizards*, Doyen Records CD022.

Telemann, Georg Phillip. *Three Chorale Preludes*. Arr. William Schmidt. Western International Music. Euphonium and two tubas. 1985. $7. 5:30. IV. Part I: d–f', Part II: D–c', Part III: G₁–f. Three movements: Kom, heiliger Geist, Herr Gott; Vater unser im Himmelreich; Herr Jesu Christ, Dich zu uns Wend. Interesting arrangements with the melodies in the top part and inventive writing in the second and third parts. No articulation marks are included, so players will need to coordinate phrasing and articulations. Parts may be doubled for a large ensemble.

Tignor, Scott. *Boats & Ships*. Cimarron Music. Euphonium, tuba, and piano. $18. Three movements: I. Tug Boat; II. Sail Boat; III. Battleship.

Turrin, Joseph. *Arabesque*. Rosehill Music. Two euphoniums and piano. 1997. IV. Part I: A♭–d♭″, Part II: (E♭₁)F♯–b♭'. For the Childs Brothers. A fun, exciting showpiece that highlights the instrument's virtuosity. Technically demanding.

Tye, Christopher. *In Nomine*. Arr. R. P. Block. Philharmonia Music. Two euphoniums and organ. $14.50.

Uber, David. *Acrobatics*. Tuba-Euphonium Press. Two euphoniums or euphonium, tuba, and piano. 1994. $10. 3:30. II–III. Part I: d–a', Part II: G–f'. For Thomas Juzwiak and Robert Kenny. May be performed with any combination of euphoniums and tubas. A piece in ternary form with compound meter in the outer sections and simple meter in the middle. Both parts are challenging and interesting.

Uccelinni, Marco. *Sonata No. 1*. Arr. John Glenesk Mortimer. Editions Marc Reift. Flute or oboe or violin or clarinet or trumpet and euphonium with keyboard accompaniment. 1996. €13.30. III.

Uccelinni, Marco. *Sonata No. 2*. Arr. John Glenesk Mortimer. Editions Marc Reift. Flute or oboe or violin or clarinet or trumpet and euphonium with keyboard accompaniment. 1996. €13.30. III.

Vazzana, Anthony. *Partita for Euphonium, Piano, and Percussion*. Tuba-Euphonium Press. Euphonium, piano, and percussion. $40.

Vivaldi, Antonio. *Vivaldi Trio Sonata*. Ed. Paul Schmidt. Heavy Metal Music. Two euphoniums and one tuba. 1997. $7. Part I: c–g', Part II: E♭–c', Part III: B♭₁–a♭. Based on *Diverse Concerto in G Minor*, this transcription is transposed to C minor. The second part may be performed on

tuba. Reviewed in the Summer 1998 issue of the *TUBA Journal*, Vol. 25, No. 4.

Vun Kannon, Raymond. *Ragtime: Op. 14i*. American Music Center. Trumpet, euphonium, and tuba. 1986. 2:30.

Wagner, Richard. *Bridal Chorus*. Arr. Dennis Armitage. Editions Marc Reift. Euphonium, tuba, and piano or two euphoniums and piano or trumpet, euphonium, and piano. 1999. €14. Also available with CD playback accompaniment for €21. This arrangement comes in a set of five pieces: Wedding March (Mendelssohn); Trumpet Voluntary (Clarke); Aria (Bach); Trumpet Tune (Purcell); Bridal Chorus (Wagner).

Wallner, Alarich. *In Modo Classico*. Blasmusilkverlag Fritz Schulz. Two clarinets and euphonium. III. E♭–a♭'. Two movements: Allegro and Allegro Vivace. A fun, simple trio in two movements.

Walton, William. *Façade Suite: Fanfare*. Arr. Maurice Bale. Godiva Music. Euphonium, tuba, percussion. V. For Steven Mead and Pat Sheridan. Difficult.

Warren, Frank E. *Suite for Three Tubas, Op. 3a*. Frank E. Warren Music Service. Euphonium and two tubas. 1976. 6:00. IV. Part I: C₁–e', Part II: E₁–f', Part III: C₁–d♭'. Extreme range and technical demands in all parts. Several tempo changes and mixed meter throughout.

Weelkes, Thomas. *Three Madrigals*. Arr. Paul Schmidt. Heavy Metal Music. Two euphoniums and one tuba. 1990. $7. 4:00. IV. Part I: e♭–f', Part II: B♭–e♭', Part III: E♭–f. Three movements: Come, Sirrah Jack, Ho!; Since Robin Hood; Strike It Up, Tabor. Three spirited madrigals. No score available; parts may be doubled.

Wilhelm, Rolf. *Duett-Concertino*. Trio Musik Edition. Trumpet, euphonium, and piano. 2000.

Four Players

Alder, Jim. *Autumn Leaves*. MMI Music. Two cornets, horn, euphonium. £15.

Alder, Jim. *Springtime Fantasy*. MMI Music. Two cornets, horn, euphonium. £15.

Anderson, Leroy. *Sleigh Ride*. Arr. Ray Rosario. Brassworks 4. Two cornets, trombone, euphonium. 2003. $11. III. c–b♭'. A fun arrangement appropriate for high school players. This Christmas classic is sure to be an audience favorite.

Anderson, Mark, arr. *Old Hundreth*. TAP Music. Two trumpets, horn, euphonium. $4. Very easy arrangement suitable for younger players.

Arndt, Felix. *Nola*. Arr. Scott Ramsey. Brassworks 4. Two cornets, trombone, euphonium. 2002. $11. III. A♭–g♭'. Fun arrangement with the melody primarily in the trumpet parts. Extended triplet rhythmic patterns. Moderate technical difficulty.

Ayres, Richard. *No. 35: Overture*. MuziekGroep Nederland. Euphonium, two pianos, and timpani. 2000. 12:00. V. F1–e″. Commissioned by the piano duo Post and Mulder with financial support form the "Fonds voor de Scheppende Toonkunst." Dedicated to Roland and Carmen. An extremely difficult contemporary work that explores the full technical and musical capabilities of the instrument. Mixed meter, angular leaps, half-valve technique, glissandi, wide rhythmic vibrato. Tessitura moves from extremely high to extremely low. The euphoniumist is also called to play a melodica for a brief section. The timpanist also plays an ocarina, electronic megaphone, and thundersheet.

Bach, Johann Sebastian. *Air on G String*. Arr. Mick Hesse. Brassworks 4. Two cornets, trombone, euphonium. 2002. $13. 4:27. IV. C♯–d′. The euphonium part is characterized by large leaps and a low tessitura. Recorded by Brassworks 4, *Play!*, Brassworks 4 BW 4002.

Bach, Johann Sebastian. *Bach for Brass*. Arr. Walter Singg. Obrasso Musikverlag. Two cornets, horn, euphonium. CHF 30. Two movements: I. Air from Suite in D and II. Two Gavottes.

Bach, Johann Sebastian. *Brandenburg Concerto, No. 2—Movement 1*. Arr. Paul Bara. Brassworks 4. Piccolo trumpet, E♭ trumpet, trombone, euphonium. 2002. $26. IV. E–b♭′. An excellent college-level recital piece. Technically challenging. Appropriate for various occasions.

Bach, Johann Sebastian. *Fuga II from the Well Tempered Clavier*. Arr. Scott Ramsey. Brassworks 4. Two cornets, trombone, euphonium. 2002. $13. III–IV. E♭–e♭′. A short but solid arrangement of a classic fugue. Appropriate for good high school players. Recorded by Brassworks 4, *Play!*, Brassworks 4 BW 4002.

Bach, Johann Sebastian. *Fugue in G Minor*. Arr. Connie Schultz. Brassworks 4. Two cornets, trombone, euphonium. 2002. $16. IV. D–d′. A technically challenging arrangement of this four-voice fugue. Low tessitura in the euphonium part. The trombone part includes some tenor clef.

Bach, Johann Sebastian. *Jesu, Joy of Man's Desiring*. Arr. Scott Ramsey. Brassworks 4. Two cornets, trombone, euphonium. 2002. $11. III. E♭–e♭′. An accessible arrangement appropriate for high school players. The euphonium primarily plays the bass line.

Bale, Maurice, arr. *The Twelve Days of Christmas*. Godiva Music. Two cornets, tenor horn, euphonium.

Bara, Paul, arr. *All Creatures of Our God and King*. Brassworks 4. Two cornets, trombone, euphonium. 2002. $11. III. E–e′. A simple arrangement of this well-known hymn. Appropriate for high school players. Recorded by Brassworks 4, *Chalice Hymnal Song of Praise*, Brassworks 4 BW 4003.

Bara, Paul, arr. *Beer Belly Polka*. Brassworks 4. Two cornets, trombone, euphonium. 2002.

Bara, Paul. *Brassworks Fanfare*. Brassworks 4. Piccolo trumpet, cornet, trombone, euphonium.

2002. $7. III. F♯–f′. A short fanfare suitable for various occasions.

Bara, Paul, arr. *Just a Closer Walk with Thee*. Brassworks 4. Cornet (doubles piccolo trumpet), cornet, trombone, euphonium. 2002. $11. III. E–d′. A traditional arrangement that includes a piccolo trumpet descant on the final refrain. Recorded by Brassworks 4, *Chalice Hymnal Song of Praise*, Brassworks 4 BW 4003.

Bara, Paul, arr. *Mine Eyes Have Seen the Glory*. Brassworks 4. Two cornets, trombone, euphonium. 2002. $16. III. E–a♭′. A fun arrangement suitable for high school players. Recorded by Brassworks 4, *Chalice Hymnal Song of Praise*, Brassworks 4 BW 4003.

Bara, Paul, arr. *Tis the Gift to Be Simple*. Brassworks 4. Cornet, flugelhorn, trombone, euphonium. 2002. $11. III–IV. C–d′. This fun arrangement of the well-known melody begins with euphonium playing the tune alone. A short arrangement that is more suitable to ensemble performances than in recital.

Bara, Paul, arr. *Variations on Amazing Grace*. Brassworks 4. Cornet, cornet/flugelhorn, trombone, euphonium. 2002. $21. III. F–f′. An original set of variations on this familiar tune. Appropriate for high school players. Mutes are required for all players.

Bara, Paul, arr. *Wassailing*. Brassworks 4. Two cornets, trombone, euphonium. 2002. $11. III. G–d′. A fun take on this Christmas favorite. The first half of the piece is in a traditional style while the second is in a jazz style. Recorded by Brassworks 4, *Christmas Palette*, Brassworks 4 BW 4001.

Bara, Paul, Mick Hesse, Scott Ramsey, and Connie Schultz, arr. *The Star Spangled Banner*. Brassworks 4. Two cornets, trombone, euphonium. 2002. $7. II. F–b♭. Simple arrangement appropriate for younger players.

Barber, Clarence. *Royal Variations*. Ludwig Music Publishing. Two trumpets, euphonium, percussion. $9. Changing meters, some accidentals, easy ranges.

Baron, Samuel. *Impression of a Parade*. Arr. Scott Ramsey. Brassworks 4. Two cornets, trombone, euphonium. 2002. $21. IV. C–d′. A fun and challenging march in 12/8 meter. All parts call for mutes; trumpets need both straight and whisper mutes.

Bassano, Giovanni. *Canzona per Sonare on C. de Rore*. Arr. R. P. Block. Philharmonia Music. Two cornets, euphonium, tuba. $19.50.

Baxley, W. S. *Chorale in E Major*. Clark-Baxley Publications. Horn, trombone, euphonium, and tuba. $7.25.

Bayliss, Colin. *Ale & Arty*. Da Capo Music Limited. One euphonium and two tubas with narrator. £10. Narrator performs poems and tales about beer drinking. Recorded by Tubalaté on the compact disc *Earth and Moon*.

Beethoven, Ludwig van. *Drei Equali*. Arr. Clifford P. Barnes. Ludwig Music Publishing. Two cornets, trombone, euphonium. $15.95.

Beethoven, Ludwig van. *Equali No. 1*. Arr. Paul Bara. Brassworks 4. Two cornets, trombone, euphonium. 2002. $7. II. A–c'. A simple chorale that is musically challenging though not technically difficult. Appropriate for various occasions.

Beethoven, Ludwig van. *Ode to Joy*. Arr. Connie Schultz. Brassworks 4. Two cornets, trombone, euphonium. 2002. $13. III. F–c'. A simple arrangement consisting of three strains of the famous melody. The second setting features a trombone countermelody and the third features a trumpet countermelody. The euphonium primarily plays the bass line.

Berlin, Irving. *Puttin' on the Ritz*. Arr. Alan Fernie. Obrasso Musikverlag. Two cornets, horn, euphonium. CHF 30.

Bizet, George. *Carmen for Brass*. Arr. Ray Woodfield. Obrasso Musikverlag. Two cornets, horn, euphonium. CHF 41. Three movements: Overture; Habañera; Toreador Song.

Bradbury, William B. *Just As I Am*. Arr. Gordon A. Adnams. Sonate Publications. Cornet, flugelhorn, euphonium, and tuba. 1982. $5.50. 1:20. I–II. A very easy devotional piece arranged for conical instruments.

Bradbury, William B. *Sweet Hour of Prayer*. Arr. Scott Ramsey. Brassworks 4. Two cornets, trombone, euphonium. 2002. $11. II. A–g. A simple hymn tune arrangement appropriate for younger players. Descant parts included in treble and bass clef. Recorded by Brassworks 4, *Chalice Hymnal Songs of Praise*, Brassworks 4 BW 4003.

Brahms, Johannes. *Lo, How a Rose E'er Blooming*. Arr. Connie Frerich. Brassworks 4. Two cornets, trombone, euphonium. 2002. $11. III. G–d'. Gorgeous lyrical arrangement of Brahms's take on a traditional melody. Not technically difficult. Includes some simple meter changes.

Brody, Martin. *Divertimento d.C.* Martin Brody. Violin, viola, flute, euphonium. 2000.

Brugk, Hans Melchior. *Festlich-Feierlich: Intradan und Chorale für 4 Bläser*. Musikverlag Elisabeth Thomi-Berg. Flexible brass quartet with euphonium. III. F–a'. Four movements: I. Intrada; II. Chorale; III. Chorale; IV. Intrada. Appropriate for high school students. Could work well for solo and ensemble contests. Parts in treble and bass clef included.

Brugk, Hans Melchior. *Vier Kleine Turmmusiken*. Musikverlag Elisabeth Thomi-Berg. Flexible brass quartet with euphonium. II. A♭–f'. Four movements: Nr. 1; Nr. 2; Nr. 3; Nr. 4. Ideal for introducing young players to chamber music. Parts provided in treble and bass clef.

Bull, John. *The King's Hunting Jig*. Arr. Simon Kerwin. Obrasso Musikverlag. Two cornets, horn, euphonium. CHF 30.

Campra, André. *Rigaudon*. Arr. Manfred Obrecht. Obrasso Musikverlag. Two cornets, horn, euphonium. CHF 30.

Capdenat, Philippe. *Spargens Sonum, Op. 42*. Gérard Billaudot. Euphonium, tuba, and two percussion. 1993. €22.23. This chaconne was written for the Concours du C.N.S.M. de Paris in 1993.

Caravelli, Romuald. *Let Me Try Again*. Arr. Simon Kerwin. Obrasso Musikverlag. Two cornets, horn, euphonium. CHF 30.

Christophe, J. *4 Quators*. Tierolff Muziekcentrale. Two trumpets, trombone, euphonium.

Cimarosa, Domenico. *The Impresario*. Arr. Simon Kerwin. Obrasso Musikverlag. Two cornets, horn, euphonium. CHF 30.

Clarke, Herbert L. *Cousins*. Arr. Paul Bara. Brassworks 4. Two cornets, trombone, euphonium. 2002. $17. IV. F–c''. An excellent arrangement featuring cornet and euphonium. Technically challenging for the soloists. Multiple tonguing is required. Good choice for a collegiate recital.

Clarke, Jeremiah. *Trumpet Voluntary*. Arr. Connie Schultz. Brassworks 4. Two cornets, trombone, euphonium. 2002. $7. III. F–d'. An accessible arrangement of this wedding favorite.

Corwell, Neal. *Drum Taps*. Tuba-Euphonium Press. Tuba, horn, euphonium, and drums. 2002. $15. 11:45. IV. F–c''. Written for Velvet M. Brown and Julianne Fish. Inspired by "Drum Taps," a collection of poems penned by Walt Whitman based upon his experiences during the American Civil War. The tuba plays the solo role for most of the piece, but all parts of the ensemble are prominent and challenging. Extensive use of double tonguing technique in all parts. An exciting recital piece.

Couperin, Francois. *L'Apotheose de Lully*. Arr. R. P. Block. Philharmonia Music. Euphonium, two trumpets, and organ. $27.50.

Cresswell, Tony. *Melodie Semplice*. Mostyn Music. Two cornets, horn, euphonium. £4.50.

Danielsson, Christer. *Little Suite for Four Brass*. Throre Ehrling Musik AB. Trombone, trombone (or horn), euphonium (or trombone), and tuba (or bass trombone). 1972. $22.50. 8:00. III–IV. Part I: d–c'', Part II: d♭–a', Part III: A♭–d', Part IV: A₁–e♭. Three movements: Moderato; Lento; Scherzo. Tuneful work with pop and jazz influences. High tessitura in all parts. Suitable for various combinations of instruments.

Daquin, Louis Claude. *Le Coucou*. Arr. Alan MacRae. MMI Music. Two cornets, horn, euphonium. £15.

Davis, Mike. *Suite for Brass Quartet*. Hallamshire Music. Flexible brass quartet with euphonium. £15.95. 9:15.

Debussy, Claude. *Golliwog's Cakewalk*. Arr. Peter Tutak. Brassworks 4. Two cornets, trombone, euphonium. 2002. $19. III. G♭–d♭'. An accessible arrangement playable by good high school students. Extensive syncopated rhythmic patterns and some technical challenges. The trumpet parts require straight and Harmon mutes, the trombone part requires a plunger mute, and the euphonium part requires a straight mute.

Dukas, Paul. *L'Apprenti Sorcier.* Arr. Scott Ramsey. Brassworks 4. Two cornets, trombone, euphonium. 2002. $26. IV. F–g'. Great four-part arrangement of this orchestral classic. An audience favorite appropriate for recital performances. Challenging for all players.

Dvořák, Antonin. *Slavonic Dance No. 5.* Arr. Paul Bara. Brassworks 4. Two cornets, trombone, euphonium. 2002. $20. IV. E♭–b♭'. Challenging for all players.

Dvořák, Antonin. *Slavonic Dance No. 4.* Arr. Paul Bara. Brassworks 4. Two cornets, trombone, euphonium. 2002. $20. IV. D–c''. Challenging for all players.

Dykes, John. *Holy, Holy, Holy.* Arr. Paul Bara. Brassworks 4. Two cornets, trombone, euphonium. 2002. $13. II. E–e'. A short, traditional arrangement of this classic hymn. Appropriate for younger players. Recorded by Brassworks 4, *Chalice Hymnal Songs of Praise,* Brassworks 4 BW 4003.

Edwards, David. *When You Do This, Remember Me.* Brassworks 4. Two cornets, trombone, euphonium. 2002. $11. II. F–b. A simple hymn tune appropriate for younger players. Descant parts included in treble and bass clef. Recorded by Brassworks 4, *Chalice Hymnal Song of Praise,* Brassworks 4 BW 4003.

Elgar, Edward. *Land of Hope and Glory from Pomp and Circumstance March No. 1.* Arr. Roy Newsome. Obrasso Musikverlag. Two cornets, horn, euphonium. CHF 30.

Fernie, Alan, arr. *Four Negro Spirituals.* Obrasso Musikverlag. Two cornets, horn, euphonium. CHF 41. Four movements: I. Peter, Go Ring Dem Bells; II. Go Down, Moses; III. Joshua Fit De Battle; IV. Swing Low, Sweet Chariot.

Fernie, Alan, arr. *Four Negro Spirituals, Vol. 2.* Obrasso Musikverlag. Two cornets, horn, euphonium. CHF 41. Four movements: I. Heav'n Heav'n!!; II. Dem Bones; III. Steal Away; IV. Sometimes I Feel Like a Motherless Child.

Fernie, Alan, arr. *Music from the 16th Century.* Obrasso Musikverlag. Two cornets, horn, euphonium. CHF 41. Three movements: I. Villanella; II. The Earl of Salisbury's Pavan; III. The Battle.

Fernie, Alan, arr. *Oh, Happy Day.* Obrasso Musikverlag. Two cornets, horn, euphonium. CHF 30.

Fernie, Alan, arr. *Shenandoah.* Obrasso Musikverlag. Two cornets, horn, euphonium. CHF 30.

Fernie, Alan, arr. *A Southern Gospel Suite.* Obrasso Musikverlag. Two cornets, horn, euphonium. CHF 41. Three movements: I. Kum-Ba-Yah; II. Deep River; III. Down by the Riverside.

Fernie, Alan. *Three Pieces for Brass Quartet.* Obrasso Musikverlag. Two cornets, horn, euphonium.

CHF 30. Three movements: I. A Song for Kathryn; II. Elegy; III. March of the Toy Soldiers.

Fernie, Alan, arr. *Three Renaissance Pieces.* Obrasso Musikverlag. Two cornets, horn, euphonium. CHF 30. Three movements: I. Pavan; II. His Rest; III. Rondo.

Fernie, Alan, arr. *Three Sea Songs.* Obrasso Musikverlag. Two cornets, horn, euphonium. CHF 38. Three movements: I. Drunken Sailor; II. Blow the Man Down; III. Hornpipe.

Fernie, Alan, arr. *Two Rags for Four, Vol. 1.* Obrasso Musikverlag. Two cornets, horn, euphonium. CHF 38. Two movements: I. Cracked Ice Rag and II. Black and White Rag.

Fernie, Alan, arr. *Two Rags for Four, Vol. 2.* Obrasso Musikverlag. Two cornets, horn, euphonium. CHF 38. Two movements: I. Ragtime Nightmare and II. Ragtime Dance.

Fernie, Alan, arr. *When the Saints Go Marching In.* Obrasso Musikverlag. Two cornets, horn, euphonium. CHF 30.

Fillmore, Henry. *Lassus Trombone.* Arr. Scott Ramsey. Brassworks 4. Two cornets, trombone, euphonium. 2002. $16. 2:17. III. F–f'. A fun arrangement featuring the trombone player. A moderate technical challenge with some syncopated rhythms. Recorded by Brassworks 4, *Play!,* Brassworks 4 BW 4002.

Fillmore, Henry. *Teddy Trombone.* Arr. Mick Hesse. Brassworks 4. Two cornets, trombone, euphonium. 2002. $16. III. F–d'. A fun arrangement featuring the trombone player. A moderate technical challenge with some syncopated rhythms.

Foster, Stephen. *Stephen Foster Medley.* Arr. Scott Ramsey. Brassworks 4. Two cornets, trombone, euphonium. 2002. $16. III. B♭–e♭'. Appropriate for high school players.

Franz, R. *Request.* Arr. Dan Rager. Ludwig Music Publishing. Two trumpets, horn, euphonium. $10. A beautiful melody that is scored well for the beginning quartet. Key of F in a 2/2 meter with largo as the tempo marking.

Frerich, Connie, arr. *Hark! The Herald Angels Sing.* Brassworks 4. Two cornets, trombone, euphonium. 2002. $11. III. D–c'. A fun arrangement that follows a traditional setting of the famous carol with a rock version. Includes some simple syncopation. Not technically difficult. The euphonium's lower pitches may be played up an octave to make this arrangement accessible to younger students. Recorded by Brassworks 4, *Christmas Palette,* Brassworks 4 BW 4001.

Frerich, Connie, arr. *Joy to the World.* Brassworks 4. Two cornets, trombone, euphonium. 2002. $11. III. E♭–f'. A creative arrangement suitable for high school players. Recorded by Brassworks 4, *Christmas Palette,* Brassworks 4 BW 4001.

Frerich, Connie, arr. *O Come All Ye Faithful.* Brassworks 4. Two cornets, trombone, euphonium. 2002. $11. II. G–d'. Appropriate for younger players. Not technically difficult. Recorded by

Brassworks 4, *Christmas Palette,* Brassworks 4 BW 4001.

Frerich, Connie. *What Child Is This?* Brassworks 4. Two cornets, trombone, euphonium. 2002. $16. III. E♭–f′. Features the euphonium in the first half of the arrangement. Recorded by Brassworks 4, *Christmas Palette,* Brassworks 4 BW 4001.

Frescobaldi, Girolamo. *Gagliarda.* Arr. Henry Aaron. G. Schirmer. Two trumpets, euphonium, trombone. 1953. Out of Print.

Friedman, Stanley. *Zephyr Dances.* Editions BIM. Two trumpets, horn, euphonium. 2001. 10:35.

Friedrich, Kenneth. *Circus Suite.* Cimarron Music. Trumpet, horn, euphonium, tuba. $24. Four movements: I. A Grand Entrance; II. Artists in the Air; III. Defiers of Mortality; IV. A View from Goodbye.

Gabrieli, Giovanni. *Canzona.* Arr. Manfred Obrecht. Obrasso Musikverlag. Two cornets, horn, euphonium. CHF 30.

Gabrieli, Giovanni. *Canzona per Sonare.* Arr. R. P. Block. Philharmonia Music. Euphonium and three tubas. $12.50.

Gabrieli, Giovanni. *Canzona Venezia.* Arr. Manfred Obrecht. Obrasso Musikverlag. Two cornets, horn, euphonium. CHF 30.

Galuppi, Baldassare. *Sonata.* Arr. Connie Schultz. Brassworks 4. Two cornets, trombone, euphonium. 2002. $11. IV. C–c′. A slow, lyrical piece that features the two cornet parts. The euphonium plays the bass line. Cornet parts include sextuplet rhythmic figures with large intervallic leaps.

Gershwin, George. *Porgy and Bess.* Arr. Walter Zingg. Obrasso Musikverlag. Two cornets, horn, euphonium. CHF 41. Three movements: I. It Ain't Necessarily So; II. Summertime; III. I Got Plenty.

Gervaise, Claude. *Four Renaissance Dances.* Arr. Manfred Obrecht. Obrasso Musikverlag. Two cornets, horn, euphonium. CHF 30. Four movements: I. Branle de Champagne; II. Branle de Champagne; III. Branle de Champagne; IV. Allemande.

Glière, Rheinhold. *Russian Sailor's Dance.* Arr. Simon Kerwin. Obrasso Musikverlag. Two cornets, horn, euphonium. CHF 30.

Golland, John. *Bagatelles.* Hallamshire Music. Two cornets, horn, euphonium. £11.95. For advanced players.

Golland, John. *Divertimento.* Kirklees Music. Two cornets, horn, euphonium. £10.50.

Golland, John. *Phantasie.* Kirklees Music. Two cornets, horn, euphonium. £10.50.

Graham, Peter. *Timepiece.* Gramercy Music. Two cornets, horn, euphonium. £12.95. Commissioned for the Swiss Quartet Championships.

Greenwood, Philip H. *En Vacances.* Obrasso Musikverlag. Two cornets, horn, euphonium. CHF 46.

Grieg, Edvard. *Aase's Death.* Arr. Scott Ramsey. Brassworks 4. Two cornets, trombone, euphonium. 2002. 11:00. III. F–d′. A short, effective arrangement of this famous dirge. Appropriate for high school players.

Grieg, Edvard. *Anitra's Dance.* Arr. Scott Ramsey. Brassworks 4. Two cornets, trombone, euphonium. 2002. $11. IV. A–a′. A technically challenging arrangement that is fun for audience and performers alike.

Grieg, Edvard. *In the Hall of the Mountain King.* Arr. Scott Ramsey. Brassworks 4. Two cornets, trombone, euphonium. 2002. $16. III. F–d♭′. A fun arrangement appropriate for various occasions that is sure to be an audience favorite. A moderate technical challenge.

Gruber, Franz. *Silent Night.* Arr. Scott Ramsey. Brassworks 4. Cornet, flugelhorn, trombone, and euphonium. 2002. $11. II. G–f′. A traditional setting of this famous carol. Recorded by Brassworks 4, *Christmas Palette,* Brassworks 4 BW 4001.

Hakenberg, Stefan. *Small Craft.* Tonos Musikverlag. Flute, violin, viola, euphonium. 2001. €15.90. 6:00.

Hall, Nigel, arr. *Agnus Dei.* MMI Music. Two cornets, horn, euphonium. £15.

Hall, Percy. *Air and March.* Ludwig Music Publishing. Two trombones, euphonium, tuba. 1994.

Hammond, Albert, and John Bettis. *One Moment in Time.* Arr. Alan Fernie. Obrasso Musikverlag. Two cornets, horn, euphonium. CHF 30.

Handel, George Frederic. *Air—Water Music.* Arr. Connie Schultz. Brassworks 4. Two cornets, trombone, euphonium. 2002. $9. II. F–b♭. A short, easy arrangement appropriate for younger players.

Handel, George Frederic. *Allegro Maestoso—Water Music.* Arr. Connie Schultz. Brassworks 4. Two cornets, trombone, euphonium. 2002. $10. III.

Handel, George Frederic. *Aria—Concerto Grosso, Op. 6, No. 12.* Arr. Connie Schultz. Brassworks 4. Two cornets, trombone, euphonium. 2002. $9. III. E–g′. An effective arrangement suitable for various occasions.

Handel, George Frederic. *La Rejouissance: Allegro from Royal Fireworks Music.* Arr. Scott Ramsey. Brassworks 4. Two cornets, trombone, euphonium with optional timpani part. 2002. $11. III. D–d′. A fun arrangement suitable for various occasions.

Handel, George Frederic. *Music for the Royal Fireworks.* Arr. Walter Zingg. Obrasso Musikverlag. Two cornets, horn, euphonium. CHF 41.

Handel, George Frederic. *Thine Is the Glory.* Arr. Scott Ramsey. Brassworks 4. Two cornets, trombone, euphonium. 2002. $11. II. G–c′. A simple hymn arrangement appropriate for younger players. Descant parts included in treble and bass clef. Recorded by Brassworks 4, *Chalice Hymnal Song of Praise,* Brassworks 4 BW 4003.

Handel, George Frederic. *Water Music Suite*. Arr. Simon Kerwin. Obrasso Musikverlag. Two cornets, horn, euphonium. CHF 41.

Harris, Floyd O. *Vesper Moods*. Ludwig Music Publishing. Two trumpets, trombone, euphonium. $7.95.

Hartley, Walter. *Quartet for Low Brass and Piano*. Tuba-Euphonium Press. Trombone, euphonium, tuba, and piano. 2003. $24. III–IV. Four movements: Allegro Moderato; Scherzando; Adagio; Vivace.

Hesse, Mick, arr. *Angels We Have Heard on High*. Brassworks 4. Cornet (doubles on piccolo trumpet), cornet, trombone, euphonium. 2002. $9. II. F–e'. Simple arrangement of this familiar carol. Recorded by Brassworks 4, *Christmas Palette*, Brassworks 4 BW 4001.

Hesse, Mick, arr. *Donna Nobis Pacem*. Brassworks 4. Cornet (piccolo trumpet), cornet (flugelhorn), trombone, euphonium. 2002. $6. II. B♭–c'. Effective arrangement in which each voice enters with the eight-measure melody until all parts are playing. Appropriate for younger players. Optional piccolo trumpet part for advanced ensembles. Recorded by Brassworks 4, *Christmas Palette*, Brassworks 4 BW 4001.

Holden, Oliver. *All Hail the Power of Jesus' Name*. Arr. Scott Ramsey. Brassworks 4. Two cornets, trombone, euphonium. 2002. $11. II. A–a. Simple hymn tune arrangement appropriate for younger players. Recorded by Brassworks 4, *Chalice Hymnal Songs of Praise*, Brassworks 4 BW 4003.

Holst, Gustav. *In the Bleak Midwinter*. Arr. Paul Bara. Brassworks 4. Two cornets, trombone, euphonium. 2002. $11. II. F–f'. An easy and traditional arrangement of this classic carol. Recorded by Brassworks 4, *Christmas Palette*, Brassworks 4 BW 4001.

Hovhaness, Alan. *Sharagan and Fugue*. Robert King Music Sales, Inc. Two trumpets, horn, euphonium. 1950. $18.80. 4:00. III–IV. B–a'. A well-written original quartet in Hovhaness's unique style. The first part is a slow, lyrical pallete of tonal color. The second half of the work is a spritely allegro fugue. Good recital material.

Hügli, Albrecht. *L O G O S*. Obrasso Musikverlag. Two cornets, horn, euphonium. CHF 30.

Hulton, James. *Brass*. Scottish Music Information Centre. Two cornets, baritone, euphonium. 1974.

Joplin, Scott. *The Entertainer*. Arr. Paul Bara. Brassworks 4. Piccolo trumpet, cornet, trombone, euphonium. 2002. $13. III–IV. C–f'.

Joplin, Scott. *Maple Leaf Rag*. Arr. David Werden. Cimarron Music. Two cornets, horn, euphonium. $13. 4:00.

Joplin, Scott. *The Rose-Bud March*. Arr. Scott Ramsey. Brassworks 4. Two cornets, trombone, euphonium. 2002. $16. 1:30. II–III. E♭–d'. A

fun march in 6/8 time. Recorded by Brassworks 4, *Play!*, Brassworks 4 BW 4002.

Joplin, Scott. *The Sycamore Rag*. Arr. Alan Fernie. Obrasso Musikverlag. Two cornets, horn, euphonium. CHF 30.

Kabalevsky, Dimitri. *Comedian's Gallup*. Arr. Scott Ramsey. Brassworks 4. Two cornets, trombone, euphonium. 2002. $16. IV. A♭–a'. A fun arrangement of this familiar piece that works well as a concert opener or closer. Some technical challenges. Double tonguing required of all players.

Kabalevsky, Dimitri. *Comedian's Gallup*. Arr. Simon Kerwin. Obrasso Musikverlag. Two cornets, horn, euphonium. CHF 30.

Kerwin, Simon. *Brass Quartet in Three Movements*. Mostyn Music. Two cornets, horn, euphonium. £10.50.

Kerwin, Simon, arr. *Classical Brass*. Obrasso Musikverlag. Two cornets, horn, euphonium. CHF 41. Collection of four famous classical works: Rondo Alla Turk (Mozart); Nimrod (Elgar); Slavonic Dance (Dvořák); Intermezzo (Mascagni).

Kerwin, Simon, arr. *Festive Brass*. Obrasso Musikverlag. Two cornets, horn, euphonium. CHF 41. Collection of festive tunes by various composers: Rondeau (Mouret); Fanfare and Chorus (Buxtehude); Pastime with Good Company (Henry VIII).

Kerwin, Simon, arr. *Four Marches*. Obrasso Musikverlag. Two cornets, horn, euphonium. CHF 41. Collection of four marches by various composers: Fehrbelliner Reitermarsch; Zurich March; March Militaire; Radetzky March.

Kerwin, Simon, arr. *Six Melodious Pieces*. Obrasso Musikverlag. Two cornets, horn, euphonium. CHF 41. Collection of six singable tunes: Drink to Me Only; Jeannie with the Light Brown Hair; Two Versets on Love Divine; Etude (Chopin); All through the Night; All in the April Evening.

Kerwin, Simon, arr. *Six Sacred Tunes*. Obrasso Musikverlag. Two cornets, horn, euphonium. CHF 41. Collection of six sacred works by various composers: Du bist die Ruh; Panis Angelicus; Nearer My God to Thee; Deep Harmony; Ich hatt einen Kameraden; Ave Verum.

Khachaturian, Aram. *Sabre Dance*. Arr. Scott Ramsey. Brassworks 4. Two cornets, trombone, euphonium. 2002. $16. IV. F–g'. An exciting, challenging arrangement. The euphonium is featured in the "b" section, playing the lyrical melody.

Kitto, Gordon. *Allegro, Andante & Scherzo*. Mostyn Music. Two cornets, horn, euphonium. £10.50.

Leech, Brian Jeffrey. *Come Share the Lord*. Arr. Paul Bara. Brassworks 4. Two cornets, trombone, euphonium. 2002. $13. IV. D–d'. Great arrangement of this well-known hymn suitable for various occasions. Recorded by Brassworks 4,

Chalice Hymnal Song of Praise, Brassworks 4 BW 4003.

Legrand, Michel. *The Summer Knows: From the Summer of '42*. Arr. Ray Rosario. Brassworks 4. Cornet, flugelhorn, trombone, euphonium. 2003. $11. 3:20. III. F–g'. Features the flugelhorn and euphonium. Recorded by Brassworks 4, *Play!*, Brassworks 4 BW 4002.

Lennon, John, and Paul McCartney. *Beatles for Four*. Arr. Alan Fernie. Obrasso Musikverlag. Two cornets, horn, euphonium. CHF 41.

Lennon, John, and Paul McCartney. *Hey Jude*. Arr. Alan Fernie. Obrasso Musikverlag. Two cornets, horn, euphonium. CHF 30.

Lennon, John, and Paul McCartney. *Yesterday*. Arr. Alan Fernie. Obrasso Musikverlag. Two cornets, horn, euphonium. CHF 30.

Loewe, Frederick. *My Fair Lady Collection*. Arr. Walter Zingg. Obrasso Musikverlag. Two cornets, horn, euphonium. CHF 41. Collection of popular tunes: On the Street Where You Live; With a Little Bit; Wouldn't It Be Loverly; Ascot Gavotte; I Could Have Danced All Night; Get Me to the Church on Time.

Lowry, Robert. *Shall We Gather at the River*. Arr. Scott Ramsey. Brassworks 4. Two cornets, trombone, euphonium. 2002. $11. II. A–g. An easy hymn tune arrangement. Descant parts included in treble and bass clef.

MacDowell, Edward. *To a Wild Rose*. Arr. Alan Fernie. Obrasso Musikverlag. Two cornets, horn, euphonium. CHF 30.

Mahaffey, Jim, arr. *Wedding Favorites*. Southern Music Company. Flexible brass quartet with euphonium. $20. Collection of wedding favorites: Ode to Joy (Beethoven); Trumpet Tune (Clarke); Trumpet Voluntary (Purcell); Canon (Pachelbel); Bridal March (Wagner); Water Music (Handel); Wedding March (Mendelssohn); Jesu, Joy of Man's Desiring (Bach); Spring, from *The Four Seasons* (Vivaldi); Rondeau (Mouret).

Maker, Frederick. *Beneath the Cross of Jesus*. Arr. Connie Schultz. Brassworks 4. Two cornets, trombone, euphonium. 2002. $11. III. F–g'. A simple hymn tune arrangement appropriate for high school players and various occasions. Recorded by Brassworks 4, *Chalice Hymnal Song of Praise*, Brassworks 4 BW 4003.

Marcello, Benedetto. *Psalm XIX: The Heavens Declare*. Arr. Connie Schultz. Brassworks 4. Piccolo trumpet, cornet, trombone, euphonium. 2002. $16. III. E–g'. Recorded by Brassworks 4, Christmas *Palette*, Brassworks 4 BW 4001.

Mascagni, Pietro. *Intermezzo and Easter Hymn*. Arr. Maurice Bale. Godiva Music. Two cornets, E♭ tenor horn, euphonium. 1999. £6. IV. (B♭₁)E♭–e♭'. Musically challenging but not technically difficult. The euphonium functions as the bass voice in this ensemble.

Mendelssohn, Felix. *Fanfare and Wedding March*. Arr. Alan Fernie. Obrasso Musikverlag. Two cornets, horn, euphonium. CHF 30.

Mendelssohn, Felix. *The Wedding March*. Arr. Scott Ramsey. Brassworks 4. Two cornets, trombone, euphonium. 2002. $11. F–f. A simple arrangement appropriate for high school players.

Meyer, Hannes. *Schanfigger Bauernhochzeit*. Arr. Alan Fernie. Obrasso Musikverlag. Two cornets, horn, euphonium. CHF 30.

Michel, Jean-François, arr. *32 Christmas Carols*. Editions Marc Reift. Two trumpets, trombone, and euphonium or two cornets, horn, and euphonium. 1993. €27.30. A collection of carols suitable for younger players. Includes: Good King Wenceslas; Alle Jahre wieder; Les Angesdans nos campagnes; Lasst uns froh und munter sein; In Dulci Jubilo; We wish You a Merry Christmas; Süsser die Glocken nie klingen; March of the Three Kings; O Little Town of Bethlehem; Silent Night; The First Noel; Deck the Halls; Jingle Bells; Still, Still, Still; We Three Kings; O Tannenbaum; Adeste Fideles; Kommet, Ihr Hirten; While Shepherds Watched; O du Fröhliche; God Rest You; The Holly and the Ivy; O Holy Night; Hark, the Herald Angels; Joy to the World; Ihr Kinderlein kommet; Kling, Glöcklein, kling; Am Weihnachtsbaum; Es ist ein Ros entsprungen; Il est né le divin enfant; Vom Himmel hoch; Leise rieselt der Schnee.

Miles, C. Austin. *In the Garden*. Arr. Paul Bara. Brassworks 4. Two cornets, trombone, euphonium. 2002. $13. III. D–d♭'. A lilting hymn in 6/8 meter. Recorded by Brassworks 4, *Chalice Hymnal Songs of Praise*, Brassworks 4 BW 4003.

Miller, Glenn. *Glenn Miller Medley*. Arr. Scott Ramsey. Brassworks 4. Two cornets, trombone, euphonium. 2000. $21. III–IV. F–d'. A fun medley featuring four classic Miller tunes: "Little Brown Jug," "Tuxedo Junction," "String of Pearls," "In the Mood." The euphonium plays the bass line throughout. The cornet and trombone parts all call for a plunger and present some technical challenges.

Miserendino, Joe. *Lighthearted and Lowpitched*. Joe Miserendino. Baritone, two euphoniums, tuba. 2003. $5. 4:00. III. Part I: B♭–g', Part II: E♭–a', Part III: B♭₁–g', Part IV: A₁–a. A fun original piece suitable for high school players. The first part may be played on euphonium.

Moore, Colin. *The Drunken Sailor*. Mostyn Music. Two cornets, horn, euphonium. £5.95.

Morton, John. *Avenues*. Mostyn Music. Cornet, horn, euphonium, tuba. £7.95.

Mouret. *Rondeau*. Arr. Paul Bara. Brassworks 4. Two cornets, trombone, euphonium. 2002. $9. 0:57. II. c–c'. A simple arrangement appropriate for younger students. Recorded by Brassworks 4, *Play!*, Brassworks 4 BW 4002.

Mozart, Wolfgang Amadeus. *Ave verum Corpus.* Arr. Connie Schultz. Brassworks 4. Two cornets, trombone, euphonium. 2002. $9. II. G♯–b. A short, simple arrangement appropriate for younger students and various occasions.

Mozart, Wolfgang Amadeus. *The Magic Flute Overture.* Arr. Maurice Bale. Godiva Music. Two cornets (trumpets), tenor horn (horn), euphonium.

Mozart, Wolfgang Amadeus. *Overture: Marriage of Figaro.* Arr. Scott Ramsey. Brassworks 4. Two cornets, trombone, euphonium, 2002. $26. IV. E♭–g'. A technically challenging arrangement that is fun for audience and performers alike.

Mozart, Wolfgang Amadeus. *Twinkle, Twinkle Little Star.* Arr. David Werden. Cimarron Music. Two cornets, horn, euphonium. $13.50. 3:30.

Mucci, John C. *The Chambered Nautilus.* American Music Center. Euphonium, two F tubas, CC tuba. 1977. 17:00.

Newsome, Roy, arr. *Three Great Hymns.* Obrasso Musikverlag. Two cornets, horn, euphonium. CHF 38. Three movements: I. Richmond/ Eventide/Praise; II. My Soul; III. The King of Heaven.

Obrecht, Manfred, arr. *Two Old French Dances.* Obrasso Musikverlag. Two cornets, horn, euphonium. CHF 30.

Pachelbel, Johann. *Canon in D.* Arr. Connie Schultz. Brassworks 4. Two cornets, trombone, euphonium. 2002. $16. III–IV. G–b♭'. This arrangement features the first cornet and euphonium. Presents some technical challenges.

Pollack, Lew. *That's a Plenty.* Arr. Scott Ramsey. Brassworks 4. Two cornets, trombone, euphonium. 2002. $16. III. F–f'.

Pollack, Lew. *That's a Plenty.* Arr. Alan Fernie. Obrasso Musikverlag. Two cornets, horn, euphonium. CHF 30.

Purcell, Henry. *Music for Queen Mary.* Arr. Manfred Obrecht. Obrasso Musikverlag. Two cornets, horn, euphonium. CHF 30. Three movements: I. Hymn; II. Anthem; III. Canzona.

Rager, Dan. *Baroque Brass.* Ludwig Music Publishing. Two trumpets, horn, euphonium. $9. A single cantabile movement in the baroque style, this technically easy work presents musical challenges. Written in Dorian mode, this work provides opportunities to develop phrasing, breathing, ensemble, and legato style.

Ramsey, Scott, arr. *Beer Belly Polka.* Brassworks 4. Two cornets, trombone, euphonium. 2002. $12. III–IV. E♭–e♭'. A fun arrangement that calls for the second cornet and trombone to sing a verse. Moderate technical difficulty.

Ramsey, Scott, arr. *Danny Boy.* Brassworks 4. Two cornets, trombone, euphonium. 2002. $13. III. E♭–a'. All parts have a chance to play the melody in this traditional arrangement. Not technically difficult. Appropriate for high school players.

Ramsey, Scott, arr. *God Rest Ye Merry Foom Foom.* Brassworks 4. Two cornets, trombone, euphonium. 2002. $16. III. G–e♭'. A fun arrangement combining "God Rest Ye Merry Gentlemen" and "Foom, Foom, Foom." Recorded by Brassworks 4, *Christmas Palette,* Brassworks 4 BW 4001.

Ramsey, Scott, arr. *The Irish Washerperson.* Brassworks 4. Two cornets, trombone, euphonium. 2002. $16. III. G–d'. A fun setting of this traditional tune in which all parts have a chance to play the melody.

Ramsey, Scott. *Lana Dolores Melendres.* Brassworks 4. Two cornets, trombone, euphonium. 2002. $16. III. G–f'. A fun up-tempo Latin tune. Includes extensive meter changes and some syncopated rhythms. Moderate technical difficulty.

Ramsey, Scott, arr. *Morning Has Broken.* Brassworks 4. Two cornets, trombone, euphonium. 2002. $11. II. F–c'. A simple hymn arrangement. Includes descant parts in treble and bass clef. Recorded by Brassworks 4, *Chalice Hymnal Song of Praise,* Brassworks 4 BW 4003.

Ramsey, Scott, arr. *Of the Father's Love Begotten.* Brassworks 4. Two cornets, trombone, euphonium. 2002. $11. III. E♭–b♭. A plainsong arrangement written in one-measure phrases of irregular meter. Recorded by Brassworks 4, *Chalice Hymnal Song of Praise,* Brassworks 4 BW 4003.

Ramsey, Scott, arr. *Riu, Riu, Chiu.* Brassworks 4. Two cornets, trombone, euphonium. 2002. $11. II. A–a. A simple, fun arrangement of this Spanish carol. Employs simple changing meters and some syncopation. Optional tambourine part included.

Ramsey, Scott, arr. *Saints.* Brassworks 4. Piccolo trumpet, cornet, trombone, euphonium. 2002. $11. III. F–c'. This classic Dixieland arrangement begins with a slow introduction followed by an up-tempo swing in cut time.

Ramsey, Scott. *A Suite for Clowns.* Brassworks 4. Two cornets, trombone, euphonium. 2002. $26. 4:30. III–IV. F–g'. Three movements: I. Clown Dance; II. Clown at Rest; III. Clown Act. A fun original work for brass quartet. Third movement is technically challenging for the first cornet and euphonium. Fun to play. Recorded by Brassworks 4, *Play!*, Brassworks 4 BW 4002.

Ramsey, Scott, arr. *Tin Roof Blues.* Brassworks 4. Two cornets, trombone, euphonium. 2002. $16. III. F–a♭. A medium tempo blues that includes improvised solo sections for each player.

Ravel, Maurice. *Pavane for a Dead Princess.* Arr. Paul Bara. Brassworks 4. Two cornets, trombone, euphonium. 2002. $21. III–IV. E–c". The euphonium begins this great arrangement of Ravel's famous melody that is suitable for recitals and other occasions. Not technically difficult. Some tenor clef in the euphonium part.

Ravel, Maurice. *Ravel's Pavane.* Arr. Steven Booth. SB Music. Flexible quartet with euphonium.

Reiche, Johann Gottfried. *Turmsonate.* Arr. Paul Cadow. Musikverlag Elisabeth Thomi-Berg. Trumpet, horn, euphonium, tuba. 1993. II. c–e♭'. Not technically difficult. Appropriate for younger players.

Rimsky-Korsakov, Nicolai. *Dance of the Tumblers.* Arr. Simon Kerwin. Obrasso Musikverlag. Two cornets, horn, euphonium. CHF 30.

Rimsky-Korsakov, Nicolai. *Flight of the Bumblebee.* Arr. Scott Ramsey. Brassworks 4. Two cornets, trombone, euphonium. 2002. $16. IV–V. G–g'. A technically challenging arrangement in which the bee flies amongst the ensemble. Double tonguing required in the trombone part. Careful rehearsal is needed for ensemble timing and clarity.

Ringgenberg, Jörg. *444 (Four for Four).* Obrasso Musikverlag. Two cornets, horn, euphonium. CHF 38.

Risher, Tim. *4*4.* American Music Center. Two trumpets, horn, euphonium or trombone. 1988.

Robertson, Donna N. *Fanfare for the Prince of Darkness.* American Music Center. Four part low brass ensemble. 1983. 6:00.

Rossini, Gioacchino. *La Danza.* Arr. Simon Kerwin. Obrasso Musikverlag. Two cornets, horn, euphonium. CHF 30.

Rossini, Gioacchino. *Overture: Barber of Seville.* Arr. Scott Ramsey. Brassworks 4. Two cornets, trombone, euphonium. 2002. $26. IV. D–g'. A challenging arrangement that is fun to play.

Rossini, Gioacchino. *Overture: An Italian in Algiers.* Arr. Scott Ramsey. Brassworks 4. Two cornets, trombone, euphonium. 2002. $26. 4:18. IV. C–g'. A fun arrangement of this classic overture. Technically challenging. Recorded by Brassworks 4, *Play!,* Brassworks 4 BW 4002.

Rossini, Gioacchino. *Overture: William Tell.* Arr. Scott Ramsey. Brassworks 4. Two cornets, trombone, euphonium. 2002. $26. IV. E♭–g'. An exciting arrangement suitable for various occasions. Technically challenging for all players.

Rossini, Gioacchino. *Quando Corpus from Stabat Mater.* Arr. Clifford P. Barnes. Ludwig Music Publishing. Two trumpets, trombone, euphonium. $9.95.

Rossini, Gioacchino. *William Tell Overture.* Arr. Simon Kerwin. Obrasso Musikverlag. Two cornets, horn, euphonium. CHF 30.

Roth, Elton. *In My Heart There Rings a Melody.* Arr. Scott Ramsey. Brassworks 4. Two cornets, trombone, euphonium. 2002. $11. II. A♭–a♭. A short and simple hymn tune arrangement appropriate for younger players. Includes descant parts in both treble and bass clefs. Recorded by Brassworks 4, *Chalice Hymnal Songs of Praise,* Brassworks 4 BW 4003.

Rüedi, Thomas. *Brass Quartet No. 2.* Obrasso Musikverlag. Two cornets, horn, euphonium. CHF 38.

Rüti, Carl. *En Plein Air.* Obrasso Musikverlag. Two cornets, horn, euphonium. CHF 41. Four movements: I. Brins d'Herbe; II. La Sauterelle; III. Le Petit Nuage; IV. Jet d'Eau.

Satie, Erik. *Gymnopedie I.* Arr. R. P. Block. Philharmonia Music. Two trumpets, horn, euphonium. $12.50.

Schmutz, Albert D. *Chorale Prelude on From Heaven Above to Earth I Come.* Ludwig Music Publishing. Two trumpets, trombone, euphonium. $10.95.

Schultz, Connie, arr. *Auld Lang Syne.* Brassworks 4. Two cornets, trombone, euphonium. 2002. $11. III–IV. B♭–g'. A great arrangement of this traditional Scottish New Year's tune. High tessitura in the trombone part.

Schultz, Connie, arr. *Boogie Woogie Bugle Boy.* Brassworks 4. Two cornets, trombone, euphonium. 2002. $16. 1:51. Recorded by Brassworks 4, *Play!,* BW 4002.

Schultz, Connie, arr. *Coventry Carol/We Three Kings.* Brassworks 4. Two cornets, trombone, euphonium. 2002. $11. III–IV. D–f'. A creative arrangement pairing these two traditional carols. All parts have a chance to play the melody. The low tessitura of the euphonium part may cause difficulty for high school players. Recorded by Brassworks 4, *Christmas Palette,* Brassworks 4 BW 4001.

Schultz, Connie, arr. *Deck the Halls.* Brassworks 4. Two cornets, trombone, euphonium. 2002. $11. A cute arrangement of this classic carol in which all parts have a chance to play the melody. Included is a 6/8 blues section that features the second trumpet doubling on flugelhorn. Recorded by Brassworks 4, *Christmas Palette,* Brassworks 4 BW 4001.

Schultz, Connie, arr. *I Wonder as I Wander.* Brassworks 4. Two cornets, trombone, euphonium. 2002. $11. III. F–f'. A traditional hymn tune arrangement appropriate for various occasions. Suitable for high school players.

Schultz, Connie, arr. *Jingle Bells.* Brassworks 4. Two cornets, trombone, euphonium. 2002. $11. III. F–b. A fun and short arrangement in which the euphonium part plays the bass line.

Schultz, Connie, arr. *Sing Noel.* Brassworks 4. Two cornets, trombone, euphonium. 2002. $7. II. G–b. An easy arrangement of a traditional French carol. Includes optional parts for finger cymbal and drum. Recorded by Brassworks 4, *Christmas Palette,* Brassworks 4 BW 4001.

Schultz, Connie, arr. *Spiritual Offerings.* Brassworks 4. Two cornets, trombone, euphonium. 2002. $26. 4:30. III. D–g'. Recorded by Brassworks 4, *Play!,* Brassworks 4 BW 4002.

Scott, Steve. *Quartet for Brass.* Cimarron Music. Two trumpets, horn, euphonium. $14.

Sibelius, Jean. *Finlandia-Hymni, Op. 26.* Arr. Mark Anderson. TAP Music. Two trumpets, horn, euphonium. $5. Appropriate for younger players.

Sleeth, Natalie. *Hymn of Promise (In the Bulb There Is a Flower)*. Arr. Scott Ramsey. Brassworks 4. Two cornets, trombone, euphonium. 2002. $11. II. F–c'. This simple hymn arrangement also includes optional descant parts in treble and bass clef. Recorded by Brassworks 4, *Chalice Hymnal Songs of Praise*, Brassworks 4 BW 4003.

Sousa, John Philip. *A Sousa Collection*. Arr. Alan Fernie. Obrasso Musikverlag. Two cornets, horn, euphonium. CHF 38.

Sparke, Philip. *Divertimento*. Studio Music Company. Two cornets, E♭ horn, euphonium. 1985. IV–V. D♭–g'. Commissioned and specially published for the Swiss Solo and Quartet Contest, 1985. A fun but difficult ensemble piece that is lyrical in nature and technically demanding. Extensive rapid double tonguing passages in all parts.

Stähli, Urs, arr. *Amen*. Obrasso Musikverlag. Two cornets, horn, euphonium. CHF 30.

Stanley. *Trumpet Voluntary*. Arr. Mick Hesse. Brassworks 4. Two cornets, trombone, euphonium. 2002. $7. III. F♯–d'.

Sturzenegger, Kurt, arr. *11 Pieces*. Editions Marc Reift. Two trumpets, trombone, euphonium. 1997. €24.50. A collection of eleven short pieces: Schütz: Choral; Praetorious: Choral; Pezel: Intrada; Pezel: Sarabande; Pezel: Bal; Reiche: Intrada; Schein: Allemande; Anonymous: Air; Susato: Pavane; Morley: Three English Madrigals; Charpentier: Entrée. Suitable for younger players.

Szkutko, John. *Four Frogs and a Fly*. SZK Music. Trumpet, horn, euphonium, tuba. The frogs introduce themselves one by one, singing their own little melody. Just as the fourth frog (Grommet) is about to finish singing, a pesky little fly interrupts the party. Within a couple of bars, however, the frogs manage to resolve and finish. This is the cue for the fly's eventual downfall. Success! They got him. Being the frogs that they are, they give the fly a dignified death by singing a funeral march in memory of their dinner. Finally, the frogs ride off into the sunset, happily ever after!

Taupin, Tom. *Harlem Rag March*. Arr. Alan Fernie. Obrasso Musilverlag. Two cornets, horn, euphonium. CHF 30.

Thompson, Malachi Richard. *Chorale and Fanfare*. American Music Center. Two trumpets, euphonium, bass trombone.

Tomer, William G. *God Be with You 'Till We Meet Again*. Arr. Mick Hesse. Brassworks 4. Two cornets, trombone, euphonium. 2002. $6. II. G–g. A short and simple hymn tune arrangement. Recorded by Brassworks 4, *Chalice Hymnal Songs of Praise*, Brassworks 4 BW 4003.

Ulf, Otto, arr. *Sechs alte Tanzweisen*. Musikverlag Elisabeth Thomi-Berg. Two trumpets,

horn, euphonium. II. F–d'. Six movements: I. Allemande (Scheidt); II. Basse dance (Attaignant); III. Altdeutscher Tanz (Hausmann); IV. Galliarda (M. Franck); V. Aufzug (Staden); VI. Courante (Staden). Ideal for younger players.

Ulf, Otto, arr. *Two Canzonas from the Old Masters (16th Cent.)*. Musikverlag Elisabeth Thomi-Berg. Two trumpets, trombone, euphonium. II. B♭–d♭'. Two movements: I. La Leonora (Claudio Merulo) and II. La Feliciana (Adriano Banchieri). A good piece with which to introduce younger players to chamber music. Parts included in treble and bass clef.

Van de Vate, Nancy. *Diversion*. American Music Center. Horn, two trumpets, euphonium. 1964. 3:30.

Various. *Ludwig Brass Quartette Edition, Vol. 5*. Ludwig Music Publishing. Flexible brass quartet with euphonium. $7.95. A collection of easy quartets: Londonderry Air (Old Irish Melody); Poem (Fibich); Come Where My Love Lies Dreaming (Foster).

Various. *Ludwig Brass Quartette Edition, Vol. 4*. Ludwig Music Publishing. Flexible brass quartet with euphonium. $7.95. A collection of easy quartets: Fanfare from "La Reine de Saba" (Gounod); Original Fanfare (Mastinelli); Original Fanfare (Grossman); Two Marches (Fischer); Choral "Ach Herr, laz dein lieb' Engelein" (Bach); Turm Sonata (Pezel).

Various. *Ludwig Brass Quartette Edition, Vol. 1*. Ludwig Music Publishing. Flexible brass quartet with euphonium. $7.95. A collection of easy quartets: Song of India (Rimsky-Korsakov); Sweet and Low (Barnby); O Sole Mio (Capua); La Golondrina (Serradell).

Various. *Ludwig Brass Quartette Edition, Vol. 3*. Ludwig Music Publishing. Flexible brass quartet with euphonium. $7.95. A collection of easy quartets: Sailor's Song; Heart Wounds; To Spring.

Various. *Ludwig Brass Quartette Edition, Vol. 2*. Ludwig Music Publishing. Flexible brass quartet with euphonium. $7.95. A collection of easy quartets: Away to the Mountain Brow (Rev. L. L. Balogh); Drink to Me Only with Thine Eyes (Old English Tune); Sally in Our Alley (Carey); Cherry Ripe (Horn).

Vasconi, Eugene. *Promenade*. Southern Music Company. Two trumpets, euphonium (trombone), and tuba. $5. A good piece of traditional harmonic writing without technical challenges. Melody resembles a fugue subject. May work well for a larger ensemble with parts doubled.

Vesterinen, Vilijo. *Sakkijarven Polkka*. Arr. Scott Ramsey. Brassworks 4. Two cornets, trombone, euphonium. 2002. $16. 2:05. IV. G–b♭. A fast polka that is technically challenging for all players. Recorded by Brassworks 4, *Play!*, Brassworks 4 BW 4002.

Vinter, Gilbert. *Alla Burlesca*. Studio Music. Two cornets, tenor horn, euphonium. 1968.

Vinter, Gilbert. *Elegy and Rondo*. Studio Music. Two cornets, tenor horn, euphonium. 1966.

Voegelin, Fritz. *Divertimento*. Obrasso Musikverlag. Two cornets, horn, euphonium. CHF 46.

Von Tilzer, Albert. *Take Me Out to the Ballgame*. Arr. Paul Bara. Brassworks 4. Two cornets, trombone, euphonium. 2002. $11. III. A♭–e♭'. Recorded by Brassworks 4, *Play!*, Brassworks 4 BW 4002.

Wagner, Richard. *Bridal Chorus*. Arr. Connie Schultz. Brassworks 4. Two cornets, trombone, euphonium. 2002. $7. III. F–b. Effective arrangement of this classic wedding tune.

Warren, George G. *God of Our Fathers*. Arr. Scott Ramsey. Brassworks 4. Two cornets, trombone, euphonium. 2002. $11. II. A♭–d'. An easy arrangement of this well-known hymn. Appropriate for younger players. Recorded by Brassworks 4, *Chalice Hymnal Songs of Praise*, Brassworks 4 BW 4003.

Weber, Beat. *Promenade*. Obrasso Musikverlag. Two cornets, horn, euphonium. CHF 30.

Weber, Beat. *Slawische Impressionen*. Obrasso Musikverlag. Two cornets, horn, euphonium. CHF 30.

Weber, Beat. *Swingy*. Obrasso Musikverlag. Two cornets, horn, euphonium. CHF 30.

White, B. F. *Restless Weaver*. Arr. Scott Ramsey. Brassworks 4. Two cornets, trombone, euphonium. 2002. $11. II. F–f. An easy hymn tune arrangement. Includes descant parts in treble and bass clef. Recorded by Brassworks 4, *Chalice Hymnal Songs of Praise*, Brassworks 4 BW 4003.

Wiggins, Christopher. *Four by Four*. Kirklees Music. Two cornets, horn, euphonium. £10.50.

Wood, Christopher. *Quartet for Brass (Resignation)*. Christopher Wood. Two cornets, tenor horn, euphonium.

Woodfield, Ray, arr. *Classical Album*. Obrasso Musikverlag. Two cornets, horn, euphonium. CHF 41. A collection of arrangements appropriate for various occasions: From Symphony No. 40; From Prince Igor; From *The Nutcracker Suite*.

Woodfield, Ray, arr. *Festival Album*. Obrasso Musikverlag. Two cornets, horn, euphonium. CHF 41. A collection of arrangements appropriate for various occasions: Trumpet Voluntary; Ave Maria; Barcarolle; Czardas from *Coppélia*.

Woodfield, Ray, arr. *Hymns for All Seasons*. Obrasso Musikverlag. Two cornets, horn, euphonium. CHF 41. Collection of hymn arrangements: Angelus; Nottingham; Holy, Holy, Holy; Greensleeves; Scarborough Fair; Sweet and Low.

Woodfield, Ray, arr. *Three Swiss Tunes*. Obrasso Musikverlag. Two cornets, horn, euphonium. CHF 41. Three movements: I. Vo Luzärn uf Wäggis zue; II. L'inverno è passato; III. S'Ramseyers wei go grase.

Woodfield, Ray, arr. *Two Folksongs*. Obrasso Musikverlag. Two cornets, horn, euphonium.

CHF 38. Two movements: I. Navah Nagilah and II. Kalinka.

Woodfield, Ray, arr. *Wedding Album*. Obrasso Musikverlag. Two cornets, horn, euphonium. CHF 41. A collection of arrangements appropriate for wedding ceremonies: Wedding March; Bridal Chorus; Largo; Trumpet Tune; Amazing Grace.

Wright, Denis. *Romantica*. Weinberger. Two cornets, E♭ saxhorn, euphonium. 1961.

Youngman, R. *Dragon's Green Suite*. Mostyn Music. Two cornets, horn, euphonium. £5.95.

Zurwerra, Eduardo. *Rondo*. Obrasso Musikverlag. Two cornets, horn, euphonium. CHF 30.

Five Players

Albinoni, Tomaso. *Adagio in G Minor*. Arr. R. P. Block. Philharmonia Music. Euphonium solo and string quartet. $42.50. IV. c–a'.

Albinoni, Tomaso. *Adagio in G Minor*. Arr. R. P. Block. Philharmonia Music. Two soprano saxophones, alto saxophone, euphonium, tuba. $52.50. IV. f–b♭'.

Albinoni, Tomaso. *Adagio in G Minor*. Arr. R. P. Block. Philharmonia Music. Four euphoniums and tuba. $17.50. IV–V. B♭–e♭".

Aud, Jean, arr. *The Twelve Days of Christmas*. Philharmonia Music. Euphonium and string quartet. $37.50.

Bach, Johann Sebastian. *Jesu, Joy of Man's Desiring*. Arr. R. P. Block. Philharmonia Music. Euphonium and string quartet. $37.50.

Bach, Johann Sebastian. *March*. Arr. Scott Richards. Editions Marc Reift. Four euphoniums and piano or organ. 1997. €12.60. Parts available in both treble and bass clef.

Bach, Johann Sebastian. *Sheep May Safely Graze*. Arr. Ken Smith. MMI Music. Cornet, flugelhorn, horn, euphonium, tuba. £15.

Barcos, George. *Suite Para Quinteto*. Editions BIM. Two trumpets, horn, trombone, euphonium. $20.

Barnett, Carol. *The Mysterious Brass Band*. American Music Center. Two trumpets, horn, euphonium, tuba. 1990. 8:00.

Bassano, Giovanni. *Canzona per Sonare on C. de Rore*. Arr. R. P. Block. Philharmonia Music. Euphonium and string quartet. $52.50. Also available with two alternate instrumentations: three euphoniums and tuba; two cornets, euphonium, and tuba.

Bellon, Jean. *Quintet No. 1*. Editions BIM. Two cornets, horn, trombone, euphonium. 2000.

Bellstedt, Herman, and Donald Hunsberger. *Napoli Variations*. Arr. Maurice Bale. Godiva Music. Solo euphonium and four trombones. 2003. £5. Recorded by Steven Mead, *4 Valves 4 Slides*, Bocchino Music.

Benker, Heinz. *Dingolfinger Intraden*. Musikverlag Elisabeth Thomi-Berg. Two trumpets, horn, euphonium, timpani. II. B♭–c′. Two movements: I and II. Ideal for introducing younger players to chamber music.

Bizet, George. *Gipsy Dance from Carmen*. Arr. Maurice Bale. Godiva Music. Solo euphonium and four trombones. 2003. £5. V. B♭–e♭″. Recorded by Steven Mead, *4 Valves 4 Slides*, Bocchino Music.

Block, R. P., arr. *Villancico: Riu, riu, chiu*. Philharmonia Music. Euphonium and string quartet. $27.50.

Boedecker, P. F. *Christmas Concerto*. Arr. W. and J. Boswell. Philharmonia Music. Euphonium and string quartet. $57.50.

Bramson, Neil. *The Old Bailey–An Entertainment*. Da Capo Music Limited. Violin, two euphoniums, two tubas. £16.

Campra, André. *Rigaudon*. Arr. Scott Richards. Editions Marc Reift. Four euphoniums and piano or organ. 1997. €12.60. Parts available in treble or bass clef.

Clarke, Jeremiah. *Fanfare*. Arr. Scott Richards. Editions Marc Reift. Four euphoniums and piano or organ. 1997. €12.60. Parts available in treble or bass clef.

Clarke, Jeremiah. *The Prince of Denmark's March*. Arr. R. P. Block. Philharmonia Music. Four euphoniums and tuba. $18.50.

Clarke, Jeremiah. *Trumpet Voluntary*. Arr. Ken Smith. MMI Music. Two cornets, horn, euphonium, tuba. £15.

Debussy, Claude. *The Girl with the Flaxen Hair*. Arr. Maurice Bale. Godiva Music. Solo euphonium and four trombones. 2003. £5. Recorded by Steven Mead, *4 Valves 4 Slides*, Bocchino Music.

Elgar, Edward. *Land of Hope and Glory from Pomp and Circumstance March No. 1*. Arr. Roy Newsome. Obrasso Musikverlag. Two cornets, horn, euphonium, organ. CHF 41.

Erskine, Robin. *Canon, Op. 56, No. 5*. Scottish Music Information Centre. Two trumpets, trombone, euphonium, and tuba.

Ewald, Victor. *Quintett I in B-Flat Minor (authentic edition)*. Arr. R. P. Block. Philharmonia Music. Two cornets, horn, euphonium, and tuba. $22.50.

Fraser, Bruce, arr. *Greensleeves*. Obrasso Musikverlag. Two cornets, horn, euphonium, organ. CHF 41.

Furlong, Gregory J. *Quintet for Euphonium and Strings*. Greg Furlong. Solo euphonium, two violins, viola, cello. 2003. 27:00. V. G♭₁–b♭′. Three movements: I. Allegro Moderato; II. Adagio; III. Circus Finale. An intriguing, well-written work that is a great addition to the repertoire. The piece is technically challenging and calls for multi-phonics in the second movement. Given their length and thorough composition, single movements may be performed separately. The string parts are difficult and the piece requires careful rehearsal for ensemble cohesiveness.

Germani, Ferruccio. . . . *and so much time has passed . . . why have you come* . . . Cimarron Music. Flute, clarinet, horn, euphonium, piano. $20.

Gervaise, Claude. *Three Dances*. Arr. Roy Newsome. Obrasso Musikverlag. Two cornets, horn, euphonium, organ. CHF 41.

Gladwin, Walter, arr. *The Day of Resurrection*. TAP Music. Two trumpets, two euphoniums, tuba. $12. 2:30. An excellent prelude for Easter services, this arrangement of the familiar hymn begins in a chorale style, drifts into polyphonic fantasy, and returns modulated with a rousing descant ending.

Glinka, Mikhail. *Overture: Russlan & Ludmilla*. Arr. Ken Smith. MMI Music. Two cornets, horn, euphonium, tuba. £15.

Gow, Niel. *Four Tunes*. Arr. Robin Erskine. Scottish Music Information Centre. Two trumpets, horn, trombone, euphonium.

Guedry, Donnie. *Evening Rain*. TAP Music. Trumpet, horn, euphonium, tuba, percussion. $10.

Handel, George Frederic. *All We Like Sheep Have Gone Astray from Messiah*. Arr. David Marlatt. Eighth Note Publications. Two trumpets, horn, euphonium, and tuba. 1996. $15. III. A♭–g′. An allegro moderato from the famous oratorio.

Handel, George Frederic. *Comfort Ye My People and Every Valley Shall Be Exalted from Messiah*. Arr. David Marlatt. Eighth Note Publications. Solo euphonium, piccolo trumpet, E♭ trumpet, horn, tuba. 1996. $15. III. e–a′. A beautiful melodic solo that features the instrument's rich sound. Good recital material.

Handel, George Frederic. *Halleluja*. Arr. Jean-François Michel. Editions Marc Reift. Four euphoniums and piano. 1991. €21. Part of a collection of four popular classics: Halleluja (Handel); Rondeau (Mouret); Overture from Water Music (Handel); Hochzeitsmarsch (Haydn).

Handel, George Frederic. *He Shall Feed His Flock from Messiah*. Arr. David Marlatt. Eighth Note Publications. Two trumpets, horn, euphonium, and tuba. 1996. $15. III. c–g′. A slow, lyrical movement in 12/8 from the famous oratorio.

Handel, George Frederic. *His Yoke Is Easy from Messiah*. Arr. David Marlatt. Eighth Note Publications. Two trumpets, horn, euphonium, and tuba. 1996. $15. III. B♭–f′. A brief allegro from the famous oratorio.

Handel, George Frederic. *Overture from Water Music*. Arr. Jean-François Michel. Editions Marc Reift. Four euphoniums and piano. 1991. €21. Part of a collection of four popular classics: Halleluja (Handel); Rondeau (Mouret); Overture from Water Music (Handel); Hochzeitsmarsch (Haydn).

Handel, George Frederic. *Pifa from Messiah*. Arr. David Marlatt. Eighth Note Publications. Two trumpets, horn, euphonium, and tuba. 1996.

$15. III. e–e♭'. A slow, lyrical movement from the famous oratorio.

Handel, George Frederic. *Rejoice Greatly, O Daughter of Zion from Messiah*. Arr. David Marlatt. Eighth Note Publications. Two trumpets, horn, euphonium, and tuba. 1996. $15. III. e♭–f'. A good arrangement suitable for high school players. The trumpet parts have most of the technical challenges.

Handel, George Frederic. *Sinfony from Messiah*. Arr. David Marlatt. Eighth Note Publications. Piccolo trumpet, trumpet, horn, euphonium, and tuba. 1996. $15. III. A–g'. Good arrangement of this overture from the famous oratorio. Appropriate for high school players.

Handel, George Frederic. *The Trumpet Shall Sound from Messiah*. Arr. David Marlatt. Eighth Note Publications. Two trumpets, horn, euphonium, and tuba. 1996. $15. III. F–d'. While the tuba is featured, euphonium would work equally well as the solo voice. The written euphonium part plays the bass line.

Handel, George Frederic. *Worthy Is the Lamb That Was Slain*. Arr. David Marlatt. Eighth Note Publications. Two trumpets, horn, euphonium, and tuba. 1996. $15. III. F–g'. Effective arrangement of the finale of *Messiah*. Fun to play. Appropriate for high school ensembles.

Haydn, Franz Joseph. *Hochzeitzmarsch*. Arr. Jean-François Michel. Editions Marc Reift. Four euphoniums and piano. 1991. €21. Part of a collection of four popular classics: Halleluja (Handel); Rondeau (Mouret); Overture from Water Music (Handel); Hochzeitsmarsch (Haydn).

Ito, Yasuhide. *A la Suite Classique for Five Players*. Ito Music. Four euphoniums and accordion. 1995. IV–V. Seven movements: I. Prélude; II. Allemande en forme de Tango; III. Sarabande en forme de Chaconne; IV. Interlude l'imitation de Mr. Couperin; V. Gavotte en forme de Habanera; VI. Menuet en forme de Musette; VII. Gigue en forme de Zapateado. An intriguing work that prominently features the accordion in addition to the euphonium. The first three movements are scored for two E♭ baritones, two euphoniums, and accordion. The fourth and fifth movements are scored for four euphoniums and accordion. The sixth movement is an accordion solo and the last movement is scored as the first three.

Ito, Yasuhide. *Four Euphoniums for You*. Ito Music. Four euphoniums and harpsichord or piano. 2005.

Jørgensen, Axel Borup. *Quintet for Brass Instruments*. Hansen. Cornet, trumpet, horn, euphonium, tuba. 1976.

Koetsier, Jan. *Skurrile Elegie auf Richard W. Op. 86/2*. Donemus Amsterdam. Euphonium and string quartet. 1981. 8:00. V. D–e♭". For Herman Jeurissen. A challenging lyrical work for advanced players. High tessitura in the euphonium part. Requires flutter tonguing and

presents some technical challenges. Features an extended solo cadenza with *ossia* parts for advanced players.

Levy, Jules. *Grand Russian Fantasia*. Arr. Maurice Bale. Godiva Music. Solo euphonium and four trombones. 2003. £5. IV–V. G–b♭'. Recorded by Steven Mead, *4 Valves 4 Slides*, Bocchino Music.

Mantia, Simone. *Believe Me if All Those Endearing Young Charms*. Arr. Henry Howey. Cimarron Music. Solo euphonium, two trumpets, horn, trombone. $17.

Meechan, Pete. *Funk Theory*. Prima Vista Musikk. Solo euphonium and trombone quartet. 2003. 4:30. IV–V. A₁–d". Commissioned by and dedicated to David Childs. A fun but difficult solo written in a funk style. Technically challenging with syncopated rhythmic figures and extreme range requirements. Also available from the composer with CD accompaniment.

Mendelssohn, Felix. *Wedding March*. Arr. Scott Richards. Editions Marc Reift. Four euphoniums and piano or organ. 1997. €14. Parts available in both treble and bass clefs.

Michel, Jean-François, arr. *32 Christmas Carols*. Editions Marc Reift. Two trumpets, trombone, euphonium, tuba. 1993. €27.30. A collection of carols suitable for younger players. Includes Good King Wenceslas; Alle Jahre wieder; Les Angesdans nos campagnes; Lasst uns froh und munter sein; In Dulci Jubilo; We Wish You a Merry Christmas; Süsser die Glocken nie klingen; March of the Three Kings; O Little Town of Bethlehem; Silent Night; The First Noel; Deck the Halls; Jingle Bells; Still, Still, Still; We Three Kings; O Tannenbaum; Adeste Fideles; Kommet, Ihr Hirten; While Shepherds Watched; O du Fröhliche; God Rest You; The Holly and the Ivy; O Holy Night; Hark, the Herald Angels; Joy to the World; Ihr Kinderlein kommet; Kling, Glöcklein, kling; Am Weihnachtsbaum; Es ist ein Ros entsprungen; Il est né le divin enfant; Vom Himmel hoch; Leise rieselt der Schnee.

Mortimer, John Glenesk, arr. *Christmas Carols*. Editions Marc Reift. Four euphoniums and piano. 1996. €21.

Mouret, Jean-Joseph. *Rondeau*. Arr. Jean-François Michel. Editions Marc Reift. Four euphoniums and piano. 1991. €21. Part of a collection of four popular classics: Halleluja (Handel); Rondeau (Mouret); Overture from Water Music (Handel); Hochzeitsmarsch (Haydn).

Mozart, Wolfgang Amadeus. *Allegro from Bassoon Concerto in B-Flat, K. 191*. Arr. Bill Bjornes, Jr. Eighth Note Publications. Solo euphonium, two trumpets, horn, tuba. 2004. $15. IV. C–b♭'. A refreshing arrangement of the first movement from this classic concerto. The solo part is technically challenging and requires a careful stylistic interpretation. Requires strong ensemble players. A good college-level recital piece.

Mozart, Wolfgang Amadeus. *Don Giovanni*. Arr. Ken Smith. MMI Music. Two cornets, horn, euphonium, tuba. £15.

Mutter, Gerbert. *Two Miniatures*. Musikverlag Elisabeth Thomi-Berg. Two trumpets, two horns, euphonium. I–II. G–b♭. Two movements: I. Spielerisch-beschwingt and II. Mit schlichter Sanglichkeit. Ideal for younger players.

Nerijnen, J. V. *3 Inventionen*. Molenaar Editions BV. Three trumpets, horn, euphonium.

Newsome, Roy, arr. *Pastime with Good Company*. Obrasso Musikverlag. Two cornets, horn, euphonium, organ. CHF 41.

Pachelbel, Johann. *Canon*. Arr. R. P. Block. Philharmonia Music. Euphonium, vibraphone, guitar, bass, drums. $52.50.

Presser, William. *Folk Song Fantasy*. Composers Press. Two trumpets, trombone, euphonium, tuba. 5:00.

Puccini, Giacomo. *Nessun Dorma*. Arr. Maurice Bale. Godiva Music. Solo euphonium and four trombones. 2003. £5. Recorded by Steven Mead, *4 Valves 4 Slides,* Bocchino Music.

Puccini, Giacomo. *Recondita Armonia from Tosca*. Arr. Maurice Bale. Godiva Music. Solo euphonium and four trombones. 2003. £5. Recorded by Steven Mead, *4 Valves 4 Slides,* Bocchino Music.

Rimsky-Korsakov, Nicolai. *Flight of the Bumblebee*. Arr. R. P. Block. Philharmonia Music. Four euphoniums and tuba. $19.50.

Rimsky-Korsakov, Nicolai. *The Flight of the Bumble Bee*. Arr. Maurice Bale. Godiva Music. Solo euphonium and four trombones. 2003. £6. Recorded by Steven Mead, *4 Valves 4 Slides,* Bocchino Music.

Satie, Erik. *Gymnopedie I*. Arr. R. P. Block. Philharmonia Music. Euphonium, vibraphone, guitar, bass, drum set. $39.50.

Senaille, Jean-Baptiste. *Allegro Spiritoso from Sonata No. 5*. Arr. Bill Bjornes, Jr. Eighth Note Publications. Solo euphonium, two flugelhorns, horn, tuba. 2004. $15. IV. G–a'. A great arrangement of this traditional baroque piece that works well in recital.

Sousa, John Philip. *The Gladiator*. Arr. R. P. Block. Philharmonia Music. Four euphoniums and tuba. $17.50.

Sousa, John Philip. *Manhattan Beach*. Arr. R. P. Block. Philharmonia Music. Four euphoniums and tuba. $18.50.

Sousa, John Philip. *The Stars and Stripes Forever.* Arr. R. P. Block. Philharmonia Music. Four euphoniums and tuba. $18.50.

Sousa, John Philip. *The Washington Post*. Arr. R. P. Block. Philharmonia Music. Euphonium and string quartet. $32.50.

Stockhausen, Karlheinz. *Zungenspitzentanz (Tip-of-the-Tongue-Dance)*. Stockhausen Verlag. Piccolo, dancer, two euphoniums, percussionist. 1983. 9:00. V. Difficult contemporary work.

The following sound equipment is needed for performance: one transmitter, five microphones, two loudspeakers, mixing console, and sound projector.

Sturzenegger, Kurt, arr. *11 Pieces*. Editions Marc Reift. Four euphoniums and piano. 1997. €24.50. A collection of eleven short pieces: Schütz: Choral; Praetorious: Choral; Pezel: Intrada; Pezel: Sarabande; Pezel: Bal; Reiche: Intrada; Schein: Allemande; Anonymous: Air; Susato: Pavane; Morley: Three English Madrigals; Charpentier: Entrée. Suitable for younger players.

Tchaikovsky, Peter Ilyich. *March from 6th Symphony*. Arr. Ken Smith. MMI Music. Two cornets, horn, euphonium, tuba. £15.

Tye, Christopher. *In Nomine*. Arr. R. P. Block. Philharmonia Music. Four euphoniums and tuba. $17.50.

Verdi, Giuseppi. *Quartet from "Rigoletto."* Arr. Akihiko Ito. Akihiko Ito. Four euphoniums and piano. ¥1,600 (.pdf version, ¥1,100).

Wagner, Richard. *Prelude to "The Mastersingers of Nuremberg."* Arr. Ken Smith. MMI Music. Two cornets, horn, euphonium, tuba. £15.

Wagner, Richard. *Wedding March from Act III of "Lohengrin."* Arr. John Glenesk Mortimer. Editions Marc Reift. Four euphoniums and piano or organ. 1996. €14.

Warlock, Peter. *Pieds-en-L'air from Capriol Suite*. Arr. David Marlatt. Eighth Note Publications. Trumpet, flugelhorn, horn, euphonium, tuba. 2001. $15. III. B♭–e♭'. A beautiful slow, lyrical tune in 9/8 meter. Appropriate for high school ensembles.

Six Players

Angell, Michael. *Concertino for Euphonium and Winds*. Tuba-Euphonium Press. Euphonium solo, two flutes, oboe, two clarinets. 1991. $20. IV–V. G₁–g♯'. Three movements: I. Allegro Moderato; II. Muezzin; III. Fugue and Funeral. A challenging work for a unique ensemble. Extensive use of mixed meter in the first and third movements as the meter seems to change virtually every measure. Utilizes half-valve technique and the removal of the main tuning slide as an effect. Requires a strong low range. Careful rehearsal needed to achieve ensemble cohesiveness.

Bach, Johann Sebastian. *Air from Suite in D*. Arr. Ray Woodfield. Obrasso Musikverlag. Two trumpets, horn, trombone, euphonium, tuba. CHF 46.

Bach, Johann Sebastian. *Canzona, BWV 588*. Arr. Gary Bricault. Solid Brass Music. Two trumpets, horn, trombone, baritone, euphonium. $15.

Bach, Johann Sebastian. *Jauchzet Gott in allen Landen from Cantata #51*. Arr. David Marlatt. Eighth Note Publications. Two E♭ trumpets, horn, euphonium, and tuba. 1996.

Baldwin, David. *Concerto for Al's Breakfast*. David Baldwin. Solo euphonium and brass quintet. Three movements: I. Coffee, Tea, or Banana?; II. The Special; III. Eat Your Load and Hit the Road. Written for Dr. Mary Ann Craig. Al's Breakfast is a small diner in Minneapolis that is open from 6 A.M. to 1 P.M. daily and serves only eggs and pancakes. The work is intended to be light, yet virtuosic in nature. The first movement is in sonata form, the second is a passacaglia, and the last a theme and variations.

Bashmakov, Leonid. *Flibarium*. Finnish Music Information Centre. Euphonium, flute, English horn, clarinet, piano, and percussion.

Beethoven, Ludwig van. *March from Fidelio*. Arr. G. E. Holmes. C. L. Barnhouse. Two trumpets, horn, trombone, euphonium, tuba. $12.50.

Bizet, George. *March from Carmen*. Arr. Michael Stewart. Solid Brass Music. Two trumpets, horn, trombone, euphonium, and tuba.

Bloch, Ernest. *Chanty*. G. Schirmer. Two trumpets, horn, trombone, euphonium, tuba. $25.

Böhm, Oscar. *Largo from Trumpet Concerto*. Arr. Mick Hesse. Brassworks 4. Solo euphonium and brass quintet. 2004.

Böhm, Oscar. *Sextet, Op. 30*. Arr. Robert King. Robert King Music Sales, Inc. Two trumpets, horn, trombone, euphonium, tuba. $53.95.

Chase, A. *Sextet*. Cor Publishing Company. Two trumpets, horn, trombone, euphonium, tuba. $7.

Clarke, Jeremiah. *Trumpet Voluntary*. Arr. Ray Woodfield. Obrasso Musikverlag. Two trumpets, horn, trombone, euphonium, tuba. CHF 46.

Cummings, Barton. *Three Sketches from Antioch*. Solid Brass Music. Two trumpets, Two horns, euphonium, tuba.

Debussy, Claude. *The Girl with the Flaxen Hair*. Arr. Ray Woodfield. Obrasso Musikverlag. Two trumpets, horn, trombone, euphonium, tuba. CHF 46.

De Filippi, A. *Two Hymn-Tune Preludes*. Robert King Music Sales, Inc. Two trumpets, horn, trombone, euphonium, tuba. $7.65.

Dvořák, Antonin. *Finale from Serenade in D Minor, Op. 44*. Arr. Paul Luhring. PEL Music Publications. Two trumpets, horn, trombone, euphonium, and tuba. 1993. $12.50. F–g'. A fun arrangement suitable for high school players.

Everson, Dana, arr. *Old Time Religion*. Solid Brass Music. Two trumpets, horn, trombone, euphonium, tuba.

Fauré, Gabriel. *Berceuse*. Arr. Prater. Solid Brass Music. Horn, three euphoniums, bass trombone, tuba.

Friedrich, Kenneth D. *Petite Suite for Six*. Kenneth D. Friedrich. Two trumpets, horn, trombone, euphonium, tuba.

Friedrich, Kenneth D. *Suite No. 2 for Sextet*. Kenneth D. Friedrich. Two trumpets, horn,

trombone, euphonium, tuba. 2005. $18.50. 9:20. III. F–f'. Three movements: I. Fanfare; II. Lento; III. Allegro. A rhythmically based work suitable for good high school players.

Gershwin, George. *Love Walked In*. Arr. Ray Woodfield. Obrasso Musikverlag. Two trumpets, horn, trombone, euphonium, tuba. CHF 46.

George, Thom Ritter. *Sextet*. Tuba-Euphonium Press. Euphonium, flute, oboe, clarinet, horn, and bassoon. 1993. $30. IV. E–ab'. Three movements: Allegretto alla Marcia; Pastorale: Lento e mesto; Theme and Variations on an Old English Song. An important, though little-known, part of the repertoire that was originally composed in 1981. The euphonium is featured in places but is treated more as part of the ensemble. Challenging for all players and fun to play. The second movement calls for a mute. Recorded by Steven Mead, *Classic Quintet*, volume 1.

Gossec, J. F. *Tambourin*. Arr. Ray Woodfield. Obrasso Musikverlag. Two trumpets, horn, trombone, euphonium, tuba. CHF 46.

Grieg, Edvard. *Spring*. Arr. Ray Woodfield. Obrasso Musikverlag. Two trumpets, horn, trombone, euphonium, tuba. CHF 46.

Hall, Percy, arr. *Two Civil War Songs*. Ludwig Music Publishing. Two trumpets, horn, trombone, euphonium, tuba. 1997. $12. II. G–d'. Two movements: Aura Lee and Dixie. A fun arrangement appropriate for younger players. Not technically difficult.

Handel, George Frederic. *Classic March*. Arr. F. Erickson. Belwin-Mills. Two trumpets, horn, trombone, euphonium, tuba. $7.50.

Hartley, Walter S. *Sextet*. Tuba-Euphonium Press. Euphonium solo and woodwind quintet. 1994. $24. IV. A₁–bb'. Five movements: I. Allegro moderato; II. Allegretto Grazioso; III. Presto; IV. Lento; V. Vivace. An outstanding work for an effective combination of instruments. Each member of the ensemble plays an important role. Extensive double tonguing in the third movement. Fifth movement written in a fast 5/8. Winner of the 1993 TUBA Composition Contest for Euphonium in Mixed Ensemble.

Hartzell, Doug. *Strange One*. Cimarron Music. Two trumpets, horn, trombone, euphonium, tuba. $15.

Haubiel, C. *Ballade*. Opus Music Publishers. Two trumpets, horn, trombone, euphonium, tuba. $3.50.

Haydn, Franz Joseph. *Capriccio*. Arr. R. E. Foster. Belwin-Mills. Two trumpets, horn, trombone, euphonium, tuba. $4.95.

Haydn, Franz Joseph. *Divertimento*. Arr. Ian Lamb. MMI Music. Two cornets, horn, baritone, euphonium, tuba. £15. Movements I, II, and IV of this classical favorite.

Haydn, Franz Joseph. *Minuetto-Trio (Op. 70, No. 1)*. Arr. Ian Lamb. MMI Music. Two cornets, horn, baritone, euphonium, tuba. £15.

Hilfiger, John. *Prelude on O God, Our Help*. Wehr House Music. Two trumpets, horn, trombone, euphonium, tuba. $6.50.

Hounsell, Clare, arr. *When Johnny Comes Marching Home*. PEL Music Publications. Two trumpets, horn, trombone, euphonium, tuba. 1993. $8.95. I–II. A–g. An easy arrangement appropriate for younger players. A good teaching tool suitable for concert performance.

Howe, M. C., ed. *Three Madrigals*. Theodore Presser Company. Two trumpets, horn, trombone, euphonium, tuba. $2.50.

Hughes, John. *Guide Me, O Thou Great Jehovah*. Solid Brass Music. Two trumpets, horn, trombone, euphonium, tuba.

Ippolitov-Ivanov, Mikhail. *Alleluia*. Arr. F. Erickson. Belwin-Mills. Two trumpets, horn, trombone, euphonium, tuba. $6.95.

Joplin, Scott. *The Entertainer*. Arr. Ray Woodfield. Obrasso Musikverlag. Two trumpets, horn, trombone, euphonium, tuba. CHF 46.

Joplin, Scott. *The Sycamore Rag*. Arr. Ray Woodfield. Obrasso Musikverlag. Two trumpets, horn, trombone, euphonium, tuba. CHF 46.

Jurrens, J. *Moderne*. Southern Music Company. Two trumpets, horn, trombone, euphonium, tuba. $7.

Kabalevsky, Dmitri . *Sonatina*. Arr. C. P. Barnes. Ludwig Music Publishing. Two trumpets, horn, trombone, euphonium, tuba. $13.95.

Kazdin, A., arr. *The Twelve Days of Christmas*. Robert King Music Sales, Inc. Two trumpets, horn, trombone, euphonium, tuba. $6.65.

Kroeger, K. *Canzona #2*. Theodore Presser. Two trumpets, horn, trombone, euphonium, tuba. $14.95.

Lamb, Ian. *Scherzo for Brass Sextet*. MMI Music. Two cornets, horn, baritone, euphonium, tuba. £15.

Lennon, John, and Paul McCartney. *Eleanor Rigby*. Arr. Richard Sesco. TAP Music. Two trumpets, flugelhorn, trombone, euphonium, tuba. $12.

Leybourne, George. *Artiste Aerienne (The Man on the Flying Trapeze)*. Arr. Clare Hounsell. PEL Music Publications. Two trumpets, horn, trombone, euphonium, and tuba. 1995. $9.50. II. Bb–d'. A simple arrangement suitable for younger players. Not technically difficult.

Massenet, Jules. *Meditation from Thais*. Arr. Robert Collison. Mostyn Music. Two trumpets, horn, trombone, euphonium, tuba. £11.50.

Mehul, E. N. *Joseph in Egypt*. Carl Fischer. Two trumpets, horn, trombone, euphonium, tuba. $7.50.

Mendelssohn, Felix. *Prelude and Fugue*. Arr. C. P. Barnes. Ludwig Music Publishing. Two trumpets, horn, trombone, euphonium, tuba. $13.95.

Meyerbeer, Giacomo. *Coronation March*. Arr. Clare Hounsell. PEL Music Publications. Two trumpets, horn, trombone, euphonium, tuba. 1981. $8.95. III. Ab–db'. A march in the classical style suitable for high school players.

Milford, Gene, arr. *Two Western Songs*. Ludwig Music Publishing. Two trumpets, horn, trombone, euphonium, tuba. $9. Two movements: I. Red River Valley and II. She'll Be Comin' Around the Mountain. Appropriate for middle school students.

Miserendino, Joe. *Canzona della notte scura (Songs of the Dark Night)*. Joe Miserendino. Solo euphonium, two violins, viola, cello, bass. 2003. $10. III. A–bb'. A beautiful, haunting melody scored for a sonorous combination of instruments. Also available with piano accompaniment.

Miserendino, Joe. *Canzona della notte scura (Songs of the Dark Night)*. Solid Brass Music. Cornet, flugelhorn, tenor horn, baritone, euphonium, tuba. 2003. $16. III. A–bb'. A beautiful haunting melody with little technical difficulty. The euphonium begins and ends this piece as the prominent solo voice and functions as an accompaniment voice throughout.

Miserendino, Joe. *Keystone Kapers*. Solid Brass Music. Cornet, flugelhorn, tenor horn, baritone, euphonium, tuba. $18.

Miserendino, Joe. *Music of the Seasons: Autumn Moods*. Joe Miserendino. Solo euphonium, two violins, viola, cello, bass. 2003. $10. IV. F#–d". For Charley Brighton. A fun piece depicting the moods of autumn. Moderate technical difficulty. Can be performed alone or as part of the *Music of the Seasons* suite. Also available with piano accompaniment.

Miserendino, Joe. *Music of the Seasons: Summer Celebration*. Joe Miserendino. Solo euphonium, two violins, viola, cello, bass. 2003. $15. IV. G–c". For Charley Brighton. A fun, jaunty dance in 6/8 meter. Challenging and fun for the whole ensemble. May be performed alone or as part of the *Music of the Seasons* suite. Also available with piano accompaniment.

Miserendino, Joe. *Music of the Seasons: Winter Songs and Spring Dances*. Joe Miserendino. Solo euphonium, two violins, viola, cello, bass. 2002. $10. IV. Db–c". For Charley Brighton. A fun original work inspired by Vivaldi. The piece is in two sections, the first being a lyrical 6/8 and the second a fast, technically challenging vivace. May be performed alone or as part of the *Music of the Seasons* suite. Solo part includes some tenor clef. Also available with piano accompaniment.

Miserendino, Joe. *The Revelers*. Solid Brass Music. Cornet, flugelhorn, tenor horn, baritone, euphonium, tuba. $18.

Miserendino, Joe. *Strollin'*. Solid Brass Music. Cornet, flugelhorn, tenor horn, baritone, euphonium, tuba. $22.

Miserendino, Joe. *Summer Celebration*. Solid Brass Music. Two trumpets, flugelhorn, horn, euphonium, tuba. 2003. $16.

Moszkowski, M. *Spanish Dance*. Arr. G. E. Holmes. Rubank, Inc. Two trumpets, horn, trombone, euphonium, tuba. $5.

Mozart, Wolfgang Amadeus. *Concerto in E-Flat Major (K. 417)*. Arr. Robert Madeson. Solid Brass Music. Two trumpets, horn, trombone, euphonium, tuba.

Mozart, Wolfgang Amadeus. *Divertimento No. 5*. Arr. C. W. Johnson. Rubank, Inc. Two trumpets, horn, trombone, euphonium, tuba. $5.95.

Mozart, Wolfgang Amadeus. *Divertimento No. 5, K. 187*. Solid Brass Music. Two trumpets, horn, trombone, euphonium, tuba.

Mutter, Gerbert. *Sarabande for Six Brass Instruments*. Musikverlag Elisabeth Thomi-Berg. Three trumpets, trombone, euphonium, tuba. II. B♭–d′. A great piece with which to introduce younger players to chamber music. Parts included in treble and bass clef.

Osmon, L. *Prelude*. Southern Music Company. Two trumpets, horn, trombone, euphonium, tuba. $6.50.

Ostransky, L. *Passacaglia and Scherzo*. Rubank, Inc. Two trumpets, horn, trombone, euphonium, tuba. $6.50.

Pachelbel, Johann. *Canon*. Arr. R. P. Block. Philharmonia Music. Two trumpets, horn, trombone, euphonium, tuba. $22.50.

Palestrina, Giovanni. *Exaltabo Te, Domine*. Arr. A. Wise. Western International Music. Two trumpets, horn, trombone, euphonium, tuba. $12.

Parker, H. *Deep Harmony*. Arr. Ray Woodfield. Obrasso Musikverlag. Two trumpets, horn, trombone, euphonium, tuba. CHF 46.

Pergolesi, Giovanni Battista. *Two Further Movements from "Stabat Mater."* Arr. Ian Lamb. MMI Music. Two cornets, horn, baritone, euphonium, tuba. £15.

Pergolesi, Giovanni Battista. *Two Movements from "Stabat Mater."* Arr. Ian Lamb. MMI Music. Two cornets, horn, baritone, euphonium, tuba. £15.

Purcell, Henry. *March and Fanfare*. Arr. Clifford P. Barnes. Ludwig Music Publishing. Two trumpets, horn, trombone, euphonium, tuba. $13.95.

Purcell, Henry. *Trumpet Tune & Air*. Arr. L. F. Brown. Rubank, Inc. Two trumpets, horn, trombone, euphonium, tuba. $5.95.

Rimsky-Korsakov, Nicolai. *Dance of the Tumblers*. Brelmat Music. Two trumpets, horn, trombone, euphonium, tuba. $12.50.

Saruya, Toshiro. *Dawn Pink*. Toshiro Saruya. Violin, viola, flute, oboe, horn, euphonium, and video accompaniment. 2000.

Scheidt, S. *Canzon Cornetto*. Arr. Ray Woodfield. Obrasso Musikverlag. Two trumpets, horn, trombone, euphonium, tuba. CHF 46.

Schubert, Franz. *Military March*. Arr. R. E. Foster. Belwin-Mills. Two trumpets, horn, trombone, euphonium, tuba. $6.50.

Schubert, Franz. *2nd Movement from String Quartet (D804)*. Arr. Ian Lamb. MMI Music. Two cornets, horn, baritone, euphonium, tuba. £15.

Short, M. *Jazz Preludes*. Boosey & Hawkes. Two trumpets, two trombones, horn, euphonium. £9.99.

Siekmann, F. H. *Discourse*. Seesaw Music Corp. Two trumpets, horn, trombone, euphonium, tuba. $27.50.

Smart. *Lead On O King Eternal*. Arr. Dana Everson. Solid Brass Music. Two trumpets, horn, trombone, euphonium, tuba.

Solomon, E. S. *Trumpets of Castile*. Southern Music Co. Two trumpets, horn, trombone, euphonium, tuba. $15.

Steinohrt, W. *Procession and Festival*. MS Publications. Two trumpets, horn, trombone, euphonium, tuba. $7.

Tchaikovsky, Peter Ilyich. *Finale from Violin Concerto*. Arr. Henry Howey. Solid Brass Music. Euphonium solo with brass quintet accompaniment. $28.

Uber, David. *Bugle Call Parade*. Solid Brass Music. Two trumpets, horn, trombone, euphonium, tuba.

Uber, David. *Pantomime*. Encore Music Publishers. Two trumpets, horn, trombone, euphonium, tuba. $24.75.

Various. *Brass Recital for Brass Sextet*. Rubank, Inc. Two trumpets, horn, trombone, euphonium, tuba. $37.60. A collection of arrangements by various composers suitable for a recital: A Day of Joy Op. 63, No. 5; Andante and Allegro (Mozart, K. 188); Canciones Mexicanas; Canzone No. 4; Cordoba Op.232 No. 4 (Albeniz); Ecce Sacerdos; Intrada No. 7; Passamezzo Brillante; Processional for Brass; Retrospection; Scherzino; The Earle of Oxford's Marche (Byrd); Two Dialogues.

Various. *Concert Repertoire for Brass Sextet*. Rubank, Inc. Two trumpets, horn, trombone, euphonium, tuba. $37.60. A collection of arrangements by various composers suitable for a recital: Allerseelen (Strauss); Ballade (Shelukov); Chanson Triste; Chorale; Christmas Serenade (C. W. Johnson); Jubilee (C. W. Johnson); Marche Vaillant (Koepke); Moon Meadows (Koepke); Night Watch #2 (Brahms); Overture for Brass (F. L. Frank); Panis Angelicus (O Lord Most Holy); Pizza-Party (H. L. Walters); Prelude & Caprice (F. D. Cofield); Secrecy (Wolf); Spanish Dance; Triumphal March; Trumpet Voluntary.

Vaughan Williams, Ralph. *Turtle Dove*. Arr. Michael Stewart. Cimarron Music. Two trumpets, horn, trombone, euphonium, tuba. $16.

Verdi, Giuseppe. *Grand March from Aida*. Arr. L. B. Smith. Belwin-Mills. Two trumpets, horn, trombone, euphonium, tuba. $6.95.

Webster, Gerald, arr. *Christmas for Six*. Hoyt Editions. Two trumpets, horn, trombone, euphonium, tuba. $28. A set of traditional Christmas carols that work well on their own or as sing-alongs.

Weiner, L. *Second Suite*. Southern Music Company. Two trumpets, horn, trombone, euphonium, tuba. $10.

Woodson, Thomas C "Bear." *In Memoriam for the Fallen Victims of the September 11, 2001, Attack.* Bear Woodson Music. Solo euphonium, two violins, viola, cello, bass. 2001. 6:53. IV–V. G–d♭″. Dedicated to Dr. Karen McGale Fiehler. A difficult six-voice double fugue in a contemporary harmonic language. Some treble clef in the solo part.

Woodson, Thomas C "Bear." *Our Horn Shall Be Exalted (Psalm 89:17)*. Bear Woodson Music. Solo euphonium, two violins, viola, cello, bass. 2001. 7:13. IV–V. A–c″. Dedicated to Dr. Karen McGale Fiehler. An interesting contemporary work consisting of a complex harmonic structure and difficult rhythmic figures. This slow contrapuntal piece begins with a stretto fugato, is interrupted by a short solo cadenza, and ends with an inversion of the opening canon theme. Some treble clef in the solo part.

Seven Players

Anderson, Mark. *Oh, Mary, Don't You Weep*. TAP Music. Two trumpets, two horns, trombone, euphonium, tuba. $3. Simple arrangement with room for improvisation.

Bowder, Jerry, arr. *Three Folk Songs for Brass Ensemble*. Accura Music. Two trumpets, two horns, trombone, euphonium, and tuba. $21.50.

Buonamente, G. *Sonata*. Arr. Robert King. Robert King Music Sales, Inc. Two trumpets, two horns, trombone, euphonium, tuba. $11.85.

Chesnokov, Pavel. *Salvation Is Created*. Joseph Wood Music Co. Two trumpets, two horns, trombone, euphonium, tuba. $7.50.

Corwell, Neal. *Black Moon Rising*. Nicolai Music. Solo euphonium, flute, oboe, clarinet in A, bassoon, string bass, timpani. 1997. $35. 7:00. IV. F–b′. Commissioned by the Deep Creek Symphony. A programmatic contemporary work that makes a welcome recital addition. The piece is meant to depict a reaction to witnessing a black moon rising. The moon is rising on a dark, cloudy, nearly starless night, and it appears to be backlit with the resulting halo lighting up swirling dark clouds. The soloist presents the primary thematic material and the winds develop related material. The string bass functions as the ensemble foundation while the timpani adds color and dramatic effect. Moderate technical and range demands. Mute required. Also available for euphonium and CD accompaniment and euphonium and piano. Recorded by Neal Corwell, *Heart of a Wolf,* Nicolai Music. See listings under Music for Euphonium and Electronic Media and Euphonium and Keyboard.

Corwell, Neal. *Denali*. Tuba-Euphonium Press. Euphonium, tuba, string quartet, and piano.

1998. $35. 12:00. IV. A♭₁–e″. Commissioned by the Garrett Lakes Arts Festival, Erick Friedman, music director. Inspired by Mt. McKinley, this work is a programmatic depiction of the awestruck experience of contemplating such a magnificent mountain. Difficult due to technical demands, extreme range, and ensemble considerations. A free ad-lib section in the middle of the piece calls for careful timing and rehearsal, particularly in the string parts. There are two muted section near the end of the work.

Cottrell, Jeff, arr. *Depart, Depart*. Cimarron Music. Two trumpets, two horns, trombone, euphonium, tuba. $18.

Elgar, Edward. *From "Pomp and Circumstance" for Brass Ensemble*. Arr. Yasuhide Ito. Ito Music. Three cornets, horn, trombone, euphonium, percussion. 2001.

Kimmell, Jack Normain. *Suite of Short Pieces for Brass Septet*. Manduca Music. Three trumpets, two trombones, euphonium, tuba. $20. 11:30. Thirteen well-written contemporary vignettes. A satisfying workout for the players and readily accessible good listening for the audience.

Lamb, Joseph. *Reindeer Rag*. Arr. John Beyrent. Brassworks 4. Two trumpets, horn, trombone, euphonium, tuba, and drum set. 2003. $20. III. F–f′. A fun holiday ragtime. Moderate technical difficulty. Extensive syncopation.

Mantia, Simone. *Believe Me if All Those Endearing Young Charms*. Arr. Henry Howey. Solid Brass Music. Euphonium solo and brass sextet.

Serraioco, Steven G. *Concertino for Euphonium and Chamber Ensemble*. Tuba-Euphonium Press. Solo euphonium, clarinet, bassoon, violin, viola, cello, piano. 1996. IV. B♭₁–b′. Three movements: Toccata; Tema can Variazione; Scherzo. A unique work with rhythmic intensity. The opening movement features mixed meter and chromatic writing. The second movement is an extended theme and variations on several dances (gavotte–theme; valse–variation I; gigue–variation II; aria–variation III), which ends with a lively molto piu vivo section. The final movement requires a mute and is technically challenging with numerous accidentals and rapid runs.

Stimpson, Des. *Starlight Carol (A New Original Christmas Piece)*. MMI Music. Three cornets, flugelhorn, horn, euphonium, tuba. £15.

Theobald, Jim. *Concerto for Euphonium, Strings, and Percussion*. Solo euphonium, two violins, viola, cello, bass, and percussion. 2003.

Eight Players

Adler, S. *Praeludium*. Robert King Music Sales, Inc. Two trumpets, two horns, two trombones, euphonium, tuba. $23.35.

Armitage, Denis. *Let's All Take It Easy-Going Home-Complaining Blues-Sweet and Mellow-Happy Go*

Lucky Rag. Editions Marc Reift. Four euphoniums with optional piano, guitar, bass, and drums. 1991. €22.40. A suite of five original jazz tunes: Let's All Take It Easy; Going Home; Complaining Blues; Sweet and Mellow; Happy Go Lucky Rag. Parts are written in treble clef. See listing under Music for Multiple Euphoniums.

Bach, Johann Sebastian. *Prelude & Fugue (BWV 546).* Arr. R. Nakagawa. Theodore Presser Co. Three trumpets, horn, two trombones, euphonium, tuba. $20.

Bach, Johann Sebastian. *Psalm 19.* Arr. Thayne Tolle. Cimarron Music. Three trumpets, three trombones, euphonium, tuba. $15.

Cottrell, Jeff. *Fanfare for Brass Choir.* Cimarron Music. Two trumpets, two horns, trombone, euphonium, two tubas. $12.

Cunningham, M. *Motet for Brass, Op. 67B.* Seesaw Music Corp. Two trumpets, two horns, two trombones, euphonium, tuba. $10.50.

Cunningham, M. *Remembering Helen Keller.* Seesaw Music Corp. Two trumpets, two horns, two trombones, euphonium, tuba. $15.

Frederick, D., ed. *Four Pieces.* Shawnee Press. Two trumpets, two horns, two trombones, euphonium, tuba. $20.

Friedrich, Kenneth. *Of Bells and Brass.* Cimarron Music. Two trumpets, horn, two trombones, euphonium, tuba, bells. $19.

Gabrieli, Giovanni. *Antiphony No. 2.* Arr. G. W. Anthony. Theodore Presser Co. Two cornets, two horns, two trombones, euphonium, and tuba. $10.95.

Gabrieli, Giovanni. *Sonata pian' e forte.* Arr. John Beyrent. Brassworks 4. Two cornets, two horns, two trombones, euphonium, and tuba. 2003. $23. III. B♭–d'.

George, Thom Ritter. *Two Interplays.* Thom Ritter George. Three trombones, bass trombone, two euphoniums, two tubas. 1985. $15.

Gershwin, George. *Rhapsody in Blue for Brass Octet.* Arr. Yasuhide Ito. Ito Music. Two trumpets, two horns, two trombones, euphonium, tuba. 1993.

Gregson, Edward. *Three Dance Episodes.* Studio Music. Three trumpets, horn, two trombones, euphonium, tuba. 1974. 9:00. IV. G–b♭'. Three movements: I. Molto Allegro; II. Andante con espressione; III. Vivace. Commissioned by the James Shepherd Versatile Brass. Recorded by the Hallé Brass, *Hallé Brass Plays Gregson,* Doyen Records DOYCD038.

Holst, Gustav. *First Movement from "First Suite in E♭."* Arr. Yasuhide Ito. Ito Music. Flute, clarinet, two saxophones, trumpet, horn, trombone, euphonium. 1998.

Horvit, M. *Antique Suite.* Shawnee Press. Two trumpets, two horns, two trombones, euphonium, tuba. $20.

Janáček, Leoš. *Capriccio.* Editio Supraphon Praha. Flute, two trumpets, tenor tuba, three trombones, piano. 1974. 22:00. V. F–b♭'. Four movements: I. Allegro; II. Adagio; III. Allegretto; IV. Andante. Originally written in 1926, this is the first known chamber work to include euphonium (tenor tuba). Technically challenging for all players, this work displays contemporary chamber music writing at its best. Despite its technical challenges, *Capriccio* is a lyrical work in a romantic style. Extensive use of accidentals in the euphonium part. Mixed meter, awkward rhythmic patterns, and frequent tempo changes call for careful preparation and rehearsal. Recorded by members of L'Orchestre de l'Opéra National de Paris, Sir Charles Mackerras, conductor, EMI CDC5 55585-2.

Le June, Claude. *Revecy vinir du printans.* Arr. Gary Barrow. TAP Music. Two trumpets, two horns, two trombones, euphonium, tuba. $24. A rhythmically challenging piece in mixed meter. Gives all voices a piece of the technical action while prominently featuring the euphonium.

Luckhardt, Hilmar. *Octet for Brass.* Mills Music Library, University of Wisconsin–Madison. Two trumpets, two horns, two trombones, euphonium, tuba. 1977. 11:00. Three movements: I. Preamble; II. Arioso; III. Finale. With special emphasis on the euphonium part, for Barry Kilpatrick. An interesting piece displaying baroque-style characteristics within a contemporary tonal setting. The euphonium is prominently featured throughout. Recorded by Barry Kilpatrick, *American Music for Euphonium,* Mark Records 2535-MCD.

Mahler, Gustav. *Adagio from Symphony No. 3.* Arr. Maurice Bale. Godiva Music. Four euphoniums and four trombones. 2003. Written for the British Euphonium Quartet and Bones Apart.

Mendelssohn, Felix. *Scherzo.* Arr. M. Shiner. Kendor Music, Inc. Three trumpets, two horns, trombone, euphonium, tuba. $10.

Morgan, Thomas, arr. *Coventry Carol.* MMI Music. Three cornets, flugelhorn, horn, trombone, euphonium, tuba. £15.

Nagel, Robert. *Songs of Faith and Praise.* Mentor Music. Three trumpets, two horns, three trombones, euphonium, tuba. $19.

Pishny-Floyd, Monte Keene. *Euphonism: A Divertimento-Concertino.* Tuba-Euphonium Press. Euphonium, flute, clarinet, two violins, viola, bass, piano. 1994. $24. IV. E♭₁–c". A challenging, playful work for a unique combination of instruments. Includes mixed meter and calls for extensive multiple tonguing. The solo cadenza near the end of the work is technically difficult, containing large intervallic leaps and extreme range demands. Good collegiate recital material.

Rognoni-Taeggi, Giocomo. *Canzona per Sonare.* Arr. R. P. Block. Philharmonia Music. Four trombones, three euphoniums, and tuba. $47.50.

Schutte, Daniel L. *Here I Am, Lord.* Arr. Paul Bara. Brassworks 4. Two cornets, flugelhorn, two horns, trombone, bass trombone, euphonium. 2002. $26. III. E♭–f'. A simple yet effective arrangement that makes the most of the sonorous capabilities of a double quartet. Not technically difficult. Some extreme range demands in the trombone and horn parts may cause difficulties for younger players. Recorded by Brassworks 4, *Chalice Hymnal Songs of Praise*, Brassworks 4 BW 4003.

Sibelius, Jean. *Tiera*. Edition Fazer. Three cornets, tenor horn, baritone, euphonium, tuba, percussion. 1967.

Szkutko, John. *Goliath Suite*. SZK Music. Three trumpets, horn, two trombones, euphonium, and tuba. Four movements: Ode Magnifique; Fairground Frolics; Love's Enchantment; Goliath. The first movement is an intense allegro with contrasting softer sections. The second movement is a carefree waltz. The third movement features the horn and euphonium. Finally, Goliath arrives in the fourth movement as two contrasting continual motion sections build to a massive climax. Alternate parts included for C trumpet, E♭ horn, T.C. trombone, euphonium, and E♭ tuba.

Turner, K. *Ghost Riders*. Editions BIM. Two trumpets, two horns, two trombones, euphonium, tuba. $33.

Uber, David. *Tides of Destiny, Op. 380*. TAP Music. Two trumpets, two horns, two trombones, euphonium, tuba. $16. 3:25.

Wagner, Richard. *Introduction to Act III of Die Meistersinger*. Arr. Robert King. Robert King Music Sales, Inc. Two trumpets, horn, three trombones, euphonium, tuba or two trumpets, three trombones, two euphoniums, tuba. $7.65.

Wilby, Philip. *Concert Music for Eight Instruments*. Chester Music. Flute, oboe, clarinet, horn, trumpet, trombone, euphonium, and percussion. £19.45.

Zuercher, D. *All Creatures of Our God and King*. Sound Ideas Publications. Two trumpets, two horns, two trombones, euphonium, tuba. $9.

Nine Players

Anderson, Eugene. *Quintuple Overlays*. Cimarron Music. Two euphoniums and two tubas with two trumpets and percussion. 1997. $15. 3:00. III–IV. Part I: G–a♭', Part II: G–a♭', Part III: D♯–c♯', Part IV: D1–g. This original work for brass choir features a tuba/euphonium quartet with two trumpets and three percussion parts: snare drum, cymbal, and timpani. Syncopation, chromatic lines, and large intervals are challenging elements of each part. First two parts also available in treble clef. Works well as a concert opener.

Arban, Jean-Baptiste. *The Carnival of Venice*. Arr. Yasuhide Ito. Ito Music. Solo euphonium, four euphoniums, four tubas. V. A fresh take on this classic virtuosic solo.

Aud, Jean, arr. *The Twelve Days of Christmas*. Philharmonia Music. Flute, oboe, clarinet, bassoon, two cornets, horn, euphonium, tuba. $47.50.

Censhu, Jiro. *The Noble Mirror*. Jiro Censhu. Baritone vocalist and eight euphoniums. 1993. IV. Part I: B♭–b', Part II: E–b♭', Part III: F♯–a', Part IV: F♯–b♭', Part V: G–b♭', Part VI: F–g', Part VII: D–c', Part VIII: A₁–c'. For Toru Miura and the Euphonium Company. A unique work for large euphonium choir. The vocal part is not difficult; however, the text is in Japanese and euphonium may be a viable substitute. Some technical challenges in all parts. See listing under Music for Multiple Euphoniums.

Corwell, Neal. *Meditation and Finale: A Chamber Concerto in Two Movements*. Tuba-Euphonium Press. Euphonium, three violins, two violas, two celli, and piano. 1995. $35. G₁–c''. Two movements: 1. Meditation and 2. Finale. Commissioned by the Garrett Lakes Art Festival, Erick Friedman, music director. The first movement is slow, lyrical, and reflective. The second movement begins slowly, with a quasi cadenza in the euphonium that leads to a brisk allegro. The second movement is technically challenging. Requires careful rehearsal for ensemble cohesiveness.

Gabrieli, Giovanni. *Jubilate Deo*. Arr. Donald O. Braatz. PEL Music Publications. Four trumpets, two horns, trombone, euphonium, tuba. 1995. $9.95. II. G–c'. A simple arrangement appropriate for younger players. A great introduction to the music of Gabrieli.

Girolamo. *Alix Avoit*. Arr. Johnson. Medici Music Press. Solo trumpet, two trumpets, two horns, two trombones, euphonium, and tuba. $14.50.

Guerrero, Francisco. *Canite Tuba in Sion*. Arr. R. P. Block. Philharmonia Music. Four trumpets, three trombones, euphonium, and tuba. $34.50.

Monteverdi, Claudio. *Sonata Sopra Sancta Maria*. Arr. Robert King. Robert King Music Sales, Inc. Four trumpets, horn, two trombones, two euphoniums. $6.65.

Pachelbel, Johann. *Canon*. Arr. R. P. Block. Philharmonia Music. Four trumpets, horn, two trombones, euphonium, tuba. $52.50.

Shulman, A. *Two Chorales*. Alexander Broude. Two trumpets, two horns, two trombones, two euphoniums, tuba. $8.50.

Stewart, Michael. *Chorale for O.M.S.* Cimarron Music. Three trumpets, two horns, two trombones, euphonium, tuba. $11.50. Appropriate for younger students.

Stewart, Michael. *Chorales and Imitations*. Cimarron Music. Three trumpets, two horns, two trombones, euphonium, tuba. $16.

Stewart, Michael. *Heritage*. Cimarron Music. Three trumpets, two horns, two trombones, euphonium, tuba. $19.

Stewart, Michael. *Tristus*. Cimarron Music. Three trumpets, two horns, two trombones, euphonium, tuba. $22.50.

Stockhausen, Karlheinz. *Oberlippentanz (PRO-TEST)*. Stockhausen Verlag. Piccolo trumpet, euphonium, four or eight horns, two percussion, and sound engineer. 1983. 14:30. V. Difficult contemporary work. The following sound equipment is needed for performance: two transmitters, ten microphones, two loudspeakers, mixing console, and sound projector.

Veeman, Arnold. *Carcassonne: From Might to Secrecy*. Donemus Amsterdam. Boy soprano, recorder, trumpet, horn, euphonium, vibraphone, timpani, thunder machine, double bass. 2000. 10:00. IV–V. D–a♯'. An interesting work for an eclectic ensemble. All parts require strong players. The euphonium plays a soloistic role in addition to adding color to the ensemble.

Whyte, Ian. *Ode: For Brass and Organ*. Scottish Music Information Centre. Trumpet, two horns, three trombones, euphonium, db, organ.

Ten Players

Aagaard-Nilsen, Torstein. *Feber Fantasy (Fever Fantasy)*. Taan-Band Music. Euphonium solo and nine cornets. V. B♭–f''. An intriguing piece that is challenging for both the soloist and ensemble. The work unfolds through the development of a four-note motive present in the opening cornet fanfare. Technically difficult. Recorded by Steven Mead, *The World of the Euphonium*, volume 4.

Beethoven, Ludwig van. *Adagio*. Arr. Denzil Stephens. Sarnia Music. Four cornets, tenor horn, euphonium, trombone, bass trombone, tuba, drum set. £11.45. A "pop ballad" take on this classical masterpiece.

Boellman, Léon. *Prière à Notre-Dame from Suite Gothique*. David Marlatt. Eighth Note Publications. Ten-piece brass. 1999.

Coakley, Donald, and David Marlatt, arr. *A La Claire Fontaine*. Eighth Note Publications. Three trumpets, two horns, two trombones, euphonium, tuba, percussion. 2003.

Corwell, Neal. *Tribes*. Tuba-Euphonium Press. Solo euphonium, E♭ trumpet, three B♭ trumpets, horn, three trombones, tuba. 2002. $30. V. C–d♭''. A difficult one-movement work challenging for the soloist and ensemble alike. Contains angular lines and large intervallic leaps; extensive, rapid multiple tonguing; and tricky meter changes.

Elgar, Edward. *Enigma Variations No. 9 (Nimrod)*. Arr. David Marlatt. Eighth Note Publications. Two trumpets, two cornets, two horns, euphonium, trombone, two tubas. 1999. $20. III. A–g'. An excellent abbreviated arrangement of Elgar's famously haunting melody. The euphonium starts the piece with a solo and is featured at

various points throughout. Not technically difficult. Appropriate for good high school players.

Flowers, Herbie. *Great Balloon Race*. Sarnia Music. Four cornets, tenor horn, euphonium, trombone, bass trombone, tuba, drum set. £11.45. Appropriate for younger players.

Flowers, Herbie *Lady and the IMP*. Sarnia Music. Four cornets, tenor horn, euphonium, trombone, bass trombone, tuba, drum set. £11.45. Appropriate for younger players. Light concert piece.

Hakenberg, Stefan, and Theo Lipfert. *The Displacement Map: A Documentary without Words*. Stefan Hakenberg. Flute, oboe, horn, flugelhorn, euphonium, koto, guitar, two violins, cello. 2002. 18:00. V. F♯–a'. Four movements: I. War; II. Howling Wolves; III. Monochrome; IV. Return. An interesting and intriguing modern work composed with film to present an artistic depiction of historical interdependency. The piece uses visual and musical means to narrate an almost universal story of war and displacement, concentrating on Aleut relocation to southeast Alaska during the Second World War. The euphonium part is of moderate technical difficulty, yet the piece is a unique challenge as an ensemble. In the first two movements, the euphonium plays a coloration and punctuating role. In movement four, the euphonium first states the primary melodic material and is featured at times throughout. The euphonium part is tacit in the third movement. A mute is required in the last movement.

Hounsell, Clare, arr. *Civil War Medley–The Confederacy*. PEL Music Publications. Nine-piece brass and snare drum. 1995. $10.95. II. B♭–d'. Appropriate for younger players.

Hounsell, Clare, arr. *Civil War Medley–The Union*. PEL Music Publications. Nine-piece brass and snare drum. 1995. $9.95. II. A♭–e♭'. Appropriate for younger players.

Key, Gareth. *Brass Bandinerie*. Sarnia Music. Four cornets, tenor horn, euphonium, trombone, bass trombone, tuba, drum set. £11.45. Appropriate for younger players.

Key, Gareth. *Calypso*. Sarnia Music. Four cornets, tenor horn, euphonium, trombone, bass trombone, tuba, drum set. £11.45. Appropriate for younger players.

Klein. *Cranberry Corners USA*. Sarnia Music. Four cornets, tenor horn, euphonium, trombone, bass trombone, tuba, drum set. £11.45. A foot-tapping folk tune.

Leslie. *Night Flight to Madrid*. Sarnia Music. Four cornets, tenor horn, euphonium, trombone, bass trombone, tuba, drum set. £11.45.

Mahler, Gustav. *Symphony No. 1, Movement II*. Arr. David Marlatt. Eighth Note Publications. Ten-piece brass. 1997.

Naulais, Jérôme. *Triangle Austral*. Editions M. Combre. Three trumpets, horn, two trombones, euphonium, tuba, marimba, percussion. $62.55.

Pachelbel, Johann. *Canon*. Arr. R. P. Block. Philharmonia Music. Nine euphoniums and one tuba. $57.50.

Pownall, Claire. *Great Budworth Fanfare & Meditation*. MMI Music. Three cornets, two horns, baritone, two trombones, euphonium, tuba. £15.

Prokofiev, Sergei. *Opus 99*. Sarnia Music. Four cornets, tenor horn, euphonium, trombone, bass trombone, tuba, drum set. £11.45.

Sousa, John Philip. *Semper Fideles*. Arr. Denzil Stephens. Sarnia Music. Four cornets, tenor horn, euphonium, trombone, bass trombone, tuba, drum set. £11.45.

Stephens, Denzil. *Aces High*. Sarnia Music. Four cornets, tenor horn, euphonium, trombone, bass trombone, tuba, drum set. £11.45. A light concert march.

Stephens, Denzil. *Boy from Dundee*. Sarnia Music. Four cornets, tenor horn, euphonium, trombone, bass trombone, tuba, drum set. £11.45. Written in treble clef.

Stephens, Denzil. *Bubbling Brass*. Sarnia Music. Four cornets, tenor horn, euphonium, trombone, bass trombone, tuba, drum set. £11.45. Written in treble clef.

Stephens, Denzil. *Carnival*. Sarnia Music. Solo euphonium, four cornets, tenor horn, two trombones, tuba, drum set. £11.45. Written in treble clef.

Stephens, Denzil. *Dance of the Little Fairies*. Four cornets, tenor horn, euphonium, trombone, bass trombone, tuba, drum set. £11.45. Written in treble clef.

Stephens, Denzil. *Dizzy Fingers*. Sarnia Music. Solo euphonium, four cornets, tenor horn, two trombones, tuba, drum set. 1999. £11.45. V. F₁–b♭'. A showpiece in the truest sense of the word. A formidable technical challenge written in ABA form. The piece begins and ends in a flurry of 32nd notes interrupted by a flowing melodic section. Fun for audience and performers alike. Written in treble clef.

Stephens, Denzil, arr. *Drigo's Serenade*. Sarnia Music. Solo euphonium, four cornets, tenor horn, two trombones, tuba, drum set. £11.45. IV. c–a'. A beautiful melody that works exceptionally well with this instrumentation. Not technically difficult, but requires musical maturity from the soloist. High tessitura in the solo part. Written in treble clef.

Stephens, Denzil, arr. *Fanfares and National Anthem*. Sarnia Music. Four cornets, tenor horn, euphonium, trombone, bass trombone, tuba, drum set. £11.45. A great setting of the British national anthem. Written in treble clef.

Stephens, Denzil, arr. *Frere Jacques*. Sarnia Music. Four cornets, tenor horn, euphonium, trombone, bass trombone, tuba, drum set. £11.45. Written in treble clef.

Stephens, Denzil. *Gameplan*. Sarnia Music. Solo euphonium, four cornets, tenor horn, two trombones, tuba, drum set. £11.45. Written in treble clef.

Stephens, Denzil, arr. *Myfanwy*. Sarnia Music. Solo euphonium, four cornets, tenor horn, two trombones, tuba, drum set. £11.45. III. Wonderful arrangement of this famous Welsh melody. Not technically difficult. Written in treble clef.

Stephens, Denzil. *Promenade*. Sarnia Music. Four cornets, tenor horn, euphonium, trombone, bass trombone, tuba, drum set. £11.45. Written in treble clef.

Stephens, Denzil. *Quintessence*. Sarnia Music. Solo euphonium, four cornets, tenor horn, two trombones, tuba, drum set. £11.45. IV. B♭1–c". An up-tempo original work in 5/4 time that showcases the soloist's technical and musical prowess. Some technical challenges and a high tessitura in the solo part. Written in treble clef.

Stephens, Denzil. *Rondino*. Sarnia Music. Solo euphonium, four cornets, tenor horn, two trombones, tuba, drum set. £11.45. IV. An original solo in a classic brass band style. A dance-like 6/8 preceded by a lyrical introduction. Written in treble clef.

Stephens, Denzil. *Solo Rhapsody for Euphonium*. Solo euphonium, four cornets, tenor horn, two trombones, tuba, drum set. 1989. £13.45. IV. A fun original work that showcases the lyrical quality and technical ability of the performer. Written in treble clef.

Stephens, Denzil. *Spring Fever*. Sarnia Music. Solo euphonium, four cornets, tenor horn, two trombones, tuba, drum set. 2004. £11.45. IV. A–c". A playful showpiece in 6/8 meter that is fun for performers and audience alike. Technically challenging for the soloist. Written in treble clef.

Tignor, Scott. *Circus Elephant Fanfare*. Cimarron Music. Three trumpets, two horns, three trombones, euphonium, tuba. $32.

Eleven Players

Corelli, Arcangelo. *Adagio*. Arr. Denis Wilby. Mostyn Music. Solo euphonium and ten-piece brass ensemble. £13.50.

Gardner, Alexandra. *Tamarak*. Alexandra Gardner. Two violins, viola, cello, bass, flute, horn, trombone, euphonium, koto, mandolin. 2000.

Puccini, Giacomo. *Nessun Dorma*. Arr. Denzil Stephens. Sarnia Music. Solo euphonium, four cornets, tenor horn, euphonium, two trombones, tuba, percussion. £11.45. 3:00. IV. e♭–c". A great arrangement of this classic melody that showcases the rich sound of the euphonium and brass ensemble to its fullest potential. High tessitura in the solo part. Written in treble clef.

Stephens, Denzil, arr. *Catari, Catari*. Sarnia Music. Euphonium solo and ten-piece brass ensemble. 1985. £11.45. III. g–b♭'. A beautiful lyrical solo. Not technically difficult. Written in treble clef.

Twelve Players

Bizet, George. *Duo (Petit Marie)*. Arr. Denzil Stephens. Sarnia Music. Solo cornet, solo euphonium, four cornets, tenor horn, euphonium, trombone, bass trombone, tuba, drum set. £11.45.

Epstein, Marti. *Chant*. Marti Epstein. Voice, three violins, viola, cello, bass, two flutes, horn, trombone, euphonium, etc. 2001.

First, Craig. *The Eternal Return*. Craig First. Violin, viola, cello, flute, oboe, clarinet, horn, trombone, euphonium, drums, vibraphone, guitar. 2002.

Forbes, Michael. *Lullaby*. Tuba-Euphonium Press. Euphonium and tuba duet with brass tenet. 2001. $12. 5:30. IV. Part I: c–c", Part II: B♭–f'. For Siiri. A light and effective piece that consists of several expressive lyrical themes dispersed amongst the soloists and ensemble. Not technically difficult.

Gershwin, George. *Porgy and Bess in 15 Minutes*. Arr. Yasuhide Ito. Ito Music. Eleven euphoniums and piano. 1997. IV–V. A medley of highlights from *Porgy and Bess*. All parts are challenging and require mutes. Difficult piano part.

Vivaldi, Antonio. *Viva Vivaldi*. Arr. Thomas Wyss. Mostyn Music. Two euphoniums and ten-piece brass ensemble. £18.60.

Zdechlik, John P. *Balade*. John P. Zdechlik. Solo euphonium, three trumpets, four horns, three trombones, tuba. 2004. IV. A–b♭'. A tuneful, lyrical work that is a welcome addition to the repertoire. Appropriate for college-level players, this piece is a good recital addition. Moderate technical difficulty. High tessitura in the solo part.

Thirteen Players

Bach, Johann Sebastian. *Aria-Duet from Cantata No. 78*. Arr. David Werden. Cimarron Music. Euphonium and tuba duet, two flutes, two oboes, three clarinets, two bassoons, horn, double bass. $55.

Fourteen Players

Blumenthaler, Volker. *SPEC*. Volker Blumenthaler. Erhu, four violins, viola, cello, bass, flute, horn, trombone, euphonium, koto, mandolin. 2000.

Constantinides, Dino. *Landscape III*. Magni Publications. Solo euphonium, twelve-part brass ensemble, and one percussion. 2001. 6:15. IV. F♯–c". A challenging contemporary piece that presents lyrical thematic material and develops the material with virtuosic solo passages. Characterized by polychords and sudden harmonic shifts. Difficult rhythmic figures and extensive use of accidentals.

Ross, Walter. *Concerto for Euphonium, Symphonic Brass, and Timpani*. Tuba-Euphonium Press. Solo euphonium, brass, and timpani. 1993. $40. 13:00. IV. G–a♭. Three movements: I. Fantasia; II. Chorale Variations; III. Scherzo. Commissioned by the Kennesaw College Brass Ensemble, William Hill, director. The first movement opens with a dramatic introduction followed by a cadenza in the solo euphonium. The principal idea is then heard in the euphonium and the movement continues in a series of episodes and developments of the main idea. The second movement is a theme and three variations on the old hymn "Der Alte Jahr Vergangen ist." The last movement is a scherzo, so called because of the humorous interplay between the rhythm and the meter.

7. Music for Unaccompanied Euphonium

Neal Corwell

Unaccompanied works offer the soloist great artistic freedom: freedom to experiment with phrasing, tempi, and other musical nuances in a spontaneous and liberating fashion, without the necessity of maintaining synchronization or balance with an accompanying instrument. Because of the inherent rhythmic freedom of the medium, it is common for compositions to be improvisational in nature, often lacking bar lines or a time signature. However, along with the freedom comes additional musical responsibilities for the performer. The absence of an accompaniment means the soloist is required, without the support of another instrument, to create a musically complete whole. Another consideration, quite practical in nature, is that demands on endurance are generally increased for performers of unaccompanied works because there are no accompaniment interludes, and therefore no rests of any length, to aid the soloist in rejuvenating the embouchure.

The lack of an accompaniment also means a decrease in the number of harmonic possibilities and tonal colors available to the composer. The harmonic limitations of a single-line wind instrument, such as the euphonium, are addressed in a couple of ways. The more traditional approach is to create the illusion of harmony through the use of arpeggiated patterns. Another method, called multi-phonic technique, requires the performer to sing one pitch while playing another, thereby creating harmony, and/or other unusual effects. The performer is often called upon to compensate for the limitations of timbre by using mutes to vary the color of the instrument, or by utilizing non-traditional sound production techniques such as flutter tonguing, pitch bending, glissandi, half-valving, valve rattling, foot stomping, blowing air through the horn, or tapping on various objects or parts of the horn to create percussive effects.

The body of literature currently available for euphonium solo runs the gamut from conservative and traditional to experimental and avant-garde, with quality compositions to be found at both ends of the spectrum. Although not all works are necessarily worthy of being considered as recital material, most do offer at the very least pedagogical benefits to those patient enough to master their challenges. The practice and experience obtained by learning the non-traditional techniques just described, along with lessons about utilizing musical and rhythmic freedom while maintaining coherence and intelligibility, are valuable enough in their own right to merit the study of the literature included in this chapter. Most of the works included are original compositions, but some arrangements/adaptations are also listed. Clearly there are numerous unaccompanied solos intended originally for other instruments that may easily be adapted for use by the euphonium. However, only those designated by the arranger or publisher as being suitable for the euphonium have been included in this chapter.

The publisher for several works included in this chapter is listed as the "TUBA GEM Series" or "ITEA GEM Series." This indicates that the piece was printed or included as an enclosure within a *TUBA Journal* or *ITEA Journal* during the year listed. The practice of featuring works that could be fit onto one or two pages as a bonus to subscribers to these journals was begun in 1982 and revived again in 2003. Although printed in the journal, the organization does not claim copyright ownership, which still belongs to the composers. Some works are currently published and available elsewhere. I would like to thank all that assisted me in finding the unaccompanied works listed, with special thanks to Brian Bowman and Angie Hunter for their assistance in locating some of the more difficult to obtain literature.

Aagaard-Nilsen, Torstein. *4 Lyriske Stykker (Four Lyric Pieces)*. Nordic Sounds. 2000. $19.50. 6:10. IV–V. B2–e♭″. Four movements: Poco parlando sempre; Recitative e molto rubato; Energico; Adagio. For Egil Magnussen. Although a variety of tempi and styles are used, a lyrical quality is maintained throughout all four pieces. An atonal language is used, but thematic unity gives a clear cohesiveness to the music, and the composer creates numerous exciting and dramatic musical moments without making excessive demands on the performer's range or technique. Technical and expressive challenges, though numerous, are well suited to the idiomatic capabilities of the euphonium. A list of technical hurdles would include mixed meters, complex rhythms, a few rhythmically tricky grace notes, and flutter tonguing.

Aagaard-Nilsen, Torstein. *Svart Regn (Black Rain)*. Nordic Sounds. 1990. 7:00. IV. D–c″. One movement. This solo, which uses contemporary musical language but no unusual avant-garde techniques, is musically coherent and, despite its difficulty level, should be accessible for many audiences and performers. The composer uses arch form to construct a well-balanced mix of dramatic and lyrical elements, replete with numerous exciting fast passages. Good single tonguing speed is essential if the performer is to play the many repeated-note passages at the designated tempi. Although double tonguing could be used, multiple tonguing would be problematic for some passages, making it difficult to add the proper rhythmic and melodic accentuation. Although primarily in bass clef, tenor clef is used for passages in the higher registers.

Aho, Kalevi. *Solo VIII*. 2003. $20. 9:00. V. E1–d″. One movement. For Lieska Brass Week. This composition can perhaps best be described as being relentless. Demands on endurance are high because, from start to finish, no breaks or rests are provided for the soloist. Most of the piece is notated in bass clef, but tenor clef is used for passages that linger in the high range. No time signatures are provided, but bar lines and the grouping of note staves make clear the composer's intent with regard to rhythmic subdivisions. The rhythms are not extremely complex, but the ever-changing measure lengths and shifting rhythmic emphases, along with the persistent forward-driving nature of the piece, provide an extreme challenge for the performer. The repetitiveness of the piece makes it a challenge for the listener as well. The piece served well its purpose as a demanding work for professional level soloists in the 2004 ITEA euphonium soloist competition, but most listeners will find, because of its lack of melodic or thematic variety, that musically it is more of an etude than a true concert piece.

Anderson, Tommy Joe. *Petite Suite*. Dorn Publications. 1981 (written in 1972). 4:00. IV. F–b′. Four movements: Prelude; Elegie; Etude; Waltz. For Mary Larson. The five brief movements of this composition are mostly playful in nature, and the atonal melodic lines move freely between the high and low registers. Although only the final Waltz features bar lines or a time signature, rhythms are not extremely complex. Because of the rhythmic freedom granted the performer,

phrasing will require good judgment if the piece is to be presented in a musically coherent fashion. However, the melodic nature of the work makes this an easier task than one might expect. The Etude, with its fast tempo, chromatic running eighth notes, wide interval leaps, and only one space to breathe, is the most technically challenging movement.

Anonymous. *Hijazker Longa*. Arr. Gary Buttery. Cimarron Music. 1973. $4.50. 4:00. III. D–c. One movement. This transcription of a traditional Syrian Ode concert piece is entertaining and, if played with appropriate enthusiasm, can be quite exciting. The opening cadenza is rhythmically free and improvisational in character, but the remainder of the piece features simple rhythmic and melodic patterns that gradually gather momentum, regularly increasing in tempo. Near the end of the composition, some double tonguing is required, but because this rapid passage is idiomatically well suited to the euphonium, the articulation pattern is not difficult. Because this arrangement works well as either a euphonium or tuba solo, it makes use, particularly in the opening bars, of the register below the bass clef staff. The euphonium soloist will therefore need a solid low register to effectively perform the piece as written.

Anonymous. *Sakura, Sakura*. Arr. N. Yamamoto. 1984. 1:30. II. F–a′. One movement. For Brian Bowman. This arrangement, both simple and elegant, is an appropriate setting for the famous Japanese melody about cherry blossoms. Graceful arpeggiated patterns are used occasionally to enhance the melody.

Bach, Johann Sebastian. *Sarabande and Preludio*. Arr. Neal Corwell. Nicolai Music. 2004. $10. 8:00. IV–V. D–b♭′. Two movements: Sarabande and Preludio. Two complementary movements were extracted from separate Bach compositions, and transposed into the idiomatically facile key of B♭, to create a recital piece displaying both the lyrical and technical capabilities of the euphonium. The lyrical opening movement is from Bach's final solo cello suite, a suite often neglected by brass players because of its awkward original key and high tessitura. The Sarabande is not technically difficult, but fluid and expressive phrasing, plus the ability to slur smoothly upward into the high register, are requirements for an effective performance. The Preludio is from Bach's third partita for solo violin. It features a steady stream of sixteenth notes, and the energy and exuberance of the movement make it as exciting for the audience as it is challenging for the performer. The judicious omission of carefully selected notes makes it possible to perform this movement without resorting to circular breathing. As the movement nears its close, some license is taken by the arranger with phrasing and tempi. These changes are both practical and musical, giving the soloist some brief rest and creating added momentum for the final push toward the finale.

Bach, Johann Sebastian. *Six Short Solo Suites.* Arr. Robert King. Robert King/Alphonse Leduc. 1989. $9. II–III. F–a'. This is a collection of selected movements extracted from each of Bach's six solo cello suites. In an effort to make the pieces easier for less-advanced performers, the arranger has chosen the shortest movements, transposed them into keys that are well suited to a b♭ instrument, and sometimes simplified Bach's melodic lines. The low fourth-valve range below the bass clef staff is avoided by the choice of keys that lie in the mid-range of the euphonium. Sometimes the simplification of solo lines results in a sanitized melodic line lacking the character of the Bach original, but many of the movements are hardly altered at all. These suites are a good source of study and recital material for the younger performer.

Bach, Johann Sebastian. *Solo Cello Suites Nos. 4, 5, 6.* Arr. Robert Marsteller. Southern Music Company. 1963. $14. III–IV. C–c''. The same annotation given below for the first three suites applies to this collection of the last of Bach's cello suites. The fourth and fifth suites are just as well arranged and useful as recital and practice material as are the first three suites described below. Unfortunately, the original key and octave placement are retained for the sixth and final suite, making it awkward and impractical for performance on euphonium because of its high tessitura.

Bach, Johann Sebastian. *Solo Cello Suites Nos. 1, 2, 3.* Arr. Robert Marsteller. Southern Music Company. 1963. $10. III. C–a'. Dedicated to Emory Remington. This collection contains arrangements of Bach's first three cello suites. All are presented in their entirety and in the original keys. Because of the extensive use of range below the bass clef staff, these suites are excellent study material for developing facility with the fourth valve. In these arrangements, melodic lines are sometimes arbitrarily oversimplified for no clear technical reason, thus detracting from the beauty of Bach's original melodic line. Fortunately, the arranger usually gives the performer the option of performing Bach's original cello figuration or a simplified version. The articulation choices are also sometimes questionable and inconsistent. These suites are a good source of study and recital material, but I would recommend that the serious performer also study the Keith Brown arrangement of the suites (for trombone, published by International Music), as well as Bach's original cello score. The ideal euphonium presentation of the suites would be an amalgamation of these three sources.

Bachelder, Daniel F. *Lyric Piece for Euphonium.* Tuba-Euphonium Press. 1994. $8. 5:00. III–IV. E–c''. One movement. As the title suggests, this piece is generally, although not exclusively, lyrical in nature. Although time signatures are provided, with frequently changing meters, an improvisatory character is retained throughout the work. One brief passage features a "free section" in which, at the discretion of the performer, notes may be repeated ad-lib using any rhythmic pattern desired. There are no extraordinary demands on range or endurance, and the piece is not technically difficult. However, there is limited use of multi-phonic technique. Both bass and treble clef parts are provided.

Baxley, Wayne. *Ronald McDifficult.* T.A.P. Music Sales. 1989. 2:30. IV–V. G1–b'. One movement. This brief solo, with its conventional melodic opening, could be labeled as traditional and conservative if it were not for its extreme reliance upon multi-phonic effects. Multi-phonic use is not limited to a few short passages, nor confined to uses that are relatively easy to perform. Instead, quite difficult maneuvers are called for, which make this a very demanding, though not musically substantive, work.

Bittinger, Musser, and Wittekind. *Four Island Fantasies.* Pocono Mountain Music Publishing. 1994. $4. 12:00 (ca. 3:00 each). II. F–b♭'. Four Movements: Cairns Island Phantasy; Burns Island Phantasy; Kipp Island Phantasy; Epply Island Phantasy. This collection of compositions by three composers (all three are listed as co-composers for each piece) may be performed as a suite or as four separate individual solos. The pieces are clearly designed for young players and, although marketed as euphonium solos, were not written specifically with one type of instrument in mind. Versions for everything from flute to mallet percussion are available from the publisher. Despite the fanciful titles, the little studies are generally lacking in musical character or melodic interest.

Blatter, Alfred. *Eulogy.* TUBA GEM Series. 1976. 2:30. IV. E–c''. One movement. For Bob Gale in memory of Jay Ahrens. This companion piece to Blatter's *Eunique* is both atonal and lyrically expressive. The slow tempo and sustained passages, some in the high register, are demanding, but not ridiculously so. A somber mood dominates this work, which can be an effective and moving concert piece if performed by a musically mature soloist.

Blatter, Alfred. *Eunique.* TUBA GEM Series. 1976. 4:00. IV. A1–e'' (A1–c'' with optional *ossia*). One movement. For Bob Gale. The dramatic solo line of this composition fluctuates between bursts of vigorous activity and slower sustained passages with wide interval leaps. No non-traditional performance techniques are used, but the melodic lines are clearly atonal in origin. Both double and triple tonguing are called for, but only briefly and in simple patterns. In performance, *Eunique* may be paired with its companion piece, *Eulogy.*

Brustad, Karsten. *"Wrsh."* Norsk Musikkinformasion. 1999. 15:00. V. B♭1–c''. "Wrsh" is Egyptian for "to spend the time," and any soloist that wishes to perform this avant-garde work should expect to spend a great amount of time preparing for the performance. The part of the composition that is to be played on the euphonium using conventional sound production techniques is complex and difficult, but not prohibitively so. However, the plethora of extramusical demands of the work present a great, and some would say ridiculous, challenge for the performer. Many unconventional sound production techniques are called for such as bending the pitch up or down by specified quarter tone intervals, singing consonants through the horn, using "jaws-harp technique," using alternate fingerings, mouth pops, hand pops, and making a "pig's noise." The difficulty of these techniques is compounded by the fact that they often must be performed while also sustaining a pitch on the euphonium. There is extensive use of multi-phonic technique, most of it quite difficult. During one passage, the soloist is required to sing a rapid pattern of notes while simultaneously playing a different melodic pattern on the euphonium itself. A special mute is required (directions for creating it are provided), as is a bass drum. The drum is used for muting and special effects. As if this weren't enough to keep the performer's head spinning, the soloist is required to literally spin in circles and also rotate between four stage positions to make use of four different music stands that are placed in a diamond shape onstage. Although much of the euphonium part is in the low register, the piece is notated almost exclusively in tenor clef.

Clinard, Fred L. *Sonata.* Shawnee Press. 1978. $5. 7:00. IV. F–c″. Three movements: Introduction and Allegro; Song; Finale. For Alan M. Clark. The three movements of the *Sonata* are well crafted and clearly varied in mood. The first is dramatic, the second lyrical, and the final movement is energetic and exciting. The writing is tonal and melodic. The work presents enough challenges to make it interesting, but it is not extremely difficult from a technical standpoint. The Song provides a good opportunity to showcase lyrical expressiveness and should be played without metronomic rigidity. The Finale, by contrast, with its mixed meters and syncopated rhythms, demands rhythmic precision. During the concluding movement the performer is often required to rapidly jump between the low and mid registers to present, nearly simultaneously, both the melody and its supporting baseline. This technique, reminiscent of methods used by J. S. Bach in his solo cello suites, is quite effective.

Constantinides, Dinos. *Fantasy for Solo Euphonium.* Cimarron Music. 1978. $7. 12:30. V. G1–d″. One movement. For Larry Campbell. This *Fantasy,* as the name implies, is very free in form. However, unlike many works of the same name, it is not at all lyrical or melodic in nature. The

work is built upon a series of atonal motivic fragments that are presented and developed, often in dramatic fashion, through repetition and rapid or gradual shifts in volume and/or tempo. Extreme dynamic contrasts and wide interval leaps are the norm throughout the work, so control and consistency while jumping between registers is necessary. Endurance is also needed, in particular to negotiate passages that require the repetition of an awkward passage several times while increasing the volume and intensity. The task of shaping the contrasting, fragmented, and unmelodic musical elements into a unified whole is the primary musical challenge of the piece. Individual performances of the composition could vary widely in detail because the burden of many of the musical decisions, such as how long to sustain a pitch, or how fast a passage should be played, is placed upon the shoulders of the soloist. When performed by a mature performer, able to make the most of its creative possibilities, this can be very exciting work.

Constantinides, Dinos. *Piece for Solo Tuba or Euphonium.* T.A.P. 1979. $5. 4:00. IV. F–c″. Apparently this work was originally written for tuba, and select passages were then raised one octave to make it suitable for euphonium. Like Constantinides's *Fantasy* (see above), this work is comprised of a series of fragmented atonal musical ideas, with many passages that contain repeated notes that speed up and then decelerate in a dramatic fashion. However, unlike the *Fantasy,* a time signature is used and a clear traditional overall structure (ABA form) may be discerned. Rhythms are complex and the work contains many arpeggiated patterns and some wide leaps. Musical maturity is required to pull the piece together into a musically coherent whole.

Cope, David. *BTRB.* Brass Music Ltd. 1974. $7. IV. One movement. For Tom Everett. Foot stomps and bassoon reeds are among the special effects used for this theatrical work, which relies heavily on extramusical sounds. Although originally written for bass trombone, the composer has specified that it may be adapted for any brass instrument.

Corwell, Neal. *Four Short Narratives.* Tuba-Euphonium Press. 1981 (revised 1996). $8. 6:00. III–IV. A♭1–b′. Four movements: Morning; Day of Celebration; Dusk; Night. This composition was first published as part of the *TUBA Journal* GEM Series. Each narrative is a miniature tone painting of a particular time of day. All movements begin with a descriptive theme, which, not coincidentally, contains as many notes as there are letters in the movement's title. The correspondence exists because the composer, using a personally developed system, assigned letters of the alphabet to musical pitches. During the unfolding of each narrative, the opening theme or motive is subsequently developed using techniques borrowed from the "serial method" of composition. *Morning* and *Dusk* are lyrical and generally quiet, the latter movement calling for use of a mute. *Day of Celebration,* by contrast, is vigorous and, at times, fanfare-like. *Night,* which depicts the eerie and frightening aspects of nighttime, is the most dramatic and least melodic or tonal movement. It makes use of flutter tonguing, half-valve glissandi, and harsh dynamic changes. It does, however, end softly and peacefully, bringing the work to a quiet conclusion.

Corwell, Neal. *Improvisations on a Bach Sarabande.* Nicolai Music & ITEA GEM Series (2005). 2003. $25. 6:30. IV. D1–d″ (*ossia* F–bb′). One movement. Although this work comes with recorded accompaniment, it is designed so that it may also be performed as an unaccompanied solo. The soloist is also given the option of performing with or without a mute. The *Sarabande* from J. S. Bach's *Cello Suite No. 2* is the source for the melodic ideas that constitute the substance of this composition. The written solo, if performed effectively, sounds as though it is improvised. A wide range from high to low registers is required, but no passages could be classified as technically difficult. If the reduced range offered in the *ossia* passages is utilized, the difficulty level is significantly reduced. See listing under Music for Euphonium and Electronic Media.

Coryn, Roland. *Inquieto.* CeBeDeM-Brussels. 1991. 8:00. V. G♯1–c♯″. One movement. A clear and balanced arch form structure is used to hold together the dramatic elements of this composition. Although rhythms are notated conventionally, no time signature or bar lines are provided, so the soloist has much interpretative freedom. A great number of challenges are presented to include wide interval leaps, extreme and sudden dynamic contrasts, lip trills, passages requiring multiple tonguing, and a chromatic language that adds to the difficulty of the many rapidly accelerating runs. The most difficult, and perhaps most exciting, portion of the work is the central section, which is built upon a relentless succession of rapid hard-driving quintuplets.

Coryn, Roland. *In Un Tempo per Tenor-Tuba.* 1987. 4:00. IV. Bb1–c″. Five contiguous movements: Lento; L'istesso tempo; Vivo; Lento; L'istesso tempo. The work begins with a quiet, but dramatic, opening thematic idea, which is subsequently developed during the rest of the piece. Rhythm, melodic shape, and dynamics all work together to create many effective climactic moments during the unfolding of the work. The overall structure is an arch form with the central contrasting section, the Vivo, presenting most of the technical challenges. The fervent leaps of the second movement are mirrored in the fourth movement, and the final movement is a recap of the opening, although at a different pitch level. Wide interval leaps, dramatic

dynamic contrasts, a chromatic tonal language, and complex rhythms used to create the feeling of acceleration are the primary technical hurdles the soloist must master.

Croley, Randell. *Sonata.* Philharmonia Corporation. 1983. 7:00. IV–V. E–g′. Three movements: Moderato; Fast; Marcato. This is an atonal twelve-tone work. The three movements are similar in tempo but divergent in style. The first movement, using a rounded form, begins with accented and rhythmic material, which is followed by contrasting sustained and legato themes before returning to the opening material. The second movement uses a similar formal structure, but thematic material is more slurred and connected. The final Marcato, which opens with a fanfare-like passage, is the most awkward and disjunctive movement. The composition is not particularly well suited to the euphonium, or a significant addition to the repertoire, but it could serve as an introductory study to twelve-tone music.

DeFotis, William. *Euphoniana.* American Composers Alliance. 1972. 5:00. V. G1–d″. One movement. For Mark Sikorski. This work makes extensive use of avant-garde techniques. The performer is required to whisper random syllables through the horn, click the valves, and sing using specified tongue positions. Extremes in range and dynamics are prevalent, and rhythms are sometimes so complex as to be nearly indiscernible. Hints at modified arch form are barely detectable, and most listeners, on first hearing, would judge the piece to be random and unorganized.

Dragonetti, D. *Concert Etude.* Arr. Randall Block. Musical Evergreen. 1975. $4. 3:10. III. E–g′. One movement. This transcription is often performed on F tuba and lies within a very comfortable register for the euphonium. It is a spirited work, full of sixteenth note runs intertwined with pleasant melodies. The rapid running passages are based on predictable diatonic patterns, with the biggest challenge being some octave leaps in the coda. The musical language is what one would expect of a composer of the same generation as Mozart. It is a delightful piece, fun to play, but perhaps a little too brief to stand on its own as a recital selection.

Erdman-Abele, Veit. *Es war ein König in Thule.* Blasmusikverlag Schulz GmbH. 1987. $9.50. 3:30. III. c–c″. One movement. After a statement of the simple title theme, a nineteenth-century melody by Carl Friedrich Zelter, six variations are presented. Both musical examples and text (in German) are used to illustrate the relationship of these variations to the theme. However, because of the numerous awkward and abrupt shifts in rhythm and tonality, the listener and performer will probably have a difficult time aurally discerning the stated relationships to the source material. The technical difficulties are few.

The performer only needs to negotiate several slurred sixteenth note passages and some wide interval leaps. However, the musical challenge of presenting the work in a coherent fashion is daunting because the piece, as written on the page, seems disjointed and lacking in musical direction or flow.

Falcone, Nicholas D. *Mazurka*. Tuba-Euphonium Press. 1964. $10. 4:00. III–IV. F–bb'. One movement. For Glenn P. Smith. Written by the brother of baritone horn virtuoso Leonard Falcone, this solo is very melodic and sounds as though it was written during the romantic era. In fact, it is reminiscent of the violin caprices of Paganini. The rapid sixteenth note passages, interspersed with other melodic fragments, are impressive, but not actually technically difficult to any great extent. The piece could serve well as an encore piece because it is fun to listen to and perform, particularly if a generous portion of playful and expressive rubato is used.

Fisher, Eric. *Bagatelle 1 & 2*. 4:30. III. Eb–ab'. Two movements: Adagio and Allegro. As one would expect from the title, both pieces are short and unpretentious. The slow opening movement is very simple melodically and makes use of a somewhat chromatic harmonic language. The second *Bagatelle* is clearly diatonic and very repetitive. Although the second movement proceeds at a rapid tempo, the only true technical challenges to be found are the rapid meter changes and occasional mixed meter passages. The simplistic melodic lines and lack of variety do not offer much to hold the listener's attention, making it difficult for the pieces to stand on their own as recital material without the addition of a complementary musical accompaniment.

Frackenpohl, Arthur. *Sonata for Solo Euphonium*. Tuba-Euphonium Press. 1994. $8. 9:15. III–IV. A1–bb'. Three movements: Intrada; Aria; Scherzo. For Brian Bowman. Syncopated rhythms and arpeggiated melodic patterns are the principal characteristics of the Intrada. The Aria begins with a gracefully arching melodic line that subsequently goes through several rhythmic transformations before returning in its original form near the end of the movement. The biggest technical hurdles are saved for the Scherzo, which features rapid sixteenth note runs, wide interval leaps, syncopated rhythms, and many sudden shifts in meter. Overall, the work is conservative in approach and light in nature.

Frackenpohl, Arthur. *Suite for Unaccompanied Bass Trombone or Euphonium*. Anglo American Music Publishers. 1983. 7:30. IV. G1–a'. Four movements: Aria; Scherzo; Recitative; Allegro. For Donald Knaub. Although originally intended for bass trombone, this suite also works well as a euphonium solo. The composer specifically names the euphonium as an alternate instrument choice, and addresses the one non-idiomatic feature of the work by specifying in the score that when playing "on euphonium, glisses may be done as chromatic grace notes or rips." One finds a variety of styles within this interesting work, from the simple and rich melodic lines of the Aria, to the rapid staccato prancing of the Scherzo. Although contemporary in style and chromatic in harmonic language, no avant-garde techniques are used. There are, however, numerous technical challenges in the form of mixed meters, free declamatory rhythms, syncopations, wide interval leaps, sudden dynamic changes, and brief passages that require double tonguing. Because of the emphasis on the low range, both a strong low register and good facility with the fourth valve are prerequisites for an effective performance of the work.

Gabrieli, Domenico. *Ricercare*. Arr. Sarro. 2:20. III–IV. A–b'. One movement. This transcription is intelligently edited, with well-placed breath markings and articulation choices that work well for a brass instrument. Because of the moderate tempo and diatonic nature of the work, the sixteenth note patterns are not difficult. However, the high tessitura makes this a challenging work for one without a strong embouchure. Because of the high range, the transcriber has wisely chosen to notate the composition entirely in tenor clef for ease of reading. This *Ricercare* is a good stereotypical musical example of Renaissance instrumental music, but because of its short duration, it would be more useful as concert repertoire if paired with another movement or included in a suite of pieces from that era.

Garcia, D. Manuel. *Suite for Solo Euphonium*. TUBA GEM Series. 1977. 5:00. IV. Eb–e''. Five movements: Molto leggiero; Slow, with rubato; Faster; Tempo ad lib with rubato; Fast. For Mark A. Dennis. This suite is actually a theme and variations solo, with movements two through five being variants of the first movement, each progressively more difficult and further removed from the original thematic material. All the movements are brief, between forty and eighty seconds in duration. The writing is in some ways traditional, but with a contemporary twist in the form of a chromatic tonal language that results in unexpected melodic turns. It is the non-diatonic melodic patterns, along with some syncopation, complex rhythms, and sudden dynamic changes, that make this a more challenging work than one might suspect at first glance.

Gillingham, David R. *Blue Lake Fantasies*. Tuba-Euphonium Press. 1999. $10. 11:00. IV–V. Bb1–f''. Five movements: Firefly; Moonlight Across the Water; All That Jazz; Ancient Air; Party-Antics. For Leonard Falcone International Euphonium Festival. This suite is both entertaining and challenging. Each movement portrays an image associated with the Blue Lake Fine Arts Camp at Twin Lake, Michigan. The musically painted images range from the simulation of the varied flight patterns of a firefly to a personal reflection on the beauty of moonlight on a shimmering lake. It is apparent that the composer has a good grasp of the capabilities and strengths of the euphonium because, although numerous technical challenges are offered, all are idiomatically feasible. Lightning-fast technique is required for the Firefly, while a more fluid dexterity is needed for Moonlight Across the Water. A good grasp of "swing style" is a must for a convincing rendition of All That Jazz (which is muted throughout), and the Ancient Air calls for mastering of basic multi-phonic technique plus a good lung capacity. The concluding Party-Antics, as one would expect from the title, is playful, fast, and fun.

Globokar, Vinko. *Echanges.* Henry Litolff's Verlag/ C. F. Peters. 1975. $28. Indeterminate duration, difficulty, and range. One movement. This work is intended for performance by any brass instrument. It is avant-garde in nature and uses no traditional notation. Instead, the performer is presented with four pages of graphic notation symbols, which may be interpreted by referencing explanatory notes (entirely in German). A tone row, presented in the explanatory notes, also plays a role in the interpretation of the symbols. A microphone is to be placed near specific slide and valve openings, and loudspeakers are to be placed behind the audience. Other extended techniques include pitch bends, flutter tonguing, glissandi, trills, mutes, various mouthpieces, and reeds. See listing under Music for Euphonium and Electronic Media.

Grady, Michael T. *Soliloquy.* Tuba-Euphonium Press. 1992. $8. 3:00. IV. E1–b'. One movement. The lyrical reflective mood of this work's opening lines gives way to a fast tempo and agitated style a minute or two into the piece. From that point on, the tempo generally increases with each brief section. Although some of the thematic ideas show promise, the general impression is one of a few scattered musical statements, some brief flurries of activity, and then a conclusion that is abrupt and unsatisfying. The writing is traditional in nature and the technical difficulties, arpeggiated patterns and some syncopations, are only difficult when taken at the breakneck speeds specified by the metronome markings the composer has provided within the score.

Grant, James. *Stuff.* Tuba-Euphonium Press, Grantwood Music Press. $6. 5:00. III–IV. G–bb'. Eight movements: Theme; Lullaby; Insistent; Cartoon Music; Gregarious; Urgent; More Urgent; Swing It! For Solstice/Equinox Commissioning Consortium. This light work, commissioned as a tuba solo by a large consortium of tubists, has been arranged for euphonium by the composer. The range of this version suits the euphonium well, although the character of some portions of the composition is clearly geared more toward the tuba. The theme, a rhythmically simple and melodically interesting idea stated at the start of the work, is treated to seven variations, each given a descriptive title. None of the variations are very long, and some are only a few seconds in duration. The musical language is harmonically conservative, and the overall mood is playful, with some mock seriousness thrown in occasionally for good measure. The piece ends with a restatement of the theme and a brief humorous codetta. The variety of moods and styles presented within such a small time frame will provide a challenge to the musical versatility of the soloist, as will a few of the rhythmic and articulation patterns, but no extreme technical hurdles are presented.

Haas, Wolfgang G. *St. Anthony's Choral mit 5 Variationen und Finale, op. 21.* Wolfgang G. Haas-Musikverlag Köln. 2001. $8. 3:00. II. Bb–g'. Seven movements: Theme; Moderato; Allegro; Andante; Scherzando; Allegro; Finale. The piece begins with a statement of the title theme, which is subsequently followed by five brief variations, all in different tempi and styles. The chorale melody then returns, presented in the manner of a stately march, to bring the work to a close. Triplet and sixteenth note passages at a brisk tempo, but utilizing basic diatonic patterns, are the biggest challenge. For the younger or less-advanced player, this work could serve as a good introduction to theme and variations form.

Hewitt, Harry. *Sonatina, Op. 275. No. 10.* 1979. 8:30. III–IV. F–b'. Three movements: Moderato; Legato; Finale. The first two movements both begin with a simple melodic idea that appears to be folk-like in character. In the first prelude, the theme is followed by a series of disjointed musical statements in various tempos, which are generally devoid of musical interest and do not appear to bear any relationship to one another. The second movement stays in one slow tempo throughout, again lacking an engaging musical flow. The final movement is fast and includes many awkward fingering patterns built upon half steps and major triads. When considered as a whole, the *Sonatina* lacks musical cohesiveness and offers little for either performers or audiences.

Hoch, Peter. *From the Quiet . . .* Tuba-Euphonium Press. 1996. $8. 14:00. V. F1–c''. Five contiguous movements: Free; Con Moto; Speech; Fast; Final. For Angie Hunter. This composition calls for the use of the euphonium in many non-traditional ways. However, because the unusual techniques employed work well idiomatically, it appears that the composer is either well acquainted with the instrument or sought detailed input from a euphonium player. In addition to removing two valve slides, reciting text, and blowing air in various prescribed ways through the horn, the soloist is also required to play two other instruments: crotales and a small organ pipe. The organ pipe is to be used as a whistle and "should be placed in the corner of the mouth and played together with the euphonium tone." The stage directions and performance instructions (in both German and English) are stated clearly and concisely. The euphonium part is notated on a standard staff, but bar lines and time signatures are lacking for much of the piece. Fast passages, because they are not built upon familiar diatonic patterns, are sometimes non-intuitive, but they are, nevertheless, quite playable. Although there is extensive use of extramusical effects, the work is surprisingly lyrical, and contains some haunting tonal melodic passages. Unlike many works of similar avant-garde description, this work is actually a very effective and moving concert piece in the hands of a competent performer.

Hunt, Clyde E. *Chacone.* B-Flat Music Production. 1992. $10. 4:00. IV–V. A1–e♭". Six movements: I; II; III; IV; V; VI. For Willian Booth Best. The piece consists of a simple theme followed by five variations. The variations follow the general pattern found in many old-style cornet solos but lack the ingenuity, variety, and spirit found within the famous solos by Clarke, Bellstedt, and Arban. None of the variations require multiple tonguing, but extremely wide interval leaps are called for in the final variation, and the penultimate variation is a study in adding arpeggiated grace notes to a melodic line. Though computer-generated, the score is rather sloppy, and there are discrepancies in pitch and articulation between the treble and bass clef versions of the solo part.

Israel, Brian. *Dance Suite.* Tritone Press/Theodore Presser. 1977. $6. 4:30. III. E–b'. Three movements: Polka; Waltz; Tarantella. The three brief movements of this suite are all light in character. The Polka provides a merry start to the composition, and the lively Tarantella brings it to an energetic close. The middle movement, Waltz, offers some surprising and sudden deviations from the standard triple meter, to keep both performer and audience alert. Though not profound, this can be an enjoyable little piece.

Mutter, Gerbert. *Monodie: 4 Kleine Skizzen.* Moseler Verlag. 1974. $3.50. 5:00. II–III. B♭–f'. Four movements: Berüßung; Synkopia; Ernste Melodie; Abmarsch. These four short musical sketches are interesting and well-crafted pieces of music that should be useful to young performers as both study and performance material. Although some passages are not as simple as they first appear, the difficulty level is low. Syncopations in the second movement are the primary rhythmic challenge, and good single tonguing technique is required to play the triplets cleanly in the final study.

Nelson, Gary. *Verdigris.* Tuba-Euphonium Press. 1995. $8. 7:15. III–IV. A1–ab'. One movement. This work was created "with the aid of a computer program which emphasized certain intervallic structures." The language is atonal, and no bar lines or time signatures are provided. Rhythms, however, are not complex, and are notated in standard fashion. A poem, related to the varied definitions of the composition's title, is presented in piecemeal fashion during the unfolding of the work. *Verdigris* is not complex and, other than the reciting of text and a few glissandos, is rather conventional.

Paganini, Niccolo. *Caprice No. 24.* Arr. David Werden. Cimarron Music. 1983. $5.50. 3:00. IV. D–c". One movement. This version of one of Paganini's most famous violin caprices, a theme with variations, works well for euphonium because of the good choices made by the arranger. Since it was conceived as a showpiece, it is, not surprisingly, a technically challenging piece. The performer must negotiate many rapid scale and arpeggio patterns and have a mastery of double tonguing to present an effective performance. Expressive maturity is required to tie the variations together musically and to occasionally add rubato without disrupting the flow of the music.

Paganini, Niccolo. *Four Caprices.* Arr. David Werden. Cimarron Music. 1983. $6.50. IV. D–c". Four Caprices: Nos. 13, 17, 20, 24. This collection of arrangements of violin caprices includes *Caprice No. 24* (see entry above), plus three other technical showpieces. All are transposed into simple keys, and have been edited to make them idiomatically feasible, without removing the energy and flavor of the originals. The difficulties presented by the various pieces is diverse and includes wide interval leaps, fast scale passages and arpeggios, and double tonguing.

Pantalone, Gordie. *Suite for Unaccompanied Euphonium.* 1981. 5:30. IV. D♯–c". Four movements: Andante; Alla Marcia; Cantibile; Rondo and Finale. A balanced mixture of lyricism and energy may be found within the four interesting and well-crafted movements of this suite. Though not exceptionally difficult, mixed meters, frequent time signature changes, and rapid shifts between duple and triplet-based rhythms may be found in the two fast movements. The opening Andante, dramatic in nature, has no bar lines, but uses standard rhythmic values. The final movement, with its sixteenth note patterns and occasional sextuplets, is the most challenging, but the moderate tempo substantially lessens the difficulty level.

Patterson, Merlin. *Episodes.* TUBA GEM Series. 1979. 3:00. IV–V. A1–c". Three contiguous movements: Recitative; Slow and Relaxed; Fast and Furious. This work relies heavily on avant-garde techniques and uses a contemporary musical language. The Recitative is soft and creates a mysterious mood for the opening of the piece. A mute is gradually removed and re-inserted while sustaining pitch, thereby gradually raising and lowering the pitch. The section that follows, although slow and generally melodic, contains some harsh outbursts and extremes of register, to include a high and loud passage that is the dramatic climax of the work. Some difficult multi-phonic passages are found within this central section. The fast tempo, driving rhythms, and mixed meters of the final section are accented by foot stomps. After some building of intensity, the energy subsides into a soft concluding finale, which is reminiscent of the opening sustained section and again employs multi-phonic technique. Some practice will be required to master required physical techniques such as the adjusting of the mute and the stomping of one's feet while playing, but the demands on coordination are not unreasonable.

Remson, Michael. *Fanfare and Air.* Tuba-Euphonium Press. 1997. $8. 6:20. III–IV. C♯–b'. One movement. This composition is in basic ternary ABA form, with the *Air* serving as the contrasting middle section. The opening and closing sections, labeled *Fanfare* by the composer, do not actually sound very fanfare-like. The main motive is a rising crescendo and glissando leading from one sustained pitch to another. Eventually some marcato statements are presented that one would associate with a fanfare. The central section is lyrical and song-like, featuring a melody that is folk-like in its simplicity. The piece features wide interval leaps, high articulated passages, much use of the range below the bass clef staff, and some mixed meter passages. However, overall, the work is not extremely complex rhythmically or otherwise.

Schneider, Willy. *Fünf Epigramme.* Moseler Verlag. 1982. $6.75. 6:30. III. B♭1–c". Five movements: Feierlich, nicht zu langsam; Lebhaft; Etwas fließend; capriziös; Sehr lebhaft. For Hermann Egner. The five movements are brief, simplistic, and comprised largely of conventional and predictable melodic and rhythmic patterns, although a few unexpected harmonic shifts are thrown in on occasion. When seeking out recital repertoire, a performer advanced enough to have the embouchure strength for the required range, and enough agility to accurately negotiate the wide leaps, is likely to prefer other works of more musical substance.

Schulz, Patrick. *Constellation.* TubaQuartet.com. 1999. 10:00. IV–V. F1–c♯". Five movements: Cassiopeia; Eridanus; Sagittarius; Gemini; Scorpius. For Scott Anderson. The five movements are each meant to be descriptive of a particular constellation found in the night sky. They are classified as "concert etudes," meaning they could be used either for private study or as public recital material. Motivic materials for each movement are built around a specific set of intervals (which are given in parentheses underneath the etude title), and they appear to be arranged in progressive order with the final etude, Scorpius,

being the most difficult. Although originally intended for trombone solo, the pieces are very well suited to the euphonium, and despite the atonal language and angular disjunct melodic contours, the work is quite playable and should be accessible to most audiences. Recorded by Demondrae Thurman.

Steiger, Daniel. *New Generated Norms.* Tuba-Euphonium Press. 1985. $8. 7:00. IV. A1–c". Four movements: A True Beginning; Space without Time; Is It Really Life?; A Frightening Reality! For Anatol Eberhard. The composer states that this work is derived "from the knowledge gained about the present scientific theories of the origins of life on earth and the origins of our solar system." The music is basically tonal with no use of avant-garde techniques, and the movements are varied in style and in mood, in keeping with the various descriptive titles. During A True Beginning, silence is given a role almost equal to that of sound as the movement unfolds from a single short motive. Space without Time, a slow and sustained movement, is dominated by long note values and dependent upon close attention to dynamics and other markings for musical direction. Unity is derived from recurring thematic material in the fast and furious Is It Really Life?, the first movement to present technical challenges to the performer. The final movement, A Frightening Reality!, is the most difficult and features a fast tempo and a mixture of meters and rhythmic patterns. The variety and good musical flow and direction of this movement make it the highlight of the work.

Stevens, John. *Elegy.* ITEA GEM Series. 2004. 5:00. III. F–b♭' (*ossia* F–a'). One movement. Despite the title, this work is not dark or somber in nature. Instead, the focus is on neo-romantic melodic lines, built around a four-note motive stated at the opening of the piece. The sustained nature of the piece is somewhat demanding in regard to endurance, but the range requirements are moderate and the clearly expressive nature of the piece allows the soloist liberties regarding breathing, phrasing, tempi, dramatic pauses, and so forth. Although lyrical and song-like throughout, some complex rhythms may be found. Sometimes they are no more than notated melodic ornamentations, and at other times these rhythms propel the melodic line forward, adding momentum to the expressive and beautiful lyrical lines. When printed in the *ITEA Journal,* a notational system was used whereby the composition may be read in either bass clef or b♭ treble clef, with the bass clef version (a perfect fifth lower in actual pitch) intended for tubists.

Stevens, John. *Soliloquies for Solo Euphonium.* Tuba-Euphonium Press. 2001. $10. 9:00. IV–V. A1–b♭'. Three movements: Maestoso; Adagio; Vivace. For Demondrae Thurman. This multi-movement work is a well-crafted and musically cohesive concert piece, full of exciting and interesting thematic material. The first movement is a study in contrasts, vacillating between bold declamatory statements and fast, somewhat delicate, rhythmic motives. The middle movement features the development of a haunting and angular melodic line. The concluding Vivace features a fast tempo, mixed meters with odd metric shifts, sudden dynamic contrasts, wide interval leaps, and rapid chromatic passages. The technical and expressive demands of this work are numerous, but the effort is worth the reward. Recorded by Demondrae Thurman.

Vazzana, Anthony. *Euphonisms*. 1994. 16:00. V. C♯–d♭″. Five movements: Dialogue; Wistful Song; Upward Mobility; Remembrance; Kinesis. The programmatic titles of the five movements match well the character of each movement. The Dialogue, for example, creates the illusion of two euphoniums in conversation with one another, and for Upward Mobility, the soloist negotiates rapid passages throughout, which begin in the low register and gradually work upward toward the highest register. The composer suggests that any movement may be performed separately as an individual concert piece, or paired or grouped with other movements in a number of ways. Because of the length of movements, lack of rests, and generally high tessitura for all the movements, the demands on endurance are enormous. In addition, the constant streams of awkward atonal sixteenth note runs place tremendous mental and technical demands upon the soloist. This difficulty is magnified by the fact that the score, which is handwritten, is often crowded and difficult to decipher.

Vetter, K. *Music for Euphonium*. The Musical Evergreen. 1975. 3:15. IV–V. D–e♭″. One movement. The opening theme is rhythmically simple and based on a basic melodic pattern that rises up by the interval of a third and then descends by a half step. This opening motive seems to be the basis for the entire work, and it is not developed in an interesting or imaginative fashion. Therefore *Music for Euphonium* appears to be more of a method book study than concert piece. The rhythms are basic and simple, but the demands on the high range are extensive. The switch from bass to tenor clef for much of the final section is appropriate because of the very high tessitura.

Wiggins, Christopher. *Soliloquy IX*. Neuschel Music. 1997. $12. 4:00. IV. B♭–d♭″. One movement. The work begins with the bold statement of a three-note motive, which is subsequently developed in an interesting and imaginative fashion throughout the entire composition. Although the meter and tempo are constant during the moderately fast opening portion of the piece, the pace is varied by rhythmic means. The central contrasting lyrical section, yet another variant of the opening motive, features a slower tempo and calls for use of a mute. The bold and dramatic spirit of the opening section, with its rhythms that often create the feeling of acceleration or deceleration, then returns to bring the work to its conclusion. A good sense of rhythm is needed if the complex rhythms are to serve their function of propelling the music forward. If performed in a mechanical fashion, they could hinder the musical flow of the piece. Most of the work lies within the comfortable mid-register, and it is only in the final bars that the soloist is asked to play above high b♭.

Wood, Gareth. *Three Pieces*. G&M Brand Publications. $5.50. 6:00. III. B♭–f′. Three movements: Fantasia; Aubade; Capriccio. The work is conservative in range and tonality, making it quite playable. In the opening and closing movements, the melodic patterns are simple, but the brisk tempi and quirky syncopations suffice to make them interesting for the performer and amusing for the audience. Double tonguing is required to perform the Capriccio at the indicated tempo, and triple tonguing is required for the optional ending. The central contrasting movement has some unexpected tonal shifts and is dominated by quintuplet-based rhythms.

Woodsen, Thomas. *Musings*. Available from composer. 2000. 7:00. Fantasy form.

Zoelen, Andreas van. *Tzigane Mansarda-Sintra*. 2002. $9. 1:45. IV. G1–b♭′. One movement. For Steven Mead. This piece begins and ends with sections devoted to repetition of a short fanfare-like motive. The brief contrasting central section features pedal tones and one use of multi-phonic technique. Challenges include numerous high trills, ascending glissandi, and rapid descending arpeggiated patterns, sometimes requiring multiple tonguing. The short length, coupled with the lack of variety and the absence of a satisfying conclusion, is a weakness that makes it difficult for the work to stand on its own as a concert piece.

8. Music for Euphonium and Electronic Media

Neal Corwell

In the not so distant past, this chapter would have been titled "Solos with Tape," but such a designation is no longer accurate. Today's modern digital audio storage mediums, with the exception of DAT (digital audio tape), are tapeless. And although several works included in this chapter were initially recorded onto analog tape (reel-to-reel or cassette), digital storage media is now the norm, with CD (compact disc) being the current preferred medium. It should also be noted that numerous works call for the use of electronic sound processors in real time during live performance, hence the enhanced accuracy of the updated chapter title. The word "solo" is not included in the chapter title because, although most of the works listed are indeed solos, compositions in the electronic idiom calling for euphonium in combination with other instruments, such as tuba/euphonium duo with CD accompaniment, are also included.

The Performance Medium

Works with recorded accompaniments offer many potential benefits to a performer. In a recital situation, the primary accompaniment instrument of choice is, with good reason, the piano. It is a marvelously flexible instrument and, in the hands of a talented pianist, capable of creating many nuances of color and texture. However, electronic instruments are capable of creating an even wider variety of timbres, attacks, and effects, and when paired with modern multi-track recording and mixing techniques, the sonic possibilities are virtually endless. Adding a solo with recorded accompaniment and/or live electronics to one's repertoire is a relatively simple way of adding variety and contrast to a recital program. With the push of a button, a novel and exciting audio environment may be created, and the musical horizons of both audience and performer expanded.

Another benefit to using a recorded accompaniment is that many questions the performer may have concerning phrasing, tempos, dynamics, articulations, and other interpretive nuances are likely to be answered by simply listening to the recording. The composer has recorded the accompaniment as it is intended to be performed, and this provides a clear guide for the soloist. This is particularly true when there is interaction between the live and recorded voices, because the live soloist may imitate the interpretive shadings heard in the recorded performance. The fact that one begins preparing the work by listening to the final version of the electronic performance is a help, but it can also be a hindrance. The tempos, for example, are usually inflexible, and this rigidity of tempo restricts the creative flexibility of the artist. A performer's interpretation of a particular work usually changes during the course of repeated performances, but this evolutionary process is severely restricted when working with an inflexible recording. The recording's consistency is reassuring, but its unyielding nature can be frustrating. Most composers are aware of this limitation and plan their compositions so as to allow the soloist some freedom of expression, often by including cadenzas or extensive un-metered sections. This brings us to a cautionary statement that I believe should be made to all who intend to perform a work with recorded accompaniment: "Don't forget to make music!" In order to stay in synchronization with the accompaniment, much concentration is necessarily devoted to listening to the playback of the recording, and this often distracts soloists from the finer details of their own performance. Although it is important that the performer be aware of the whereabouts of the recording at all times, since it will certainly not alter its playback to accommodate the soloist, it is also crucial that the soloist concentrate on listening to, and fine-tuning, his or her own live performance. It should appear to the audience that the soloist is in charge and leading the way, as would be the case if a pianist were providing the accompaniment. Careful preparation and numerous thorough rehearsals with the recording are vital if one wishes to avoid this pitfall, because when worries over "keeping up" with the accompaniment disappear, the mind is free to focus on more important matters such as the subtleties of musical expression.

Performance Preparation Advice

When practicing with a recording, one of the chief challenges is finding ways to cope with the inflexibility of tempos. The live and recorded components cannot be combined until the solo part has been worked up to performance tempo, so until this level of proficiency on the part of the soloist is achieved, it may be difficult to get a feel for how the composition fits together as a musical whole. If the soloist has access to a recording of the composition with solo part added, repeated listening will be a beneficial first step. As a courtesy to the soloist, reference recordings of this nature are often included as an extra track on the accompaniment CD. However, to acquire a true feel for a piece of music, merely listening is not as beneficial as physically performing with the accompaniment. Sometimes the composer or arranger will supply various so-called "practice versions" of a piece at slower tempi than the final performance version. Having slower versions to work with gives the soloist the opportunity of performing with the accompaniment before full technical proficiency has been attained, and even when technical problems are not an issue, slowing the tempo of a piece is a good strategy for thoroughly observing and absorbing all the elements of a musical composition. It is also a good strategy for memorizing music, if that is one of your goals.

Current technology has made available several affordable devices for creating your own variable-speed versions of works with recorded accompaniment. The manufacturer Stereoscope makes a CD deck, model PSD-220, that will alter the speed of a playback, faster or slower and by small or large increments, without changing the pitch of the accompaniment. The option of automatically repeating selected sections of a piece (called A-B repeat) is another capability of this device. For slightly more money, the PSD-230 has the additional capability of changing the pitch without altering the tempo, although it cannot alter speed and pitch at the same time. The PSD-300 has the same capability of the PSD-230 but is twice as expensive because it features a second CD drive and CD recording capability. Even more affordable than the Stereoscope PSD-220 are the various Tascam practice devices, models CD-GT1, CD-BT1, and CD-VT1. Although less expensive, the Tascam machines are only capable

of slowing down the tempo, and fewer tempo increment choices are available. I should caution you that the aforementioned devices by Tascam and Stereoscope are affordable because their digital processing components are not of the caliber that you would find in high-end professional studio equipment. Some distortion is likely to be evident when altering the speed (or pitch) of the playback. The degree of distortion will be in proportion to the amount of the tempo change and dependent on the nature and complexity of the audio source material. Despite their small audio shortcomings, these devices are quite useful as practice aids.

In addition to the musical benefits already mentioned, works utilizing recorded accompaniments also offer some practical advantages. First of all, because one is not working with a live accompanist, there are no scheduling problems. The soloist may rehearse whenever and wherever it is convenient. All that is needed is a playback device plus speakers or headphones with which to hear the accompaniment. There is also no need to worry whether the technical demands of the piece exceed the skills of your pianist. There is a financial bonus as well, because you do not need to pay an accompanist for his or her time and services. For the guest artist performing at several venues and usually arriving the day of the performance, the advantages are clear. When performing a work with your recorded accompaniment, there is no need to send the music ahead, worry about the skills or preparedness of your accompanist, or rush through a pre-performance rehearsal, which can be stressful and always drains time and energy from the soloist.

Along with the advantages come disadvantages. All components in the audio chain need to function properly for any sound to be heard at all, so you need to familiarize yourself with the specific equipment to be used as far in advance as possible to avoid potential problems. You will also need to schedule advance preparation time in the performance hall to set up your equipment or test and familiarize yourself with equipment and personnel that may be supplied to you by the performance venue. If you are provided with on-site quality equipment and competent staff to operate the sound system, preparation will be simple. A sound check to ensure proper balance between soloist and recording should be all that is required. To avoid problems, be sure to communicate clearly with the staff prior to your arrival to ensure that they understand your technical needs. You should also bear in mind that even well-equipped halls are sometimes surprisingly limited in their playback and monitoring capabilities, plus unexpected problems caused by equipment failure or lack of a quality technical assistant can wreak havoc with a performance and the performer's nerves.

To avoid such problems, I prefer bringing my own sound system to performance venues when possible. I then need only roll the equipment into the hall, make a few connections, and do a quick sound check. This saves time and avoids stressful situations. An additional benefit to this approach is that, because I'm using my own equipment with which I'm very familiar, it is not likely that unexpected technical glitches will occur during a live performance. Also, if issues do come up, my familiarity with the gear will make it more likely that I will be able to solve the problem quickly and with little or no perceivable interruption in the flow of the program. Assembling a personal system might not be as complicated or expensive as you may think. A basic equipment setup would require only a playback deck and two speakers with built in amplifiers. My personal traveling performance gear consists of only a cart on wheels plus two speakers. The cart contains rack-mounted and pre-connected gear to include a mixer, amplifier, effects module, and two playback decks: one for CDs and another for mini-discs. Only one playback deck would be needed, but as a safety measure I have two different playback media available. The mixer and effects module are needed in my setup only because I sometimes use a microphone and other devices to perform works that involve live sound processing. For safety's sake, you should make two or more backup copies of the recorded accompaniment. When arriving at a performance venue, I usually have on hand two CD copies plus two mini-disc copies of all the works I will be performing. It is also advisable to have spare cables on hand, as well as adapters and other miscellaneous gear, in the event of any last-minute equipment malfunctions.

If your recorded accompaniment happens to be stored in an analog format (cassette or reel-to-reel tape), you have an additional potential problem on your hands: the inconsistency of tape-playback speed. Even properly functioning quality tape players often operate at slightly different speeds, and variations in speed equal variations in pitch center. To avoid surprises with regard to intonation, it is absolutely crucial that you test the playback deck in advance. Many high-end machines offer a solution by allowing you to adjust the speed of tape playback. To avoid such problems altogether, I recommend transferring tapes to your preferred form of digital media, all of which are immune from pitch variation problems.

Conclusion

Since the 1952 premiere of the first composition for live soloist and electronic music recorded on tape (*Musica su due dimensioni I* for flute and tape by Maderna), many composers, both major and minor, have written pieces for the combination. The potential of the electronic medium as a complement to the euphonium is enormous. With the quality and affordability of current digital recording equipment and the versatility of today's synthesizers, samplers, and sound processing equipment, the creative possibilities open to most musicians and composers would seem to be endless. Nevertheless, there currently seems to be only a small number of individuals interested in writing music for this genre. Hopefully this is a trend that will reverse itself in the near future.

Anonymous. *House of the Rising Sun*. Arr. Neal Corwell. Nicolai Music. Solo with CD. 2001. $25. 4:45. III. D–e″(D–a′ with optional *ossia*). CD includes accompaniment with recorded reference performance of the work and a printed part that includes essential accompaniment cues. After a leisurely introduction and two contrasting statements of this traditional blues/folk tune, the arranger has written out a challenging "improvised" solo to be performed over the rhythmic ostinato pattern of the accompaniment. The soloist is encouraged to write or improvise his or her own solo for this section, and is also given the option of playing the written solo with octave changes ad-lib. When the high range and rapid passages of the aforementioned "improvised" solo are extracted, few technical difficulties remain. The accompaniment consists primarily of recorded acoustic guitar, and an ensemble of horns (real, not synthesized) enters in support of the soloist for the final chorus.

Bach, Johann Sebastian. *Largo & Allegro*. Arr. Neal Corwell. Nicolai Music. Solo with CD (plus optional live treble instrument of choice). 2001. $25. 8:00. IV. F–c″. Two movements: Largo and Allegro. Largo is dedicated to victims of September 11, 2001. Two contrasting movements have been extracted from different Bach compositions. The Largo is from the *Harpsichord Concerto in f minor, BWV 1056*, and the Allegro is from his *Brandenburg Concerto No. 3*. The accompaniment for the opening lyrical movement is quiet and ethereal. The soloist is given Bach's original melodic line, and an obbligato countermelody has been added by the arranger. For the accompaniment CD, the obbligato is performed on classical guitar. The option of adding it live during actual performance has been made available by the inclusion of a printed part for the obbligato instrument (which need not be guitar) and an extra recorded accompaniment with the obbligato line extracted. For the Allegro, the soloist plays the prominent melodic lines of the ensemble work upon which the arrangement is based. The tempo is brisk, but no multiple tonguing is required. The rapid interval leaps that dominate the movement are the principal difficulty.

Boda, John. *Sonatina*. Cimarron Music. Solo with tape. 1970. 8:00. IV. E–b♭′. For Earle Louder. In the most recent available version, the accompaniment is on a cassette tape. The printed part includes a separate line for accompaniment cues. The accompaniment is an electronic realization of a tonal homophonic keyboard accompaniment (the composer published a piano version of the accompaniment in 1972). A Moog synthesizer is the principal sound source, but some euphonium lines (performed by Earle Louder) may be heard on the accompaniment tape. A traditional fast-slow-fast solo sonata format is used. The three brief movements are connected by cadenzas that give the soloist opportunities for personal expression, free from the inflexible tempos of the tape. Technical difficulties are not extraordinary, but the soloist will need to adjust to some unexpected tempo inconsistencies and learn to accurately space the cadenzas, and also the melodic phrases of the brief middle movement, over the allotted time. The composition's distinction as the first composition for euphonium and tape make it historically significant. Recorded by Brian Bowman.

Carastathis, Aris. *Differentia*.

Corwell, Neal. *Aboriginal Voices*. Nicolai Music. Solo with CD. 1994. $25. 7:30. III–IV. G1–a♭′. For Mark Nelson and Pete Hommel. CD includes accompaniment plus recorded reference performance of the work, and printed part includes essential accompaniment cues. This work is intended as a solo for tuba, euphonium, or bass trombone, and the soloist is permitted to take chosen passages up an octave at his or her own discretion. The accompaniment features a didjeridoo, simple percussion sounds, and an array of animalistic sounds created by sampling the composer's voice. An introductory cadenza creates a mystical atmosphere, preparing the way for a primal dance. Once the dance begins, its strong rhythmic drive persists through the remainder of the composition. A strong low range and crisp consistent single tonguing are required for an effective performance. Some meter changes are likely to offer difficulties, and multi-phonics are used briefly during the introduction. Recorded by Velvet Brown, Mark Nelson.

Corwell, Neal. *Black Moon Rising*. Nicolai Music. Solo with CD. 1997. $25. 6:45. III. F–b′.

Dedicated to Nick, the composer's dog. CD includes accompaniment plus recorded reference performance of the work, and printed part includes separate line for accompaniment cues. This work was originally composed for solo euphonium accompanied by a small chamber ensemble (wind quartet, string bass, and timpani). The electronic version features not only sampled voices in imitation of the original acoustic instruments but also added electronic effects and textures. Because the artistic goal of the composition is to depict an eerie surreal landscape, the overall tone is dark and the harmony, though tonal, is largely dissonant. There are no technical difficulties, but endurance is required because most of the melodic lines are in the medium to high range of the instrument and there are few rests. Recorded by Neal Corwell. See listing under Music for Euphonium in Mixed Ensemble.

Corwell, Neal. *Dandy Noodles*. Nicolai Music. Solo with CD. 2001. $25. 5:00. IV. F1–c″. CD includes accompaniment plus recorded reference performance of the work, and printed part includes essential accompaniment cues. This tongue-in-cheek tribute to old-time cornet solos of 100 years ago features three variations on the patriotic tune *Yankee Doodle*. The accompaniment includes humorous acoustic additions such as duck calls and tap dancing, in addition to more conventional instruments. The soloist is given the option of using a homemade instrument (comprised of two plastic pipes and played like a trombone) for the opening and closing bars, and the middle blues-like movement may be made even more entertaining through the optional use of a plunger-like mute (a large plastic bowl is suggested). Wide interval leaps and triple tonguing head the list of technical difficulties. The concluding variation is reminiscent of the finales of the famous variations on *Carnival of Venice* by Arban and Clarke. Recorded by Neal Corwell. See listing under Music for Euphonium and Wind Band.

Corwell, Neal. *Distant Images*. Nicolai Music. Solo with CD. 1992. $25. 9:00. III. D–c″. For Ray Chaney. CD includes accompaniment plus recorded reference performance of the work, and printed part includes essential accompaniment cues. This work was designed as a solo for either trombone or euphonium. The unique tonal palette of the accompaniment was created by digitally sampling two primary sources: the voice of the composer, and the sound of a hammer striking various metallic objects. The influence of minimalism is apparent in the use of repetitive accompaniment patterns and sustained drones in support of the solo's melodic lines, in which two simple motivic ideas are continually developed and interwoven. The work begins with two cadenza-like sections, giving the soloist opportunity for freedom of expression. The pace then picks up for the remaining "images," which require the soloist to be rhythmically precise in order to maintain synchronization with the simple but intricate accompaniment patterns. The soloist uses both a straight mute and plunger-like mute to vary tone colors. There are no striking technical difficulties, and clear instructions regarding muting of the euphonium are provided. Recorded by Neal Corwell.

Corwell, Neal. *The Dream*. Tuba-Euphonium Press. Tuba/Euphonium duo with CD. 1995. $20. 6:45. IV. A1–d″. For Velvet Brown. CD includes accompaniment plus recorded reference performance of the work, and both duo parts are on the same page for easy ensemble reference. The work opens with dissonant tone clusters droning underneath a cadenza by the duo partners. The majority of the piece is fast in tempo with the rhythm of the accompaniment punctuated by percussive sounds and driving ostinato patterns. A martial atmosphere is created at key moments as field drums enter into the mix. The live duo is given the role of presenting and developing the thematic materials. Brisk slurred runs, double tonguing, and intricate rhythmic dovetailing between tuba and euphonium are the primary technical difficulties. The euphonium also needs to confidently pop out isolated high notes and play strongly in the pedal register to match the intensity of the tubist.

Corwell, Neal. *Fantasy on "Night."* Nicolai Music. Solo with CD and optional live electronics. 2004. $25. 11:00. V. E♭1–e″. CD includes accompaniment plus recorded reference performance of the work, and printed part includes essential accompaniment cues. This work is built upon thematic material drawn from the composer's earlier piece *Night,* the final movement of his *Four Short Narratives* for unaccompanied euphonium. The accompaniment is comprised of a mixture of tone clusters and various arpeggiated patterns, created by processing various vocal utterances through an effects module. After an unaccompanied opening exposition of source material, the accompaniment enters and the soloist begins developing the ideas thus far presented. Optional live effects may be added to the solo part, and instructions for doing so are included in the score. Effects range from simple reverb to ring modulation and pitch shifting: standard effects included in most effects modules. The soloist is called upon several times to blow air through the horn to create a wind sound, flutter tonguing is required, and one section requires a mute. Technical difficulties include disjunct angular chromatic patterns, wide leaps, rapid slurs from high pitches down to the pedal register, and sudden dynamic changes.

Corwell, Neal. *Heart of a Wolf.* Nicolai Music. Solo with CD. 1998. $25. 7:00. V. A1–d″. CD includes accompaniment plus recorded reference performance of the work, and printed part includes separate line for accompaniment cues. A series of episodes based upon the life of a wolf pack are the basis of this composition. The accompaniment is aggressive, atonal, rhythmic, and percussive. Challenges for the soloist include frequent meter changes, disjunct angular atonal melodic patterns, and rapid interval leaps. The work is brought to a close by a lengthy solo cadenza that can best be described as wild. As the pace of the cadenza slows near its conclusion, half-valve glissandos are used to imitate the howling of a wolf. Recorded by Neal Corwell.

Corwell, Neal. *Improvisations on a Bach Sarabande.* Nicolai Music. Solo with CD. 2003. $25. 6:30. III–IV. D1–d″. CD includes accompaniment plus recorded reference performance of the work, and printed part includes essential accompaniment cues. This work may be performed with or without accompaniment, and use of a mute is optional. The *Sarabande* from J. S. Bach's *Cello Suite No. 2* is the source material for the improvisatory melodic ideas that constitute the substance of this composition. The accompanying recording is comprised of additional improvisations based on the *Sarabande*'s thematic material, as performed by Corwell with a muted euphonium. The written solo, if performed effectively, sounds as though it is also improvised. A wide range from high to low registers is required, but no passages could be classified as technically difficult. See listing under Music for Unaccompanied Euphonium.

Corwell, Neal. *Meditation.* Nicolai Music. Solo with CD or live electronic keyboard accompaniment. 1992. $25. 7:00. III. C–c″. CD includes accompaniment plus recorded reference performance of the work. A printed part with essential cues is provided for the soloist, and a keyboard score is also included. If performed with live accompanist instead of CD accompaniment, an acoustic piano is not the composer's preferred instrument. Instead, an electronic keyboard or synthesizer should be used: one that features a standard patch, commonly found, that combines the sound of an acoustic piano with a sustained sound such as strings (usually referred to as a string or synth "pad"). As one would expect from the title, the work is quiet and introspective in nature. The harmony, based on the interval of a fourth instead of traditional thirds, is wandering and restless in nature. Although not technically difficult, there are some occasional wide slurred leaps, and good endurance is required. This composition later became the first movement of a euphonium concerto. Recorded by Neal Corwell. See listing (*Meditation & Finale: A Chamber Concerto in Two Movements*) under Music for Euphonium in Mixed Ensemble.

Corwell, Neal. *New England Reveries.* Nicolai Music. Solo with CD. 1990. $25. 9:15. IV. D–b′. For Mark Nelson. CD includes accompaniment plus recorded reference performance of the work. This work was designed as a solo for either euphonium or tuba, so parts for both instruments are included. This programmatic work is intended to evoke images of the New England landscapes. The work is primarily lyrical and the soloist is sometimes given elaborate and somewhat intricate countermelodies. Most technical challenges, which are moderate, come in the central sections, which are sprightly and dance-like in character. Recorded by Neal Corwell, Mark Nelson.

Corwell, Neal. Tuba-Euphonium Press. Solo with CD. 1989. $21. 9:30. III. D1–b′. CD includes accompaniment plus recorded reference performance of the work, and printed part includes essential accompaniment cues. The accompaniment uses many timbres and devices associated with "new age" music. The solo begins with a cadenza, during which principal thematic materials are presented. A lyrical song then ensues and continues, interrupted occasionally by contrasting melodic statements at the same tempo, until the conclusion of the work. Recorded by Neal Corwell.

Corwell, Neal. *Odyssey.* Nicolai Music. Solo with CD. 1990. $25. 13:15. IV–V. D–db″. Three contiguous movements: Theme with Variations; Lento; Presto. For Brian Bowman. CD includes accompaniment plus recorded reference performance of the work, and printed part includes separate line for accompaniment cues. The entire work is based on a simple lyrical motive presented in the introduction. The primary sections that follow echo the three movements of a traditional solo sonata. The first movement is a set of variations, and the second is slow and lyrical, based upon a whole-tone version of the primary theme. The finale is a presto in which new material is rapidly spun out from fragments of the original lyrical theme. Technical challenges are presented in many sections of the work, particularly in the finale, in which double tonguing is required. Much of the accompaniment uses timbres and devices associated with "new age" music. Recorded by Neal Corwell, Robin Taylor.

Corwell, Neal. *Quiet Mountain.* Nicolai Music. Duo for trombone and euphonium (or tuba) with CD or trio for two euphoniums, trombone with CD. 2000. $25. 8:00. III. F1–d′. CD includes accompaniment plus recorded reference performance of the work, and both duo parts are on the same page for easy ensemble reference. This piece is a tone poem inspired by a scene of natural beauty in the mountains of Hokkaido, Japan. Although originally intended as a duo for trombone and tuba, the nature of the piece makes the euphonium a viable substitute for the tuba. The composer has also made available a version in which two euphoniums join the trombone to form a trio. All incarnations of the work use the same CD accompaniment. Technical challenges

are few because the emphasis is on free lyrical expression. As the accompaniment provides a sustained and subtly shifting backdrop, the live performers answer one another freely and unhurriedly. For only one brief section in the middle of the piece is there a regular metered pulse, and drum beats heard during this section make it easy for the performers to synchronize with the recorded accompaniment. There is a loud dramatic climax at the end of the metered section, but all else is quiet and ethereal.

Corwell, Neal. *Ritual.* Nicolai Music. Tuba/euphonium duo with CD. 1997. $25. 9:30. V. F1–db″. For Velvet Brown. CD includes accompaniment plus recorded reference performance of the work, and both duo parts are on the same page for easy ensemble reference. The euphonium and tuba share equally challenging roles in this tumultuous duo. After the opening chant-like meditative section, the accompaniment becomes rhythmically forceful and percussive, and a "primal" atmosphere is created through the use of shouting and chanting voices. The duo parts are also aggressive. In addition to flutter tonguing and valve tremolos, other technical challenges include triple tongued arpeggiated patterns and slurred sextuplet patterns. The euphonium player also needs a strong high range and good endurance to successfully navigate the entire composition. Recorded by Neal Corwell, Velvet Brown.

Corwell, Neal. *Simyeh.* Nicolai Music. Solo with CD. 1994. $25. 12:30. V. D1–c″. Three contiguous movements: Prologue; Love Song; Celebration. CD includes accompaniment plus recorded reference performance of the work, and printed part includes essential accompaniment cues. Intended as a tribute to Native Americans, thematic material is based on authentic songs of the Blackfeet tribe, of which Simyeh was a tribal chief. The source of the songs was the book *The Old North Trail* by Walter McClintock. This work relies heavily on the sound of acoustic instruments, in particular a vessel flute, which appears in each movement. The Prologue is a relatively simple controlled cadenza, and the ensuing Love Song is lyrical with some long sustained passages in the high register. The conclusion, titled Celebration, offers technical challenges such as meter changes, rapid interval leaps, fast slurred passages, lip glissandi between high and low registers, and double and triple tonguing. Recorded by Neal Corwell.

Corwell, Neal. *2 AM.* Nicolai Music. Solo with CD. 1998. $25. 6:00. III. G–bb′. Dedicated to the memory of Otis Wilson. CD includes accompaniment plus recorded reference performance of the work, and printed part includes separate line for accompaniment cues. An acoustic guitar is the principal sound source for accompaniment, with some additional vocal interjections, such as whispers, also added. The guitar is often used percussively to provide rhythmic underpinnings for the solo. The composition is a portrayal of a quiet middle-of-the-night mood, and the soloist plays muted throughout to help create the proper atmosphere. Technical demands are not great, but a steady sense of tempo and its varied subdivisions is essential to stay in synchronization with the accompaniment, and a lyrical connected style is called for during most of the piece. Recorded by Neal Corwell.

Corwell, Neal. *Venetian Carnival Animals*. Nicolai Music. Solo with CD. 1994. $25. 7:15. IV–V. E♭–b♭' (optional E1♭–e♭"). Dedicated to Chitate Kagawa and Hokkaido Tuba-Euphonium Camp. CD includes accompaniment plus recorded reference performance of the work, and printed part includes essential accompaniment cues. A humorous set of theme and variations, this composition is based closely upon the Arban variations on *The Carnival of Venice*. There are, however, two themes instead of one. In addition to the *Carnival of Venice* theme, we also hear a treatment of "The Elephant" song from Saint-Saens's *Carnival of the Animals*. As a matter of fact, elephant calls, along with other animal sounds, are heard during the finale. Technical challenges are what one would expect for a solo of this type and include double and triple tonguing, wide interval leaps, and some unexpected meter shifts. Recorded by Neal Corwell. See listing under Music for Euphonium and Wind Band.

Foster, Ruben. *Spooky Kids*. Available from composer. Solo with live sound processing plus CD accompaniment. 2002. $10. 6:30. III–IV. B♭1–a♭'. CD includes accompaniment plus recorded reference performance of the work, and printed part includes explanatory notes. The accompaniment CD was created by digitally processing the sound of euphonium and several other electronic sources. The performer has the option of adding sound processing, such as digital delay and detuning, to the euphonium during live performance. Instructions in the score are specific to the device used (a Lexicon MPX 100), but other devices could replicate the results. The composer labels this as an "ambient" work and encourages experimentation so that each performance is unique. The solo part is written in traditional notation, but there are no bar lines or meters. The work is in three through-composed sections and appears to be loosely built upon the five-note motive stated by the soloist at the start of the piece. There are few technical difficulties, but double tonguing is required.

Globokar, Vinko. *Echanges*. Henry Litolff's Verlag/ C. F. Peters. Solo with live electronics. 1975. $28. Indeterminate duration, difficulty, and range. This work is intended for performance by any brass instrument. It is avant-garde in nature and uses no traditional notation. Instead, the performer is presented with four pages of graphic

notation symbols, which may be interpreted by referencing the explanatory notes provided by the composer (which are entirely in German). A tone row, also presented in the explanatory notes, plays a role in the interpretation of the symbols. Deciphering the symbols and translating them into a coherent musical statement are the primary challenges of the work. A microphone is to be placed near specific slide and valve openings, and loudspeakers are to be placed behind the audience. Other extended techniques include pitch bends, flutter tonguing, glissandi, trills, mutes, various mouthpieces, and reeds. See listing under Music for Unaccompanied Euphonium.

Grieg, Edvard. *Solveig's Song Fantasy*. Arr. Neal Corwell. Nicolai Music. Solo with CD. 1994. $25. 7:45. III. A1–a'. For Kristen Byler. CD includes accompaniment plus recorded reference performance of the work, and printed part includes essential accompaniment cues. The accompaniment is mostly quiet and ethereal. This arrangement of the bittersweet song from Grieg's *Peer Gynt* includes much additional melodic material based upon thematic motives of the original song. The introduction and epilogue are cadenzas and may be played muted if the soloist desires. The most technically challenging portion is the soloist's countermelody added to the second full statement of the Grieg song. It includes some slurred and single tongued sextuplets, plus ascending arpeggios, all at a moderate tempo.

Heussenstamm, George. *Alter Ego*. Available from composer. Solo with recording created by performer. 1978. $25. 17:00. IV. E♭1–d". Written for Loren Marsteller. Calculation of the performance duration given above is based upon an omission, permitted by the composer, of the printed repeat of the central section of the composition. The accompaniment is a monaural recording of a single euphonium to be prepared by the soloist, and instructions for creating the recording are included in the score. The work is essentially a duet between the live and recorded euphonium. The work begins and ends with humorous theatrics as the soloist and audio speaker interact. The central core of the piece is a serious and intriguing atonal duet. Some contemporary performance techniques such as alternation of fingerings to vary tone color, multi-phonics, and tapping on the horn with fingernails are called for, and technical challenges include complex rhythms, awkward atonal melodic patterns, and passages in the extreme low register. In addition to a little acting, the soloist must be willing to do a small amount of speaking and singing. Several props are required, and a good deal of planning and preparation must be undertaken before the performance.

Liszt, Franz. *Hungarian Hallucination*. Arr. Neal Corwell. Nicolai Music. Solo with CD or tuba/ euphonium duo with CD. 2000. $25. 5:00.

IV–V. C–c″. CD includes accompaniment plus recorded reference performance of the work, and printed parts for both solo and duo versions are provided. Humor is the intent of this composition, which is ostensibly an arrangement of Liszt's *Hungarian Rhapsody No. 2.* As the piece progresses, numerous other well-known classical themes gradually intrude upon Liszt's melodies, occasionally pushing the rhapsody aside completely. The accompaniment provides a synthesizer-created orchestra plus bird calls, whistles, and other humorous effects. Difficulties include rapid leaps between the high and low registers and double tonguing. If performing the solo version, endurance may also be a factor. Recorded by Neal Corwell.

Magnuson, Roy D. *The Clock Tower.* Tuba-Euphonium Press. Solo with CD. 2003. $22. 5:45. III–IV. c–a′. Written for Brandon Hopkins. CD includes accompaniment only, and printed part includes a few accompaniment cues plus extensive performance notes. The piece begins and ends with cadenzas, and the central core of the work is in a regular meter in strict synchronization with the accompaniment. For one time period of approximately one minute the soloist is instructed to create a personal mixture of random ambient noise through the use of any combination of techniques such as growling, whispering, and blowing air through the horn, or tapping on the horn's bell with fingernails or a coin. A generally dark and eerie atmosphere prevails, and the accompaniment textures range from sustained drones with chimes, bells, and random animal-like noises, to repetitive tonal piano patterns. The solo part is not difficult, with the exception of several bars leading into the dramatic climax of the piece. These technically challenging bars are at a fast tempo and some double tonguing is required to execute the sixteenth note runs with the proper articulation.

Nagano, Mitsuhiro. *Matrix.* Available from composer. Solo with CD. 1989. $80. 9:30. IV–V. B♭–c″. A complete score is provided in addition to the solo part. The composer describes this piece as "environmental music" comprised of minimalist elements and designed to be "soothing music for the home and workplace." Sample-based synthesizer patches in imitation of acoustic instruments such as piano, drums, flutes, and voices are the primary sound sources for the recording, which is strictly a homophonic accompaniment. The composition is comprised of three contiguous movements in a fast-slow-fast format. The first movement is built around a central rhythmic point of origin called a "matrix," hence the title. The middle movement is free and lacks a rhythmic pulse in the accompaniment, so for proper synchronization, the soloist must work to acquire a feel for the proper pace. The final movement, built upon a rhythmic ostinato pattern, builds to

a strong conclusion through the use of dynamics, key changes, and increasing complexity of the solo line. The numerous difficult sixteenth note slurred passages, generally high tessitura, numerous key changes, and relative absence of rests make this a challenging work. Recorded by Toru Miura.

Patterson, Merlin. *Dream Sequence* (originally published as *Landscapes*). Available from composer. Solo with CD. 1981. $50 14:00. V. A1–c″. Printed part includes separate lines for accompaniment cues, time-line references, and complete performance instructions including the explanation of various notation symbols. The recorded synthesizer is an equal partner with the euphonium, and both present melodic and rhythmic materials, sometimes passing them back and forth in a pointilistic style. The work is divided into three main sections. The first is a monologue in which the unaccompanied euphonium presents all the thematic materials. The synthesizer enters for the central development section, which is quite complex and at times frenzied. The sound of falling rain provides a constant and calming backdrop for the final section, subtitled Pastorale. Soft, distant, and slightly fragmented statements of earlier materials are presented by both euphonium and synthesizer, bringing the work to a hushed and haunting close. "Proportional notation" (whereby note-heads are connected to horizontal lines that approximate note durations) is used for this avant-garde work, which calls for two mutes (straight and plunger) and the mastery of several contemporary brass techniques such as multi-phonics, flutter tonguing, trilled glissandi, alternate fingerings, and tongue clicks. Synchronizing solo with recorded part is difficult during the central section, and wide interval leaps, awkward atonal passages, and extremes of range and dynamics are difficult technical hurdles.

Rimsky-Korsakov, Nicolai. *Flight of the Bumble Bee.* Arr. Neal Corwell. Tuba-Euphonium Press. Solo with CD. 1994. $22. 1:40–2:00. IV. E–b♭′. The accompaniment CD also includes several different versions of the accompaniment at different tempi, ranging from a slow "practice" tempo to a brisk version with the quarter note at m.m. = 178. This arrangement of the well-known encore piece features an introduction with a "fat bee-like" sound, a few brief excursions away from the central key, and an additional unexpected coda. Double tonguing and rapid chromatic passages are the primary technical challenges. Recorded by Neal Corwell. See listing under Euphonium with Piano in chapter 10.

Schulz, Patrick. *Wet Metal Music.* Available from composer. Solo with computer-generated tape environment. 1996. $20. 4:30. II–III. E1–a♭′. CD includes accompaniment plus recorded reference performance of the work, and printed part includes accompaniment time-line references.

The audio source material for the accompaniment was created by recording various sounds of water and metal, hence the title of the work. The source material was then manipulated via computer to create an original soundscape. The solo lines, created using "pitch sets," are atonal but quite playable. Although standard notation is used and rhythms are not complex, the rhythms sound quite free because there is no set tempo. The soloist will need to refer to a stopwatch in order to stay close to the approximate passage timings indicated in the score, but there is much flexibility in how the accompaniment and solo may mesh together.

Suzuki, Ryati. *Psalm for Euphonium and Synthesizer.* Solo with tape. 1992. 7:45 III. C–b♭'. Written for Toru Miura. Although premiered by Toru Miura at the 1992 ITEC in Lexington, Kentucky, this work was never published or otherwise made available to the public. With the exception of a few rubato bars in the middle of this composition, the tempo and meter of this composition never vary from a steady moderato pace. The accompaniment uses nine different voices, all of which appear to be standard synthesizer factory-loaded patches. There are few dynamic, articulation, or expression markings to guide the soloist, but it appears that the solo part should be interpreted as being song or chant-like. There is little rhythmic variation, and the many sixteenth note step-wise patterns given to the soloist are not difficult. Endurance is a challenge because the soloist consistently plays in the medium-high register of the instrument with little opportunity for rest.

9. Music for Multiple Euphoniums

Seth D. Fletcher

What could be better than the beautiful, rich sound of a euphonium? How about the resonant sonority of eight, nine, or ten euphoniums! The combination of two or more euphoniums together produces a striking and unique sound that combines richness, clarity, and a palette of colors unavailable to other like-instrument ensembles. In recent years, composers have slowly started to recognize the vast possibilities of the euphonium ensemble due to the instrument's unmatched versatility and the rapid advancement of musicianship and technical prowess among euphonium artists and students alike.

Euphonium ensembles are beginning to appear professionally (the British Euphonium Quartet, Euphoniums Unlimited), at colleges and universities across the globe (notably at the University of North Texas and the Royal Northern College of Music in Manchester, England), and at summer festivals and camps, a trend that will likely continue with the development of literature and an increase in the number of euphoniumists pursuing a career in music.

The large euphonium ensemble can be traced back to Toru Miura and the Euphonium Company, which first appeared in Japan in the early 1990s, presenting several concerts and broadcasts internationally and generating numerous arrangements and transcriptions. More recently, Steven Mead's incredible multi-track *Euphonium Magic* series of recordings have pushed the limits of what the euphonium is capable of, providing an array of first-class arrangements and bringing a new audience to the euphonium ensemble. Still, 2004 marked the world's first euphonium choir recording, by Euphoniums Unlimited, a project that produced a wealth of original new literature from accomplished composers that will hopefully further the interest in music for euphonium choir.

This chapter lists only works that have been scored for two or more euphoniums, with the exception of works that have optional parts (such as piano or percussion) that are not necessary for performance. Pieces that are scored for two

or more euphoniums and combinations of other instruments (such as two euphoniums and piano or eight euphoniums and voice) and cannot be performed by multiple euphoniums alone can be found under Euphonium in Mixed Ensemble. For navigational purposes, the listings in this chapter are organized alphabetically by number of parts.

The intention of this chapter is to provide a reference resource of music specifically composed for multiple euphoniums and to encourage the proliferation of such ensembles by guiding them in developing a repertoire. However, the versatility of the euphonium allows for the "borrowing" of literature written for other instruments, and while the goal is to create an original repertoire for euphonium ensembles, other options should not be totally ignored.

Thanks to all the publishers, composers, and international consultants who provided information and examination materials for this project. This resource would not be available without their support. Unfortunately, due to the widespread practice of illegal copying, several publishers have been unable to provide the materials necessary for review. All listings in this chapter include all verifiable information available for each piece. Legally purchasing music from publishers and composers allows for the continued development of the euphonium repertoire and prevents the loss of current literature.

While progress has been made in this genre, much more still needs to be done to develop the repertoire available, particularly in creating music specifically written for the younger euphoniumist and creating new original repertoire in general. It is the hope of this publication to provide the impetus to do just that.

Two Part

Arban, Jean-Baptiste. *Play Along Easy Duets*. Arr. Steven Mead. De Haske. Two euphoniums with CD accompaniment. $15.95. 52 pp. III. Play-along duets of twenty essential Arban studies for the intermediate-level player. CD accompaniment includes tracks with each part plus accompaniment and accompaniment only for each piece.

Armitage, Dennis. *Eight Happy Pieces*. Editions Marc Reift. Two euphoniums. 1994. €12.60. III. Eight original duets of medium difficulty.

Ashbridge, David. *Time, Eagles and Mists*. Da Capo Music Limited. Two euphoniums. £6.00.

Bach, Johann Sebastian. *Five Arias from the Magnificat*. Arr. Norman J. Nelson. Bocal Music Company. Out of Print. Two euphoniums. IV. Part I: B♭1–b♭'. Part II: B♭1–g'. Five movements: I. Et exultavit spiritus meus; II. Quia respexit humilitatem; III. Quai fecit mihi magna; IV. Deposuit potentes de sede; V. Esurientes implevit bonis. Well-done arrangement appropriate for college-level recitals. Technically challenging for both parts. Parts alternate between bass and tenor clef.

Bayliss, Colin. *Greetings, Rehearsal and Farewells*. Da Capo Music Limited. Two euphoniums. £6.00.

Block, R.P., arr. *Sumer Is Icumen In*. Philharmonia Music. Two euphoniums. $8.50.

Bramson, Neil. *Two Euphonium Duos*. Da Capo Music Limited. £6.00.

Braun, Yehezkel. *Four Pieces*. Israeli Music Institute. Two euphoniums. 1974. $4.

Braun, Yehezkel. *Three Easy Pieces*. Israeli Music Institute. Two euphoniums. 1974. $4.

Buckley, Lewis J. *Fanfare for a New Beginning*. Cimarron Music. Two euphoniums. $10.

Conley, Lloyd, arr. *Christmas for Two, No. 3*. Kendor Music, Inc. Two euphoniums. $10. III. Easy arrangements of familiar Christmas carols. Appropriate for high school concerts, church services, and any other Christmas occasion.

Conley, Lloyd, arr. *Christmas for Two, No. 2*. Kendor Music, Inc. Two euphoniums. $10. III. Easy arrangements of familiar Christmas carols. Appropriate for high school concerts, church services, and any other Christmas occasion.

Deason, David. *Concert Etudes*. David Deason. Two euphoniums. 1997.

DeFries, Byron. *Bon March*. PEL Music Publications. Two euphoniums. 1998. $8.50. 1:10. II. Part I: f–f', Part II: A–c'. A fun, easy duet appropriate for younger players.

Frackenpohl, Arthur. *R3E2: Rumba, Refrain, and Romp for Two Euphoniums*. Tuba-Euphonium Press. Two euphoniums. 1994. $10. 8:35. IV. Part I: D–c'', Part II: Al–a'. Three movements: I. Rumba; II. Refrain; III. Romp. For Brian, David, Roger, and Sharie. The first movement is a Latin dance, the rumba, in a fast 4/4 meter. The second movement is slow and lyrical. The final movement is in a ragtime style. Both parts are equally important and challenging.

Friedrich, Kenneth D. *Concordium Suite*. Cimarron Music. Two euphoniums. 1992. $10.

Three movements: I. Moderato; II. Lento; III. Andante.

Friedrich, Kenneth D. *Euphantasies*. Cimarron Music. Two euphoniums. 1992. $10. Three movements: I. Euphantasy; II. Euphrenzy; III. Euphoria.

Friedrich, Kenneth D. *Six Etudes for Duet*. Cimarron Music. Two euphoniums. 2002. $12. Six movements: I. Allegro; II. Andante; III. Largo; IV. Andante con moto; V. Adagio; VI. Presto.

Friedrich, Kenneth D. *Suite No. 5*. Cimarron Music. Two euphoniums. $12. Four movements: I. Adagio; II. Andante/Allegro; III. Andante; IV. Andante.

Friedrich, Kenneth D. *Suite No, 4*. Cimarron Music. Two euphoniums. $10. Three movements: I. Allegro; II. Adagio; III. Allegro con brio.

Friedrich, Kenneth D. *Suite No. 6*. Cimarron Music. Two euphoniums. $11. Four movements: I. Allegro; II. Adagio; III. Moderato; IV. Allegro.

Friedrich, Kenneth D. *Suite No. 3*. Cimarron Music. Two euphoniums. $10. Three movements: I. Allegro; II. Andante Lugubre; III. Allegro Energico.

Glick, Andrew. *Six Duodecant Duets for Two Euphoniums*. Tuba-Euphonium Press. Two euphoniums. 2002. $10. 16 pp. IV. Part I: D–g', Part II: E♭–g'. Six movements: I. Inclusively Yours; II. J. S. Lived Here; III. Holy Whole-Tone, Batman!; IV. Mode Indigo; V. Igor Here, Igor There; VI. I Cannot Tell a Fib(onacci). This collection of duets is intended to introduce performers to various compositional techniques. Movement I derives pitch material from the two all-inclusive tetrachord pitch sets (0, 1, 4, 6) and (0, 1, 3, 7). Movement II uses the B-A-C-H collection (0, 11, 2, 1). The third movement, a reverse theme and variations, uses pitch material from the whole-tone scale. The fourth movement is bimodal, consisting of the D-Phrygian and G-Mixolydian modes, and written in a tricky 4/4 +3/8 meter. Movement V derives its pitch material from Stravinsky's octatonic rotational arrays. The final movement borrows its pitch classes from the numbers of the Fibonacci sequence. Extended techniques include glissandi, half-valve technique, double tonguing, trills, and flutter tonguing. Mixed meter is common, as are angular leaps. Some technical challenges.

Goble, Joseph. *Abrelatas*. Tuba-Euphonium Press. Two euphoniums with optional percussion. 1996. $10. IV. Part I: F>N>b♭', Part II: F–f'. For Mark and Tim. A short, fun duet in a Latin style. The first part primarily plays the melody while the second plays a funky bass line. Syncopation is used extensively. Optional percussion parts include cabasa, claves, timbales, and castanets. Parts included in both treble and bass clef. See listing under Euphonium in Mixed Ensemble.

Harris, Floyd O. *Flower of the Orient*. Ludwig Music Publishing. Two euphoniums. $4.95. I–II. Appropriate for younger players.

Holmes and Smith. *Call of the Sea*. C. L. Barnhouse. Two euphoniums. $12. Appropriate for younger players.

Holmes and Smith. *Massa's in the Cold, Cold Ground*. C. L. Barnhouse. Two euphoniums. $12. Appropriate for younger players.

Holmes and Smith. *Through Shadowed Vales*. C. L. Barnhouse. Two euphoniums. $12. Appropriate for younger players.

Israel, Brian. *Parita Piccola Canonica*. Tritone Press. Two euphoniums. $7.95.

Israel, Brian. *Parita Piccola Canonica Secunda*. Tritone Press. Two euphoniums. $7.95.

Kiefer, Will H. *Elena Polka*. C. L. Barnhouse. Two euphoniums. Appropriate for younger players.

King, Karl L. *A Night in June*. C. L. Barnhouse. Two euphoniums. $12. Appropriate for younger players.

Knight, Steve. *Conversations*. Cimarron Music. Two euphoniums. $10.

Liszt, Franz. *Liebestraum*. Arr. Clay Smith. C. L. Barnhouse. Two euphoniums. Appropriate for younger players.

Loup, Christophe. *11 Petits Duos*. Gérard Billaudot. 13:35. Two euphoniums.

Mead, Steven, ed. *Play Along Duets*. De Haske. Two euphoniums with CD accompaniment. $14.95. 56 pp. Collection of duets by various composers. Available in both treble and bass clef parts. CD accompaniment includes tracks with each part plus accompaniment and accompaniment only for each piece.

Mead, Steven, ed. *Play Along Easy Duets*. De Haske. Two euphoniums with CD accompaniment. £12.50. Collection of duets by various composers. Available in both treble and bass clef parts. CD includes three versions of each piece: one track of each part with accompaniment to play along with and a track with accompaniment only.

Mead, Steven, ed. *Play Along Jazz Duets & Solos*. De Haske. Two euphoniums with CD accompaniment. $14.95. 44 pp. III–IV. A♭–b♭'. Collection of four jazz duets and two solos by Fons van Gorp. Some technical challenges and difficult rhythmic figures. Available in both treble and bass clef parts. CD accompaniment includes tracks with each part plus accompaniment and accompaniment only for each piece.

Michel, Jean-François, arr. *Duett Album Vol. 4*. Editions Marc Reift. Two euphoniums. €14.00. A collection of thirty short and easy arrangements of well-known folk tunes and melodies by famous composers. The most advanced of the four volumes.

Michel, Jean-François, arr. *Duett Album Vol. 1*. Editions Marc Reift. Two euphoniums. €14.00. A collection of thirty short and easy arrangements

of well-known folk tunes and melodies by famous composers. Suitable for younger players.

Michel, Jean-François, arr. *Duett Album Vol. 3*. Editions Marc Reift. Two euphoniums. €14.00. A collection of thirty short and easy arrangements of well-known folk tunes and melodies by famous composers. More advanced than volumes 1 and 2. Suitable for younger players.

Michel, Jean-François, arr. *Duett Album Vol. 2*. Editions Marc Reift. Two euphoniums. €14.00. A collection of 31 short and easy arrangements of well-known folk tunes and melodies by famous composers. More advanced than volume 1. Suitable for younger players.

Michel, Jean-François, arr. *32 Christmas Carols*. Editions Marc Reift. Two euphoniums. 1993. €9.80. A collection of carols suitable for younger players. Includes: Good King Wenceslas; Alle Jahre wieder; Les Angesdans nos campagnes; Lasst uns froh und munter sein; In Dulci Jubilo; We Wish You a Merry Christmas; Süsser die Glocken nie klingen; March of the Three Kings; O Little Town of Bethlehem; Silent Night; The First Noel; Deck the Halls; Jingle Bells; Still, Still, Still; We Three Kings; O Tannenbaum; Adestes Fideles; Kommet, Ihr Hirten; While Shepherds Watched; O du Fröhliche; God Rest You; The Holly and the Ivy; O Holy Night; Hark, the Herald Angels; Joy to the World; Ihr Kinderlein kommet; Kling, Glöcklein, kling; Am Weihnachtsbaum; Es ist ein Ros entsprungen; Il est né le divin enfant; Vom Himmel hoch; Leise rieselt der Schnee.

Nevin, Ethelbert, and Floyd O. Harris. *The Rosary*. Ludwig Music Publishing. Two euphoniums. $4.95. I–II. Appropriate for younger players.

Roark, Larry. *Primordial Suite*. Kiwi Music Publishers. Two euphoniums.

Schmidt, William. *Variations on a Theme of Prokofieff*. Western International Music. Two euphoniums. 1990. $5. 5:00. IV. Part I: B–g', Part II: D♯–e'. High tessitura in the second part allows it also to be played on euphonium. Contemporary harmonic language.

Smith, Clay. *Among the Sycamores*. C. L. Barnhouse. Two euphoniums. Appropriate for younger players.

Smith, Clay. *Italiana*. C. L. Barnhouse. Two euphoniums. $12. Appropriate for younger players.

Smith, Clay. *Milady's Pleasure*. C. L. Barnhouse. Two euphoniums. Appropriate for younger players.

Smith, Clay. *Rainbow Hues*. C. L. Barnhouse. Two euphoniums. Appropriate for younger players.

Smith, Clay. *Smithsonian*. C. L. Barnhouse. Two euphoniums. Appropriate for younger players.

Smith, Clay. *The Trumpeter*. C. L. Barnhouse. Two euphoniums. $12. Appropriate for younger players.

Smith, Clay, and Guy E. Holmes. *The Wayfarer.* C. L. Barnhouse. Two euphoniums. Appropriate for younger players.

Stouffer, Paul, arr. *Easy Classics for Two.* Kendor Music, Inc. Two euphoniums. 1993. $6. II. Part I: G–d', Part II: G–d'. Six movements: Andante (Mozart); Bourrée (Telemann); Dance (Haydn); Andantino (Schubert); Minuet (Purcell); Imitation (Baton). No technical or range difficulties. Ideal for younger players.

Sturzenegger, Kurt, arr. *11 Pieces.* Editions Marc Reift. Two euphoniums. 1997. €24.50. A collection of eleven short pieces: Schütz: Choral; Praetorious: Choral; Pezel: Intrada; Pezel: Sarabande; Pezel: Bal; Reiche: Intrada; Schein: Allemande; Anonymous: Air; Susato: Pavane; Morley: Three English Madrigals; Charpentier: Entrée. Suitable for younger players.

Sturzenegger, Kurt, arr. *Twelve Duets from the Old Masters.* Editions Marc Reift. Two euphoniums. 1996. €12.60. A collection of twelve simple polyphonic duets by composers from varying time periods. Suitable for younger players.

Telemann, Georg Philipp. *Six Canonic Duets.* Mike Forbes. Tuba-Euphonium Press. Two euphoniums. 1998. $12. 26 pp. III–IV. Part I: F–f', Part II: F–f'. A collection of six canonic sonatas with three movements each. Each movement is a two-voice canon in unison. The second player begins where indicated and ends at the fermata, which the first player ignores. Some technical challenges exist and the piece is fun to play. Appropriate for performance and study.

Uber, David. *Three Picaresque Duos.* Kendor Music, Inc. Out of Print. Two euphoniums.

Uber, David. *Twentieth-Century Duets.* The Brass Press. Two euphoniums.

Three Part

Bach, Johann Sebastian. *Sinfonia No. 9 in F Minor.* Arr. Andrei Strizek. Tuba-Euphonium Press. Three euphoniums. 2003. $10. IV. Part I: E♭–a', Part II: C–a', Part III: C–a'. Great arrangement that would be effective in recital. Parts are equally challenging.

Banco, Gerhart. *9 Miniaturen.* Doblinger. Three euphoniums. 1980. €19.30. III. Part I: f–b♭', Part II: A–f', Part III: E♭–c'. Nine movements: I. Praeludium; II. Fughette; III. Air; IV. Scherzo; V. Hymnus; VI. Rondo; VII. Ländler; VIII. Marsch; IX. Kehraus. Short, fun to play trios that may be performed in various combinations. Appropriate for high school players. Parts may be doubled for a large ensemble.

Gershwin, George. *Gershwin-Medley.* Arr. Denis Armitage. Editions Marc Reift. Three euphoniums. 1993. €13.30.

Hall, Percy, arr. *College Glee Club.* Ludwig Music Publishing. Three euphoniums. 1999. $10. II. Part I: A♭–e♭', Part II: A♭–c', Part III: F–b♭. Two movements: I. Aura Lee; II. Good Night Ladies. Dedicated to Doug Bennett, band director, Wooster City Schools, Wooster, Ohio. Simple arrangements of these two classic tunes. Appropriate for younger players. Parts are provided in treble and bass clef.

Hall, Percy. *Dance Suite.* Ludwig Music Publishing. Three euphoniums. 1999. $10. IV. Part I: F–c'', Part II: F–g', Part III: F–f'. Three movements: I. Gavotte; II. Sarabande; III: Gigue a la Canon. Dedicated to Dan Adams, director of bands and orchestra, Wooster Ohio Schools. Three original contrasting movements in the style of eighteenth-century French dances. Treble and bass clef parts included.

Hall, Percy. *Olde Tyme Songs.* Ludwig Music Publishing. Three euphoniums. 1999. $10. II–III. Part I: B♭–f', Part II: B♭–e♭', Part III: F–c'. Two movements: I. Sentimental Waltz; II. Rambunctious Rag. Dedicated to Mike Grady, Mansfield, Ohio. Fun arrangement suitable for younger players. Not technically difficult, but the second movement introduces some syncopation that may challenge inexperienced players. Treble and bass clef parts are included.

Hall, Percy. *Reflecting and Rejoicing.* Ludwig Music Publishing. Three euphoniums. 1999. $8. III. Part I: B♭–b♭', Part II: B♭–g', Part III: F–g'. Two movements: I. Reflecting; II. Rejoicing. Dedicated to John Hall, Worthington, Ohio. Two exact canons in contrasting moods and styles. A good recital addition appropriate for high school players. Treble and bass clef parts included.

Hall, Percy, arr. *Spirituals of the Old South.* Great Works Publishing. Three euphoniums. 1999. $8. II. Part I: e♭–f', Part II: c–d', Part III: E–b♭. Dedicated to Jason Hall, West Hartford, Connecticut. A simple medley of three spirituals: My Lord, What a Mornin'; King Jesus Is a' Listenin'; My Lord Delivered Daniel. Appropriate for younger players. Not technically difficult, with a few simple syncopated rhythmic patterns. Treble and bass clef parts included.

Hall, Percy, arr. *Steal Away, Little David.* Ludwig Music Publishing. Three euphoniums. 1999. $10. II. Part I: e♭–f', Part II: c–d', Part III: F–a. Two movements: I. Steal Away; II. Little David, Play on Your Harp. Dedicated to Doug Bennett, band director, Wooster City Schools, Wooster, Ohio. Easy arrangement of two familiar tunes. Appropriate for younger players. Treble and bass clef parts included.

Hawlin, Jan. *12 Intonations-Fugen.* Editions Marc Reift. Three euphoniums. €21.00. Twelve movements of interesting fugal writing.

Haydn, Franz Joseph. *Divertimento No. 70.* Arr. Paul Droste. Ludwig Music Publishing. Three euphoniums. 1981. $9.95. 13:00. III–IV. Part I: G–c', Part II: c–b♭', Part III: E–d'. Three movements: I. Scherzo; II. Andante; III. Menuet. The first movement is a rollicking scherzo in 3/8 that presents some technical challenges. The second movement is slow and lyrical in a 4/8 meter that should be counted in four. The first part primarily has the melody in this movement. The final movement is a light minuet. Appropriate for advanced high school or college students. Good recital material.

Hazelgrove, Bernard. *Jazz Suite.* Mostyn Music. Three euphoniums. £4.50. Appropriate for younger players.

Hazelgrove, Bernard. *Mood Swings.* Mostyn Music. Three euphoniums. £7.95. Appropriate for younger players.

Isomura, Yukiko. *The Four Seasons Suite.* Athens Music Publishing. Three euphoniums. 2003. $35. 19:00. IV. Part I: E♭–b♭', Part II: E♭–b♭', Part III: E♭–a'. Four movements: I. The Start in Season; II. Water Lily; III. Storm of Autumn; IV. Noel Arpeggio. An interesting addition to the repertoire that would work well in a variety of settings. New age in style and audience accessible. Parts are equally challenging. Movements may be performed separately or together as a suite in any combination. Parts may be doubled for a large ensemble.

James, Ifor. *6 Fanfares.* Editions Marc Reift. Three euphoniums. 1999. €12.60.

Michel, Jean-François, arr. *32 Christmas Carols.* Editions Marc Reift. Three euphoniums. 1993. €14.70. A collection of carols suitable for younger players. Includes thirty-two carols: Good King Wenceslas; Alle Jahre wieder; Les Angesdans nos campagnes; Lasst uns froh und munter sein; In Dulci Jubilo; We Wish You a Merry Christmas; Süsser die Glocken nie klingen; March of the Three Kings; O Little Town of Bethlehem; Silent Night; The First Noel; Deck the Halls; Jingle Bells; Still, Still, Still; We Three Kings; O Tannenbaum; Adestes Fideles; Kommet, Ihr Hirten; While Shepherds Watched; O du Fröhliche; God Rest You; The Holly and the Ivy; O Holy Night; Hark, the Herald Angels; Joy to the World; Ihr Kinderlein kommet; Kling, Glöcklein, kling; Am Weihnachtsbaum; Es ist ein Ros entsprungen; Il est né le divin enfant; Vom Himmel hoch; Leise rieselt der Schnee.

Michel, Jean-François, arr. *Trio Album—Feierliche Musik.* Editions Marc Reift. Three euphoniums. 1989. €21.00. Fifteen movements: March from Judas Maccabaeus (Handel); Overture from Water Music (Handel); Grosser Gott wir preisen Dich; Heilig, Heilig, Heilig (Schubert); Trumpet Tune (Purcell); Overture from Te Deum (Charpentier); Andante (Haydn); Hochzeitsmarsch (Mendelssohn); March in the Occasional Oratorio (Handel); Hochzeitsmarsch (Haydn); Hymne à la joie (Beethoven); Jesus bleibt meine Freud (Bach); Plus près de toi Mon Dieu; The Rejoicing from Fireworks Music (Handel); Moderato-Menuetto (Purcell).

Michel, Jean-François, arr. *Trio Album–Golden Hits.* Editions Marc Reift. Three euphoniums. 1997. €24.50. Fifteen movements: Muss i denn, muss i denn . . . ; Nobody Knows; Glory, Glory, Alleluja; Kalinka; I Got Rhythm (Gershwin); Amazing Grace; Funicula Funiculi; O When the Saints; The Entertainer (Joplin); Go Down Moses; El Condor Pasa; La cucuracha; Joshua Fit the Battle of Jericho; Hava Nagila; Auld Lang Syne.

Sturzenegger, Kurt, arr. *7 Trios from 16th–18th Centuries.* Editions Marc Reift. Three euphoniums. 1996. €14.00.

Uber, David. *Carnival.* Belwin-Mills Publishing Corp. Three euphoniums.

Uber, David. *Characteristic Trios.* Tuba-Euphonium Press. Three euphoniums. 1991. $18. IV. Part I: e–c″, Part II: A–g', Part III: A1–e'. Nine movements: I. Poco allegretto; II. Moderato; III. Allegro moderato; IV. Andante; V. Allegretto; VI. Poco allegretto; VII. Allegro barbaro; VIII. Lento; IX. Allegro. A collection of nine short trios useful for study or recital purposes. The movements vary greatly in style and offer several challenges to the performer while being accessible to an audience as well.

Uber, David. *Modern Trios.* Editions Musicus. Three euphoniums.

Four Part

Altenburg, Johann Ernst. *Suite.* Arr. Kurt Sturzenegger. Editions Marc Reift. Four euphoniums with optional timpani part. 1996. €13.30. Parts are written in treble clef.

Armitage, Denis. *Four Golden Bells.* Editions Marc Reift. Four euphoniums. 1996. €10.50. Employs mixed meter but utilizes homophonic rhythms. Parts are available in both treble and bass clefs.

Armitage, Denis, arr. *Happy Birthday Fantasy for Euphonium Quartet.* Editions Marc Reift. Four euphoniums. 1997. €14.00. Several stylistic variations on this festive tune. Parts are available in both treble and bass clefs.

Armitage, Denis. *Let's All Take It Easy-Going Home-Complaining Blues-Sweet and Mellow-Happy Go Lucky Rag.* Editions Marc Reift. Four euphoniums with optional piano, guitar, bass, and drums. 1991. €22.40. A suite of five original jazz tunes. Parts are written in treble clef. See listing under Euphonium in Mixed Ensemble.

Bach, J. S., and Charles Gounod. *Ave Maria.* Arr. John Glenesk Mortimer. Editions Marc Reift. Four euphoniums. 1996. €10.50.

Bach, Johann Sebastian. *Chorale, Fugue, Prelude, and Fantasy.* Arr. Kurt Sturzenegger. Editions Marc Reift. Four euphoniums. 1996. €14.00.

Bach, Johann Sebastian. *Jesus bleibet meine Fruede.* Arr. Akihiko Ito. Akihiko Ito. Four euphoniums. ¥1,000 (.pdf version ¥600).

Bale, Maurice, arr. *David of the White Rock*. Godiva Music. Four euphoniums. 2003. £6.00. IV. Part I: B♭–b♭', Part II: A–a♭', Part III: G–f', Part IV: G1–d. A wonderful arrangement of this traditional Welsh melody. Not technically difficult, but subtle tempo changes require careful rehearsal. Extremely low tessitura in the fourth part. Parts available in treble or bass clef.

Bale, Maurice, arr. *Oh Dear, What Can the Matter Be?* Godiva Music. Four euphoniums. 1998. £6.00. IV. Part I: A♭–a♭', Part II: A♭–f', Part III: A♭–e♭', Part IV: A♭1–d♭'. A great arrangement of this traditional English folk song. Parts available in treble or bass clef.

Beethoven, Ludwig van. *Three Equali*. Arr. Maurice Bale. Godiva Music. Four euphoniums. 2003. £5.00. III. Part I: g–g', Part II: d–e♭', Part III: B♭–c', Part IV: D–b♭. Three movements: Poco adagio; Poco sostenuto; Andante. A simple arrangement of this work originally scored for trombones. Three short chorales that are not technically difficult. Fourth part requires a good low register. Parts available in treble or bass clef.

Chopin, Frederick. *Waltz, Op. 64, No. 2*. Arr. Maurice Bale. Godiva Music. Four euphoniums. 2004. £6.00. IV–V. Part I: e♭–e♭", Part II: B♭–a♭', Part III: E♭–e♭', Part IV: B♭1–c'. A good, difficult arrangement of this piano classic. High tessitura in the first part and extreme range demands throughout. Parts are available in treble or bass clef.

Chopin, Frederick. *Waltz, Op. 69, No. 1*. Arr. Maurice Bale. Godiva Music. Four euphoniums. 2004. £6.00. V. Part I: e–a♭", Part II: c–f', Part III: A–e♭', Part IV: C–b♭. Very difficult. Extremely high tessitura in the first part. Parts are available in treble or bass clef.

Chopin, Frederick. *Fantasy Impromptu*. Arr. Maurice Bale. Godiva Music. Four euphoniums. 2004. £8.00. IV–V. Part I: C–b♭', Part II: C♯–d", Part III: D–f', Part IV: C–e♭'. First two parts have the lead and are technically difficult in the first section while the bottom two parts are prominent and lyrical in the second half of the piece. Parts are available in treble or bass clef.

Corelli, Arcangelo. *Suite*. Arr. Kurt Sturzenegger. Editions Marc Reift. Four euphoniums or three euphoniums and one tuba. 1996. €16.80.

Debussy, Claude. *The Girl with the Flaxen Hair*. Arr. Maurice Bale. Godiva Music. Four euphoniums. £5.00. 2:00. Great arrangement of this classic melody. Parts are available in treble or bass clef. Recorded by Steven Mead, *Euphonium Magic*, volume 1.

Debussy, Claude. *Le petit nègre*. Arr. Akihiko Ito. Akihiko Ito. Four euphoniums. ¥1,000 (.pdf version ¥600).

Debussy, Claude. *Le petit nègre*. Arr. John Glenesk Mortimer. Editions Marc Reift. Four euphoniums. 1996. €13.30.

Desloges, Jacques. *6 Pieces Faciles—Volume 1*. Gérard Billaudot. Four euphoniums. €4.76.

Eid, Krister. *Nøtteliten Variations*. Encore Music Publishers. Out of Print. Four euphoniums. 1985.

Friedrich, Kenneth D. *Drive!!*. Kenneth D. Friedrich. Four euphoniums. 2005. $14. 4:00. IV. Part I: F–b♭', Part II: c–g', Part III: B♭–f', Part IV: F–b♭'. Written for the 2005 International Euphonium Institute. A driving rhythmic piece that would work well as a recital opener. The first and fourth parts primarily share the melody while the middle voices provide a gradual rising and falling rhythmic ostinato. Extensive syncopation.

Hall, Percy, arr. *Gaudeamus Igitur*. Ludwig Music Publishing. Four euphoniums. 1999. $12. III. Part I: d–a', Part II: A–f', Part III: B♭–c', Part IV: F–c'. Dedicated to David Leyerle, band director, Ontario High School, Ontario, Ohio. A short set of variations on this traditional European college song. The theme is played first in a marcato style in 3/4 meter. A slightly faster variation in 4/4 follows. Next comes a fast dance in 6/8 time. The piece ends with a return to the original tempo and style in a brief coda. Parts included in both treble and bass clef.

Handel, George Frederic. *Halleluja*. Arr. Jean-François Michel. Editions Marc Reift. Four euphoniums. 1991. €21.00. Part of a collection of four popular classics: Halleluja (Handel); Rondeau (Mouret); Overture from Water Music (Handel); Hochzeitsmarsch (Haydn).

Handel, George Frederic. *Overture from Water Music*. Arr. Jean-François Michel. Editions Marc Reift. Four euphoniums. 1991. €21.00. Part of a collection of four popular classics: Halleluja (Handel); Rondeau (Mouret); Overture from Water Music (Handel); Hochzeitsmarsch (Haydn).

Haydn, Franz Joseph. *Hochzeitsmarsch*. Arr. Jean-François Michel. Editions Marc Reift. Four euphoniums. 1991. €21.00. Part of a collection of four popular classics: Halleluja (Handel); Rondeau (Mouret); Overture from Water Music (Handel); Hochzeitsmarsch (Haydn).

Hewitt, Harry. *24 Preludes*. Harry Hewitt. Four euphoniums.

Ito, Akihiko, arr. *Italian Song Medley: Il giocatore nel carnevale*. Akihiko Ito. Four euphoniums. ¥1,400 (.pdf version ¥1,000).

Ito, Yasuhide. *Euphonium Parfait: Suite for 4 Euphoniums*. Ito Music. Four euphoniums. 2002. 10:00. V. Part I: F–d", Part II: E♭–a', Part III: D♯–g', Part IV: C–f'. Four movements: I. Fruits Parfait; II. Milonga di Malone; III. Cioccolata d'amore; IV. Gelato con caffè. A fantastic original work that is fun for audience and performers alike. Technically challenging with a high tessitura in the first part. Recorded by Steven Mead, *Euphonium Magic*, volume 2.

Joplin, Scott. *The Easy Winners.* Arr. John Glenesk Mortimer. Editions Marc Reift. Four euphoniums. 1997. €12.60.

Joplin, Scott. *The Entertainer.* Arr. Maurice Bale. Godiva Music. Four euphoniums. 1998. £6.00. Parts are available in treble or bass clef.

Lennon, John, and Paul McCartney. *The Beatles.* Arr. John Glenesk Mortimer. Editions Marc Reift. Four euphoniums. €19.60. IV. Part I: f–c″, Part II: B–a′, Part III: G–f′, Part IV: G1–c′. A suite of four classic Beatles tunes: "Michelle"; "Eleanor Rigby"; "Yesterday"; "Ob-la-di. Ob-la-da." Not technically difficult. Extremely low tessitura in the fourth part. Available in both treble and bass clefs.

Machaut, Guillaume de. *Messe Notre Dame.* Arr. Dan Rager. Ludwig Music Publishing. Four euphoniums. 1992. $9. II. Part I: c–d′, Part II: A–e′, Part III: A–c′, Part IV: A–d′. Dedicated to Walter Motter. A short, easy arrangement of this fourteenth-century masterpiece. The third and fourth parts are easier than the first two parts.

Mancini, Henry. *The Pink Panther.* Arr. Denis Armitage. Editions Marc Reift. Four euphoniums. €13.30. Parts are written in treble clef.

Meechan, Pete. *Rite.* Pete Meechan. Four euphoniums. 2003. 5:00. V. Part I: C1–c″, Part II: C–c″, Part III: C–c″, Part IV: C–c″. Commissioned by the British Euphonium Ensemble. A creative and exciting original work for euphonium quartet. The piece tells the story of the Semdeij Cendet tribe of dwarfs who lived on the Spanish side of the Pyrenees. In order to remain dwarfs the tribe would sacrifice the tallest member every full moon. Eventually, the tribe dwindled until only one remained. A bit of acting adds to the effect and makes this an audience favorite. Works best if quartet has at least one very short member. Technically difficult. Written in treble clef.

Mendelssohn, Felix. *The Bee's Wedding.* Arr. Maurice Bale. Godiva Music. Four euphoniums. 2004. £6.00. IV–V. Part I: f–g″, Part II: B–c″, Part III: A–g′, Part IV: G1–eb′. One of the *Songs without Words,* also known as "The Spinning Song." Technically demanding.

Mendelssohn, Felix. *Wedding March.* Arr. Scott Richards. Editions Marc Reift. Four euphoniums with optional piano or organ. 1997. €14.00. Parts available in both treble and bass clefs.

Michel, Jean-François, arr. *Quarttet Album.* Editions Marc Reift. Four euphoniums. 1995. €21.00. A collection of eight arrangements: Marche (Lully); Ave Verum (Mozart); Allemande (Phalèse); Intrada (Franck); O vos Omnes (Victoria); Ave Maria (Schubert); Trumpet Voluntary (Clarke); Trumpet Tune & March (Clarke).

Michel, Jean-François, arr. *Three Spirituals.* Editions Marc Reift. Four euphoniums. 1993. €16.10. Three movements: Joshua Fit the Battle of Jericho; O When the Saints; Go Down Moses.

Michel, Jean-François, arr. *Three Traditionals.* Editions Marc Reift. Four euphoniums. 1994. €16.10. Three movements: Kalinka; El Condor Pasa; Funiculi Funicula.

Miserendino, Joe. *Hussar's Hurrah.* Joe Miserendino. Four euphoniums. 2003. $5. 3:00. III–IV. Part I: Bb–bb′, Part II: Bb–ab′, Part III: Bb–a′, Part IV: Eb–c♯′. A fun concert original for euphonium quartet. Each part is equally difficult. Available in treble clef.

Mortimer, John Glenesk, arr. *Christmas Carols.* Editions Marc Reift. Four euphoniums with optional piano part. 1996. €21.00.

Mouret, Jean-Joseph. *Rondeau.* Arr. Jean-François Michel. Editions Marc Reift. Four euphoniums. 1991. €21.00. Part of a collection of four popular classics: Halleluja (Handel); Rondeau (Mouret); Overture from Water Music (Handel); Hochzeitsmarsch (Haydn).

Mozart, Wolgang Amadeus. *March of the Priests.* Arr. Donald M. Sherman. Tuba-Euphonium Press. Four euphoniums. 1989. $10. III. Part I: eb–ab′, Part II: eb–f′, Part III: Bb–eb′, Part IV: Eb–ab. A brief, simple arrangement of this classical melody. The first two parts share the melody while the third and fourth provide the accompaniment. Parts provided in both treble and bass clef.

Mozart, Wolgang Amadeus. *Rondo a la Turca.* Arr. Thomas Wyss. Mostyn Music. Four euphoniums. £7.60.

Rimsky-Korsakov, Nicolai. *Notturno.* Arr. Steven Mead. Studio Music. Four euphoniums. 1997. £4.50. 2:30. III–IV. Part I: bb–bb′, Part II: f–g′, Part III: Bb–db′, Part IV: Eb–eb′. A great lyrical arrangement suitable for various occasions. Not technically difficult but has a high tessitura in the first part. Recorded by Steven Mead, *The World of the Euphonium,* volume 3.

Roberton, Hugh. *All in the April Evening.* Arr. Maurice Bale. Godiva Music. Four euphoniums. 2000. £5.00. 3:00. II–III.

Robertson, Donna N. *Fanfare for the Prince of Darkness.* American Music Center. Four euphoniums. 1983. 6:00.

Satie, Eric. *Le Piccadilly.* Arr. Akihiko Ito. Akihiko Ito. Four euphoniums. ¥600 (.pdf version ¥400).

Scheidemann, Heinrich. *Präambulum.* Editions Marc Reift. Four euphoniums or three euphoniums and tuba. 1996. €14.00. Parts available in both treble and bass clefs.

Schoendorff, Matthew. *Adagio for Four Euphoniums.* Tuba-Euphonium Press. Four euphoniums. 1999. $8. 4:45. III–IV. Part I: d–ab′, Part II: Ab–g′, Part III: G–b′, Part IV: C–f. A lyrical, tonal work in ABA form that features flowing, folk-like melodies and rich harmonies. No technical difficulties. Mutes required for all parts. Parts may be doubled for a large ensemble.

Sciortino, Patrice. *Figures.* Gérard Billaudot. Four euphoniums. €51.00.

Sherwin, Manning, and Gene Puerling. *A Nighten-gale Sang in Berkeley Square*. Arr. Darin Cochran. Manuscript. Four euphoniums. 4:30. IV. Part I: e♭–c″, Part II: e♭–g′, Part III: c–d′, Part IV: A1–b♭. This beautiful, lush arrangement for four-part euphonium choir highlights the rich, velvety sound of the euphonium to its fullest potential. Homophonic writing in a free-flowing style. High tessitura in the first part. Fourth part requires a strong low register. Playable as a quartet or parts may be doubled for a large ensemble. Recorded by Euphoniums Unlimited, *Music for Euphonium Choir*.

Smalley, Peter. *Ball of Fire: Toccata for Euphonium Quartet*. Studio Music. Four euphoniums. 1996. £10.50. 4:00. IV–V. Part I: F–b♭′, Part II: F–b♭′, Part III: E♭–g′, Part IV: C–g′. An exciting and mesmerizing minimalist original that belongs in every euphonium quartet library. The piece has four distinct sections of repetitive material, ending with a restatement of the opening material with an added melodic bass line. Technically difficult. Parts are written in treble clef. Recorded by Steven Mead, *The World of the Euphonium*, volume 2.

Sousa, John Phillip. *Sempre Fideles*. Arr. Maurice Bale. Godiva Music. Four euphoniums. 2003. £7.00. IV. Part I: d–b♭′(e♭′), Part II: c–b♭′, Part III: E♭(B♭1)–g′, Part IV: E♭(B♭1)–g′. A fantastic arrangement of this classic march. Fun to play and challenging for all parts. Optional octaves for pitches in the extreme ranges. Parts are available in treble or bass clef.

Sousa, John Phillip. *The Washington Post*. Arr. Scott Richards. Editions Marc Reift. Four euphoniums. 1999. €13.30. Parts are available in both treble and bass clefs.

Sturzenegger, Kurt, arr. *11 Pieces*. Editions Marc Reift. Four euphoniums with optional piano part. 1997. €24.50. A collection of eleven short pieces: Schütz: Choral; Praetorious: Choral; Pezel: Intrada; Pezel: Sarabande; Pezel: Bal; Reiche: Intrada; Schein: Allemande; Anonymous: Air; Susato: Pavane; Morley: Three English Madrigals; Charpentier: Entrée. Suitable for younger players.

Sturzenegger, Kurt. *Frühlingsstimmen*. Arr. Akihiko Ito. Akihiko Ito. Four euphoniums. ¥2,600 (.pdf version ¥2,000).

Sturzenegger, Kurt, arr. *7 Quarttets*. Editions Marc Reift. Four euphoniums. 1996. €17.50. Seven movements: Motet (Franck); Intrada (Schein); Ave Verum (Mozart); Entrée (Dandrieu); Prélude et Fugue (Telemann); Cantique (Bruckner); Zum Abendsegen (Mendelssohn).

Sturzenegger, Kurt, arr. *10 Noëls*. Editions Marc Reift. Four euphoniums. 1998. €14.00.

Templeton, Alec. *Bach Goes to Town*. Arr. Maurice Bale. Godiva Music. Four euphoniums. £6.00.

Uber, David. *Shadow-Graph, Op. 356*. Tuba-Euphonium Press. Four euphoniums. 2002. $12.

6:00. IV. Part I: B♭–c″, Part II: B♭1–g′, Part III: A–e♭′, Part IV: A1–b♭. For Shinya Suzuki and Ikuko Miura. An interesting original work for euphonium quartet that evokes the mysteriousness of shadows and shadow puppets. Each part has several brief solos. Parts may be doubled for a large ensemble.

Uber, David. *A Vermont Gathering, Op. 406*. Tuba-Euphonium Press. Four euphoniums. 2001. $10. 3:00. III. Part I: f♯–g′, Part II: c♯–f′, Part III: B–f′, Part IV: E♭–a♭. A fun original work appropriate for high school players. Not technically difficult. Parts may be doubled for a large ensemble.

Van Valkenburg, Jamie. *Fantasia on "God of Our Fathers."* Tuba-Euphonium Press. Four euphoniums. 1999. $12. IV. Part I: B1–d♭″, Part II: D–d♭″, Part III: A1–c″, Part IV: B♭1–c♯″. Composed for the George Mason University Euphonium Quartet. A challenging original composition based on the famous hymn using a contemporary harmonic language. All parts alternate between tenor and bass clef. Interspersed mixed meter measures require careful counting. The piece begins with a solo recitative followed by an allegro section characterized by repeated rising sixteenth note patterns. A brief pause connects to a chorale-like section in which the theme is first recognized. The remainder of the work combines ideas from the two previous sections, ending with a flourish.

Verdi, Giuseppi. *Quartet from "Rigoletto."* Arr. Akihiko Ito. Akihiko Ito. Four euphoniums and piano. ¥1,600 (.pdf version ¥1,100).

Wagner, Richard. *Hochzeitmarsch (from "Lohengrin")*. Arr. Akihiko Ito. Akihiko Ito. Four euphoniums. ¥600 (.pdf version ¥400).

Wagner, Richard. *Wedding March from Act III of "Lohengrin."* Arr. John Glenesk Mortimer. Editions Marc Reift. Four euphoniums with optional piano or organ. 1996. €14.

Five Part

Censhu, Jiro. *Traveling Clouds*. Jiro Censhu. Five euphoniums. 2002. IV. Part I: G–c″, Part II: c–b♭′, Part III: A–b♭′, Part IV: A♭–f′, Part V: C–g′. A single-movement work that dreamily depicts the graceful movement of clouds through the sky. Isolated technical challenges. High tessitura in the first part. Parts may be doubled for a large ensemble.

Corwell, Neal. *In the Cathedral*. Nicolai Music. Solo euphonium and four-part euphonium ensemble. 2004. 10:00. V. Solo part: C1–c′, Part I: D–b♭′, Part II: D–b♭′, Part III: A1–a′, Part IV: D1–a′. Commissioned by Brian Bowman and R. Winston Morris. Written for Brian Bowman, euphonium soloist, for performance with Euphoniums Unlimited under the direction of R. Winston Morris. A programmatic piece inspired by the majesty and awe of a cathedral, this work captures the reverence, beauty, and exhilaration one is likely to sense upon entering a grand place of worship. Allusions to cantors, chants, and bells are easily recognized in this welcome addition to the repertoire. The piece begins and ends in a lyrical, contemplative style with a fervent and pleading faster section in the middle interrupted by a virtuosic cadenza displaying the full range of the instrument. High tessitura in the solo part and extreme low range demands. All the ensemble parts require a mute. Parts may be doubled for a large ensemble. Recorded by Brian Bowman and Euphoniums Unlimited, *Music for Euphonium Choir.*

Forte, Aldo Rafael, and Carolyn Ruth Moser. *Moser Cameos.* Aldo Forte. Five euphoniums and narrator. 2004. 8:45. V. Part I: c–c″, Part II: G–bb′, Part III: G–f♯′, Part IV: E–e′, Part V: A1–bb. Five movements: I. Harmony; II. Bacchus; III. Tennis?; IV. Thunder Shower; V. Hats. Dedicated to R. Winston Morris and Euphoniums Unlimited, narrator Raymond Jones, and producer Mark Morette. A well-written suite of short musical vignettes that is fun for audience and performers alike. The composition's five contrasting movements feature five poems from the collection titled *Rhythms of the Heart* by Carolyn Ruth Moser. Harmony opens with unaccompanied narration of the entire poem followed by slow expressive music. In Bacchus, the music depicts many moods while maintaining the same tempo. Tennis?, like the racquet sport, is driven by several repetitive patterns. In the dramatic Thunder Shower, the ensemble's vast "orchestrational" possibilities are further explored. Hats closes the work with whimsical overtones and features syncopated, jazzy rhythms with a Latin Caribbean flavor. Parts may be doubled for a large ensemble. Extreme low register demands in the bottom part. Recorded by Euphoniums Unlimited, *Music for Euphonium Choir.*

Frederick, Donald, arr. *Hymns, Carols, and Spirituals for Low Brass.* Accura Music. Four euphoniums. $16. Fourteen well-known pieces arranged for quartet.

Hauser, Joshua. *EuPhunk.* Joshua Hauser. Euphonium solo and four-part euphonium ensemble with optional drum set accompaniment. 2004. 3:30. V. Part I: Bb–f″, Part II: Bb–f″, Part III: A–c″, Part IV: G–f′, Part V: F1–c′. An original funk tune that is a guaranteed crowd favorite. The solo part features an extended improvised solo section where the performer is given chord changes only. The first two parts are in a high tessitura. The lowest part requires a strong low register and is fun to play. Recorded by Joshua Hauser and Euphoniums Unlimited, *Music for Euphonium Choir.*

Mendelssohn, Felix. *Auf Flügeln des Gesanges.* Arr. Akihiko Ito. Akihiko Ito. Euphonium solo and

four-part euphonium ensemble. ¥1,300 (.pdf version ¥900).

Rimsky-Korsakov, Nicolai. *The Flight of the Bumblebee.* Arr. Akihiko Ito. Akihiko Ito. Euphonium solo and four-part euphonium ensemble. ¥1,600 (.pdf version ¥1,100).

Sturzenegger, Kurt, arr. *7 Quintets.* Editions Marc Reift. Five euphoniums. 1996. €19.60. Seven movements of arrangements of mostly well-known works: Balletto (Gstoldi); Coro di Spiriti (Monteverdi); Sinfonia (Schütz); Préambule (Kindermann); Intrada (Pezel); Sonata (Speer); Two Chorales (Bach).

Takumi, Hidetoshi. *Suite for Five Euphoniums.* Tuba-Euphonium Press. Five euphoniums. 1996. V. Part I: Bb–c″, Part II: Gb–bb′, Part III: F–g′, Part IV: Gb–a′, Part V: Bb1–f′. Four movements: I. Lively; II. Andante cantabile; III. Agitato; IV. Adagio elegioco. The first movement is a playful dance in 6/8. The second movement is slow and lyrical. The third movement is a rhythmical and technical challenge utilizing mixed meters as well as half-valve and flutter tongue techniques. The final movement begins with a haunting melody that yields to a lively allegro finish. High tessitura in the first part.

Uber, David. *Exhibitions, Op. 98.* Tuba-Euphonium Press. Euphonium solo and four-part euphonium ensemble. 1993. $17. 3:25. IV. Part I: eb–b″, Part II: e–g′, Part III: c–e′, IV: Ab–eb′, Part V: Ab1–c′. A short, fun to play recital piece. The work is in three sections: a playful 6/8 allegretto; a tuneful, expressive andante; and a march-like 2/4 allegretto ending with a brief coda alluding to the opening section. Each ensemble part is featured with brief solos. Parts may be doubled for a large ensemble. Recorded by Brian Bowman and Euphoniums Unlimited, *Music for Euphonium Choir.*

Six Part

Censhu, Jiro. *Forest Harmony.* Jiro Censhu. Six euphoniums. 1994. IV. Part I: Bb–c″, Part II: G–a′, Part III: D–e′, Part IV: Bb–bb′, Part V: Eb–g′, Part VI: Bb1–e′. Two movements: I. Con brio ma non troppo; II. Andante con moto. The first movement is a playful scherzo. The second movement begins with a slow and lyrical section followed by a rousing mixed meter dance, which returns to the opening melody. The piece ends with a return of the dance in a brief coda. Technically challenging. High tessitura in the first part.

Debussy, Claude. *Clair de Lune.* arr. Maurice Bale. Godiva Music. Six euphoniums. 2003. £8.00. 4:00. Recorded by Steven Mead, *Euphonium Magic,* volume 1.

Debussy, Claude. *Golliwog's Cakewalk.* Arr. Maurice Bale. Godiva Music. Six euphoniums. 2003. £8.00. V. Part I: ab–bb″, Part II: db–bb′,

Part III: G♭–g′, Part IV: G–b♭′, Part V: E♭–c♭, Part 6: E♭1–a♭. A great arrangement of the best-known tune from Children's Corner. Extreme range demands in the first and sixth parts. Challenging and fun to play. Recorded by Steven Mead, *Euphonium Magic,* volume 1.

Lemeland, Aubert. *Le Tombeau de Paul Hindemith.* Gérard Billaudot. Six euphoniums. €151.24.

Lintinen, Kirmo. *Lampi.* Finnish Music Information Centre. Solo euphonium and five-part euphonium ensemble. 2004. 5:30. V. Solo part: c♯–d″, Part I: c♯–f♯′, Part II: G–f′, Part III: F–g′, Part IV: B1–c♯′, Part V: A♭1–e♭. Commissioned by Jukka Myllys and the Finnish Trombone and Tuba Association (SuPaTuS). "Lampi" is a Finnish word for a pond or a small lake. The term gives the impression of eternal serenity, but also that wet ground is alive, swarming with different creatures. The solo part is quite difficult with a high tessitura throughout and large, angular intervals as well as difficult rhythmic figures and rapid double tonguing passages. Challenging for the entire ensemble. Rhythmic complexity requires careful rehearsal. Solo part is written in tenor clef while the ensemble parts are in bass clef. Additionally, the first and second parts contain brief sections written in tenor clef. Parts may be doubled for a large ensemble. Recorded by Jukka Myllys and Euphoniums Unlimited, *Music for Euphonium Choir.*

Strauss, Johann. *Perpetuum Mobile.* Arr. Maurice Bale. Godiva Music. Six euphoniums. 2004. £6.00. V. Part I: c–b♭″, Part II: F–b♭′, Part III: F–g′, Part IV: F–f′, Part V: F–b♭′, Part VI: A1–d″. Extremely high first part, low sixth part. Technically challenging.

Tchaikovsky, Piotr Illyich. *Humoreske.* Arr. Maurice Bale. Godiva Music. Six euphoniums. 1996. £8.00. 2:30. Recorded by Steven Mead, *Euphonium Magic,* volume 1.

Eight Part

Berlioz, Hector. *Le Carnival Romain.* Arr. Akihiko Ito. Akihiko Ito. Eight euphoniums. ¥7,500 (.pdf version ¥5,500).

Bizet, Georges. *Carmen in 15 Minutes.* Arr. Yasuhide Ito. Ito Music. Eight euphoniums. 1991. 15:00. IV–V. A medley of highlights from *Carmen.* Fun for audience and performers alike. High tessitura in the first two parts, low tessitura in the bottom part. Challenging for all players.

Brandon, Sy. *Echoes.* Co-op Press. Eight euphoniums. 2005. $10. 6:00. Commissioned by Adam Frey for the 2005 International Euphonium Institute. A tonal, one-movement piece in four sections. The first and last sections are marked "allegro," exploring antiphonal choir echoes and pyramids. The second section is an adagio that continues the antiphonal echoes between choirs with an added fading effect. The third section explores echoes in a scherzo style.

Brusick, William R. *By the Waters of Babylon: A Psalmody Tone Poem for Euphonium Choir.* William Brusick. Eight euphoniums. 2004. 9:15. V. Part I: A–d″, Part II: B♭–a′, Part III: F–b♭′, Part IV: D–g′, Part V: E♭–a′, VI: E♭–d′, VII: D–a′, VIII: B♭1–b♭. Commissioned by Clifford and Mary Van Eaton, Dr. William and Patty Applegate, Dr. Donald and Betty Lambert, Mark Vinzant, Bill and Shirley Hart, and Bill and Nancy Page. Written for R. Winston Morris and Euphoniums Unlimited. An inspiring and moving programmatic work based on Psalm 137 that depicts the Israelites' shouts and songs as they are held captive in Babylon. Technically challenging for all parts as rapidly running sixteenth notes portray the flowing river. High tessitura in the first part. Difficult rhythmic figures require careful counting and thorough rehearsal as ensemble cohesiveness may be difficult due to the complexity of the piece. Some sections have optional parts for singing. Mutes are required for parts three, five, six, seven, and eight. Recorded by Euphoniums Unlimited, *Music for Euphonium Choir.*

Censhu, Jiro. *The Noble Mirror.* Jiro Censhu. Baritone vocalist and eight euphoniums. 1993. IV. Part I: B♭–b′, Part II: E–b♭′, Part III: F♯–a′, Part IV: F♯–b♭′, Part V: G–b♭′, Part VI: F–g′, Part VII: D–c′, Part VIII: A1–c′. For Toru Miura and the Euphonium Company. A unique work for large euphonium choir. The vocal part is not difficult; however, the text is in Japanese and euphonium may be a viable substitute. Some technical challenges exist in all parts. See listing under Euphonium in Mixed Ensemble.

Danner, Greg. *Runnin' with Bydlo.* Greg Danner. Eight euphoniums. 2003. 6:15. V. Part I: f–c″, Part II: d♭–a♭′, Part III: F–e′, Part IV: F–d′, Part V: f–c″, Part VI: d♭–a♭′, Part VII: F–e′, Part VIII: F–d′. A "tour de force" based on the well-known movement from Mussorgsky's *Pictures at an Exhibition,* this is an exciting up-tempo work composed as an energetic characterization of the euphonium to contrast the slow and ponderous nature of the original "Bydlo." The work de- and then reconstructs the essential musical elements of the original, focusing on intervallic, harmonic, and rhythmic motives. Requires strong players on all parts. Technically challenging with frequent meter changes, double tonguing, and extensive use of syncopation. High tessitura in the first and fifth parts. Mutes are required for all parts except one and two. Recorded by Euphoniums Unlimited, *Music for Euphonium Choir.*

Elgar, Edward. *Pomp and Circumstance.* Arr. S. Yamazato. Akihiko Ito. Eight euphoniums. ¥4,000.

Gabrieli, Giovanni. *Sonata Pian' e Forte.* Arr. Maurice Bale. Godiva Music. Eight euphoniums or four baritones and four euphoniums. 1998.

£8.00. 3:30. III–IV. Effective arrangement of this baroque masterpiece for antiphonal quartets.

Hartley, Walter. *Intrada and Gigue for Eight Euphoniums.* Tuba-Euphonium Press. Eight euphoniums. 1998. $15. 1:45. IV. Part I: E♭–c♯″, Part II: G–f♯′, Part III: G♭–b♭′, Part IV: C–e♭′, Part V: F–f′, Part VI: E♭–d′, Part VII: C–f′, Part VIII: A♭1–b♭. Two movements: I. Intrada; II. Gigue. For Barry Kilpatrick. A fun piece that would work well as a concert opener. The first movement begins with a slow introduction followed by a lyrical allegro. The second movement is a short, spirited dance. Not technically difficult. Parts one and two are written in tenor clef. High tessitura in the first part. Part eight requires a strong low register.

Mendelssohn, Felix. *Scherzo from A Midsummer Night's Dream.* Arr. Maurice Bale. Godiva Music. Eight euphoniums. 2003. £12.00. 4:00. V. Written for the Royal Northern College of Music euphonium choir. A difficult piece with extensive range demands. Recorded by Steven Mead, *Euphonium Magic,* volume 1.

Mozart, Wolgang Amadeus. *Divertimento I.* Arr. Akihiko Ito. Akihiko Ito. Eight euphoniums. ¥5,500 (.pdf version ¥4,000).

Raum, Elizabeth. *A Little Monster Music.* Elizabeth Raum. Eight euphoniums. 2004. 12:30. IV–V. Part I: A♭–b′, Part II: A♭–b′, Part III: C–g′, Part IV: A♭1–f′, Part V: G1–e′, Part VI: B♭1–e, Part VII: A♭1–c♯′, Part VIII: F1–b♭. Four movements: I. Hydra; II. Nessie; III. Fafner; IV. St. George and the Dragon. Commissioned by Roger Bobo for STUBA. This version for eight euphoniums was especially adapted from the original tuba ensemble version by the composer for Euphoniums Unlimited. The first movement, Hydra, depicts the nine-headed beast from Greek mythology that ravaged the country of Argos. The second movement, Nessie, characterizes a much gentler beast, Scotland's mystery and mist-enshrouded monster of Loch Ness. Fafner, the dragon from Richard Wagner's *Siegfried,* is aptly portrayed in the third movement with direct Wagnerian quotes as well as subtle allusions to Wagner's scoring. The final movement, St. George and the Dragon, portrays the epic battle between the patron saint of England and a fierce dragon in Selena, Libya. An excellent composition that audiences will enjoy. High tessitura in the first part. Extended low register in the bottom four parts, particularly part VIII. Some technical challenges. Parts may be doubled for a large ensemble. Recorded by Euphoniums Unlimited, *Music for Euphonium Choir.*

Rossini, Giocchino. *L'Italiana in Algeri—Sinfonia.* Arr. Akihiko Ito. Akihiko Ito. Eight euphoniums. ¥4,100 (.pdf version ¥3,000).

Self, Jim. *Euphoniums Unlimited: Reggae for Eu-uns.* Basset Hound Music. Eight euphoniums. 2003. $35. 5:00. V. Part I: B♭1–f″, Part II: C–d♭″, Part III: C–c″, Part IV: C–a′, Part V: C–c″,

VI: C–a′, VII: F1–c″, VIII: F1–a′. Commissioned by Winston Morris and Euphoniums Unlimited. For Winston. This exciting and challenging work begins with a unison fanfare that leads into a recurring "reggae groove" section. The several statements of the reggae have pentatonic melodies traded around in all of the parts. These sections are punctuated by odd meter (2/8, 3/8, 5/16, etc.) interludes, modulations, a modified return of the fanfare, and a final coda section that propels the "groove" to the end. Very difficult rhythmic patterns, angular leaps, and extreme range demands on all parts. Technically challenging and great fun to play. High tessitura in the first two parts. Recorded by Euphoniums Unlimited, *Music for Euphonium Choir.*

Uber, David. *Music for Euphonium Choir.* David Uber. Eight euphoniums.

Uber, David. *Octet.* David Uber. Eight euphoniums.

Wagner, Richard. *Der Hochzeitzug zum Münster (from "Lohengrin").* Arr. Akihiko Ito. Akihiko Ito. Eight euphoniums. ¥2,000 (.pdf version ¥1,500).

Nine Part

Glinka, Mikhail. *Overture from "Ruslan and Ludmila."* Arr. Akihiko Ito. Available from Akihiko Ito. Nine euphoniums or two baritones and seven euphoniums. ¥5,500 (.pdf version ¥4,100). Technically very difficult.

MacMillan, Duncan J. *In Memoriam: September 11th, 2001.* Duncan J. MacMillan. Solo euphonium and eight-part euphonium ensemble. 2003. 8:10. V. Solo part: f–g″, Part I: d–d″, Part II: d–c″, Part III: c–a♭′, Part IV: B♭–f♯′, Part V: F–f′, Part VI: F–c♭′, Part VII: E♭1–f, Part VIII: B♭2–e♭. Commissioned by Adam Frey. Dedicated to the memory of the victims of the terrorist attacks on the World Trade Center, September 11, 2001. This moving elegy, based on motives from *America the Beautiful,* is an expression of both profound grief and great strength. Written shortly after the events of September 11, 2001, it is a tonal work that begins quietly and achieves power through use of "Ivesian" dissonance and motivic development. Its heroically triumphant climax is followed by a quiet reprise of opening materials. Extremely difficult due to range, intonation, and endurance demands on all performers, particularly the soloist and lower parts. Not technically difficult. Brief muted section near the end in the first euphonium part. Recorded by Adam Frey and Euphoniums Unlimited, *Music for Euphonium Choir.*

Twelve Part

Ross, Walter. *Contrasts!* Nichols Music Company. Twelve euphoniums. IV–V. Written for Toru

Miura and the Euphonium Company. This large ensemble piece is a one-movement work in four sections. A slow introduction begins the piece, in which the beautiful sonority of the ensemble is emphasized. The following allegro is in three sections, ABA', in which the group of twelve euphoniums is often divided and treated as three quartets. The work is intended to display the agile musical ability, range, and sonority of the instrument. Modal and pandiatonic harmonic language.

10. Recommended Repertoire Written for Other Instruments

Sharon Huff

This chapter on recommended works for the euphonium that were originally written for other instruments has proven to be somewhat problematical. First, it must be stated that euphoniumists take for granted the fact that they must borrow literature from other instruments. Like the tuba, which was also invented in the relatively recent nineteenth century, the euphonium did not exist when many of music history's finest composers were at work. Because of this omission in the literature, the euphoniumist frequently borrows literature originally written for the bassoon, cello, trombone, and trumpet. In fact, literature of these four instruments lends itself quite readily to adaptation for the euphonium since the soloist can often read directly from the original parts, providing one can read the necessary clefs.

Transcriptions of compositions for violin, voice, horn, or other instruments are also available to the euphoniumist. Borrowing literature from these instruments just entails a bit more transposition and editing on the part of the performer. Of course, there may also be some techniques idiomatic to each instrument that would render a particular composition less usable to the euphoniumist, such as trombone glissandi or cello double stops.

The intended scope of this chapter is to provide a list of some basic repertoire that was originally composed for an instrument other than the euphonium, but works well and has often been used by today's euphoniumists. It would be impossible and impractical to list all such repertoire, so it must be noted that this list is by no means comprehensive.

For works that have been transcribed for several different instruments, the most challenging aspect has been determining which arrangement to include in each citation. I have attempted to list an arrangement that is readily usable by the euphoniumist; one for trombone, for example, even though the piece was not necessarily composed for trombone. One must take into consideration the intent of this chapter, and it seems

that detailed listings of compositions that would not be readily usable by the euphoniumist would be a somewhat wasted effort. This is what posed the most difficulty–trying to make a judgment of which version of each composition to list. In many cases, the availability of the music has guided my selection. It appears that some of the Herbert L. Clarke pieces for cornet, for example, are not always available in arrangements for trombone because many are out of print. Thus, I have listed the cornet sheet music, as most euphonium performers should be able to read directly from these parts. It should be noted that many of the pieces listed in this chapter have been arranged specifically for the euphonium, making it unnecessary to use a version written for some other instrument. These arrangements can be found in chapter 2. However, there may be some instances where the performer would prefer to see the original composition.

I would like to thank the following people for assisting me with the formulation and accuracy of this chapter: Gail Robertson, David Werden, Alan Hawkins, and Kent White (from Stanton's Sheet Music), who possesses a staggering amount of knowledge about publishers.

Euphonium with Piano

Arban, Jean Baptiste. *Carnival of Venice*. Rev. and rearr. Eric Leidzen. Belwin/Alfred Publishing Company. Cornet. 1961. $5.95. 7:39. IV. Recorded by Mark Fisher, Mary Ann Craig, Harold Brasch, Stef Pillaert, Robert Childs, David Childs, Alexandre Gagnaux, Sho-ichiro Hokazono, Chris Mallett, Morgan Griffiths, John Clough, Trevor Groom, Derick Kane, Glynn Parry, Brian Warrington, Steven Mead, Lyndon Baglin, David Moore, Arthur Lehman.

Arban, Jean Baptiste. *Fantaisie and Variation on Carnival of Venice*. Rev. Edwin Franko Goldman. Carl Fischer, Inc. Cornet. 1912. $9.50. III–IV.

Arban, Jean Baptiste. *Fantaisie Brillante*. Cundy-Bettoney/Carl Fischer, Inc. Out of Print. Trombone. $4.25. 7:00. III. A♭–g♭[1]. This is one of the characteristic studies from the *Arban's Famous Method for Trombone,* which was originally written for cornet. Recorded by David Moore, Steven Booth, Manfred Heidler, Sho-ichiro Hokazono.

Bach, Johann Sebastian. *Aria (Bist du Bei Mir).* Arr. R. Bernard Fitzgerald. Belwin/Alfred Publishing Company. Trombone. 1952. $4.50. II. Bb–eb.

Bach, Johann Sebastian. *Ave Maria.* Arr. Charles Gounod. Philharmusica Corp. Trombone and organ. $8.50. III. Originally written for voice. Recorded by David Childs; an arrangement by Denny recorded by Riki McDonnell and Mike Kilroy; an arrangement by Denton recorded by Adam Frey; an arrangement by Falcone recorded by Leonard Falcone; an arrangement by Porret recorded by Alexandre Gagnaux.

Bach, Johann Sebastian. *Meditation on Prelude in C.* Arr. James Christensen. Kendor Music, Inc. Out of Print. Trombone. 1978. $1.50. 2:50. III.

Bach, Johann Sebastian. *Sonata No. 3.* Arr. Robert Marsteller. Southern Music Company. Trombone. 1974. $12. IV. Recorded by Loren Marsteller.

Bach, Johann Sebastian. *Sonata No. 2.* Arr. Robert Marsteller. Southern Music Company. Trombone. 1975. $9.95. IV.

Bach, Johann Sebastian. *3 Viola da Gamba Sonatas.* Ed. Keith Brown. International Music Company. Trombone. 1972. $12.75. IV. Originally written for Viola da Gamba.

Bach, Vincent. *Hungarian Melodies.* PP Music. Cornet. $7.50. III–IV. E–bb[1]. Recorded by Elva Kay Tims, Harold Brasch.

Barat, J., ed. *Andante and Allegro.* Alphonse Leduc. Trombone. $14.90. 6:40 (4:30, 2:10). III. F–bb[1]. Recorded by Raymond G. Young.

Barat, J., ed. *Andante and Scherzo.* Alphonse Leduc. Trombone. $14.90. 5:59. III.

Barat, J., ed. *Fantaisie En Mi Bemol.* Alphonse Leduc. Trumpet. 1958. $16.70. III.

Barat, J., ed. *Introduction and Dance.* Alphonse Leduc. Bb bass saxhorn. $13.35. 4:20. III–IV. Also edited for euphonium by Glenn Smith, published by Southern Music Company. Recorded by Raymond G. Young, Masanori Fukuda, Toru Miura.

Barat, J., ed. *Lento et Scherzo.* Alphonse Leduc. Trumpet. 1949. $14.90. III.

Barat, J., ed. *Morceau de Concours.* Alphonse Leduc. Out of Print. $12.20. 7:25. III. G–bb. Recorded by Roger Behrend.

Barat, J., ed. *Orientale.* Alphonse Leduc. Trumpet. 1957. $14.90. III.

Barat, J., ed. *Piece En Mi Bemol.* Alphonse Leduc. Trombone. 1923. $14.90. III. Recorded by Raymond G. Young.

Barat, J., ed. *Reminiscences De Navarre.* Alphonse Leduc. Tuba or saxhorn. 1950. $16.70. III.

Beethoven, Ludwig van. *Adagio Cantabile.* Arr. Albert J. Andraud. Southern Music Company. Horn. 1958. $3.50. III.

Beethoven, Ludwig van. *12 Variations on a Theme from Judas Maccabeus.* Arr. Keith Brown. International Music Company. Trombone. $6.50. III. Originally written for cello.

Bellstedt, Herman. *Napoli.* Arr. Simon. Southern Music Company. Trombone. 1932. $7.95. 5:15. III–IV. F–Bb[1]. Originally written for cornet/ trumpet. Recorded by Leonard Falcone, Roger Behrend, Brian Bowman, John Storey, Tamao Araki, Michael Dodd, Euphoniums of University of Illinois, Toru Miura; an arrangement by Geoffrey Brand recorded by Steven Mead; an arrangement by Childs recorded by Robert Childs; an arrangement by Owenson recorded by Ian Craddock.

Bellstedt, Herman. *The Student's Sweetheart.* Arr. Simon. Southern Music Company. Cornet. 1962. $2.50. III.

Bennett, Robert Russell. *Rose Variations.* Ed. Thom Proctor. Belwin/Alfred Publishing Company. Trumpet. 1955. $15.00. IV.

Berghmans, Jose. *Concertino.* Alphonse Leduc. Trombone. 1954. $38.95. IV.

Berghmans, Jose. *La Femme A Barbe.* Alphonse Leduc. Trombone. 1958. $14.90. III.

Berlioz, Hector. *"Recitative and Prayer" from Grand Symphony for Band.* Ed. Vern Kagarice. Kagarice Brass Editions. Trombone. 1947. $10.00. 5:12. IV. A–a[2]. Recorded by Henry Charles Smith on trombone.

Bizet, Georges. *"The Flower Song" from Carmen.* Boosey & Hawkes. Voice. $6.50. III. Also arranged for euphonium by Maurice Bale, published by Studio Music. Recorded by Steven Mead, Leonard Falcone, Roger Behrend, Riki McDonnell and Mike Kilroy, Earle Louder, Nicholas Childs, and the Euphonium Section.

Blazewitch, B. M. *Concert Piece No. 5.* Belwin/ Alfred Publishing Company. Out of Print. Trombone. 1939. $7.95. III. F–bb.

Bourgeois, Derek. *Concerto for Trombone, Op. 114.* G & M Brand. Trombone. $24.95. 20:25 (9:06, 6:09, 5:13). IV–V. G1–d[2]. Allegro; Adagio; Presto. Recorded by Steven Mead, Angie Hunter.

Bozza, Eugene. *Ballad.* Alphonse Leduc. Trombone. $16.70. IV.

Bozza, Eugene. *Burlesque.* Alphonse Leduc. Bassoon. 1957. $14.90. IV.

Bozza, Eugene. *Ciaccona.* Alphonse Leduc. Trombone. 1967. $14.90. IV.

Bozza, Eugene. *Hommage A Bach.* Alphonse Leduc. Trombone. 1957. $11.85. IV.

Brahms, Johannes. *Four Serious Songs.* Ed. Don Little. Kagarice Brass Editions. Trombone. $25. IV.

Brandt, Vassily. *Concertpiece No. 2, Op. 12.* Ed. Robert Nagel. International Music Company. Trumpet. 1960. $12. III–IV.

Bruckner, Anton. *Ave Maria.* Edition Musicus. Trombone. 1951. $3.25. III.

Busser, Henri. *Variations in D♭, Op. 53.* Cundy-Bettoney/Carl Fischer, Inc. Trumpet. $5.50. III.

Capuzzi, Antonio. *Andante and Rondo from Concerto for Double Bass.* Arr. Philip Catelinet. Hinrichsen Edition. Tuba or Euphonium. 1967. $14. 8:09 (4:22, 3:47). III–IV. F–g¹. Recorded by Brian Bowman, Tyrone Breuninger, Takashi Yamamoto, Masanori Fukuda, Mary Ann Craig; an arrangement by R. Childs recorded by Robert Childs. Originally written for double bass.

Cassadó, Gaspar. *Toccata in the Style of Frescobaldi.* Arr. Keith Brown. International Music Company. Trombone. 1967. $7.25. III.

Castérède, Jacques. *Fantaisie Concertante.* Alphonse Leduc. Bass trombone. 1960. $21.95. 8:16. IV. Recorded by Steven Mead, Paul Droste, Sho-ichiro Hokazono.

Castéréde, Jacques. *Sonatine.* Alphonse Leduc. Trombone. 1958. $23.90. IV.

Charlier, Theo. *Second Solo de Concours.* Ed. Marty Winkler. Edwin F. Kalmus & Co., Inc. Trumpet. $8.95. IV.

Chopin, Frédéric. *The Minute Waltz.* Alfred Publishing Company. Piano. $2.50. III–IV. Also arranged for euphonium by Steven Mead, published by Studio Music.

Clarke, Herbert L. *Bride of the Waves.* Arr. Arthur Brandenburg. Warner Bros. Publications, Inc. Trombone. 1943. $6.95. III–IV. G–b♭¹ (c²). Recorded by Brian Bowman, Steven Mead, David Werden. Originally written for cornet.

Clarke, Herbert L. *Carnival of Venice.* Warner Bros. Publications, Inc. Cornet. 1938. $5.95. 3:55. III. Recorded by Brian Bowman, David Werden, Ken Wood, Earle Louder, Masanori Fukuda, Euphonium Quartet; an arrangement by Brandenburg recorded by Frederick Boyd; an arrangement by Brasch recorded by Harold Brasch.

Clarke, Herbert L. *The Debutante.* Arr. Arthur Brandenburg. Warner Bros. Publications, Inc. Trombone. 1942. $5.95. 6:30. III–IV. F–b♭2. Originally written for cornet. Recorded by Steven Booth, John Swallow.

Clarke, Herbert L. *From the Shores of the Mighty Pacific.* Warner Bros. Publications, Inc. Trombone/baritone. $5.95. 6:27. III. F–b♭¹. Originally written for cornet. Recorded by Leonard Falcone, Steven Mead, Frederick Boyd.

Clarke, Herbert L. *King Neptune.* Charles Colin. Cornet. 1941. $5.95. III–IV.

Clarke, Herbert L. *Maid of the Mist.* Arr. Arthur Brandenburg. Warner Bros. Publications, Inc. Trombone. 1912. $5.95. III. Originally written for cornet.

Clarke, Herbert L. *Sounds from the Hudson.* Arr. Robert Geisler. Southern Music Company. Cornet or baritone treble clef. 1992. $8.50. III. A–f (a♭¹). Also arranged for baritone bass clef, published by Southern Music Company.

Clarke, Herbert L. *The Southern Cross.* Arr. Arthur Brandenburg. Warner Bros. Publications, Inc. Trombone. 1942. $5.95. III. E–d². Originally written for cornet.

Clarke, Herbert L. *Stars in a Velvety Sky.* Carl Fischer, Inc. Cornet. 1939. $5.95. III–IV. d–a♭¹.

Cools, Eugene. *Allegro de Concert.* Editions Billaudot. Trumpet. $10.75. 4:23. III. Recorded by Leonard Falcone.

Cords, Gustav. *Concert Fantasie.* Carl Fischer, Inc. Out of Print. Trumpet. $11.50. 11:17. III. Was also transcribed for trombone or baritone. Recorded by Roger Behrend, Fred Dart.

Cords, Gustav. *Romanze.* Carl Fischer, Inc. Out of Print. Trumpet. $4.95. 5:52. III. Was also transcribed for baritone bass clef. Recorded by Raymond Young; an arrangement by Fabrizio recorded by Roger Behrend.

Corelli, Arcangelo. *Sonata in F Major.* Ed. Keith Brown. International Music Company. Trombone. 1965. $7.75. 6:00. III–IV. G–c². Preludio; Allemanda; Sarabanda; Gavotta; Giga. Originally written for violin and continuo.

Creston, Paul. *Fantasy, Op. 42.* G. Schirmer, Inc. Trombone. 1951. $14.95. IV–V.

Curnow, James. *Fantasy for Trombone.* Rosehill Music Publishing Company. Trombone. 1992. $13.25. II.

Danzi, Franz. *Concerto in F Major.* Ed. Robert Munster. Masters Music Publications, Inc. Bassoon. $13.95. III. Recorded by Jean-Pierre Chevailler.

David, Ferdinand. *Concertino for Trombone in E♭, Op. 4.* Ed. William Gibson. International Music Company. Trombone. 1961. $11.25. 16:32 (7:45, 4:30, 4:17). III–IV. F–c². Allegro Maestoso; Andante Marcia Funebre; Allegro Maestoso.

Davison, John. *Sonata.* Shawnee Press, Inc. Trombone. 1966. $12. 10:20. III–IV. B♭–b¹. Fantasia; After an English Folk Song; Rondo with Chorale.

Dawes, Charles G. *Melody in A Major.* Arr. Jerry Sears. Briar Music Press. Trombone. 1950. $12.00. III–IV.

De La Nux, P. V. *Concert Piece.* Southern Music Company. Trombone. 1958. $6.25. 5:45. III. G–b♭¹. Recorded by Leonard Falcone, Raymond G. Young, Masanori Fukuda.

Demersseman, Jules. *Introduction and Polonaise, Op. 30.* Edwin F. Kalmus & Co., Inc. Trombone. $7.95. IV.

Ewald, Victor. *Romance, Op. 2.* Ed./trans. David Reed. Edition Musicus, Inc. Trombone. 1984. $5.50. III. Recorded by Tyrone Breuninger.

Ewazen, Eric. *Sonata for Trombone.* Southern Music Company. Trombone. 1998. $20. IV–V.

Fasch, Johann Friedrich. *Sonata.* Arr. A. Fromme. McGinnis & Marx Music Publishers. Trombone. 1964. $7. Originally written for bassoon or cello. Recorded by Henry Charles Smith.

Fauré, Gabriel Urbain. *Après un Rêve.* Arr. Allen Ostrander. International Music Company.

Trombone. 1953. $7.75. III–IV. Originally written for cello. Also edited for euphonium by Steven Mead, published by Studio Music. Recorded by Steven Mead.

Fauré, Gabriel Urbain. *Faure Melody*. Arr. Richard Fote. Kendor Music, Inc. Out of Print. Trombone. $3. 3:00. III–IV. f–b♭[1].

Fauré, Gabriel Urbain. *Sicilienne, Op. 78*. Arr. Keith Brown. International Music Company. Trombone. 1917. $8.25. 3:35. IV. G–b[1]. Originally written for cello.

Frackenpohl, Arthur. *Pastorale*. Accura Music. Trombone. 1952. $7. 3:30. III. G–a[1] (d♭[2]).

Franck, César. *Panis Angelicus*. Arr. R. C. Dishinger. Medici Music Press. Trombone. $5. 4:00. III. Originally written for voice. Recorded by Paul Droste, Robert Childs, Brian Bowman, Riki McDonnell, Mike Kilroy.

Frescobaldi, Girolamo. *Canzone*. Arr. Eddie Koopman. Warwick Music. Bass trombone. 2001. $35.95. III. Includes a CD.

Galliard, Johann Ernst. *Six Sonatas for Bassoon or Cello, Vols. 1 and 2*. Ed. Josef Marx. McGinnis & Marx. Bassoon/cello/trombone. 1946. $8 each. III.

Gedalge, Andre. *Contest Piece*. Ed. Christopher Jones. International Music Company. Trombone. 1973. $7.25. III–IV.

Goedicke, Alexander. *Concert Etude, Op. 49*. Universal Edition (MCA Solo Series). Trumpet. 1946. $4.95. III.

Goeyens, Alphonse. *Introduction and Scherzo*. Carl Fischer, Inc. Trumpet. 1937. $5. III.

Goldman, Edwin Franko. *My Old Kentucky Home*. Arr. Theo M. Tobani. Carl Fischer, Inc. Out of Print. Cornet. 1914. III–IV. An arrangement by Rimmer recorded by Derek Deacon, Walter Appleton, Norihisa Yamamoto, Len Withington, Alan Jones.

Goltermann, Georg. *Concerto No. 4, Op. 65*. Ed. Leonard Rose. International Music Company. Cello. 1956. $13. IV.

Graefe, Friedebald. *Grand Concerto*. Carl Fischer, Inc. Trombone/bassoon. 1944. $7.95. III.

Guilmant, Alexandre. *Morceau Symphonique Op. 88*. Arr. E. Falaguerra. Kalmus/ Warner Bros. Publications, Inc. Trombone. 1937. $8.95. 6:24. III. Recorded by Leonard Falcone, Fred Dart, Earle Louder, David Werden.

Haddad, Don. *Suite for Tuba*. Shawnee Press, Inc. Tuba. 1979. $10. 9:00. III. B♭–c[2]. Also transcribed for baritone, published by Shawnee Press, Inc.

Handel, George Frederick. *Adagio and Allegro Marziale*. Arr. Bernard Fitzgerald. Theodore Presser Company. Trumpet. $4.95. III.

Handel, George Frederick. *Andante and Allegro*. Arr. Harry Gee. Southern Music Company. Trombone. 1971. $4. II–III. D–a[1].

Handel, George Frederick. *Aria Con Variazioni*. Trans. Bernard Fitzgerald. Belwin/Alfred

Publishing Company. Trumpet. 1969. $6.95. 5:19. III. G–a[1]. Recorded by Paul Droste.

Handel, George Frederick. *Concerto in F Minor*. Arr. K. H. Fussl/Keith Brown. International Music Company. Trombone. 1964. $9.95. 9:23 (3:30, 1:50, 2:57, 2:06). III. Grave; Allegro; Sarabande-Largo; Allegro. Originally written for oboe. Recorded by Jean-Pierre Chevailler, Henry Charles Smith, Douglas Nelson.

Handel, George Frederick. *Harmonious Blacksmith*. Carl Fischer, Inc. Trombone. $9.95. III. Includes a CD of the piano accompaniment. Also arranged for euphonium by K. Wilkinson, published by Studio Music. An arrangement by Hume recorded by Trevor Groom, Arthur Lehman, Barrie Perrins, Glynn Parry.

Handel, George Frederick. *Honor and Arms*. Arr. Allen Ostrander. Edition Musicus. Trombone. $4.25. III. Originally written for voice.

Handel, George Frederick. *Sonata in A Minor Opus I, No. 4*. Trans. Keith Brown. International Music Company. Trombone. 1970. $8.25. III–IV.

Handel, George Frederick. *Sonata No. 3 in F Major*. Trans. Keith Brown. International Music Company. Trombone. 1968. $8.25. III–IV.

Harris, Floyd O. *The Fairy Princess*. Ludwig Music Publishing Company. Trombone. 1952. $3.50. 3:00. II. B–f[1]. Originally written for cornet/trumpet.

Hartmann, John. *Facilita*. Tromba Publications. Cornet. 1932. $7. IV. Recorded by Arthur Lehman, Steven Mead, Ben Haemhouts; an arrangement by Mortimer recorded by Morgan Griffiths, Steven Mead, Marrie Perrins.

Hartmann, John. *Fantasia Brilliante (Pretty Jane)*. Wright & Round Ltd. Cornet. $17.95. IV.

Hartmann, John. *Fantasia Brilliante (Rule Britannia)*. Wright & Round Ltd. Cornet. $17.95. IV.

Hartmann, John. *Grand Fantasia Brillante (La Belle Americaine)*. Wright & Round Ltd. Cornet. $17.95. IV.

Howarth, Elgar. *The Amazing Mr. Arban*. Shawnee Press, Inc. Trumpet. 1982. $21.95. IV. Recorded by Steven Mead.

Jacob, Gordon. *Concerto for Bassoon and Strings or Band*. Galaxy Music Corp. Bassoon. 1948. $11.25. IV.

Jacob, Gordon. *Concerto for Trombone and Orchestra*. Galaxy Music Corp./E. C. Schirmer. Trombone. 1956. $14.55. 6:14. IV. B♭2–d[2](f[2]). Maestoso/ Allegro Molto; Adagio Molto/Misterioso; Alla Marcia Vivace.

Kelly, Brian. *Sonatina*. Josef Weinberger Ltd./ Boosey & Hawkes/Hal Leonard Publishing Corporation. Trombone. 1980. $26.95. III. G–b♭[1]. Agitato; Con Dvolo; Allegro Giocoso.

Klengel, Julius. *Concertino No. 1 in C, Op. 7*. Breitkopf and Härtel. Cello. $14. III. Also arranged for euphonium in the key of B♭ by Leonard Falcone, published by Tuba/Euphonium Press.

Recorded by Steven Mead, Champions of the Leonard Falcone Festival 1986–2000, Fred Dart, Brian Bowman, Masanori Fukuda.

Klengel, Julius. *Sonatina No. 1 in C Minor, Op. 48.* International Music Company. Cello. 1953. $10.50. IV.

Kreisler, Alexander von. *Sonatina for Trombone and Piano.* Southern Music Company. Trombone. 1967. $7.50. 6:10. III. Recorded by Douglas Nelson.

Kreisler, Fritz. *Liebesfreud.* Carl Fischer, Inc. Violin. $7.95. III. Also arranged for euphonium by David Werden, published by Cimarron Music Press. Recorded by Steven Mead.

Kreisler, Fritz. *Liebesleid.* Carl Fischer, Inc. Violin. $7.95. 3:20. III. Also available transcribed for trumpet by Timofei Dokshitser, published by Editions Marc Reift.

Kryl, Bohumir. *Josephine Waltz.* Carl Fischer, Inc. Trumpet. $4. III.

Kuhne, J.C. *Concertino in E♭ Major.* Kalmus/Warner Bros. Publications, Inc. Trombone. $8.95. III–IV.

Lake, M. L. *Annie Laurie Fantasia.* Carl Fischer, Inc. Out of Print. Cornet. 1922. III. b♭–a♭[1].

Larsson, Lars-Erik. *Concertino Op. 45, No. 7.* Gehrmans Musikförlag. Trombone. $26.95. III–IV.

Leclercq, Edgard. *First Concertino.* Rev. Albert J. Andraud. Southern Music Company. Trombone. 1958. $4. III.

Levy, Jules. *Carnival of Venice.* Arr. Richard Thurston. Southern Music Company. Trumpet/cornet. 1991. $7.95. III–IV. Also arranged for baritone bass clef and treble clef, published by Southern Music Company.

Llewellyn, Edward. *My Regards.* Ed. Clifford P. Lillya. Warner Bros. Publications, Inc. Trombone. 1940. $4.95. 5:36. III. Originally written for cornet. Recorded by Leonard Falcone; Ken Wood.

Magnan, G. *Concerto.* Arr. Allen Ostrander. Cundy-Bettoney/Carl Fischer, Inc. Out of Print. Trombone. 1969. $4.95. 6:47. III–IV. A♭–c[2]. Recorded by Leonard Falcone.

Marcello, Benedetto. *Adagio and Allegro.* Arr. Lyle Merriman. Southern Music Company. Bassoon. 1968. $5. 2:55 (1:10, 1:45). II–III. G–g[1].

Marcello, Benedetto. *Largo and Allegro.* Arr. Lyle Merriman. Southern Music Company. Bassoon. 1968. $5. III.

Marcello, Benedetto. *Sonata III in A Minor.* Arr. Richard Fote. Kendor Music, Inc. Trombone. 1967. $7. III.

Marcello, Benedetto. *Sonata in A Minor.* Arr. Allen Ostrander. International Music Company. Trombone. 1961. $8.50. III. An arrangement by Flaten recorded by Tormod Flaten.

Marcello, Benedetto. *Sonata in C Major.* Trans. Keith Brown. International Music Company. Trombone. 1969. $10. III.

Marcello, Benedetto. *Sonata in D Major.* Trans. Keith Brown. International Music Company. Trombone. 1968. $9. III.

Marcello, Benedetto. *Sonata in F Major.* Trans. Allen Ostrander. International Music Company. Trombone. 1978. $8.25. 7:05 (1:40, 2:29, 1:11, 1:45). III. Largo; Allegro; Largo; Presto. Recorded by Steven Mead, Tamao Araki.

Marcello, Benedetto. *Sonata in G Major.* Trans. Keith Brown. International Music Company. Trombone. 1979. $8.25. III.

Mendelssohn, Felix. *If with All Your Hearts.* Arr. Allen Ostrander. Southern Music Company. Trombone. 1973. $4. 2:25. II. d♯–e[1]. Recorded by Henry Charles Smith, David Childs, Brian Bowman, Mary Ann Craig.

Mendez, Rafael. *Danse Boheme.* Carl Fischer, Inc. Out of Print. Trumpet. $5.95. III–IV.

Monti, Vittorio. *Csárdás.* Arr. Marc Reift/Branimir Slokar. Editions Marc Reift. Trombone. $15.50. 4:30. III–IV. Recorded by David Childs, Shoichiro Hokazono, Jukka Myllys, Steven Mead, the Childs Brothers, Hugo Verweij, Steven Booth, Ivan Milhiet.

Monti, Vittorio. *Czárdás.* Arr. Rafael Méndez. Carl Fischer, Inc. Trumpet. 1953. $6.95. III–IV.

Morel, Florentin. *Piece in F Minor.* Editions Billaudot. Trombone. 1933. $9.75. III. Recorded by Toru Miura, Raymond G. Young, Masanori Fukuda.

Mozart, Wolfgang Amadeus. *Concerto in B♭, K. 191.* Ed./arr. Bernard Garfield. Edition Musicus. Bassoon. 1954. $10.50. 16:11 (6:09, 6:01, 4:01). III–IV. Allegro; Andante; Rondo. Recorded by Jean-Pierre Chevailler.

Mozart, Wolfgang Amadeus. *Concerto in B♭, K. 191 (Rondo).* Arr. Richard Fote. Kendor Music, Inc. Trombone. 1925. $7. III. Originally written for bassoon.

Mozart, Wolfgang Amadeus. *Sonata in B♭ Major, K. 292* Trans. Keith Brown. International Music Company. Trombone. 1968. $8.50. Originally written for bassoon and cello.

Paganini, Niccolo. *Moto Perpetuo, Op. 11.* Ed. Leonard Rose. International Music Company. Cello. 1951. $9.50. IV–V. Originally written for violin. An arrangement by Chabloz recorded by Eran Levi; an arrangement by Snell recorded by Steven Mead, the Childs Brothers, Wendy Picton.

Peaslee, Richard. *Arrows of Time.* Margun Music, Inc. Trombone. 1997. $18. V.

Ponce, Manuel. *Estrellita.* Arr. Mayhew Lake. Carl Fischer, Inc. Out of Print. 3:36. III. Originally for voice. Recorded by Steven Mead, Adam Frey, Leonard Falcone.

Pryor, Arthur. *Air Varie.* Arr. Vern Kagarice. Kagarice Brass Editions. Trombone. $15. III–V.

Pryor, Arthur. *Annie Laurie.* Arr. Glenn P. Smith. Ludwig Music Publishing Company. Trombone. 1963. $6.95. III. B♭1–c[2].

Pryor, Arthur. *Blue Bells of Scotland*. Carl Fischer, Inc. Trombone. 1939. $8.95. 5:30. III–IV. G1–c². Also arranged for euphonium by Philip Sparke, published by Studio Music. Recorded by Paul Droste, Leonard Falcone, Roger Behrend, Nicholas Childs, Brian Bowman, Thomas Runty, Michael Dodd; an arrangement by Sparke recorded by Ueli Kipfer; an arrangement by Pearson recorded by Marcus Dickman.

Pryor, Arthur. *Fantastic Polka*. Carl Fischer, Inc. Trombone. 1939. $12.95 III. Includes a CD.

Pryor, Arthur. *La Petite Suzanne*. Carl Fischer, Inc. Out of Print. Trombone. 1937. $4.95. III.

Pryor, Arthur. *Love's Enchantment*. Editions Marc Reift. Trombone. $19.50. III. Recorded by Harold Brasch.

Pryor, Arthur. *Starlight*. Carl Fischer, Inc. Trombone. 1939. $7.50. III.

Pryor, Arthur. *Thoughts of Love*. Carl Fischer, Inc. Trombone. 1904. $7.50. III. Bb–c².

Pryor, Arthur. *The Whistler and His Dog*. Arr. G. Key. Virgo Music Publishers. Trombone. 1988. $9. III.

Puccini, Giacomo. *"Nessun Dorma" from Turandot*. G. Ricordi & Co., Ltd. Tenor voice. $4.95. 2:57. III. Also arranged for euphonium by Joseph Spaniola, published by Tuba-Euphonium Press, and Adam Frey, published by euphonium.com. Recorded by Adam Frey, Steven Mead, Steven Booth, Riki McDonnell and Mike Kilroy, David Childs.

Puccini, Giacomo. *"O Mio Babbino Caro" from Gianni Schicchi*. G. Ricordi & Co., Ltd. Soprano voice. $4.95. 2:18. III. Recorded by Michael J. Colburn.

Rachmaninoff, Sergei. *Vocalise*. Trans. Keith Brown. International Music Company. Trombone. 1972. $8.25. 5:12. III. Also edited for euphonium by Steven Mead, published by Studio Music. Recorded by Steven Mead, Adam Frey, Mary Ann Craig, Masanori Fukuda; an arrangement by Langford recorded by John Clough, Anders Lundin, Morgan Griffiths.

Ravel, Maurice. *Pavane pour une Infante défunte*. Arr. R. Dishinger. Medici Music Press. Trombone. $5. III. Originally written for piano.

Ravel, Maurice. *Pièce en Forme de Habanera*. Trans. Fernand Oubradous. Alphonse Leduc. Bassoon. 1926. $9.90. 3:09. IV. Also arranged for euphonium/trombone by Ramsay/Dishinger, published by Medici Music Press; originally written for piano. Recorded by Leonard Falcone, Matthew Murchinson.

Reiche, Eugen. *Concerto #2 in A Major*. Edwin F. Kalmus & Co., Inc. Trombone. $6.95. III–IV. (Eb)F#–c².

Rimsky-Korsakov, Nikolai. *Concerto for Trombone and Band*. Ed. Davis Schuman. MCA Music/Hal Leonard Publishing Corporation. Trombone. 1962. $6.95. III. Recorded by Raymond G. Young.

Rimsky-Korsakov, Nikolai. *Flight of the Bumble Bee*. Trans. Gerardo Iasilli. Carl Fischer, Inc. Cornet. 1932. $6.75. 2:00. IV. Also arranged for euphonium (with CD) by Neal Corwell, published by Tuba-Euphonium Press; by Davis, published by Ludwig Music Publishing Company; and by Maurice Bale, published by Studio Music. Recorded by Steven Mead, David Childs, Alexandre Gagnaux, the Childs Brothers, Adam Frey.

Romberg, Bernhard. *Sonata in Bb Major, Op. 43, No. 1*. Arr. F. G. Jansen. International Music Company. Cello. 1953. $10.50. III.

Romberg, Sigmund. *"Serenade" from The Student Prince*. Ed. Carol Cuellar. Warner Bros. Publications, Inc. Voice. 1926. $12.95. 3:37. III. Also arranged for euphonium by David Werden, published by Cimarron Music Press. An arrangement by Godfrey recorded by Brian Bowman, Mary Ann Craig, Harold Brasch, Norihisa Yamamoto; an arrangement by Oswin recorded by Riki McDonnell and Mike Kilroy.

Ropartz, J. Guy. *Andante et Allegro*. Arr. A. Shapiro. Carl Fischer, Inc. Trombone. $7.50. 6:21. III–IV. Originally written for cornet/trumpet. Recorded by Raymond G. Young.

Ropartz, J. Guy. *Piece in E Flat Minor* (incorrectly titled *Piece in B Flat Minor* on the cover—publisher error). Edwin F. Kalmus & Co., Inc. Trombone. $7.95. 5:30. IV. Ab–c² (eb²). Recorded by Nicolas Pfeifle.

Rossini, Gioacchino. *"Largo al Factotum" from The Barber of Seville*. G. Schirmer, Inc. Baritone voice. $4.50. II–III. Edited for euphonium by Bert Sullivan, published by Boosey & Hawkes. Recorded by Raymond G. Young, the Childs Brothers, Nicolas Pfeifle, Riki McDonnell and Mike Kilroy; an arrangement by Langford recorded by John Clough, Ian Craddock, Fred Dart, Morgan Griffiths.

Saint-Saëns, Camille. *Cavatine, Op. 144*. Elkan-Vogel/Theodore Presser Company. Trombone. 1915. $9.95. 4:52. III–IV. Ab–db².

Saint-Saëns, Camille. *Morceau de Concert Op. 94*. Warner Bros. Publications, Inc. Horn. $5.95. 8:30. III–IV. Also arranged for euphonium by Douglas A. Nelson, published by Shawnee Press, Inc. Recorded by Douglas Nelson, Earle Louder.

Saint-Saëns, Camille. *"The Swan" from Carnival of the Animals*. Ed. Keith Brown. International Music Company. Trombone. 1974. $7.25. 3:01. III. d–c². Also arranged for euphonium by Steven Mead, published by Studio Music. Originally written for cello. Recorded by Angie Hunter, Leonard Falcone, Steven Mead, David Childs, Adam Frey, Glynn Parry, David Woollam, the Childs Brothers, Derick Kane, E. Codd, John Clough, Lyndon Baglin.

Schubert, Franz. *An Die Musik*. G. Schirmer, Inc. $3.95. Voice. III. Also arranged for euphonium by David Werden, published by Cimarron Music Press.

Schumann, Robert. *Five Pieces in Folk Style, Op. 102.* Breitkopf & Härtel. Violoncello. $10. 16:01. IV. With Humor; Slow; Not Fast, but Freely; Not Too Fast; Intense and Marked. Recorded by Paul Droste. Also arranged for euphonium by Paul Droste, published by Ludwig Music Publishing Company.

Schumann, Robert. *Traumerei.* Schott Music Company. Cello. $5.95. 2:30. II. Also arranged for euphonium by Richard Thurston, published by Southern Music Company. Originally for piano. Recorded by Manfred Heidler.

Serocki, Kazimierz. *Sonatina für Posaune und Klavier.* Ed. Hermann Moeck. Hermann Moeck Verlag. Trombone. 1985. $20.50. 6:58 (2:15, 2:43, 2:00). IV. G–c♭². Allegro; Andante molto sostenuto; Allegro vivace. Recorded by Henry Charles Smith on trombone.

Simons, Gardell. *Atlantic Zephyrs.* Carl Fischer, Inc. Out of Print. Trombone or baritone. 1915. 5:17. III. e♭–g¹ (b♭¹). Recorded by Leonard Falcone, Steven Mead.

Simons, Gardell. *The Volunteer.* Arr. M. L. Lake. Carl Fischer, Inc. Trombone. $3.25. IV. Recorded by Brian Bowman, Harold Brasch, Arthur Lehman.

Smith, Claude T. *Fantasy for Trumpet.* Wingert-Jones Publishing, Inc. Trumpet. 1967. $10. IV.

Smith, Claude T. *Rondo for Trumpet.* Wingert-Jones Publishing, Inc. Trumpet. 1969. $10. 6:19. IV–V. G–e♭². Recorded by David Werden, Ramond G. Young.

Smith, Clay. *Castles in the Air.* Carl Fischer, Inc. Out of Print. Trumpet, cornet, trombone, or baritone. 1915. $4.95. III. A♭–a¹.

Smith, Clay. *Thoughts of Yesterday.* Carl Fischer, Inc. Out of Print. Trumpet. 1919. $5.50. III. A♭–a♭¹.

Stevens, Halsey. *Sonatina.* Peer International Corporation. Trombone or tuba. 1968. $16. 9:00. IV. G–f².

Still, William Grant. *Romance.* Trans. Douglas Yeo. International Music Company. Bass trombone. 1990. $8.95. III.

Stojowski, Sigismond. *Fantasy.* Ed. Keith Brown. International Music Company. Trombone. 1972. $10. 6:25. IV.

Sulek, Stjepan. *Sonata Vox Gabrieli.* Brass Press. Trombone. 1975. $14.25. III–IV. Recorded by Christian Lindbergh on trombone.

Telemann, Georg Philipp. *Sonata in A Minor.* Ed. Keith Brown. International Music Company. Trombone. 1957. $8.25. III.

Telemann, Georg Philipp. *Sonata in F Minor.* Ed. Allen Ostrander/Veryon-Lacroix. International Music Company. Trombone. 1968. $10. 10:17 (2:13, 3:54, 1:55, 2:15). III. Andante Cantabile; Allegro; Andante; Vivace. Originally written for bassoon. Recorded by Mark Fisher, Roger Behrend.

Vaughan Williams, Ralph. *"Romanza" from Tuba Concerto.* Oxford University Press. Tuba. $19.95.

III–IV. The second movement of this concerto works nicely for euphonium.

Vaughan Williams, Ralph. *Six Studies in English Folksong.* Galaxy Music Corp./E. C. Schirmer. Cello. 1927. $12.50. 9:32 (1:40, 1:23, 1:48, 1:52, 2:02, 0:47). III–IV. E–b♭¹. Adagio; Andante Sostenuto; Larghetto; Lento; Andante Tranquillo; Allegro Vivace. Also arranged for euphonium treble clef and trombone bass clef by Paul Droste, published by Ludwig Music Publishing Company. Recorded by Paul Droste.

Verdi, Giuseppe. *Cavatine et Variations sur Nabucco.* Editions Billaudot. Trumpet. 1995. $12.95. IV.

Verdi, Giuseppe. *Fantaisie No. 1 sur Le Trouvere.* Editions Billaudot. Trumpet. 1995. $19.50. III.

Verdi, Giuseppe. *Fantaisie No. 2 sur Le Trouvere.* Editions Billaudot. Trumpet. 1995. $19.50. III.

Verdi, Giuseppe. *Fantaisie sur La Force Du Destin.* Editions Billaudot. Trumpet. 1995. $19.50. III.

Verdi, Giuseppe. *Fantaisie sur Simon Boccanegra.* Editions Billaudot. Trumpet. 1995. $12.50. III.

Vivaldi, Antonio. *Concerto in A Minor.* Arr. Allen Ostrander. Edition Musicus. Trombone. 1958. $10.50. 10:58 (3:37, 4:46, 2:35). III. G–f¹(a¹). Allegro molto; Andante molto; Allegro. Originally written for bassoon.

Vivaldi, Antonio. *Sonata No. 5 in E Minor.* Ed. Allen Ostrander. International Music Company. Trombone. 1955. $8.75. IV. Originally written for cello.

Vivaldi, Antonio. *Sonata No. 4 in B♭ Major.* Ed. Allen Ostrander. International Music Company. Trombone. 1955. $8.25. IV. Originally written for cello.

Vivaldi, Antonio. *Sonata No. 1 in B♭ Major.* Ed. Allen Ostrander. International Music Company. Trombone. 1955. $8.25. IV. Originally written for cello. Recorded by Ivan Milhiet.

Vivaldi, Antonio. *Sonata No. 6 in B♭ Major.* Ed. Leonard Rose. International Music Company. Trombone. 1955. $8.25. 7:48. IV. Largo; Allegro; Largo; Allegro. Originally written for cello. Recorded by Henry Charles Smith; an arrangement by Mortimer recorded by Ueli Kipfer.

Vivaldi, Antonio. *Sonata No. 3 in A Minor.* Ed. Allen Ostrander. International Music Company. Trombone. 1955. $8.25. IV. Originally written for cello.

Vivaldi, Antonio. *Sonata No. 2 in F Major.* ed. Allen Ostrander. International Music Company. Trombone. 1955. $8.25. IV. Originally written for cello.

Weber, Carl Maria von. *Concertino in E♭ Major, Op. 26.* Trans. Simon Kovar. International Music Company. Bassoon. 1949. $12. IV.

Weber, Carl Maria von. *Romance.* Edwin F. Kalmus & Co., Inc. Trombone. $9.95. 8:00. IV. (C₁) F–a¹(c²).

Weber, Carl Maria von. *"Rondo" from Concerto for Bassoon.* Arr. Himie Voxman. Rubank, Inc. Bassoon. 1938. $4.95. III.

Weide, William. *Fantasia Brilliante on the Air "My Love Is Like a Red Red Rose."* Spaeth/Schmid Brass Wind Notes. Cornet. $10.50. IV.

Weide, William. *Fantasia Brilliante on the Air "Sweet Spirit, Hear My Prayer."* Spaeth/Schmid Brass Wind Notes. Cornet. $5. IV.

White, Donald. *Sonata.* Southern Music Company. Trombone. 1967. $12. IV. E–b^1. Quietly and Sustained/Allegro; Andante sostenuto; Very Spirited.

Williams, Ernest S. *Concerto #2.* Charles Colin. Trumpet or tuba. 1937. $5.95. III–IV.

Unaccompanied Solos

Arnold, Malcolm. *Fantasy for Trombone.* Faber Music. Trombone. 1969. $9.95. 3:30. III–IV. B♭1–d^2.

Bach, Johann Sebastian. *Six Cello Suites.* Arr. Keith Brown. International Music Company. Trombone. 1972. $13.50. III–IV. Originally written for cello.

Bourgeois, Derek. *Fantasy Pieces for Tenor Trombone.* Warwick Music. Trombone. $19.95. IV.

Frackenpohl, Arthur. *Bonebits.* Anglo-American Music Publishers. Trombone. 1983. 7:55 (1:05, 2:05, 1:30, 1:45, 1:30). IV. E♭–c^2.

Gabrieli, Domenico. *Ricercare.* Arr. Davis Shuman. Southern Music Company. Trombone. $5.95. III–IV.

Grainger, Percy. *Irish Tune from County Derry.* Philharmusica Corp. Trumpet. $7.50. III. Also known as the folk song "Londonderry Air" or "Danny Boy."

Hidas, Frigyes. *Fantasia.* Editio Musica Budapest. Trombone. $8.95. IV.

Ketting, Otto. *Intrada.* Theodore Presser Company/Donemus. Trumpet. 1977. $12.95. IV.

Paganini, Niccolo. *Caprices.* Ed. Carl Flesch. C. F. Peters. Violin. $11.95. IV. Several of the *Caprices* have been arranged for euphonium by David Werden, published by Cimarron Music Press. *Caprice No. 17* recorded by Jae-Young Heo.

Persichetti, Vincent. *Parable, Op. 133.* Theodore Presser Company. Trombone. $4.50. III–IV.

Persichetti, Vincent. *Parable, Op. 127.* Theodore Presser Company. Trumpet. $4.95. III–IV.

Plog, Anthony. *Postcards.* Editions BIM. Trombone. $16.95. IV.

Vizzutti, Allen. *Cascades.* Brass Press. Trumpet. 1981. $9.95. IV. Recorded by Sho-ichiro Hokazono.

Collections

Arnold, J. *Cello Solos.* Amsco Publications. Cello. 1940. $15.95. 128 pp. II–IV.

Bach, Johann Sebastian. *Six Suites for Violoncello Solo.* Rev. Frits Gaillard. G. Schirmer. Violoncello. 1939. $12.30. 53 pp. III–IV.

Bellstedt, Herman. *Herman Bellstedt Jr. Twelve Famous Technical Studies.* Ed. Frank Simon. Southern Music Company. 1960. Trombone. $7. 18 pp. III. Originally written for cornet or trumpet.

Clarke, Herbert L. *The Best of Herbert L. Clarke.* Warner Bros. Publications, Inc. Cornet. $10.95. III–IV.

Clarke, Herbert L. *Collection of Ten Solos.* Carl Fischer, Inc. Out of Print. Cornet. 1919. $11.50. III.

Clarke, Herbert L. *The Herbert L. Clarke Collection.* Carl Fischer, Inc. Cornet. $22.95. III–IV.

Clarke, Herbert L. *The Music of Herbert L. Clarke, Books 1 and 2.* Warner Bros. Publications, Inc. Out of Print. Cornet. 1977. III–IV.

Fillmore, Henry. *Lassus Trombone Plus 14 Hot Trombone Rags.* Carl Fischer, Inc. Trombone. $13.50. III–IV.

Hunsberger, Donald, arr. *Carnaval.* Carl Fischer, Inc. Out of Print. Trumpet. 1990. $24.95. 48 pp. III–IV.

Mendez, Rafael. *The Rafael Mendez Collection.* Carl Fischer, Inc. Trumpet. 1996. $34.95. III–IV.

Morrison, Timothy, ed. *Solos for Trumpet.* Carl Fischer, Inc. Trumpet. 2003. $19.95. III–IV.

Price, S. J. *Let Us Have Music for Cornet.* Carl Fischer, Inc. Out of Print. Cornet. 1940. II–III.

Pryor, Arthur. *Solos for Trombone.* Carl Fischer, Inc. Trombone. 2002. $14.95. III–IV.

Puccini, Giacomo. *Play Puccini for Trombone: 10 Arias Transcribed for Solo Instrument & Piano.* Ricordi/ Hal Leonard Publishing Corporation. Trombone. $16.95. 40 pp. III. Includes a CD.

Raph, Alan, ed. *Famous Coloratura Arias for Instrumental Solo.* Carl Fischer, Inc. Bass clef instruments. 1990. $11.95. III.

Raph, Alan, ed. *Recital Pieces for Unaccompanied Trombone.* Carl Fischer, Inc. Trombone. 1990. $10.95. III.

Raph, Alan, ed. *Solos for Trombone.* Carl Fischer, Inc. Trombone. 2000. $17.95. II–IV.

Rubank Book of Trumpet Solos. Hal Leonard Publishing Corporation. Trumpet. 1943. $7.95. 48 pp. II–III.

Selected Trumpet Solos. Amsco Publications. Trumpet. 1960. $17.95. 128 pp. II–IV.

Smith, Henry Charles, ed. *Solos for the Trombone Player.* G. Schirmer, Inc. Trombone. 1963. $15.95. II–IV.

Telemann, Georg Philipp. *Twelve Fantasies for Unaccompanied Trombone.* Ed./trans. Alan Raph. Carl Fischer, Inc. Trombone. $8.95. III–IV.

Vandercook, H. A. *Trombone Gems.* Rubank, Hal Leonard Publishing Corporation. Trombone. 2001. $12.95. III. Includes a CD.

Vandercook, H. A. *Trumpet Stars.* Rubank, Hal Leonard Publishing Corporation. Trumpet. 2001. $12.95. 24 pp. III. Includes a CD.

Vivaldi, Antonio. *6 Sonatas.* Ed. Leonard Rose. International Music Company. Cello. 1955. $17.75. 64 pp. IV–V.

Voxman, Himie. *Concert and Contest Collection.* Rubank, Inc. Trombone. $4.95. II–IV.

Williams, Ernest S. *Trumpet Solo Collection.* Charles Colin. Out of Print. Trumpet. 1936. $7.50. III–IV.

Method Books

Arban, Jean Baptiste. *Arban's Famous Method for Trombone.* Arr. C. L. Randall/Simone Mantia. Carl Fischer, Inc. Trombone. 1936. $28.95. 261 pp. I–IV. Originally written for cornet.

Bitsch, Marcel. *Quinze Etudes de Rythme.* Alphonse Leduc. Trombone. 1956. $18.80. IV–V.

Blazhevich, Vladislav. *Sequences.* Ed. Keith Brown. International Music Company. Trombone. $13. 17 pp. IV–V.

Blazhevich, Vladislav. *70 Studies for BB♭ Tuba, Vols. I and II.* Robert King Music Sales, Inc. Tuba. 1965. $8.75 each. III–IV.

Blazhevich, Vladislav. *Studies in Clefs.* Ed. Allen Ostrander. International Music Company. Trombone. 1957. $17.75. 78 pp. III–IV.

Bleger, Michel. *10 Caprices.* Arr. Allen Ostrander. International Music Company. Trombone. $7. III.

Bleger, Michel. *31 Studies.* Arr. Allen Ostrander. International Music Company. Trombone. $7.50. III.

Blume, O. *36 Studies for Trombone.* Carl Fischer, Inc. $10.95. Trombone. 1962. 45 pp. III–IV.

Bordogni, Marco. *Melodious Etudes for Performance.* Trans./arr. Alan Raph. Carl Fischer, Inc. Trombone. 2002. $12.95. 32 pp. IV.

Bordogni, Marco. *Melodious Etudes for Trombone Books I–III.* Trans./arr. Joannes Rochut. Carl Fischer, Inc. Trombone. 1928. $13.95 each. 65 pp. III–V. Originally written for voice.

Bourgeois, Derek. *Bone of Contention (Fifteen Studies for Trombone).* Brass Wind Publications. 1990. Trombone. $10. 15 pp. III.

Bousquet, Narcisse. *36 Celebrated Studies.* Rev. Edwin Franko Goldman. Carl Fischer, Inc. Trumpet. $9.95. 39 pp. III–IV.

Boutry, Roger. *12 Etudes de Haute Perfectionnement.* Alphonse Leduc. Trombone. $20.85. IV.

Bozza, Eugène. *13 Etudes-Caprices.* Alphonse Leduc. Trombone. $18.80. IV. Originally written for saxophone.

Campbell, Charles J. *30 Contemporary Etudes.* Sam Fox Publishing Co., Inc. Trombone. 1974. $6. 36 pp. III–IV.

Charlier, Théo. *Etudes de Perfectionnement.* Henry Lemoine. Trombone. $37.95. IV–V.

Charlier, Théo. *Trente-six Etudes Transcendante.* Alphonse Leduc. Trumpet. $65. IV–V.

Cimera, Jaroslav. *221 Progressive Studies.* Belwin/Alfred Publishing Company. Trombone. 1942. $9.95. 48 pp. II.

Clarke, Herbert L. *Technical Studies.* Arr. Claude Gordon. Carl Fischer, Inc. Trombone. 1976. $14.50. 53 pp. III–IV. Originally written for cornet.

Clodomir, Pierre François. *Methode Complete, Books I and II.* Alphonse Leduc. Trombone. $38.35. III–IV.

Clodomir, Pierre François. *70 Little Studies.* Friedrich Hofmeister. Trombone. $13.25. III–IV. Originally written for trumpet.

Colin, Charles. *Advanced Lip Flexibilities, Vols. 1–3.* Charles Colin. Trombone. 1980. $15. 80 pp. III–IV. Originally written for trumpet.

Colin, Charles. *Melodious Fundamentals.* Charles Colin. Trombone. 1975. $6.95. 40 pp. III–IV. Originally written for trumpet.

Colin, Charles. *Original Warm-Ups.* Charles Colin. Trombone. 1975. $6.95. 24 pp. III–IV. Originally written for trumpet.

Colin, Charles. *Progressive Technique.* Charles Colin. Trombone. 1988. $6.95. 24 pp. III–IV. Originally written for trumpet.

Colin, Charles. *Scales and Chords.* Charles Colin. Trombone. 1991. $6.95. 24 pp. III–IV. Originally written for trumpet.

Concone, Giuseppe. *15 Vocalises Op. 12.* Arr./ed. W. F. Cramer. Robert King Music Sales, Inc. Trombone. $3.55. 27 pp. IV–V.

Concone, Giuseppe. *Legato Etudes.* Arr. J. Shoemaker. Carl Fischer, Inc. Trombone. $11.95. III.

Cornette, Victor. *Method for Trombone.* Rev. Jerome N. Procter. Cundy-Bettoney/Carl Fischer, Inc. Trombone. 1937. $24.95. 123 pp. III–IV.

Couillaud, Henri. *Modern Etudes.* Alphonse Leduc. Trombone. $30.10. IV.

Fink, Reginald H. *Introducing the Alto Clef.* Accura Music. Trombone. 1968. $10. 32 pp. III–IV.

Fink, Reginald H. *Introducing the F Attachment.* Accura Music. Trombone. 1968. $14. III.

Fink, Reginald H. *Introducing the Tenor Clef.* Accura Music. Trombone. 1968. $10. III–IV.

Fink, Reginald H. *Studies in Legato.* Carl Fischer, Inc. Trombone. 1969. $13.95. 46 pp. II–III.

Gaetke, Ernst. *School of Etudes.* Musikverlag Wilhelm Zimmermann. Trombone. 1933. $16. 39 pp. IV.

Gaetke, Ernst. *Studies in Scales and Arpeggios.* Musikverlag Wilhelm Zimmermann. Trombone. 1928. $13.95. 40 pp. IV.

Galindo, Jeff, and the Berklee Faculty. *Berklee Practice Method.* Berklee Press. Trombone. 2002. $14.95. 157 pp. III–IV.

Hering, Sigmund. *Progressive Etudes.* Carl Fischer, Inc. Trombone. $12.95. III–IV.

Hering, Sigmund. *Recreational Studies.* Carl Fischer, Inc. Trombone. $10.95. III–IV.

Hering, Sigmund. *32 Etudes.* Carl Fischer, Inc. Trombone. $11.50. III–IV.

Hickman, David R. *Music Speed Reading for Beginners.* Trigram Music Inc. Trumpet. 1986. $9.95. 48 pp. II–IV.

Kahila, Kauko. *Advanced Studies (Alto and Tenor Clef)*. Robert King Music Sales, Inc. Trombone. 1948. $8.75. 16 pp. IV–V.

Kopprasch, Carl. *Selected Kopprasch Studies for Trombone with F Attachment*. Ed. Richard Fote. Kendor Music, Inc. Trombone. 1964. $4.75. 31 pp. IV.

Kopprasch, Carl. *60 Studies for Trombone, Books I and II*. Carl Fischer, Inc. Trombone. 1905. $8.95 each. 27 pp. each. III–IV. Originally for horn.

Kreutzer, Rodolphe. *10 Famous Etudes*. Arr. Aug. H. Schaefer. Carl Fischer, Inc. Out of Print. Trombone. 1935. $4.50. 16 pp. III. Originally written for violin.

LaFosse, André. *Méthode Complete, Vols. 1–3*. Alphonse Leduc. Trombone. $29.30 each. III–IV.

LaFosse, André. *School of Sight Reading and Style, Books A–E*. M. Baron Company. Trombone. $7.95 each. II–V.

Milde, Ludwig. *25 Studies in Scales and Chords*. Ed. Simon Kovar. International Music Company. Bassoon. 1950. $12.50. 27 pp. IV–V.

Ostrander, Allen. *Shifting Meter Studies*. Robert King Music Sales, Inc. Trombone/bass trombone. $9.65. III–IV.

Paudert, Ernst. *24 Studies*. Ed. Allen Ostrander. International Music Company. Trombone. 1961. $11.25. 34 pp. III–IV.

Pederson, Tommy. *Elementary Etudes for Bass Trombone*. Belwin-Mills Publishing Corp. Bass trombone. 1972. $7.95. 56 pp. II–III.

Pederson, Tommy. *Unaccompanied Solos for Tenor Trombone. Vol. 1—Melodic Exercises*. Kendor Music, Inc. Trombone. 1977. $9. 18 pp. III–IV.

Peres, Gabriel. *Scales*. Rev./ed. Harvey S. Whistler. Rubank, Inc. Trombone. 1943. $6.50. 48 pp. III.

Remington, Emory. *Warm-Up Exercises*. Arr. Donald Hunsberger. Accura Music. Trombone. $12.50. 63 pp. II–IV.

Remington, Emory. *Warm-Up Exercises*. Accura Music. Manuscript. Trombone. $5.50. II–IV.

Reynolds, Verne. *48 Etudes*. G. Schirmer, Inc. Trumpet. 1971. $12.95. 53 pp. III–IV.

Rode, (Jacques) Pierre. *15 Caprices for Bass Trombone or Trombone with F attachment*. Ed. Keith Brown. International Music Company. Trombone. 1971. $4. 24 pp. IV–V. Originally written for bassoon.

Schlossberg, Max. *Daily Drills and Technical Studies*. M. Baron Co. Trombone. 1947. $15.95. 72 pp. III–IV. Originally for trumpet.

Slama, Anton. *Melodic Technique*. Ed. Reginald H. Fink. Accura Music. Trombone. 1991. $11. 48 pp. III–IV.

Slama, Anton. *66 Basic Studies*. Ed. Keith Brown. International Music Company. Trombone. 1970. $11.50. 37 pp. III–IV.

Slama, Anton. *66 Etudes in all Major and Minor Keys*. Carl Fischer, Inc. Trombone. 1922. $12.50. 45 pp. III–IV.

Slokar, Branimir, and Marc Reift. *Double and Triple Tonguing* Editions Marc Reift. Trombone. 1990. $32. 99 pp. III–IV.

Tyrrell, H. W. *40 Progressive Studies*. Boosey & Hawkes, Inc. Trombone. 1927. $12.50. 40 pp. III. Also spelled "Tyrell."

Vobaron, Edmond. *32 Celebrated Melodies*. Carl Fischer, Inc. Out of Print. Trombone. $11.95. III–IV.

Vobaron, Felix. *34 Etudes*. Carl Fischer, Inc. Out of Print. Trombone/bassoon. $8.50. 41 pp. III–IV.

Voxman, Himie. *Selected Studies*. Rubank, Inc. Trombone. 1952. $6.95. 72 pp. III.

Werner, Fritz. *38 Studies*. Ed. Keith Brown. International Music Company. Trombone. 1965. $13. 40 pp. IV.

Two Euphoniums

Most compositions written for two trombones, bassoons, cellos, or trumpets can be used by two euphoniumists, as can combinations of the aforementioned instruments (i.e. trombone and trumpet, bassoon and cello, etc.) This is not intended as a comprehensive list, just a few possible options.

Amsden, Arthur. *Amsden's Celebrated Practice Duets*. C. L. Barnhouse Company. 1918. Two cornets, clarinets, baritones, saxophones, horns, bassoons, and so forth. $15.95. 70 pp. II–IV.

Bach, Johann Sebastian. *Bach for Two Trumpets*. Ed. Sigmund Hering. Carl Fischer, Inc. Two trumpets. 1972. $14.95. II–III.

Bach, Johann Sebastian. *Fifteen Two-Part Inventions for Two Bassoons*. Arr. Alan Hawkins. Bocal Music. Two bassoons. 1990. $16. 31 pp. III–IV. Originally written for harpsichord.

Beethoven, Ludwig van. *Three Sonatas*. Trans. Alan Hawkins. Bocal Music. Two bassoons. 1990. $12. 25 pp. III–IV. Originally written for clarinet and bassoon.

Belcke, Friedrich August. *Duo Concertant, Op. 55*. Editions BIM. Two trombones. $15. III–IV.

Blavet, Michel. *Seven Easy Duets for Two Bassoons*. Arr. Alan Hawkins. Bocal Music. Two bassoons. 1997. $6. 4 pp. II–III. Originally written for violin and cello.

Blazhevich, Vladislav. *Concert Duets for Trombone*. International Music Company. Out of Print. Two trombones. $14. III–IV.

Bleger, Michel. *12 Duets*. Arr. Allen Ostrander. International Music Company. Two trombones. $11.25. III–IV.

Bleger, Michel. *12 Duos Concertants.* Alphonse Leduc. Two trombones. $20.85. III–IV.

Blume, O. Ed. William Gibson. *12 Duets, Vols. 1 and 2.* International Music Company. Two trombones. 1959. $11.75 (volume 1), $13.50 (volume 2). III–IV.

Boismortier, Joseph Bodin de. *Baroque Duos.* Arr. Thompson. Shawnee Press, Inc. Two bassoons. $8. III–IV.

Bower, Bugs, and Steve Bulla. *Bop Duets, Complete.* 3 volumes. Charles Colin. Two trombones. 1981. $18. 92 pp. III–IV.

Clodomir, Pierre François. *Twelve Duets.* Ed. Eugene Foveau. International Music Company. Two trumpets. 1959. $14. 24 pp. III.

Concone, Guiseppe. *5 Duets.* Arr. Allen Ostrander. Kendor Music, Inc. Two trombones. $7. III.

Cooper, Lewis Hugh. *Thirteen Duets and Etudes for Two Bassoons.* Bocal Music. Two bassoons. 1995. $12. 24 pp. III–IV.

Cornette, Victor. *Six Concert Duets.* Carl Fischer, Inc. Out of Print. Two trombones. $6. III–IV.

Devienne, François. *Eighteen Easy Duets.* Arr. Alan Hawkins. Bocal Music. Two bassoons. 1991. $6. 14 pp. II–III.

Dotzauer, Friedrich. *Three Sonatas, Op. 103.* Ed. Schroeder. International Music Company. Two cellos. 1954. $10. 28 pp. III–IV.

15 Top Jazz Duets. Hal Leonard Publishing Corporation. Two trombones. $6.95. 32 pp. III.

Gale, Jack. *12 Jazz Duets.* Music Express. Two trombones. 1997. $16.95. 27 pp. III–IV. Includes play-along CD.

Hartzell, Doug. *Diggin' Doug's Duos: Ten Duets for Trombones.* Shawnee Press, Inc. Two trombones. 1977. $8. III.

Hartzell, Doug. *Ten Jazz Duos and Solos.* Shawnee Press, Inc. 1974. Two trumpets. $7. III.

Hartzell, Doug. *Twelve Jazz Duets.* Shawnee Press, Inc. Two trombones. $10. III.

Jazz Duets–Standards for Trombone. Hal Leonard Publishing Corporation. Two trombones. $5.95. 31 pp. III.

Kummer, Friedrich August. *Three Duets, Op. 22.* Ed. Julius Klengel. International Music Company. Two cellos. 1953. $12. 32 pp. IV.

Lee, Sebastian. *Three Duets, Op. 37.* Ed. Bernhardt Schmidt. International Music Company. Two cellos. 1953. $10.50. 24 pp. IV.

Miller, Ernest R. *Brass Duet Notebook from the Works of J. S. Bach, Vols. I and II.* Southern Music Company. Two trombones. 1988. $8.50. III.

Mozart, Wolfgang Amadeus. *Concerto in B♭ Major, K. 191 for Two Bassoons.* Arr. Alan Hawkins. Bocal Music. Two bassoons. 1989. $12. 12 pp. III–IV. Originally written for bassoon and orchestra.

Mozart, Wolfgang Amadeus. *Sixteen Duets.* Arr. Alan R. Hawkins. Bocal Music. Two bassoons. 1991. $6. 16 pp. II–III. Originally written for violin and cello.

Mozart, Wolfgang Amadeus. *Sonata Amabile in F Major for Two Bassoons.* Arr. Alan Hawkins. Bocal Music. Two bassoons. 1995. $8. 5 pp. III. Originally written for two flutes.

Mozart, Wolfgang Amadeus. *Sonata in B♭ Major, K. 292.* Ed. Alan R. Hawkins. Bocal Music. Two bassoons. 1992. $7. 8 pp. III. Originally written for bassoon and cello.

Mozart, Wolfgang Amadeus. *Twelve Duets.* Arr. Alan R. Hawkins. Bocal Music. Two bassoons. 1993. $6. 12 pp. II–III. Originally written for two violins.

Music for Two Trombones, Vol. 1. (Duets in a Jazzy and Classical Style). Last Resort Music Publishing. Two trombones. 2001. $16. III.

Nelson, Bob. *Advanced Duets Phase I and Phase II, Books A and B.* Charles Colin. Two trumpets. 1971. $15. each. 84 pp. IV.

Nelson, Bob, and Aaron Harris. *35 Original Duets.* Charles Colin. Two trombones. 1975. $8.95. 68 pp. III–IV.

Niehaus, Lennie. *10 Jazz Inventions.* Kendor Music, Inc. Two trombones. 1983. $9.50. III.

Ozi, Etienne. *14 Duets.* Ed. R. C. Dishinger. Medici Music Press. Two trombones. $10. III–IV.

Ozi, Etienne. *Six Sonatinas Books 1 and 2.* Ed. Alan Hawkins. Bocal Music. Two bassoons. 1993. $6. 19 pp. II–III.

Pederson, Tommy. *Ten Duets for Tenor and Bass Trombone.* Kendor Music, Inc. Tenor and bass trombone. 1976. $10. IV–V.

Pederson, Tommy. *Ten Tenor Trombone Duets.* Kendor Music, Inc. Two trombones. 1980. $10. IV.

Rimsky-Korsakoff, Nicholai. *Flight of the Bumblebee for Two Bassoons.* Arr. Alan Hawkins. Bocal Music. Two bassoons. 1998. $8. 4 pp. IV. Originally written for orchestra.

Rossini, Gioacchino. *Sonata in C Major.* Arr. Alan R. Hawkins. Bocal Music. Two bassoons. 1993. $7. 15 pp. III–IV. Originally written for cello and contrabass.

Snell, Keith. *Belwin Master Duets, Advanced, Books 1 and 2.* Belwin/Alfred Publishing Company. 1991. Two trombones. $6.50. IV.

Stouffer, Paul, ed. *Easy Six for Two (Short Classical Pieces).* Kendor Music, Inc. Two trombones. $6. II–III.

Telemann, Georg Philipp. *Six Canonic Sonatas.* Ed. Keith Brown. International Music Company. Two trombones. 1981. $8.75. III–IV.

Vandercook, H. A. *Vandercook Progressive Duets.* Rubank, Inc. Two trumpets. 1958. $7.95. 32 pp. II.

Vivaldi, Antonio. *Concerto in G Minor, RV531.* Ed. Janos Starker. International Music Company. Two cellos. 1975. $11.25. III.

Voxman, Himie, ed. *Selected Duets, Books 1 and 2.* Rubank, Inc. Two trombones. $8.95 each. III–IV.

Voxman, Himie, ed. *Selected Duets, Books 1 and 2*. Rubank, Inc. Two trumpets. $8.95 each. III–IV.

Wienandt, Elvyn A., ed. *Dozen Plus One*. Southern Music Company. Two bassoons. 1990. $6.50. II. Also published for two trombones.

Three Euphoniums

Most compositions written for three trombones, bassoons, cellos, or trumpets can be used by three euphoniumists, as can combinations of the aforementioned instruments (i.e., two trumpets and a trombone, two bassoons and a cello, etc.). However, one must take into consideration any idiomatic techniques that might be employed, such as trombone glissandi or cello harmonics. Naturally, these techniques are not easily duplicated by the euphoniumist. The list below is not intended to be comprehensive, but rather, a list of a few possible options.

Albinoni, Tomaso. *Trio Sonata*. Arr. Doug Yeo. Southern Music Company. Three trombones. $10. III–IV.

Bach, Johann Sebastian. *Eight Easy Trios for Three Bassoons*. Arr. Alan Hawkins. Bocal Music. Three bassoons. 1993. $12. III. Originally written for harpsichord.

Bach, Johann Sebastian. *Sinfonias, Vols. 1–3*. Arr. Ralph Sauer. Williams Music Publishing Company. Three trombones. $16 each. III–IV.

Bach, Johann Sebastian. *"Wachet Auf" from Cantata No. 140*. Arr. Vern Kagarice. Williams Music Publishing Company. Three trombones. $15.50. III–IV.

Beethoven, Ludwig van. *Rondo*. Trans. Mark Prater. Wehr's Music House. Three trombones. 2001. $9. IV.

Beethoven, Ludwig van. *Trio in G Major for Three Bassoons*. Arr. Alan Hawkins. Bocal Music. Three bassoons. $12. III–IV. Originally written for two oboes and English horn.

Big Book of Trombone Trios. Arr. David Nikkel. Mark Tezak Musikverlag. Three trombones. $16. III.

Blazhevich, Vladislav. *Suite 1 and 2*. Briar Music Press. Three trombones. $18 each. III–IV.

Bruckner, Anton. *Two Equale*. Arr. Keith Brown. International Music Company. Three trombones. $11.25. III–IV.

Byrd, William. *Earle of Oxford's Marche*. Arr. R. C. Dishinger. Medici Music Press. Three trombones. $6.50. III.

Corelli, Arcangelo. *Trio Sonata, Op. 1, No. 10*. Arr. George Osborn. Ensemble Publications. Three trombones. $5. III–IV.

Cornette, Victor. *Trios, Books 1–3*. Ensemble Publications. Three trombones. $6 each. III–IV.

Frescobaldi, Girolamo. *Canzona I*. Arr. David Fetter. Ensemble Publications. Three trombones. $5. III–IV.

Gershwin, George. *Gershwin for Three*. Arr. Dennis Armitage. Editions Marc Reift. Three trombones. $26. IV.

Handel, George Frederick. *Gigue*. Arr. George Osborn. Ensemble Publications. Three trombones. $5. III.

Handel, George Frederick. *"Menuet" from Concerto, Op. 6, No. 5*. Arr. R. C. Dishinger. Medici Music Press. Three trombones. $5. III.

Handel, George Frederick. *Suite for Three Trombones*. Arr. Allen Ostrander. Edition Musicus. Three trombones. $16. III.

Hartzell, Doug. *March of the T-Bones*. Grand Mesa Music. Three trombones. $3.95. III.

Haydn, Franz Joseph. *Trio in C Major for Three Bassoons*. Arr. Alan Hawkins. Bocal Music. Three bassoons. $8. III–IV. Originally written for two violins and cello.

Haydn, Franz Joseph. *Trio from String Quartets 63 and 37*. Arr. Paul Delisse. Ensemble Publications. Three trombones. $5. IV.

Houston, Rudy. *Avant Garde Trios*. Ed. Charles Colin. Charles Colin. Out of Print. Three trombones. 1968. $2.50. III.

Jones, Robert W. *Three by Three*. Shawnee Press, Inc. Three trombones. 1972. $5. III.

Kreisler, Alexander von. *Two Sketches*. Southern Music Company. Three trombones. 1969. $6. III.

Lo Presti, Ronald. *Trombone Trio*. Carl Fischer, Inc. Out of Print. Three trombones. 1958. $6. III.

Marcellus, John, arr. *Trios for Brass, Vol. 1, Easy-Intermediate, and Advanced*. Ed. Thom Proctor. CPP/Belwin/Alfred Publishing Company. Three trombones. $6.95 each. II–IV. Published in bass or treble clef.

Mendelssohn, Felix. *Elijah Favorites for Trombone Trio*. Arr. Hall. Great Works Publishing, Inc. $10. III.

Mozart, Wolfgang Amadeus. *Divertimento No. 1 in F Major for Three Bassoons*. Arr. Alan Hawkins. Bocal Music. Three bassoons. 1990. $10. 4 pp. II–III. Originally written for two violins and cello.

Mozart, Wolfgang Amadeus. *Divertimento No. 1 in G Major for Three Bassoons*. Arr. Alan Hawkins. Bocal Music. Three bassoons. 1990. $10. 4 pp. II–III. Originally written for two violins and cello.

Mozart, Wolfgang Amadeus. *Fourteen Easy Trios for Three Bassoons*. Arr. Alan Hawkins. Bocal Music. Three bassoons. 1997. $14. 8 pp. II. Originally written for two violins and cello.

Mozart, Wolfgang Amadeus. *Suite*. Arr. Allen Ostrander. Edition Musicus. Three trombones. $8. III.

Mozart, Wolfgang Amadeus. *Twelve Variations for Three Bassoons*. Arr. Alan Hawkins. Bocal Music. Three bassoons. 1989. $10. 4 pp. III. Originally written for piano.

Niehaus, Lennie. *Ten Jazz Sketches Vols. 1–3 Trombone Trio.* Kendor Music, Inc. Three trombones. $11 each. III–IV.

Ostransky, Leroy. *Contest Trio #1.* Hal Leonard Publishing Corporation. Three trombones and piano. $3. III.

Pederson, Tommy. *Tenor Trombone Trios Vols. 1 and 3.* Kendor Music, Inc. Three trombones. $12 each. IV.

Purcell, Henry. *"Gavotte" from Harpsichord Suite No. 5.* Arr. A. Vedeski. Medici Music Press. Three trombones. $6. III.

Purcell, Henry. *Three Fantasias.* Arr. D. Miller. Ensemble Publications. Three trombones. $5. III.

Rathgeber, Valentin. *Five Pastorales.* Arr. Alan Hawkins. Bocal Music. Three bassoons. 1991. $6. 8 pp. II–III. Originally written for two flutes and cello.

Speer, Daniel. *2 Sonatas.* Arr. Anthony Baines. Musica Rara. Three trombones. $11.50. IV.

Stouffer, Paul. *Contrupuntal Six for Three.* Kendor Music, Inc. Three trombones. $11. III–IV.

Stouffer, Paul. *Six for Three.* Kendor Music, Inc. Three trombones. $9. III.

Telemann, Georg Philipp. *Trio Sonata in C Minor.* Arr. Richard Bailey. Wehr's Music House. Three trombones. $9. III–IV.

Vivaldi, Antonio. *Trio in B♭ Major for Three Bassoons.* Arr. Alan Hawkins. Bocal Music. Three bassoons. 1990. $8. 4 pp. III. Originally written for two violins and cello.

Vivaldi, Antonio. *Trio in C Major.* Arr. Alan Hawkins. Bocal Music. Three bassoons. 1993. $6. 4 pp. III. Originally written for two violins and cello.

Vivaldi, Antonio. *Trio in D Minor for Three Bassoons.* Arr. Alan Hawkins. Bocal Music. Three bassoons. 1993. $8. 4 pp. III. Originally written for two violins and cello.

Vivaldi, Antonio. *Trio in F Major for Three Bassoons.* Arr. Alan Hawkins. Bocal Music. Three bassoons. 1993. $8. 4 pp. III. Originally written for two violins and cello.

Four Euphoniums

Many compositions written for four trombones, bassoons, cellos, or trumpets can be used by four euphoniumists, as can combinations of the aforementioned instruments (i.e., two trumpets and two trombones, two bassoons and two cellos, etc.). However, one must take into consideration any idiomatic techniques that might be employed, such as trombone glissandi or cello harmonics. Naturally, these techniques are not easily duplicated by the euphoniumist. When using compositions written for unlike instruments, one

must take into account the differences in timbre and pitch in order to avoid selecting pieces with voicing that would be too close in range when played by four euphoniumists or four of any like instrument. The list below is not intended to be comprehensive, but rather, a list of a few possible options.

Bach, Johann Sebastian. *Air from Suite #3.* Arr. Patrick McCarty. Ensemble Publications. Four trombones. $8. III.

Bach, Johann Sebastian. *Fugue in G Minor.* Arr. Hiroyuki Odagiri. Editions Mark Reift. Four trombones. $18. III–IV.

Bach, Johann Sebastian. *Sixteen Chorales.* Ed. Robert King. Robert King Music Sales, Inc. Four trombones. 1958. $4.25. 16 pp. III. In score form.

Beethoven, Ludwig van. *3 Equali.* Arr. Robert King. Robert King Music Sales, Inc. Four trombones. $11.70. III.

Berlioz, Hector. *Excerpts from Damnation of Faust.* Arr. Allen Ostrander. Edition Musicus. Four trombones. $12.50. III–IV.

Blahnik, Joel. *New Prague Trombones.* Hal Leonard Publishing Corporation. Four trombones. $12. III.

Brahms, Johannes. *O Cast Me Not Away Op. 29 # 2.* Arr. Ernest Williams. Kendor Music, Inc. Four trombones. $7. III.

Bruckner, Anton. *Three Motets for Four Trombones.* Arr. Ralph Sauer. Western International Music Company. Four trombones. $9. III–IV.

Byrd, William. *Earle of Oxford's Marche.* Arr. R. C. Dishinger. Medici Music Press. Four trombones. $8.50. III.

Chopin, Frédéric. *Chorale and Prelude.* Kendor Music, Inc. Four trombones. 1978. $4. 2:30. III.

Cooper, Lewis Hugh. *Bassoon Quartet.* Bocal Music. Four bassoons. 1991. $8. 12 pp. IV.

Curnow, James, arr. *Three Madrigals.* Medici Music Press. Four trombones. $11.50. III–IV.

Forbes, Mike, arr. *Just a Closer Walk.* Music Express. Four trombones. $12. III–IV.

Franck, César. *Panis Angelicus.* Arr. Rod Miller. Rod Miller Music/Kagarice Brass Editions. Four trombones. $12. III.

Frescobaldi, Girolamo. *Toccata.* Arr. David Vining. Kagarice Brass Editions. Four trombones. $10. III–IV.

Fucik, Julius. *The Grouchy Old Bear.* Arr. Alan Hawkins. Bocal Music. Four bassoons. 1990. $10. 4 pp. III. Originally written for bassoon and orchestra.

Gabrieli, Andrea. *Ricercare.* Arr. Howard J. Buss. Brixton Publications. Four trombones. $7.95. III–IV.

Gabrieli, Andrea. *Ricercar del Duodecimi Tono.* Arr. A. Cauthen. Kagarice Brass Editions. Four trombones. $12. III–IV.

Gabrieli, Giovanni. *Sonata*. Arr. Keith Brown. International Music Company. Four trombones. $9.50. III–IV.

Gearhart, Livingston, arr. *Bass Clef Sessions*. Shawnee Press, Inc. Four bass clef instruments. $10. III. Contains solos, duets, and trios as well.

Glière, Reinhold. *Russian Sailor's Dance*. Arr. Frank Siekmann. C. L. Barnhouse Company. Four trombones. $12. III–IV.

Grieg, Edvard. *In the Hall of the Mountain King*. Trans. Michael Brenner. Wehr's Music House. Four trombones. $8. III.

Haddad, Donald. *T-Bone Party*. Shawnee Press, Inc. Four trombones. $10. III.

Handel, George Frederick. *"Largo" from Xerxes*. Arr. Ernest Williams. Southern Music Company. Four trombones. $5. III.

Handel, George Frederick. *Music for the Royal Fireworks*. Arr. Dave Thomas. Music Express. Four trombones. $15. III–IV.

Hawkins, Alan, arr. *Sixteen Christmas Carols for Bassoon Quartets*. Bocal Music. Four bassoons. 1991. $16. 4 pp. II. Originally written for chorus.

Haydn, Franz Joseph. *"Achieved Is Thy Glorious Work" from The Creation*. Arr. Ernest Miller. Ensemble Publications. Four trombones. $8. III.

Haydn, Franz Joseph. *Largo*. Arr. Ernest Miller. Southern Music Company. Four trombones. $7.95. III.

Kreisler, Fritz. *Liebesleid*. Arr. Michael Brenner. Wehr's Music House. Four trombones. $11. III.

Marcellus, John, arr. *Quartets for Brass, Vol. 1, Easy-Intermediate, and Advanced*. Ed. Thom Proctor. CPP/Belwin/Alfred Publishing Company. Four trombones. $6.95 each. II–IV. Published in bass or treble clef.

Mendelssohn, Felix. *Equale #3 for Four Trombones*. Arr. Glenn Smith. Ludwig Music Publishing Company. Four trombones. $8.95. III–IV.

Mendelssohn, Felix. *Hunter's Farewell*. Arr. Allen Ostrander. Edition Musicus. Four trombones. $4.50. III–IV.

Monti, Vittorio. *Csárdás*. Arr. Marc Reift. Editions Marc Reift. Four trombones. $19.50. IV.

Mouret, Jean Joseph. *Fanfare-Rondeau*. Arr. Marc Reift. Editions Marc Reift. Four trombones. $15.50. III–IV.

Mozart, Wolfgang Amadeus. *Adagio and Fugue for Four Bassoons*. Arr. Alan Hawkins. Bocal Music. Four bassoons. 1994. $12. 4 pp. III–IV. Originally written for string orchestra.

Mozart, Wolfgang Amadeus. *Eine Kleine Nachtmusik for Four Bassoons*. Arr. Alan Hawkins. Bocal Music. Four bassoons. 1994. $12. 8 pp. III–IV. Originally written for string orchestra.

Mozart, Wolfgang Amadeus. *Presto*. Arr. Jean Thilde. Editions Billaudot. Four trombones. $9.25. III–IV.

Mozart, Wolfgang Amadeus. *Quartet in F Major for Four Bassoons*. Arr. Alan Hawkins. Bocal Music. Four bassoons. 1991. $10. 20 pp. III–IV. Originally written for piano four hands.

Pachelbel, Johannes. *Three Magnificat Fugen*. Arr. Ernest Miller. Ludwig Music Publishing Company. Four trombones. $12. III–IV.

Palestrina, Giovanni Pierluigi da. *Ricercar del 1. Tuono*. Arr. Kurt Sturzenegger. Editions Marc Reift. Four trombones. $17. III–IV.

Purcell, Henry. *Gavotte & Hornpipe*. Arr. R. C. Dishinger. Medici Music Press. Four trombones. $6.50. III.

Quartet Repertoire for Trombone. Hal Leonard Publishing Corporation. Four trombones. $4.95. III.

Quartet Repertoire for Trumpet. Hal Leonard Publishing Corporation. Four trumpets. $4.95. III.

Reichenbach, Bill, arr. *Scarborough Fair*. Virgo Music Publishers. Four trombones. $8. III–IV.

Rimsky-Korsakoff, Nicolai. *Flight of the Bumblebee for Bassoon Quartet*. Arr. Alan Hawkins. Bocal Music. Four bassoons. 1991. $12. 2 pp. IV. Originally written for orchestra.

Saint-Saëns, Camille. *Adagio from Symphony No. 3*. Arr. Ken Murley. Ensemble Publications. Four trombones. 1959. $9. III. Originally written for orchestra.

Scheidt, Samuel. *Canzona Bergamasca*. Arr. Dave Thomas. Music Express. Four trombones. $12. III–IV.

Scheidt, Samuel. *Galliard Battaglia*. Arr. Dave Thomas. Music Express. Four trombones. $15. III–IV.

Schubert, Franz. *Andante Con Moto*. Arr. Ernest R. Miller. Southern Music Company. Four trombones. 1990. $5. III.

Shaw, Lowell. *Fripperies Books 1–9*. The Hornists' Nest. Four trombones. $8. Originally written for four horns.

Sibelius, Jean. *Finlandia*. Arr. Mark McDunn. Neil A. Kjos Music Company. Four trombones. 1970. $9. III. Originally written for orchestra.

Smith, Claude T. *In Dulci Jubilo*. Wingert-Jones Music, Inc. Four trombones. $7.50. III.

Speer, Daniel. *Sonata for Four Trombones*. Ensemble Publications. Four trombones. $8. IV.

Tchaikovsky, Peter. *"Andante Cantabile" from the Fifth Symphony*. Arr. G. E. Holmes. C. L. Barnhouse, Inc. Four trombones. 1951. $7.50. III. Originally written for orchestra.

Telemann, Georg Philipp. *Quartet in C Major for Four Bassoons*. Arr. Alan Hawkins. Bocal Music. Four bassoons. 1991. $12. 4 pp. III–IV. Originally written for string orchestra.

Telemann, Georg Philipp. *Quartet in F Major for Four Bassoons*. Arr. Alan Hawkins. Bocal Music. Four bassoons. 1991. $12. 4 pp. IV. Originally written for string orchestra.

Telemann, Georg Philipp. *Quartet in G Major for Four Bassoons*. Arr. Alan Hawkins. Bocal Music.

Four bassoons. 1991. $12. 4 pp. III–IV. Originally written for string orchestra.

Vivaldi, Antonio. *Concerto in B♭ Major.* Arr. Alan Hawkins. Bocal Music. Four bassoons. 1991. $12. 3 pp. IV. Originally written for string orchestra.

Vivaldi, Antonio. *Concerto in D Minor for Four Bassoons.* Arr. Alan Hawkins. Bocal Music. Four bassoons. 1992. $12. 4 pp. III–IV. Originally written for string orchestra.

Vivaldi, Antonio. *Concerto in E Minor for Four Bassoons.* Arr. Alan Hawkins. Bocal Music. Four bassoons. 1991. $12. 4 pp. III–IV. Originally written for string orchestra.

Vivaldi, Antonio. *Concerto in F Major for Four Bassoons.* Arr. Alan Hawkins. Bocal Music. Four bassoons. 1993. $12. 4 pp. III–IV. Originally written for string orchestra.

Wagner, Richard. *Elsa's Procession to the Cathedral.* Arr. Jack Gale. Music Express. Four trombones. $12. III–IV. Originally written for orchestra.

Zipoli, Domenico. *Festival Prelude for Bassoon Quartet.* Arr. Alan Hawkins. Bocal Music. Four bassoons. 1991. $10. 2 pp. III–IV. Originally written for wind band.

11. Methods and Studies

Brian Bowman

Historically method and study materials have not been written exclusively for the euphonium. The majority of study methods were written in the twentieth century for the combination of trombone/baritone horn (euphonium). Since the euphonium and baritone horn commonly read both bass and treble clefs, many trumpet and cornet methods were also used. In addition to utilizing methods from other brass instruments, study materials were also borrowed from the violoncello and bassoon. This chapter will include materials that were written with euphonium/baritone horn specifically mentioned in the title or supporting materials. A few band methods have also been included, especially those that include CD examples of euphonium playing for the student.

There are methods published for the French tuba and saxhorn, which are similar instruments to the euphonium. Some but not all of these methods are included in this chapter. Further information can be found in the 1994 Indiana Press publication *French Music for Low Brass Instruments: An Annotated Bibliography* written by J. Mark Thompson.

In the past ten years there has been a growth of method books and especially etude study books specifically written for the euphonium. The majority of these materials have been generated in response to competitions sponsored by the Tubists Universal Brotherhood Association (now named the International Tuba-Euphonium Association [ITEA]). A debt of gratitude is due to the ITEA for sponsoring several specific euphonium etude competitions for all levels.

Catalogs from various music publishers and online sources were used in preparing this chapter, in addition to the extensive music library at the University of North Texas and the personal library of Brian Bowman. The inclusion of many older items is important in documenting early methods for the euphonium. Many of these early materials may be permanently out of print. Availability of all the materials has been verified where possible and permanently out of print notations

have been used. However, lack of an out of print notation does not guarantee that the item is currently available. The prices given are current as of time of verification and usually given in U.S. currency. For out of print materials or where no other source is given, the cover price on the item is listed. Items without notation and/or with incomplete bibliographic information were not made available to the editor for examination. Particular thanks go to the Tuba-Euphonium Press and David Miles for being the major publisher of specific materials for the euphonium during the last quarter of the twentieth century. The editor appreciates the supplying of review copies of all Tuba-Euphonium Press materials. Thanks also to other publishers and composers who assisted in supplying review copies.

Special thanks are given to doctoral candidates Elena Hansen Johnson and Brian Meixner for their assistance in gathering and evaluating materials for this chapter.

Anderson, Eugene D. *Musically Mastering the Low Range of the Tuba and Euphonium.* Anderson's Arizona Originals. 1991. $20. 87 pp. III–IV. This book contains a foreword about low-register playing by Sam Pilafian and many etudes in contrasting styles in sets of three gradually working lower. Also, there are fingering charts, three tuba and euphonium duets, and written information on intonation and a clinic for the beginning tubist by Eugene Anderson. These etudes are a good source of material for low-register development.

Arban, J. B. *Arban Complete Method for Trombone & Euphonium.* Ed./notated by Joseph Alessi and Dr. Brian L. Bowman. Encore Music Publishers. 2000. $56.95. 394 pp. II–V. A complete rework of the original Arban's method in bass clef including all materials in previous versions edited and corrected. The book also contains instructions and comments from the editors on practice and performance techniques. Additionally, it is spiral bound to facilitate opening flat on the music stand and to encourage longevity.

Arban, J. B. *Arban Prescott, First and Second Year.* Carl Fischer. 1936. $15.95. 79 pp. II–IV. This book was designed for use with the first two years of the Prescott Technic System. It was published to make the studies of the famed Arban's complete method available to the first- and second-year student at a lower cost. All material contained in the book is taken directly from the complete Arban's method.

Arban, J. B. *Arban Scales for Euphonium.* Arr. Wesley Jacobs. Encore Music now distributed by Tuba-Euphonium Press. 1999. $17. 46 pp. An arrangement of the familiar scale patterns in the Arban's complete method differing in that each individual exercise is presented in all the keys before progressing to the next pattern.

Arban, J. B. *Arban's Famous Method for Slide and Valve Trombone and Baritone in Bass Clef.* Adapted by and issued under the editorial supervision of Charles L. Randall and Simone Mantia. Carl Fischer. 1936. $28.95. 261 pp. II–V. For many years the only version of the Arban's method in bass clef, it contains much of the same material from the treble clef version missing the song and duet sections. There are also many differences in notes and dynamics from the edited Carl Fischer treble clef version of the same book.

Arban, J. B. *Mead Meets Arban.* De Haske. 1999. $17.95. 60 pp. IV–V. Available in both treble and bass clef, this book contains a reprinting of eight of the solos at the end of the complete Arban's method. Also included is a CD of Steven Mead performing these solos with piano accompaniment. Publisher numbers are baritone/euphonium treble clef, 991435; baritone/euphonium bass clef, 991689; piano accompaniment, 991690. The piano accompaniment is permanently out of print.

Archimede, Alexander. *Foundation to Baritone Playing.* In collaboration with Edwin Franko Goldman. Carl Fischer. Out of Print. 1918. 109 pp. I–II. This text is a very early elementary method specifically written for the baritone horn/euphonium. It contains many diagrams and explanations of how to play, including explanations of the baritone and the euphonium. Out of print for some time, it is a historical book from the early part of the twentieth century.

Beeler, Walter. *Method for the Baritone, Book I.* Warner Bros. 1956. $8.95. 74 pp. I–II. A specific and most effective book for teaching the young euphonium player, this method book includes exercises and concepts for the early learner and is especially effective in private study. The book contains a foreword introducing the basics of euphonium playing, a list of musical terms and definitions, and a fingering chart.

Bernard, Paul. *Méthode Complète pour Trombone Basse, Tuba, Saxhorns Basses et Contrebasses.* Alphonse Leduc. 1960. $47.40. III–IV. This complete method written in French includes translations in English, German, and Spanish. The material

covers exercises similar to the Arban's method along with studies in transposition, studies on Bach, modern studies, and orchestral works.

Blank, Allan. *Sixteen Studies for Solo Euphonium.* Tuba-Euphonium Press. 1991 $10. 19 pp. IV. This collection can be used as etudes or separate unaccompanied solo works. Many of these studies alternate between the bass and tenor clefs. Performance suggestions by the composer are included.

Blazhevich, V. *Blazhevich Etudes for Trombone and Euphonium.* Ed. Reginald H. Fink. Accura Music. $19.50. 1991. 154 pp. This volume is an edition of the original Blazhevich clef studies without the clef changes, all in bass clef. While the original clef studies for trombone have long been a standard text for both trombone and euphonium, this volume removes the clef reading requirement while maintaining the musical content of the etudes.

Bléger, Michel. *Méthode Complète de Saxhorn-Basse.* Alphonse Leduc. 1948. $38.35. III–IV. The first exercises of this method include interval studies and basic scales. They quickly advance to more complex major and minor scales, etudes, and concert duets.

Boosey & Hawkes. *The Complete Boosey & Hawkes Trombone and Euphonium Scale and Arpeggios Book.* Boosey & Hawkes. 1995. $8.25. 49 pp. II–III. This book includes all major and minor scales in varying patterns, arpeggios, and ranges.

Brandon, Sy. *Dance Etudes for Euphonium.* Tuba-Euphonium Press. 2002. $10. 23 pp. IV–V. More advanced etudes than the earlier etudes by Sy Brandon; these fifteen etudes in dance forms begin in the baroque styles and proceed through various nationalistic dances including the zortziko, flamenco, polonaise, and barcarolle. There are very challenging non-traditional harmonic treatments in these etudes.

Brandon, Sy. *Stylistic Etudes for Euphonium.* Tuba-Euphonium Press. 1996. $10. 26 pp. II–III. Etudes for the developing student to help develop a sense of style of different dance types. Designed to not go beyond the level of a third-year student, some etudes have two version, A and B, with the A version being a simplified version of the B version.

Brasch, Harold. *The Euphonium and 4-Valve Brasses.* Tuba-Euphonium Press. $20. 178 pp. III–V. A very specific book on the compensating four-valve euphonium with sections on fingerings and special techniques, including perhaps one of the most extensive chapters on multi-phonics of any method book. Containing much advice on solo playing by one of the twentieth-century's finest euphonium soloists, including examples of vintage solo repertoire, this book is a must for the serious euphonium student.

Charlier, T. *32 etudes of perfectionment.* Lemoire. 1988. $37.95 55 pp. Arranged somewhat progressively, these 32 etudes each have individual and specific goals. They have been transcribed for trumpet and are available in B♭ treble clef.

Clarke, Herbert L. *Technical Studies for Bass Clef Instruments*. Ed. Claude Gordon, trans. into bass clef by Willima B. Knevitt. Carl Fischer. 1976. $14.50. 53 pp. II–V. A series of studies and etudes that have been standard exercises for developing technical fluency on valved brass instruments, this bass clef version is an accurate transcription of the original work for cornet.

Clodomir, Pierre. *Méthode Complète pour tous les Saxhorns en Clé de Fa et le Trombone à Pistons*. Alphonse Leduc. 1954. $38.35. II–IV. This book is now available in a complete version rather than in two volumes.

Clodomir, Pierre. *Méthode Complète pour tous les Saxhorns en Clé de Fa et le Trombone à Pistons eu deux volumes*. Alphonse Leduc.1948. $23.75. 56 pp. II–III. This is the first of the two-volume work. The introduction is in French and does not include an English translation. The first studies focus on basic technique and then advance to ornamentation and melodic duets.

Clodomir, Pierre. *Méthode Complète pour tous les Saxhorns en Clé de Fa et leTrombone à Pistons eu deux volumes*. Alphonse Leduc. 1954. $23.75. 56 pp. III–IV. Volume two includes more advanced studies, including major and minor scales, melodic duets, and theme and variations.

Colin, Charles. *Advanced Lip Flexibilities*. Volumes I, II, and III. Charles Colin Publications. 1975. $15. 80 pp. Excellent material for developing extensive legato lip flexibilities, transposed from the original trumpet method of the same name. Extensive material is included on lip trills and upper range flexibility.

Concone, Giuseppe. *Donald S. Reinhardt's Selection of Concone Studies*. Comp./arr. by Donald S. Reinhardt. Elkan-Vogel. 1943. $7.50. 16 pp. II–III. This work is a collection of fifteen vocal studies by Concone edited and arranged progressively by Donald Reinhardt.

Corina, John. *25 Progressive Euphonium Etudes*. Tuba-Euphonium Press. 1994. $12. 30 pp. I–II. This collection was the winner of the 1995 TUBA composition contest for euphonium etudes at the elementary level. Each etude is fairly short in length and contains a limited range of keys. Beginning at the half note and whole note level, these etudes progress rather quickly into sixteenth note rhythm patterns in 6/8 and 9/8 time signatures.

Corwell, Neal. *Sixteen Etudes for Euphonium*. Tuba-Euphonium Press. 1990. $8. 16 pp. III–IV. This book contains four different series of exercises covering single, double, and triple tonguing as well as changing meters, tenor clef, whole tone scales, intervals, and lyrical playing. These are very specific exercises that would benefit the college euphonium student.

Daniels, M. L. *Eighteen Etudes for Euphonium*. Tuba-Euphonium Press. 1992. $10. 14 pp. III–IV. These etudes are in various keys and meters, not neglecting the more difficult ones, and they contain various technical and musical challenges.

De Ville, Paul. *The Eclipse Instructor for Baritone*. Carl Fischer. Out of Print. 1950. 65 pp. II–III. This book includes a lengthy introduction on music rudiments and proper posture. The exercises begin with scale exercises and move through rhythmic, melodic, and articulation exercises.

Dufresne, Gaston. *Develop Sight Reading, Vol. 1 & 2 for All Bass Clef Instruments*. Ed. Roger Voisin. Charles Colin Music. 1954. $12.50. 59 pp. III–V. A combination of these two volumes develops sight-reading skills that progress to a high level of difficulty. These etudes combine the bass and tenor clefs and involve complex intervallic relationships, rhythms, and meters.

Ellis, James L. *Back to Basics for Baritone*. LS Publications. 2002. $10. 57 pp. This book is a collection of basic warm-ups and major scale studies.

Ferone, Steiner. *Baritone ABC*. 2001. $20.95. 55 pp. I–III. Ranging in difficulty for the beginner through the intermediate player, this book contains a routine of daily exercises as well as a set of solos with piano accompaniment.

Fink, Reginald H. *From Treble Clef to Bass Clef Baritone*. Accura Music. 1972. $11. 31 pp. I–III. As the title suggests, these are graduated, short etudes introducing the bass clef to a treble clef reader. The etudes are identical to those found in Fink's other books introducing the tenor and alto clefs.

Fritze, Gregory. *Twenty-five Characteristic Etudes*. Tuba-Euphonium Press. 1992. $14. 50 pp. IV–V. The same composer transcribed the first twenty etudes in this collection from *Twenty Characteristic Etudes for Tuba*. The last five were written specifically for the euphonium. Many of the etudes contain quotes from symphonic wind and orchestral literature with inherent stylistic characteristics present.

Froseth, James O. *Do It! Play Euphonium, Book I*. GIA Publications, Inc. $6.95. 48 pp. I. Part of a complete beginning band method. The book comes with a compact disc recording of Dr. Brian Bowman performing each selection on euphonium with professional studio backgrounds. This book is available in both the bass and treble clefs.

Froseth, James O. *Do It! Play Euphonium, Book II*. GIA Publications, Inc. $6.95. Part of a complete band method for second-year players. This book is available in both the bass and treble clefs.

Froseth, James O. *The Individualized Instructor: Sing, Drum, and Play*. GIA Publications, Inc. The series of books is as follows: *Preliminary*

Book ($6.50), *Book I* ($5.50), *Book II* ($5.50), *Book III* ($5.50), *Supplementary Book I, Solos and Ensembles* ($5.50), *Supplementary Book II, Tunes for Developmental Technique* ($4.50). This book is available in both the bass and treble clefs.

Froseth, James O. *Listen, Move, Sing, and Play.* GIA Publications, Inc. The series of books is as follows: *Book I* ($5.50), *Book II* ($5.50), *Book III* ($5.50), *Supplementary Book I* ($4.50), *Supplementary Book II* ($5.50). This book is available in both the bass and treble clefs.

Fuentes, David. *Mail-Order Etudes, A Catalog for Euphonium.* Manuscript available from David Fuentes, 1260 Broadway, Flat 2, Somerville, Massachusetts 02144. 617-776-2042. 29 pp. This book available in manuscript only is an inventive group of etudes utilizing the fourth-valve range, challenging intervals, and keys centers.

Gallay, Jacques. *15 Etudes de style pour Trombone, Tuba, Euphonium.* Gérard Billaudot Éditeur. Rev. Edmond Leloir. 1974. $14.75. 14 pp. III–IV. This book would serve advanced high school students and college students.

Gause, Charles F. *Learn to Play the Baritone, B.C., Book One.* Alfred Music Co., Ltd. $7.50. 48 pp. I. This is a beginning method containing appropriate exercises and etudes.

Gause, Charles F. *Learn to Play the Baritone, B.C., Book Two.* Ed. J. David Abt. Alfred Music Co., Ltd. $5.95. 48 pp. II. These etudes are a continuation from *Book One,* designed for the second-year player.

Gendron, Denise A. *How to Play Trombone and Baritone—23 Easy Lessons.* Ed. Tony Santorella. Santorella Publications, Ltd. 2002. $7.95. 32 pp. I. This method is intended for the beginner. It includes a foreword with pictures showing proper playing position and technique, a glossary of terms, and a fingering chart. The book alternates pages between playing exercises for the beginner and theory worksheets and exercises.

Gendron, Denise A. *Learn from a Pro—23 Easy Lessons.* Ed. Tony Santorella. Santorella Publications, Ltd. 2002. $12.95. 32 pp. I. This book is exactly the same as Gendron's *How to Play Trombone and Baritone—23 Easy Lessons,* but includes a compact disc of a professional euphoniumist performing the examples in the book.

Girard, Anthony. *15 Études de Concours.* Gérard Billaudot Éditeur. 2000. $11.95. 41 pp. IV–V. This is volume 8 of the series of competition etudes specifically written for euphonium. These etudes pose a good challenge both technically and musically for college and professional players.

Girard, Anthony. *15 Études sur le phrase et la vélocité pour saxhorn basse ou euphonium.* Gérard Billaudot Éditeur. 2000. $11.95. 33 pp. III–IV. This is volume 7 of the Girard series of method books. It focuses on phrasing and velocity with varying styles and range and includes passages in tenor clef.

Gower, Wm., and H. Voxman. *Advanced Method for Trombone or Baritone, Volume I.* Hal Leonard. $6.95. 76 pp. II–III. Rubank Educational Library No. 96. Significant portions of this book are dedicated to scale and arpeggio routines, duets, and technical etudes and exercises. Six simple solos are included at the end of the book. Exercises in flexibility and ornamentation, along with a glossary of terms, are included as well.

Gower, Wm., and H. Voxman. *Advanced Method for Trombone or Baritone, Volume II.* Hal Leonard. $6.95. 96 pp. III. Rubank Educational Library No. 179. The final method book in the Rubank series. Significant portions of this book are dedicated to scale and arpeggio routines, duets, and technical etudes and exercises. Seven solos of increasing difficulty are included at the end of the book. Exercises in flexibility, ornamentation, multiple tonguing, and the tenor clef are included as well.

Grunow, Richard F., Edwin E. Gordon, and Christopher D. Azzara. *Jump Right In: The Instrumental Series, Book I.* GIA Publications, Inc. $6.50. Part of a complete band method for beginning band. The book is accompanied by a compact disc recording (additional $10) of each selection played on euphonium. This is available in both the bass and treble clef.

Grunow, Richard F., Edwin E. Gordon, and Christopher D. Azzara. *Jump Right In: The Instrumental Series, Book II.* GIA Publications, Inc. $6.50. Part of a complete band method for the second-year player. The book is accompanied by a compact disc recording (additional $10) of each selection played on euphonium. This is available in both the bass and treble clef.

Haynie, John. *Development and Maintenance of Techniques for All Brass Instruments in Bass Clef.* Charles Colin. $3.50. 48 pp. III. This book includes an introduction on developing technique. Each of the exercises uses major and minor scales, arpeggios, tone studies, and interval studies. The exercises are organized by key signatures.

Heller, Duane. *Nocturne Etudes.* Tuba-Euphonium Press. 1991. $10. 12 pp. These etudes are actually a progressive theme and variations work. The composer suggests that they may be played in their entirety and then should be played in the written order. A variety of performance techniques are used in the variations to include valve alternations on repeated notes.

Hindsley, Mark H. *Carl Fischer Basic Method for the Baritone.* Carl Fischer. Out of Print. 1938. $5. 48 pp. I–II. This book includes forty lessons arranged progressively for the beginning student, including an introduction to reading the staff.

Hutchison, Warner. *30 Etudes for the Young Euphonium Player.* Tuba-Euphonium Press. 1997. $10. 28 pp. I–II. As the title suggests, these thirty etudes are designed for the younger student. Many of these creatively named etudes are humorous in nature and contain an ample variety of keys, articulations, and styles.

Irons, Earl D. *Twenty-Seven Groups of Exercises for Trombone or Baritone.* Southern Music Company. 1964. $11.50. 32 pp. This collection of exercises is intended to be a warm-up routine for players of varying abilities. Most prominent are the long tones, lip flexibilities, chromatic patterns, and multiple tonguing exercises.

Jacobs, Wesley. *Etudes for Euphonium, Volume 5.* Encore Music, now distributed by Tuba-Euphonium Press. 1991. $13. 27 pp. IV–V. This is a collection of etudes similar to earlier volumes, with each etude being present three times in different keys and notations.

Jacobs, Wesley. *Etudes for Euphonium, Volume 4.* Encore Music, now distributed by Tuba-Euphonium Press. 1994. $13. 20 pp. III–IV. This is a collection of etudes similar to earlier volumes, with each etude being present three times in different keys and notations.

Jacobs, Wesley. *Etudes for Euphonium, Volume 1.* Encore Music, now distributed by Tuba-Euphonium Press. 1989. $13. 15 pp. III. Actually this is a collection of only five distinct etudes, each etude being presented three times and each time in a different key. In the sample examined, etude thirteen was missing.

Jacobs, Wesley. *Etudes for Euphonium, Volume 3.* Encore Music, now distributed by Tuba-Euphonium Press. 1994. $13. 20 pp. III–IV. This is a collection of etudes similar to earlier volumes, with each etude being present three times in different keys and notations.

Jacobs, Wesley. *Etudes for Euphonium, Volume 2.* Encore Music, now distributed by Tuba-Euphonium Press. $13. 39 pp. III. This is a collection similar to volume one in that the same basic etude is presented several times in different keys and different notations.

Jacobs, Wesley. *Technical Studies for Euphonium.* Encore Music, now distributed by Tuba-Euphonium Press. 1994. $16. 16 pp. II–IV. This is a collection of warm-up type exercises including articulation and slurring studies, arpeggios, and tone quality studies.

Johnson, Keith. *Progressive Studies for the Higher Register (Trombone or Baritone).* Harold Gore Publishing. 1991. $10. 35 pp. III–IV. A series of slurred exercises that develop the high register, these systematic slur patterns are progressive and make for excellent supplementary material. This book provides a systematic approach to developing the upper register.

Kenfield, Leroy. *The New and Modern Method for Baritone or Euphonium.* Cundy-Bettoney Company. Out of Print. 1910. 104 pp. II–III. This method includes a variety of exercises designed for advanced younger players. Many of the exercises resemble those in the Arban's method.

Laas, Bill, and Fred Weber. *Studies and Melodious Etudes for Baritone.* Belwin-Mills. 1969. $5.50. 32 pp. II. This method includes 59 etudes with supplementary scale and arpeggio exercises. It also includes a fingering chart.

Laas, Bill, and Major Herman Vincent, in collaboration with James Ployhar. *Student Instrumental Course, A Method for Individual Instruction, Book III-Advanced-Intermediate.* Belwin-Mills. 1970. $6.95. 40 pp. II–III. This book is a part of the complete band method. This third book in the series is intended for the third-year player. A 32-page supplemental technique book is also available.

Langey, Otto. *New and Revised Edition of Celebrated Tutors for Baritone.* Carl Fischer. Out of Print. 113 pp. II–III. This method resembles the structure of the Arban's method with exercises more accessible to younger players.

Lelong, Fernand. *Methode Pour Euphonium-Saxhorn-Tuba.* Volumes I, II, III. Billaudot Editions. 1997. $19.95. I–III. 49 pp. (volume I). A method for all three instruments with color pictures of the instruments. All instructions and comments are in French and English.

Lin, Bai. *Lip Flexibilities for All Brass Instruments.* Balquhidder Music (distributed by Carl Fischer). 1996. $13.95. 40 pp. This is a book of lip flexibility exercises applicable to all brass instruments. Published only in treble clef, this book has proved to be valuable to all low-brass players as well as trumpet players.

Little, Lowell. *Embouchure Builder for the Trombone or Baritone.* Belwin-Mills. 1954—renewed 1982. $5.95. 16 pp. I–III. This volume contains a series of simple to moderately difficult lip flexibility exercises.

Long, Newell H. *Elementary Method for Trombone or Baritone.* Hal Leonard. $5.50. 52 pp. I–II. Rubank Educational Library No. 39. This method is a book for the young player containing etudes, duets, trios, and a fingering chart.

Mead, Steven, ed. *New Concert Studies for Euphonium Vol. 1.* De Haske Publications. 1999. $14.95. 48 pp. III–IV. This volume contains nineteen concert studies written by various composers specifically for euphonium and this publication. The studies focus on lyrical and technical playing; some etudes are better suited for the advanced player. The book includes a CD of Steven Mead performing nine of the studies. It is available in both treble and bass clefs.

Mead, Steven, ed. *New Concert Studies for Euphonium Vol. 2.* De Haske Publications. $16.95. III–IV. A continuation of etudes from volume one. Contains a CD similar to volume one. It is available in both bass and treble clefs.

Michel, Jean-François. *Méthode Volume 1 for Cornet and Treble Clef Euphonium.* Editions Marc Reift. €31.5. 104 pp. II. This book presents lessons on theory, technical exercises, memorizing, and composing.

Müller, Robert. *Dreißig leichte Etüden für Bariton.* Veb Friedrich Hofmeister. 19 pp. III. This method includes thirty etudes in major and minor keys. Etudes 21–30 are written in tenor clef.

Nairn, Ron. *Improvisation, Bridging the Gap.* Mel Bay Publications, Inc. 2001 $19.95. 103 pp. This is a one book fits all instruments on developing improvisation skills. It includes a compact disk containing exercises and accompaniments.

Nauert, Paul. *Sixteen Etudes for Euphonium.* Tuba-Euphonium Press. 1992. $10. 17 pp. III–IV. Published in manuscript, these etudes are particularly difficult in their use of rhythm and meter. A variety of styles, including swing, are incorporated. The special playing techniques of half-valving, flutter tonguing, multiple tonguing, and mute use are required.

Parés, Gabriel. *Pares Scales.* Ed. Harry Whistler. Rubank Inc. 1968. $6.50. 48 pp. II–III. This book presents scale exercises in C, F, G, B♭, D, E♭, A, A♭, D♭, and a, d, e, g, b, c, f♯, f, b♭, including arpeggios, chromatic exercises, and lip slurs as well as an artist etude.

Paudert, Ernest. *24 Studies for Trombone or Baritone.* Ed. Henry Howey. Southern Music Company. 1983. $6. 49 pp. III–IV. These 24 etudes are organized progressively and include two etudes with parts in tenor clef. They present a wide range of rhythms and range.

Pethel, Stan. *Twenty-one Etudes for Euphonium.* Tuba-Euphonium Press. 1991. $12. 51 pp. II–III. These etudes are appropriate for the intermediate student, although many of the selections are written in tenor clef. A significant number of these etudes are in the blues and jazz style.

Presser, William. *Sixteen Studies for Euphonium.* Tuba-Euphonium Press. 1997. $10. 21 pp. IV–V. These studies are written in both the bass and tenor clefs. Many of the studies are unified by the development and variation of common themes. Significant challenges are presented, especially in the areas of dexterity and flexibility.

Reger, Wayne M. *The Talking Twins.* Charles Colin Music. 1975. $6.95. 27 pp. This book is intended to be an aid in developing strong fundamentals in the trombone and euphonium player. Each page contains exercises stressing the basic ideas of brass playing, including tone production and quality, articulation, lip flexibility, vibrato, rhythm, and breathing, among others. Reger uses cartoon characters and illustrations throughout the book to emphasize these concepts.

Reinhardt, Dr. Donald S. *Graduated Studies for the Brass Player.* Pivot Publishing. 2004. $11.95. 38 pp. I–II. These studies are intended for the younger brass player. The book contains informational instruction for the beginner, fingering charts, scales, exercises, and short etudes.

Salvo, Victor. *241 Double and Triple Tonguing Exercises Progressively Arranged for Trombone, Baritone, Tuba.* Pro Art Publications. 1973. $2. 36 pp. III–IV. The exercises in this book serve as an introduction to double and triple tonguing. The exercises stay in the mid to upper register.

Schaefer, August. *Kreutzer's 10 Famous Etudes Transcribed for the Slide Trombone or Baritone.* Fillmore Music House through Carl Fischer. Out of Print. 1935. $4.50. 16 pp. III–IV. The Kreutzer etudes, originally for violin, present trombone and euphonium students with material meant to increase their technique and musicality.

Schaefer, August. *The Professional's Key to Double-Triple-Fanfare Tonguing.* Fillmore Music House through Carl Fischer. Out of Print. 1938. $2. 35 pp. II–III. This method provides original exercises designed to help students master double and triple tonguing.

Seidel, Eduard. *24 Etüden für Posaune oder Bariton.* Musikverlag Hans Sikorski. 19 pp. II–III. These etudes serve as supplementary material for the younger students who have mastered the rudiments of playing in different keys.

Shapiro, Aaron. *Modern Universal Method for the Baritone and Slide Trombone Part I.* Cundy-Bettoney Co. (now owned by Carl Fischer). Out of Print. 1946. $8. 144 pp. II–III. This book compiles studies from Arban, Vobaron, Collinet, and St. Jacome. Part I includes rudimentary exercises, major and minor scales, interval exercises, and slurs. It also includes sections on articulation, duets, and 120 progressive scale studies.

Shapiro, Aaron. *Modern Universal Method for the Baritone and Slide Trombone Part III.* Cundy-Bettoney Co. (now owned by Carl Fischer). Out of Print. 1946. $8. 126 pp. III–IV. Part III features the art of phrasing; studies by Dieppo, Kopprasch, Cornett, St. Jacome; and seven solos.

Shapiro, Aaron. *Modern Universal Method for the Baritone and Slide Trombone Part II.* Cundy-Bettoney Co. (now owned by Carl Fischer). Out of Print. 1946. $8. 127 pp. III–IV. Part II focuses on chromatic studies, ornamentation, lyrical recitative melodies, major and minor chords, and multiple tonguing.

Shiner, Matty. *Matty Shiner's Lip Builder.* Progressive Music Inc. 1974. $4.95. 31 pp. II–IV. This book contains a collection of warm-up studies developed by Matty Shiner, long-time low-brass pedagogue at Duquesne University in Pittsburgh, Pennsylvania. In addition to a variety of exercises developing articulation and flexibility, there is introductory material with diagrams of the tongue position and breathing apparatus.

Shoemaker, John R. *Legato Etudes for Euphonium.* Roger Dean Publishing. 1975. $6. 32 pp. III–IV. This book is a collection of 24 lyrical etudes, based on the vocalises of Guiseppe Concone. A wide variety of keys are implemented, along with the bass, treble, and tenor clefs.

Siekmann, Frank. *Playable Jazz Etudes for Euphonium.* Brelmat Music. 1997. $8. 12 pp. III. A collection of thirteen etudes in the jazz style specifically written for the euphonium. As the title suggests, these etudes are quite playable for the more experienced student, but each etude develops the swing style.

Skornicka, J. E., and E. G. Boltz. *Intermediate Method for Trombone or Baritone.* Hal Leonard. $5.50. 48 pp. II. Rubank Educational Library No. 65. This book includes etudes for technical and musical development. Trios, duets, and scales are also included throughout the book.

Slama, Anton. *66 Studies for Bass Clef Trombone and Euphonium.* Ed. Reginald Fink. Accura Music. 1991. $11. 47 pp. III–IV. The exercises in this book incorporate diatonic patterns, arpeggios, and sequential motifs in order to develop greater flexibility and intonation. All major and minor keys are included in these studies.

Slama, Anton. *66 Studies in All Major and Minor Keys.* Carl Fischer. 1922. $12.50. 45 pp. III–IV. The exercises in this book incorporate diatonic patterns, arpeggios, and sequential motifs in order to develop greater flexibility and intonation. All major and minor keys are included in these studies.

Spaniola, Joseph T. *Sixteen Etudes for Euphonium.* Tuba-Euphonium Press. 1991. $10. 21 pp. IV–V. Published in manuscript type, these studies are especially difficult sight-reading material, although the technique necessary for accurate performance requires diligent preparation for even the advanced player.

Sparke, Philip. *Skilful Studies (40 Progressive Studies),* Anglo Music Press. 2004. II. The second book of a series geared to take the beginner to an accomplished musical level.

Sparke, Philip. *Starter Studies (65 Progressive Studies),* Anglo Music Press (distributed by Hal Leonard). 2004. $7.95 47 pp. I. A wonderful beginning method in the first of a series geared to take the beginner to an accomplished musical level. This book and all of the series are written in both treble and bass clef, the first half of the book in treble clef and the same material repeated in bass clef.

Sparke, Philip. *Super Studies (35 Progressive Studies),* Anglo Music Press. 2004. $9.95. III. The third book of a series geared to take the beginner to an accomplished musical level.

Stegmann, Richard. *Elementarschule für Posaune und Bariton.* Würzberg. 1970. 122 pp. II. This elementary method is designed to help the student develop embouchure, time, and technique using scales and melodic etudes. For each section Stegmann includes an explanation of the proper technique needed. The text is in German with an English translation at the end of the book.

Steiner, F. *Baritone ABC.* Edito Musica Budapest. $20.95. Available from Robert King Music.

Uber, David. *Intermediate-Advanced Etudes, for Euphonium or Trombone.* Tuba-Euphonium Press. 1999. $12. 22 pp. III–V. This volume comprises good etudes in a variety of keys and styles. The high school and college student will be challenged, especially in the areas of range and facility.

Uber, David. *Symphonic Studies in Alto Clef for Trombone or Euphonium.* Rebu Music. 1992. $8. 23 pp. IV–V. These etudes are written for the advanced student who already proficiently reads the alto clef. The etudes include a variety of tonalities, metric changes, intervallic skips, and rhythmic patterns with some emphasis on the high register.

Uber, David. *Twenty-Two Etudes.* Tuba-Euphonium Press. 1991. $12. 44 pp. IV–V. Winner of the 1990 TUBA etude contest, these etudes present a challenge to the advanced player. Each etude is two pages in length, containing a wide variety of keys, meters, rhythmic structures, and tempi.

Uffelen, P. C. *Voordrachtstukken en Etudes voor Baryton-Tenorhorn.* Molenaar N. V. Out of Print. 1963. 18 pp. II–III. This book contains thirty etudes in treble clef taken from various composers such as Uffelen, Blazevich, and Hanze. The introduction is in Dutch.

Vincent, Major Herman, in collaboration with James Ployhar. *Studies and Melodious Etudes for Baritone.* Belwin-Mills. 1970. $5.95. 32 pp. I–II. Supplemental technique book for the Belwin *Student Instrumental Course,* including a fingering chart, commonly used major and minor scales, exercises, and simple etudes.

Vizutti, Allen. *20 Dances for Euphonium.* De Haske Publications. 2001. $12.95. 39 pp. III–IV. Written by trumpet virtuoso Allen Vizutti, these dances blend technical and lyrical material based on classical music and dance styles. The book includes a CD of Steven Mead performing all twenty dances. It is available in bass and treble clefs.

Vobaron, E. *34 Etudes, Trombone or Baritone Solo.* Cundy-Bettony Co. Out of Print. $5. 41 pp. IV. This etude collection involves fairly challenging exercises, mainly technical in nature. Three duets are included in the volume as well.

Vobaron, E. *32 Celebrated Melodies for Trombone (Baritone or Bassoon).* Carl Fischer. Out of Print. $8.50. 40 pp. III–IV. These etudes would present challenging material for an advanced high school student, but may be better suited for college students. These etudes are technically complex and similar to the etudes found in Tyrell's *40 Progressive Etudes for Trombone.*

Voxman, H. *Selected Studies for Baritone.* Rubank Inc. 1952. $6.95. 72 pp. III. This frequently used method includes advanced etudes and scales and arpeggios in all major and minor keys. This book has been used for all-state auditions in the state of Texas for many years.

Watelle, Jules. *Grande Méthode de Basse et Tuba.* Éditions Salabert. Out of Print. 1913. 196 pp. III–IV. This method is comparable to the Arban's method. It includes various exercises in all keys and concert solos.

Weber, Fred. *Student Instrumental Course, A Method for Individual Instruction, Book I—Elementary.* Belwin-Mills. 1970. $6.95. 40 pp. I. This book is a part of the complete band method. This beginning book includes basic exercises for the beginner along with a fingering chart.

Weber, Fred. *Student Instrumental Course, A Method for Individual Instruction, Book II—Intermediate.* Belwin-Mills. 1970. $6.95. 40 pp. II. This book is a part of the complete band method. This intermediate book includes slightly more advanced exercises for the second-year player.

Weber, Fred. *Tunes for Baritone Technic.* Belwin-Mills. 1970. $5.50. 32 pp. I–III. Available in elementary, intermediate, and advanced-intermediate difficulty levels, these books primarily consist of well-known melodies in simple keys.

Webster, Melville. *The Ludwig Elementary Baritone Instructor.* Ludwig Music Publishing. Out of Print. 1938. $1. 56 pp. I–II. This method is designed for the beginning student, with the lessons arranged progressively. It includes a lengthy introduction to the baritone with photographs included.

Whistler, Harvey. *Modern Arban-St. Jacome Comprehensive Course for Trombone or Baritone.* Rubank Inc. 1966. $8.95. 104 pp. I–II. This method compiles and reorganizes material found in the Arban's and St. Jacome method books. The material is presented progressively.

White's Elementary Method for the Baritone. Jean White Publications, Boston. 1884. 63 pp. A complete facsimile is available in the Library of Congress, call number M2.3.U6A44, and on the website American Memory, http://memory.loc.gov/ammem/index.html. A very similar book in style and content to the Arban's complete method, this item is one of the earliest examples of a specific euphonium method.

Wiggins, Bram. *First Tunes and Studies for the Trombone or Euphonium.* Oxford University Press. 1976. $8.75. 39 pp. I–II. This method provides elementary studies and melodies for beginners. The melodies represent a variety of different sources from orchestral pieces to folk songs.

Williams, Ernest. *Method for Trombone or Bass Clef Baritone.* Charles Colin. 1956. $18. 95 pp. II. This method includes progressive exercises divided into twelve chapters. It focuses on tone quality, scales, syncopation, interval studies, and melodic etudes.

Winslow, Roger. *30 Original Easy Etudes for Trombone-Euphonium.* Harold Gore Publishing. 2000. $8. 21 pp. I–II. A collection of thirty simple etudes that do not progress beyond a middle school level. It is good supplementary material for the young player.

Winslow, Roger. *30 Original Moderately Difficult Etudes for Trombone-Euphonium.* Harold Gore Publishing. 2000. $10. 33 pp. III–IV. A continuation of the etudes in Winslow's *30 Original Easy Etudes.* These studies involve a much more expanded range and incorporate mixed meters.

Woude, Mary Vander. *Pre-Virtuoso Studies.* Charles Colin. Out of Print. 1964. $1.50. 23 pp. III. This book includes 37 etudes and two sets of arpeggio exercises. The etudes cover a wide range of time signatures, rhythmic patterns, and harmony. Published now in a complete set of three volumes in one for trumpet by Charles Colin for $8.95. The publisher states, "The book opens with a series of 'pre-virtuoso' studies designed to prepare the student for the virtuoso works that follow. With each succeeding volume, conventional musical restrictions have been gradually removed until the player is permitted almost complete freedom from traditional form. A mode of writing—explained in the appendices—not used before in composition, has been created to allow for this liberation from usual technical restraints. The pieces themselves are marvels of rhythmic complexity and interpretive sophistication."

12. Band and Orchestral Excerpts

Brian Bowman

The euphonium in orchestra has traditionally occupied the role of the "tenor tuba." There are few if any orchestral scores that use the term "euphonium." Roy Harris changes from using the term "tenor tuba" in his first few symphonies to using the term "baritone horn" in his later symphonies to indicate the usual instrument used to play the tenor tuba part in the score. While there is not sufficient repertoire to create permanent positions in the symphony and operatic orchestra, there are major parts in many major works. The euphonium is often substituted for other instruments in the orchestral score. It has sometimes been used in place of the bass trumpet and fliccorno tenore. The nomenclature is often confusing, as different names are used for the euphonium in different countries: baryton (German for euphonium), fliccorno basso (Italy), saxhorn basse (France), clarion-basse (French), kleine bass (German), and bass flugelhorn (Britain).

The following is a list of works usually played on euphonium. This first list contains works written specifically for the euphonium or baritone horn.

Barber, Samuel: *Third Essay for Orchestra*
Bernstein, Leonard: *Divertimento for Orchestra*
Birtwhistle, Harrison: *Gawain's Journey*
Halbrooke, Joseph: *The Children of Don, Dylan, Bronwen, Symphony No. 2, Op. 51, No. 3, Op. 90*
Harris, Roy: *Celebration Variations*
Harris, Roy: *Give Me the Splendid Silent Sun*
Harris, Roy: *Ode to Friendship*
Harris, Roy: *The Quest*
Harris, Roy: *Symphonies 1, 3, 5, 7–12*
Havergal, Brian: *Gothic Symphony* (two parts), *Symphonies 8, 10, 11, 12, 13, 14, 15, 17, 19*
Kay, Hershey: *Stars and Stripes* (ballet)
Kay, Hershey: *Western Symphony* (ballet)
Maazel, Lorin: *Music for Flute, Op. 11*
Shostakovich, Dmitri: *Age of Gold*
Shostakovich, Dmitri: *The Bolt*
Turnage, Mark-Anthony: *Three Screaming Popes*
Wood, Henry: *The Saucy Arethusa* from *Fantasia on British Sea Songs*
Yardumium, Richard: *Symphony No. 2*

These pieces were written for tenor tuba and are played on euphonium.

Barber, Samuel: *Symphony No. 2*
Bartok, Bela: *Kossuth* (two parts)
Bax, Arnold: *Symphony No. 2*
Elgar, Edward: *Cockaigne Overture*
Holst, Gustav: *The Planets*
Janacek, Leos: *Capriccio* (small group)
Janacek, Leos: *Sinfonietta*
Schuman, William: *Credendum*
Strauss, Richard: *Don Quixote*
Strauss, Richard: *Ein Heldenleben*

These works are often played on euphonium today. The original instrument is listed following the excerpt.

Bax, Arnold: *Overture to Picaresque Comedy* (tuba)
Berlioz, Hector: *Benvenuto Cellini* (ophicleide)
Berlioz, Hector: *Les francs-juges* (ophicleide)
Elgar, Edward: *Wand of Youth: First and Second Suites* (tuba)
Mahler, Gustav: *Symphony No. 7* (tenor horn)
Mendelssohn, Felix: *Overture to a Midsummer's Night Dream* (ophicleide)
Mussorgsky, Modeste (orch. Ravel): *Pictures at an Exposition* (French tuba)
Respighi, Ottorino: *Pines of Rome* (fliccorno offstage part)
Stravinsky, Igor: *Petrushka* (tuba)
Stravinsky, Igor: *Sacre du Printemps* (Wagner tuba)

Orchestral Excerpt Sources

Brown, Keith, ed. *Orchestral Excerpts from the Symphonic Repertoire for Trombone—Strauss.* International Music Company. 1969. $9. 28 pp. This book contains trombone, tenor, and bass tuba excerpts. The tenor tuba parts are from *Ein Heldenleben* and *Don Quixote* and are in the B♭ bass clef notation.

Complete Low Brass Excerpt Collection, The. Cherry, https://www.cherry-classics.com/. Package #5, $15. Contents: Strauss, Richard: *Alpine Symphony, Aus Italien, Dance Suite, Death and Transfiguration, Der Rosenkavalier Suite* from the opera, *Die Frau Ohne Schatten Suite* from the opera, *Don Quixote* (including the tenor tuba part transposed into C), *Ein Heldenleben* (including the tenor tuba part transposed into C), *Intermezzo, Macbeth* (including the bass trumpet part), *Salome's Dance of the Seven Veils* from the opera, *Symphonia Domestica, Till Eulenspiegel*.

Orchestra Musician's CD-ROM Library, volume 2. Hal Leonard Publishing Corp. $19.95. CD-ROM with printable parts for tenor tuba from Mahler *Symphony No. 7* and all of the Bruckner symphonies. Many other works for trombone and tuba are included in this product. Contents: Bizet: *Symphony No. 1 in C; Carmen Suites Nos. 1 and 2; L'Arlesienne Suites Nos. 1 and 2;* Bruch: *Violin Concerto, Op 1/26; Kol Nidrei for Cello and Orchestra, Op 47; Scottish Fantasy for Violin and Orchestra, Op 46;* Bruckner: *Symphonies Nos. 1 through 9; Te Deum;* Busoni: *Turandot Suite;* Debussy: *Images Nos. 1, 2, and 3; Jeux; La Mer; Nocturnes; Petite Suite; Prelude to the Afternoon of a Fawn; Printemps; Rhapsody for Clarinet; Sacred and Profane Dances;* Faure: *Pavane, Op 50; Pelleas and Melisande, Op 80; Requiem, Op 48;* Grieg: *Piano Concerto in A Minor; Holberg Suite, Op 40; Peer Gynt Suite No. 1, Op 46; Peer Gynt Suite No. 2, Op 55; Symphonic Dances, Op 64;* Mahler: *all nine symphonies; Kindertotenlieder; Das Klagende Lied; Das Knaben Wunderhorn; Das Lied von der Erde; Lieder Eines Fahrenden Gesellen; 6 Lieder (Revelge; Der Tamboursg'sell; Blicke mir nicht in die Lieder; Ich atmet' einen Linden Duft; Ich bin der Welt abhanden; Un Mitternacht);* Reger: *Variations and Fugue on a Theme of Mozart, Op 132;* Saint-Saens: *Symphony No. 3 in C Minor, Op 78; Cello Concerto No. 1 in A Minor, Op 33; Piano Concerto No. 2 in G Minor, Op 22; Carnival of the Animals; Christmas Oratorio; Dance Macabre, Op 40; Introduction and Rondo Capriccioso, Op 28.*

Shifrin, Ken. *The Professional's Handbook of Orchestral Excerpts for Euphonium and Bass Trumpet.* Ed. Ken Hanlon. Virgo Music Publishers. 1995. $24.95. 65 pp. This volume is one of the most comprehensive published editions of works for euphonium (tenor tuba) and bass trumpet. This text includes the complete concert pitch bass clef parts to *Don Quixote* and *Ein Heldenleben* by Richard Strauss. There is an extensive text on the history and use of the euphonium in the orchestral repertoire with many illustrations.

Articles, Books, and Papers on the Orchestral Use of the Euphonium

Bowman, Brian. "The Bass Trumpet and Tenor Tuba in Orchestral and Operatic Literature." D.M.A. diss., Catholic University of America, 1975.

Roust, Colin. "Heavy Metal: The Orchestral History of the Euphonium." *TUBA Journal,* Vol. 28, No. 3 (Spring 2001).

Scowcroft, Phillip. "The Euphonium and British Music." http://www.musicweb-international. com/classrev/2001/July01/euphonium.htm.

Stewart, M. Dee. "The Tenor Tuba Trauma." *The School Musician* 57 (May 1986): 12–15

Some information on the euphonium in orchestra for this chapter is credited to Nikk Pilato's web site at http://www.nikknakks.net/ Euphonium/.

Band Excerpts

Payne, Barbara, comp. *Euphonium Excerpts from the Standard Band and Orchestra Library.* Ed. Brian Bowman, David Werden. Cimarron Press. 1992. $39. 88 pp. Third Edition. Currently, this is the only available published book of euphonium excerpts of band/wind ensemble literature in print. This edition contains five sections: Marches, Transcriptions, Original Works for Band, Orchestral Excerpts, and a Service Band Primer. This volume also contains the Richard Strauss works *Ein Heldenleben* and *Don Quixote* transcribed into concert pitch bass clef. Contents: Alford, arr: *The World Is Waiting for the Sunrise;* Arnold-Paynter: *Four Scottish Dances;* Bach-Leidzen: *Toccata and Fugue in D Minor;* Bagley, E. E: *National Emblem;* Barber, Samuel: *Commando March;* Barber, Samuel: *Overture to the School for Scandal;* Bennett, R. R.: *Suite of Old American Dances;* Bennett, R. R.: *Symphonic Songs;* Berlioz-Safranek: *Roman Carnival Overture;* Chambers-Smith: *The Boys of the Old Brigade;* Creston, Paul: *Celebration Overture;* Dahl, Ingolf: *Sinfonietta;* De Nardis-Cafarella: *The Universal Judgement;* Dvorak-Leidzen: *New World Symphony* Finale; Fillmore-Fennell: *Rolling Thunder March;* Giordano-Richards: *Andre Chenier;* Gould, Morton: *Symphony for Band* Movement I; Grainger, Percy: *Children's March;* Grainger-Goldman: *Handel in the Strand;* Grainger, Percy: *Irish Tune from County Derry;* Grainger, Percy: *Lincolnshire Posy;* Grainger, Percy: *Molly on the Shore;* Hanson-Maddy: *Nordic Symphony* Movement II; Hindemith-Wilson: *Symphonic Metamorphosis* March; Holst, Gustav: *First Suite in E♭;* Holst, Gustav: *Marching Song;* Holst, Gustav: *The Planets* (band version); Holst, Gustav: *The Planets* (orchestral version); Holst, Gustav: *Second Suite in F;* Kabalevsky-Hunsberger: *Colas Breugnon Overture;* King-Bainum: *Barnum and Bailey's Favorite;* King, K. L.: *The Melody Shop;* Mendelssohn-Seredy: *Fingal's Cave;* Menin, Paul: *Canzona;* Milhaud, Darius: *Suite Francaise;* Moussorgsky-Ravel: *Pictures at an Exhibition* Bydlo; Nixon, Roger: *Fiesta del Pacifico;* Orf, Carl: *Carmina Burana;* Persichetti, Vincent: *Symphony No. 6 for Band;* Rismsky-Korsakov-Leidzen: *Procession of the Nobles;*

Rossini-Moses-Tobani: *Italian in Algiers Overture;* Rossini-Meyrelles-Kent: *La Gazza Ladra;* Schoenberg, Arnold: *Theme and Variations;* Schuman-Owen: *Circus Overture;* Schumann, William: *When Jesus Wept;* Shostakovich-Hunsberger: *Festive Overture;* Shostakovich-Hunsberger: *Moscow Cheremushky* Galap; Smith, Claude T: *Festival Variations;* Sousa, John Philip: *El Capitan;* Sousa, John Philip: *The Fairest of the Fair;* Sousa, John Philip: *George Washington Bicentennial;* Sousa, John Philip: *The Invincible Eagle;* Sousa, John Philip: *Nobles of the Mystic Shrine;* Sousa, John Philip: *The Stars and Stripes Forever;* Strauss, Richard: *Don Quixote, Op 35;* Strauss, Richard: *Ein Heldenleben, Op 40;* Sullivan-Mackerras: *Pineapple Poll;* Tchaikowsky-Laurendeau: *Caprice Italien;* Tchaikowsky-Safranek: *Symphony in F Minor* Finale; Wagner-Grabel: *The Flying Dutchman Overture;* Wagner-Grabel: *Overture to Rienzi;* Walton, William: *Crown Imperial;* Weinberger-Bainum: *Schwanda* Polka and Fugue; Williams, R. Vaughn: *Sea Songs.* Service Band Primer.

In the early part of the twentieth century there was a series of baritone (euphonium) band excerpt books called the *Baritonist's Studio: A Collection of Baritone Parts,* edited by Hugo Wagner and published by Carl Fischer. There were at least five volumes of music. The majority of music included was complete band parts rather than excerpts, and the music consisted of mainly orchestral transcriptions. These books have been out of print for nearly 100 years but copies are still in some libraries.

Wagner, Hugo, ed. *Baritonist's Studio: A Collection of Baritone Parts Volume V.* $2.50. 159 pp. Bazzini, A.: *Serenade;* Beethoven, Ludwig von: *Coriolan Overture;* Beethoven, Ludwig von: *Moonlight Sonata;* Chaminade, C.: *Air de Ballet* Pierette; Chaminade, C.: *Serenade;* Chapi, R.: *Moorish Suite* Courts of Granada; Donizetti, G.: *Lucia* Sextette; Eilenberg, R.: *First Heart Throbs;* Friedemann, C.: *Slavonic Rhapsody;* Glinka, M.: *La Vie Pour Le Tsar;* Gottschalk, L. M.: *The Dying Poet;* Herold, L. J. F.: *Zampa Overture;* Jungmann, A.: *Morceau, Op. 366* Espanola; Kalliwoda: *Overture in F;* Kéler-Béla: *Rakoczy Overture;* Lachner, Vincenz: *Fest Overture in C;* Lange, G.: *Idylle, Op. 31* Pure as Snow; Liszt, Franz: *Dreams of Love;* Liszt, Franz: *Mazeppa* Finale; Liszt, Franz: *Hungarian Rhapsody No. 1;* Liszt, Franz: *Hungarian Rhapsody No. 6;* Liszt, Franz: *Hungarian Rhapsody No. 12;* Liszt, Franz: *Les Preludes;* Marenco-Millars: *Excelsior;* Massenet, J.: *Herodiade* Ballet Movement; Mendelssohn, Felix: *Fingal's Cave;* Mendelssohn, Felix: *Midsummer Night's Dream* Nocturne; Meyerbeer, G.: *L'Africaine* Marche Indienne; Meyerbeer, G.: *Les Huguenots*

Dedication and Benediction; Mozart, W. A.: *Don Juan;* Nesvadba: *Die Loreley;* Offenbach, J.: *Les Contes D'Hoffmann;* Ponchielli, A.: *La Gioconda* Dance of the Hours; Roberts, Chas J.: *Old Folks at Home and in Foreign Lands;* Rubinstein, A.: *The Bride of Kaschmir* Torchlight Dance; Rubinstein, A.: *Triomphale Overture Fantasie;* Rubinstein, A.: *Valse Caprice;* Safranek, V. F.: *Atlantis the Lost Continent;* Safranek, V. F.: *Don Quixote;* Saint-Saëns, C.: *Algerian Suite* Marche Militaire Francaise; Schumann, Robert: *Traumerei;* Sousa, John Philip: *International Congress;* Suppé, Franz von: *La Burlesque;* Suppé-Kerssen: *Miner's Dream Overture;* Svendsen, J. S.: *Swedish Coronation March, Op. 13;* Strauss, J.: *Die Fledermaus* The Bat; Strauss, J. and J.: *Pizzicato Polka;* Tschaikowsky, P.: *Symphony in F Minor* Finale; Tschaikowsky, P.: *Ballet Suite Sleeping Beauty* Waltz; Voelker: *Hunt in the Black Forest;* Verdi, G.: *Il Trovatore;* Wagner, Richard: *Flying Dutchman Selection;* Wagner, Richard: *Lohengrin Selection;* Wagner, Richard: *Tannhäuser Overture;* Wallace, W. V.: *Lurline Overture;* Westmeyer, Wilhelm: *Kaiser Overture.*

Wagner, Hugo, ed. *Baritonist's Studio: A Collection of Baritone Parts Volume IV.* $2.50. 148 pp. Balfe, William: *Siege of Rochelle;* Beethoven-Tobani: *Fidelio;* Bellini-Laurendeau: *La Sonnambula;* Bizet, G.: *L'Arlesienne;* Boccalari, Ed: *Dance of the Serpents;* Boccalari, Ed: *Mauresque Caprice;* Chabrier, Em: *Espana Rhapsodie;* German, Edward: *Henry VIII* Three Dances; Goldmark, Carl: *Sakuntala Overture;* Gounod, Charles: *Faust* Ballet Music; Humperdinck-Safranek: *Haensel and Gretel;* Johnson, Lee: *The Battle of Big Horn:* Kretschmer, W. F.: *American Festival Overture;* Kretschmer, W. F.: *Highlanders Overture;* Lacome, P.: *Suite Espagnole* La Feria; Langey, Otto: *Schumann Suite;* Liszt, Franz: *Hungarian Rhapsody;* Marschner, H.: *Hans Heiling;* Massenet-Tobani: *Don Cèsar de Bazan;* Massenet-Tobani: *Herodias;* Mendelssohn, F.: *Calm Sea and Happy Voyage;* Mendelssohn, F.: *Military Overture;* Meyerbeer, G.: *The North Star;* Moszkowsky, M.: *Three Spanish Dances;* Safranek, V. F.: *Operatic Masterpieces;* Saint-Saëns, C.: *Poème Symphonique* Le Rouet D'omphale; Saint-Saëns, C.: *Poème Symphonique* Phaéton; Saint-Saëns, C.: *Prélude du Déluge;* Saint-Saëns-Laurendeau: *Henry VIII* Ballet-Divertissement; Saint-Saëns-Laurendeau: *Sampson and Delilah;* Schubert, Franz: *Unfinished Symphony;* Suppé, Franz von: *Die Frau Meisterin;* Suppé, Franz von: *Tantalusqualen;* Thomas, A.: *The Queen's Secret* Raymond; Tobani, Theo M.: *America Forever, Op. 459* Grand American Fantasia; Tobani, Theo M.: *Fantasia on German Songs* German Liederkranz No. 1; Tobani, Theo M.: *Grand International Fantasia, Op. 503* Hands Across the Sea; Tobani, Theo M.: *The Opera Mirror;* Tschakoff, Ivan: *Dance Suite;* Tschaikowsky-Safranek: *Eugène*

Onéquine; Tschaikowsky, P.: *March Slave;* Verdi-Laurendeau: *Aida;* Verdi-Laurendeau: *I Lombardi;* Wagner, Richard: *The Flying Dutchman;* Wagner-Laurendeau: *Die Walküre* Ride of the Valkyries; Wagner-Safranek: *Die Walküre* Wotan's Abschied und Feuerzauber.

Wagner, Hugo, ed. *Baritonist's Studio: A Collection of Baritone Parts Volume I.* $2.50. 145 pp. Auber, D. F. E: *Crown Diamonds;* Auber, D. F. E: *Fra Diavolo Overture;* Auber, D. F. E.: *Zanetta;* Bernstein, J.: *Tally-Ho Gallop;* Bishop, H.: *Guy Mannering Overture;* Boettger, E.: *Offenbachiana No.2;* Conradi, A.: *Musical Panorama;* Fahrbach, Ph.: *Musician's Strike;* Flotow, Franz von: *Martha Overture;* Gounod, Charles: *Funeral March of a Marionet;* Gounod, Charles: *La Colombe* Ariette; Gounod, Charles: *La Reine de Saba* Marche et Cortege; Gounod, Charles: *Mirella Overture;* Hamm, J. V.: *Musical Jokes;* Handel, G. F.: *Largo;* Hartman, John: *A Night in Berlin;* Haydn, Joseph: *Surprise Symphony* Andante; Herold, F.: *Zampa Overture;* Jakobowsky, Ed: *Erminie;* Kappey, J. A.: *Yule-Tide;* Kéler-Béla: *On the Beautiful Rhine;* Lumbye, H. E.: *Traumbilder;* Mercadante, C.: *Stabat Mater;* Meyerbeer, G.: *Coronation March;* Meyerbeer, G.: *Fackeltanz;* Meyerbeer, G.: *The Huguenots;* Meyrelles, M. C.: *Bouquet of Melodies;* Meyrelles, M. C.: *Musical Review;* Meyrelles, M. C.: *Reveille Portuguese;* Meyrelles, M. C.: *Offenbachiana No. 1;* Meyrelles, M. C.: *Reminiscences from Wagner's Operas;* Meyrelles, M. C.: *Selection on Spanish National Melodies;* Meyrelles, M. C.: *The Yeoman of the Guard;* Milloecker, Carl: *The Army Chaplain;* Milloecker, Carl: *The Beggar Student;* Moses, Theo: *Simplicity;* Offenbach, Jacq: *Monsieur Choufleuri;* Petrella, E.: *Ione;* Rossini, G.: *Barber of Seville;* Rossini, G.: *La Gazza Ladra;* Rossini, G.: *Semiramide Overture;* Rossini, G.: *William Tell Overture;* Strauss, J.: *Egyptian March;* Sullivan, A.: *Mikado;* Suppé, Franz von: *Journey through Africa;* Suppé, Franz von: *Poet and Peasant Overture;* Titl, A. E.: *Serenade;* Tobani, Thomas M.: *A Trip to Coney Island;* Tobani, Thomas M.: *Gems from the Popular Comic Operas;* Thomas, Amb: *Mignon* Grand Polonaise; Thomas, Amb: *Raymond;* Wagner, Richard: *Tannhäeuser March;* Wagner, Richard: *Tannhäeuser Overture;* Wagner, Richard: *Tannhäeuser Selection;* Weber, Carl Maria von: *Freischuetz;* Weber, Carl Maria von: *Invitation to Dance;* Wernthal, A.: *Grand Musical Divertissement;* Wiegand, Geo: *Cavalleria Rusticana.*

Wagner, Hugo, ed. *Baritonist's Studio: A Collection of Baritone Parts Volume III.* $2.50. 149 pp. Beethoven-Tobani: *Allegretto Scherzando, from Eighth Symphony;* Beethoven-Tobani: *Andante from Fifth Symphony;* Beethoven, Ludwig: *Egmont Overture;* Beethoven-Tobani: *Fidelio;* Bizet, G.: *L'Arlesienne Suite* Intermezzo; Boito-Tobani: *Mefistofele;* Brooks, Ellis: *In the Great Beyond;*

Chaminade, C.: *Ballet Symphonique Callirhoë* Pas des Echarpes; Chaminade, C.: *Ballet Symphonique Callirhoë* Variation; Chaminade, C.: *La Lisonjera;* Delibes-Laurendeau: *Sylvia;* Dvorak, A.: *Slavonic Dance No. 1;* Erkel, Franz: *Hunyady Làszlo;* Godfrey, Fred: *Reminiscences of Scotland;* Godfrey, Fred: *Reminiscences of Verdi;* Gomez, Carlo A.: *Il Guarany;* Gottschalk, L. M.: *The Last Hope;* Haydn, Joseph: *Military Symphony;* Keler-Bela-Kretschmer: *Roumanian Festival Overture;* Kücken, F.: *Warrior's Return;* Langey, Otto: *Sounds from England;* Laurendeau, Leoncavallo: *Il Pagliacci* Minuetto e Gavotta; Leutner, A.: *Fest Overture;* Liszt, Franz: *Second Polonaise;* Luigini, Alexandre: *Ballet Egyptien;* Massenet, J.: *Phèdre;* Massenet, J.: *Scènes Pittoresques;* Nessler-Laurendeau: *The Ratcharmer of Hameln* Wedding March; Ponchielli-Tobani: *La Gioconda;* Raff-Tobani: *Symphony Leonore* Parting; Reissiger, C. G.: *Yelva Overture;* Rossini-Tobani: *William Tell;* Rubenstein, A.: *Rêve Angélique;* Rubenstein, A.: *Romance;* Saint-Saëns, Camille: *Danse Macabre;* Scharwenka, X.: *Polish Dance No. 1;* Schubert, Franz: *Rosamunde;* Stücken, Frank van der: *St. Louis World's Fair March* Louisiana; Suppé, Franz von: *Isabella;* Tobani, Theo M.: *Alpine Fantasia;* Tobani, Theo M.: *Auld Lang Syne;* Tobani, Theo M.: *Crême de la Crême;* Tobani, Theo M.: *Echoes from the Metropolitan Opera House;* Tobani, Theo M.: *Old Heidelberg;* Tobani, Theo M.: *Russian Fantasia;* Tobani, Theo M.: *Souvenir de Meyerbeer;* Tschaikowsky, P.: *Caprice Italien;* Tschaikowsky, P.: *1812 Overture;* Verdi-Tobani: *Attila;* Verdi-Tobani: *Ernani;* Verdi-Tobani: *Macbeth;* Wagner-Tobani: *Die Goetterdaemmerung;* Wagner-Tobani: *Die Meistersinger von Nürnberg;* Wagner-Tobani: *Parsifal;* Wagner-Tobani: *Rienzi* Grand War March and Battle Hymn.

Wagner, Hugo, ed. *Baritonist's Studio: A Collection of Baritone Parts Volume II.* $2.50. 143 pp Ackermann: *Aria Concertante;* Auber, D. F. E.: *Lac des Fees;* Baetens, Charles: *Albion;* Balfe, W.: *Bohemian Girl;* Beethoven, Ludwig von: *Leonore Overture;* Bizet, G.: *Carmen;* Bizet, G.: *Suite L'Arlésienne* Intermezzo; De Koven: *The Highwaymen;* Delibes, L.: *Coppélia* Entr'acte and Valse; Delibes, L.: *Nalia* Pas de Fleurs; Donizetti, G.: *Lucia di Lammermor;* Flotow, F.: *Martha;* Flotow, F.: *Stradella Overture;* Grieg, E.: *Peer Gynt Suite;* Gounod, Charles: *Faust;* Herman, Andrew: *Columbus;* Keler-Bela: *Hugarian Lustspiel;* Kontski, A.: *Le Reveil du Lion;* Kücken, F.: *The Warrior's Return;* Lassen, E.: *Fest-Overture;* Liszt, Franz: *Second Hungarian Rhapsody;* Litolff, Henry: *Robespierre;* Luscomb, F.: *A Trip to the Country;* Mendelssohn, Felix: *Ruy Blas;* Moszkowski, M.: *From Foreign Lands;* Reissiger, C. G.: *The Mill on the Cliff;* Rossini, G.: *The Italian in Algeria;* Rossini, G.: *Tancred Overture;* Rubenstein, A.: *Bal Costumé* Toreador et Andalouse; Rubenstein, A.: *Bal Costumé*

Royal Tambour et Vivandiere" Smetana, F.: *The Bartered Bride;* Suppé, Franz von: *Morning, Noon and Night Overture;* Suppé, Franz von: *Pique Dame Overture* Thomas, A.: *Mignon Overture;* Tobani, Theo M.: *An American Battle Scene;* Tobani, Theo M.: *Hungarian Fantasia;* Tobani, Theo M.: *Nautical Fantasia;* Tobani, Theo M.: *Providence;* Tobani, Theo M.: *The Sleeping Beauty;* Tobani, Theo M.: *Souvenir de Beethoven;* Tobani, Theo M.: *Souvenir de Richard Wagner;* Verdi, G.: *Un Ballo in Maschera;* Wagner, Richard: *Album Leaf;* Wagner, Richard: *Die Walküre;* Wagner, Richard: *Lohengrin;* Wagner, Richard: *Rienzi Overture;* Wagner, Richard: *Siegfried;* Wagner, Richard: *Tristan and Isolde* Nachtgesang and Isoldes Liebestod; Wallace, W. V.: *Maritana Grand Fantasia;* Wallace, W. V.: *Maritana Overture;* Weber, Carl Maria von: *Freischutz Overture;* Weber, Carl Maria von: *Jubel Overture;* Weber, Carl Maria von: *Oberon Overture.*

13. Recommended Basic Repertoire

Carroll Gotcher and Atticus Hensley

For the High School Student

The two writers' experience in teaching high school euphonium players, playing the literature themselves, and preparing students for auditions at regional, state, national, and international levels has provided them with valuable insights into the capabilities and difficulties of the developing euphonium player. With the invaluable assistance of publishers, composers, and *ESB* international consultants, the following lists of solos, method books, and supplemental materials were compiled. These lists represent the best and most readily available materials for students of the euphonium.

One of the most challenging aspects of teaching high school euphonium players is helping them achieve a level of musicianship and skill equal to that of other instruments in the concert band. The authors of this section have noted that a great percentage of euphonium students do not start out as euphonium players. Whether they came to euphonium as frustrated trumpet players, trombone doublers, or members of the marching band who played non-marching instruments, we are charged with accelerating their learning to prepare them for full performance in the concert setting. For this reason, we have dispensed with the usual music grading techniques of first year, second year, and so forth, and opted for beginner, intermediate, advanced, and very advanced.

The list of recommended method books is by no means an exhaustive list of every book published, but one of the most tested, trusted, and readily available at this time. The books help to develop scales, arpeggios, articulations, phrasing, rhythm, dynamic control, accuracy, and velocity. These concepts form the basis of routines that are critical to the advancement of the euphonium player. These methods are not graded by level of ability because most cross one or more categories in their scope.

Also included in the list are supplemental materials used by the authors in their teaching. These materials are not stand-alone method books but are invaluable in the teaching studio. Duets, trios, and other small ensembles are indispensable in helping to establish balance, blend, timing, tuning, melodic prominence, and individual responsibilities in a group. Specific exercises are included in the list to address technical weaknesses, as well as exercises to strengthen any range deficiencies.

The study of appropriate solo literature is critical at every level of ability, as this is where the real musicality of the student can develop. Euphonium parts in band literature, while often more musically satisfying than tuba parts, do not fulfill the need for development of soloistic concepts such as phrasing, stylistic details, timing/tuning with an accompanist, and extended exposed passages. The solos that follow represent literature that is readily available and written with euphonium in mind. Some limited works originally intended for other instruments are included. The solos are divided into four levels and the technical and musical demands gradually increase. The student will encounter ever more complicated rhythms, expanding ranges, and greater endurance challenges with higher levels of music.

We would like to express our appreciation and thanks to the following distributors, publishers, and composers for providing materials instrumental in the compilation of this list: Franco Albian, Allans Publishing—Australia, Belwin (Warner Bros.), Sy Brandon, Brelmat Music, Carl Fischer, Inc., Cimarron Music Press (David Werden), Editions Billaudot, Editions M. Combre, Great Works Publishing, Hal Leonard, Heavy Metal Music, Heilman Music, Kjos Music, Ludwig Music Publishing, Medici Music Press (Ronald Dishinger), Shawnee Press, Southern Music, TUBA Press (David Miles), Western International Music, Zen—On Music (Jiro Censhu)—Japan.

Title	Composer	Arranger	Publisher	Notes
VERY ADVANCED				
Andante et Allegro	J. Guy-Ropartz	A. Shapiro	Carl Fischer, Inc.	
Concert Piece	P. V. De la Nux		Southern Music Company	
Contest Piece, Opus 57	G. Alary	P. X. Laube	Carl Fischer, Inc.	Contained in *Contest Album*
Allegro Moderato from "Arpeggione Sonata"	Franz Schubert	Sharon Davis/ Ray Herberer	Western International Music	
Andante and Rondo from "Concerto for Double Bass"	Antonio Capuzzi	Philip Catelinet	Hinrichsen editions	
As Wonderful Things Drift By	Jiro Censhu 1990		Zen-On Music Company	
Believe Me if All Those Endearing Young Charms	Simone Mantia	David Werden	Cimarron Music	
Blue Bells of Scotland	Arthur Pryor		Carl Fischer, Inc.	More similar titles available
Concert Fantasie	Gustav Cords	P. X. Laube	Carl Fischer, Inc.	Contained in *Contest Album*
Concerto in A Minor, BWV 1041	Johann S. Bach Dishinger	Ronald C. Dishinger	Medici Music Press	Conductor's Series
Concerto No. 3–Diran (The Religious Singer)	Alan Hovaness		Alphonse Leduc (Robert King Music)	For baritone and string orchestra
Eidólons	William P. Latham		Shawnee Press, Inc.	Some "non-standard" notation
Fantasia di Concerto	E. Boccalari		Carl Fischer, Inc. (Tuba-Euphonium Press)	
Fantasie Heroique	Heinrich Gottwald	P. X. Laube	Carl Fischer, Inc.	Contained in *Contest Album*
Fantasy	Philip Sparke		Studio Music	Also available for euphonium and band
Grand Concerto	Friedebald Gräfe	P. X. Laube	Carl Fischer, Inc.	Contained in *Contest Album*
Lyric Suite	Donald White		G. Schirmer	
New Concert Studies Vol. 1	Stephen Bulla et al	Steven Mead	De Haske Publications	Collection of 19 pieces by various composers
Piece en Forme de Habanera	Maurice Ravel	Neal Ramsay/ Ronald C. Dishinger	Medici Music Press	Many, many similar titles available
Sonata	Fred L. Clinard, Jr.		Shawnee Press, Inc.	Unaccompanied euphonium
Sonata for Solo Euphonium	Arthur Frackenpohl		Tuba-Euphonium Press	Unaccompanied euphonium
Thoughts of Love	Arthur Pryor		Carl Fischer, Inc.	Valse de Concert

Vocalise	Rachmaninoff	Steven Mead	De Haske Publications	
Willow Echoes	Frank Simon		Fillmore Music House (Carl Fischer, Inc.)	

ADVANCED

Clay Smith Solos	Clay Smith		C. L. Barnhouse	Collection of 19 original compositions and arrangements
Concertino No. 1 in B Flat Major, Opus 7– First Movement	Julius Klengel	Leonard Falcone	Belwin (Warner Bros) Tuba-Euphonium Press	
Legende Heroique, Opus 27	Jules Mouquet	P. X. Laube	Carl Fischer, Inc.	Contained in *Contest Album*
Six Studies in English Folksong	Ralph Vaughan Williams	Paul Droste	Galaxy Music	
Concert and Contest	various authors	Himie Voxman	Rubank Collection	
20 Dances for Euphonium	Allen Vizzutti	Steven Mead	De Haske Publications	
Alla Siciliana (Aria and Variations for Euphonium and Symphonic Band)	Franco Albian		Albian Publishing	Piano accompaniment is also available
Andante et Allegro	J. Ed. Barat		Southern Music	
Arioso from "Cantata No. 156"	J. S. Bach	R. Kent	Carl Fischer, Inc.	Many more similar titles available
Ave Maria	Franz Schubert	Clarence Barber	Great Works Publ.	Also for voice w/ band
Beautiful Colorado	Joseph De Luca		Carl Fischer, Inc.	Also available for band
Bride of the Waves, The Concerto	Herbert L. Clarke David Uber		Warner Bros. Publ. Tuba-Euphonium Press	Polka Brilliante
Concerto No. 1 in D Major	F. J. Haydn	Ronald C. Dishinger	Medici Music Press	Originally for horn and orchestra
Contest Piece (Morceau de Concours Op. 57)	G. Alary		Carl Fischer, Inc.	Many more similar titles available
Desert Star	Albert O. Davis		Ludwig Music	Also available for symphonic band
Èlégie	Gabriel Fauré	Robert L. Marsteller	Southern Music Company	
Fantasy	Hiroshi Hoshina		Tuba-Euphonium Press	
Five Pieces in Folk Style	Robert Schumann	Paul Droste	Ludwig Music	
From the Shores of the Mighty Pacific	Herbert L. Clarke		Warner Bros.	Rondo Caprice

Continued

Title	Composer	Arranger	Publisher	Notes
Girl with the Flaxen Hair, The Claude Debussy	Neal Ramsay	Medici Music		
La Fille aux Introduction and Allegro Spiritoso	J. B. Senaille	Philip Catelinet	Hinrichsen Editions	
Introduction et Serenade	J. Ed. Barat		Alphonse Leduc (Paris)	
Liebesfreud	Fritz Kreisler	David Werden	Cimarron Music	
Mirror Lake	Edward Montgomery	Ludwig Music		Also available for symphonic band
Moderation	Marcel Querat		Editions Combre (Paris)	
Morceau de Concert	Camille Saint-Saens	Douglas A. Nelson	Shawnee Press, Inc.	Originally for horn in F
Morceau de Concours	J. Ed. Barat		Alphonse Leduc (Paris)	
Morceau de Concours	Edmond Missa	H. Voxman	Rubank/Hal Leonard	Concert and Contest Collection
Morceau Symphonique	Alexandre Guilmant	E. Falaguerra	Warner Bros. Publications	
Napoli	Herman Bellstedt	Frank Simon	Southern Music Company	
Petite Pièce Concertante	Guillaume Balay	G. Mager/ A. Andraud	Southern Music Company	
Phantasy on an American Spiritual	William Schmidt		Western International Music	
Reflections	Frank H. Siekmann		(Pro Art Publications)- Brelmat Music	
Rhapsody for Euphonium	James Curnow		Curnow Music	Also available for symphonic band and brass band
Romance	Mari Miura		Tuba-Euphonium Press	
Romanze in F, Opus 50	Ludwig v. Beethoven	Ronald C. Dishinger	Medici Music Press	Many, many more similar titles available
Sicilienne	Gabrielle Faure	Sharon Davis	Western International Music	
Sonata from "Sonata for Violin and Bass"	Tomaso Albinoni	Ronald C. Dishinger	Medici Music Press	Figured bass by J. S. Bach and H. N. Gerber
Sonatina	Warner Hutchison		Carl Fischer, Inc.	
Suite for Baritone	Don Haddad		Shawnee Press, Inc.	Arranged by the composer from Suite for Tuba, also available for band
Vocalise	John Schooley		Heilman Music	Orchestra version can be rented

INTERMEDIATE

Master Solos	various authors	Larry Campbell	Hal Leonard	
Adagio and Allegro	Bendetto Marcello	Lyle Merriman	Southern Music Company	
Angel's Serenade	Gaetano Braga	Albert O. Davis	Great Works Publishing	
Arcane	Max Mereaux		Editions Combre (Paris)	
Ballade	Jan Krzywicki		Heilman Music	
Bolero	Hector Berlioz	Ronald C. Dishinger	Medici Music Press	
Eight Bel Canto Songs	various	Harry I. Phillips	Shawnee Press, Inc.	Bononcini, Caccini, Caladra, Durante, Marcello, Pergolesi, Scarlatti, Stradella
Encore	Quincy C. Hilliard		Carl Fischer, Inc.	Extracted from *Concerto for Young Artist(s) and Band*
Evening in the Country	Bela Bartok	Floyd O. Harris	Ludwig Music	
Fantasy Jubiloso	Douglas Court		Curnow Music	Also available for symphonic band and brass band
Gavotte in Rondeau	Jean Babtiste Lully	Ronald C. Dishinger	Medici Music Press	Many, many more similar titles available
Idylle	Robert Clérisse	Glenn Smith	Southern Music Company	
My Johann	Edvard Grieg	Neal Corwell	Kendor Music	
O King of Kings	Handel	D. F. Bachelder	Tuba-Euphonium Press	Many other similar titles available
On Wings of Song	Felix Mendelssohn	David Werden	Cimarron Music	
Petit Concerto pour Alexandre	Francois Thullier		Editions Combre (Paris)	
Prelude and Minuet	Arcangelo Corelli	Richard E. Powell	Southern Music Company	
Prelude No. 7	Dmitri Shastakovich	Sharon Davis	Western International Music	
Reverie from "Pieces for Piano"	Claude Debussy	Ronald C. Dishinger	Medici Music Press	Many, many more similar titles available
Serenade from "The Student Prince"	Sigmund Romberg	David Werden	Cimarron Music	
Sonata in F, Opus 17 (Horn and Piano)	Ludwig v. Beethoven	Ronald C. Dishinger	Medici Music Press	Many, many more similar titles available
Three Pieces from "Album for the Young"	Robert Schumann	Sharon Davis	Western International Music	
Thrice Happy the Monarch from "Alexander Balus"	G. F. Handel	R. Winston Morris	Ludwig Music	

Continued

Title	Composer	Arranger	Publisher	Notes
To a Wild Rose	Edward MacDowell	Merle J. Isaac	Carl Fischer, Inc.	Many, many more similar titles available
Variations on a Theme of Robert Schumann	William Davis		Southern Music Company	
What if I Never Speed	John Dowland	Michael Fischer	Tuba-Euphonium Press	

EASY

Title	Composer	Arranger	Publisher	Notes
Festival Performance Solos	various authors	Andrew Ballent	Carl Fischer	Volumes I and II
Brass–Series 1	various authors	Gary McPherson	Allans Publishing	Method book for Australian Music Examination Board– 1st &2nd Grades/ 3rd & 4th Grades
Classic Festival Solos	various authors	various arrangers	Belwin Mills	Piano Volumes 1 and 2 accompaniment book available
Euphonium– Series 1	various	Joe Cook	Allans Publishing	Method book for Australian Music Examination Board– 1st &2nd Grades/ 3rd & 4th Grades
Solos for the Baritone Player	various	Henry C. Smith	G. Schirmer	16 solos
First Recital Series for Euphonium	various	various	Curnow Music Distributors	
A Minor Etude	Ed Solomon		Southern Music Company	
Allegro from "Trio No. 12"	George Druschetzky	Ronald C. Dishinger	Medici Music Press	Many, many similar titles available
An die Musik	Franz Schubert	David Werden	Cimarron Music	
Argonaut Waltz	Forrest l. Buchtel		Kjos Music	
Arioso from "Cantata No. 156"	J. S. Bach	Leonard B. Smith	Warner Bros. Publications	
Conqueror	Leonard B. Smith	Leonard V. Falcone	Warner Bros. Publications	
Happy Bugler	Forrest L. Buchtel		Kjos Music	
Piece in Classic Style	Leonard B. Smith		Warner Bros.	Many other titles included in *Classic Festival Solos Vol. 2 Collection*
Pièces Classiques	various authors	Patrice Sciortino	Editions Billaudot (Paris)	Volume 1 (très facile)
Sailor's Song from "Book III for Clavier"	Francois Couperin	Ronald C. Dishinger	Medici Music Press	Many, many similar titles available
Song of the Woods	Paul Tanner		Belwin (Warner Bros)	
Two Arias	W. A. Mozart	Elwyn Wienandt	Southern Music Company	
Two Little Stars	Floyd O. Harris		Ludwig Music	

Weather Vane	Paul Tanner		Warner Bros.	Many other titles included in *Classic Festival Solos Vol. 1 Collection*
Where'er You Walk	George F. Handel	Ronald C. Dishinger	Medici Music Press	

METHODS AND SUPPLEMENTAL MATERIALS

32 Etudes	Sigmund Hering		Carl Fischer	
40 Progressive Studies	H. W. Tyrrell		Boosey & Hawkes	
66 Studies	Anton Slama	Reginald H. Fink	Accura Music	
Elementary Method	Newell H. Long		Rubank/Hal Leonard	Method also available *Intermediate Method and Advanced Method* Vol. I and II
Famous Method	Jean Baptiste Arban	Charles L. Randall/ Simone Mantia	Carl Fischer, Inc.	
Legato Etudes for Euphonium	John R. Shoemaker		Roger Dean Publishing	Based on vocalises of Giuseppe Concone
Selected Studies	H. Voxman		Rubank/ Hal Leonard	
Sixty Selected Studies	C. Kopprasch		Carl Fischer, Inc.	Books I & II
Thirty-six Studies	O. Blume	Reginald H. Fink	Carl Fischer, Inc.	
Vander Cook Etudes	H. A. Vander Cook	Walter C. Welke	Rubank/ Hal Leonard	
12 Grand Etudes Brillantes	J. F. Gallay	E. Leloir	Alphonse Leduc	Also 15 more etudes
1st Book of Practical Studies	Gerald Bordner	Thom Proctor	Belwin	Also 2nd book
20 Solo Studies	Marco Bordogni	Wayne S. Clark	Southern Music	Etudes with piano
30 Studies in Bass and Tenor Clefs	David Uber		Southern Music Company	
50 Mini Etudes	Francois Thullier		Editions Combre (Paris)	Also available *Gammes*
Arban Complete Method	Jean Baptiste Arban	Brian Bowman/ Joe Alessi	Encore Music Publishers	
Belwin Master Duets	various	Keith Snell	Belwin (Warner Bros)	
Chansons et Rondes Enfantines	various	Fernand Lelong	Editions Billaudot	Easy French folksong melodies
Clef Studies	Vladislav Blazevich	Donald Hunsberger	MCA Music	Bass, treble, and tenor clefs
Dance Etudes for Euphonium	Sy Brandon		Tuba-Euphonium Press	Also available *Stylistic Etudes* for *Euphonium* and *Twenty-Two Etudes*
Embouchure Builder	Lowell Little		Belwin-Mills	
Encyclopedia of Jazz Duets	Bugs Bower / Rudy Houston	Charles Colin		

Continued

Title	Composer	Arranger	Publisher	Notes
Euphonium Excerpts	various	Barbara Payne, Paul Droste, Brian Bowman, David Werden	Cimarron Music	Band and orchestra excerpts
Favorite Encore Folio	Clay Smith		C. L. Barnhouse	Duets with piano
From Treble Clef to Bass Clef Baritone	Reginald H. Fink		Accura Music	
Jeux de Tubes a Essayer	Phillipe Legris		Editions Combre	Available in two progressive volumes
Leviathan Love	various	Paul Schmidt	Heavy Metal Music	Unusual and stimulating duets
Pares Scales	Gabriel Parès	Harvey S. Whistler	Rubank/ Hal Leonard	
Pieces Classiques (Classical Pieces)	various	Patrice Sciortino	Editions Billaudot (Paris)	Available in 5 progressive volumes
Practical Hints on Playing Baritone	Brian Bowman/ James D. Ployhar	Thom Proctor	Belwin	Text
Rhythmical Articulation	Pasquale Bona	William D. Fitch	Carl Fischer, Inc.	
Selected Duets	various	Himie Voxman	Rubank, Inc.	Volumes I and II
Starter Studies	Philip Sparke		Dehaske	Available in Volumes 1, 2, and 3
Technical Studies	H. L. Clarke	Claude Gordon	Carl Fischer	Transposition of trumpet book
The Art of Tuba and Euphonium	Harvey Phillips/ Winkle Phillips	Judi Gowe	Warner Bros	Text
Treble Clef Duets	Ellen Levy-Ryan		Southern Music	For clef study also available in bass clef
Twelve Duets	Johann J. Quantz	Paul Schmidt	Heavy Metal Music	Duets, Opus No. 2 and Opus No. 5
Twenty Counterparts	Bordogni-Rochut	Tom Ervin	Tom Ervin	Duets– accompaniments to Bordogni-Rochut *Melodious Etudes*
Twenty Duets from Symphonic Masterworks	Various	Alan Hawkins	Shawnee Press, Inc.	
Twenty-Two Etudes	David Uber		Tuba-Euphonium Press	Also available– *Intermediate-Advanced Etudes*
Warm-up Studies	Emory Remington	Donald Hunsberger	Accura Music	

For the University Student

BRIAN BOWMAN

The materials in this section are graded into five levels of ability, encompassing four years of undergraduate, graduate, and post-graduate/professional level. Of course these levels are suggested and it may be possible to jump from one to another in both directions to find the appropriate material to study for each student. These lists were compiled from many different sources, including the editor's personal experience, and from suggested curricula at many different universities and schools of music. Much credit is given to the accessibility of such materials on the world wide web. The list is by no means comprehensive but should present a good cross section of available materials and current curriculum materials. For more study material, the editor suggests looking carefully at the Methods and Studies chapter of this volume for specific euphonium etudes to include in the college curriculum.

It may be noticed that study materials and solos are taken from other instruments in the brass area. As the euphonium is closely related in range and clef to the trombone, many books from the trombone area are especially appropriate for euphonium study, especially in the advanced levels. Very few university students have the opportunity to actually study with a specialist in euphonium. Most students are now assigned to the tuba, trombone, or trumpet teacher. It is hoped that this suggested list would be of value to those teaching euphonium who do not have extensive euphonium repertory background.

Thanks to the following for sharing information via the world wide web: John Tuinstra, University of Wisconsin–Whitewater School of Music; Skip Gray, University of Kentucky; Jeffrey Funderburk, University of Northern Iowa; Jeff Macomber, Missouri South State University; David Zerkel, University of Georgia; John Manning, University of Iowa; Raul Rodriguez, Texas State University–San Marcos; Michael Smith, Luther College; Charles Guy, Crane School of Music, SUNY–Potsdam; Steven Mead, Royal Northern College of Music; Thomas Stein, University of Missouri–Kansas City Conservatory of Music; Thomas Zugger, Capital University; Michael Dunn, University of Alabama; Jerry Young, University of Wisconsin–Eau Claire; Chris Hosmer, Jacksonville State University; Fritz Kaenzig, University of Michigan; Jimmy Clark, Texas A&M–Commerce; Loren Marstellar, California State University–Long Beach. A very special thanks to Roger Behrend, euphonium soloist with the United States Navy Band and Adjunct Professor of Euphonium and Tuba at George Mason University, for a final review and suggestions on this chapter.

The materials are graded as follows: Level I, College Freshman; Level II, College Sophomore; Level III, College Junior; Level IV, College Senior-Graduate; Level V, DMA-Professional.

Etudes and Studies

Arban, J. B. *Arban Complete Method for Trombone & Euphonium*. Ed./notated Joseph Alessi and Dr. Brian L. Bowman. Encore Music Publishers. II–V. A complete rework of the original Arban's method in bass clef, including all materials in previous versions edited and corrected. The book also contains instructions and comments from the editors on practice and performance techniques. Additionally, it is spiral bound to facilitate opening flat on the music stand and to encourage longevity.

Beeler, Walter. *Method for the Baritone, Book I*. I–II. A specific and most effective book for teaching the young euphonium player, this method book includes exercises and concepts for the early learner and is especially effective in helping the remedial college student.

Bitsch, Marcel. *Fifteen Rhythmical Studies*. Leduc. IV–V. These etudes contain advanced challenges in reading rhythms and styles as well as technical challenges of range, large intervals, and articulation speed and clarity.

Blazevich, Vladimir. *Clef Studies for Trombone*. III–IV. These etudes utilize bass, tenor, and alto clefs throughout. The value of these etudes is more than the clef reading, as the etudes are really musical gems with a large variety of styles and interpretive challenges presented.

Blume, O. *36 Studies for Trombone with f Attachment*. Carl Fischer. III–IV. These are the same etudes written for tenor trombone, just transposed downward, making excellent studies for developing the use of the lower fourth-valve register.

Bordogni, Marco. *Melodious Etudes for Trombone*, Volumes I, II, and III. Trans./progressively arr. Johannes Rochut. Carl Fischer, 1928. I–V. A standard in developing lyrical legato vocal style of playing, these books are a must for every euphonium student.

Bower, Bugs. *Rhythms and Improvisations. Trombone Rhythms*. Charles Colin. II–IV. Both of these books contain excellent materials for teaching sight-reading rhythmic acuity. For all students they are a resource to define basic rhythm patterns.

Bozza, Eugene. *13 Etudes Caprices*. V. Very difficult etudes utilizing both alto and tenor clef. These etudes are complex rhythmically and have a lot of unusual intervals.

Brasch, Harold. *The Euphonium and 4-Valve Brasses*. Tuba-Euphonium Press. III–V. A very specific book on the compensating four-valve euphonium with sections on fingerings and special techniques, including perhaps one of the most extensive chapters on multi-phonics of any method book. Also contains much advice on solo playing by one of the twentieth century's finest euphonium soloists, including examples of vintage solo repertoire. This book is a must for the serious euphonium student.

Charlier, T. *32 Etudes de Perfectionneme.* Lemoire. IV–V. These studies are arranged progressively and are available in both a bass clef and treble clef version. Each etude in the volume emphasizes a different playing challenge and technique.

Clarke, Herbert. *Technical Studies.* Carl Fischer. III–IV. Printed in both bass clef and treble clef editions, this book is the standard for developing finger technique. There are excellent finger exercises through scales and repeated patterns to develop virtuoso technique.

Colin, Charles. *Advanced Lip Flexibilities.* Volumes I, II, and III. Charles Colin Publications. Excellent material for developing extensive legato lip flexibilities, transposed from the original trumpet method of the same name. Extensive material is included on lip trills and upper range flexibility.

Fink. *Studies in Legato.* Carl Fischer. I–II. Good preparatory exercises to prepare the student for the more challenging Bordogni/Rochut books.

Gower, W. M., and H. Voxman. *Advanced Method for Trombone or Baritone, Volume I and II.* Hal Leonard. I–III. Rubank Educational Library No. 96. Significant portions of these books are dedicated to scale and arpeggio routines, duets, and technical etudes and exercises. This is an excellent book for early or remedial college students.

Johnson, Keith. *Progressive Studies for the Higher Register (Trombone or Baritone).* Harold Gore Publishing. III–IV. A series of slurred exercises that develop the high register, these systematic slur patterns are progressive and make for fine supplementary material. This book provides a systematic approach to developing the upper register.

Kopprasch C. *Sixty Etudes for Trombone.* Carl Fischer. I–III. Published in two volumes, these groups of etudes are among the most frequently used in college euphonium study. They contain a few etudes in tenor and alto clef.

Lin, Bai. *Lip Flexibilities for All Brass Instruments.* Balquhidder Music (distributed by Carl Fischer). This is a book of lip flexibility exercises applicable to all brass instruments. Published only in treble clef, this book has proved to be valuable to all low-brass players as well as trumpet players.

Mead, Steven. *New Concert Studies for Euphonium Volume I.* De Haske Publications. III–IV. This volume contains nineteen concert studies written specifically for euphonium and this publication. The studies focus on lyrical and technical playing; some etudes are better suited for the advanced player. The book includes a CD of Steven Mead performing nine of the studies.

Mead, Steven. *New Concert Studies for Euphonium Volume II.* De Haske Publications. IV. Composed by various excellent writers, these etudes are useful in developing a variety of skills. Composed with the contemporary demands of the euphonium player in mind, they are particularly valuable.

Remington, Emory. *The Remington Warm-Up Studies.* Ed. Donald Hunsberger. I–V. Accura Music. These exercises have become a standard routine for euphonium players as well as trombone players since the middle of the twentieth century. Highly recommended for developing tone quality and flexibility control.

Reynolds, Verne. *Forty-eight Etudes.* IV–V. Originally written for horn, these 48 etudes have been transcribed for trumpet and are very challenging rhythmically and technically. They are available only in treble clef and both the horn and trumpet versions can be used, although the trumpet version is more compatible with the euphonium.

Shoemaker, John R. *Legato Etudes for Euphonium.* Roger Dean Publishing. 1975. $6. 32 pp. III–IV. This book is a collection of 24 lyrical etudes, based on the vocalises of Guiseppe Concone. A wide variety of keys are implemented, along with the bass, treble, and tenor clefs.

Tyrrell, H. W. *40 Progressive Studies.* Boosey & Hawkes. I–III. Usually an advanced high school etude book, these etudes are also useful for the younger student.

Uber, David. *Twenty-two Etudes.* Tuba-Euphonium Press. IV–V.

Vizutti, Allen. *20 Dances for Euphonium.* De Haske Publications. III–IV. Written by trumpet virtuoso Allen Vizutti, these dances blend technical and lyrical material based on classical music and dance styles. The book includes a CD of Steven Mead performing all twenty dances. Winner of the 1990 TUBA etude contest, these etudes present a challenge to the advanced player. Each etude is two pages in length, containing a wide variety of keys, meters, rhythmic structures, and tempi.

Excerpt Books

Payne, Barbara, comp. *Euphonium Excerpts from the Standard Band and Orchestra Library.* Ed. Brian Bowman, David Werden. Cimarron Press. 1992. Third Edition. Newly re-released in a fully corrected version, this is the only published volume of band excerpts available.

Shifrin, Ken. *The Professional's Handbook of Orchestral Excerpts for Euphonium and Bass Trumpet.* Ed. Ken Hanlon. Virgo Music Publishers. 1995. One of the most complete published editions of works for euphonium (tenor tuba) and bass trumpet, including the complete, transposed parts to *Don Quixote* and *Ein Heldenleben* by Richard Strauss. There is an extensive text on the history and use of the euphonium in the orchestral repertoire, with many illustrations.

Solo Literature

Level I

Barat, J. E.	*Introduction and Dance*	Southern
Barat, J. E.	*Introduction and Serenade*	Leduc
Barat, J. E.	*Andante et Allegro*	Southern
Bellstedt, H	*Napoli*	Southern
Capuzzi, Antonio	*Andante and Rondo*	Hinrichsen
Clarke, Herbert	*Bride of the Waves*	Witmark
Clarke, Herbert	*From the Shores of the Mighty Pacific*	Witmark
Curnow, James	*Rhapsody*	Tuba-Euphonium Press
DeLuca, Joseph	*Beautiful Colorado*	Carl Fischer
Galliard, Ernest	*Sonatas 1–6*	International
Grafe, F.	*Grand Concerto*	Cundy-Bettoney
Guilmant, Alexander	*Morceau Symphonique*	Belwin
Hutchison, Warner	*Sonatina*	Carl Fischer
Marcello	*Sonata in F Major*	International
Nux, De La	*Concertpiece*	Southern
Rachmaninoff	*Vocalise*	various

Level II

Clarke, Herbert	*Carnival of Venice*	Witmark
Cord, Gustav	*Concert Fantasie*	Carl Fischer
Corwell, Neal	*Night Song* (with CD)	Nicolai
Falcone, Nicolas	*Mazurka*	Tuba-Euphonium Press
George, Thom Ritter	*Sonata*	Tuba-Euphonium Press
Handel, G. F./laFosse	*Concerto in F Minor*	Leduc
Israel, Brian	*Dance Suite*	Tritone/Presser
Jones, Roger	*Dialogues*	Tuba-Euphonium Press
Klengel, Jules/Falcone	*Concertino No. 1 in B♭*	Tuba-Euphonium Press
Ravel, Maurice	*Piece en Forme de Habanera*	Leduc
Saint-Saens/Falcone	*The Swan*	Southern
Senaille, J. B.	*Allegro Spiritoso*	Southern
Shepherd	*Nocturne and Rondolette*	Southern
Spears, Jared	*Rondo Capriccioso*	Barnhouse
Telemann, Georg Philipp	*Sonata in f Minor*	International
Vaughan Williams, R./ Paul Droste	*Six Studies in English Folksong*	Galaxy Music Corp.

Level III

Barat, J. E.	*Morceau de Concours*	B. Crampon
Bizet, Georges	*Flower Song from Carmen*	Rosehill
Boda, John	*Sonatina* (with CD)	Cimarron
Brahms, Johannes/Little	*Four Serious Songs*	Kagarice Music
Casterede, Jaques	*Fantasia Concertante*	Alphonse Leduc
Clinard, Fred	*Sonata*	Shawnee
Cord, Gustav	*Concert Fantasie*	Carl Fischer
David, Ferdinand	*Concertino, Op 4*	Carl Fischer
Frachenpohl, Arthur	*Sonata*	Dorn
Handel/ Fitzgerald	*Aria con Variazioni*	Belwin
Hartley	*Sonata Euphonica*	Presser
Hindemith, Paul	*Sonata for Bassoon*	Schott
Jacob, Gordon	*Fantasia*	Boosey & Hawkes
Mantia, Simone	*Endearing Young Charms*	Tuba-Euphonium Press

Pryor, Arthur	*Blue Bells of Scotland*	Carl Fischer
Puccini, Giacomo	Nessum Dorma	Tuba-Euphonium Press
Rachmaninoff, Sergei	*Vocalise*	Schirmer
Ross, Walter	*Partita*	Boosey & Hawkes
Rossini, Gioachino	*Largo al Factotum*	Boosey & Hawkes
Schmidt, Hugo	*The Devil's Tongue*	Tuba-Euphonium Press
Schumman, Robert/ Paul Droste	*Five Pieces in Folk Song Style, Op 102*	Ludwig Music
Sparke, Philip	*Fantasy*	Studio
Sparke, Philip	*Song for Ina*	Studio
Takacs, J.	*Sonata, Op 59*	Sidemton Verlag
White, Donald	*Lyric Suite*	Schirmer
Wilder, Alec	*Sonata*	Margun Music

Level IV

Bach, J. S.	*Cello Suites*	various
Boccolari, Ed	*Fantasia di ConcertoBourgeois*	Tuba-Euphonium Press
Bourgeois, Derek	*Concerto for Trombone* (euph)	R. Smith
Bowen, Brian	*Euphonium Music*	Rosehill
Butterworth	*Partita*	Comus
Censu, J.	*As Wonderful Things Drift By*	Zen-On Music
Corwell, Neal	*Odyssey* (with CD)	Nicolai
Curnow, James	*Symphonic Variants*	Tuba-Euphonium Press
Gillingham, David	*Blue Lake Fantasies*	Tuba-Euphonium Press
Gillingham	*Vintage*	Tuba-Euphonium Press
Horovitz	*Concerto*	Novello
Hoshina, H.	*Fantasy for Euphonium and Piano*	Tuba-Euphonium Press
Hovhaness, Alan	*Symphony #29*	Mount Tahoma
Jager, Robert	*Concerto for Euphonium*	Leonard
Lathan, William P.	*Eidolons*	Shawnee
Mantia, Simone	*Auld Lang Syne*	Tuba-Euphonium Press
Mozart, W. A.	*Concerto for Bassoon K 191*	various
Picchi/Mantia	*Fantasia Originale*	Tuba-Euphonium Press
Ponchielli, Amilcare	*Concerto per Flicorno Basso*	Tuba-Euphonium Press
Raum, Elizabeth	*Faustbach*	Tuba-Euphonium Press
Richards, Goff	*Rangitoto*	Studio
Rogers, Walter	*The Volunteer*	Tuba-Euphonium Press
Saint Saens, Camille	*Morceau de Concert*	Shawnee
Sparke, Philip	*Concerto*	Studio
Sparke, Philip	*Pantomime*	Studio PR
Stevens, John	*Soliloquies*	Tuba-Euphonium Press
Uber, David	*Sonata*	Dorn
Vivaldi, Antonio	*Sonatas* (six for cello)	Schirmer
Weber	*Concerto for Bassoon*	various
Wiggins, C.	*Soliloquy No. 9*	Studio
Wilhelm, Rolf	*Concertino for Euphonium*	Trio Musik Edition

Level V

Aagard-Nilsen, Torstein	*4 Lyric Pieces*	Norsk MF
Aagard-Nilsen, Torstein	*Euphonium Concerto*	Norsk MF
Adler, Sam	*Four Dialogs* (with marimba)	Carl Fischer
Bach, Jan	*Concert Variations*	Tuba-Euphonium Press
Bach, Jan	*Concerto*	Tuba-Euphonium Press
Bach, J. S.	*Sonata 1–3*	Southern
Bourgeois, Derek	*Euphoria*	Vanderbeek & Imrie, Ltd.

Cosma, Vladimir	*Concerto*	Lam largo
Ellerby, Martin	*Concerto*	Studio
Gallaher, Christopher	*Sonata*	Tuba-Euphonium Press
Golland, John	*Concerto #1*	Chester
Golland, John	*Concerto #2*	Studio
Linkola, Jukka	*Concerto for Euphonium*	FMIC
Nagano, Mitsuhiro	*Matrix* (with CD)	Manu
Nehleybel, Vaclav	*Concerto for Euphonium*	Tuba-Euphonium Press
Szentpali, Roland	*Pearls*	Bim
Vazzana, Anthony	*Partita for Euph, Piano and Percussion*	Tuba-Euphonium Press
Weber, Carl Maria Von	*Concertino* (for clarinet)	various
Wilby, Philip	*Concerto*	Rosehill

Euphonium Texts

Bowman, Brian, and J. D. Ployhar. *Practical Hints on Playing the Baritone*. Belwin-Mills.

Lehman, Art. *The Art of Euphonium Playing, Volume I* (book only). Tuba-Euphonium Press.

Lehman, Art. *The Art of Euphonium Playing, Volume II* (book and record). Tuba-Euphonium Press.

Lehman, Art, and David Werden. *The Brass Musician*. Cimarron Music Press.

Miles, David. *An Annotated Bibliography of Selected Contemporary Euphonium Solo Literature by American Composers*. Tuba-Euphonium Press. $20.

Phillips, Harvey, and Winkle. *The Art of Tuba and Euphonium*. Summy-Birchard.

Rose, William. *Studio Class Manual*. Tuba-Euphonium Press. $16.

Werden, David. *Scoring for Euphonium*. Tuba-Euphonium Press. $8.

Werden, David, and Denis Winter. *Euphonium Music Guide*. Tuba-Euphonium Press. $16.

For U.S. Military Band Auditions

BRIAN BOWMAN

Each branch of the U.S. military maintains at least two levels of professional bands. These are the line, base, or field bands and the premiere bands. The two types of organizations differ in size, personnel, permanency, and mission scope. Premiere bands are generally larger in size, provide permanent duty stations, and have national and international performance venue and mission scope. They also have an accelerated promotion schedule with earlier opportunity for higher rank and pay than the line, base, or field bands. Line, field, or base bands are smaller with some additional duties usually required. Their performance arena and mission scope are more regional in nature. In addition to these bands the Army and Air Force have reserve and National Guard bands.

The premiere bands of the Army, Navy, Marines, and Air Force are located in Washington, D.C. The Army has a second premiere band, The United States Army Field Band, which is primarily a touring organization based in Fort Meade, Maryland, near Washington, D.C. The official band of the Coast Guard is in New London, Connecticut, at the Coast Guard Academy. There are also special bands at the other service academies, West Point (Army), Annapolis (Navy), and in Colorado at the Air Force Academy. These special bands hold auditions for vacancies as they occur. Vacancies are advertised in the Musicians Union paper and on the individual websites of each band. There are slight differences in procedures between the bands. Most of the bands require an application recording (with the exception of the Marine Band and the Navy Band). Auditions consist of prepared materials to include solo or other prepared piece, band excerpts, sight-reading, and in some cases scales. Most of the band excerpts are from standard literature, although there may be some special arrangements not generally available.

Preparation for the audition for a premiere band will also prepare the applicant for auditions for the regular line, field, or base bands maintained by each of the services. All the military services have line or base bands both in the United States and abroad. The Army, Navy, and Marine Corps have training programs in the Armed Forces School of Music. After being accepted into the music program for any of the field, line, or base bands of these three services and completing basic training, there is a term of study at this school prior to being assigned to a band. The Air Force often will audition for each line or base band in a similar manner to the special bands, and following basic training, the performer will go directly to the band without further training.

Prior to 1980, there were no required lists of literature for the premiere band auditions. The candidates would perform a prepared solo and then read from an audition book of excerpts prepared by each band. At that time, the entire audition could be considered sight-reading depending upon the candidate's knowledge of band literature. As there were no euphonium excerpts books generally available, those wishing to prepare for auditions would accumulate personal copies of as much band literature as possible, for use in developing sight-reading skills. The availability of published excerpt books is still lacking and several of the bands have changed their audition policy to require lists of materials to be prepared for the auditions. In many cases, they will have these works available in an audition packet that is sent to the candidates for preparation. In the last part of the twentieth century, the Marine, Air Force, and Army Field bands have followed this procedure.

The United States Army Band, Fort Myer, Virginia, has a slightly different audition procedure. After an opening is announced, applicants may submit an audition. The material for the tape is chosen by the performer, and should be indicative of his/her playing, preferably displaying different styles and strengths: lyrical, technical, and so forth. The audition committee in the band hears these tapes anonymously and approximately fifteen candidates are chosen to participate in the live audition at Fort Myer.

For the first round, participants play the following:

- One solo, or solo excerpt, of their choice, which must be less than three minutes in duration.
- Two prepared short contrasting pieces, one lyrical, one of a more technical nature (although not prohibitively so). For the 2001 audition, the pieces required were both etudes: Rochut #69 and Kopprasch #14.
- The remainder of the audition is comprised of sight-reading.

For the final round, three to six are chosen, and the round consists entirely of sight-reading.

There is no supplied "repertoire list" as you may find with other auditions. The sight-reading is comprised of euphonium excerpts from marches, transcriptions, and original works from both symphonic band and brass band literature. Although a few well-known standard excerpts are chosen for the reading, an emphasis is placed on lesser-known works (or lesser-known versions of works, in the

case of transcriptions) so that the participants are more likely to be truly "sight-reading" material that they have never seen previously.

The United States Marine Band, Washington, D.C., does not have a taped screening round. All applicants complete an application, which must be returned to the band prior to the audition. Candidates check in the day of the audition and are assigned audition times in accordance with the order in which they appear and register. Often the final rounds of the auditions may be heard in a second day.

Recent Marine Band Audition Materials:

Believe Me if All Those Endearing Young Charms–Mantia (solo)
The Stars and Stripes Forever–Sousa
March from Suite in F for Military Band, Opus 28, No. 2–Holst
Overture to "Benvenuto Cellini"–Berlioz/Patterson
The Roman Carnival Overture, Opus 9–Berlioz/Godfrey II
Chanconne from Suite in E♭ for Military Band, Opus 28, No. 1–Holst
Fiesta del Pacifico–Nixon
Theme and Variations, Opus 43a–Schoenberg
Aegean Festival Overture–Makris/Rogers
The Pines Near a Catacomb from "The Pines of Rome"–Respighi/Duker
Molly on the Shore–Grainger/Rogers
Toccata Marziale–Vaughan Williams
Marche Hongroise from "La Damnation de Faust," Opus 24–Berlioz/Bowlin
Rocky Point Holiday–Nelson
Colonial Song–Grainger
Jupiter from "The Planets," Opus 32–Holst/Smith

Audition Excerpts Used Prior to 1991:

Le Maschere–P. Mascagni
Florentiner March–Julius Fucik
Finale from Symphony No. 4–P. Tschaikowsky
Academic Festival Overture–Johannes Brahms
American Overture for Band–J. W. Jenkins
Colas Breugnon Overture–Dmitri Kabalevsky/trans. Beeler
Concerto for Orchestra–Bartok/trans. Knox
The Corsair Overture–Berlioz
Crown Imperial–William Walton
Dance of the Tumblers–N. Rimsky-Korsakov
Espana Rhapsodie–Emmanuel Chabrier/Safranek
Farandole from Suite No. 2 from l'Arlesienne–Bizet/Finck

Festival Variations–Claude T. Smith
Firebird–Stravinsky/Knox
The Flying Dutchman–Wagner/Hindsley
Francesco da Rimini–Tschaikowsky/
    Patterson
The Judges of the Secret Court–Berlioz/Knox
Legend–Paul Creston
Lohengrin, Intro to Act III–Wagner/
    Hindsley
Looking Upward–Sousa
Luisa Miller–Verdi
Pineapple Poll–Arthur Sullivan
Rakoczy March–Berlioz/Bowlin
Russlan & Ludmilla–M. Glinka/
    Winterbottom
Spitfire Fugue–William Walton/arr. Wallace
Symphony for Band–Gould
Symphony No. 3 "Slavyanskaya"–Boris Koz-
    hevnikov
Tannhauser Overture–Wagner/Winter-
    bottom
Thunder and Blazes–J. Fucik/ Laurendeau/
    Seredy
Tunbridge Fair–W. Piston
Witches' Sabbath from *Symphonie Fantastique*–
    Berlioz/Kline

The United States Air Force Band requires a current resume and preliminary audition recording, which should include a three- to five-minute solo portion and a performance of designated repertoire from the packet of excerpts provided. Those candidates passing the screening recording are then invited to audition in person.

USAF Band Audition Materials, 1998 and 2001:

Characteristic Study #1 from "Method"–Arban
Overture to Colas Breugnon–Kabalesvsky/
    Beeler
Festive Overture–Shostakovich/Hunsberger
Rolling Thunder–Fillmore
Commando March–Barber
The World Is Waiting for the Sunrise–Alford
Festival Variations–Smith
Euryanthe Overture–Von Weber/Safranek
Pineapple Poll–Sullivan/Mackerra
Theme and Variations–Schoenberg (Var-
    iation V)
Universal Judgment–De Nardis
The Roman Carnival–Berlioz/Safranek
Euphonium Music–Bowen (prepared solo)
Lincolnshire Posey–Grainger
Suite in F–Holst
El Capitan March–Sousa

Danse Slave–Chabrier/Odom
The Warriors–Grainger/Papajohn
Scales: all major and minor (harmonic,
    melodic, and natural)
Two octaves
Quarter note–100

The United States Army Field Band requires a recording of ten to fifteen minutes in length. Those accepted and invited to audition will need to visit an Army recruiter to begin paperwork and take the needed mental and physical exams required prior to the live audition. Travel expenses to this audition may be provided and arranged by the Army. In addition to the audition additional reading with chamber music groups including a tuba/euphonium quartet may be required.

The United States Army Field Band Audition Lists:

Characteristic Study No. 1–Arban
Barnum and Baileys–King
George Washington Bicentennial–Sousa
Melody Shop–King
Rolling Thunder–Filmore
The Stars and Stripes–Sousa
Festive Overture–Shostakovitch/Hunsberger
Procession of the Nobles–Rimsky-Korsakov
Festival Variations–Smith
Second Suite in F–Holst
Suite of Old American Dances–Bennett
Theme and Variations–Schoenberg
The Official West Point March–Egner
Finale from Symphony in f Minor No. 4–
    Tschaikovsky/Safranek
Roman Carnival Overture–Berlioz/Safranek
Euryanthe Overture–von Weber/Safranek
Pocahontas Suite–Merken-Schwartz/
    McClung
Salute to the Big Bands–arr. Roberts

Suggested Prepared Solos:

All Those Endearing Young Charms–Mantia
Pantomime–Philip Sparke

The United States Navy Band has a similar prepared list of excerpts to the other premiere bands as well as a choice of prepared solo. The auditions are not screened through tape auditions and are open to all. All auditions are held behind a screen.

Below are listed websites for the bands and music programs in the U.S. Armed Forces. The latest information on auditions and requirements will be listed on these sites.

World Wide Web Links for Premiere Bands:

The United States Army Band, Washington, D.C.
  http://www.army.mil/armyband/
The United States Marine Band, Washington, D.C.
  http://www.marineband.usmc.mil/
The United States Navy Band, Washington, D.C.
  http://www.navyband.navy.mil/
The United States Air Force Band, Washington, D.C.
  http://www.usafband.com/
The United States Army Field Band, Fort Meade, Maryland
  http://www.army.mil/fieldband/
The United States Coast Guard Band, New London, Connecticut
  http://www.uscg.mil/band/
The United States Military Academy Band, West Point, New York
  http://www.usma.army.mil/band/
The United States Naval Academy Band, Annapolis, Maryland
  http://www.nadn.navy.mil/USNABand/
The United States Air Force Academy Band, Peterson Air Force Base, Colorado
  http://www.usafacademyband.com/index.html

Information on all military bands including active duty, reserve, and National Guard bands can be found at the following sites:

Army: http://bands.army.mil/default.asp
Air Force: http://www.af.mil/band/
Navy Bands: https://www.npc.navy.mil/CommandSupport/NavyMusic/NavyBands/
Marine Corp Bands: http://www.marines.com/about_marines/marinecorpsbands.asp

The editor expresses gratitude to the following for help with this chapter: Roger Behrend (the United States Navy Band), Will Jones and Dan Helseth (The United States Air Force Band), Neal Corwell (The United States Army Band), and Mark Jenkins (The United States Marine Band).

For High School and College Tuba/Euphonium Quartets

SHARON HUFF

These recommendations have been extracted from work done by Kenyon D. Wilson. To locate more information on these quartets and on many

others, please consult his chapter on Music for Multiple Tubas in the book *Guide to the Tuba Repertoire: The New Tuba Source Book*, also published by Indiana University Press.

Recommended Tuba/Euphonium Quartets (Two Euphoniums and Two Tubas), High School Level

Arcadelt, Jacob. *Ave Maria*. Arr. James Self. Wimbledon Music Incorporated. 1979. $7. 2:30. III–IV.
Ayers, Jesse. *Into the Magical Rain Forest for Tuba/Euphonium Ensemble and Tape*. Tuba-Euphonium Press. Two euphoniums, two tubas, and tape. 1993. $15. 5:30. III–IV.
Bach, Johann Sebastian. *Bist Du Bei Mir*. Arr. David Werden. Whaling Music Publishers. 1978. $5. 2:30. III–IV.
Bach, Johann Sebastian. *Contrapunctus IX*. Arr. Mike Forbes. Tuba-Euphonium Press. 1999. $10. 3:00. III.
Bach, Johann Sebastian. *Prelude and Fugue in G Minor, BWV 558*. Arr. Kenyon D. Wilson. Tuba-Euphonium Press. 1997. $8. 3:15. III.
Brahms, Johannes. *Four Brahms Folk Songs*. Trans. Frank Ferriano. Tuba-Euphonium Press. 2000. $8. 5:30. I–II.
Bullet, William. *Greensleeves*. Arr. Gary A. Buttery. Whaling Music Publishers. 1978. $5. 2:00. III–IV.
Dempsey, Ray. *Now Hear This!* Tuba-Euphonium Press. 1998. $10. 3:00. III.
De Vittoria, Tomas Luis. *O Magnum Misterium*. Arr. Barton Cummings. Solid Brass Music Co. 1998. $9. 4:00. II.
Drobnak, Ken, arr. *Renaissance Choral Music, Vol. I and II*. Tuba-Euphonium Press. 2001. $15. 16 pp. II.
Forbes, Michael. *Cosmic Voyage*. Editions BIM. 2003. CHF 25. 5:45. III–IV.
Fucik, Julius. *Entry of the Gladiators (Thunder and Blazes)*. Arr. J. Kelly Diamond. Tuba-Euphonium Press. 1996. $8. 3:00. III.
Gabrieli, Giovanni. *Canzona per sonare No. 2*. Arr. Benjamin Roundtree. Roundtree Music. 2002. $12. 2:15. III.
Garrett, James, arr. *Wabash Cannon Ball for Tuba-Euphonium Ensemble*. Ludwig Music Publishing Company. 1987. $15.50. 1:45. III–IV.
Gervaise, Claude. *Dance Suite*. Arr. David R. Werden. Whaling Music Publishers. 1979. $8.50. 5:00. III–IV.
Gliere, Reinhold. *Russian Sailor's Dance*. Arr. J. Kelly Diamond. Tuba-Euphonium Press. 2000. $12. 4:00. III.
Grim, Ray, arr. *St. Paul Waltz*. Cimarron Music and Productions. 1996. $9.50. 3:00. III.
Hall, Percy. *Waltz and March*. Great Works Publishing, Inc. Three euphoniums and one tuba. 1999. $10. 2:30. II.

Handel, George Frederic. *Sarabande and Variations.* Arr. Richard Barth. Music Arts Company. 1978. $10. 5:00. III.

Handel, George Frederic. *Two Baroque Dances.* Arr. Grady Greene. Music Arts Company. 1987. $15. 2:30. III–IV.

Haydn, Franz Joseph. *Achieved Is the Glorious Work.* Arr. Mike Forbes. Tuba-Euphonium Press. 1999. $8. 2:45. III–IV.

Hutchinson, Terry. *Tuba Juba Duba.* Brass Press. 1974. $5. 3:10. III.

Joplin, Scott. *The Entertainer.* Arr. David Schanke. Music Arts Publishing Company. 1996. $16. 4:15. III.

Kotscher, Edmund, and Rudi Lindt. *Liechtensteiner Polka.* Arr. Gail Robertson. Tuba-Euphonium Press. 1999. $14. 2:30. III.

Kresin, Willibald. *Tuba Rodeo.* Editions Marc Reift. Two euphoniums and two tubas with drums. 2001. $17.50. 3:00. III.

Lasso, Orlando di. *I Know a Young Maiden.* Arr. Barton Cummings. Solid Brass Music Co. 1996. $9. 1:30. III.

Lasso, Orlando di. *Mon Coeur se Recommende á Vous: Madrigal for Tuba Quartet.* Arr. Jack Robinson. Whaling Music Publishers. 1979. $5. 2:00. III.

Lasso, Orlando di. *Two Madrigals.* Arr. Frank Ferriano. Tuba-Euphonium Press. 2001. $10. 3:00. III.

Mancini, Henry. *The Pink Panther.* Arr. Jay Krush. Northride Music, Incorporated/Kendor Music, Incorporated. 1982. $8.50. 3:45. III–IV.

Mozart, Wolfgang Amadeus. *Adoramus Te, Christe.* Arr. Mark Nelson. Whaling Music Publishers. 1991. $8. 1:30. III.

Mozart, Wolfgang Amadeus. *Ave Verum Corpus (K. 618).* Arr. Rudy Emilson. Kendor Music, Inc. 2000. $7. 2:35. III.

Mozart, Wolfgang Amadeus. *Allegro from Eine Kleine Nachtmusik, K. 525.* Arr. Albert Peoples. Southern Music Company. 1990. $12.50. 5:00. III.

Mozart, Wolfgang Amadeus. *Marriage of Figaro.* Arr. Al Fabrizio. Tuba-Euphonium Press. 1994. $12. 3:45. III.

Pezold. *Menuet from Anna Magdalena's Notebook.* Arr. Stephen Shoop. Cimarron Music and Productions. 1995. $9. 1:45. II.

Puccini, Giacomo. *March from "La Boheme.."* Arr. David Butler. Tuba-Euphonium Press. 1998. $12. 2:15. III.

Renwick, Wilke. *Dance* Arr. Kenyon D. Wilson. Tromba Music Publishers. 1994. 1:00. III.

Rimsky-Korsakov, Nicolai. *Dance of the Tumblers.* Arr. Al Fabrizio. Tuba-Euphonium Press. 2000. $12. 3:30. III.

Robertson, Gail, arr. *Amazing Grace.* Tuba-Euphonium Press. 1998. $10. 2:00. III.

Saint-Saëns, Camille. *Adagio from Symphony #3.* Arr. Steve Hanson. KIWI Music Press. $5. 3:00. III–IV.

Schubert, Franz. *Serenade.* Arr. Gail Robertson. Tuba-Euphonium Press. 1999. $10. 2:45. III–IV.

Singleton, Kenneth, arr. *Three 16th Century Flemish Pieces.* Queen City Brass Publications. 1984. $7.50. 3:00. III.

Sousa, John Philip. *The Liberty Bell.* Arr. Gail Robertson. Tuba-Euphonium Press. 1999. $12. 3:30. III.

Sousa, John Philip. *Semper Fidelis.* Arr. R. Winston Morris. Ludwig Music Publishing Company. 1988. $15.50. 2:30. III.

Sousa, John Philip. *Thunderer, The.* Arr. Peter Smalley. Studio Music Company. 1996. III.

Stevens, John. *Ballade.* Available from the composer. 1990. 2:00. III.

Strauss, Johann. *Pizzacato Polka.* Arr. Ray Grim. Cimarron Music and Productions. 1996. $9. 1:15. III.

Tchaikovsky, Peter. *Andante Cantabile from String Quartet No. 1.* Arr. Ken Drobnak. Tuba-Euphonium Press. 2002. $10. 2:45. III.

Tchaikovsky, Peter. *Dance of the Little Tubas (Swans).* Arr. Joseph Goble. Tuba-Euphonium Press. 1993. $8. 1:30. III.

Uber, David. *Suite for Four Bass Tubas, Op. 67.* Almitra Music Company (Kendor Music, Incorporated). 1976. $11. 5:30. III–IV.

Vaughan, Rodger, arr. *American Favorites: Tuba Euphonium Quartets.* Tuba-Euphonium Press. 1992. $15. 14 pp. II–III.

Verdi, Giuseppe. *La donna é mobile.* Arr. Benjamin Roundtree. Roundtree Music. 2002. $12. 2:00. III.

Victoria, Thomas Luis de. *O Vos Omnes (Motet).* Arr. James Self. Wimbledon Music Incorporated. 1979. $7. 2:30. III.

Werden, David, arr. *Good Cheer Collection.* Cimarron Music and Productions. $45. III.

Wilder, Alec, and Norlan Bewley, arr. *Carols for a MERRY TUBACHRISTMAS, Volume II.* Harvey Phillips Foundation. 1992. $6. 66 pp. II–III.

Wilder, Alec, arr. *Carols for a MERRY TUBACHRISTMAS.* Harvey Phillips Foundation. 1977. $5. 20 pp. II–III.

Recommended Tuba/Euphonium Quartets (Two Euphoniums and Two Tubas), College/University Level

Bach, Johann Sebastian. *Fugue in G Minor (Little).* Arr. Skip Gray. Shawnee Press, Incorporated. 1984. $9. 3:15. III–IV.

Bach, Johann Sebastian. *Jesu, Joy of Man's Desiring.* Arr. David Werden. Whaling Music Publishers. 1978. $5. 2:10. III–IV.

Bach, Johann Sebastian. *Toccata and Fugue in D Minor.* Arr. Todd Fiegel. Celluloid Tubas. 2000. $25. IV.

Bach, Johann Sebastian. *Wachet Auf.* Arr. Gary A. Buttery. Whaling Music Publishers. 1978. $9. 3:20. IV.

Bartles, Alfred H. *When Tubas Waltz.* Kendor Music, Incorporated. 1976. $11. 4:20. IV.

Bulla, Stephen. *Celestial Suite.* Rosehill Music Publishing Company. 1989. $14.95. 8:00. IV.

Bulla, Stephen. *Quartet for Low Brass.* Kendor Music, Incorporated (Out of Print). 1978. 4:00. IV.

DiGiovanni, Rocco. *Tubas at Play.* Available from the composer. 1978. $18. 3:30. IV–V.

Frackenpohl, Arthur. *Pop Suite.* Kendor Music, Incorporated. 1974. $10.50. 7:00. IV.

Frackenpohl, Arthur. *Suite for Tuba Quartet.* Horizon Press. 1991. $16. 6:50. IV.

Fritze, Gregory. *Prelude and Dance.* Tuba-Euphonium Press. 1990. $18. 9:00. IV.

George, Thom Ritter. *TUBASONATINA.* Available from the composer. 1977. $13. 8:20. IV.

Gounod, Charles Francois. *Funeral March of a Marionette.* Arr. Arthur Frackenpohl. Almitra Music Company, Incorporated (Kendor Music, Incorporated). 1992. $11. 4:00. IV.

Grieg, Edward. *In the Hall of the Mountain King.* Arr. David R. Werden. Whaling Music Publishers. 1992. $9. 3:00. III–IV.

Handel, George Frederic. *The Hallelujah Chorus.* Arr. David Sabourin. Touch of Brass Music Corporation. 1981. $10. 3:00. IV.

Hill, William H. *Fantasia on "Dies Irae" for Tuba Ensemble.* Neil A. Kjos Music Company. 1980. $7. 5:00. IV.

Holmes, Paul. *Quartet for Tubas.* TRN Music Publishers. 1980. $20. 10:00. IV.

Joplin, Scott. *Maple Leaf Rag.* Arr. Karl Humble. T.A.P. Music. 1989. $6. 3:20. IV.

Joplin, Scott. *Swipesy.* Arr. David R. Werden. Whaling Music Publishers. 1981. $7. 3:00. IV.

Kern, Jerome. *They Didn't Believe Me.* Arr. Bill Holcombe. Musicians Publications. 1991. $12. 2:45. III–IV.

King, Karl. *The Melody Shop.* Arr. David R. Werden. Whaling Music Publishers. 1987. $8. 2:30. IV.

Liszt, Franz. *Hungarian Rhapsodie No. 2.* Arr. Bruno Seitz. Musikverlag Martin Scherbacher. 1990. $13.50. 2:30. IV.

Lyon, Max J. *Suite for Four Bass Instruments.* Shawnee Press, Incorporated. 1975. $10. 5:00. IV.

Mancini, Henry. *Baby Elephant Walk.* Arr. Eugene Anderson. Anderson's Arizona Originals. 1988. $5. 2:45. III–IV.

Martino, Ralph. *Fantasy for Tuba/Euphonium Quartet.* PP Music. 1992. $11. 5:00. IV–V.

Massenet, J. E. F. *Aragonaise from "Le Cid."* Arr. M. S. Erickson. PP Music. 1986. $6. 1:45. IV.

Mehlan, Keith. *Bottoms Up Rag.* Horizon Press. 1991. $8. 2:45. III–IV.

Minerd, Doug, arr. *Sea Tubas.* Whaling Music Publishers. 1982. $12.50. 5:10. IV.

Mozart, Wolfgang Amadeus. *Turkish March K. 331.* Arr. Keith Mehlan. PP Music. 1986. $8. 3:30. IV.

Niehaus, Lennie. *Keystone Chops.* Kendor Music, Incorporated. 1986. $9. 3:10. IV.

Payne, Frank Lynn. *Quartet for Tubas.* Shawnee Press, Incorporated. 1971. $18. 11:00. IV.

Powell, Baden. *Bocoxe.* Arr. Gary Buttery. Whaling Music Publishers. 1978. $5. 1:45. IV.

Ramsoe, Wilhelm. *Quartet for Brass.* Arr. Gary Buttery. Whaling Music Publishers. 1978. $12. 9:00. IV.

Rimsky-Korsakov, Nicholai. *Procession of the Nobles.* Arr. David Butler. Tuba-Euphonium Press. 1993. $15. 3:30. III–IV.

Robertson, Gail, arr. *All Things Bright and Beautiful.* Tuba-Euphonium Press.1998. $12. 3:00. IV.

Rossini, Gioacchino. *Petit Caprice: In the Style of Offenbach.* Arr. Ron Davis. Tuba-Euphonium Press. 1993. $5. 3:20. IV.

Schumann, Robert. *Piece in Folk Style.* Arr. David R. Werden. Whaling Music Publishers. Three euphoniums and one tuba. 1981. $5. 2:20. IV.

Sousa, John Philip. *Hands Across the Sea.* Arr. David R. Werden. Whaling Music Publishers. 1983. $8. 3:30. IV.

Sousa, John Philip. *The Stars and Stripes Forever.* Arr. David R. Werden. Whaling Music Publishers. 1992. $8. 2:00. IV.

Sousa, John Philip. *Washington Post.* Arr. David Sabourin. Touch of Brass Music Corporation. 1981. $8.50. 2:30. III–IV.

Stevens, John. *Dances.* Peer International Corporation. Solo tuba and three tubas. 1978. $12. 7:30. IV.

Stevens, John. *Manhattan Suite.* Southern Music Publishing Company Incorporated. 1979. $12. 15:20. IV.

Stevens, John. *Music 4 Tubas.* Peer International Corporation. 1978. $12. 8:00. IV.

Stevens, John. *Power for Four Tubas.* Peer International Corporation. 1978. $12. 2:10. III–IV.

Taylor, Jeff. *Fanfare No. 1.* Horizon Press. 1991. $6. 2:30. IV.

Victoria, Thomas Luis de. *O Regem Coeli for Tuba Quartet.* Arr. Joseph Schwartz. Unicorn Music Company, Incorporated. 1990. 4:30. IV.

Wagner, Richard. *Elsa's Procession to the Cathedral.* Arr. Gail Robertson. Tuba-Euphonium Press. 1998. $14. 4:00. III–IV.

Wagner, Richard. *Pilgrim's Chorus from Tannhäuser.* Arr. Paul Schmidt. Heavy Metal Music. 1991. $7. 3:20. III–IV.

Wilson, Kenyon D. *Dance No. 1.* Tuba-Euphonium Press. 1993. $5. 2:00. IV.

14. Discography

Eric Paull

This chapter is a detailed listing of over 880 sound recordings that feature the euphonium as a prominent solo instrument. This project is intended to create a reference index of significant euphonium recordings by cataloging as many long-playing records, cassettes tapes, and compact discs as possible. Incorporated within this chapter are recordings for solo euphonium, euphonium and piano or tape, duets, trios, tuba/euphonium ensembles, and euphonium with band, orchestra, and jazz ensembles. In order to provide a thorough listing of material, three major divisions have been developed in this index, and these categories are detailed listings by artist, composer, and title of composition. In addition, there is a separate publisher address list that contains contact information for many of the record labels and distributors.

This discography is as comprehensive as possible, not accounting for recordings that may be released after printing deadlines. In addition, it is neither agreeable nor realistic to include every recording that includes euphonium performance. Certain restrictions have been made. Recordings with the use of the euphonium as a section instrument with wind band, orchestra, and brass ensemble have been excluded from this project because these mediums are too vast and numerous to include.

Among the reasons for compiling this information is an attempt to overcome a lack of both public and professional awareness in regard to the euphonium. In order to advance the euphonium's role as a viable musical outlet, the instrument must have support from other professionals in the field of music. Thus, it is necessary to collect and catalog euphonium recordings to inform both amateurs and professionals of the available worldwide resources. The main intention is to provide a reference tool that can enrich the body of knowledge of artists, composers, and compositions by way of recordings in the area of euphonium music.

When doing a project that is based on historical research and put forth in "reference index style," there are few pitfalls. However, the most troubling problem thus far has been in locating these recordings. Some of the older recordings are now out of print and difficult to obtain. A major concern in this research effort has been to confirm the veracity of printed material about the recordings. Some record label jackets appear in print with many misspellings and typographical errors. Common mistakes are composer's names and the titles of their compositions. The most severe of these errors occur in misprinting the catalog number assigned to the recording by the publisher. Incorrect catalog numbers make it all that much harder to locate or purchase particular recordings.

The material collected for this discography has been cataloged in the most logical manner possible. A database was designed with a total of forty-six different fields. They are broken down as follows: *Artist* field, listing the name(s) of the performer(s) on each particular recording; a field for the *Title* of the album; another field designated *Personnel* for the names of individuals, along with their instruments, who assisted the major euphonium artist; and the *Label* field includes the record company, year, catalog number, and the classification of long-playing record (LP), cassette tape (CS), or compact disc (CD). There are twenty-one fields each in the area of *Composer* and *Composition*. All of the information contained in these fields will be broken down into the three major divisions previously mentioned and will be listed in alphabetical order.

There is a great deal of potential for this project to be beneficial to many people throughout the world. Historically, the euphonium Discography will provide a foundation for others to build from and improve upon. Educationally, this chapter is useful in the fact that it will give students and professionals a definitive reference index, one that will aid them in finding euphonium recordings to enjoy, study, and add to their aesthetic experience.

Much appreciation goes to the countless sources that contributed to the creation of this

discography. There have been several previously
published discographies as well as numerous private collectors who have generously provided
information. I wish to express my gratitude to
everyone involved in this project.

Euphonium Recordings by Artist

Aho, Eric. *See* Droste, Paul
Albertasaurus Tuba Quartet
  Title: *Albertasaurus*
  Personnel: John McPherson, David Reid,
    euphonium; Scott Whetham, Michael
    Eastep, tuba
  Label: Arktos, CD: 2044 TUAL02
  Massenet: *Aragonaise*
  Bach, Johann Sebastian: *Vivace from "Trio
    Sonata in c for Organ"*
  Beethoven, Ludwig van: *Pathetique Sonata*
  Mozart, Wolfgang Amadeus: *Turkish March
    from "Piano Sonata in A"*
  Mozart, Wolfgang Amadeus: *Andante
    Cantabile from "Piano Sonata in C"*
  McPherson, John: *Hugo Hugo*
  Chopin, Frederic: *Minute Waltz*
  Verdi, Giuseppi: *Two Selections from "La
    Traviata"*
  Ketelby, Albert: *A Night in a Persian Caravan*
  Shearing, George: *Lullaby of Birdland*
  Joplin, Scott: *Strenuous Life, The*
  Turpin, Tom: *Harlem Rag*
Albiez, Cédric
  Album Title: *Country Scene*
  Personnel: Thierry Margairaz, cornet; Ensemble
    de Cuivres Melodia, Guy Michel, conductor
  Label: Artlab, 1995 CD: 9684-1
  Curnow, James: *Rhapsody for Euphonium*
  Richards, Goff: *Country Scene*
Alchemy (previously Atlantic Tuba Quartet)
  Album Title: *Village Dances*
  Personnel: Danny Vinson, James Jackson,
    euphonium; Gary Buttery, Joanna Hersey,
    tuba
  Label: Alchemy, CD: TUAL20 Buttery, Gary:
    Fanfare for the Millennium
  Buttery, Gary: *Fantasia of Eastern European
    Village Dances*
  Gautier, L./Werden: *Le Secret*
  Gibbons, O./Campbell: *Tuba Voluntary*
  Hart, Bill/Buttery: *Brass Cuckoo*
  Koetsier, Jan: *Wolkenschatten fur Tubaquartett,
    Op. 136*
  Mozart, Wolfgang Amadeus/Werden: *Ah! Vous
    Dirai-Je, Maman*
  Powell, Baden/Aquino/Buttery: *Bocoxe*
  Susato, Tielman/Buttery: *Shepherd's Dance*
  Traditional/Buttery: *Christmas Tubas of the
    British Isles*
  Traditional/Buttery: *Sponger Money*

  Traditional/Buttery: *While Soft Winds Shake
    the Barley*
  Vinson, Danny: *Memoirs of the American
    Civil War*
  Villa-Lobos, Hector/Buttery: *Danza: Martello*
Alexander, Ashley
  Album Title: *Power Slide*
  Personnel: Ashley Alexander Big Band
  Label: Pausa Records, LP: PR 7178
  Mantooth, Frank: *Belgrade Hangover*
Alexander, Ashley. *See* Matteson-Phillips Tubajazz
Consort
Allison, Gordon
  Album Title:
  Personnel: Worthing Citadel Band
  Label: Boosey & Hawkes Sound, 1984 LP:
    BHSS0115
  Unknown: *My Christ Is in All, in All*
Allred, John
  Album Title: *In The Beginning*
  Personnel: Allred Jazz Ensemble
  Label: Arbors Records, 2001 CD: ARCD
    19115
Anderson, Eric
  Album Title: *Steven Seward, "The Virtuoso Tuba"*
  Personnel: Steven Seward, tuba; Vicki
    Bereking, piano
  Label: Golden Crest Records, 1979 LP:
    RE-7083
  Vivaldi, Antonio: *Concerto for Two Trumpets*
Andresen, Mogens
  Album Title: *Danish Romantic Brass Music*
  Personnel: Royal Danish Orchestra
  Label:
  Jorgensen, Axel: *Caprice Oriental*
Andrews, Paul
  Album Title:
  Personnel: Paul Lawler, euphonium; Leyland
    DAF Band, Richard Evans, conductor
  Label: Triton, 1987 LP: TRM8103
  Bizet, George/Wilkinson: *Duet from "Pearl-
    fishers"*
Anonymous
  Album Title: *Australian Fantasy*
  Personnel: Hawthorn Band
  Label:
  Curnow, James: *Rhapsody for Euphonium*
Anonymous
  Album Title: *Blitz*
  Personnel: Black Dyke Mills Band
  Label: Black Dyke Mills Band
  Himes, William: *Journey into Freedom*
Anonymous
  Album Title: *Evening with Brighouse and
    Rastrick*
  Personnel: Brighouse and Rastrick Band
  Label: Brighouse and Rastrick
  Horovitz, Joseph: *Lento from "Euphonium
    Concerto"*
Anonymous
  Album Title: *Facets of Glass*

Personnel: Brassband De Bazuin
Label: Brassband De Bazuin
Unknown: *Variations for Euphonium*
Anonymous
Album Title: *Flying High*
Personnel: Melbourne Staff Band of the
Salvation Army
Label:
Curnow, James: *Rhapsody for Euphonium*
Anonymous
Album Title: *Music of Thy Name*
Personnel: Norwich Citadel Band of the
Salvation Army
Label: Monti, Vittorio: *Czárdás*
Anonymous
Album Title: *Polished*
Personnel: Foothills Brass Band
Label: Foothills Brass Band
Mozart, Wolfgang Amadeus/Thompson:
Allegro from "Concerto, K 191"
Anonymous
Album Title: *Scenes for Band*
Personnel: Koninklijk Militaire Kapel Royal
Military Band
Label: Great Lakes Music Enterprises, VBEB 010
Stanek, P.: *Nocturno for Euphonium*
Anonymous
Album Title:
Personnel:
Label: Crest, 1981: INC-81-13
Jacob, Gordon: *Fantasia*
Anthony, Phil. *See* Euphonium Quartet
Appleton, Walter
Album Title: *The Virtuoso Band*
Personnel: The Royal Artillery Band, Sidney V.
Hays, conductor
Label: Vanguard, 1960 LP: VSD 2093
Foster, Stephen/Rimmer: *My Old Kentucky
Home*
Araki, Tamao
Album Title: *Vivid Colours!*
Personnel: Vivid Brass, Masanori Fukuda,
conductor; Akiko Kato, piano
Label: Blue Lights, CD: BLCD-0125
Richards, Goff: *Vivid Colours*
Marcello, Benedetto: *Sonata in F Major*
Ross, Walter: *Partita*
Senshu, Jiro: *Fantasy*
Sparke, Philip: *Euphonium Concerto*
Golland, John: *Peace*
Bellstadt, Herman: *Napoli*
Narita, Tamezo: *Song of the Seashore*
Araki, Tamao. *See* Ushigami, Ryuji
Archer, Stephen
Album Title:
Personnel:
Label: Pye Records, 1975 LP: TB 3002
Doughty, George, arr.: *Old Rustic Bridge, The*
Ashworth, Tom. *See* Symphonia
Atlantic Tuba Quartet, The
Album Title: *Euphonic Sounds*

Personnel: David Werden, Denis Winter, eupho-
nium; Gary Buttery, David Chaput, tuba
Label: Golden Crest Records Inc., 1978 LP:
CRSQ-4173
Susato, Tielman/Winter: *Ronde and Saltarelle*
Bach, Johann Sebastian/Myers: *Toccata in d
Minor (Allegro)*
Bach, Johann Sebastian/Werden: *Bist Du
Bei Mir*
Lyon, Max: *Suite for Low Brass*
Traditional/Buttery: *Greensleeves*
Joplin, Scott/Werden: *Euphonic Sounds*
Sousa, John Philip/Werden: *Stars and Stripes
Forever*
Bach, Johann Sebastian/Werden: *"Air" from
Suite No. 3*
Ramsöe, Emilio/Buttery: *Quartet No. 4*
Byrd, William/Winter: *John, Come Kisse
Me Now*
Hartley, Walter: *Miniatures for Four Valve
Instruments*
Collins, Judy/Buttery: *Since You've Asked*
Powell, Baden/Buttery: *Bocoxe*
Best, Denzil/Buttery: *Move*
Baglin, Lyndon
Album Title: *Lyndon Baglin's Best of Brass*
Personnel: Cory Band, Arthur Kenny,
conductor
Label: Saydisc Records, 1985 LP: SDL 347
Mantia, Simone/Boddington: *Believe Me if All
Those Endearing Young Charms*
Baglin, Lyndon
Album Title: *Recorded Delivery*
Personnel: Sun Life Band
Label: Stanshaw, STA 001
Rossini, Gioacchino: *Prelude, Theme and
Variations*
Baglin, Lyndon
Album Title: *Showcase for the Euphonium*
Personnel: Geoffrey Spratt, Gavin Ashenden,
flute; Meinir Heulyn, harp; Olwyn Wonncott,
piano; William Thomas, conductor
Label: Saydisc Records, 1975 LP: SDC 269
Traditional: *Spanish Dance*
Squire, W. H.: *Tarantella*
Arban, Jean Baptiste: *Carnival of Venice, The*
Godfrey/Herbert: *Lucy Long*
Handel, George Frederic/Anonymous: *Ombra
mai fu from "Xerses"*
Lennon, John/Lucena: *Yesterday*
Martini, Giovanni/Lucena: *Plaisir D'Amour*
Rossini, Gioacchino/Anonymous: *Prelude,
Theme and Variations*
Saint-Saëns, Camille/Anonymous: *Le Cygne
from "The Carnival of the Animals"*
Simon, Paul/Lucena: *Scarborough Fair*
Handel, George Frederic: *Largo*
Baglin, Lyndon
Album Title:
Personnel: CWS Manchester Band, Alex Mor-
timer, conductor

Label: Fontana, 1961 LP: STFL 5158
Hartmann, John: *La Belle Americaine*
Baglin, Lyndon
  Album Title:
  Personnel: CWS Manchester Band, Alex
    Mortimer, conductor
  Label: Fontana, 1962 LP: TL 680988
  Mozart, Wolfgang Amadeus/Wright: *Rondo
    from "Concerto No. 4"*
Baglin, Lyndon
  Album Title:
  Personnel: CWS Manchester Band, Alex
    Mortimer, conductor
  Label: Fontana, 1963 LP: TL 5199
  Senaille, Jean Baptiste/Wright: *Allegro Spiritoso*
Baglin, Lyndon
  Album Title:
  Personnel: CWS Manchester Band, Alex
    Mortimer, conductor
  Label: Fontana, 1963 LP: FJL 507
  Sutton, Eddie: *Cavalier, The*
Baglin, Lyndon
  Album Title:
  Personnel: Brighouse and Rastrick Band,
    Walter Hargreaves, conductor
  Label: Pye Records, 1968 LP: GSGL 10407
  Rimmer, William: *Variations on Jenny Jones*
Baglin, Lyndon
  Album Title:
  Personnel: Brighouse and Rastrick Band, Walter
    Hargreaves, conductor
  Label: Studio 2 Stereo TWO, 1969 LP: 253
  Arban, Jean Baptiste: *Caprice and Variations*
Baglin, Lyndon
  Album Title:
  Personnel: Brighouse and Rastrick Band, Walter
    Hargreaves, conductor
  Label: Polydor, 1969 LP: 583047
  Traditional/Boddington: *Long, Long Ago*
Baglin, Lyndon
  Album Title:
  Personnel: Stanshawe Band, Walter Hagreaves,
    conductor
  Label: Decca, 1976 LP: SB 322
  Doughty, George: *Grandfather's Clock*
Baglin, Lyndon
  Album Title: *Foursome for Brass*
  Personnel: CWS Manchester Band Brass
    Quartet
  Label: Saydisc, CD: SDL 254
  Spurgin, Anthony: *Foursome for Brass*
  Traditional/Mortimer: *An Eriskay Love Lilt*
  Vinter, Gilbert: *Alla Burlesca*
  Vinter, Gilbert: *Fancy's Knell*
Baker, Buddy. *See* Matteson-Phillips Tubajazz
  Consort
Bargeron, Dave
  Album Title: *Gravity!!!*
  Personnel: J. Daley, E. McIntyre, euphonium;
    C. Kleinsteuber, T. Malone, tuba; H. Johnson,

pennywhistle; G. Wadenius, guitar; P. Shaffer,
  piano; M. Slocum, electric bass; K. Washing-
  ton, drums; V. S. Yuen, percussion
  Label: Verve Recording Co., 1996 CD:
    31453-10212
  Perkinson, Coleridge Taylor: *'Way 'Cross
    Georgia*
Bates, Clifford. *See* Euphonium Quartet
Baumgartner, Stephane
  Album Title: *Diamond Heritage*
  Personnel: Diablement Brass Band
  Label: Diablement Brass, 2002 CD
  Traditional/Roberts: *Carrickfergus*
Bazsinka Tuba Octet
  Album Title: *Waves*
  Personnel: Andras Fejer, Ferenc Koczias, Balint
    I. Perter, Sandor Balogh, euphonium; Laszlo
    Szabo, Zsolt Szekely, Roland Szentpali,
    Tamas Kelemen, tuba
  Label: Hungaroton, 1996 CD: 31642
  Stevens, John: *Liberation of Sisyphus, The*
Behrend, Roger
  Album Title: *Centennial Celebration*
  Personnel: Michigan State University Wind
    Symphony
  Label: Blue Hyacinth Productions
  Bizet, George/Harding: *Flower Song from
    "Carmen"*
  Giordano/Curnow: *Finale from "Andre
    Chenier"*
  Picchi, Ermano/Mantia: *Fantaisie Originale*
  Smith, Robert: *Willson Suite*
Behrend, Roger
  Album Title: *The Compositions of Alfred Reed*
  Personnel: Michigan State University Sym-
    phonic Band, Kenneth Bloomquist, director;
    Thad Hegerberg, conductor
  Label: Golden Crest Records, Inc., 1978 LP:
    ATH-5057
  Reed, Alfred: *Seascape*
Behrend, Roger
  Album Title: *Elegance*
  Personnel: Richard Donn, piano/harpsichord;
    William Wiedrich, piano
  Label: Coronet Recording Co., CD: COR-
    400-0
  Barat, J. Ed.: *Morceau de Concours*
  Telemann, Georg: *Sonata in f Minor*
  Schumann, Robert/Bowman: *Ich grolle nicht*
  Cords, Gustav: *Concert Fantasie*
  Uber, David: *Sonata for Euphonium and Piano*
  Wiedrich, William: *Reverie for Euphonium and
    Piano*
  Bellstedt, Herman: *Napoli*
Behrend, Roger
  Album Title: *1990 Mid-West International
    Band and Orchestra Clinic*
  Personnel: Dave Porter, tuba; Lake Braddock
    Secondary School Symphonic Band, Roy
    Holder, conductor

Label: Mark Custom Recording Service, 1990
CD: MW-90MCD-19
Frackenpohl, Arthur: *Song and Dance*
Behrend, Roger
Album Title: *Roger Behrend, Euphonium*
Personnel: Caryl Conger, piano; Emily Fisher,
harp
Label: Roger Behrend, CD
Senaille, Jean Baptiste: *Allegro Spiritoso*
Ito, Yasuhide: *Fantasy Variations*
Frackenpohl, Arthur: *Sonata for Euphonium*
Bach, Johann Sebastian/Falcone: *Two Pieces*
Traditional/Taylor, Jeff: *Nautical Variations*
Curnow, James: *Rhapsody for Euphonium*
Falcone, Nicholas: *Mazurka for Unaccompanied
Euphonium*
Mantia, Simone: *Believe Me if All Those
Endearing Young Charms*
Pryor, Arthur: *Blue Bells of Scotland, The*
Behrend, Roger
Album Title: *A Shared Vision of Excellence*
Personnel: George Mason University Wind
Ensemble, Anthony Maiello, conductor
Label: CAMPRO Custom Recording, 1993 CD
Curnow, James: *Symphonic Variants for Eupho-
nium and Band*
Reed, Alfred: *Seascape*
Brubaker, Jerry: *Rhapsody for Euphonium and
Piano*
Martino, Ralph: *Introspect*
Cords, Gustav/Frabrizio: *Romanze*
Gillingham, David: *Vintage*
Nelhybel, Vaclav: *Concerto for Euphonium and
Band*
Behrend, Roger. *See* Coast Guard Tuba-Eupho-
nium Quartet
Behrend, Roger. *See* United States Armed Forces
Tuba-Euphonium Ensemble
Belvin, Cory. *See* Euphoniums Unlimited
Benedict, Lesley
Album Title: *Hometown Saturday Night,
Mr. Jack Daniel's Original Silver Cornet Band*
Personnel: Mr. Jack Daniel's Original Silver
Cornet Band, Dave Fulmer, conductor
Label: GNP/Crescendo Record Co., Inc., 1993
CD: GNPD 524
Traditional/McRitchie: *Shenandoah*
Bewley, Norlan. *See* TubaCompany of Harvey
Phillips
Bewley, Norlan. *See* TubaShop Quartet
Biffle, Ronnie
Album Title: *1973 Mid-West National Band
and Orchestra Clinic*
Personnel: Marvin King, trumpet, Jonesboro
Junior High School Symphonic Band, Julian
Creamer, conductor
Label: Silver Crest Records, 1973 LP: MID-
73-12
Stauffer, Donald: *Rube and Boob, for Trumpet,
Euphonium and Band*

Bjørge, Rolf. *See* Flaten, Tormond
Bjorkland, Michael. *See* Schultz, Karl
Blackburn, Robert
Album Title: *The Music of Arthur Butterworth*
Personnel: Lesley Howie, tenor horn; Black
Dyke Mills Band, Nicholas Childs, conductor
Label: Doyen Recordings Ltd., 2001 CD: DOY
CD130
Butterworth, Arthur: *"Sinfonia Concertante"
Op. 111 for Tenor Horn and Baritone*
Bogetvedt, Bjorn
Album Title: *Blowing*
Personnel: Royal Norwegian Navy Band
Label: Et Pro Music, PPC 9019
Bergh, Sverre: *Introduction, Theme and
Variations*
Jacob, Gordon: *Fantasia*
Bondt de, Fan. *See* Haemhouts, Ben
Bone, Lloyd. *See* Euphoniums Unlimited
Bone, Lloyd. *See* Tennessee Technological Univer-
sity Alumni Tuba-Euphonium Ensemble
Booth, Steven
Album Title: *Brassband de Vooruitgang Meets
Steven Booth*
Personnel: Brassband de Vooruitgang
Label:
Arban, Jean Baptiste: *Fantasy Brilliante*
Puccini, Giacomo: *Nessun Dorma*
Clarke, Herbert L.: *Debutante, The*
Anonymous: *Way We Are, The*
Anonymous: *Carnival Duet*
Booth, Steven
Album Title: *The Essential Dyke*
Personnel: Black Dyke Mills Band, James
Watson, conductor
Label: Doyen Recordings Ltd., 1994 CD: DOY
CD 034
MacMurrough, D./Hume: *Macushla*
Booth, Steven
Album Title: *Nova Scotia International Tat-
too—1996*
Personnel: Woods Manufacturing Brass Band
Label:
Monti, Vittorio: *Czárdás*
Booth, Steven
Album Title: *Reflections—Listen to the Band*
Personnel: Leyland Band
Label:
Anonymous: *Broken Melody*
Borrie, Bob
Album Title:
Personnel: Luton Band, Albert Coupe, con-
ductor
Label: Saga, 1969 LP: 8127
Hartmann, John: *Robin Adair*
Bos, Arjen. *See* Dutch Tuba Quartet
Bouise, Mark
Album Title: *American Landscapes*
Personnel: Sellers International Band, Phillip
McCann, conductor

Label: Doyen Recordings, 2003 CD: DOY
CD185
Foster, Stephen: *Jeanie with the Light Brown Hair*
Bowden, Ray
Album Title:
Personnel: Saint Sythians Band, E. Floyd, conductor
Label: Sentinel, 1970 LP: 1004
MacDowell, Edward/Ball: *To a Wild Rose*
Bowman, Brian
Album Title: *American Variations*
Personnel: Cincinnati Conservatory Wind Symphony, Eugene Corporon, conductor
Label: Klavier Recording Co., CD: KCD-11060
Clarke, Herbert L.: *Carnival of Venice, The*
Picchi, Ermano/Mantia: *Fantaisie Originale*
Romberg, Sigmund/Godfrey: *Serenade from "The Student Prince"*
Goldman, Edwin Franko: *Scherzo*
Bellstedt, Herman/Simon: *Napoli Variations*
Rogers, Walter: *Volunteer, The*
Bowman, Brian
Album Title: *The Brass Band of Columbus, Ohio*
Personnel: Brass Band of Columbus, Paul Droste, director
Label: Mark Records, 1988 CS: MW88-MC-20
Sparke, Philip: *Fantasy*
Bowman, Brian
Album Title: *Brian Bowman, Euphonium*
Personnel: Gordon Stout, marimba; Marjorie Lee, piano
Label: Crystal Records Co., 1978 LP: S393
Adler, Samuel: *Four Dialogs for Euphonium and Marimba*
Ross, Walter: *Partita for Euphonium and Piano*
Capuzzi, Antonio: *Andante and Rondo from "Doublebass Concerto"*
Boda, John: *Sonatina for Euphonium and Synthesizer*
Bowman, Brian
Album Title: *The Compositions of Alec Wilder*
Personnel: University of South Florida Wind Ensemble, James Croft, conductor; Frederick Fennell, guest conductor
Label: Golden Crest Records LP: ATH-5070
Wilder, Alec: *Concerto for Euphonium and Wind Ensemble*
Bowman, Brian
Album Title: *Forty-Third Mid-West Band and Orchestra Clinic*
Personnel: United States Armed Forces Tuba-Euphonium Ensemble
Label: Mark Records, 1989 CD: MW89MCD-8
Traditional/Garret: *Londonderry Air*
Bowman, Brian
Album Title: *The Henderson High School Wind Ensemble, 1987 Mid-West*
Personnel: Henderson High School Wind Ensemble

Label: Mark Records, 1987 CS: MW87-MC-8
Bellstedt, Herman: *Napoli*
Bowman, Brian
Album Title: *Live in Chicago*
Personnel: Tokyo Kosei Wind Orchestra, Douglas Bostock, conductor
Label: Mark Custom Recording Service, CD: MCD 4341
Ito, Yasuhide: *Fantasy Variations*
Bowman, Brian
Album Title: *1981 Mid-West National Band and Orchestra Clinic*
Personnel: The United States Air Force Band, Arnold Gabriel, conductor
Label: Silver Crest Records, 1981 LP: MID-81-5
Smith, Claude T.: *Concert Piece for Euphonium*
Bowman, Brian
Album Title: *1990 Mid-West International Band and Orchestra Clinic*
Personnel: Victor Bowman, cornet; The United States Air Force Band, Steven Grimo, conductor
Label: Mark Custom Recording Service, 1991 CD: MW-90MCD-7
Barnes, James: *Duo Concertante*
Bowman, Brian
Album Title: *1978 North Central Missouri Bandmasters Association Honors Band*
Personnel: Honors Band
Label: Audio House, 1978 LP: AHCI 138F78
Picchi, Ermano/Mantia: *Fantasia Originale*
Rimmer, William: *Hailstorm*
Bowman, Brian
Album Title: *On Tour*
Personnel: The United States Air Force Band
Label: United States Air Force Band. Public service, not for sale
Curnow, James: *Symphonic Variants for Euphonium and Band*
Bowman, Brian
Album Title: *On Winged Flight*
Personnel: Victor Bowman, cornet; The United States Air Force Band
Label: United States Air Force, BOL-8902ac
Barnes, James: *Duo Concertante*
Bowman, Brian
Album Title: *The Sacred Euphonium*
Personnel: James Welch, organ
Label: Mark Records, 1985 LP/CD: MRS-37883
Mendelssohn, Felix: *If with All Your Hearts*
Franck, Cesar: *Panis Angelicus*
O'Hara, Geoffrey: *I Walked Today Where Jesus Walked*
Adams, Stephen: *Holy City, The*
Yon, Pietro: *Gesu Bambino*
Malotte, Albert: *Lord's Prayer, The*
Brahe, May: *Bless This House*
Bizet, George: *Agnus Dei*
Bach, Johann Sebastian/Foote: *Air from "Suite No. 3 in D"*

Mendelssohn, Felix: *O Rest in the Lord*
Knapp, Mrs. Joseph/Henneman: *Open the Gates of the Temple*
Gounod, Charles: *O Divine Redeemer*
Bowman, Brian
  Album Title: *Spotlight–Outstanding Solo Performances*
  Personnel: The United States Air Force Band
  Label: United States Air Force Band. Public service, not for sale
  Boccalari, Ed/Kent-Akers: *Fantasia di Concerto*
Bowman, Brian
  Album Title: *St. Mary's College of Maryland Wind Ensemble*
  Personnel: St. Mary's College of Maryland Wind Ensemble, Robert Cameron, conductor
  Label: St. Mary's College, 1982 LP: KM 10222
  Curnow, James: *Symphonic Variants for Euphonium and Band*
Bowman, Brian
  Album Title: *Timpview High School Symphonic Band*
  Personnel: Timpview High School Symphonic Band
  Label: Mark Records, MW94MCD-17
  Clarke, Herbert L.: *Bride of the Waves, The*
  Pryor, Arthur: *Blue Bells of Scotland, The*
Bowman, Brian
  Album Title: *The United States Air Force Band*
  Personnel: The United States Air Force Band
  Label: Crest Records, 1978 LP: MENC-78-3
  Klengel, Julius/Odom: *Concertino No. 1, Op. 7*
Bowman, Brian
  Album Title: *The United States Air Force Band*
  Personnel: The United States Air Force Band
  Label: Crest Records, 1979 LP: MYSSMA-12279
  Boccalari, Ed/Kent-Akers: *Fantasia di Concerto*
Bowman, Brian
  Album Title: *U.S. Air Force Band on Tour*
  Personnel: The United States Air Force Band
  Label: United States Air Force. Public service, not for sale
  Curnow, James: *Symphonic Variants for Euphonium and Band*
Bowman, Brian. *See* Euphonium Section, The
Bowman, Brian. *See* Euphoniums Unlimited
Bowman, Brian. *See* Symphonia
Bowman, Brian. *See* United States Armed Forces Tuba-Euphonium Ensemble
Boyd, Frederick
  Album Title: *The Forty-Third American Bandmasters Association, 1977*
  Personnel: Sarasota Concert Band, Arthur Rohr, conductor
  Label: Silver Crest Records, 1977 LP: ABA-77-2
  Clarke, Herbert L.: *From the Shores of the Mighty Pacific*
  Clarke, Herbert L./Brandenburg: *Carnival of Venice, The*

Brasch, Harold
  Album Title: *Harold Brasch*
  Personnel: Band Accompaniment
  Label: H.B., LP: 001
  Rogers, Walter: *Volunteer, The*
Brasch, Harold
  Album Title: *Heritage of the March*
  Personnel: National Concert Band, Edmond DeMattia, conductor
  Label: Volume pppp
  Tchaikovsky, Piotr: *Dance of the Swans from "Swan Lake"*
  Romberg, Sigmund: *Serenade from "The Student Prince"*
Brasch, Harold
  Album Title: *International Music Camp Bands, Featuring Harold Brasch*
  Personnel: International Music Camp Bands, Merton Utgard, conductor
  Label: Mark Records, 1969 LP: UMC 2818; Century Records, 1976 LP: 35776
  Bach, Vincent: *Hungarian Melodies*
  Romberg, Sigmund: *Serenade from "The Student Prince"*
  Schmidt, Hugo: *Devil's Tongue, The*
  Rimmer, William: *Hailstorm*
  Arban, Jean Baptiste/Brasch: *Carnival of Venice, The*
  Mantia, Simone: *Believe Me if All Those Endearing Young Charms*
  Wren, Jenny/Davis: *Concert Polka*
  Pryor, Arthur: *Love's Enchantment*
Brasch, Harold
  Album Title: *Mr. Euphonium, in Actual Performance*
  Personnel:
  Label: Harold Brasch
  Clarke, Herbert/Manning/Brasch: *Carnival of Venice, The*
  Wren, Jenny/Davis: *Concert Polka*
  Bellstedt, Herman: *La Coquette*
  Romberg, Sigmund: *Serenade from "The Student Prince"*
  Schmidt, Hugo: *Devil's Tongue, The*
  Brahe, May: *Bless This House*
  Bellstedt, Herman: *La Mandolinata*
  Brasch, Harold: *Weber's Last Waltz Fantasie*
Brasch, Harold
  Album Title: *Neptune's Court*
  Personnel: Jane Rathburn, piano
  Label: H.B., LP: 003
Bray, Mark
  Album Title:
  Personnel: Horbury Victoria Band, Elgar Howarth, conductor
  Label: Horbury Victoria Band, 1982 LP: HVB 1001
  Foster, Stephen/Howarth: *Jeannie with the Light Brown Hair*
Breuninger, Tyrone
  Album Title: *The Classical Euphonium*

Personnel: David Booth, pianist
Label: Tyrone Breuninger, 1999 CD: RG28512
Traditional/Drover: *Wee Cooper of Fire*
Capuzzi, Antonio: *Andante and Rondo from "Doublebass Concerto"*
Sparke, Philip: *Aubade*
Horovitz, Joseph: *Euphonium Concerto*
Ewald, Victor/Reed: *Romance, Op. 2*
Curnow, James: *Rhapsody for Euphonium*
Saint-Saëns, Camille/Larendeau: *My Heart at Thy Sweet Voice*
Sparke, Philip: *Fantasy*
Bridge, Kenneth
  Album Title:
  Personnel: Slaithwaite Band, Roy Newsome, conductor
  Label: Look, LP: 6028
  Mantia, Simone/Langford: *Believe Me if All Those Endearing Young Charms*
Brighton, Charley
  Album Title:
  Personnel: Alder Valley Aldershot Brass, Clive Rubery, conductor
  Label: Alder Valley, 1986 LP: AV 001
  Foster, Stephen/Howarth: *Jeannie with the Light Brown Hair*
British Tuba Quartet, The
  Album Title: *Boosey and Hawkes National Brass Band Championships of Great Britain, 1991*
  Personnel: Steven Mead, Michael Howard, euphonium; Ken Ferguson, Stuart Birnie, tuba
  Label: Polyphonic Reproductions Ltd., 1991 CD: QDRL 049D
  Frackenpohl, Arthur: *Pop Suite* (last movement)
British Tuba Quartet, The
  Album Title: *Elite Syncopations*
  Personnel: Steven Mead, Michael Howard, euphonium, Ken Ferguson, Stuart Birnie, tuba
  Label: Polyphonic Reproductions Ltd., 1993 CD: QPRZ 012D
  Glinka/Ferguson/Smalley: *Russlan and Ludmila*
  Rossini, Gioacchino/Smalley: *La Danza*
  Chopin, Frédéric/Mead: *Minute Waltz*
  Martino, Ralph: *Fantasy*
  Bull, John/Howard: *King's Hunt, The*
  Gabrieli, Giovanni/Rauch: *Canzona, La Spiritata*
  Tchaikovsky, Piotr/Smalley: *Trepak*
  Strauss, Johann/Smalley: *Chit Chat Polka*
  Gershwin, George/Ferguson: *Fascinatin' Gershwin*
  Sherwin, Manning/Smalley: *A Nightingale Sang in Berkeley Square*
  Dubin and Warren/Minard: *42nd Street*
  Schönberg, Claude-Michel/Mead: *On My Own*
  Joplin, Scott/Picher: *Elite Syncopations*
  Horovitz, Joseph: *Rumpole of the Bailey*
  Berlin, Irving/Gout: *Puttin' on the Ritz*

Dempsey, arr.: *Three Movements from "Quatre Chansons"*
Niehaus, Lennie: *Grand Slam*
Wolking, Henry: *Tuba Blues*
British Tuba Quartet, The
  Album Title: *Euphonic Sounds*
  Personnel: Steven Mead, Michael Howard, euphonium; Stuart Birnie, Ken Ferguson, tuba
  Label: Polyphonic Reproductions Ltd., 1992 CD: QPRZ 009D
  Bulla, Stephen: *Celestial Suite*
  Diero/Ferguson: *Il Ritorno*
  Kern, Jerome/Holcombe: *They Didn't Believe Me*
  Ramsöe, Emilio/Buttery: *Quartet for Brass*
  Di Lasso/Robinson: *Mon Coeur Se Recommende a Vous*
  Byrd, William/Winter: *John, Come Kisse Me Now*
  Powell, Baden/Buttery: *Bocoxe*
  Joplin, Scott/Sabourin: *Favorite Rag, The*
  Traditional/Niehaus: *Spiritual Jazz Suite*
  Traditional/Buttery: *Greensleeves*
  Lemer and Loewe/Belshaw: *Get Me to the Church on Time*
  Bach, Johann Sebastian/Werden: *Air from "Suite No. 3 in D"*
  Mancini, Henry/Krush: *Pink Panther, The*
  Joplin, Scott/Werden: *Euphonic Sounds*
  Manaco/Holcombe: *You Made Me Love You*
  Rossini, Gioacchino/Smalley: *William Tell Overture*
British Tuba Quartet, The
  Album Title: *Fireworks*
  Personnel: Steven Mead, Michael Howard, euphonium; Ken Ferguson, Stuart Birnie, tuba
  Label: Polyphonic Reproductions Ltd., 1997 CD: QDRL 20
  Taylor, Jeffrey: *Fanfare No. 1*
  Nicolai, Otto: *Merry Wives of Windsor Overture*
  Delibes: *Flower Duet from "Lakme"*
  Dempsey, Ray: *Now Hear This*
  Purcell, Henry: *Distressed Innocence Overture*
  Amos, Keith: *Flander's Cauldron*
  Verdi, Giuseppi: *Force of Destiny Overture*
  Ridout, Alan: *Pigs*
  Forsyth, Kieran: *Westminster Intrada*
  Kupferman, Meyer: *Kierkegaard*
  Frith, John: *Fireworks*
  Rossini, Gioacchino: *Petit Caprice in the Style of Offenbach*
  Prokofiev, Sergey: *Montagues and Capulets*
  Strauss, Johann: *Perpetuum Mobile*
  Smalley, Peter: *A Cool Suite*
  Traditional: *Bavarian Polka*
British Tuba Quartet, The
  Album Title: *In at the Deep End*
  Personnel: Steven Mead, Michael Howard, euphonium; Ken Ferguson, Stuart Birnie, tuba

Label: Heavyweight Records Ltd., 1991 CD:
HR008/D
Bulla, Stephen: *Quartet for Low Brass*
Sousa, John Philip/Morris: *Semper Fidelis*
Frackenpohl, Arthur: *Pop Suite*
Saint-Saëns, Camille/Murley: *Adagio from
"Symphony No. 3"*
Bach, Johann Sebastian/Werden: *Jesu, Joy of
Man's Desiring*
Mozart, Wolfgang Amadeus/Ferguson: *Over-
ture from the "Marriage of Figaro"*
Rimsky-Korsakov, Nicolai: *Notturno*
Heusen, Van/Barton: *Here's That Rainy Day*
Bach, Johann Sebastian/Gray: *Fugue from
"Fantasia and Fugue in g Minor"*
Sousa, John Philip/Morris: *El Capitan*
Cheetham, John: *Consortium*
Joplin, Scott/Sabourin: *Cascades, The*
Anonymous/Baker: *Lute Dances*
Holmes, Paul: *Quartet for Tubas*
Hook, J./Garrett: *Rondo*
Bach, Johann Sebastian/Howard: *Rondo*
Traditional/Garrett: *Wabash Cannonball*
Traditional/Trippet/Howard: *Steal Away*
Sousa, John Philip/Sabourin: *Washington Post*
British Tuba Quartet, The
Album Title: *March to the Scaffold*
Personnel: Steven Mead, Michael Howard,
euphonium; Ken Ferguson, Stuart Birnie,
tuba
Label: Polyphonic Reproductions Ltd., 1994
CD: QPRZ 013D
Sousa, John Philip: *Thunderer, The*
Traditional: *Havah Nagilah*
Tchaikovsky, Piotr: *Danse of the Sugar Plum
Fairy*
McHugh, Jimmy: *On the Sunny Side of the Street*
Smalley, Peter: *Glyder Landscape, The*
Lefébure, Louis-François: *Sortie in Eb*
Lundquist, Trobjörn: *Triplet for Four Tubas*
Bach, Johann Sebastian/Gray: *Fugue from
"Fantasia and Fugue in g Minor"*
Jewell: *Battle Royal*
Purcell, Henry: *Dido's Lament from "Dido and
Aeneas"*
Hartley, Walter: *Miniatures for Four Valve
Instruments*
Mozart, Wolfgang Amadeus: *Turkish March*
Premru: *In Memoriam*
Morley, Thomas: *April Is in My Mistress' Face*
Reeman: *Sonatina for Tuba Quartet*
Berlioz, Hector: *March to the Scaffold*
Brown, William
Album Title:
Personnel: Canadian Staff Band, Norman Bear-
croft, conductor
Label: Salvation Army Label, 1971 LP: CSB2
Bowes, R.: *Song of Triumph*
Brown, William
Album Title:
Personnel: Canadian Staff Band, Robert Red-
head, conductor

Label: Festival Records, 1977 LP: CSB27707
Himes, William: *My Christ*
Brunner, Stefan
Album Title: *Crazy Little Things*
Personnel: Nderegg Raphael, euphonium;
Beraagauer Brass Band
Label: Obrasso, CD: 865
Anonymous: *To All the Girls I've Loved Before*
Anonymous: *As Long As He Needs Me*
Bulter, James
Album Title:
Personnel: Kirbymoorside Town Band, L.
Maw, conductor
Label: Look, 1980 LP: LP 6471
Langford, Gordon: *Blaydon Races, The*
Burba, Malte
Album Title: *Le vertige des profondeurs*
Personnel:
Label: Thorofon, CTH 2198
Sell, Michael: *Death and Rebirth*
Hlszky, Adriana: *Corners of the World*
Burgess, Gary. *See* Euphonium Section, The
Burghgraef, Frans Aert
Album Title: *Impressive Brass*
Personnel: Provinciale Brassband Groningen,
Siemen Hoekstra, conductor
Label: World Wind Music, 2002 CD: WWM
500.083
Dewhurst, Robin: *Panache*
Burleson, Don
Album Title: *The United States Army Field Band*
Personnel: The United States Army Field Band
Label: United States Army Field Band. Public
service, not for sale
Wren, Jenny/Davis/Brasch: *Concert Polka*
Butler, John
Album Title: *The Salvation Army Melbourne
Territorial Staff Band*
Personnel: Melbourne Territorial Staff Band of
the Salvation Army Southern Australia Head-
quarters, Norman K. McLeod, conductor
Label: Fidelity Sound Recordings, 1959 LP:
FSR-1218
Kjellgren, G.: *My Light and Song*
Campbell, Larry
Album Title: *Master Solos—Intermediate Level,
Baritone*
Personnel:
Label: Hal Leonard Publishing Co.
Arcadelt, Jacob: *Credo*
Carissmi: *Vittoria! Vittoria!*
Handel, George Frederic: *Sarabande and
Minuet*
Arcadelt, Jacob: *Gloria*
Saint-Saëns, Camille: *Swan, The*
Haydn, Franz Josef: *Two Classical Themes*
Wilson: *Three Miniatures*
Campbell, Larry. *See* Symphonia
Cant, Ken. *See* Williams, Glyn
Cay-Lennart
Album Title: *CAndY Stompers Big Band*
Personnel: CAndY Stompers Big Band

Label: GMH Records, Sundbyberg, Sweden
Cay-Lennart: *Gotlandsk Sommarnatt*
Cay-Lennart: *Joshua Fought the Battle of Jeriko*
Champions of the Leonard Falcone Festival 1986–2000
   Album Title: *The Legacy*
   Personnel: Angie Hunter, David Lang, Ken-ichi Watanabe, Marc Dickman, Robin Taylor, David Cleveland, Matthew Tropman, Takeshi Hatano, Jeremy VanHoy, Adam Frey, Benjamin Pierce, Jamie Van Valkenberg, euphonium
   Label: Bernel Music, 2000 CD: 10014
   Bourgeois, Derek: *Allegro from "Concerto, Op. 114"*
   White, Donald: *Lyric Suite*
   Ito, Yasuhide: *Fantasy Variations*
   Smith, Robert: *Willson Suite*
   Corwell, Neal: *Odyssey*
   Bourgeois, Derek: *Euphoria*
   Fauré, Gabriel: *Papillon, Op. 77*
   Picchi, Ermano/Mantia/Falcone: *Fantaisie Originale*
   Klengel, Julius: *Concerto No. 1*
   Bach, Johann Sebastian: *Courante from "Suite No. 4"*
   Sandoval, Migul: *Sin tu Amor*
   Flotow von, Friedrich: *Last Rose of Summer, The*
   Cosma, Vladimir: *Finale from "Euphonium Concerto"*
   Ponchielli, Amilcare/Howey: *Concerto per Flicorno Basso*
Cherry, Bill. *See* Tennessee Tech Tuba-Euphonium Quintet
Chevailler, Jean-Pierre
   Album Title: *The Classic Euphonium*
   Personnel: City of London Sinfonia, George Lloyd, conductor
   Label: Albany Records, 1989 CD: TROY 201-2
   Handel, George Frederic: *Concerto in f Minor*
   Mozart, Wolfgang Amadeus: *Concerto in B♭, K-191*
   Danzi: *Concerto in F Major*
Childs Brothers
   Album Title: *Brass Band "De Bazuin," Oenkerk*
   Personnel: Robert Childs, Nicholas Childs, euphonium; Brass Band "De Bazuin," Klaas Van Der Woude, conductor
   Label: Stemra, 1989 CD: KRO/NOB
   Bryce, F.: *Rondoletto*
   Fraser, Bruce: *Fantastic Fast Finger Fandango, The*
   Graham, Peter: *Brilliante*
   DeVita, Alfred/Catherall: *Softly As I Leave You*
   Rimsky-Korsakov, Nikolai/Woude: *Flight of the Bumble Bee, The*
Childs Brothers
   Album Title: *British Bandsman Centenary Concert*
   Personnel: Robert Childs, Nicholas Childs, euphonium; various brass bands

Label: Chandos Records Ltd., CD: CHAN 8571
Graham, Peter: *Brilliante*
Paganini, Niccolo/Snell: *Moto Perpetuo*
Childs Brothers
   Album Title: *Childs Play*
   Personnel: Robert Childs, Nicholas Childs, euphonium; various brass bands
   Label: Doyen Recordings Ltd., 1989 CD: DOY CD 001
   Arban, Jean Baptiste/Farr: *Carnival of Venice, The*
   Wilkinson, Keith, arr.: *Deep inside the Sacred Temple*
   Handel, George Frederic/Wilson, arr.: *Arrival of the Queen of Sheba*
   Jenkins, Alan, arr.: *Myfanwy*
   Wyss, Thomas, arr.: *Rondo Alla Turca*
   Woodfield, Ray: *Double Brass*
   Snell, Howard, arr.: *Moto Perpetuo*
   DeVita, Alfred/Catherall: *Softly As I Leave You*
   Golland, John: *Childs Play*
   Fraser, Bruce, arr.: *Perhaps Love*
   Ball, Eric, arr.: *Calon Lan*
   Childs, Nicholas, arr.: *Parade of the Tin Soldiers*
   Howarth, Elgar, arr.: *Grand Study No. 13*
   Graham, Peter: *Brilliante*
Childs Brothers
   Album Title: *CWS Glasgow Band Meet the Sovereign Soloists*
   Personnel: Robert Childs, Nicholas Childs, euphonium; CWS Glasgow Band, Frank Renton, conductor
   Label: Doyen Recordings Ltd., CD: DOY CD 012
   Bizet, George/Wilkinson: *Deep inside the Sacred Temple*
   Woodfield, Ray: *Varied Mood*
   Rossini, Gioacchino: *Largo Al Factotum*
Childs Brothers
   Album Title: *Euphonium Music*
   Personnel: Nicholas Childs, Robert Childs, euphonium; Britannia Building Society Band, Howard Snell, conductor
   Label: Doyen Recordings Ltd., 1990 CD: DOY CD002
   Bowen, Brian: *Euphonium Music*
   Curnow, James: *Rhapsody*
   Phillips, John: *Romance*
   Stephens, Denzil: *Solo Rhapsody for Euphonium*
   Golland, John: *Euphonium Concerto No. 1, Op. 64*
   Howarth, Elgar: *Cantabile for John Fletcher*
   Sparke, Philip: *Fantasy for Euphonium*
Childs Brothers
   Album Title: *1984 Brass Band Festival*
   Personnel: Robert Childs, Nicholas Childs, euphonium; combined bands
   Label: Chandos Records Lyd., BBRD 1028
   Arban, Jean Baptiste/Farr: *Carnival of Venice, The*

DeVita, Alfred/Catherall: *Softly As I Leave You*
Childs Brothers
Album Title: *The Song of the Brother*
Personnel: Robert Childs, Nicholas Childs, euphonium; London Citadel Band of the Salvation Army
Label: Salvationist Supplies & Publishing, 1993 CD: SPSLCB 18
Larson, John/Bosanko: *I'll Not Turn Back*
Bearcroft, Norman: *Better World*
Bearcroft, Norman: *Timepiece*
Foster, Stephen/Steadman-Allen: *My Story and Song*
Gregson, Edward: *Symphonic Rhapsody for Euphonium and Band*
Leidzen, Erik: *Song of the Brother, The*
Marshall, George: *Ransomed*
Saint-Saëns, Camille/Steadman-Allen: *Swan, The*
Steadman-Allen, Ray: *Conqueror, The*
Twitchen, Bert: *Silver Threads*
Childs Brothers
Album Title: *Sovereign Soloists, Volume 1*
Personnel: Robert Childs, Nicholas Childs, euphonium; Rochdale Band, Richard Evans, conductor
Label: Doyen Recordings Ltd., 1990 CD: DOY CD 003
Mantia, Simone/Boddington: *Believe Me if All Those Endearing Young Charms*
Hamlisch/Barry: *Way We Were, The*
Sparke, Philip: *Two-Part Invention*
Cardillo/Stephens: *Catari, Catari*
Sparke, Philip: *Pantomime*
Childs Brothers
Album Title: *Stars in Brass*
Robert Childs, Nicholas Childs, euphonium; Grimethorpe Colliery Band, Frank Renton, conductor
Label: Doyen Recordings Ltd., 1994 CD: DOY CD 035
Arban, Jean Baptiste/Farr: *Carnival of Venice, The*
DeVita, Alfred/Catherall: *Softly As I Leave You*
Childs Brothers
Album Title: *Sun Burst*
Personnel: Robert Childs, Nicholas Childs, euphonium; The United States Army Brass Band, Thomas H. Palmatier, conductor
Label: The United States Army Brass Band, 1993. Public service, not for sale
Graham, Peter: *Brilliante*
Denver, John/Fraser: *Perhaps Love*
Fraser, Bruce: *Fantastic Fast Fingered Fandango, The*
Childs Brothers
Album Title: *Welsh Wizards*
Personnel: Robert Childs, Nicholas Childs, euphonium; Tredegar Band, EYMS (Hull) Band

Label: Doyen Recordings Ltd., 1993 CD: DOY CD 022
Barry, Darrol: *Fascinating Euphs.*
Brodsky, Nicholas/Farr: *Be My Love*
Fraser, Bruce: *Fantastic Fast Fingered Fandango, The*
Catherall, Alan, arr.: *Elfriede*
Elgar, Edward/Wilson: *Salut d'amour*
Powell, T. J.: *Duo for Euphoniums*
Catherall, Alan, arr.: *Song of the Seashore*
Sparke, Philip: *Pantomime*
Rimsky-Korsakov, Nikolai/Newsome: *Flight of the Bumble Bee, The*
Catherall, Alan, arr.: *Only Love*
Newsome, Roy: *A Piece of Cake*
Rossini, Gioacchino: *Largo Al Factotum*
Ball, Eric, arr.: *Calon Lan*
Monti, Vittorio/Wilson: *Czárdás*
Yamada, Kosaku/Yamamoto: *Aka Tonbi*
Sparke, Philip: *Two-Part Invention*
Childs Brothers
Album Title:
Personnel: Robert Childs, Nicholas Childs, euphonium; Yorkshire Imperial Band, Ray Farr, conductor
Label:
Arban, Jean Baptiste/Farr: *Carnival of Venice, The*
Childs Brothers
Album Title:
Personnel: Robert Childs, Nicholas Childs, euphonium; Besses o' th' Barn Band, Roy Newsome, conductor; Yorkshire Imperial Band, John Childs, conductor
Label: Chandos Records Ltd., LP: BBRD 1035
DeVita, Alfred/Catherall: *Softly As I Leave You*
Paganini, Niccolo/Snell: *Moto Perpetuo*
Childs, David
Album Title: *Brass Band Classics, Volume 2*
Personnel: Buy As You View Cory Band, Robert Childs, conductor
Label: Doyen Recordings, 2003 CD: DOY CD155
Wright, Frank, arr.: *Le Roi d'Ys*
Childs, David
Album Title: *Hear My Prayer*
Personnel: Hendon Band of the Salvation Army; Philip Wilby, organ; Georgina Wells, harp
Label: Doyen Recordings, 2003 CD: DOY CD166
Lyte: *Abide with Me*
Bach, Johann Sebastian/Gounod: *Ave Maria*
Jenkins: *Hymn from "Adiemus"*
Mascagni: *Easter Hymn*
Bizet, George: *Pearl Fishers Duet*
Adam: *O Holy Night*
Jenkins: *Benedictus*
Mendelssohn, Felix: *Hear My Prayer*
Sullivan: *Lost Chord, The*
Traditional: *Swedish Hymn*
Bennard: *Old Rugged Cross, The*

Brahe, May: *Bless This House*
Godard: *Angels Guard Thee*
Mendelssohn, Felix: *If with All Your Heart*
Redhead, Robert: *Comfort My People*
Saint-Saëns, Camille: *Softly Awakes My Heart*
Webster/Brodsky: *I'll Walk with God*
Childs, David
   Album Title: *Metamorphosis*
   Personnel: The Royal Northern College of
     Music Wind and Symphony Orchestras,
     James Gourlay, conductor
   Label: Doyen Recordings Ltd., 2001 CD:
     DOY CD 134
   Wilby, Philip: *Concerto for Euphonium*
   Monti, Vittorio/D. Childs: *Czárdás*
   Morricone, Ennio/D. Childs: *Gabriel's Oboe*
   Alfén, Hugo/R. Childs: *Dance of the Herd-
     maiden*
   Clarke, Nigel: *City in the Sea*
   Arban, Jean Baptiste/G. Kingston: *Carnival of
     Venice, The*
   Stamford, Charles Villes/R. Childs: *Caoine*
   Rimsky-Korsakov, Nikolai/D. Childs: *Flight of
     the Bumble Bee, The*
   Graham, Peter/D. McGiboney: *Brilliante*
   Rutti, Carl: *Metamorphosis*
Childs, David
   Album Title: *Prodigy*
   Personnel: Brighouse and Rastrick Band, Rob-
     ert Childs, guest conductor; Jo Sealy, John
     Wilson, piano; Tiziana Tagliani, harp; Helena
     Roques, Stephen Cordiner, violin; Fran
     Higgs-Strange, Katy Miller, viola; Burak,
     double bass
   Label: Doyen Recordings Ltd., 2000 CD:
     DOY CD 104
   Newton, Rodney: *Caelidh*
   Saint-Saëns, Camille/D. Childs: *Swan, The*
   Arban, Jean Baptiste/D. Childs: *Carnival of
     Venice, The*
   Glennie, Evelyn/R. Childs: *A Little Prayer*
   Squire, W. H./R. Childs: *Tarantella*
   Traditional/J. Iveson: *Londonderry Air*
   Traditional/P. Graham: *Swedish Hymn*
   Hartmann, John: *La Belle Americaine*
   Traditional/Stephens: *Carrickfergus*
   Golland, John: *Peace*
   Puccini, Giacomo/D. Childs: *Nessun Dorma*
   Traditional/Baker: *Spread Your Wide Wings*
   Doughty, George: *Grandfather's Clock*
   Bach, Johann Sebastian/D. Childs: *Air from
     "Suite in D"*
   Lusher, Don: *Concert Variations*
   DeVita, Alfred/Catherall: *Softly As I Leave You*
   Woodfield, Ray: *Varied Mood*
Childs, David
   Album Title: *2003 European Championships*
   Personnel: Buy As You View Cory Band, Rob-
     ert Childs, conductor
   Label: Doyen Recordings, 2003 CD: DOY
     CD153

Arban, Jean Baptiste/Catherall: *Carnival of
     Venice, The*
Childs, David. *See* Mead, Steven
Childs, Nicholas
   Album Title: *Grimethorpe Entertains*
   Personnel: Grimethorpe Colliery Band, David
     James, conductor
   Label: Strawberry Studios, 1986: NMS 402/
     MM0624
   Pryor, Arthur: *Blue Bells of Scotland, The*
Childs, Nicholas
   Album Title: *King Size Brass*
   Personnel: Grimethorpe Colliery Band, Ray
     Farr, conductor
   Polyphonic Reproductions, Ltd., 1980:
     PRL 004
   Hartmann, John: *La Belle Americane*
Childs, Nicholas
   Album Title: *Master Brass, Volume 3*
   Personnel: various brass bands
   Label: Polyphonic Reproductions, Ltd.
   Sparke, Philip: *Pantomime*
Childs, Nicholas
   Album Title: *Mountain Song*
   Personnel: Brass Band Berner Oberland, James
     Gourlay, conductor
   Label: Doyen Recordings Ltd., CD: DOY CD
     025
   Traditional/Collins/French/Newsome: *Moun-
     tains of Mourne, The*
Childs, Nicholas
   Album Title: *Rule Britannia*
   Personnel: Britannia Building Society Band,
     Howard Snell, conductor
   Label: Doyen Recordings Ltd., 1990 CD:
     DOY CD 004
   Bizet, George: *Flower Song from "Carmen"*
Childs, Nicholas
   Album Title: *The Year of the Dragon*
   Personnel: Robert Childs, Nicholas Childs,
     euphonium; Britannia Building Society
     Band, Howard Snell, conductor
   Label: Doyen Recordings Ltd., CD: DOY CD
     021
   DeVita, Alfred/Catherall: *Softly As I Leave You*
Childs, Nicholas. *See* Childs Brothers
Childs, Nicholas. *See* Mead, Steven
Childs, Robert
   Album Title: *Arrivederci Grimethorpe*
   Personnel: Grimethorpe Colliery Band, Ray
     Farr, conductor
   Label: Look Records, 1980: LK/LP-6482
   Mantia, Simone/Stanley: *Believe Me if All Those
     Endearing Young Charms*
Childs, Robert
   Album Title: *Cathedral Brass*
   Personnel: Black Dyke Mills Band, James Wat-
     son, conductor
   Label: Doyen Recordings Ltd., CD: DOY
     CD 060
   Franck, Cesar: *Panis Angelicus*

Childs, Robert
Album Title: *Concerto*
Personnel: Black Dyke Mills Band, Major Peter
Parkes, conductor
Label: Chandos Records Ltd., 1989 CD:
CHAN 8793
Horovitz, Joseph: *Euphonium Concerto*
Childs, Robert
Album Title: *The Essential Dyke*
Personnel: Black Dyke Mills Band, James Watson, conductor
Label: Doyen Recordings Ltd., 1994 CD:
DOY CD 034
Hartmann, John/Stephens: *Rule Britannia*
Childs, Robert
Album Title: *The Great Revival*
Personnel: Black Dyke Mills Band, James Watson, conductor
Label: De Haske Music Records
Evenepoel, Johan: *Rhapsody for Euphonium*
Childs, Robert
Album Title: *Live, at the World Music Contest 1997*
Personnel: Brass Band du Conservatoire d'Esch-sur-Alzette
Label: World Music Contest, 1997
Sparke, Philip: *Fantasy for Euphonium*
Wilby, Philip: *Paganini Variations*
Childs, Robert
Album Title: *On the Bandstand*
Personnel: Brighouse and Rastrick Band
Label: Polyphonic Reproductions, Ltd., PRL 031D
Arban, Jean Baptiste/Catherall: *Carnival of Venice, The*
Childs, Robert
Album Title: *Première*
Personnel: Black Dyke Mills Band, James Watson, conductor
Label: Doyen Recordings Ltd., 1997 CD:
DOY CD 061
Hummel, Johann Nepomuk/R. Childs: *Fantasy*
Capuzzi, Antonio/R. Childs: *Andante and Rondo*
Mozart, Wolfgang Amadeus/R. Childs: *Adagio and Rondo*
Fiocco, Joseph Hector/R. Childs: *Arioso and Allegro*
Clarke, Nigel: *City in the Sea*
Wilby, Philip: *Concerto for Euphonium*
Childs, Robert
Album Title: *Prestige*
Personnel: Royal Norwegian Navy Band, Nigel Boddice, conductor
Label: Doyen Recordings Ltd., CD: DOY CD 107
Bellstedt, Herman/Childs: *Napoli*
Golland, John/Ashmore: *Peace*
Woodfield, Ray: *Varied Mood*
Drigo, Riccardo/Wright: *Serenade from "Millions d'Arlequin"*

Mantia, Simone/Moore: *Believe Me if All Those Endearing Young Charms*
DeLuca, Joseph/Roberts: *Beautiful Colorado*
Templeton, Alec/Childs: *Sonia*
Wilby, Philip: *Song and Greek Dance from "Concerto for Euphonium"*
Jacob, Gordon: *Fantasia*
Horovitz, Joseph: *Concerto for Euphonium*
Childs, Robert
Album Title: *Revelations*
Personnel: Black Dyke Mills Band, James Watson, conductor
Label: Doyen Recordings Ltd., 1996 CD:
DOY CD 046
Arban, Jean Baptiste/Camerata/Catherall: *Carnival of Venice, The*
Childs, Robert
Album Title: *Sacred Symphonies*
Personnel: Black Dyke Mills Band, James Watson, conductor
Label Doyen Recordings Ltd., 1996 CD: DOY CD 053
Wilby, Philip: *Concert Galop*
Childs, Robert
Album Title: *Sir Edward Elgar, Volume III*
Personnel: Desford Colliery Band and Feden O.T.S. Band
Label: Polyphonic Reproductions, Ltd., EHS 002D
Elgar, Edward/Bourgeois: *Adagio and Allegro from "Cello Concerto"*
Childs, Robert
Album Title:
Personnel: Tredegar Band, T. Williams, conductor
Label: Decca, 1975 LP: SB 320
Gheel, Henry, arr.: *Watching the Wheat*
Childs, Robert. *See* Childs Brothers
Childs, Robert. *See* Mead, Steven
Christian, Peter
Album Title: *The Great British Tradition*
Personnel: Black Dyke Mills Band, Major Peter Parkes, conductor
Label: Chandos Records Ltd., BBRD-1024
Langford, Gordon: *Sally in Our Alley*
Church, David
Album Title: *Crossover*
Personnel: Pasadena Tabernacle Band
Label: Pasadena Tabernacle Band, 1997 CD:
PTB1997
Bulla, Stephen: *Euphonium Fantasia*
Gordon, William: *Gospel Crossover*
Church, David
Album Title: *Monuments of Brass Band Literature*
Personnel: National Capital Band
Label: National Capital Band, CD: CR009
Chaulk, David: *Variants on St. Francis*
Clark, Alan. *See* Tennessee Tech Tuba-Euphonium Quintet

Clark, Trevor
  Album Title:
  Personnel: Hamilton Citadel Band
  Label: Priceless Treasure, 1985 LP: PRA51
  Steadman-Allen, Ray: *Love Lifted Me*
Cleveland, David
  Album Title: *"To The Fore," Percy Grainger's Great Symphonic Band Music*
  Personnel: Michigan State University Symphonic Band, Keith Brion, conductor
  Label: Delos Records, LP: 3101; CD: DE 3101
  Faure, Gabriel/Grainger: *Tuscan Serenade*
Cleveland, David. *See* Champions of the Leonard Falcone Festival 1986–2000
Clough, John
  Album Title: *Black Dyke Plays Rossini*
  Personnel: Black Dyke Mills Band, Trevor Walmsley, conductor
  Label: Chandos Records Ltd., 1983 LP: BBRD 1021; 1992 CD: CHAN 4505
  Rossini, Gioacchino/Langford: *Largo Al Factotum*
Clough, John
  Album Title: *The Champions*
  Personnel: Black Dyke Mills Band, Roy Newsome, conductor
  Label: Pye Records, GSGL 10410
  Doughty, George: *Grandfather's Clock*
Clough, John
  Album Title: *Kings of Brass*
  Personnel: Black Dyke Mills Band, Michael Antrobus, associate conductor
  Label: Chandos Records, 1979 LP: BBR 1011
  Drigo/Wright: *Serenade*
Clough, John
  Album Title: *150 Years of Black Dyke Mills Band*
  Personnel: Black Dyke Mills Band
  Label: Chandos Records, Ltd. CD
  Toselli, Enrico: *Serenata*
Clough, John
  Album Title: *A Russian Festival*
  Personnel: Black Dyke Mills Band, Michael Antrobus, associate conductor
  Label: Chandos Records Ltd., 1981, 1992 CD: CHAN 4519
  Rachmaninov, Sergei/Langford: *Vocalise Op. 34, No. 14*
Clough, John
  Album Title: *Traditionally British*
  Personnel: Black Dyke Mills Band
  Label: Chandos Records, Ltd. CD
  Langford, Gordon: *Blaydon Races, The*
Clough, John
  Album Title: *The Virtuosi Brass Band of Great Britain, Volume V*
  Personnel: Trevor Groom, euphonium; The Virtuosi Brass Band of Great Britain
  Label: Kirklees Music, CD: KRCD 1024
  Saint-Saëns, Camille/Mott: *Le Cygne, Euphonium Duet*

Clough, John
  Album Title: *The Virtuosi Brass Band of Great Britain, Volume I*
  Personnel: Trevor Groom, euphonium; The Virtuosi Brass Band of Great Britain
  Label: Kirklees Music, CD: KRCD 1020
  Bryce, F.: *Rondoletto for Two Euphoniums*
Clough, John
  Album Title:
  Personnel: Black Dyke Mills Band, Roy Newsome, conductor
  Label: Pye Records, GSGL 10391
  Arban, Jean Baptiste/Remington: *Carnival of Venice, The*
Clough, John
  Album Title:
  Personnel: Black Dyke Mills Band, Roy Newsome, conductor
  Label: RCA, 1975 LP: LSA 3186
  Hartmann, John: *Rule Britannia*
Clough, John
  Album Title:
  Personnel: Black Dyke Mills Band, Roy Newsome, conductor
  Label: Decca, 1973 LP: SB 305
  Traditional/Collins/French/Newsome: *Mountains of Mourne, The*
Clough, John
  Album Title:
  Label: Pye Records, 1971 LP: GSGL 10477
  Mozart, Wolfgang Amadeus/Henstridge: *Allegro from "Bassoon Concerto"*
Clough, John. *See* Groom, Trevor
Coast Guard Tuba-Euphonium Quartet
  Album Title: *The Musical Sounds of the Seasons*
  Personnel: David Werden, Roger Behrend, euphonium; Gary Buttery, John Banker, tuba
  Label: United States Coast Guard Band, 1981 LP. Public service, not for sale
  Buttery, Gary, arr.: *An English Folk Christmas*
Coast Guard Tuba-Euphonium Quartet
  Album Title: *The United States Coast Guard Band, Soloists and Chamber Players*
  Personnel: David Werden, Denis Winter, euphonium; Gary Buttery, David Chaput, tuba
  Label: The United States Coast Guard, LP: USCG122678. Public service, not for sale
  Ramsöe, Emilio: *Quartet for Brass*
Cochran, Darin. *See* Tennessee Technological University Alumni Tuba-Euphonium Ensemble
Cochran, Darin. *See* Top Brass
Codd, E.
  Album Title:
  Personnel: Barton upon Humber Salvation Army Band, D. Woodcock, conductor
  Label: Deroy Records, LP: 1263
  Saint-Saëns, Camille/Steadman-Allen: *Swan, The*
Colburn, Michael
  Album Title: *The Golden Age of Brass, Volume 3*

Personnel: American Serenade Band, Henry
  Charles Smith, conductor
Label: Summit Records, 1993 CD: DCD 150
Mantia, Simone/Branson: *Auld Lang Syne*
Ponchielli, Amilcare/Howey: *Concerto per
  Flicorno basso*
Puccini, Giacomo/Colburn: *O, Mio Babbino
  Caro*
Schmidt, Hugo: *Devil's Tongue, The*
Foster, Stephen: *Gentle Annie*
Mantia, Simone/Eichner: *Believe Me if All
  Those Endearing Young Charms*
Sousa, John Philip: *I've Made Plans for the
  Summer*
Bellstedt, Herman: *Betty Lee*
Fauré, Gabriel/Grainger: *Tuscan Serenade*
DeLuca, Joseph/Hazes: *Thoughts of Gold*
Picchi, Ermano/Mantia: *Fantaisie Originale*
Colburn, Michael. *See* United States Armed Forces
Tuba-Euphonium Ensemble
Colliard, Corrado
  Album Title: *Exercices de Style*
  Personnel: Roberta Menegotto, pianoforte
  Label: Editions L'Eubage, 2001 CD: 2/2001
Sanson, Davide: *T-Tango*
Dougherty, William: *Duo for Euphonium and
  Marimba*
Hirano, Mitsuru: *Fantasia di foresta*
Bach, Johann Sebastian: *Sonata No. 3 in sol
  minore*
Manfrin, Paolo: *Interferenze per euphonium solo*
Ross, John: *Concertino for Euphonium, Piano,
  and Percussion*
Barbera, Beppe: *Ca suffit!*
Colonial Tuba Quartet, The
  Album Title: *Spectraphonics*
  Personnel: Mary Ann Craig, Jay Hildebrandt,
    euphonium; Gary Bird, Gregory Fritze,
    tuba
  Label: Mark Custom Recording Service, 1995
    CD: MCD-1909
Stamp, Jack: *Colonial Express, The*
Frackenpohl, Arthur: *Suite for Tuba Quartet*
Bernie, Pinkard, and Casey/Fragomeni: *Sweet
  Georgia Brown*
Fritz, Gregory: *Prelude and Dance*
Traditional/Fritze/Hildebrandt: *Colonial
  Suite, The*
Melillo, Stephen: *Erich!*
Cummings, Barton: *In Darkness Dreaming*
Mozart, Wolfgang Amadeus: *Allegro from
  "Eine Kleine Nacht Music"*
Picchi, Ermano/Craig: *Fantaisie Originale*
Arlen, Harold/Fritze: *Over the Rainbow*
Pullig, Kenneth: *Dances; Four Tubas*
Banchieri, Adriano/Fritze: *Two Fantasias*
Traditional/Fritze: *Edelweiss*
Sousa, John Philip/Morris: *Washington Post
  March*
Contraband
  Album Title: *Swingin' Low*

Personnel: Martin Kym, Martin Meier, eupho-
  nium; David LeClair, Ernest May, tuba;
  Andy Lüscher, drums; Thomas Thüring,
  piano
Label: Marcophon, 1993 CD: CD 940-2
LeClair, David: *Heidentüblein*
Willibald, Kresin, arr.: *Swing Low*
Schubert, Franz Peter/LeClair: *Ständchen*
Carmichael, Hoagy/LeClair: *Georgia on My
  Mind*
Bartles, Alfred: *When Tubas Waltz*
Niehaus, Lennie: *Sleeping Giants*
Schmidt, Dankwart, arr.: *Tuba Muckl*
Traditional/Lohmann, George/Schmidt:
  Bayerische Polka
Arban, Jean Baptiste/LeClair: *Carnival of
  Venice, The*
Schubert, Franz Peter/LeClair: *Militärmarsch*
Kresin, Willibald: *Chin Up!*
Sousa, John Philip/Werden: *Washington Post
  March*
LeClair, David: *Growing Up Together*
Joplin, Scott/LeClair: *Easy Winners, The*
Clarke, Herbert L./LeClair: *Cousins*
Contraband Tuba Quartet
  Album Title: *The Dragon's Dance*
  Personnel: Martin Kym, Martin Meier, eupho-
    nium; David LeClair, Ernest May, tuba; Andy
    Lüscher, drums; Thomas Thüring, piano
  Label: Marcophon, CD: CD 7031
LeClair, David: *Dragon's Dance, The*
Schubert, Franz: *Die Forelle*
Willibald, Kresin: *Movin Groovin/Tuba Rodeo/
  Tango*
Templeton, Alec: *Mr. Bach Goes to Town*
Templeton, Alec: *On a Rocky Road*
Gershwin, George: *Impromptu in 2 Keys*
Gershwin, George: *Three Preludes*
Monti, Vittorio: *Czárdás*
Conway, Sean
  Album Title: *Honest Toil*
  Personnel: David Woodward, euphonium;
    Marsden Silver Prize Band, Alan Widdop,
    conductor
  Label: Harmonic Discovery Studios, CD
Bizet, George/Wilkinson: *Deep inside the
  Sacred Temple*
Cooper, Lyndon
  Album Title: *A Touch More Spice*
  Personnel: William Davis Construction Group
    Band, Keith Wilkinson, conductor
  Label: Polyphonic Reproductions, Ltd., CPRL
    042D
Sparke, Philip: *Party Piece*
Corwell, Neal
  Album Title: *Distant Images*
  Personnel:
  Label: Nicolai Music, 1994 CD: NIC 119
Corwell, Neal: *New England Reveries*
Corwell, Neal: *Simyeh*
Corwell, Neal: *Meditation*

Corwell, Neal: *Distant Images*
Corwell, Neal: *Odyssey*
Corwell, Neal: *Night Song*
Corwell, Neal
   Album Title: *Festival Fanfares*
   Personnel: Triangle Brass Band
   Label: Triangle Brass Band
   Gregson, Edward: *Symphonic Rhapsody for Euphonium and Brass Band*
Corwell, Neal
   Album Title: *Heart of a Wolf*
   Personnel: Velvet Brown, tuba
   Label: Nicolai Music, 2000 CD: NC 6400
   Corwell, Neal: *Ritual*
   Corwell, Neal: *2:00:00*
   Corwell, Neal: *Black Moon Rising*
   Corwell, Neal: *Heart of a Wolf*
   Corwell, Neal: *Furies, The*
   Corwell, Neal: *Arctic Dream*
Corwell, Neal
   Album Title: *Out Sitting in His Field*
   Personnel:
   Label: Nicolai Music, 2004 CD: NM 5946
   Mantia, Simone/Corwell: *Believe Me if All Those Endearing Young Charms*
   Corwell, Neal: *Hungarian Hallucination*
   Corwell, Neal: *Venetian Carnival Animals*
   Corwell, Neal, arr.: *Lassus Trombone*
   Corwell, Neal: *Scherzo*
   Corwell, Neal: *At the Far Side of the Pasture*
   Corwell, Neal: *Bumble Bee*
   Corwell, Neal: *Dandy Noodles*
Corwell, Neal. *See* Symphonia
Craddock, Ian
   Album Title: *Checkmate*
   Personnel: The Band of Yorkshire Imperial Metals, Denis Carr, conductor
   Label: Two-Ten Records, 1979 LP: TT003
   Sparke, Philip: *Fantasy for Euphonium and Brass Band*
Craddock, Ian
   Album Title:
   Personnel: Yorkshire Imperial Metals Band, Trevor Walmsley, conductor
   Label: Pye Records, 1972 LP: GSGL 10488
   Mozart, Wolfgang Amadeus/Wright: *Rondo from "Horn Concerto No. 4"*
Craddock, Ian
   Album Title:
   Personnel: Yorkshire Imperial Metals Band, Trevor Walmsley, conductor
   Label: Decca, 1973 LP: SB 306
   Bellstedt, Herman/Owenson: *Napoli*
Craddock, Ian
   Album Title:
   Personnel: Yorkshire Imperial Metals Band, Trevor Walmsley, conductor
   Label: Silverline, 1975 LP: DJSL 034
   Traditional/Gheel: *Watching the Wheat*
Craddock, Ian
   Album Title:
   Personnel: Yorkshire Imperial Metals Band, Trevor Walmsley, conductor

Label: Pye Records, 1976 LP: TBX 3008
   Rossini, Gioacchino/Langford: *Largo Al Factotum*
Craddock, Ian
   Album Title:
   Personnel: Yorkshire Imperial Metals Band, Dennis Carr, conductor
   Label: Two Ten Records, 1979 LP: TT003
   Sparke, Philip: *Fantasy for Euphonium*
Craig, Mary Ann
   Album Title: *Euphonium, Out on a Limb*
   Personnel: James Staples, piano; Jack Stamp, marimba; Faculty Brass Quintet at Indiana University of Pennsylvania
   Label: Mark Records, 1995 CD: MCD-1794
   Curnow, James: *Symphonic Variants*
   Frite, Gregory: *Euphonistic Dance*
   Baldwin, David: *Concerto for Al's Breakfast*
   Cummings, Barton: *Spring Suite*
   Romberg, Sigmund: *Serenade from "The Student Prince"*
   George, Thom Ritter: *Sonata for Baritone Horn and Piano*
Craig, Mary Ann
   Album Title: *Mary Ann Craig, Euphonium*
   Personnel: James Staples, piano
   Label: Saints and Sinners LP: WRA1-476
   Capuzzi, Antonio: *Andante and Rondo from "Doublebass Concerto"*
   Rachmaninov, Sergei: *Vocalise Op. 34, No. 14*
   Schmidt, Hugo: *Devil's Tongue, The*
   Jacob, Gordon: *Fantasia*
   Mendelssohn, Felix: *If with All Your Heart*
   Arban, Jean Baptiste/Brasch/Clarke/Craig/Straigers: *Carnival of Venice, The*
Craig, Mary Ann. *See* Colonial Tuba Quartet
Cranson, Colin
   Album Title:
   Personnel: Fodens Motor Works Band, Rex Mortimer, conductor
   Label: Polydor, 1971 LP: 2485 015
   Sutton, Eddie: *Cavalier, The*
Cranson, Colin
   Album Title:
   Personnel: Fodens Motor Works Band, James Scott, conductor
   Label: Decca, 1977 LP: SB 330
   Bellini, Vincenzo/Adolphe: *La Sonnambula*
Crespo, Enrique. *See* Gerhard Meinl's Tuba Sextet
Cresswell, John
   Album Title:
   Personnel: Newhall Band, Earnest Woodhouse, conductor
   Label: Midland, LP: MSR 1408
   Rimmer, William: *Variations on Jenny Jones*
Crompton, Carole
   Album Title: *Variations*
   Personnel: Desford Colliery Caterpillar Band
   Label: Polyphonic Reproductions, Ltd., CPRL 041D
   Bennett: *Rutland Water*
Crookes, Brian
   Album Title: *The Music of Philip Sparke*

Personnel: Leyland Band
Label: Triton Records, 1986 LP: TRMB 68101
Sparke, Philip: *Fantasy for Euphonium*
Crossley, Peter
Album Title:
Personnel: Thurlstone Band, Eric Crossley, conductor
Label: Northern Light, 1979 LP: NLR012
Prietro/Siebert: *Wedding, The*
Cunliffe, Stuart
Album Title:
Personnel: Greenalls Band, C. Fradley, conductor
Label: Canon, 1977 LP: VAR 5952
Doughty, George: *Grandfather's Clock*
Cutts, Marcus
Album Title: *Brass Favorites*
Personnel: The Fairey Band, Kenneth Dennison, conductor
Label: Chandos Records Ltd., 1971, 1991 CD: 6530
Mantia, Simone/Langford: *Believe Me if All Those Endearing Young Charms*
MacDowell, Edward/Langford: *To a Wild Rose*
Cutts, Marcus
Album Title:
Personnel: Fairey Band, Harry Mortimer, conductor
Label: E. M. I., 1969 LP: CSD 3668
Foulds, John: *A Keltic Lament*
Cutts, Marcus
Album Title:
Personnel: Fairey Band, Kenneth Dennison, conductor
Label: Camden, 1970 LP: INTS 1158
MacDowell, Edward/Ball: *To a Wild Rose*
Cutts, Marcus
Album Title:
Personnel: Fairey Band, Kenneth Dennison, conductor
Label: RCA, 1971 LP: INTS 1331
Mantia, Simone/Langford: *Believe Me if All Those Endearing Young Charms*
Cutts, Marcus
Album Title:
Personnel: Fairey Band, Richard Evans, conductor
Label: BBC, 1978 LP: REC 302
Golland, John: *Peace*
Dale, Kevin
Album Title:
Personnel: United Co-Op Crewe Band, Roy Sparkes, conductor
Hollick and Taylor, 1987 LP: HTLPS 1723
Corbett, Stephen, arr.: *Solitaire*
Dart, Fred
Album Title: *Euphonium Solos*
Personnel: Gertrude Kuehefuhs, piano
Label: Coronet Recording Co., LP: SR4M-7275
Haydn, Franz Josef: *Adagio*
Klengel, Julius: *Concertino No. 1, Op. 7*
Guilmant, Alexander: *Morceau Symphonique*

Bakaleinikov, Vladimir: *Meditation*
Selmer: *Barcarolle et Chanson Bachique*
Cords: *Concert Fantasie*
Takács, Jenö: *Sonata*
Rossini, Gioacchino/Langford: *Largo Al Factotum*
Davies, Russell
Album Title:
Personnel: Camberwell Salvation Army Band of Australia, B. Davies, conductor
Label: Salvationist Publishing & Supplies Ltd., 1982 LP: SPS022
Redhead, Robert: *Euphony*
Davis, George
Album Title:
Personnel: Cory Band, John Harrison, conductor
Label: Music for Pleasure, 1969 LP: MFP 1313
Chester, Barie: *Arabella*
Davis, George
Album Title:
Personnel: Cory Band, Arthur Kenny, conductor
Label: Polydor, 1971 LP: 2485014
Zutano/Rimmer: *Spanish Serenade*
Davis, George
Album Title:
Personnel: Cory Band, Arthur Kenny, conductor
Label: Decca, 1974 LP: SB 319
Mantia, Simone/Langford: *Believe Me if All Those Endearing Young Charms*
Davis, George
Album Title:
Personnel: Cory Band, Bram Gay, conductor
Label: Grosvenor, 1977 LP: GRS 1052
Foster, Stephen/Howarth: *Jeannie with the Light Brown Hair*
Deacon, Derek
Album Title:
Personnel: Royal Doulton Band, Edward Gray, conductor
Label: Pye Records, 1976 LP: TBX 3005
MacDowell, Edward/Ball: *To a Wild Rose*
Deacon, Derek
Album Title:
Personnel: Royal Doulton Band, Edward Gray, conductor
Label: Pye Records, 1978 LP: TB 3015
Foster, Stephen/Rimmer: *My Old Kentucky Home*
Dempster, Stuart
Album Title: *American Sampler*
Personnel: Elizabeth Suderburg, vocals; Victor Steinhardt, Robert Suderburg, piano
Label: Olympic Recording, University of Washington Press, 1975 LP: OLY 104
Mantia, Simone: *Priscilla*
Jacobs Bond, Carrie: *I Love You Truly*
Jacobs Bond, Carrie: *A Perfect Day*
Denys, Marnik
Album Title: *The Comedians—Works for Symphonic Band*

Personnel: Belgian Air Force Symphonic Band,
  Alain Crpin, conductor
Label: Rene Gailly Records, CD: 87–036
Curnow, James: *Symphonic Variants for Eupho-
  nium and Band*
Dickman, Marcus
  Album Title: *College Band Directors National
    Association—Southern Division Biennial
    Conference, 1982*
  Personnel: Troy State University Symphony
    Band, John Long, conductor
  Label: Silver Crest Records, 1982 LP: CBSD-
    82-1
  Pryor, Arthur/Pearson: *Blue Bells of Scotland,
    The*
Dickman, Marcus
  Album Title: *A Weaver of Dreams*
  Personnel: Bill Prince, trumpet, clarinet, flute,
    flugelhorn, tenor sax; Kevin Bales, piano;
    Rick Kirkland, drums; Ben Tucker, bass
  Label: Note-Able Music, 2004 CD: FMS 2391
  Young, Victor/Elliot, Jack: *A Weaver of Dreams*
  Dickman, Marcus: *Bee-Bo*
  Ellington, Duke: *Cotton Tail*
  Rollins, Sonny/Dickman: *Doxy*
  Giuffre, Jimmy/Prince: *Four Brothers*
  Wrubel, Allie/Magidson, Herb: *Gone with the
    Wind*
  Waller, Fats: *Jitterbug Waltz*
  Jordon, Duke: *Jordu*
  Norton, George/Burnett, Ernie: *My Melan-
    choly Baby*
  Coltrane, John: *Mr. P.C.*
  Dickman, Marcus: *Patrice Elaine*
  Prince, Bill: *Something Happy*
Dickman, Marcus. *See* Champions of the Leonard
  Falcone Festival 1986–2000
Dickman, Marcus. *See* Modern Jazz Tuba Project
Dickman, Marcus. *See* Symphonia
Dodd, Michael
  Album Title: *Grimethorpe in Concert*
  Personnel: Grimethorpe Colliery Band, Garry
    Cutt, conductor
  Label: Egon Records, 2002 CD: SFZ 105
  Pryor, Arthur: *Blue Bells of Scotland, The*
Dodd, Michael
  Album Title: *Music from the Park*
  Personnel: Grimethorpe Colliery Band, Garry
    Cutt, conductor
  Label: Grimethorp Colliery Band, 1999 CD:
    GCB 002
  Bellstedt, Herman: *Napoli*
Drewitt, Adrian
  Album Title: *Celebration*
  Personnel: Drewent Brass, Keith Leonard, con-
    ductor
  Label: Amadeus Recordings, 2002 CD: AMS
    045
  Traditional/Roberts: *Carrickfergus*
Droste, Paul
  Album Title: *Euphonium Favorites for Recital
    and Contest*

Personnel: Anne Droste, piano; Laura Line-
  berger, Eric Aho, euphonium; Robert
  LaBlanc, tuba
Label: Coronet Recording Co., LP: LPS 3203
Vaughan Williams, Ralph/Droste: *Six Studies
  in English Folk Song*
Haydn, Franz Josef/Droste: *Divertimento
  No. 70*
Dougherty, William: *Meditation and Celebra-
  tion*
Franck, Cesar/Smith: *Panis Angelicus*
Pryor, Arthur: *Blue Bells of Scotland, The*
Hartley, Walter: *Bivalve Suite*
Droste, Paul
  Album Title: *Euphonium Solos*
  Personnel: Anne Droste, piano
  Label: Coronet Recording Co., LP: LPS 3026
  Handel, George Frederic/Fitzgerald: *Aria con
    Variazioni*
  McBride, Robert: *Way-Out, but Not Too Far*
  Castéréde: *Fantaisie Concertante*
  Vaughan Williams, Ralph: *Romanza*
  Schumann, Robert/Droste: *Five Pieces in Folk
    Style, Op. 102*
Droste, Paul
  Album Title: *Ohio State Plays Ed Montgomery*
  Personnel: Ohio State University Wind Band
  Label: Fidelity Sound Records, 1978 LP:
    FSRS-1316
  Montgomery, Ed: *Mirror Lake Suite*
Droste, Paul. *See* Symphonia
Dunstan, John
  Album Title:
  Personnel: St. Dennis Band, E. J. Williams,
    conductor
  Label: Fanfare, 1971 LP: 2485010
  Gheel/Wiggins, arr.: *Watching the Wheat*
Dutch Tuba Quartet
  Album Title: *Escape from "Oompah-Land"*
  Personnel: Arjen Bos, Hugo Verweij, eupho-
    nium; Jan van de Sanden, Ron Antens, tuba
  Label: World Wind Music
  Wilkinson, Robert: *Happy Soul, The*
  Hawkins/Luis: *Tuxedo Junction*
  Sousa, John Philip/Smalley: *Thunderer, The*
  Hidas, Frigyes: *Tuphonium*
  Payne, Frank Lynn: *Quartet for Tubas*
  Stevens, John: *Dances*
  Bruckner/Sabourin: *Locus Iste*
  Joplin, Scott/Sabourin: *Pleasant Moments*
  Gale, Jack, arr.: *Tiger Rag*
  Uber, David: *Music for the Stage*
  Gabrieli/Gray: *Canzone per Sonare*
  Alexander, Lois, arr.: *Swing Low, Sweet Chariot*
  Mancini, Henry/Gale: *Pink Panther, The*
Dutch Tuba Quartet
  Album Title: *Four Keen Guys*
  Personnel: Arjen Bos, Hugo Verweij, eupho-
    nium; Jan van de Sanden, Ron Antens, tuba
  Label: World Wind Music
  Beal, Keith: *Three Movements for Four Tubas*
  Berlioz, Hector/Werden: *Hungarian March*

Frackenpohl, Arthur: *Pop Suite*
Lew, Gillis: *Four Kuehn Guys*
Handy/Holcombe: *St. Louis Blues*
Jacob, Gordon: *Four Pieces for Tuba Quartet*
Joplin, Scott/Werden: *Easy Winners*
Mertens, Hardy: *Scyths*
Stevens, John: *Manhattan Suite*
Dutch Tuba Quartet
Album Title: *Wolkenschatten*
Personnel: Arjen Bos, Hugo Verweij, euphonium; Jan van de Sanden, Ron Antens, tuba
Label: World Wind Music
Gourlay, James: *Eagle Thunders, The*
Nordhagen, Stig: *Nocturne*
Debussy, Claude: *Golliwog's Cakewalk*
Koetsier, Jan: *Wolkenschatten*
Stevens, John: *Moondance*
Williams, John/Dawson: *March from "1941"*
Traditional/Verweij: *Freylekhs fun der Khupe*
Traditional/Verweij: *Der Khusid geyt Tantsn*
Brown, Clifford/Wilkinson: *Daahoud*
Kleine Schaars, Peter: *Wolf the Cat*
Edwards, Bryce. *See* Euphoniums Unlimited
Entwistle, Heather
Album Title:
Personnel: Hatherleigh Silver Band
Label: Sentinel Records, 1980 LP: SENLPP 602
Doughty, George: *Grandfather's Clock*
Euphonium Quartet
Album Title: *Texas Tech Concert Band—1963*
Personnel: Marlin Lindsey, Bill Patterson, Clifford Bates, Phil Anthony, euphonium; Texas Tech Concert Band, Dean Killion, conductor
Label: Austin, 1963 LP: 6388
Clarke, Herbert L.: *Carnival of Venice, The*
Euphonium Section, The
Album Title: *The Revelli Years*
Personnel: Brian Bowman, Gary Burgess, William Johnson, Robert Sreckfus, Charles Wolgamott, euphonium; The University of Michigan Symphony Band, William Revelli, conductor
Label: Golden Crest Records, Inc., 1981 LP: CRS-4211
Bizet, George: *Flower Song from "Carmen"*
Euphoniums of University of Illinios
Album Title:
Personnel: University of Illinois Symphony Band, Harry Begian, conductor
Label: CD: 125
Bellstedt, Herman: *Napoli*
Euphoniums Unlimited
Album Title: *Euphoniums Unlimited*
Personnel: Brian Bowman, Adam Frey, Jukka Myllys, Cory Belvin, Lloyd Bone, Bryce Edwards, Seth Fletcher, Josh Hauser, Ashley Sample, Jimmie Self, Kelly Thomas, Mark Walker, euphonium; R. Winston Morris, conductor

Label: Mark Custom Recording Service, Inc., 2004 CD: 5543-MCD
Sherwin, Manning/Puerling/Cochran: *A Nightingale Sang in Berkeley Square*
Uber, David: *Exhibitions*
Danner, Gregory: *Runnin' with Bydlo*
Forte, Aldo Rafael: *Moser Cameos*
Lintinen, Kirmo: *Lampi*
Raum, Elizabeth: *A Little Monster Music*
Corwell, Neal: *In the Cathedral*
Brusick, William: *By the Waters of Babylon*
MacMillan, Duncan: *"In Memoriam" Sept. 11, 2001*
Self, James: *Euphoniums Unlimited*
Hauser, Joshua: *EuPhunk*
European Tuba Octet
Album Title: *Tuba Libera, Roger Bobo*
Personnel: European Tuba Octet
Label: Crystal Records, 1994 CD: CD690
Stevens, John: *Liberation of Sisyphus, The*
Evans, Jonathon
Album Title: *Music for a Joyful Occasion*
Personnel: Egon Virtuosi Brass
Label: Egon Music, CD: EGN 102
Leidzen, Erik: *Home on the Range*
Falcone, Leonard
Album Title: *Leonard Falcone, Baritone Horn, Volume 4*
Personnel: Joseph Evans, piano; 1962 Pennsylvania Inter-Collegiate Band, James Dunlop, conductor; Pontiac High School Band, Dale Harris, conductor; Royal Canadian Regiment Band, Derek Stannard, conductor
Label: Michigan State University, LP/CS: CA-MSU 8984B, Falcone Competition
Clarke, Herbert L.: *From the Shores of the Mighty Pacific*
DiCapua: *O, Sole Mio*
Schubert, Franz: *Serenade*
Bach, Johann Sebastian/Gounod/Falcone: *Ave Maria*
Picchi, Ermano/Mantia/Falcone: *Fantasia Originale*
Bizet, George/Harding: *Flower Song from "Carmen"*
Toselli, Enrico: *Serenade*
Falcone, Leonard
Album Title: *Leonard Falcone and His Baritone, Volume 1*
Personnel: Joseph Evans, piano
Label: Golden Crest Records Inc., LP/CS: RE 7001, Falcone Competition, CA 7001
Clarke, Herbert L.: *From the Shores of the Mighty Pacific*
Ponce, Manuel: *Estrellita*
Bach, Johann Sebastian: *Bourree I and II from "Suite III for Cello"*
DeLuca, Joseph: *Beautiful Colorado*
Simons, Guardell: *Atlantic Zephyrs*
Ravel, Maurice: *Piece en Forme de Habanera*
Senaille, Jean Baptiste: *Allegro Spiritoso*
Guilmant, Alexander: *Morceau Symphonique*

Falcone, Leonard
Album Title: *Leonard Falcone and His Baritone, Volume 3*
Personnel: Joseph Evans, piano
Label: Golden Crest Records Inc., LP/CS: RE 7036, Falcone Competition, CA 7036
Llwellyn, Edward: *My Regards*
Donizetti, Gaetano/Harvey: *Una Furtiva Lacrima*
DeLuca, Joseph: *Sentimentale "Danse Caprice"*
Nux, P. V. de la: *Concert Piece*
Cools, Eugene: *Allegro De Concert*
Barat, J. Ed.: *Andante et Allegro*
Haydn, Franz Josef/Shuman: *Adagio from "Concerto for Cello"*
Bellstedt, Herman: *Napoli*
Falcone, Leonard
Album Title: *Leonard Falcone and His Baritone, Volume 2*
Personnel: Joseph Evans, piano
Label: Golden Crest Records Inc., LP/CS: RE 7016, Falcone Competition, CA 7016
Magnan, G.: *Concerto*
Squire, W. H.: *Tarantella*
Picchi, Ermano/Mantia: *Fantasia Originale*
Combelle, F.: *Premier Solo de Concert*
Granados, Enrique/Falcone: *Playera "Danse Espagnole"*
Saint-Saëns, Camille: *Swan, The*
Pryor, Arthur: *Blue Bells of Scotland, The*
Faro, Michael
Album Title:
Personnel: St. Dennis Band, E. J. Williams, conductor
Label: Pye Records, 1976 LP: TB3009
MacDowell, Edward/Ball: *To a Wild Rose*
Farrington, Christopher
Album Title:
Personnel: Holme Silver Band, David Hirst, conductor
Label: Look Records, 1980 LP: 6500
Heath, Reginald: *Springtime*
Fawbert, Andrew
Album Title: *Tournament for Brass*
Personnel: The Jones and Crossland Band, Roy Curran, conductor
Label: Grosvenor Recording Studios, 1981 LP: GRS 1099
Hartmann, John: *La Belle Americaine*
Fawbert, Andrew
Album Title:
Personnel: Market Rasen Band, Keith Edwards, conductor
Label: Midland Sound Records, LP: MSRS 1387
Code, Percy: *Zelda*
Brown, Norman, arr.: *Catari*
Ferguson, Maynard
Album Title: *Chameleon*
Personnel: Maynard Ferguson Orchestra

Label: Columbia Records, 1974 LP: KC 33007
Ferguson, Maynard, arr.: *Gospel John*
Ferguson, Maynard
Album Title: *Swingin' My Way through College*
Personnel: Maynard Ferguson Orchestra
Label: Roulette Records, LP: SR 25058
Ferguson, Maynard, arr.: *It's a Pity to Say Goodnight*
Finch, Peter
Album Title:
Personnel: Chalk Farm Salvation Army Band, M. Clack, conductor
Label: Salvationist Publishing & Supplies Ltd., 1980 LP: SPS005
Senaille, Jean Baptiste: *Allegro Spiritoso*
Fisher, Mark
Album Title: *Eufish*
Personnel: Mark Lawson, piano
Label: Albany Records, 1995 CD: TROY162
Bach, Johann Sebastian: *Sonata for Flute in E♭ Major*
Brahms, Johannes/Reynolds: *Hornsongs*
Jacob, Gordon: *Fantasia*
Telemann, Georg: *Sonata in f Minor for Bassoon and Continuo*
Bach, Jan: *Concert Variations*
Arban, Jean Baptiste/Leidzen: *Fantasia, Theme and Variations on Carnival of Venice*
Fisher, Mark
Album Title: *Introducing the Asbury Brass Quintet*
Personnel: Bœhme Sextet-Asbury Brass Quintet; Adolph Herseth, guest soloist
Label: Forte Records
Fisher, Mark. See Symphonia
Flaten, Tormond
Album Title: *Art of the States*
Personnel: Rolf Bjørge, euphonium; Eikanger Bjørsik Band, Reid Gilje, conductor
Label: Doyen Recordings, 2002 CD: DOY CD152
Dreyer/Jolson/Rydland: *Me and My Shadow*
Flaten, Tormod
Album Title: *Flight*
Personnel: Daniel Beskow, piano; Brass Band from Eikanger-Bjørsvik; Thor-Arne Pedersen, euphonium; Mangus Brandseth, Hogne Aarflot, tuba
Label: Tormod Flaten, 2002 CD
Alfén, Hugo/Olsrud/Rydland: *Vallflickans Dans*
Aagaard-Nilsen, Torstein: *Two Insects*
Marcello, Benedetto/Flaten: *Sonata in a Minor*
Barnby, Joseph/Farr: *Sweet and Low*
Wilby, Philip: *Flight*
Golland, John: *Peace*
Linkola, Jukka: *Third Movement of "Euphonium Concerto"*
Mason, John/Rydland: *Rev. Archie Beaton*
Jacob, Gordon: *Fantasia*

Massenet, Jules/Flaten: *Meditation from "Thaïs"*
Bach, Johann Sebastian/Flaten: *Suite No. 4 in Eb Major*
Farr, Craig: *Larghetto for Euphonium*
Snell, Howard: *Variations on Drink to Me Only*
Fletcher, Seth. *See* Euphoniums Unlimited
Fletcher, Seth. *See* Tennessee Technological University Tuba-Euphonium Ensemble
Follis, Joan. *See* United States Armed Forces Tuba-Euphonium Ensemble
Fox, Mike
Album Title: *Prelude*
Personnel: Pennine Brass, Ian Porthouse, conductor
Label: Amadeus, CD: AMSCD057
Golland, John: *Peace*
Franke, Philip
Album Title: *In Concert, University of Illinois Symphonic Band*
Personnel: University of Illinois Symphonic Band, Harry Begian, conductor
Label: University of Illinois Bands, LP: 103
Curnow, James: *Symphonic Variants for Euphonium and Band*
French, John. *See* Thorton, David
Frey, Adam
Album Title: *Collected Dreams*
Personnel: Damon Denton, piano
Label: Euphonium Enterprises Inc., and Damon Denton, 2003 CD
Traditional/Denton: *Londonderry Air*
Bach, Johann Sebastian/Denton: *Arioso*
Traditional/Denton: *Shenandoah*
Traditional/Denton: *Last Rose of Summer, The*
Traditional/Denton: *Ye Banks and Braes*
Bach, Johann Sebastian/Gounod/Denton: *Ave Maria*
Traditional/Denton: *Over Yandro*
Saint-Saëns, Camille/Denton: *Swan, The*
Traditional/Denton: *O Waly Waly*
Traditional/Denton: *Shall We Gather at the River*
Traditional/Denton: *Amazing Grace*
Frey, Adam
Album Title: *Family Portrait*
Personnel: Point of Ayr Band, Michael Fowles, conductor
Label: Polyphonic Reproductions Ltd., 2000 CD: QPRL 204D
Picchi, Ermano/Mantia/Bale: *Fantaisie Originale*
Frey, Adam
Album Title: *Listen to THIS!*
Personnel: Damon Denton, piano
Label: Euphonium Enterprises Inc., 1999 CD
Sparke, Philip: *Pantomime*
Rachmaninov, Sergei: *Vocalise Op.34, No. 14*
Ito, Yasuhide: *Fantasy Variations*
Puccini, Giacomo: *Nessun Dorma*
Cosma, Vladimir: *Euphonium Concerto*

Fauré, Gabriel: *Elegié in c Minor, Op. 24*
Rimsky-Korsakov, Nikolai: *Flight of the Bumble Bee, The*
Ponce, Manuel: *Estrellita*
Picchi, Ermano/Mantia: *Fantaisie Originale*
Frey, Adam
Album Title: *Little Buckaroos*
Personnel: Scott Hartmann, trombone; Metropolitan Wind Symphony, Lawrence Isaacson, conductor
Label: Euphonium.com, CD: 2005
Ellerby, Martin: *Euphonium Concerto*
Reed, Alfred: *Seascape*
Hartmann John/Frey: *Rule Britannia*
Puccini, Giacomo: *Un Bel Di*
Delibus, Leo/Curnow: *Flower Song from "Lakme"*
Smith, Arthur/Frey: *Duelin' Banjos*
Frey, Adam. *See* Champions of the Leonard Falcone Festival 1986–2000
Frey, Adam. *See* Euphoniums Unlimited
Fukuda, Masanori
Album Title: *Peace, Piece*
Personnel: Tomomi Sato, piano
Label: Power House, CD: SBPCD-5017
Barat, J. Ed.: *Introduction and Dance*
Toda, Akira: *Student's Concertino*
Klengel, J.: *Concertino No. 1, Movement 1*
Nux, P. V. de la: *Concert Piece*
Capuzzi, Antonio: *Andante and Rondo from "Doublebass Concerto"*
Rachmaninov, Sergei: *Vocalise Op. 34, No. 14*
Mozart, Wolfgang Amadeus: *Aria*
Webber, C. W.: *Romanta Passonata*
Morel, Florentin: *Piece in fa mineur*
Fujita, Genma: *Glowing Spirit*
Barat, J. Ed.: *Andante and Allegro*
Clarke, Herbert L.: *Variations on Carnival of Venice*
Puccini, Giacomo: *Turandoto*
Gagnaux, Alexandre
Album Title: *Euphonium in Sight*
Personnel: Orchestre Symphonique de Lettonie, Vigo Racevskis, conductor; Orchestre d'Harmonie de Fribourg, Carlo Balmelli, conductor; La Landwehr de Fribourg, Herve Klopfenstein, conductor; Dominique Schweizer, piano
Label: ARTLAB, CD: 02513
Cosma, Vladimir: *Euphonium Concerto*
Golland, John: *Peace*
Curnow, James: *Symphonic Variants for Euphonium and Band*
Thingnaes, Frode: *Peace, Please*
Wilby, Philip: *Euphonium Concerto, Part I*
Traditional/Snell: *Variations on Drink to Me Only*
Sarasate, Pablo de/Buitenhuis: *Gypsy Airs*
Bohme, Oskar/Smith: *Russian Dance*
Gagnaux, Alexandre
Album Title: *Trilogie*

Personnel: Le Corps de Musique de Landwehr
de Fribourg, Herve Klopfenstein, conductor;
Dominique Schweizer, piano; The Flying
Brass Ensemble, Blaise Heritier, conductor
Label: Alexandre Gagnaux, CD
Bearcroft, Norman: *Better World, The*
Jenkinson, Ezra: *Elfentanz*
Wiggins, Brian: *Trilogy for Euphonium*
Redhead, Robert: *Euphony*
Wilby, Philip: *Danse Grecque: Zeibekikos*
Arban, Jean Baptiste/Catherall: *Carnival of
Venice, The*
Richards, Goff: *Rangitoto*
Sparke, Philip: *Mace*
Rimsky-Korsakov, Nikolai/James: *Flight of the
Bumble Bee, The*
Legrand, Michel/Drover: *What Are You Doing
with the Rest of Your Life?*
Bach, Johann Sebastian/Gounod/Porret: *Ave
Maria*
Woodfield, Ray: *Varied Mood*
Sparke, Philip: *Fantasy for Euphonium and
Concert Band*
Garden State Tuba Ensemble
Album Title: *Karl I. Megules, Tuba*
Personnel: John Swallow, James Kala, eupho-
nium; Toby Hanks, Bruce Jones, Paul
Mayberry, Karl Megules, Harry Weil, tuba;
Bernie Leighton, piano
Label: Recorded Publications Company, 1976
LP: Z434471
Bach, Johann Sebastian/Sauter: *Komm Susser
Tod from "Die geistlichen Leider und Arien,"
BWV 478*
Butts, Carrol M.: *Ode for Low Brass*
Croft: *Duet for Tenor Tuba and Bass Tuba*
Frackenpohl, Arthur: *Pop Suite*
Tarlow, Lawrence: *Quintet for Tubas*
Garnon, Barry
Album Title:
Personnel: Sydney Congress Hall Band, Barry
Gott, conductor
Label: Private label, 1980
Senaille, Jean Baptiste: *Allegro Spiritoso*
Garrett, Guy
Album Title:
Personnel: Lydbrook Silver Band, Lyndon
Baglin, conductor
Label: Saydisc, 1981 LP: CP 122
Traditional/Siebert, Edrich: *Edelweiss*
Gerhard Meinl's Tuba Sextet
Album Title: *Tuba! A Six-Tuba Musical Romp*
Personnel: Enrique Crespo, Dankwart Schimdt,
euphonium; Warren Deck, Walter Hilgers,
Samuel Pilafian, Jonathan Sass, tuba
Label: EMI Records Ltd., 1992 CD: CDC 7
54729 2
Mozart, Wolfgang Amadeus: *Divertimento #2
in B♭*
Bach, Johann Sebastian: *Fugue in g Minor*
Couperin, François: *Les Baricades Misterieuses*

DiLasso, Orlando: *Oia, O che bon Eccho!*
Rosler, J. J.: *Partita-Polacca*
Hilgers, Walter: *Praeludium*
Crespo, Enrique: *Bruckner Etude*
Crespo, Enrique: *Three Milongas*
Denson, Frank: *Three Folksongs for Four Brass*
Sass, Jon: *Meltdown*
Watz, F.: *Melton Marsch*
Traditional: *Bayrische Zell*
Traditional: *Bayrische Polka*
Giles, Mark
Album Title: *Majesty*
Personnel: Norwich Citadel Band
Label:
Redhead, Robert: *Euphony*
Goddard, Don. *See* Groom, Joe
Gosney, Richard
Album Title: *Brass Dynamics*
Personnel: Desford Colliery Caterpillar Band
Label: De Haske Music Records, CD
Bulla, Stephen: *Euphonium Fantasia*
Gosney, Richard
Album Title: *Desford Colliery Caterpillar Band*
Personnel: Desford Colliery Caterpillar Band
Label: Polyphonic Reproductions, Ltd., CD
Sparke, Philip: *Pantomime*
Gosney, Richard
Album Title:
Personnel: Jayess Queensbury Band, James
Shepherd, conductor
Label: CJS Records, 1985 LP
Woodfield, Ray: *Caprice*
Grainger, Andre
Album Title: *Andre Grainger*
Personnel:
Label: Artifice Records
Curnow, James: *Rhapsody for Euphonium*
Handel, George Frederic: *Musizure pur un
Feu o'*
Green, Barry. *See* Modern Jazz Tuba Project
Griffiths, Morgan
Album Title: *Cry of the Celts*
Personnel: Yorkshire Building Society Band
Label:
MacMurrough, D.: *Macushla*
Griffiths, Morgan
Album Title: *Essence of Time*
Personnel: Black Dyke Mills Band
Label: Polyphonic Reproductions Ltd., CD:
QPRL 048D
Arban, Jean Baptiste/Manning/Remmington:
Carnival of Venice, The
Griffiths, Morgan
Album Title: *Highlights from the European
Brass Band Championships, 1998*
Personnel: various brass bands
Label: World Wind Music, CD: WWM-
500.038
Hartmann, John/Greenwood: *Rule Britannia*
Griffiths, Morgan
Album Title: *Introduction*

Personnel: Yorkshire Building Society Band,
David King, conductor
Label: Polyphonic Reproductions Ltd., 1995
CD: QPRL 074D
Hartmann, John/Mortimer: *Facilita*
Griffiths, Morgan
Album Title: *That's a Plenty*
Personnel: Ian Yates, euphonium; The York-
shire Building Society Band, Nicholas Childs,
conductor
Label: Obrasso Records, CD
Hudec, Adam: *Golden Euphoniums*
Griffiths, Morgan
Album Title: *Virtuosi*
Personnel: Fairey Band, Howard Snell, Bryan
Hurdley, conductors
Label: Egon Recordings, 2002 CD: SFZ 115
Bulla, Stephen: *Euphonium Fantasia*
Drigo, R.: *Serenade from "Les Millions
D'Arlequin"*
Lear, Thos: *Shylock*
Griffiths, Morgan
Album Title: *The Voice of the Euphonium*
Personnel: Yorkshire Building Society Band,
David King, conductor
Label: Polyphonic Reproductions Ltd., 1999
CD: QPRL 098D
Redhead, Robert: *Euphony*
Brodsky/Farr: *Be My Love*
Hartmann, John: *Rule Britannia*
Davis, Trevor: *Shepherd Song*
Mozart, Wolfgang Amadeus/Henstridge: *Alle-
gro from "Bassoon Concerto"*
Mendez/Freeh: *Valse*
Graham, Peter: *Holy Well, The*
Fernie, Alan: *Introduction and Allegro*
Leoncavallo/Langford: *Mattinata*
Rossini, Gioacchino/Langford: *Largo Al
Factotum*
Rachmaninov, Sergei/Langford: *Vocalise Op.
34, No. 14*
Gregson, Edward: *Symphonic Rhapsody*
Groom, Joe
Album Title:
Personnel: Don Goddard with the British Air-
ways Band, Stan Tamplin, conductor
Label: Rediffusion Records, 1975 LP: WR
101
Maclean, Don/Greenwood: *And I Love You So*
Groom, Trevor
Album Title: *Celebration Golden Jubilee*
Personnel: G.U.S. Footwear Band, Stanley
Boddington, conductor
Label: Chandos, BBRD 1019
Handel, George Frederic/Hume: *Harmonious
Blacksmith, The*
Groom, Trevor
Album Title: *European Journey*
Personnel: G.U.S. Footwear Band, Stanley
Boddington, conductor
Label: Krestrel Records, KES 8204

Arban, Jean Baptiste/Remington: *Carnival of
Venice, The*
Groom, Trevor
Album Title: *Quartets for Brass*
Personnel: G.U.S. Footwear Band, Keith
Wilkinson, conductor
Label: Polyphonic Reproductions Ltd., LP:
PRL 003
Vinter, Gilbert: *Alla Burlesca*
Vinter, Gilbert: *Elegy and Rondo*
Vinter, Gilbert: *Fancy's Knell*
Groom, Trevor
Album Title:
Personnel: G.U.S. Footwear Band, Stanley
Boddington, conductor
Label: Studio Two Records, 1969 LP: TWO
282
DeLuca, Joseph/Boddington: *Beautiful Colo-
rado*
Groom, Trevor
Album Title:
Personnel: G.U.S. Footwear Band, Joseph
Horovitz, conductor
Label: Studio Two Records, 1973 LP: TWO
418
Horovitz, Joseph: *Euphonium Concerto*
Groom, Trevor
Album Title:
Personnel: John Clough, euphonium; Virtuosi
Band, James Scott, conductor
Label: Philips, 1976 LP: SON 025
Bryce, Frank: *Rondoletto for Two Euphoniums*
Groom, Trevor
Album Title:
Personnel: G.U.S. Footwear Band, Keith
Wilkinson, conductor
Label: Chandos Records, 1983 LP: BBRD 1019
Handel, George Frederic/Hume/Wilkinson:
Harmonious Blacksmith, The
Groom, Trevor
Album Title:
Personnel: G.U.S. Footwear Band, Keith
Wilkinson, conductor
Label: Kestrel, 1984 LP: KES 8203
Puccini, Giacomo/Wilkinson: *Nessun Dorma*
Groom, Trevor
Album Title:
Personnel: G.U.S. Footwear Band, Keith
Wilkinson, conductor
Label: Kestrel, 1985 LP: KES 8204
Arban, Jean Baptiste/Remmington: *Carnival
of Venice, The*
Groom, Trevor
Album Title:
Personnel: Kettering Salvation Army Band,
D. Manning, conductor
Label: Banners and Bonnetts, 1979 LP:
BAB3510
Leizden, Erik: *Home on the Range*
Groom, Trevor
Album Title:

Personnel: Kettering Salvation Army Band,
D. Manning, conductor
Label: Salvationist Publishing & Supplies Ltd.,
1982 LP: SPS010
Steadman-Allen, Ray: *Ransomed Host, The*
Groom, Trevor. *See* Clough, John
Haas, Uli. *See* Melton Tuba-Quartett
Haemhouts, Ben
Album Title: *Serenades, Variations and More*
Personnel: Fan De Bondt, euphonium; Brass
Band of St. Cecilia Hombeek, Michel
Leveugle, conductor
Label: Beriato Music, CD: SSR 002
Doughty, George: *Grandfather's Clock*
Hartmann, John: *Facilita*
Drigo, R.: *Serenade from "Les Millions
D'Arlequin"*
Tosselli, E./Pierce: *Serenata*
Sparke, Philip: *Aubade*
Puccini, Giacomo/Moreau: *Oh, My Beloved
Father*
Denver, John/Fraser: *Perhaps Love*
Hallas, David
Album Title:
Personnel: Hade Edge Band, J. C. Fisher,
conductor
Label: Look Records, 1981 LP: LP7027
Sutton, Eddie: *Cavalier, The*
Hammarberg, Ake
Album Title:
Personnel: Sodetalje Salvation Army Band of
Stockholm
Label: Festival Records, 1978 LP: FLP124
Steadman-Allen, Ray: *Love Lifted Me*
Hanson, Scott
Album Title: *Alive! (and Kickin') Mr. Jack
Daniel's Original Silver Cornet Band*
Personnel: Bernard Walker, David Hobbs,
Chuck Bond, Stephen K. Charpie, cornet;
Cathy Caldwell, Noble Rawls, alto horn;
Tom Lundberg, tenor horn; Mike Dunn,
tuba; John R. Beck, percussion; Perry Hines,
drums; Bob Stephens, banjo; Marcus Arnold,
conductor
Label: Silver Cornet Productions, Inc., 1993
CD: SCP1
Mantia, Simone/McRitchie: *Believe Me if All
Those Endearing Young Charms*
Hardick, Caspar
Album Title: *Best of Brass, 1986*
Personnel: various brass bands
Label:
Saint-Saëns, Camille: *Swan, The*
Harewood, Ern
Album Title:
Personnel: David Harvey, euphonium;
Melbourne Salvation Army Staff Band, C.
Woods, conductor
Label: Klarion Records, 1978 LP: SF307
Bearcroft, Norman: *Timepiece*
Harvey, David. *See* Harewood, Ern

Hatano, Takeshi. *See* Champions of the Leonard
Falcone Festival 1986–2000
Hauser, Josh. *See* Euphoniums Unlimited
Hawkey, Vivian
Album Title:
Personnel: St. Austrell Band, Fred Roberts,
conductor
Label: Carnival, 1972 LP: 2928012
Doughty, George: *Scherzo for Four*
Heidler, Manfred
Album Title: *Exotenkonzert, Volume 1*
Personnel: Nicholas Pfeifle, euphonium;
Thomas Turek, Eriko Takezawa, piano
Label: Rodney Records, 1998 CD: LC 4148
Belcke, Friedrich August: *Etüde Nr. 2*
Belcke, Friedrich August: *Etüde Nr. 5*
Belcke, Friedrich August: *Etüde Nr. 7*
Rex: *Concertino*
Schumann, Robert: *"Träumerei" aus Kinder-
szenen Op. 15*
Mühlfeld, W.: *Conzertstück Op. 7*
Arban, Jean Baptiste: *Fantasy Brilliante*
Ponchielli, Amilcare: *Concerto per Flicorno basso*
Vancura, Adolf: *Canzonetta amorosa Op. 202*
Dräxelmeier, Xaver: *Konzertstück für Tenorhorn*
Turek, Thomas: *". . . im Stillen berauschter
Regen"*
Heo, Jae-Young
Album Title: *Euphonium Recital "Live"*
Personnel: Ji-Hee Shin, piano; Nam-Ho Kim,
Young-Sun Kwoen, Heon-Kyu Lim, tuba
Label: Mizentertainment Records, 2002 CD
Mozart, Wolfgang Amadeus/Blaauw: *Horn
Concerto No. 4 in E♭ Major*
Vivaldi, Antonio/Maganini: *Bassoon Concerto
No. 7 in a Minor*
Frackenpohl, Arthur: *Sonata for Euphonium
and Piano*
Paganini, Niccolo/Werden: *Caprice No. 17*
Leidzén, Erik/Field: *Song of the Brother, The*
Horner, James/Heo: *Titanic*
Mantia, Simone/Hunsberger: *Believe Me if All
Those Endearing Young Charms*
Hildebrandt, Jay. *See* Colonial Tuba Quartet
Hildreth, Gordon
Album Title: *Eventide—The Salvation Army
Wellington Citadel Band*
Personnel: Wellington Citadel Band, Bert
Neeve, conductor
Fidelity Sound Recordings, 1962 LP: FSR-
1235
Audoire, Norman: *We'll All Shout Hallelujah*
Hildreth, Gordon
Album Title:
Personnel: Wellington Salvation Army Band,
B. Neeve, conductor
Label: Fidelity Records, 1968 LP: LPS1263
Mozart, Wolfgang Amadeus/Rive: *Rondo from
"Horn Concerto in E♭"*
Himes, William
Album Title: *Atlanta Brass*

Personnel: Atlanta Temple Band of the Salvation Army, Richard Holz, conductor
Label: Salvation Army, 1981 LP: ASA 32481
Bowes, Ray: *Song of Triumph*
Clayton, Norman/Broughton: *Now I Belong to Jesus*
Senaille, J. B./Himes: *Allegro Spiritoso*
Hokazono, Sho-ichiro
Album Title: *Euphology*
Personnel: Mitsutaka Shiraishi, piano
Label: Toshiba EMI, CD: TOCE-55067
Poulenc, Frank/Isoda: *Suite Francaise*
Piazzolla, A./Hokazono: *Tango-Etudes*
Bozza, Eugene: *Aria*
Casterede, J.: *Fantasie Concertante*
Gillingham, David: *Blue Lake Fantasy*
Poulenc, F.: *Les Chemins L'Amour*
Hokazono, Sho-ichiro
Album Title: *Euphonium Dream*
Personnel: Ami Fukjiwara, piano
Label: Exton, CD: OVCL-00120
Bach, Johann Sebastian: *Sonata for Flute*
Arban, Jean Baptiste: *Fantasy Brilliante*
Yuste, Miguel: *Solo De Concurso*
Saegusa, Shigeaki: *Journey to Cornwell*
Traditional: *Last Rose of Summer, The*
Tomasi: *Sacred Dance Music*
Yoshimatsu, Takashi: *Dream Song*
Takemitsu, Toru/Fukjiwara: *Song of March*
Bosanko, Ivor: *Heart in Heart*
Wilby, Philip: *Concerto for Euphonium*
Hokazono, Sho-ichiro
Album Title: *Family Tree*
Personnel: Rei Egnchi, piano; Koichiro Yamamoto, trombone
Label: Kosei Publishers, CD: KOCD-2513
Bourgeois, Derek: *Euphoria*
Arban, Jean Baptiste: *Characteristic Study No. 1*
Vizzuti, Paul: *Cascade*
Kenswich, Marcel: *Legento*
Davis, Michael: *Family Tree*
Hokazono, Sho-ichiro
Album Title: *Fantastic Euphonium*
Personnel: Makoto Kanai, Yumi Sato, piano
Label: Nippon Crown, 1995 CD: CRCI-35012
Bolling, C.: *Rag-Polka from "Toot Suite"*
Arban, Jean Baptiste/Hunsberger: *Carnival of Venice, The*
Narita, Tamezo: *Hamabe no uta*
Harline, L./Kanai: *When You Wish upon a Star*
Sparke, Philip: *Pantomime*
Weber, Andrew Lloyd/Kanai: *Music of the Night*
Monti, Vittorio/Kanai: *Czárdás*
Martini, Giovanni/Kanai: *Plaisir D'Amour*
Sibelius, Jean: *Spruce, The*
Curnow, James: *Symphonic Variants*
Hokazono, Sho-ichiro
Album Title: *Hello, Mr. Ammonite!*
Personnel: Takeshi Inomata, piano
Label: Basic Video Arts, CD: BCD 20201

Carmichael, Hoagy: *Stardust*
Mancini, Henry: *Sunflower*
Inomata, Takeshi: *My Sweet Love*
Rodgers and Hammerstein: *My Favorite Things*
Webber, Andrew Lloyd: *Music of the Night*
Debussy, Claude: *My Reverie*
Monk/Williams: *'Round Midnight*
Pestalozza, A.: *Ciribribin*
Maeda, Norio: *Chim Chim Che-ree*
Hokazono, Sho-ichiro
Album Title: *New Band Music '98*
Personnel: Minako Ishibashi, euphonium; Tokyo Kosei Wind Orchestra, Yasuhiko Shiozawa, conductor
Label: Sony Records, CD: SRCS 2204
Sparke, Philip: *Two-Part Invention*
Hokazono, Sho-ichiro
Album Title: *Vintage–Fantastic Euphonium II*
Personnel: Kazuhiko Kohiruimaki, euphonium; The Central Band of the Japan Air Self Defense Forces, Katsuo Mizushima, conductor
Label: Crown Japan, CD: 35020
Reed, Alfred: *Seascape*
Fauré, Gabriel/Grainger: *Tuscan Serenade*
Boccalari, Ed/Kent-Akers: *Fantasia di Concerto*
Sparke, Philip: *Two Part Invention*
Jacob, Gordon: *Fantasia*
Gillingham, David: *Vintage*
Lacalle, G. J. M./Kosugi: *Amapola*
Howard, Michael. *See* British Tuba Quartet
Howell, Colin
Album Title:
Personnel: Woodfalls Band, Courtney Bosanko, conductor
Label: Hassell, 1975 LP: LP 3049
Mozart, Wolfgang Amadeus/Henstridge: *Allegro from "Bassoon Concerto"*
Huber, Billy. *See* Modern Jazz Tuba Project
Hunley, William. *See* Tennessee Technological University Tuba-Euphonium Ensemble
Hunter, Angie
Album Title: *Collage*
Personnel: Uwe Zeutzheim, piano
Label: Bernel CDs Ltd, 1998 CD: CD 10003
Sparke, Philip: *Pantomime*
Saint-Saëns, Camille: *Swan, The*
Curnow, James: *Symphonic Variants*
Picchi, Ermano/Mantia: *Fantaisie Originale*
Gordon, Harry/Conner, Tommie: *Down in the Glen*
Bourgeois, Derek: *Concerto, Op. 114*
Traditional: *How Great Thou Art*
Hunter, Angie
Album Title: *University of Illinois Brass Band*
Personnel: University of Illinois Brass Band
Label: University of Illinois, LP: #111
Steadman-Allen, Ray: *Ransomed Host, The*
Hunter, Angie. *See* Champions of the Leonard Falcone Festival 1986–2000
Ishibashi, Minako. *See* Hokazono, Sho-ichiro

Jackson, James. *See* Alchemy
Johnson, Frank
  Album Title:
  Personnel: Besses o' th' Barn Band, Igor James,
    conductor
  Label: Pye Records, 1973 LP: GSGL 10510
  Handel, George Frederic/Brockway: *Sonata in
    g Minor*
Johnston, Leon
  Album Title:
  Personnel: St. Keverne Band, Derek Johnston,
    conductor
  Label: Look Records, 1981 LP: 6583
  Corbett, Stephen, arr.: *Solitaire*
Jones, Alan
  Album Title: *Abbey Brass*
  Personnel: Abbey Brass
  Label: Abbey Brass
  Foster, Stephen: *My Old Kentucky Home*
Jordan, Jill
  Album Title: *1971 Mid-West National Band
    and Orchestra Clinic*
  Personnel: Round Lake Junior High School
    Band, Barbara Buehlman, conductor
  Label: Silver Crest Records, 1971 LP: MID-
    73-13
  Barat, J. Ed./Marsteller: *Andante et Allegro for
    Trombone and Band*
Jose, Robert
  Album Title: *Full Spectrum*
  Personnel: Kevin Mackenzie, euphonium;
    Mount Charles Band, Bryan Hurdley, con-
    ductor
  Label: Mount Charles Band, 2002 CD:
    MCBCD 1
  Graham, Peter: *Brilliante*
Jous, Christian. *See* Steckar Tubapack
Kane, Derick
  Album Title: *Blazon*
  Personnel: International Staff Band of the
    Salvation Army
  Label: Salvationist Supplies & Publishing, Ltd.,
    CD: SPS 091
  Himes, William: *Journey into Peace*
Kane, Derick
  Album Title: *Bridgewater Hall Live, 2001*
  Personnel: Great Northern Brass Arts Festi-
    val—Various Bands
  Label: CD: 2001
  Arban, Jean Baptiste/Remmington: *Carnival
    of Venice, The*
  Glennie/Childs: *A Little Prayer*
Kane, Derick
  Album Title: *The Derick Kane Euphonium
    Album*
  Personnel: International Staff Band of the
    Salvation Army; Richard Phillips, piano
  Label: Salvationist Publishing & Supplies Ltd.,
    CD: 2005
  Bearcroft, Norman: *Better World, The*
  Catherwood, David: *Spirit of Life*

Traditional/Downie: *My Love Is Like a Red
    Red Rose*
Mallet, Chris: *Travelling Along*
Steadman-Allen, Ray: *Lyric Variations*
Phillips, Richard: *There Will Be God*
Bosanko, Ivor: *To Live Right*
Pearce: *Welsh Fantasy*
Bearcroft, Norman: *Jesus I Come to Thee*
Rance, Ernest: *Ochills*
Blyth: *Compelled by Love*
Kane, Derick: *A New Direction*
Bizet, George/Norbury: *Menuet*
Bearcroft, Norman: *Timepiece*
Kane, Derick
  Album Title: *International Brass Spectacular*
  Personnel: International Staff Band of the Sal-
    vation Army, R. Bowes, conductor
  Label: Banners and Bonnetts, 1977 LP:
    BAB3505
  Leizden, Erik: *Song of the Brother, The*
Kane, Derick
  Album Title: *International Staff Band of the
    Salvation Army*
  Personnel: International Staff Band of the
    Salvation Army
  Label: Salvationist Publishing & Supplies Ltd.,
    1982 LP: SPS021
  Audoire, Norman: *We'll All Shout Hallelujah*
Kane, Derick
  Album Title: *ISB USA 1980*
  Personnel: International Staff Band of the Sal-
    vation Army, R. Bowes, conductor
  Label: Banners and Bonnetts, 1980 LP:
    BAB3525
  Camsey, Terry: A Joy Untold
Kane, Derick
  Album Title: *The Kingdom Triumphant*
  Personnel: International Staff Band of the Sal-
    vation Army, Stephen Cobb, conductor
  Label: Salvationist Supplies & Publishing, Ltd.,
    2002 CD: SPS 169
  Graham, Peter: *Bravura*
Kane, Derick
  Album Title: *Lyric Variations*
  Personnel: International Staff Band of the Sal-
    vation Army, Stephen Cobb, conductor
  Label: Salvationist Publishing & Supplies Ltd.,
    1999 CD: SPS 127 CD
  Ball, Eric/Birkett: *A Song of Faith*
  Rance, Ernest: *Ochills*
  Bearcroft, Norman: *Harbour Light*
  Bearcroft, Norman: *Timepiece*
  Steadman-Allen, Ray: *Conqueror, The*
  Gordon, William: *Saved by Grace*
  Steadman-Allen, Ray: *Lyric Variations*
  Phillips, Richard: *There Will Be God*
  Saint-Saëns, Camille/Steadman-Allen: *Swan, The*
  Bearcroft, Norman: *Better World, The*
  Catherwood, David: *Annie Laurie*
Kane, Derick
  Album Title: *Manuscripts*

Personnel: International Staff Band of the
    Salvation Army
Label: Salvationist Supplies & Publishing, Ltd.
Bosanko, Ivor: *My Unchanging Friend*
Kane, Derick
    Album Title: *New York Central Citadel*
    Personnel: International Staff Band Quartette
    Label: Salvationist Publishing & Supplies Ltd.
    Bearcroft, Norman: *Better World, The*
Kane, Derick
    Album Title: *Odyssey*
    Personnel: International Staff Band of the
        Salvation Army
    Label: Salvationist Supplies & Publishing, Ltd.
    Catherwood, David: *Spirit of Life*
Kane, Derick
    Album Title: *Perspectives*
    Personnel: International Staff Band of the
        Salvation Army
    Label: Salvationist Supplies & Publishing, Ltd.,
        1990
    Redhead, Robert: *Euphony*
Kane, Derick
    Album Title: *Trumpet Call*
    Personnel: International Staff Band of the
        Salvation Army
    Label: Salvationist Supplies & Publishing, Ltd.
    Bearcroft, Norman: *Locomotion*
Kane, Derick
    Album Title:
    Personnel: International Staff Band of the Sal-
        vation Army, R. Bowes, conductor
    Label: Banners and Bonnetts, 1977 LP:
        BAB3509
    Steadman-Allen, Ray: *Conqueror, The*
Kane, Derick
    Album Title:
    Personnel: International Staff Band of the Sal-
        vation Army, R. Bowes, conductor
    Label: Banners and Bonnetts, 1978 LP:
        BAB3519
    Bearcroft, Norman: *Better World, The*
Kane, Derick
    Album Title:
    Personnel: International Staff Band of the Sal-
        vation Army, R. Bowes, conductor
    Label: Salvationist Publishing & Supplies Ltd.,
        1987 LP: SPS055
    Bearcroft, Norman: *Jesus, I Come to Thee*
Kane, Derick
    Album Title:
    Personnel: International Staff Band of the Sal-
        vation Army, R. Bowes, conductor
    Label: Salvationist Publishing & Supplies Ltd.,
        1988 LP: SPS063
    Catherwood, David: *Everybody Should Know*
Kane, Derrick. *See* Mead, Steven
Keene, Ian
    Album Title:
    Personnel: Aldbourne Band, Don Keene,
        conductor

Label: TFW Records, 1980 LP: TJ 8004
Mantia, Simone/Boddington: *Believe Me if All
    Those Endearing Young Charms*
Kellens, Chris
    Album Title: *The Golden Eight*
    Personnel: Kenny Clarke, Francy Boland and
        Company
    Label: Blue Note Records, Inc.
Kershaw, Ronnie. *See* Warrington, Brian
Kilpatrick, Barry
    Album Title: *American Music for Euphonium*
    Personnel: Phyllis East, piano; Grant Cooper,
        Wade Weast, trumpet; Marc Guy, Pauline
        Emilson, horn; Scott Hull, Jeffrey Nelson,
        trombone; Rudolph Emilson, tuba
    Label: Mark Records LP: MRS-37882
    Wilder, Alec: *Sonata for Euphonium and
        Piano*
    Hartley, Walter: *Two Pieces for Euphonium and
        Piano*
    Hartley, Walter: *Sonata Euphonica*
    Wilder, Alec: *Concerto for Euphonium and
        Wind Orchestra (1971)*
    Luckhardt, Hilmar: *Octet for Brass (1977)*
Kilroy, Mike
    Album Title: *Diamond Heritage*
    Personnel: Brighouse and Rastrick Band, David
        Hurst, conductor
    Label: PACD, 2003 CD: 01
    Horner/Velde: *My Heart Will Go On*
Kilroy, Mike
    Album Title: *French Bon Bons*
    Personnel: Jonothan Beatty, trombone; Gri-
        methorpe Colliery Band, Major Peter Parkes,
        conductor
    Label: Chandos, 1996: CHAN 4542
    Bizet, George/Wilkinson: *Duet from
        "Pearlfishers"*
Kilroy, Mike
    Album Title: *Grimethorpe*
    Personnel: Grimethorpe Colliery Band, Garry
        Cutt, conductor
    Label: Chandos, 1996: CHAN 4545
    Skyes, Steven, arr.: *Carnival Cocktail*
Kilroy, Mike
    Album Title: *Let's Go!*
    Personnel: Williams Fairey Engineering Band,
        Peter Parkes, conductor
    Label: Obrasso Records, CD
    Rossini, Gioacchino/Newsome: *Prelude, Theme
        and Variations*
Kilroy, Mike
    Album Title: *Master Brass Volume 8*
    Personnel: Grimethorpe Colliery Band, Major
        Peter Parkes, conductor
    Label: Polyphonic Reproductions Ltd., 1997:
        QPRL 088D
    Skyes, Steven, arr.: *Carnival Cocktail*
Kilroy, Mike
    Album Title: *Romance in Brass*
    Personnel: Leyland DAF Band

Label: Polyphonic Reproductions Ltd., CPRL
043D
Weber, A.: *All I Ask of You*
Weber, A.: *Anything But Lovely*
Kilroy, Mike
Album Title:
Personnel: Mirlees Works Band, Ken Dennison,
conductor
Label: Grosvenor, 1978 LP: GRS 1069
Langford, Gordon: *Blaydon Races, The*
Kilroy, Mike. *See* McDonnell, Riki
Kipfer, Ueli
Album Title: *Air Varie*
Personnel: Beat Schafer, piano
Label: Ueli Kipfer, CD
Vivaldi, Antonio/Mortimer: *Sonata No. 6 in
B♭ Major*
Fiocco, Joseph Hector/Childs/Wilby: *Arioso
and Allegro*
Paganini, Niccolo/Wuthrich: *La Campanella
from "Violin Concerto No. 2"*
Golland, John: *Rhapsody No. 2*
Klose, Hyacinthe/Kipfer: *Air Varie, Op. 21*
Golland, John: *Peace*
Gillingham, David: *Blue Lake Fantasies*
Pryor, Arthur/Sparke: *Blue Bells of Scotland, The*
Kipfer, Ueli
Album Title: *The Music of John Golland*
Personnel: Brass Band Berner Oberland
Label: MF Records
Golland, John: *Euphonium Concerto No. 2*
Kohiruimaki, Kazuhiko. *See* Hokazono, Sho-ichiro
Kym, Martin. *See* Contraband
LaDuke, Lance
Album Title: *Take a Walk*
Personnel: Tyson Friar, guitar; Tim Thelen,
drums; Rich Ridenour, bandoneon in a box;
Susie Wing, vocals
Label: Lance LaDuke, CD: LL9097
LaDuke, Lance: *Take a Walk*
Traditional/LaDuke: *I Wonder What's Keeping
My True Love Tonight*
Traditional/LaDuke: *Nine Points of Roguery/
Murphy's Reel*
Traditional/LaDuke: *Arran Boat/Untitled Air*
Traditional/LaDuke: *May Morning Dew/
Strawaway Child/Conlon's Jig*
LaDuke, Lance: *Victor Hugo*
Pilafian, Sam: *Relentless Grooves II, Armenia*
Foster, Stephen/Pilafian: *Slumber My Darling*
Foster, Stephen/LaDuke: *My Wife Is a Most
Knowing Woman*
Piazzolla, Astor/LaDuke: *Cafè 1930*
Piazzolla, Astor/LaDuke: *Nightclub 1960*
Scott, Casey/LaDuke: *Cry (If You Want To)*
LaDuke, Lance. *See* Murchinson, Matthew
Lake Highlands Euphonium Section
Album Title: *1979 Mid-West National Band
and Orchestra Clinic*
Personnel: David Mills, Carl Wehe, Kit Mac-
Donald, euphonium; Malcolm Helm,
conductor

Label: Silver Crest Records, 1979 LP: MID-
79-15
Bellstedt, Herman: *La Mandolinata*
Lang, David. *See* Champions of the Leonard Fal-
cone Festival 1986–2000
Lawler, Paul. *See* Andrews, Paul
Lawrence, Mark
Album Title: *The Golden Age of Brass
Volume 2*
Personnel: American Serenade Band, Henry
Charles Smith, conductor
Label: Summit Records, 1991 CD: DCD 121
Mattei, Tito: *Non e Ver'*
Lawrie, Lindsay
Album Title:
Personnel: Fodens Motor Works Band, Derek
Garside, conductor
Label: Decca, 1980 LP: SB 341
Rimmer, William: *Variations on Jenny Jones*
Lean, David
Album Title:
Personnel: Mount Charles Band, W. H. Mag-
inn, conductor
Label: MSRS, LP: 1437
DeLuca, Joseph/Boddington: *Beautiful Colo-
rado*
Lehman, Arthur
Album Title: *The Art of Euphonium Playing,
Volume 1*
Personnel:
Label: Robert Hoe, 1977 LP: PDB 116
Mantia, Simone: *Auld Lang Syne*
Mantia, Simone: *Believe Me if All Those Endear-
ing Young Charms*
Picchi, Ermano/Mantia: *Fantasia Originale*
Hartmann, John: *Facilita*
Schmidt, Hugo: *Devil's Tongue, The*
Rogers, Walter: *Volunteers, The*
Kryl, Bohumir: *King Carneval*
King, Karl L.: *A Night in June*
Kemp: *Fantasia Capriccioso*
Short, T.V.: *Emmett's Lullaby*
Lehman, Arthur
Album Title: *The Art of Euphonium Playing,
Volume 2*
Personnel:
Label: Robert Hoe, 1979 LP: PDB 816
Schumann/Bell: *Jolly Farmer, The*
Anonymous/Godfrey: *Lucy Long*
Foster, Stephen: *Gentle Annie*
Rimmer, William: *Hailstorm*
Arban, Jean Baptiste: *Carnival of Venice, The*
Brasch, Harold: *Five Octave Stunt, The*
Windsor: *Alpine Echoes*
Handel, George Frederic/Hume: *Harmonious
Blacksmith, The*
Liberati, Allesandro: *Remembrance of Switzer-
land*
DeLuca, Joseph: *Beautiful Colorado*
Hartmann, John: *Robin Adair*
Lehman, Arthur
Album Title: *Euphonium Soloist*

Personnel: Buddy Burroughs, euphonium;
United States Marine Band
Label: Robert Hoe, 1976 LP
Anonymous/Clifton: *We Won't Go Home
Until Morning (The Bear Went Over the
Mountain)*
Godfrey/Herbert: *Lucy Long*
Arban, Jean Baptiste: *Carnival of Venice, The*
Bellstedt, Herman: *La Manodoinata*
DeLuca, Joseph: *Beautiful Colorado*
Foster, Stephen/Godfrey: *Gentle Annie*
Handel, George Frederic/Hume: *Harmonious
Blacksmith, The*
Liberati, Allesandro: *Remembrance of
Switzerland*
Mozart, Wolfgang Amadeus/Wright: *Rondo
from "Concerto No. 4 in Eb Major for Horn
and Orchestra"*
Rimmer, William: *Hailstorm*
Windsor, Basil: *Alpine Echoes*
Lehman, Arthur
Album Title: *Heritage of the March, Volume 70*
Personnel: National Concert Band of America,
Edmond DeMattia, conductor
Label: National Concert Band of America, LP:
PDB-443
Swift, George: *Elfriede*
Lehman, Arthur
Album Title: *A Night in June, Euphonium
Solos*
Personnel: Jimmy Basta, organ
Label: Robert Hoe, 1973 LP: NR 3646
Anonymous: *Best There Are, The*
Mantia, Simone: *Believe Me if All Those Endear-
ing Young Charms*
Hartmann, John: *Facilita*
King, Karl L.: *A Night in June*
Kryl, Bohumir: *King Carneval*
Mantia, Simone: *Auld Lang Syne*
Orff, Carl: *Ego Sum Abbas from "Carmina
Burana"*
Picchi, Ermano/Mantia: *Fantasia Originale*
Rogers, Walter: *Volunteer, The*
Levi, Eran
Album Title: *Levitation*
Personnel: Ensemble de Cuivres Melodia,
Olivier Chabloz, conductor
Label: Artlab, 1999 CD
Horovitz, Joseph: *Euphonium Concerto*
Paganini, Niccolo/Chabloz: *Moto Perpetuo*
Lidsle, Harri
Album Title: *Northern Light Tuba Quartet*
Personnel: Northern Light Tuba Quartet
Label: Northern Light Tuba Quartet
Stevens, John: *Power*
Traditional/Minerd: *Sea Tubas*
Sousa, John Philip/Werden: *Stars and Stripes
Forever*
Schooley, John: *Cherokee*
Niehaus, Lennie: *Brass Tracks*
Bach, Johann Sebastian/Sabourin: *Preludium*
Stevens, John: *Dances*

Sousa, John Philip/Werden: *Hands Across the
Sea*
Wolking, Henry: *Tuba Blues*
Mancini, Henry: *Pink Panther, The*
Offenbach, Jacques/Fletcher: *Orpheus in the
Underworld*
Lindsey, Marlin. *See* Euphonium Quartet
Lineberger, Laura. *See* Droste, Paul
Lineberger, Laura. *See* Wilkins, Richard
Lloyd, G.
Album Title:
Personnel: Tintwistle Band, Norman Ashcroft,
conductor
Label: TB Records, 1981 LP: SRTX/81/
WS1183
Foster, Stephen/Howarth: *Jeannie with the
Light Brown Hair*
Lord, Stephen
Album Title: *The Brighouse and Rastrick Band,
"In Concert"*
Personnel: The Brighouse and Rastrick Band,
James Scott, conductor
Label: Polyphonic Reproductions Ltd., 1980
LP: PRL 008
Woodfield, Ray: *Varied Mood*
Louder, Earle
Album Title: *The Florida State University Band
Presents Bach, Rock, and All That Jazz on
Record*
Personnel: Florida State University Band
Label: Custom Records, 1975 LP: USR 8770
Adams/Louder: *Bravura Variations*
Rodgers and Hart: *With a Song in My Heart*
Louder, Earle
Album Title: *Gems of the Concert Band, Volume 4*
Personnel: Detroit Concert Band
Label: H & L Records, 1981 LP: HL 80885-S
Adams/Louder: *Bravura Variations*
Louder, Earle
Album Title: *Gems of the Concert Band,
Volume 17*
Personnel: Detroit Concert Band
Label: H & L Records, 1988 LP: HL 71387-S
Verdi, Giuseppe: *Euphonium Solo from "Man-
zoni Requiem"*
Louder, Earle
Album Title: *Gems of the Concert Band, Volume 6*
Personnel: Detroit Concert Band
Label: H & L Records, LP: HL 82820-S
(41366)
DeLuca, Joseph: *Beautiful Colorado*
Louder, Earle
Album Title: *Gems of the Concert Band,
Volume 10*
Personnel: Detroit Concert Band
Label: H & L Records, 1984 LP: 83817-S
Rodgers and Hart: *With a Song in My Heart*
Louder, Earle
Album Title: *Greenville Senior High School
Concert Band*
Personnel: Greenville Senior High School
Concert Band

Label: Mark Records, 1970 LP: UMC 2424
Mantia, Simone: *Believe Me if All Those Endearing Young Charms*
Louder, Earle
Album Title: *Gunnison Music Camp, Volume 4*
Personnel: Gunnison Music Camp Bands
Label: Century Records, 1962 LP
Saint-Saëns, Camille: *Swan, The*
Louder, Earle
Album Title: *Holmes Symphonic Band*
Personnel: Holmes Symphonis Band
Label: Century Records, 1969 LP: 35226
Guilmant, Alexandre: *Morceau Symphonique*
Mantia, Simone: *Believe Me if All Those Endearing Young Charms*
Louder, Earle
Album Title: *Morehead State University Director's Band*
Personnel: Morehead State University Symphony Band
Label: Audicom, 1973 LP: USR 5211
Bizet, George: *Flower Song from "Carmen"*
Senaille, Jean Baptiste: *Allegro Spiritoso*
Louder, Earle
Album Title: *Morehead State University Symphony Band, Volume III*
Personnel: Morehead State University Symphony Band, Robert Hawkins, conductor
Label: Mark Custom Records, LP: UMC-2123
Mueller, Frederick: *Concerto for Euphonium and Band*
Louder, Earle
Album Title: *Morehead State University Symphony Band, Volume 12*
Personnel: Morehead State University Symphony Band
Label: Audicom, 1973 LP: USR 7260
Mantia, Simone: *Believe Me if All Those Endearing Young Charms*
Louder, Earle
Album Title: *Music from America's Golden Age*
Personnel: New Columbian Brass Band
Louder, Earle
Album Title: *1970 MENC BiAnnual Convention*
Personnel: Holmes High School Band
Label: Silver Crest Records, 1970 LP: 70MENC6
Guilmant, Alexandre: *Morceau Symphonique*
Louder, Earle
Album Title: *1979 Mid-West National Band and Orchestra Clinic*
Personnel: Northshore Concert Band, John Paynter, conductor
Label: Silver Crest Records, 1979 LP: MID-79-8
Saint-Saëns, Camille/Nelson: *Morceau de Concert, Op. 94*
Louder, Earle
Album Title: *Soloists of the Detroit Concert Band*

Personnel: The Detroit Concert Band, Leonard Smith, conductor
Label: H & L Records, LP: HL-121061-S (30662)
Mantia, Simone: *Believe Me if All Those Endearing Young Charms*
Donizetti, Gaetano: *Lucia Di Lammermoor*
Verdi, Giuseppe: *Bella Figlia from "Rigoletto"*
Louder, Earle
Album Title: *Sunny Hill High School Band*
Personnel: Sunny Hill High School Band
Label: Audio Engineering Association, 1979 LP: AEA 1259
Clarke, Herbert L.: *Carnival of Venice, The*
Adams/Louder: *Bravura Variations*
Traditional/Ades: *Londonderry Air*
Louder, Earle
Album Title: *Sunny Hill High School Band*
Personnel: Sunny Hill High School Band
Label: Audio Engineering Association, 1983 LP: AEA 1391
DeLuca, Joseph: *Beautiful Colorado*
Louman: *Carioca*
Mantia, Simone: *Believe Me if All Those Endearing Young Charms*
Louder, Earle. *See* Symphonia
Lowry, Benny
Album Title:
Personnel: Carlton Main Frickley Colliery Band, Robert Oughton, conductor
Label: Pye Records, 1970 LP: GSGL 10454
Brahms, Johannes/Ruffles: *Lullaby*
Lundin, Anders
Album Title: *World Champions*
Personnel: Gothenburg Brass Band
Label: Intim Musik, IMC 4
Rachmaninov, Sergei/Langford: *Vocalise Op. 34, No. 14*
Mack, Thomas
Album Title: *Digital Brass*
Personnel: New York Salvation Army Staff Band, Derek Smith, conductor
Label: Triumphonic, 1980 LP: TRLPS-33
Camsey, Terry: *A Joy Untold*
Mack, Thomas
Album Title: *Profile II—The Music of Colonel Albert H. Jakeway*
Personnel: New York Staff Band of the Salvation Army, Albert H. Jakeway, guest conductor
Label: Triumphonic, 1980 LP: TRLPS-32
Jakeway, Albert H.: *Land Beyond the Blue*
Mack, Thomas
Album Title: *Return to England*
Personnel: New York Staff Band of the Salvation Army, Derek Smith, conductor
Label: Triumphonic, 1985 LP: TRLPS-44
Mack, Thomas: *Tell the World*
Mack, Thomas
Album Title:
Personnel: New York Salvation Army Staff Band, Derek Smith, conductor

Label: Banners and Bonnetts, 1978 LP:
  BAB3512
Mack, Thomas: *Covenant, The*
Mack, Thomas
  Album Title:
  Personnel: New York Salvation Army Staff
    Band, Derek Smith, conductor
  Label: Pilgrim Records, 1986 LP: PRA55
  Mack, Thomas: *Tell the World*
Mackenzie, Kevin. *See* Jose, Robert
Mackie, Kevin
  Album Title: *Varsity Variations*
  Personnel: Morrells Concert Brass
  Label:
  Doe, Phillip: *Lullaby*
Mallett, Chris
  Album Title: *Chris Mallett and Friends*
  Personnel: Ivor Bosanko, piano; Terry Camsey,
    cornet; Fay Mallett, vocals; Brass Band, Ivor
    Bosanko, conductor
  Label: Salvationist Supplies & Publishing, Ltd.
  Smith, Bernard: *Glorious Fountain*
  Camsey, Terry: *A Joy Untold*
  Arban, Jean Baptiste/Mallet: *Carnival of
    Venice, The*
  Davies, Howard/Catherwood: *Search for a
    New World*
  Krinjak, Karen/Bosanko: *I Have No Claim on
    Grace*
  Mantia, Simone/Langford: *Believe Me if All
    Those Endearing Young Charms*
  Larson, John/Bosanko: *I'll Not Turn Back*
  Senaille, Jean Baptiste/Himes: *Allegro Spiritoso*
  Graham, Peter: *Glorious Ventures*
  Bosanko, Ivor: *Glorious Liberation*
Mallett, Chris
  Album Title: *On a Mission*
  Personnel: Household Troops of the Salvation
    Army, John Mott, conductor
  Label: Salvationist Supplies & Publishing, 2002
    CD: SPS 168
  Anonymous: *Traveling Along*
Mancuso, Gus
  Album Title: *Gus Mancuso and Special Friends*
  Personnel: B. Douglas, C. Tjader, B. Greve,
    drums; G. Wiggins, V. Guaraldi, P. Jolly,
    piano; G. Wright, R. Mitchell, bass; R.
    Kamuca,
    J. Romano, tenor saxophone
  Label: Fantasy Records, 2001 CD: FCD
    24762-2
  Dorsey, Tommy/Madeira: *I'm Glad There
    Is You*
  Mancuso, Gus: *Brother Aintz*
  Martin/Blane: *Ev'ry Time*
  Wiggins, Gerald: *Ruble and the Yen, The*
  Young/Pollack/Lewis/White: *By the Way*
  Tjader, Patricia: *And Baby Makes Three*
  Mercer/Malenck: *Goody Goody*
  Cahn/Brodszky: *How Do You Like Your Eggs in
    the Morning?*

Guaraldi, Vince: *A Hatful of Dandruff*
Porter, Cole: *Ev'ry Time We Say Goodbye*
Carroll/Siegal: *Love Is a Simple Thing*
Carroll/Siegal: *Monotonous*
Spinelli, Joseph: *Scratch My Back*
Mancuso, Gus: *O-Fayces*
Harnick, Sheldon: *Boston Beguine, The*
Grand/Boyd: *Guess Who I Saw Today?*
Brown/Fain: *Love Is Never Out of Season*
Graham: *I'm in Love with Miss Logan*
Mancuso, Gus
  Album Title: *Introducing Gus Mancuso*
  Personnel: Gus Mancuso Ensemble
  Label: Fantasy Records, 3233
Marsteller, Loren
  Album Title: *Geronimo: An American Legend*
  Personnel:
  Label: Columbia Records, LP: 475645-2
  Cooder, Ry: *Train to Florida*
Marsteller, Loren
  Album Title: *Loren Marsteller, Euphonium*
  Personnel: Stephen Harlos, piano
  Label: Sawday Instruments, CD: 8107
  Hill, William: *Concerto for Euphonium*
  Bach, Johann Sebastian/Marsteller: *Sonata
    No. 3*
Marsteller, Loren. *See* Mighty Tubadours
Marsteller, Robert
  Album Title: *Sounds for Success, Baritone*
  Personnel: Max Ervin, piano; George DeGre-
    gori, narrator
  Label: Century Records Co., 1963 LP: 32721
Mather, Harry
  Album Title:
  Personnel: Cammell Laird Band, James Scott,
    conductor
  Label: Fontana, 1970 LP: STL 5531
  Godfrey/Herbert: *Lucy Long*
Matteson, Rich
  Album Title: *The Art of Improvisation, Volume 1*
  Personnel: Rich Matteson, euphonium and
    piano
  Label: Music Minus One, 1973 LP: Includes
    method books
Matteson, Rich
  Album Title: *The Art of Improvisation, Volume 2*
  Personnel: Rich Matteson, euphonium and
    piano
  Label: Music Minus One, 1974 LP: Includes
    method books
Matteson, Rich
  Album Title: *Do Your Own Thing*
  Personnel: Rich Matteson, euphonium and
    piano
  Label: Music Minus One, 1968 LP: Includes
    method books
Matteson, Rich
  Album Title: *Easy Street*
  Personnel: Ulf Andersson, tenor sax; Kjell
    Öhman, piano; Sture Nordin, bass; Egil
    Johansen, drums

Label: Four Leaf Records, 1980 LP: FLC 5051
Parker, Charlie: *Donna Lee*
Jones, Alan: *Easy Street*
Joel, Billy: *Just the Way You Are*
Matteson, Rich: *Mikki's Blues*
Huesen van, J.: *I Thought About You*
Petersen, Jack: *Dan's Blues*
Haerle, Dan: *Crib Chimp*
Youman/Rose/Eliscu: *Without a Song*
Matteson, Rich
   Album Title: *Groovey*
   Personnel: Phil Wilson, trombone; Jim Riggs,
      alto sax; Jack Petersen, guitar; Ben Hallberg,
      piano; Red Mitchell, bass; Egil Johansen,
      drums
   Label: Four Leaf Records, 1982 LP: FLC 5060
Petersen, Jack: *Skippin'*
Petersen, Jack: *Kokomo*
Wilson, Phil: *Budda Eastern Bebop*
Matteson, Rich: *Tahoe*
Haerle, Dan: *Magic Morning*
Petersen, Jack: *Groovey*
Matteson, Rich
   Album Title: *The Jazz Ambassadors, Live on Tour*
   Personnel: The United States Army Field Band
   Label: United States Army Band. Public ser-
      vice, not for sale
Matteson, Rich
   Album Title: *Jazz Journey, Pete Petersen and the
      Collection Jazz Orchestra*
   Personnel: Pete Petersen and the Collection
      Jazz Orchestra
   Label: Chase Music Group, 1984 CD: CMD
      8042
Joel, Billy/Matteson: *Just the Way You Are*
Matteson, Rich
   Album Title: *Life's a Take*
   Personnel: Stefan Karlsson, piano; Red Mitch-
      ell, bass; Peter Östlund, drums
   Label: Four Leaf Records, 1985 LP, 1993
      CD: 123
Mitchell, Red: *Life's a Take*
Robbin, L./Rainger: *Easy Living*
Porter, Cole: *I Love You*
Gershwin, George: *Our Love Is Here to Stay*
Kahn, G./Jones: *You Stepped Out of a Dream*
Symes, M./Jones: *There Is No Greater Love*
Webster, P./Mandel: *Shadow of Your Smile, The*
Matteson, Rich
   Album Title: *Pardon Our Dust, We're Making
      Changes, Rich Matteson Sextet*
   Personnel: John Allred, euphonium; Shelly
      Berg, piano; Jack Petersen, guitar; Lou
      Fischer, bass; Louie Bellson, drums
   Label: Four Leaf Records, 1990, 1995 CD: 131
Bellson, Louie: *Hawk Talks, The*
Rollins, Sonny: *St. Thomas*
Ellington, Duke: *In a Mellow Tune*
Hamm, F./Bennet/Lown/Gray: *Bye, Bye Blues*
Woode, H./Hines: *Rosette*
Cohn, Al: *Travissimo*

Matteson, Rich: *A Very Special Love*
Matteson, Rich: *Ira's Tune*
Braham, P./Furber: *Limehouse Blues*
Matteson, Rich
   Album Title: *Rich Matteson*
   Personnel:
   Label: Crest Records, LP: MID-72-13
Legrand/Slater: *Summer of '42*
Matteson, Rich/Peterson: *Shout, The*
Pape: *For Richer or Poorer*
Matteson, Rich
   Album Title: *The Sound of the Wasp*
   Personnel: Rich Matteson, euphonium, valve
      trombone, tuba; Phil Wilson, slide trom-
      bone; Jack Petersen, guitar; Lyle Mays,
      piano; Ed Soph, drums; Kirby Stewart, bass
   Label: ASI Records, 1975 LP: ASI-203
Wilson, Phil: *What Wasp?*
Petersen, Jack: *Hey Man!*
Matteson, Rich: *Hassels*
Wilson, Phil: *Another Balance*
Wilson, Phil: *Red Flannel Hash*
Wilson, Phil: *Sound of the Wasp, The*
Wilson, Phil: *Hills and Valleys*
Matteson, Rich: *Carrob*
Petersen, Jack: *A Breath of Fresh Air*
Wilson, Phil: *What's Her Name?*
Mays, Lyle: *Kilgore Trout*
Wilson, Phil: *That Wasp*
Matteson, Rich
   Album Title: *Texas State of Mind*
   Personnel: Pete Petersen and the Collection
      Jazz Orchestra
   Label: Pause Records, 1983 LP
Matteson, Rich
   Album Title: *Thurs Night Dues*
   Personnel: The Summer Jazz Band, Rich
      Matteson, leader
   Label: SJC Productions, 1973 LP: SJC81673
Matteson, Rich: *Archie's Back*
McPartland, Marian/Wilson: *Time and Time
   Again*
Wilson, Phil: *Three Friends*
Wilson, Phil: *Colonel Corn*
Matteson, Rich: *I Got No Bread*
Matteson, Rich
   Album Title: *Tuba-Euphonium Legacy Project,
      Volume I*
   Personnel: Various Ensembles
   Label: Mark Custom Recording Service, Inc.,
      2003 CD: 4580 MCD
Wilson, Phil: *What's Her Name?*
Wilson, Phil: *Sound of the Wasp, The*
Anonymous: *Apple Strudel and Cheese*
Carmichael, Hoagy/Matteson: *Georgia on My
   Mind*
Anonymous: *Blue Bossa*
Anonymous: *Stella by Starlight*
Anonymous: *Undecided*
Matteson, Rich: *Shuckin' and Jivin'*
Schooley, John: *Cherokee*

Braham, P./Furber: *Limehouse Blues*
Wilson, Phil: *That Wasp*
Matteson-Phillips Tubajazz Consort
  Album Title: *Matteson-Phillips Tubajazz Consort*
  Personnel: Rich Matteson, Ashley Alexander, Buddy Baker, euphonium; Harvey Phillips, Winston Morris, Dan Perantoni, tuba; Jack Petersen, guitar; Dan Haerle, Tom Ferguson, piano; Rufus Reid, Kelly Sills, bass; Ed Soph, drums
  Label: A & R Records, 1976 LP
  Silver, Horace: *Gregory Is Here*
  Jarrett, Keith: *Lucky Southern*
  Gershwin, George: *Summertime*
  Rollins, Sonny: *Oleo*
  Matteson, Rich: *Spoofy*
Matteson-Phillips TubaJazz Consort
  Album Title: *Perantoni Plays Perantoni*
  Personnel: Matteson-Phillips TubaJazz Consort
  Label: Mark Custom Recording Service, CD: 2433-MCD
  Matteson, Rich: *Little Ole Softy*
Matteson-Phillips Tubajazz Consort
  Album Title: *Superhorn*
  Personnel: Rich Matteson, Ashley Alexander, Buddy Baker, euphonium; Harvey Phillips, Winston Morris, Dan Perantoni, tuba; Jack Petersen, guitar; Dan Haerle, Tom Ferguson, piano; Rufus Reid, Kelly Sills, bass; Ed Soph, drums
  Label: Mark Records, 1988 CD: MJS-57626CD (combined LPs *SUPERHORN and Matteson-Phillips Tubajazz Consort*)
  Sampson/Racaf/Foodman/Webb: *Stompin' at the Savoy*
  Matteson, Rich: *Little Ole Softy*
  Peterson, Oscar/J. Peterson: *Noreen's Nocturn*
  Ellington, Duke/Matteson: *Things Ain't What They Used to Be*
  Carmichael, Hoagy/Matteson: *Georgia on My Mind*
  Matteson, Rich; arr.: *Waltzing Matilda*
  Silver, Horace: *Gregory Is Here*
  Jarrett, Keith: *Lucky Southern*
  Gershwin, George: *Summertime*
  Rollins, Sonny: *Oleo*
  Matteson, Rich: *Spoofy*
Matteson-Phillips Tubajazz Consort
  Album Title: *SUPERHORN*
  Personnel: Rich Matteson, Ashley Alexander, Buddy Baker, euphonium; Harvey Phillips, Winston Morris, Dan Perantoni, tuba; Jack Petersen, guitar; Dan Haerle, Tom Ferguson, piano; Rufus Reid, Kelly Sills, bass; Ed Soph, drums
  Label: Mark Records, 1982 LP: MJS-57591
  Sampson/Racaf/Foodman/Webb: *Stompin' at the Savoy*
  Matteson, Rich: *Little Ole Softy*
  Peterson, Oscar/J. Peterson: *Noreen's Nocturn*

Ellington, Duke/Matteson: *Things Ain't What They Used to Be*
Carmichael, Hoagy/Matteson: *Georgia on My Mind*
Matteson, Rich; arr.: *Waltzing Matilda*
Matteson-Phillips Tubajazz Consort
  Album Title: *Tubajazz Superhorns*
  Personnel: Matteson-Phillips Tubajazz Consort
  Label: HPF-TJ-CD 3
Matteson-Phillips Tubajazz Consort
  Album Title: *Tubajazz Superhorns Live!!!*
  Personnel: Matteson-Phillips Tubajazz Consort
  Label: HPF-TJ-CD 4
Matthew, Gee
  Album Title: *Blues in Orbit*
  Personnel: Duke Ellington Orchestra
  Label: Columbia, LP: CS 8241
  Ellington, Duke: *Swingers Get the Blues Too*
Matti, Jean-Claude
  Album Title: *Brass Band Berner Oberland*
  Personnel: Daniel von Siebenthal, euphonium
  Label: Amos Records, 1982 LP
  Bryce, Frank: *Rondolette fur zwei Euphonium*
McCrea, Melvin
  Album Title:
  Personnel: Ever Ready Band, Eric Cunningham, conductor
  Label: Decca, 1977 LP: SB 329
  Gheel, Henry: *Romanza*
McDonnell, Riki, and Mike Kilroy
  Album Title: *The Euphonium Songbook*
  Personnel: Robert Childs, euphonium; Peter Gratrix, tuba; Maxine Mollins, piano; Pamela Harrop, harp; The Marple Band, Garry Cutt, conductor
  Label: Polyphonic Reproductions Ltd., 1999 CD: QPRL 097D
  Brodsky/Farr: *Be My Love*
  Richards, Goff: *Jean-Elizabeth*
  Mandel/Maunder: *Shadow of Your Smile, The*
  Brahe, May: *Bless This House*
  Romberg, Sigmund/Oswin: *Serenade from "The Student Prince"*
  Kern/Maunder: *All the Things You Are*
  Paganini, Niccolo/Richards: *Cantabile*
  Parry/Maunder: *Myfanwy*
  Rimmer, William/Kerwin: *In Dixieland*
  Bach, Johann Sebastian/Gounod/Denny: *Ave Maria*
  Traditional/Maunder: *Hine e Hine*
  Catelinet, Philip: *Call of the Seasons*
  Foster, Stephen/Howarth: *Jeannie with the Light Brown Hair*
  Webber, Andrew Lloyd/Mowat: *All I Ask of You*
  Johnstone, Helen: *Anna Karenina*
  Balfe/Kerwin: *I Dreamt I Dwelt in Marble Halls*
  Traditional/Denny: *Turn Your Eyes upon Jesus*
McDonnell, Riki, and Mike Kilroy
  Album Title: *Midnight Euphonium*

Personnel: Lynne Daniell, piano; Williams
Fairey Band, Major Peter Parkes, conductor
Label: Polyphonic Reproductions Ltd., 1994
CD: QPRL 064D
Richards, Goff: *Midnight Euphonium*
Sparke, Philip: *Euphonism*
Fiocco, Jean-Joseph/McKenzie/Maunder:
Arioso
Mancini, Henry/Maunder: *How Soon*
Schönberg, Claude-Michel/Barry: *On My Own*
Brandt: *Concerto No. 1*
Puccini, Giacomo/Stephens: *Nessun Dorma*
Puccini, Giacomo: *Your Tiny Hand Is Frozen*
Sparke, Philip: *Ina*
Richards, Goff: *Love Is Forever*
Bizet, George/Wilkinson: *Deep inside the
Sacred Temple*
Foster, Stephen/Howarth: *Jeanie with the Light
Brown Hair*
Sykes, Steven, arr.: *Carnival Cocktail*
Gounod, Charles/Snell: *Hail, Ancient Walls*
Bernstein, Leonard/Adams: *Somewhere*
Fiocco, Jean-Joseph/Smith: *Allegro*
Tomoana/Maunder: *Pokarekareana*
McDonnell, Riki, and Mike Kilroy
Album Title: *Operatic Euphonium*
Personnel: Grimethorpe Colliery Band, Garry
Cutt, conductor
Label: Polyphonic Reproductions Ltd., CD:
QPRL 072D
Verdi, Guiseppe: *Celeste Aida*
Verdi, Guiseppe: *La Donna e Mobile*
Verdi, Guiseppe: *Quartet from "Rigoletto"*
Verdi, Guiseppe: *La Miserere from "Il
Travatore"*
Delibes, Léo: *Flower Duet*
Cardillo: *Catari, Catari*
Rossini, Gioacchino: *Largo Al Factotum*
Donizetti, Gaetano: *Duet from "Don Pasquale"*
Humperdinck, Engelbert: *Evening Prayer from
"Hansel and Gretel"*
Mozart, Wolfgang Amadeus: *Marriage of Figaro*
Mozart, Wolfgang Amadeus: *Papageo Papagena*
Bizet, George: *Flower Song from "Carmen"*
Leoncavallo, Ruggero: *On with the Motley*
Saint-Saëns, Camille: *Softly Awakes My Heart*
Puccini, Giacomo: *Recondita Armonia*
Puccini, Giacomo: *Oh My Beloved Father*
Puccini, Giacomo: *One Fine Day*
Puccini, Giacomo: *Nessun Dorma*
Franck, César: *Panis Angelicus*
Wagner, Richard: *Introduction to Act Three
from "Lohengrin"*
Lehár, Franz: *U Are My Heart's Delight*
Strauss, Richard: *Nun's Chorus*
McEnvoy, Graham
Album Title: *Besses in Australia*
Personnel: Besses o' th' Barn Band, Roy New-
some, conductor
Label: Chandos, 1979 LP: BBR 1002
Newsome, Roy, arr.: *Dublin's Fair City*

McEnvoy, Graham
Album Title: *Heritage of the March, Volume IV,
Besses o' th' Barn Band*
Personnel: Besses o' th' Barn Band, Roy New-
some, conductor
Label: Besses o' th' Barn Band
Gheel, Henry, arr.: *Watching the Wheat*
McEnvoy, Graham
Album Title:
Personnel: Peter Read, cornet; Besses o' th'
Barn Band, Roy Newsome, conductor
Label: Chandos, 1979 LP: BBR 1003
Newsome, Roy, arr.: *Foxtrot between Friends*
McGlashan, Don
Album Title: *The Mutton Birds*
Personnel: The Mutton Birds
Label: Bag Records, 8282612
McKinney, Bernard
Album Title: *The Cool Sound of Pepper Adams*
Personnel: Pepper Adams, baritone sax; George
Duvivier, bass; Hank Jones, piano; Elvin
Jones, drums
Label: Savoy Jazz
Unknown: *Bloos*
Unknown: *Booze*
Unknown: *Blues*
Unknown: *Settin' Red*
Unknown: *Like What Is This?*
Unknown: *Skippy*
McKinney, Bernard
Album Title: *First Flight*
Personnel: Donald Byrd, trumpet; Barry Har-
ris, piano; Kenny Clark, drums; Frank Foster,
Yusaf Lateef, tenor sax; Paul Chambers, Alvin
Jackson, bass
Label: Delmark
Unknown: *Blues*
Unknown: *Tortion Level*
Unknown: *Woodyn' You*
Unknown: *Dancing in the Dark*
McKinney, Bernard
Album Title: *The Futuristic Sounds of Sun Ra*
Personnel: Sun Ra, piano; John Gilmore, tenor
sax, bass clarinet; Marshall Allen, tenor sax,
alto sax, flute; Pat Patrick, baritone sax; Ron-
ald Boykins, bass; Willie Jones, drums; Ricky
Murray, vocals; Leah Ananda, conga
Label: Savoy Jazz, SV-213
Sun Ra: *Bassism*
Sun Ra: *Of Wounds and Something Else*
Sun Ra: *What's That?*
Sun Ra: *Where Is Tomorrow?*
Sun Ra: *Beginning, The*
Sun Ra: *New Day*
Sun Ra: *Tapestry from an Asteroid*
Sun Ra: *Jet Flight*
Sun Ra: *Looking Outward*
Sun Ra: *Space Jazz Reverie*
Young/Adamson: *China Gates*
McKinney, Bernard
Album Title: *Ready for Freddie*

Personnel: Freddie Hubbard Band
Label: Blue Note Records, Inc., LP: 32094
McKinney, Bernard
Album Title: *Sister Salvation*
Personnel: The Slide Hampton Octet
Label: Collectables, CD: COL-CD 6173
Hampton, Slide: *Sister Salvation*
Ellington, Duke/Gaines: *Just Squeeze Me*
Weston, Randy: *Hi-Fi*
Hampton, Slide: *Asseveration*
Gryce, Gigi: *Conversation Piece*
Hampton, Slide: *A Little Night Music*
McNally, Robert
Album Title: *Christmas with the Salvation Army*
Personnel: New York Salvation Army Staff
Band, Richard E. Holz, conductor
Label: Westminster: WP 6096 (WST 15015)
Adam, Adolphe/Anonymous: *Cantique de Noel*
McNally, Robert
Album Title: *Star Spangled Band Music*
Personnel: New York Staff Band of the Salva-
tion Army, Richard E. Holz, conductor
Label: Triumphonic, 1960 LP: LP-5
Leidzen, Erik: *Home on the Range*
McNally, Robert
Album Title: *Symphony in Brass*
Personnel: New York Staff Band of the Salva-
tion Army, Richard E. Holz, conductor
Label: Word, 1965 LP: WST 8137 (W-3252)
Steadman-Allen, Ray: *Ransomed Host, The*
McPherson, John. *See* Albertasaurus Tuba Quartet
Mead, Steven
Album Title: *Bella Italia—Beautiful Italy*
Personnel: Italian Army Band, Fulvio Creux,
conductor
Label: Bocchino Music, 2004 CD: BOCC 102
Koper, Karl-Heinz: *Dulcamarata for Eupho-
nium and Symphonic Band*
Giordani, Giuseppe/Bona: *Caro mio ben*
Stradella, Alessandro/Barbagallo: *Aria di chiesa*
Bellini, Vincenzo/Bona: *Vaga luna che
inargenti*
Bellini, Vincenzo/Bona: *Vi ravviso, o luoghi
ameni*
Bellini, Vincenzo/Bona: *Ah, non credea mirarti*
Bellini, Vincenzo/Bona: *Ah, non giunge from
"La Sonnambula"*
Verdi,Giuseppe/Creux: *A fors' è lui from "la
Traviata"*
Verdi, Giuseppe/Creux: *Di Provenza il mar, il
suol from "la Traviata"*
Verdi, Giuseppe/Creux: *Ave Maria from
"Otello"*
Puccini, Giacomo/Bona: *Vissi d'arte from
"Tosca"*
Toselli, Enrico/Rüedi: *Serenata*
Feliciangeli, Francesco/Creux: *Preghiera from
"Lo Scudiero del Re"*
Orsomando, Giovanni/Creux: *Alla Czárdás*
Arban, Jean Baptiste/Hunsberger: *Variations
on "Carnival of Venice"*

Mead, Steven
Album Title: *Best of Brass, 1986*
Personnel: Desford Colliery Caterpillar Band,
Howard Snell, conductor
Label: Polyphonic Reproductions Ltd., 1986
CPRL 026D
Saint-Saëns, Camille/Snell: *Swan, The*
Mead, Steven
Album Title: *Brass Pins*
Personnel: Brass Band Bürgermusik Luzern
Label: Obrasso Records, CD
Curnow, James: *Rhapsody for Euphonium*
Richards, Goff: *Pilatus*
Mead, Steven
Album Title: *Bravura*
Personnel: William Fairey Band, Howard Snell,
conductor
Label: Polyphonic Reproductions Ltd., QPRL
217D
Gounod/Snell: *Hail Ancient Walls*
Golland, John: *Euphonium Concerto No. 2*
Hartmann, John: *Arbucklenian Polka*
Paradies/Snell: *Sicilienne*
Cosma, Vladimir/Meredith: *Concerto*
Elgar, Edward/Bourgeois: *Lento from "Cello
Concerto"*
Paganini, Niccolo/Snell: *Moto Perpetuo*
Graham, Peter: *Bravura Variations for Eupho-
nium Quartet*
Mead, Steven
Album Title: *Brilliante*
Personnel: Egon Virtuosi Brass and Salvation
Army Brass Band, J. Williams, P. Graham,
conductors
Label: EGON, CD: 118
Graham, Peter: *Glorious Ventures*
Graham, Peter: *Brilliante Fantasy on Rule
Britannia*
Mead, Steven
Album Title: *Britain and Brass*
Personnel: Brass Band of Battle Creek
Label: Brass Band of Battle Creek
Picchi, Ermano/Bale: *Fantaisie Originale*
Mead, Steven
Album Title: *The Canadian Staff Band, featur-
ing Steven Mead*
Personnel: Salvation Army Canadian Staff Band
Label: Salvation Army, CD: CSB WRC8-7193
Graham, Peter: *Brilliante*
Hartmann, John: *Facilita*
Redhead, Robert: *Euphony*
Harline/Kanai: *When You Wish upon a Star*
Mead, Steven
Album Title: *Classic Quintet Volume 1*
Personnel: Woodwind Quintet
Label: Newport, CD: 572-004-2
Wilhelm, Rolf: *Concertino*
George, Thom Ritter: *Sextet*
Prinz: *Merry Black Widow, The*
Mantia, Simone/Brasch/Maldonado: *Believe
Me if All Those Endearing Young Charms*

Puccini, Giacomo: *Nessun Dorma*
Woodfield, Ray: *Varied Mood*
Mead, Steven
  Album Title: *Classic Quintet Volume 2*
  Personnel: Woodwind Quintet
  Label: ProCultura, CD: 0377
  Holst, Gustav: *Wind Quintet in A♭*
  Graham, Peter/Veit: *Brilliante*
  Iturralde/Veit: *Pequeña Czárdás*
  Monti, Vittorio/Veit: *Czárdás*
  Picchi, Ermano/Veit: *Fantaisie Originale*
  Traditional/Catherwood/Veit: *Lark in the Clear Air, The*
  Bimboni/Veit: *Concerto Brilliante on "Carnival of Venice"*
Mead, Steven
  Album Title: *Concertino*
  Personnel: The Lillestrøm Musikkorps, Gert Buitenhuis, conductor
  Label: Polyphonic Reproductions Ltd., 1999 CD: QPRM 131D
  Wilhelm, Rolf: *Concertino*
  Thingnaes, Frode: *Peace, Please*
  Sparke, Philip: *Fantasy*
  Gillingham, David: *Vintage*
  Horovitz, Joseph: *Lento from "Euphonium Concerto"*
  Böhme, Oskar/Smith: *Russian Dance*
  Bourgeois, Derek: *Concerto*
Mead, Steven
  Album Title: *Continental Brass*
  Personnel: Desford Colliery Caterpillar Band
  Label: DHM 3002.3
  Schoonenbeek, Kees: *Twilight Serenade*
Mead, Steven
  Album Title: *Die Druiden*
  Personnel: Landesblasorchester Baden-Württemberg
  Label: Great Lakes Music Enterprises, CD: ACD 6014-3
  Curnow, James: *Symphonic Variants*
Mead, Steven
  Album Title: *Dreamscapes, Great British Music for Wind Band, Volume 8*
  Personnel: The Royal Northern College of Music Wind Orchestra, James Gourlay, conductor
  Label: Polyphonic Reproductions Ltd., CD: QPRM 143D
  Ellerby, Martin: *Euphonium Concerto*
Mead, Steven
  Album Title: *The Essential Steven Mead*
  Personnel: Williams Fairey Band, Howard Snell, conductor
  Label: Polyphonic Reproductions Ltd., 1998 CD: QPRL 095D
  Webber, Andrew Lloyd/Graham: *Variations*
  Drigo/Stephens: *Serenade*
  Heaton, Wilfred: *Variations on Annie Laurie*
  Schubert, Franz/Wilkinson: *Serenade*
  Leidzén, Erik: *Home on the Range*

Woodfield, Ray: *Varied Mood*
Doughty, George: *Grandfather's Clock*
Puccini, Giacomo/Smith: *O My Beloved Father*
Arban, Jean Baptiste/Remmington: *Carnival of Venice, The*
Bruch/Gay: *Kol Nidrei*
Snell, Howard: *Variations on Drink to Me Only*
Golland, John: *Peace*
Mead, Steven
  Album Title: *Euphonium Magic*
  Personnel:
  Label: Bocchino Music, 2003 CD: BOCC 101
  Tchaikovsky, Piotr/Bale: *Humoreske*
  Gabrieli, Giovanni/Bale: *Sonata Pian 'e forte*
  Schumman, William/Mahlknecht: *Erinnerung*
  Bach, Johann Sebastian/Taylor: *Toccata and Fugue in d Minor*
  Garfunkel/Reichenbach: *Scarborough Fair*
  Dukas/Bale: *Sorcerer's Apprentice, The*
  Debussy, Claude/Bale: *Golliwogg's Cakewalk*
  Debussy, Claude/Bale: *Clair de Lune*
  Mendelssohn, Felix/Bale: *Scherzo from "Midsummer Nights Dream"*
  Debussy, Claude/Bale: *Girl with the Flaxen Hair, The*
  Wagner, Richard/Hall: *Ride of the Valkyries, The*
  Traditional/Roberts: *Frankie and Johnny*
  Howard, B./Hughes: *Fly Me to the Moon*
  Prima, L./Vinson: *Jump, Jive an' Wail*
Mead, Steven
  Album Title: *Euphonium Magic 2, Music of Life*
  Personnel:
  Label: Bocchino Music, 2005 CD
  Elfman/Robertson: *What's This?*
  Beethoven/Bale: *Finale of 5th Symphony*
  Chopin/Bale: *Waltz, Op. 64, No. 2*
  Wagner/Ito: *Processional to the Minster*
  Ito, Yasuhide: *Euphoniums Parfait*
  Grieg/Harris: *Ase's Death*
  Harline/Robertson: *When You Wish upon a Star*
  Desmond/Luis: *Take Five*
  Traditional/Olcott: *Shenandoah*
  Elfman/Harris: *The Simpsons*
  Ellington/Paul: *Come Sunday*
  Thomas/Dos: *A la Romanesc*
  Andresen: *And Soon It Will Be Blossom Time*
  Fucik/Carrol/Maldonado: *Entrance and Polka of the Euphonium Players*
  Vejvoda/Zelch: *Rosamunde*
Mead, Steven
  Album Title: *Euphony*
  Personnel: The Royal Northern College of Music Brass Band, Howard Snell, conductor
  Label: Polyphonic Reproductions Ltd., 1996 CD: QPRL 082D
  Sparke, Philip: *Euphonium Concerto*
  Traditional/Roberts: *Carrickfergus*
  Redhead, Robert: *Euphony*
  Sparke, Philip: *Aubade*
  Curtis, De/Roberts: *Return to Sorrento*

Bowen, Brian: *Euphonium Music*
Bellstedt, Herman/Brand: *Napoli*
Richards, Goff: *Midnight Euphonium*
Bearcroft, Norman: *Better World, The*
Mead, Steven
Album Title: *Euphoria*
Personnel: Christine Jones, piano
Label: SJM Music, 1989 CS: SJM 262
Woodfield, Ray: *Varied Mood*
Saint-Saëns, Camille: *Swan, The*
Bosanko, Ivor: *Heart in Heart*
Elgar, Edward/Wilson: *Romance Op. 62*
Mantia, Simone/Boddington: *Believe Me if All Those Endearing Young Charms*
Horovitz, Joseph: *Euphonium Concerto*
Arban, Jean Baptiste: *Carnival of Venice, The*
Bourgeois, Derek: *Euphoria*
Mead, Steven
Album Title: *Excalibur*
Personnel: Breeze Brass Band, Kazuyoshi Uemura
Label: Kosei Publishing Co., 1993 CD: KOCD-2503
Golland, John: *Euphonium Concerto, No. 1, Op. 64*
Rossini, Gioacchino/Brennan: *Introduction, Theme and Variations*
Sparke, Philip: *Pantomime*
Mead, Steven
Album Title: *Fireworks*
Personnel:
Label: Polyphonic Reproductions Ltd., QPRZ 020D
Mead, Steven
Album Title: *4 Valves 4 Slides*
Personnel: Trombonisti Italiani
Label: ProCultura, CD: 0405
Bizet, George/Bale: *Gypsy Dance from "Carmen"*
Debussy, Claude/Bale: *Girl with the Flaxen Hair, The*
Bellstedt, Herman/Bale: *Napoli Variations*
Puccini, Giacomo/Bale: *Recondita Armosia from "Tosca"*
Howard, Bart/Hughes: *Fly Me to the Moon*
Levy, Jules/Bale: *Grand Russian Fantasia*
Jobim, Antonio Carlos/Dittmar: *One Note Samba*
Rimsky-Korsakov, Nikolai/Bale: *Flight of the Bumble Bee, The*
Hart, Lorenzo; Rodgers, Richard/Pirone: *My Funny Valentine*
Parker, Charlie/Pirone: *Au Privave*
Traditional/Stuckelschweiger: *Pcelinca*
Mead, Steven
Album Title: *Great British Music for Wind Band, Volume 3*
Personnel: Royal Air Force Central Band, Rob Wiffin, conductor
Label: Polyphonic Reproductions Ltd., QPRM 124D

Sparke, Philip: *Pantomime*
Mead, Steven
Album Title: *Highlights from the BBC Television Brass Band Contest*
Personnel: Sun Life Band, Barry Pope, conductor
Label: Polyphonic Records, 1983, PRL 022
Langford, Gordon: *Blaydon Races, The*
Mead, Steven
Album Title: *Highlights from the European Brass Band Championships, 1998*
Personnel: various brass bands
Label: World Wind Music, CD: WWM-500.038
Sarasate/Snell: *Ziegunerweisen*
Mead, Steven
Album Title: *Holst, Vaughan Williams, Jacob*
Personnel: The Keystone Wind Ensemble, Jack Stamp, conductor
Label: Not in print
Jacob, Gordon: *Fantasia for Euphonium*
Mead, Steven
Album Title: *Joseph Horovitz, Music for Brass*
Personnel: CSW (Glasgow), Joseph Horovitz, conductor
Label: Serendipity, 1994 CD: SERCD 1900
Horovitz, Joseph: *Euphonium Concerto*
Mead, Steven
Album Title: *Jubilee Brass, Highlights of the 2002 National Finals Gala Concert*
Personnel: David Thorton, Derrick Kane, David Childs, Robert Childs, Nicholas Childs, euphonium; Black Dyke Mills Band, International Staff Band, Don Lusher Big Band
Label: Salvationist Supplies & Publishing, Ltd., CD: SPS 165
Graham, Peter: *Bravura Variations on British Folksongs*
Mead, Steven
Album Title: *Love Songs in Brass*
Personnel: CWS Glasgow Band, Frank Renton, conductor
Label: Obrasso Records, CD
Garner, Errol/Fernie: *Misty*
Mead, Steven
Album Title: *Mead IN(N)—Brass*
Personnel: Sound-INN-Brass Austria, Howard Snell, conductor
Label: Weinberg Records, CD: SW010183-2
Doss, Thomas: *Sir "EU"*
Arban, Jean Baptiste/Howarth/Gurtner: *Amazing Mr. Arban, The*
Schumann, Robert/Gurtner: *Adagio and Allegro*
Richards, Goff/Mead: *Midnight Euphonium*
Foster, Stephen/Harvey: *Jeannie with the Light Brown Hair*
Mead, Steven
Album Title: *The Mighty Voice*
Personnel: Central Band of the Royal Air Force, R. K. Whiffin, conductor

Label: Polyphonic Reproductions Ltd., QORM
124D
Sparke, Philip: *Pantomime*
Mead, Steven
Album Title: *National Brass Band Festival,
1986*
Personnel: combined brass bands
Label: Polyphonic Reproductions Ltd., CPRL
001D
Gregson, Edward: *Symphonic Rhapsody for
Euphonium and Band*
Mead, Steven
Album Title: *Norge moter England*
Personnel: Norwegian Army Military Band,
Ray Farr, conductor
Label: FDMT, Bernel Music
Gregson, Edward: *Symphonic Rhapsody for
Euphonium*
Gillingham, David: *Vintage*
Mead, Steven
Album Title: *Oration*
Personnel: Williams Fairey Band, Howard
Snell, conductor
Label: Polyphonic Reproductions Ltd., 2001
CD: QPRL 209D
Iturralde, Pedro/van der Woude: *Pequeña
Czárdás*
Bozza, Eugene/van der Woude: *Aria*
Wilby, Philip: *Euphonium Concerto*
Wagner, Richard/Bale: *Walther's Prize Song*
Boccalari, Eduardo/Meredith: *Fantasia di
Concerto*
Traditional/Catherwood: *Lark in the Clear
Air, The*
Moren, Bertrand: *Mr. Euphonium*
Rossini, Gioacchino/Brennan: *Introduction,
Theme and Variations*
Snell, Howard: *Oration*
Mead, Steven
Album Title: *Rondo*
Personnel: Rigid Containers Group Band,
Robert Watson, conductor
Label: Heavyweight Records, 1990 CD:
HR004/D
Catelinet, Philip: *Call of the Seasons*
Gounod, Charles/Snell: *Hail Ancient Walls*
Sparke, Philip: *Pantomime*
Ponce, Manuel/Bennett: *Estrellita*
Bourgeois, Derek: *Euphoria*
Sarasate, Pablo de/Snell: *Gypsy Airs*
Puccini, Giacomo/Wilkinson: *Nessun Dorma*
Hartmann, John/Stephens: *Rule Britannia*
Rimsky-Korsakov, Nikolai/James/Freeh: *Flight
of the Bumble Bee, The*
Smith/Freeh: *Rondo*
Mead, Steven
Album Title: *Sing, Sing, SING*
Personnel: Brass Band of Battle Creek, K. C.
Bloomquist, conductor
Label: Brass Band of Battle Creek
Sparke, Philip: *Party Piece*

Mead, Steven
Album Title: *Symphonic Variants*
Personnel: J.W.F. Military Band, Alex Schil-
lings, conductor
Label: DeHaske, CD: DHR 4.008
Curnow, James: *Rhapsody for Euphonium and
Band*
Curnow, James: *Concerto for Euphonium and
Band*
Curnow, James: *Symphonic Variants for Eupho-
nium and Band*
Mead, Steven
Album Title: *Timepiece*
Personnel: Brass Band des Posses, Switzerland
Label: ArtLab, CD: 99917
Woodfield, Ray: *Varied Mood*
Traditional/Roberts: *Carrickfergus*
Sykes, Steven, arr.: *Carnival Cocktails*
Mantia, Simone/Boddington: *Believe Me if All
Those Endearing Young Charms*
Mead, Steven
Album Title: *Tribute*
Personnel: Michigan State University Wind
Symphony, Kenneth Bloomquist, conductor
Label: Polyphonic Reproductions Ltd., CD:
QPRM 118D
Picchi, Ermano/Mantia: *Fantasie Originale*
King, Karl L.: *A Night in June*
Clarke, Herbert L.: *From the Shores of the
Mighty Pacific*
Curnow, James: *Rhapsody*
DeLuca, Joseph/Roberts: *Beautiful Colorado*
Klengel, Julius/Falcone: *Concertino No. 1 in B♭*
Boccalari, Ed/Kent-Akers: *Fantasia Di Con-
certo*
Ponce, Manuel/Lake: *Estrellita*
Simons: *Atlantic Zephyrs*
Mantia, Simone/Brasch/Maldanado: *Believe
Me if All Those Endearing Young Charms*
Bizet, George/ Harding: *Flower Song from
"Carmen"*
Mantia, Simone: *Auld Lang Syne*
Mead, Steven
Album Title: *Trittico*
Personnel: Desford Colliery Caterpillar Band
Label: DHM 3003.3
Ponce, Manuel/Bennett: *Estralita*
Mead, Steven
Album Title: *Variations*
Personnel: Desford Colliery Caterpillar Band,
James Watson, conductor
Label: Polyphonic Reproductions Ltd., QPRL
041D
Hartmann, John/Mortimer: *Facilita*
Mead, Steven
Album Title: *Vistas, the Music of Martin Ellerby*
Personnel: The Royal Northern College of
Music Brass Band, James Gourlay, conductor
Label: Polyphonic Reproductions Ltd., 1997
CD: QPRL 085D
Ellerby, Martin: *Euphonium Concerto*

Mead, Steven
  Album Title: *The Waters of Myth*
  Personnel: Tennessee Technological University
    Symphony Band, Joseph Hermann,
    conductor
  Label: TTU Recording Services, 1994 CD
  Sparke, Philip/Maldonado: *Pantomime*
Mead, Steven
  Album Title: *The World of the Euphonium,*
    Volume 4
  Personnel: Nicoletta Mezzini, piano; cornet
    section of Williams Fairey Band, Howard
    Snell, conductor
  Label: Polyphonic Reproductions Ltd., QPRZ
    023D
  Cosma, Vladimir: *Euphonium Concerto*
  Paganini, Niccolo/Richards: *Cantabile*
  Snell, Howard: *Fever Fantasy*
  Piazolla, Astor/Mead: *Café 1930*
  Reeman, John: *Sonata for Euphonium*
  Kassatti, Tadeuz: *By Gaslight*
  Sparke, Philip: *Birthday Tribute*
  Brahams, Johann/Gotoh: *Es ist Eine Rose*
    Entsprungen
  Szentpali, Roland: *Pearls*
  Puccini, Giacomo/Mead: *Vissi D'Arte*
  Alen, Hugo/Olsrud: *Herbmaiden's Dance*
Mead, Steven
  Album Title: *The World of the Euphonium,*
    Volume 1
  Personnel: Joyce Woodhead, Richard Phillips,
    piano
  Label: Polyphonic Reproductions Ltd., 1994
    CD: QPRZ 014D
  Marcello, Benedetto: *Sonata in F Major*
  Butterworth, Arthur: *Partita Op. 89*
  Rachmaninov, Sergei: *Vocalise, Op. 34,*
    No. 14
  Wiggins, Christopher: *Soliloquy IX*
  Hoshina, Hiroshi: *Fantasy for Euphonium*
  Kummer, Friedrich: *Variations for Ophicleide*
  Hartley, Walter: *Sonata Euphonica*
  Fauré, Gabriel: *Après Un Rêve*
  Rimmer, William: *Weber's Last Waltz*
  Bosanko, Ivor: *Heart in Heart*
  Offenbach, J.: *Bacarolle*
  Stevens, Thomas: *A New Carnival of Venice*
Mead, Steven
  Album Title: *The World of the Euphonium,*
    Volume 3
  Personnel: Stewart Death, piano
  Label: Polyphonic Reproductions Ltd., 1996
    CD: QPRZ 019D
  Leidzen, Erik: *Song of the Brother, The*
  Wilby, Philip: *Flight*
  Elgar, Edward/Wilson: *Romance*
  Sparke, Philip: *Party Piece*
  Narita/Kanai: *Song of the Seashore*
  Ito, Yasuhide: *Fantasy Variations*
  Roper: *Sonata for Euphonium*
  Schmid/Bacon: *Im Tiefsten Walde Notturno*

Ponchielli, Amilcare/Howey: *Concerto per*
    Flicorno Basso
Mead, Steven
  Album Title: *The World of the Euphonium,*
    Volume 2
  Personnel: Stewart Death, Richard Phillips,
    piano
  Label: Polyphonic Reproductions Ltd., 1995
    CD: QPRZ 017D
  Wilby, Philip: *Concert Gallop*
  Yuste, Miguel: *Solo De Concurso*
  Jacob, Gordon: *Fantasia*
  Saint-Saëns, Camille/Mead: *Swan, The*
  Casterede, Jacques: *Fantaisie Concertante*
  Sparke, Philip: *Song for Ina*
  Marshall, George: *Ransomed*
  Kreisler, Fritz: *Liebesfreud*
  Golland, John: *Largo Elegaico from "Eupho-*
    nium Concerto No. 2"
  Dewhurst, Robin: *Panache*
  Fauré, Gabriel/Mead: *Two Fauré Duets*
  Smalley, Peter: *Ball of Fire*
  Dinicu-Heifitz: *Hora Staccato*
Mead, Steven
  Album Title:
  Personnel: Desford Colliery Caterpillar Band,
    Howard Snell, conductor
  Label: Music for Pleasure, 1987 LP: MFP
    5782
  Saint-Saëns, Camille/Snell: *Swan, The*
Mead, Steven
  Album Title:
  Personnel: Young Ambassadors Brass Band,
    Ray Farr, conductor
  Label: U.K.M.A. Records, 1983 LP
  Hartmann, John: *Rule Britannia*
Mead, Steven
  Album Title:
  Personnel: Young Ambassadors Brass Band,
    Roy Newsome, conductor
  Label: Y.A.B.B., 1988 LP: 003
  Doughty, George: *Grandfather's Clock*
Mead, Steven. *See* British Tuba Quartet
Meier, Martin. *See* Contraband
Meixner, Brian
  Album Title: *Genesis*
  Personnel: Caryl W. Conger, piano; the Uni-
    versity of Kentucky Wind Ensemble, Richard
    Clary, conductor; University of Kentucky
    Tuba-Euphonium Ensemble, Skip Gray,
    conductor
  Label: Bernel CDs Ltd., CD: CD 10011
  Ellerby, Martin: *Euphonium Concerto*
  Martino, Ralph: *Introspect*
  Sibbing, Robert: *Reverie and Frolic*
  Traditional/James A.Garrett: *Londonderry Air*
  Gillingham, David R.: *Vintage*
  Dewhurst, Robin: *Panache*
  Rimmer, William: *Hailstorm*
Meli, Renato
  Album Title: *At the Contests*

Personnel: Brass Band Limburg
Label:
Woodfield, Ray: *Varied Mood*
Meli, Renato
Album Title: *Demelza*
Personnel: Brass Band Limburg
Label: Brass Band Limburg, CD: CDL2020
Picchi, Ermano: *Fantaisie Originale*
Meli, Renato
Album Title: *I Himmelen*
Personnel: Brass Band Limburg
Label:
Sparke, Philip: *Pantomime*
Meli, Renato
Album Title: *Swiss Entertainment Contest*
Personnel: Brass Band Limburg
Label: Brass Band Limburg
Sparke, Philip: *Fantasy for Euphonium and
Brass Band*
Melton Tuba-Quartett
Album Title: *Lazy Elephants*
Personnel: Uli Haas, euphonium; Heiko
Triebener, Henrik Tietz, Hartmut Müller,
tuba
Label: Diavolo Records, 1993 CD: 003
Bach, Johann Sebastian/Hermann: *Badinerie*
Gabrieli, Giovanni/Gray: *Canzone per Sonare
No. 4*
Victoria, Thomas Luis de/Self: *O Vos Omnes*
Mozart, Wolfgang Amadeus/Doerner: *Das
Butterbrot*
Liszt, Franz/Seitz: *Hungarian Rhapsody No. 2*
Hidas, Frigyas: *Tuba Quartett*
Strauss, Johann/Seitz: *Tritsch-Tratsch Polka*
Fucik, Julius/Watz: *Florentiner March*
Rimsky-Korsakov, Nicolai/Watz: *Flight of the
Bumble Bee, The*
Khatchaturian/Seitz: *Sabre Dance*
Kalke, Ernst-Thilo: *Requiem to a Dead Little
Cat*
Kalke, Ernst-Thilo: *Jumbo's Holiday*
Schooley, John: *Cherokee*
Barrozo, Ary/Weichselbaumer: *Brazil*
Hawkins, Erskin/Luis: *Tuxedo Junction*
Desmond, Paul/Luis: *Take Five*
Luis, Ingo: *Lazy Elephant Blues*
Melton Tuba-Quartett
Album Title: *Melton Tuba-Quartett
"Premiere"*
Personnel: Uli Haas, euphonium; Heiko
Triebener, Henrik Tietz, Hartmut Müller,
tuba
Label: Diavolo Records, 1993 CD: DR-D-93-
C-001
Sousa, John Philip/Sabourin: *Washington Post
March*
Frackenpohl, Arthur: *Ragtime*
Handy, W.C./Holcombe: *St. Louis Blues*
Mozart, Wolfgang Amadeus/Fletcher: *Eine
kleine Nachtmusik*
Ramsöe, Wilhelm/Buttery: *Andante Quasi
Allegretto*

Payne, Frank Lynn: *Quartet for Tubas*
Bach, Johann Sebastian/Arcadelt/Self: *Ave
Maria*
Garrett, James Allen: *Miniature Jazz Suite*
Mancini, Henry/Luis: *Baby Elephant Walk*
Stevens, John: *Dances*
Bach, Johann Sebastian/Werden: *Bist Du Bei
Mir*
Schumann, Robert/Seitz: *Träumerei*
Mancini, Henry/Krush: *Pink Panther, The*
Hutchinson, Terry: *Tuba Juba Duba*
Melton Tuba-Quartett
Album Title: *Power*
Personnel: Uli Haas, euphonium; Heiko
Triebener, Henrik Tietz, Hartmut Müller,
tuba
Label: Diavolo Records, 1993 CD
Stevens, John: *Power*
Stevens, John: *Moondance*
Traditional: *Londonderry Air*
Traditional: *Greensleeves*
Traditional: *Old Star*
Dempsey, Ray: *Quatre Chansons*
Luis, Ingo: *Little Lullabye*
Wolking, Henry: *Tuba Blues Melody*
Powell, Baden: *Bocoxe*
Roblee, Richard: *Four Tuba Blues*
Wilhelm, Rolf: *Bavarian Stew*
Watz, Franz: *Melton Marsch*
Membury, Clive
Album Title:
Personnel: Royal Doulton Band, Ted Gray,
conductor
Label: Bandleader, 1986 LP: BNB2009
Gheel, Henry, arr.: *Watching the Wheat*
MacDowell, Edward/Ball: *To a Wild Rose*
Merkin, Geoffrey
Album Title:
Personnel: Dodsworth Band, Graham
O'Connor, conductor
Label: Northern Sound, 1979 LP: RES 200
Webber, Andrew Lloyd/Woodfield: *Don't Cry
for Me Argentina*
Metcalf, Curtis
Album Title: *Canadian Impressions*
Personnel: Hannaford Street Silver Band
Label: CBC Records, LP: 5136
Irvine, Scott: *Concertino for Euphonium*
Metcalf, Curtis
Album Title: *Tour of Europe*
Personnel: Canadian Staff Band, Robert Red-
head, conductor
Label: Salvation Army of Canada, LP:
CSB27909
Redhead, Robert: *Euphony*
Metcalf, Curtis
Album Title:
Personnel: Canadian Staff Band, Robert Red-
head, conductor
Label: Boosey & Hawkes Sound, 1983 LP:
BHSS091
Himes, William: *Journey into Peace*

Meyer, Donald
Album Title: *Chicago Staff Band of the Salvation Army*
Personnel: Chicago Staff Band, Tom Gabrielsen, conductor
Label: Fidelity Sound Recordings, LP: FSRS-1269
Himes, William: *My Christ*
Middleburg, Marco
Album Title: *On Top—25 Years of De Waldsang*
Personnel: Brass Band of De Waldsang, Rieks van der Velde, conductor
Label: World Wind Music, CD: WWM 500.007
Miesenberger, Anton
Album Title: *Faces Live*
Personnel: Heavy Tuba, Heimo Schmid, leader
Label: Atemmusik, 1994 CD: 94004, LC 7352
Pecha, Antonin: *Hvezdonicka*
Miles, David. *See* Monarch Tuba-Euphonium
Quartet
Milhiet, Ivan
Album Title: *Inouï . . .*
Personnel: Frédéric Guérouet, accordion; François Desforges, Cyril Landriau, percussion
Label: Sacem, 1998 CD: SDRM
Monti, Vittorio: *Czárdás*
Piazzola, Astor: *Suite Lumière*
Nissim, Mico: *Symphonie des regards*
Escaich, Thierry: *Ground*
Vivaldi, Antonio: *Sonata No.1 en Si b majeur*
Cosma, Vladimir: *Euphonium Concerto*
Piazzola, Astor: *Libertango*
Millar, Billy
Album Title: *Romance in Brass, Volume II*
Personnel: BNFL Band
Label: Polyphonic Reproductions, Ltd. CD
Sparke, Philip: *Aubade*
Millar, Billy
Album Title:
Personnel: James Shepherd Versatile Brass, Ray Farr, conductor
Label: Polyphonic Reproductions Ltd., 1983 LP: PRL 019
Hartmann, John/Hopkinson: *Rule Britannia*
Miraphone Tuba Quartet
Album Title: *International Marschparade*
Personnel: Patrick Couttet, Philippe Wendling, euphonium; Philippe Gallet, Olivier Galmant, tuba
Label: Koch International, CD: 324199
Fucik, Julius: *Entry of the Gladiators*
Unknown: *Under the Admirals Flag*
Sousa, John Philip: *Washington Post March*
Unknown: *Yorkscher March*
Unknown: *Graf Zeppelin March*
Fucik, Julius: *Florentiner March*
Unknown: *Bayerischer Defiliermarsch*
Unknown: *Mes Sana in Corpore Sano*
Unknown: *Castaldo March*
Unknown: *Alte Kameraden*
Unknown: *Petersburger March*
Strauss, Johann: *Radetzky March*

Unknown: *Preussens Gloria*
Sousa, John Philip: *Stars and Stripes Forever, The*
Miraphone Tuba Quartet
Album Title: *Miraphone Tuba Quartet*
Personnel: Patrick Couttet, Philippe Wendling, euphonium; Philippe Gallet, Olivier Galmant, tuba
Label: Koch International, CD: 323759
Frackenpohl, Arthur: *Pop Suite*
Glinka, Michael: *Overture to "Russlan and Ludmila"*
Agrell, Jeffrey: *Gospel Tune*
Joplin, Scott/Walter: *Strenuous Life, The*
Lennon, John/Luis: *Hey Jude*
Martino, Ralph: *Fantasy*
Mozart, Wolfgang Amadeus: *Overture from the "Magic Flute"*
Neihaus, Lennie: *Tubalation*
Shaw, Lowell: *Frippery*
Steckar, Marc: *Bassa Cat*
Stevens, John: *Manhattan Suite*
Traditional/Buttery: *Greensleeves*
Miraphone Tuba Quartet
Album Title: *Pictural*
Personnel: Patrick Couttet, Philippe Wendling, euphonium; Philippe Gallet, Olivier Galmant, tuba
Label: Koch International, CD: 324653
Rossini, Gioacchino/Smalley: *La Danza*
Unknown: *Casbah of Tetouan, The*
Unknown: *Pictural*
Unknown: *Entrevue/Tribal*
Schönberg, Claude-Michel: *On My Own*
Stevens, John: *Power*
Unknown: *Under the Sea*
King, Karl/Werden: *Melody Shop, The*
Traditional/Lohmann, George: *Bayrische Polka*
Miura, Toru
Album Title: *Contest Band Music Selections '76*
Personnel: Philharmonia Wind Ensemble
Label: CBS/Sony Inc., 1976 LP: 22AG 3
Jacob, Gordon: *Fantasia*
Miura, Toru
Album Title: *Invitation to Playing Instruments—Euphonium/Trombone*
Personnel:
Label: CBS Sony, CD: 36AG622-3
Bellstedt, Herman: *Napoli*
Morel, Florentin: *Piece in fa mineur*
Miura, Toru
Album Title: *Sempre Italiano*
Personnel: Tokyo Kosei Wind Orchestra, Fredrick Fennell, conductor
Label: KOCD, CD: 3573
Boccalari, Ed/Kent-Akers: *Fantasia di Concerto*
Miura, Toru
Album Title: *Solo Album for Wind Instruments, Euphonium*
Personnel:
Label: Denon Records, 1990 CD: COCG-6535
Arban, Jean Baptiste/Ito: *Variations from "Carnival of Venice"*

Youmans, V./Ito: *Carioca*
Rossini, Gioacchino/Ito: *La Danza*
Traditional/Ito: *Greensleeves*
Hoshina, Hiroshi: *Fantasy for Euphonium and Piano*
Yamada, Kosaku/Ito: *Akatombow*
Offenbach, J./Ito: *Bacarolle*
Barat, J. Ed.: *Introduction et Serenade*
Nagano, Mitsuhiro: *Matrix for Euphonium and Synthesizer*
Anderson, Leroy/Ito: *Anderson's Toy-box*
Handel, George Frederic/Ito: *Xerxes, Ombra mai fu (Largo)*
Miura, Toru
    Album Title: *Tokyo Kosei Wind Ensemble Plays Alfred Reed*
    Personnel: Tokyo Kosei Wind Ensemble, Fredrick Fennell, conductor
    Label: KOCD, CD: 3012
    Reed, Alfred: *Seascape*
Modern Jazz Tuba Project
    Album Title: *Favorite Things*
    Personnel: Marcus Dickman, Billy Huber, Barry Green, euphonium; Joe Murphy, Richard Perry, Winston Morris, tuba; Paul Carrol Binkley, guitar; Jim Ferguson, bass; Bob Mater, drums; Steve Willets, Kevin Mandill, keyboards
    Label: Heartdance Music, Inc., 2003 CD: HDM-1120
    Rodgers and Hammerstein/Madill: *My Favorite Things*
    Brown, David/Williamson: *Theme for Malcolm*
    Russell, Leon/Florance: *Strange Thing*
    Petersen, Jack/Perry: *Hey Man!*
    Silver, Horace/Matteson: *Gregory Is Here*
    Martin, Glenn: *Pearl Casters*
    Russell, Leon/Madill: *This Masquerade*
    Carmichael, Hoagy/Matteson: *Georgia on My Mind*
    Duncan/Ball/McIntryre/Gorrie/Stuart/McIntosh/Murphy: *Pick Up the Pieces*
    Perry, Richard: *Kool Kube*
    Prima, Louis/Murphy: *Sing, Sing, Sing*
Modern Jazz Tuba Project
    Album Title: *Live at the Bottom Line*
    Personnel: Marcus Dickman, Billy Huber, Barry Green, euphonium; Joe Murphy, Richard Perry, Winston Morris, tuba; Marty Crum, guitar; Tony Nagy, bass; Jeff Lloyd, drums; Steve Willets, keyboards
    Label: Heartdance Music, Inc., 2001 CD: HDM-1090
    Matteson, Rich, arr.: *Cherokee*
    Martin, Glenn: *Valvin' On a Riff*
    Carmichael, Hoagy/Matteson: *Skylark*
    Toledo, Rene Luis/Murphy: *Rene's Song*
    Silver, Horace/Perry: *Cookin' at the Continental*
    Brown, Clifford/Perry: *Sandu*

Legrand, Michel/Williamson: *Summer Knows*
Brubeck, Dave/Esleck/Murphy: *Blue Rondo alla Turk*
Esleck, David: *I-95*
Rollins, Sonny/Matteson: Oleo
Mølgård, Torolf. *See* Scandinavian Tuba Jazz
Monarch Tuba-Euphonium Quartet
    Album Title: *Metamorphosis*
    Personnel: Roger Behrend, David Miles, euphonium; Martin Erickson, Keith Mehlan, tuba
    Label: Campro Productions, 1993 CD: MPS
    Rossini, Gioacchino/Davis: *Petit Caprice in the Style of Offenbach*
    Mehlan, Keith: *Bottoms Up Rag*
    Mozart, Wolfgang Amadeus/Fabrizio: *Overture from the "Marriage of Figaro"*
    Singleton, arr.: *Three Sixteenth Century Flemish Pieces*
    Mozart, Wolfgang Amadeus/Mehlan: *Turkish Rondo*
    Martino, Ralph: *Fantasy*
    Sherwin, Manning/Mehlan: *A Nightingale Sang in Berkeley Square*
    Sousa, John Philip/Morris: *El Capitan*
    Dempsey, Raymond; arr.: *Quatre Chansons*
    Massenet, Jules/Erickson, Margaret: *Argonaise from "Le Cid"*
    Dempsey, Raymond: *Now Here This!*
    Arban, Jean Baptiste/LeClair, David: *Carnival of Venice, The*
    Traditional/Mehlan: *Londonderry Air*
    Taylor, Jeffery: *Fanfare No. 1*
    Mehlan, Keith: *Eine kleine Schreckens Musik (A Little Fright Music)*
Moore, David
    Album Title: *The Best of James Shepherd*
    Personnel: James Shepherd Versatile Brass
    Label: Doyen Recordings Ltd., CD: DOY CD 031
    Arban, Jean Baptiste: *Fantasy Brilliante*
Moore, David
    Album Title: *Endeavour*
    Personnel: IMI Yorkshire Imperial Band, David Hirst, conductor
    Label: Doyen Recordings Ltd., CD: DOY CD 006
    Arban, Jean Baptiste: *Fantasy Brilliante*
Moore, David
    Album Title: *Solo Reflections*
    Personnel: James Shepherd Versatile Brass, James Shepherd, conductor
    Label: Kirklees Music, 2002 CD: KRCD 1041
    Woodfield, Ray: *Caprice*
Moore, David
    Album Title: *Sounds of Brass*
    Personnel: James Shepherd Versatile Brass, Elgar Howarth, conductor
    Label: Decca, 1976 LP: SB 325
    Foster, Stephen/Howarth: *I Dream of Jeannie*
Moore, David
    Album Title:

Personnel: Grimethorpe Colliery Band, George
  Thompson, conductor
Label: Pye Records, 1967 LP: GSGL 10392
Hartmann, John: *La Belle Americaine*
Moore, David
  Album Title:
  Personnel: Grimethorpe Colliery Band, George
    Thompson, conductor
  Label: Pye Records, 1968 LP: GSGL 10418
  Smith: *Invincible*
Moore, David
  Album Title:
  Personnel: Grimethorpe Colliery Band, George
    Thompson, conductor
  Label: SAGA, 1970 LP: 8147
  Heath, Reginald: *Springtime*
Moore, David
  Album Title:
  Personnel: Grimethorpe Colliery Band, George
    Thompson, conductor
  Label: Polydor, 1970 LP: 2661003
  Sutton, Eddie: *Cavalier, The*
Moore, David
  Album Title:
  Personnel: James Shepherd Versatile Brass,
    Dennis Wilby, conductor
  Label: Kennedy, 1973 LP: 2
  Rimmer, William: *Variations on Jenny Jones*
Moore, David
  Album Title:
  Personnel: James Shepherd Versatile Brass,
    Dennis Wilby, conductor
  Label: Decca, 1974 LP: SB 314
  Arban, Jean Baptiste: *Carnival of Venice, The*
Moore, David
  Album Title:
  Personnel: James Shepherd Versatile Brass, Ray
    Woodfield, conductor
  Label: Decca, 1975 LP: SB 321
  Relton, William: *Chevailler D'Honneur*
Moore, David
  Album Title:
  Personnel: James Shepherd Versatile Brass, Ray
    Woodfield, conductor
  Label: Decca, 1978 LP: SB 331
  Woodfield, Ray: *Varied Mood*
Moore, David
  Album Title:
  Personnel: James Shepherd Versatile Brass,
    Frank Renton, conductor
  Label: Look Records, 1978 LP: 6343
  Foster, Stephen/Howarth: *I Dream of
    Jeannie*
Moore, David
  Album Title:
  Personnel: James Shepherd Versatile Brass,
    Frank Renton, conductor
  Label: Decca, 1979 LP: SB 337
  Woodfield, Ray: *Caprice*
Morgan, Gareth
  Album Title:

Personnel: Morris Motors Band, Harry
  Mortimer, conductor
Label: Columbia Records, 1968 LP: CSD 3650
Rimmer, William: *Hailstorm*
Morgan, Gareth
  Album Title:
  Personnel: Morris Motors Band, Harry Mor-
    timer, conductor
  Label: Music for Pleasure, 1970 LP: MFP 1387
  Heath, Reginald: *Springtime*
Morgan, Gareth
  Album Title:
  Personnel: Morris Motors Band, Harry Mor-
    timer, conductor
  Label: Music for Pleasure, 1975 LP: MFP
    50201
  MacDowell, Edward/Ball: *To a Wild Rose*
Morgan, Gareth
  Album Title:
  Personnel: Malcolm Teasdale, Nicholas Russell;
    All Star Brass, Harry Mortimer, conductor
  Label: EMI, 1978 LP: NTS 145
  Doughty, George: *Grandfather's Clock*
Mortimer, Alex
  Album Title: *Centenary Brass*
  Personnel: Fodens Motor Works Band, Fred
    Mortimer, conductor
  Traditional/Mortimer: *Drinking Song*
Mortimer, Alex
  Album Title: *Vintage Brass*
  Personnel: Fodens Motor Works Band, Fred
    Mortimer, conductor
  Label: Two Ten Records, 1979 LP: TTV 099
  Traditional/Mortimer: *Drinking Song*
Morton, Hugh
  Album Title: *Shades of Blue*
  Personnel: Andrew Keachie, conductor
  Label: Chandos, 1983 LP: BBRD 1022
  Foster, Stephen/Howarth: *Jeanie with the Light
    Brown Hair*
Moss, John
  Album Title:
  Personnel: Barrie Tupper; William Davis Band,
    Keith Wilkinson, conductor
  Label: Polyphonic Reproductions Ltd., 1987
    LP: PRL 034D
  Bizet, George/Wilkinson: *Deep inside the
    Sacred Temple*
Moss, John
  Album Title:
  Personnel: Adrian Nurney, euphonium; William
    Davis Band, John Berryman, conductor
  Label: AVS, 1981 LP: ALM 4007
  Bryce, Frank: *Rondoletto for Two Euphoniums*
Mountain, Wilfrid
  Album Title: *From Hollywood . . . Pleasure in
    His Service*
  Personnel: The Hollywood Tabernacle Band of
    the Salvation Army
  Label: The Salvation Army
  Catelinet, Philip: *Call of the Seasons*

Mueller, John
  Album Title: *Euphonic Sounds*
  Personnel: Joseph Holt, piano; Woody English,
    cornet; Steve Fidyk, drums; Jim Roberts,
    bass
  Label: John Mueller, 1999 CD
  Davis, William Mac: *Rondo Concertante*
  Joplin, Scott/Milburne: *Euphonic Sounds*
  Joplin, Scott/Milburne: *Solace*
  DeLuca, Joseph: *Beautiful Colorado*
  Boccalari, Ed/Kent-Akers: *Fantasia di Concerto*
  Wilder, Alec: *Sonata for Euphonium*
  Truax, Bert: *Love Song*
  Tomaro, Mike: *Excursion*
Mueller, John. *See* United States Armed Forces
Tuba-Euphonium Ensemble
Muggeridge, Keith
  Album Title: *Diamond Jubliee*
  Personnel: Williams Fairey Brass Band
  Label: Doyen Recordings Ltd., CD: DOYCD
    052
  Traditional/Roberts: *Carrickfergus*
Mulcahy, Michael
  Album Title: *Orchestral Excerpts for Bass Trom-
    bone, Tenor Tuba and Bass Trumpet*
  Personnel:
  Label: Summit Records, 1995 CD: DCD 158
  Moussorgsky, Modeste: *Bydlo*
  Mahler, Gustav: *Symphony No. 7*
  Holst, Gustav: *Planets*
  Strauss, Richard: *Don Quixote*
  Strauss, Richard: *Ein Heldenleben*
Murchinson, Matthew
  Album Title: *Everyone but Me*
  Personnel: Lance LaDuke, euphonium; Donna
    Amato, piano; Tim Adams, marimba
  Label: MURCH, CD: 2607
  Gershwin, George/Heifetz/Murchinson: *Three
    Preludes*
  Mussorgsky, Modest: *Where Are You, My Little
    Star?*
  Bach, Jan: *Concert Variations*
  Ravel, Maurice: *Piece en forme de habanera*
  Adler, Samuel: *Four Dialogs for Euphonium and
    Marimba*
  Sargent, Fred/Gedris: *Remember Your Dreams*
  Bourgeois, Derek: *Euphoria*
  Murchinson, Charles/Murchinson: *Ev'ryone
    but Me*
  Mahler, Gustav: *Ich bin der welt abbanden
    gekommen*
  Fennell, Drew: *Prescott Poem*
  Aagaad-Nielsen, Torstein: *Lokk from the Green
    Island*
Myers, Timothy
  Album Title: *St. Louis Symphony Orchestra*
  Personnel: St. Louis Symphony Orchestra,
    Leonard Slatlain, conductor
  Label: Angel EMI, 1988 CD: CDC-7 494632
  Barber, Samuel: *Three Essays for Orchestra*
Myllys, Jukka
  Album Title: *Finnish Euphonium*

Personnel: Oulu Symphony Orchestra, Arvo
    Volmer, conductor; Hannu Hirvelä, piano;
    Aki Virtanen, percussion
  Label: Alba Records Oy, 1998 CD: ABCD 118
  Linkola, Jukka: *Euphonium Concerto*
  Koskinen, Juha T.: *Destination*
  Kohlenberg, Oliver: *Blue Gleam of Arctic
    Hysteria*
Myllys, Jukka
  Album Title: *Jubilee*
  Personnel: The Pohja Military Band, Elias
    Seppälä, conductor
  Label: Pohja Military Band, CD: SAMCD-3
  Monti, Vittorio/Seppälä: *Czárdás*
  Sparke, Philip/Maldonado: *Pantomime*
Myllys, Jukka. *See* Euphoniums Unlimited
Narita, Yuko
  Album Title: *The New Style of the Euphonium*
  Personnel:
  Label: Yuko Narita, CD: EUP01-1023
  Isomura, Yukiko: *I'm Waiting Alone*
  Isomura, Yukiko: *Four Seasons Suite, The*
  Isomura, Yukiko: *Suite of Spring Wind*
  Isomura, Yukiko: *Merry Christmas to All of the
    World*
  Chopin, Fredrick: *Prelude*
  Fauré, Gabriel: *Pavane*
  Debussy, Claude: *Dream*
  Isomura, Yukiko; Narita, Yuko: *Orange Shores*
Nash, Dick
  Album Title: *Oklahoma Crude*
  Personnel: Mancini Orchestra
  Label: RCA Victor, APL 1-0271
  Mancini, Henry: *Lightfinger*
Nash, Dick
  Album Title: *The Theme Scene*
  Personnel: Mancini Orchestra
  Label: RCA Victor, AQLI-3052
  Mancini, Henry: *Heaven Can Wait*
Nash, Dick
  Album Title: *What Did You Do in the War,
    Daddy?*
  Personnel: Mancini Orchestra
  Label: RCA Victor, LSP-3648
  Mancini, Henry: *Tender Thieves, The*
Nelson, Douglas
  Album Title: *Recital Music for Euphonium*
  Personnel: Robin Stone, piano
  Label: Mark Educational Recordings, 1980 LP:
    MES-37878
  Handel, George Frederic: *Concerto in f Minor*
  Saint-Saëns, Camille: *Morceau de Concert,
    Op. 94*
  Templeton, Alec: *Elegie*
  Kreisler von, Alexander: *Sonatina*
  Uber, David: *Montage, Op. 84*
  George, Thom Ritter: *Sonata for Baritone
    Horn and Piano*
Nerland, Eldfrid
  Album Title: *Velomme med Aera*
  Personnel: Krohnengen Brass Band, Ray Farr,
    conductor

Label: Krohnengen Brass Band, 2002 CD:
KBB001
Grieg, Edward/Farr: *Jeg Elsker Dig*
Nurney, Adrian. *See* Moss, John
Nygvist, Rune
Album Title: *Stockholm VII Band of the Salvation Army*
Personnel: Stockholm VII Band, Erland Beijer,
conductor
Label: Fidelity Sound Recordings, 1964 LP:
FSR-1236
Leidzen, Erik: *Song of the Brother, The*
Oates, John
Album Title:
Personnel: Easington Colliery Band
Label: Look Records, 1981 LP: 7018
Heath, Reginald: *Andante and Scherzo*
O'Brien, Robert
Album Title: *Brass Encounters*
Personnel: Sydney Congress Hall Band, Robert
Prussing, conductor
Label: SCH/8, 1985
Redhead, Robert: *Euphony*
O'Hara, Betty
Album Title: *Horns A'Plenty*
Personnel: Betty O'Hara, euphonium, trumpet,
flugel horn, trombone, vocals; Johnny
Varro, piano; Morty Cobb, bass; Gene Estes,
percussion
Label: Delmark, 1995 CD: DD-482
O'Hara, Betty: *Euphonics*
Ellington, Duke: *It Don't Mean a Thing*
Sampson, Edgar: *If Dreams Come True*
Carmichael, Hoagy: *Stardust*
Rodgers, Richard; Hart, Lorenz: *My Heart
Stood Still*
Robinson, Willard: *Pigeon Toed Joad*
Brown, Nacio Herb: *You Stepped Out of
a Dream*
Waller, Thomas "Fats": *Alligator Crawl*
Arlen, Harold: *A Sleeping Bee*
Bernstein, Leonard: *Medley from "On the Town"*
O'Hara, Betty
Album Title: *A Woman's Intuition*
Personnel: Betty O'Hara Ensemble
Label: Sea Breeze, 1997 CD: SB 3025
Ellington, Duke: *Mood Indigo*
Gershwin, George: *But Not for Me*
Carmichael, Hoagy: *Skylark*
Gershwin, George: *Someone to Watch Over Me*
Arlen, Harold: *Out of This World*
Smith, H.: *It's Wonderful*
Youmans, Vincent: *More Than You Know*
Jones, Quincy: *Medley from "Stockholm Sweet-
nin'" and "You Leave Me Breathless"*
Young and Washington: *A Woman's Intuition*
Ellington, Duke: *All Too Soon*
Rodgers, Richard; Hart, Lorenz: *It's Easy to
Remember*
Arlen, Harold: *One for My Body*
Olsrud, Sverre Stakston
Album Title: *Sverre Stakston Olsrud, Euphonium*

Personnel: Yngvild Storaekre Henning, piano
Label: Sverre Stakston Olsrud, CD: 001
Aagaard-Nilsen, Torstein: *Black Rain*
Boccalari, Ed/Kent-Akers: *Fantasia di Concerto*
Butterworth, Arthur: *Partita for Euphonium
and Piano, Op. 89*
Kjerulf, Halfdan: *I sode blege Kinder*
Kjerulf, Halfdan: *Mit Hjerte og min Lyre,
Op. 16, No. 2*
Kjerulf, Halfdan: *Ved Sjoen den morke, Op. 6,
No. 2*
Plagge, Wolfgang: *Sonata Op. 64, for Eupho-
nium and Piano*
Ponchielli, Amilcare/Howey: *Concerto per
Flicorno Basso*
Schumann, Robert: *Fantasiestucke Op. 73*
Orosz, Josef
Album Title: *Opera without Singing*
Personnel: Boston Pops Orchestra, Arthur
Fiedler, conductor
Label: Victrola, CS: AIK 15382 (previously
RCA LM 1906)
Wagner, Richard: *Song to the Evening Star*
Ost, Nick
Album Title: *Euphonic Moods*
Personnel: Revitat Scaldis Chamber Ensemble
Label: Revitat Scaldis Fanfare, CD: GS88353-2
Glorieux, F.: *Sunrise on the River*
Glorieux, F.: *Orchestra Scheldt*
Glorieux, F.: *Concerto for Euphonium*
Glorieux, F.: *Regrets*
Glorieux, F.: *Waltz*
Glorieux, F.: *Contemplation*
Glorieux, F.: *Elegy*
Glorieux, F.: *Euphonic Moods*
Glorieux, F.: *Desolation*
Glorieux, F.: *Fantasy*
Glorieux, F.: *Farewell*
Owen, Mark
Album Title:
Personnel: Royal Doulton Band, Edward Gray,
conductor
Label: Parade, 1980 LP: PRD 2013
Golland, John: *Peace*
Parry, Glynn
Album Title:
Personnel: Hammonds Sauce Works Band,
Geoffrey Witham, conductor
Label: Pye Records, 1973 LP: GSGL 10498
Arban, Jean Baptiste/Remmington: *Carnival
of Venice, The*
Parry, Glynn
Album Title:
Personnel: Hammonds Sauce Works Band,
Harry Mortimer, conductor
Label: One Up, 1976 LP: OU 2146
Handel, George Frederic/Hume: *Harmonious
Blacksmith, The*
Parry, Glynn
Album Title:
Personnel: Hammonds Sauce Works Band,
Geoffrey Witham, conductor

Label: Decca, 1977 LP: SB 327
Saint-Saëns, Camille/Mott: *Swan, The*
Parton, Jack
    Album Title: *The Salvation Army Los Angeles Congress Hall Band*
    Personnel: Los Angeles Congress Hall Band, Harry Stillwell, conductor
    Label: Fidelity Sound Recordings, 1964 LP: FSR-1237
    Fischer, William/Kippax: *I Love to Tell the Story*
Pascuzzi, Todd
    Album Title: *Joseph Wagner Works for Concert Band*
    Personnel: Kiltie Symphony Band, Carnegie Mellon University, Richard E. Strange, conductor
    Label: Orion, 1973 LP: ORS 73118
    Wagner, Joseph: *Concerto Grosso*
Patterson, Bill. *See* Euphonium Quartet
Paull, Eric. *See* Symphonia
Paull, Eric. *See* Tennessee Technological University Alumni Tuba-Euphonium Ensemble
Pederson, Thor-Arne
    Album Title: *Tribute—American and Norwegian Music for Brass Band*
    Personnel: Manger Mussiklag, Helge Haukas, conductor
    Label: Manger Mussiklag, CD: GRCD004
    King, Karl L./Braten: *A Night in June*
Perrins, Barrie
    Album Title: *The Hendon Way*
    Personnel: The Hendon Band, Donald Morrison, conductor
    Label: Pye Records, 1976 LP: TB 3011
    Mozart, Wolfgang Amadeus/Henstridge: *Bassoon Concerto*
Perrins, Barrie
    Album Title: *Spectacular*
    Personnel: The Hendon Band, Donald Morrison, conductor
    Label: Musical Rendezvous, 1971 LP: 2870135
    Hartmann, John/Mortimer: *Facilita*
Perrins, Barrie
    Album Title:
    Personnel: The Hendon Band, Donald Morrison, conductor
    Label: Musical Rendezvous, 1973 LP: 2870343
    Handel, George Frederic/Hume: *Harmonious Blacksmith, The*
Peters, Neil
    Album Title:
    Personnel: Camborne Town Band, Derek Johnston, conductor
    Label: Rainbow, 1973 LP: RSR 1015
    Prieto, J./Siebert: *Wedding, The*
Pfeifle, Nicolas
    Album Title: *Tango Mortale*
    Personnel: Eriko Takezawa, piano
    Label: Nicolas Pfeilfe Label
    Turek, Thomas: *Tango Mortale*

Pagannini, Niccolo: *Moses-Fantasie*
Massenet, Jules: *Meditation*
Mozart, Leopold: *Concerto*
Rossini, Gioacchino: *Largo Al Factotum*
Ropartz, Guy: *Piece en mi bemol mineur*
Dvorak, Antonin/Pfeifle: *Romantische Stucke, Op. 7*
Turek, Thomas: *Walzer Nr. 1*
Pfeifle, Nicolas. *See* Heidler, Manfred
Pickard, Norman
    Album Title:
    Personnel: St. Gennys Silver Band
    Label: Sentinel Records, 1979 LP: SENLPP 601
    Prieto, J./Siebert: *Wedding, The*
Picton, Wendy
    Album Title: *Wendy Picton, Young Virtuoso*
    Personnel:
    Label: Miraphone Co., 1984 CS
    Paganini, Niccolo: *Moto Perpetuo*
    Shelukov, Vyacheslav: *Etude No. 1*
    Weber von, C.M.: *Bassoon Concerto*
    Jacob, Gordon: *Fantasia*
    Rimmer, William: *Grand Fantasia on Jenny Jones*
Pierce, Benjamin. *See* Champions of the Leonard Falcone Festival 1986–2000
Pillaert, Stef
    Album Title: *European Brass Band Championships 2002*
    Personnel: Black Dyke Mills Band, Nicholas Childs, conductor
    Label: Doyen Recordings, 2002 CD: DOY CD136
    Arban, Jean Baptiste/Briccialdi: *Carnival of Venice, The*
Poole, Sydney
    Album Title:
    Personnel: C.W.S. Manchester Band, Alex Mortimer, conductor
    Label: Fontana, 1960 LP: STFL 529
    Hartmann, John: *Robin Adair*
Postma, Simon
    Album Title: *Of Men and Mountains*
    Personnel: Soli Deo Gloria
    Label: De Haske Music Records, CD
    Golland, John: *Peace*
Postma, Simon
    Album Title: *Soli Solo*
    Personnel: Soli Deo Gloria
    Label: De Haske Music Records, CD
    Traditional: *Lark in the Clear Air, The*
    Ares, Rob: *Memory*
    Traditional: *Londonderry Air*
Pratt, Mike
    Album Title:
    Personnel: York Railway Institute Band, G. E. Pratt, conductor
    Label: Look Records, LP: 6467
    Langford, Gordon: *Blaydon Races, The*
Psarakis, Dean. *See* Robertson, Gail
Pugh, Joel
    Album Title: *The Champions*

Personnel: Brass Band of Columbus, Paul
   Droste, conductor
Label: Blimp Recording Co., CD: BRCD 02
Sparke, Philip: *Party Piece*
Pugh, Joel
   Album Title: *Metamorphoses*
   Personnel: Cuyahoga Valley Brass Band
   Label: World Records
   Sparke, Philip: *Pantomime*
Raphael, Nderegg. *See* Brunner, Stefan
Reid, David. *See* Albertasaurus Tuba Quartet
Reifsnyder, Robert
   Album Title: *The Versatile Trombonist*
   Personnel: Karl Paulnack, piano
   Label: Five Oaks Recordings, 1987 LP: KM
     14385
   DeLuca, Joseph: *Beautiful Colorado*
Richards, Dean
   Album Title:
   Personnel: Warrington Youth Band, Len
     Andrews, conductor
   Label: Crow Records, LP: PPC005
   Mozart, Wolfgang Amadeus/Wright: *Rondo
     from "Horn Concerto"*
Richards, Kelvin
   Album Title: *Newton Citadel Band*
   Personnel: Newton Citadel Band, James
     Denny, conductor
   Label: Fidelity Sound Recordings, 1979 LP:
     FSRS-1288
   Himes, William: *My Christ Is All*
Richards, Robert
   Album Title:
   Personnel: Derek Garside, cornet; Ian Richards,
     trombone; C.W.S. Manchester Band, Alex
     Mortimer, conductor
   Label: Fontana, 1968 LP: STL 5466
   Wright, Dennis: *Trio Concerto*
Richards, Robert
   Album Title:
   Personnel: C.W.S. Manchester Band, Derek
     Garside, conductor
   Label: Decca, 1973 LP: SB 309
   Martini/Rimmer: *Plaisir D'Amour*
Roberts, David
   Album Title:
   Personnel: Point of Ayr Band, Denzil Stephens,
     conductor
   Label: Polyphonic Reproductions Ltd., 1986
     LP: PRL 029D
   Traditional/Stephens: *Myfanwy*
Roberts, Roy
   Album Title:
   Personnel: Cory Band, Denzil Stephens,
     conductor
   Label: Pye Records, 1980 LP: TB 3023
   Saint-Saëns, Camille/Stephens: *Swan, The*
Robertson, Gail
   Album Title: *Brass A-Peel*
   Personnel: Dean Psarakis, euphonium; Brass
     Band of Central Florida, Michael Garasi,
     conductor

Label: Full Sail Studio Recordings, 2002 CD:
   BBCF 1
Graham, Peter: *Gaelforce*
Robyr, Dominique
   Album Title: *La Chasse Au Dragon*
   Personnel: Ensemble de Cuivres Valaisan,
     Christopher Jeanbourquin, conductor
   Label: FAB Recordings, 2002 CD: 08
   Sparke, Philip: *Two-Part Invention*
Royall, Dennis
   Album Title: *The Compositions of William
     H. Hill*
   Personnel: The California State University Los
     Angeles Wind Ensemble, William H. Hill,
     conductor
   Label: Golden Crest Records, LP: ATH 5053
   Hill, William H.: *Concerto for Euphonium*
Royall, Dennis
   Album Title: *The Golden Sound of Euphoniums*
   Personnel: Carolyn Bridger, piano
   Label: Mirafone Music Co.
   Benedetto, Marcello: *Largo from "Sonata,
     Op. 4, No. 2"*
   Jones, Roger: *Dialogue for Euphonium and Piano*
Royall, Dennis
   Album Title: *Kendor Brass Ensembles*
   Personnel: Delta State University Euphonium
     Quartet
   Label: Evatone Sound Sheets (available with
     purchase of music)
   Uber, David: *Exhibitions*
Rüedi, Thomas
   Album Title: *Elégie*
   Personnel: Brassband Bürgermusik Luzern,
     Ludwig Wicki, conductor
   Label: Obrasso Records, 2000 CD: CD 875
   Vieuxtemps, Henri/Rüedi: *Elégie Op. 30*
   Sarasate, Pablo de/Rüedi: *Gypsy Airs*
   Tchaikovsky, Piotr/Rüedi: *Variations on a
     Rocco Theme Op. 33*
   Lalo, Edouard/Rüedi: *Chants russes Op. 29*
   Picchi, Ermano/Bale: *Fantaisie Originale*
   Tchaikovsky, Piotr/Rüedi: *Nocturne Op. 19*
   Kroll, William/Rüedi: *Banjo and Fiddle*
   Bridge, Frank: *Meditation*
   Cassadó, Gaspar/Rüedi: *Danse du Diable vert*
   Hahn, Reynaldo: *L'Huere exquise*
Rüedi, Thomas
   Album Title: *Go for It*
   Personnel: Nobody's Brass
   Label: MF Records, CD: 6913
   Graham, Peter: *Brilliante*
   Hamlisch/Barry: *Way We Were, The*
Rüedi, Thomas
   Album Title: *Montreux 1999*
   Personnel: BB Bürgermusik Luzern
   Label: Pro Music, CD
   Wilby, Philip: *Concerto for Euphonium*
Rüedi, Thomas
   Album Title: *Montreux 1996*
   Personnel: BB Bürgermusik Luzern
   Label: Pro Music, CD: PM737

Schramm, Robert
  Album Title:
  Personnel: National Citadel Band of the
    Salvation Army, A. Campbell Robinson,
    conductor
  Label: Private label, 1978 LP: 780679
  Gheel, Henry: *Watching the Wheat*
Schultz, Karl
  Album Title: *The Spirit of Victory*
  Personnel: Michael Bjorkland, euphonium, the
    United States Continental Army Band
  Label: The United States Continental Army
    Band. Public service, not for sale
  Sparke, Philip: *Pantomime*
  DeVita, Alfred/Catherall: *Softly As I Leave You*
Schulz, Patrick. *See* Sotto Voce Quartet
Schwarz, Gerard
  Album Title: *Turn of the Century Cornet
    Favorites*
  Personnel: Columbia Chamber Ensemble,
    Gunther Schuller, conductor
  Label: Columbia Records, 1977 LP: M 34553
  Dede, Edmond: *Mephisto Masque*
Self, Jimmie. *See* Euphoniums Unlimited
Sewell-Jones, Adam
  Album Title: *Timepiece*
  Personnel: Gary Smith, euphonium; East Lon-
    don Youth Band
  Label: SAELYB1
  Bearcroft, Norman: *Timepiece*
Shepherd, Ken
  Album Title:
  Personnel: Carlton Main Frickley Colliery
    Band, Robert Oughton, conductor
  Label: Grosvenor, 1973 LP: GRS 1020
  MacDowell, Edward/Ball: *To a Wild Rose*
Shepherd, Ken
  Album Title:
  Personnel: Carlton Main Frickley Colliery
    Band, Robert Oughton, conductor
  Label: Grosvenor, 1976 LP: GRS 1043
  Drigo/Oughton: *Serenade*
Shipp, Charles
  Album Title:
  Personnel: Cambridge Band, Davis Read,
    conductor
  Label: Pye Records, 1980 LP: TB 3020
  Handel, George Frederic/Greenwood: *Where
    E're You Walk*
Shrum, Ken. *See* United States Armed Forces Tuba-
  Euphonium Ensemble
Siebenthal, von Daniel. *See* Matti, Jean-Claude
Singleton, Stephen
  Album Title: *Brass with Class*
  Personnel: Fodens Motor Works Band, How-
    ard Snell, conductor
  Label: Polyphonic Reproductions Ltd., 1988
    LP: PRL 037D
  MacDowell, Edward/Ball: *To a Wild Rose*
Singleton, Stephen
  Album Title: *By Request*

  Personnel: BNFL Band
  Label: Polyphonic Reproductions Ltd., CD:
    QPRL 078D
  Godfrey/Herbert: *Lucy Long*
Smith, Christopher
  Album Title:
  Personnel: Portsmouth Junior Band of the
    Salvation Army, J. Bird, conductor
  Label: Hassell Records, 1973 LP: HAS
    LP3001
  Pattison: *Gladsome Call, The*
Smith, Gary. *See* Sewell-Jones, Adam
Smith, Henry Charles
  Album Title: *Henry Charles Smith Plays Baritone*
  Personnel: Gertrude Kuehefuhs, piano
  Label: Coronet Recording Co., 1969 LP:
    COR1714 (Z4RS-5075)
  Vivaldi, Antonio: *Sonata No. 6*
  Pergolesi, Giovanni: *Nina*
  Handel, George Frederic: *Concerto in f Minor*
  Haydn, Franz Josef: *With Verdure Clad from
    "The Creation"*
  Mendelssohn, Felix: *If with All Your Heart*
  Mendelssohn, Felix: *Lord God of Abraham*
  Moussorgsky, Modeste: *Bydlo from "Pictures at
    an Exibition"*
  Fasch, J. F.: *Sonata for Trombone and Piano*
Sobotta, Uli
  Album Title: *Blechente*
  Personnel:
  Label: Alles, CD: AR 40242
  Sobotta, Uli: *Metal Love*
  Sobotta, Uli: *M—Virus*
  Sobotta, Uli: *Sprechstunde*
  Sobotta, Uli: *Erinnert Sich Der Hund*
  Sobotta, Uli: *Bellamira*
  Sobotta, Uli: *Das A & O Der Gegenwart*
  Sobotta, Uli: *Blechente*
  Sobotta, Uli: *Nice Guys These Beatles*
  Sobotta, Uli: *Riedl Polka*
  Sobotta, Uli: *Das Tier, Das Gemuse*
  Sobotta, Uli: *Good Morning My Head*
  Sobotta, Uli: *Das Mirakel*
  Sobotta, Uli: *Don Quichotte*
  Sobotta, Uli: *Ins Blaue Licht*
  Sobotta, Uli: *Within/Without*
  Sobotta, Uli: *Drunken Early Morning Song*
Sobotta, Uli
  Album Title: *Blue Fish Blue*
  Personnel: Mike Klagge, electric guitar
  Label: Starfish Music, CD: 01801-6
  Sobotta, Uli: *Safety Pin*
  Sobotta, Uli: *Blue Fish Blue*
  Sobotta, Uli: *Good Morning My Head*
  Sobotta, Uli: *Koslowski*
  Sobotta, Uli: *Zugvogel*
  Sobotta, Uli: *Pickle Song*
  Sobotta, Uli: *Dibbuk*
  Sobotta, Uli: *Blue and Yellow—Beach Behind*
  Sobotta, Uli: *Zum Schuls das Ende*
  Sobotta, Uli: *It's Good to Know*

Sobotta, Uli: *Slow Biker*
Sobotta, Uli: *To Cross the Mountain*
Sotto Voce Quartet
   Album Title: *Consequences*
   Personnel: Demondrae Thurman, Patrick
     Schulz, euphonium; Michael Forbes, Nat
     McIntosh, tuba
   Label: Summit Records, 2002 CD: DCD 322
   Forbes, Michael: *Consequences*
   Gasparini, Quirino: *Adoramus te*
   Bach, Johann Sebastian: *Contrapunctus 9 from
     "Die Kunst der Fuge"*
   Kupferman, Meyer: *Kierkegaard*
   Haydn, Franz Josef: *Achieved Is the Glorious
     Work from "Die Schöpfung"*
   Grovlez, Gabriel: *Petites Litanies de Jésus*
   Schulz, Patrick: *Profiles*
   Forbes, Michael: *Auburn Is the Colour*
   Handel, George Frederic: *Harmonious Black-
     smith, The*
   Malotte, Albert Hay: *Lord's Prayer, The*
   Primrose, Joe: *St. James Infirmary Blues*
   Williams, Clarence; Williams, Spencer: *Royal
     Garden Blues*
Sotto Voce Quartet
   Album Title: *Viva Voce! The Quartets of John
     Stevens*
   Personnel: Demondrae Thurman, Patrick
     Schulz, euphonium; Michael Forbes, Nat
     McIntosh, tuba
   Label: Summit Records, 2004 CD: DCD 388
   Stevens, John: *Power*
   Stevens, John: *Music 4 Tubas*
   Stevens, John: *Manhattan Suite*
   Stevens, John: *Diversions*
   Stevens, John: *Moondance*
   Stevens, John: *Fanfare for a Friend*
   Stevens, John: *Viva Voce!*
   Stevens, John: *Benediction*
Spencer, Graham. *See* Wilkinson, Harry
Squibb, Christian
   Album Title: *Promenade*
   Personnel: Bournemouth Concert Brass, Nigel
     Taken, conductor
   Label: Harleqiun Recordings, CD:
     HAR0105CD
   Richards, Goff: *Midnight Euphonium*
Sreckfus, Robert. *See* Euphonium Section, The
Steckar Elephant Tuba Horde
   Album Title: *Steckar Elephant Tuba Horde*
   Personnel: Jean-Jacques Justafre, tuben;
     Jean-Louis Damant, Christian Jous, Michel
     Nicolle, Marc Steckar, tenor tuba; Philippe
     Legris, Phillippe Fritsch, Thierry Thibault,
     bass tuba; Bernard Lienard, Daniel Landreat,
     Didier Havet, contrabass tuba
   Label: IDA Records, 1987 LP: IDA 011/
     OMD 520
   Steckar, Franck: *Rouleaux de Printemps*
   Cugny, Laurent: *Molloy*
   Michel, Marc: *Le Jour ou les Tubas*

Elmer, Andy: *Gicael Mibbs*
Vigneron, Louis: *Stabillo Steckardello*
Steckar, Marc: *Tubas au Fujiyama*
Goret, Didier: *Detournement Mineur*
Steckar, Marc
   Album Title: *Kantation*
   Personnel: Bernard Arcadio, piano
   Label: JAM, LP: 1281/SA 023
   Steckar, Marc: *Batubop*
   Arcadio, Bernard: *Leleo*
   Steckar, Marc: *Megalo Fanfare*
   Arcadio, Bernard: *Splash*
   Steckar, Marc; Arcadio, Bernard: *Tubach*
   Arcadio, Bernard: *Felinesquement*
   Steckar, Marc; Arcadio, Bernard: *Konservato-
     rium*
Steckar, Marc. *See* Steckar Tubapack
Steckar Tubapack
   Album Title: *Steckar Tubapack*
   Personnel: Marc Steckar, Christian Jous,
     euphonium, tuba; Michel Godard, Daniel
     Landréat, tuba; Alain Bouchaux, drums
   Label: JAM, 1982 LP: 0681/MS 019
   Steckar, Franck: *Hurry Up*
   Steckar, Marc: *Série Noire*
   Jeanneau, François: *Paul et Mike*
   Steckar, Franck: *In a Digital Mood*
   Caratini, Patrice: *Demain il fera jour*
   Steckar, Franck: *Tubapack Blues*
   Fosset, Marc: *3 à 5*
   Quibel, Robert: *Danse Bizarre n 3*
   Arcadio, Bernard/Steckar, Marc: *Forét Vierge*
   Steckar, Marc: *Dynozophorium*
   Steckar, Marc: *Vendredi 13*
Steckar Tubapack
   Album Title: *Suite à Suivre*
   Personnel: Marc Steckar, Christian Jous, tuba
     and euphonium; Michel Godard, Daniel
     Landreat, tuba; Alain Bouchaux, drums
   Label: JAM, 1982 LP: 0183/MS036
   Steckar, Marc; Steckar, Franck: *Suite à
     Suivre*
   Monk, Thelonius: *Blue Monk*
   Godard, Michel/Steckar, Marc: *Et Le Klaxon
     Retentit Derechef Comme Un Lézard
     Hongrois Enrhumé*
   Steckar, Franck: *Danse Pour Un Kangourou*
   Bolognesi, Jacques: *Maria alm*
   Solal, Martial: *For Tuba Only*
Steckar Tubapack
   Album Title: *Tubakoustic*
   Personnel: Marc Steckar, Christian Jous,
     euphonium; Michael Godard, Daniel Lan-
     dreat, tuba
   Label: IDA Records, 1989 CD
Steen, Grierson
   Album Title:
   Personnel: Scottish C.W.S. Band, Geoffrey
     Brand, conductor
   Label: Pye Records, 1969 LP: GSGL 10430
   Heath, Reginald: *Andante and Scherzo*

Steen, Grierson
Album Title:
Personnel: Scottish CWS Band, Geoffrey
  Witham, conductor
Label: Polydor, 1971 LP: 2928003
Greenwood: *Bonny Mary of Argyle*
Stewart, Dee
Album Title: *Stewart Sounds*
Personnel: Diane Birr, piano
Label: Hal Leonard
Tomasi, Henri: *Danse Sacrée*
White, Donald H.: *Lyric Suite*
Storey, John
Album Title: *On Her Majesty's Service*
Personnel: Regimental Band of Coldstream
  Guard, Graham Jones, conductor
Label: Egon Recordings, CD: SFZ 111
Bellstedt, Herman: *Napoli*
Stowe, David
Album Title: *The First International Conference
  for Symphonic Bands and Wind Ensembles,
  1981*
Personnel: Surrey County Wind Ensemble,
  David Hamilton, conductor
Label: Silver Crest Records, 1981 LP: IC-
  81-13
Jacob, Gordon: *Fantasia*
Sullivan, Bert
Album Title: *Championship Bandstand*
Personnel: The G.U.S. Footwear Band, Harry
  Mortimer and Stanley Boddington,
  conductors
Label: EMI Records Ltd., 1960 LP: ONCR
  514
Mantia, Simone/Boddington: *Believe Me if All
  Those Endearing Young Charms*
Sullivan, Bert
Album Title:
Personnel: Munn and Feltons Footwear Band,
  Stanley Boddington, conductor
Label: Columbia, 1959 LP: 33SX 1184
Traditional/Boddington: *Long, Long Ago*
Svoboda, Michael
Album Title: *Music for Trombone and Eupho-
  nium*
Personnel: Andreas Boettger, percussion;
  Simon Stockhausen, synthesizer; Karlheinz
  Stockhausen, sound projection
Label: Stockhausen, 1989 CD: 44
Stockhausen, Karlheinz: *Chin-Dance*
Swallow, John
Album Title: *New England Conservatory Wind
  Ensemble*
Personnel: New England Conservatory Wind
  Ensemble
Label: New England Conservatory Wind
  Ensemble, 1973
Wilder, Alec: *Concerto for Euphonium and
  Wind Ensemble*
Swallow, John
Album Title: *Sousa Concert*

Personnel: Yale University Band
Label: Yale University Band Department
Clarke, Herbert L.: *Debutante, The*
Swallow, John
Album Title: *Stars and Stripes and Cakewalk*
Personnel: Boston Pops Orchestra
Label: RCA Victor, LP: 09026-61501-2
Kay, Hershy: *Stars and Stripes Ballet Suite*
Swallow, John
Album Title: *Turn of the Century Cornet
  Favorites*
Personnel: Columbia Chamber Ensemble,
  Gunther Schuller, conductor
Label: Columbia Records, 1977 LP: M 34553
Clarke, Herbert L.: *Side Partners*
Swallow, John. *See* American Brass Band Journal
Swiss Tuba Quartet
Album Title: *Power*
Personnel: Marcel Bossert, Rolf Aebersold
Label: Pro Music, SA-PM 736
Joplin, Scott: *Elite Syncopations*
Rimsky-Korsakov, Niccolo: *Flight of the Bumble
  Bee, The*
Rossini, Gioacchino: *La Gazza Ladra*
Sousa, John Philip: *Stars and Stripes Forever, The*
Stevens, John: *Power*
Strauss, Johann: *Impressario, The*
Traditional: *Greensleeves*
Jewell: *Battle Royal*
Gourlay, James: *Eagle Thunders, The*
Unknown: *Fughetta*
Unknown: *Hallelijah Drive*
Unknown: *Prelude and Dance*
Steckar, Marc; Arcadio, Bernard: *Tubach*
Unknown: *Wassermusik*
Symphonia
Album Title: *. . . a Super Sonic Ensemble in the
  Alternate Clef*
Personnel: Tom Ashworth, Brian Bowman,
  Larry Campbell, Neal Corwell, Paul Droste,
  Mark Fisher, Earle Louder, Denis Winter,
  euphonium; Martin Erickson, Hank Feld-
  man, Jeff Funderburk, Fritz Kaenzig, Rex
  Martin, Dan Perantoni, Sam Pilafian, John
  Stevens, Scott Watson, Jerry Young, tuba; R.
  Winston Morris, conductor
Label: Mark Custom Recording Service, Inc.,
  1996 CD: MCD-1982
Forte, Aldo Rafael: *Sequidillas*
Forte, Aldo Rafael: *Adagio and Rondo*
Welcher, Dan: *Hauntings*
George, Thom Ritter: *Tubamobile*
Stevens, John: *Adagio*
Corwell, Neal: *Furies, The*
Holst, Gustav/Butler: *Mars from "The
  Planets"*
Bach, Johann Sebastian/Garrett: *Passacaglia
  and Fugue in c Minor*
Pegram, Wayne: *Broadway Brash*
Kerbs, Jesse: *Jesse's Jump*
Feldman, Hank C.: *Freedom*

Symphonia
  Album Title: *La Morte dell' Oom (No Pah
    Intended)*
  Personnel: Tom Ashworth, Brian Bowman,
    Larry Campbell, Neal Corwell, Paul Droste,
    David Werden, Earle Louder, Denis Winter,
    euphonium; Martin Erickson, Hank Feld-
    man, Jeff Funderburk, Fritz Kaenzig, Rex
    Martin, Tim Northcut, Dan Perantoni, Sam
    Pilafian, John Stevens, Scott Watson, Jerry
    Young, tuba;
    R. Winston Morris, conductor
  Label: Mark Custom Recording Service, Inc.,
    1998 CD: MCD-2808
  Holst, Gustav/Werden: *Second Suite in F for
    Military Band*
  Daugherty, Michael: *Timbuktuba*
  Self, James: *La Morte dell' Oom*
  Stevens, John: *Talisman*
  Barnes, James: *Yorkshire Ballad*
  Duruflé, Maurice; Renwick, Wilke/Wilson: *Ubi
    Caritas/Dance*
  Shostakovich, Dimitri/Oliver: *Festive Overture*
  Puccini, Giacomo/Williams: *La Tregenda from
    "Le villi"*
  Jager, Robert: *Three Ludes for Tuba*
  Williams, John/Fiegel: *March from "1941"*
  Sherwin, Manning/Manhattan Transfer/Fun-
    derburk/Jones: *A Nightingale Sang in
    Berkley Square*
  Mingus, Charles/Feldman: *Freedom*
  Stevens, John: *Cookie's Revenge*
Symphonia
  Album Title: *SYMPHONIA FANTASTIQUE!*
  Personnel: Tom Ashworth, Brian Bowman,
    Larry Campbell, Neal Corwell, Paul Droste,
    Earle Louder, Eric Paull, Gail Robertson,
    David Werden, euphonium; Martin Erickson,
    Hank Feldman, John Jones, Fritz Kaenzig,
    Rex Martin, Mark Nelson, Timothy North-
    cut, Dan Perantoni, John Stevens, Scott Wat-
    son, tuba; Wilber T. England, Bryson Kern,
    Stacey Duggan, percussion; R. Winston
    Morris, conductor
  Label: Mark Custom Recording Service, Inc.,
    2001 CD: MCD-3883
  Rossini, Gioacchino/Dawson: *Overture to Wil-
    liam Tell*
  Bach, Johann Sebastian/Barnes: *Prelude and
    Fugue in d Minor*
  Berlioz, Hector/Fiegel: *Dream of a Witches
    Sabbath from "Symphonie Fantastique"*
  Corwell, Neal: *Wasteland, The*
  Barnes, James: *Tangents, Op. 109*
  Barber, Samuel/Stevens: *Adagio*
  Verdi, Giuseppe/Cole: *Dies Irae from "Requiem"*
  Raum, Elizabeth: *Jason and the Golden Fleece*
  Mendez, Rafel/Cole: *La Virgin De La
    Macarena*
  Bartles, Alfred: *New "When Tubas Waltz," The*
  Kosma, J./Prevert, J./Mercer, J./Perry:
    Autumn Leaves

Taylor, Barbara
  Album Title: *Solo!*
  Personnel: Air Combat Command Heritage of
    America Band, Lowell E. Graham, conductor
  Label: Air Combat Command Band, 1995 CD:
    0013. Public service, not for sale
  Forte, Aldo: *Canzonetta for Euphonium and
    Band*
Taylor, Brian
  Album Title:
  Personnel: Aldershot Brass Ensemble, Ronald
    Binge, conductor
  Label: Gold Star, 1975 LP: 1540
  Binge, Ronald: *Variations on Alouette*
Taylor, Philip
  Album Title:
  Personnel: Scissett Youth Band, Pat France,
    conductor
  Label: SYB1
  Heath, Reginald: *Springtime*
Taylor, Robin
  Album Title: *Metaeuphosis*
  Personnel: Recorded synthesizer
  Label: Huntcliff Recording Services, 1993 CD:
    HRSCD 382
  Boda, John: *Sonatina*
  Brustad, Karsten: *Initiation*
  Corwell, Neal: *Odyssey*
  Corwell, Neal: *Simyeh*
  Nagano, Mitsuhiro: *Matrix for Euphonium and
    Synthesizer*
  Suzuki, Ryuta: *Psalm*
Taylor, Robin
  Album Title: *Robin Taylor, Euphonium*
  Personnel: The Grimethorpe Colliery Band,
    Garry Cutt, conductor; Joseph Horovitz,
    guest conductor
  Label: Huntcliff Recording Services, 1993 CD:
    HRSCD 310
  Curnow, James/Bryant: *Symphonic Variants for
    Euphonium and Brass*
  Jacob, Gordon/Bryant: *Fantasia for Eupho-
    nium and Brass*
  Horovitz, Joseph: *Euphonium Concerto*
  Bowen, Brian: *Euphonium Music*
Taylor, Robin. See Champions of the Leonard
Falcone Festival 1986–2000
Teasdale, Malcolm
  Album Title: *The City of Coventry Band Cel-
    ebrates Its 40th Anniversary*
  Personnel: The City of Coventry Band
  Label: Pye Records, TB 3019
  Saint-Saëns, Camille: *Swan, The*
Teasdale, Malcolm
  Album Title:
  Personnel: The City of Coventry Band
  Label: Grosvenor, 1977 LP: GRE 1053
  Mantia, Simone/Dennison: *Believe Me if All
    Those Endearing Young Charms*
Teasdale, Malcolm. See Morgan, Gareth
Tennessee Technological University Alumni Tuba-
Euphonium Ensemble

Album Title: *Tubalogy 601*
Personnel: Darin Cochran, Kelly Thomas, Eric Paull, Lloyd Bone, euphonium; Joe Murphy, Richard Perry, Joe Skillen, Marcus Arnold, David Brown, tuba; R. Winston Morris, conductor
Label: Mark Custom Recording Service, Inc., 1999 CD: MCD-3051
Porter, Cole: *It's All Right with Me*
Moten, Bennie: *Moten Swing*
Lowe, Frederick: *Almost Like Being in Love*
Mandel, Johnny: *A Time for Love*
Gronick, Don: *Pools*
Arlen, Harold: *That Old Black Magic*
Silver, Horace: *Señor Blues*
Brown, Clifford: *Sandu*
Ellington, Duke: *In a Mellowtone*
Monk, Thelonius: *'Round Midnight*
Gillespie, Dizzy: *Manteca*

Tennessee Technological University and Alumni Tuba-Euphonium Ensemble
Album Title: *For the Kings of Brass*
Personnel: Tennessee Technological University Tuba-Euphonium Ensemble, R. Winston Morris, conductor
Label: Mark Custom Recording Service, Inc., 2001 CD: MCD-3713
Clinard, Fred: *Diversion for Seven Bass Clef Instruments*
Spears, Jared: *Divertimento for Tuba Ensemble*
Boone, Daniel: *Three Moods*
Krol, Bernhard: *Feiertagsmusik, Op. 107b*
Canter, James: *Siamang Suite*
Holmes, Paul: *Quartet for Tubas*
Camphouse, Mark: *Ceremonial Sketch*
Wilson, Kenyon: *Dance No. 1*
Rodgers, Thomas: *Air for Tuba Ensemble*
Canter, James: *Appalachian Carol*
Brusick, William: *For the Kings of Brass*

Tennessee Technological University and Alumni Tuba-Euphonium Ensemble
Album Title: *Pierre Garbáge*
Personnel: William Hunley, solo euphonium; Tennessee Technological University and Alumni Tuba-Euphonium Ensemble, R. Winston Morris, conductor
Label: Mark Custom Recording Service, Inc., 2000 CD: MCD-3471
Garrett, James Allen: *Chaser #1*
Garrett, James Allen: *Bullfrog Rag*
Garrett, James Allen: *Pop-Rock Medley*
Traditional/Garrett, James Allen: *Londonderry Air*
Garrett, James Allen: *Mystical Music*
Garrett, James Allen: *Sousa Surrenders*
Garrett, James Allen: *Wabash Cannon Ball*
Garrett, James Allen: *Gay 50's Medley*
Garrett, James Allen: *Songs in the Fight Against Rum*
Garrett, James Allen: *A Pierre Soliloquy: Ode to Pierre*

Tennessee Technological University Tuba-Euphonium Ensemble
Album Title: *All That Jazz*
Personnel: Tennessee Technological University Tuba-Euphonium Ensemble, R. Winston Morris, conductor
Label: Mark College Jazz Series, LP: MES 20608
Garrett, James Allen, arr.: *Just a Closer Walk with Thee*
Garrett, James Allen, arr.: *Won't You Come Home Bill Bailey*
Garrett, James Allen, arr.: *Chimes Blues*
Ahbez, Eden/Cherry: *Nature Boy*
Harrison, Wayne: *Beneath the Surface*
Green, Freddie/Esleck: *Corner Pocket*
Morrison, Van/Kile: *Moondance*
Brown, Nacio Herb/Sample: *Two Tunes (You Stepped Out of a Dream; Temptation)*
Martin, Glenn: *Chops!*
Correa, Chick: *Spain*
Zawinul, Josef/Arnold: *Birdland*

Tennessee Technological University Tuba-Euphonium Ensemble
Album Title: *Carnegie VI*
Personnel: Seth Fletcher, solo euphonium; Tennessee Technological University Tuba-Euphonium Ensemble, R. Winston Morris, conductor
Label: Mark Custom Recording Service, Inc., 2003 CD: MCD-4769
Handel, George Frederic/Hauser: *Arrival of the Queen of Sheba*
Vivaldi, Antonio/Beaver: *Winter*
Fauré, Gabriel/Wilson: *Pavane, Op. 50*
Dvorak, Antonin/Butler: *Slavonic Dances, Op. 46, No. 1*
Prokofiev, Sergei/Butler: *Troika from "Lieutenant Kije"*
Danner, Gregory/Vaden: *Scherzo*
Cosma, Vladimir/Fletcher: *Giocoso from "Euphonium Concerto"*
Mobberley, James: *On Thin Ice*
Osmon, Larry: *Frescos De Bonampak*
Tull, Fisher: *Tubular Octad*

Tennessee Technological University Tuba-Euphonium Ensemble
Album Title: *Fifty-First Meeting Music Educators National Conference*
Personnel: Tennessee Technological University Tuba-Euphonium Ensemble, R. Winston Morris, conductor
Label: Mark Custom Recording Service, 1988 CS: MENC88-1-4
Tchaikovsky, Piotr/O'Conner: *Serenade for Tubas*
Camphouse, Mark: *Ceremonial Sketch*
Werle, Floyd: *Variations on an Old Hymn Tune*
O'Hara, Betty: *Euphonics*
Brubeck, David/Esleck: *Blue Rondo alla Turk*
Hancock, Herbie/Perry: *Chameleon*

Tennessee Technological University Tuba-Euphonium Ensemble
  Album Title: *Heavy Metal*
  Personnel: Tennessee Technological University Tuba-Euphonium Ensemble, R. Winston Morris, conductor
  Label: Mark Custom Recording Service, 1987 LP: MES 20759
  Pegram, Wayne: *Howdy!*
  Gates, Crawford: *Tuba Quartet, Op. 59*
  Lamb, Marvin: *Heavy Metal*
  Shearing, George/Perry: *Lullaby of Birdland*
  Wilson, Ted: *Wot Shigona Dew*
  Garrett, James Allen: *Miniature Jazz Suite*
  Martin, Glenn: *Bluesin' Tubas*
  Jarreau, Al/Murphy: *Boogie Down*
Tennessee Technological University Tuba-Euphonium Ensemble
  Album Title: *Live!!!*
  Personnel: Tennessee Technological University Tuba-Euphonium Ensemble, R. Winston Morris, conductor
  Label: KM Educational Library, 1980 LP: KM 5661
  Konagaya, Soichi: *Illusion*
  Knox, Charles: *Scherzando for Tubular Octet*
  Ruth, Matthew: *Exigencies*
  DiGiovanni, Rocco: *Tuba Magic*
  Gershwin, George/Sample/Corazon: *Gershwin Medley*
Tennessee Technological University Tuba-Euphonium Ensemble
  Album Title: *Merry Christmas from Tennessee Tech*
  Personnel: Tennessee Technological University Tuba-Euphonium Ensemble, R. Winston Morris, conductor
  Label: Mark Records, 1985 LP: MC-20632
  Gottschalk, arr.: *Silent Night*
  Hancock, arr.: *First Noel, The*
  Canter, James: *Twelve Days of Housetops*
Tennessee Technological University Tuba-Euphonium Ensemble
  Album Title: *Music of Jared Spears*
  Personnel: Tennessee Technological University Tuba-Euphonium Ensemble, R. Winston Morris, conductor
  Label: KM Records, 1981 LP: KM 6549
  Spears, Jared: *Divertimento for Tuba Ensemble*
Tennessee Technological University Tuba-Euphonium Ensemble
  Album Title: *Play That Funky Tuba Right, Boy!*
  Personnel: Tennessee Technological University Tuba-Euphonium Ensemble, R. Winston Morris, conductor
  Label: Mark Custom Recording Service, Inc., 2003 CD: MCD-4757
  Jarreau, Al/Murphy: *Boogie Down*
  Parissi, Rob/Kortyka: *Play That Funky Tuba Right, Boy!*
  Jackson, Michael/Rose: *Beat It*

King/Laypread/Mcclary/Orange/Richie/Williams/Murphy: *Brick House*
  Correa, Chick/Arnold: *Spain*
  Carpenter, Richard/Esleck: *Walkin'*
  Morgan, Lee/Hauser: *Sidewinder*
  Rodgers and Hammerstein/Cherry: *Favorite Things*
  Cherry, Bill: *Musings*
  Monk, Thelonius/Walker: *'Round Midnight*
  Green, Freddie/Esleck: *Until I Met You*
  Silver, Horace/Hauser: *Sister Sadie*
  Hayes, Isaac/Gottschalk: *Shaft*
  Hancock, Herbie/Perry: *Chameleon*
Tennessee Technological University Tuba-Euphonium Ensemble
  Album Title: *The Tennessee Technological University Tuba Ensemble*
  Personnel: Tennessee Technological University Tuba-Euphonium Ensemble, R. Winston Morris, conductor
  Label: KM Educational Library, 1980 LP: 4631
  Cheetham, John: *Consortium*
  George, Thom Ritter: *Tubasonatina*
  Dodson, John: *Out of the Depths*
  Porter, Cole/Sample: *Cole Porter Medley*
  Bernie, Pinkard, and Casey/Garrett: *Sweet Georgia Brown*
  Nyro, Laura/Cherry: *Eli's Coming*
  Garrett, James Allen: *A Tubalee Jubalee*
  Rodgers, Richard/Cherry: *My Favorite Things*
Tennessee Technological University Tuba-Euphonium Ensemble
  Album Title: *Tennessee Tech Tuba Ensemble Presents Their Carnegie Recital Hall Program*
  Personnel: Tennessee Technological University Tuba-Euphonium Ensemble, R. Winston Morris, conductor
  Label: Golden Crest, 1976 LP: CRS 4152
  Beale, David: *Reflections on a Park Bench*
  Bach, Johann Sebastian/Phillips: *Air from "Suite No. 3 in D Major for Orchestra"*
  Stroud, Richard: *Treatments for Tuba*
  Sample, Steve: *Nostalgia Medley*
Tennessee Technological University Tuba-Euphonium Ensemble
  Album Title: *Tennessee Tech Tuba Ensemble, Volume I*
  Personnel: Tennessee Technological University Tuba-Euphonium Ensemble, R. Winston Morris, conductor
  Label: Golden Crest, 1975 LP: CRS 4139
  Bartles, Alfred: *When Tubas Waltz*
  Barroso, Ary/Morris: *Brazil*
  Hutchinson, Terry: *Tuba Juba Duba*
  Lecuona, Ernesto/Morris: *Malagueña*
  Ellington, Duke/Sample: *Tribute to Duke Ellington*

Bach, Johann Sebastian/Morris: *Toccata and Fugue in d Minor*
Ross, Walter: *Concerto Basso*
Bach, Johann Sebastian/Sauter: *Come, Sweet Death*
Tennessee Technological University Tuba-Euphonium Ensemble
  Album Title: *Unleash the Beast!!!*
  Personnel: Tennessee Technological University Tuba-Euphonium Ensemble, R. Winston Morris, conductor
  Label: Mark Custom Recording Service, Inc., 1995 CD: MCD-1800
  Kamen, Michael/Oliver: *Robin Hood Fanfare*
  Bach, Johann Sebastian/Beckman: *St. Anne's Fugue*
  Wilson, Kenyon D.: *Tuba Quartet No. 1 in c Minor, Op. 3*
  Danner, Gregory: *Beast!*
  Forte, Aldo: *Tubas Latinas*
  Lockhart-Seitz/Butler: *World Is Waiting for the Sunrise, The*
  Johnston, Bruce/O'Connor: *Sunrise Lady*
  Davis, Miles/Perry: *So What*
  Davis, Miles/Esleck: *Walkin'*
  James, Bob/O'Connor: *Courtship*
  Foster, Frank/Perry: *Shiny Stockings*
  Hancock, Herbie/Perry: *Chameleon*
  Correa, Chick/Arnold: *La Fiesta*
Tennessee Tech Tuba-Euphonium Quintet
  Album Title: *The Golden Sound of Euphoniums*
  Personnel: Bill Cherry, Alan Clark, euphonium; R. Winston Morris, Bill Acuff, Myron Stringer, tuba
  Label: Mirafone, flexible 33⅓ (promotional)
  Bach, Johann Sebastian/Morris: *Contrapuntus I*
  Joplin, Scott/Self: *Entertainer, The*
Thingnäs, Frode. *See* Scandinavian Tuba Jazz
Thomas, Kelly. *See* Euphoniums Unlimited
Thomas, Kelly. *See* Tennessee Technological University Alumni Tuba-Euphonium Ensemble
Thomas, Shaun
  Album Title: *The Music of Roy Newsome*
  Personnel: The Sun Life Band, Roy Newsome, conductor
  Label: Obrasso Records, CD
  Newsome, Roy: *Fantasy on Swiss Airs*
Thompson, Kevin
  Album Title: *Euphonic Bach, Solo Suites and Partitas*
  Personnel:
  Label: Janus Musiek, 1997 CD: JANP10
  Bach, Johann Sebastian: *Suite No.1 in G Major*
  Bach, Johann Sebastian: *Partita in a Minor*
  Bach, Johann Sebastian: *Suite No. 5 in c Minor*
  Bach, Johann Sebastian: *Partita No. 2 in d Minor*
Thorton, David
  Album Title: *Call of the Cossacks*

Personnel: John French, euphonium soloist; Black Dyke Mills Band, Nicholas Childs, conductor
  Label: Doyen Recordings, 2002 CD: DOY CD138
  Graham, Peter: *Celtic Dream from "Windows of the World"*
  Graham, Peter: *Cossack Wedding Dance from "Call of the Cossacks"*
Thorton, David
  Album Title: *Epic Brass*
  Personnel: Highlight Bands of the 2001 Nationals Finals Gala Concert from the Royal Albert Hall
  Label: Salvationist Supplies & Publishing, 2001 CD: SPS 153
  Graham, Peter: *Brilliante*
Thorton, David. *See* Mead, Steven
Thurman, Demondrae. *See* Sotto Voce Quartet
Timlin, Christopher
  Album Title:
  Personnel: Lingdale Band, Alan Morrison, conductor
  Label: Sound News Studio, LP: SM199
  Mantia, Simone/Langford: *Believe Me if All Those Endearing Young Charms*
Tims, Elva Kay
  Album Title: *Mississippi State University Clarinet Choir*
  Personnel: Mississippi State University Clarinet Choir, Warren Lutz, conductor
  Label: United Sound, 1974 LP: US 7365
  Bach, Vincent/Lutz: *Hungarian Melodies*
Tokyo Bari-Tuba Ensemble
  Album Title: *Tokyo Bari-Tuba Ensemble*
  Personnel: Tokyo Bari-Tuba Ensemble, Toru Miura, conductor
  Label: Toshiba EMI, CD
  Harrison, George: *Something with Tokyo*
Top Brass
  Album Title: *Top Brass, Distinctly American*
  Personnel: Darin Cochran, euphonium; David Coleman, trumpet; Ted Hale, trombone; Norlan Bewley, tuba
  Label: The Brass Chamber Music Foundation, Inc., CD: TB 001, DIDX 006150
  Baker, David: *Soleil Impromptu*
  Lennon, John/McCartney: *Eleanor Rigby*
  Brubeck, Dave: *Blue Rondo alla Turk*
  Anonymous: *Jinny Jinkins*
  Baker, David: *Harlem Pipes*
  Baker, David: *Pastorale*
  Baker, David: *To Dizzy with Love*
  Baker, David: *Jean Marie at the Picture Show*
  Baker, David: *Folklike*
  Baker, David: *Stickin'*
  Baker, David: *Wait's Barbershop*
  Niehaus, Lennie: *Saxidentally*
  Arlen, Harold: *Over the Rainbow*
  Anonymous: *Black Jack Davie*
  Traditional: *Amazing Grace*

Gershwin, George: *A Woman Is a Sometime Thing*
Chaplin, Charlie: *Smile*
Tropman, Matt
   Album Title: *Continuum*
   Personnel: Alice Mikolajewski, piano; Dom Moio, percussion
   Label: Summit Records, 2000 CD: DCD 279
   Alfén, Hugo/Olsrud: *Vallflickans Dans*
   Picchi, Ermano/Mantia: *Fantaisie Originale*
   Gillingham, David: *Blue Lake Fantasies*
   Gluck, von C.W./Winter: *Dance of the Blessed Spirits*
   Fauré, Gabriel: *Papillon and Sicilienne*
   Anonymous/Buttery: *Hijazker Longa*
   Pilafian, Sam: *Relentless Grooves*
   Sondheim, Stephen: *Send in the Clowns*
Tropman, Matt
   Album Title: *From the Balcony*
   Personnel: Gail Novak, piano; Chris Rose, percussion; Eric Sabo, bass
   Label: Summit Records, 2002 CD: DCD 316
   Bernstein, Leonard/Fettig: *West Side Story: Prologue*
   Bernstein, Leonard/Fettig: *Scherzo*
   Bernstein, Leonard/Fettig: *Mambo*
   Bernstein, Leonard/Fettig: *Cha-cha*
   Bernstein, Leonard/Fettig: *Maria*
   Bernstein, Leonard/Fettig: *Tonight*
   Bernstein, Leonard/Fettig: *One Hand, One Heart*
   Bernstein, Leonard/Fettig: *Cool-Fugue*
   Bernstein, Leonard/Fettig: *Somewhere*
   Bernstein, Leonard/Fettig: *I Have a Love*
   Bernstein, Leonard/Fettig: *Finale*
   Prokofiev, Sergei/Fettig: *Romeo and Juliet: Introduction*
   Prokofiev, Sergei/Fettig: *Masks*
   Prokofiev, Sergei/Fettig: *Montagues and Capulets, The*
   Prokofiev, Sergei/Fettig: *Young Juliet, The*
   Prokofiev, Sergei/Fettig: *City Awakens, The*
   Prokofiev, Sergei/Fettig: *Public Merryment*
   Prokofiev, Sergei/Fettig: *Mercutio-Fight*
   Prokofiev, Sergei/Fettig: *Romeo and Juliet at Parting*
   Prokofiev, Sergei/Fettig: *Juliet's Funeral and Death*
Tropman, Matt. *See* Champions of the Leonard Falcone Festival 1986–2000
Tuba Christmas Ensemble
   Album Title: *Merry TubaChristmas*
   Personnel: Euphonium/Tuba Ensembles; Bloomington, Chicago, Dallas, Los Angeles, New York; Harvey Phillips, conductor
   Label: Harvey Phillips Foundation, 1980 LP: NR-1111-4
   Traditional: *O Come All Ye Faithful*
   Traditional: *Deck the Halls*
   Traditional: *First Noel, The*

Traditional: *Go Tell It on the Mountain*
Traditional: *O Little Town of Bethlehem*
Traditional: *O Come, O Come Immanuel*
Traditional: *We Three Kings*
Traditional: *Joy to the World*
Traditional: *Angels We Have Heard on High*
Traditional: *Good King Wenceslas*
Traditional: *It Came upon a Midnight Clear*
Traditional: *God Rest Ye Merry Gentlemen*
Bach, Johann Sebastian/Sauter: *Komm Süsser Tod*
Traditional: *Silent Night*
TubaCompany of Harvey Phillips
   Album Title: *Harvey Phillips TubaCompany*
   Personnel: Jim Williams, Norlan Bewley, euphonium; Harvey Phillips, Gary Tirey, tuba; Tubashop Quartet and Friends
   Label: HPF Recordings and Tapes, 1999 CD: HFP 002
   Bewley, Norlan, arr.: *Octubafest Medley*
   Bewley, Norlan, arr.: *Tubafiesta Medley*
   Bewley, Norlan, arr.: *Tubarock Medley*
   Bewley, Norlan, arr.: *Tubaswing Medley*
Tubadours
   Album Title: *The Mighty Tubadours Merry Christmas Album*
   Personnel: Loren Marsteller, Gilbert Zimmerman, euphonium; Norman Pearson, Albert Harclerode, tuba
   Label: Crystal Records Co., 1984 LP: S422
   Herbert, Victor/Vaughan: *March of the Toy Soldiers*
   Vaughan, Rodger, arr.: *Oh Little Town of Bethlehem*
   Vaughan, Rodger, arr.: *Hail to the Lord's Annointed*
   Harclerode, Albert, arr.: *March of the Kings/O Come Little Children*
   Harclerode, Albert/Lycan: *We Three Kings*
   Vaughan, Rodger, arr.: *Away in a Manger*
   Harclerode, Albert, arr.: *Good King Wenceslas*
   Falconer, Leigh: *Von Himmel Hoch*
   Harclerode, Albert, arr.: *Gloucestershire Wassail Song, The/Il Est Ne*
   Vaughan, Rodger, arr.: *O Come Emmanuel*
   Tchaikovsky, Piotr/Self: *Dance of the Reed Pipes*
   Charlton, Philip: *March-Overture*
   Vaughan, Rodger, arr.: *Coventry Carol*
   Harclerode, Albert, arr.: *O Tannanbaum*
   Kingsbury, Craig/Harclerode: *Infant Holy*
   Vaughan, Rodger, arr.: *Break Forth Oh Beauteous Light*
   Harclerode, Albert, arr.: *It Came upon a Midnight Clear*
   Vaughan, Rodger, arr.: *God Rest Ye Merry Gentlemen*
   Charlton, Frederick: *First Noel, The*
   Vaughan, Rodger, arr.: *White Christmas*
   Harclerode, Albert: *O Sanctissmus*

Vaughan, Rodger, arr.: *Santa Claus Is Coming to Town*

Tubadours

Album Title: *Ve Iss Da Mighty Tubadours, Ya?*

Personnel: Frank Berry, Loren Marsteller, Gilbert Zimmerman, euphonium; Norman Pearson, Albert Harclerode, Adi Hershko, David Lusher, Timothy Reilly, tuba

Label: Crystal Records Co., 1991 CD: CD 420 (combined *The Mighty Tubadours Merry Christmas Album* and *Ya, Ve Iss Da Mighty Tubadours*)

Vaughan, Rodger: *Jingle Bell Waltz*

Tubadours

Album Title: *Ya, Ve Iss Da Mighty Tubadours*

Personnel: Frank Berry, euphonium; Albert Harclerode, Adi Hershko, David Lusher, Timothy Reilly, tuba

Label: Crystal Records Co., 1978 LP: S421

Herbert, Victor/Vaughan: *March of the Toy Soldiers*

Strauss, Johann/Berry: *Waltz from "Die Fledermaus"*

King, Karl/Berry: *Barnum and Bailey's Favorite March*

Bartles, Alfred: *When Tubas Waltz*

Mouret, Jean/Self: *Rondeau*

Vaughan, Rodger, arr.: *Down by the Old Mill Stream*

Tchaikovsky, Piotr/Self: *Dance of the Reed Pipes*

Gounod, Charles/Berry: *March of the Marionettes*

Bach, Johann Sebastian/Berry: *Fugue in g Minor*

Lusher, David, arr.: *Come Dearest, the Daylight Is Gone*

Kabalevsky, Dmitri/Berry: *Comedian's Gallop*

Beethoven, Ludwig van/Berry: *Bagatelle*

Ellington, Duke/Vaughan: *Mood Indigo*

Ellington, Duke/Vaughan: *Satin Doll*

Richardson and Maclean/Whitcomb: *Too Fat Polka*

Mozart, Wolfgang Amadeus/Self: *Eine Kleine Nachtmusik*

Tuba Laté

Album Title: *Earth and Moon*

Personnel: John Powell, Paul Walton, euphonium; Ryan Breen, Leslie Neis, tuba

Label: Horizon, 2000 CD: TCD 4

McQueen, Ian: *Heights of Halifax, The*

Roper, Anthony: *A String of Tones*

Scott, Stuart: *Fellscape*

Seivewright, Andrew: *Gowbarrow Gavotte*

Bousted, Donald: *Tears*

Crump, Peter: *March of the Hare, The*

Solomons, David: *Pieces of Eight*

Parfrey, Raymond: *Tributes to Tunesmiths*

Puw, Guto Pryderi: *Visages*

Regan, Michael J.: *Quartet*

Bayliss, Colin: *Tuba Quartet No, 2: Ale and Arty*

Parfrey, Raymond: *Male Voice for Brass*

Rice, Hugh Collins: *Earth and Moon*

Wood, Derek: *Tubafusion*

Tuba Laté

Album Title: *Episodes*

Personnel: John Powell, Paul Walton, euphonium; Ryan Breen, Leslie Neis, tuba

Label: ASC CS, 1999 CD: CD 12

Hinchley, John: *Boogie Woogie Tuba Boy*

Bach, Johann Sebastian/Wood: *Air from "Suite in D"*

Mitchell-Davidson, Paul: *Tubafication*

Traditional/Forbes: *Scarborough Fair*

Kerwin, Simon: *Illustrations for Tubas*

Parker, Handel/Walton: *Deep Harmony*

Reeman, John: *Episodes*

Schifrin, Lalo/Smalley: *Mission Impossible*

Tuba Laté

Album Title: *Light Metal*

Personnel: John Powell, Paul Walton, euphonium; Ryan Breen, Leslie Neis, tuba

Label: TUBA CD, 1995 CD: 001

Sousa, John Philip: *Thunder, The*

Frackenpohl, Arthur: *Pop Suite*

Saint-Saëns, Camille/Minchin: *Swan, The*

Saint-Saëns, Camille/Minchin: *Elephant, The*

Traditional/Werden: *English Country Airs*

Ivanovici, J./Konagaya: *Wave of the Danube*

Khatchaturian, Aram/Seitz: *Sabre Dance*

Proctor, S.: *Light Metal-I Talatasco*

Kreisler, Fritz/Woodcock: *Liebeslied*

Edgar, M./Powell: *Three Ha'Pence a Foot*

Moore, T.: *Three Piece Suite*

Lennon, John/McCartney, Paul/Miyagawa: *Yesterday*

Sousa, John Philip/Morris: *El Capitan*

Tchaikovsky, Piotr/Butler: *Neopolitan Song*

Tuba Laté

Album Title: *Move*

Personnel: John Powell, Paul Walton, euphonium; Ryan Breen, Leslie Neis, tuba

Label: ASC CS, 2000 CD: CD 21

Kerwin, Simon: *March-Frot*

Skempton, Howard: *Rest and Recreation*

Traditional/Moore: *3 Negro Spirituals*

Naftel, Frederick: *Pascal's Victim*

Traditional/Plakidis: *Aija Zuzu*

Bach, Johann Sebastian/Smalley: *Fugue in g Minor*

Primrose/Forbes: *St. James Infirmary*

Davidson, Matthew: *Move*

Gasparini/Miller: *Adoramus Te Christe*

Newsome, Roy: *Basics, The*

Traditional/Forbes: *Just a Closer Walk*

Solomons, David: *Prayer Before the Close of Day*

TubaShop Quartet

Album Title: *TubaShop Quartet, Featuring the Music of TubaChristmas and TubaSantas*

Personnel: Jim Williams, Norlan Bewley, euphonium; Harvey Phillips, Gary Tirey, tuba

Label: Harvey Phillips Foundation, 1991 CS:
1000-1
Bewley, Norlan: *Santa Wants a Tuba for
Christmas*
Martin, Blaine/Bewley: *Have Yourself a Merry
Little Christmas*
Torme, Mel/Bewley: *Christmas Song, The*
Bewley, Norlan, arr.: *TubaChristmas Suite*
Bewley, Norlan, arr.: *Fum, Fum, Fum*
Bewley, Norlan, arr.: *Good Christian Men
Rejoice*
Bewley, Norlan, arr.: *Greensleeves*
Bewley, Norlan, arr.: *Bring a Torch, Jeanette,
Isabella*
Bewley, Norlan, arr.: *Pat-A-Pan*
Bewley, Norlan, arr.: *Carol of the Bells*
Wilder, Alec: *Carols for a Merry TubaChristmas*
United States Armed Forces Tuba-Euphonium
Ensemble
Album Title: *Forty-Third Annual Mid-West
International Band and Orchestra Clinic*
Personnel: Brian Bowman, John Mueller, Car-
lyle Weber, David Werden, Michael Colburn,
Joan Follis, Roger Behrend, Ken Shrum,
euphonium; Bob Daniel, Jeff Arwood, Tim
Loehr, Gary
Buttery, Ike Evans, Joe Roccaro, Marty
Erickson, Scott Tarabour, tuba; Tim Hues-
gen, drums; R. Winston Morris, conductor
Label: Mark Custom Recording Services, 1989
CD: MW89MCD-8
Pegram, Wayne: *Howdy!*
Mozart, Wolfgang Amadeus/Gottschalk: *Over-
ture to the "Marriage of Figaro"*
Rossini, Gioacchino/Kile: *Overture to the "Bar-
ber of Seville"*
Cheetham, John: *Consortium*
Traditional/Garrett: *Londonderry Air*
Garrett, James: *A Tubalee Jubalee*
Gershwin, George/Sample: *Gershwin Medley*
King, Karl L./Werden: *Melody Shop, The*
King, Karl L./Morris: *Barnum and Bailey's
Favorite*
United States Army Band Tuba-Euphonium Ensem-
ble and Massed Ensemble, The
Album Title: *The United States Army Band
Tuba-Euphonium Conference*
Personnel: The United States Army Band
Tuba-Euphonium Ensemble and Massed
Ensemble,
R. Winston Morris, conductor
Label: United States Army Band, CS. Public
service, not for sale. Also released by Mark
Custom Recording Services, 1989 CD:
MW89MCD-8
Bach, Johann Sebastian/Beckman: *St. Anne's
Fugue*
Saint-Saëns, Camille/Cohen: *Marche Militaire
Francaise*
Werle, Floyd: *Variations on an Old Hymn*
Camphouse, Mark: *Ceremonial Sketch*

Bach, Johann Sebastian/Werden: *Bist Du
Bei Mir*
Frank, Marcel: *Lyric Poem*
Canter, James: *Appalachian Carol*
DiGiovanni, Rocco: *Tuba Magic*
Joplin, Scott/Self: *Entertainer, The*
Huffine, G. H.: *Them Basses*
United States Coast Guard Tuba-Euphonium
Quartet
Album Title: *The Musical Sounds of the Seasons*
Personnel: Roger Behrend, David Werden,
euphonium; John Banker, Gary Buttery, tuba
Label: United States Coast Guard, 1984 LP.
Public service, not for sale
Buttery, Gary: *An English Folk Christmas*
United States Coast Guard Tuba-Euphonium
Quartet
Album Title: *The United States Coast Guard
Band, Soloists and Chamber Players*
Personnel: David Werden, Dennis Winter,
euphonium; Gary Buttery, David Chaput,
tuba
Label: The United States Coast Guard, 1978
LP: USGC122678
Ramsöe, Emilio/Buttery: *Quartet for Brass*
United States Navy Band Tuba-Euphonium
Quartet
Album Title: *The United States Navy Band
Presents the Tuba Quartet*
Personnel: Roger Behrend, John Bowman,
euphonium; Keith Mehlan, Martin Erickson,
tuba
Label: United States Navy Band, 1986 CS.
Public service, not for sale
Bulla, Stephen: *Quartet for Low Brass*
Ramsöe, Emilio/Buttery: *Quartet for Brass
(third movement)*
Massenet, Jules/Erickson, Margaret: *Argonaise
from "Le Cid"*
Joplin, Scott/Werden: *Ragtime Dance*
University of Miami Tuba Ensemble
Album Title: *University of Miami Tuba
Ensemble Greatest Hits*
Personnel: University of Miami Tuba Ensem-
ble, Constance Weldon, director
Label: Miami United Tuba Ensemble Society,
LP: 14568
Payne, Frank: *Quartet for Tubas (The
Condor)*
Frank, Marcel G.: *Lyric Poem for Five Tubas*
Hastings, Ross: *Little Madrigal for Big Horns*
Rogers, Thomas: *Music for Tuba Ensemble*
Boone, Dan: *Three Moods*
Donaldson, W./Self: *Carolina in the Morning*
Gould, Morton/Woo: *Pavanne from "Latin
American Suite"*
Frackenpohl, Arthur: *Pop Suite for Barituba
Ensemble*
Jones, Roger: *Duet No. 12 from "21 Distinctive
Duets"*
Davis, Akst/Woo: *Baby Face*

University of Michigan Tuba and Euphonium Ensemble
Album Title: *The Brass Menagerie*
Personnel: University of Michigan Tuba and Euphonium Ensemble, Abe Torchinsky, director
Label: University of Michigan School of Music Records, 1979 LP: SM0011
Byrd, William: *Agnus Dei*
Payne, Frank: *Quartet for Tubas*
Holmes, Paul: *Quartet for Tubas*
Stevens, John: *Manhattan Suite*
Mozart, Wolfgang Amadeus/Gottschalk: *Overture from the "Marriage of Figaro"*
University of Michigan Tuba and Euphonium Ensemble
Album Title: *University of Michigan Percussion and Tuba Ensembles*
Personnel: University of Michigan Tuba and Euphonium Ensemble, Abe Torchinsky, director; Uri Mayer, conductor
Label: Golden Crest Records Inc., 1975 LP: CRS 4145
Iannaccone, Anthony: *"Hades" for Two Euphoniums and Two Tubas*
Pressor, William: *Serenade for Four Tubas (Allegro, 3rd Movement)*
Iannaccone, Anthony: *Three Mythical Sketches for Four Tubas*
Gottschalk, Arthur: *Substructures for Ten Tubas*
Ushigami, Ryuji
Album Title: *Euphoria*
Personnel: Tamao Araki, euphonium; Tomomi Sato, Piano
Label: Victor Entertainment, CD: NCS-193
Sparke, Philip: *Party Piece*
Bourgeois, Derek: *Euphoria*
Sparke, Philip: *Song for Ina*
Kassatti, T.: *Kino Concertino*
Senshu, Jiro: *Window Opens Toward the Ocean, The*
Golland, John: *Euphonium Concerto*
Ushigami, Ryuji
Album Title: *Obsessions*
Personnel:
Label:
Vanderweele, Aaron
Album Title: *Air 'N Variations*
Personnel: New York Staff Band of the Salvation Army
Label: Salvationist Supplies & Publishing, Ltd., CD: 2005
Phillips, Richard: *There Will Be God*
Audoire, Norman: *We'll All Shout Hallelujah*
Bearcroft, Norman: *The Great Adventure*
Scott/Bulla: *Commitment*
Redhead, Robert: *Ochills*
Catelinet: *Larghetto Semplice from "Call of the Seasons"*
Leidzen, Erik: *Song of the Brother, The*
Dinicu/Heifetz/Gates: *Hora Staccato*

Gates: *Shadowed*
Mallet, Chris: *Travelling Along*
Lovland/Gates: *You Raised Me Up*
Norbury: *Joyous Service*
Bulla, Stephen: *Air 'N Variations*
Camsey, Terry: *A Joy Untold*
Vanderweele, Aaron
Album Title: *Down Under*
Personnel: Preston Citadel Band of the Salvation Army
Label: Salvation Army Label, CD: DCD 0077
Bearcroft, Norman: *Harbour Light*
Bearcroft, Norman: *Jesus, I Come to Thee*
Camsey, Terry: *Promises*
Catherwood, David: *All I Have I Am Bringing to Thee*
VanHoy, Jeremy. *See* Champions of the Leonard Falcone Festival 1986–2000
Van Lier, Bart
Album Title: *First Brass*
Personnel: Allan Botschinsky, Derek Watkins, trumpet and fluegelhorn; Erik Van Lier, tuba
Label: M-A Music, 1986 LP
Botschinsky, Allan: *Interlude No. 4*
Botschinsky, Allan: *October Sunshine*
Botschinsky, Allan: *Kubismus 502*
Brahms, Johannes: *Wiegenlied*
Botschinsky, Allan: *Don't Shoot the Banjo Player ('Cause We've Done It Already)*
Botschinsky, Allan: *Toot Your Roots*
Botschinsky, Allan: *Lady in Blue, The*
Botschinsky, Allan: *Alster Promenade*
Botschinsky, Allan: *Chops a la Salsa*
Botschinsky, Allan: *Love Waltz*
Van Valkenberg, Jamie. *See* Champions of the Leonard Falcone Festival 1986–2000
Vernon, Ken
Album Title:
Personnel: Burton Construction Band, Earnest Woodhouse, conductor
Label: Pye Records, 1976 LP: TB 3008
Catelinet, Phillip, arr.: *Twinkle, Twinkle Little Star*
Verweij, Hugo
Album Title: *Euphonica*
Personnel: Carlos Moerdijk, piano
Label: Mirasound, CD: 399072
Jacob, Gordon: *Fantasia*
Ross, Walter: *Partita*
Monti, Vittorio/Wilson: *Czárdás*
Elgar/Wilson: *Romance*
Boutry, Roger: *Tubacchanale*
Bitsch, Marcel: *Intermezzo*
Toebosch, Louis: *Variaties voor Euphonium en Piano*
Bozza, Eugene: *New Orleans*
Verweij, Hugo. *See* Dutch Tuba Quartet
Vinson, Danny. *See* Alchemy
Vydra, Jiri
Album Title: *The Music of David Gaines*

Personnel: Moravian Philharmonic Orchestra,
Vit Micka, conductor
Label: MMC Recordings, Ltd., 2001 CD:
MMC2113
Gaines, David: *Concerto for Euphonium and
Orchestra 1987*
Walker, Mark. *See* Euphoniums Unlimited
Walton, Paul
Album Title: *Champion Sound*
Personnel: Britannia Building Society Band,
Howard Snell, conductor
Label: Obrasso Records, CD
Newsome, Roy: *A Piece of Cake, Duet for
Euphoniums*
Walton, Paul
Album Title: *Saddleworth Festival*
Personnel: Dobcross Silver Band
Label: BobX Music, CD: DCCD01
Rimmer, William: *Jenny Jones*
Warrington, Brian
Album Title:
Personnel: Ronnie Kershaw, euphonium; Roch-
dale Band, Norman Ashcroft, conductor
Label: Decca, 1974 LP: SB 316
Powell, Tom: *Duo for Euphoniums*
Warrington, Brian
Album Title:
Personnel: Rochdale Band, Norman Ashcroft,
conductor
Label: Grosvenor, 1977 LP: GRS 1054
Hartmann, John: *Robin Adair*
Warrington, Brian
Album Title:
Personnel: Goodshaw Band, Kevin Bolton,
conductor
Label: Midland Sound Recordings, 1979 LP:
MSRS 1436
Arban, Jean Baptiste/Remmington: *Carnival
of Venice, The*
Watanabe, Ken-ichi. *See* Champions of the Leonard
Falcone Festival 1986–2000
Waterworth, Ken
Album Title:
Personnel: Melbourne Staff Band of the Salva-
tion Army, C. Woods, conductor
Label: Regency Records, 1984 LP: MWB11
Himes, William: *Journey into Peace*
Weber, Carlyle. *See* United States Armed Forces
Tuba-Euphonium Ensemble
Webster, Jonathan. *See* Walton, Paul
Welsh, David
Album Title: *Double Champions*
Personnel: Williams Fairey Band, Peter Parkes,
conductor
Label: Polyphonic Reproductions Ltd., 1994
CD: QPRL 065D
Curnow, James: *Rhapsody for Euphonium*
Werden, David
Album Title: *Coast Guard Bicentennial*
Personnel: The United States Coast Guard
Band
Label: The United States Coast Guard, 1990
CD. Public service, not for sale

Clarke, Herbert L.: *Bride of the Waves, The*
Werden, David
Album Title: *Live from Leamy Hall*
Personnel: The United States Coast Guard
Band, Lewis Buckley, conductor
Label: The United States Coast Guard, 1980
LP: CG-32183
Smith, Claude T.: *Rondo*
Werden, David
Album Title: *Robert Hoe V: In Memoriam*
Personnel: The United States Coast Guard
Band, Lewis Buckley, conductor
Label: Mark Custom Recording Service, 1983
LP: MC 20443
Owen, Jerry: *Variations*
Werden, David
Album Title: *This Was the Bicentennial!*
Personnel: The United States Coast Guard
Band, Lewis Buckley, conductor
Label: The United States Coast Guard Band,
1977 LP: USCG8177
Clarke, Herbert: *Carnival of Venice, The*
Werden, David
Album Title: *The United States Coast Guard
Band at Mid-West*
Personnel: The United States Coast Guard Band
Label: Mark Custom Recording Service,
1991 CS
Sparke, Philip: *Fantasy for Euphonium and Band*
Werden, David
Album Title: *The United States Coast Guard
Band at Mid-West, 1984*
Personnel: The United States Coast Guard
Band, Lewis Buckley, conductor
Label: Crest, LP: MID84–5
Owen, Jerry: *Variations*
Werden, David
Album Title: *The United States Coast Guard
Band, Soloists and Chamber Players*
Personnel: The United States Coast Guard
Band, Lewis Buckley, conductor
Label: The United States Coast Guard, 1978
LP: USGC122678
Guilmant, Alexandre: *Morceau Symphonique*
Werden, David. *See* Atlantic Tuba Quartet
Werden, David. *See* Coast Guard Tuba-Euphonium
Quartet
Werden, David. *See* Symphonia
Werden, David. *See* United States Armed Forces
Tuba-Euphonium Ensemble
Wharton, Andrew
Album Title:
Personnel: Skipton Band, D. Robbins,
conductor
Label: Look Records, 1981 LP: 7001
Sutton, Eddie: *Cavalier, The*
Wilkins, Richard
Album Title: *Firestorm*
Personnel: Laura Lineberger, euphonium; The
United States Army Brass Band, Bryan
Shelburne, conductor
Label: The United States Army Brass Band,
1991. Public service, not for sale

DeVita, Alfred/Catherall: *Softly As I Leave You*
Wilkinson, Harry
    Album Title:
    Personnel: Markham Main Colliery Band, Allan
        Street, conductor
    Label: Pye Records, 1966 LP: GSGL 10395
    Chester, Barry: *Arabella*
Wilkinson, Harry
    Album Title:
    Personnel: Graham Spencer, euphonium;
        Hammonds Sauce Works Band, Geoffrey
        Witham, conductor
    Label: Pye Records, 1969 LP: GSGL 10439
    Powell, Tom: *Duo for Euphoniums*
Wilkinson, Harry
    Album Title:
    Personnel: Hammonds Sauce Works Band,
        Geoffrey Witham, conductor
    Label: Pye Records, 1970 LP: GSGL 10455
    Mozart, Wolfgang Amadeus/Rimmer: *Non Piu
        Andrai*
Wilkinson, Mark. *See* Williams, Glyn
Willems, John
    Album Title: *I Himmelen*
    Personnel: Brass Band Limburg
    Label: Brass Band Limburg
    Golland, John: *Meiso*
Williams, Glyn
    Album Title: *Brass in Concert*
    Personnel: Fodens Motor Works Band, Bryan
        Hurdley, Bramwell Tovey
    Label: Doyen Recordings, 2002 CD: DOY
        CD139
    Traditional/Fernie: *Air Varie*
Williams, Glyn
    Album Title: *Brass Night*
    Personnel: Ken Cant, euphonium; Fodens
        Motor Works Band
    Label: Fodens Motor Works Band
    Trenet, Paul: *I Wish You Love*
Williams, Glyn
    Album Title: *From North to South*
    Personnel: Fodens Motor Works Band
    Label: Egon, CD: EGN-CD 120
    Graham, Peter: *Brilliante*
Williams, Glyn
    Album Title: *Music from inside the Lighthouse*
    Personnel: Geno White
    Label: Clear Ear Publishing
    White, Geno: *Bend to the Horizon*
Williams, Glyn
    Album Title: *The Music of William Rimmer*
    Personnel: Fodens Motor Works Band
    Label: Fodens Motor Works Band
    Rimmer, William: *Jenny Jones*
Williams, Glyn
    Album Title: *On Stage*
    Personnel: Mark Wilkinson, euphonium;
        Fodens Motor Works Band
    Label: Fodens Motor Works Band
    Hudec, Adam: *Slavonic Impressions*
    Rüedi, Thomas: *Winter Dream*
Williams, Glyn

Album Title: *Whitsun Wakes*
    Personnel: Fodens Motor Works Band
    Label: Fodens Motor Works Band
    Graham, Peter: *Brilliante*
Williams, Jim. *See* TubaCompany of Harvey Phillips
Williams, Jim. *See* TubaShop Quartet
Williams, Joseph
    Album Title:
    Personnel: Warrington Youth Band, Len
        Andrews, conductor
    Label: Pad Records, LP: PAD016
    Round, H.: *Scenes that are Brightest*
Williams, Kate
    Album Title: *Something 2 Celebrate*
    Personnel: Staffordshire Band, David Maple-
        stone, conductor
    Label: Harlequin Recordings, Ltd., CD: 2002
        HAR 0103
    Golland, John: *Peace*
Willis, Simon
    Album Title: *Celebration*
    Personnel: BT Band
    Label: Doyen Recordings Ltd., CD: DOY
        CD026
    Doughty, George: *Grandfather's Clock*
Winter, Denis. *See* Atlantic Tuba Quartet
Winter, Denis. *See* Coast Guard Tuba-Euphonium
    Quartet
Winter, Denis. *See* Symphonia
Winterbottom, D.
    Album Title:
    Personnel: Mossley Band
    Label: Midland Sound Recordings, 1974 LP:
        MSRS 1384
    Heath, Reginald: *Andante and Scherzo*
Wise, Peter
    Album Title: *The Enfield Citadel Band*
    Personnel: The Enfield Citadel Band
    Label: Salvationist Publishing & Supplies Ltd.,
        SPS 004
    Redhead, Robert: *Euphony*
Wise, Peter
    Album Title:
    Personnel: International Staff Band of the Sal-
        vation Army, B. Adams, conductor
    Label: Salvationist Publishing & Supplies Ltd.,
        1976 LP: SA6
    Marshall, George: *Ransomed*
Wise, Peter
    Album Title:
    Personnel: International Staff Band of the Sal-
        vation Army, James Williams, conductor
    Label: EMI, 1980 LP: PRA 1026
    Redhead, Robert: *Euphony*
Withington, Len
    Album Title: *The National Champions*
    Personnel: Wingates Temperance Band
    Label: Phonodisc, NSPL-15048
    Prieto, J.: *Wedding, The*
Withington, Len
    Album Title:
    Personnel: Wingates Temperance Band, Hugh
        Parry, conductor

Label: Music for Pleasure, 1966 LP: MFP
1099
Rimmer, William: *Weber's Last Waltz*
Withington, Len
Album Title:
Personnel: Wingates Temperance Band, Dennis
Smith, conductor
Label: Pye Records, 1970 LP: GSGL 10461
Foster, Stephen/Rimmer: *My Old Kentucky
Home*
Withington, Len
Album Title:
Personnel: Wingates Temperance Band, Dennis
Smith, conductor
Label: Pye Records, 1972 LP: GSGL 10482
Prieto, J.: *Wedding, The*
Withington, Len
Album Title:
Personnel: Wingates Temperance Band, Rich-
ard Evans, conductor
Label: Grosvenor, 1976 LP: GRS 1045
Massenet, Jules: *Meditation from "Thais"*
Withington, Len
Album Title:
Personnel: Wingates Temperance Band, Dennis
Wilby, conductor
Label: Decca, 1979 LP: SB 338
Sedaka: *Solitaire*
Wolgamott, Charles. *See* Euphonium Section, The
Wood, Ken
Album Title: *Presenting Ken Wood, Euphonium
Soloist, with an All-Star Band*
Personnel: The All-Star Band
Label: TBR Publications, 1982 LP: NR13487
Clarke, Herbert L.: *Carnival of Venice, The*
Llewellyn: *My Regards*
Rodgers, Thomas: *If I Love You from "Carousel"*
Goldman, Richard: *Tramp, Tramp, Tramp*
Mantia, Simone: *Believe Me if All Those Endear-
ing Young Charms*
Doughty, George: *Grandfather's Clock*
Wood: *Drink to Me Only with Thine Eyes*
King, Karl L.: *A Night in June*
Woodland, Shaun
Album Title:
Personnel: Bodmin Town Band
Label: Look Records, 1981 LP: LKLP 7012
Heath, Reginald: *Springtime*
Woodward, David. *See* Conway, Sean
Woollam, David
Album Title: *Roberts Bakery in Concert,
Volume 3*
Personnel: Roberts Bakery Band
Label: Boosey & Hawkes Sound Recordings
Saint-Saëns, Camille/Snell: *Swan, The*
Woollam, David
Album Title: *Roberts Bakery in Concert,
Volume 2*
Personnel: Roberts Bakery Band
Label: Boosey & Hawkes Sound Recordings
Doughty, George: *Grandfather's Clock*
Yamamoto, Norihisa

Album Title: *Concerto for Band, Volume 2*
Personnel:
Label: Victor, LP: SKX-25056
Foster, Stephen/Rimmer: *My Old Kentucky
Home*
Romberg, Sigmond: *Serenade from "The Stu-
dent Prince"*
Yamamoto, Takashi
Album Title: *Takashi Yamamoto, Euphonium
Concert in Casals Hall*
Personnel: Chieko Ito, piano; Marakio Yama-
moto, marimba
Label: Euphonic Sound, R-900169
Capuzzi, Antonio: *Andante and Rondo from
"Doublebass Concerto"*
Boccalari, Ed/Kent-Akers: *Fantasia di Concerto*
Adler, Samuel: *Four Dialogs for Euphonium and
Marimba*
Janalek, Loes: *Capriccio*
Yates, Ian. *See* Griffiths, Morgan
Young, R. *See* Scannell, A. J.
Young, Raymond G.
Album Title: *CBDNA Southern Division
Conference*
Personnel: New Orleans Concert Band
Label: Mark Records, 1988 LP: CBDNA88-10
Smith, Claude T.: *Rondo*
Young, Raymond G.
Album Title: *Clinician Series, Raymond Young*
Personnel:
Label: Golden Crest Records, LP: CR 1009
Young, Raymond G.
Album Title: *College Band Directors National
Association—Fifteenth National Conference,
1969*
Personnel: The University of Southern Missis-
sippi Symphonic Band, Alan Drake,
conductor
Label: Silver Crest Records, 1969 LP: CBD-
69-4
Barat, J. Ed./Berryman: *Piece en Mi Bemol for
Tenor Trombone*
Young, Raymond G.
Album Title: *1977 Mid-West National Band
and Orchestra Clinic*
Personnel: Plymouth Centennial High School
Band, James Griffith, conductor
Label: Silver Crest Records, 1977 LP: MID-
77-14
Rimsky-Korsakov, Nicolai/Ivallin: *Concerto for
Trombone and Band*
Young, Raymond G.
Album Title: *Raymond G. Young, Baritone Horn*
Personnel: Tom Fraschillo, piano
Label: Golden Crest Records, LP: RE 7025
Barat, J. Ed.: *Andante et Allegro*
Beach: *Suite for Baritone Horn and Piano*
Hutchison: *Sonatina for Baritone Horn and
Piano*
Morel, Florentin: *Piece en Fa mineur*
Martin, David: *Suite for Euphonium and
Piano*

Gower, A. E.: *Three Short Pieces for Baritone Horn and Piano*
Young, Raymond G.
  Album Title: *Raymond G. Young, Euphonium Soloist*
  Personnel:
  Label: Century, 17647
  Barat, J. Ed.: *Andante and Scherzo*
  Nux, de la P. V.: *Concert Piece*
  Shepherd, Arthur: *Nocturne and Rondolette*
  Barat, J. Ed.: *Introduction and Dance*
  Ropartz, Guy: *Andante and Allegro*
  Cords: *Romanze*
  Rossini, Gioacchino: *Largo Al Factotum*
Young, Ron
  Album Title: *TRI uni EUPH, Euphonium Performance*
  Personnel: Hendon Band of the Salvation Army, Stephen Cobb, conductor; Central Band of the Royal Air Force, Rob Wiffin, conductor; June Collin, piano
  Label: Ron Young Label, CD: RY001
  Bozza, Eugene: *Allegro et Finale*
  Spohr, Louis: *Benediction*
  Vaughan Williams, Ralph: *Romanza*
  Grieg, Edward: *Spring*
  Leidzen, Erik: *Home on the Range*
  Leidzen, Erik: *Song of the Brother, The*
  Rimmer, William: *Weber's Last Waltz*
  Senaille, Jean Baptiste/Catelnet: *Introduction and Allegro Spiritoso*
  Langford, Gordon/Grand: *Blaydon Races, The*
  Jacob, Gordon: *Fantasia*
Zawadi, Kiane
  Album Title: *Blue Spirits*
  Personnel:
  Label: Blue Note Records Inc., BLP 4196
Zawadi, Kiane
  Album Title: *Harold Vick, Don't Look Back*
  Personnel: Harold Vick, tenor sax, flute; Virgil Jones, trumpet, flugelhorn; George Davis, alto flute; Joe Bonner, piano, tuba, guitar; Sam Jones, bass; Billy Hart, drums
  Label: Strata-East Records, 1974 LP: SES-7431
  Vick, Harold: *Don't Look Back*
  Vick, Harold: *Melody for Bu*
  Vick, Harold: *Señor Zamora*
Zawadi, Kiane
  Album Title: *Last Chance for Common Sense*
  Personnel:
  Label: Verve, 531 536-2
  Kendrick, Rodney: *Rodney's Rhythm, Part One*
Zawadi, Kiane
  Album Title: *New Jersey Jazz Festival*
  Personnel: Ted Harris Octet
  Label: Harris and Dyer Records
Zawadi, Kiane
  Album Title: *Ready for Fredie*
  Personnel:
  Label: Blue Note Records Inc., BLP 4085
Zawadi, Kiane
  Album Title: *Slide Hampton: Sister Salvation*

  Personnel: Slide Hampton Ensemble
  Label: Atlantic, 1339
Zawadi, Kiane
  Album Title: *Slide Hampton and His Horn of Plenty*
  Personnel: Slide Hampton Ensemble
  Label: Strand, 1006
Zawadi, Kiane
  Album Title: *Ted Harris Presents More Giants of Jazz*
  Personnel: Ted Harris Septet
  Label: Harris and Dyer Records
Zuback, Joseph
  Album Title: *Concert in the Park*
  Personnel: River City Brass Band, Robert Bernat, conductor
  Label: River City Brass Band Inc., 1992 CD: BB192A
  Mantia, Simone/Boddington: *Believe Me if All Those Endearing Young Charms*
Zuback, Joseph
  Album Title: *Star Spangled Brass*
  Personnel: River City Brass Band, Robert Bernat, conductor
  Label: River City Brass Band, Inc., 1989 CD: BB289A
  Curnow, James: *Rhapsody for Euphonium and Brass Band*

Euphonium Recordings by Title

A fors' è lui from "la Traviata," Verdi, Giuseppe/Creux: Mead, Steven
A la Romanesc, Thomas/Dos: Mead, Steven
Abide with Me, Lyte: Childs, David
Achieved Is the Glorious Work from "Die Schöpfung," Haydn, Franz Josef: Sotto Voce Quartet
Adagio and Allegro from "Cello Concerto," Elgar, Edward/Bourgeois: Childs, Robert
Adagio and Allegro, Schumann, Robert/Gurtner: Mead, Steven
Adagio and Rondo, Forte, Aldo Rafael: Symphonia
Adagio and Rondo, Mozart, Wolfgang Amadeus/R. Childs: Childs, Robert
Adagio from "Concerto for Cello," Haydn, Franz Josef/Shuman: Falcone, Leonard; Dart, Fred
Adagio from "Symphony No. 3," Saint-Saëns, Camille/Murley: British Tuba Quartet, The
Adagio, Barber, Samuel/Stevens: Symphonia
Adagio, Stevens, John: Symphonia
Adoramus Te Christe, Gasparini, Quirino/Miller: Tuba Laté; Sotto Voce Quartet
Agnus Dei, Bizet, George: Bowman, Brian
Agnus Dei, Byrd, William: University of Michigan Tuba and Euphonium Ensemble
Ah! Vous Dirai-Je, Maman, Mozart, Wolfgang Amadeus/Werden: Alchemy (previously Atlantic Tuba Quartet)
Ah, non credea mirarti, Bellini, Vincenzo/Bona: Mead, Steven

Ah, non giunge from "La Sonnambula," Bellini, Vincenzo/Bona: Mead, Steven

Aija Zuzu, Traditional/Plakidis: Tuba Laté

Air 'N Variations, Bulla, Stephen: Vanderweele, Aaron

Air for Tuba Ensemble, Rodgers, Thomas: Tennessee Technological University and Alumni Tuba-Euphonium Ensemble

Air from "Suite No. 3 in D," Bach, Johann Sebastian/D. Childs: Childs, David

Air from "Suite No. 3 in D," Bach, Johann Sebastian/Foote: Bowman, Brian

Air from "Suite No. 3 in D," Bach, Johann Sebastian/Phillips: Tennessee Technological University Tuba-Euphonium Ensemble

Air from "Suite No. 3 in D," Bach, Johann Sebastian/Werden: Atlantic Tuba Quartet, The; British Tuba Quartet, The

Air from "Suite No. 3 in D," Bach, Johann Sebastian/Wood: Tuba Laté

Air Varie, Op. 21, Klose, Hyacinthe/Kipfer: Kipfer, Ueli

Air Varie, Traditional/Fernie: Williams, Glyn

Aka Tonbi, Yamada, Kosaku/Yamamoto: Childs Brothers

Akatombow, Yamada, Kosaku/Ito: Miura, Toru

All Blues, Davis, Miles: Scandinavian Tuba Jazz

All I Ask of You, Webber, Andrew Lloyd/Mowat: McDonnell, Riki, and Mike Kilroy

All I Ask of You, Webber, Andrew Lloyd: Schmidli, Erich; Kilroy, Mike

All I Have I Am Bringing to Thee, Catherwood, David: Vanderweele, Aaron

All the Things You Are, Kern, Jerome/Maunder: McDonnell, Riki, and Mike Kilroy

All Too Soon, Ellington, Duke: O'Hara, Betty

Alla Burlesca, Vinter, Gilbert: Groom, Trevor; Baglin, Lyndon

Alla Czárdás, Orsomando, Giovanni/Creux: Mead, Steven

Allegro De Concert, Cools, Eugene: Falcone, Leonard

Allegro et Finale, Bozza, Eugene: Young, Ron

Allegro from "Bassoon Concerto," Mozart, Wolfgang Amadeus/Henstridge: Griffiths, Morgan; Perrins, Barrie; Howell, Colin; Clough, John

Allegro from "Concerto in B♭, K 191," Mozart, Wolfgang Amadeus/Thompson: Anonymous

Allegro from "Concerto, Op. 114," Bourgeois, Derek: Champions of the Leonard Falcone Festival 1986–2000

Allegro Spiritoso, Senaille, Jean Baptiste/Catelnet: Young, Ron

Allegro Spiritoso, Senaille, Jean Baptiste/Himes: Himes, William; Mallett, Chris

Allegro Spiritoso, Senaille, Jean Baptiste/Wright: Baglin, Lyndon

Allegro Spiritoso, Senaille, Jean Baptiste: Falcone, Leonard; Behrend, Roger; Finch, Peter; Garnon, Barry; Louder, Earle

Allegro, Fiocco, Joseph Hector/Smith: McDonnell, Riki, and Mike Kilroy

Alligator Crawl, Waller, Thomas "Fats": O'Hara, Betty

Almost Like Being in Love, Lowe, Frederick: Tennessee Technological University Alumni Tuba-Euphonium Ensemble

Alpine Echoes, Windsor, Basil: Lehamn, Arthur

Alster Promenade, Botschinsky, Allan: Van Lier, Bart

Alte Kameraden, Unknown: Miraphone Tuba Quartet

Amapola, Lacalle, G.J.M./Kosugi: Hokazono, Sho-ichiro

Amapola, Lacalle, G.J.M.: Rustic Bari-Tuba Ensemble

Amazing Grace, Traditional/Denton: Frey, Adam

Amazing Grace, Traditional: Top Brass

Amazing Mr. Arban, The, Arban, Jean Baptiste/Howarth/Gurtner: Mead, Steven

American Tuba Patrol, Meacham, Frank: Rustic Bari-Tuba Ensemble

Andante and Allegro, Ropartz, Guy: Young, Raymond G.

Andante and Rondo from "Doublebass Concerto," Capuzzi, Antonio/R. Childs: Childs, Robert

Andante and Rondo from "Doublebass Concerto," Capuzzi, Antonio: Bowman, Brian; Breuninger, Tyrone; Yamamoto, Takashi; Fukuda, Masanori; Craig, Mary Ann

Andante and Scherzo, Heath, Reginald: Steen, Grierson; Oates, John; Winterbottom, D.

Andante Cantabile from "Piano Sonata in C," Mozart, Wolfgang Amadeus: Albertasaurus Tuba Quartet

Andante Cantabile, Tchaikovsky, Piotr/Rüedi: Rüedi, Thomas

Andante et Allegro for Trombone and Band, Barat, J. Ed./Marsteller: Jordan, Jill

Andante et Allegro, Barat, J. Ed.: Young, Raymond G.; Falcone, Leonard; Fukuda, Masanori

Andante Quasi Allegretto, Ramsöe, Emilio/Buttery: Melton Tuba-Quartett

And Baby Makes Three, Tjader, Patricia: Mancuso, Gus

Anderson's Toy-box, Anderson, Leroy/Ito: Miura, Toru

And I Love You So, Maclean, Don/Greenwood: Groom, Joe

And Soon It Will Be Blossom Time, Andresen: Mead, Steven

An English Folk Christmas, Buttery, Gary, arr.: United States Coast Guard Tuba-Euphonium Quartet

An English Folk Christmas, Buttery, Gary; arr.: Coast Guard Tuba-Euphonium Quartet

An Eriskay Love Lilt, Traditional/Mortimer: Baglin, Lyndon

Angels Guard Thee, Godard, Michael: Childs, David

Angels We Have Heard on High, Traditional: Tuba Christmas Ensemble

Anna Karenina, Johnstone, Helen: McDonnell, Riki, and Mike Kilroy

Annie Laurie, Catherwood, David: Kane, Derick

Another Balance, Wilson, Phil: Matteson, Rich

Anything But Lovely, Webber, Andrew Lloyd: Kilroy, Mike

Appalachian Carol, Canter, James: Tennessee Technological University and Alumni Tuba-Euphonium Ensemble; United States Army Band Tuba-Euphonium Ensemble and Massed Ensemble

Apple Strudel and Cheese, Anonymous: Matteson, Rich

Après Un Rêve, Fauré, Gabriel: Mead, Steven

April Is in My Mistress' Face, Morley, Thomas: British Tuba Quartet, The

Arabella, Chester, Barry: Wilkinson, Harry; Davis, George

Arbucklenian Polka, Hartmann, John: Mead, Steven

Archie's Back, Matteson, Rich: Matteson, Rich

Arctic Dream, Corwell, Neal: Corwell, Neal

Argonaise from "Le Cid," Massenet, Jules/ Margaret Erickson: United States Navy Band Tuba-Euphonium Quartet; Monarch Tuba-Euphonium Quartet; Albertasaurus Tuba Quartet

Aria con Variazioni, Handel, George Frederic/ Fitzgerald: Droste, Paul

Aria di chiesa, Stradella, Alessandro/Barbagallo: Mead, Steven

Aria, Bozza, Eugene/van der Woude: Mead, Steven; Hokazono, Sho-ichiro

Aria, Mozart, Wolfgang Amadeus: Fukuda, Masanori

Arioso and Allegro, Fiocco, Joseph Hector/Childs/ Wilby: Kipfer, Ueli

Arioso and Allegro, Fiocco, Joseph Hector/Childs: Childs, Robert

Arioso, Bach, Johann Sebastian/Denton: Frey, Adam

Arioso, Fiocco, Joseph Hector/McKenzie/ Maunder: McDonnell, Riki, and Mike Kilroy

Arran Boat/Untitled Air, Traditional/LaDuke: LaDuke, Lance

Arrival of the Queen of Sheba, Handel, George Frederic/Hauser: Tennessee Technological University Tuba-Euphonium Ensemble

Arrival of the Queen of Sheba, Handel, George Frederic/Wilson; arr.: Childs Brothers

As Long As He Needs Me, Anonymous: Brunner, Stefan

Ase's Death, Grieg/Harris: Mead, Steven

Assevervation, Hampton, Slide: McKinney, Bernard

Atlantic Zephyrs, Simons, Guardell: Falcone, Leonard; Mead, Steven

At the Far Side of the Pasture, Corwell, Neal: Corwell, Neal

Au Privave, Parker, Charlie/Pirone: Mead, Steven

Aubade, Sparke, Philip: Mead, Steven; Haemhouts, Ben; Breuninger, Tyrone; Millar, Billy

Auburn Is the Colour, Forbes, Michael: Sotto Voce Quartet

Auld Lang Syne, Mantia, Simone: Lehman, Arthur; Mead, Steven; Colburn, Michael

Autumn Leaves, Kosma, J./Prevert, J./Mercer, J/ Perry: Symphonia

Ave Maria from "Otello," Verdi, Giuseppe/Creux: Mead, Steven

Ave Maria, Bach, Johann Sebastian/Arcadelt/Self: Melton Tuba-Quartett

Ave Maria, Bach, Johann Sebastian/Gounod/ Denny: McDonnell, Riki; and Mike Kilroy

Ave Maria, Bach, Johann Sebastian/Gounod/ Denton: Frey, Adam

Ave Maria, Bach, Johann Sebastian/Gounod/ Falcone: Falcone, Leonard

Ave Maria, Bach, Johann Sebastian/Gounod/ Porret: Gagnaux, Alexandre

Ave Maria, Bach, Johann Sebastian/Gounod: Childs, David

Away in a Manger, Vaughan, Rodger, arr.: Tubadours

Baby Elephant Walk, Mancini, Henry/Luis: Melton Tuba-Quartett

Baby Face, Davis, Akst/Woo: University of Miami Tuba Ensemble

Bacarolle, Offenbach, Jacques/Ito: Miura, Toru; Mead, Steven

Badinerie, Bach, Johann Sebastian/Hermann: Melton Tuba-Quartett

Bagatelle, Beethoven, Ludwig van/Berry: Tubadours

Ball of Fire, Smalley, Peter: Mead, Steven

Banjo and Fiddle, Kroll, William/Rüedi: Rüedi, Thomas

Barcarolle et Chanson Bachique, Selmer: Dart, Fred

Barnum and Bailey's Favorite, King, Karl L./Berry: Tubadours

Barnum and Bailey's Favorite, King, Karl L./ Morris: United States Armed Forces Tuba-Euphonium Ensemble

Basics, The, Newsome, Roy: Tuba Laté

Bassa Cat, Steckar, Marc: Miraphone Tuba Quartet

Bassism, Sun Ra: McKinney, Bernard

Bassoon Concerto No. 7 in a Minor, Vivaldi, Antonio/Maganini: Heo, Jae-Young

Bassoon Concerto, Weber von, C.M.: Picton, Wendy

Battle Royal, Jewell: British Tuba Quartet, The; Swiss Tuba Quartet

Batubop, Steckar, Marc: Steckar, Marc

Bavarian Polka, Traditional: British Tuba Quartet, The

Bavarian Stew, Wilhelm, Rolf: Melton Tuba-Quartett

Bayerischer Defiliermarsch, Unknown: Miraphone Tuba Quartet

Bayrische Polka, Traditional/Lohmann, George/ Schmidt: Contraband; Miraphone Tuba Quartet

Bayrische Polka, Traditional: Gerhard Meinl's Tuba Sextet

Bayrische Zell, Traditional: Gerhard Meinl's Tuba Sextet

Be My Love, Brodsky, Nicholas/Farr: Childs Brothers; Griffiths, Morgan; McDonnell, Riki, and Mike Kilroy

Beach Song, Narita, Tamezo: Araki, Tamao

Beast!, Danner, Gregory: Tennessee Technological University Tuba-Euphonium Ensemble

Beat It, Jackson, Michael/Rose: Tennessee Technological University Tuba-Euphonium Ensemble

Beautiful Colorado, DeLuca, Joseph/Boddington: Groom, Trevor; Lean, David

Beautiful Colorado, DeLuca, Joseph/Roberts: Mead, Steven; Childs, Robert

Beautiful Colorado, DeLuca, Joseph: Louder, Earle; Reifsnyder, Robert; Falcone, Leonard; Lehamn, Arthur; Mueller, John

Bee-Bo, Dickman, Marcus: Dickman, Marcus

Beginning, The, Sun Ra: McKinney, Bernard

Belgrade Hangover, Mantooth, Frank: Alexander, Ashley

Believe Me if All Those Endearing Young Charms Mantia, Simone/Dennison: Teasdale, Malcolm

Believe Me if All Those Endearing Young Charms, Mantia, Simone/Boddington: Baglin, Lyndon; Mead, Steven; Zuback, Joseph; Sullivan, Bert; Keene, Ian; Childs Brothers

Believe Me if All Those Endearing Young Charms, Mantia, Simone/Brasch/Maldanado: Mead, Steven

Believe Me if All Those Endearing Young Charms, Mantia, Simone/Corwell: Corwell, Neal

Believe Me if All Those Endearing Young Charms, Mantia, Simone/Eichner: Colburn, Michael

Believe Me if All Those Endearing Young Charms, Mantia, Simone/Hunsberger: Heo, Jae-Young

Believe Me if All Those Endearing Young Charms, Mantia, Simone/Langford: Bridge, Kenneth; Mallett, Chris; Timlin, Christopher; Davis, George; Cutts, Marcus

Believe Me if All Those Endearing Young Charms, Mantia, Simone/McRitchie: Hanson, Scott

Believe Me if All Those Endearing Young Charms, Mantia, Simone/Moore: Childs, Robert

Believe Me if All Those Endearing Young Charms, Mantia, Simone/Stanley: Childs, Robert

Believe Me if All Those Endearing Young Charms, Mantia, Simone: Louder, Earle; Lehman, Arthur; Wood, Ken; Brasch, Harold; Behrend, Roger

Bella Figlia from "Rigoletto," Verdi, Giuseppe: Louder, Earle

Bellamira, Sobotta, Uli: Sobotta, Uli

Bend to the Horizon, White, Geno: Williams, Glyn

Beneath the Surface, Harrison, Wayne: Tennessee Technological University Tuba-Euphonium Ensemble

Benediction, Spohr, Louis: Young, Ron

Benediction, Stevens, John: Sotto Voce Quartet

Benedictus, Jenkins: Childs, David

Best There Are, The, Anonymous: Lehman, Arthur

Better World, The, Bearcroft, Norman: Kane, Derick; Gagnaux, Alexandre; Childs Brothers; Mead, Steven

Betty Lee, Bellstedt, Herman: Colburn, Michael

Birdland, Zawinul, Josef/Arnold: Tennessee Technological University Tuba-Euphonium Ensemble

Birthday Tribute, Sparke, Philip: Mead, Steven

Bist Du Bei Mir, Bach, Johann Sebastian/Werden: United States Army Band Tuba-Euphonium Ensemble and Massed Ensemble; Atlantic Tuba Quartet, The; Melton Tuba-Quartett

Bivalve Suite, Hartley, Walter: Droste, Paul

Black Jack Davie, Anonymous: Top Brass

Black Moon Rising, Corwell, Neal: Corwell, Neal

Black Rain, Aagaard-Nilsen, Torstein: Olsrud, Sverre Stakston

Blaydon Races, The, Langford, Gordon/Grand: Young, Ron

Blaydon Races, The, Langford, Gordon: Clough, John; Bulter, James; Rüedi, Thomas; Pratt, Mike; Mead, Steven; Kilroy, Mike

Blechente, Sobotta, Uli: Sobotta, Uli

Bless This House, Brahe, May: McDonnell, Riki, and Mike Kilroy; Brasch, Harold; Bowman, Brian; Childs, David

Bloos, Unknown: McKinney, Bernard

Blue and Yellow—Beach Behind, Sobotta, Uli: Sobotta, Uli

Blue Bells of Scotland, The, Pryor, Arthur/Pearson: Dickman, Marcus

Blue Bells of Scotland, The, Pryor, Arthur/Sparke: Kipfer, Ueli

Blue Bells of Scotland, The, Pryor, Arthur: Childs, Nicholas; Behrend, Roger; Falcone, Leonard; Droste, Paul; Bowman, Brian; Runty, Thomas; Dodd, Michael

Blue Bossa, Anonymous: Matteson, Rich

Blue Fish Blue, Sobotta, Uli: Sobotta, Uli

Blue Gleam of Arctic Hysteria, Kohlenberg, Oliver: Myllys, Jukka

Blue Lake Fantasies, Gillingham, David: Tropman, Matt; Hokazono, Sho-ichiro; Kipfer, Ueli

Blue Monk, Monk, Thelonius: Steckar Tubapack

Blue Rondo a la Turk, Brubeck, Dave/Esleck/Murphy: Modern Jazz Tuba Project; Tennessee Technological University Tuba-Euphonium Ensemble; Top Brass

Blues, Unknown: McKinney, Bernard

Bluesin' Tubas, Martin, Glenn: Tennessee Technological University Tuba-Euphonium Ensemble

Bocoxe, Powell, Baden/Aquino/Buttery: Alchemy (previously Atlantic Tuba Quartet); Melton Tuba-Quartett; British Tuba Quartet, The

Bonny Mary of Argyle, Greenwood: Steen, Grierson

Boogie Down, Jarreau, Al/Murphy: Tennessee Technological University Tuba-Euphonium Ensemble

Boogie Woogie Tuba Boy, Hinchley, John: Tuba Laté

Booze, Unknown: McKinney, Bernard

Boston Beguine, The, Harnick, Sheldon: Mancuso, Gus

Bottoms Up Rag, Mehlan, Keith: Monarch Tuba-Euphonium Quartet

Bourree I and II from "Suite III for Cello," Bach, Johann Sebastian: Falcone, Leonard

Brass Cuckoo, Hart, Bill/Buttery: Alchemy (previously Atlantic Tuba Quartet)

Brass Tracks, Niehaus, Lennie: Lidsle, Harri

Bravura Variations for Euphonium Quartet, Graham, Peter: Mead, Steven

Bravura Variations on British Folksongs, Graham, Peter: Mead, Steven; Kane, Derick

Bravura Variations, Adams/Louder: Louder, Earle

Brazil, Barroso, Ary/Morris: Tennessee Technological University Tuba-Euphonium Ensemble

Brazil, Barrozo, Ary/Weichselbaumer: Melton Tuba-Quartett

Break Forth Oh Beauteous Light, Vaughan, Rodger, arr.: Tubadours

Breath of Fresh Air, A, Petersen, Jack: Matteson, Rich

Brick House, King/Lapread/Mcclary/Orange/ Richie/Williams/Murphy: Tennessee Technological University Tuba-Euphonium Ensemble

Bride of the Waves, The, Clarke, Herbert L.: Bowman, Brian; Werden, David

Brilliante Fantasy on Rule Britannia, Graham, Peter: Mead, Steven

Brilliante, Graham, Peter/D. McGiboney: Childs, David

Brilliante, Graham, Peter/Veit: Mead, Steven

Brilliante, Graham, Peter: Childs Brothers; Jose, Robert; Mead, Steven; Rüedi, Thomas; Thorton, David; Williams, Glyn

Bring a Torch, Jeanette, Isabella, Bewley, Norlan, arr.: TubaShop Quartet

Broadway Brash, Pegram, Wayne: Symphonia

Broken Melody, Anonymous: Booth, Steven

Brother Aintz, Mancuso, Gus: Mancuso, Gus

Bruckner Etude, Crespo, Enrique: Gerhard Meinl's Tuba Sextet

Budda Eastern Bebop, Wilson, Phil: Matteson, Rich

Bullfrog Rag, Garrett, James Allen: Tennessee Technological University and Alumni Tuba-Euphonium Ensemble

Bumble Bee, Corwell, Neal: Corwell, Neal

But Not for Me, Gershwin, George: O'Hara, Betty

Buttercrunch, Wilson, Phil: Matteson, Rich

By Gaslight, Kassatti, Tadeuz: Mead, Steven

By the Waters of Babylon, Brusick, William: Euphoniums Unlimited

By the Way, Young/Pollack/Lewis/White: Mancuso, Gus

Bydlo from "Pictures at an Exhibition," Moussorgsky, Modeste: Smith, Henry Charles; Mulcahy, Michael

Bye, Bye Blues, Hamm, F./Bennet/Lown/Gray: Matteson, Rich

Ca suffit!, Barbera, Beppe: Colliard, Corrado

Caelidh, Newton, Rodney: Childs, David

Café 1930, Piazzolla, Astor/LaDuke: LaDuke, Lance

Café 1930, Piazzolla, Astor/Mead: Mead, Steven

Call of the Seasons, Catelinet, Philip: McDonnell, Riki, and Mike Kilroy; Mountain, Wilfrid; Mead, Steven, Vanderweele, Aaron

Calon Lan, Ball, Eric; arr.: Childs Brothers

Cantabile for John Fletcher, Howarth, Elgar: Childs Brothers

Cantabile, Paganini, Niccolo/Richards: McDonnell, Riki, and Mike Kilroy; Mead, Steven

Cantique de Noel, Adam, Adolphe/Anonymous: McNally, Robert

Canzona, La Spiritata, Gabrieli, Giovanni/Rauch: British Tuba Quartet, The

Canzone per Sonare No. 4, Gabrieli, Giovanni/Gray: Melton Tuba-Quartett; Dutch Tuba Quartet

Canzonetta amorosa, Op. 202, Vancura, Adolf: Heidler, Manfred

Canzonetta for Euphonium and Band, Forte, Aldo Rafael: Taylor, Barbara

Caoine, Stamford, Charles Villes/R. Childs: Childs, David

Capriccio, Janalek, Loes: Yamamoto, Takashi

Caprice and Variations, Arban, Jean Baptiste: Baglin, Lyndon

Caprice No. 17, Paganini, Niccolo/Werden: Heo, Jae-Young

Caprice Oriental, Jorgensen, Axel: Andresen, Mogens

Caprice, Woodfield, Ray: Gosney, Richard; Moore, David

Carioca, Louman: Louder, Earle

Carioca, Youmans, Vincent/Ito: Miura, Toru

Carnival Cocktail, Sykes, Steven, arr.: McDonnell, Riki, and Mike Kilroy; Mead, Steven

Carnival Duet, Anonymous: Booth, Steven

Carnival of Venice, The, Arban, Jean Baptiste/Brasch/ Clarke/Craig/Straigers: Craig, Mary Ann

Carnival of Venice, The, Arban, Jean Baptiste/ Brasch: Brasch, Harold

Carnival of Venice, The, Arban, Jean Baptiste/ Briccialdi: Pillaert, Stef

Carnival of Venice, The, Arban, Jean Baptiste/ Camerata/Catherall: Childs, Robert

Carnival of Venice, The, Arban, Jean Baptiste/ Catherall: Childs, David

Carnival of Venice, The, Arban, Jean Baptiste/ Catherall: Childs, Robert

Carnival of Venice, The, Arban, Jean Baptiste/ D. Childs: Childs, David

Carnival of Venice, The, Arban, Jean Baptiste/ Farr: Childs Brothers

Carnival of Venice, The, Arban, Jean Baptiste/ G. Kingston: Childs, David

Carnival of Venice, The, Arban, Jean Baptiste/ Hunsberger: Hokazono, Sho-ichiro

Carnival of Venice, The, Arban, Jean Baptiste/ LeClair, David: Monarch Tuba-Euphonium Quartet

Carnival of Venice, The, Arban, Jean Baptiste/ LeClair: Contraband

Carnival of Venice, The, Arban, Jean Baptiste/ Mallet: Mallett, Chris

Carnival of Venice, The, Arban, Jean Baptiste/Manning/Remmington: Griffiths, Morgan

Carnival of Venice, The, Arban, Jean Baptiste/Remington: Clough, John; Groom, Trevor; Kane, Derick; Parry, Glynn; Warrington, Brian; Mead, Steven

Carnival of Venice, The, Clarke, Herbert L./ Brandenburg: Boyd, Frederick

Carnival of Venice, The, Clarke, Herbert L./ Manning/Brasch: Brasch, Harold

Carnival of Venice, The, Clarke, Herbert L.: Bowman, Brian; Werden, David; Wood, Ken; Louder, Earle; Fukuda, Masanori; Euphonium Quartet

*Carnival of Venice, The,*Arban, Jean Baptiste/ Catherall: Gagnaux, Alexandre

*Carnival of Venice, The,*Arban, Jean Baptiste: Baglin, Lyndon; Moore, David; Lehman, Arthur; Mead, Steven

Caro mio ben, Giordani, Giuseppe/Bona: Mead, Steven

Carol of the Bells, Bewley, Norlan, arr.: TubaShop Quartet

Carolina in the Morning, Donaldson, W./Self: University of Miami Tuba Ensemble

Carols for a Merry TubaChristmas, Wilder, Alec: TubaShop Quartet

Carrickfergus, Traditional/Roberts: Rüedi, Thomas; Drewitt, Adrian; Mead, Steven; Baumgartner, Stephane; Muggeridge, Keith

Carrickfergus, Traditional/Stephens: Childs, David

Carrob, Matteson, Rich: Matteson, Rich

Casbah of Tetouan, The, Unknown: Miraphone Tuba Quartet

Cascade, Vizzuti, Paul: Hokazono, Sho-ichiro

Cascades, The, Joplin, Scott/Sabourin: British Tuba Quartet, The

Castaldo March, Unknown: Miraphone Tuba Quartet

Catari, Brown, Norman, arr.: Fawbert, Andrew

Catari, Catari, Cardillo/Stephens: Childs Brothers; McDonnell, Riki, and Mike Kilroy

Cavalier, The, Sutton, Eddie: Baglin, Lyndon; Wharton, Andrew; Moore, David; Hallas, David; Cranson, Colin

Celeste Aida, Verdi, Guiseppe: McDonnell, Riki, and Mike Kilroy

Celestial Suite, Bulla, Stephen: British Tuba Quartet, The

Celtic Dream from "Windows of the World," Graham, Peter: Thorton, David

Ceremonial Sketch, Camphouse, Mark: Tennessee Technological University Tuba-Euphonium Ensemble; United States Army Band Tuba-Euphonium Ensemble and Massed Ensemble

Cha-cha, Bernstein, Leonard/Fettig: Tropman, Matt

Chameleon, Hancock, Herbie/Perry: Tennessee Technological University Tuba-Euphonium Ensemble

Chants russes Op. 29, Lalo, Edouard/Rüedi: Rüedi, Thomas

Characteristic Study No. 1, Arban, Jean Baptiste: Hokazono, Sho-ichiro

Chaser #1, Garrett, James Allen: Tennessee Technological University and Alumni Tuba-Euphonium Ensemble

Cherokee, Schooley, John/Matteson: Modern Jazz Tuba Project

Cherokee, Schooley, John: Rustic Bari-Tuba Ensemble; Melton Tuba-Quartett; Matteson, Rich; Lidsle, Harri

Chevailler D'Honneur, Relton, William: Moore, David; Schmidli, Erich

Childs Play, Golland, John: Childs Brothers

Chim Chim Che-ree, Maeda, Norio: Hokazono, Sho-ichiro

Chimes Blues, Garrett, James Allen, arr.: Tennessee Technological University Tuba-Euphonium Ensemble

Chin Up!, Kresin, Willibald: Contraband

China Gates, Young/Adamson: McKinney, Bernard

Chin-Dance, Stockhausen, Karlheinz: Svoboda, Michael

Chit Chat Polka, Strauss, Johann/Smalley: British Tuba Quartet, The

Chops a la Salsa, Botschinsky, Allan: Van Lier, Bart

Chops!, Martin, Glenn: Tennessee Technological University Tuba-Euphonium Ensemble

Christmas Song, The, Torme, Mel/Bewley: TubaShop Quartet

Christmas Tubas of the British Isles, Traditional/ Buttery: Alchemy (previously Atlantic Tuba Quartet)

Ciribribin, Pestalozza, A.: Hokazono, Sho-ichiro

City Awakens, The, Prokofiev, Sergei/Fettig: Tropman, Matt

City in the Sea, Clarke, Nigel: Childs, Robert; Childs, David

Clair de Lune, Debussy, Claude/Bale: Mead, Steven

Cole Porter Medley, Porter, Cole/Sample: Tennessee Technological University Tuba-Euphonium Ensemble

Colonel Corn, Wilson, Phil: Matteson, Rich

Colonial Express, The, Stamp, Jack: Colonial Tuba Quartet, The

Colonial Suite, The, Traditional/Fritze/ Hildebrandt: Colonial Tuba Quartet, The

Come Dearest, the Daylight Is Gone, Lusher, David, arr.: Tubadours

Come Sunday, Ellington/Paul: Mead, Steven

Come, Sweet Death, Bach, Johann Sebastian/ Sauter: Tennessee Technological University Tuba-Euphonium Ensemble

Comedian's Gallop, Kabalevsky, Dmitri/Berry: Tubadours

Comfort My People, Redhead, Robert: Childs, David

Commitment, Scott/Bulla: Vanderweele, Aaron

Compelled by Love, Blyth: Kane, Derick

Concert Fantasie, Cords, Gustav: Behrend, Roger; Dart, Fred

Concert Gallop, Wilby, Philip: Childs, Robert; Mead, Steven

Concertino, Rex: Heidler, Manfred

Concertino, Wilhelm, Rolf: Mead, Steven

Concertino for Euphonium, Irvine, Scott: Metcalf, Curtis

Concertino for Euphonium, Piano, and Percussion, Ross, John: Colliard, Corrado

Concertino No. 1, Op. 7 in B♭, Klengel, Julius/ Falcone: Mead, Steven; Champions of the Leonard Falcone Festival 1986–2000; Dart, Fred

Concertino No. 1, Op. 7 in B♭, Klengel, Julius/ Odom: Bowman, Brian

Concertino No. 1, Op. 7 in B♭, Mvt. 1, Klengel, Julius: Fukuda, Masanori

Concerto, Magnan, G.: Falcone, Leonard

Concerto, Mozart, Leopold: Pfeifle, Nicolas

Concerto Basso, Ross, Walter: Tennessee Technological University Tuba-Euphonium Ensemble

Concerto Brillante on "Carnival of Venice," Bimboni/ Veit: Mead, Steven

Concerto for Al's Breakfast, Baldwin, David: Craig, Mary Ann

Concerto for Euphonium and Band, Curnow, James: Mead, Steven

Concerto for Euphonium and Band, Mueller, Frederick: Louder, Earle

Concerto for Euphonium and Band, Nelhybel, Vaclav: Behrend, Roger

Concerto for Euphonium and Orchestra 1987, Gaines, David: Vydra, Jiri

Concerto for Euphonium and Wind Ensemble, Wilder, Alec: Swallow, John; Bowman, Brian; Kilpatrick, Barry

Concerto for Euphonium, Glorieux, F.: Ost, Nick

Concerto for Euphonium, Hill, William H.: Royall, Dennis; Marsteller, Loren

Concerto for Euphonium, Wilby, Philip: Rüedi, Thomas; Childs, David; Childs, Robert; Gagnaux, Alexandre; Mead, Steven; Hokazono, Sho-ichiro

Concerto for Trombone and Band, Rimsky-Korsakov, Nikolai/Ivallin: Young, Raymond G.

Concerto for Two Trumpets, Vivaldi, Antonio: Anderson, Eric

Concerto Grosso, Wagner, Joseph: Pascuzzi, Todd

Concerto in B♭, K-191, Mozart, Wolfgang Amadeus: Chevailler, Jean-Pierre

Concerto in F Major, Danzi: Chevailler, Jean-Pierre

Concerto in f Minor, Handel, George Frederic: Chevailler, Jean-Pierre; Smith, Henry Charles; Nelson, Douglas

Concerto No. 1, Brandt: McDonnell, Riki, and Mike Kilroy

Concerto per Flicorno Basso, Ponchielli, Amilcare/ Howey: Olsrud, Sverre Stakston; Heidler, Manfred; Champions of the Leonard Falcone Festival 1986–2000; Mead, Steven; Colburn, Michael

Concerto, Op. 114, Bourgeois, Derek: Hunter, Angie; Mead, Steven

Concert Piece for Euphonium, Smith, Claude T.: Bowman, Brian

Concert Piece, Nux, P.V. de la: Falcone, Leonard; Young, Raymond G.; Fukuda, Masanori

Concert Polka, Wren, Jenny/Davis/Brasch: Brasch, Harold; Burleson, Don

Concert Variations, Bach, Jan: Murchinson, Matthew; Fisher, Mark

Concert Variations, Lusher, Don: Childs, David

Conqueror, The, Steadman-Allen, Ray: Kane, Derick; Childs Brothers

Consequences, Forbes, Michael: Sotto Voce Quartet

Consortium, Cheetham, John: Tennessee Technological University Tuba-Euphonium Ensemble; United States Armed Forces Tuba-Euphonium Ensemble; British Tuba Quartet, The

Contemplation, Glorieux, F.: Ost, Nick

Contrapunctus 9 from "Die Kunst der Fuge," Bach, Johann Sebastian: Sotto Voce Quartet

Contrapuntus I, Bach, Johann Sebastian/Morris: Tennessee Tech Tuba-Euphonium Quintet

Conversation Piece, Gryce, Gigi: McKinney, Bernard

Conzertstück, Op. 7, Mühlfeld, W.: Heidler, Manfred

Cookie's Revenge, Stevens, John: Symphonia

Cookin' at the Continental, Silver, Horace/Perry: Modern Jazz Tuba Project

Cool-Fugue, Bernstein, Leonard/Fettig: Tropman, Matt

Cool Suite, A, Smalley, Peter: British Tuba Quartet, The

Corner Pocket, Green, Freddie/Esleck: Tennessee Technological University Tuba-Euphonium Ensemble

Corners of the World, Hlszky, Adriana: Burba, Malte

Cossack Wedding Dance from "Call of the Cossacks," Graham, Peter: Thorton, David

Cotton Tail, Ellington, Duke: Dickman, Marcus

Country Scene, Richards, Goff: Albiez, Cédric

Courante from "Suite No. 4," Bach, Johann Sebastian: Champions of the Leonard Falcone Festival 1986–2000

Courtship, James, Bob/O'Connor: Tennessee Technological University Tuba-Euphonium Ensemble

Cousins, Clarke, Herbert L./LeClair: Contraband

Covenant, The, Mack, Thomas: Mack, Thomas

Coventry Carol, Vaughan, Rodger, arr.: Tubadours

Credo, Arcadelt, Jacob: Campbell, Larry

Crib Chimp, Haerle, Dan: Matteson, Rich

Cry (If You Want To), Scott, Casey/LaDuke: LaDuke, Lance

Czárdás, Monti, Vittorio/D. Childs: Childs, David

Czárdás, Monti, Vittorio/Kanai: Hokazono, Sho-ichiro

Czárdás, Monti, Vittorio/Seppälä: Myllys, Jukka

Czárdás, Monti, Vittorio/Veit: Mead, Steven

Czárdás, Monti, Vittorio/Wilson: Childs Brothers; Verweij, Hugo

Czárdás, Monti, Vittorio: Anonymous; Booth, Steven; Milhiet, Ivan; Contraband Tuba Quartet

Daahoud, Brown, Clifford/Wilkinson: Dutch Tuba Quartet

Dance No. 1, Wilson, Kenyon: Tennessee Technological University and Alumni Tuba-Euphonium Ensemble

Dance of the Blessed Spirits, Gluck, von C.W./Winter: Tropman, Matt

Dance of the Herdmaiden, Alfén, Hugo/R. Childs: Childs, David

Dance of the Reed Pipes, Tchaikovsky, Piotr/Self: Tubadours

Dance of the Sugar Plum Fairy, Tchaikovsky, Piotr: British Tuba Quartet, The

Dance of the Swans from "Swan Lake," Tchaikovsky, Piotr: Brasch, Harold

Dances, Stevens, John: Rustic Bari-Tuba Ensemble; Dutch Tuba Quartet; Lidsle, Harri; Melton Tuba-Quartett

Dances; Four Tubas, Pullig, Kenneth: Colonial Tuba Quartet, The

Dancing in the Dark, Unknown: McKinney, Bernard

Dandy Noodles, Corwell, Neal: Corwell, Neal

Dan's Blues, Petersen, Jack: Matteson, Rich

Danse Bizarre n 3, Quibel, Robert: Steckar Tubapack

Danse du Diable vert, Cassadó, Gaspar/Rüedi: Rüedi, Thomas

Danse Grecque: Zeibekikos, Wilby, Philip: Gagnaux, Alexandre

Danse Pour Un Kangourou, Steckar, Franck: Steckar Tubapack

Danse Sacrée, Tomasi, Henri: Stewart, Dee; Hokazono, Sho-ichiro

Danza: Martello, Villa-Lobos, Hector/Buttery: Alchemy (previously Atlantic Tuba Quartet)

Das A & O Der Gegenwart, Sobotta, Uli: Sobotta, Uli

Das Butterbrot, Mozart, Wolfgang Amadeus/Doerner: Melton Tuba-Quartett

Das Mirakel, Sobotta, Uli: Sobotta, Uli

Das Tier, Das Gemuse, Sobotta, Uli: Sobotta, Uli

Dead End, McDermot, Ragni, and Rado/Bergmann: Scandinavian Tuba Jazz

Death and Rebirth, Sell, Michael: Burba, Malte

Debutante, The, Clarke, Herbert L.: Booth, Steven; Swallow, John

Deck the Halls, Traditional: Tuba Christmas Ensemble

Deep Harmony, Parker, Handel/Walton: Tuba Laté

Deep inside the Sacred Temple, Bizet, George/Wilkinson: McDonnell, Riki, and Mike Kilroy; Moss, John; Conway, Sean; Childs Brothers

Demain il fera jour, Caratini, Patrice: Steckar Tubapack

Der Khusid geyt Tantsn, Traditional/Verweij: Dutch Tuba Quartet

Desolation, Glorieux, F.: Ost, Nick

Destination, Koskinen, Juha T.: Myllys, Jukka

Detournement Mineur, Goret, Didier: Steckar Elephant Tuba Horde

Devil's Tongue, The, Schmidt, Hugo: Brasch, Harold; Craig, Mary Ann; Colburn, Michael; Lehman, Arthur

Di Provenza il mar, il suol from "la Traviata," Verdi, Giuseppe/Creux: Mead, Steven

Dialogue for Euphonium and Piano, Jones, Roger: Royall, Dennis

Dibbuk, Sobotta, Uli: Sobotta, Uli

Dido's Lament from "Dido and Aeneas," Purcell, Henry: British Tuba Quartet, The

Die Forelle, Schubert, Franz: Contraband Tuba Quartet

Dies Irae from "Requiem," Verdi, Giuseppe/Cole: Symphonia

Distant Images, Corwell, Neal: Corwell, Neal

Distressed Innocence Overture, Purcell, Henry: British Tuba Quartet, The

Diversion for Seven Bass Clef Instruments, Clinard, Fred: Tennessee Technological University and Alumni Tuba-Euphonium Ensemble

Diversions, Stevens, John: Sotto Voce Quartet

Divertimento for Tuba Ensemble, Spears, Jared: Tennessee Technological University and Alumni Tuba-Euphonium Ensemble; Tennessee Technological University Tuba-Euphonium Ensemble

Divertimento No. 70, Haydn, Franz Josef/Droste: Droste, Paul

Divertimento No. 2 in B♭, Mozart, Wolfgang Amadeus: Gerhard Meinl's Tuba Sextet

Don Quichotte, Sobotta, Uli: Sobotta, Uli

Don Quixote, Strauss, Richard: Mulcahy, Michael

Donna Lee, Parker, Charlie: Matteson, Rich

Don't Cry for Me Argentina, Webber, Andrew Lloyd/Woodfield: Merkin, Geoffrey

Don't Look Back, Vick, Harold: Zawadi, Kiane

Don't Shoot the Banjo Player ('Cause We've Done It Already), Botschinsky, Allan: Van Lier, Bart

Double Brass, Woodfield, Ray: Childs Brothers

Down by the Old Mill Stream, Vaughan, Rodger, arr.: Tubadours

Down in the Glen, Gordon, Harry; Conner, Tommie: Hunter, Angie

Doxy, Rollins, Sonny/Dickman: Dickman, Marcus

Dragon's Dance, The, LeClair, David: Contraband Tuba Quartet

Dream, Debussy, Claude: Narita, Yuko

Dream of a Witches Sabbath from "Symphonie Fantastique," Berlioz, Hector/Fiegel: Symphonia

Dream Song, Yoshimatsu, Takashi: Hokazono, Sho-ichiro

Drinking Song, Traditional/Mortimer: Mortimer, Alex

Drink to Me Only with Thine Eyes, Wood: Wood, Ken

Drunken Early Morning Song, Sobotta, Uli: Sobotta, Uli

Dublin's Fair City, Newsome, Roy, arr.: McEnvoy, Graham

Duelin' Banjos, Smith, Arthur/Frey: Frey, Adam

Duet for Tenor Tuba and Bass Tuba, Croft: Garden State Tuba Ensemble

Duet from "Don Pasquale," Donizetti, Gaetano: McDonnell, Riki, and Mike Kilroy

Duet from "Pearlfishers," Bizet, George/Wilkinson: Andrews, Paul; Kilroy, Mike; Childs, David

Duet No. 12 from "21 Distinctive Duets," Jones, Roger: University of Miami Tuba Ensemble

Dulcamarata for Euphonium and Symphonic Band, Koper, Karl-Heinz: Mead, Steven

Duo Concertante, Barnes, James: Bowman, Brian

Duo for Euphonium and Marimba, Dougherty, William: Colliard, Corrado

Duo for Euphoniums, Powell, Tom: Warrington, Brian; Childs Brothers; Wilkinson, Harry

Dynozophorium, Steckar, Marc: Steckar Tubapack

Eagle Thunders, The, Gourlay, James: Dutch Tuba Quartet; Swiss Tuba Quartet

Earth and Moon, Rice, Hugh Collins: Tuba Laté

Easter Hymn, Mascagni: Childs, David

Easy Living, Robbin, L./Rainger: Matteson, Rich

Easy Street, Jones, Alan: Matteson, Rich

Easy Winners, Joplin, Scott/LeClair: Contraband

Easy Winners, Joplin, Scott/Werden: Dutch Tuba Quartet

Edelweiss, Traditional/Fritze: Colonial Tuba Quartet, The

Edelweiss, Traditional/Siebert, Edrich: Garrett, Guy

Ego Sum Abbas from "Carmina Burana," Orff, Carl: Lehman, Arthur

Ein Heldenleben, Strauss, Richard: Mulcahy, Michael

Eine Kleine Nachtmusik, Mozart, Wolfgang Amadeus/Fletcher: Melton Tuba-Quartett

Eine Kleine Nachtmusik, Mozart, Wolfgang Amadeus/Self: Tubadours; Colonial Tuba Quartet, The

Eine kleine Schreckens Musik (A Little Fright Music), Mehlan, Keith: Monarch Tuba-Euphonium Quartet

El Capitan, Sousa, John Philip/Morris: British Tuba Quartet, The; Tuba Laté; Monarch Tuba-Euphonium Quartet

Eleanor Rigby, Lennon, John/McCartney: Top Brass

Elegié in c Minor, Op. 24, Fauré, Gabriel: Frey, Adam

Elégie Op. 30, Vieuxtemps, Henri/Rüedi: Rüedi, Thomas

Elegie, Templeton, Alec: Nelson, Douglas

Elegy and Rondo, Vinter, Gilbert: Groom, Trevor

Elegy, Glorieux, F.: Ost, Nick

Elephant, The, Saint-Saëns, Camille/Minchin: Tuba Laté

Elfentanz, Jenkinson, Ezra: Gagnaux, Alexandre

Elfriede, Swift, George/Catherall: Childs Brothers

Elfriede, Swift, George: Lehman, Arthur

Eli's Coming, Nyro, Laura/Cherry: Tennessee Technological University Tuba-Euphonium Ensemble

Elite Syncopations, Joplin, Scott/Picher: British Tuba Quartet, The; Swiss Tuba Quartet

Emmett's Lullaby, Short, T.V.: Lehman, Arthur

English Country Airs, Traditional/Werden: Tuba Laté

Entertainer, The, Joplin, Scott/Self: United States Army Band Tuba-Euphonium Ensemble and Massed Ensemble; Tennessee Tech Tuba-Euphonium Quintet

Entrance and Polka of the Euphonium Players, Fucik/Carrol/Maldonado: Mead, Steven

Entrevue/Tribal, Unknown: Miraphone Tuba Quartet

Entry of the Gladiators, Fucik, Julius: Miraphone Tuba Quartet

Episodes, Reeman, John: Tuba Laté

Erich!, Melillo, Stephen: Colonial Tuba Quartet, The

Erinnert Sich Der Hund, Sobotta, Uli: Sobotta, Uli

Erinnerung, Schumman, William/Mahlknecht: Mead, Steven

Es ist Eine Rose Entsprungen, Brahams, Johann/Gotoh: Mead, Steven

Estrellita, Ponce, Manuel/Bennett: Mead, Steven

Estrellita, Ponce, Manuel/Lake: Mead, Steven

Estrellita, Ponce, Manuel: Falcone, Leonard; Frey, Adam

Et Le Klaxon Retentit Derechef Comme Un Lézard Hongrois Enrhumé, Godard, Michael/Steckar, Marc: Steckar Tubapack

Etude No. 1, Shelukov, Vyacheslav: Picton, Wendy

Etüde Nr. 2, Belcke, Friedrich August: Heidler, Manfred

Etüde Nr. 5, Belcke, Friedrich August: Heidler, Manfred

Etüde Nr. 7, Belcke, Friedrich August: Heidler, Manfred

Euphonic Moods, Glorieux, F.: Ost, Nick

Euphonic Sounds, Joplin, Scott/Milburne: Mueller, John

Euphonic Sounds, Joplin, Scott/Werden: Atlantic Tuba Quartet, The; British Tuba Quartet, The

Euphonics, O'Hara, Betty: Tennessee Technological University Tuba-Euphonium Ensemble

Euphonism, Sparke, Philip: McDonnell, Riki, and Mike Kilroy

Euphonistic Dance, Frite, Gregory: Craig, Mary Ann

Euphonium Concerto No. 2, Golland, John: Mead, Steven; Kipfer, Ueli

Euphonium Concerto, Cosma, Vladimir/Meredith: Mead, Steven

Euphonium Concerto, Cosma, Vladimir: Mead, Steven; Milhiet, Ivan; Frey, Adam; Gagnaux, Alexandre; Champions of the Leonard Falcone Festival 1986–2000

Euphonium Concerto, Ellerby, Martin: Frey, Adam; Mead, Steven; Meixner, Brian

Euphonium Concerto, Horovitz, Joseph/Rüedi: Rüedi, Thomas

Euphonium Concerto, Horovitz, Joseph: Levi, Eran; Rüedi, Thomas; Childs, Robert; Groom, Trevor; Mead, Steven; Taylor, Robin; Breuninger, Tyrone

Euphonium Concerto, Linkola, Jukka: Myllys, Jukka

Euphonium Concerto, Mvt. 3, Linkola, Jukka: Flaten, Tormod

Euphonium Concerto, No. 1, Op. 64, Golland, John: Mead, Steven; Childs Brothers; Ushigami, Ryuji

Euphonium Concerto, Sparke, Philip: Mead, Steven; Araki, Tamao

Euphonium Fantasia, Bulla, Stephen: Church, David; Gosney, Richard; Griffiths, Morgan

Euphonium Music, Bowen, Brian: Childs Brothers; Taylor, Robin; Mead, Steven

Euphonium Solo from "Manzoni Requiem," Verdi, Giuseppe: Louder, Earle

Euphonium Tuba Quartet, Toda, Akira: Rustic Bari-Tuba Ensemble

Euphoniums Parfait, Ito, Yasuhide: Mead, Steven

Euphoniums Unlimited, Self, James: Euphoniums Unlimited

Euphony, Redhead, Robert: Mead, Steven; Gagnaux, Alexandre; Wise, Peter; O'Brien, Robert; Metcalf, Curtis; Kane, Derick; Griffiths, Morgan; Giles, Mark; Davies, Russell

Euphoria, Bourgeois, Derek: Hokazono, Shoichiro; Ushigami, Ryuji; Mead, Steven; Champions of the Leonard Falcone Festival 1986–2000; Murchinson, Matthew

EuPhunk, Hauser, Joshua: Euphoniums Unlimited

Evening Prayer from "Hansel and Gretel," Humperdinck, Engelbert: McDonnell, Riki, and Mike Kilroy

Everybody Should Know, Catherwood, David: Kane, Derick

Ev'ry Time We Say Goodbye, Porter, Cole: Mancuso, Gus

Ev'ry Time, Martin, Glenn/Blane: Mancuso, Gus

Ev'ryone but Me, Murchinson, Charles/Murchinson: Murchinson, Matthew

Excursion, Tomaro, Mike: Mueller, John

Exhibitions, Uber, David: Euphoniums Unlimited; Royall, Dennis

Exigencies, Ruth, Matthew: Tennessee Technological University Tuba-Euphonium Ensemble

Facilita, Hartmann, John/Mortimer: Griffiths, Morgan; Mead, Steven; Perrins, Barrie

Facilita, Hartmann, John: Lehman, Arthur; Mead, Steven; Haemhouts, Ben

Family Tree, Davis, Michael: Hokazono, Sho-ichiro

Fancy's Knell, Vinter, Gilbert: Groom, Trevor; Baglin, Lyndon

Fanfare for a Friend, Stevens, John: Sotto Voce Quartet

Fanfare for the Millennium, Buttery, Gary: Alchemy (previously Atlantic Tuba Quartet)

Fanfare No. 1, Taylor, Jeffery: Monarch Tuba-Euphonium Quartet; British Tuba Quartet, The

Fantaisie Concertante, Castéréde, Jacques: Mead, Steven; Hokazono, Sho-ichiro; Droste, Paul

Fantaisie Originale, Picchi, Ermano/Craig: Colonial Tuba Quartet, The

Fantaisie Originale, Picchi, Ermano/Mantia/Bale: Rüedi, Thomas; Mead, Steven; Frey, Adam

Fantaisie Originale, Picchi, Ermano/Mantia/Falcone: Falcone, Leonard; Champions of the Leonard Falcone Festival 1986–2000

Fantaisie Originale, Picchi, Ermano/Mantia: Bowman, Brian; Mead, Steven; Behrend, Roger; Falcone, Leonard; Lehman, Arthur; Hunter, Angie; Tropman, Matt; Frey, Adam; Colburn, Michael; Meli, Renato

Fantaisie Originale, Picchi, Ermano/Veit: Mead, Steven

Fantasia Capriccioso, Kemp: Lehman, Arthur

Fantasia di Concerto, Boccalari, Ed/Kent-Akers: Bowman, Brian; Hokazono, Sho-ichiro; Miura, Toru; Yamamoto, Takashi; Mueller, John; Mead, Steven; Olsrud, Sverre Stakston

Fantasia di Concerto, Boccalari, Ed/Meredith: Mead, Steven

Fantasia di foresta, Hirano, Mitsuru: Colliard, Corrado

Fantasia for Euphonium and Brass, Jacob, Gordon/Bryant: Taylor, Robin

Fantasia of Eastern European Village Dances, Buttery, Gary: Alchemy (previously Atlantic Tuba Quartet)

Fantasia, Jacob, Gordon: Mead, Steven; Anonymous; Miura, Toru; Runty, Thomas; Stowe, David; Verweij, Hugo; Bogetvedt, Bjorn; Fisher, Mark; Craig, Mary Ann; Picton, Wendy; Hokazono, Sho-ichiro; Childs, Robert; Flaten, Tormod; Young, Ron

Fantasia, Theme and Variations on Carnival of Venice, Arban, Jean Baptiste/Leidzen: Fisher, Mark

Fantasiestucke Op. 73, Schumann, Robert: Olsrud, Sverre Stakston

Fantastic Fast Fingered Fandango, The, Fraser, Bruce: Childs Brothers

Fantasy Brilliante, Arban, Jean Baptiste: Moore, David; Booth, Steven; Heidler, Manfred; Hokazono, Sho-ichiro

Fantasy for Euphonium and Piano, Hoshina, Hiroshi: Miura, Toru; Mead, Steven

Fantasy for Euphonium, Sparke, Philip: Childs, Robert; Childs Brothers; Bowman, Brian; Craddock, Ian; Crookes, Brian; Meli, Renato; Werden, David; Mead, Steven; Gagnaux, Alexandre; Breuninger, Tyrone

Fantasy on Swiss Airs, Newsome, Roy: Thomas, Shaun

Fantasy Variations, Ito, Yasuhide: Bowman, Brian; Behrend, Roger; Champions of the Leonard Falcone Festival 1986–2000; Frey, Adam; Mead, Steven

Fantasy, Glorieux, F.: Ost, Nick

Fantasy, Hummel, Johann Nepomuk/R. Childs: Childs, Robert

Fantasy, Martino, Ralph: British Tuba Quartet, The; Miraphone Tuba Quartet; Monarch Tuba-Euphonium Quartet

Fantasy, Senshu, Jiro: Araki, Tamao

Farewell, Glorieux, F.: Ost, Nick

Fascinatin' Gershwin, Gershwin, George/Ferguson: British Tuba Quartet, The

Fascinating Euphs., Barry, Darrol: Childs Brothers

Favorite Rag, The, Joplin, Scott/Sabourin: British Tuba Quartet, The

Favorite Things, Rodgers and Hammerstein/Cherry: Tennessee Technological University Tuba-Euphonium Ensemble

Feiertagsmusik, Op. 107b, Krol, Bernhard: Tennessee Technological University and Alumni Tuba-Euphonium Ensemble

Felinesquement, Arcadio, Bernard: Steckar, Marc

Fellscape, Scott, Stuart: Tuba Laté

Festive Overture, Shostakovich, Dimitri/Oliver: Symphonia

Fever Fantasy, Snell, Howard: Mead, Steven

Finale from "Andre Chenier," Giordano/Curnow: Behrend, Roger

Finale of 5th Symphony, Beethoven, Ludwig van/Bale: Mead, Steven

Finale, Bernstein, Leonard/Fettig: Tropman, Matt

Fink Finster, Thingäs, Frode: Scandinavian Tuba Jazz

Fireworks, Frith, John: British Tuba Quartet, The

First Noel, The, Charlton, Frederick, arr.: Tubadours

First Noel, The, Hancock; arr.: Tennessee Technological University Tuba-Euphonium Ensemble

First Noel, The, Traditional: Tuba Christmas Ensemble

Five Octave Stunt, The, Brasch, Harold: Lehman, Arthur

Five Pieces in Folk Style, Op. 102, Schumann, Robert/Droste: Droste, Paul

Flander's Cauldron, Amos, Keith: British Tuba Quartet, The

Flight of the Bumble Bee, The, Rimsky-Korsakov, Nikolai/Bale: Mead, Steven

Flight of the Bumble Bee, The, Rimsky-Korsakov, Nikolai/D. Childs: Childs, David

Flight of the Bumble Bee, The, Rimsky-Korsakov, Nikolai/James/Freeh: Mead, Steven

Flight of the Bumble Bee, The, Rimsky-Korsakov, Nikolai/James: Gagnaux, Alexandre

Flight of the Bumble Bee, The, Rimsky-Korsakov, Nikolai/Newsome: Childs Brothers

Flight of the Bumble Bee, The, Rimsky-Korsakov, Nikolai/Watz: Melton Tuba-Quartett

Flight of the Bumble Bee, The, Rimsky-Korsakov, Nikolai/Woude: Childs Brothers

Flight of the Bumble Bee, The, Rimsky-Korsakov, Nikolai: Frey, Adam; Swiss Tuba Quartet

Flight, Wilby, Philip: Mead, Steven; Flaten, Tormod

Florentiner March, Fucik, Julius/Watz: Melton Tuba-Quartett; Miraphone Tuba Quartet

Flower Duet from "Lakme," Delibes, Léo: McDonnell, Riki, and Mike Kilroy; British Tuba Quartet, The; Frey, Adam

Flower Song from "Carmen," Bizet, George/Harding: Falcone, Leonard; Mead, Steven; Behrend, Roger

Flower Song from "Carmen," Bizet, George: McDonnell, Riki, and Mike Kilroy; Louder, Earle; Childs, Nicholas; Euphonium Section, The

Fly Me to the Moon, Howard, Bart/Hughes: Mead, Steven

Folklike, Baker, David: Top Brass

Force of Destiny Overture, Verdi, Giuseppe: British Tuba Quartet, The

Forêt Vierge, Arcadio, Bernard/Steckar, Marc: Steckar Tubapack

For Richer or Poorer, Pape: Matteson, Rich

For the Kings of Brass, Brusick, William: Tennessee Technological University and Alumni Tuba-Euphonium Ensemble

For Tuba Only, Solal, Martial: Steckar Tubapack

42nd Street, Dubin and Warren/Minard: British Tuba Quartet, The

Four Brothers, Giuffre, Jimmy/Prince: Dickman, Marcus

Four Dialogs for Euphonium and Marimba, Adler, Samuel: Bowman, Brian; Yamamoto, Takashi; Murchinson, Matthew

Four Kuehn Guys, Lew, Gillis: Dutch Tuba Quartet

Four Pieces for Tuba Quartet, Jacob, Gordon: Dutch Tuba Quartet

Four Seasons Suite, The, Isomura, Yukiko: Narita, Yuko

Foursome for Brass, Spurgin, Anthony: Baglin, Lyndon

Four Tuba Blues, Roblee, Richard: Melton Tuba-Quartett

Foxtrot between Friends, Newsome, Roy, arr.: McEnvoy, Graham

Frankie and Johnny, Traditional/Roberts: Mead, Steven

Freedom, Feldman, Hank C.: Symphonia

Freedom, Mingus, Charles/Feldman: Symphonia

Frescos De Bonampak, Osmon, Larry: Tennessee Technological University Tuba-Euphonium Ensemble

Freylekhs fun der Khupe, Traditional/Verweij: Dutch Tuba Quartet

Frippery, Shaw, Lowell: Miraphone Tuba Quartet

From the Shores of the Mighty Pacific, Clarke, Herbert L.: Falcone, Leonard; Mead, Steven; Boyd, Frederick

Fughetta, Unknown: Swiss Tuba Quartet

Fugue from "Fantasia and Fugue in g Minor," Bach, Johann Sebastian/Gray: British Tuba Quartet, The

Fugue in g Minor, Bach, Johann Sebastian/Berry: Tubadours

Fugue in g Minor, Bach, Johann Sebastian/Smalley: Tuba Laté

Fugue in g Minor, Bach, Johann Sebastian: Gerhard Meinl's Tuba Sextet

Fum, Fum, Fum, Bewley, Norlan, arr.: TubaShop Quartet

Furies, The, Corwell, Neal: Corwell, Neal; Symphonia

Gabriel's Oboe, Morricone, Ennio/D. Childs: Childs, David

Gaelforce, Graham, Peter: Robertson, Gail

Gay 50's Medley, Garrett, James Allen: Tennessee Technological University and Alumni Tuba-Euphonium Ensemble

Gentle Annie, Foster, Stephen/Godfrey: Lehamn, Arthur; Colburn, Michael

Georgia on My Mind, Carmichael, Hoagy/LeClair: Contraband

Georgia on My Mind, Carmichael, Hoagy/Matteson: Matteson, Rich; Matteson-Phillips Tubajazz Consort; Modern Jazz Tuba Project

Gershwin Medley, Gershwin, George/Sample/Corazon: Tennessee Technological University Tuba-Euphonium Ensemble; United States Armed Forces Tuba-Euphonium Ensemble

Gesu Bambino, Yon, Pietro: Bowman, Brian

Get Me to the Church on Time, Lemer and Loewe/Belshaw: British Tuba Quartet, The

Gicael Mibbs, Elmer, Andy: Steckar Elephant Tuba Horde

Giocoso from "Euphonium Concerto," Cosma, Vladimir/Fletcher: Tennessee Technological University Tuba-Euphonium Ensemble

Girl with the Flaxen Hair, The, Debussy, Claude/Bale: Mead, Steven

Gladsome Call, The, Pattison: Smith, Christopher

Gloria, Arcadelt, Jacob: Campbell, Larry

Glorious Fountain, Smith, Bernard: Mallett, Chris

Glorious Liberation, Bosanko, Ivor: Mallett, Chris

Glorious Ventures, Graham, Peter: Mead, Steven; Mallett, Chris

Glousteshire Wassail Song, The/Il Est Ne, Harclerode, Albert, arr.: Tubadours

Glowing Spirit, Fujita, Genma: Fukuda, Masanori

Glyder Landscape, The, Smalley, Peter: British Tuba Quartet, The

Go Tell It on the Mountain, Traditional: Tuba Christmas Ensemble

God Rest Ye Merry Gentlemen, Traditional: Tuba Christmas Ensemble

God Rest Ye Merry Gentlemen, Vaughan, Rodger, arr.: Tubadours

Golden Euphoniums, Hudec, Adam: Griffiths, Morgan

Golliwogg's Cakewalk, Debussy, Claude/Bale: Mead, Steven

Golliwogg's Cakewalk, Debussy, Claude: Dutch Tuba Quartet

Gone with the Wind, Wrubel, Allie; Magidson, Herb: Dickman, Marcus

Good Christian Men Rejoice, Bewley, Norlan, arr.: TubaShop Quartet

Good King Wenceslas, Harclerode, Albert, arr.: Tubadours

Good King Wenceslas, Traditional: Tuba Christmas Ensemble

Good Morning My Head, Sobotta, Uli: Sobotta, Uli

Goody Goody, Mercer/Malenck: Mancuso, Gus

Gospel Crossover, Gordon, William: Church, David

Gospel John, Ferguson, Maynard; arr.: Ferguson, Maynard

Gospel Tune, Agrell, Jeffrey: Miraphone Tuba Quartet

Gotlandsk Sommarnatt, Cay-Lennart: Cay-Lennart

Gowbarrow Gavotte, Seivewright, Andrew: Tuba Laté

Graf Zeppelin March, Unknown: Miraphone Tuba Quartet

Grand Russian Fantasia, Levy, Jules/Bale: Mead, Steven

Grand Slam, Niehaus, Lennie: British Tuba Quartet, The

Grand Study No. 13, Howarth, Elgar; arr.: Childs Brothers

Grandfather's Clock, Doughty, George: Baglin, Lyndon; Clough, John; Cunliffe, Stuart; Entwistle, Heather; Haemhouts, Ben; Mead, Steven; Morgan, Gareth; Willis, Simon; Woollam, David; Wood, Ken; Childs, David

Great Adventure, The, Bearcroft, Norman: Vanderweele, Aaron

Greensleeves, Traditional/Bewley: TubaShop Quartet

Greensleeves, Traditional/Buttery: Atlantic Tuba Quartet, The; Miraphone Tuba Quartet; British Tuba Quartet, The; Rustic Bari-Tuba Ensemble

Greensleeves, Traditional/Ito: Miura, Toru

Greensleeves, Traditional: Melton Tuba-Quartett; Swiss Tuba Quartet

Gregory Is Here, Silver, Horace/Matteson: Matteson-Phillips Tubajazz Consort; Modern Jazz Tuba Project

Groovey, Petersen, Jack: Matteson, Rich

Ground, Escaich, Thierry: Milhiet, Ivan

Growing Up Together, LeClair, David: Contraband Tuba Quartet

Guess Who I Saw Today?, Grand/Boyd: Mancuso, Gus

Gypsy Airs, Sarasate, Pablo de/Buitenhuis: Gagnaux, Alexandre

Gypsy Airs, Sarasate, Pablo de/Rüedi: Rüedi, Thomas

Gypsy Airs, Sarasate, Pablo de/Snell: Mead, Steven

Gypsy Dance from "Carmen," Bizet, George/Bale: Mead, Steven

"Hades" for Two Euphoniums and Two Tubas, Iannaccone, Anthony: University of Michigan Tuba and Euphonium Ensemble

Hail Ancient Walls, Gounod, Charles/Snell: Mead, Steven; McDonnell, Riki, and Mike Kilroy

Hail to the Lord's Annointed, Vaughan, Rodger, arr.: Tubadours

Hailstorm, Rimmer, William: Bowman, Brian; Lehamn, Arthur; Meixner, Brian; Brasch, Harold; Morgan, Gareth

Hallelijah Drive, Unknown: Swiss Tuba Quartet

Hamabe no uta, Narita, Tamezo: Hokazono, Sho-ichiro

Hands Across the Sea, Sousa, John Philip/Werden: Lidsle, Harri

Happy Soul, The, Wilkinson, Robert: Dutch Tuba Quartet

Harbour Light, Bearcroft, Norman: Kane, Derick; Vanderweele, Aaron

Harlem Pipes, Baker, David: Top Brass

Harlem Rag, Turpin, Tom: Albertasaurus Tuba Quartet

Harmonious Blacksmith, The, Handel, George Frederic/Hume/Wilkinson: Groom, Trevor

Harmonious Blacksmith, The, Handel, George Frederic/Hume: Groom, Trevor; Lehamn, Arthur; Perrins, Barrie; Parry, Glynn

Harmonious Blacksmith, The, Handel, George Frederic: Sotto Voce Quartet

Hassels, Matteson, Rich: Matteson, Rich

Hatful of Dandruff, A, Guaraldi, Vince: Mancuso, Gus

Hatschichacha, Sobotta, Uli: Sobotta, Uli

Hauntings, Welcher, Dan: Symphonia

Havah Nagilah, Traditional: British Tuba Quartet, The

Have Yourself a Merry Little Christmas, Martin, Blaine/Bewley: TubaShop Quartet

Hawk Talks, The, Bellson, Louie: Matteson, Rich

Hear My Prayer, Mendelssohn, Felix: Childs, David

Heart in Heart, Bosanko, Ivor: Mead, Steven; Hokazono, Sho-ichiro

Heart of a Wolf, Corwell, Neal: Corwell, Neal

Heaven Can Wait, Mancini, Henry: Nash, Dick

Heaven, Plett, Danny: Schmidli, Erich

Heavy Metal, Lamb, Marvin: Tennessee Technological University Tuba-Euphonium Ensemble

Heidentüblein, LeClair, David: Contraband Tuba Quartet

Heights of Halifax, The, McQueen, Ian: Tuba Laté

Herbmaiden's Dance, Alen, Hugo/Olsrud: Mead, Steven

Here's That Rainy Day, Heusen, Van/Barton: British Tuba Quartet, The

Hey Jude, Lennon, John/Luis: Miraphone Tuba Quartet

Hey Man!, Petersen, Jack/Perry: Modern Jazz Tuba Project

Hey Man!, Petersen, Jack: Matteson, Rich

Hi-Fi, Weston, Randy: McKinney, Bernard

Hijazker Longa, Anonymous/Buttery: Tropman, Matt

Hills and Valleys, Wilson, Phil: Matteson, Rich

Hine e Hine, Traditional/Maunder: McDonnell, Riki, and Mike Kilroy

Holy City, The, Adams, Stephen: Bowman, Brian

Holy Well, The, Graham, Peter: Griffiths, Morgan

Home on the Range, Leidzén, Erik: Mead, Steven; Groom, Trevor; Young, Ron; McNally, Robert; Evans, Jonathon

Hora Staccato, Dinicu-Heifitz/Gates: Vanderweele, Aaron

Hora Staccato, Dinicu-Heifitz: Mead, Steven

Horn Concerto No. 4 in E♭ Major, Mozart, Wolfgang Amadeus/Blaauw: Heo, Jae-Young

Hornsongs, Brahms, Johannes/Reynolds: Fisher, Mark

How Deep Is the Ocean, Berlin, Irving/Windfeld: Scandinavian Tuba Jazz

How Do You Like Your Eggs in the Morning?, Cahn/Brodszky: Mancuso, Gus

How Great Thou Art, Traditional: Hunter, Angie

How Soon, Mancini, Henry/Maunder: McDonnell, Riki, and Mike Kilroy

Howdy!, Pegram, Wayne: Tennessee Technological University Tuba-Euphonium Ensemble; United States Armed Forces Tuba-Euphonium Ensemble

Hugo Hugo, McPherson, John: Albertasaurus Tuba Quartet

Humoreske, Tchaikovsky, Piotr/Bale: Mead, Steven

Hungarian Hallucination, Corwell, Neal: Corwell, Neal

Hungarian March, Berlioz, Hector/Werden: Dutch Tuba Quartet

Hungarian Melodies, Bach, Vincent/Lutz: Tims, Elva Kay

Hungarian Melodies, Bach, Vincent: Brasch, Harold

Hungarian Rhapsody No. 2, Liszt, Franz/Seitz: Melton Tuba-Quartett

Hurry Up, Steckar, Franck: Steckar Tubapack

Hvezdonicka, Pecha, Antonin: Miesenberger, Anton

Hymn from "Adiemus," Jenkins: Childs, David

I Dreamt I Dwelt in Marble Halls, Balfe/Kerwin: McDonnell, Riki, and Mike Kilroy

I Got No Bread, Matteson, Rich: Matteson, Rich

I Have a Love, Bernstein, Leonard/Fettig: Tropman, Matt

I Have No Claim on Grace, Krinjak, Karen/Bosanko: Mallett, Chris

I Love to Tell the Story, Fischer, William/Kippax: Parton, Jack

I Love You Truly, Jacobs Bond, Carrie: Dempster, Stuart

I Love You, Porter, Cole: Matteson, Rich

I sode blege Kinder, Kjerulf, Halfdan: Olsrud, Sverre Stakston

I Thought About You, Huesen van, J.: Matteson, Rich

I Walked Today Where Jesus Walked, O'Hara, Geoffrey: Bowman, Brian

I Wish You Love, Trenet, Paul: Williams, Glyn
I Wonder What's Keeping My True Love Tonight, Traditional/LaDuke: LaDuke, Lance
I-95, Esleck, David: Modern Jazz Tuba Project
Ich bin der welt abbanden gekommen, Mahler, Gustav: Murchinson, Matthew
Ich grolle nicht, Schumann, Robert/Bowman: Behrend, Roger
If Dreams Come True, Sampson, Edgar: O'Hara, Betty
If I Love You from "Carousel," Rodgers, Thomas: Wood, Ken
If with All Your Heart, Mendelssohn, Felix: Smith, Henry Charles; Childs, David; Bowman, Brian; Craig, Mary Ann
Il Ritorno, Diero/Ferguson: British Tuba Quartet, The
I'll Not Turn Back, Larson, John/Bosanko: Mallett, Chris, Childs Brothers
I'll Walk with God, Webster/Brodsky: Childs, David
Illusion, Konagaya, Soichi: Tennessee Technological University Tuba-Euphonium Ensemble
Illustrations for Tubas, Kerwin, Simon: Tuba Laté
I'm Glad There Is You, Dorsey, Tommy/Madeira: Mancuso, Gus
I'm in Love with Miss Logan, Graham: Mancuso, Gus
. . . im Stillen berauschter Regen, Turek, Thomas: Heidler, Manfred
Im Tiefsten Walde, Schmid/Bacon: Mead, Steven
I'm Waiting Alone, Isomura, Yukiko: Narita, Yuko
Impressario, The, Strauss, Johann: Swiss Tuba Quartet
Impromptu in 2 Keys, Gershwin, George: Contraband Tuba Quartet
In a Digital Mood, Steckar, Franck: Steckar Tubapack
In a Mellow Tune, Ellington, Duke: Matteson, Rich; Tennessee Technological University Alumni Tuba-Euphonium Ensemble
In Darkness Dreaming, Cummings, Barton: Colonial Tuba Quartet, The
In Dixieland, Rimmer, William/Kerwin: McDonnell, Riki, and Mike Kilroy
In Memoriam, Premru: British Tuba Quartet, The
"In Memoriam" Sept. 11, 2001, MacMillan, Duncan: Euphoniums Unlimited
In the Cathedral, Corwell, Neal: Euphoniums Unlimited
Infant Holy, Kingsbury, Craig/Harclerode: Tubadours
Initiation, Brustad, Karsten: Taylor, Robin
Ins Blaue Licht, Sobotta, Uli: Sobotta, Uli
Interferenze per euphonium solo, Manfrin, Paolo: Colliard, Corrado
Interlude No. 4, Botschinsky, Allan: Van Lier, Bart
Intermezzo, Bitsch, Marcel: Verweij, Hugo
Introduction and Allegro, Fernie, Alan: Griffiths, Morgan

Introduction and Dance, Barat, J. Ed.: Young, Raymond G.; Fukuda, Masanori; Miura, Toru
Introduction to Act Three from "Lohengrin," Wagner, Richard: McDonnell, Riki, and Mike Kilroy
Introduction, Theme and Variations, Bergh, Sverre: Bogetvedt, Bjorn
Introduction, Theme and Variations, Rossini, Gioacchino/Brennan: Mead, Steven; Baglin, Lyndon
Introduction, Theme and Variations, Rossini, Gioacchino/Newsome: Kilroy, Mike
Introspect, Martino, Ralph: Behrend, Roger; Meixner, Brian
Invincible, Smith: Moore, David
Ira's Tune, Matteson, Rich: Matteson, Rich
It Came upon a Midnight Clear, Harclerode, Albert, arr.: Tubadours
It Came upon a Midnight Clear, Traditional: Tuba Christmas Ensemble
It Don't Mean a Thing, Ellington, Duke: O'Hara, Betty
It's a Pity to Say Goodnight, Ferguson, Maynard; arr.: Ferguson, Maynard
It's All Right with Me, Porter, Cole: Tennessee Technological University Alumni Tuba-Euphonium Ensemble
It's Easy to Remember, Rodgers, Richard; Hart, Lorenz: O'Hara, Betty
It's Good to Know, Sobotta, Uli: Sobotta, Uli
It's Wonderful, Smith, H.: O'Hara, Betty
I've Made Plans for the Summer, Sousa, John Philip: Colburn, Michael
Jason and the Golden Fleece, Raum, Elizabeth: Symphonia
Jean Marie at the Picture Show, Baker, David: Top Brass
Jean-Elizabeth, Richards, Goff: McDonnell, Riki, and Mike Kilroy
Jeannie with the Light Brown Hair, Foster, Stephen/Harvey: Mead, Steven
Jeannie with the Light Brown Hair, Foster, Stephen/Howarth: Bray, Mark; Davis, George; Lloyd, G.; Moore, David; Morton, Hugh; McDonnell, Riki, and Mike Kilroy; Brighton, Charley; Bouise, Mark
Jeg Elsker Dig, Grieg, Edward/Farr: Nerland, Eldfrid
Jenny Jones, Rimmer, William: Baglin, Lyndon; Cresswell, John; Lawrie, Lindsay; Moore, David; Walton, Paul; Williams, Glyn; Picton, Wendy
Jesse's Jump, Kerbs, Jesse: Symphonia
Jesu, Joy of Man's Desiring, Bach, Johann Sebastian/Werden: British Tuba Quartet, The
Jesus, I Come to Thee, Bearcroft, Norman: Kane, Derick; Vanderweele, Aaron
Jet Flight, Sun Ra: McKinney, Bernard
Jingle Bell Waltz, Vaughan, Rodger: Tubadours
Jinny Jinkins, Anonymous: Top Brass
Jitterbug Waltz, Waller, Fats: Dickman, Marcus
John, Come Kiss Me Now, Byrd, William/Winter: Atlantic Tuba Quartet, The; British Tuba Quartet, The

Jolly Farmer, The Schumann/Bell: Lehman, Arthur

Jordu, Jordon, Duke: Dickman, Marcus

Joshua Fought the Battle of Jeriko, Cay-Lennart: Cay-Lennart

Journey into Freedom, Himes, William: Anonymous

Journey into Peace, Himes, William: Kane, Derick; Waterworth, Ken; Metcalf, Curtis

Journey to Cornwell, Saegusa, Shigeaki: Hokazono, Sho-ichiro

Joyous Service, Norbury: Vanderweele, Aaron

Joy to the World, Traditional: Tuba Christmas Ensemble

Joy Untold, A, Camsey, Terry: Kane, Derick; Mack, Thomas; Mallett, Chris, Vanderweele, Aaron

Juliet's Funeral and Death, Prokofiev, Sergei/Fettig: Tropman, Matt

Jumbo's Holiday, Kalke, Ernst-Thilo: Melton Tuba-Quartett

Jump, Jive an' Wail, Prima, L./Vinson: Mead, Steven

Just a Closer Walk with Thee, Garrett, James Allen, arr.: Tennessee Technological University Tuba-Euphonium Ensemble

Just a Closer Walk with Thee, Traditional/Forbes: Tuba Laté

Just Squeeze Me, Ellington, Duke/Gaines: McKinney, Bernard

Just the Way You Are, Joel, Billy/Matteson: Matteson, Rich

Keltic Lament, A, Foulds, John: Cutts, Marcus

Kierkegaard, Kupferman, Meyer: Sotto Voce Quartet; British Tuba Quartet, The

Kilgore Trout, Mays, Lyle: Matteson, Rich

King Carneval, Kryl, Bohumir: Lehman, Arthur

King's Hunt, The, Bull, John/Howard: British Tuba Quartet, The

Kino Concertino, Kassatti, T.: Ushigami, Ryuji

Kokomo, Petersen, Jack: Matteson, Rich

Kol Nidrei, Bruch/Gay: Mead, Steven

Komm Süsser Tod from "Die geistlichen Leider und Arien," BWV 478, Bach, Johann Sebastian/Sauter: Garden State Tuba Ensemble; Tuba Christmas Ensemble

Konservatorium, Steckar, Marc; Arcadio, Bernard: Steckar, Marc

Konzertstück für Tenorhorn, Dräxelmeier, Xaver: Heidler, Manfred

Kool Kube, Perry, Richard: Modern Jazz Tuba Project

Korn Blues, Hermann, Heinz: Scandinavian Tuba Jazz

Koslowski, Sobotta, Uli: Sobotta, Uli

Kubismus 502, Botschinsky, Allan: Van Lier, Bart

La Belle Americane, Hartmann, John: Childs, Nicholas; Childs, David; Fawbert, Andrew; Moore, David; Baglin, Lyndon

La Campanella from "Violin Concerto No. 2," Paganini, Niccolo/Wuthrich: Kipfer, Ueli

La Coquette, Bellstedt, Herman: Brasch, Harold

La Danza, Rossini, Gioacchino/Ito: Miura, Toru

La Danza, Rossini, Gioacchino/Smalley: British Tuba Quartet, The; Miraphone Tuba Quartet

La Donna e Mobile, Verdi, Guiseppe: McDonnell, Riki, and Mike Kilroy

Lady in Blue, The, Botschinsky, Allan: Van Lier, Bart

La Fiesta, Correa, Chick/Arnold: Tennessee Technological University Tuba-Euphonium Ensemble

La Fille aux Cheveux de lin, Debussy, Claude: Rustic Bari-Tuba Ensemble

La Gazza Ladra, Rossini, Gioacchino: Swiss Tuba Quartet

La Manodoinata, Bellstedt, Herman: Brasch, Harold; Lehamn, Arthur; Lake Highlands Euphonium Section

La Miserere from "Il Travatore," Verdi, Guiseppe: McDonnell, Riki, and Mike Kilroy

La Morte dell' Oom, Self, James: Symphonia

Lampi, Lintinen, Kirmo: Euphoniums Unlimited

Land Beyond the Blue, Jakeway, Albert H.: Mack, Thomas

Largo, Handel, George Frederic: Baglin, Lyndon

Largo Al Factotum, Rossini, Gioacchino/Langford: Clough, John; Craddock, Ian; Dart, Fred; Griffiths, Morgan

Largo Al Factotum, Rossini, Gioacchino: Childs Brothers; Pfeifle, Nicolas; McDonnell, Riki, and Mike Kilroy; Young, Raymond G.

Largo from "Sonata, Op. 4, No. 2," Benedetto, Marcello: Royall, Dennis

Larghetto for Euphonium, Farr, Craig: Flaten, Tormod

Lark in the Clear Air, The, Traditional/Catherwood/Veit: Mead, Steven

Lark in the Clear Air, The, Traditional/Catherwood: Mead, Steven

Lark in the Clear Air, The, Traditional: Postma, Simon

La Sonnambula, Bellini, Vincenzo/Adolphe: Cranson, Colin

Lassus Trombone, Corwell, Neal, arr.: Corwell, Neal

Last Rose of Summer, The, Traditional/Denton: Frey, Adam

Last Rose of Summer, The, Traditional/Flotow von: Champions of the Leonard Falcone Festival 1986–2000

Last Rose of Summer, The, Traditional: Hokazono, Sho-ichiro

La Tregenda from "Le villi," Puccini, Giacomo/Williams: Symphonia

La Virgin De La Macarena, Mendez, Rafel/Cole: Symphonia

Lazy Elephant Blues, Luis, Ingo: Melton Tuba-Quartett

Le Cygne from "The Carnival of the Animals," Saint-Saëns, Camille/Mott: Clough, John; Baglin, Lyndon

Legento, Kenswich, Marcel: Hokazono, Sho-ichiro

Le Jour ou les Tubas, Michel, Marc: Steckar Elephant Tuba Horde

Leleo, Arcadio, Bernard: Steckar, Marc

Lento from "Cello Concerto," Elgar, Edward/Bourgeois: Mead, Steven

Lento from "Euphonium Concerto," Horovitz, Joseph: Mead, Steven; Anonymous

Le Roi d'Ys, Wright, Frank, arr.: Childs, David

Les Baricades Misterieuses, Couperin, François: Gerhard Meinl's Tuba Sextet

Les Chemins L'Amour, Poulenc, F.: Hokazono, Sho-ichiro

Le Secret, Gautier, L./Werden: Alchemy (previously Atlantic Tuba Quartet)

Let Me Try Again, Caravelli/Fernie: Rüedi, Thomas

L'Huere exquise, Hahn, Reynaldo: Rüedi, Thomas

Liberation of Sisyphus, The, Stevens, John: Bazsinka Tuba Octet; European Tuba Octet

Libertango, Piazzola, Astor: Milhiet, Ivan

Liebesfreud, Kreisler, Fritz: Mead, Steven

Liebeslied, Kreisler, Fritz/Woodcock: Tuba Laté

Life's a Take, Mitchell, Red: Matteson, Rich

Light Metal-I Talatasco, Proctor, S.: Tuba Laté

Lightfinger, Mancini, Henry: Nash, Dick

Like What Is This?, Unknown: McKinney, Bernard

Limehouse Blues, Braham, P./Furber: Matteson, Rich

Little Lullabye, Luis, Ingo: Melton Tuba-Quartett

Little Madrigal for Big Horns, Hastings, Ross: University of Miami Tuba Ensemble

Little Monster Music, A, Raum, Elizabeth: Euphoniums Unlimited

Little Night Music, A, Hampton, Slide: McKinney, Bernard

Little Ole Softy, Matteson, Rich: Matteson-Phillips Tubajazz Consort

Little Prayer, A, Glennie, Evelyn/R. Childs: Childs, David; Kane, Derick

Locomotion, Bearcroft, Norman: Kane, Derick

Locus Iste, Bruckner/Sabourin: Dutch Tuba Quartet

Lokk from the Green Island, Aagaad-Nielsen, Torstein: Murchinson, Matthew

Londonderry Air, Traditional/Ades: Louder, Earle

Londonderry Air, Traditional/Denton: Frey, Adam

Londonderry Air, Traditional/Garrett, James Allen: Tennessee Technological University and Alumni Tuba-Euphonium Ensemble; United States Armed Forces Tuba-Euphonium Ensemble; Bowman, Brian; Meixner, Brian

Londonderry Air, Traditional/J. Iveson: Childs, David

Londonderry Air, Traditional/Mehlan: Monarch Tuba-Euphonium Quartet

Londonderry Air, Traditional: Melton Tuba-Quartett; Postma, Simon

Long, Long Ago, Traditional/Boddington: Baglin, Lyndon; Sullivan, Bert

Looking Outward, Sun Ra: McKinney, Bernard

Lord God of Abraham, Mendelssohn, Felix: Smith, Henry Charles

Lord's Prayer, The, Malotte, Albert: Bowman, Brian; Sotto Voce Quartet

Lost Chord, The, Sullivan: Childs, David

Love Changes Everything, Webber, Andrew Lloyd: Schmidli, Erich

Love Is a Simple Thing, Carroll/Siegal: Mancuso, Gus

Love Is Forever, Richards, Goff: McDonnell, Riki, and Mike Kilroy

Love Is Never Out of Season, Brown/Fain: Mancuso, Gus

Love Lifted Me, Steadman-Allen, Ray: Clark, Trevor; Hammarberg, Ake

Love Song, Truax, Bert: Mueller, John

Love Waltz, Botschinsky, Allan: Van Lier, Bart

Love's Enchantment, Pryor, Arthur: Brasch, Harold

Lucia Di Lammermoor, Donizetti, Gaetano: Louder, Earle

Lucky Southern, Jarrett, Keith: Matteson-Phillips Tubajazz Consort

Lucy Long, Godfrey/Herbert: Mather, Harry; Singleton, Stephen; Lehamn, Arthur; Baglin, Lyndon

Lullaby of Birdland, Shearing, George/Perry: Tennessee Technological University Tuba-Euphonium Ensemble

Lullaby of Birdland, Shearing, George: Albertasaurus Tuba Quartet

Lullaby, Brahms, Johannes/Ruffles: Lowry, Benny

Lullaby, Doe, Phillip: Mackie, Kevin

Lute Dances, Anonymous/Baker: British Tuba Quartet, The

Lyric Poem for Five Tubas, Frank, Marcel G.: University of Miami Tuba Ensemble; United States Army Band Tuba-Euphonium Ensemble and Massed Ensemble

Lyric Suite, White, Donald H.: Stewart, Dee; Champions of the Leonard Falcone Festival 1986–2000

Lyric Variations, Steadman-Allen, Ray: Kane, Derick

Mace, Sparke, Philip: Gagnaux, Alexandre

Macushla, MacMurrough, D./Hume: Booth, Steven; Griffiths, Morgan

Magic Morning, Haerle, Dan: Matteson, Rich

Malagueña, Lecuona, Ernesto/Morris: Tennessee Technological University Tuba-Euphonium Ensemble

Male Voice for Brass, Parfrey, Raymond: Tuba Laté

Mambo, Bernstein, Leonard/Fettig: Tropman, Matt

Mancushla, Mcmurrough, D.: Schmidli, Erich

Manhattan Suite, Stevens, John: University of Michigan Tuba and Euphonium Ensemble; Miraphone Tuba Quartet; Dutch Tuba Quartet; Sotto Voce Quartet

Manteca, Gillespie, Dizzy: Tennessee Technological University Alumni Tuba-Euphonium Ensemble

March from "1941," Williams, John/Dawson: Dutch Tuba Quartet

March from "1941," Williams, John/Fiegel: Symphonia

March of the Hare, The, Crump, Peter: Tuba Laté

March of the Kings/O Come Little Children, Harclerode, Albert, arr.: Tubadours

March of the Marionettes, Gounod, Charles/Berry: Tubadours

March of the Toy Soldiers, Herbert, Victor/Vaughan: Tubadours

March to the Scaffold, Berlioz, Hector: British Tuba Quartet, The

Marche Militaire Francaise, Saint-Saëns, Camille/Cohen: United States Army Band Tuba-Euphonium Ensemble and Massed Ensemble

March-Frot, Kerwin, Simon: Tuba Laté

March-Overture, Charlton, Philip: Tubadours

Maria alm, Bolognesi, Jacques: Steckar Tubapack

Maria, Bernstein, Leonard/Fettig: Tropman, Matt

Marriage of Figaro, Mozart, Wolfgang Amadeus: McDonnell, Riki, and Mike Kilroy

Mars from "The Planets," Holst, Gustav/Butler: Symphonia

Masks, Prokofiev, Sergei/Fettig: Tropman, Matt

Matrix for Euphonium and Synthesizer, Nagano, Mitsuhiro: Miura, Toru; Taylor, Robin

Mattinata, Leoncavallo, Ruggero/Langford: Griffiths, Morgan

May Morning Dew/Strawaway Child/Conlon's Jig, Traditional/LaDuke: LaDuke, Lance

Mazurka for Unaccompanied Euphonium, Falcone, Nicholas: Behrend, Roger

Me and My Shadow, Dreyer/Jolson/Rydland: Flaten, Tormond

Meditation and Celebration, Dougherty, William: Droste, Paul

Meditation from "Thaïs," Massenet, Jules/Flaten: Flaten, Tormod

Meditation from "Thaïs," Massenet, Jules: Withington, Len; Pfeifle, Nicolas

Meditation, Bakaleinikov, Vladimir: Dart, Fred

Meditation, Bridge, Frank: Rüedi, Thomas

Meditation, Corwell, Neal: Corwell, Neal

Medley from "On the Town," Bernstein, Leonard: O'Hara, Betty

Medley from "Stockholm Sweetnin'" and "You Leave Me Breathless," Jones, Quincy: O'Hara, Betty

Megalo Fanfare, Steckar, Marc: Steckar, Marc

Meiso, Golland, John: Willems, John

Melody for Bu, Vick, Harold: Zawadi, Kiane

Melody Shop, The, King, Karl L./Werden: United States Armed Forces Tuba-Euphonium Ensemble; Miraphone Tuba Quartet

Meltdown, Sass, Jon: Gerhard Meinl's Tuba Sextet

Melton Marsch, Watz, Franz: Melton Tuba-Quartett; Gerhard Meinl's Tuba Sextet

Memoirs of the American Civil War, Vinson, Danny: Alchemy (previously Atlantic Tuba Quartet)

Memory, Ares, Rob: Postma, Simon

Menuet, Bizet, George/Norbury: Kane, Derick

Mephisto Masque, Dede, Edmond: Schwarz, Gerard

Mercutio-Fight, Prokofiev, Sergei/Fettig: Tropman, Matt

Merry Black Widow, The, Prinz: Mead, Steven

Merry Christmas to All of the World, Isomura, Yukiko: Narita, Yuko

Merry Wives of Windsor Overture, Nicolai, Otto: British Tuba Quartet, The

Mes Sana in Corpore Sano, Unknown: Miraphone Tuba Quartet

Metal Love, Sobotta, Uli: Sobotta, Uli

Metamorphosis, Rutti, Carl: Childs, David

Midnight Euphonium, Richards, Goff/Mead: Mead, Steven

Midnight Euphonium, Richards, Goff: McDonnell, Riki, and Mike Kilroy; Squibb, Christian; Mead, Steven

Mikki's Blues, Matteson, Rich: Matteson, Rich

Militärmarsch, Schubert, Franz Peter/LeClair: Contraband

Miniature Jazz Suite, Garrett, James Allen: Tennessee Technological University Tuba-Euphonium Ensemble; Melton Tuba-Quartett

Miniatures for Four Valve Instruments, Hartley, Walter: British Tuba Quartet, The; Atlantic Tuba Quartet, The

Minute Waltz, Chopin, Frédéric/Mead: British Tuba Quartet, The

Minute Waltz, Chopin, Frédéric: Albertasaurus Tuba Quartet

Mirror Lake Suite, Montgomery, Ed: Droste, Paul

Mission Impossible, Schifrin, Lalo/Smalley: Tuba Laté

Misty, Garner, Errol/Fernie: Mead, Steven

Mit Hjerte og min Lyre, Op. 16, No. 2, Kjerulf, Halfdan: Olsrud, Sverre Stakston

Molloy, Cugny, Laurent: Steckar Elephant Tuba Horde

Mon Coeur Se Recommende a Vous, Di Lasso/Robinson: British Tuba Quartet, The

Monotonous, Carroll/Siegal: Mancuso, Gus

Montage, Op. 84, Uber, David: Nelson, Douglas

Montagues and Capulets, The, Prokofiev, Sergei/Fettig: Tropman, Matt

Montagues and Capulets, The, Prokofiev, Sergei: British Tuba Quartet, The

Mood Indigo, Ellington, Duke/Vaughan: Tubadours

Mood Indigo, Ellington, Duke: O'Hara, Betty

Moondance, Morrison, Van/Kile: Tennessee Technological University Tuba-Euphonium Ensemble

Moondance, Stevens, John: Dutch Tuba Quartet; Melton Tuba-Quartett; Sotto Voce Quartet

Morceau de Concert, Op. 94, Saint-Saëns, Camille/Nelson: Nelson, Douglas; Louder, Earle

Morceau de Concours, Barat, J. Ed.: Behrend, Roger

Morceau Symphonique, Guilmant, Alexander: Dart, Fred; Falcone, Leonard; Louder, Earle; Werden, David

More Than You Know, Youmans, Vincent: O'Hara, Betty

Moser Comeos, Forte, Aldo Rafael: Euphoniums Unlimited

Moses-Fantasie, Paganini, Niccolo: Pfeifle, Nicolas

Moten Swing, Moten, Bennie: Tennessee Technological University Alumni Tuba-Euphonium Ensemble

Moto Perpetuo, Paganini, Niccolo/Chabloz: Levi, Eran

Moto Perpetuo, Paganini, Niccolo/Snell: Childs Brothers; Mead, Steven; Picton, Wendy

Mountains of Mourne, The, Traditional/Collins/French/Newsome: Clough, John; Childs, Nicholas

Move, Best, Denzil/Buttery: Atlantic Tuba Quartet, The

Move, Davidson, Matthew: Tuba Laté

Movin Groovin/Tuba Rodeo/Tango, Willibald, Kresin: Contraband Tuba Quartet

Mr. Bach Goes to Town, Templeton, Alec: Contraband Tuba Quartet

Mr. Euphonium, Moren, Bertrand: Mead, Steven

Mr. P. C., Coltrane, John: Dickman, Marcus

Music 4 Tubas, Stevens, John: Sotto Voce Quartet

Music for the Stage, Uber, David: Dutch Tuba Quartet

Music for Tuba Ensemble, Rogers, Thomas: University of Miami Tuba Ensemble

Music of the Night, Webber, Andrew Lloyd/Kanai: Hokazono, Sho-ichiro

Musings, Cherry, Bill: Tennessee Technological University Tuba-Euphonium Ensemble

Musizure pur un Feu o', Handel, George Frederic: Grainger, Andre

M—Virus, Sobotta, Uli: Sobotta, Uli

My Christ Is All, Himes, William: Richards, Kelvin; Meyer, Donald; Brown, William

My Christ Is in All, in All, Unknown: Allison, Gordon

Myfanwy, Traditional/Jenkins: Childs Brothers

Myfanwy, Traditional/Maunder: McDonnell, Riki, and Mike Kilroy

Myfanwy, Traditional/Stephens: Roberts, David

My Favorite Things, Rodgers and Hammerstein/Cherry: Tennessee Technological University Tuba-Euphonium Ensemble

My Favorite Things, Rodgers and Hammerstein/Madill: Modern Jazz Tuba Project

My Favorite Things, Rodgers and Hammerstein: Hokazono, Sho-ichiro

My Funny Valentine, Hart, Lorenzo; Rodgers, Richard/Pirone: Mead, Steven

My Heart at Thy Sweet Voice, Saint-Saëns, Camille/Larendeau: Breuninger, Tyrone

My Heart Stood Still, Rodgers, Richard; Hart, Lorenz: O'Hara, Betty

My Heart Will Go On, Horner, James/Velde: Kilroy, Mike

My Light and Song, Kjellgren, G.: Butler, John

My Love Is Like a Red Red Rose, Traditional/Downie: Kane, Derick

My Melancholy Baby, Norton, George; Burnett, Ernie: Dickman, Marcus

My Old Kentucky Home, Foster, Stephen/Rimmer: Deacon, Derek; Appleton, Walter; Yamamoto, Norihisa; Withington, Len; Jones, Alan

My Regards, Llwellyn, Edward: Falcone, Leonard; Wood, Ken

My Reverie, Debussy, Claude: Hokazono, Sho-ichiro

Mystical Music, Garrett, James Allen: Tennessee Technological University and Alumni Tuba-Euphonium Ensemble

My Story and Song, Foster, Stephen/Steadman-Allen: Childs Brothers

My Sweet Love, Inomata, Takeshi: Hokazono, Sho-ichiro

My Unchanging Friend, Bosanko, Ivor: Kane, Derick

My Wife Is a Most Knowing Woman, Foster, Stephen/LaDuke: LaDuke, Lance

Napoli Variations, Bellstedt, Herman/Bale: Mead, Steven

Napoli Variations, Bellstedt, Herman/Simon: Bowman, Brian

Napoli, Bellstedt, Herman/Brand: Mead, Steven

Napoli, Bellstedt, Herman/Childs: Childs, Robert

Napoli, Bellstedt, Herman/Owenson: Craddock, Ian

Napoli, Bellstedt, Herman: Falcone, Leonard; Bowman, Brian; Storey, John; Araki, Tamao; Dodd, Michael; Euphoniums of University of Illinios; Miura, Toru; Behrend, Roger

Nature Boy, Ahbez, Eden/Cherry: Tennessee Technological University Tuba-Euphonium Ensemble

Nautical Variations, Traditional/Taylor, Jeff: Behrend, Roger

Neopolitan Song, Tchaikovsky, Piotr/Butler: Tuba Laté

Nessun Dorma, Puccini, Giacomo/D. Childs: Childs, David

Nessun Dorma, Puccini, Giacomo/Stephens: McDonnell, Riki, and Mike Kilroy

Nessun Dorma, Puccini, Giacomo/Wilkinson: Groom, Trevor; Mead, Steven

Nessun Dorma, Puccini, Giacomo: Mead, Steven; Booth, Steven; Frey, Adam; McDonnell, Riki, and Mike Kilroy

New Carnival of Venice, A, Stevens, Thomas: Mead, Steven

New Day, Sun Ra: McKinney, Bernard

New Direction, A, Kane, Derick: Kane, Derick

New England Reveries, Corwell, Neal: Corwell, Neal

New Orleans, Bozza, Eugene: Verweij, Hugo

New "When Tubas Waltz," The, Bartles, Alfred: Symphonia

Nice Guys These Beatles, Sobotta, Uli: Sobotta, Uli

Nightclub 1960, Piazzolla, Astor/LaDuke: LaDuke, Lance

Night in a Persian Caravan, A, Ketelby, Albert: Albertasaurus Tuba Quartet

Nightingale Sang in Berkeley Square, A, Sherwin, Manning/Manhattan Transfer/Funderburk/ Jones: Symphonia

Nightingale Sang in Berkeley Square, A, Sherwin, Manning/Mehlan: Monarch Tuba-Euphonium Quartet

Nightingale Sang in Berkeley Square, A, Sherwin, Manning/Puerling/Cochran: Euphoniums Unlimited

Nightingale Sang in Berkeley Square, , A, Sherwin, Manning/Smalley: British Tuba Quartet, The

Night in June, A, King, Karl L./Braten: Pederson, Thor-Arne

Night in June, A, King, Karl L.: Mead, Steven; Wood, Ken; Lehman, Arthur

Night Song, Corwell, Neal: Corwell, Neal

Nina, Pergolesi, Giovanni: Smith, Henry Charles

Nine Points of Roguery/Murphy's Reel, Traditional/LaDuke: LaDuke, Lance

Nocturne and Rondolette, Shepherd, Arthur: Young, Raymond G.

Nocturne Op. 19, Tchaikovsky, Piotr/Rüedi: Rüedi, Thomas

Nocturne, Nordhagen, Stig: Dutch Tuba Quartet

Nocturno for Euphonium, Stanek, P.: Anonymous

Non e Ver', Mattei, Tito: Lawrence, Mark

Non Piu Andrai, Mozart, Wolfgang Amadeus/Rimmer: Wilkinson, Harry

Noreen's Nocturn, Peterson, Oscar/J. Peterson: Matteson-Phillips Tubajazz Consort

Nostalgia Medley, Sample, Steve: Tennessee Technological University Tuba-Euphonium Ensemble

Notturno, Rimsky-Korsakov, Nikolai/Mead: Mead, Steven; British Tuba Quartet, The

Now Here This!, Dempsey, Raymond: Monarch Tuba-Euphonium Quartet; British Tuba Quartet, The

Now I Belong to Jesus, Clayton, Norman/Broughton: Himes, William

Nun's Chorus, Strauss, Richard: McDonnell, Riki, and Mike Kilroy

Ochills, Rance, Ernest: Kane, Derick

Ochills, Redhead, Robert: Vanderweele, Aaron

O Come All Ye Faithful, Traditional: Tuba Christmas Ensemble

O Come Emmanuel, Vaughan, Rodger, arr.: Tubadours

O Come, O Come Immanuel, Traditional: Tuba Christmas Ensemble

Octet for Brass (1977), Luckhardt, Hilmar: Kilpatrick, Barry

October Sunshine, Botschinsky, Allan: Van Lier, Bart

Octubafest Medley, Bewley, Norlan, arr.: TubaCompany of Harvey Phillips

Ode for Low Brass, Butts, Carrol M.: Garden State Tuba Ensemble

O Divine Redeemer, Gounod, Charles: Bowman, Brian

Odyssey, Corwell, Neal: Corwell, Neal; Champions of the Leonard Falcone Festival 1986–2000; Taylor, Robin

Of Wounds and Something Else, Sun Ra: McKinney, Bernard

O-Fayces, Mancuso, Gus: Mancuso, Gus

Oh Little Town of Bethlehem, Vaughan, Rodger, arr.: Tubadours

Oh, My Beloved Father, Puccini, Giacomo/Moreau: Haemhouts, Ben

Oh, My Beloved Father, Puccini, Giacomo/Smith: Mead, Steven

Oh, My Beloved Father, Puccini, Giacomo: McDonnell, Riki, and Mike Kilroy

O Holy Night, Adam: Childs, David

Oia, O che bon Eccho!, Di Lasso, Orlando: Gerhard Meinl's Tuba Sextet

Old Rugged Cross, The, Bennard: Childs, David

Old Rustic Bridge, The, Doughty, George, arr.: Archer, Stephen

Old Star, Traditional: Melton Tuba-Quartett

Oleo, Rollins, Sonny/Matteson: Matteson-Phillips Tubajazz Consort; Modern Jazz Tuba Project

O Little Town of Bethlehem, Traditional: Tuba Christmas Ensemble

Ombra mai fu from "Xerses," Handel, George Frederic/Anonymous: Baglin, Lyndon

Ombra mai fu from "Xerses," Handel, George Frederic/Ito: Miura, Toru

O, Mio Babbino Caro, Puccini, Giacomo/Colburn: Colburn, Michael

On a Rocky Road, Templeton, Alec: Contraband Tuba Quartet

One Fine Day, Puccini, Giacomo: McDonnell, Riki, and Mike Kilroy

One for My Body, Arlen, Harold: O'Hara, Betty

One Hand, One Heart, Bernstein, Leonard/Fettig: Tropman, Matt

One Note Samba, Jobim, Antonio Carlos/Dittmar: Mead, Steven

Only Love, Catherall, Alan; arr.: Childs Brothers

On My Own, Schönberg, Claude-Michel/Barry: McDonnell, Riki, and Mike Kilroy

On My Own, Schönberg, Claude-Michel/Mead: British Tuba Quartet, The

On My Own, Schönberg, Claude-Michel: Miraphone Tuba Quartet

On the Sunny Side of the Street, McHugh, Jimmy: British Tuba Quartet, The

On Thin Ice, Mobberley, James: Tennessee Technological University Tuba-Euphonium Ensemble

On with the Motley, Leoncavallo, Ruggero: McDonnell, Riki, and Mike Kilroy

Open the Gates of the Temple, Knapp, Mrs. Joseph/ Henneman: Bowman, Brian

Orange Shores, Isomura, Yukiko/Narita: Narita, Yuko

Oration, Snell, Howard: Mead, Steven

Orchestra Scheldt, Glorieux, F.: Ost, Nick

O Rest in the Lord, Mendelssohn, Felix: Bowman, Brian

Orpheus in the Underworld, Offenbach, Jacques/ Fletcher: Lidsle, Harri

O Sanctissmus, Harclerode, Albert: Tubadours

O, Sole Mio, DiCapua: Falcone, Leonard

O Tannanbaum, Harclerode, Albert, arr.: Tubadours

Our Love Is Here to Stay, Gershwin, George: Matteson, Rich

Out of the Depths, Dodson, John: Tennessee Technological University Tuba-Euphonium Ensemble

Out of This World, Arlen, Harold: O'Hara, Betty

Over the Rainbow, Arlen, Harold/Fritze: Colonial Tuba Quartet, The

Over the Rainbow, Arlen, Harold: Top Brass

Overture from the "Magic Flute," Mozart, Wolfgang Amadeus: Miraphone Tuba Quartet

Overture from the "Marriage of Figaro," Mozart, Wolfgang Amadeus/Fabrizio: Monarch Tuba-Euphonium Quartet

Overture from the "Marriage of Figaro," Mozart, Wolfgang Amadeus/Ferguson: British Tuba Quartet, The

Overture from the "Marriage of Figaro," Mozart, Wolfgang Amadeus/Gottschalk: University of Michigan Tuba and Euphonium Ensemble; United States Armed Forces Tuba-Euphonium Ensemble

Overture to "Russlan and Ludmila," Glinka, Michael: Miraphone Tuba Quartet

Overture to the "Barber of Seville," Rossini, Gioacchino/Kile: United States Armed Forces Tuba-Euphonium Ensemble

Overture to William Tell, Rossini, Gioacchino/Dawson: Symphonia

Over Yandro, Traditional/Denton: Frey, Adam

O Vos Omnes, Victoria, Thomas Luis de/Self: Melton Tuba-Quartett

O Waly Waly, Traditional/Denton: Frey, Adam

Paganini Variations, Wilby, Philip: Childs, Robert

Panache, Dewhurst, Robin: Burghgraef, Frans Aert; Meixner, Brian; Mead, Steven

Panis Angelicus, Franck, Cesar/Smith: Droste, Paul; Childs, Robert; Bowman, Brian; McDonnell, Riki, and Mike Kilroy

Pantomime, Sparke, Philip/Maldonado: Mead, Steven; Myllys, Jukka

Pantomime, Sparke, Philip: Childs, Nicholas; Frey, Adam; Gosney, Richard; Hunter, Angie; Mead, Steven; Meli, Renato; Pugh, Joel; Schultz, Karl; Childs Brothers; Hokazono, Sho-ichiro

Papageo Papagena, Mozart, Wolfgang Amadeus: McDonnell, Riki, and Mike Kilroy

Papillon and Sicilienne, Fauré, Gabriel: Tropman, Matt

Papillon, Op. 77, Fauré, Gabriel: Champions of the Leonard Falcone Festival 1986–2000

Parade of the Tin Soldiers, Childs Nicholas; arr.: Childs Brothers

Parisian Thoroughfare, Unknown: McKinney, Bernard

Partita for Euphonium and Piano, Op. 89, Butterworth, Arthur: Olsrud, Sverre Stakston; Mead, Steven

Partita for Euphonium and Piano, Ross, Walter: Bowman, Brian; Verweij, Hugo; Araki, Tamao

Partita in a Minor, Bach, Johann Sebastian: Thompson, Kevin

Partita No. 2 in d Minor, Bach, Johann Sebastian: Thompson, Kevin

Partita—Polacca, Rosler, J.J.: Gerhard Meinl's Tuba Sextet

Pascal's Victim, Naftel, Frederick: Tuba Laté

Passacaglia and Fugue in c Minor, Bach, Johann Sebastian/Garrett: Symphonia

Pastorale, Baker, David: Top Brass

Pat-A-Pan, Bewley, Norlan, arr.: TubaShop Quartet

Pathetique Sonata, Beethoven, Ludwig van: Albertasaurus Tuba Quartet

Patrice Elaine, Dickman, Marcus: Dickman, Marcus

Paul et Mike, Jeanneau, François: Steckar Tubapack

Pavane, Op. 50, Fauré, Gabriel/Wilson: Tennessee Technological University Tuba-Euphonium Ensemble

Pavane, Op. 50, Fauré, Gabriel: Narita, Yuko

Pavanne from "Latin American Suite," Gould, Morton/Woo: University of Miami Tuba Ensemble

Pcelinca, Traditional/Stuckelschweiger: Mead, Steven

Peace, Golland, John/Ashmore: Childs, Robert

Peace, Golland, John: Cutts, Marcus; Fox, Mike; Owen, Mark; Postma, Simon; Williams, Kate; Gagnaux, Alexandre; Araki, Tamao; Flaten, Tormod; Kipfer, Ueli; Mead, Steven; Childs, David

Peace, Please, Thingäs, Frode: Mead, Steven; Gagnaux, Alexandre

Pearl Casters, Martin, Glenn: Modern Jazz Tuba Project

Pearls, Szentpali, Roland: Mead, Steven

Pequeña Czárdás, Iturralde, Pedro/van der Woude: Mead, Steven

Pequeña Czárdás, Iturralde, Pedro/Veit: Mead, Steven

Perfect Day, A, Jacobs Bond, Carrie: Dempster, Stuart

Perhaps Love, Denver, John/Fraser: Childs Brothers; Haemhouts, Ben

Perpetuum Mobile, Strauss, Johann: British Tuba Quartet, The

Petersburger March, Unknown: Miraphone Tuba Quartet

Petit Caprice in the Style of Offenbach, Rossini, Gioacchino/Davis: British Tuba Quartet, The; Monarch Tuba-Euphonium Quartet

Petites Litanies de Jésus, Grovlez, Gabriel: Sotto Voce Quartet

Pick Up the Pieces, Duncan/Ball/McIntryre/ Gorrie/Stuart/McIntosh/Murphy: Modern Jazz Tuba Project

Pickle Song, Sobotta, Uli: Sobotta, Uli

Pictural, Unknown: Miraphone Tuba Quartet

Piece en Forme de Habanera, Ravel, Maurice: Falcone, Leonard; Murchinson, Matthew

Piece en Mi Bemol for Tenor Trombone, Barat, J. Ed./ Berryman: Young, Raymond G.

Piece en mi bemol mineur, Ropartz, Guy: Pfeifle, Nicolas

Piece in fa mineur, Morel, Florentin: Miura, Toru; Young, Raymond G.; Fukuda, Masanori

Piece of Cake, A, Duet for Euphoniums, Newsome, Roy: Walton, Paul; Childs Brothers

Pieces of Eight, Solomons, David: Tuba Laté

Pierre Soliloquy, A: Ode to Pierre, Garrett, James Allen: Tennessee Technological University and Alumni Tuba-Euphonium Ensemble

Pigeon Toed Joad, Robinson, Willard: O'Hara, Betty

Pigs, Ridout, Alan: British Tuba Quartet, The

Pilatus, Richards, Goff: Mead, Steven; Schmidli, Erich

Pink Panther, The, Mancini, Henry/Gale: Dutch Tuba Quartet

Pink Panther, The, Mancini, Henry/Krush: British Tuba Quartet, The; Melton Tuba-Quartett

Pink Panther, The, Mancini, Henry: Lidsle, Harri

Plaisir D'Amour, Martini, Giovanni/Kanai: Hokazono, Sho-ichiro

Plaisir D'Amour, Martini, Giovanni/Lucena: Baglin, Lyndon

Plaisir D'Amour, Martini, Giovanni/Rimmer: Richards, Robert

Planets, Holst, Gustav: Mulcahy, Michael

Play That Funky Tuba Right, Boy!, Parissi, Rob/ Kortyka: Tennessee Technological University Tuba-Euphonium Ensemble

Playera "Danse Espagnole," Granados, Enrique/ Falcone: Falcone, Leonard

Pleasant Moments, Joplin, Scott/Sabourin: Dutch Tuba Quartet

Pokarekareana, Tomoana/Maunder: McDonnell, Riki, and Mike Kilroy

Pools, Gronick, Don: Tennessee Technological University Alumni Tuba-Euphonium Ensemble

Pop Suite, Frackenpohl, Arthur: Miraphone Tuba Quartet; British Tuba Quartet, The; Colonial Tuba Quartet, The; Tuba Laté; Dutch Tuba Quartet; Garden State Tuba Ensemble; Rustic Bari-Tuba Ensemble; University of Miami Tuba Ensemble

Pop-Rock Medley, Garrett, James Allen: Tennessee Technological University and Alumni Tuba-Euphonium Ensemble

Power, Stevens, John: Melton Tuba-Quartett; Lidsle, Harri; Sotto Voce Quartet; Swiss Tuba Quartet; Miraphone Tuba Quartet

Praeludium, Hilgers, Walter: Gerhard Meinl's Tuba Sextet

Prayer Before the Close of Day, Solomons, David: Tuba Laté

Preghiera from "Lo Scudiero del Re," Feliciangeli, Francesco/Creux: Mead, Steven

Prelude and Dance, Fritz, Gregory: Colonial Tuba Quartet, The

Prelude and Dance, Unknown: Swiss Tuba Quartet

Prelude and Fugue in d Minor, Bach, Johann Sebastian/Barnes: Symphonia

Prelude, Chopin, Frédéric: Narita, Yuko

Preludium, Bach, Johann Sebastian/Sabourin: Lidsle, Harri

Premier Solo de Concert, Combelle, F.: Falcone, Leonard

Prescott Poem, Fennell, Drew: Murchinson, Matthew

Preussens Gloria, Unknown: Miraphone Tuba Quartet

Priscilla, Mantia, Simone: Dempster, Stuart

Processional to the Minster, Wagner/Ito: Mead, Steven

Profiles, Schulz, Patrick: Sotto Voce Quartet

Promises, Camsey, Terry: Vanderweele, Aaron

Psalm, Suzuki, Ryuta: Taylor, Robin

Public Merryment, Prokofiev, Sergei/Fettig: Tropman, Matt

Puttin' on the Ritz, Berlin, Irving/Gout: British Tuba Quartet, The

Quartet for Brass No. 4, Ramsöe, Emilio/Buttery: Atlantic Tuba Quartet, The; United States Coast Guard Tuba-Euphonium Quartet; United States Navy Band Tuba-Euphonium Quartet; British Tuba Quartet, The; Coast Guard Tuba-Euphonium Quartet

Quartet for Low Brass, Bulla, Stephen: United States Navy Band Tuba-Euphonium Quartet; British Tuba Quartet, The

Quartet for Tubas (The Condor), Payne, Frank Lynn: University of Miami Tuba Ensemble; Melton Tuba-Quartett; Dutch Tuba Quartet; University of Michigan Tuba and Euphonium Ensemble

Quartet for Tubas, Holmes, Paul: Tennessee Technological University and Alumni Tuba-Euphonium Ensemble; British Tuba Quartet, The; University of Michigan Tuba and Euphonium Ensemble

Quartet from "Rigoletto," Verdi, Guiseppe: McDonnell, Riki, and Mike Kilroy

Quartet, Regan, Michael J.: Tuba Laté

Quatre Chansons, Dempsey, Raymond: Melton Tuba-Quartett; British Tuba Quartet, The; Monarch Tuba-Euphonium Quartet

Quintet for Tubas, Tarlow, Lawrence: Garden State Tuba Ensemble

Radetzky March, Strauss, Johann: Miraphone Tuba Quartet

Rag-Polka from "Toot Suite," Bolling, C.: Hokazono, Sho-ichiro

Ragtime Dance, Joplin, Scott/Werden: United States Navy Band Tuba-Euphonium Quartet

Ragtime, Frackenpohl, Arthur: Melton Tuba-Quartett

Rangitoto, Richards, Goff: Gagnaux, Alexandre

Ransomed Host, The, Steadman-Allen, Ray: Groom, Trevor; Hunter, Angie; McNally, Robert

Ransomed, Marshall, George: Childs Brothers; Wise, Peter; Mead, Steven

Recondita Armosia from "Tosca," Puccini, Giacomo/Bale: Mead, Steven

Recondita Armosia from "Tosca," Puccini, Giacomo: McDonnell, Riki, and Mike Kilroy

Red Flannel Hash, Wilson, Phil: Matteson, Rich

Reflections on a Park Bench, Beale, David: Tennessee Technological University Tuba-Euphonium Ensemble

Regrets, Glorieux, F.: Ost, Nick

Relentless Grooves II, Armenia, Pilafian, Sam: LaDuke, Lance

Relentless Grooves, Pilafian, Sam: Tropman, Matt

Remember Your Dreams, Sargent, Fred/Gedris: Murchinson, Matthew

Remembrance of Switzerland, Liberati, Allesandro: Lehamn, Arthur

Rene's Song, Toledo, Rene Luis/Murphy: Modern Jazz Tuba Project

Requiem to a Dead Little Cat, Kalke, Ernst-Thilo: Melton Tuba-Quartett

Rest and Recreation, Skempton, Howard: Tuba Laté

Return to Sorrento, Curtis, De/Roberts: Mead, Steven

Rev. Archie Beaton, Mason, John/Rydland: Flaten, Tormod

Reverie and Frolic, Sibbing, Robert: Meixner, Brian

Reverie for Euphonium ans Paino, Wiedrich, William: Behrend, Roger

Rhapsody for Euphonium and Piano, Brubaker, Jerry: Behrend, Roger

Rhapsody for Euphonium, Curnow, James: Albiez, Cédric; Mead, Steven; Anonymous; Grainger, Andre; Welsh, David; Zuback, Joseph; Childs Brothers; Behrend, Roger; Breuninger, Tyrone

Rhapsody for Euphonium, Evenepoel, Johan: Childs, Robert

Rhapsody No. 2, Golland, John: Kipfer, Ueli

Ride of the Valkyries, The, Wagner, Richard/Hall: Mead, Steven

Riedl Polka, Sobotta, Uli: Sobotta, Uli

Ritual, Corwell, Neal: Corwell, Neal

Robin Adair, Hartmann, John: Lehman, Arthur; Borrie, Bob; Poole, Sydney; Warrington, Brian

Robin Hood Fanfare, Kamen, Michael/Oliver: Tennessee Technological University Tuba-Euphonium Ensemble

Rodney's Rhythm, Part One, Kendrick, Rodney: Zawadi, Kiane

Romance Op. 62, Elgar, Edward/Wilson: Mead, Steven; Verweij, Hugo

Romance, Op. 2, Ewald, Victor/Reed: Breuninger, Tyrone

Romance, Phillips, John: Childs Brothers

Romanta Passonata, Weber von, C.M.: Fukuda, Masanori

Romantische Stucke, Op. 7, Dvorak, Antonin/Pfeifle: Pfeifle, Nicolas

Romanza, Gheel, Henry: McCrea, Melvin

Romanza, Vaughan Williams, Ralph: Young, Ron; Droste, Paul

Romanze, Cords, Gustav/Frabrizio: Behrend, Roger

Romanze, Cords, Gustav: Young, Raymond G.

Romeo and Juliet at Parting, Prokofiev, Sergei/Fettig: Tropman, Matt

Romeo and Juliet: Introduction, Prokofiev, Sergei/Fettig: Tropman, Matt

Ronde and Saltarelle, Susato, Tielman/Winter: Atlantic Tuba Quartet, The

Rondeau, Mouret, Jean/Self: Tubadours

Rondo Alla Turca, Wyss, Thomas; arr.: Childs Brothers

Rondo Concertante, Davis, William Mac: Mueller, John

Rondo from "Concerto No. 4 in E♭ Major for Horn and Orchestra," Mozart, Wolfgang Amadeus/Rive: Hildreth, Gordon

Rondo from "Concerto No. 4 in E♭ Major for Horn and Orchestra," Mozart, Wolfgang Amadeus/Wright: Lehamn, Arthur; Richards, Dean; Craddock, Ian; Baglin, Lyndon

Rondo, Bach, Johann Sebastian/Howard: British Tuba Quartet, The

Rondo, Hook, J./Garrett: British Tuba Quartet, The

Rondo, Smith, Claude T./Freeh: Mead, Steven

Rondo, Smith, Claude T.: Werden, David; Young, Raymond G.

Rondoletto for Two Euphoniums, Bryce, Frank: Groom, Trevor; Childs Brothers; Clough, John; Matti, Jean-Claude; Moss, John

Rosamunde, Vejvoda/Zelch: Mead, Steven

Rosette, Woode, H./Hines: Matteson, Rich

Rouleaux de Printemps, Steckar, Franck: Steckar Elephant Tuba Horde

'Round Midnight, Monk, Thelonius/Walker: Tennessee Technological University Alumni Tuba-Euphonium Ensemble; Tennessee Technological University Tuba-Euphonium Ensemble

'Round Midnight, Monk, Thelonius/Williams: Hokazono, Sho-ichiro

Royal Garden Blues, Williams, Clarence; Williams, Spencer: Sotto Voce Quartet

Rube and Boob, for Trumpet, Euphonium and Band, Stauffer, Donald: Biffle, Ronnie

Ruble and the Yen, The, Wiggins, Gerald: Mancuso, Gus

Rule Britannia, Hartmann, John/Frey: Frey, Adam

Rule Britannia, Hartmann, John/Greenwood: Griffiths, Morgan

Rule Britannia, Hartmann, John/Hopkinson: Millar, Billy

Rule Britannia, Hartmann, John/Stephens: Childs, Robert; Mead, Steven

Rule Britannia, Hartmann, John: Clough, John; Mead, Steven; Griffiths, Morgan

Rumpole of the Bailey, Horovitz, Joseph: British Tuba Quartet, The

Runnin' with Bydlo, Danner, Gregory: Euphoniums Unlimited

Russian Dance, Böhme, Oskar/Smith: Mead, Steven; Gagnaux, Alexandre

Russlan and Ludmila, Glinka, Michael/Ferguson/Smalley: British Tuba Quartet, The

Rutland Water, Bennett: Crompton, Carole

Sabre Dance, Khatchaturian, Aram/Seitz: Tuba Laté; Melton Tuba-Quartett

Safety Pin, Sobotta, Uli: Sobotta, Uli

Sally in Our Alley, Langford, Gordon: Christian, Peter

Salut d'amour, Elgar, Edward/Wilson: Childs Brothers

Samba Loco, Thingäs, Frode: Scandinavian Tuba Jazz

Sandu, Brown, Clifford/Perry: Modern Jazz Tuba Project; Tennessee Technological University Alumni Tuba-Euphonium Ensemble

Santa Claus Is Coming to Town, Vaughan, Rodger, arr.: Tubadours

Santa Wants a Tuba for Christmas, Bewley, Norlan: TubaShop Quartet

Sarabande and Minuet, Handel, George Frederic: Campbell, Larry

Satin Doll, Ellington, Duke/Vaughan: Tubadours

Saved by Grace, Gordon, William: Kane, Derick

Saxidentally, Niehaus, Lennie: Top Brass

Scarborough Fair, Garfunkel/Simon/Reichenbach: Mead, Steven

Scarborough Fair, Simon/Garfunkel/Lucena: Baglin, Lyndon

Scarborough Fair, Traditional/Forbes: Tuba Laté

Scenes That Are Brightest, Round, H.: Williams, Joseph

Scherzando for Tubular Octet, Knox, Charles: Tennessee Technological University Tuba-Euphonium Ensemble

Scherzo for Four, Doughty, George: Hawkey, Vivian

Scherzo from "Midsummer Nights Dream," Mendelssohn, Felix/Bale: Mead, Steven

Scherzo, Bernstein, Leonard/Fettig: Tropman, Matt

Scherzo, Corwell, Neal: Corwell, Neal

Scherzo, Danner, Gregory/Vaden: Tennessee Technological University Tuba-Euphonium Ensemble

Scherzo, Goldman, Edwin Franko: Bowman, Brian

Scratch My Back, Spinelli, Joseph: Mancuso, Gus

Scyths, Mertens, Hardy: Dutch Tuba Quartet

Sea Tubas, Traditional/Minerd: Lidsle, Harri

Search for a New World, Davies, Howard/Catherwood: Mallett, Chris

Seascape, Reed, Alfred: Behrend, Roger; Hokazono, Sho-ichiro; Miura, Toru

Second Suite in F for Military Band, Holst, Gustav/Werden: Symphonia

Semper Fidelis, Sousa, John Philip/Morris: British Tuba Quartet, The

Send in the Clowns, Sondheim, Stephen: Tropman, Matt

Señor Blues, Silver, Horace: Tennessee Technological University Alumni Tuba-Euphonium Ensemble

Señor Zamora, Vick, Harold: Zawadi, Kiane

Sequidillas, Forte, Aldo Rafael: Symphonia

Serenade for Four Tubas (Allegro, 3rd Movement), Pressor, William: University of Michigan Tuba and Euphonium Ensemble

Serenade for Tubas, Tchaikovsky, Piotr/O'Conner: Tennessee Technological University Tuba-Euphonium Ensemble

Serenade from "Millions D'Arlequin," Drigo, Riccardo/Oughton: Shepherd, Ken

Serenade from "Millions D'Arlequin," Drigo, Riccardo/Stephens: Mead, Steven

Serenade from "Millions D'Arlequin," Drigo, Riccardo/Wright: Childs, Robert; Clough, John

Serenade from "Millions D'Arlequin," Drigo, Riccardo: Griffiths, Morgan; Haemhouts, Ben

Serenade from "The Student Prince," Romberg, Sigmund/Godfrey: Bowman, Brian; Yamamoto, Norihisa; Brasch, Harold; Craig, Mary Ann

Serenade from "The Student Prince," Romberg, Sigmund/Oswin: McDonnell, Riki, and Mike Kilroy

Serenade, Schubert, Franz/Wilkinson: Mead, Steven

Serenade, Schubert, Franz: Falcone, Leonard

Serenata, Toselli, Enrico/Pierce: Haemhouts, Ben

Serenata, Toselli, Enrico/Rüedi: Mead, Steven

Serenata, Toselli, Enrico: Clough, John; Falcone, Leonard

Série Noire, Steckar, Marc: Steckar Tubapack

Settin' Red, Unknown: McKinney, Bernard

Sextet, George, Thom Ritter: Mead, Steven

Shadow of Your Smile, The, Mandel, Johnny/Maunder: McDonnell, Riki, and Mike Kilroy

Shadow of Your Smile, The, Webster, P./Mandel: Matteson, Rich

Shadowed, Gates: Vanderweele, Aaron

Shaft, Hayes, Isaac/Gottschalk: Tennessee Technological University Tuba-Euphonium Ensemble

Shall We Gather at the River, Traditional/Denton: Frey, Adam

Shaw Nuff, Unknown: McKinney, Bernard

Shenandoah, Traditional/Denton: Frey, Adam

Shenandoah, Traditional/McRitchie: Benedict, Lesley

Shenandoah, Traditional/Olcott: Mead, Steven

Shepherd Song, Davis, Trevor: Griffiths, Morgan

Shepherd's Dance, Susato, Tielman/Buttery: Alchemy (previously Atlantic Tuba Quartet)

Shiny Stockings, Foster, Frank/Perry: Tennessee Technological University Tuba-Euphonium Ensemble

Shout, The, Matteson, Rich/Peterson: Matteson, Rich

Shuckin' and Jivin', Matteson, Rich: Matteson, Rich

Shylock, Lear, Thos: Griffiths, Morgan

Siamang Suite, Canter, James: Tennessee Technological University and Alumni Tuba-Euphonium Ensemble

Sicilienne, Paradies/Snell: Mead, Steven

Side Partners, Clarke, Herbert L.: Swallow, John

Sidewinder, Morgan, Lee/Hauser: Tennessee Technological University Tuba-Euphonium Ensemble

Silent Night, Gottschalk, Arthur, arr.: Tennessee Technological University Tuba-Euphonium Ensemble

Silent Night, Traditional: Tuba Christmas Ensemble

Silver Threads, Twitchen, Bert: Childs Brothers

Simpsons, The, Elfman/Harris: Mead, Steven

Simyeh, Corwell, Neal: Corwell, Neal; Taylor, Robin

Sin tu Amor, Sandoval, Migul: Champions of the Leonard Falcone Festival 1986–2000

Since You've Asked, Collins, Judy/Buttery: Atlantic Tuba Quartet, The

Sinfonia Concertante, Op. 111 for Tenor Horn and Baritone, Butterworth, Arthur: Blackburn, Robert

Sing, Sing, Sing, Prima, Louis/Murphy: Modern Jazz Tuba Project

Sir "EU," Doss, Thomas: Mead, Steven

Sister Sadie, Silver, Horace/Hauser: Tennessee Technological University Tuba-Euphonium Ensemble

Sister Salvation, Hampton, Slide: McKinney, Bernard

Six Studies in English Folk Song, Vaughan Williams, Ralph/Droste: Droste, Paul

Skippin', Petersen, Jack: Matteson, Rich

Skippy, Unknown: McKinney, Bernard

Skylark, Carmichael, Hoagy/Matteson: Modern Jazz Tuba Project; O'Hara, Betty

Slavonic Dances, Op. 46, No. 1, Dvorak, Antonin/Butler: Tennessee Technological University Tuba-Euphonium Ensemble

Slavonic Impressions, Hudec, Adam: Williams, Glyn

Sleeping Bee, A, Arlen, Harold: O'Hara, Betty

Sleeping Giants, Niehaus, Lennie: Contraband

Slow Biker, Sobotta, Uli: Sobotta, Uli

Slumber My Darling, Foster, Stephen/Pilafian: LaDuke, Lance

Smile, Chaplin, Charlie: Top Brass

Softly As I Leave You, DeVita, Alfred/Catherall: Childs Brothers; Childs, Nicholas; Childs, David; Wilkins, Richard; Schultz, Karl

Softly Awakes My Heart, Saint-Saëns, Camille: McDonnell, Riki, and Mike Kilroy; Childs, David

Solace, Joplin, Scott/Milburne: Mueller, John

Soleil Impromptu, Baker, David: Top Brass

Soliloquy IX, Wiggins, Christopher: Mead, Steven

Solitaire, Corbett, Stephen, arr.: Johnston, Leon; Dale, Kevin

Solitaire, Sedaka: Withington, Len

Solo De Concurso, Yuste, Miguel: Mead, Steven; Hokazono, Sho-ichiro

Solo Rhapsody for Euphonium, Stephens, Denzil: Childs Brothers

Someone to Watch Over Me, Gershwin, George: O'Hara, Betty

Something Happy, Prince, Bill: Dickman, Marcus

Something with Tokyo, Harrison, George: Tokyo Bari-Tuba Ensemble

Somewhere, Bernstein, Leonard/Adams: McDonnell, Riki, and Mike Kilroy

Somewhere, Bernstein, Leonard/Fettig: Tropman, Matt

Sonata Euphonica, Hartley, Walter: Mead, Steven; Kilpatrick, Barry

Sonata for Baritone Horn and Piano, George, Thom Ritter: Craig, Mary Ann; Nelson, Douglas

Sonata for Euphonium, Frackenpohl, Arthur: Behrend, Roger; Heo, Jae-Young

Sonata for Euphonium, Reeman, John: Mead, Steven

Sonata for Euphonium, Roper, Anthony: Mead, Steven

Sonata for Euphonium and Piano, Bach, Johann Sebastian: Fisher, Mark, Hokazono; Sho-ichiro

Sonata for Euphonium and Piano, Uber, David: Behrend, Roger

Sonata for Trombone and Piano, Fasch, J. F.: Smith, Henry Charles

Sonata in a Minor, Marcello, Benedetto/Flaten: Flaten, Tormod

Sonata in F Major, Marcello, Benedetto: Mead, Steven; Araki, Tamao

Sonata in f Minor, Telemann, Georg: Behrend, Roger; Fisher, Mark

Sonata in g Minor, Handel, George Frederic/Brockway: Johnson, Frank

Sonata No. 3 in sol minore, Bach, Johann Sebastian: Colliard, Corrado

Sonata No. 3, Bach, Johann Sebastian/Marsteller: Marsteller, Loren

Sonata No. 6 in B♭ Major, Vivaldi, Antonio/Mortimer: Kipfer, Ueli

Sonata No. 6 in B♭ Major, Vivaldi, Antonio: Smith, Henry Charles

Sonata No.1 en Si b majeur, Vivaldi, Antonio: Milhiet, Ivan

Sonata Op. 64, for Euphonium and Piano, Plagge, Wolfgang: Olsrud, Sverre Stakston

Sonata Pian 'e forte, Gabrieli, Giovanni/Bale: Mead, Steven

Sonata, Takács, Jenö: Dart, Fred

Sonatina for Baritone Horn and Piano, Hutchison: Young, Raymond G.

Sonatina for Euphonium and Synthesizer, Boda, John: Bowman, Brian; Taylor, Robin

Sonatina for Tuba Quartet, Reeman, John: British Tuba Quartet, The

Sonatina, Kreisler von, Alexander: Nelson, Douglas

Song and Dance, Frackenpohl, Arthur: Behrend, Roger

Song for Ina, Sparke, Philip: Mead, Steven; Ushigami, Ryuji; McDonnell, Riki, and Mike Kilroy

Song of Faith, A, Ball, Eric/Birkett: Kane, Derick

Song of March, Takemitsu, Toru/Fukjiwara: Hokazono, Sho-ichiro

Song of the Brother, The, Leidzén, Erik/Field: Heo, Jae-Young

Song of the Brother, The, Leidzén, Erik: Mead, Steven; Kane, Derick; Young, Ron; Childs Brothers; Schmidli, Erich; Nygvist, Rune, Vanderweele, Aaron

Song of the Seashore, Catherall, Alan; arr.: Childs Brothers

Song of the Seashore, Narita, Tamezo/Kanai: Mead, Steven

Song of Triumph, Bowes, Ray: Himes, William; Brown, William

Song to the Evening Star, Wagner, Richard: Orosz, Josef

Songs in the Fight Against Rum, Garrett, James Allen: Tennessee Technological University and Alumni Tuba-Euphonium Ensemble

Sonia, Templeton, Alec/Childs: Childs, Robert

Sorcerer's Apprentice, The, Dukas/Bale: Mead, Steven

Sortie in E♭, Lefébure, Louis-François: British Tuba Quartet, The

Sound of the Wasp, The, Wilson, Phil: Matteson, Rich

Sousa Surrenders, Garrett, James Allen: Tennessee Technological University and Alumni Tuba-Euphonium Ensemble

So What, Davis, Miles/Perry: Tennessee Technological University Tuba-Euphonium Ensemble

Space Jazz Reverie, Sun Ra: McKinney, Bernard

Spain, Correa, Chick/Arnold: Tennessee Technological University Tuba-Euphonium Ensemble

Spanish Dance, Traditional: Baglin, Lyndon

Spanish Serenade, Zutano/Rimmer: Davis, George

Spirit of Life, Catherwood, David: Kane, Derick

Spiritual Jazz Suite, Traditional/Niehaus: British Tuba Quartet, The

Splash, Arcadio, Bernard: Steckar, Marc

Sponger Money, Traditional/Buttery: Alchemy (previously Atlantic Tuba Quartet)

Spoofy, Matteson, Rich: Matteson-Phillips Tubajazz Consort

Spread Your Wide Wings, Traditional/Baker: Childs, David

Sprechstunde, Sobotta, Uli: Sobotta, Uli

Spring Suite, Cummings, Barton: Craig, Mary Ann

Spring, Grieg, Edward: Young, Ron

Springtime, Heath, Reginald: Morgan, Gareth; Woodland, Shaun; Moore, David; Farrington, Christopher; Taylor, Philip

Spruce, The, Sibelius, Jean: Hokazono, Sho-ichiro

St. Anne's Fugue, Bach, Johann Sebastian/Beckman: United States Army Band Tuba-Euphonium Ensemble and Massed Ensemble; Tennessee Technological University Tuba-Euphonium Ensemble

St. James Infirmary Blues, Primrose, Joe/Forbes: Sotto Voce Quartet; Tuba Laté

St. Louis Blues, Handy, W.C./Holcombe: Melton Tuba-Quartett; Dutch Tuba Quartet

St. Thomas, Rollins, Sonny: Matteson, Rich

Stabillo Steckardello, Vigneron, Louis: Steckar Elephant Tuba Horde

Ständchen, Schubert, Franz Peter/LeClair: Contraband

Stardust, Carmichael, Hoagy: O'Hara, Betty; Hokazono, Sho-ichiro

Starry Crown, A, Boon, Brindley: Schramm, Robert

Stars and Stripes Ballet Suite, Kay, Hershy: Swallow, John

Stars and Stripes Forever, Sousa, John Philip/Werden: Atlantic Tuba Quartet, The; Lidsle, Harri

Stars and Stripes Forever, Sousa, John Philip: Miraphone Tuba Quartet; Swiss Tuba Quartet

Steal Away, Traditional/Trippet/Howard: British Tuba Quartet, The

Stella by Starlight, Anonymous: Matteson, Rich

Stickin', Baker, David: Top Brass

Stompin' at the Savoy, Sampson/Racaf/Foodman/Webb: Matteson-Phillips Tubajazz Consort

Strange Thing, Russell, Leon/Florance: Modern Jazz Tuba Project

Strenuous Life, The, Joplin, Scott/Walter: Miraphone Tuba Quartet; Albertasaurus Tuba Quartet

String of Tones, A, Roper, Anthony: Tuba Laté

Student's Concertino, Toda, Akira: Fukuda, Masanori

Substructures for Ten Tubas, Gottschalk, Arthur: University of Michigan Tuba and Euphonium Ensemble

Suite à Suivre, Steckar, Marc; Franck Steckar: Steckar Tubapack

Suite for Baritone Horn and Piano, Beach: Young, Raymond G.

Suite for Euphonium and Piano, Martin, David: Young, Raymond G.

Suite for Low Brass, Lyon, Max: Atlantic Tuba Quartet, The

Suite Francaise, Poulenc, Frank/Isoda: Hokazono, Sho-ichiro

Suite Lumière, Piazzola, Astor: Milhiet, Ivan

Suite No. 4 in E♭ Major, Bach, Johann Sebastian/Flaten: Flaten, Tormod

Suite No. 5 in c Minor, Bach, Johann Sebastian: Thompson, Kevin

Suite No. 1 in G Major, Bach, Johann Sebastian: Thompson, Kevin

Suite of Spring Wind, Isomura, Yukiko: Narita, Yuko

Summer Knows, Legrand, Michel/Williamson: Modern Jazz Tuba Project

Summer of '42, Legrand/Slater: Matteson, Rich

Summertime, Gershwin, George: Matteson-Phillips Tubajazz Consort

Sunflower, Mancini, Henry: Hokazono, Sho-ichiro

Sunrise Lady, Johnston, Bruce/O'Connor: Tennessee Technological University Tuba-Euphonium Ensemble

Sunrise on the River, Glorieux, F.: Ost, Nick

Surely We, Matteson, Rich: Matteson, Rich

Swan, The, Saint-Saëns, Camille/D. Childs: Childs, David

Swan, The, Saint-Saëns, Camille/Denton: Frey, Adam

Swan, The, Saint-Saëns, Camille/Mead: Mead, Steven

Swan, The, Saint-Saëns, Camille/Minchin: Tuba Laté

Swan, The, Saint-Saëns, Camille/Mott: Parry, Glynn

Swan, The, Saint-Saëns, Camille/Snell: Mead, Steven; Woollam, David

Swan, The, Saint-Saëns, Camille/Steadman-Allen: Childs Brothers; Kane, Derick; Codd, E;

Swan, The, Saint-Saëns, Camille/Stephens: Roberts, Roy

Swan, The, Saint-Saëns, Camille: Hardick, Caspar; Falcone, Leonard; Campbell, Larry; Schmidli, Erich; Mead, Steven; Hunter, Angie; Teasdale, Malcolm; Louder, Earle

Swedish Hymn, Traditional/P. Graham: Childs, David

Sweet and Low, Barnby, Joseph/Farr: Flaten, Tormod

Sweet Georgia Brown, Bernie, Pinkard, and Casey/Garrett: Tennessee Technological University Tuba-Euphonium Ensemble

Sweet Georgia Brown, Bernie, Pinkard; and Casey/Fragomeni: Colonial Tuba Quartet, The

Swing Low, Sweet Chariot, Alexander, Lois; arr.: Dutch Tuba Quartet

Swing Low, Sweet Chariot, Willibald, Kresin; arr.: Contraband

Swingers Get the Blues Too, Ellington, Duke: Matthew, Gee

Symphonic Rhapsody for Euphonium and Band, Gregson, Edward: Mead, Steven; Corwell, Neal; Childs Brothers; Griffiths, Morgan

Symphonic Variants for Euphonium and Band, Curnow, James: Bowman, Brian; Behrend, Roger; Craig, Mary Ann; Denys, Marnik; Franke, Philip; Mead, Steven; Gagnaux, Alexandre; Hunter, Angie; Hokazono, Sho-ichiro

Symphonic Variants for Euphonium and Brass, Curnow, James/Bryant: Taylor, Robin

Symphonie des regards, Nissim, Mico: Milhiet, Ivan

Symphony No. 7, Mahler, Gustav: Mulcahy, Michael

Tahoe, Matteson, Rich: Matteson, Rich

Take a Walk, LaDuke, Lance: LaDuke, Lance

Take Five, Desmond, Paul/Luis: Melton Tuba-Quartett

Talisman, Stevens, John: Symphonia

Tangents, Op. 109, Barnes, James: Symphonia

Tango Mortale, Turek, Thomas: Pfeifle, Nicolas

Tango-Etudes, Piazzolla, Astor/Hokazono: Hokazono, Sho-ichiro

Tapestry from an Asteroid, Sun Ra: McKinney, Bernard

Tarantella, Squire, W. H./R. Childs: Childs, David

Tarantella, Squire, W.H.: Falcone, Leonard; Baglin, Lyndon

Tears, Bousted, Donald: Tuba Laté

Tell the World, Mack, Thomas: Mack, Thomas

Tender Thieves, The, Mancini, Henry: Nash, Dick

That Old Black Magic, Arlen, Harold: Tennessee Technological University Alumni Tuba-Euphonium Ensemble

That Wasp, Wilson, Phil: Matteson, Rich

Them Basses, Huffine, G.H.: United States Army Band Tuba-Euphonium Ensemble and Massed Ensemble

Theme for Malcolm, Brown, David/Williamson: Modern Jazz Tuba Project

There Is No Greater Love, Symes, M./Jones: Matteson, Rich

There Will Be God, Phillips, Richard: Kane, Derick, Vanderweele, Aaron

They Didn't Believe Me, Kern, Jerome/Holcombe: British Tuba Quartet, The

Things Ain't What They Used to Be, Ellington, Duke/Matteson: Matteson-Phillips Tubajazz Consort

This Masquerade, Russell, Leon/Madill: Modern Jazz Tuba Project

Thoughts of Gold, DeLuca, Joseph/Hazes: Colburn, Michael

3 à 5, Fosset, Marc: Steckar Tubapack

Three Essays for Orchestra, Barber, Samuel: Myers, Timothy

Three Folksongs for Four Brass, Denson, Frank: Gerhard Meinl's Tuba Sextet

Three Friends, Wilson, Phil: Matteson, Rich

Three Ha'Pence a Foot, Edgar, M./Powell: Tuba Laté

Three Ludes for Tuba, Jager, Robert: Symphonia

Three Milongas, Crespo, Enrique: Gerhard Meinl's Tuba Sextet

Three Miniatures, Wilson: Campbell, Larry

Three Moods, Boone, Daniel: Tennessee Technological University and Alumni Tuba-Euphonium Ensemble; University of Miami Tuba Ensemble

Three Movements for Four Tubas, Beal, Keith: Dutch Tuba Quartet

Three Mythical Sketches for Four Tubas, Iannaccone, Anthony: University of Michigan Tuba and Euphonium Ensemble

Three Piece Suite, Moore, T.: Tuba Laté

Three Preludes, Gershwin, George/Heifetz/Murchinson: Murchinson, Matthew

Three Preludes, Gershwin, George: Contraband Tuba Quartet

Three Short Pieces for Baritone Horn and Piano, Gower, A. E.: Young, Raymond G.

Three Sixteenth Century Flemish Pieces, Singleton; arr.: Monarch Tuba-Euphonium Quartet

Thunderer, The, Sousa, John Philip/Smalley: Dutch Tuba Quartet

Thunderer, The, Sousa, John Philip: British Tuba Quartet, The; Tuba Laté

Tiger Rag, Gale, Jack; arr.: Dutch Tuba Quartet

Timbuktuba, Daugherty, Michael: Symphonia

Time and Time Again, McPartland, Marian/Wilson: Matteson, Rich

Time for Love, A, Mandel, Johnny: Tennessee Technological University Alumni Tuba-Euphonium Ensemble

Timepiece, Bearcroft, Norman/Rockey: Scannell, A.J.

Timepiece, Bearcroft, Norman: Childs Brothers; Kane, Derick; Sewell-Jones, Adam; Harewood, Ern

Titanic, Horner, James/Heo: Heo, Jae-Young

To a Wild Rose, MacDowell, Edward/Ball: Faro, Michael; Singleton, Stephen; Shepherd, Ken; Morgan, Gareth; Deacon, Derek; Cutts, Marcus; Bowden, Ray; Membury, Clive

To a Wild Rose, MacDowell, Edward/Langford: Cutts, Marcus

To All the Girls I've Loved Before, Anonymous: Brunner, Stefan

Toccata and Fugue in d Minor, Bach, Johann Sebastian/Morris: Tennessee Technological University Tuba-Euphonium Ensemble

Toccata and Fugue in d Minor, Bach, Johann Sebastian/Taylor: Mead, Steven

Toccata in d Minor (Allegro), Bach, Johann Sebastian/Myers: Atlantic Tuba Quartet, The

To Cross the Mountain, Sobotta, Uli: Sobotta, Uli

To Dizzy with Love, Baker, David: Top Brass

To Live Right, Bosanko, Ivor: Kane, Derick

Tonight, Bernstein, Leonard/Fettig: Tropman, Matt

Too Fat Polka, Richardson and Maclean/Whitcomb: Tubadours

Toot Your Roots, Botschinsky, Allan: Van Lier, Bart

Tortion Level, Unknown: McKinney, Bernard

Train to Florida, Cooder, Ry: Marsteller, Loren

Tramp, Tramp, Tramp, Goldman, Richard: Wood, Ken

Träumerei aus Kinderszenen, Op. 15, Schumann, Robert/Seitz: Melton Tuba-Quartett

Träumerei aus Kinderszenen, Op. 15, Schumann, Robert: Heidler, Manfred

Traveling Along, Anonymous: Mallett, Chris, Vanderweele, Aaron, Kane, Derick

Travissimo, Cohn, Al: Matteson, Rich

Treatments for Tuba, Stroud, Richard: Tennessee Technological University Tuba-Euphonium Ensemble

Trepak, Tchaikovsky, Piotr/Smalley: British Tuba Quartet, The

Tribute to Duke Ellington, Ellington, Duke/Sample: Tennessee Technological University Tuba-Euphonium Ensemble

Tributes to Tunesmiths, Parfrey, Raymond: Tuba Laté

Trilogy for Euphonium, Wiggins, Brian: Gagnaux, Alexandre

Trio Concerto, Wright, Dennis: Richards, Robert

Triplet for Four Tubas, Lundquist, Trobjörn: British Tuba Quartet, The

Tritsch-Tratsch Polka, Strauss, Johann/Seitz: Melton Tuba-Quartett

Troika from "Lieutenant Kije," Prokofiev, Sergei/Butler: Tennessee Technological University Tuba-Euphonium Ensemble

T-Tango, Sanson, Davide: Colliard, Corrado

Tuba Blues Melody, Wolking, Henry: Melton Tuba-Quartett; British Tuba Quartet, The; Lidsle, Harri

Tubacchanale, Boutry, Roger: Verweij, Hugo

Tubach, Steckar, Marc; Arcadio, Bernard: Steckar, Marc; Swiss Tuba Quartet

TubaChristmas Suite, Bewley, Norlan, arr.: TubaShop Quartet

Tubafication, Mitchell-Davidson, Paul: Tuba Laté

Tubafiesta Medley, Bewley, Norlan, arr.: TubaCompany of Harvey Phillips

Tubafusion, Wood, Derek: Tuba Laté

Tuba Juba Duba, Hutchinson, Terry: Tennessee Technological University Tuba-Euphonium Ensemble; Melton Tuba-Quartett

Tubalation, Niehaus, Lennie: Miraphone Tuba Quartet

Tubalee Jubalee, A, Garrett, James Allen: Tennessee Technological University Tuba-Euphonium Ensemble; United States Armed Forces Tuba-Euphonium Ensemble

Tuba Magic, DiGiovanni, Rocco: Tennessee Technological University Tuba-Euphonium Ensemble; United States Army Band Tuba-Euphonium Ensemble and Massed Ensemble

Tubamobile, George, Thom Ritter: Symphonia

Tuba Muckl, Schmidt, Dankwart; arr.: Contraband

Tubapack Blues, Steckar, Franck: Steckar Tubapack

Tuba Quartet No, 2: Ale and Arty, Bayliss, Colin: Tuba Laté

Tuba Quartet No. 1 in c Minor, Op. 3, Wilson, Kenyon D.: Tennessee Technological University Tuba-Euphonium Ensemble

Tuba Quartet, Op. 59, Gates, Crawford: Tennessee Technological University Tuba-Euphonium Ensemble

Tuba Quartett, Hidas, Frigyas: Melton Tuba-Quartett

Tubarock Medley, Bewley, Norlan, arr.: TubaCompany of Harvey Phillips

Tubas au Fujiyama, Steckar, Marc: Steckar Elephant Tuba Horde

Tubas Latinas, Forte, Aldo Rafael: Tennessee Technological University Tuba-Euphonium Ensemble

Tubasonatina, George, Thom Ritter: Tennessee Technological University Tuba-Euphonium Ensemble

Tubaswing Medley, Bewley, Norlan, arr.: TubaCompany of Harvey Phillips

Tuba Voluntary, Gibbons, O./Campbell: Alchemy (previously Atlantic Tuba Quartet)

Tubular Octad, Tull, Fisher: Tennessee Technological University Tuba-Euphonium Ensemble

Tuphonium, Hidas, Frigyes: Dutch Tuba Quartet

Turandoto, Puccini, Giacomo: Fukuda, Masanori

Turkish March from "Piano Sonata in A," Mozart, Wolfgang Amadeus: Albertasaurus Tuba Quartet; British Tuba Quartet, The

Turkish Rondo, Mozart, Wolfgang Amadeus/ Mehlan: Monarch Tuba-Euphonium Quartet

Turn Your Eyes upon Jesus, Traditional/Denny: McDonnell, Riki, and Mike Kilroy

Tuscan Serenade, Fauré, Gabriel/Grainger: Colburn, Michael; Hokazono, Sho-ichiro; Cleveland, David

Tuxedo Junction, Hawkins, Erskin/Luis: Melton Tuba-Quartett; Dutch Tuba Quartet

Twelve Days of Housetops, Canter, James: Tennessee Technological University Tuba-Euphonium Ensemble

Twilight Serenade, Schoonenbeek, Kees: Mead, Steven

Twinkle, Twinkle Little Star, Catelinet, Phillip, arr.: Vernon, Ken

2:00:00, Corwell, Neal: Corwell, Neal

Two Classical Themes, Haydn, Franz Josef: Campbell, Larry

Two Fantasias, Banchieri, Adriano/Fritze: Colonial Tuba Quartet, The

Two Fauré Duets, Fauré, Gabriel/Mead: Mead, Steven

Two Insects, Aagaard-Nilsen, Torstein: Flaten, Tormod

Two Pieces for Euphonium and Piano, Hartley, Walter: Kilpatrick, Barry

Two Pieces, Bach, Johann Sebastian/Falcone: Behrend, Roger

Two Selections from "La Traviata," Verdi, Giuseppe: Albertasaurus Tuba Quartet

Two Tunes (You Stepped Out of a Dream; Temptation), Brown, Nacio Herb/Sample: Tennessee Technological University Tuba-Euphonium Ensemble

Two-Part Invention, Sparke, Philip: Childs Brothers; Hokazono, Sho-ichiro; Robyr, Dominique

U Are My Heart's Delight, Lehár, Franz: McDonnell, Riki, and Mike Kilroy

Ubi Caritas/Dance, Duruflé, Maurice; Renwick, Wilke/Wilson: Symphonia

Una Furtiva Lacrima, Donizetti, Gaetano/Harvey: Falcone, Leonard

Undecided, Anonymous: Matteson, Rich

Under the Admirals Flag, Unknown: Miraphone Tuba Quartet

Under the Sea, Unknown: Miraphone Tuba Quartet

Until I Met You, Green, Freddie/Esleck: Tennessee Technological University Tuba-Euphonium Ensemble

Vaga luna che inargenti, Bellini, Vincenzo/Bona: Mead, Steven

Vallflickans Dans, Alfén, Hugo/Olsrud/Rydland: Flaten, Tormod

Vallflickans Dans, Alfén, Hugo/Olsrud: Tropman, Matt

Valse, Mendez/Freeh: Griffiths, Morgan

Valvin' on a Riff, Martin, Glenn: Modern Jazz Tuba Project

Variants on St. Francis, Chaulk, David: Church, David

Variaties voor Euphonium en Piano, Toebosch, Louis: Verweij, Hugo

Variations for Euphonium, Unknown: Anonymous

Variations for Ophicleide, Kummer, Friedrich: Mead, Steven

Variations from "Carnival of Venice," Arban, Jean Baptiste/Ito: Miura, Toru

Variations on "Carnival of Venice," Arban, Jean Baptiste/Hunsberger: Mead, Steven

Variations on a Rocco Theme Op. 33, Tchaikovsky, Piotr/Rüedi: Rüedi, Thomas

Variations on Alouette, Binge, Ronald: Taylor, Brian

Variations on an Old Hymn Tune, Werle, Floyd: Tennessee Technological University Tuba-Euphonium Ensemble; United States Army Band Tuba-Euphonium Ensemble and Massed Ensemble

Variations on Annie Laurie, Heaton, Wilfred: Mead, Steven

Variations on Drink to Me Only, Traditional/Snell: Gagnaux, Alexandre; Mead, Steven; Flaten, Tormod

Variations, Owen, Jerry: Werden, David

Variations, Webber, Andrew Lloyd/Graham: Mead, Steven

Varied Mood, Woodfield, Ray: Lord, Stephen; Childs, Robert; Mead, Steven; Meli, Renato; Moore, David; Childs Brothers; Gagnaux, Alexandre; Childs, David

Ved Sjoen den morke, Op. 6, No. 2, Kjerulf, Halfdan: Olsrud, Sverre Stakston

Vendredi 13, Steckar, Marc: Steckar Tubapack

Venetian Carnival Animals, Corwell, Neal: Corwell, Neal

Very Special Love, A, Matteson, Rich: Matteson, Rich

Vi ravviso, o luoghi ameni, Bellini, Vincenzo/Bona: Mead, Steven

Victor Hugo, LaDuke, Lance: LaDuke, Lance

Vintage, Gillingham, David: Mead, Steven; Meixner, Brian; Behrend, Roger; Hokazono, Sho-ichiro

Visages, Puw, Guto Pryderi: Tuba Laté

Vissi d'arte from "Tosca," Puccini, Giacomo/Bona: Mead, Steven

Vissi d'arte from "Tosca," Puccini, Giacomo/Mead: Mead, Steven

Vittoria! Vittoria!, Carissmi: Campbell, Larry

Viva Voce!, Stevens, John: Sotto Voce Quartet

Vivace from Trio Sonata in c for Organ, Bach, Johann Sebastian: Albertasaurus Tuba Quartet

Vivid Colours, Richards, Goff: Araki, Tamao

Vocalise, Op. 34, No. 14, Rachmaninov, Sergei/Langford: Clough, John; Lundin, Anders; Griffiths, Morgan

Vocalise, Op. 34, No. 14, Rachmaninov, Sergei: Fukuda, Masanori; Craig, Mary Ann; Frey, Adam; Mead, Steven

Volunteer, The, Rogers, Walter: Brasch, Harold; Lehman, Arthur; Bowman, Brian

Von Himmel Hoch, Falconer, Leigh: Tubadours

Wabash Cannonball, Traditional/Garrett: British Tuba Quartet, The; Tennessee Technological University and Alumni Tuba-Euphonium Ensemble

Wait's Barbershop, Baker, David: Top Brass

Walkin', Carpenter, Richard/Esleck: Tennessee Technological University Tuba-Euphonium Ensemble

Walkin', Davis, Miles/Esleck: Tennessee Technological University Tuba-Euphonium Ensemble

Walther's Prize Song, Wagner, Richard/Bale: Mead, Steven

Waltz from "Die Fledermaus," Stauss, Johann/Berry: Tubadours

Waltz, Glorieux, F.: Ost, Nick

Waltz, Op. 64, No. 2, Chopin/Bale: Mead, Steven

Waltzing Matilda, Matteson, Rich; arr.: Matteson-Phillips Tubajazz Consort

Walzer Nr. 1, Turek, Thomas: Pfeifle, Nicolas

Washington Post March, Sousa, John Philip/Morris: Colonial Tuba Quartet, The

Washington Post March, Sousa, John Philip/Sabourin: Melton Tuba-Quartett; British Tuba Quartet, The

Washington Post March, Sousa, John Philip/Werden: Contraband

Washington Post March, Sousa, John Philip: Miraphone Tuba Quartet

Wassermusik, Unknown: Swiss Tuba Quartet

Wasteland, The, Corwell, Neal: Symphonia

Watching the Wheat, Gheel, Henry, arr.: Childs, Robert; McEnvoy, Graham; Schramm, Robert; Dunstan, John; Membury, Clive; Craddock, Ian

Wave of the Danube, Ivanovici, J./Konagaya: Tuba Laté

'Way 'Cross Georgia, Perkinson, Coleridge Taylor: Bargeron, Dave

Way-Out, but Not Too Far, McBride, Robert: Droste, Paul

Way We Are, The, Anonymous: Booth, Steven

Way We Were, The, Hamlisch/Barry: Rüedi, Thomas; Childs Brothers

Weaver of Dreams, A, Young, Victor; Elliot, Jack: Dickman, Marcus

Weber's Last Waltz Fantasie, Brasch, Harold: Brasch, Harold

Weber's Last Waltz, Rimmer, William: Mead, Steven; Withington, Len; Young, Ron

Wedding, The, Prieto, J./Siebert: Peters, Neil; Crossley, Peter; Withington, Len; Pickard, Norman

Wee Cooper of Fire, Traditional/Drover: Breuninger, Tyrone

We'll All Shout Hallelujah, Audoire, Norman: Hildreth, Gordon; Kane, Derick, Vanderweele, Aaron

Welsh Fantasy, Pearce: Kane, Derick

Wenn Friede mit Gott, Bliss, P.: Schmidli, Erich

West Side Story: Prologue, Bernstein, Leonard/Fettig: Tropman, Matt

Westminster Intrada, Forsyth, Kieran: British Tuba Quartet, The

We Three Kings, Traditional/Harclerode/Lycan: Tubadours

We Three Kings, Traditional: Tuba Christmas Ensemble

We Won't Go Home Until Morning (The Bear Went Over the Mountain), Anonymous/Clifton: Lehamn, Arthur

What Are You Doing with the Rest of Your Life?, Legrand, Michel/Drover: Gagnaux, Alexandre

What Wasp?, Wilson, Phil: Matteson, Rich

What's Her Name?, Wilson, Phil: Matteson, Rich

What's That?, Sun Ra: McKinney, Bernard

What's This?, Elfman/Robertson: Mead, Steven

When Tubas Waltz, Bartles, Alfred: Tennessee Technological University Tuba-Euphonium Ensemble; Rustic Bari-Tuba Ensemble; Tubadours; Contraband

When You Wish upon a Star, Harline, L./Kanai: Hokazono, Sho-ichiro; Mead, Steven

When You Wish upon a Star, Narita, Tamezo/Kanai: Mead, Steven

Where Are You, My Little Star?, Moussorgsky, Modeste: Murchinson, Matthew

Where E're You Walk, Handel, George Frederic/Greenwood: Shipp, Charles

Where Is Tomorrow?, Sun Ra: McKinney, Bernard

While Soft Winds Shake the Barley, Traditional/Buttery: Alchemy (previously Atlantic Tuba Quartet)

White Christmas, Vaughan, Rodger, arr.: Tubadours

Wiegenlied, Brahms, Johannes: Van Lier, Bart

William Tell Overture, Rossini, Gioacchino/Smalley: British Tuba Quartet, The

Willson Suite, Smith, Robert: Champions of the Leonard Falcone Festival 1986–2000; Behrend, Roger

Wind Quintet in A♭, Holst, Gustav: Mead, Steven

Window Opens Toward the Ocean, The, Senshu, Jiro: Ushigami, Ryuji

Winter Dream, Rüedi, Thomas: Williams, Glyn

Winter, Vivaldi, Antonio/Beaver: Tennessee Technological University Tuba-Euphonium Ensemble

With a Song in My Heart, Rodgers and Hart: Louder, Earle

With Verdure Clad from "The Creation," Haydn, Franz Josef: Smith, Henry Charles

Within/Without, Sobotta, Uli: Sobotta, Uli

Without a Song, Youmans, Vincent/Rose/Eliscu: Matteson, Rich

Wolf the Cat, Kleine Schaars, Peter: Dutch Tuba Quartet

Wolkenschatten fur Tubaquartett, Op. 136, Koetsier, Jan: Alchemy (previously Atlantic Tuba Quartet); Dutch Tuba Quartet

Woman Is a Sometime Thing, A, Gershwin, George: Top Brass

Woman's Intuition, A, Young and Washington: O'Hara, Betty

Won't You Come Home Bill Bailey, Garrett, James Allen, arr.: Tennessee Technological University Tuba-Euphonium Ensemble

Woodyn' You, Unknown: McKinney, Bernard

World Is Waiting for the Sunrise, The, Lockhart-Seitz/Butler: Tennessee Technological University Tuba-Euphonium Ensemble

Wot Shigona Dew, Wilson, Ted: Tennessee Technological University Tuba-Euphonium Ensemble

Y Luego, Hermann, Heinz: Scandinavian Tuba Jazz

Ye Banks and Braes, Traditional/Denton: Frey, Adam

Yesterday, Lennon, John; McCartney, Paul/Lucena: Baglin, Lyndon

Yesterday, Lennon, John; McCartney, Paul/Miyagawa: Tuba Laté

Yorkscher March, Unknown: Miraphone Tuba Quartet

Yorkshire Ballad, Barnes, James: Symphonia

You Made Me Love You, Manaco/Holcombe: British Tuba Quartet, The

You Raised Me Up, Lovland/Gates: Vanderweele, Aaron

You Stepped Out of a Dream, Brown, Nacio Herb: O'Hara, Betty

You Stepped Out of a Dream, Kahn, G./Jones: Matteson, Rich

Young Juliet, The, Prokofiev, Sergei/Fettig: Tropman, Matt

Your Tiny Hand Is Frozen, Puccini, Giacomo: McDonnell, Riki, and Mike Kilroy

Yusef, Unknown: McKinney, Bernard

Zeitvergleich, Sobotta, Uli: Sobotta, Uli

Zelda, Code, Percy: Fawbert, Andrew

Ziegunerweisen, Sarasate, Pablo de/Snell: Mead, Steven

Zugvogel, Sobotta, Uli: Sobotta, Uli

Zum Schuls das Ende, Sobotta, Uli: Sobotta, Uli

Euphonium Recordings by Composer

Aagaad-Nielsen, Torstein, *Lokk from the Green Island:* Murchinson, Matthew

Aagaard-Nilsen, Torstein, *Black Rain:* Olsrud, Sverre Stakston

Aagaard-Nilsen, Torstein, *Two Insects:* Flaten, Tormod

Adam, Adolphe/Anonymous, *Cantique de Noel:* McNally, Robert

Adam, *O Holy Night:* Childs, David

Adams, Stephen, *Holy City, The:* Bowman, Brian

Adams/Louder, *Bravura Variations:* Louder, Earle

Adler, Samuel, *Four Dialogs for Euphonium and Marimba:* Bowman, Brian; Yamamoto, Takashi; Murchinson, Matthew

Agrell, Jeffrey, *Gospel Tune:* Miraphone Tuba Quartet

Ahbez, Eden/Cherry, *Nature Boy:* Tennessee Technological University Tuba-Euphonium Ensemble

Alen, Hugo/Olsrud, *Herbmaiden's Dance:* Mead, Steven

Alexander, Lois; arr., *Swing Low, Sweet Chariot:* Dutch Tuba Quartet

Alfén, Hugo/Olsrud/Rydland, *Vallflickans Dans:* Flaten, Tormod

Alfén, Hugo/Olsrud, *Vallflickans Dans:* Tropman, Matt

Alfén, Hugo/R. Childs, *Dance of the Herdmaiden:* Childs, David

Amos, Keith, *Flander's Cauldron:* British Tuba Quartet, The

Anderson, Leroy/Ito, *Anderson's Toy-box:* Miura, Toru

Andresen, *And Soon It Will Be Blossom Time:* Mead, Steven

Anonymous, *Apple Strudel and Cheese:* Matteson, Rich

Anonymous, *As Long As He Needs Me:* Brunner, Stefan

Anonymous, *Best There Are, The:* Lehman, Arthur

Anonymous, *Black Jack Davie:* Top Brass

Anonymous, *Blue Bossa:* Matteson, Rich

Anonymous, *Broken Melody:* Booth, Steven

Anonymous, *Carnival Duet:* Booth, Steven

Anonymous, *Jinny Jinkins:* Top Brass

Anonymous, *Stella by Starlight:* Matteson, Rich

Anonymous, *To All the Girls I've Loved Before:* Brunner, Stefan

Anonymous, *Traveling Along:* Mallett, Chris

Anonymous, *Undecided:* Matteson, Rich

Anonymous, *Way We Are, The:* Booth, Steven

Anonymous/Baker, *Lute Dances:* British Tuba Quartet, The

Anonymous/Buttery, *Hijazker Longa:* Tropman, Matt

Anonymous/Clifton, *We Won't Go Home Until Morning (The Bear Went Over the Mountain):* Lehamn, Arthur

Arban, Jean Baptiste, *Caprice and Variations:* Baglin, Lyndon

Arban, Jean Baptiste, *Carnival of Venice, The:* Baglin, Lyndon; Moore, David; Lehman, Arthur; Mead, Steven

Arban, Jean Baptiste, *Characteristic Study No. 1:* Hokazono, Sho-ichiro

Arban, Jean Baptiste, *Fantasy Brilliante:* Moore, David; Booth, Steven; Heidler, Manfred; Hokazono, Sho-ichiro

Arban, Jean Baptiste/Brasch/Clarke/Craig/Straigers, *Carnival of Venice, The:* Craig, Mary Ann

Arban, Jean Baptiste/Brasch, *Carnival of Venice, The:* Brasch, Harold

Arban, Jean Baptiste/Briccialdi, *Carnival of Venice, The:* Pillaert, Stef

Arban, Jean Baptiste/Camerata/Catherall, *Carnival of Venice, The:* Childs, Robert

Arban, Jean Baptiste/Catherall, *Carnival of Venice, The:* Childs, David

Arban, Jean Baptiste/Catherall, *Carnival of Venice, The:* Childs, Robert

Arban, Jean Baptiste/Catherall, *Carnival of Venice, The:* Gagnaux, Alexandre

Arban, Jean Baptiste/D. Childs, *Carnival of Venice, The:* Childs, David

Arban, Jean Baptiste/Farr, *Carnival of Venice, The:* Childs Brothers

Arban, Jean Baptiste/G. Kingston, *Carnival of Venice, The:* Childs, David

Arban, Jean Baptiste/Howarth/Gurtner, *Amazing Mr. Arban, The:* Mead, Steven

Arban, Jean Baptiste/Hunsberger, *Carnival of Venice, The:* Hokazono, Sho-ichiro

Arban, Jean Baptiste/Hunsberger, *Variations on "Carnival of Venice":* Mead, Steven

Arban, Jean Baptiste/Ito, *Variations from "Carnival of Venice":* Miura, Toru

Arban, Jean Baptiste/LeClair, David, *Carnival of Venice, The:* Monarch Tuba-Euphonium Quartet

Arban, Jean Baptiste/LeClair, *Carnival of Venice, The:* Contraband

Arban, Jean Baptiste/Leidzen, *Fantasia, Theme and Variations on Carnival of Venice:* Fisher, Mark

Arban, Jean Baptiste/Mallet, *Carnival of Venice, The:* Mallett, Chris

Arban, Jean Baptiste/Manning/Remmington, *Carnival of Venice, The:* Griffiths, Morgan

Arban, Jean Baptiste/Remington, *Carnival of Venice, The:* Clough, John; Groom, Trevor; Kane, Derick; Parry, Glynn; Warrington, Brian; Mead, Steven

Arcadelt, Jacob, *Credo:* Campbell, Larry

Arcadelt, Jacob, *Gloria:* Campbell, Larry

Arcadio, Bernard/Steckar, Marc, *Forêt Vierge:* Steckar Tubapack

Arcadio, Bernard, *Felinesquement:* Steckar, Marc

Arcadio, Bernard, *Leleo:* Steckar, Marc

Arcadio, Bernard, *Splash:* Steckar, Marc

Ares, Rob, *Memory:* Postma, Simon

Arlen, Harold, *One for My Body:* O'Hara, Betty

Arlen, Harold, *Out of This World:* O'Hara, Betty

Arlen, Harold, *Over the Rainbow:* Top Brass

Arlen, Harold, *A Sleeping Bee:* O'Hara, Betty

Arlen, Harold, *That Old Black Magic:* Tennessee Technological University Alumni Tuba-Euphonium Ensemble

Arlen, Harold/Fritze, *Over the Rainbow:* Colonial Tuba Quartet, The

Audoire, Norman, *We'll All Shout Hallelujah:* Hildreth, Gordon; Kane, Derick, Vanderweele, Aaron

Bach, Jan, *Concert Variations:* Murchinson, Matthew; Fisher, Mark

Bach, Johann Sebastian, *Bourree I and II from "Suite III for Cello":* Falcone, Leonard

Bach, Johann Sebastian, *Contrapunctus 9 from "Die Kunst der Fuge":* Sotto Voce Quartet

Bach, Johann Sebastian, *Courante from "Suite No. 4":* Champions of the Leonard Falcone Festival 1986–2000

Bach, Johann Sebastian, *Fugue in g Minor:* Gerhard Meinl's Tuba Sextet

Bach, Johann Sebastian, *Partita in a Minor:* Thompson, Kevin

Bach, Johann Sebastian, *Partita No. 2 in d Minor:* Thompson, Kevin

Bach, Johann Sebastian, *Sonata for Flute in Bb Major:* Fisher, Mark, Hokazono; Sho-ichiro

Bach, Johann Sebastian, *Suite No. 5 in c Minor:* Thompson, Kevin

Bach, Johann Sebastian, *Suite No. 1 in G Major:* Thompson, Kevin

Bach, Johann Sebastian, *Sonata No. 3 in sol minore:* Colliard, Corrado

Bach, Johann Sebastian, *Vivace from Trio Sonata in c for Organ:* Albertasaurus Tuba Quartet

Bach, Johann Sebastian/Arcadelt/Self, *Ave Maria:* Melton Tuba-Quartett

Bach, Johann Sebastian/Barnes, *Prelude and Fugue in d Minor:* Symphonia

Bach, Johann Sebastian/Beckman, *St. Anne's Fugue:* United States Army Band Tuba-Euphonium Ensemble and Massed Ensemble; Tennessee Technological University Tuba-Euphonium Ensemble

Bach, Johann Sebastian/Berry, *Fugue in g Minor:* Tubadours

Bach, Johann Sebastian/D. Childs, *Air from "Suite No. 3 in D":* Childs, David

Bach, Johann Sebastian/Denton, *Arioso:* Frey, Adam

Bach, Johann Sebastian/Falcone, *Two Pieces:* Behrend, Roger

Bach, Johann Sebastian/Flaten, *Suite No. 4 in Eb Major:* Flaten, Tormod

Bach, Johann Sebastian/Foote, *Air from "Suite No. 3 in D":* Bowman, Brian

Bach, Johann Sebastian/Garrett, *Passacaglia and Fugue in c Minor:* Symphonia

Bach, Johann Sebastian/Gounod/Denny, *Ave Maria:* McDonnell, Riki, and Mike Kilroy

Bach, Johann Sebastian/Gounod/Denton, *Ave Maria:* Frey, Adam

Bach, Johann Sebastian/Gounod/Falcone, *Ave Maria:* Falcone, Leonard

Bach, Johann Sebastian/Gounod/Porret, *Ave Maria:* Gagnaux, Alexandre

Bach, Johann Sebastian/Gounod, *Ave Maria:* Childs, David

Bach, Johann Sebastian/Gray, *Fugue from "Fantasia and Fugue in g Minor":* British Tuba Quartet, The

Bach, Johann Sebastian/Hermann, *Badinerie:* Melton Tuba-Quartett

Bach, Johann Sebastian/Howard, *Rondo:* British Tuba Quartet, The

Belcke, Friedrich August, *Etüde Nr. 5:* Heidler, Manfred

Belcke, Friedrich August, *Etüde Nr. 7:* Heidler, Manfred

Bellini, Vincenzo/Adolphe, *La Sonnambula:* Cranson, Colin

Bellini, Vincenzo/Bona, *Ah, non credea mirarti:* Mead, Steven

Bellini, Vincenzo/Bona, *Ah, non giunge from "La Sonnambula":* Mead, Steven

Bellini, Vincenzo/Bona, *Vaga luna che inargenti:* Mead, Steven

Bellini, Vincenzo/Bona, *Vi ravviso, o luoghi ameni:* Mead, Steven

Bellson, Louie, *Hawk Talks, The:* Matteson, Rich

Bellstedt, Herman, *Betty Lee:* Colburn, Michael

Bellstedt, Herman, *La Coquette:* Brasch, Harold

Bellstedt, Herman, *La Manodoinata:* Brasch, Harold; Lehamn, Arthur; Lake Highlands Euphonium Section

Bellstedt, Herman, *Napoli:* Falcone, Leonard; Bowman, Brian; Storey, John; Araki, Tamao; Dodd, Michael; Euphoniums of University of Illinios; Miura, Toru; Behrend, Roger

Bellstedt, Herman/Bale, *Napoli Variations:* Mead, Steven

Bellstedt, Herman/Brand, *Napoli:* Mead, Steven

Bellstedt, Herman/Childs, *Napoli:* Childs, Robert

Bellstedt, Herman/Owenson, *Napoli:* Craddock, Ian

Bellstedt, Herman/Simon, *Napoli Variations:* Bowman, Brian

Benedetto, Marcello, *Largo from "Sonata, Op. 4, No. 2":* Royall, Dennis

Bennard, *Old Rugged Cross, The:* Childs, David

Bennett, *Rutland Water:* Crompton, Carole

Bergh, Sverre, *Introduction, Theme and Variations:* Bogetvedt, Bjorn

Berlin, Irving/Gout, *Puttin' on the Ritz:* British Tuba Quartet, The

Berlin, Irving/Windfeld, *How Deep Is the Ocean:* Scandinavian Tuba Jazz

Berlioz, Hector/Fiegel, *Dream of a Witches Sabbath from "Symphonie Fantastique":* Symphonia

Berlioz, Hector/Werden, *Hungarian March:* Dutch Tuba Quartet

Berlioz, Hector, *March to the Scaffold:* British Tuba Quartet, The

Bernie, Pinkard, and Casey/Garrett, *Sweet Georgia Brown:* Tennessee Technological University Tuba-Euphonium Ensemble

Bernie, Pinkard; and Casey/Fragomeni, *Sweet Georgia Brown:* Colonial Tuba Quartet, The

Bernstein, Leonard, *Medley from "On the Town":* O'Hara, Betty

Bernstein, Leonard/Adams, *Somewhere:* McDonnell, Riki, and Mike Kilroy

Bernstein, Leonard/Fettig, *Cha-cha:* Tropman, Matt

Bernstein, Leonard/Fettig, *Cool-Fugue:* Tropman, Matt

Bernstein, Leonard/Fettig, *Finale:* Tropman, Matt

Bernstein, Leonard/Fettig, *I Have a Love:* Tropman, Matt

Bernstein, Leonard/Fettig, *Mambo:* Tropman, Matt

Bernstein, Leonard/Fettig, *Maria:* Tropman, Matt

Bernstein, Leonard/Fettig, *One Hand, One Heart:* Tropman, Matt

Bernstein, Leonard/Fettig, *Scherzo:* Tropman, Matt

Bernstein, Leonard/Fettig, *Somewhere:* Tropman, Matt

Bernstein, Leonard/Fettig, *Tonight:* Tropman, Matt

Bernstein, Leonard/Fettig, *West Side Story: Prologue:* Tropman, Matt

Best, Denzil/Buttery, *Move:* Atlantic Tuba Quartet, The

Bewley, Norlan, *Santa Wants a Tuba for Christmas:* TubaShop Quartet

Bewley, Norlan, arr., *Bring a Torch, Jeanette, Isabella:* TubaShop Quartet

Bewley, Norlan, arr., *Carol of the Bells:* TubaShop Quartet

Bewley, Norlan, arr., *Fum, Fum, Fum:* TubaShop Quartet

Bewley, Norlan, arr., *Good Christian Men Rejoice:* TubaShop Quartet

Bewley, Norlan, arr., *Octubafest Medley:* TubaCompany of Harvey Phillips

Bewley, Norlan, arr., *Pat-A-Pan:* TubaShop Quartet

Bewley, Norlan, arr., *TubaChristmas Suite:* TubaShop Quartet

Bewley, Norlan, arr., *Tubafiesta Medley:* TubaCompany of Harvey Phillips

Bewley, Norlan, arr., *Tubarock Medley:* TubaCompany of Harvey Phillips

Bewley, Norlan, arr., *Tubaswing Medley:* TubaCompany of Harvey Phillips

Bimboni/Veit, *Concerto Brillante on "Carnival of Venice":* Mead, Steven

Binge, Ronald, *Variations on Alouette:* Taylor, Brian

Bitsch, Marcel, *Intermezzo:* Verweij, Hugo

Bizet, George, *Agnus Dei:* Bowman, Brian

Bizet, George, *Flower Song from "Carmen":* McDonnell, Riki, and Mike Kilroy; Louder, Earle; Childs, Nicholas; Euphonium Section, The

Bizet, George/Bale, *Gypsy Dance from "Carmen":* Mead, Steven

Bizet, George/Harding, *Flower Song from "Carmen":* Falcone, Leonard; Mead, Steven; Behrend, Roger

Bizet, George/Norbury, *Menuet:* Kane, Derick

Bizet, George/Wilkinson, *Deep inside the Sacred Temple:* McDonnell, Riki, and Mike Kilroy; Moss, John; Conway, Sean; Childs Brothers

Bizet, George/Wilkinson, *Duet from "Pearlfishers"*: Andrews, Paul; Kilroy, Mike; Childs, David

Bliss, P., *Wenn Friede mit Gott*: Schmidli, Erich

Blyth, *Compelled by Love*: Kane, Derick

Boccalari, Ed/Kent-Akers, *Fantasia di Concerto*: Bowman, Brian; Hokazono, Sho-ichiro; Miura, Toru; Yamamoto, Takashi; Mueller, John; Mead, Steven; Olsrud, Sverre Stakston

Boccalari, Ed/Meredith, *Fantasia di Concerto*: Mead, Steven

Boda, John, *Sonatina for Euphonium and Synthesizer*: Bowman, Brian; Taylor, Robin

Böhme, Oskar/Smith, *Russian Dance*: Mead, Steven; Gagnaux, Alexandre

Bolling, C., *Rag-Polka from "Toot Suite"*: Hokazono, Sho-ichiro

Bolognesi, Jacques, *Maria alm*: Steckar Tubapack

Boon, Brindley, *A Starry Crown*: Schramm, Robert

Boone, Daniel, *Three Moods*: Tennessee Technological University and Alumni Tuba-Euphonium Ensemble; University of Miami Tuba Ensemble

Bosanko, Ivor, *Glorious Liberation*: Mallett, Chris

Bosanko, Ivor, *Heart in Heart*: Mead, Steven; Hokazono, Sho-ichiro

Bosanko, Ivor, *My Unchanging Friend*: Kane, Derick

Bosanko, Ivor, *To Live Right*: Kane, Derick

Botschinsky, Allan, *Alster Promenade*: Van Lier, Bart

Botschinsky, Allan, *Chops a la Salsa*: Van Lier, Bart

Botschinsky, Allan, *Don't Shoot the Banjo Player ("Cause We've Done It Already)*: Van Lier, Bart

Botschinsky, Allan, *Interlude No. 4*: Van Lier, Bart

Botschinsky, Allan, *Kubismus 502*: Van Lier, Bart

Botschinsky, Allan, *Lady in Blue, The*: Van Lier, Bart

Botschinsky, Allan, *Love Waltz*: Van Lier, Bart

Botschinsky, Allan, *October Sunshine*: Van Lier, Bart

Botschinsky, Allan, *Toot Your Roots*: Van Lier, Bart

Bourgeois, Derek, *Allegro from "Concerto, Op. 114"*: Champions of the Leonard Falcone Festival 1986–2000

Bourgeois, Derek, *Concerto, Op. 114*: Hunter, Angie; Mead, Steven

Bourgeois, Derek, *Euphoria*: Hokazono, Sho-ichiro; Ushigami, Ryuji; Mead, Steven; Champions of the Leonard Falcone Festival 1986–2000; Murchinson, Matthew

Bousted, Donald, *Tears*: Tuba Laté

Boutry, Roger, *Tubacchanale*: Verweij, Hugo

Bowen, Brian, *Euphonium Music*: Childs Brothers; Taylor, Robin; Mead, Steven

Bowes, Ray, *Song of Triumph*: Himes, William; Brown, William

Bozza, Eugene/van der Woude, *Aria*: Mead, Steven; Hokazono, Sho-ichiro

Bozza, Eugene, *Allegro et Finale*: Young, Ron

Bozza, Eugene, *New Orleans*: Verweij, Hugo

Braham, P./Furber, *Limehouse Blues*: Matteson, Rich

Brahams, Johann/Gotoh, *Es ist Eine Rose Entsprungen*: Mead, Steven

Brahe, May, *Bless This House*: McDonnell, Riki, and Mike Kilroy; Brasch, Harold; Bowman, Brian; Childs, David

Brahms, Johannes/Reynolds, *Hornsongs*: Fisher, Mark

Brahms, Johannes/Ruffles, *Lullaby*: Lowry, Benny

Brahms, Johannes, *Wiegenlied*: Van Lier, Bart

Brandt, *Concerto No. 1*: McDonnell, Riki, and Mike Kilroy

Brasch, Harold, *Five Octave Stunt, The*: Lehman, Arthur

Brasch, Harold, *Weber's Last Waltz Fantasie*: Brasch, Harold

Bridge, Frank, *Meditation*: Rüedi, Thomas

Brodsky, Nicholas/Farr, *Be My Love*: Childs Brothers; Griffiths, Morgan; McDonnell, Riki, and Mike Kilroy

Brown, Clifford/Perry, *Sandu*: Modern Jazz Tuba Project; Tennessee Technological University Alumni Tuba-Euphonium Ensemble

Brown, Clifford/Wilkinson, *Daahoud*: Dutch Tuba Quartet

Brown, David/Williamson, *Theme for Malcolm*: Modern Jazz Tuba Project

Brown, Nacio Herb/Sample, *Two Tunes (You Stepped Out of a Dream; Temptation)*: Tennessee Technological University Tuba-Euphonium Ensemble

Brown, Nacio Herb, *You Stepped Out of a Dream*: O'Hara, Betty

Brown, Norman, arr., *Catari*: Fawbert, Andrew

Brown/Fain, *Love Is Never Out of Season*: Mancuso, Gus

Brubaker, Jerry, *Rhapsody for Euphonium and Piano*: Behrend, Roger

Brubeck, Dave/Esleck/Murphy, *Blue Rondo a la Turk*: Modern Jazz Tuba Project; Tennessee Technological University Tuba-Euphonium Ensemble; Top Brass

Bruch/Gay, *Kol Nidrei*: Mead, Steven

Bruckner/Sabourin, *Locus Iste*: Dutch Tuba Quartet

Brusick, William, *By the Waters of Babylon*: Euphoniums Unlimited

Brusick, William, *For the Kings of Brass*: Tennessee Technological University and Alumni Tuba-Euphonium Ensemble

Brustad, Karsten, *Initiation*: Taylor, Robin

Bryce, Frank, *Rondoletto for Two Euphoniums*: Groom, Trevor; Childs Brothers; Clough, John; Matti, Jean-Claude; Moss, John

Bull, John/Howard, *King's Hunt, The*: British Tuba Quartet, The

Bulla, Stephen, *Air'N Variations*: Vanderweele, Aaron

Bulla, Stephen, *Celestial Suite:* British Tuba Quartet, The

Bulla, Stephen, *Euphonium Fantasia:* Church, David; Gosney, Richard; Griffiths, Morgan

Bulla, Stephen, *Quartet for Low Brass:* United States Navy Band Tuba-Euphonium Quartet; British Tuba Quartet, The

Butterworth, Arthur, *Partita for Euphonium and Piano, Op. 89:* Olsrud, Sverre Stakston; Mead, Steven

Butterworth, Arthur, *Sinfonia Concertante, Op. 111 for Tenor Horn and Baritone:* Blackburn, Robert

Buttery, Gary, arr., *An English Folk Christmas:* United States Coast Guard Tuba-Euphonium Quartet

Buttery, Gary, *Fanfare for the Millennium:* Alchemy (previously Atlantic Tuba Quartet)

Buttery, Gary, *Fantasia of Eastern European Village Dances:* Alchemy (previously Atlantic Tuba Quartet)

Buttery, Gary; arr., *An English Folk Christmas:* Coast Guard Tuba-Euphonium Quartet

Butts, Carrol M., *Ode for Low Brass:* Garden State Tuba Ensemble

Byrd, William/Winter, *John, Come Kiss Me Now:* Atlantic Tuba Quartet, The; British Tuba Quartet, The

Byrd, William, *Agnus Dei:* University of Michigan Tuba and Euphonium Ensemble

Cahn/Brodszky, *How Do You Like Your Eggs in the Morning?:* Mancuso, Gus

Camphouse, Mark, *Ceremonial Sketch:* Tennessee Technological University Tuba-Euphonium Ensemble; United States Army Band Tuba-Euphonium Ensemble and Massed Ensemble

Camsey, Terry, *A Joy Untold:* Kane, Derick; Mack, Thomas; Mallett, Chris, Vanderweele, Aaron

Camsey, Terry, *Promises:* Vanderweele, Aaron

Canter, James, *Appalachian Carol:* Tennessee Technological University and Alumni Tuba-Euphonium Ensemble; United States Army Band Tuba-Euphonium Ensemble and Massed Ensemble

Canter, James, *Siamang Suite:* Tennessee Technological University and Alumni Tuba-Euphonium Ensemble

Canter, James, *Twelve Days of Housetops:* Tennessee Technological University Tuba-Euphonium Ensemble

Capuzzi, Antonio/R. Childs, *Andante and Rondo from "Doublebass Concerto":* Childs, Robert

Capuzzi, Antonio, *Andante and Rondo from "Doublebass Concerto":* Bowman, Brian; Breuninger, Tyrone; Yamamoto, Takashi; Fukuda, Masanori; Craig, Mary Ann

Caratini, Patrice, *Demain il fera jour:* Steckar Tubapack

Caravelli/Fernie, *Let Me Try Again:* Rüedi, Thomas

Cardillo/Stephens, *Catari, Catari:* Childs Brothers; McDonnell, Riki, and Mike Kilroy

Carissmi, *Vittoria! Vittoria!:* Campbell, Larry

Carmichael, Hoagy/LeClair, *Georgia on My Mind:* Contraband

Carmichael, Hoagy/Matteson, *Georgia on My Mind:* Matteson, Rich; Matteson-Phillips Tubajazz Consort; Modern Jazz Tuba Project

Carmichael, Hoagy/Matteson, *Skylark:* Modern Jazz Tuba Project; O'Hara, Betty

Carmichael, Hoagy, *Stardust:* O'Hara, Betty; Hokazono, Sho-ichiro

Carpenter, Richard/Esleck, *Walkin':* Tennessee Technological University Tuba-Euphonium Ensemble

Carroll/Siegal, *Love Is a Simple Thing:* Mancuso, Gus

Carroll/Siegal, *Monotonous:* Mancuso, Gus

Cassadó, Gaspar/Rüedi, *Danse du Diable vert:* Rüedi, Thomas

Castéréde, Jacques, *Fantaisie Concertante:* Mead, Steven; Hokazono, Sho-ichiro; Droste, Paul

Catelinet, Philip, *Call of the Seasons:* McDonnell, Riki, and Mike Kilroy; Mountain, Wilfrid; Mead, Steven, Vanderweele, Aaron

Catelinet, Philip, arr., *Twinkle, Twinkle Little Star:* Vernon, Ken

Catherall, Alan; arr., *Elfriede:* Childs Brothers

Catherall, Alan; arr., *Only Love:* Childs Brothers

Catherall, Alan; arr., *Song of the Seashore:* Childs Brothers

Catherwood, David, *All I Have I Am Bringing to Thee:* Vanderweele, Aaron

Catherwood, David, *Annie Laurie:* Kane, Derick

Catherwood, David, *Everybody Should Know:* Kane, Derick

Catherwood, David, *Spirit of Life:* Kane, Derick

Cay-Lennart, *Gotlandsk Sommarnatt:* Cay-Lennart

Cay-Lennart, *Joshua Fought the Battle of Jeriko:* Cay-Lennart

Chaplin, Charlie, *Smile:* Top Brass

Charlton, Frederick, *First Noel, The:* Tubadours

Charlton, Philip, *March-Overture:* Tubadours

Chaulk, David, *Variants on St. Francis:* Church, David

Cheetham, John, *Consortium:* Tennessee Technological University Tuba-Euphonium Ensemble; United States Armed Forces Tuba-Euphonium Ensemble; British Tuba Quartet, The

Cherry, Bill, *Musings:* Tennessee Technological University Tuba-Euphonium Ensemble

Chester, Barry, *Arabella:* Wilkinson, Harry; Davis, George

Childs Nicholas; arr., *Parade of the Tin Soldiers:* Childs Brothers

Chopin, Frédéric, *Minute Waltz:* Albertasaurus Tuba Quartet

Chopin, Frédéric, *Prelude:* Narita, Yuko

Chopin, Frédéric /Bale, *Waltz, Op. 64, No. 2:* Mead, Steven

Chopin, Frédéric/Mead, *Minute Waltz:* British Tuba Quartet, The

Clarke, Herbert L./Brandenburg, *Carnival of Venice, The:* Boyd, Frederick

Clarke, Herbert L./LeClair, *Cousins:* Contraband

Clarke, Herbert L./Manning/Brasch, *Carnival of Venice, The:* Brasch, Harold

Clarke, Herbert L., *Bride of the Waves, The:* Bowman, Brian; Werden, David

Clarke, Herbert L., *Carnival of Venice, The:* Bowman, Brian; Werden, David; Wood, Ken; Louder, Earle; Fukuda, Masanori; Euphonium Quartet

Clarke, Herbert L., *Debutante, The:* Booth, Steven; Swallow, John

Clarke, Herbert L., *From the Shores of the Mighty Pacific:* Falcone, Leonard; Mead, Steven; Boyd, Frederick

Clarke, Herbert L., *Side Partners:* Swallow, John

Clarke, Nigel, *City in the Sea:* Childs, Robert; Childs, David

Clayton, Norman/Broughton, *Now I Belong to Jesus:* Himes, William

Clinard, Fred, *Diversion for Seven Bass Clef Instruments:* Tennessee Technological University and Alumni Tuba-Euphonium Ensemble

Code, Percy, *Zelda:* Fawbert, Andrew

Cohn, Al, *Travissimo:* Matteson, Rich

Collins, Judy/Buttery, *Since You've Asked:* Atlantic Tuba Quartet, The

Coltrane, John, *Mr. P.C.:* Dickman, Marcus

Combelle, F., *Premier Solo de Concert:* Falcone, Leonard

Cooder, Ry, *Train to Florida:* Marsteller, Loren

Cools, Eugene, *Allegro De Concert:* Falcone, Leonard

Corbett, Stephen, arr., *Solitaire:* Johnston, Leon; Dale, Kevin

Cords, Gustav/Frabrizio, *Romanze:* Behrend, Roger

Cords, Gustav, *Concert Fantasie:* Behrend, Roger; Dart, Fred

Cords, Gustav, *Romanze:* Young, Raymond G.

Correa, Chick/Arnold, *La Fiesta:* Tennessee Technological University Tuba-Euphonium Ensemble

Correa, Chick/Arnold, *Spain:* Tennessee Technological University Tuba-Euphonium Ensemble

Corwell, Neal, *2:00:00:* Corwell, Neal

Corwell, Neal, *Arctic Dream:* Corwell, Neal

Corwell, Neal, *At the Far Side of the Pasture:* Corwell, Neal

Corwell, Neal, *Black Moon Rising:* Corwell, Neal

Corwell, Neal, *Bumble Bee:* Corwell, Neal

Corwell, Neal, *Dandy Noodles:* Corwell, Neal

Corwell, Neal, *Distant Images:* Corwell, Neal

Corwell, Neal, *Furies, The:* Corwell, Neal; Symphonia

Corwell, Neal, *Heart of a Wolf:* Corwell, Neal

Corwell, Neal, *Hungarian Hallucination:* Corwell, Neal

Corwell, Neal, *In the Cathedral:* Euphoniums Unlimited

Corwell, Neal, *Meditation:* Corwell, Neal

Corwell, Neal, *New England Reveries:* Corwell, Neal

Corwell, Neal, *Night Song:* Corwell, Neal

Corwell, Neal, *Odyssey:* Corwell, Neal; Champions of the Leonard Falcone Festival 1986–2000; Taylor, Robin

Corwell, Neal, *Ritual:* Corwell, Neal

Corwell, Neal, *Scherzo:* Corwell, Neal

Corwell, Neal, *Simyeh:* Corwell, Neal; Taylor, Robin

Corwell, Neal, *Venetian Carnival Animals:* Corwell, Neal

Corwell, Neal, *Wasteland, The:* Symphonia

Corwell, Neal, arr., *Lassus Trombone:* Corwell, Neal

Cosma, Vladimir/Fletcher, *Giocoso from "Euphonium Concerto":* Tennessee Technological University Tuba-Euphonium Ensemble

Cosma, Vladimir/Meredith, *Euphonium Concerto:* Mead, Steven

Cosma, Vladimir, *Euphonium Concerto:* Mead, Steven; Milhiet, Ivan; Frey, Adam; Gagnaux, Alexandre; Champions of the Leonard Falcone Festival 1986–2000

Couperin, François, *Les Baricades Misterieuses:* Gerhard Meinl's Tuba Sextet

Crespo, Enrique, *Bruckner Etude:* Gerhard Meinl's Tuba Sextet

Crespo, Enrique, *Three Milongas:* Gerhard Meinl's Tuba Sextet

Croft, *Duet for Tenor Tuba and Bass Tuba:* Garden State Tuba Ensemble

Crump, Peter, *March of the Hare, The:* Tuba Laté

Cugny, Laurent, *Molloy:* Steckar Elephant Tuba Horde

Cummings, Barton, *In Darkness Dreaming:* Colonial Tuba Quartet, The

Cummings, Barton, *Spring Suite:* Craig, Mary Ann

Curnow, James, *Concerto for Euphonium and Band:* Mead, Steven

Curnow, James, *Rhapsody for Euphonium:* Albiez, Cédric; Mead, Steven; Anonymous; Grainger, Andre; Welsh, David; Zuback, Joseph; Childs Brothers; Behrend, Roger; Breuninger, Tyrone

Curnow, James, *Symphonic Variants for Euphonium and Band:* Bowman, Brian; Behrend, Roger; Craig, Mary Ann; Denys, Marnik; Franke, Philip; Mead, Steven; Gagnaux, Alexandre; Hunter, Angie; Hokazono, Sho-ichiro

Curnow, James/Bryant, *Symphonic Variants for Euphonium and Brass:* Taylor, Robin

Curtis, De/Roberts, *Return to Sorrento:* Mead, Steven

Danner, Gregory/Vaden, *Scherzo:* Tennessee Technological University Tuba-Euphonium Ensemble

Danner, Gregory, *Beast!:* Tennessee Technological University Tuba-Euphonium Ensemble

Danner, Gregory, *Runnin' with Bydlo:* Euphoniums Unlimited

Danzi, *Concerto in F Major:* Chevailler, Jean-Pierre

Daugherty, Michael, *Timbuktuba:* Symphonia

Davidson, Matthew, *Move:* Tuba Laté

Davies, Howard/Catherwood, *Search for a New World:* Mallett, Chris

Davis, Akst/Woo, *Baby Face:* University of Miami Tuba Ensemble

Davis, Michael, *Family Tree:* Hokazono, Sho-ichiro

Davis, Miles/Esleck, *Walkin':* Tennessee Technological University Tuba-Euphonium Ensemble

Davis, Miles/Perry, *So What:* Tennessee Technological University Tuba-Euphonium Ensemble

Davis, Miles, *All Blues:* Scandinavian Tuba Jazz

Davis, Trevor, *Shepherd Song:* Griffiths, Morgan

Davis, William Mac, *Rondo Concertante:* Mueller, John

Debussy, Claude, *Dream:* Narita, Yuko

Debussy, Claude, *Golliwogg's Cakewalk:* Dutch Tuba Quartet

Debussy, Claude, *La Fille aux Cheveux de lin:* Rustic Bari-Tuba Ensemble

Debussy, Claude, *My Reverie:* Hokazono, Sho-ichiro

Debussy, Claude/Bale, *Clair de Lune:* Mead, Steven

Debussy, Claude/Bale, *Girl with the Flaxen Hair, The:* Mead, Steven

Debussy, Claude/Bale, *Golliwogg's Cakewalk:* Mead, Steven

Dede, Edmond, *Mephisto Masque:* Schwarz, Gerard

Delibes, Léo, *Flower Duet from "Lakme":* McDonnell, Riki, and Mike Kilroy; British Tuba Quartet, The; Frey, Adam

DeLuca, Joseph, *Beautiful Colorado:* Louder, Earle; Reifsnyder, Robert; Falcone, Leonard; Lehamn, Arthur; Mueller, John

DeLuca, Joseph/Boddington, *Beautiful Colorado:* Groom, Trevor; Lean, David

DeLuca, Joseph/Hazes, *Thoughts of Gold:* Colburn, Michael

DeLuca, Joseph/Roberts, *Beautiful Colorado:* Mead, Steven; Childs, Robert

Dempsey, Raymond, *Now Here This!:* Monarch Tuba-Euphonium Quartet; British Tuba Quartet, The

Dempsey, Raymond, *Quatre Chansons:* Melton Tuba-Quartett; British Tuba Quartet, The; Monarch Tuba-Euphonium Quartet

Denson, Frank, *Three Folksongs for Four Brass:* Gerhard Meinl's Tuba Sextet

Denver, John/Fraser, *Perhaps Love:* Childs Brothers; Haemhouts, Ben

Desmond, Paul/Luis, *Take Five:* Melton Tuba-Quartett, Mead, Steven

DeVita, Alfred/Catherall, *Softly As I Leave You:* Childs Brothers; Childs, Nicholas; Childs, David; Wilkins, Richard; Schultz, Karl

Dewhurst, Robin, *Panache:* Burghgraef, Frans Aert; Meixner, Brian; Mead, Steven

Di Lasso, Orlando, *Oia, O che bon Eccho!:* Gerhard Meinl's Tuba Sextet

Di Lasso/Robinson, *Mon Coeur Se Recommende a Vous:* British Tuba Quartet, The

DiCapua, *O, Sole Mio:* Falcone, Leonard

Dickman, Marcus, *Bee-Bo:* Dickman, Marcus

Dickman, Marcus, *Patrice Elaine:* Dickman, Marcus

Diero/Ferguson, *Il Ritorno:* British Tuba Quartet, The

DiGiovanni, Rocco, *Tuba Magic:* Tennessee Technological University Tuba-Euphonium Ensemble; United States Army Band Tuba-Euphonium Ensemble and Massed Ensemble

Dinicu-Heifitz, *Hora Staccato:* Mead, Steven

Dinicu-Heifitz/Gates, *Hora Staccato:* Vanderweele, Aaron

Dodson, John, *Out of the Depths:* Tennessee Technological University Tuba-Euphonium Ensemble

Doe, Phillip, *Lullaby:* Mackie, Kevin

Donaldson, W./Self, *Carolina in the Morning:* University of Miami Tuba Ensemble

Donizetti, Gaetano/Harvey, *Una Furtiva Lacrima:* Falcone, Leonard

Donizetti, Gaetano, *Duet from "Don Pasquale":* McDonnell, Riki, and Mike Kilroy

Donizetti, Gaetano, *Lucia Di Lammermoor:* Louder, Earle

Dorsey, Tommy/Madeira, *I'm Glad There Is You:* Mancuso, Gus

Doss, Thomas, *Sir "EU":* Mead, Steven

Dougherty, William, *Duo for Euphonium and Marimba:* Colliard, Corrado

Dougherty, William, *Meditation and Celebration:* Droste, Paul

Doughty, George, *Grandfather's Clock:* Baglin, Lyndon; Clough, John; Cunliffe, Stuart; Entwistle, Heather; Haemhouts, Ben; Mead, Steven; Morgan, Gareth; Willis, Simon; Woollam, David; Wood, Ken; Childs, David

Doughty, George, *Scherzo for Four:* Hawkey, Vivian

Doughty, George, arr., *Old Rustic Bridge, The:* Archer, Stephen

Dräxelmeier, Xaver, *Konzertstück für Tenorhorn:* Heidler, Manfred

Dreyer/Jolson/Rydland, *Me and My Shadow:* Flaten, Tormond

Drigo, Riccardo/Oughton, *Serenade from "Millions D'Arlequin":* Shepherd, Ken

Drigo, Riccardo/Stephens, *Serenade from "Millions D'Arlequin":* Mead, Steven

Drigo, Riccardo/Wright, *Serenade from "Millions D'Arlequin":* Childs, Robert; Clough, John

Drigo, Riccardo, *Serenade from "Millions D'Arlequin":* Griffiths, Morgan; Haemhouts, Ben

Dubin and Warren/Minard, *42nd Street:* British Tuba Quartet, The

Dukas/Bale, *Sorcerer's Apprentice, The:* Mead, Steven

Duncan/Ball/McIntryre/Gorrie/Stuart/McIntosh/Murphy, *Pick Up the Pieces:* Modern Jazz Tuba Project

Duruflé, Maurice; Renwick, Wilke/Wilson, *Ubi Caritas/Dance:* Symphonia

Dvorak, Antonin/Butler, *Slavonic Dances, Op. 46, No. 1:* Tennessee Technological University Tuba-Euphonium Ensemble

Dvorak, Antonin/Pfeifle, *Romantische Stucke, Op. 7:* Pfeifle, Nicolas

Edgar, M./Powell, *Three Ha'Pence a Foot:* Tuba Laté

Elfman/Harris, *The Simpsons:* Mead Steven

Elfman/Robertson, *What's This?:* Mead Steven

Elgar, Edward/Bourgeois, *Adagio and Allegro from "Cello Concerto":* Childs, Robert

Elgar, Edward/Bourgeois, *Lento from "Cello Concerto":* Mead, Steven

Elgar, Edward/Wilson, *Romance Op. 62:* Mead, Steven; Verweij, Hugo

Elgar, Edward/Wilson, *Salut d'amour:* Childs Brothers

Ellerby, Martin, *Euphonium Concerto:* Frey, Adam; Mead, Steven; Meixner, Brian

Ellington/Paul, *Come Sunday:* Mead, Steven

Ellington, Duke, *All Too Soon:* O'Hara, Betty

Ellington, Duke, *Cotton Tail:* Dickman, Marcus

Ellington, Duke, *In a Mellow Tune:* Matteson, Rich; Tennessee Technological University Alumni Tuba-Euphonium Ensemble

Ellington, Duke, *It Don't Mean a Thing:* O'Hara, Betty

Ellington, Duke, *Mood Indigo:* O'Hara, Betty

Ellington, Duke, *Swingers Get the Blues Too:* Matthew, Gee

Ellington, Duke/Gaines, *Just Squeeze Me:* McKinney, Bernard

Ellington, Duke/Matteson, *Things Ain't What They Used to Be:* Matteson-Phillips Tubajazz Consort

Ellington, Duke/Sample, *Tribute to Duke Ellington:* Tennessee Technological University Tuba-Euphonium Ensemble

Ellington, Duke/Vaughan, *Mood Indigo:* Tubadours

Ellington, Duke/Vaughan, *Satin Doll:* Tubadours

Elmer, Andy, *Gicael Mibbs:* Steckar Elephant Tuba Horde

Escaich, Thierry, *Ground:* Milhiet, Ivan

Esleck, David, *I-95:* Modern Jazz Tuba Project

Evenepoel, Johan, *Rhapsody for Euphonium:* Childs, Robert

Ewald, Victor/Reed, *Romance, Op. 2:* Breuninger, Tyrone

Falcone, Nicholas, *Mazurka for Unaccompanied Euphonium:* Behrend, Roger

Falconer, Leigh, *Von Himmel Hoch:* Tubadours

Farr, Craig, *Larghetto for Euphonium:* Flaten, Tormod

Fasch, J. F., *Sonata for Trombone and Piano:* Smith, Henry Charles

Fauré, Gabriel, *Après Un Rêve:* Mead, Steven

Fauré, Gabriel, *Elegié in c Minor, Op. 24:* Frey, Adam

Fauré, Gabriel, *Papillon and Sicilienne:* Tropman, Matt

Fauré, Gabriel, *Papillon, Op. 77:* Champions of the Leonard Falcone Festival 1986–2000

Fauré, Gabriel, *Pavane, Op. 50:* Narita, Yuko

Fauré, Gabriel/Grainger, *Tuscan Serenade:* Colburn, Michael; Hokazono, Sho-ichiro; Cleveland, David

Fauré, Gabriel/Mead, *Two Fauré Duets:* Mead, Steven

Fauré, Gabriel/Wilson, *Pavane, Op. 50:* Tennessee Technological University Tuba-Euphonium Ensemble

Feldman, Hank C., *Freedom:* Symphonia

Feliciangeli, Francesco/Creux, *Preghiera from "Lo Scudiero del Re":* Mead, Steven

Fennell, Drew, *Prescott Poem:* Murchinson, Matthew

Ferguson, Maynard; arr., *It's a Pity to Say Goodnight:* Ferguson, Maynard

Ferguson, Maynard; arr., *Gospel John:* Ferguson, Maynard

Fernie, Alan, *Introduction and Allegro:* Griffiths, Morgan

Fiocco, Joseph Hector/Childs/Wilby, *Arioso and Allegro:* Kipfer, Ueli

Fiocco, Joseph Hector/Childs, *Arioso and Allegro:* Childs, Robert

Fiocco, Joseph Hector/McKenzie/Maunder, *Arioso:* McDonnell, Riki, and Mike Kilroy

Fiocco, Joseph Hector/Smith, *Allegro:* McDonnell, Riki, and Mike Kilroy

Fischer, William/Kippax, *I Love to Tell the Story:* Parton, Jack

Forbes, Michael, *Auburn Is the Colour:* Sotto Voce Quartet

Forbes, Michael, *Consequences:* Sotto Voce Quartet

Forsyth, Kieran, *Westminster Intrada:* British Tuba Quartet, The

Forte, Aldo Rafael, *Adagio and Rondo:* Symphonia

Forte, Aldo Rafael, *Canzonetta for Euphonium and Band:* Taylor, Barbara

Forte, Aldo Rafael, *Moser Comeos:* Euphoniums Unlimited

Forte, Aldo Rafael, *Sequidillas:* Symphonia

Forte, Aldo Rafael, *Tubas Latinas:* Tennessee Technological University Tuba-Euphonium Ensemble

Fosset, Marc, *3 à 5:* Steckar Tubapack

Foster, Frank/Perry, *Shiny Stockings:* Tennessee Technological University Tuba-Euphonium Ensemble

Foster, Stephen/Godfrey, *Gentle Annie:* Lehamn, Arthur; Colburn, Michael

Foster, Stephen/Harvey, *Jeannie with the Light Brown Hair:* Mead, Steven

Foster, Stephen/Howarth, *Jeannie with the Light Brown Hair:* Bray, Mark; Davis, George; Lloyd, G.; Moore, David; Morton, Hugh; McDonnell, Riki, and Mike Kilroy; Brighton, Charley; Bouise, Mark

Foster, Stephen/LaDuke, *My Wife Is a Most Knowing Woman:* LaDuke, Lance

Foster, Stephen/Pilafian, *Slumber My Darling:* LaDuke, Lance

Foster, Stephen/Rimmer, *My Old Kentucky Home:* Deacon, Derek; Appleton, Walter; Yamamoto, Norihisa; Withington, Len; Jones, Alan

Foster, Stephen/Steadman-Allen, *My Story and Song:* Childs Brothers

Foulds, John, *A Keltic Lament:* Cutts, Marcus

Frackenpohl, Arthur, *Pop Suite:* Miraphone Tuba Quartet; British Tuba Quartet, The; Colonial Tuba Quartet, The; Tuba Laté; Dutch Tuba Quartet; Garden State Tuba Ensemble; Rustic Bari-Tuba Ensemble; University of Miami Tuba Ensemble

Frackenpohl, Arthur, *Ragtime:* Melton Tuba-Quartett

Frackenpohl, Arthur, *Sonata for Euphonium:* Behrend, Roger; Heo, Jae-Young

Frackenpohl, Arthur, *Song and Dance:* Behrend, Roger

Franck, Cesar/Smith, *Panis Angelicus:* Droste, Paul; Childs, Robert; Bowman, Brian; McDonnell, Riki, and Mike Kilroy

Frank, Marcel G., *Lyric Poem for Five Tubas:* University of Miami Tuba Ensemble; United States Army Band Tuba-Euphonium Ensemble and Massed Ensemble

Fraser, Bruce, *Fantastic Fast Fingered Fandango, The:* Childs Brothers

Frite, Gregory, *Euphonistic Dance:* Craig, Mary Ann

Frith, John, *Fireworks:* British Tuba Quartet, The

Fritz, Gregory, *Prelude and Dance:* Colonial Tuba Quartet, The

Fucik, Julius, *Entry of the Gladiators:* Miraphone Tuba Quartet

Fucik, Julius/Carrol/Maldonado, *Entrance and Polka of the Euphonium Players:* Mead, Steven

Fucik, Julius/Watz, *Florentiner March:* Melton Tuba-Quartett; Miraphone Tuba Quartet

Fujita, Genma, *Glowing Spirit:* Fukuda, Masanori

Gabrieli, Giovanni/Bale, *Sonata Pian 'e forte:* Mead, Steven

Gabrieli, Giovanni/Gray, *Canzone per Sonare No. 4:* Melton Tuba-Quartett; Dutch Tuba Quartet

Gabrieli, Giovanni/Rauch, *Canzona, La Spiritata:* British Tuba Quartet, The

Gaines, David, *Concerto for Euphonium and Orchestra 1987:* Vydra, Jiri

Gale, Jack; arr., *Tiger Rag:* Dutch Tuba Quartet

Garfunkel/Reichenbach, *Scarborough Fair:* Mead, Steven

Garner, Errol/Fernie, *Misty:* Mead, Steven

Garrett, James Allen, *Bullfrog Rag:* Tennessee Technological University and Alumni Tuba-Euphonium Ensemble

Garrett, James Allen, *Chaser #1:* Tennessee Technological University and Alumni Tuba-Euphonium Ensemble

Garrett, James Allen, arr., *Chimes Blues:* Tennessee Technological University Tuba-Euphonium Ensemble

Garrett, James Allen, *Gay 50's Medley:* Tennessee Technological University and Alumni Tuba-Euphonium Ensemble

Garrett, James Allen, arr., *Just a Closer Walk with Thee:* Tennessee Technological University Tuba-Euphonium Ensemble

Garrett, James Allen, *Miniature Jazz Suite:* Tennessee Technological University Tuba-Euphonium Ensemble; Melton Tuba-Quartett

Garrett, James Allen, *Mystical Music:* Tennessee Technological University and Alumni Tuba-Euphonium Ensemble

Garrett, James Allen, *A Pierre Soliloquy: Ode to Pierre:* Tennessee Technological University and Alumni Tuba-Euphonium Ensemble

Garrett, James Allen, *Pop-Rock Medley:* Tennessee Technological University and Alumni Tuba-Euphonium Ensemble

Garrett, James Allen, *Songs in the Fight Against Rum:* Tennessee Technological University and Alumni Tuba-Euphonium Ensemble

Garrett, James Allen, *Sousa Surrenders:* Tennessee Technological University and Alumni Tuba-Euphonium Ensemble

Garrett, James Allen, *A Tubalee Jubalee:* Tennessee Technological University Tuba-Euphonium Ensemble; United States Armed Forces Tuba-Euphonium Ensemble

Garrett, James Allen, arr., *Won't You Come Home Bill Bailey:* Tennessee Technological University Tuba-Euphonium Ensemble

Gasparini, Quirino/Miller, *Adoramus Te Christe:* Tuba Laté; Sotto Voce Quartet

Gates, *Shadowed:* Vanderweele, Aaron

Gates, Crawford, *Tuba Quartet, Op. 59:* Tennessee Technological University Tuba-Euphonium Ensemble

Gautier, L./Werden, *Le Secret:* Alchemy (previously Atlantic Tuba Quartet)

George, Thom Ritter, *Sextet:* Mead, Steven

George, Thom Ritter, *Sonata for Baritone Horn and Piano:* Craig, Mary Ann; Nelson, Douglas

George, Thom Ritter, *Tubamobile:* Symphonia

George, Thom Ritter, *Tubasonatina:* Tennessee Technological University Tuba-Euphonium Ensemble

Gershwin, George, *A Woman Is a Sometime Thing:* Top Brass

Gershwin, George, *But Not for Me:* O'Hara, Betty

Gershwin, George, *Impromptu in 2 Keys:* Contraband Tuba Quartet

Gershwin, George, *Our Love Is Here to Stay:* Matteson, Rich

Gershwin, George, *Someone to Watch Over Me:* O'Hara, Betty

Gershwin, George, *Summertime:* Matteson-Phillips Tubajazz Consort

Gershwin, George, *Three Preludes:* Contraband Tuba Quartet

Gershwin, George/Ferguson, *Fascinatin' Gershwin:* British Tuba Quartet, The

Gershwin, George/Heifetz/Murchinson, *Three Preludes:* Murchinson, Matthew

Gershwin, George/Sample/Corazon, *Gershwin Medley:* Tennessee Technological University Tuba-Euphonium Ensemble; United States Armed Forces Tuba-Euphonium Ensemble

Gheel, Henry, arr., *Watching the Wheat:* Childs, Robert; McEnvoy, Graham; Schramm, Robert; Dunstan, John; Membury, Clive; Craddock, Ian

Gheel, Henry, *Romanza:* McCrea, Melvin

Gibbons, O./Campbell, *Tuba Voluntary:* Alchemy (previously Atlantic Tuba Quartet)

Gillespie, Dizzy, *Manteca:* Tennessee Technological University Alumni Tuba-Euphonium Ensemble

Gillingham, David, *Blue Lake Fantasies:* Tropman, Matt; Hokazono, Sho-ichiro; Kipfer, Ueli

Gillingham, David, *Vintage:* Mead, Steven; Meixner, Brian; Behrend, Roger; Hokazono, Sho-ichiro

Giordani, Giuseppe/Bona, *Caro mio ben:* Mead, Steven

Giordano/Curnow, *Finale from "Andre Chenier":* Behrend, Roger

Giuffre, Jimmy/Prince, *Four Brothers:* Dickman, Marcus

Glennie, Evelyn/R. Childs, *A Little Prayer:* Childs, David; Kane, Derick

Glinka, Michael/Ferguson/Smalley, *Russlan and Ludmila:* British Tuba Quartet, The

Glinka, Michael, *Overture to "Russlan and Ludmila":* Miraphone Tuba Quartet

Glorieux, F., *Concerto for Euphonium:* Ost, Nick

Glorieux, F., *Contemplation:* Ost, Nick

Glorieux, F., *Desolation:* Ost, Nick

Glorieux, F., *Elegy:* Ost, Nick

Glorieux, F., *Euphonic Moods:* Ost, Nick

Glorieux, F., *Fantasy:* Ost, Nick

Glorieux, F., *Farewell:* Ost, Nick

Glorieux, F., *Orchestra Scheldt:* Ost, Nick

Glorieux, F., *Regrets:* Ost, Nick

Glorieux, F., *Sunrise on the River:* Ost, Nick

Glorieux, F., *Waltz:* Ost, Nick

Gluck, von C.W./Winter, *Dance of the Blessed Spirits:* Tropman, Matt

Godard, Michael/Steckar, Marc, *Et Le Klaxon Retentit Derechef Comme Un Lézard Hongrois Enrhumé:* Steckar Tubapack

Godard, Michael, *Angels Guard Thee:* Childs, David

Godfrey/Herbert, *Lucy Long:* Mather, Harry; Singleton, Stephen; Lehamn, Arthur; Baglin, Lyndon

Goldman, Edwin Franko, *Scherzo:* Bowman, Brian

Goldman, Richard, *Tramp, Tramp, Tramp:* Wood, Ken

Golland, John/Ashmore, *Peace:* Childs, Robert

Golland, John, *Childs Play:* Childs Brothers

Golland, John, *Euphonium Concerto No. 2:* Mead, Steven; Kipfer, Ueli

Golland, John, *Euphonium Concerto, No. 1, Op. 64:* Mead, Steven; Childs Brothers; Ushigami, Ryuji

Golland, John, *Meiso:* Willems, John

Golland, John, *Peace:* Cutts, Marcus; Fox, Mike; Owen, Mark; Postma, Simon; Williams, Kate; Gagnaux, Alexandre; Araki, Tamao; Flaten, Tormod; Kipfer, Ueli; Mead, Steven; Childs, David

Golland, John, *Rhapsody No. 2:* Kipfer, Ueli

Gordon, Harry; Conner, Tommie, *Down in the Glen:* Hunter, Angie

Gordon, William, *Gospel Crossover:* Church, David

Gordon, William, *Saved by Grace:* Kane, Derick

Goret, Didier, *Detournement Mineur:* Steckar Elephant Tuba Horde

Gottschalk, Arthur, arr., *Silent Night:* Tennessee Technological University Tuba-Euphonium Ensemble

Gottschalk, Arthur, *Substructures for Ten Tubas:* University of Michigan Tuba and Euphonium Ensemble

Gould, Morton/Woo, *Pavanne from "Latin American Suite":* University of Miami Tuba Ensemble

Gounod, Charles, *O Divine Redeemer:* Bowman, Brian

Gounod, Charles/Berry, *March of the Marionettes:* Tubadours

Gounod, Charles/Snell, *Hail Ancient Walls:* Mead, Steven; McDonnell, Riki, and Mike Kilroy

Gourlay, James, *Eagle Thunders, The:* Dutch Tuba Quartet; Swiss Tuba Quartet

Gower, A. E., *Three Short Pieces for Baritone Horn and Piano:* Young, Raymond G.

Graham, *I'm in Love with Miss Logan:* Mancuso, Gus

Graham, Peter, *Bravura Variations for Euphonium Quartet:* Mead, Steven

Graham, Peter, *Bravura Variations on British Folksongs:* Mead, Steven; Kane, Derick

Graham, Peter, *Brilliante:* Childs Brothers; Jose, Robert; Mead, Steven; Rüedi, Thomas; Thorton, David; Williams, Glyn

Graham, Peter, *Brilliante Fantasy on Rule Britannia:* Mead, Steven

Graham, Peter, *Celtic Dream from "Windows of the World":* Thorton, David

Graham, Peter, *Cossack Wedding Dance from "Call of the Cossacks":* Thorton, David

Graham, Peter, *Gaelforce:* Robertson, Gail

Graham, Peter, *Glorious Ventures:* Mead, Steven; Mallett, Chris

Graham, Peter, *Holy Well, The:* Griffiths, Morgan

Graham, Peter/D. McGiboney, *Brilliante:* Childs, David

Graham, Peter/Veit, *Brilliante:* Mead, Steven

Granados, Enrique/Falcone, *Playera "Danse Espagnole"*: Falcone, Leonard

Grand/Boyd, *Guess Who I Saw Today?*: Mancuso, Gus

Green, Freddie/Esleck, *Corner Pocket*: Tennessee Technological University Tuba-Euphonium Ensemble

Green, Freddie/Esleck, *Until I Met You*: Tennessee Technological University Tuba-Euphonium Ensemble

Greenwood, *Bonny Mary of Argyle*: Steen, Grierson

Gregson, Edward, *Symphonic Rhapsody for Euphonium and Band*: Mead, Steven; Corwell, Neal; Childs Brothers; Griffiths, Morgan

Grieg, Edward, *Spring*: Young, Ron

Grieg, Edward/Farr, *Jeg Elsker Dig*: Nerland, Eldfrid

Grieg, Edward/Harris, *Ase's Death*: Mead, Steven

Gronick, Don, *Pools*: Tennessee Technological University Alumni Tuba-Euphonium Ensemble

Grovlez, Gabriel, *Petites Litanies de Jésus*: Sotto Voce Quartet

Gryce, Gigi, *Conversation Piece*: McKinney, Bernard

Guaraldi, Vince, *A Hatful of Dandruff*: Mancuso, Gus

Guilmant, Alexander, *Morceau Symphonique*: Dart, Fred; Falcone, Leonard; Louder, Earle; Werden, David

Haerle, Dan, *Crib Chimp*: Matteson, Rich

Haerle, Dan, *Magic Morning*: Matteson, Rich

Hahn, Reynaldo, *L'Huere exquise*: Rüedi, Thomas

Hamlisch/Barry, *Way We Were, The*: Rüedi, Thomas; Childs Brothers

Hamm, F./Bennet/Lown/Gray, *Bye, Bye Blues*: Matteson, Rich

Hampton, Slide, *A Little Night Music*: McKinney, Bernard

Hampton, Slide, *Asseveration*: McKinney, Bernard

Hampton, Slide, *Sister Salvation*: McKinney, Bernard

Hancock, Herbie/Perry, *Chameleon*: Tennessee Technological University Tuba-Euphonium Ensemble

Hancock; arr., *First Noel, The*: Tennessee Technological University Tuba-Euphonium Ensemble

Handel, George Frederic, *Concerto in f Minor*: Chevailler, Jean-Pierre; Smith, Henry Charles; Nelson, Douglas

Handel, George Frederic, *Harmonious Blacksmith, The*: Sotto Voce Quartet

Handel, George Frederic, *Largo*: Baglin, Lyndon

Handel, George Frederic, *Musizure pur un Feu o'*: Grainger, Andre

Handel, George Frederic, *Sarabande and Minuet*: Campbell, Larry

Handel, George Frederic/Anonymous, *Ombra mai fu from "Xerses"*: Baglin, Lyndon

Handel, George Frederic/Brockway, *Sonata in g Minor*: Johnson, Frank

Handel, George Frederic/Fitzgerald, *Aria con Variazioni*: Droste, Paul

Handel, George Frederic/Greenwood, *Where E're You Walk*: Shipp, Charles

Handel, George Frederic/Hauser, *Arrival of the Queen of Sheba*: Tennessee Technological University Tuba-Euphonium Ensemble

Handel, George Frederic/Hume/Wilkinson, *Harmonious Blacksmith, The*: Groom, Trevor

Handel, George Frederic/Hume, *Harmonious Blacksmith, The*: Groom, Trevor; Lehamn, Arthur; Perrins, Barrie; Parry, Glynn

Handel, George Frederic/Ito, *Ombra mai fu from "Xerses"*: Miura, Toru

Handel, George Frederic/Wilson; arr., *Arrival of the Queen of Sheba*: Childs Brothers

Handy, W.C./Holcombe, *St. Louis Blues*: Melton Tuba-Quartett; Dutch Tuba Quartet

Harclerode, Albert, arr., *Glousteshire Wassail Song, The/Il Est Ne*: Tubadours

Harclerode, Albert, arr., *Good King Wenceslas*: Tubadours

Harclerode, Albert, arr., *It Came upon a Midnight Clear*: Tubadours

Harclerode, Albert, arr., *March of the Kings/O Come Little Children*: Tubadours

Harclerode, Albert, arr., *O Tannanbaum*: Tubadours

Harclerode, Albert, *O Sanctissmus*: Tubadours

Harline, L./Kanai, *When You Wish upon a Star*: Hokazono, Sho-ichiro; Mead, Steven

Harnick, Sheldon, *Boston Beguine, The*: Mancuso, Gus

Harrison, George, *Something with Tokyo*: Tokyo Bari-Tuba Ensemble

Harrison, Wayne, *Beneath the Surface*: Tennessee Technological University Tuba-Euphonium Ensemble

Hart, Bill/Buttery, *Brass Cuckoo*: Alchemy (previously Atlantic Tuba Quartet)

Hart, Lorenzo; Rodgers, Richard/Pirone, *My Funny Valentine*: Mead, Steven

Hartley, Walter, *Bivalve Suite*: Droste, Paul

Hartley, Walter, *Miniatures for Four Valve Instruments*: British Tuba Quartet, The; Atlantic Tuba Quartet, The

Hartley, Walter, *Sonata Euphonica*: Mead, Steven; Kilpatrick, Barry

Hartley, Walter, *Two Pieces for Euphonium and Piano*: Kilpatrick, Barry

Hartmann, John, *Arbucklenian Polka*: Mead, Steven

Hartmann, John, *Facilita*: Lehman, Arthur; Mead, Steven; Haemhouts, Ben;

Hartmann, John, *La Belle Americane*: Childs, Nicholas; Childs, David; Fawbert, Andrew; Moore, David; Baglin, Lyndon

Hartmann, John, *Robin Adair*: Lehman, Arthur; Borrie, Bob; Poole, Sydney; Warrington, Brian

Hartmann, John, *Rule Britannia:* Clough, John; Mead, Steven; Griffiths, Morgan

Hartmann, John/Frey, *Rule Britannia:* Frey, Adam

Hartmann, John/Greenwood, *Rule Britannia:* Griffiths, Morgan

Hartmann, John/Hopkinson, *Rule Britannia:* Millar, Billy

Hartmann, John/Mortimer, *Facilita:* Griffiths, Morgan; Mead, Steven; Perrins, Barrie

Hartmann, John/Stephens, *Rule Britannia:* Childs, Robert; Mead, Steven

Hastings, Ross, *Little Madrigal for Big Horns:* University of Miami Tuba Ensemble

Hauser, Joshua, *EuPhunk:* Euphoniums Unlimited

Hawkins, Erskin/Luis, *Tuxedo Junction:* Melton Tuba-Quartett; Dutch Tuba Quartet

Haydn, Franz Josef, *Achieved Is the Glorious Work from "Die Schöpfung":* Sotto Voce Quartet

Haydn, Franz Josef, *Two Classical Themes:* Campbell, Larry

Haydn, Franz Josef, *With Verdure Clad from "The Creation":* Smith, Henry Charles

Haydn, Franz Josef/Droste, *Divertimento No. 70:* Droste, Paul

Haydn, Franz Josef/Shuman, *Adagio from "Concerto for Cello":* Falcone, Leonard; Dart, Fred

Hayes, Isaac/Gottschalk, *Shaft:* Tennessee Technological University Tuba-Euphonium Ensemble

Heath, Reginald, *Andante and Scherzo:* Steen, Grierson; Oates, John; Winterbottom, D.

Heath, Reginald, *Springtime:* Morgan, Gareth; Woodland, Shaun; Moore, David; Farrington, Christopher; Taylor, Philip

Heaton, Wilfred, *Variations on Annie Laurie:* Mead, Steven

Herbert, Victor/Vaughan, *March of the Toy Soldiers:* Tubadours

Hermann, Heinz, *Korn Blues:* Scandinavian Tuba Jazz

Hermann, Heinz, *Y Luego:* Scandinavian Tuba Jazz

Heusen, Van/Barton, *Here's That Rainy Day:* British Tuba Quartet, The

Hidas, Frigyas, *Tuba Quartett:* Melton Tuba-Quartett

Hidas, Frigyes, *Tuphonium:* Dutch Tuba Quartet

Hilgers, Walter, *Praeludium:* Gerhard Meinl's Tuba Sextet

Hill, William H., *Concerto for Euphonium:* Royall, Dennis; Marsteller, Loren

Himes, William, *Journey into Freedom:* Anonymous

Himes, William, *Journey into Peace:* Kane, Derick; Waterworth, Ken; Metcalf, Curtis

Himes, William, *My Christ Is All:* Richards, Kelvin; Meyer, Donald; Brown, William

Hinchley, John, *Boogie Woogie Tuba Boy:* Tuba Laté

Hirano, Mitsuru, *Fantasia di foresta:* Colliard, Corrado

Hlszky, Adriana, *Corners of the World:* Burba, Malte

Holmes, Paul, *Quartet for Tubas:* Tennessee Technological University and Alumni Tuba-Euphonium Ensemble; British Tuba Quartet, The; University of Michigan Tuba and Euphonium Ensemble

Holst, Gustav, *Planets:* Mulcahy, Michael

Holst, Gustav, *Wind Quintet in A♭:* Mead, Steven

Holst, Gustav/Butler, *Mars from "The Planets":* Symphonia

Holst, Gustav/Werden, *Second Suite in F for Military Band:* Symphonia

Hook, J./Garrett, *Rondo:* British Tuba Quartet, The

Horner, James/Heo, *Titanic:* Heo, Jae-Young

Horner, James/Velde, *My Heart Will Go On:* Kilroy, Mike

Horovitz, Joseph/Rüedi, *Euphonium Concerto:* Rüedi, Thomas

Horovitz, Joseph, *Euphonium Concerto:* Levi, Eran; Rüedi, Thomas; Childs, Robert; Groom, Trevor; Mead, Steven; Taylor, Robin; Breuninger, Tyrone

Horovitz, Joseph, *Lento from "Euphonium Concerto":* Mead, Steven; Anonymous

Horovitz, Joseph, *Rumpole of the Bailey:* British Tuba Quartet, The

Hoshina, Hiroshi, *Fantasy for Euphonium and Piano:* Miura, Toru; Mead, Steven

Howard, Bart/Hughes, *Fly Me to the Moon:* Mead, Steven

Howarth, Elgar, *Cantabile for John Fletcher:* Childs Brothers

Howarth, Elgar; arr., *Grand Study No. 13:* Childs Brothers

Hudec, Adam, *Golden Euphoniums:* Griffiths, Morgan

Hudec, Adam, *Slavonic Impressions:* Williams, Glyn

Huesen van, J., *I Thought About You:* Matteson, Rich

Huffine, G. H., *Them Basses:* United States Army Band Tuba-Euphonium Ensemble and Massed Ensemble

Hummel, Johann Nepomuk/R. Childs, *Fantasy:* Childs, Robert

Humperdinck, Engelbert, *Evening Prayer from "Hansel and Gretel":* McDonnell, Riki, and Mike Kilroy

Hutchinson, Terry, *Tuba Juba Duba:* Tennessee Technological University Tuba-Euphonium Ensemble; Melton Tuba-Quartett

Hutchison, *Sonatina for Baritone Horn and Piano:* Young, Raymond G.

Iannaccone, Anthony, *"Hades" for Two Euphoniums and Two Tubas:* University of Michigan Tuba and Euphonium Ensemble

Iannaccone, Anthony, *Three Mythical Sketches for Four Tubas:* University of Michigan Tuba and Euphonium Ensemble

Inomata, Takeshi, *My Sweet Love:* Hokazono, Sho-ichiro

Irvine, Scott, *Concertino for Euphonium:* Metcalf, Curtis

Isomura, Yukiko, *Four Seasons Suite, The:* Narita, Yuko

Isomura, Yukiko, *I'm Waiting Alone:* Narita, Yuko

Isomura, Yukiko, *Merry Christmas to All of the World:* Narita, Yuko

Isomura, Yukiko, *Suite of Spring Wind:* Narita, Yuko

Isomura, Yukiko; Narita, Yuko, *Orange Shores:* Narita, Yuko

Ito, Yasuhide, *Euphoniums Parfait:* Mead, Steven

Ito, Yasuhide, *Fantasy Variations:* Bowman, Brian; Behrend, Roger; Champions of the Leonard Falcone Festival 1986–2000; Frey, Adam; Mead, Steven

Iturralde, Pedro/van der Woude, *Pequeña Czárdás:* Mead, Steven

Iturralde, Pedro/Veit, *Pequeña Czárdás:* Mead, Steven

Ivanovici, J./Konagaya, *Wave of the Danube:* Tuba Laté

Jackson, Michael/Rose, *Beat It:* Tennessee Technological University Tuba-Euphonium Ensemble

Jacob, Gordon/Bryant, *Fantasia for Euphonium and Brass:* Taylor, Robin

Jacob, Gordon, *Fantasia:* Mead, Steven; Anonymous; Miura, Toru; Runty, Thomas; Stowe, David; Verweij, Hugo; Bogetvedt, Bjorn; Fisher, Mark; Craig, Mary Ann; Picton, Wendy; Hokazono, Sho-ichiro; Childs, Robert; Flaten, Tormod; Young, Ron

Jacob, Gordon, *Four Pieces for Tuba Quartet:* Dutch Tuba Quartet

Jacobs Bond, Carrie, *A Perfect Day:* Dempster, Stuart

Jacobs Bond, Carrie, *I Love You Truly:* Dempster, Stuart

Jager, Robert, *Three Ludes for Tuba:* Symphonia

Jakeway, Albert H., *Land Beyond the Blue:* Mack, Thomas

James, Bob/O'Connor, *Courtship:* Tennessee Technological University Tuba-Euphonium Ensemble

Janalek, Loes, *Capriccio:* Yamamoto, Takashi

Jarreau, Al/Murphy, *Boogie Down:* Tennessee Technological University Tuba-Euphonium Ensemble

Jarrett, Keith, *Lucky Southern:* Matteson-Phillips Tubajazz Consort

Jeanneau, François, *Paul et Mike:* Steckar Tubapack

Jenkins, Alan; arr., *Myfanwy:* Childs Brothers

Jenkins, *Benedictus:* Childs, David

Jenkins, *Hymn from "Adiemus":* Childs, David

Jenkinson, Ezra, *Elfentanz:* Gagnaux, Alexandre

Jewell, *Battle Royal:* British Tuba Quartet, The; Swiss Tuba Quartet

Jobim, Antonio Carlos/Dittmar, *One Note Samba:* Mead, Steven

Joel, Billy/Matteson, *Just the Way You Are:* Matteson, Rich

Johnston, Bruce/O'Connor, *Sunrise Lady:* Tennessee Technological University Tuba-Euphonium Ensemble

Johnstone, Helen, *Anna Karenina:* McDonnell, Riki, and Mike Kilroy

Jones, Alan, *Easy Street:* Matteson, Rich

Jones, Quincy, *Medley from "Stockholm Sweetnin'" and "You Leave Me Breathless":* O'Hara, Betty

Jones, Roger, *Dialogue for Euphonium and Piano:* Royall, Dennis

Jones, Roger, *Duet No. 12 from "21 Distinctive Duets":* University of Miami Tuba Ensemble

Joplin, Scott/LeClair, *Easy Winners:* Contraband

Joplin, Scott/Milburne, *Euphonic Sounds:* Mueller, John

Joplin, Scott/Milburne, *Solace:* Mueller, John

Joplin, Scott/Picher, *Elite Syncopations:* British Tuba Quartet, The; Swiss Tuba Quartet

Joplin, Scott/Sabourin, *Cascades, The:* British Tuba Quartet, The

Joplin, Scott/Sabourin, *Favorite Rag, The:* British Tuba Quartet, The

Joplin, Scott/Sabourin, *Pleasant Moments:* Dutch Tuba Quartet

Joplin, Scott/Self, *Entertainer, The:* United States Army Band Tuba-Euphonium Ensemble and Massed Ensemble; Tennessee Tech Tuba-Euphonium Quintet

Joplin, Scott/Walter, *Strenuous Life, The:* Miraphone Tuba Quartet; Albertasaurus Tuba Quartet

Joplin, Scott/Werden, *Easy Winners:* Dutch Tuba Quartet

Joplin, Scott/Werden, *Euphonic Sounds:* Atlantic Tuba Quartet, The; British Tuba Quartet, The

Joplin, Scott/Werden, *Ragtime Dance:* United States Navy Band Tuba-Euphonium Quartet

Jordon, Duke, *Jordu:* Dickman, Marcus

Jorgensen, Axel, *Caprice Oriental:* Andresen, Mogens

Kabalevsky, Dmitri/Berry, *Comedian's Gallop:* Tubadours

Kahn, G./Jones, *You Stepped Out of a Dream:* Matteson, Rich

Kalke, Ernst-Thilo, *Jumbo's Holiday:* Melton Tuba-Quartett

Kalke, Ernst-Thilo, *Requiem to a Dead Little Cat:* Melton Tuba-Quartett

Kamen, Michael/Oliver, *Robin Hood Fanfare:* Tennessee Technological University Tuba-Euphonium Ensemble

Kassatti, Tadeuz, *Kino Concertino:* Ushigami, Ryuji

Kassatti, Tadeuz, *By Gaslight:* Mead, Steven

Kay, Hershy, *Stars and Stripes Ballet Suite:* Swallow, John

Kemp, *Fantasia Capriccioso:* Lehman, Arthur

Kendrick, Rodney, *Rodney's Rhythm, Part One:* Zawadi, Kiane

Kenswich, Marcel, *Legento:* Hokazono, Sho-ichiro

Kerbs, Jesse, *Jesse's Jump:* Symphonia

Kern, Jerome/Holcombe, *They Didn't Believe Me:* British Tuba Quartet, The

Kern, Jerome/Maunder, *All the Things You Are:* McDonnell, Riki, and Mike Kilroy

Kerwin, Simon, *Illustrations for Tubas:* Tuba Laté

Kerwin, Simon, *March-Frot:* Tuba Laté

Ketelby, Albert, *A Night in a Persian Caravan:* Albertasaurus Tuba Quartet

Khatchaturian, Aram/Seitz, *Sabre Dance:* Tuba Laté; Melton Tuba-Quartett

King, Karl L./Berry, *Barnum and Bailey's Favorite:* Tubadours

King, Karl L./Braten, *A Night in June:* Pederson, Thor-Arne

King, Karl L./Morris, *Barnum and Bailey's Favorite:* United States Armed Forces Tuba-Euphonium Ensemble

King, Karl L./Werden, *Melody Shop, The:* United States Armed Forces Tuba-Euphonium Ensemble; Miraphone Tuba Quartet

King, Karl L., *A Night in June:* Mead, Steven; Wood, Ken; Lehman, Arthur

King/Lapread/Mcclary/Orange/Richie/Williams/Murphy, *Brick House:* Tennessee Technological University Tuba-Euphonium Ensemble

Kingsbury, Craig/Harclerode, *Infant Holy:* Tubadours

Kjellgren, G., *My Light and Song:* Butler, John

Kjerulf, Halfdan, *I sode blege Kinder:* Olsrud, Sverre Stakston

Kjerulf, Halfdan, *Mit Hjerte og min Lyre, Op. 16, No. 2:* Olsrud, Sverre Stakston

Kjerulf, Halfdan, *Ved Sjoen den morke, Op. 6, No. 2:* Olsrud, Sverre Stakston

Kleine Schaars, Peter, *Wolf the Cat:* Dutch Tuba Quartet

Klengel, Julius/Falcone, *Concertino No. 1, Op. 7 in B♭:* Mead, Steven; Champions of the Leonard Falcone Festival 1986–2000; Dart, Fred

Klengel, Julius/Odom, *Concertino No. 1, Op. 7 in B♭:* Bowman, Brian

Klengel, Julius, *Concertino No. 1, Op. 7 in B♭, Mvt. 1:* Fukuda, Masanori

Klose, Hyacinthe/Kipfer *Air Varie, Op. 21:* Kipfer, Ueli

Knapp, Mrs. Joseph/Henneman, *Open the Gates of the Temple:* Bowman, Brian

Knox, Charles, *Scherzando for Tubular Octet:* Tennessee Technological University Tuba-Euphonium Ensemble

Koetsier, Jan, *Wolkenschatten fur Tubaquartett, Op. 136:* Alchemy (previously Atlantic Tuba Quartet); Dutch Tuba Quartet

Kohlenberg, Oliver, *Blue Gleam of Arctic Hysteria:* Myllys, Jukka

Konagaya, Soichi, *Illusion:* Tennessee Technological University Tuba-Euphonium Ensemble

Koper, Karl-Heinz, *Dulcamarata for Euphonium and Symphonic Band:* Mead, Steven

Koskinen, Juha T., *Destination:* Myllys, Jukka

Kosma, J./Prevert, J./Mercer, J/Perry, *Autumn Leaves:* Symphonia

Kreisler von, Alexander, *Sonatina:* Nelson, Douglas

Kreisler, Fritz/Woodcock, *Liebeslied:* Tuba Laté

Kreisler, Fritz, *Liebesfreud:* Mead, Steven

Kresin, Willibald, *Chin Up!:* Contraband

Krinjak, Karen/Bosanko, *I Have No Claim on Grace:* Mallett, Chris

Krol, Bernhard, *Feiertagsmusik, Op. 107b:* Tennessee Technological University and Alumni Tuba-Euphonium Ensemble

Kroll, William/Rüedi, *Banjo and Fiddle:* Rüedi, Thomas

Kryl, Bohumir, *King Carneval:* Lehman, Arthur

Kummer, Friedrich, *Variations for Ophicleide:* Mead, Steven

Kupferman, Meyer, *Kierkegaard:* Sotto Voce Quartet; British Tuba Quartet, The

Lacalle, G.J.M./Kosugi, *Amapola:* Hokazono, Sho-ichiro

Lacalle, G.J.M., *Amapola:* Rustic Bari-Tuba Ensemble

LaDuke, Lance, *Take a Walk:* LaDuke, Lance

LaDuke, Lance, *Victor Hugo:* LaDuke, Lance

Lalo, Edouard/Rüedi, *Chants russes Op. 29:* Rüedi, Thomas

Lamb, Marvin, *Heavy Metal:* Tennessee Technological University Tuba-Euphonium Ensemble

Langford, Gordon/Grand, *Blaydon Races, The:* Young, Ron

Langford, Gordon, *Blaydon Races, The:* Clough, John; Bulter, James; Rüedi, Thomas; Pratt, Mike; Mead, Steven; Kilroy, Mike

Langford, Gordon, *Sally in Our Alley:* Christian, Peter

Larson, John/Bosanko, *I'll Not Turn Back:* Mallett, Chris; Childs Brothers

Lear, Thos, *Shylock:* Griffiths, Morgan

LeClair, David, *Dragon's Dance, The:* Contraband Tuba Quartet

LeClair, David, *Growing Up Together:* Contraband Tuba Quartet

LeClair, David, *Heidentüblein:* Contraband Tuba Quartet

Lecuona, Ernesto/Morris, *Malagueña:* Tennessee Technological University Tuba-Euphonium Ensemble

Lefébure, Louis-François, *Sortie in E♭:* British Tuba Quartet, The

Legrand, Michel/Drover, *What Are You Doing with the Rest of Your Life?:* Gagnaux, Alexandre

Legrand, Michel/Williamson, *Summer Knows:* Modern Jazz Tuba Project

Legrand/Slater, *Summer of '42:* Matteson, Rich

Lehár, Franz, *U Are My Heart's Delight:* McDonnell, Riki, and Mike Kilroy

Leidzén, Erik/Field, *Song of the Brother, The:* Heo, Jae-Young

Leidzén, Erik, *Home on the Range:* Mead, Steven; Groom, Trevor; Young, Ron; McNally, Robert; Evans, Jonathon

Leidzén, Erik, *Song of the Brother, The:* Mead, Steven; Kane, Derick; Young, Ron; Childs Brothers; Schmidli, Erich; Nygvist, Rune, Vanderweele, Aaron

Lemer and Loewe/Belshaw, *Get Me to the Church on Time:* British Tuba Quartet, The

Lennon, John/Lucena, *Yesterday:* Baglin, Lyndon

Lennon, John/Luis, *Hey Jude:* Miraphone Tuba Quartet

Lennon, John/McCartney, *Eleanor Rigby:* Top Brass

Lennon, John; McCartney, Paul/Miyagawa, *Yesterday:* Tuba Laté

Leoncavallo, Ruggero/Langford, *Mattinata:* Griffiths, Morgan

Leoncavallo, Ruggero, *On with the Motley:* McDonnell, Riki, and Mike Kilroy

Levy, Jules/Bale, *Grand Russian Fantasia:* Mead, Steven

Lew, Gillis, *Four Kuehn Guys:* Dutch Tuba Quartet

Liberati, Allesandro, *Remembrance of Switzerland:* Lehamn, Arthur

Linkola, Jukka, *Euphonium Concerto:* Myllys, Jukka

Linkola, Jukka, *Euphonium Concerto, Mvt. 3:* Flaten, Tormod

Lintinen, Kirmo, *Lampi:* Euphoniums Unlimited

Liszt, Franz/Seitz, *Hungarian Rhapsody No. 2:* Melton Tuba-Quartett

Llwellyn, Edward, *My Regards:* Falcone, Leonard; Wood, Ken

Lockhart-Seitz/Butler, *World Is Waiting for the Sunrise, The:* Tennessee Technological University Tuba-Euphonium Ensemble

Louman, *Carioca:* Louder, Earle

Lovland/Gates, *You Raised Me Up:* Vanderweel, Aaron

Lowe, Frederick, *Almost Like Being in Love:* Tennessee Technological University Alumni Tuba-Euphonium Ensemble

Luckhardt, Hilmar, *Octet for Brass (1977):* Kilpatrick, Barry

Luis, Ingo, *Lazy Elephant Blues:* Melton Tuba-Quartett

Luis, Ingo, *Little Lullabye:* Melton Tuba-Quartett

Lundquist, Trobjörn, *Triplet for Four Tubas:* British Tuba Quartet, The

Lusher, David, arr., *Come Dearest, the Daylight Is Gone:* Tubadours

Lusher, Don, *Concert Variations:* Childs, David

Lyon, Max, *Suite for Low Brass:* Atlantic Tuba Quartet, The

Lyte, *Abide with Me:* Childs, David

MacDowell, Edward/Ball, *To a Wild Rose:* Faro, Michael; Singleton, Stephen; Shepherd, Ken; Morgan, Gareth; Deacon, Derek; Cutts, Marcus; Bowden, Ray; Membury, Clive

MacDowell, Edward/Langford, *To a Wild Rose:* Cutts, Marcus

Mack, Thomas, *Covenant, The:* Mack, Thomas

Mack, Thomas, *Tell the World:* Mack, Thomas

Maclean, Don/Greenwood, *And I Love You So:* Groom, Joe

MacMillan, Duncan, *"In Memoriam" Sept. 11, 2001:* Euphoniums Unlimited

MacMurrough, D./Hume, *Macushla:* Booth, Steven; Griffiths, Morgan

Maeda, Norio, *Chim Chim Che-ree:* Hokazono, Sho-ichiro

Magnan, G., *Concerto:* Falcone, Leonard

Mahler, Gustav, *Ich bin der welt abbanden gekommen:* Murchinson, Matthew

Mahler, Gustav, *Symphony No. 7:* Mulcahy, Michael

Mallet, Chris, *Travelling Along:* Vanderweele, Aaron; Kane, Derick

Malotte, Albert, *Lord's Prayer, The:* Bowman, Brian; Sotto Voce Quartet

Manaco/Holcombe, *You Made Me Love You:* British Tuba Quartet, The

Mancini, Henry, *Heaven Can Wait:* Nash, Dick

Mancini, Henry, *Lightfinger:* Nash, Dick

Mancini, Henry, *Pink Panther, The:* Lidsle, Harri

Mancini, Henry, *Sunflower:* Hokazono, Sho-ichiro

Mancini, Henry, *Tender Thieves, The:* Nash, Dick

Mancini, Henry/Gale, *Pink Panther, The:* Dutch Tuba Quartet

Mancini, Henry/Krush, *Pink Panther, The:* British Tuba Quartet, The; Melton Tuba-Quartett

Mancini, Henry/Luis, *Baby Elephant Walk:* Melton Tuba-Quartett

Mancini, Henry/Maunder, *How Soon:* McDonnell, Riki, and Mike Kilroy

Mancuso, Gus, *Brother Aintz:* Mancuso, Gus

Mancuso, Gus, *O-Fayces:* Mancuso, Gus

Mandel, Johnny/Maunder, *Shadow of Your Smile, The:* McDonnell, Riki, and Mike Kilroy

Mandel, Johnny, *A Time for Love:* Tennessee Technological University Alumni Tuba-Euphonium Ensemble

Manfrin, Paolo, *Interferenze per euphonium solo:* Colliard, Corrado

Mantia, Simone, *Auld Lang Syne:* Lehman, Arthur; Mead, Steven; Colburn, Michael

Mantia, Simone, *Believe Me if All Those Endearing Young Charms:* Louder, Earle; Lehman, Arthur; Wood, Ken; Brasch, Harold; Behrend, Roger

Mantia, Simone, *Priscilla:* Dempster, Stuart

Mantia, Simone/Boddington, *Believe Me if All Those Endearing Young Charms:* Baglin, Lyndon; Mead, Steven; Zuback, Joseph; Sullivan, Bert; Keene, Ian; Childs Brothers

Mantia, Simone/Brasch/Maldanado, *Believe Me if All Those Endearing Young Charms:* Mead, Steven

Mantia, Simone/Corwell, *Believe Me if All Those Endearing Young Charms:* Corwell, Neal

Mantia, Simone/Dennison, *Believe Me if All Those Endearing Young Charms:* Teasdale, Malcolm

Mantia, Simone/Eichner, *Believe Me if All Those Endearing Young Charms:* Colburn, Michael

Mantia, Simone/Hunsberger, *Believe Me if All Those Endearing Young Charms:* Heo, Jae-Young

Mantia, Simone/Langford, *Believe Me if All Those Endearing Young Charms:* Bridge, Kenneth; Mallett, Chris; Timlin, Christopher; Davis, George; Cutts, Marcus

Mantia, Simone/McRitchie, *Believe Me if All Those Endearing Young Charms:* Hanson, Scott

Mantia, Simone/Moore, *Believe Me if All Those Endearing Young Charms:* Childs, Robert

Mantia, Simone/Stanley, *Believe Me if All Those Endearing Young Charms:* Childs, Robert

Mantooth, Frank, *Belgrade Hangover:* Alexander, Ashley

Marcello, Benedetto/Flaten, *Sonata in a Minor:* Flaten, Tormod

Marcello, Benedetto, *Sonata in F Major:* Mead, Steven; Araki, Tamao

Marshall, George, *Ransomed:* Childs Brothers; Wise, Peter; Mead, Steven

Martin, Blaine/Bewley, *Have Yourself a Merry Little Christmas:* TubaShop Quartet

Martin, David, *Suite for Euphonium and Piano:* Young, Raymond G.

Martin, Glenn/Blane, *Ev'ry Time:* Mancuso, Gus

Martin, Glenn, *Bluesin' Tubas:* Tennessee Technological University Tuba-Euphonium Ensemble

Martin, Glenn, *Chops!:* Tennessee Technological University Tuba-Euphonium Ensemble

Martin, Glenn, *Pearl Casters:* Modern Jazz Tuba Project

Martin, Glenn, *Valvin' on a Riff:* Modern Jazz Tuba Project

Martini, Giovanni/Kanai, *Plaisir D'Amour:* Hokazono, Sho-ichiro

Martini, Giovanni/Lucena, *Plaisir D'Amour:* Baglin, Lyndon

Martini, Giovanni/Rimmer, *Plaisir D'Amour:* Richards, Robert

Martino, Ralph, *Fantasy:* British Tuba Quartet, The; Miraphone Tuba Quartet; Monarch Tuba-Euphonium Quartet

Martino, Ralph, *Introspect:* Behrend, Roger; Meixner, Brian

Mascagni, *Easter Hymn:* Childs, David

Mason, John/Rydland, *Rev. Archie Beaton:* Flaten, Tormod

Massenet, Jules/Flaten, *Meditation from "Thaïs":* Flaten, Tormod

Massenet, Jules/Margaret Erickson, *Argonaise from "Le Cid":* United States Navy Band Tuba-Euphonium Quartet; Monarch Tuba-Euphonium Quartet; Albertasaurus Tuba Quartet

Massenet, Jules, *Meditation from "Thaïs":* Withington, Len; Pfeifle, Nicolas

Mattei, Tito, *Non e Ver':* Lawrence, Mark

Matteson, Rich/Peterson, *Shout, The:* Matteson, Rich

Matteson, Rich, *A Very Special Love:* Matteson, Rich

Matteson, Rich, *Archie's Back:* Matteson, Rich

Matteson, Rich, *Carrob:* Matteson, Rich

Matteson, Rich, *Hassels:* Matteson, Rich

Matteson, Rich, *I Got No Bread:* Matteson, Rich

Matteson, Rich, *Ira's Tune:* Matteson, Rich

Matteson, Rich, *Little Ole Softy:* Matteson-Phillips Tubajazz Consort

Matteson, Rich, *Mikki's Blues:* Matteson, Rich

Matteson, Rich, *Shuckin' and Jivin':* Matteson, Rich

Matteson, Rich, *Spoofy:* Matteson-Phillips Tubajazz Consort

Matteson, Rich, *Surely We:* Matteson, Rich

Matteson, Rich, *Tahoe:* Matteson, Rich

Matteson, Rich; arr., *Cherokee:* Modern Jazz Tuba Project

Matteson, Rich; arr., *Waltzing Matilda:* Matteson-Phillips Tubajazz Consort

Mays, Lyle, *Kilgore Trout:* Matteson, Rich

McBride, Robert, *Way-Out, but Not Too Far:* Droste, Paul

McDermot, Ragni, and Rado/Bergmann, *Dead End:* Scandinavian Tuba Jazz

McHugh, Jimmy, *On the Sunny Side of the Street:* British Tuba Quartet, The

Mcmurrough, D., *Mancushla:* Schmidli, Erich

McPartland, Marian/Wilson, *Time and Time Again:* Matteson, Rich

McPherson, John, *Hugo Hugo:* Albertasaurus Tuba Quartet

McQueen, Ian, *Heights of Halifax, The:* Tuba Laté

Meacham, Frank, *American Tuba Patrol:* Rustic Bari-Tuba Ensemble

Mehlan, Keith, *Bottoms Up Rag:* Monarch Tuba-Euphonium Quartet

Mehlan, Keith, *Eine kleine Schreckens Musik (A Little Fright Music):* Monarch Tuba-Euphonium Quartet

Melillo, Stephen, *Erich!:* Colonial Tuba Quartet, The

Mendelssohn, Felix, *Hear My Prayer:* Childs, David

Mendelssohn, Felix, *If with All Your Heart:* Smith, Henry Charles; Childs, David; Bowman, Brian; Craig, Mary Ann

Mendelssohn, Felix, *Lord God of Abraham:* Smith, Henry Charles

Mendelssohn, Felix, *O Rest in the Lord:* Bowman, Brian

Mendelssohn, Felix/Bale, *Scherzo from "Midsummer Nights Dream":* Mead, Steven

Mendez, Rafel/Cole, *La Virgin De La Macarena:* Symphonia

Mendez/Freeh, *Valse:* Griffiths, Morgan

Mercer/Malenck, *Goody Goody:* Mancuso, Gus

Mertens, Hardy, *Scyths:* Dutch Tuba Quartet

Michel, Marc, *Le Jour ou les Tubas:* Steckar Elephant Tuba Horde

Mingus, Charles/Feldman, *Freedom:* Symphonia

Mitchell, Red, *Life's a Take:* Matteson, Rich

Mitchell-Davidson, Paul, *Tubafication:* Tuba Laté

Mobberley, James, *On Thin Ice:* Tennessee Technological University Tuba-Euphonium Ensemble

Monk, Thelonius, *Blue Monk:* Steckar Tubapack

Monk, Thelonius/Walker, *'Round Midnight:* Tennessee Technological University Alumni Tuba-Euphonium Ensemble; Tennessee Technological University Tuba-Euphonium Ensemble

Monk, Thelonius/Williams, *'Round Midnight:* Hokazono, Sho-ichiro

Montgomery, Ed, *Mirror Lake Suite:* Droste, Paul

Monti, Vittorio, *Czárdás:* Anonymous; Booth, Steven; Milhiet, Ivan; Contraband Tuba Quartet

Monti, Vittorio/D. Childs, *Czárdás:* Childs, David

Monti, Vittorio/Kanai, *Czárdás:* Hokazono, Sho-ichiro

Monti, Vittorio/Seppälä, *Czárdás:* Myllys, Jukka

Monti, Vittorio/Veit, *Czárdás:* Mead, Steven

Monti, Vittorio/Wilson, *Czárdás:* Childs Brothers; Verweij, Hugo

Moore, T., *Three Piece Suite:* Tuba Laté

Morel, Florentin, *Piece in fa mineur:* Miura, Toru; Young, Raymond G.; Fukuda, Masanori

Moren, Bertrand, *Mr. Euphonium:* Mead, Steven

Morgan, Lee/Hauser, *Sidewinder:* Tennessee Technological University Tuba-Euphonium Ensemble

Morley, Thomas, *April Is in My Mistress' Face:* British Tuba Quartet, The

Morricone, Ennio/D. Childs, *Gabriel's Oboe:* Childs, David

Morrison, Van/Kile, *Moondance:* Tennessee Technological University Tuba-Euphonium Ensemble

Moten, Bennie, *Moten Swing:* Tennessee Technological University Alumni Tuba-Euphonium Ensemble

Mouret, Jean/Self, *Rondeau:* Tubadours

Moussorgsky, Modeste, *Bydlo from "Pictures at an Exibition":* Smith, Henry Charles; Mulcahy, Michael

Moussorgsky, Modeste, *Where Are You, My Little Star?:* Murchinson, Matthew

Mozart, Leopold, *Concerto:* Pfeifle, Nicolas

Mozart, Wolfgang Amadeus, *Andante Cantabile from "Piano Sonata in C":* Albertasaurus Tuba Quartet

Mozart, Wolfgang Amadeus, *Aria:* Fukuda, Masanori

Mozart, Wolfgang Amadeus, *Concerto in B♭, K-191:* Chevailler, Jean-Pierre

Mozart, Wolfgang Amadeus, *Divertimento No. 2 in B♭:* Gerhard Meinl's Tuba Sextet

Mozart, Wolfgang Amadeus, *Marriage of Figaro:* McDonnell, Riki, and Mike Kilroy

Mozart, Wolfgang Amadeus, *Overture from the "Magic Flute":* Miraphone Tuba Quartet

Mozart, Wolfgang Amadeus, *Papageo Papagena:* McDonnell, Riki, and Mike Kilroy

Mozart, Wolfgang Amadeus, *Turkish March from "Piano Sonata in A":* Albertasaurus Tuba Quartet; British Tuba Quartet, The

Mozart, Wolfgang Amadeus/Blaauw, *Horn Concerto No. 4 in E♭ Major:* Heo, Jae-Young

Mozart, Wolfgang Amadeus/R. Childs, *Adagio and Rondo:* Childs, Robert

Mozart, Wolfgang Amadeus/Doerner, *Das Butterbrot:* Melton Tuba-Quartett

Mozart, Wolfgang Amadeus/Fabrizio, *Overture from the "Marriage of Figaro":* Monarch Tuba-Euphonium Quartet

Mozart, Wolfgang Amadeus/Ferguson, *Overture from the "Marriage of Figaro":* British Tuba Quartet, The

Mozart, Wolfgang Amadeus/Fletcher, *Eine Kleine Nachtmusik:* Melton Tuba-Quartett

Mozart, Wolfgang Amadeus/Gottschalk, *Overture from the "Marriage of Figaro":* University of Michigan Tuba and Euphonium Ensemble; United States Armed Forces Tuba-Euphonium Ensemble

Mozart, Wolfgang Amadeus/Henstridge, *Allegro from "Bassoon Concerto":* Griffiths, Morgan; Perrins, Barrie; Howell, Colin; Clough, John

Mozart, Wolfgang Amadeus/Mehlan, *Turkish Rondo:* Monarch Tuba-Euphonium Quartet

Mozart, Wolfgang Amadeus/Rimmer, *Non Piu Andrai:* Wilkinson, Harry

Mozart, Wolfgang Amadeus/Rive, *Rondo from "Horn Concerto in E♭":* Hildreth, Gordon

Mozart, Wolfgang Amadeus/Self, *Eine Kleine Nacht-musik:* Tubadours; Colonial Tuba Quartet, The

Mozart, Wolfgang Amadeus/Thompson, *Allegro from "Concerto in B♭, K 191":* Anonymous

Mozart, Wolfgang Amadeus/Werden, *Ah! Vous Dirai-Je, Maman:* Alchemy (previously Atlantic Tuba Quartet)

Mozart, Wolfgang Amadeus/Wright, *Rondo from "Concerto No. 4 in E♭ Major for Horn and Orchestra":* Lehamn, Arthur; Richards, Dean; Craddock, Ian; Baglin, Lyndon

Mueller, Frederick, *Concerto for Euphonium and Band:* Louder, Earle

Mühlfeld, W., *Conzertstück op. 7:* Heidler, Manfred

Murchinson, Charles/Murchinson, *Ev'ryone but Me:* Murchinson, Matthew

Naftel, Frederick, *Pascal's Victim:* Tuba Laté

Nagano, Mitsuhiro, *Matrix for Euphonium and Synthesizer:* Miura, Toru; Taylor, Robin

Narita, Tamezo/Kanai, *Song of the Seashore:* Mead, Steven

Narita, Tamezo/Kanai, *When You Wish upon a Star:* Mead, Steven

Narita, Tamezo, *Beach Song:* Araki, Tamao

Narita, Tamezo, *Hamabe no uta:* Hokazono, Sho-ichiro

Nelhybel, Vaclav, *Concerto for Euphonium and Band:* Behrend, Roger

Newsome, Roy, arr., *Dublin's Fair City:* McEnvoy, Graham

Newsome, Roy, arr., *Foxtrot between Friends:* McEnvoy, Graham

Newsome, Roy, *A Piece of Cake, Duet for Euphoniums:* Walton, Paul; Childs Brothers

Newsome, Roy, *Basics, The:* Tuba Laté

Newsome, Roy, *Fantasy on Swiss Airs:* Thomas, Shaun

Newton, Rodney, *Caelidh:* Childs, David

Nicolai, Otto, *Merry Wives of Windsor Overture:* British Tuba Quartet, The

Niehaus, Lennie, *Brass Tracks:* Lidsle, Harri

Niehaus, Lennie, *Grand Slam:* British Tuba Quartet, The

Niehaus, Lennie, *Saxidentally:* Top Brass

Niehaus, Lennie, *Sleeping Giants:* Contraband

Niehaus, Lennie, *Tubalation:* Miraphone Tuba Quartet

Nissim, Mico, *Symphonie des regards:* Milhiet, Ivan

Norbury, *Joyous Service:* Vanderweele, Aaron

Nordhagen, Stig, *Nocturne:* Dutch Tuba Quartet

Norton, George; Burnett, Ernie, *My Melancholy Baby:* Dickman, Marcus

Nux, P.V. de la, *Concert Piece:* Falcone, Leonard; Young, Raymond G.; Fukuda, Masanori

Nyro, Laura/Cherry, *Eli's Coming:* Tennessee Technological University Tuba-Euphonium Ensemble

Offenbach, Jacques/Fletcher, *Orpheus in the Underworld:* Lidsle, Harri

Offenbach, Jacques/Ito, *Bacarolle:* Miura, Toru; Mead, Steven

O'Hara, Betty, *Euphonics:* Tennessee Technological University Tuba-Euphonium Ensemble

O'Hara, Geoffrey, *I Walked Today Where Jesus Walked:* Bowman, Brian

Orff, Carl, *Ego Sum Abbas from "Carmina Burana":* Lehman, Arthur

Orsomando, Giovanni/Creux, *Alla Czárdás:* Mead, Steven

Osmon, Larry, *Frescos De Bonampak:* Tennessee Technological University Tuba-Euphonium Ensemble

Owen, Jerry, *Variations:* Werden, David

Paganini, Niccolo, *Moses-Fantasie:* Pfeifle, Nicolas

Paganini, Niccolo/Chabloz, *Moto Perpetuo:* Levi, Eran

Paganini, Niccolo/Richards, *Cantabile:* McDonnell, Riki, and Mike Kilroy; Mead, Steven

Paganini, Niccolo/Snell, *Moto Perpetuo:* Childs Brothers; Mead, Steven; Picton, Wendy

Paganini, Niccolo/Werden, *Caprice No. 17:* Heo, Jae-Young

Paganini, Niccolo/Wuthrich, *La Campanella from "Violin Concerto No. 2":* Kipfer, Ueli

Pape, *For Richer or Poorer:* Matteson, Rich

Paradies/Snell, *Sicilienne:* Mead, Steven

Parfrey, Raymond, *Male Voice for Brass:* Tuba Laté

Parfrey, Raymond, *Tributes to Tunesmiths:* Tuba Laté

Parissi, Rob/Kortyka, *Play That Funky Tuba Right, Boy!:* Tennessee Technological University Tuba-Euphonium Ensemble

Parker, Charlie, *Donna Lee:* Matteson, Rich

Parker, Charlie/Pirone, *Au Privave:* Mead, Steven

Parker, Handel/Walton, *Deep Harmony:* Tuba Laté

Parry/Maunder, *Myfanwy:* McDonnell, Riki, and Mike Kilroy

Pattison, *Gladsome Call, The:* Smith, Christopher

Payne, Frank Lynn, *Quartet for Tubas (The Condor):* University of Miami Tuba Ensemble; Melton Tuba-Quartett; Dutch Tuba Quartet; University of Michigan Tuba and Euphonium Ensemble

Pearce, *Welsh Fantasy:* Kane, Derick

Pecha, Antonin, *Hvezdonicka:* Miesenberger, Anton

Pegram, Wayne, *Broadway Brash:* Symphonia

Pegram, Wayne, *Howdy!:* Tennessee Technological University Tuba-Euphonium Ensemble; United States Armed Forces Tuba-Euphonium Ensemble

Pergolesi, Giovanni, *Nina:* Smith, Henry Charles

Perkinson, Coleridge Taylor, *'Way 'Cross Georgia:* Bargeron, Dave

Perry, Richard, *Kool Kube:* Modern Jazz Tuba Project

Pestalozza, A., *Ciribiribin:* Hokazono, Sho-ichiro

Petersen, Jack, *A Breath of Fresh Air:* Matteson, Rich

Petersen, Jack, *Dan's Blues:* Matteson, Rich

Petersen, Jack, *Groovey:* Matteson, Rich

Petersen, Jack, *Hey Man!:* Matteson, Rich

Petersen, Jack, *Kokomo:* Matteson, Rich

Petersen, Jack, *Skippin':* Matteson, Rich

Petersen, Jack/Perry, *Hey Man!:* Modern Jazz Tuba Project

Peterson, Oscar/J. Peterson, *Noreen's Nocturn:* Matteson-Phillips Tubajazz Consort

Phillips, John, *Romance:* Childs Brothers

Phillips, Richard, *There Will Be God:* Kane, Derick, Vanderweele, Aaron

Piazzolla, Astor, *Libertango:* Milhiet, Ivan

Piazzolla, Astor, *Suite Lumière:* Milhiet, Ivan

Piazzolla, Astor/Hokazono, *Tango-Etudes:* Hokazono, Sho-ichiro

Piazzolla, Astor/LaDuke, *Café 1930:* LaDuke, Lance

Piazzolla, Astor/LaDuke, *Nightclub 1960:* LaDuke, Lance

Piazzolla, Astor/Mead, *Café 1930:* Mead, Steven

Picchi, Ermano/Craig, *Fantaisie Originale:* Colonial Tuba Quartet, The

Picchi, Ermano/Mantia/Bale, *Fantaisie Originale:* Rüedi, Thomas; Mead, Steven; Frey, Adam

Picchi, Ermano/Mantia/Falcone, *Fantaisie Originale:* Falcone, Leonard; Champions of the Leonard Falcone Festival 1986–2000

Picchi, Ermano/Mantia, *Fantaisie Originale:* Bowman, Brian; Mead, Steven; Behrend, Roger; Falcone, Leonard; Lehman, Arthur; Hunter, Angie; Tropman, Matt; Frey, Adam; Colburn, Michael; Meli, Renato

Picchi, Ermano/Veit, *Fantaisie Originale:* Mead, Steven

Pilafian, Sam, *Relentless Grooves:* Tropman, Matt

Pilafian, Sam, *Relentless Grooves II, Armenia:* LaDuke, Lance

Plagge, Wolfgang, *Sonata Op. 64, for Euphonium and Piano:* Olsrud, Sverre Stakston

Plett, Danny, *Heaven:* Schmidli, Erich

Ponce, Manuel/Bennett, *Estrellita:* Mead, Steven

Ponce, Manuel/Lake, *Estrellita:* Mead, Steven

Ponce, Manuel, *Estrellita:* Falcone, Leonard; Frey, Adam

Ponchielli, Amilcare/Howey, *Concerto per Flicorno Basso:* Olsrud, Sverre Stakston; Heidler, Manfred; Champions of the Leonard Falcone Festival 1986–2000; Mead, Steven; Colburn, Michael

Porter, Cole, *Ev'ry Time We Say Goodbye:* Mancuso, Gus

Porter, Cole, *I Love You:* Matteson, Rich

Porter, Cole, *It's All Right with Me:* Tennessee Technological University Alumni Tuba-Euphonium Ensemble

Porter, Cole/Sample, *Cole Porter Medley:* Tennessee Technological University Tuba-Euphonium Ensemble

Poulenc, F., *Les Chemins L'Amour:* Hokazono, Shoichiro

Poulenc, Frank/Isoda, *Suite Francaise:* Hokazono, Sho-ichiro

Powell, Baden/Aquino/Buttery, *Bocoxe:* Alchemy (previously Atlantic Tuba Quartet); Melton Tuba-Quartett; British Tuba Quartet, The

Powell, Tom, *Duo for Euphoniums:* Warrington, Brian; Childs Brothers; Wilkinson, Harry

Premru, *In Memoriam:* British Tuba Quartet, The

Pressor, William, *Serenade for Four Tubas (Allegro, 3rd Movement):* University of Michigan Tuba and Euphonium Ensemble

Prieto, J./Siebert, *Wedding, The:* Peters, Neil; Crossley, Peter; Withington, Len; Pickard, Norman

Prima, Louis/Vinson, *Jump, Jive an' Wail:* Mead, Steven

Prima, Louis/Murphy, *Sing, Sing, Sing:* Modern Jazz Tuba Project

Primrose, Joe/Forbes, *St. James Infirmary Blues:* Sotto Voce Quartet; Tuba Laté

Prince, Bill, *Something Happy:* Dickman, Marcus

Prinz, *Merry Black Widow, The:* Mead, Steven

Proctor, S., *Light Metal-I Talatasco:* Tuba Laté

Prokofiev, Sergei, *Montagues and Capulets:* British Tuba Quartet, The

Prokofiev, Sergei/Butler, *Troika from "Lieutenant Kije":* Tennessee Technological University Tuba-Euphonium Ensemble

Prokofiev, Sergei/Fettig, *City Awakens, The:* Tropman, Matt

Prokofiev, Sergei/Fettig, *Juliet's Funeral and Death:* Tropman, Matt

Prokofiev, Sergei/Fettig, *Masks:* Tropman, Matt

Prokofiev, Sergei/Fettig, *Mercutio-Fight:* Tropman, Matt

Prokofiev, Sergei/Fettig, *Montagues and Capulets, The:* Tropman, Matt

Prokofiev, Sergei/Fettig, *Public Merryment:* Tropman, Matt

Prokofiev, Sergei/Fettig, *Romeo and Juliet at Parting:* Tropman, Matt

Prokofiev, Sergei/Fettig, *Romeo and Juliet, Introduction:* Tropman, Matt

Prokofiev, Sergei/Fettig, *Young Juliet, The:* Tropman, Matt

Pryor, Arthur, *Blue Bells of Scotland, The:* Childs, Nicholas; Behrend, Roger; Falcone, Leonard; Droste, Paul; Bowman, Brian; Runty, Thomas; Dodd, Michael

Pryor, Arthur, *Love's Enchantment:* Brasch, Harold

Pryor, Arthur/Pearson, *Blue Bells of Scotland, The:* Dickman, Marcus

Pryor, Arthur/Sparke, *Blue Bells of Scotland, The:* Kipfer, Ueli

Puccini, Giacomo, *Nessun Dorma:* Mead, Steven; Booth, Steven; Frey, Adam; McDonnell, Riki, and Mike Kilroy

Puccini, Giacomo, *Oh, My Beloved Father:* McDonnell, Riki, and Mike Kilroy

Puccini, Giacomo, *One Fine Day:* McDonnell, Riki, and Mike Kilroy

Puccini, Giacomo, *Recondita Armosia from "Tosca":* McDonnell, Riki, and Mike Kilroy

Puccini, Giacomo, *Turandoto:* Fukuda, Masanori

Puccini, Giacomo, *Your Tiny Hand Is Frozen:* McDonnell, Riki, and Mike Kilroy

Puccini, Giacomo/Bale, *Recondita Armosia from "Tosca":* Mead, Steven

Puccini, Giacomo/Bona, *Vissi d'arte from "Tosca":* Mead, Steven

Puccini, Giacomo/Colburn, *O, Mio Babbino Caro:* Colburn, Michael

Puccini, Giacomo/D. Childs, *Nessun Dorma:* Childs, David

Puccini, Giacomo/Mead, *Vissi d'arte from "Tosca":* Mead, Steven

Puccini, Giacomo/Moreau, *Oh, My Beloved Father:* Haemhouts, Ben

Puccini, Giacomo/Smith, *Oh, My Beloved Father:* Mead, Steven

Puccini, Giacomo/Stephens, *Nessun Dorma:* McDonnell, Riki, and Mike Kilroy

Puccini, Giacomo/Wilkinson, *Nessun Dorma:* Groom, Trevor; Mead, Steven

Puccini, Giacomo/Williams, *La Tregenda from "Le villi":* Symphonia

Pullig, Kenneth, *Dances; Four Tubas:* Colonial Tuba Quartet, The

Purcell, Henry, *Dido's Lament from "Dido and Aeneas":* British Tuba Quartet, The

Purcell, Henry, *Distressed Innocence Overture:* British Tuba Quartet, The

Puw, Guto Pryderi, *Visages:* Tuba Laté

Quibel, Robert, *Danse Bizarre n 3:* Steckar Tubapack

Rachmaninov, Sergei/Langford, *Vocalise, Op. 34, No. 14:* Clough, John; Lundin, Anders; Griffiths, Morgan

Rachmaninov, Sergei, *Vocalise, Op. 34, No. 14:* Fukuda, Masanori; Craig, Mary Ann; Frey, Adam; Mead, Steven

Ramsöe, Emilio/Buttery, *Andante Quasi Allegretto:* Melton Tuba-Quartett

Ramsöe, Emilio/Buttery, *Quartet for Brass No. 4:* Atlantic Tuba Quartet, The; United States Coast Guard Tuba-Euphonium Quartet; United States Navy Band Tuba-Euphonium Quartet; British Tuba Quartet, The; Coast Guard Tuba-Euphonium Quartet

Rance, Ernest, *Ochills:* Kane, Derick

Raum, Elizabeth, *A Little Monster Music:* Euphoniums Unlimited

Raum, Elizabeth, *Jason and the Golden Fleece:* Symphonia

Ravel, Maurice, *Piece en Forme de Habanera:* Falcone, Leonard; Murchinson, Matthew

Redhead, Robert, *Comfort My People:* Childs, David

Redhead, Robert, *Euphony:* Mead, Steven; Gagnaux, Alexandre; Wise, Peter; O'Brien, Robert; Metcalf, Curtis; Kane, Derick; Griffiths, Morgan; Giles, Mark; Davies, Russell

Redhead, Robert, *Ochills:* Vanderweele, Aaron

Reed, Alfred, *Seascape:* Behrend, Roger; Hokazono, Sho-ichiro; Miura, Toru

Reeman, John, *Episodes:* Tuba Laté

Reeman, John, *Sonata for Euphonium:* Mead, Steven

Reeman, John, *Sonatina for Tuba Quartet:* British Tuba Quartet, The

Regan, Michael J., *Quartet:* Tuba Laté

Relton, William, *Chevailler D'Honneur:* Moore, David; Schmidli, Erich

Rex, *Concertino:* Heidler, Manfred

Rice, Hugh Collins, *Earth and Moon:* Tuba Laté

Richards, Goff/Mead, *Midnight Euphonium:* Mead, Steven

Richards, Goff, *Country Scene:* Albiez, Cédric

Richards, Goff, *Jean-Elizabeth:* McDonnell, Riki, and Mike Kilroy

Richards, Goff, *Love Is Forever:* McDonnell, Riki, and Mike Kilroy

Richards, Goff, *Midnight Euphonium:* McDonnell, Riki, and Mike Kilroy; Squibb, Christian; Mead, Steven

Richards, Goff, *Pilatus:* Mead, Steven; Schmidli, Erich

Richards, Goff, *Rangitoto:* Gagnaux, Alexandre

Richards, Goff, *Vivid Colours:* Araki, Tamao

Richardson and Maclean/Whitcomb, *Too Fat Polka:* Tubadours

Ridout, Alan, *Pigs:* British Tuba Quartet, The

Rimmer, William/Kerwin, *In Dixieland:* McDonnell, Riki, and Mike Kilroy

Rimmer, William, *Hailstorm:* Bowman, Brian; Lehamn, Arthur; Meixner, Brian; Brasch, Harold; Morgan, Gareth

Rimmer, William, *Jenny Jones:* Baglin, Lyndon; Cresswell, John; Lawrie, Lindsay; Moore, David; Walton, Paul; Williams, Glyn; Picton, Wendy

Rimmer, William, *Weber's Last Waltz:* Mead, Steven; Withington, Len; Young, Ron

Rimsky-Korsakov, Nikolai, *Flight of the Bumble Bee, The:* Frey, Adam; Swiss Tuba Quartet

Rimsky-Korsakov, Nikolai/Bale, *Flight of the Bumble Bee, The:* Mead, Steven

Rimsky-Korsakov, Nikolai/D. Childs, *Flight of the Bumble Bee, The:* Childs, David

Rimsky-Korsakov, Nikolai/Ivallin, *Concerto for Trombone and Band:* Young, Raymond G.

Rimsky-Korsakov, Nikolai/James/Freeh, *Flight of the Bumble Bee, The:* Mead, Steven

Rimsky-Korsakov, Nikolai/James, *Flight of the Bumble Bee, The:* Gagnaux, Alexandre

Rimsky-Korsakov, Nikolai/Mead, *Notturno:* Mead, Steven; British Tuba Quartet, The

Rimsky-Korsakov, Nikolai/Newsome, *Flight of the Bumble Bee, The:* Childs Brothers

Rimsky-Korsakov, Nikolai/Watz, *Flight of the Bumble Bee, The:* Melton Tuba-Quartett

Rimsky-Korsakov, Nikolai/Woude, *Flight of the Bumble Bee, The:* Childs Brothers

Robbin, L./Rainger, *Easy Living:* Matteson, Rich

Robinson, Willard, *Pigeon Toed Joad:* O'Hara, Betty

Roblee, Richard, *Four Tuba Blues:* Melton Tuba-Quartett

Rodgers, Richard/Cherry, *My Favorite Things:* Tennessee Technological University Tuba-Euphonium Ensemble

Rodgers, Richard; Hart, Lorenz, *It's Easy to Remember:* O'Hara, Betty

Rodgers, Richard; Hart, Lorenz, *My Heart Stood Still:* O'Hara, Betty

Rodgers, Thomas, *Air for Tuba Ensemble:* Tennessee Technological University and Alumni Tuba-Euphonium Ensemble

Rodgers, Thomas, *If I Love You from "Carousel":* Wood, Ken

Rodgers and Hammerstein, *My Favorite Things:* Hokazono, Sho-ichiro

Rodgers and Hammerstein/Cherry, *Favorite Things:* Tennessee Technological University Tuba-Euphonium Ensemble

Rodgers and Hammerstein/Madill, *My Favorite Things:* Modern Jazz Tuba Project

Rodgers and Hart, *With a Song in My Heart:* Louder, Earle

Rogers, Thomas, *Music for Tuba Ensemble:* University of Miami Tuba Ensemble

Rogers, Walter, *Volunteer, The:* Brasch, Harold; Lehman, Arthur; Bowman, Brian

Rollins, Sonny/Dickman, *Doxy:* Dickman, Marcus

Rollins, Sonny/Matteson, *Oleo:* Matteson-Phillips Tubajazz Consort; Modern Jazz Tuba Project

Rollins, Sonny, *St. Thomas:* Matteson, Rich

Romberg, Sigmund/Godfrey, *Serenade from "The Student Prince":* Bowman, Brian; Yamamoto, Norihisa; Brasch, Harold; Craig, Mary Ann

Romberg, Sigmund/Oswin, *Serenade from "The Student Prince"*: McDonnell, Riki, and Mike Kilroy

Ropartz, Guy, *Andante and Allegro:* Young, Raymond G.

Ropartz, Guy, *Piece en mi bemol mineur:* Pfeifle, Nicolas

Roper, Anthony, *A String of Tones:* Tuba Laté

Roper, Anthony, *Sonata for Euphonium:* Mead, Steven

Rosler, J.J., *Partita—Polacca:* Gerhard Meinl's Tuba Sextet

Ross, John, *Concertino for Euphonium, Piano, and Percussion:* Colliard, Corrado

Ross, Walter, *Concerto Basso:* Tennessee Technological University Tuba-Euphonium Ensemble

Ross, Walter, *Partita for Euphonium and Piano:* Bowman, Brian; Verweij, Hugo; Araki, Tamao

Rossini, Gioacchino, *La Gazza Ladra:* Swiss Tuba Quartet

Rossini, Gioacchino, *Largo Al Factotum:* Childs Brothers; Pfeifle, Nicolas; McDonnell, Riki, and Mike Kilroy; Young, Raymond G.

Rossini, Gioacchino/Brennan, *Introduction, Theme and Variations:* Mead, Steven; Baglin, Lyndon

Rossini, Gioacchino/Davis, *Petit Caprice in the Style of Offenbach:* British Tuba Quartet, The; Monarch Tuba-Euphonium Quartet

Rossini, Gioacchino/Dawson, *Overture to William Tell:* Symphonia

Rossini, Gioacchino/Ito, *La Danza:* Miura, Toru

Rossini, Gioacchino/Kile, *Overture to the "Barber of Seville":* United States Armed Forces Tuba-Euphonium Ensemble

Rossini, Gioacchino/Langford, *Largo Al Factotum:* Clough, John; Craddock, Ian; Dart, Fred; Griffiths, Morgan

Rossini, Gioacchino/Newsome, *Introduction, Theme and Variations:* Kilroy, Mike

Rossini, Gioacchino/Smalley, *La Danza:* British Tuba Quartet, The; Miraphone Tuba Quartet

Rossini, Gioacchino/Smalley, *William Tell Overture:* British Tuba Quartet, The

Round, H., *Scenes That Are Brightest:* Williams, Joseph

Rüedi, Thomas, *Winter Dream:* Williams, Glyn

Russell, Leon/Florance, *Strange Thing:* Modern Jazz Tuba Project

Russell, Leon/Madill, *This Masquerade:* Modern Jazz Tuba Project

Ruth, Matthew, *Exigencies:* Tennessee Technological University Tuba-Euphonium Ensemble

Rutti, Carl, *Metamorphosis:* Childs, David

Saegusa, Shigeaki, *Journey to Cornwell:* Hokazono, Sho-ichiro

Saint-Saëns, Camille, *Softly Awakes My Heart:* McDonnell, Riki, and Mike Kilroy; Childs, David

Saint-Saëns, Camille, *Swan, The:* Hardick, Caspar; Falcone, Leonard; Campbell, Larry; Schmidli, Erich; Mead, Steven; Hunter, Angie; Teasdale, Malcolm; Louder, Earle

Saint-Saëns, Camille/Cohen, *Marche Militaire Francaise:* United States Army Band Tuba-Euphonium Ensemble and Massed Ensemble

Saint-Saëns, Camille/D. Childs, *Swan, The:* Childs, David

Saint-Saëns, Camille/Denton, *Swan, The:* Frey, Adam

Saint-Saëns, Camille/Larendeau, *My Heart at Thy Sweet Voice:* Breuninger, Tyrone

Saint-Saëns, Camille/Mead, *Swan, The:* Mead, Steven

Saint-Saëns, Camille/Minchin, *Elephant, The:* Tuba Laté

Saint-Saëns, Camille/Minchin, *Swan, The:* Tuba Laté

Saint-Saëns, Camille/Mott, *Le Cygne from "The Carnival of the Animals":* Clough, John; Baglin, Lyndon

Saint-Saëns, Camille/Mott, *Swan, The:* Parry, Glynn

Saint-Saëns, Camille/Murley, *Adagio from "Symphony No. 3":* British Tuba Quartet, The

Saint-Saëns, Camille/Nelson, *Morceau de Concert, Op. 94:* Nelson, Douglas; Louder, Earle

Saint-Saëns, Camille/Snell, *Swan, The:* Mead, Steven; Woollam, David

Saint-Saëns, Camille/Steadman-Allen, *Swan, The:* Childs Brothers; Kane, Derick; Codd, E;

Saint-Saëns, Camille/Stephens, *Swan, The:* Roberts, Roy

Sample, Steve, *Nostalgia Medley:* Tennessee Technological University Tuba-Euphonium Ensemble

Sampson, Edgar, *If Dreams Come True:* O'Hara, Betty

Sampson/Racaf/Foodman/Webb, *Stompin' at the Savoy:* Matteson-Phillips Tubajazz Consort

Sandoval, Migul, *Sin tu Amor:* Champions of the Leonard Falcone Festival 1986–2000

Sanson, Davide, *T-Tango:* Colliard, Corrado

Sarasate, Pablo de/Buitenhuis, *Gypsy Airs:* Gagnaux, Alexandre

Sarasate, Pablo de/Rüedi, *Gypsy Airs:* Rüedi, Thomas

Sarasate, Pablo de/Snell, *Gypsy Airs:* Mead, Steven

Sarasate, Pablo de/Snell, *Ziegunerweisen:* Mead, Steven

Sargent, Fred/Gedris, *Remember Your Dreams:* Murchinson, Matthew

Sass, Jon, *Meltdown:* Gerhard Meinl's Tuba Sextet

Schifrin, Lalo/Smalley, *Mission Impossible:* Tuba Laté

Schmid/Bacon, *Im Tiefsten Walde:* Mead, Steven

Schmidt, Dankwart; arr., *Tuba Muckl:* Contraband

Schmidt, Hugo, *Devil's Tongue, The:* Brasch, Harold; Craig, Mary Ann; Colburn, Michael; Lehman, Arthur

Schönberg, Claude-Michel/Barry, *On My Own* McDonnell, Riki, and Mike Kilroy

Schönberg, Claude-Michel/Mead, *On My Own:* British Tuba Quartet, The

Schönberg, Claude-Michel, *On My Own:* Miraphone Tuba Quartet

Schooley, John, *Cherokee:* Rustic Bari-Tuba Ensemble; Melton Tuba-Quartett; Matteson, Rich; Lidsle, Harri

Schoonenbeek, Kees, *Twilight Serenade:* Mead, Steven

Schubert, Franz, *Die Forelle:* Contraband Tuba Quartet

Schubert, Franz, *Serenade:* Falcone, Leonard

Schubert, Franz/Wilkinson, *Serenade:* Mead, Steven

Schubert, Franz Peter/LeClair, *Militärmarsch:* Contraband

Schubert, Franz Peter/LeClair, *Ständchen:* Contraband

Schulz, Patrick, *Profiles:* Sotto Voce Quartet

Schumann/Bell, *Jolly Farmer, The:* Lehman, Arthur

Schumann, Robert, *Fantasiestucke Op. 73:* Olsrud, Sverre Stakston

Schumann, Robert, *Träumerei aus Kinderszenen op. 15:* Heidler, Manfred

Schumann, Robert/Bowman, *Ich grolle nicht:* Behrend, Roger

Schumann, Robert/Droste, *Five Pieces in Folk Style, Op. 102:* Droste, Paul

Schumann, Robert/Gurtner, *Adagio and Allegro:* Mead, Steven

Schumann, Robert/Seitz, *Träumerei aus Kinderszenen op. 15:* Melton Tuba-Quartett

Schumman, William/Mahlknecht, *Erinnerung:* Mead, Steven

Scott/Bulla, *Commitment:* Vanderweele, Aaron

Scott, Casey/LaDuke, *Cry (If You Want To):* LaDuke, Lance

Scott, Stuart, *Fellscape:* Tuba Laté

Sedaka, *Solitaire:* Withington, Len

Seivewright, Andrew, *Gowbarrow Gavotte:* Tuba Laté

Self, James, *Euphoniums Unlimited:* Euphoniums Unlimited

Self, James, *La Morte dell' Oom:* Symphonia

Sell, Michael, *Death and Rebirth:* Burba, Malte

Selmer, *Barcarolle et Chanson Bachique:* Dart, Fred

Senaille, Jean Baptiste/Catelnet, *Allegro Spiritoso:* Young, Ron

Senaille, Jean Baptiste/Himes, *Allegro Spiritoso:* Himes, William; Mallett, Chris

Senaille, Jean Baptiste/Wright: *Allegro Spiritoso:* Baglin, Lyndon

Senaille, Jean Baptiste, *Allegro Spiritoso:* Falcone, Leonard; Behrend, Roger; Finch, Peter; Garnon, Barry; Louder, Earle

Senshu, Jiro, *Fantasy:* Araki, Tamao

Senshu, Jiro, *Window Opens Toward the Ocean, The:* Ushigami, Ryuji

Shaw, Lowell, *Frippery:* Miraphone Tuba Quartet

Shearing, George/Perry, *Lullaby of Birdland:* Tennessee Technological University Tuba-Euphonium Ensemble

Shearing, George, *Lullaby of Birdland:* Albertasaurus Tuba Quartet

Shelukov, Vyacheslav, *Etude No. 1:* Picton, Wendy

Shepherd, Arthur, *Nocturne and Rondolette:* Young, Raymond G.

Sherwin, Manning/Manhattan Transfer/Funderburk/Jones, *A Nightingale Sang in Berkley Square:* Symphonia

Sherwin, Manning/Mehlan, *A Nightingale Sang in Berkeley Square:* Monarch Tuba-Euphonium Quartet

Sherwin, Manning/Puerling/Cochran, *A Nightingale Sang in Berkeley Square:* Euphoniums Unlimited

Sherwin, Manning/Smalley, *A Nightingale Sang in Berkeley Square:* British Tuba Quartet, The

Short, T.V., *Emmett's Lullaby:* Lehman, Arthur

Shostakovich, Dimitri/Oliver, *Festive Overture:* Symphonia

Sibbing, Robert, *Reverie and Frolic:* Meixner, Brian

Sibelius, Jean, *Spruce, The:* Hokazono, Sho-ichiro

Silver, Horace/Hauser, *Sister Sadie:* Tennessee Technological University Tuba-Euphonium Ensemble

Silver, Horace/Matteson, *Gregory Is Here:* Matteson-Phillips Tubajazz Consort; Modern Jazz Tuba Project

Silver, Horace/Perry, *Cookin' at the Continental:* Modern Jazz Tuba Project

Silver, Horace, *Señor Blues:* Tennessee Technological University Alumni Tuba-Euphonium Ensemble

Simon, Paul/Lucena, *Scarborough Fair:* Baglin, Lyndon

Simons, Guardell, *Atlantic Zephyrs:* Falcone, Leonard; Mead, Steven

Singleton; arr., *Three Sixteenth Century Flemish Pieces:* Monarch Tuba-Euphonium Quartet

Skempton, Howard, *Rest and Recreation:* Tuba Laté

Smalley, Peter, *A Cool Suite:* British Tuba Quartet, The

Smalley, Peter, *Ball of Fire:* Mead, Steven

Smalley, Peter, *Glyder Landscape, The:* British Tuba Quartet, The

Smith, Arthur/Frey, *Duelin' Banjos:* Frey, Adam

Smith, Bernard, *Glorious Fountain:* Mallett, Chris

Smith, Claude T./Freeh, *Rondo:* Mead, Steven

Smith, Claude T., *Concert Piece for Euphonium:* Bowman, Brian

Smith, Claude T., *Rondo:* Werden, David; Young, Raymond G.

Smith, H., *It's Wonderful:* O'Hara, Betty

Smith, Robert, *Willson Suite:* Champions of the Leonard Falcone Festival 1986–2000; Behrend, Roger

Smith, *Invincible:* Moore, David

Snell, Howard, *Fever Fantasy:* Mead, Steven

Snell, Howard, *Oration:* Mead, Steven

Sobotta, Uli, *Bellamira:* Sobotta, Uli

Sobotta, Uli, *Blechente:* Sobotta, Uli

Sobotta, Uli, *Blue and Yellow—Beach Behind:* Sobotta, Uli

Sobotta, Uli, *Blue Fish Blue:* Sobotta, Uli

Sobotta, Uli, *Das A & O Der Gegenwart:* Sobotta, Uli

Sobotta, Uli, *Das Mirakel:* Sobotta, Uli

Sobotta, Uli, *Das Tier, Das Gemuse:* Sobotta, Uli

Sobotta, Uli, *Dibbuk:* Sobotta, Uli

Sobotta, Uli, *Don Quichotte:* Sobotta, Uli

Sobotta, Uli, *Drunken Early Morning Song:* Sobotta, Uli

Sobotta, Uli, *Erinnert Sich Der Hund:* Sobotta, Uli

Sobotta, Uli, *Good Morning My Head:* Sobotta, Uli

Sobotta, Uli, *Hatschichacha:* Sobotta, Uli

Sobotta, Uli, *Ins Blaue Licht:* Sobotta, Uli

Sobotta, Uli, *It's Good to Know:* Sobotta, Uli

Sobotta, Uli, *Koslowski:* Sobotta, Uli

Sobotta, Uli, *M—Virus:* Sobotta, Uli

Sobotta, Uli, *Metal Love:* Sobotta, Uli

Sobotta, Uli, *Nice Guys These Beatles:* Sobotta, Uli

Sobotta, Uli, *Pickle Song:* Sobotta, Uli

Sobotta, Uli, *Riedl Polka:* Sobotta, Uli

Sobotta, Uli, *Safety Pin:* Sobotta, Uli

Sobotta, Uli, *Slow Biker:* Sobotta, Uli

Sobotta, Uli, *Sprechstunde:* Sobotta, Uli

Sobotta, Uli, *To Cross the Mountain:* Sobotta, Uli

Sobotta, Uli, *Within/Without:* Sobotta, Uli

Sobotta, Uli, *Zeitvergleich:* Sobotta, Uli

Sobotta, Uli, *Zugvogel:* Sobotta, Uli

Sobotta, Uli, *Zum Schuls das Ende:* Sobotta, Uli

Solal, Martial, *For Tuba Only:* Steckar Tubapack

Solomons, David, *Pieces of Eight:* Tuba Laté

Solomons, David, *Prayer Before the Close of Day:* Tuba Laté

Sondheim, Stephen, *Send in the Clowns:* Tropman, Matt

Sousa, John Philip, *I've Made Plans for the Summer:* Colburn, Michael

Sousa, John Philip, *Stars and Stripes Forever:* Miraphone Tuba Quartet; Swiss Tuba Quartet

Sousa, John Philip, *Thunderer, The:* British Tuba Quartet, The; Tuba Laté

Sousa, John Philip, *Washington Post March:* Miraphone Tuba Quartet

Sousa, John Philip/Morris, *El Capitan:* British Tuba Quartet, The; Tuba Laté; Monarch Tuba-Euphonium Quartet

Sousa, John Philip/Morris, *Semper Fidelis:* British Tuba Quartet, The

Sousa, John Philip/Morris, *Washington Post March:* Colonial Tuba Quartet, The

Sousa, John Philip/Sabourin, *Washington Post March:* Melton Tuba-Quartett; British Tuba Quartet, The

Sousa, John Philip/Smalley, *Thunderer, The:* Dutch Tuba Quartet

Sousa, John Philip/Werden, *Hands Across the Sea:* Lidsle, Harri

Sousa, John Philip/Werden, *Stars and Stripes Forever:* Atlantic Tuba Quartet, The; Lidsle, Harri

Sousa, John Philip/Werden, *Washington Post March:* Contraband

Sparke, Philip, *Aubade:* Mead, Steven; Haemhouts, Ben; Breuninger, Tyrone; Millar, Billy

Sparke, Philip, *Birthday Tribute:* Mead, Steven

Sparke, Philip, *Euphonism:* McDonnell, Riki, and Mike Kilroy

Sparke, Philip, *Euphonium Concerto:* Mead, Steven; Araki, Tamao

Sparke, Philip, *Fantasy for Euphonium:* Childs, Robert; Childs Brothers; Bowman, Brian; Craddock, Ian; Crookes, Brian; Meli, Renato; Werden, David; Mead, Steven; Gagnaux, Alexandre; Breuninger, Tyrone

Sparke, Philip, *Mace:* Gagnaux, Alexandre

Sparke, Philip, *Pantomime:* Childs, Nicholas; Frey, Adam; Gosney, Richard; Hunter, Angie; Mead, Steven; Meli, Renato; Pugh, Joel; Schultz, Karl; Childs Brothers; Hokazono, Sho-ichiro

Sparke, Philip, *Song for Ina:* Mead, Steven; Ushigami, Ryuji; McDonnell, Riki, and Mike Kilroy

Sparke, Philip, *Two-Part Invention:* Childs Brothers; Hokazono, Sho-ichiro; Robyr, Dominique

Sparke, Philip/Maldonado, *Pantomime:* Mead, Steven; Myllys, Jukka

Spears, Jared, *Divertimento for Tuba Ensemble:* Tennessee Technological University and Alumni Tuba-Euphonium Ensemble; Tennessee Technological University Tuba-Euphonium Ensemble

Spinelli, Joseph, *Scratch My Back:* Mancuso, Gus

Spohr, Louis, *Benediction:* Young, Ron

Spurgin, Anthony, *Foursome for Brass:* Baglin, Lyndon

Squire, W. H./R. Childs, *Tarantella:* Childs, David

Squire, W.H., *Tarantella:* Falcone, Leonard; Baglin, Lyndon

Stamford, Charles Villes/R. Childs, *Caoine:* Childs, David

Stamp, Jack, *Colonial Express, The:* Colonial Tuba Quartet, The

Stanek, P., *Nocturno for Euphonium:* Anonymous

Stauffer, Donald, *Rube and Boob, for Trumpet, Euphonium and Band:* Biffle, Ronnie

Stauss, Johann/Berry, *Waltz from "Die Fledermaus":* Tubadours

Steadman-Allen, Ray, *Conqueror, The:* Kane, Derick; Childs Brothers

Steadman-Allen, Ray, *Love Lifted Me:* Clark, Trevor; Hammarberg, Ake

Steadman-Allen, Ray, *Lyric Variations:* Kane, Derick

Steadman-Allen, Ray, *Ransomed Host, The:* Groom, Trevor; Hunter, Angie; McNally, Robert

Steckar, Franck, *Danse Pour Un Kangourou:* Steckar Tubapack

Steckar, Franck, *Hurry Up:* Steckar Tubapack

Steckar, Franck, *In a Digital Mood:* Steckar Tubapack

Steckar, Franck, *ouleaux de Printemps:* Steckar Elephant Tuba Horde

Steckar, Franck, *ubapack Blues:* Steckar Tubapack

Steckar, Marc, *Bassa Cat:* Miraphone Tuba Quartet

Steckar, Marc, *Batubop:* Steckar, Marc

Steckar, Marc, *Dynozophorium:* Steckar Tubapack

Steckar, Marc, *Megalo Fanfare:* Steckar, Marc

Steckar, Marc, *Série Noire:* Steckar Tubapack

Steckar, Marc, *Tubas au Fujiyama:* Steckar Elephant Tuba Horde

Steckar, Marc, *Vendredi 13:* Steckar Tubapack

Steckar, Marc; Arcadio, Bernard, *Konservatorium:* Steckar, Marc

Steckar, Marc; Arcadio, Bernard, *Tubach:* Steckar, Marc; Swiss Tuba Quartet

Steckar, Marc; Franck Steckar, *Suite à Suivre:* Steckar Tubapack

Stephens, Denzil, *Solo Rhapsody for Euphonium:* Childs Brothers

Stevens, John, *Adagio:* Symphonia

Stevens, John, *Benediction:* Sotto Voce Quartet

Stevens, John, *Cookie's Revenge:* Symphonia

Stevens, John, *Dances:* Rustic Bari-Tuba Ensemble; Dutch Tuba Quartet; Lidsle, Harri; Melton Tuba-Quartett

Stevens, John, *Diversions:* Sotto Voce Quartet

Stevens, John, *Fanfare for a Friend:* Sotto Voce Quartet

Stevens, John, *Liberation of Sisyphus, The:* Bazsinka Tuba Octet; European Tuba Octet

Stevens, John, *Manhattan Suite:* University of Michigan Tuba and Euphonium Ensemble; Miraphone Tuba Quartet; Dutch Tuba Quartet; Sotto Voce Quartet

Stevens, John, *Moondance:* Dutch Tuba Quartet; Melton Tuba-Quartett; Sotto Voce Quartet

Stevens, John, *Music 4 Tubas:* Sotto Voce Quartet

Stevens, John, *Power:* Melton Tuba-Quartett; Lidsle, Harri; Sotto Voce Quartet; Swiss Tuba Quartet; Miraphone Tuba Quartet

Stevens, John, *Talisman:* Symphonia

Stevens, John, *Viva Voce!:* Sotto Voce Quartet

Stevens, Thomas, *A New Carnival of Venice:* Mead, Steven

Stockhausen, Karlheinz, *Chin-Dance:* Svoboda, Michael

Stradella, Alessandro/Barbagallo, *Aria di chiesa:* Mead, Steven

Strauss, Johann, *Impressario, The:* Swiss Tuba Quartet

Strauss, Johann, *Perpetuum Mobile:* British Tuba Quartet, The

Strauss, Johann, *Radetzky March:* Miraphone Tuba Quartet

Strauss, Johann/Seitz, *Tritsch-Tratsch Polka:* Melton Tuba-Quartett

Strauss, Johann/Smalley, *Chit Chat Polka:* British Tuba Quartet, The

Strauss, Richard, *Don Quixote:* Mulcahy, Michael

Strauss, Richard, *Ein Heldenleben:* Mulcahy, Michael

Strauss, Richard, *Nun's Chorus:* McDonnell, Riki, and Mike Kilroy

Stroud, Richard, *Treatments for Tuba:* Tennessee Technological University Tuba-Euphonium Ensemble

Sullivan, *Lost Chord, The:* Childs, David

Sun Ra, *Bassism:* McKinney, Bernard

Sun Ra, *Beginning, The:* McKinney, Bernard

Sun Ra, *Jet Flight:* McKinney, Bernard

Sun Ra, *Looking Outward:* McKinney, Bernard

Sun Ra, *New Day:* McKinney, Bernard

Sun Ra, *Of Wounds and Something Else:* McKinney, Bernard

Sun Ra, *Space Jazz Reverie:* McKinney, Bernard

Sun Ra, *Tapestry from an Asteroid:* McKinney, Bernard

Sun Ra, *What's That?:* McKinney, Bernard

Sun Ra, *Where Is Tomorrow?:* McKinney, Bernard

Susato, Tielman/Buttery, *Shepherd's Dance:* Alchemy (previously Atlantic Tuba Quartet)

Susato, Tielman/Winter, *Ronde and Saltarelle:* Atlantic Tuba Quartet, The

Sutton, Eddie, *Cavalier, The:* Baglin, Lyndon; Wharton, Andrew; Moore, David; Hallas, David; Cranson, Colin

Suzuki, Ryuta, *Psalm:* Taylor, Robin

Swift, George, *Elfriede:* Lehman, Arthur

Sykes, Steven, arr., *Carnival Cocktail:* McDonnell, Riki, and Mike Kilroy; Mead, Steven

Symes, M./Jones, *There Is No Greater Love:* Matteson, Rich

Szentpali, Roland, *Pearls:* Mead, Steven

Takács, Jenö, *Sonata:* Dart, Fred

Takemitsu, Toru/Fukjiwara, *Song of March:* Hokazono, Sho-ichiro

Tarlow, Lawrence, *Quintet for Tubas:* Garden State Tuba Ensemble

Taylor, Jeffery, *Fanfare No. 1:* Monarch Tuba-Euphonium Quartet; British Tuba Quartet, The

Tchaikovsky, Piotr, *Dance of the Sugar Plum Fairy:* British Tuba Quartet, The

Tchaikovsky, Piotr, *Dance of the Swans from "Swan Lake":* Brasch, Harold

Tchaikovsky, Piotr/Bale, *Humoreske:* Mead, Steven

Tchaikovsky, Piotr/Butler, *Neopolitan Song:* Tuba Laté

Tchaikovsky, Piotr/O'Conner, *Serenade for Tubas:* Tennessee Technological University Tuba-Euphonium Ensemble

Tchaikovsky, Piotr/Rüedi, *Andante Cantabile:* Rüedi, Thomas

Tchaikovsky, Piotr/Rüedi, *Nocturne Op. 19:* Rüedi, Thomas

Tchaikovsky, Piotr/Rüedi, *Variations on a Rocco Theme Op. 33:* Rüedi, Thomas

Tchaikovsky, Piotr/Self, *Dance of the Reed Pipes:* Tubadours

Tchaikovsky, Piotr/Smalley, *Trepak:* British Tuba Quartet, The

Telemann, Georg, *Sonata in f Minor:* Behrend, Roger; Fisher, Mark

Templeton, Alec, *Elegie:* Nelson, Douglas

Templeton, Alec, *Mr. Bach Goes to Town:* Contraband Tuba Quartet

Templeton, Alec, *On a Rocky Road:* Contraband Tuba Quartet

Templeton, Alec/Childs, *Sonia:* Childs, Robert

Thingäs, Frode, *Fink Finster:* Scandinavian Tuba Jazz

Thingäs, Frode, *Peace, Please:* Mead, Steven; Gagnaux, Alexandre

Thingäs, Frode, *Samba Loco:* Scandinavian Tuba Jazz

Thomas/Dos, *A la Romanesc:* Mead, Steven

Tjader, Patricia, *And Baby Makes Three:* Mancuso, Gus

Toda, Akira, *Euphonium Tuba Quartet:* Rustic Bari-Tuba Ensemble

Toda, Akira, *Student's Concertino:* Fukuda, Masanori

Toebosch, Louis, *Variaties voor Euphonium en Piano:* Verweij, Hugo

Toledo, Rene Luis/Murphy, *Rene's Song:* Modern Jazz Tuba Project

Tomaro, Mike, *Excursion:* Mueller, John

Tomasi, Henri, *Danse Sacrée:* Stewart, Dee; Hokazono, Sho-ichiro

Tomoana/Maunder, *Pokarekareana:* McDonnell, Riki, and Mike Kilroy

Torme, Mel/Bewley, *Christmas Song, The:* TubaShop Quartet

Toselli, Enrico/Pierce, *Serenata:* Haemhouts, Ben

Toselli, Enrico/Rüedi, *Serenata:* Mead, Steven

Toselli, Enrico, *Serenata:* Clough, John; Falcone, Leonard

Traditional, *Amazing Grace:* Top Brass

Traditional, *Angels We Have Heard on High:* Tuba Christmas Ensemble

Traditional, *Bavarian Polka:* British Tuba Quartet, The

Traditional, *Bayrische Polka:* Gerhard Meinl's Tuba Sextet

Traditional, *Bayrische Zell:* Gerhard Meinl's Tuba Sextet

Traditional, *Deck the Halls:* Tuba Christmas Ensemble

Traditional, *First Noel, The:* Tuba Christmas Ensemble

Traditional, *Go Tell It on the Mountain:* Tuba Christmas Ensemble

Traditional, *God Rest Ye Merry Gentlemen:* Tuba Christmas Ensemble

Traditional, *Good King Wenceslas:* Tuba Christmas Ensemble

Traditional, *Greensleeves:* Melton Tuba-Quartett; Swiss Tuba Quartet

Traditional, *Havah Nagilah:* British Tuba Quartet, The

Traditional, *How Great Thou Art:* Hunter, Angie

Traditional, *It Came upon a Midnight Clear:* Tuba Christmas Ensemble

Traditional, *Joy to the World:* Tuba Christmas Ensemble

Traditional, *Lark in the Clear Air, The:* Postma, Simon

Traditional, *Last Rose of Summer, The:* Hokazono, Sho-ichiro

Traditional, *Londonderry Air:* Melton Tuba-Quartett; Postma, Simon

Traditional, *O Come All Ye Faithful:* Tuba Christmas Ensemble

Traditional, *O Come, O Come Immanuel:* Tuba Christmas Ensemble

Traditional, *Old Star:* Melton Tuba-Quartett

Traditional, *O Little Town of Bethlehem:* Tuba Christmas Ensemble

Traditional, *Silent Night:* Tuba Christmas Ensemble

Traditional, *Spanish Dance:* Baglin, Lyndon

Traditional, *We Three Kings:* Tuba Christmas Ensemble

Traditional/Ades, *Londonderry Air:* Louder, Earle

Traditional/Baker, *Spread Your Wide Wings:* Childs, David

Traditional/Bewley, *Greensleeves:* TubaShop Quartet

Traditional/Boddington, *Long, Long Ago:* Baglin, Lyndon; Sullivan, Bert

Traditional/Buttery, *Christmas Tubas of the British Isles:* Alchemy (previously Atlantic Tuba Quartet)

Traditional/Buttery, *Greensleeves:* Atlantic Tuba Quartet, The; Miraphone Tuba Quartet; British Tuba Quartet, The; Rustic Bari-Tuba Ensemble

Traditional/Buttery, *Sponger Money:* Alchemy (previously Atlantic Tuba Quartet)

Traditional/Buttery, *While Soft Winds Shake the Barley:* Alchemy (previously Atlantic Tuba Quartet)

Traditional/Catherwood/Veit, *Lark in the Clear Air, The:* Mead, Steven

Traditional/Catherwood, *Lark in the Clear Air, The:* Mead, Steven

Traditional/Collins/French/Newsome, *Mountains of Mourne, The:* Clough, John; Childs, Nicholas

Traditional/Denny, *Turn Your Eyes upon Jesus:* McDonnell, Riki, and Mike Kilroy

Traditional/Denton, *Amazing Grace:* Frey, Adam

Traditional/Denton, *Last Rose of Summer, The:* Frey, Adam

Traditional/Denton, *Londonderry Air:* Frey, Adam

Traditional/Denton, *O Waly Waly:* Frey, Adam

Traditional/Denton, *Over Yandro:* Frey, Adam

Traditional/Denton, *Shall We Gather at the River:* Frey, Adam

Traditional/Denton, *Shenandoah:* Frey, Adam

Traditional/Denton, *Ye Banks and Braes:* Frey, Adam

Traditional/Downie, *My Love Is Like a Red Red Rose:* Kane, Derick

Traditional/Drover, *Wee Cooper of Fire:* Breuninger, Tyrone

Traditional/Fernie, *Air Varie:* Williams, Glyn

Traditional/Flotow von, *Last Rose of Summer, The:* Champions of the Leonard Falcone Festival 1986–2000

Traditional/Forbes, *Just a Closer Walk:* Tuba Laté

Traditional/Forbes, *Scarborough Fair:* Tuba Laté

Traditional/Fritze/Hildebrandt, *Colonial Suite, The:* Colonial Tuba Quartet, The

Traditional/Fritze, *Edelweiss:* Colonial Tuba Quartet, The

Traditional/Garrett, *Londonderry Air:* Tennessee Technological University and Alumni Tuba-Euphonium Ensemble; United States Armed Forces Tuba-Euphonium Ensemble; Bowman, Brian; Meixner, Brian

Traditional/Garrett, *Wabash Cannonball:* British Tuba Quartet, The; Tennessee Technological University and Alumni Tuba-Euphonium Ensemble

Traditional/Harclerode/Lycan, *We Three Kings:* Tubadours

Traditional/Ito, *Greensleeves:* Miura, Toru

Traditional/J. Iveson, *Londonderry Air:* Childs, David

Traditional/LaDuke, *Arran Boat/Untitled Air:* LaDuke, Lance

Traditional/LaDuke, *I Wonder What's Keeping My True Love Tonight:* LaDuke, Lance

Traditional/LaDuke, *May Morning Dew/Strawaway Child/Conlon's Jig:* LaDuke, Lance

Traditional/LaDuke, *Nine Points of Roguery/Murphy's Reel:* LaDuke, Lance

Traditional/Lohmann, George/Schmidt, *Bayrische Polka:* Contraband; Miraphone Tuba Quartet

Traditional/Maunder, *Hine e Hine:* McDonnell, Riki, and Mike Kilroy

Traditional/McRitchie, *Shenandoah:* Benedict, Lesley

Traditional/Mehlan, *Londonderry Air:* Monarch Tuba-Euphonium Quartet

Traditional/Minerd, *Sea Tubas:* Lidsle, Harri

Traditional/Moore, *3 Negro Spirituals:* Tuba Laté

Traditional/Mortimer, *An Eriskay Love Lilt:* Baglin, Lyndon

Traditional/Mortimer, *Drinking Song:* Mortimer, Alex

Traditional/Niehaus, *Spiritual Jazz Suite:* British Tuba Quartet, The

Traditional/Olcott, *Shenandoah:* Mead, Steven

Traditional/P. Graham, *Swedish Hymn:* Childs, David

Traditional/Plakidis, *Aija Zuzu:* Tuba Laté

Traditional/Roberts, *Carrickfergus:* Rüedi, Thomas; Drewitt, Adrian; Mead, Steven; Baumgartner, Stephane; Muggeridge, Keith

Traditional/Roberts, *Frankie and Johnny:* Mead, Steven

Traditional/Siebert, Edrich, *Edelweiss:* Garrett, Guy

Traditional/Snell, *Variations on Drink to Me Only:* Gagnaux, Alexandre; Mead, Steven; Flaten, Tormod

Traditional/Stephens, *Carrickfergus:* Childs, David

Traditional/Stephens, *Myfanwy:* Roberts, David

Traditional/Stuckelschweiger, *Pcelinca:* Mead, Steven

Traditional/Taylor, Jeff, *Nautical Variations:* Behrend, Roger

Traditional/Trippet/Howard, *Steal Away:* British Tuba Quartet, The

Traditional/Verweij, *Der Khusid geyt Tantsn:* Dutch Tuba Quartet

Traditional/Verweij, *Freylekhs fun der Khupe:* Dutch Tuba Quartet

Traditional/Werden, *English Country Airs:* Tuba Laté

Trenet, Paul, *I Wish You Love:* Williams, Glyn

Truax, Bert, *Love Song:* Mueller, John

Tull, Fisher, *Tubular Octad:* Tennessee Technological University Tuba-Euphonium Ensemble

Turek, Thomas, *. . . im Stillen berauschter Regen:* Heidler, Manfred

Turek, Thomas, *Tango Mortale:* Pfeifle, Nicolas

Turek, Thomas, *Walzer Nr. 1:* Pfeifle, Nicolas

Turpin, Tom, *Harlem Rag:* Albertasaurus Tuba Quartet

Twitchen, Bert, *Silver Threads:* Childs Brothers

Uber, David, *Exhibitions:* Euphoniums Unlimited; Royall, Dennis

Uber, David, *Montage, Op. 84:* Nelson, Douglas

Uber, David, *Music for the Stage:* Dutch Tuba Quartet

Uber, David, *Sonata for Euphonium and Piano:* Behrend, Roger

Unknown, *Alte Kameraden:* Miraphone Tuba Quartet

Unknown, *Bayerischer Defiliermarsch:* Miraphone Tuba Quartet

Unknown, *Bloos:* McKinney, Bernard

Unknown, *Blues:* McKinney, Bernard

Unknown, *Booze:* McKinney, Bernard

Unknown, *Casbah of Tetouan, The:* Miraphone Tuba Quartet

Unknown, *Castaldo March:* Miraphone Tuba Quartet

Unknown, *Dancing in the Dark:* McKinney, Bernard

Unknown, *Entrevue/Tribal:* Miraphone Tuba Quartet

Unknown, *Fughetta:* Swiss Tuba Quartet

Unknown, *Graf Zeppelin March:* Miraphone Tuba Quartet

Unknown, *Hallelijah Drive:* Swiss Tuba Quartet

Unknown, *Like What Is This?:* McKinney, Bernard

Unknown, *Mes Sana in Corpore Sano:* Miraphone Tuba Quartet

Unknown, *My Christ Is in All, in All:* Allison, Gordon

Unknown, *Parisian Thoroughfare:* McKinney, Bernard

Unknown, *Petersburger March:* Miraphone Tuba Quartet

Unknown, *Pictural:* Miraphone Tuba Quartet

Unknown, *Prelude and Dance:* Swiss Tuba Quartet

Unknown, *Preussens Gloria:* Miraphone Tuba Quartet

Unknown, *Settin' Red:* McKinney, Bernard

Unknown, *Shaw Nuff:* McKinney, Bernard

Unknown, *Skippy:* McKinney, Bernard

Unknown, *Tortion Level:* McKinney, Bernard

Unknown, *Under the Admirals Flag:* Miraphone Tuba Quartet

Unknown, *Under the Sea:* Miraphone Tuba Quartet

Unknown, *Variations for Euphonium:* Anonymous

Unknown, *Wassermusik:* Swiss Tuba Quartet

Unknown, *Woodyn' You:* McKinney, Bernard

Unknown, *Yorkscher March:* Miraphone Tuba Quartet

Unknown, *Yusef:* McKinney, Bernard

Vancura, Adolf, *Canzonetta amorosa op. 202:* Heidler, Manfred

Vaughan Williams, Ralph/Droste, *Six Studies in English Folk Song:* Droste, Paul

Vaughan Williams, Ralph, *Romanza:* Young, Ron; Droste, Paul

Vaughan, Rodger, arr., *Away in a Manger:* Tubadours

Vaughan, Rodger, arr., *Break Forth Oh Beauteous Light:* Tubadours

Vaughan, Rodger, arr., *Coventry Carol:* Tubadours

Vaughan, Rodger, arr., *Down by the Old Mill Stream:* Tubadours

Vaughan, Rodger, arr., *God Rest Ye Merry Gentlemen:* Tubadours

Vaughan, Rodger, arr., *Hail to the Lord's Annointed:* Tubadours

Vaughan, Rodger, *Jingle Bell Waltz:* Tubadours

Vaughan, Rodger, arr., *O Come Emmanuel:* Tubadours

Vaughan, Rodger, arr., *Oh Little Town of Bethlehem:* Tubadours

Vaughan, Rodger, arr., *Santa Claus Is Coming to Town:* Tubadours

Vaughan, Rodger, arr., *White Christmas:* Tubadours

Vejvoda/Zelch, *Rosamunde:* Mead, Steven

Verdi, Giuseppe, *Bella Figlia from "Rigoletto":* Louder, Earle

Verdi, Giuseppe, *Euphonium Solo from "Manzoni Requiem":* Louder, Earle

Verdi, Giuseppe, *Force of Destiny Overture:* British Tuba Quartet, The

Verdi, Giuseppe, *Two Selections from "La Traviata":* Albertasaurus Tuba Quartet

Verdi, Guiseppe, *Celeste Aida:* McDonnell, Riki, and Mike Kilroy

Verdi, Guiseppe, *La Donna e Mobile:* McDonnell, Riki, and Mike Kilroy

Verdi, Guiseppe, *La Miserere from "Il Travatore":* McDonnell, Riki, and Mike Kilroy

Verdi, Guiseppe, *Quartet from "Rigoletto":* McDonnell, Riki, and Mike Kilroy

Verdi, Giuseppe/Cole, *Dies Irae from "Requiem":* Symphonia

Verdi, Giuseppe/Creux, *A fors' è lui from "la Traviata":* Mead, Steven

Verdi, Giuseppe/Creux, *Ave Maria from "Otello":* Mead, Steven

Verdi, Giuseppe/Creux, *Di Provenza il mar, il suol from "la Traviata":* Mead, Steven

Vick, Harold, *Don't Look Back:* Zawadi, Kiane

Vick, Harold, *Melody for Bu:* Zawadi, Kiane

Vick, Harold, *Señor Zamora:* Zawadi, Kiane

Victoria, Thomas Luis de/Self, *O Vos Omnes:* Melton Tuba-Quartett

Vieuxtemps, Henri/Rüedi, *Elégie Op. 30:* Rüedi, Thomas

Vigneron, Louis, *Stabillo Steckardello:* Steckar Elephant Tuba Horde

Villa-Lobos, Hector/Buttery, *Danza, Martello:* Alchemy (previously Atlantic Tuba Quartet)

Vinson, Danny, *Memoirs of the American Civil War:* Alchemy (previously Atlantic Tuba Quartet)

Vinter, Gilbert, *Alla Burlesca:* Groom, Trevor; Baglin, Lyndon

Vinter, Gilbert, *Elegy and Rondo:* Groom, Trevor

Vinter, Gilbert, *Fancy's Knell:* Groom, Trevor; Baglin, Lyndon

Vivaldi, Antonio, *Concerto for Two Trumpets:* Anderson, Eric

Vivaldi, Antonio, *Sonata No. 6 in B♭ Major:* Smith, Henry Charles

Vivaldi, Antonio, *Sonata No.1 en Si b majeur:* Milhiet, Ivan

Vivaldi, Antonio/Beaver, *Winter:* Tennessee Technological University Tuba-Euphonium Ensemble

Vivaldi, Antonio/Maganini, *Bassoon Concerto No. 7 in a Minor:* Heo, Jae-Young

Vivaldi, Antonio/Mortimer *Sonata No. 6 in B♭ Major:* Kipfer, Ueli

Vizzuti, Paul, *Cascade:* Hokazono, Sho-ichiro

Wagner, Joseph, *Concerto Grosso:* Pascuzzi, Todd

Wagner, Richard, *Introduction to Act Three from "Lohengrin":* McDonnell, Riki, and Mike Kilroy

Wagner, Richard, *Song to the Evening Star:* Orosz, Josef

Wagner, Richard/Bale, *Walther's Prize Song:* Mead, Steven

Wagner, Richard/Hall, *Ride of the Valkyries, The:* Mead, Steven

Wagner, Richard/Ito, *Processional to the Minster:* Mead, Steven

Waller, Fats, *Jitterbug Waltz:* Dickman, Marcus

Waller, Thomas "Fats," *Alligator Crawl:* O'Hara, Betty

Watz, Franz, *Melton Marsch:* Melton Tuba-Quartett; Gerhard Meinl's Tuba Sextet

Webber, Andrew Lloyd, *All I Ask of You:* Schmidli, Erich; Kilroy, Mike

Webber, Andrew Lloyd, *Anything But Lovely:* Kilroy, Mike

Webber, Andrew Lloyd, *Love Changes Everything:* Schmidli, Erich

Webber, Andrew Lloyd/Graham, *Variations:* Mead, Steven

Webber, Andrew Lloyd/Kanai, *Music of the Night:* Hokazono, Sho-ichiro

Webber, Andrew Lloyd/Mowat, *All I Ask of You:* McDonnell, Riki, and Mike Kilroy

Webber, Andrew Lloyd/Woodfield, *Don't Cry for Me Argentina:* Merkin, Geoffrey

Weber von, C.M., *Bassoon Concerto:* Picton, Wendy

Weber von, C.M., *Romanta Passonata:* Fukuda, Masanori

Webster, P./Mandel, *Shadow of Your Smile, The:* Matteson, Rich

Webster/Brodsky, *I'll Walk with God:* Childs, David

Welcher, Dan, *Hauntings:* Symphonia

Werle, Floyd, *Variations on an Old Hymn Tune:* Tennessee Technological University Tuba-Euphonium Ensemble; United States Army Band Tuba-Euphonium Ensemble and Massed Ensemble

Weston, Randy, *Hi-Fi:* McKinney, Bernard

White, Donald H., *Lyric Suite:* Stewart, Dee; Champions of the Leonard Falcone Festival 1986–2000

White, Geno, *Bend to the Horizon:* Williams, Glyn

Wiedrich, William, *Reverie for Euphonium ans Paino:* Behrend, Roger

Wiggins, Brian, *Trilogy for Euphonium:* Gagnaux, Alexandre

Wiggins, Christopher, *Soliloquy IX:* Mead, Steven

Wiggins, Gerald, *Ruble and the Yen, The:* Mancuso, Gus

Wilby, Philip, *Concert Gallop:* Childs, Robert; Mead, Steven

Wilby, Philip, *Concerto for Euphonium:* Rüedi, Thomas; Childs, David; Childs, Robert; Gagnaux, Alexandre; Mead, Steven; Hokazono, Sho-ichiro

Wilby, Philip, *Danse Grecque, Zeibekikos:* Gagnaux, Alexandre

Wilby, Philip, *Flight:* Mead, Steven; Flaten, Tormod

Wilby, Philip, *Paganini Variations:* Childs, Robert

Wilder, Alec, *Carols for a Merry TubaChristmas:* TubaShop Quartet

Wilder, Alec, *Concerto for Euphonium and Wind Ensemble:* Swallow, John; Bowman, Brian; Kilpatrick, Barry

Wilder, Alec, *Sonata for Euphonium and Piano:* Kilpatrick, Barry; Mueller, John

Wilhelm, Rolf, *Bavarian Stew:* Melton Tuba-Quartett

Wilhelm, Rolf, *Concertino:* Mead, Steven

Wilkinson, Robert, *Happy Soul, The:* Dutch Tuba Quartet

Williams, Clarence; Williams, Spencer, *Royal Garden Blues:* Sotto Voce Quartet

Williams, John/Dawson, *March from "1941":* Dutch Tuba Quartet

Williams, John/Fiegel, *March from "1941":* Symphonia

Willibald, Kresin, *Movin Groovin/Tuba Rodeo/Tango:* Contraband Tuba Quartet

Willibald, Kresin; arr., *Swing Low:* Contraband

Wilson, Kenyon, *Tuba Quartet No. 1 in c Minor, Op. 3:* Tennessee Technological University Tuba-Euphonium Ensemble

Wilson, Kenyon, *Dance No. 1:* Tennessee Technological University and Alumni Tuba-Euphonium Ensemble

Wilson, Phil, *Another Balance:* Matteson, Rich

Wilson, Phil, *Budda Eastern Bebop:* Matteson, Rich

Wilson, Phil, *Buttercrunch:* Matteson, Rich

Wilson, Phil, *Colonel Corn:* Matteson, Rich

Wilson, Phil, *Hills and Valleys:* Matteson, Rich

Wilson, Phil, *Red Flannel Hash:* Matteson, Rich

Wilson, Phil, *Sound of the Wasp, The:* Matteson, Rich

Wilson, Phil, *That Wasp:* Matteson, Rich

Wilson, Phil, *Three Friends:* Matteson, Rich

Wilson, Phil, *What Wasp?:* Matteson, Rich

Wilson, Phil, *What's Her Name?:* Matteson, Rich

Wilson, Ted, *Wot Shigona Dew:* Tennessee Technological University Tuba-Euphonium Ensemble

Wilson, *Three Miniatures:* Campbell, Larry

Windsor, Basil, *Alpine Echoes:* Lehamn, Arthur

Wolking, Henry, *Tuba Blues Melody:* Melton Tuba-Quartett; British Tuba Quartet, The; Lidsle, Harri

Wood, Derek, *Tubafusion:* Tuba Laté

Wood, *Drink to Me Only with Thine Eyes:* Wood, Ken

Woode, H./Hines, *Rosette:* Matteson, Rich

Woodfield, Ray, *Caprice:* Gosney, Richard; Moore, David

Woodfield, Ray, *Double Brass:* Childs Brothers

Woodfield, Ray, *Varied Mood:* Lord, Stephen; Childs, Robert; Mead, Steven; Meli, Renato; Moore, David; Childs Brothers; Gagnaux, Alexandre; Childs, David

Wren, Jenny/Davis/Brasch, *Concert Polka:* Brasch, Harold; Burleson, Don

Wright, Dennis, *Trio Concerto:* Richards, Robert

Wright, Frank, arr., *Le Roi d'Ys:* Childs, David

Wrubel, Allie; Magidson, Herb, *Gone with the Wind:* Dickman, Marcus

Wyss, Thomas; arr., *Rondo Alla Turca:* Childs Brothers

Yamada, Kosaku/Ito, *Akatombow:* Miura, Toru

Yamada, Kosaku/Yamamoto, *Aka Tonbi:* Childs Brothers

Yon, Pietro, *Gesu Bambino:* Bowman, Brian

Yoshimatsu, Takashi, *Dream Song:* Hokazono, Sho-ichiro

Youmans, Vincent/Ito, *Carioca:* Miura, Toru

Youmans, Vincent/Rose/Eliscu, *Without a Song:* Matteson, Rich

Youmans, Vincent, *More Than You Know:* O'Hara, Betty

Young and Washington, *A Woman's Intuition:* O'Hara, Betty

Young, Victor; Elliot, Jack, *A Weaver of Dreams:* Dickman, Marcus

Young/Adamson, *China Gates:* McKinney, Bernard

Young/Pollack/Lewis/White, *By the Way:* Mancuso, Gus

Yuste, Miguel, *Solo De Concurso:* Mead, Steven; Hokazono, Sho-ichiro

Zawinul, Josef/Arnold, *Birdland:* Tennessee Technological University Tuba-Euphonium Ensemble

Zutano/Rimmer, *Spanish Serenade:* Davis, George

Addresses of Recording Companies/ Distributors

A & R Records, Euphonium Concerts, 14274 Crystal Cove Drive South, Jacksonville, FL, 32224

Abbey Brass. E-mail: info@abbeybrass.com.

ACA Digital Recording, Department BR-T. PO Box 450727, Atlanta, GA, 30345, USA.

Accura Recordings, PO Box 4260, Athens, OH, 45701-4260, USA.

Accurate Records, 117 Columbia Street, Cambridge, MA, 02139, USA.

Activ.

ACUM.

Adelphi Records, Box 7688, Silver Springs, MD, 20907, USA.

Adi Hershko, 123 Stern Street, Kiron 55.000, Israel.

AHO.

Al Opland Recording Service, 1006 5th Ave S., W. Pipestone, MN, 56164, USA.

Al Teare Digital Recordings, 9076 Willoughby Road, Pittsburgh, PA, 15237, USA. 412-367-1526.

Alba Records Oy, POBox 549 Fin-33101, Tampere, Finland. Tel int +358-3-345 1387. Fax int +358-3-345 1384. E-mail: timo@alba.fi. Web site: www.alba.fi.

Albany Records, 915 Broadway, Albany, NY, 12207, USA. Tel: 518-436-8814. E-mail: infoalbany@aol.com. Web site: www.albanyrecords.com.

Alchemy. Web site: www.alchemyrecords.com.

ALCRA.

Alles Records, Beim Sandschuster 11, 29640 Schneverdingen, Tel.: (05199) 98880. Fax: (05199) 988899. E-mail: db@allesrecords.de.

Altrisuoni. Web site: www.altrisuoni.com.

Amadeo, dist. PolyGram Group Distribution.

Amadeus Recording Studios, 59100 Prato (PO) Italy. Tel: +39 0574 692475. Fax: +39 0574 590918.

AMIGA, Deutsche Schallplatten GmbH, Berlin, 1080, Reichstagsuger.

Amos.

Angel, CEMA Distribution, 21700 Oxnard St. #700, Woodland Hills, CA, 91367, USA.

Antilles, dist. PolyGram Group Distribution.

AppleJazz Records, 10825 Wheaton Court, Orlando, FL, 32821, USA. Tel: 888-241-2464. E-mail: info@applejazz.com. Web site: www.applejazz.com.

AR University.

Arabesque Recordings, Arabesque Recordings, LLC, 420 Lexington Avenue Suite 340, New York, NY, 10170, USA. Tel: 800-966-1416. E-mail: info@arabesquerecords.com. Web site: www.arabesquerecordings.com.

Arbors Records, 2189 Cleveland Street, Suite 225, Clearwater, FL, 33765, USA.

Argo, dist PolyGram Group Distribution.

Ariola., Division of BMG and Arista Records.

Arista Records, Inc., 6 West 57th Street, New York, NY, 10019, USA.

Arktos, 18432—55 Avenue, Edmonton, Alberta, Canada. T6M 1Y7. Tel: 780 469-2192. Fax: 780-469-2192. E-mail: arktos@arktosrecordings.com. Web site: www.arktosrecordings.com.

Artifice Records.

Artlab. Web site: www.artlab.ch.

The Army Ground Forces Band, 1777 Hardee Avenue SW Ft. McPherson, GA, 30330-1062, USA. Tel: 404-464-6381. E-mail: afcs-pa@forscom. army. mil. Web site: www.forscom.army.mil/band/.

Artra, Artist management for Pat Sheridan.

Arts Music.

Aru Musici.

ASC CS.

ASI Records, 711 West Broadway, Minneapolis, MN, 55411, USA.

ASV Living Era, Distributed by Bournemouth Classic Compact. Web site: http://www.bcc-classics.co.uk.

Atemmusik Records, Brucknerstraße 12 A—4501 Neuhofen/Krems, Austria, Europe.

Atlantic Jazz, dist. Warner-Electra-Atlantic Corp.

Atlantic Records. Web site: www.atlanticrecords.com.

ATS Records. Web site: www.members.aon.at/ats/.

Audicom Corporation, 4950 Nome Street, Unit C, Denver, CO, 80239, USA.

Audio Fidelity, dist. Leisure Audio.

Audio House, dist. Strange Attractors. E-mail: info@strange-attractors.com.

Audite, Koch International, 177 Cantiague Rock Road, Westbury, NY, 11590, USA.

Austin.

Avant, dist. Western International Music.

AVS.

Bag Records.

Band Leader.

Banners and Bonnetts, dist. Salvationist Supplies & Publishing, Ltd.

Barbirolli Society, 8 Tunnel Road, Retford Notts, Dn 22 7 TA, England.

Basic Video Arts.

Basset Hound Records, 2139 Kress Street, Los Angeles, CA, 90046, USA.

Bayrischen Rundfunk, Qualition Imports, 24-02 40th Ave., Long Island City, NY, 11101, USA.

BBC.

Bear Productions.

Beriato Music. Web site: www.beriato.com.

Bernel Music Ltd., PO Box 2438, Cullowhee, NC, 28723, USA.

BES.

Besses o' th' Barn Band. Web site: www.besses. co.uk.

BISRecords, Stationsvägen 20, SE-184 50 Åkersberga, Sweden. Tel. +46-8-544 102-30. Fax +46-8-544 102-40. E-mail: info@bis.se. Web site: www.bis.se.

Black Eagle.

Black Saint, Sphere Marketing, PO Box 771, Manhassett, NY, 11030, USA.

Blimp Recording Co.

Blue Groove Records, Liebhartstal Strasse 15-5, A-1160 Vienna, Austria.

Blue Hyacinth Productions.

Blue Note Records, Inc., 150 5th Ave., New York, NY, 10011, USA. Tel. 212-786-8600. Fax 212-786-8613.

BMG Entertainment, 1540 Broadway, New York, NY, 10036, USA.

BobX Music, USA.

Bocchino Music, Steven Mead, 10 Old Forge Road, Fenny Drayton, Nr. Nuneaton, Warks, CV13 6BD, UK. Web site: www.euphonium.net.

Boosey and Hawkes Sound Recordings, Boosey & Hawkes Music Publishers Limited, Aldwych House, 71-91 Aldwych, London, WC2B 4HN. Web site: www.boosey.com.

Borgen Records, Henning Christiansen, Bakkehojgaard, 4792 Askeby, Denmark.

Brain Music.

Brass Band Limburg, Provincialeweg-Zuid 52, 6438 BG Oirsbeek, Broekstraat 44, 6247 BS Gronsveld. Tel. 046-4422345, 043-408351, 0655-128470. Web site: http://cm19806-a.maast1.lb.home.nl/.

The Brass Chamber Music Foundation, Inc.

Brazzology Productions, Jazz group with Richard Murrow.

Broadway, PO Box 100, Brighton, MI, 48116, USA.

BVHaast Records BVHAAST, Prinseneiland 99, 1013 LN Amsterdam, Holland. Tel: +31 20 6239799. Fax +31 20 6243534. E-mail: bvhaast@xs4all.nl. Web site: www.xs4all.nl/~wbk/BVHAAST.html.

C&CC.

Cadence, dist. North Country.

Caedmon.

Cala Records. Web site: www.calarecords.com.

Camden. E-mail: info@camdenrecords.com.

Campro Productions, 70 Route 202 North, Petersborough, NH, 03458, USA.

Candid. Web site: www.candidrecords.com.

Canon.

Capital Records, 1750 N. Vine Street, Hollywood, CA, 90028, USA.

Capra.

Capriccio. Web site: http://www.capricciousa. com/capriccio.html.

Caprice, Svenska Rikskonserter, Box 1225, 111 27 Stockholm, Sweden.

Carnival Records, Att: Anders Ohlin, Kronborgs vägen 8 b, 217 42 Malmö, Sweden. Web site: www.carnivalrecords.com. E-mail: info@carnival-records.com.

CBC. Web site: http://www.cbcrecords.ca/. Canadian classical label.

CBS Inc., CBS Masterworks, 51 W. 52nd Street, New York, NY, 10019, USA.

Century Custom Recording Service, dist. Century Records.

Century of Chicago, dist. Century Records.

Century Records, 303 North Pine Street, Prospect Heights, IL, USA.

Chandos Records, LTD., 41 Charing Cross Road, London WC2HOAR, England.

Chase Music Group, PO Box 11178, Glendale, CA, 91226, USA. E-mail: cmgrec@earthlink.net. Tel. 800-724-2730.

Children's Records of America.

CH-Records.

Circle Records, Collector's Record Club, GHB Jazz Foundation Building, 1206 Decatur St., New Orleans, LA, 70116, USA.

CJS Records. Web site: www.cjs.co.uk.

Clean-feed Records. Web site: http://www. cleanfeed-records.com/.

Clear Ear Publishing.

CMP Records. Web site: http://www.artist-shop. com/cmp/.

College Presentation Series, dist. University of Illinois Band.

Colosseum Records, Qualition Imports, 24-02 40th Ave., Long Island City, NY, 11101, USA.

Columbia Records, dist. CBS Inc.

Columbia.Columbia Legacy, dist. Sony Music Distribution.

Composer's Recordings, Inc., 73 Spring Street, Room 506, New York, NY, 10012, USA.

Concord Records, PO Box 845, Concord, CA, 94522, USA.

Cornell University Wind Ensemble, Band Office, Lincoln Hall, Cornell University, Ithaca, NY, 14850, USA.

Coronet Recording Co., 4971 N. High Street, Columbus, OH, 43214, USA.

CPO Records.

CR.

Crest Music, 33 Chambers Bridge Road, Lakewood, NJ, 08901, USA.

Crest Records, dist. Golden Crest Records.

Cricket Records.

Crow Records, PO Box 600188, Dallas, TX, 75360, USA. Web site: www.crowrecords.com.

Crown Records, Reissued on Red Records, PO Box 750, Reseda, CA, 91335, USA.

Crystal Records, 28818 NE Hancock Road, Camas, WA, 98607, USA.

D Flat Records.

Dana Recording Project, Dana School of Music, Youngstown State University, Youngstown, OH, 44555, USA.

Dance Opus.

Dave Gannett, 82452 US Hwy 231 Arab, AL, 35016, USA.

Daybreak Express Records, PO Box 250, Van Brunt Station, Brooklyn, NY, 11215, USA.

De Haske Music Records, De Haske Music (UK) Ltd., Fleming Road, Corby NN17 4SN, England. Tel: 01536 260981. Fax: 01536 401075. E-mail music@dehaske.co.uk.

Decca, Decca Personality Series, dist. MCA Records.

Delos Records, Suite 200, El Capitan Building, 6834 Hollywood Blvd., Hollywood, CA, 90028, USA. Tel: (323) 962-2626, (800) 364-0645, (323) 962-2636 (fax). Web site: www.delosmus.com.

Denon. Web site: http://www.usa.denon.com/.

Deroy Records. Web site: www.deroyrecords. co.uk.

Deutsche Grammophon, dist. PolyGram Group Distribution.

Deutsche Schallplatten, DEUTSCHE SCHALLPLATTEN GMBH BERLIN Reichstagsufer 4-5 01080 Berlin. Tel.: (0049)(030) 2209-0. Fax.: (0049)(030) 2209-218. Web site: http://www.discogs.com/label/Deutsche+Schallplatten.

DHM.

Diablement Brass, dist. Artlab.

Diavolo Records, Schmid & Galke GbR, Kaiser Friedrich Strausse 4, Dusseldorf, Germany.

Digitally Encoded Cassette Classics, dist. Mr. Cassette, 360 Supertest Road, Ontario, Canada M3J 2M2.

Disc BIM, dist. North Country.

Discophon, Calle Cardenal Tedeschini, 14–22. Esca: A—2o, 4a, Barcelona–27, Spain.

Disneyland Records, Disneyland Productions, 350 S. Buena Vista, Burbank, CA, 91521, USA.

D'Note Classics, D'Note Records. Web site: http://www.dnote.com/mainframe.htm.

Doyen Recordings, LTD., Doyen House, 17 Coupland Close, Moorside, Oldham, Lancs., England 0L4 2TQ.

DPT.

East Coasting.

ECM, dist. PolyGram.

Ed. RZ. Web site: http://www.justjazz.net.nz/index.html.

Edipan. Web site: http://www.edipan.com/.

Edition Wilhelm Hansen, Ole Schmidt, Brokbjergstrand 12.4583 Sj, Odde, Denmark.

Educational Brass Recordings. Web site: http://www.windsongpress.com.

Egon Recordings. Web site: www.4barsrest.com

Electrecord, Allegro Imports, 3434 S. E. Milwaukie Ave, Portland, OR, 97202, USA.

Elf Records. Web site: http://www.ludwigmusic. com.

EMI Angel EMI Records. Web site: http://www. emigroup.com/.

ENJA. Web site: http://www.enjarecords.com/.

Epic, Epic Soundtrax, dist. Sony Music Distribution.

Equilibrium Records. Web site: http://www. equilibri.com/.

Et Pro Music.

Euphonia. Web site: http://www.euphonia.it/.

Euphonium Concerts, 14274 Crystal Cove Drive South, Jacksonville, FL, 32224, USA.

Euphonium Enterprises Inc., dist. Euphonium.com. Web site: www.euphonium.com.

Euphony.

Evatone Sound Sheets. Web site: www.evatone. com.

Excerpt Recording Company, PO Box 231, Kingsbridge Station, Bronx, NY, 10463, USA.

Extraplatte. Web site: http://www.extraplatte.at/.

FAB Recordings.

Fanfare, Intersound International, PO Box 1724, Roswell, GA, 30077, USA.

Fantasy Records, Tenth and Parker, Berkeley, CA, 94710, USA. Web site: www.fantasyjazz.com.

Fenox.

Festival Records. Web site: www.festivalrecords. com.au.

Fidelity Sound Records, PO Box 152, Hillsdale, NJ, 07642, USA. Web site: www.fidelityrecords.net.

Five Oaks Recordings.

Flying Fish Records, 1304 W. Schubert, Chicago, IL, 60614, USA.

Fodens Motor Works Band. Web site: www. fodensband.co.uk.

Fonit-Cetra, Allegro Imports, 3434 S. E. Milwaukee Ave, Portland, OR, 97202, USA.

Fontana, dist. Dutch Phillips Co.

Forces Command, Ft. McPherson, U.S. Army Ground Forces Band, Fort McPherson, GA, 30330-5000, USA.

Forte Records. Web site: www.allrecordlabels.com.

Four Leaf Records, Box 1231, 172 24 Sundbyberg, Sweden.

Fresh Sound Records, dist. Jazz Workshop S. L. Barcelona, Spain.

Friendly Bull Recordings.

Full Sail Studio Recordings. Web site: www.fullsail. com.

Furious Artisans. Web site: http://www. furiousartisans.com/.

GAR Music. Web site: http://members.aol.com/ ny91st/sound.html.

Gary Buttery Label.

Gasparo Records, PO Box 600, Jaffrey, NH, 03452, USA.

Geffen Records, 9130 Sunset Blvd., Los Angeles, CA 90069, USA.

German Brass Productions. Web site: http://www. german-brass.de/german_brass/contact/indexe. php.

GHB Records. Web site: http://www.jazzology. com/ghb_records.php.

GM Recordings, Gun Mar Music, 167 Dudley Road, Newton Centre, MA, 02159, USA.

GMH Records, Sundbyberg, Sweden.

GNP Crescendo, 8400 Sunset Blvd., Los Angeles, CA, 90069, USA.

Gold Star.

Golden Crest Records, Inc., 220 Broadway, Huntington Station, NY, 11746, USA.

Golden Records, 250 W. 57th Street, New York, NY, 10019, USA.

Grammofonfirma BIS, Varingavagen 6, 182 63 Djursholm, Sweden.

Grand Award. Web site: http://www.bsnpubs. com/abc/grandaward.html.

Grasmere. Web site: http://www.crazyjazz.co.uk/ labels/misc/miscgk.htm.

Grimethorpe Colliery Band. Web site: www. grimethorpeband.com.

Grosvenor, 16 Grosvenor Road, Handsworth Wood, Birmingham B20 3NP, England.

H & L Records.

Hal Leonard, 7777 West Bluemound Road, PO Box 13818, Milwaukee, WI, 53213, USA.

Harlequin Recording, Elgar House, Rufford, Tamworth, Staffordshire, England. E-mail: info@harlequinrecords.com.

Harmonic Discovery Studios, 38 Manningham Lane, Bradford. BD1 3EA. Web site: www. harmonic-discovery.net.

Harold T. Brasch.

Harris and Dyer Records. Web site: www.hdrecords. com.

Harvey Phillips Foundation, PO Box 933, Bloomington, IN, 47402, USA.

Hassell Records.

Hat Art Records, Im Muhleboden 54, CH-4106 Therwil, Switzerland.

Heartdance Music, 1(800) 884-8422. Web site: hdance@mindspring.com.

Heavyweight Records, PO Box 57, Kettering, Northants NN15 5PL, England.

Hemisphere Records, PO Box 3578, New York, NY, 10185, USA.

Hermitage. Web site: http://www.bluesland productions.com/roadrecords/ngtb/.

Himpsl Records, Zwergerstrasse 2c D-85579 Neubiberg. Tel./Fax: (089) 637 27. E-mail: kontakt@ unterbiberger.de.

Hollick and Taylor, 16 Grosvenor Road, Handsworth Wood, Birmingham B20 3NP, England.

Horbury Victoria Band.

Horizon. Web site: http://www. horizonrecords.net.

HPF Records and Tapes, PO Box 933, Bloomington, IN, 47402, USA.

Hungaroton, Hungaroton Classics. Web site: http://www.hungaroton.hu.

Huntcliff Recording Services.

Hypnos Recordings. Web site: http://www.hypnos. com/.

I WANNA Records. Web site: http://www. weewanna.com/main.

IDA Records, dist. North Country. Web site: http://www.brittensmusic.co.uk/norway1. asp?label=IDA%20Records.

Idielle Music.

Impulse Records, dist. UNI. Web site: http://www. vervemusicgroup.com.

Impulse, dist. MCA. Web site: http://www. vervemusicgroup.com.

India Navigation, 177 Franklin St., New York, NY, 10013, USA.

Innove Records. Web site: http://www.tomheasley. com/buycds.html.

Innowo, Viale Verdi 1, 22037, Ponte Lambro, Italy.

Intim Musik. Web site: www.intim-musik.se.

Invisible Music. Web site: http://www. invisiblemusicrecords.com/.

IRIDA. Web site: http://www.deeplistening.org/ dlc/95irida.html.

JAM DISC. Web site: http://www.jamrecordings. com/catalog.php?alpha=vz.

Janus Musiek.

Janz Team.

Jazz Heritage, 914 Lanyard Avenue, Kirkwood, MO, 63122, USA.

JazzHausMusik. Web site: http://www.jazzhausmusik.de/.

Jecklin Red Note. Web site: http://www. swiss-music-news.ch.

JMT, dist. PolyGram Group Distribution. Web site: http://new.umusic.com.

John Fletcher Trust Fund, 14 Hamilton Terrace, London NW8 UG.

John Mueller, University of Memphis. E-mail: jtmueller@memphis.edu.

Kendor, PO Box 278, Delvan, NY, 14042, USA.

Kennedy.

Kestrel.

Kirklees Music, 609 Bradford Rd., Bailiff Bridge, Brighouse, West Yorkshire, HD6 4DN England. Web site: www.kirkleesmusic.co.uk.

Kitty Jazz, dist. Polydor Japan. Web site: http:// www.polydor.co.uk.

Klarion Records.

Klavier Recording Co., Klavier Records, PO Box 177, San Juan Capistrano, CA, 92675, USA.

Kleos. Web site: http://www.heliconrecords. com.

KM Educational Library, 2980 N. Ontario, Burbank, CA, 91504, USA.

KM Records, dist. KM Educational Library.

Koch International, 177 Cantiague Rock Road, Westbury, NY, 11590, USA.

KoDa. E-mail: dwaskew@uncg.edu.

Kompost Rekords, Beat Blaser, Steinenstrasse 28, CH-5406 Baden-Rutihof.

Kosei Publishing Co., ELF Music, Ludwig Music Publishing Co., 557 East 140th Street, Cleveland, OH, 44110, USA.

Krestrel Records.

KRO Records. Web site: http://allimportmusic. com/KRO-LAJ.html.

Krohnengen Brass Band. Web site: www.kbb.no.

Laurel. Web site: http://www.laurelrecord.com.

Legacy, Sony Music Entertainment.

Legend Record Co., 12055 Burbank Blvd, N. Hollywood, CA, 91607, USA.

Leisure Audio, PO Box 56757, New Orleans, LA, 70156-6757, USA. (800) 321-1499.

Leo Records, Box 193, 00101 Helsinki, Finland.

Loft Records, Schlehecker Str. 114.5064, Roesrath-Durbusch, Germany.

London Records, dist. PolyGram Group Distribution.

Look Records. Web site: www.lookrecords.com.

Lynx. Web site: http://www.lynxrecords.com.

M-A Music, K-tel International, 15535 Medina Road, Plymouth, MN, 55447, USA.

Made in Sweden.

Magna Graphic Jazz Productions.

Mama Foundation, 555 E. Easy Street, Simi Valley, CA, 93065, USA.

Manger Mussiklag, Norway.

Marc Dickman. E-mail: mdickmanjz@aol.com.

Marcophon, Im Schwantenmos 15, CH-8126 Zumikon, Switzerland.

Mark College Jazz Series, dist. Mark Recordings.

Mark Custom Recording Services, dist. Mark Recordings.

Mark Educational Recordings, dist. Mark Recordings.

Mark Nelson. Web site: http://members.aol.com/ mnelson921/.

Mark Recordings, 10815 Bodine Road, PO Box 406, Clarence, NY14031-0406, USA.

Martin-PM Sound. Web site: http://www.cmc. ie/composers.

MCA Records International, 70 Universal City Plaza, Universal City, CA, 91608, USA.

MD&G Records. Web site: http://www.dvdpacific. com/audio.

Mercury, dist. PolyGram Group Distribution.

MF Records. Web site: www.backtrackrecords.com.

MGM Children's Series, dist. PolyGram Group Distribution.

MGM, dist. PolyGram Group Distribution.

Miami United Tuba Ensemble Society.

Michigan State University.

Midland Sound Recordings.

Milestone.Fantasy, Inc., 10th & Parker, Berkley, CA, 94710, USA.

MILS. E-mail: mils@netti.fi. Web site: http://www. tks.pp.fi/ecdlp.html.

Mirafone. Web site: http://www.miraphone.de/.

Mizentertainment Records.

MMC.

MMM. Web site: http://www.nuloop.com.

Mole Records., dist. North Country. Web site: http://members.aol.com/molerecords206/ mole.htm.

Mood Records, DA Music, 362 Pinehurst Lane, Marietta, GA, 30068, USA.

Morehead State University Book Store, 4950 Nome Street, Unit C, Denver, CO, 80239, USA.

Mount Charles Band. Web site: www.mountcharles-band.co.uk.

Move Records. Web site: http://www.move.com. au/index.cfm.

MPS Records, dist. PolyGram Group Distribution.

mSi, Austria. Web site: http://www. rockdiscography.com.

MSRS.

MURCH.

Music for Pleasure. Web site: www.musicforpleasure. com.

Music Minus One. Web site: http://www. musicminusone.com.

Música Chilena de Siglo. Web site: http://www. latinoamerica-musica.net.

Música de Arte. Web site: http://www.hellion. com.br.

Musica Helvetica, Swiss Broadcasting Coporation, Swiss Radio International, 3000 Berne 15 – Switzerland.

Musical Heritage Society Orpheus, 1991 Broadway, New York, NY, 10023, USA.

Musical Rendezvous.

My Pal God. Web site: www.mypalgodrecords.com.

National Concert Band of America, PO Box 386, Oxon Hill, MD, 20745, USA. Web site: www. nationalconcertband.org.

Navigation, dist. India Navigation.

New Age Sight and Sound, (404) 956-7956.

New Columbian Brass Band.

New England Conservatory Wind Ensemble.

Nicolai Music, PO Box 253, Clear Spring, MD, 21722, USA. E-mail: nicolaimusic@erols.com.

Nicolas Pfeilfe Label, Germany.

Nippon Columbia Co. LTD.. Web site: www. columbia.jp.

Nippon Crown, Japan.

Norman Records, Unit 1 Armley Park Court, Stanningley Road, Leeds, LS12 2AE, UK. Phone/Fax: +44 0113 2311114. E-mail: phil@normanrecords.com. Web site: www. normanrecords.com.

North Country, Cadence Building, Redwood, NY, 13679, USA. Tel: 315-287-2852. Fax: 315-287-2860. E-mail: cadence@cadencebuilding.com. Web site: www.cadencebuilding.com.

Northern Sound.

Northern Tuba Lights, Harri Lidsle, Lautamiehen-katu 10B13, 15100 Lahti, Finland.

NOVA, Deutsche Schallplatten GmbH, Berlin, 1080, Reichstagsuger.

Nueve Composiciones de Camara.

Nurnichtnur, Dieter Schlensog GbR Gnadenthal 8, 47533 Kleve, Germany. Tel: +49 2821 18666. Fax: +49 2821 24780. E-mail: info@nurnichtnur.com. Web site: www.nurnichtnur.com.

NVA Production.

Obrasso Records. Web site: www.4barsrest.com.

Odyssey, dist. Sony Music Distribution.

Olufsen Records, Skt. Knudsvej 8.1903 Frederiks-berg C, Denmark.

Olympic Recording, University of Washington Press.

One Up.

Opera House Records.

Opus One, 212 Lafayette Street, New York, NY, 10012, USA.

Orion.

Ozone Music, Tel: 212-247-1596. Web site: www.ozonemusic.com.

PACD.

Pad Records. Web site: www.allrecordlabels.com.

Parade.

Pasadena Tabernacle Band. Web site: www.pasadenatab.org.

Pause Records. Web site: www.pauserecord.com.

Periferic. Web site: www.pefericrecords.com.

Peter Pan Records, Peter Pan Industries, 88 St. Francis Street, Newark, NJ, 07105, USA.

Philips, dist. PolyGram Group Distribution.

Phonodisc. Web site: www.collectable-records.ru.

Pierre Verany. Web site: www.arion-music.com.

Pilgrim Records. Web site: www.pilgrimrecords.com.

Plaene.

Plainsong.

Polydor, dist. PolyGram Group Distribution.

PolyGram Group Distribution, Worldwide Plaza, 825 Eighth Avenue, New York, NY, 10019, USA.

Polyphonic, 77-79 Dudden Hill Lane, London NW10 1BD, England.

Postcards.

Prestige, Fantasy Records, Inc. 10th & Parker, Berk-ley, CA, 94710, USA. E-mail: info@fantasyjazz.com. Web site: www.fantasyjazz.com.

Priceless Treasure.

Pro Musica.

Proviva, Deutsche Austrophon, GMBH.D-2840 Diepholz, Bestell Nr.: ISPV 102.

Pye Records. Web site: www.answers.com/topic/pye-records.

QCA Red Mark, Liben Records, Liben Music Publishers, 6265 Dawes Lane, Cincinnati, OH, 45230, USA.

Rainbow, dist. Collectables Records Corp. and Alpha Video Distributors.

Random Acoustics, Haager Str. 5, D-81671 Munchen, Germany. Tel: 49 89 45769190. Fax: 49 89 457691996. Web site: www.randomacous-tics.de.

RCA Red Seal, Bertelsman Music Group, 1133 Avenue of the Americas, New York, NY, 10036, USA.

RCA Victor, Bertelsman Music Group, 1133 Avenue of the Americas, New York, NY, 10036, USA.

RCA, RCA Red Seal, RCA Victor, dist. BMG Enter-tainment.

Recorded Publications Company, 1100 State Street, Camden, NJ, 08105, USA.

Red Lehr, Rural Route 1, Box 90, New Athens, IL, 62264, USA.

Rediffusion Records. Web site: http://www.vinylvulture.co.uk/pages/rediffusion.htm.

Regency Records. Web site: www.abbcyrecords.com.

Rene Gailly.

ReR, 79 Beulah Rd., Thornton Heath, Sur-rey CR7 8JG, UK. Tel: 44 (0)20 8771 1063. Fax: 44 (0)20 8771 3138. Web site: www.rermegacorp.com.

Ricordi, One World Records, 1250 W. Northwest Hwy., Suite 505, Palatine, IL, 60067, USA.

Righteous Babe.

River City Brass Band, Inc., 885 Progress Street #2, Pittsburgh, PA, 15212, USA. Tel: (800) 292-7222 (412) 322-7222. Web site: www.rcbb.com.

Robert Hoe.

Rodney Records.

Rofo Records.

Roger Behrend, Monarch Tuba/Euphonium Quartet, 9069 Northedge Drive, Springfield, VA, 22153, USA.

Ron Young Label.

Rondo Grammofon & Danish Brass Publishing, Indepent Music OH. PO Box 49.2680 Solrod Strand, Denmark.

Roulette Records. Web site: http://www.crazyjazz.co.uk/Labels/R/ROULETTE.htm.

Rounder Records, 1 Camp Street, Cam-bridge, MA, 02140, USA. Tel: 800-768-6337. E-mail: info@rounder.com. Web site: www.rounder.com.

Saarländischer Rundfunk. Web site: www.sr-online.de.

Sacem.

SAGA, Saga Records Limited, 326 Kensal Road, London W10, England.

Saints and Sinners.

Salvation Army Label, dist. Salvationist Supplies & Publishing, Ltd.

Salvation Army of Canada, dist. Salvationist Sup-plies & Publishing, Ltd.

Salvationist Supplies & Publishing, Ltd., 1 Tiver-ton Street, London, SE1 6NT, England. Tel: 020 7367 6570. Mail Order Hotline: 020 7367 6580. Fax: 020 7367 6589. Web site: http//:web.salva-tionarmy.org.uk.

Saskatchewan Arts Board, 2135 Broad Street, Regina, Saskatchewan S4P 1Y6. Tel: 306-787-4056. Fax: 306-787-4199. E-mail: sab@artsboard. sk.ca. Web site: www.artsboard.sk.ca.

Sawday Instruments. Web site: http://www. snhmusic.com.

Saydisc Records, c/o Gef Lucena, Saydisc Records, The Barton, Inglestone Common, Badminton, S. Glos., GL9 1BX, England. Fax: +44 (0)1454 299 858. Web site: www.saydisc.com. E-mail: saydisc@ aol.com.

SCH/8, 1985.

School of Music LP Records, University of Michigan, Ann Arbor, MI, 48109, USA.

SEM Gramophone.

Sentinel Records. Web site: www.sentinelireland. com.

Serendipity.

Seven Seas Records.

Sica-Sound-Music, Steinamangererstrasse 187, A-7400 Oberwart, Austria.

Silver Cornet Productions, PO Box 2699, Murfreesboro, TN, 37133, USA. Tel: (615) 890-7506. Web site: www.silvercornet.com.

Silver Crest, 408 Carew Tower, Cincinnati, OH, 45202, USA. *See* Golden Crest.

Silverline. Web site: http://www.silverlinerecords. com.

SIMAX-PSC, ProMusica AS, Boks 4379, Torshov, N-0402 Oslo, Norway.

Simon Says, Record Guild of America, 144 Milbar Blvd., Farmingdale, NY, 11735, USA.

Sion Records.

SJC Productions.

SJM Music.

SoCal.

Sony Music Entertainment, 550 Madison Avenue, New York, NY, 10022-3211, USA. Web site: www.sonymusic.com.

Soul Notes, Sphere Marketing, PO Box 771, Manhassett, NY, 11030, USA.

Sound Aspects, Cai Sound Aspects, Pedro R. de Freitas, Im Bluetengarten 14, 7150 Backnang, Germany.

Sound Mark, 4950-C Nome Street, Denver, CO, 80239, USA.

Sound News Studio.

SPLASC(H), Via Roma 11—PO Box 97, 21051 Arcisate, Italy.

St. Mary's College. Web site: www.saintmarys. edu.

Stanshaw. Web site: www.stanshawe.fsnet.co.uk.

Starfish Music. Web site: www.starfish-music.de.

Stash Records, 140 W. 22nd St., New York, NY, 10011, USA. Tel: 212-243-4321.

Stemra Records, Holland.

Sterling Productions, 20 W. Verde Lane Tempe, AZ, 85284, USA. Tel: 480-838-8292. Fax: 480-413-0483. Web site: www.sterlingproductions. com.

Stockhausen. Web site: http://www.newalbion. com/artists/stockhausenk/.

Stolat, Arista Records, Inc., 65 West 55th Street, New York, NY, 19919, USA.

Stomp Off, Box 342, Dept. C., York, PA, 17405, USA. Web site: www.stompoffrecords.com.

Strand.

Strata-East Records, PO Box 36, G. C. S., New York, NY, 10163, USA. Web site: www. serecs.com.

Strawberry Studios, 3 Waterloo Road, Stockport, SK1 3BD, England.

Studio fur Angewandte Musik, dist. Extraplatte.

Studio 2 Stereo Records. Web site: http://www. vinylvulture.co.uk/pages/studio-2-a.htm.

Summit Records, PO Box 26850, Tempe, AZ, 85285, USA. Tel: 480-921-5212. Fax: 480-491-6433. Web site: www.summitrecords.com.

Sunrise Record, 4069 Gordon Baker Rd., Toronto, Ontario M1W 2P3. Tel: 416-498-6601. Fax: 416-494-8467. Web site: www.sunriserecords.com.

Sverre Stakston Olsrud.

Swedish Society Discofil, Allegro Imports, 3434 S. E. Milwaukee Ave., Portland, OR, 97202, USA.

SWF.

SYB.

T.A.P. Music Sales, 1992 Hunter Ave. Newton, IA, 50208, USA. Tel: 641-792-0352. E-mail: tapmusic@tapmusic.com. Web site: www. tapmusic.com.

TB Records. Web site: http://www. tbrecordslimited.com.

TBR Publications.

Telarc International Corporation, 23307 Commerce Park Road, Cleveland, OH, 44122, USA. Web site: www.telarc.com.

Teldec, BMG Direct Marketing, 6550 East 30th Street, Indianapolis, IN, 46219, USA.

TFW Records.

ThorofonTime Records, Time Jazz Series, 2 West 45 Street, New York 36, NY, USA.

TMK Köln. Web site: www.tmk-gruppe.de.

Tomato Records, CEMA Distribution, 21700 Oxnard St. #700, Woodland Hills, CA, 91367, USA. E-mail: info@tomatorecords.com. Web site: www.tomatorecords.com.

Tomorrow River Music, PO Box 165, Madison, WI, 53701, USA. Tel: 608-423-3095.

Tontraeger.

Tormod Flaten.

Toshiba EMI. Web site: http://www.emigroup. com/.

Tower, Phone: 916-373-3050 Fax: 916-373-2930. Web site: www.towerrecords.com.

Trend Records-Discovery Records, PO Box 48081, Los Angeles, CA, 90048, USA.

Triangle Brass Band. Web site: http://www. trianglebrass.org/.

Triton Recordings. Web site: http://www. thestaffordshireband.com.

Triumphonic. Web site: http://www.triumphonic. com/audserve.html.

Troy Records.

Tryfan.

TTT Music.

TTU Recording Services, Tennessee Technological University, Bryan Fine Arts, Cookeville, TN, 38505, USA.

TUBA CD.

Tuba-Euphonium Press, 3811 Ridge Road, Annandale, VA, 22003-1832, USA. Fax: 703-916-0711. Web site: www.tubaeuphoniumpress.com.

Two-Ten Records. Web site: http://www.yorkshireimps.co.uk/recordings.asp.

Twoten.

Tyrone Breuninger.

U.K.M.A. Records.

UMG Recordings. E-mail: communications@umusic.com. Web site: www.umusic.com.

UNI Distribution Corp, 10 Universal City Plaza, Universal City, CA, 91608, USA.

Unit Records, Beat Blaser, Steinenstrasse 28, CH-5406 Baden-Rutihof, Switzerland.

United Artists. Web site: www.unitedartists.com.

United Sound.

United States Air Force Band, 201 McChord Street, Bolling AFB, DC, 20032-0202, USA. Web site: www.usafband.com.

United States Air Force of Mid-America, 900 Chapman Dr., Scott Air Force Base, IL, 62225-5115, USA. Tel: 618-229-8188. Fax: 681-229-0284. E-mail: amc-ba@scott.af.mil. Web site: public.amc.af.mil/band/.

United States Army Band, 204 Lee Ave., Fort Myer, VA, 22211-1199, USA. Web site: www.army.mil/armyband/.

United States Army Brass Band, 204 Lee Ave., Fort Myer, VA, 22211-1199, USA. Web site: www.army.mil/armyband/.

United States Coast Guard, 15 Mohegan Ave., New London, CT, 06320, USA. E-mail: alyman@cga.uscg.mil. Web site: www.uscg.mil/band/.

United States Navy Band, 617 Warrington Ave., S.E. Washington Navy Yard, DC, 20374-5054, USA. Tel: 202-433-6090. E-mail: NavyBand.Public.Affairs@navy.mil. Web site: www.navyband.navy.mil.

University Brass Recording Series, PO Box 2374 Station A, Champaign, IL, 61820, USA.

University of Illinois Band, 140 Harding Band Building, 1103 S. 6th Street, Champaign, IL, 61820, also: 2134 Music Building 1114 W. Nevada Street Urbana, IL, 61801, USA. Tel: 217-333-2620. Web site: www.bands.uiuc.edu

University of Kansas, Lawrence, 1530 Naismith Drive, Lawrence, KS, 66045-3102. Tel: 785-864-3436. Fax: 785-864-5866. Web site: www.ku.edu.

University of Michigan School of Music Records, School of Music LP Records, University of Michigan, Ann Arbor, MI, 48109, USA.

Vanguard. Web site: http://www.vanguardrecords.com/.

Varese-Sarabande, 13006 Saticoy Street, North Hollywood, CA 91605; 11846 Ventura Boulevard, Suite 130 Studio City, CA, 91604, USA. Tel: (800) 827-3734 or (818) 753-4143. Fax: (818) 753-7596. Web site: www.varesesarabande.com.

VDE-Gallo, Qualition Imports, 24-02 40th Ave., Long Island City, NY, 11101, USA. In Switzerland. Web site: www.vdegallo.ch. The American distributor is Albany Music Distributors, Inc. 915 Boadway, Albany, NY, 12207, USA. Tel: 518.436.8814. Fax: 518.436.0643. E-mail: LPAlbany@aol.com.

Verve, dist. UMG Recordings.

Viper Records, Viper Records 230 Mott St., New York, NY, 10012, USA. Tel: 212-873-4415. E-mail: info@viperrecords.com. Web site: www.viperrecords.com.

Volume pppp.

Walking Frog Records, PO Box 680, Oskaloosa, IA, 52577, USA. Tel: 641-673-8397. Fax: 888-673-4718. Web site: www.walkingfrog.com.

Warner Brothers, 3300 Warner Blvd., Burbank, CA, 91510, USA. Tel: 818-846-9090. Web site: www.warnerbrosrecords.com/.

Warner-Electra-Atlantic Corp, 111 N. Hollywood Way, Burbank, CA, 91505, USA. Web site: www.wea.com.

Watt Works, dist. PolyGram Group Distribution.

Weltmelodie, dist. Borgen Records.

Western International Music, 3707 65th Avenue, Greeley, CO, 80634-9626, USA. Tel: (970) 330-6901. Fax: (970) 330-7738. E-mail: wimbo@wiminc.com. Web site: www.wiminc.com.

Westmark Tapes, Opland Recordings, R. R. 10 Box 403, Sioux Falls, SD, 57104, USA.

Westminster.

Wheaton Municipal Band, City Hall, 303 W. Wesley Street Wheaton, IL, 60187. Web site: http://www.wheatonmunicipalband.org/.

White Line.

Willson, DEG Music, N3475 Springfield Road, Lake Geneva, WI, 53147, USA. Tel: 800-558-9416 or 262-248-8314. Web site: www.willsonbrass.com.

Winchester Music School.

Wonderland, AA Wonderland Records, 12 Gelb Ave., Union, NJ, 07083, USA; also: 2 Moores Valley Road, Homedale PO Box 30-831 Wainuiomata, Wellington New Zealand. Phone/fax: +64 4 939 7581.

Woong-Jin Records. E-mail: webmaster@woongjinmedia.com. Web site: www.woongjinmedia.com.

Word.

World Music Contest.

World Records.

World Wide Music. Web site: www.worldwidemusic.com.

World Wind Music, Ariane 6 3824 MB Amersfoort The Netherlands. Tel: +31-(0)33.4555004. Fax: +31-(0)33.4552730. E-mail: wwm@mirasound.nl. Web site: www.mirasound.nl/wwm/.

Y.A.B.B., Yale University Band Department, PO Box 208246, New Haven, CT, 06520-8246, USA. Web site: http://www.yale.edu/schmus/. Young People's.

ZERX, 725 Van Buren Place, SE Albuquerque, NM, 87108, USA. Web site: www.zerxrecords.com/.

Zuk Records, D-27568 Bremerhaven (Germany) Bürgermeister-Smidt-Straße 102 Tel.: +49 (0471) 49481—Fax: +49 (0471) 415378. E-mail: zuk-records@t-online.de. Web site: www.zuk-records.de/.

15. Bibliography

Kenneth R. Kroesche

This chapter is dedicated to providing a comprehensive listing of every book, article, and research document written about, or relating to, the euphonium. What follows represents countless hours of national online computer searches, as well as time spent reviewing the sources firsthand. For this, I am grateful to the staffs of the Kresge Library of Oakland University and Britton Library of the University of Michigan for their guidance and assistance with this project. Thanks must also be given to David Miles of the Tuba-Euphonium Press and David Sivant of Hickey's Music, who provided review copies of the most current publications and editions of books and texts. Deep appreciation is extended to my Oakland University colleague David Kidger for his support and insight in providing the most up-to-date research methods for this project. A special thanks goes to my undergraduate research assistant, Robert Benton, for his help in reviewing articles and books, as well as to Laura Kroesche, who helped in the final proofreading of the chapter.

In this section, every effort has been made to uncover, evaluate, and cite all books pertaining specifically to the euphonium, baritone horn, and tenor tuba. Special care has been taken to provide the most current citation of the book's edition and publisher.

Abbreviations: N.p. = no place, n.p. = no publisher, n.d. = no date.

Books

Bailey, Wayne, Patrick Miles, Alan Siebert, William Stanley, and Thomas Stein. *Teaching Brass: A Resource Manual.* New York: McGraw-Hill, Inc., 1992.

Cummings, Barton. *Teaching Technique on Brass Instruments.* Troy, Michigan: Encore Music Publishers, 1997.

Fasman, Mark J. *Brass Bibliography: Sources on the History, Literature, Pedagogy, Performance, and Acoustics of Brass Instruments.* Bloomington: Indiana University Press, 1990.

Griffiths, John R. *Low Brass Guide.* Hackensack, New Jersey: Jerona Music Corp., 1980. 2nd ed.

Roswell, Georgia: E. Williams Music Publishing Co., 1999.

Morris, R. Winston, and Edward R. Goldstein. *The Tuba Source Book.* Bloomington: Indiana University Press, 1996.

Rasmussen, Mary. *A Teacher's Guide to the Literature of Brass Instruments.* Durham, New Hampshire: Appleyard Publications, 1968.

Robertson, James. *The Low Brass Book: A Method for Private or Group Instruction.* Dubuque, Iowa: Wm. C. Brown Publishers, 1990.

Whitener, Scott. *A Complete Guide to Brass: Instruments and Technique.* New York: Schirmer Books, 1990. 2nd ed. Belmont, California: Schirmer and Thomson Learning, Inc., 1997.

Biography

Bridges, Glenn D. *Pioneers in Brass.* Rev. ed. Detroit: Glenn D. Bridges, 1968.

Meckna, Michael. *Twentieth-Century Brass Soloists.* Westport, Connecticut: Greenwood Press, 1994.

Discography

Bahr, Edward R. *Trombone/Euphonium Discography.* Stevens Point, Wisconsin: Index House, 1988.

Bailey, Wayne, Patrick Miles, Alan Siebert, William Stanley, and Thomas Stein. *Teaching Brass: A Resource Manual.* New York: McGraw-Hill, Inc., 1992.

Cummings, Barton. *Teaching Technique on Brass Instruments.* Troy, Michigan: Encore Music Publishers, 1997.

Griffiths, John R. *The Low Brass Guide.* Hackensack, New Jersey: Jerona Music Corp., 1980.

Louder, Earle L., and David R. Corbin. *Euphonium Music Guide.* Evanston, Illinois: Instrumentalist Co., 1978.

Morris, R. Winston, and Edward R. Goldstein. *The Tuba Source Book.* Bloomington: Indiana University Press, 1996.

Sloan, Gerald. *Orchestral Recordings for Low Brass Players.* Troy, Michigan: Encore Music, 1997.

Werden, David, and Denis Winter. *Euphonium Music Guide.* New London, Connecticut: Whaling Music Publishers, 1990.

Whitener, Scott. *A Complete Guide to Brass: Instruments and Technique.* New York: Schirmer Books, 1990. 2nd ed. Belmont, California: Schirmer and Thomson Learning, Inc., 1997.

Equipment

Bailey, Wayne, Patrick Miles, Alan Siebert, William Stanley, and Thomas Stein. *Teaching Brass: A Resource Manual.* New York: McGraw-Hill, Inc., 1992.

Bevan, Clifford. *The Tuba Family.* New York: Charles Scribner's Sons, 1978. 2nd ed. Winchester, Hampshire, England: Piccolo Press, 2000.

Bowman, Brian L. *Practical Hints on Playing the Euphonium/Baritone.* Practical Hints Series. Melville, New York: Belwin-Mills Publishing Corp., 1984.

Brasch, Harold T. *The Brass Clinic.* New York: C. Bruno & Son, 1958.

Draper, F. C. *The Besson Compensating System Fully Explained.* London: Besson, 1953.

Draper, F. C. *The Besson Compensating System Further Explained.* London: Besson, 1953.

Draper, F. C. *The Besson Compensating System Simply Explained.* London: Besson, 1953.

Draper, F. C. *Notes on the Boosey & Hawkes System of Automatic Compensation of Valved Brass Wind Instruments.* Rev. ed. London: Boosey & Hawkes, 1954.

Draper, F. C. *Report on Tone Projection Relative to Bell Front and Upright Bell Instruments.* New York: C. Bruno, 1957.

Robertson, James. *The Low Brass Book: A Method for Private or Group Instruction.* Dubuque, Iowa: Wm. C. Brown Publishers, 1990.

Whitener, Scott. *A Complete Guide to Brass: Instruments and Technique.* New York: Schirmer Books, 1990. 2nd ed. Belmont, California: Schirmer and Thomson Learning, Inc., 1997.

General References

Bailey, Wayne, Patrick Miles, Alan Siebert, William Stanley, and Thomas Stein. *Teaching Brass: A Resource Manual.* New York: McGraw-Hill, Inc., 1992.

Baines, Anthony. *Brass Instruments: Their History and Development.* New York: Charles Scribner's Sons, 1981. Reprint ed. Mineola, New York: Dover Publications, Inc., 1993.

Griffiths, John R. *Low Brass Guide.* Hackensack, New Jersey: Jerona Music Corp., 1980. 2nd ed. Roswell, Georgia: E. Williams Music Publishing Co., 1999.

Lehman, Arthur W. *The Art of Euphonium Playing.* Vol. I. Ed. Robert Hoe. Poughkeepsie, New York: n.p., n.d. N.p.: Tuba-Euphonium Press, 1992.

Lehman, Arthur W. *The Art of Euphonium Playing.* Vol. II. Ed. Robert Hoe. Poughkeepsie, New York: n.p., n.d.

Phillips, Harvey, and William Winkle. *The Art of Tuba and Euphonium.* Secaucus, New Jersey: Summy-Birchard Music, 1992.

Robertson, James. *The Low Brass Book: A Method for Private or Group Instruction.* Dubuque, Iowa: Wm. C. Brown Publishers, 1990.

Rose, William H. *Studio Class Manual for Tuba and Euphonium.* Houston, Texas: Iola Publications, 1980.

University of Iowa, School of Music. *University of Iowa Music Source Book: Wind and Percussion Materials.* Iowa City, Iowa: Paul Anderson, 1986.

History

Baines, Anthony. *Brass Instruments: Their History and Development.* New York: Charles Scribner's Sons, 1981. Reprint ed. Mineola, New York: Dover Publications, Inc., 1993.

Bevan, Clifford. *The Tuba Family.* New York: Charles Scribner's Sons, 1978. 2nd ed. Winchester, Hampshire, England: Piccolo Press, 2000.

Carse, Adam. *Musical Wind Instruments.* New York: Da Capo Press, 1965.

Droste, Paul. *The Euphonium Handbook.* Grand Rapids, Michigan: Yamaha Music Corporation, 1987.

Mason, J. Kent. *The Tuba Handbook.* Toronto, Ontario: Sonante Publications, 1977.

Morris, R. Winston, and Edward R. Goldstein. *The Tuba Source Book.* Bloomington: Indiana University Press, 1996.

Phillips, Harvey, and William Winkle. *The Art of Tuba and Euphonium.* Secaucus, New Jersey: Summy-Birchard Music, 1992.

Robertson, James. *The Low Brass Book: A Method for Private or Group Instruction.* Dubuque, Iowa: Wm. C. Brown Publishers, 1990.

Whitener, Scott. *A Complete Guide to Brass: Instruments and Technique.* New York: Schirmer Books, 1990. 2nd ed. Belmont, California: Schirmer and Thomson Learning, Inc., 1997.

Literature

Bailey, Wayne, Patrick Miles, Alan Siebert, William Stanley, and Thomas Stein. *Teaching Brass: A Resource Manual.* New York: McGraw-Hill, Inc. 1992.

Bevan, Clifford. *The Tuba Family.* New York: Charles Scribner's Sons, 1978.

Brisse, Hervé. *10 ans avec le tuba: catalogue raisonné.* Paris: Cité de la musique, Centre de ressources musique et danse, 1999. French.

Cummings, Barton. *Teaching Technique on Brass Instruments.* Troy, Michigan: Encore Music Publishers, 1997.

Griffiths, John R. *Low Brass Guide.* Hackensack, New Jersey: Jerona Music Corp., 1980. 2nd ed. Roswell, Georgia: E. Williams Music Publishing Co., 1999.

King, Robert D. *Brass Player's Guide*. North Easton, Massachusetts: Robert King Music, 1993.

Louder, Earle L., and David R. Corbin. *Euphonium Music Guide*. Evanston, Illinois: Instrumentalist Co., 1978.

Miles, David Royal. *An Annotated Bibliography of Selected Contemporary Euphonium Solo Literature by American Composers*. Annandale. Virginia: Tuba-Euphonium Press, 1992

Morris, R. Winston. *Tuba Music Guide*. Evanston, Illinois: Instrumentalist Co., 1973.

Preinsperger, Ewald. *Solo-Tenorhorn und Blasorchester: Verzeichnis von über 500 Solowerken für ein oder mehrere Tenorhörner/Euphonien und Blasorchester*. Wien: J. Kliment, 1995.

Rasmussen, Mary. *A Teacher's Guide to the Literature of Brass Instruments*. Durham, New Hampshire: Appleyard Publications, 1968.

Robertson, James. *The Low Brass Book: A Method for Private or Group Instruction*. Dubuque, Iowa: Wm. C. Brown Publishers, 1990.

Thompson, Mark, and Jeffrey Jon Lemke. *French Music for Low Brass Instruments: An Annotated Bibliography*. Bloomington: Indiana University Press, 1994.

Werden, David, and Denis W. Winter. *Euphonium Music Guide*. Dallas: Cimarron Music & Productions, 1997.

Whitener, Scott. *A Complete Guide to Brass: Instruments and Technique*. New York: Schirmer Books, 1990. 2nd ed. Belmont, California: Schirmer and Thomson Learning, Inc. 1997.

Orchestration

Kunitz, Hans. *Die Instrumentation*. Teil 9: Tuba. Leipzig, Germany: Breitkopf & Härtel, 1968.

Morris, R. Winston, and Edward R. Goldstein. *The Tuba Source Book*. Bloomington: Indiana University Press, 1996.

Werden, David. *Scoring for Euphonium*. New London, Connecticut: Whaling Music Publishers, 1989.

Pedagogy

Bailey, Wayne, Patrick Miles, Alan Siebert, William Stanley, and Thomas Stein. *Teaching Brass: A Resource Manual*. New York: McGraw-Hill, Inc., 1992.

Baker, Buddy. *The Buddy Baker Trombone Handbook*. Kevin Carroll, ed. Austin, Texas: International Trombone Association Manuscript Press, 2001.

Barker, Norman. *Sight-Reading and Technique: For Students, Teachers and Performers on Trumpet; French Horn; Cornet; Flugel Horn; Tenor Horn; Euphonium*. Middlesex, England: Moorcroft Publications, 1981.

Bellamah, Joseph L. *A Survey of Modern Brass Teaching Philosophies: of Today's Leading Brass Specialists Including Trumpet, Cornet, Horn, Trombone, Euphonium and Tuba: Also Including Jazz Approaches to Brass Playing by the Leading Performers*. San Antonio, Texas: Southern Music Co., 1976.

Bowman, Brian L. *Practical Hints on Playing the Euphonium/Baritone*. Practical Hints Series. Melville, New York: Belwin-Mills Publishing Corp., 1984.

Brasch, Harold T. *The Brass Clinic*. New York: C. Bruno & Son, 1958.

Brasch, Harold T. *The Euphonium and 4-Valve Brasses: An Advanced Tutor*. Arlington, Virginia: H. T. Brasch, 1971. N.p.: TUBA Press, 1997.

Brown, Merrill E. *Teaching the Successful High School Brass Section*. West Nyack, New York: Parker Publishing Company, 1981.

Cummings, Barton. *Teaching Technique on Brass Instruments*. Troy, Michigan: Encore Music Publishers, 1997.

Droste, Paul. *The Euphonium Handbook*. Grand Rapids, Michigan: Yamaha Music Corporation, 1987.

Fink, Reginald H. *The Trombonist's Handbook*. Athens, Ohio: Accura Music, 1977.

Griffiths, John R. *Low Brass Guide*. Hackensack, New Jersey: Jerona Music Corp., 1980. 2nd ed. Roswell, Georgia: E. Williams Music Publishing Co., 1999.

Hunt, Norman J. *Brass Ensemble Method*. 3rd ed. Dubuque, Iowa: Wm. C. Brown Company Publishers, 1974.

Hunt, Norman J. *Guide to Teaching Brass*. 3rd ed. Dubuque, Iowa: Wm. C. Brown Company Publishers, 1984.

Lehman, Arthur W. *The Art of Euphonium Playing*. Vol. I. Ed. Robert Hoe. Poughkeepsie, New York: n.p., n.d. N.p.: Tuba-Euphonium Press, 1992.

Lehman, Arthur W. *The Art of Euphonium Playing*. Vol. II. Ed. Robert Hoe. Poughkeepsie, New York: n.p., n.d.

Maddy, Joseph E., and Thaddeus P. Giddings. *Instrumental Technique for Orchestras and Bands*. Cincinnati, Ohio: Willis Music Co., 1926.

Mueller, Herbert C. *Learning to Teach through Playing: A Brass Method*. Reading, Massachusetts: Addison-Wesley Publishing Company, 1968.

Phillips, Harvey, and William Winkle. *The Art of Tuba and Euphonium*. Secaucus, New Jersey: Summy-Birchard Music, 1992.

Ployhar, James D. *I Recommend*. Tuning-Warm Up by Harold Brasch. Miami, Florida: Warner Bros. Publications, Inc., 1972.

Reinhardt, Donald S. *The Encyclopedia of the Pivot System for All Cupped Mouthpiece Brass Instruments*. New York: Charles Colin, 1964.

Robertson, James. *The Low Brass Book: A Method for Private or Group Instruction.* Dubuque, Iowa: Wm. C. Brown Publishers, 1990.

Rose, William H. *Studio Class Manual for Tuba and Euphonium.* Houston, Texas: Iola Publications, 1980.

Roznoy, Richard T. *Trombone—Low Brass Techniques and Pedagogy.* Boulder, Colorado: n.p., 1978.

Rusch, Harold W. *Hal Leonard Advanced Band Method for Baritone.* Special Studies by Butler R. Eitel. Winona, Minnesota: Hal Leonard Music, Inc., 1963.

Sax, Adolphe. *Méthode compléte pour saxhorn et saxtromba soprano, alto, ténor, baryton, basse et contrebasse á 3, 4 et 5 cylindres; suivie d' exercises pour l' emploi du compensatuer.* Paris, France: Brandus & Dufour, n.d.

Whitener, Scott. *A Complete Guide to Brass: Instruments and Technique.* New York: Schirmer Books, 1990. 2nd ed. Belmont, California: Schirmer and Thomson Learning, Inc., 1997.

Miscellaneous

Hunt, Norman J. *Brass Ensemble Method.* 3rd ed. Dubuque, Iowa: Wm. C. Brown Company Publishers, 1974.

Hunt, Norman J. *Guide to Teaching Brass.* 3rd ed. Dubuque, Iowa: Wm. C. Brown Company Publishers, 1984.

Severson, Paul, and Mark McDunn. *Brass Wind Artistry: Master Your Mind, Master Your Instrument.* Athens, Ohio: Accura, 1983.

KENNETH R. KROESCHE

In searching for dissertations and theses, the single, authoritative source still remains Dissertation Abstracts International (DAI), which is published by University Microfilms Inc. (UMI) of Ann Arbor, Michigan. Researching and obtaining dissertations and theses is now easier than it has ever been with the rapidly changing advances in technology. By accessing the UMI ProQuest Digital Dissertations at http://il.proquest.com/brand/umi, anyone can view a database of Dissertation Abstracts from the most current two years for free. Most university libraries subscribe to UMI's online service, making it possible to search all citations dating before the current two-year period. Offered in PDF format, each entry will include a full citation, abstract, the first 24 pages of the manuscript if dated from 1997 to the present, as well as the convenient option of ordering the dissertation online. Presently, all dissertations and theses dated prior to 1997 may be obtained by ordering them through Dissertation Express, which is also available through the UMI website.

Dissertations, Theses, and Research Projects

Bibliography

Thompson, John Mark. "An Annotated Bibliography of French Literature for Bass Trombone, Tuba, and Bass Saxhorn Including Solos and Pedagogical Materials." D.M.A. diss., University of Iowa, 1991.

Overview: Within the scope of the literature for low brass, the researcher quickly finds that there is a very limited selection of solo literature and pedagogical materials. A particularly noteworthy series of reference works began to emerge in 1963 in which prominent brass educators have attempted to keep teachers and students informed of what literature is available for their instruments. Some texts list solos by composer, title, and publisher; others include a simple grading system, an upper range stipulation, or short annotation. Only five texts provide extended annotations to include clefs, full range indications, duration, and additional information concerning mutes, mixed meter, and special performance techniques. Jeffrey J. Lemke's dissertation ["French Tenor Trombone Solo Literature and Pedagogy Since 1836." D.M.A. diss., University of Arizona, 1983] annotates French literature for tenor trombone only. While many of these publications are useful, they say little about the French literature for bass trombone, tuba, and bass saxhorn. This body of literature is essential because it alone constitutes approximately two-fifths of the entire body of published music composed for the bass trombone and a substantial portion of the available literature for tuba and bass saxhorn.

Purpose: It is the purpose of this essay to present the low brass teacher and student with an evaluation of the body of existing French literature for bass trombone, tuba, and bass saxhorn. Through the compilation of this bibliography, it is my desire to promote the use of more French solos and pedagogical materials by teachers and performers of low brass instruments. This will also serve as a companion guide to Lemke's dissertation; when combined, these two documents will yield a comprehensive discussion of French music for tenor trombone, bass trombone, tuba, and bass saxhorn. Because of the nature of some materials in this discussion, an occasional overlap may occur with Lemke's dissertation (e.g., items identified for trombone may be appropriate for both tenor and bass trombone).

Limitations: The musical material examined for this study includes French solos and pedagogical materials composed specifically for the bass trombone, French tuba, or bass saxhorn. Works written for tenor trombone with optional bass trombone parts have also been identified.

This study is primarily concerned with developments in low brass literature at the *Conservatoire National Supérieur de Musique de Paris* (hereafter called the Paris Conservatory) and other regional French conservatories. Examined works also contain pieces commissioned from non-French composers for use in the annual *concours* [contest] at the Paris Conservatory. Through techniques that will be discussed later, a comprehensive list of solo and study literature has been compiled. Out-of-print materials are listed because they might be found in school or private libraries, the International Trombone Association Resource Library, or occasionally in music stores that stock large inventories.

Biography

Dickman, Marcus, Jr. "Richmond Matteson: Euphonium Innovator, Teacher and Performer (Jazz)." D.M.A. diss., University of North Texas (0158), 1997, 97 pp. Advisor: Don Little; Source: DAI, 58, no. 07A, p. 2449; Accession No: AAG9801376; Subject: Music Biography.

Abstract: An examination is conducted of the life, career and musical styles of Richmond Matteson, an influential jazz euphonium and tuba performer of the twentieth century. The study includes a brief history of the euphonium's role in concert bands. A description of Matteson's background as a musician and clinician including education, influences and career changes will also be discussed.

Analysis of Matteson's improvisational style and a transcription from the recording Dan's Blues is included. A formal analysis of Claude T. Smith's Variations for Baritone is provided, as well as a brief biography of the composer. Matteson's stylistic traits which Smith employed for the composition of Variations for Baritone are illustrated. The conclusion calls for further study of jazz styles by euphoniumists with more frequent performances of Variations for Baritone. Appendices include lists of Matteson's compositions and arrangements, a selected discography and a list of clinics and performances from 1982–1992.

Good, Richard Deforrest. "A Biography of Earle L. Louder: Euphonium Performer and Educator (Louder, Earle L.)." D.M.A. diss., Arizona State University (0010), 1996, 91 pp. Advisor: Gail Eugene Wilson; Source: DAI, 57, no. 10A, p. 4182; Accession No: AAG9710356; Subject: Music Education, Music Biography.

Abstract: Earle L. Louder is a famous euphonium performer and respected low brass educator. The purpose of the study is to determine the influence of Earle L. Louder on current euphonium educators and performers. The information gathered on the life and influence of Earle Louder was organized in chronological order, beginning with his birth in 1932 and ending with his retirement from the teaching profession in 1996. Within this format, data was organized according to the following topics: Louder's early childhood through high school graduation, his experiences as a student of Leonard Falcone, his years with the United States Navy Band, and his tenure as a faculty member at Morehead State University.

Information gathered for the study was derived from a variety of sources. Louder's own recollections uncovered through personal interviews provided the most beneficial material.

Telephone interviews with colleagues, students and family were conducted. Transcripts, letters, concert programs and articles were reviewed.

The study revealed that Louder provides an essential transition between two schools of euphonium performance and acts as the catalyst for a contemporary sound. He also influenced a number of students on a personal level due to his humanistic, educational approach.

Huff, Sharon Elise. "The Life and Career Contributions of Brian L. Bowman through 1991 (Euphonium, Brass Pedagogy)." D.M.A. diss., University of Illinois at Urbana–Champaign (0090), 1994, 523 pp. Advisor: Blaine Edlefsen; Source: DAI, 55, no. 12A, p. 3678; Accession No: AAI9512407; Subject: Music Education, Music Biography.

Abstract: The purpose of this study was to present biographical data on the life and career of one of the United States' most prominent euphonium performer[s] and teacher[s], Dr. Brian L. Bowman, and to demonstrate how he has influenced the musical world. Bowman began his career as a soloist very early in his life and continued being featured throughout his 21-year career as a United States military bandsman in Washington, D.C. Bowman's high profile as a soloist with the United States Navy Band, the United States Bicentennial Band, and the United States Air Force Band has brought greater recognition to his instrument, the euphonium.

Chapter I of the study contains the introduction, statement of purpose, questions to be explored, delimitations, need for the study, procedure of the study, and related literature. Utilizing mainly primary source materials, Chapter II describes Bowman's early background, family life, musical influences, and training. A chronological description of Bowman's professional career while he was in the military service comprises Chapter III. Chapter IV outlines many of Bowman's teaching methods and philosophies. Eight of his former euphonium students, all of whom are also professional euphoniumists, were interviewed, and the results are compiled in this chapter.

Chapter V delves into how Bowman affected the design and manufacture of several models of euphoniums, including the Yamaha, Hirsbrunner, Marzan, and Willson euphoniums. A description of Bowman's involvement in the international organization for tuba and euphonium players, known as T.U.B.A., is presented in Chapter VI. Chapter VII contains information concerning the genesis and popularization of euphonium literature that was a direct result of Bowman's efforts or prominence as a musical artist. A summary of the study is contained in Chapter VIII, as are conclusions and suggestions for further study. A section of appendices is located just before the bibliography, which concludes the study.

Discography

Bahr, Edward Richard. "A Discography of Classical Trombone/Euphonium Music on Long-Playing Records Distributed in the United States." D.M.A. diss., University of Oklahoma (0169), 1980, 324 pp. Source: DAI, 41, no. 02A, p. 0451; Accession No: AAG8016922; Subject: Music.

Abstract: Purpose of the Study. The purpose of this study was to provide a comprehensive list of trombone and euphonium recordings in order that performers, teachers, students, composers, record collectors, and librarians might become better acquainted with the repertoire. The discography was particularly intended to make performers, teachers, and students of the trombone and euphonium aware of pertinent compositions that have and have not been recorded and also might serve toward broadening an individual's knowledge of and possible exposure to various interpretations of the trombone and euphonium repertoire.

Procedures/Conclusions. The procedure for the completion of this project began with the compilation of a list of the author's own records and of records available within local libraries in order to establish what information was to be included in the listing of recordings. Through study of this list it became obvious that specific elements were necessary for the compilation of the discography. As a result, the format of Part II was designed to include the elements pertinent to this discography. Thus, Part II includes a main listing of trombone and euphonium solo and ensemble recordings released commercially and categorical cross-reference listings of compositions. Included in these listings are the album title, the performer's or ensemble's name, other soloists or ensembles, the accompanist's name or the accompanying ensemble, the ensemble conductor's name, and the number of sides, record size, record label and number, and mono, stereo, or quadraphonic designation followed by the composer's name and the title of the

composition recorded. In order to allow for verification of each listing presented in this project, the basic source from which the information was obtained was also listed.

The descriptive section of the document, Part I, was designed after the fact to explain how the research was approached, conducted, and concluded; to suggest potential uses of the discography listing; and finally to recommend additions to the available body of recordings.

Performance

Cottrell, Jeffrey S. "A Historical Survey of the Euphonium and Its Future in Non-Traditional Ensembles Together with Three Recitals of Selected Works by Jan Bach, Neal Corwell, Vladimir Cosma, and Others (Romania)." D.M.A. diss., University of North Texas (0518), 2004, 59 pp. Advisor: Brian Bowman; Source: DAI-A, 65/03, p. 749; Accession No.: AAT 3126563; Subject: Music, Music Education.

Abstract: The euphonium has been a respected member of military bands, brass bands, and civilian concert (wind) bands since its invention in 1843. These bands were very visible to the public, and often performed popular music of the day. Since then, the euphonium has had occasional use in orchestral works, jazz, and in brass chamber groups as well. However, by the middle of the 20th century, its traditional use as an instrument of the wind band resulted in a prevailing attitude of the music world toward the euphonium as an instrument strictly for that purpose. This attitude, along with changing popular tastes in music, has over time caused professional opportunities for euphoniumists to become very limited. This lack of public exposure [sic] for the instrument has therefore resulted in people outside of wind band experience being unaware of the euphonium's existence. There have been, however, positive signs in the last thirty years that changes are taking place in prevailing attitudes toward the euphonium. The formation of the Tubists Universal Brotherhood Association (renamed the International Tuba Euphonium Association in 2000) as a supportive professional organization, the emergence of the tuba/euphonium ensemble as chamber music, new solo works by major composers, and the use of euphonium in nontraditional ensembles have all served to promote the instrument. The future of the euphonium will depend on exploring the possibilities of using the instrument in nontraditional ensembles, and on changing the way euphonium is taught in a way that will adjust to the changing musical climate.

Dickman, Marcus, Jr. "Richmond Matteson: Euphonium Innovator, Teacher and Performer (Jazz)." See listing under Biography, above.

Graves, Jeffrey Philip. "Three Programs of Euphonium and Tuba Music (Performance)." D.M.A. diss., University of Michigan (0127), 2000, Advisor: Fritz Kaenzig; Source: DAI, 61, no. 03A, p. 811; Accession No: AAI0801263; Subject: Music.

Abstract: Three euphonium and tuba recitals were given in lieu of a written dissertation.

The repertory for these recitals was chosen to represent the past, present, and future of literature for the modern euphonium and tuba. References to the past were made through performances of transcriptions heard in the second recital. The present state of repertory was represented through performances of British euphonium and tuba literature heard in the first recital. For the third recital, one composition was commissioned and premiered in an attempt to expand the compositional depth of the euphonium repertory. The third recital featured virtuosic works for euphonium from the past and present.

Friday, December 12, 1999, 8:00 P.M., School of Music Recital Hall, The University of Michigan. Assisted by Aldon Mazzoni, piano and Lara Coppler, piano. John Golland Euphonium Concerto, Op. 64; Arthur Butterworth Partita, Op. 89; Ralph Vaughan Williams Six Studies in English Folk Song; Philip Wilby Concert Gallop; Derek Bourgeois Euphoria, Op. 75; Brian Bowen Euphonium Music.

Friday, January 28, 2000, 8:00 P.M., School of Music Recital Hall, The University of Michigan. Assisted by Aldon Mazzoni, piano, Lara Coppler, piano and Anthony Halloin, Tuba. Georg Philipp Telemann Sonata in A Minor arranged by Keith Brown; Edward Gregson Tuba Concerto; Franz Joseph Haydn Trio XXII transcribed by Jeffrey Graves; Johann Nepomuk Hummel Bassoon Concerto.

Friday, March 17, 2000 8:00 P.M., School of Music McIntosh Theatre. Assisted by Aldon Mazzoni, piano and Rochelle Sennet, piano. Paul Hindemith Sonata for Tuba and Piano; Chingchu Hu Of Thee I Scream (premiere); Martin Ellerby Euphonium Concerto; Simone Mantia Variations on Auld Lang Syne.

Kroesche, Kenneth Ray. "Summary of Dissertation Recitals: Three Programs of Euphonium Music (Performance)." D.M.A. diss., University of Michigan (0127), 1994, Advisor: Fritz Kaenzig; Source: DAI, 55, no. 12A, p. 3679; Accession No: AAI0575628; Subject: Music.

Abstract: Three euphonium recitals were given in lieu of a written dissertation.

The repertory for these recitals was chosen to represent the past, present, and future of literature for the modern euphonium. References to the past were made through the performance of transcriptions heard in the first and second recitals. Further, this was the premise of the second recital which explored the legacy of early virtuoso euphoniumists. During the first and third recitals, a total of three compositions were premiered as an attempt to perpetuate the future euphonium repertory. The present state of the repertory was represented in all the recitals through the performance of what has become standard literature for the euphonium.

Sunday, February 28, 1993, 7:00 P.M., School of Music Recital Hall, The University of Michigan. Assisted by Howard Watkins, piano and Jeanine Sefton, marimba. Georg Philipp Telemann "Fantasy No. 2 in A Minor" from Zwolf Fantasien fur Querflote ohne Bass, transcribed by Kenneth Kroesche; William W. Wiedrich Reverie No. 3 (premiere); James Curnow Symphonic Variants for Euphonium and Piano; Samuel Adler Four Dialogues for Euphonium and Marimba; Robert Schumann Funf Stucke im Volkston, Op. 102, transcribed by Paul Droste.

Sunday, April 25, 1993, 6:00 P.M., School of Music McIntosh Theatre, The University of Michigan. Lecture-Recital: "The Euphonium Soloists of the John Philip Sousa Band." This performance was accompanied by a 37 piece band conducted by William W. Wiedrich. It was funded in part by a Dissertation Grant from the Horace H. Rackham School of Graduate Studies. Simone Mantia Believe Me if All Those Endearing Young Charms; Richard Wagner "Evening Star" from Tannhauser arranged by Mayhew Lake; Joseph DeLuca Beautiful Colorado; Gaetano Donizetti "Sextet" from Lucia di Lammermoor arranged by Leonard Smith; Edoardo Boccalari Fantasia di Concerto "Sounds of the Riviera."

Sunday, October 2, 1994, 1:00 P.M., School of Music Recital Hall, The University of Michigan. Assisted by Howard Watkins, piano. Stuart Folse Sonata for Euphonium and Piano (premiere); Walter S. Hartley Sextet for Euphonium and Woodwind Quintet (premiere); Jan Bach Concerto for Euphonium and Piano.

Krueger, T. Howard. "The Employment of Orchestral of Brass by Richard Strauss." M.M. thesis, Eastman School of Music, 1948. No abstract available.

Maldonado, Luis. "Three Programs of Euphonium Music (Performance)." A.MUS.D. diss., University of Michigan (0127), 1992, Advisor: Fritz Kaenzig; Source: DAI, 53, no. 05A, p. 1318; Accession No: AAG0571982; Subject: Music.

Abstract: Three recitals were presented in lieu of a written dissertation. Most of the music for the recitals were selected due to their importance as serious euphonium works. Also taken into consideration was the fact that these works were recently composed and these recitals were presented for the first Doctor of Musical Arts degree in Euphonium Performance at the University of Michigan.

The first recital was presented on Tuesday, January 14, 1992 at 8:00 P.M. at the School of Music Recital Hall at the University of Michigan. The program consisted of Sonata C-Dur by Johann Friedrich Fasch, one of the most significant German contemporaries of Bach; Brian Bowen's Euphonium Music (1978), which stresses the cello-like expressive qualities of the euphonium; Samuel Adler's Four Dialogues for Euphonium and Marimba (1974), the result of the first commission by the Tubists Universal Brotherhood Association (T.U.B.A.); William W. Wiedrich's Reverie (1978), which was written for Roger L. Behrend, principal euphoniumist with the United States Navy Band; and Jan Bach's Concert Variations (1977), also a commissioned work by T.U.B.A.

The second recital consisted of two compositions for solo euphonium and band. The performance was presented on Saturday, February 1, 1992 at 7:30 P.M. in Brucker Hall at Fort Myer, Virginia during the Ninth Annual United States Army Band Tuba-Euphonium Conference as part of the Grand Concert with the United States Army Band. The compositions were David R. Gillingham's Vintage (1990) for solo euphonium and symphonic band, and Philip Sparke's Pantomime (1986) for euphonium and concert band, which was adapted from brass band to concert band accompaniment by Luis Maldonado.

The final recital was presented on Thursday, March 14, 1992 at 8:00 P.M. at the School of Music Recital Hall at the University of Michigan. The program consisted of Hiroshi Hoshina's Fantasy (1986), commissioned by Toru Miura, Japan's most noted euphoniumist; Alec Wilder's Sonata for Baritone Horn (1959); Neal Corwell's Odyssey (1990) for euphonium and taped synthesizer accompaniment, written for Brian Bowman, United States' most noted euphoniumist; and Wilhelm Ramsoe's Quartet No. 4, Op. 37 (1888). The quartet was performed on original instrumentation: cornet, trumpet, tenor horn and tuba.

McCready, Matthew. "Euphonium/Trombone Doubling among Service Band Euphoniumists and Orchestral Trombonists in the United States." D.MUS. diss., Indiana University (0093), 1989, Source: ADD, X1989, p. 0215; Accession No: AAG0381041; Subject: Music.

Sherburne, Earl Larson. "An Analysis of the Blowing Pressure Used for Trombone and Euphonium Tone Production." Ph.D. diss., University of Minnesota (0130), 1981, 118 pp. Source: DAI, 42, no. 10A, p. 4197; Accession No: AAG8206423; Subject: Music.

Abstract: The purpose of this study was to test whether the euphonium required less blowing pressure than the trombone. To test whether various brands of instruments require different amounts of blowing pressure, three different trombones and three different euphoniums were used. Hypothesis I states that there is no difference in the blowing pressure used by a skilled performer to play the trombone and the euphonium. To test whether mouthpieces of various sizes require different blowing pressures to achieve the desired tone, five mouthpieces of different sizes were used in a separate test. Hypothesis II states that there is no difference in the blowing pressure used by a skilled performer to play a trombone using five mouthpieces of different size cups and/or throats.

One performer played three notes selected at random, representative of the low, middle, and high registers at three dynamic levels—p, mf, and f. A tube was attached to each mouthpiece and inserted into the performer's mouth. This tube was connected to an electronic transducer. The transducer transformed the blowing pressure used by the performer into a voltage, and the voltage produced was recorded on a chart recorder. The information was plotted on a grid, transformed to a scattergram, and then transferred to computer cards and put into the BMDPZV computer program entitled: "Analysis of Variance and Covariance Including Repeated Measures."

Data gathered from the first test indicate that null hypothesis I is rejected. The subject in this study used more air pressure to play the trombone than the euphonium. The brand of instruments had no significant effect on the results of the test, nor did the pitch, dynamics, or the pitch and dynamics together.

Data gathered from the second test indicates that null hypothesis II is accepted. Mouthpieces of different dimensions do not significantly affect the blowing pressure used for each pitch. The pitch, dynamics, and pitch and dynamics together did not significantly affect this conclusion.

The data also indicates that blowing pressure increases with higher pitches and with louder dynamics. This is qualitatively consistent with results documented from previous studies.

Shrum, Kenneth Earl. "An Analytical Commentary on the Euphonium and Tuba Music of Jan Bach." D.M.A. diss., Arizona State University (0010), 1989, 151 pp. Source: DAI, 50, no. 06A, p. 1479; Accession No: AAG8919653; Subject: Music.

Abstract: This paper presents an analytical commentary on the euphonium and tuba music of Jan Bach. The rationale for this essay is that an understanding of the structural elements of a musical work is necessary for a convincing performance. The works represented are Concert

Variations (1977, euphonium and piano) and Quintet for Tuba and Strings (1978, tuba and string quartet), and they are analyzed according to the criteria of form, melody, harmony, rhythm, dynamics, and performance problems.

The information in this study reveals that Bach utilizes basically simple formal structures which often closely model traditional formal structures, such as scherzo and fugue. Both works utilize a number of scalar formations, but the Concert Variations features a synthetic variant of the Lydian mode known as the overtone scale as its major unifying concept; the Quintet, on the other hand, utilizes the chromatic scale as its structural basis. In addition, there is a strong tendency toward contrapuntal writing in both compositions.

Bach's concept of harmony features pervasive use of tertian, extended tertian, and compound structures in a non-traditional context. The interval of the tritone permeates the Concert Variations, while the Quintet features the third as an underlying harmonic concept. In terms of rhythm and dynamics, neither work strays far from the boundaries of convention, utilizing standard and dynamic markings.

Both works present considerable performance challenges in the areas of range, endurance, valve technique, breath control, special effects, and ensemble relationships. Both are virtuosic, but in contrasting styles. The Concert Variations utilizes a number of contemporary effects, including: the bend, the alternate valve tremolo, the alternate valve scale in quartertones, multiphonic technique, and the fan valves glissando. The tuba solo, however uses no special techniques save for one muted passage, and is virtuosic in a more traditional sense, with extreme range, valve technique, and endurance demands.

Equipment

Droste, Paul. "An Acoustical Study of the Euphonium." M.M. thesis, Eastman School of Music, 1961. No abstract available.

Mallett, Edward Keith. "The Double Bell Euphonium: Design and Literature Past and Present." Ph.D. diss., Michigan State University (0128), 1996, 442 pp. Advisor: Philip N. Sinder; Source: DAI, 57, no. 05A, p. 1904; Accession No: AAI963131; Subject: Music.

Abstract: Relegated to museums, attics, and bar room walls, the double bell euphonium is often thought of as a forgotten oddity in the family of brass instruments. In reality, this instrument enjoyed unprecedented popularity during the "Golden Age of Bands," when double bell euphonium soloists such as Simone Mantia, Joseph DeLuca, and Joseph Michele Raffayola performed with the bands of John Philip Sousa, Arthur Pryor, Herbert Clarke and others, achieving a celebrity status that parallels that of present era pop music stars.

While the C. G. Conn company of Elkhart, Indiana was the dominant manufacturer of double bell euphoniums from the 1880s through the 1950s, nearly all American instrument makers, as well as several European companies, included double bell euphoniums in their product offerings at some time. An examination by the author of 49 instruments, representing eleven instrument companies and a time span of nearly 70 years, was conducted to study instrument design and construction. Of primary interest was the shape of the bell flare of both sides of the instrument, with other measurements including bore, valve casing, height, and weight. Photographs were taken of all instruments studied.

Using information from these studies as well as a consideration of late twentieth century euphonium aesthetics, a new double bell euphonium was designed and built by the author, attempting to remove deficiencies found in older instruments and include new features and capabilities previously untried. The design and manufacturing process is documented, including photographs.

Finally, literature for the double bell euphonium was studied: original works written and notated for the instrument, including a piece composed by the author for the new instrument; works which were originally played on the instrument but not specifically notated for it; and, works written for other instruments which are suited to the double bell euphonium.

It is hoped that a renewal of interest in the double bell euphonium will result in the commissioning of new literature and continued performances for the instrument, as well as a more thorough understanding of the double bell euphonium and its place in the history of instruments.

Winslow, Stephen P. "A Comparative Study of the Euphonium and Baritone Horn." M.M. thesis, North Texas State University. No abstract available.

History

Gould, Olive. "A Study of the Increased Technical Facilities of Orchestral Instruments Due to Mechanical Improvements Since the 18th Century." M.M. thesis, Eastman School of Music, 1932. No abstract available.

Jones, Charleen. "The Euphonium and Euphonium Playing." M.M.Ed. thesis, University of Michigan, June 1951. No abstract available.

Louder, Earle Leroy. "An Historical Lineage of the Modern Baritone Horn and Euphonium." D.MUS. diss., Florida State University (0071), 1976, Source: ADD, X1976, p. 0215; Accession No: AAG0317001; Subject: Music.

Nash, E. W. "The Euphonium: Its History, Literature, and Use in American Schools." Master's thesis, University of Southern California—Berkley. No abstract available.

Perry, Richard Henry. "The Tennessee Technological University Tuba Ensemble: A Short History and Summary of Original Contributions to Tuba/Euphonium Ensemble Literature (R. Winston Morris)." D.M.A. diss., University of Wisconsin–Madison (0262), 1996, 123 pp. Advisor: John D. Stevens; Source: DAI, 57, no. 09A, p. 3867; Accession No: AAG9703669; Subject: Education, Music Biography.

Abstract: The Tennessee Technological University Tuba Ensemble, founded in 1967 by R. Winston Morris, is considered to be one of the leading tuba/euphonium ensembles in the world today. The ensemble has made appearances at conventions and festivals throughout the eastern United States, including five appearances at Weill Recital Hall (formerly Carnegie Recital Hall). The ensemble has also issued seven commercial recordings on three labels.

Prior to the formation of the Tennessee Tech Tuba Ensemble there was very little precedent for the concept of music for multiple tubas. Consequently, there were very few works available for such a group, and almost none of them were available in published form. Therefore the Tech Tuba Ensemble had to generate most of its literature itself. Over the years the ensemble has been responsible for over two hundred compositions and arrangements for tuba/euphonium ensembles, many of which have been published and are widely performed today. These compositions and arrangements have come from several sources: students, faculty, and graduates of Tennessee Tech; commissions; and composers interested in the ensemble and in composing for a relatively new medium.

The principal aim of this project is to document the sixty-one original compositions that have been generated by the Tennessee Tech Tuba Ensemble between 1967 and 1995. Included in this paper will be an annotated list of the compositions as well as a discussion of the various ways of generating composition, sources of funding, and a brief history of the ensemble itself.

Literature

Bowman, Brian Leslie. "The Bass Trumpet and Tenor Tuba in Orchestral and Operatic Literature." D.M.A. diss., Catholic University of America (0043), 1975. No abstract available.

Bristol, Douglas Spencer. "The Composition and Analysis of a New Fantasy for Euphonium and Orchestra with Analysis of Jan Bach's Concerto for Euphonium and Orchestra." D.A. diss., University of Northern Colorado (0161), 2002, 169 pp. Advisor: Robert Ehle; Source: DAI, 63, no. 11A, p. 3781; Accession No: AAI3071855; Subject: Music; Standard No: ISBN: 0-493-91462-5.

Abstract: Invented approximately one hundred and sixty-five years ago, the euphonium has enjoyed widespread use in concert and military bands, but its use in orchestral settings has been minimal. Today, orchestral parts for tenor horn, tenor tuba, and baritone horn are performed on the euphonium, though the use of the euphonium was not necessarily the original intent of the composer. During the twentieth century, its reputation as a suitable orchestral instrument has had modest growth, as evidenced in works by Holst, Janacek, Harris, and Shostakovich. The last quarter of the twentieth century has seen reasonable growth in all styles and types of compositions featuring the euphonium, although compositions featuring the combination of solo euphonium and orchestra did not appear until the 1960s. These initial works have generated continuing interest in the composition of original large-scale works for the euphonium with orchestra. The euphonium has a long journey to equal the quantity and quality of literature written for trumpet, horn, and trombone.

This study offers a new composition for solo euphonium and orchestra that requires advanced technique and proficiency of the soloist and includes contemporary performance techniques, such as multiphonics and jazz improvisation. Fantasy is the first work of its type to incorporate improvisation by the soloist. The author provides an analysis of the new work.

In addition to the original composition and analysis, the author provides an analysis of Concerto for Euphonium and Orchestra by Jan Bach. Bach's Concerto, composed in 1990, is held in high regard by many euphonium soloists around the world. Bach is the recipient of numerous commissions and his works have been recommended six times for the Pulitzer Prize in music.

Corwell, Neal Lynn. "Original Compositions for Solo Euphonium with Tape (Electronic Music)." D.M.A. diss., University of Maryland College Park (0117), 1997, 53 pp. Advisor: John Wakefield; Source: DAI, 58, no. 06A, p. 2125; Accession No: AAG9736677; Subject: Education, Music.

Abstract: This project, which includes both a recording and an accompanying document, is a survey of all the literature currently available for the medium of solo euphonium with tape. The recording contains performances, with Mr. Corwell as soloist, of all the works included in the survey. Background information and musical analyses for the various compositions is provided in the accompanying document, which also includes current publication information and factual information concerning equipment used to create the accompanying tapes. Composer biographies are also provided, as is a general discussion of the medium (solos with tape).

The determination that the works included in the project currently constitute the whole of the literature available in the medium was made only after making numerous international inquiries and consulting all known available sources. Information concerning individual works was gathered primarily through consultation with the composers. All completed and returned a questionnaire, were additionally contacted by Mr. Corwell by phone or mail for clarification of their answers, and received drafts of articles concerning their works for possible revisions and corrections. Tape recordings of Mr. Corwell's performances of their compositions were also offered for evaluation purposes. Because the author of this project is also the composer of several of the works included in the survey, these information-gathering steps were obviously not necessary for the compositions penned by Mr. Corwell.

Graves, Jeffrey Philip. "Three Programs of Euphonium and Tuba Music (Performance)." See listing under Performance, above.

Jones, Charleen. "The Euphonium and Euphonium Playing." See listing under History, above.

Kroesche, Kenneth Ray. "Summary of Dissertation Recitals: Three Programs of Euphonium Music (Performance)." See listing under Performance, above.

Lonnman, Gregory George. "The Tuba Ensemble: Its Organization and Literature." D.M.A. diss., University of Miami (0125), 1974, 63 pp. Source: DAI 35/12A, p. 7947; Publication No.: AAC7512870; Subject: Music (0413).

Abstract: The major purpose of this study is to develop a guideline for those individuals who are interested in organizing a tuba ensemble. The information included in the project was collected from a number of sources; however, the motivational force, as well as many of the ideas presented, was gained by the writer while attending the University of Miami School of Music and working as a graduate assistant with Constance Weldon, tuba instructor and founder and director of the University of Miami Tuba Ensemble.

The tuba ensemble is a relatively new addition to the ensemble offerings in many universities. Thus, this report reflects present-day practice at the University of Miami, as well as at a selected group of music schools with lower brass enrollments large enough to enable them to offer specialized tuba instruction. The information for this segment of the study was gained by means of a questionnaire sent to the forty-three largest schools of music as indicated by the 1972 directory of the National Association of Schools of Music.

Tuba ensemble activity in the United States colleges and universities began to flourish around 1970. Because of its infancy, few people are familiar with the sound, purpose, and literature of this medium. Only two brief articles have been published on the subject of tuba ensemble—one by Constance Weldon of the University of Miami and the other by Fred Marzan of Shenandoah Valley Conservatory at Winchester, Virginia. This study is intended to enlighten the reader on the organization and literature of the tuba ensemble and, furthermore, to demonstrate the need and performance facets for such a group in schools and colleges today.

The main types of discussion included in this project are as follows: historical background, objectives, literature and performance suggestions for the tuba ensemble, which have recently been included as standard ensembles offerings in many United States colleges and universities.

Although at first the tuba ensemble under William Bell was conceived as an enjoyable pastime for his tuba students at Indiana University, in only a decade, it has been transformed into a serious standardized ensemble, complete with its own literature. An informal survey included as part of this project indicated that twenty-six colleges and universities sponsored tuba ensembles. This number has, no doubt, grown in the past few years.

The objectives of the tuba ensemble presented by the writer are perhaps motivational in nature. They are as follows: intensified melodic playing, improved intonation, musical awareness, discussion of the tuba, teacher preparation, conducting experience, and individual responsibility to an organization. It is hoped that this information will stimulate the interest of brass teachers to form tuba ensembles at institutions where they currently do not exist. These objectives may also be helpful in providing new ideas and techniques for tuba ensembles already in existence.

The discussion of literature for the tuba ensemble should be of assistance to both composers and conductors. The suggested basic and advanced libraries represent some of the best written works for tuba ensembles and should be most helpful to anyone in the process of forming an ensemble and selecting a basic repertoire.

Because the tuba plays in such a low register, it sets off a myriad of audible overtones when a note is sounded. While these overtones are necessary in the production of the tuba's true tone quality when more than one tuba in performing, a loss of clarity results. The discussion on performance and program suggestions should provide help in overcoming these acoustical problems encountered in performance. It is hoped that this study will furnish useful material for the further development and enhancement of the tuba ensemble movement.

Maldonado, Luis. "Three Programs of Euphonium Music (Performance)." See listing under Performance, above.

Miles, David Royal. "An Annotated Bibliography of Selected Contemporary Euphonium Solo Literature by American Composers." D.M.A. diss., University of Maryland College Park (0117), 1991, 278 pp. Advisor: Emerson Head; Source: DAI, 52, no. 09A, p. 3123; Accession No: AAG 9205159; Subject: Music Education, Music.

Abstract: The purpose of this dissertation is to examine selected contemporary euphonium solo literature written by American composers. One hundred and eleven compositions are discussed and analyzed, including both published and unpublished works. Basic data listed for each piece included title, composer, instrumentation, publisher, copyright date, length, range, and relative difficulty. Published reviews and available recordings are noted. An analysis of each work is given with emphasis on helping the performer understand enough of its style and substance to decide whether the piece will meet his study or performance needs.

As an introduction to the solo listings, the history of euphonium literature is examined, with attention given to the availability of music for the euphoniumist. A scarcity of literature for the instrument soon becomes obvious, as does the need for the information about the repertoire that is available. Various attempts to address these problems are examined, including literature guides, reviews, articles, and listings of repertoire. These resources are shown to be inadequate, and it is demonstrated that more comprehensive and current materials are needed.

The mechanics, methodology, and terminology used in this investigation are discussed and defined. Limits and delineations are presented to define the scope and purpose of the study.

Criteria for selection and listing are presented and explained.

Approximately eighty percent of the text is an annotated bibliography of contemporary euphonium solos written by American composers. The future of the euphonium as a viable musical instrument is intrinsically related to the availability of an adequate quantity of appropriate literature. This dissertation assists performers and teachers in understanding and making use of the literature available to them.

Nash, E. W. "The Euphonium: Its History, Literature, and Use in American Schools." See listing under History, above.

Pollard, Louis Melvin, III. "A Transcription of Three Arias from 'The Barber of Seville,' by Gioacchino Rossini, for Solo Euphonium and Large Brass Ensemble, with Three Recitals of Selected Works by E. Bozza, A. Capuzzi, J. Koetsier, A. Ponchielli, and Others (Eugene Bozza, France, Antonio Capuzzi, Jan Koetsier, Amilcare Ponchielli, Italy)." D.M.A. diss., University of North Texas (0158), 1998, 155 pp. Advisor: Donald Little; Source: DAI, 59, no. 04A, p. 1004; Accession No: AAG9830850; Subject: Music.

Abstract: Document accompanying a transcription for solo euphonium and large brass ensemble (3 trumpets, fluegelhorn, 2 horns, 2 tenor trombones, bass trombone, euphonium, tuba) of three arias, "Ecco ridente in cielo," "Largo al factotum," and "A un dottor della mia sorte," from Gioacchino Rossini's opera The Barber of Seville. Includes overviews of the arias' texts and contexts, orchestrational techniques in the transcriptions, the history and definition of the term "euphonium," and the history of the large brass ensemble in the United States.

Reifsnyder, Robert Pennington. "The Changing Role of the Euphonium in Contemporary Band Music." D.MUS. diss., Indiana University (0093), 1980, Source: ADD, X1980, p. 0215; Accession No: AAG0359333; Subject: Music.

Steinberger, Karl Thomas. "A Performance Analysis of Five Recital Works for Euphonium." Ph.D. diss., New York University (0146), 1981, 231 pp. Source: DAI, 42, no. 02A, p. 0448; Accession No: AAG8115509; Subject: Music.

Abstract: The present study was undertaken in order to assist the utilization of the growing body of original literature for euphonium by providing information and performance suggestions for performers and teachers involved in the current euphonium/tuba renaissance. The researcher assembled a master list of works which was organized in three sections: published works for euphonium, works for French tuba, and unpublished works for euphonium. The master list was sent to a panel of five euphonium experts, each of whom listed his first ten choices from each category and who constructed a fourth list comprising the ten best compositions overall. After collating the results, the researcher selected two compositions from each of the published categories and one from the unpublished list. Works chosen for the study consisted of the following: Barat, Introduction et Danse; George, Sonata; Jacob, Fantasia; Martin, Suite; and Semler-Collery, Barcarolle et Chanson Bachique. Each of these works was analyzed in order to identify potential performance problems, based upon the researcher's performing experience.

Through historical inquiry the author traced the development of the instrument from its earliest appearances shortly after the development of the valve mechanism in the second decade of the nineteenth century. Emphasis is placed upon Aldolphe Sax's standardization of numerous early experimental types of brass instruments. The resultant family of saxhorns played a major role in the euphonium's proliferation and its inclusion in the wind ensembles of the mid-nineteenth century.

Numerous soloists of the "Golden Age" of the concert band were mentioned during discussion of the development of the solo role of the instrument. While the earliest solo literature appears to have consisted largely of transcriptions, those original works uncovered during the research process are mentioned whenever appropriate. A discussion of the instrument's role as a tenor tuba in the standard orchestral repertoire is included, as well. The historical chapter concludes with a summary of recent trends in performing opportunities in such specialized areas as euphonium-tuba choirs and jazz ensembles.

Until recently, selection of original recital literature has been a problem for the euphoniumist, often resulting in programs consisting mainly of transcriptions. Fortunately this scarcity of original literature is gradually being eliminated, largely through the Tubists Universal Brotherhood Association (T.U.B.A.) and its interest in commissioning new works. In addition, a considerable amount of literature for the French tuba is available, largely because of the annual commissioning of contest pieces by the Paris Conservatory.

A Technical Problems Checklist was constructed, listing potential performance problems in the following areas: embouchure, breath control, valve technique, articulation, and musical interpretation and style. The identification of performance problems and discussion of possible solutions was effected by means of random choice of topics selected from the Technical Problems Checklist. In order to address technical factors unique to a given composition, factors which may not have received consideration because of the random selection of topics, the researcher added to all but one of the technical analyses a concluding section entitled "Additional Suggestions for Effective Performance." Each of the selected works is also discussed in terms of historical background and style analysis.

Stern, David Wayne. "The Use of the Euphonium in Selected Wind Band Repertoire Since 1980." Ph.D. diss., Texas Tech University (0230), 2001, 313 pp. Advisor: Chairs John Cody Birdwell, Michael C. Stoune; Source: DAI, 62, no. 10A, p. 3329; Accession No: AAI3030380; Subject: Education, Music; Standard No: ISBN: 0-493-42777-5.

Abstract: During the early to mid-twentieth century, the euphonium was frequently scored in wind band works as the solo tenor instrument. Since that time, there has been a general decline in the euphonium's usage as a solo instrument and in being scored with melodic lines. The purpose of this study is to determine if that trend continues.

This dissertation is a survey of the treatment of the euphonium in twenty works for wind band composed since 1980. Several orchestration and arranging texts offer suggestions for scoring for the euphonium, and those authors' suggestions are included in the study. Although none of the works are composed for brass band, the use of the euphonium in brass bands and its influence on wind band scoring techniques is also discussed. Four noted authorities in euphonium performance were interviewed and their comments are included.

The twenty selected works are analyzed for each composer's unique and traditional scoring of the euphonium. A short biographical sketch begins each chapter and a brief summary is provided at the end of each analysis. There are many musical examples for each work that demonstrate the composers' scoring practices. Comments from the euphonium pedagogues are incorporated into the analyses.

The conclusion summarizes the observations found in the twenty analyses and provides suggestions for continued education and advocacy.

Thompson, John Mark. "An Annotated Bibliography of French Literature for Bass Trombone, Tuba, and Bass Saxhorn Including Solos and Pedagogical Materials." See listing under Bibliography, above.

Winter, Denis Ward. "The Use of the Tenorhorn and Baryton in the Brass Chamber Music of Oskar Bohme and Victor Ewald, a Lecture Recital, Together with Three Recitals of Selected Works of J. Boda, J. Brahms, G. Jacobs, G. Mahler, T. R. George, J. Casterede, A. Capuzzi and Others." D.M.A. diss., University of North Texas (0158), 1988, 70 pp. Advisor: Donald C. Little; Source: DAI, 50, no. 02A, p. 0300; Accession No: AAG8908940; Subject: Music Biography.

Abstract: The tenorhorn and baryton (euphonium), as members of the valved conical brass family, were highly regarded by Oskar Bohme (1870–1938) and Victor Ewald (1860–1935). This study examines the role the tenorhorn and baryton played in selected works by these two composers of the Russian Chamber Brass School. A chronology of the research leading to the discovery and naming of the Russian Chamber Brass School is included as well as a discussion on brass chamber music performance practice both then and now.

Pedagogy

Achilles, Darin Lyn. "Frank Crisafulli (1916–1998): A Biographical Sketch and a Profile of his Pedagogical Approaches as Related by Former Trombone Students." D.M.A. diss., University of North Carolina–Greensboro, 2004, 180 pp. Source: DAI-A 65/03, p. 871, Sep 2004; Accession No.: AAT 3126767; Subject: Music Education, Biography.

Abstract: Frank Crisafulli was born in Chicago, Illinois on 15 January 1916. Although he grew up in a musical family, Crisafulli did not begin studying the trombone until he entered high school because his older sister, a talented pianist, received all of the musical attention in the family. While in high school, he studied informally with his father, a successful trombonist with the Chicago Civic Opera Company. Although Crisafulli was successful as a young trombonist, he had trouble developing his skills due to an injury on his lip that occurred in a sledding accident as a child. After graduating from high school, he attended Northwestern University for one year and joined the Civic Orchestra of Chicago in 1934. Crisafulli became a member of the Chicago Symphony Orchestra in 1938, held the position of principal trombone from 1939 to 1955, and played second trombone from 1955 until his retirement in 1989. In addition, Crisafulli was trombonist with the Chicago Symphony Brass Quintet and an avid cellist. Crisafulli joined the faculty of Northwestern University as Instructor of Trombone and Euphonium in 1953, a position he held until shortly before his death in 1998. Due to the demands of his performance schedule with the CSO and his growing teaching demands, Art Linsner was hired in 1979 as his assistant, and they worked out a rotational system to ensure that all students studied with both teachers. A particularly unique aspect of Crisafulli's teaching methodology was his relaxed approach that was derived from his uniform treatment of all students, his non-authoritative personality, his love of teaching, and the positive feedback delivered in lessons. Due to his relaxed approach to teaching, students often recalled that their best playing of the week took place in lessons. Although Crisafulli's teaching was not sequenced, lessons were structured around the fundamental ideas of simplicity, air and musical flow, and the enjoyment of playing music. Many of Crisafulli's students continue to build on his traditions and carry on his remarkable legacy.

Bergee, Martin J. "An Application of the Facet-Factorial Approach to Scale Construction in the Development of a Rating Scale for Euphonium and Tuba Music Performance." Ph.D. diss., University of Kansas (0099), 1987, 232 pp. Advisor: John W. Grashel; Source: DAI, 49, no. 05A, p. 1086; Accession No: AAG8813388; Subject: Education, Music.

Abstract: The purpose of this study was to construct and validate a rating scale for the evaluation of euphonium and tuba performance. A facet-factorial approach to scale construction was employed in developing the rating scale.

In the preliminary phase, statements descriptive of euphonium-tuba performance were gathered from essays, adjudication sheets, and previous research. A content analysis of these materials yielded 112 statements, which were translated into items and paired with a five-option, Likert-type scale. The resulting item pool was used by 50 judges to evaluate 100 euphonium and tuba performances. The obtained data were factor analyzed, initial orthogonal factors were extracted, and the structure was rotated to a terminal solution. Five factors were identified, and 30 items were chosen to define the subscales of a Euphonium-Tuba Performance Rating Scale (ETPRS).

To examine the stability of the ETPRS structure, and to obtain data for interjudge reliability and criterion-related validity, three panels of judges rated three sets of 10 different euphonium and tuba performances using the ETPRS. The data obtained were factor analyzed and the ETPRS was revised to a four-factor structure. The four factors identified for the revised ETPRS were (a) Interpretation/Musical Effect, (b) Tone Quality/Intonation, (c) Technique, and (d) Rhythm/Tempo. Interjudge reliability estimates for the revised ETPRS total scores were .944, .985, and .975 for the three groups of judges respectively. Reliability estimates for subscales ranged from .894 to .992.

Two studies examined criterion-related validity of the revised ETPRS. In the first, revised ETPRS evaluations were compared with global ratings obtained via a magnitude estimation procedure. Zero-order correlation coefficients between revised ETPRS total scores, subscale scores, and global criterion scores ranged from .502 to .992; most were above .850. To examine the contributions of the subscale scores in predicting the global criterion, a multiple regression analysis was performed. In the second criterion-related validity study, the MENC adjudicating ballot for wind instrument solo was used as the criterion. The same procedures used in the first study were applied; correlation coefficients ranged from .823 to .992.

Jones, Charleen. "The Euphonium and Euphonium Playing." See listing under History, above.

Musella, Donald. "The Teaching of Brass Instruments in the Public Schools Using the Plan of Transferring Students of Trumpet or Cornet to the Other Brass Instruments." M.A. thesis,

Eastman School of Music, 1957. No abstract available.

Nash, E. W. "The Euphonium: Its History, Literature, and Use in American Schools." See listing under History, above.

Robertson, James David. "The Low Brass Instrumental Techniques Course: A Method Book for College Level Class Instruction." D.M.A. diss., University of Northern Colorado (0161), 1983, 280 pp. Source: DAI, 45, no. 01A, p. 0013; Accession No: AAG8408154; Subject: Music.

Abstract: The purpose of this study is to develop a method book of class instruction for low brass specifically for use at the college level. The instruments of the low brass homogeneous family groups are trombone, euphonium, baritone, bass trombone, and tuba. Typically the class is designed to help prepare students for careers in instrumental music teaching in the schools. The study is organized according to the following plan: (I) The Need for the Study; (II) The Construction of the Method; Appendix; Bibliography.

The Appendix of the dissertation consists of the method book itself. This book is entitled The Low Brass Book: A Method Book for College Level Class Instruction. This book is organized according to the following plan: Preface; (I) A Brief History of the Low Brass Instruments; (II) The Breath Supply; (III) The Embouchure; (IV) Articulation; (V) Low Brass Acoustics; (VI) Tenor Trombone; (VII) Bass Trombone; (VIII) Euphonium and Baritone; (IX) Tuba; (X) Fundamental Studies; (XI) Melodies, Duets, Trios, and Quartets; Appendix.

The text and photographs of chapters I through IX are designed to give the student a clear presentation of the fundamentals of low brass playing. With a thorough understanding of these fundamentals and the ability to apply them as a player of at least one of the low brass instruments, the chances of success of the teacher-to-be should be greater.

The fundamental etudes and musical compositions of chapters X and XI were composed by the author specifically for the method book. Additionally, they are arranged so as to provide opportunity for performance regardless of the constituency of the class. Each etude and musical composition is given in two octaves so that any of the instruments of the class can participate at the appropriate level. A suggested routine for practice outlines a course of study suitable for either a college quarter or semester time period.

Stouffer, John J. "Methods and Techniques of Teaching Brass Instruments." M.M.Ed. thesis, University of Michigan, May 1963. No abstract available.

Miscellaneous

Keathley, Gilbert Harrell. "The Tuba Ensemble." D.M.A. diss., University of Rochester, Eastman School of Music (0891), 1982, 145 pp. Source: DAI, 43, no. 08A, p. 2488; Accession No: AAG8227841; Subject: Music.

Abstract: This dissertation examines the tuba ensemble, an important experience in the training of tuba and euphonium students, and gives guidelines for composition in this medium. While the number of college tuba ensembles is rapidly increasing, the specific features of the literature and problems of composition are neither well understood nor properly documented. Composers need a resource when writing for the several members of the tuba family in ensemble, and this paper attempts to fill that void.

Background information includes the history of the tuba family from the serpent, through the Saxhorns, to the modern orchestral tuba, with a description of the range and valve requirements of each of the differently pitched tubas now in use: BB('b), CC, E('b), F, B('b), and C. Instrumentation possibilities and differing textural qualities are examined. Included is a survey of selected works of different styles from the literature, with 42 musical examples in the text, and sample programs. The last chapter addresses specific problems of composition, including range, orchestration, and acoustics. One contemporary work is analyzed briefly, and compositional features examined. The Appendix consists of statements of compositional practice from five important composers in the tuba ensemble field and comment by the author.

Metcalf, John Clayton. "The Role of the Euphonium in Selected Transcriptions for Band of Orchestral Music." D.M.A. diss., Louisiana State University and Agricultural Mechanical Col. (0107), 1989, 177 pp. Advisor: Larry B. Campbell; Source: DAI, 51, no. 07A, p. 2193; Accession No: AAG9025323; Subject: Music Education, Music.

Abstract: The purpose of this study was to explore the role of the euphonium in selected transcriptions of orchestral music for band. Part I of the monograph surveyed orchestral sources for the euphonium parts. Part II examined utilization of the instrument in the works for band.

Transcriptions in this monograph represent works from the beginning of the century to the present time and to give examples from the various periods of music. The band works span the twentieth century from 1902 through 1972.

In the first section the works were examined according to the following criteria: (1) the key of the original compared to the key of the transcription; (2) parts of the orchestral works from which the euphonium part is derived; (3) use of cuing and octave displacement in the construction of the euphonium part; and, (4) treatment of idiomatic orchestral effects. Each work was discussed and compared according to the percentage of notes representing the orchestral sources.

Part II examined the use of the instrument in melodic, countermelodic, harmonic, and rhythmic figures. Melodic and countermelodic figures were examined as used with members of the clarinet family, saxophone family, bassoon, horn, trombone, tuba, and combinations of the above.

Harmonic and rhythmic figures explored the use of the instrument as an accompanying instrument. The figures were divided into five categories. They are sustained harmonic figures, pedal point, ostinato-like patterns, arpeggiated figures, and rhythmic accompaniment figures.

Among the conclusions drawn were the following: (1) the cello consistently provided a majority of notes to the euphonium part, followed by the bassoon, horn, viola, and trombone; (2) the use of octave displacement is very important in the adaptation of string parts for performance by the euphonium in these transcriptions; (3) cued notes in the transcriptions were used less as the century progressed; (4) transcribers took liberties in the adaptation of string techniques; and, (5) versatility of the euphonium enables it to perform with many instrumental groups in a variety of melodic, countermelodic, harmonic, and rhythmic settings.

KENNETH R. KROESCHE

Articles

Acoustics

Hall, Jody. "Questions and Answers on Musical Acoustics." *Connchord* (Sept. 1959).

Horowitz, Marc David. "Tuba and Euphonium Citations in Recent Medical and Scientific Literature." *TUBA Journal*, Vol. 25, No. 1 (Spring 1997): 58–59.

Bibliography

Bevan, Clifford. "B-Flat Baritone Directory." *Sounding Brass & the Conductor* 4, No. 3 (1975): 95.

Bevan, Clifford. "B-Flat Euphonium Directory." *Sounding Brass & the Conductor* 5, No. 1 (1976): 23.

Bryant, William. "Research for Tuba and Euphonium." *TUBA Journal*, Vol. 13, No. 1 (Aug. 1985): 25–26.

Bryant, William. "Research for Tuba and Euphonium." *TUBA Journal*, Vol. 13, No. 2 (Nov. 1985): 25.

Maldonado, Luis. "A Comprehensive Bibliography on Euphonium/Baritone Horn: Part I." *TUBA Journal*, Vol. 18, No. 3 (Spring 1991): 24–25.

Maldonado, Luis. "A Comprehensive Bibliography on Euphonium/Baritone Horn: Part III." *TUBA Journal*, Vol. 19, No. 1 (Fall 1991): 40–45.

Maldonado, Luis. "A Comprehensive Bibliography on Euphonium/Baritone Horn: Part II." *TUBA Journal*, Vol. 18, No. 4 (Summer 1991): 20–23.

Peruzzini, Andrew. "Index T.U.B.A. Newsletter and Journal Volumes I–VI." *TUBA Journal*, Vol. 7, No. 1 (Summer 1979): 39–48.

Popiel, Peter. "Thirty Years of Periodical Articles Concerning the Baritone Horn and Euphonium: A Compilation Indexed by Author." *TUBA Journal*, Vol. 10, No. 3 (Winter 1983): 6–7.

"*TUBA Journal*, Vol. Index, Volume 13 No. 1–Volume 18 No. 1." *TUBA Journal*, Vol. 18, No. 2 (Winter 1990): 64–70.

Williams, Nyal. "TUBA Resource Library Holdings." *TUBA Journal*, Vol. 21, No. 4 (Summer 1994): 48–66.

Biographical

Bridges, Glenn D. "Ole June May–A Short Biography." *TUBA Journal*, Vol. 7, No. 2 (Fall 1979): 5–12.

Bridges, Glenn D. "Simone Mantia (1873–1951)—A Short Biography." *TUBA Journal*, Vol. 4, No. 3 (Spring/Summer 1977): 4–5.

Dickman, Marc. "ITEA Legacy Project—Vol. 1: The Legacy of Rich Matteson." *ITEA Journal* 30, No. 3 (Spring 2003): 36–49.

Dickman, Marc. "Rich Matteson: Portrait of an Original." *TUBA Journal*, Vol. 19, No. 2 (Winter 1991): 46–62.

Dummer, Lee. "Arthur Lehman." *TUBA Journal*, Vol. 27, No. 1 (Fall 1999): 43–47.

"Euphonium Pioneers." *Instrumentalist* 35, No. 10 (May 1981): 32.

"In Memoriam: Luis Maldonado." *TUBA Journal*, Vol. 22, No. 3 (Spring 1995): 21.

Leggett, Anthony. "Whatever Happened to Stephen Lord?" *Brass Band World* 62 (March 1997): 33.

Mathez, Jean-Pierre. "Robert Davis King." *Brass Bulletin* 109, No. 1 (2000): 118–122.

McAdams, Charles A. "Winston Morris: Teacher, Conductor, Performer and Author." Part I. *TUBA Journal*, Vol. 23, No. 4 (Summer 1996): 34–41.

McAdams, Charles A. "Winston Morris: Teacher, Conductor, Performer and Author." Part II. *TUBA Journal*, Vol. 24, No. 1 (Fall 1996): 46–53.

Mead, Steven. "Two British Euphonium Legends (Trevor Groom and John Clough)." *TUBA Journal*, Vol. 27, No. 1 (Fall 1999): 50–55.

Mueller, John. "T.U.B.A. Euphonium Profile: Harold Brasch." *TUBA Journal*, Vol. 9, No. 4 (Spring 1982): 4–6.

Mueller, John. "T.U.B.A. Euphonium Profile: Harold Brasch." *TUBA Journal,* Vol. 27, No. 1 (Fall 1999): 57–58.

Murrow, Richard. "An Interview with Ray Young." *TUBA Journal,* Vol. 19, No. 4 (Summer 1992): 28–37.

Murrow, Richard, ed. Brian Bowman, Toru Miura, William Moody, Neal Tidwell, Thomas V. Fraschillo, Joe D. Brown, Alex Cauthen. "Raymond Young: A T.U.B.A. Memorial Tribute." *TUBA Journal,* Vol. 27, No. 2 (Winter 1999): 35–39.

Sloan, Gerry. "Ramón Benítez, Colombian Bombardino Virtuoso." *ITEA Journal* 31, No. 1 (Fall 2003): 54–59.

Wilson, Peter. "John Childs' Heritage Passes Down to the Third Generation." *British Bandsman* 5008 (10 Oct. 1998): 20–21.

Yeo, Douglas. "A Tribute to Robert King (1914–1999)." *Historic Brass Society Newsletter* 13 (Summer 2000): 46–48.

Young, Jerry. "Four Unforgettable Euphoniumists." *TUBA Journal,* Vol. 27, No. 1 (Fall 1999): 41.

Discography

Bryant, William. "Recordings for the Euphoniumist." Ed. Joan Draxler. *TUBA Journal,* Vol. 13, No. 4 (May 1986): 19–22.

Maldonado, Luis. "A Comprehensive Bibliography on Euphonium/Baritone Horn: Part III." *TUBA Journal,* Vol. 19, No. 1 (Fall 1991): 40–45.

Weerts, Richard. "Educational Solo Recordings." *Instrumentalist* 23, No. 7 (Feb. 1969): 22.

Winter, Denis. "Band Director's Guide to Euphonium Recordings." *Instrumentalist* 35, No. 10 (May 1981): 27–28.

Winter, Denis. "Euphonium Recordings–A Discography of Selected Recordings of Euphonium Performances." *TUBA Journal,* Vol. 7, No. 3 (Winter 1980): 9–15.

Equipment

Apperson, Ron. "Mutes or 'What Are We Putting Down Our Bells?'" *TUBA Journal,* Vol. 6, No. 3 (Spring 1979): 12–13.

Bach, Vincent. "Know Your Brasses." *Instrumentalist* (Nov. 1950).

Bahr, Edward R. "Considerations toward Purchasing a Euphonium." *TUBA Journal,* Vol. 9, No. 3 (Winter 1982): 7–8.

Bowman, Brian L. "Euphonium/Baritone Horn Directory." *TUBA Journal,* Vol. 6, No. 1 (Fall 1978): 32–33.

Butler, Richard D. "The Upper Hand." *TUBA Journal,* Vol. 25, No. 4 (Summer 1998): 46–47.

Capper, William. "Mutes—Fabricate Your Own." *TUBA Journal,* Vol. 7, No. 3 (Winter 1980): 26–27.

Fry, Robert H. "Tuning Slide Devices for Better Euphonium Intonation." *TUBA Journal,* Vol. 13, No. 1 (Feb. 1986): 20.

Groom, Trevor. "Euphoniums Limited." *Sounding Brass and the Conductor* 1, No. 4 (1973): 41–44.

Guy, Charles. "Exploring the New Double-Bell Euphonium: A Review/Commentary of Edward Mallett's Lecture/Recital." *TUBA Journal,* Vol. 23, No. 4 (Summer 1996): 64.

Heinkel, Peggy, and Dan Vinson. "The Obvious Solution." *TUBA Journal,* Vol. 10, No. 2 (Fall 1982): 4–7.

Johnson, Tommy. "Accompaniment Technology for the Portable Tuba Studio." *TUBA Journal,* Vol. 24, No. 2 (Winter 1997): 52–54.

Kurath, Willy. "Tuba and Euphonium Today." (English, French and German.) *Brass Bulletin* 23 (1978): 41–44.

McCready, Matthew A. "Compensating Systems: A Historical View." *TUBA Journal,* Vol. 10, No. 4 (Spring 1983): 5–6.

McCready, Matthew A. "Compensating Systems: A Mathematical Comparison." *TUBA Journal,* Vol. 12, No. 3 (Feb. 1985): 11–14.

McMillen, Hugh. "The Baritone Comes of Age." *Instrumentalist* 6 (May–June 1952): 24–25.

Mead, Steven. "Steven Mead Explodes Some Myths on Mouthpieces." *British Bandsman* 4913 (14 Dec. 1996): 6–7.

Meinl, Gerhard. "Effect of Valves on the Intonation of Brass Instruments." *TUBA Journal,* Vol. 16, No. 4 (Summer 1989): 38–40.

Myers, Arnold. "Brasswind Innovation and Output of Boosey & Co. in the Blaikley Era." *Historic Brass Journal* 14 (2002): 391–424.

Myers, Arnold. "Brasswind Manufacturing at Boosey & Hawkes, 1930–1959." *Historic Brass Society Journal* 15 (2003): 55–72.

Myers, Arnold, and Raymond Park. "The Edinburgh University Collection of Historical Brass Instruments." *Brass Bulletin* 85, No. 1 (1994): 10–19.

Roberts, Chester. "Tenor, Bass and Contrabass Tubas—Comparisons and Contrasts." *T.U.B.A. Newsletter* 1, No. 3 (Spring 1974): 3–4.

Scharf, Natasha. "New Yamaha Baritone Extends Players' Choice." *British Bandsman* 4918 (18 Jan. 1997): 8.

Sluchin, Benny. "Duplex Instruments—Yesterday and Today." *Brass Bulletin* 115, No. 3 (2001): 112–115.

Tilbury, Jack. "Tuba and Euphonium heute—Von Willson—Band Instruments Flums, Schweiz." *Instrumentenbau Musik International* 31, No. 4 (1977): 375.

Werden, David R. "The Blaikley Compensating System: A Player's Perspective." *TUBA Journal,* Vol. 13, No. 1 (Aug. 1985): 17–18.

Werden, David R. "A Euphonium by Any Other Name Is Not a Baritone." *Instrumentalist* 38, No. 9 (April 1984): 62–63.

Werden, David R. "A Euphonium by Any Other Name Is Not a Baritone." *TUBA Journal,* Vol. 11, No. 4 (Spring 1984): 6–8.

Werden, David R. "Euphonium Mouthpieces—A Teacher's Guide." *Instrumentalist* 35, No. 10 (May 1981): 23–26.

Winter, James H. "Brass." *Music Educators Journal* 62, No. 2 (Oct. 1975): 34–37.

Young, Frederick J. "The Optimal Design and Fair Comparison of Valve Systems for Brass Instruments: Part IV." *TUBA Journal*, Vol. 14, No. 3 (Feb. 1987): 74–77.

Young, Frederick J. "The Optimal Design and Fair Comparison of Valve Systems for Brass Instruments: Part I." *TUBA Journal*, Vol. 13, No. 4 (May 1986): 30–33.

Young, Frederick J. "The Optimal Design and Fair Comparison of Valve Systems for Brass Instruments: Part III." *TUBA Journal*, Vol. 14, No. 2 (Nov. 1986): 36–39.

Young, Frederick J. "The Optimal Design and Fair Comparison of Valve Systems for Brass Instruments: Part II." *TUBA Journal*, Vol. 14, No. 1 (Aug. 1986): 35–39.

History

Arnsted, Jørgen. "The Euphonium and Tuba in Denmark: The State of the Art (and a Bit of History, Too . . .)." *TUBA Journal*, Vol. 28, No. 4 (Summer 2001): 50–52.

Bahr, Edward R. "Idiomatic Similarities and Differences of the Trombone and Euphonium in History and Performance." *Journal of the International Trombone Association* 6 (1978): 31–36.

Bevan, Clifford. "Background Brass." *Sounding Brass & the Conductor* 7, No. 3 (1978): 100+.

Bevan, Clifford. "The Euphonium." *Sounding Brass & the Conductor* 7, No. 4 (1978): 128–129+.

Book, Brian L. "Views of Berlioz on the Use of the Ophicleide and Tuba in His Orchestral Works." *TUBA Journal*, Vol. 10, No. 3 (Winter 1983): 10–19.

Bowman, Brian. "You Play a What?" *Brass and Percussion* 1, No. 2 (1973): 12–13+.

Davis, Ron. "Twenty-one Years of the Tuba Family." *TUBA Journal*, Vol. 27, No. 1 (Fall 1999): 59–61.

Floyd, John R. "Baritone Horn versus the Euphonium." *Woodwind World, Brass, and Percussion* 20, No. 3 (May–June 1981): 8–9.

Floyd, John R. "The Double-Bell Euphonium, Vanishing but Not Forgotten." *Woodwind World, Brass, and Percussion* 21, No. 4 (1982): 6–8.

Fox, F. "Some Thoughts on the Baritone and Tuba." *Crescendo* 2 (Nov.–Dec. 1952): 10–11.

Gotoh, Furnio. "J.E.T.A. (Japan Euphonium and Tuba Association): A Brief History." *ITEA Journal* 29, No. 4 (Winter 2002): 29.

Heidler, Manfred. "The German Tenor Horn: A Forgotten Instrument?" *TUBA Journal*, Vol. 27, No. 4 (Summer 2000): 31–37.

Heyde, Herbert. "Brass Instrument Making in Berlin from the 17th to the 20th Century: A Survey." Trans. Steven Plank. *Historic Brass Journal* 3 (1993): 43–47.

Karjalainen, Kauko. "The Brass Band Tradition in Finland." *Historic Brass Society Journal* 9 (1997): 83–96.

Lane, G. B. "Brass Instruments Used in Confederate Military Service during the American Civil War." *Historic Brass Society Journal* 4 (1992): 71–86.

Mallett, Edward K. "The Double-Bell Euphonium: The History of a Forgotten Instrument." *TUBA Journal*, Vol. 21, No. 3 (Spring 1994): 24–28.

Meucci, Renato. "The Pelitti Firm: Makers of Brass Instruments in Nineteenth-Century Milan." *Historic Brass Society Journal* 6 (1994): 304–333.

Morris, R. Winston. "The Evolution of the Tuba/ Euphonium Ensemble." *Instrumentalist* 43, No. 5 (Dec. 1988): 15–17.

Myers, Arnold. "The Living Role of Historical Instruments." *TUBA Journal*, Vol. 27, No. 3 (Spring 2000): 60–61.

Myers, Arnold. "Museums." *TUBA Journal*, Vol. 26, No. 3 (Spring 1999): 54–55.

Nash, Eugene W. "Invention of the Baritone." *Instrumentalist* 17, No. 8 (April 1963): 30, 32.

Naylor, J. J. "The English Euphonium: Its Development and Use." *TUBA Journal*, Vol. 9, No. 4 (Spring 1982): 17–18.

Nelson, Mark E. "The History and Development of the Serpent." *TUBA Journal*, Vol. 10, No. 1 (Summer 1982): 10–14.

Niemisto, Paul. "A Brief History of the Finnish Brass Band." *Historic Brass Society Newsletter* 10 (Summer 1997): 13–16.

Nilsson, Ann-Marie. "Brass Instruments in Small Swedish Wind Ensembles during the Late Nineteenth Century." *Historic Brass Journal* 13 (2001): 176–209.

Peterson, Mary. "The Arne B. Larson Collection." *TUBA Journal*, Vol. 8, No. 2 (Fall 1980): 5–7.

Peterson, Mary. "The Arne B. Larson Collection, Part II." *TUBA Journal*, Vol. 8, No. 3 (Winter 1981): 15–18.

Peterson, Mary. "Baritones and Euphoniums of European Origins in the Arne B. Larson Collection." *TUBA Journal*, Vol. 9, No. 1 (Summer 1981): 3–7.

Peterson, Mary. "A Brief History of the Euphonium." *Instrumentalist* 35, No. 10 (May 1981): 16–17.

Peterson, Mary. "Double-Bell Euphoniums in the Arne B. Larson Collection." *TUBA Journal*, Vol. 8, No. 4 (Spring 1981): 4–9.

Reynolds, George E. "Baritone—Euphonium." *School Musician* 34, No. 2 (Oct. 1962): 10, 12.

Roust, Colin. "The Orchestral History of the Euphonium." *TUBA Journal*, Vol. 28, No. 3 (Spring 2001): 33–39.

Schulz, Charles A. "Ancestors of the Tuba." *TUBA Journal*, Vol. 9, No. 2 (Fall 1981): 3–7.

Schulz, Charles A. "Ancestors of the Tuba: Part II." *TUBA Journal*, Vol. 9, No. 3 (Winter 1982): 10–12.

Smith, Wilbert, Jr. "Baritone Horn Versus Euphonium." *Woodwind World, Brass, and Percussion* 17, No. 4 (Vacation Issue 1978): 30–31, 37.

Trevor, Herbert. "Cyfartha Castle: The Origin of the Species." *Brass Bulletin* 97, No. 1 (1997): 38–44.

Weldon, Constance J., and Greg Lonnman. "The Evolution of the Tuba Ensemble." *TUBA Journal*, Vol. 7, No. 1 (Summer 1979): 2–3.

Whitham, Geoff. "Sounds of Yesterday." *TUBA Journal*, Vol. 19, No. 4 (Summer 1992): 49.

Winslow, Stephen P. "Historical Comparisons of the Euphonium and Baritone Horn." *TUBA Journal*, Vol. 5, No. 3 (Spring/Summer 1978): 5–9.

Literature

Bahr, Edward R. "Orchestral Literature Including Euphonium and Tenor Tuba." *TUBA Journal*, Vol. 7, No. 2 (Fall 1979): 5–12.

Bland, Niki. "Call for Simple 'Curnow' Solos." *British Bandsman* 4918 (18 Jan. 1997): 8.

Brown, Merrill. "Repertoire for Brass Soloists." *Instrumentalist* 31, No. 6 (Jan. 1977): 51–53.

Call, G. K. "Music for Euphonium." *School Musician* 9, No. 3 (1980): 30–31.

Chiba, Keisetsu. "Introducing Japanese Composers." *ITEA Journal* 29, No. 4 (Summer 2002): 41–43.

Corwell, Neal. "Understanding the 'New Music,' Music for Euphonium and Tape: Part One." *TUBA Journal*, Vol. 22, No. 3 (Spring 1995): 64–67.

Corwell, Neal. "Understanding the 'New Music,' Part Eight–An Introduction to Solos with Tape-Recorded Accompaniment." *TUBA Journal*, Vol. 22, No. 2 (Winter 1995): 30–32.

Corwell, Neal. "Using Lieder as Euphonium Literature." *TUBA Journal*, Vol. 9, No. 2 (Fall 1981): 20–22.

Cottrell, Jeff. "Confronting the Instrumental Canon." *ITEA Journal* 31, No. 1 (Fall 2003): 74–76.

Droste, Paul. "Arranging String Literature for Euphonium." Part 1. *TUBA Journal*, Vol. 5, No. 1 (Fall 1978): 7–9.

Droste, Paul. "Arranging String Literature for Euphonium." Part 2. *TUBA Journal*, Vol. 5, No. 2 (Winter 1978): 6–9.

Droste, Paul. "Begged, Borrowed, and Stolen Solo Euphonium Literature." *Instrumentalist* 35 (May 1981): 30–32.

Ewell, Terry B. "On Low Brass Musicians Performing Bassoon Music: A Bassoonist's Perspective." *TUBA Journal*, Vol. 23, No. 4 (Summer 1996): 66–69.

Falcone, Leonard. "An Appeal for Solos for the Baritone Horn." *Music Educators Journal* 26, No. 3 (Dec. 1939): 38.

Falcone, Leonard. "How to Choose a Solo for the Baritone." *Educational Music Magazine* (1932).

Falcone, Leonard. "If I Were Choosing a Solo for the Baritone." *School Musician* (Dec. 1939).

Fitzgerald, Bernard. "Studies for Trombone and Baritone." *Instrumentalist* 1 (May/June 1947).

Fry, Robert H. "Playing the Bach Suites for Unaccompanied Cello." *TUBA Journal*, Vol. 18, No. 3 (Spring 1990): 17+.

Green, David. "Elizabeth (Betsy) Raum: A Find for Tuba Players." *TUBA Journal*, Vol. 26, No. 4 (Summer 1999): 35–37.

Howey, Henry. "The Revival of Amilcare Ponchielli's *Concerto per flicorno basso*, Opus 155, Cremona, 1872." *TUBA Journal*, Vol. 23, No. 4 (Summer 1996): 42–49.

Kelly, Steven N. "The TUBA Press and You." *TUBA Journal*, Vol. 18, No. 4 (Summer 1991): 48–50.

Klein, Stephen. "How to Obtain the Music You Heard at the Third International Tuba-Euphonium Symposium-Workshop." *TUBA Journal*, Vol. 6, No. 3 (Spring 1979): 6–7.

Landers, Michael. "Understanding the 'New Music,' Part Seven—Other Sources of 'Hidden Repertoire.'" *TUBA Journal*, Vol. 22, No. 1 (Fall 1994): 50–52.

Landers, Michael. "Understanding the 'New Music,' Part Six—Other Sources of 'Hidden Repertoire.'" *TUBA Journal*, Vol. 21, No. 4 (Summer 1994): 32–35.

Little, Donald C. "1995 International Tuba-Euphonium Conference Competitions Information." *TUBA Journal*, Vol. 21, No. 4 (Summer 1994): 32–35.

Louder, Earle L. "Euphonium Literature–Original Solo Literature and Study Books for Euphonium." *Instrumentalist* 35, No. 10 (May 1981): 29–30.

Madeson, Robert M. "Editing Solos for Euphonium." *TUBA Journal*, Vol. 23, No. 1 (Fall 1995): 52–54.

Maldonado, Luis. "Addendum–Solo Music Literature for Junior High and High School Euphonium and Tuba Performers." *TUBA Journal*, Vol. 15, No. 2 (Nov. 1987): 24–25.

Maldonado, Luis. "Ensemble Literature for Junior High and High School Euphonium and Tuba Performers." *TUBA Journal*, Vol. 15, No. 2 (Nov. 1987): 24.

Maldonado, Luis. "The Leonard Falcone International Euphonium/Baritone Horn Festival Competition Music List 1992–1995." *TUBA Journal*, Vol. 19, No. 1 (Fall 1991): 22.

Maldonado, Luis. "Methods and Solos for Junior High and High School Euphonium Students." *TUBA Journal*, Vol. 16, No. 3 (Spring 1989): 32–35+.

Maldonado, Luis. "Solo Music Literature for Junior High and High School Euphonium and Tuba Performers." *TUBA Journal*, Vol. 14, No. 4 (May 1987): 39–41.

Mead, Steven. "Euphonium Notes." *TUBA Journal*, Vol. 23, No. 2 (Winter 1996): 44–49.

Mead, Steven. "Euphonium Repertoire—Composer's Speak." *TUBA Journal*, Vol. 19, No. 4 (Summer 1992): 44–45.

Miles, David. "Euphonium Methods and Solos." *Instrumentalist* 43, No. 9 (April 1989): 34–36.

Miles, David. "Euphonium Study Materials." *TUBA Journal*, Vol. 13, No. 4 (May 1986): 27–29, 33.

Morris, R. Winston. "Music for Multiple Tubas." *Instrumentalist* 24 (April 1970): 57–58.

Morris, R. Winston. "The United States Navy Band Tuba-Euphonium Quartet–A Review." *TUBA Journal*, Vol. 15, No. 3 (Feb. 1988): 34.

Payne, Barbara, and Jonathan D. Green. "A Critical Analysis of J. Ed. Barat's *Andante et Allegro*." *TUBA Journal*, Vol. 19, No. 2 (Winter 1991): 36–39.

Pugh, Joel. "Salvationist Euphonium Solos." *TUBA Journal*, Vol. 28, No. 3 (Spring 2001): 41–43.

Reifsnyder, Bob. "T.U.B.A. Programs: What Are They Telling Us?" *TUBA Journal*, Vol. 11, No. 2 (Fall 1983): 6–9.

Reifsnyder, Robert. "Why Have Composers Stopped Writing Melodically for the Euphonium?" *TUBA Journal*, Vol. 8, No. 4 (Spring 1981): 13–14.

Richardson, William W. "Trombone and Baritone Solos and Study Materials." *Instrumentalist* 32, No. 7 (Feb. 1987): 60–61.

Rideout, Jeffrey J. "The Annual Report of the T.U.B.A. Resource Library—1980." *TUBA Journal*, Vol. 8, No. 4 (Spring 1981): 15–22.

Rideout, Jeffrey J., and Paula Friedrich-Sandlin. "The Annual Report of the T.U.B.A. Resource Library–1979." *TUBA Journal*, Vol. 7, No. 2 (Fall 1979): 40–51.

Roust, Colin. "The Orchestral History of the Euphonium." *TUBA Journal*, Vol. 28, No. 3 (Spring 2001): 33–39.

Russell, Eileen M. "An Analysis of Movement III, John Stevens' *Soliloquies* for Solo Euphonium." *ITEA Journal* 31, No. 1 (Fall 2003): 74–76.

Schmidt, Paul. "Tuba & Euphonium Pedagogy: Potential Application of Bass Viol Literature." *TUBA Journal*, Vol. 18, No. 4 (Summer 1991): 44–47.

Shoop, Stephen. "Alec Wilder's Music for Tuba and Euphonium." *TUBA Journal*, Vol. 22, No. 3 (Spring 1995): 56–59.

Varner, J. Lesley. "Annual Report of the T.U.B.A. Resource Library." *TUBA Journal*, Vol. 6, No. 1 (Fall 1978): 8–16.

Varner, Lesley. "T.U.B.A. Resource Library." *T.U.B.A. Newsletter* 2, No. 3 (Spring 1975): 5.

Vinson, Dan S. "The Euphonium in Chamber Music." *Instrumentalist* 43, No. 5 (Dec. 1988): 18–19.

Williams, Nyal. "TUBA Resource Library Holdings." *TUBA Journal*, Vol. 21, No. 4 (Summer 1994): 48–66.

Winking, Charles R. "Solo and Etude Materials for the Low Brass Instruments (an Annotated Listing for Trombone and Bass Trombone, Euphonium, and Tuba)." *National Association of College Wind and Percussion Instructors (N.A.C.W.P.I.) Journal* (Fall 1979): 32–37.

Wyman, John. "The Euphonium Literature Archive, Part I: A Report on Its Inception, Growing Pains, and Future." *TUBA Journal*, Vol. 23, No. 4 (Summer 1996): 50–59.

Young, Jerry. "Selecting Music for Low Brass Ensemble." *Instrumentalist* 48, No. 10 (May 1994): 42–46.

Young, Raymond G. "Euphoniums–What's Happening!" *T.U.B.A. Newsletter* 1, No. 3 (Spring 1974): 10.

Young, Raymond G. "New Materials–Euphonium-Tuba." Ed. R. Winston Morris. *T.U.B.A. Newsletter* 2, No. 2 (Winter 1975): 8.

Young, Raymond G. "Some Recommended Euphonium Music." *TUBA Journal*, Vol. 1, No. 2 (Winter 1974): 5.

Orchestration

Dutton, Brent. "Interchanges." *TUBA Journal*, Vol. 7, No. 4 (Spring 1980): 19–21.

Meinl, Gerhard. "The Tenor Tuba: Richard Strauss' Orchestration and the Revival of an Instrument." Ed. Royce Lumpkin. *TUBA Journal*, Vol. 17, No. 4 (Summer 1990): 9–10.

Mueller, Frederick A. "Two Tubas for Symphony Orchestra and Chamber Music." *T.U.B.A. Newsletter* 1, No. 3 (Spring 1974): 8.

Ross, Walter. "Multiple Tuba Parts for the Orchestra." *T.U.B.A. Newsletter* 2, No. 1 (Fall 1974): 9.

Shoop, Stephen. "Arranging and Transcribing Music for the Junior High and High School Tuba Ensemble." *TUBA Journal*, Vol. 20, No. 2 (Winter 1992): 36–37.

Werden, David. "Scoring for the Euphonium." *Instrumentalist* 43, No. 5 (Dec. 1988): 33–34.

Pedagogy

Alexander, Lois. "Performance Success: A Function of Preparation—An Interview with Joseph Skillen." *TUBA Journal*, Vol. 26, No. 2 (Winter 1999): 71–73.

Anderson, Eugene. "Fourteen Ways to Improve Intonation on Tuba and Euphonium." *T.U.B.A. Newsletter* 2, No. 2 (Winter 1974): 1.

Beauregard, Cherry. "Psychology in Pedagogy." *TUBA Journal*, Vol. 9, No. 3 (Winter 1982): 18.

Bergee, Martin J. "An Alternative Approach to Evaluating Euphonium and Tuba Performance." *TUBA Journal,* Vol. 16, No. 4 (Summer 1989): 41–42.

Bough, Thomas. "Low Brass Sections in Tone and in Tune." *Instrumentalist* 54, No. 12 (July 2000): 36–46.

Bowman, Brian. "Advice for College Euphonium Applicants." *Instrumentalist* 47, No. 8 (March 1993): 40–41.

Bowman, Brian. "Developing Euphonium Tone." *Instrumentalist* 43, No. 7 (Feb. 1989): 31–32.

Bowman, Brian. "Euphonium Technique." *Instrumentalist* 47, No. 10 (May 1993): 10–14.

Bowman, Brian. "Master Class—Euphonium." *Accent* 6, No. 1 (Jan./Feb. 1978).

Bowman, Brian L., comp. and ed. Harold T. Brasch, Paul D. Droste, Leonard Falcone, Arthur Lehman, Earl L. Louder, Henry C. Smith, and Raymond G. Young. "Vibrato and the Euphonium." *TUBA Journal,* Vol. 5, No. 2 (Winter 1978): 12–21.

Brasch, Harold T. "Discriminating Use of the Tongue." *Instrumentalist* 12, No. 1 (Sept. 1957): 86.

Brasch, Harold T. "Producing Vibrato." *Instrumentalist* 12, No. 6 (Feb. 1958): 48–50.

Brasch, Harold T. "When Is a Baritone a Euphonium." *Instrumentalist* 3 (March 1949): 36–37.

Brubeck, David W. "The Pedagogy of Arnold Jacobs." *TUBA Journal,* Vol. 19, No. 1 (Fall 1991): 54–58.

Burdick, Daniel. "Overcoming Practice Boredom." *TUBA Journal,* Vol. 22, No. 2 (Winter 1995): 36–37.

Campbell, Larry D. "Why Double on Trombone and Euphonium?" *TUBA Journal,* Vol. 10, No. 4 (Spring 1983): 7–9.

Carlson, Mark. "A Finnish Virtuoso: Studies with Jukka Myllys." *TUBA Journal,* Vol. 31, No. 3 (Spring 2004): 56–61.

Childs, Robert. "The Value of Practising False Notes and Buzzing." *British Bandsman* 5160 (8 Sept. 2001): 7.

Conrey, G. "Baritone Forum." *Southwestern Brass Journal* 1 (Spring 1957): 8–11.

Corwell, Neal. "Why Practice?" *TUBA Journal,* Vol. 21, No. 2 (Winter 1994): 44–45.

Erickson, Marty. "Catching Up with . . . Jun Yamaoka." *ITEA Journal* 29, No. 4 (Summer 2002): 45–48.

Etzkorn, Cleon. "A Full Baritone Tone." *School Musician* 29, No. 8 (April 1958): 20, 53.

Falcone, Leonard. "The Euphonium—Cello of the Band." *Instrumentalist* 6, No. 6 (Nov./Dec. 1951): 22, 40–41.

Falcone, Leonard. "How to Produce a Beautiful Tone on the Baritone." *School Musician* 23 (1952).

Flor, Gloria J. "Where to Put the Left Hand while Playing the Baritone Horn." *School Musician* 36 (Feb. 1981): 36–37.

Fritze, Gregory. "The Play-Along Method of Learning Jazz Improvisation." *TUBA Journal,* Vol. 19, No. 1 (Fall 1991): 48–50.

Funderburk, Jeffrey L. "Audition Strategy." *TUBA Journal,* Vol. 18, No. 3 (Spring 1991): 52.

Gleason, Bruce. "Doubling on Euphonium." *Instrumentalist* 46, No. 10 (May 1994): 28–30.

Gleason, Gerald. "Where It All Begins." *TUBA Journal,* Vol. 26, No. 2 (Winter 1999): 65–66.

Graves, William L. "Playing the Euphonium." *Maryland Music Educator* (Summer 1971): 11.

Gray, Skip. "Getting Ready for Advanced Study—Setting a Course of Study." *Instrumentalist* 43, No. 5 (Dec. 1988): 29+.

Gray, Skip. "Organizing Your Practice: Structuring a System for Improvement." *TUBA Journal,* Vol. 16, No. 2 (Winter 1988): 40–42.

Groom, Trevor, and David Werden. "Experts Reveal Practice Routines." *TUBA Journal,* Vol. 19, No. 4 (Summer 1992): 50–51.

Heath, Fred. "Coping with Problems in Transferring to Low Brass from Trumpet." *TUBA Journal,* Vol. 7, No. 2 (Fall 1979): 16–17.

Humble, Karl. "Sound Is What It's All About." *Woodwind World, Brass, and Percussion* 21, No. 3 (March 1982): 4–5.

Johnson, Carson E. "Use That Fourth Valve." *Instrumentalist* 14, No. 8 (April 1960): 56–58.

Kaenzig, Fritz. "Tuba Pedagogy: Building a Successful Low Register." *TUBA Journal,* Vol. 13, No. 1 (Aug. 1985): 23–24.

Little, Don. "An Arnold Jacobs Clinic." *TUBA Journal,* Vol. 26, No. 2 (Winter 1999): 9–14.

Lohman, Joseph. "Does Psychology Have Anything Useful to Say to Tubists?" *TUBA Journal,* Vol. 24, No. 2 (Winter 1997): 48–51.

Louder, Earle "Master Class—Baritone." *Accent* 5, No. 4 (March 1980).

Lumpkin, Royce. "Intonation Problems of the Euphonium." *ITEA Journal* 30, No. 4 (Summer 2003): 46–51.

Maldonado, Luis. "Breathing Properly." *TUBA Journal,* Vol. 16, No. 2 (Winter 1988): 24.

Maldonado, Luis. "Checking Up on Your Intonation: Part One." *TUBA Journal,* Vol. 15, No. 3 (Feb. 1988): 31.

Maldonado, Luis. "Checking Up on Your Intonation: Part Two." *TUBA Journal,* Vol. 15, No. 4 (May 1988): 39.

Maldonado, Luis. "A Checklist for the New School Year." *TUBA Journal,* Vol. 16, No. 1 (Fall 1988): 31.

Maldonado, Luis. "A Few Guidelines on How to Practice." *TUBA Journal,* Vol. 14, No. 1 (Aug. 1986): 41+.

Maldonado, Luis. "Long Tones, Lip Slurs, and Scales–Do We Really Need Them?" *TUBA Journal,* Vol. 14, No. 2 (Nov. 1986): 35.

Maldonado, Luis. "Nervousness: What It Does and What We Can Do About It." *TUBA Journal,* Vol. 13, No. 4 (May 1986): 39.

Maldonado, Luis. "Proper Ways to Mark Your Music." *TUBA Journal,* Vol. 16, No. 4 (Summer 1989): 28–30.

Maldonado, Luis. "Response Problems. What Can I Do?" *TUBA Journal,* Vol. 15, No. 1 (Aug. 1987): 18.

Maldonado, Luis. "Selecting and Developing Young Students." *TUBA Journal,* Vol. 17, No. 2 (Winter 1989): 14–15.

Mead, Steven. "Euphonium Notes." *TUBA Journal,* Vol. 22, No. 1 (Fall 1993): 28–35.

Mead, Steven. "The Great Fourth Valve Mystery." *TUBA Journal,* Vol. 15, No. 3 (Feb. 1988): 22–24.

Mead, Steven. "Recital Preparation." *British Bandsman* No. 4494 (3 Dec. 1988).

Mead, Steven. "Recital Preparation." *TUBA Journal,* Vol. 16, No. 4 (Summer 1989): 36–37.

Meckna, Michael. "95% Human and 5% Metal: Advice from Some Tuba and Euphonium Masters." *TUBA Journal,* Vol. 21, No. 3 (Spring 1994): 36–38.

Mendoker, Scott. "Thoughts on Becoming a Performing Musician." *TUBA Journal,* Vol. 23, No. 2 (Winter 1996): 54–55.

Nelson, Mark A. "Developing the Beginning Tuba/Euphonium Ensemble." *TUBA Journal,* Vol. 9, No. 3 (Winter 1982): 14–16.

Nelson, Mark A. "Developing the College/Community Tuba/Euphonium Ensemble." *TUBA Journal,* Vol. 16, No. 1 (Fall 1988): 34–35.

Nutaitis, Raymond. "The Daily Routine—Do I Need It?" *TUBA Journal,* Vol. 8, No. 4 (Spring 1981): 24–44.

Paulson, Don H. "Improving the Low Register on the Baritone/Euphonium." *Woodwind World, Brass, and Percussion* 16, No. 6 (Holiday Issue 1977): 17, 28.

Perrins, Barrie. "Some Thoughts on Euphonium Technique." (English, French and German.) *Brass Bulletin* 22 (1978): 9+.

Popiel, Peter. "A Direct Approach to Legato on the Low Brass Instruments." *TUBA Journal,* Vol. 10, No. 3 (Winter 1983): 8–10.

Randolph, David M. "Toward Effective Performance of Multiphonics." *TUBA Journal,* Vol. 8, No. 2 (Fall 1980): 2–4.

Reed, David F. "Primer on the Breathing Process." *TUBA Journal,* Vol. 9, No. 1 (Summer 1981): 8–10.

Rees, Jonathan. "Some Thoughts on Brass Playing." *TUBA Journal,* Vol. 27, No. 2 (Winter 1999): 53–55.

Robbins, E. J. "So, You Play the Euphonium." *Instrumentalist* 21, No. 3 (Oct. 1966): 63–66.

Rohner, Traugott. "Fingering the Bass Trombone and Four-Valve Euphonium." *Instrumentalist* 8, No. 2 (Oct. 1966): 30–31.

Rohner, Traugott. "Fingering the Brasses." *Instrumentalist* (March–April 1953).

Shoop, Stephen. "The Junior High and High School Tuba Ensemble." *TUBA Journal,* Vol. 20, No. 1 (Fall 1992): 38–39.

Spiros, Lucas. "The Band Director's Approach to the Euphonium." *TUBA Journal,* Vol. 11, No. 1 (Summer 1983): 16–17.

Steiger, Daniel J. "Fundamental Problems in Young Euphonium Students." *TUBA Journal,* Vol. 19, No. 2 (Winter 1991): 42–43.

Stephenson. "Baritone Forum." *Southwestern Brass Journal* 1 (Fall 1957).

Stewart, M. Dee. "Euphonium Encumbrances and Encouragements." *TUBA Journal,* Vol. 9, No. 4 (Spring 1982): 10–12.

Stewart, M. Dee. "Some Thoughts on Posture and Holding the Euphonium." *TUBA Journal,* Vol. 8, No. 3 (Winter 1981): 13–14.

Watson, Scott. "Three Exercises for Correct Air Flow on the Tuba-Euphonium." *TUBA Journal,* Vol. 10, No. 2 (Fall 1982): 8–9.

Winter, Denis. "Technology in the Applied Studio." *TUBA Journal,* Vol. 17, No. 2 (Winter 1989): 25–26.

Young, Jerry. "Duties of Low Brass Instructors." *TUBA Journal,* Vol. 9, No. 4 (Spring 1982): 13–16.

Young, Jerry. "A Pause for Thought . . ." *TUBA Journal,* Vol. 22, No. 3 (Spring 1995): 62–63.

Young, Raymond. "Euphonium—Well-Sounding." *Instrumentalist* 18, No. 8 (March 1964): 72–73.

Performance

Arwood, Jeff, ed. "United States Military Bands." *TUBA Journal,* Vol. 14, No. 3 (Feb. 1987): 20–71.

Askew, Dennis. "ITEC 2001 Competitions Report." *ITEA Journal* 29, No. 1 (Fall 2001): 76–77.

Bach, Jan. "Jan Bach's *Concert Variations:* Observations, Insights and Suggestions for Its Performance." *TUBA Journal,* Vol. 23, No. 1 (Fall 1995): 46–49.

Bland, Niki. "Creating a Fresh Canvas for the Euphonium." *British Bandsman* 4918 (18 Jan. 1997): 13.

Bland, Niki. "A Showcase of International Stars." *British Bandsman* 4918 (18 Jan. 1997): 10–11.

Bobo, Roger. "Symposium 78: Looking Back." (English, French, and German.) *Brass Bulletin,* No. 25 (1979): 19+.

Bowman, Brian. "Euphonium-Tuba Opportunities in Service Bands." *T.U.B.A. Newsletter* 1, No. 2 (Winter 1974): 8.

Bowman, Brian. "Reflections on: Euphonium Concert Tour, Japan 1984." *TUBA Journal,* Vol. 12, No. 4 (May 1985): 17–19.

Boykin, Dan. "Things Every Performing Musician Should Think About When It Comes to Making a Living." *ITEA Journal* 31, No. 1 (Fall 2003): 66–69.

Bradley, Terry, and Danny Bradley. "1995 International Brassfest." *TUBA Journal,* Vol. 22, No. 4 (Summer 1995): 32–35.

Briggs, Vernon. "Ellerby Provides New Pinnacle for the Euphonium." *Brass Band World* 73 (April 1998): 11.

Bryant, Steven, ed. Mary Ann Feldman, John Harvey, Roy Close. "News Items—Concertos Premiered (*Symphony No. 29 for Baritone Horn and Orchestra* by Alan Hovhaness)." *TUBA Journal,* Vol. 5, No. 3 (Spring/Summer 1978): 28–31.

Bryant, Steven, J. Lesley Varner, Don Baird, Donald Little, Constance Welden, and Rex Conner. "Third International Tuba-Euphonium Symposium-Workshop—Recital Reviews." *TUBA Journal,* Vol. 6, No. 2 (Winter 1979): 19–33.

Burdick, Daniel. "The Eighth Annual Leonard Falcone International Euphonium/Baritone Horn Festival." *TUBA Journal,* Vol. 21, No. 2 (Winter 1994): 12–16.

Burdick, Daniel. "The Ninth Annual Leonard Falcone International Euphonium Festival." *TUBA Journal,* Vol. 22, No. 2 (Winter 1995): 12–15.

Buttery, Judy. "A Holiday Concert by Hot Cross Brass." *TUBA Journal,* Vol. 16, No. 3 (Spring 1989): 42–43.

Cox, Mark S. "Eleventh Annual Leonard Falcone International Euphonium and Tuba Solo Festival." *TUBA Journal,* Vol. 24, No. 3 (Spring 1997): 15–17.

"David Childs Brilliant in BBC Young Musician." *Brass Band World* 95 (June 2000): 11.

Dempster, Stuart. "Tuba Time in Tacoma: A Thoroughly Biased Report on the First Northwest Annual Tuba-Euphonium Workshop." *TUBA Journal,* Vol. 16, No. 1 (Fall 1988): 36–43.

Droste, Paul. "Brass Bands Are Back: Performing Opportunities for Euphonium and Tuba Players." *TUBA Journal,* Vol. 16, No. 3 (Spring 1989): 40–41.

Dummer, Lee. "Euphonium Performance Opportunities." *TUBA Journal,* Vol. 17, No. 4 (Summer 1990): 8+.

Dutton, Brent. "British Brass Band Championship." *TUBA Journal,* Vol. 7, No. 4 (Spring 1980): 11–15.

Dutton, Brent. "Interchanges." *TUBA Journal,* Vol. 8, No. 4 (Spring 1981): 10–12.

"The Eighteenth Annual Leonard Falcone International Euphonium and Tuba Festival." *ITEA Journal* 31, No. 1 (Fall 2003): 81–84.

Evans, Eliot D. "All You Ever Wanted to Know About the Washington D.C. Military Bands." *TUBA Journal,* Vol. 8, No. 1 (Summer 1980): 2–12.

Fletcher, John. "The Tuba in Britain." *TUBA Journal,* Vol. 5, No. 2 (Winter 1978): 22–23, 26–30.

Forbes, Mike. "Chamber Music Corner: An Introduction." *ITEA Journal* 31, No. 1 (Fall 2003): 72–73.

Goble, Joseph D. "Audition and Contest Preparation." *ITEA Journal* 29, No. 2 (Winter 2002): 79–81.

Griffiths, Morgan. "My First Year at Black Dyke." *TUBA Journal,* Vol. 19, No. 4 (Summer 1992): 56.

Guy, Charles. "Exploring the New Double-Bell Euphonium: A Review/Commentary of Edward Mallett's Lecture/Recital." *TUBA Journal,* Vol. 23, No. 4 (Summer 1996): 64.

Harris, Emily, V. Andy Anders, Gretchen R. Bowles, Brian Bowman, M. Cristina Fava, John Griffiths, John Stevens, Robert Tucci, Jerry A. Young. "International Tuba-Euphonium Conference 1997: Verso il Millennio—Reports and Reviews." *TUBA Journal,* Vol. 25, No. 1 (Spring 1997): 36–45.

Heinkel, Peggy. "Analysis for Interpretation: Samuel Adler's *Dialogues for Euphonium and Marimba.*" *TUBA Journal,* Vol. 13, No. 3 (Feb. 1986): 10–16.

Holte, Dawn. "ITEC 2002, Truly an ITEC for You." *ITEA Journal* 30, No. 1 (Fall 2002): 56–59.

"International Brass on Show (National Euphonium and Baritone Festival)." *British Bandsman* 5022 (16 Jan. 1999): 8.

"The International Tuba-Euphonium Conference 1998—Review." *TUBA Journal,* Vol. 26, No. 1 (Fall 1998): 39–76.

Jones, George W, ed. "The Second International Brass Congress." *TUBA Journal,* Vol. 12, No. 1 (Aug. 1984): 10–25.

Kaenzig, Fritz. "HETA Music Camp Report." *TUBA Journal,* Vol. 19, No. 1 (Fall 1991): 14–16.

Kaenzig, Fritz. "1992 International Tuba-Euphonium Conference Competitions Information." *TUBA Journal,* Vol. 19, No. 1 (Fall 1991): 68–71.

Keys, Stephen. "The University of Kentucky Regional Tuba-Euphonium Conference Review." *TUBA Journal,* Vol. 15, No. 2 (Nov. 1987): 20–21.

Kniffen, Anthony. "ITEA 30th Anniversary Celebration." *ITEA Journal* 30, No. 4 (Summer 2003): 40–44.

Lancto, Peter C. "1988 New England Tuba-Euphonium Symposium/Workshop: Recital Reviews." *TUBA Journal,* Vol. 16, No. 1 (Fall 1988): 53–54.

Little, Donald C. "1995 International Tuba-Euphonium Conference Competitions Information." *TUBA Journal,* Vol. 21, No. 4 (Summer 1994): 32–35.

Louder, Earle. "The Fourth Annual Leonard Falcone International Baritone Horn/Euphonium Competition." *TUBA Journal,* Vol. 17, No. 3 (Spring 1990): 23–24.

"Low Brass Scales New Depths." *Brass Band World* 60 (Dec. 1996/Jan. 1997): 12–13.

Mackim, Tom. "Tubafours: Take One—Lights . . . Camera . . . Action!" *TUBA Journal,* Vol. 25, No. 3 (Spring 1998): 34–36.

Maldonado, Luis. "Falcone Competition Finals—A Review." *TUBA Journal,* Vol. 22, No. 2 (Winter 1995): 15–16.

Maldonado, Luis. "The 1986 Japan Wind and Percussion Competition." *TUBA Journal,* Vol. 14, No. 4 (May 1987): 21–22.

Maldonado, Luis. "The 1991 Leonard Falcone International Euphonium (Baritone Horn) Competition." *TUBA Journal,* Vol. 19, No. 1 (Fall 1991): 20–21.

Maldonado, Luis. Roger Behrend, ed. "The Third Annual Leonard Falcone International Euphonium Competition." *TUBA Journal,* Vol. 16, No. 3 (Winter 1988): 11–12.

Mathez, Jean-Pierre. "Birmingham 1995—2nd Annual National Tuba and Euphonium Conference." (English, French, and German.) *Brass Bulletin* 90, No. 2 (1995): 50–57.

Mathez, Jean-Pierre, and Steven Mead. "Guebwiller France—World Competition for Tuba & Euphonium." (English, French, and German.) *Brass Bulletin* 100, No. 4 (1997): 84–92.

Mathez, Jeremy. "Lathi Brass Festival—International Tuba & Euphonium Conference." (English, French, and German.) *Brass Bulletin* 116, No. 4 (2001): 90–94.

McCready, Matthew. "Trombone Doubling Among Service Band Euphoniumists." *TUBA Journal,* Vol. 17, No. 2 (Winter 1989): 27–29.

Mead, Steven. "Around the World in 60 Days with Steven Mead." *British Bandsman* 5097 (24 June 2000): 11.

Mead, Steven. "Cutting It in the Solo CD Market with Steven Mead." *British Bandsman* (29 Nov. 2003): 12–13.

Mead, Steven. "Have Euphonium, Will Travel!" *British Bandsman* 5045 (26 June 1999): 10–11.

Mead, Steven. "The 9th Japan Wind and Percussion Competition." *TUBA Journal,* Vol. 20, No. 2 (Winter 1992): 19–20.

"Mid-South Euphonium/Tuba Symposium." *T.U.B.A. Newsletter* 3, No. 3 (Spring/Summer 1976): 8.

"Midwest Regional Tuba-Euphonium Symposium—A Report." *T.U.B.A. Newsletter* 3, No. 2 (Winter 1976): 7–8.

Miura, Toru. "Attivazione per Eufonio e Tuba in Giappone." *TUBA Journal,* Vol. 25, No. 2 (Winter 1998): 44–51.

Miura, Toru. "The Euphonium and Tuba in Japan." *TUBA Journal,* Vol. 8, No. 3 (Winter 1981): 10–12.

Morris, R. Winston. "A Guest Editorial on the U.S. Army Band Tuba-Euphonium Conference." *TUBA Journal,* Vol. 31, No. 3 (Spring 2004): 16+.

Munson, Ronald L. "Northwest 'Big Brass' Bash XI." *TUBA Journal,* Vol. 25, No. 2 (Winter 1998): 54–56.

Naylor, J. J. "The English Euphonium: Its Development and Use." *TUBA Journal,* Vol. 9, No. 4 (Spring 1982): 17–18.

Nelson, Mark. comp. and ed. "International Brassfest 1996." *TUBA Journal,* Vol. 24, No. 1 (Fall 1996): 78–83.

"1986 International Tuba-Euphonium Conference Session Reviews." *TUBA Journal,* Vol. 14, No. 1 (Aug. 1986): 11–34.

"1983 I.T.E.C.: A Wrap-Up—Part I." *TUBA Journal,* Vol. 11, No. 2 (Fall 1983): 12–20.

"1995 International Tuba-Euphonium Conference." *TUBA Journal,* Vol. 22, No. 4 (Summer 1995): 40–60.

"1991 U.S. Army Band Tuba-Euphonium Conference." (Reviews.) *TUBA Journal,* Vol. 18, No. 3 (Spring 1991): 42–50.

"1992 International Tuba-Euphonium Conference—Lexington, Kentucky, May 12–16, 1992: Concert and Clinic Reviews." *TUBA Journal,* Vol. 20, No. 1 (Fall 1992): 52–78.

"1992 U.S. Army Band Tuba-Euphonium Conference Concert Reviews." *TUBA Journal,* Vol. 19, No. 4 (Summer 1992): 8–13.

"1975 National T.U.B.A. Symposium-Workshop." *T.U.B.A. Newsletter* 1, No. 2 (Winter 1974): 12.

Northcut, Timothy, and Robert Daniel. "Region Four T.U.B.A. Regional Workshop: Review." *TUBA Journal,* Vol. 12, No. 4 (May 1985): 14–15.

Popiel, Peter. "First National Tuba-Euphonium Symposium: A Report." *T.U.B.A. Newsletter* 3, No. 1 (Fall 1975): 2+.

O'Bryant, Kelly. "An In-Depth Look at the Tuba and Euphonium Sections of the United States Military Service Academy Bands: Part Three of Three." *TUBA Journal,* Vol. 24, No. 1 (Fall 1996): 72–76.

O'Bryant, Kelly. "An In-Depth Look at the Tuba and Euphonium Sections of the United States Military Service Academy Bands: Part Two of Three." *TUBA Journal,* Vol. 24, No. 4 (Summer 1996): 60–62.

O'Bryant, Kelly. "The 16th Annual U.S. Army Band Tuba-Euphonium Conference." *TUBA Journal,* Vol. 25, No. 4 (Summer 1998): 38–42.

O'Bryant, Kelly. "The 16th Annual U.S. Army Band Tuba-Euphonium Conference." *TUBA Journal,* Vol. 26, No. 3 (Spring 1999): 29–40.

Okun, Seymour. "Falcone Festival Honors Legacy of Great Performer and Teacher." *TUBA Journal,* Vol. 20, No. 1 (Fall 1992): 13.

Pfisterer, Philippe. "1997—Tuba & Euphonium Featured at Guebwiller." (English, French, and German.) *Brass Bulletin* 93, No. 1 (1996): 28–31.

Philips, Harvey G. "The Press, the Media and Public Relations." *ITEA Journal* 29, No. 1 (Fall 2001): 78–80.

Schlabach, John. "On Connecting the Ear and Brass Performance." *ITEA Journal* 30, No. 2 (Winter 2003): 62–63.

"Second National Tuba-Euphonium Symposium-Workshop." *TUBA Journal*, Vol. 7, No. 3 (Winter 1980): 16–22.

"Second National Tuba-Euphonium Symposium-Workshop." *TUBA Journal*, Vol. 7, No. 4 (Spring 1980): 6–10.

Self, James M. "Third International Tuba-Euphonium Symposium-Workshop—An Update." *TUBA Journal*, Vol. 5, No. 3 (Spring/ Summer 1978): 20.

Shoop, Stephen. "Employment Opportunities Available to Tuba and Euphonium Players at America's Amusement-Theme Parks." *TUBA Journal*, Vol. 15, No. 3 (Feb. 1988): 20–21.

Sinder, Philip. "Twelfth Annual Leonard Falcone International Euphonium and Tuba Solo Festival." *TUBA Journal*, Vol. 25, No. 3 (Spring 1998): 13–15.

"The Sixth Annual United States Army Band/Eastern National T.U.B.A. Tuba-Euphonium Conference, February 1–4, 1989." (Review.) *TUBA Journal* 17, No. 1 (Fall 1989): 21–33.

Smith, Robert D. "A Euphonium Festival." *N.A.C.W.P.I. Journal* (Spring 1971): 40.

"SNTESW (Second National Tuba-Euphonium Symposium-Workshop)—A Wrap-Up." *TUBA Journal*, Vol. 8, No. 2 (Fall 1980): 15–40.

"SNTESW (Second National Tuba-Euphonium Symposium-Workshop)—A Wrap-Up." *TUBA Journal*, Vol. 8, No. 3 (Winter 1981): 8–10.

"Tenth Annual U.S. Army Band Tuba-Euphonium Conference—Concert Reviews." *TUBA Journal*, Vol. 19, No. 4 (Summer 1992): 8–13.

"Third International Tuba-Euphonium Symposium-Workshop." *TUBA Journal*, Vol. 5, No. 1 (Fall 1977): 17+.

"Third International Tuba-Euphonium Symposium-Workshop." *TUBA Journal*, Vol. 5, No. 2 (Winter 1978): 33.

"Third International Tuba-Euphonium Symposium-Workshop." *TUBA Journal*, Vol. 6, No. 1 (Fall 1978): 18–25.

Tilbury, Jack, David Porter, and Sally Wagner. "The United States Army Band Tuba-Euphonium Conference—February 4–7, 1987: A Summary." *TUBA Journal*, Vol. 15, No. 2 (Nov. 1987): 14–19.

"The 21st Annual U.S. Army Band Tuba-Euphonium Conference." *TUBA Journal*, Vol. 31, No. 3 (Spring 2004): 20–25.

"The United States Army Band Eastern National Tuba-Euphonium Conference." *TUBA Journal*, Vol. 17, No. 3 (Spring 1990): 18–22.

"U.S. Army Band Tuba-Euphonium Conference." *TUBA Journal*, Vol. 22, No. 3 (Spring 1995): 22–23.

Ushijima, Tomioki, Chitate Kagawa. "H.E.T.A. (Hokkaido Euphonium Tuba Association): What's Happening on Hokkaido?" *ITEA Journal* 29, No. 2 (Winter 2002): 33–36.

Vinson, Dan S. "The Euphonium in Chamber Music." *Instrumentalist* 43, No. 5 (Dec. 1988): 18–19.

Vinson, Dan S. "New England Artists Recital of the New England Tuba-Euphonium Symposium/ Workshop—A Review." *TUBA Journal*, Vol. 15, No. 4 (May 1987): 13.

Whaley, Robert, ed. "The First International Brass Congress, June 13–19, 1976, Montreux, Switzerland." *TUBA Journal*, Vol. 4, No. 1 (Fall 1976): 11+.

Whaley, Robert, ed. "The First International Brass Congress, June 13–19, 1976, Montreux, Switzerland." Part 2. *TUBA Journal*, Vol. 4, No. 2 (Winter 1977): 2+.

Wilson, Peter. "Low Brass Soars to New Heights at the RNCM." *British Bandsman* 5076 (29 Jan. 2000): 6–7.

Winter, Denis W. "The Leonard Falcone International Euphonium Competition: Another Perspective." Ed. Roger Behrend. *TUBA Journal*, Vol. 15, No. 2 (Nov. 1987): 23+.

Young, Jerry. "The Leonard Falcone International Euphonium Festival 1995." *TUBA Journal*, Vol. 23, No. 1 (Fall 1995): 12–14.

Young, Jerry. "Low Brass Hits High Spot at ITEC." *British Bandsman* 5161 (15 Sept. 2001): 5.

Young, Jerry. "Some Reflections on the 1988 Leonard Falcone International Euphonium Competition." *TUBA Journal*, Vol. 16, No. 2 (Winter 1988): 10.

Young, Jerry, ed. "ITEC 2001: Being Cool in Lahti." *ITEA Journal* 29, No. 1 (Fall 2001): 41–75.

Miscellaneous

"Ashley Alexander—1936–1988—A Tribute." *TUBA Journal*, Vol. 16, No. 1 (Fall 1988): 11–13.

Behrend, Roger L. "The Euphonium in 1988." *Instrumentalist* 43, No. 5: 40–42.

Behrend, Roger L. "In Memoriam: Dr. Leonard Falcone." *TUBA Journal*, Vol. 13, No. 1 (Aug. 1985): 7.

Behrend, Roger L, ed. "T.U.B.A. Tribute to Dr. Leonard Falcone and Harold Brasch." *TUBA Journal*, Vol. 13, No. 4 (May 1986): 14–19.

Bowman, Brian L. "1978 Annual Reports of the Euphonium Coordinator and Vice-President." *TUBA Journal*, Vol. 6, No. 3 (Spring 1979): 16–17.

Bowman, Brian L. "Report from the Euphonium Coordinator." *TUBA Journal*, Vol. 5, No. 2 (Winter 1978): 31–32.

Bowman, Brian L. "T.U.B.A. Euphonium Profile—Leonard Falcone." *TUBA Journal,* Vol. 5, No. 2 (Winter 1978): 2–5.

Brasch, Harold. "How to Play the Hose." *TUBA Journal,* Vol. 10, No. 9 (Spring 1982): 6–7.

Brasch, Harold. "The Old Man Responds." *TUBA Journal,* Vol. 10, No. 3 (Winter 1983): 33–34.

Brubeck, David, and John Olah. "Connie's Final Toot!—An Interview with Constance Weldon." *TUBA Journal,* Vol. 18, No. 4 (Summer 1991): 28–37.

Carlson, Andrew. "The United States Military Bands." *ITEA Journal* 29, No. 2 (Winter 2002): 27–78.

Corwell, Neal. "An Admirable Trio: A Look at Three Ways of Making Music Part of Your Life." *TUBA Journal,* Vol. 27, No. 3 (Spring 2000): 45–49.

Droste, Paul. "Euphonium Coordinator Report." *TUBA Journal,* Vol. 12, No. 4 (May 1985): 4.

Duckels, Ivor. "Modest Start Led to a Life of Banding Fulfillment (Profile of Eric Johnson)." *Brass Band World* 109 (Nov. 2001): 34.

Durham, Eric. "An Interview with Edward Carroll." *TUBA Journal,* Vol. 25, No. 1 (Spring 1997): 54–56.

Dutton, Brent. "Interchanges—Merle Hogg." *TUBA Journal,* Vol. 10, No. 2 (Fall 1982): 10–12.

Falcone, Leonard. "Is the Baritone Horn Dying? Let's Hope Not–But It Looks That Way." *School Musician* 46, No. 9 (May 1975): 40–41.

"Family Euphoria (David Childs)." *Brass Band World* 71 (Feb. 1998): 34.

Frey, Adam. "A British Band Experience." *TUBA Journal,* Vol. 27, No. 3 (Spring 2000): 41–44.

Fritsch, Philippe, and David Maillot. "The Saxhorn in France: From 1843 to the Present Day." *TUBA Journal,* Vol. 31, No. 3 (Spring 2004): 68–69.

Grasso, Rachel. "An Interview with Joan Follis." *TUBA Journal,* Vol. 26, No. 1 (Fall 1998): 79–81.

Heinkel-Wolfe, Peggy. "Fred Fennell on the Euphonium and Baritone—Part Three of a Series." *TUBA Journal,* Vol. 16, No. 1 (Fall 1988): 56–57.

Heinkel-Wolfe, Peggy. "A Look at the Tokyo Bari-Tuba Ensemble." *TUBA Journal,* Vol. 14, No. 2 (Nov. 1986): 18–20.

Heinkel-Wolfe, Peggy. "Marketing Your Ensemble for the Holidays." *TUBA Journal,* Vol. 19, No. 1 (Fall 1991): 64–65.

Heinkel-Wolfe, Peggy. "Sensei." *TUBA Journal,* Vol. 14, No. 3 (Feb. 1987): 23+.

Hinterbichler, Karl. "A Future for Euphonium?" *Instrumentalist* 33 (Jan. 1979): 11.

Horowitz, Marc David. "Tuba and Euphonium Citations in Recent Medical and Scientific Literature." *TUBA Journal,* Vol. 25, No. 1 (Spring 1997): 58–59.

Hvizdos, Andrew J. "The Euphonium—Dead or Alive?" *Woodwind World, Brass, and Percussion* 15, No. 2 (Spring 1976): 54.

Jaffé, Daniel. "Euphonium Champion: David Childs." *Gramophone* 79, No. 951 (March 2002): 25.

Jaffé, Daniel. "No Gain without Pain for Paul . . . (Profile of Paul Robinson)." *Brass Band World* 50 (Dec. 1995/Jan. 1996): 34.

Jenkins, Alan. "Interview with Steven Mead." *Brass Band World* (Dec. 2003).

Karjalainen, Kaudo. "Band and Brass Traditions in Finland." *TUBA Journal,* Vol. 28, No. 4 (Summer 2001): 45–49.

Larry, Don. "Reflections of an Amateur Euphoniumist." *TUBA Journal,* Vol. 26, No. 3 (Spring 1999): 62–63.

Laws, Francis H. "Euphonium Record Reviews." *T.U.B.A. Newsletter* 4, No. 2 (Winter 1977): 23–24.

Laws, Francis H. "Record Reviews—Euphonium." *T.U.B.A. Newsletter* 3, No. 2 (Winter 1976): 8.

Lewis, David. "The Story Behind Octubafest and TubaChristmas." *Instrumentalist* 43, No. 5 (Dec. 1988): 36+.

Little, Don. "T.U.B.A. Stands for Euphonium." *Instrumentalist* 35, No. 10 (May 1981): 22.

Little, Donald C. "T.U.B.A. Profile—Rich Matteson." *TUBA Journal,* Vol. 5, No. 1 (Fall 1977): 2–6.

Louder, Earle L. "My Fellow Euphoniumists." *T.U.B.A. Newsletter* 3, No. 2 (Winter 1976): 7.

Maldonado, Luis. "Contests, Foundations and Awards for Tuba and Euphonium." *TUBA Journal,* Vol. 18, No. 2 (Winter 1990): 24–27.

"The Man Who Left a Peach of a State for His Love of the Euphonium (Adam Frey)." *Brass Band World* 71 (Feb. 1998): 21.

Mathez, Jean-Pierre. "The Artistic Rise of the Euphonium." *Brass Bulletin* 103, No. 3 (1998): 32–36.

Mathez, Jean-Pierre. "Eran Levi: Top Talent on the Euphonium." *Brass Bulletin* 97, No. 1 (1997): 57–59.

Mathez, Jean-Pierre. "Fernand Lelong, Half a Century of Tuba in France." *Brass Bulletin* 106, No. 2 (1999): 98–104.

Mathez, Jean-Pierre. "Steven Mead—Mister Euphonium." *Brass Bulletin* 90, No. 2 (1995): 44–47.

Mead, Steven. "Brassed-Off Euphonium Players Now Euphoric as BBC Change Their Tune Over Banned Instrument." *TUBA Journal,* Vol. 26, No. 4 (Summer 1999): 25.

Mead, Steven. "Concerts in Russia—The Tale of a Memorable Voyage." *Brass Bulletin* 118, No. 2 (2002): 92–98.

Mead, Steven. "Euphonium Notes." *TUBA Journal,* Vol. 21, No. 1 (Fall 1993): 28–35.

Mead, Steven. "Euphonium Notes." *TUBA Journal*, Vol. 21, No. 2 (Winter 1994): 30–34.

Mead, Steven. "Euphonium Notes." *TUBA Journal*, Vol. 21, No. 4 (Summer 1994): 22–26.

Mead, Steven. "Euphonium Notes." *TUBA Journal*, Vol. 22, No. 1 (Fall 1994): 44–46.

Mead, Steven. "Have Euphonium Will Travel." *TUBA Journal*, Vol. 27, No. 4 (Summer 2000): 39–40.

Mead, Steven. "John Clough Looks Back." *TUBA Journal*, Vol. 19, No. 4 (Summer 1992): 54–55.

Mead, Steven. "Lyndon Baglin's Love Affair with the Euphonium." *TUBA Journal*, Vol. 19, No. 4 (Summer 1992): 55.

Mead, Steven. "Mead Interviews Michael Howard." *TUBA Journal*, Vol. 19, No. 4 (Summer 1992): 56.

Mead, Steven, ed. Roger Behrend, Japp Hoekstra, Luis Maldonado, Toro Miura. "Euphonium News Around the World." *TUBA Journal*, Vol. 19, No. 4 (Summer 1992): 52–53.

Miura, Toru. "Japanese Wind Band." *ITEA Journal* 29, No. 4 (Summer 2002): 30–31.

Mueller, John. "Meet the Childs Brothers—An Interview." *TUBA Journal*, Vol. 17, No. 4 (Summer 1990): 11–13.

Nelson, Mark, and Charles McAdams. "The Tuba and Euphonium on the World Wide Web." *TUBA Journal*, Vol. 24, No. 1 (Fall 1996): 54–65.

"Professional Euphoniumists in the Major U.S. Service Bands." *TUBA Journal*, Vol. 5, No. 2 (Winter 1978): 5.

Robinson, Richard. "An Interview with Ophicleide, Serpent, and Tuba Player Tony George." *Historic Brass Society Newsletter* 8 (Summer 2000): 46–48.

Robinson, Richard. "The Norwegian Star Who Was Taken by Surprise (Sverre Olsrud)." *British Bandsman* 5077 (5 Feb. 2000): 5.

Shoop, Stephen. "Tax Deductions Available to Tuba and Euphonium Players and Teachers." *TUBA Journal*, Vol. 13, No. 3 (Feb. 1986): 19.

Smith, Jason Roland. "Sotto Voce Quartet—Featured Ensemble." *TUBA Journal*, Vol. 31, No. 3 (Spring 2004): 78–79.

Stewart, M. Dee. "The Tenor Tuba Trauma." Ed. Gloria J. Flor. *School Musician* 57, No. 8 (May 1986): 25–26.

Stoddard, Hope, Simone Mantia, and Joe Tarto. "Baritones and Brasses." *International Musician* 49 (Feb. 1951): 20–21.

Torchinsky, Abe, and Roger Oyster. "Utilizing the Euphonium." *TUBA Journal*, Vol. 10, No. 1 (Summer 1982): 4–5.

Weber, Carlyle. "Roster of U.S. Army Band Personnel." *TUBA Journal*, Vol. 19, No. 2 (Winter 1991): 66–68.

Werden, David R. "Does the Euphonium Have a Future?" *TUBA Journal*, Vol. 10, No. 3 (Winter 1983): 11–12.

Wilson, John S. "The Development of the Odd Ball Brass." *Downbeat* 27, No. 1 (Jan. 1960).

Wilson, Peter. "Ambassador of the Euphonium (David Childs)." *British Bandsman* 5093 (27 May 2000): 5.

Winter, Denis. "Annual Report from the Euphonium Coordinator." *TUBA Journal*, Vol. 7, No. 4 (Spring 1980): 17–18.

Winter, Denis. "A Message from the Euphonium Coordinator." *TUBA Journal*, Vol. 7, No. 3 (Winter 1980): 49–50.

KENNETH R. KROESCHE

The books cited in this section will be found to refer to the euphonium in the broadest sense. In some cases, the euphonium, baritone horn, and tenor tuba are mentioned in as little as one sentence, while those listed above under Books refer to it with greater length. Books listed under history and other categories, may not actually make reference to the euphonium specifically, but rather to its relationship to the tuba family or its descendants (i.e., the serpent or ophicleide). This conscious decision was made to provide the reader with the most exhaustive list of references. This list expands upon the information contained in the first *Tuba Source Book*. The author is grateful to Michael Fischer for his contributions to that publication.

References

Acoustics

Anfilov, Gleb. *Physics and Music*. Translated by Boris Kuznetsov. Moscow, USSR: Mir Publishers, 1966.

Askill, John. *Physics of Musical Sounds*. New York: D. Van Nostrand Company, n.d.

Backus, John. *The Acoustical Foundations of Music*. New York: W. W. Norton & Company, Inc., 1969.

Bahnert, Heinz, Theodore Herzberg and Herbert Schramm. *Metallblasinstrumente*. Wilhelmshaven, Germany: Heinrichshofen, 1986.

Bartholomew, Wilmer T. *Acoustics of Music*. Englewood Cliffs, N.J.: Prentice Hall, Inc., 1942.

Benade, Arthur H. *Acoustics of Musical Wind Instruments*. Abstract in Research at Case. Cleveland, Ohio: Case Institute of Technology, 1961.

Benade, Arthur H. *Horns, Strings, and Harmony*. Westport, Connecticut: Greenwood Press, 1960.

Briggs, Gilbert Arthur. *Musical Instruments and Audio*. Yorkshire, England: Wharfedale Wireless Works Limited, 1965.

Campbell, Murray, and Clive A. Greated. *The Musician's Guide to Acoustics*. Oxford, England: Oxford University Press, 1998.

Clappé, Arthur A. *The Wind-Band and Its Instruments: Their History, Construction, Acoustics, Technique, and Combination*. 1911. Portland, Maine: Longwood, 1976.

Culver, Charles A. *Musical Acoustics*. 3rd ed. New York: Blakiston Company, 1951.

Eickmann, Paul E., and Nancy L. Hamilton. *Basic Acoustics for Beginning Brass*. Syracuse, New York: Center for Instructional Development, Syracuse University, 1976.

Fletcher, Neville H. and Thomas D. Rossing. *The Physics of Musical Instruments*. 2nd ed. New York: Springer, 1998.

Hamilton, Clarence G. *Sound and Its Relation to Music*. Philadelphia, Pennsylvania: Oliver Ditson Company, 1912.

Holcomb, Bruce. *Die Verbesserung der Stimmung an Ventilblasinstrumenten*. N.p.: Musikverlag Emil Katzbichler, 1981.

Kent, Earle L., ed. *Musical Acoustics*. Vol. 9. Benchmark Papers in Acoustics. Stroudsburg, Pennsylvania: Dowden, Hutchinson & Ross, Inc., 1977.

Levarie, Siegmund and Ernst Levy. *Tone: A Study in Musical Acoustics*. The Kent State University Press, 1968.

Lowery, Harry. *A Guide to Musical Acoustics*. New York: Dover Publications, Inc., 1966.

Mahillon, Victor Charles. *Elements D' accoustique*. Bruxelles, Belgian: Les Amies de la Musique, 1984.

Matzke, Hermann. *Unser Technisches Wissen von der Musik*. Lindau am Bodensee, Germany: Frisch und Preneder, 1949.

Meyer, Jürgen. *Akustik und Musikalische Aufführungspraxis*. Frankfurt am Main, Germany: Verlag Das Musikinstrument, 1980.

Meyer, Jürgen. *Acoustics and the Performance of Music*. Translated by John Bowsher and Sibylle Westphal. Frankfurt am Main, Germany: Verlag Das Musikinstrument, 1978.

Olson, Harry F. *Music, Physics and Engineering*. 2nd ed. New York: Dover Publications, Inc., 1967.

Pierce, John R. *The Science of Musical Sound*. New York: Scientific American Library, 1983.

Rigden, John S. *Physics and the Sound of Music*. 2nd ed. New York: John Wiley & Sons, Inc., 1985.

Roederer, Juan G. *Introduction to the Physics and Psychophysics of Music*. Vol. 16. Heidelberg Science Library. New York: Springer-Verlag, 1973.

Schramm, Herbert. *Mein Metallblasinstrument*. Frankfurt am Main, Germany: Verlag Das Musikinstrument, 1981.

Scientific American. *The Physics of Music*. San Francisco, California: W. H. Freeman and Company, 1978.

Vogel, Martin. *Die Intonation der Blechbläscher*. N.p.: Gesellschaft zur Förderung der Systematischen Musikwissenschaft, 1961.

Zahm, John Augustine. *Sound and Music*. 2nd ed. Chicago, Illinois: A. C. McClurg & Co., 1900.

Bibliography

Anderson, Paul G. and Larry Bruce Campbell. *Brass Music Guide: Solo and Study Material in Print*. 1985 ed. Vol. 4. Music Guide Series. Northfield, Illinois: Instrumentalist Co., 1984.

Anderson, Paul G. and Lisa Ormston Bontrager. *Brass Music Guide: Ensemble Music in Print*. Vol. 5. Music Guide Series. Northfield, Illinois: Instrumentalist Company, 1987.

Bollinger, Donald E. *Band Director's Complete Handbook*. West Nyack, New York: Parker Publishing Company, Inc., 1979.

Brüchle, Bernhard. *Music Bibliographies for all Instruments (Musik-Bibliographien für alle Instrumente)*. Munich 70 Germany, Box 700 308, D 8000: Author, 1976.

Decker, Richard G. *Music for Three Brasses; a Bibliography of Music for Three Heterogeneous Brass Instruments Alone and in Chamber Ensembles*. Oneonta, New York: Swift-Dorr Publications, 1976.

Duckles, Vincent H. and Michael A. Keller. *Music Reference and Research Materials*. 4th ed. New York: Schirmer Books, 1988.

Fasman, Mark J. *Brass Bibliography: Sources on the History, Literature, Pedagogy, Performance, and Acoustics of Brass Instruments*. Bloomington, Indiana: Indiana University Press, 1990.

Helm, Sanford M. *Catalog of Chamber Music for Wind Instruments*. Ann Arbor, Michigan: Lithoprinted by Braun-Brumfield, 1952.

Brass Anthology—A Collection of Brass Articles from "The Instrumentalist" Magazine from 1946 to 1990. 9th ed. Northfield, Illinois: Instrumentalist Publishing Company, 1991.

Morris, R. Winston. *Tuba Music Guide*. Evanston, Illinois: Instrumentalist Co., 1973.

Morris, R. Winston, and Goldstein, Edward R. *The Tuba Source Book*. Bloomington: Indiana University Press, 1996.

Thompson, J. Mark and Jeffrey J. Lemke. *French Music for Low Brass Instruments: An Annotated Bibliography*. Bloomington, Indiana: Indiana University Press, 1994.

Yeats, Robert, ed. *University of Iowa School of Music Guide to Selected Wind and Percussion Materials*. Version 2.0. Iowa City: University of Iowa and Eble Music, 1992.

Biography

Bridges, Glenn D. *Pioneers in Brass*. Rev. ed. Detroit, Michigan: Glenn D. Bridges, 1968.

Comettant, J. P. O. *Histoire d' un inventeur au XIXe siècle*. Paris, France: Pagnerre, 1860.

Frederiksen, Brian. John Taylor, ed. *Arnold Jacobs: Song and Wind*. United States: Wind Song Press, 1996.

Gilson, P. and A. Remy. *Adolphe Sax.* Brussels, Belgian: Institut National Belge de Radiodiffusion, 1938–39.

Horwood, Wally. *Adolphe Sax—His Life and Legacy.* Baldock, Herts: Egon Publishers, 1992.

Kalkbrenner, A. *Wilhelm Wieprecht, sein Leben und Wirken.* Berlin, Germany: n.p., 1882.

Meckna, Michael. *Twentieth-Century Brass Soloists.* Westport, Connecticut: Greenwood Press, 1994.

Musical Instruments and the Masters. Elkhart, Indiana: Conn Corporation, 1955.

Sousa, John Philip. *Marching Along.* Boston, Massachusetts: Hale, Cushman & Flint, 1928.

Weston, Stephen J. *Samuel Hughes, Ophicleidist.* Edinburgh: University of Edinburgh Collection of Historical Musical Instruments, 1986.

Discography

Bollinger, Donald E. *Band Director's Complete Handbook.* West Nyack, New York: Parker Publishing Company, Inc., 1979.

Brass Anthology—A Collection of Brass Articles from "The Instrumentalist" Magazine from 1946 to 1990. 9th ed. Northfield, Illinois: Instrumentalist Publishing Company, 1991.

Frederiksen, Brian. John Taylor, ed. *Arnold Jacobs: Song and Wind.* United States: Wind Song Press, 1996.

Morris, R. Winston and Goldstein, Edward R. *The Tuba Source Book.* Bloomington: Indiana University Press, 1996.

Poulton, Alan J., comp. *A Label Discography of Long-Playing Records.* Series 2—H. M. V. (Red Label) October 1952–December 1962. N.p.: Oakwood Press, n.d.

Sloan, Gerald. *Orchestral Recordings for Low Brass Players.* Troy, Michigan: Encore Music, 1997.

Equipment

Ahrens, Christian. *Eine Erfindung und ihre Folgen: Blechblasinstrumente mit Ventilen.* Kassel, Germany: Bärenreiter, 1986.

Bach, Vincent. *Embouchure and Mouthpiece Manual.* Rev. ed. Elkhart, Indiana: Selmer Company, 1979.

Bahnert, Heinz, Theodore Herzberg and Herbert Schramm. *Metallblasinstrumente.* Wilhelmshaven, Germany: Heinrichshofen, 1986.

Bollinger, Donald E. *Band Director's Complete Handbook.* West Nyack, NY: Parker Publishing Company, Inc., 1979.

Bowles, Benjamin Franklin. *Technics of the Brass Musical Instrument: A Condensed Instructive Treatise on the General Construction of Brass Musical Instruments and How to Choose Them; Care of the Instruments; and General Suggestions on Playing, Phrasing and Practicing.* New York: Carl Fischer, 1915.

Brand, Erick D. *Selmer Band Instrument Repairing Manual.* Elkhart, Indiana: H. & A. Selmer, 1959.

Brand, Erick D. *Musical Instrument Repair Tools and Supplies.* Elkhart, Indiana: Erick D. Brand, n.d.

C. G. Conn Ltd. *How to Care for Your Instrument.* Elkhart, Indiana: C. G. Conn Ltd., 1942.

Clappé, Arthur A. *The Wind-Band and Its Instruments: Their History, Construction, Acoustics, Technique, and Combination.* 1911. Portland, Maine: Longwood, 1976.

Colwell, Richard J. and Thomas Goolsby. *The Teaching of Instrumental Music.* 2nd ed. Englewood Cliffs, New Jersey: Prentice Hall, 1992.

Draper, F.C. *Notes on the Boosey & Hawkes System of Automatic Compensation of Valved Brass Wind Instruments.* Rev. ed. London: Boosey & Hawkes, 1954.

Dullat, Günter. *Blasinstrumente und Deutsche Patentschriften.* Band 1 & 2. Nanheun, Germany: 1985 (Band 1), 1986 (Band 2).

Dullat, Günter. *Metallblasinstrumentenbau.* Frankfurt am Main, Germany: Bochinsky, 1989.

Dullat, Günter. *Holz und Metallblasinstrumente.* Siegburg, Germany: Schmitt, 1986.

Duttenhöfer, Eva-Maria. *Gebrüder Alexander. 200 Jahre Musikinstrumentenbau.* Mainz, Germany: Schott, 1982.

Ferree, Cliff. *Ferree's Band Instrument Tools and Supplies.* Battle Creek, Michigan: Ferree's, P.O. Box 259, Battle Creek, MI 49016, n.d.

Franz, Oscar. *Die Musik-Instrumente der Gegenwart.* Dresdin, Germany: J. G. Seeling, 1884.

Gregory, Robin. *The Horn: A Comprehensive Guide to the Modern Instrument and Its Music.* 2nd ed. New York: Frederick A. Praeger, 1969.

Hall, Jody C. *The Proper Selection of Cup Mouthpieces.* Elkhart, Indiana: Conn Corporation, 1963.

Heyde, Herbert, Dr. *Das Ventilblasinstrument.* Leipzig, Germany: VEB Verlag deutscher Musik, 1987.

Holcomb, Bruce. *Die Verbesserung der Stimmung an Ventilblasinstrumenten.* N.p.: Musikverlag Emil Katzbichler, 1981.

Brass Anthology—A Collection of Brass Articles from "The Instrumentalist" Magazine from 1946 to 1990. 9th ed. Northfield, Illinois: Instrumentalist Publishing Company, 1991.

Kent, Earle L. *The Inside Story of Brass Instruments.* Elkhart, Indiana: C. G. Conn, 1956.

Kirachner, Frederick. *Encyclopedia of Band Instrument Repair.* New York: Music Trade Review, 1962.

Krickeberg, Dieter and Wolfgang Rauch. *Katalog der Blechblasinstrumente.* Berlin, Germany: Musikinstrumenten-Museum, 1976.

McGavin, E. comp. *A Guide to the Purchase and Care of Woodwind and Brass Instruments.* Bromley, England: Schools Music Association, 1966.

Meyer, R. F. "Peg." *The Band Director's Guide to Instrument Repair.* Edited by Willard I. Musser. Port Washington, New York: Alfred Publishing Co., Inc., 1973.

Møller, Dorthe Falcon. *Danske Instrumentbyggere 1770–1850 (Danish Instrument Factories and Builders 1770–1850).* Copenhagen, Denmark: G. E. C. Gad., 1982.

Naur, Robert. *185 är blandt blæseinstrumenter. Skitser af et dansk instrumentmagerværksted gennem 7 slægtled* (185 years between wind instruments. Telling about a Danish music instrument factory in seven generations). Copenhagen, Denmark: J. K. Gottfried, n.d.

Nödl, Karl. *Metallblasinstrumentenbau; ein Fach- und Lehrbuch über die handwerkliche Herstellung von Metallblasinstrumenten.* Frankfurt am Main, Germany: Das Musikinstrument, 1970.

Olson, R. Dale. *Sensory Evaluation of Brass Instruments.* (available from author) R. Dale Olson, 1500 Sunny Crest Drive, Fullerton, California 92635, n.d.

Pontécoulant, Adolphe Le Doulcet. *Organographie.* Vol. 1. The Netherlands: Frits Knuf, 1971.

Ridley, Edwin Alexander Keane. *European Wind Instruments.* Forward by David M. Boston. London, England: Royal College of Music, 1982.

Schlesinger, Kathleen. *The Instruments of the Modern Orchestra.* 2 vols. London, England: William Reeves, 1969.

Schramm, Herbert. *Mein Metallblasinstrument.* Frankfurt am Main, Germany: Verlag Das Musikinstrument, 1981.

Seifers, Heinrich. *Katalog der Blasinstrumente.* N.p.: Deutsches Museum, 1980.

Springer, George H. *Maintenance and Repair of Band Instruments.* Boston, Massachusetts: Allyn and Bacon, Inc., 1970.

Tiede, Clayton H. *The Practical Band Instrument Repair Manual.* Dubuque, Iowa: Wm. C. Brown Company Publishers, 1962.

Weisshaar, Otto H. *Preventive Maintenance of Musical Instruments.* Rockville Centre, New York: Belwin, 1966.

Weltausstellung 1873. *Mathematische und Physikalische Instrumente.* Gruppe XIV, Section 1 und 2. Wien, Austria: K. K. Hof- und Staatsdruckerei, 1874.

Young, T. Campbell. *The Making of Musical Instruments.* London, England: Oxford University Press, 1939.

General Reference

Ammer, Christine. *The Harper Dictionary of Music.* 2nd ed. New York: Harper & Row Publishers, 1987.

Apel, Willi, and Ralph T. Daniel. *The Harvard Brief Dictionary of Music.* Cambridge, Massachusetts: Harvard University Press, 1960.

Arnold, Denis, ed. *The New Oxford Companion to Music.* New York: Oxford University Press, 1983.

Bakaleinikoff, Vladimir and Milton Rosen. *The Instruments of the Band and Orchestra, An Encyclopedia.* New York: Boosey & Hawkes, 1940.

Basso, Alberto, ed. *Dizionario Enciclopedico Universale Della Musica E Dei Musicisti.* Vol. 2. Torino, Italy: Unione Tipografico-Editrice Torinese, 1984.

Bennwitz, Hanspeter. *Kleines Musiklexikon.* A. Francke AG Verlag Bern, 1963.

Blom, Eric. *The New Everyman Dictionary of Music.* Edited by David Cummings. 6th ed. London, England: J. M. Dent & Sons LTD, 1988.

Brousse, Joseph. *Encyclopédie de la Musique et dicationnaire du Conservatoire.* Vol. 3. Paris, France: Belgrave, 1927.

Carlton, Joseph R. *Carlton's Complete Reference Book of Music.* Studio City, California: Carlton Publications, 1980.

Cook, Kenneth, comp. *The Bandsman's Everything Within.* London, England: Hinrichsen Edition Ltd., 1950.

Cooper, Martin, ed. *The Concise Encyclopedia of Music and Musicians.* New York: Hawthorn Books Inc., 1958.

Dufourcq, Norbert. *Larousse De La Musique.* 2 vols. Paris, France: Librarie Larousse, 1957.

Dunstan, Ralph. *A Cyclopaedic Dictionary of Music.* 4th ed. New York: Da Capo Press, 1973.

Encyclopaedia Britanica. 15th ed. Chicago, Illinois: Encyclopaedia Britanica, Inc., 1986.

Herzfeld, Friedrich. *Lexikon Der Musik.* Berlin, Germany: Ullstein A. G., 1957.

Hughes, Rupert, comp. *Music Lovers' Encyclopedia.* Edited by Deems Taylor and Russell Kerr. 2nd ed. Garden City, New York: Garden City Publications Co., Inc., 1939.

Ingles, Elisabeth, ed. *Harrap's Illustrated Dictionary of Music and Musicians.* 2nd ed. Great Britain: Harrap Books Limited, 1990.

Isaacs, Alan and Elizabeth Martin, eds. *Dictionary of Music.* New York: Facts on File, Inc., 1983.

Jacquot, A., ed. *Dictionnaire des instruments de musique.* Paris, France: n.p., 1886.

Kallmann, Helmut, Gilles Potvin and Kenneth Winters, eds. *Encyclopedia of Music in Canada.* Toronto, Ontario: University of Toronto Press, 1981.

Kennedy, Michael., ed. *The Oxford Dictionary of Music.* 3rd ed. New York: Oxford University Press, 1985.

Langwill, Lyndesay Graham. *An Index of Musical Wind-Instrument Makers.* 6th ed. rev. and enl. Edinburgh, Scotland: L. G. Langwill, 1980.

Lavignac, Albert, ed. *Encyclopédie de la musique.* Vol. 3. Paris, France: Librairie Delagrave, 1927.

Lexicon der Musik. N.p.: Druck und Buchbinderei-Werkstätten May & Co Nachf., 1976.

Macmillan Encyclopedia of Music and Musicians. New York: Macmillan Company, 1938.

Marcuse, Sibyl. *Musical Instruments.* 2nd ed. New York: W. W. Norton & Company, Inc., 1975.

Marcuse, Sibyl. *A Survey of Musical Instruments.* 2nd ed. New York: Harper & Row, 1979.

Matzke, Hermann. *Unser Technisches Wissen von der Musik.* Lindau am Bodensee, Germany: Frisch und Preneder, 1949.

Mendel, Hermann. *Musikalisches Conversations-Lexikon.* Berlin, Germany: Verlag von Robert Oppenheim, 1878.

Michel, Francois. *Encyclopédie De La Musique.* Paris, France: Fasquelle, 1961.

Moore, John W. *Complete Encyclopædia of Music.* 1880. New York: AMS Press, Inc., 1973.

Moore, John W. *A Dictionary of Musical Information.* 1876. New York: Lenox Hill Pub. & Dist. Co., 1971.

Morehead, Philip D. and Anne MacNeil. *The New American Dictionary of Music.* New York: Penguin Books USA Inc., 1991.

Morin, Gösta, redaktion. *Sohlmans Musik Lexikon.* Stockholm, Sweden: Sohlmans Förlag, 1952.

Moser, Hans Joachim. *Musik Lexikon.* Hamburg, Germany: Musikverlag Hans Sikorski, 1951.

Müller-Blattau, Joseph, ed. *Höhe Schule der Musik; Handbuch der gesamten Musikpraxis.* 4 vols. Potsdam, Germany: Athenaion, 1938.

New Lexicon Webster's Dictionary of the English Language. New York: Lexicon Publications, Inc., 1991.

Parkhurst, Winthrop and L. J. de Bekker. *The Encyclopedia of Music and Musicians.* New York: Crown Publishers, 1937.

Pena, Joaquín. *Diccionario De La Música Labor.* Barcelona, Spain: Editorial Labor, S. A., 1954.

Plenckers, L. J. *Brass Instruments.* New York: Da Capo, 1970.

Posell, Elsa Z. *This Is An Orchestra.* Boston, Massachusetts: Houghton Mifflin Company, 1950.

Pratt, Waldo Selden, ed. *The New Encyclopedia of Music and Musicians.* 2nd ed. New York: MacMillan Company, 1948.

Randel, Don Michael, ed. *The New Harvard Dictionary of Music.* 3rd ed. Cambridge, Massachusetts: Belknap Press of Harvard University Press, 1986.

Riemann, Hugo. *Riemann Musik Lexikon.* Edited by Earl Dahlhaus. Mainz, Germany: B. Schott's Söhne, 1975.

Sachs, Curt. *Real-Lexicon der Musikinstrumente.* New York: Dover Publications, Inc., 1964.

Sachs, Curt. *Handbuch der Musikinstrumente.* Wiesbaden, Germany: Breitkopf & Härtel, 1979.

Sadie, Stanley, ed. *The Grove Concise Dictionary of Music.* London, England: Macmillan Press Ltd, 1988.

Sadie, Stanley, ed. *The New Grove Dictionary of Music and Musicians.* London, England: MacMillan Publishers Limited, 1980.

Sadie, Stanley, ed. *The New Grove Dictionary of Musical Instruments.* Vol. 3. London, England: Macmillan Press Limited, 1984.

Sartori, Claudio, ed. *Dizionario Ricordi.* Milano, Italy: G. Ricordi & C., 1959.

Scholes, Percy. *Oxford Companion to Music.* Edited by John Owen Ward. 10th ed. London, England: Oxford University Press, 1977.

Scholes, Percy. *The Oxford Junior Companion to Music.* London, England: Oxford University Press, 1963.

Schwartz, Harry Wayne. *Bands of America.* New York: Doubleday and Co. Inc., 1957.

Slonimsky, Nicolas. *Lectionary of Music.* New York: McGraw-Hill Publishing Company, 1989.

Stauffer, Donald W. *A Treatise on the Tuba.* Birmingham, Alabama: Stauffer Press, 1989.

Thompson, Oscar and Bruce Bohle, eds. *The International Cyclopedia of Music and Musicians.* 11th ed. New York: Dodd, Mead & Company, 1985.

Tonkunst. *Universal-Lexikon.* Edited by Eduard Bernsdorf. Offenbach, Germany: Berlag von Johann André, 1861.

University Musical Encyclopedia. New York: University Society, 1912.

Webster's Third New International Dictionary of the English Language. Springfield, Massachusetts: G. & C. Merriam Co., 1971.

Waterhouse, William. *The New Langwill Index: A Dictionary of Musical Wind-Instrument Makers and Inventors.* London: Tony Bingham, 1993.

Westrup, J. A., and F. L. Harrison. *The New College Encyclopedia of Music.* Edited by Conrad Wilson. 2nd ed. New York: W. W. Norton & Company, Inc., 1976.

Westrup, J. A., and F. L. Harrison. *Collins Music Encyclopedia.* London: William Collins Sons & Co. Ltd., 1959.

Wier, Albert E., ed. *The MacMillan Encyclopedia of Music and Musicians.* New York: Macmillan Company, 1938.

History

Abraham, Gerald. *The Concise Oxford History of Music.* London, England: Oxford University Press, 1979.

Adams, Peter H. *Antique Brass Wind Instruments.* Atglen, PA: Schiffer, 1998.

Adler, Guido. *Handbuch der Musikgeschichte.* Frankfurt am Main, Germany: Frankfurter Verlags-Anstalt A.-G., 1924.

Andresen, Mogens. *Historiske Messingblæsinstrumenter* (Historic Brass Instruments). København, Denmark: Engstrøm & Sødring Musikforlag A/S, 1988.

Andrews, George W., ed. *Musical Instruments. The American History and Encyclopedia of Music.* Toledo, Ohio: Squire Cooley Co., 1910.

Bacharach, A. L. and J. R. Pearce, eds. *A Musical Companion.* Rev. ed. London, England: Victor Gollancz Ltd., 1977.

Baines, Anthony. *Brass Instruments: Their History and Development.* New York: Charles Scribner's Sons, 1981. Reprint ed. Mineola, New York: Dover Publications, Inc., 1993.

Baines, Anthony, ed. *Musical Instruments through the Ages.* Rev. ed. London, England: Faber and Faber Limited, 1966.

Bate, Philip. *The Trumpet and Trombone.* 2nd ed. New York: W. W. Norton and Company, Inc., 1978.

Borders, James M. *European and American Wind and Percussion Instruments: Catalogue of the Stearns Collection of Musical Instruments at the University of Michigan.* Ann Arbor, Michigan: University of Michigan Press, 1988.

Boyden, David D. *An Introduction to Music.* 2nd ed. New York: Alfred A. Knopf, 1970.

Brand, Violet and Geoffrey, eds. *Brass Bands in the 20th Century.* Letchworth, Herts: Egon Publishers Ltd., 1979.

Brass Anthology—A Collection of Brass Articles from "The Instrumentalist" Magazine from 1946 to 1990. 9th ed. Northfield, Illinois: Instrumentalist Publishing Company, 1991.

Britten, Benjamin and Imogen Holst. *The Wonderful World of Music.* New York: Garden City Books, 1958.

Brown, Howard Mayer and Stanley Sadie, eds. *Performance Practice: Music After 1600.* Vol. 2. New York: W. W. Norton & Company, 1990.

Buchner, Alexander. *Musical Instruments: An Illustrated History.* New York: Crown Publishers, Inc., 1973.

Burney, Charles. *The Present State of Music in France and Italy.* 2nd ed. Vol. 1. London, England: T. Becket and Co., 1773.

Burney, Charles. *The Present State of Music in Germany, the Netherlands, and United Provinces.* London, England: T. Becket and Co., 1773.

Carse, Adam. *Musical Wind Instruments. A History of the Wind Instruments used in European Orchestras and Wind-Bands from the Middle Ages up to the Present Time.* 1939. New York: Da Capo, 1973.

Clappé, Arthur A. *The Wind-Band and Its Instruments: Their History, Construction, Acoustics, Technique, and Combination.* 1911. Portland, Maine: Longwood, 1976.

Clendenin, William R. *History of Music.* Rev. ed. Totowa, New Jersey: Littlefield, Adams & Co., 1974.

Colwell, Richard J. and Thomas Goolsby. *The Teaching of Instrumental Music.* 2nd ed. Englewood Cliffs, New Jersey: Prentice Hall, 1992.

Cselenyi, Ladislav. *Musical Instruments in the Royal Ontario Museum.* N.p.: Royal Ontario Museum, 1971.

Daubeny, Ulric. *Orchestral Wind Instruments.* Freeport, NY: Books for Libraries Press, 1970.

Diagram Group. *The Scribner Guide to Orchestral Instruments.* New York: Charles Scribner's Sons, 1983.

Dudgeon, Ralph T. *The Keyed Bugle.* Metuchen, N.J., & London: Scarecrow Press, Inc., 1993.

Dullat, Günter. *Holz und Metallblasinstrumente.* Siegburg, Germany: Schmitt, 1986.

Dundas, R. J. *Twentieth Century Brass Musical Instruments in the United States.* Cincinnati, Ohio: Queen City Brass Publications, 1986.

Duttenhöfer, Eva-Maria. *Gebrüder Alexander. 200 Jahre Musikinstrumentenbau.* Mainz, Germany: Schott, 1982.

Eliason, Robert E. *Early American Brass Makers.* Brass Research Series: No. 10. Nashville, Tennessee: Brass Press, 1979.

Engel, Carl. *Musical Instruments in the South Kensington Museum.* 2nd ed. London, England: George E. Eyre and William Spottiswoode, 1874.

Farmer, Henry George. *A History of Music in Scotland.* London, England: Hinrichsen Edition Limited, 1947.

Farmer, Henry George. *Military Music.* New York: Chanticleer Press, 1950.

Fennell, Frederick. *Time and the Winds.* Kenosha, Wisconsin: G. Leblanc Corp., 1954.

Ferguson, Donald N. *A History of Musical Thought.* 3rd ed. Westport, Connecticut: Greenwood Press Publishers, 1959.

Franz, Oscar. *Die Musik-Instrumente der Gegenwart.* Dresdin, Germany: J. G. Seeling, 1884.

Gammond, Peter. *Musical Instruments in Color.* New York: Macmillan Publishing Co., Inc., 1975.

Galpin, Francis William. *A Textbook of European Musical Instruments, Their Origin, History, and Character.* London: Williams and Norgate, 1937.

Garofalo, Robert and Mark Elrod. *A Pictorial History of Civil War Era Musical Instruments & Military Bands.* Missoula, MT: Pictorial Histories Publishing, 1985.

Geiringer, Karl. *Musical Instruments: Their History in Western Culture from the Stone Age to the Present Day.* 2nd ed. London: George Allen & Unwin, 1945.

Gregory, Robin. *The Horn: A Comprehensive Guide to the Modern Instrument and Its Music.* 2nd ed. New York: Frederick A. Praeger, 1969.

Haas, Robert. *Aufführungspraxis der Musik.* Potsdam, Germany: Akademische Verlagsgesellschaft Athenaion, 1931.

Hadow, W. H., Sir, ed. *The Oxford History of Music.* 2nd ed. New York: Cooper Square Publishers, Inc., 1973.

Haskell, Harry. *The Early Music Revival: A History*. London, England: Thames and Hudson, 1988.

Hawkins, John, Sir. *A General History of the Science and Practice of Music*. 2nd ed. London, England: Novello, Ewer & Company, 1875.

Hazen, Margaret H. and Robert M. Hazen. *The Music Men: An Illustrated History of Brass Bands in America, 1800–1920*. Washington, D.C.: Smithsonian Press, 1987.

Heinitz, Wilhelm. *Instrumentenkunde*. Wild Park-Potsdam, Germany: Akademische Verlagsgesell-schaft Athenaion, 1929.

Henderson, William James. *The Story of Music*. New York: Longmans, Green and Co., 1889.

Herbert, Trevor and John Wallace. eds. *The Cambridge Companion to Brass Instruments*. Cambridge, United Kingdom: Cambridge University Press, 1997.

Heyde, Herbert, Dr. *Das Ventilblasinstrument*. Leipzig, Germany: VEB Verlag deutscher Musik, 1987.

Hindley, Geoffrey, ed. *The Larousse Encyclopedia of Music*. New York: Crescent Books, 1989.

Hofer, Achim. *Blasmusikforschung, Eine kritische Einführung*. Darmstadt, Germany: Wissen-schaftliche Burchgesellschaft, 1992.

Kastner, Georges. *Manuel général de musique militaire à l'usage des armées françaises*. Paris, F. Didot Frères, 1848.

Kinscella, Hazel Gertrude. *Music on the Air*. New York: Viking Press, 1934.

Kirby, F. E. *An Introduction to Western Music*. New York: Free Press, 1970.

Krickeberg, Dieter and Wolfgang Rauch. *Katalog der Blechblasinstrumente*. Berlin, Germany: Musikinstrumenten-Museum, 1976.

Kunitz, Hans. *Instrumenten-Brevier*. Leipzig, Germany: n.p., 1961.

Lavoix, H. *Histoire de l'instrumentation*. Paris, France: n.p., 1878.

Lawrence, Ian. *Brass in Your School*. London, England: Oxford University Press, 1975.

Mahillon, V. C. *Catalogue descriptif et analytique du Musée instrumental du Conservatoire Royal de Musique de Bruxelles*. Vol. 2. Brussels, Belgian: n.p., 1893.

Mandel, C. *A Treatise on the Instrumentation of the Military Band*. London, England: n.p., 1859.

Mason, Daniel Gregory. *The Art of Music*. New York: National Society of Music, 1915–1917.

Mende, Emily, and Jean-Pierre Mathez. *Pictorial Family Tree of Brass Instruments in Europe Since the Early Middle Ages*. Moudon, Switzerland: Editions BIM, 1978.

Méndez, Rafael. *Prelude to Brass Playing*. New York: Carl Fischer, 1961.

Mersenne, Marin. *Harmonie universelle*. Translated by Roger E. Chapman. 2 pts. The Hague, Netherlands: Martinus Nijhoff, 1957.

Midgley, Ruth, ed. *Musical Instruments of the World*. N.p.: Paddington Press Ltd., 1976.

Moeck, Hermann, ed. *Fünf Jahrhunderte deutscher Musikinstrumenten*. Celle, Germany: Moeck, 1987.

Møller, Dorthe Falcon. *Danske Instrumentbyggere 1770–1850* (Danish Instrument Factories and Builders 1770–1850). Copenhagen, Denmark: G. E. C. Gad., 1982.

Morse, Constance. *Music and Music-Makers*. London, England: George Allen & Unwin Ltd., 1926.

Müller-Blattau, Joseph, ed. *Höhe Schule der Musik; Handbuch der gesamten Musikpraxis*. 4 vols. Potsdam, Germany: Athenaion, 1938.

Musical Instruments and the Masters. Elkhart, Indiana: Conn Corporation, 1955.

Naur, Robert. *185 år blandt blæseinstrumenter. Skitser af et dansk instrumentmagerværksted gennem 7 slægtled* (185 years between wind instruments. Telling about a Danish music instrument factory in 7 generations). Copenhagen, Denmark: J. K. Gottfried, n.d.

Paine, John Knowles. *The History of Music to the Death of Schubert*. New York: Da Capo Press, 1971.

Patton, George F. *A Practical Guide to the Arrangement of Band Music*. New York: J. F. Stratton, New York, 1875.

Pierre, Constant. *Les Facteurs D'Instruments de Musique*. Genève, Switzerland: Minkoff Reprints, 1893.

Pratt, Waldo Selden. *The History of Music*. New York: G. Schirmer, 1907.

Remnant, Mary. *Musical Instruments of the West*. New York: St. Martin's Press, 1978.

Rutz, Roland Robert. *A Brief History and Curriculum for Tuba*. N.p.: n.p., 1975.

Sachs, Curt. *Handbuch der Musikinstrumente*. Wiesbaden, Germany: Breitkopf & Härtel, 1979.

Sachs, Curt. *The History of Musical Instruments*. New York: W. W. Norton & Co. Inc., 1968.

Sachs, Curt. *Our Musical Heritage, a Short History of Music*. 2nd ed. Englewood Cliffs, New Jersey: Prentice-Hall, 1955.

Sadie, Stanley, ed. with Alison Latham. *The Cambridge Music Guide*. Cambridge, Ontario: Cambridge University Press, 1985.

Sartori, Claudio, ed. *Enciclopedia Della Musica*. 4 Vols. Milano, Italy: G. Ricordi & C., 1964.

Schlesinger, Kathleen. *The Instruments of the Modern Orchestra*. 2 vols. London, England: William Reeves, 1969.

Schwartz, Harry Wayne. *Bands of America*. New York: Doubleday and Co. Inc., 1957.

Schwartz, Harry Wayne. *The Story of Musical Instruments*. Freeport, New York: Books for Libraries Press, 1970.

Siegmeister, Elie, ed. *The New Music Lover's Handbook*. New York: Harvey House, Inc., 1973.

Sousa, John Philip. *Marching Along*. Boston, Massachusetts: Hale, Cushman & Flint, 1928.

Stoddard, Hope. *From These Comes Music.* New York: Thomas Y. Crowell Company, 1952.

Strachley, Lytton. *Queen Victoria.* New York: Harcourt, Brace and Company, 1921.

Ulrich, Homer. *Music: A Design for Listening.* New York: Harcourt, Brace and World, Inc., 1962.

Valentin, Erich. *Handbuch der Musik Instrumenten Kunde.* 2nd ed. Regensburg, Germany: Gustav Bosse Verlag, 1974.

Weckerlin, J. -B. "Le serpent." *In Dernier musiciana.* Paris, France: Garnier Frères, 1899.

Weltausstellung 1873. *Mathematische und Physihalische Instrumente. Gruppe XIV, Section 1 und 2.* Wien, Austria: K. K. Hof- und Staatsdruckerei, 1874.

Widor, C. M. *Technique de l'orchestra moderne* (sup. to Berlioz 'Traité'). London, England: n.p., 1906.

Winternitz, Emanuel. *Musical Instruments of the Western World.* New York: McGraw-Hill Book Company, n.d.

Literature

Anderson, Paul G. and Larry Bruce Campbell. *Brass Music Guide: Solo and Study Material in Print.* 1985 ed. Vol. 4. Music Guide Series. Northfield, Illinois: Instrumentalist Co., 1984.

Anderson, Paul G. and Lisa Ormston Bontrager. *Brass Music Guide: Ensemble Music in Print.* Vol. 5. Music Guide Series. Northfield, Illinois: Instrumentalist Company, 1987.

Bollinger, Donald E. *Band Director's Complete Handbook.* West Nyack, New York: Parker Publishing Company, Inc., 1979.

Brass Anthology—A Collection of Brass Articles from "The Instrumentalist" Magazine from 1946 to 1990. 9th ed. Northfield, Illinois: Instrumentalist Publishing Company, 1991.

Brüchle, Bernhard. *Music Bibliographies for all Instruments* (Musik-Bibliographien für alle Instrumente). Munich 70 Germany, Box 700 308, D 8000: Author, 1976.

Decker, Richard G. *Music for Three Brasses; a Bibliography of Music for Three Heterogeneous Brass Instruments Alone and in Chamber Ensembles.* Oneonta, New York: Swift-Dorr Publications, 1976.

Del Mar, Norman. *Orchestral Variations.* London, England: Eulenburg Books, 1981.

Dvorak, Raymond Francis. *The Band on Parade.* New York: Carl Fischer, Inc., 1937.

Ensemble Publications Catalog. Ensemble Publications, Box 98, Bidwell Station, Buffalo, New York 14222, n.d.

Famera, K. M. *Chamber Music Catalogue.* New York: Pendragon Press, 1978.

Helm, Sanford M. *Catalog of Chamber Music for Wind Instruments.* Ann Arbor, Michigan: Lithoprinted by Braun-Brumfield, 1952.

Morris, R. Winston. *Tuba Music Guide.* Evanston, Illinois: Instrumentalist Co., 1973.

Ode, James. *Brass Instruments in Church Services.* Minneapolis, Minnesota: Augsburg Pub. House, 1970.

Thompson, J. Mark and Jeffrey J. Lemke. *French Music for Low Brass Instruments: An Annotated Bibliography.* Bloomington, Indiana: Indiana University Press, 1994.

Uber, David. *New Catalogue of Unpublished Music.* Trenton, New Jersey: Dr. David Uber, Department of Music, Trenton State College, n.d.

Uber, David. *New Catalog of Published Music.* Trenton, New Jersey: Dr. David Uber, Department of Music, Trenton State College, n.d.

Weerts, Richard. ed. *Original Manuscript Music for Wind and Percussion Instruments.* Washington: Music Educators National Conference, 1964.

Orchestration

Adkins, Hector Ernest. *Treatise on the Military Band.* 2nd ed. New York: Boosey Hawkes, 1958.

Adler, Samuel. *The Study of Orchestration.* 3rd ed. New York: W. W. Norton & Company, Inc., 2002.

Anderson, A. O. *Practical Orchestration.* Boston, Massachusetts, 1929.

Bartenstein, Hans. *Hector Berlioz' Instrumentationskunst und ihre geschichtlichen Grundlagen.* Leipzig, Germany: Heitz & Co., 1939.

Bennett, Robert Russell. *Instrumentally Speaking.* Melville, New York: Belwin-Mills Publishing Corporation, 1975.

Berlioz, Hector. *Treatise on Instrumentation.* Edited by Richard Strauss. English translation by Theodore Frost. Rev. ed. New York: Edwin F. Kalmus Publishing, 1948.

Blatter, Alfred. *Instrumentation and Orchestration.* 2nd ed. New York: Schirmer Books An Imprint of Simon & Schuster Macmillan, 1997.

Burton, Stephen Douglas. *Orchestration.* Englewood Cliffs, New Jersey: Prentice-Hall, Inc., 1982.

Cacavas, John. *Music Arranging and Orchestration.* Melville, New York: Belwin-Mills Publishing Corporation, 1975.

Carse, Adam. *The History of Orchestration.* New York: E. P. Dutton & Co.,1925.

Clappé, Arthur A. *The Principles of Wind-Band Transcription.* New York: Carl Fischer, 1921.

Czerny, Carl. *School of Practical Composition.* Translated by John Bishop. New York: Da Capo Press, 1979.

Delamont, Gordon. *Modern Arranging Technique.* Delevan, New York: Kendor Music, 1965.

Dondeyne, D. and F. Robert. *Nouveau Traité d' Orchestration à l'usage des Harmonies, Fanfares et Musique Militaires.* Paris, France: H. Lemoine, 1969.

Erickson, Frank. *Arranging for the Concert Band.* Melville, New York: Belwin-Mills Publishing Corporation, 1983.

Evans, Edwin. *Method of Instrumentation.* Vol. 2. London, England: William Reeves Bookseller Limited, n.d.

Forsyth, Cecil. *Orchestration.* 2nd ed. New York: Macmillan and Co., 1946.

Gallo, Stanislao. *The Modern Band; a Treatise on Wind Instruments, Symphony Band and Military Band.* 2 vols. Boston, Massachusetts: C. C. Birchard, 1935.

Gardner, Maurice. *The Orchestrator's Handbook.* Great Neck, New York: Staff Music Publishing Company, 1948.

Hansen, Brad. *The Essentials of Instrumentation.* Mountain View, California: Mayfield Publishing Company, 1991.

Hind, Harold C. *The Brass Band.* London: Boosey & Hawkes, Ltd., 1934.

Hoby, Charles. *Military Band Instrumentation.* London, England: Oxford University Press, 1936.

Hofmann, Richard. *Practical Instrumentation.* Translated by Robin H. Legge. Leipzig, Germany: Doerffling & Franke, 1893.

Humperdinck, Engelbert. *Instrumentationslehre.* Edited by Hans-Josef Irmen. Heft 128. Beiträge zur Rheinischen Musikgeschichte. Köln, Germany: Verlag der Arbeitsgemeinschaft für rheinische Musikgeschichte, 1981.

Jacob, Gordon. *The Elements of Orchestration.* London, England: Herbert Jenkins, 1962.

Jacob, Gordon. *Orchestral Technique, A Manual for Students.* 3rd ed. London, England: Oxford University Press, 1982.

Jadassohn, S. *A Course of Instruction in Instrumentation.* Translated by Harry P. Wilkins. Leipzig, Germany: Breitkopf and Härtel, 1899.

Kennan, Kent W. and Donald Grantham. *The Technique of Orchestration.* 6th ed. Upper Saddle River, New Jersey: Prentice Hall, 2002.

Kling, H. *Modern Orchestration.* Translated by Saenger. New York: n.p., 1902.

Koechlin, Charles, ed. *Traité de l'Orchestration.* 4 vols. Paris, France: Éditions Max Eschig, 1954.

Lang, Philip J. *Scoring for the Band.* New York: Mills, 1950.

Leibowitz, René and Jan Maguire. *Thinking for Orchestra, Practical Exercises in Orchestration.* New York: G. Schirmer, Inc., 1960.

Leidzén, Erik. *An Invitation to Band Arranging.* Bryn Mawr, Pennsylvania: Theodore Presser Co., 1950.

Lockwood, Samuel Pierson. *Elementary Orchestration.* 2nd ed. Ann Arbor, Michigan: George Wahr, 1929.

Mandel, C. *A Treatise on the Instrumentation of the Military Band.* London, England: n.p., 1859.

Mason, Daniel Gregory. *The Orchestral Instruments and What They Do.* New York: H. W. Gray Co., 1937.

McKay, George Frederick. *Creative Orchestration.* Boston, Massachusetts: Allyn and Bacon, 1963.

Morris, R. Winston and Goldstein, Edward R. *The Tuba Source Book.* Bloomington, Indiana: Indiana University Press, 1996.

Müller-Blattau, Joseph, ed. *Höhe Schule der Musik; Handbuch der gesamten Musikpraxis.* 4 vols. Potsdam, Germany: Athenaion, 1938.

Nestico, Sammy. *The Complete Arranger.* Delevan, New York: Kendor Music, Inc., 1993.

Oboussier, Philippe. *Arranging Music for Young Players.* London, England: Oxford University Press, 1977.

Patterson, Frank. *Practical Instrumentation for School, Popular, and Symphony Orchestras.* 2nd ed. New York: G. Schirmer, Inc., 1923.

Piston, Walter. *Orchestration.* New York: W. W. Norton and Company, Inc., 1955.

Polansky, Larry. *New Instrumentation and Orchestration.* Oakland, California: Frog Peak Music, 1986.

Prout, Ebenezer. *The Orchestra.* Vol. 1. London, England: Augener and Co., 1897.

Prout, Ebenezer. *Instrumentation.* Boston, Massachusetts: Oliver Ditson Company, 1900.

Rauscher, Donald J. *Orchestration, Scores and Scoring.* New York: Free Press of Glencoe, 1963.

Read, Gardner. *Thesaurus of Orchestral Devices.* New York: Pitman Publishing Corporation, 1953.

Read, Gardner. *Style and Orchestration.* New York: Schirmer Books, 1979.

Rimsky-Korsakov, Nikolas. *Principles of Orchestration.* Rev. ed. Newbury Park, California: P. L. Alexander, 1989.

Rogers, Bernard. *The Art of Orchestration.* New York: Appleton-Century-Crofts, Inc., 1951.

Shatzkin, Merton. *Writing for the Orchestra: An Introduction to Orchestration.* Englewood Cliffs, New Jersey: Prentice Hall, Inc., 1993.

Skeat, William James and Harry F. Clarke. *The Fundamentals of Band Arranging.* Cleveland, Ohio: Sam Fox Publishing Co., 1938.

Skiles, Marlin. *Music Scoring for TV & Motion Pictures.* Blue Ridge Summit, Pennsylvania: Tab Books, 1976.

Stiller, Andrew. *Handbook of Instrumentation.* Berkeley, California: University of California Press, 1985.

Thomas, Eugène. *Die Instrumentation der Meistersinger von Nürnberg von Richard Wagner.* Mannheim, Germany: K. Ferd. Heckel, 1899.

Travis, F. L. *Verdi's Orchestration.* Zurich, Switzerland: n.p., 1956.

Voss, Egon. *Studien zur Instrumentation Richard Wagners.* Band 24. Studien zur Musikgeschichte des 19. Jahrhunderts. Regensburg, Germany: Gustav Bosse Verlag, 1970.

Wagner, Joseph Frederick. *Orchestration; A Practical Handbook.* New York: McGraw-Hill, 1959.

Wagner, Joseph Frederick. *Band Scoring.* New York: McGraw-Hill, 1960.

Walters, Harold L. *Arranging for the Modern Band.* New York: George F. Briegel, Inc., 1942.

White, Gary. *Instrumental Arranging.* Dubuque, Iowa: Wm. C. Brown Publishers, 1992.

White, William C. *Military Band Arranging.* New York: Carl Fischer, Inc., 1924.

Wright, Denis. *Scoring for Brass Band* 5th ed. London, England: Studio Music Company, 1986.

Yoder, Paul. *Arranging Method for School Bands.* New York: Robbins Music Corporation, 1946.

Pedagogy

Beaugeois. *Nouvelle méthode de plainchant, de musicque et de serpent.* Amiens, France: Caron-Vitet, 1827.

Belfrage, Bengt. *Uebungsmethodik für Blechbläser auf der Basis von physiologischen Faktoren.* Frankfurt am Main, Germany: Hansen, 1984.

Belfrage, Bengt. *Practice Methods for Brass Players.* Stockholm, Sweden: Ab Nordiska Musikförlaget, 1982.

Bell, William J. *A Handbook of Information on Intonation.* Elkhorn, Wisconsin: Getzen Co., 1968.

Bellamah, Joseph L. *A Survey of Modern Brass Teaching Philosophies.* San Antonio, Texas: Southern Music Company, 1976.

Bollinger, Donald E. *Band Director's Complete Handbook.* West Nyack, New York: Parker Publishing Company, Inc., 1979.

Bowles, Benjamin Franklin. *Technics of the Brass Musical Instrument: A Condensed Instructive Treatise on the General Construction of Brass Musical Instruments and How to Choose Them; Care of the Instruments; and General Suggestions on Playing, Phrasing and Practicing.* New York: Carl Fischer, 1915.

Brasch, Harold T. *The Brass Clinic.* New York: C. Bruno & Son, 1958.

Brass Anthology—A Collection of Brass Articles from "The Instrumentalist" Magazine from 1946 to 1990. 9th ed. Northfield, Illinois: Instrumentalist Publishing Company, 1991.

Brown, Merrill E. *Teaching the Successful High School Brass Section.* West Nyack, New York: Parker Publishing Company, 1981.

Clappé, Arthur A. *The Wind-Band and Its Instruments: Their History, Construction, Acoustics, Technique, and Combination.* 1911. Portland, Maine: Longwood, 1976.

Caussinus, V. *Solfège-Méthode pour l' ophicléide-basse.* Paris, France: Meissonnier, (ca. 1840).

Cornette, Victor. *Méthode d' ophicléide alto et basse.* Paris, France: Richault, (ca. 1835).

Colin, Charles. *Vital Brass Notes.* New York: Charles Colin, 1962.

Colin, Charles. *The Brass Player.* New York: Charles Colin, 1972.

Colwell, Richard J. and Thomas Goolsby. *The Teaching of Instrumental Music.* 2nd ed. Englewood Cliffs, New Jersey: Prentice Hall, 1992.

Dodworth, Allen. *Brass Band School.* New York: Harvey B. Dodworth, 1853.

Duvall, W. Clyde. *The High School Band Director's Handbook.* Englewood Cliffs, New Jersey: Prentice-Hall, Inc., 1960.

Farkas, Philip. *The Art of Brass Playing.* Bloomington, Indiana: Author, 1962.

Farkas, Philip. *The Art of Musicianship.* Rochester, New York: Wind Music Inc., 1962.

Farkas, Philip. *L' art de jouer les cuivres. Traité sur la formation et l' utilisation de l' embouchure du musicien jouant un cuivre.* Translated by Alain Maillard. Paris, France: Leduc, 1981.

Fox, Fred. *Essentials of Brass Playing.* Pittsburg, Pennsylvania: Volkwein, 1974.

Frederiksen, Brian. John Taylor, ed. *Arnold Jacobs: Song and Wind.* United States: Wind Song Press, 1996.

Gordon, Claude. *Physical Approach to Elementary Brass Playing in Bass Clef.* New York: Carl Fischer, 1979.

Garnier. *Méthode élémentaire et facile d' ophicléide à pistons ou à cylindres.* Paris, France: Schonenberger (ca. 1845–1850).

Grupp, M. *In the Name of Wind-Instrument Playing.* New York: M. Grupp Studios, 1939.

Hermenge, M. G. *Méthode élémentaire pour le serpent-forveille.* Paris, France: Forveille, (ca. 1833).

Holck, Ingrid and Mogens Andresen. *Breath Building.* Denmark: OH Music, P. O. Box 49, DK 2680 Solrød Strand, n.d.

Johnson, Don E. *A Comprehensive Practice Routine for the Aspiring Brass Player.* Markham, Canada: Mayfair Music Publications Inc., 1998.

Johnson, Keith. *Brass Performance and Pedagogy.* Upper Saddle River, New Jersey: Prentice Hall, 2002.

Kastner, J. -G. *Méthode élémentaire pour l' ophicléide.* Paris, France: Troupenas, (ca. 1845).

Kohut, Daniel L. *Musical Performance.* Englewood Cliffs, New Jersey: Prentice-Hall, Inc., 1985.

Lawrence, Ian. *Brass in Your School.* London, England: Oxford University Press, 1975.

Leidig, Vernon F. *Contemporary Brass Technique: Manual and Study Guide.* Norwalk, California: Highland Music Company, 1960.

Maddy, J. E. and T. P. Giddings. *Instrumental Technique for Orchestra and Band.* Cincinnati, Ohio: Willis Music Company, 1926.

Porter, Maurice M. *The Embouchure.* London, England: Boosey & Hawkes, 1967.

Ridgeon, John. *Brass for Beginners.* London, England: Boosey & Hawkes, 1977.

Robinson, William C. *Tone Production and Use of the Breath for Brass Instrument Playing.* Waco, Texas: Baylor University, 1972.

Stevens, Roy. *Embouchure Self Analysis and The Stevens-Costello Triple C Embouchure Technique (Complete)*. Edited by William Moriarity. New York: Stevens-Costello Embouchure Clinic, 1971.

Stewart, M. Dee. ed. *Arnold Jacobs: The Legacy of a Master.* Northfield, Illinois: Instrumentalist Publishing Company, 1987.

Sweeney, Leslie. *Teaching Techniques for the Brasses.* New York: Belwin Inc., 1953.

Thompson, J. Mark and Jeffrey J. Lemke. *French Music for Low Brass Instruments: An Annotated Bibliography.* Bloomington, Indiana: Indiana University Press, 1994.

Weast, Robert D. *Keys to Natural Performance for Brass Players.* Des Moines, Iowa: Brass World, 1979.

Whitehead, Geoffrey I. *A College Level Tuba Curriculum Developed through the Study of the Teaching Techniques of William Bell, Harvey Phillips, and Daniel Perantoni at Indiana University.* Lewiston, New York: Edwin Mellen Press, 2003.

Winslow, Robert W. and John E. Green. *Playing and Teaching Brass Instruments.* Englewood Cliffs, New Jersey: Prentice-Hall, Inc., 1961.

Winter, James H. *The Brass Instruments.* 2nd ed. Boston, Massachusetts: Allyn and Bacon, Inc., 1969.

Zorn, Jay D. *Brass Ensemble Method for Music Educators.* Belmont, California: Wadsworth Publishing Company, Inc., 1977.

Performance

Brass Anthology—A Collection of Brass Articles from "The Instrumentalist" Magazine from 1946 to 1990. 9th ed. Northfield, Illinois: Instrumentalist Publishing Company, 1991.

Dempster, Stuart. *The Modern Trombone.* Berkeley and Los Angeles, California: University of California Press, 1979.

Farkas, Philip. *The Art of Musicianship.* Rochester, New York: Wind Music Inc., 1962.

King, Robert D. *Proposals for Symphony Orchestra Brass.* N.p.: Robert D. King, 1985.

Kohut, Daniel L. *Musical Performance.* Englewood Cliffs, New Jersey: Prentice-Hall, Inc., 1985.

Olson, R. Dale. *Human Mechanisms of Brass Performance.* (available from author) R. Dale Olson, 1500 Sunny Crest Drive, Fullerton, California 92635, n.d.

Severson, Paul, and Mark McDunn. *Brass Wind Artistry: Master Your Mind, Master Your Instrument.* Athens, Ohio: Accura, 1983.

Miscellaneous

Adkins, Hector Ernest. *Treatise on the Military Band.* 2nd ed. New York: Boosey Hawkes, 1958.

Bahnert, Heinz, Theodore Herzberg and Herbert Schramm. *Metallblasinstrumente.* Wilhelmshaven, Germany: Heinrichshofen: 1986.

Bollinger, Donald E. *Band Director's Complete Handbook.* West Nyack, New York: Parker Publishing Company, Inc., 1979.

Brass Anthology—A Collection of Brass Articles from "The Instrumentalist" Magazine from 1946 to 1990. 9th ed. Northfield, Illinois: Instrumentalist Publishing Company, 1991.

Buchner, Alexander. *Musical Instruments through the Ages.* Translated by Iris Urwin. London, England: Spring Books, n.d.

Buchner, Alexander. *Musical Instruments: An Illustrated History.* New York: Crown Publishers, Inc., 1973.

Densmore, F. *Handbook of the Collection of Musical Instruments in the U. S. National Museum.* 1927. New York: n.p., 1971.

Donington, R. *The Instruments of Music.* 3rd ed. London, England: n.p., 1970.

Dullat, Günter. *Metallblasinstrumentenbau.* Frankfurt am Main, Germany: Bochinsky, 1989.

Dullat, Günter. *Holz und Metallblasinstrumente.* Siegburg, Germany: Schmitt, 1986.

Duttenhöfer, Eva-Maria. *Gebrider Alexander. 200 Jahre Musikinstrumentenbau.* Mainz, Germany: Schott, 1982.

Duvall, W. Clyde. *The High School Band Director's Handbook.* Englewood Cliffs, New Jersey: Prentice-Hall, Inc., 1960.

Dvorak, Raymond Francis. *The Band on Parade.* New York: Carl Fischer, Inc., 1937.

Engel, Carl. *Musical Instruments in the South Kensington Museum.* 2nd ed. London, England: George E. Eyre and William Spottiswoode, 1874.

Francoeur, Louis-Joseph. *Diapason Général de tous les instruments à vent.* Genève, Switzerland: Minkoff, 1971.

Gábry, György. *Old Musical Instruments.* 2nd ed. Budapest, Hungary: Corvina Press, 1969.

Goldman, Edwin Franko. *Band Betterment.* New York: Carl Fischer, 1934.

Goldman, Edwin Franko. *The Amateur Band Guide and Aid to Learners.* New York: Carl Fischer, 1916.

Heritage Music Press. *The Complete Encyclopedia of Fingering Charts.* Dayton, Ohio: HMP, 1992.

Heyde, Herbert, Dr. *Das Ventilblasinstrument.* Leipzig, Germany: VEB Verlag Deutscher Musik, 1987.

Heyde, Herbert. *Trompeten, Posaunen, Tuben.* Wiesbaden, Germany: n.p., 1985.

Hjelmervik, Kenneth and Richard C. Berg. *Marching Bands: How to Organize and Develop Them.* New York: Ronald Press Company, 1953.

King, Robert D. *Proposals for Symphony Orchestra Brass.* N.p.: Robert D. King, 1985.

Koch, Markus. *Abriß der Instrumentenkunde.* Kempten, Germany: Kösel, 1912.

Maddy, J. E. and T. P. Giddings. *Instrumental Technique for Orchestra and Band.* Cincinnati, Ohio: Willis Music Company, 1926.

Mahillon, V. C. *Catalogue descriptif et analytique du Musée instrumental du Conservatoire Royal de Musique de Bruxelles.* Vol. 2. Brussels, Belgian: n.p., 1893.

Naur, Robert. *185 år blandt blæseinstrumenter. Skitser af et dansk instrumentmagerværksted gennem 7 slægtled* (185 years between wind instruments. Telling about a Danish music instrument factory in 7 generations). Copenhagen, Denmark: J. K. Gottfried n.d.

Nickel, Ekkehart. *Der Holzblas-Instrumentenbau in der Freien Reichsstadt Nürnberg.* Munich, Germany: Katzbichler, 1971.

Nödl, Karl. *Metallblasinstrumentenbau; ein Fach- und Lehrbuch über die handwerkliche Herstellung von Metallblasinstrumenten.* Frankfurt am Main, Germany: Das Musikinstrument, 1970.

Plenckers, Leo J. *Catalogue of the Musical Instruments.* Vol. 1. New York: Da Capo Press, 1970.

Porter, Maurice M. *Dental Problems in Wind Instrument Playing.* London, England: British Dental Association, 1968.

Schlenger, Kurt. *Eignung zum Blasinstrumentenspiel. Schriften zur praktischen Psychologie.* Vol. 2. Dresden, Germany: F. Burgartz, 1935.

Schneider, Willy. *Handbuch der Blasmusik.* Mainz, Germany: Schott, 1986.

Schramm, Herbert. *Mein Metallblasinstrument.* Frankfurt am Main, Germany: Verlag Das Musikinstrument, 1981.

Stauffer, Donald W. *Intonation Deficiencies of Wind Instruments in Ensemble.* Washington D.C.: Catholic University of America Press, 1954.

Stewart, Gary M. *Keyed Brass Instruments in the Arne B. Larson Collection.* Edited by André P. Larson. Vol. 1. Shrine to Music Museum, Catalog of the Collections. Vermillion, South Dakota: Shrine to Music Museum, 1980.

Weltausstellung 1873. *Mathematische und Physikalische Instrumente.* Gruppe XIV, Section 1 und 2. Wien, Austria: K. K. Hof- und Staatsdruckerei, 1874.

Wiesner, Glenn R., Daniel R. Balbach, and Merrill A. Wilson. *Orthodontics and Wind Instrument Performance.* Washington, D.C.: Music Educators National Conference, 1973.

Zimmermann, Julius Heinrich. *Musikinstrumente.* Frankfurt am Main, Germany: Zimmermann, 1984.

16. Euphonium Composer Biographies

Mark Walker

I would be remiss if I did not immediately thank R. Winston Morris, not only for asking me to join this project but for all the guidance, musical and otherwise, since I became his student in the fall of 1990. In addition, I would like to thank Lloyd Bone and Eric Paull for their guidance, leadership, and advice in this project. My wife, Jessica, has been very helpful in the preparation and proofing of this chapter, and my friend and colleague at Troy University, Ralph Ford, has graciously encouraged my work on this chapter. In addition, Dr. Charles McAdams was instrumental in assembling the biography of the late, great James Garrett (Dr. Pierre Garbage). Finally, Jukka Myllys was very helpful in pointing me in the direction of Kirmo Lintinen's biography.

I should also mention special thanks to the Finnish Music Information Center and Music Information Center Norway, from which I gleaned material on relevant, significant composers who are not as familiar in the United States as they should be. I hope this work helps to bring their wonderful music to more euphoniumists here and throughout the world.

Much of the material for this chapter was culled from a variety of sources, including direct contact with composers, publishers, family members, and so forth. Of course, the world wide web provided much of the material in the form of biographies culled from various composer sites.

This chapter was conceived to serve primarily as a resource for euphonium students who prepare and present recitals as a part of their university matriculation. The biographies as presented are intended, hopefully, to find their way into the program notes of these recitalists. Therefore, I eschewed a "list" format that would include only the most basic information in favor of actual biographies (when possible) that provide a richer breadth and depth of detail, while maintaining a certain amount of brevity. These biographies have been culled from a variety of sources, from the internet to personal correspondence with the composers themselves. I have made a decision to omit many common biographies of composers (Bach, Handel, Vaughan Williams, etc.) and those

of arrangers for the following reasons: (1) many of these composers are very familiar and their biographies are easily found using other common resources and included in program notes, and (2) concern for the ultimate size of this chapter. Since some of the biographies are lengthier than others, I did not want to extend the chapter with composer (or arranger) biographies that readily appear in other standard reference texts.

As with any work of this kind, it will never be totally complete. As soon as this text is published, new composers will have to be added and new compositions and recordings will establish themselves as central to the euphonium repertoire. I have made every attempt to include accurate and up-to-date information on the most common composers of the standard euphonium repertoire, both established and emerging. It is my sincere hope that this resource proves useful.

Torstein Aagaard-Nilsen (1964–)

Aagaard-Nilsen's production bears witness of an un-dogmatic and playful approach to composition. After having established himself in the Bergen area by the end of the 1980s, he started composing music for brass band, for which he obtained a quick success. Gradually, his contact with the contemporary music scene in Bergen resulted in commissions from the Norwegian section of ISCM, the BIT 20 Ensemble, and festivals Music Factory and Autunnale.

At the same time, his contact with the domestic and international wind-instrument scene resulted in commissions for a large number of wind ensembles. Aagard-Nilsen completed his national service in the armed forces as a composer/arranger for the professional military bands in Norway, and he has continued his cooperation with some of these bands later on.

In the work *The Fourth Angel (for Trumpet and Sinfonietta)*, which he commenced in 1992, a line of development goes through the 1990s, in which the form endeavors to express both a narrative and a visual aspect in an attempt to reach a music with an impulsive and communicative appearance.

Samuel Adler (1928–)

Samuel Adler was born March 4, 1928, in Mannheim, Germany, and came to the United States in 1939. He was inducted into the American Academy of Arts and Letters in May 2001. He is the composer of over 400 published works, including five operas, six symphonies, twelve concerti, eight string quartets, four oratorios, and many other orchestral, band, chamber, and choral works and songs, which have been performed all over the world. He is the author of three books, *Choral Conducting* (Holt, Reinhart and Winston 1971, 2nd ed. Schirmer Books 1985), *Sight Singing* (W. W. Norton 1979, 1997), and *The Study of Orchestration* (W. W. Norton 1982, 1989, 2001). He has also contributed numerous articles to major magazines and books published in the United States and abroad.

Adler was educated at Boston University and Harvard University, and holds honorary doctorates from Southern Methodist University, Wake Forest University, St. Mary's Notre-Dame, and the St. Louis Conservatory. His major teachers were, in composition, Herbert Fromm, Walter Piston, Randall Thompson, Paul Hindemith, and Aaron Copland; and in conducting, Serge Koussevitzky.

He is professor emeritus at the Eastman School of Music, where he taught from 1966 to 1995 and served as chair of the composition department from 1974 until his retirement. Before going to Eastman, Adler served as professor of composition at the University of North Texas (1957–1977), music director at Temple Emanu-El in Dallas, Texas (1953–1966), and instructor of fine arts at the Hockaday School in Dallas, Texas (1955–1966). From 1954 to 1958 he was music director of the Dallas Lyric Theater and the Dallas Chorale. Since 1997 he has been a member of the composition faculty at the Juilliard School of Music in New York City. Adler has given master classes and workshops at over 300 universities worldwide, and in the summers has taught at major music festivals such as Tanglewood, Aspen, Brevard, and Bowdoin, as well as others in France, Germany, Israel, Spain, Austria, Poland, South America, and Korea.

Adler has been awarded many prizes, including a 1990 award from the American Academy of Arts and Letters, the Charles Ives Award, the Lillian Fairchild Award, the Music Teachers National Association (MTNA) Award for Composer of the Year (1988–1989), and a Special Citation by the American Foundation of Music Clubs (2001). In 1983 he won the Deems Taylor Award for his book, *The Study of Orchestration*. In 1988–1989

he was designated "Phi Beta Kappa Scholar." In 1989 he received the Eastman School's Eisenhard Award for Distinguished Teaching. In 1991 he was honored by being named the Composer of the Year by the American Guild of Organists. Adler was awarded a Guggenheim Fellowship (1975–1976); he has been a MacDowell Fellow for five years; and, during his second trip to Chile, he was elected to the Chilean Academy of Fine Arts (1993) "for his outstanding contribution to the world of music as a composer." In 1999, he was elected to the Akademie der Kuenste in Germany for distinguished service to music. While serving in the U.S. Army (1950–1952), Adler founded and conducted the Seventh Army Symphony Orchestra and, because of the orchestra's great psychological and musical impact on European culture, was awarded the Army's Medal of Honor.

Kalevi Aho (1949–)

Kalevi Aho entered the limelight in the early 1970s, and soon established his position as one of the leading Finnish composers of his generation. His early works are characterized by a vigorous neoclassical idiom showing the influence of Shostakovich. In the course of the 1970s, however, Aho progressively moved away from his beginnings, and his "modern" style culminated in the *Sixth Symphony* at the end of the decade. From the beginning of the 1980s, Aho's stylistic aims have varied from work to work, depending on the "content" and "message" of the music; in some pieces, Aho combines heterogeneous elements in a deliberately "postmodern" spirit; in others, his approach is either distinctly modern or more traditional.

Aho can be considered a kindred spirit of Mahler—or, among present-day composers, of Alfred Schnittke. Like Mahler, Aho seeks ambiguity—"the aesthetic of impurity"—through irony and parody, the juxtaposition of opposing emotional states (such as sublimity and banality), a mixture of styles, stylistic loans, and a stylized use of different musical genres (such as waltzes, marches, and fanfares).

Aho's works tend to take the shape of musical narratives reminiscent of psychological processes; the composer himself has used the term "abstract plot." Instead of following given formal patterns, each work sets up its own form, governed by the logic of narrative, with its own positive and negative flows of power. Characteristic of this music are magnified climaxes with something of the character of decisive battles.

Emotive content and eloquence are essential properties of music to Aho: "For me music, at least great music, is a manifestation of emotions and the soul. In music, I hear the speech of one human being to another; I hear his joy, sorrow, happiness, desperation. In a composition as a whole, I hear his attitude to life, his philosophy, his world view–his message."

Eugene Anderson

Eugene D. Anderson, composer/conductor, began his formal music studies at the age of ten playing tuba in the Brookfield, Wisconsin, schools. Having received three summer clinic music camp scholarships and winning numerous awards as a tuba soloist in high school, Anderson took up study as a music major at the University of Wisconsin, from where he graduated in 1968 with a bachelor of music.

His first teaching position as tuba instructor was at the University of Toledo. After leaving Toledo to pursue a master of music in composition, Anderson went to Arizona State University and graduated magna cum laude in 1973.

From 1975 to 1980 Anderson was director of bands at Apache Junction (Arizona) High School. Today, he composes for band, orchestra, and chamber music as well as continuing an active schedule of performing and conducting.

Anderson has performed with the Madison Civic Symphony, Toledo Orchestra, Toledo Ballet, Toledo Brass Quintet, Phoenix Symphony, and Mesa Symphony and was assistant director of bands at Arizona State University. His composition teachers were Ronald LoPresti and Grant Fletcher.

Music reviewer Barton Cummings hailed as a masterpiece one of Anderson's major compositions: *Tuba Concerto No.1 in B Minor*. In addition to this orchestral work, Anderson has nearly twenty works published and sold worldwide, including a piano reduction version of his *Tuba Concerto*.

Mogens Andresen (1945–)

Mogens Andresen is head of brass at the Royal Danish Conservatory, Copenhagen. He has composed and arranged many pieces for brass instruments in many different instrument combinations.

Jean Baptiste Arban (1825–1889)

After leaving the Paris Conservatoire in 1845, Arban played in salon orchestras and conducted at the Paris Opera before taking up a post as saxhorn professor at a military school. This eventually led to a professorship of the cornet, his favored instrument, at the Conservatoire where he had studied as a youth. There Arban remained until his death, with the exception of the years 1874–1880, when he undertook some conducting engagements outside of France. Today, he is chiefly remembered in brass circles for his cornet treatise *Grande méthode complète pour cornet à pistons et de saxhorn* (Paris, 1864) and for various bravura cornet showpieces based on popular themes from operas or well-known songs of the day.

Jacob Arcadelt (?1505–1568)

Jacob Arcadelt grew up under the influence of Josquin and the Belgian School. He began his career as a singer at the court of Florence. In 1539 he went to Rome and became singing-master of the boys' choir at St. Peter's, and the following year entered the papal choir as a singer. Here he remained till 1549. In 1555, his services having been engaged by Cardinal Charles of Lorraine, Duke of Guise, Arcadelt followed him to Paris, where he probably remained until his death. He is mentioned, at this period, as regius musicus (court musician).

Of his numerous compositions, a large proportion has been published. Foremost among these are his six books of madrigals for five voices (Venice, 1538–1556), each book containing at least forty compositions. They are his finest and most characteristic works, and, together with three volumes of masses for from three to seven voices (Paris, 1557), are perhaps his chief claim to lasting renown. An excellent copy of the first four books of the madrigals, with other selected compositions of Arcadelt, is contained in the library of the British Museum. At Paris and Lyons many of his French songs were published, including *L'excellence des chansons musicales* (Lyons, 1572) and *Chansons françaises à plusieurs parties* (Lyons, 1586).

He was one of those distinguished musicians of the Netherlands who by their efforts to advance their art in Italy, both as teachers and composers, helped to lay the foundations of the great Italian school.

Jan Bach (1937–)

Jan Bach was born in Forrest, Illinois, in 1937. He studied at the University of Illinois in Urbana, where he received the doctor of musical arts degree in composition. His performing instruments are French horn and piano. His composition teachers have included Roberto Gerhard, Aaron Copland, Kenneth Gaburo, Robert Kelly, and Thea Musgrave. From 1962 to 1965 he was associate first horn in The United States Army Band at Fort Myer in Arlington, Virginia. Upon discharge, he taught for one year at the University of Tampa, Florida, and played in the orchestras of Tampa and St. Petersburg. Since 1966 he has taught theory and composition courses at Northern Illinois University in DeKalb. In 1978 he was selected as one of three professors receiving the Excellence in Teaching award; in 1982 he was recipient of one of the first eight prestigious presidential research professorship grants instituted by the university. For six years he was Northern Illinois University's nominee for the national CASE Professor of the Year award. Although taking an early retirement in 1998, he continued to teach one course each semester at the NIU School of Music until he retired completely in the spring of 2003.

Bach has written for virtually every live medium of vocal and instrumental performance. His music has been recognized with numerous composition awards and grants since 1957 when, at the age of nineteen, he won the BMI Student Composers first prize. Other awards have included the Koussevitsky competition at Tanglewood, the Harvey Gaul composition contest, the Mannes College opera competition, the Sigma Alpha Iota choral composition award, first prize at the First International Brass Congress in Montreux, Switzerland, grants from the National Endowment for the Arts and the Illinois Arts Council, the Brown University choral composition award, first prize in the Nebraska Sinfonia chamber orchestra competition, and first prize in the New York City Opera competition. Six times his works have been recommended for a Pulitzer Prize in music. Twenty-nine works of Bach have been published by Associated, Carl Fischer, Galaxy, Boosey & Hawkes, and others. His recorded works, on LP and CD, include three of his four brass quintets *Laudes* (four recordings), *Rounds and Dances,* and *Triptych;* his work for narrator and chamber orchestra *The Happy Prince; Four Two-Bit Contraptions* for flute and horn; *Concert Variations* for euphonium and piano; *Eisteddfod* for flute, harp, and viola (three CDs); *Skizzen* for woodwind quintet, and so forth. Recordings of other works have been distributed for broadcast by NPR and the BBC.

Bach has received commissions from the Orpheus Trio, the Chicago Brass Quintet, Harvey Phillips, the Orchestra of Illinois, the International Trumpet Guild, the Greenwich Philharmonia, the Indianapolis Symphony, the Sacramento Symphony, the Biddle Trust, the Pew Memorial Trust, Chamber Music America, and many others. Performance highlights have included his trio

Eisteddfod at the Aldeburgh Festival in England; his opera *The Student from Salamanca,* produced by Beverly Sills for the New York City Opera Company; his 1991 *Anachronisms,* written for the Vermeer String Quartet and commissioned and broadcast live to 261 FM stations nationwide in its premiere by WFMT, Chicago's Fine Arts radio station; and his *Concerto for Steelpan and Orchestra,* his most-performed orchestral composition.

Vincent Bach (1890–1961)
Born Vincent Schrotenbach in Vienna during 1890, his initial musical training was received on the violin. However, young Schrotenbach preferred the majestic sounds of the trumpet and eventually switched. Also displaying an aptitude in science, Schrotenbach graduated from the Maschinenbauschule with an engineering degree. His heart remained in music, leaving an engineering career for an uncertain future in music. Success soon followed as he toured throughout Europe, adopting the stage name of Vincent Bach while in England.

Paolo Baratto (1926–)
Paolo Baratto was born in 1926 in Untersiggenthal (Argovia, Switzerland). At the age of seven he began trumpet studies with his father, Alois, and then with Paul Spörri (former principal trumpet of the Berlin Philharmonic). He did his professional studies at the Zurich Conservatory (1941–1943) while playing substitute with the Zurich Tonhalle and Opera orchestras.

From 1943 to 1953 he was the principal trumpet with the Swiss Italian Radio Orchestra, and continued his studies of various areas of music for winds. From 1943 to 1961 he played with the Swiss Festival Orchestra in Lucerne under the direction of the greatest conductors of the era. He conducted different large Swiss wind bands. From 1956 to 1983 he was a member of the Tonhalle Orchestra in Zurich.

He has composed over eighty pieces, mainly for trumpet accompanied by organ, piano, or string or wind orchestra, as well as works for choir or wind bands.

James Barnes (1949–)
As a member of the theory-composition faculty at the University of Kansas, James Barnes teaches orchestration and composition courses. His numerous publications for concert band and orchestra are extensively performed in the United States, Europe, and the Pacific Basin. His works have been performed at Tanglewood, Boston Symphony Hall, Lincoln Center, Carnegie Hall, and the Kennedy Center in Washington, D.C.

Barnes has traveled extensively as a guest composer, conductor. and lecturer throughout the United States, Europe, Australia, Japan, and Taiwan. He is a member of the American Society of Composers, Authors and Publishers (ASCAP), the American Bandmasters Association, and numerous other professional organizations and societies. Since 1984, his music has been published exclusively by Southern Music Company of San Antonio, Texas.

Darrol Barry (1956–)
Born in Salford, UK, Darrol joined the school band on E♭ bass when he was fourteen and he soon moved onto the euphonium and started to arrange music for the band.

When he left school he became an apprentice joiner but decided to study music at Salford under Roy Newsome, Goff Richards, David Loukes, and Geoff Whitham. After leaving Salford he studied composition at the Royal College of Music, London, with Joseph Horowitz.

He became a freelance composer and arranger working for several publishing houses including Studio Music, Wright and Round, Bernaerts Music, and Obrasso. Darrol also taught as a part-time lecturer on the degree courses at Salford University, Barnsley, and Accrington and Rossendale.

In March 2002 Darrol took up his position as composer- and arranger-in-residence to the Royal Guard of Oman and provides music for the bands, big band, pipe and drums, and the Royal Oman Symphony Orchestra.

Alfred Bartles (1930–)
Alfred Bartles belongs to the first generation of so-called cross-over musicians: People who feel themselves equally at home in both classical and jazz disciplines. Following piano studies with Lennie Tristano, he worked as arranger-pianist for the U.S. Army during the Korean War. He holds a masters in composition from Ohio University, where he studied with Karl Ahrendt.

He studied cello with Claus Adam and Luigi Silva, and went on to play professionally in the St. Louis Symphony, Broadway shows, and the Mantovani orchestra. In the early 1960s his compositions began to be published, among them *Music for Symphony Orchestra and Jazz Ensemble,* commissioned by the Nashville Symphony. In 1968 he founded the composition program at the Sewanee Summer Music Festival in Tennessee. Following successive residencies in Tennessee and Stuttgart, Germany, as composition student, composition professor, and cello teacher, he returned definitively to Nashville in 1997 where he's an active composer-arranger and teaches

cello. Bartles's works have been performed and recorded throughout Europe.

Steve Barton
Steven Barton is a native of western Pennsylvania. He received a master of music degree in percussion performance from Virginia Commonwealth University. He performs with the Keystone Wind Ensemble.

Herman Bellstedt (1858–1926)
Herman Bellstedt came to America in 1867 at the age of nine. His family settled in Cincinnati in 1872, where he studied the cornet with his father and Mylius Weigand. Being billed as the "Boy Wonder," he gave his debut performance on May 10, 1873. He then performed second cornet in the orchestra at Arctic Gardens, soon being promoted to first cornet and soloist. From 1874 to 1879, he performed solo cornet with the Cincinnati Reed Band under the direction of Michael Brand. In 1879, he became cornet soloist with the Red Hussar Band on Manhattan Beach, later returning to the Cincinnati Reed Band in 1883. He performed from 1889 to 1892 in Gilmore's Band sitting next to Benjamin Bent, from 1904 to 1906 in the Sousa Band (replacing Walter B. Rogers) performing next to Herbert L. Clarke, and from 1906 to 1909 in Frederick N. Innes's Band (replacing Bohumir Kryl). Bellstedt's talents extended well beyond the cornet realm, as he conducted the Bellstedt & Ballenberg Band and performed first trumpet in orchestras conducted by Theodore Thomas, Van der Stucken, and Schradieck between the years of 1892 and 1904.

Warren Benson (1924–)
Warren Benson has distinguished himself in the world of contemporary music as a composer, conductor, lecturer, and writer; he is a musician who is as interested in writing music for orchestras, singers, chamber players, and children as he is in exploring the complexities of the world of the artist.

In his compositions and international recordings, Benson is most noted for his song cycles and pioneering work in behalf of percussionists and wind ensembles. He has been invited to conduct his works in Australia, Canada, Europe, Great Britain, Mexico, Scandinavia, and South America. As an author and lecturer, Benson has also been in demand worldwide. His writings have been translated into Spanish and Japanese and he has lectured in Spanish and Greek. He also sits on the board of directors of numerous musical organizations, including the Minuscule University Press, the Chestnut Brass company, the American Wind

Ensemble Library, and the World Association for Symphonic Bands and Ensembles (WASBE).

Born in 1924 and a professional performer by the age of fourteen, Benson, early in his career, played timpani in the Detroit Symphony Orchestra, graduated from the University of Michigan, organized the first touring percussion ensemble in the eastern United States (1953), received four Fulbright grants, and was the author and director of the first pilot project of the Contemporary Music Project (funded by the Ford Foundation). More recently, he has been commissioned by more than eighty major artists and ensembles, including the United States Marine Band, the International Horn Society, the Rochester Philharmonic Orchestra, the New York Choral Society, the Bishop Ireton Symphonic Wind Ensemble, and the Kronos Quartet. He has received numerous distinguished international awards, including the John Simon Guggenheim Composer Fellowship, three National Endowment for the Arts composer commissions, and the Diploma de Honor from the Ministry of Culture of the Republic of Argentina. After fourteen years at Ithaca College, Benson became a professor of composition at the Eastman School of Music, where he was honored with an Alumni Citation for Excellence, the Kilbourn Professorship for distinguished teaching, and was named University Mentor. In 1994 he was appointed professor emeritus, completing a fifty-year teaching career that began in 1943 at the University of Michigan. As a freshman there, he was the major teacher for undergraduate and graduate percussionists and played third horn in the university orchestra. He is listed in the first edition of *Who's Who in the World of Percussion*, 1980 to the present, as well as thirty other biographical dictionaries including *Who's Who in America* and *Groves Dictionary of Music*.

Currently busy writing books, he is a commissioned and published poet and writer of humorous fiction. Almost an even dozen commissions for songs, chamber music, and large ensembles keep him "retired to, not from," as he likes to put it.

Sverre Bergh (1915–1980)
Sverre Bergh was born at Hamar a little north of Oslo. During the years 1935–1937 he studied music theory with Fartein Valen. He also had a shorter stay in Vienna. From 1937 to 1946 he worked as a freelance musician in Oslo. After that he was employed as arranger in the Norwegian Broadcasting Corporation.

From 1952 on he was conductor at various theatres; the most important one was the National Theatre of Bergen. His name is today closely linked to musical theatre. He has arranged and composed a tremendous amount of music for the stage, movies, radio, and television. His two most important works in this field are the television opera *Lyrikkens verkefinger (The Swollen Finger of the Poetry)* and the pop musical *Alice in Underworld*, utilizing the fairytale with a similar name to describe the world of advertising. ("Underworld" in Norwegian means both underworld and wonderland.)

He has also composed chamber, choral, and orchestral music. His serious compositions are mostly held in a neoclassical style, but an even stronger characteristic of his list of works is humor.

During most of his life Sverre Bergh was active as an organizer and artistic consultant. He had lots of honorary offices in Norwegian musical life, and to a great degree contributed to having contemporary music on the repertory of Norwegian performing institutions. His later years were spent as the director of the Bergen International Festival.

Alfred Blatter
Alfred Blatter is the co-founder of Media Press and the author of the definitive international reference/textbook *Instrumentation and Orchestration*, now in its second edition. His compositions are performed throughout the world, and he has received commissions from such groups as Sonneries Woodwind Quintet, Eugene (Oregon) Symphony, Champaign-Urbana (Illinois) Symphony, and the Orchestra Society of Philadelphia. He received his DMA from the University of Illinois and taught music theory at Illinois before becoming the director of performing arts at Drexel University in Philadelphia. Blatter was conductor and musical coordinator for the American Music Theater's acclaimed Philadelphia and New York City performances of Harry Partch's *Revelation in Courthouse Park*.

Eduardo Boccolari (1851–1929)
Eduardo Boccolari was an Italian composer and arranger, most notably of *Fantasia di Concerto* (see listings under Euphonium and Keyboard and Euphonium and Wind Band).

John Boda (1922–2002)
John Boda was born in Wisconsin in 1922 and received his early music training near Cleveland, Ohio. He received his bachelor's degree from Kent State University and his master's degree and doctorate from the Eastman School of Music. In 1946 he won a national competition to become

apprentice conductor to George Szell and the Cleveland Orchestra for one year.

Derek Bourgeois (1941–)

Derek Bourgeois graduated from Cambridge University in 1963 with a first-class honors degree in music, and he returned for a subsequent doctorate. He also spent two years at the Royal College of Music, where he studied composition with Herbert Howells and conducting with Sir Adrian Boult.

He has composed seven symphonies, eight concertos, several other extended orchestral works, seven major works for chorus and orchestra, two operas, and a musical. As well as a considerable quantity of chamber, vocal, and instrumental music, he has composed ten extended works for brass band and two symphonies for symphonic wind orchestra. He has also written a considerable amount of music for television productions.

From 1970 to 1984 he was a lecturer in music at Bristol University. He was the conductor of the Sun Life Band from 1980 until 1983, and during the same period was chairman of the Composers' Guild of Great Britain and a member of the Music Advisory Panel of the Arts Council.

In September 1984 he gave up his university post to become the musical director of the National Youth Orchestra of Great Britain. In 1988 he founded the National Youth Chamber Orchestra of Great Britain, which held its first course in the summer of 1989. In 1990 he was appointed artistic director of the Bristol Philharmonic Orchestra.

He left the National Youth Orchestra in 1993 to become the director of music at St. Paul's Girls' School in London.

Eugene Bozza (1905–1991)

Eugene Bozza was born in Nice and made an early impact at the Paris Conservatoire as a brilliant violinist and conductor, gaining recognition as a composer when he won the prestigious Prix de Rome in 1934. Although he went on to write five symphonies and several operas and ballets, like many French composers he spent much of his life as an academic, becoming head of the Valenciennes Conservatoire in 1948. In this capacity he wrote much of the wind chamber music for which he is now best known and of which the short *Caprice*, from 1943, is absolutely typical.

Timothy Broege (1947–)

Born and raised in Belmar, New Jersey, composer Timothy Broege studied piano and theory with Helen Antonides during his childhood years. At Northwestern University, he studied composition with M. William Karlins, Alan Stout, and Anthony Donato; piano with Frances Larimer; and harpsichord with Dorothy Lane, receiving a bachelor of music with highest honors degree in 1969. From 1969 to 1971, he taught in the Chicago Public School system, after which he served as an elementary school music teacher in Manasquan, New Jersey, until 1980. He currently holds the positions of organist and director of music at First Presbyterian Church in Belmar, a position he has held since 1972, and organist and director of music at the historic Elberon Memorial Church in Elberon, New Jersey.

The music of Broege has been performed throughout the world by, among others, the Monmouth Symphony Orchestra, the United States Military Academy Band, the Atlantic String Quartet, the Cygnus Ensemble, pianist Robert Pollock, and recorder player Jody Miller. He has received numerous grants and commissions, and his music is published by Boosey & Hawkes, Manhattan Beach Music, Hal Leonard Corporation, Bourne Company, Daehn Publications, Dorn Publications, Polyphonic Publications, Grand Mesa Music, and Allaire Music Publications. In addition to his compositional activities, Broege is an active recitalist on early keyboard instruments and recorder appearing both as a soloist and in duo recitals.

Bruce Broughton

Bruce Broughton, a composer who works in many styles and eclectic venues, is best known for film scores. He has been nominated for an Oscar, a Grammy, and twenty Emmys, having won the latter award seven times. He has composed music for many of the Disney theme park attractions throughout the world, and wrote the first orchestral score for a CD-ROM game, *Heart of Darkness*. He conducted and supervised the recording of Gershwin's *Rhapsody in Blue* for *Fantasia 2000*, and has recorded critically acclaimed performances of classic film scores such as Miklos Rozsa's *Ivanhoe* and *Julius Caesar*, as well as Bernard Herrmann's *Jason and the Argonauts*.

As a composer of concert music, he has composed a popular tuba concerto, a piccolo concerto, *Modular Music* and *Modular Music II* for the Los Angeles Chamber Orchestra, the *English Music for Horn and Strings*, and the children's fantasy *The Magic Horn* for narrator and orchestra. His *Masters of Space and Time* was jointly commissioned by the American Brass Band Association and the British Open Championship, and he recently recorded his *Fanfares, Marches, Hymns and Finale* with the Bay Brass, the ensemble that commissioned it.

Broughton is a past president of the Society of Composers and Lyricists, and has served as a governor on the boards of both the Academy of Motion Picture Arts and Sciences and the Academy of Television Arts and Sciences. He has taught film composition at the University of Southern California and has lectured at UCLA.

Jerry Brubaker (1946–)

A native of Altoona, Pennsylvania, Jerry Brubaker is a graduate of the Eastman School of Music and received a master's degree from the Catholic University of America. He served for thirty years in the United States Navy Band in Washington, D.C., as a French horn soloist and composer/arranger. He became the band's chief arranger in 1985 and held that position until his retirement from the Navy in 1998. He is well known for his arrangements of popular music and Christmas favorites. Jerry has published over 100 works for band, symphony orchestra, and chorus.

William R. Brusick (1959–)

A native Floridian, William R. Brusick received his bachelor of science degree in music education from Tennessee Technological University in 1981, studying with Robert Jager. Studies continued at North Texas State University, where in 1984, he received his master of music in composition, studying with Martin Mailman, and finally receiving his doctor of music degree in 1988 from Florida State University, studying with John Boda.

Over the years, Brusick has composed several works for chamber ensembles, as well as symphonic band and orchestra, including *For the Kings of Brass* (commissioned by the Tennessee Tech Tuba Ensemble), *Concerto for Tuba and Wind Orchestra* (commissioned by and dedicated to Timothy J. Northcut), *March of the Conch Republic* (commissioned by and dedicated to the City of Key West), *The Cookeville Herald-Citizen March* (composed for the 100th anniversary of this newspaper), *Skin and Bones,* a rousing fanfare for trombone and percussion ensembles, and, most recently, the five-movement *Concerto for Wind Ensemble* (dedicated to Joseph W. Hermann and the Tennessee Tech Wind Ensemble).

He has also composed over 150 sacred works for chorus, solos, organ, and handbells including *Come, Holy Ghost* (commissioned by the Milwaukee Children's Chorus), *A New Song* (a complete jazz setting of the Lutheran Eucharist service), *Shout for Joy!* (commissioned for the 100th anniversary of Trinity Lutheran Church in Delray Beach, Florida), and *Te Deum and Requiem: The Stride Is O'er* (for full orchestra, chorus, and soloists).

For the past sixteen years, he has served as a minister of music in the Florida-Georgia District of the Lutheran Church–Missouri Synod, as choir director, organist, composer, recitalist, clinician, and teacher. In 2002 he was named to *Who's Who Among American Teachers,* and in September of 2003 was awarded the Dr. Ben Eggers Lutheran Educator of the Year (Middle School division).

Karsten Brustad (1959–)

Karsten Brustad studied classical guitar at the Eastern Norway Conservatory of Music under Geir-Otto Nilsson and Professor Sven Lundestad. As a composer he is mainly self-taught, but he has studied instrumentation with Ragnar Söderlind and has received instruction from professor Michael Jarrell at Hochschule for Musik und darstellende Kunst i Vienna, as well as Asbjørn Schaathun and Professor Olav Anton Thommessen at the Norwegian State Academy of Music.

Brustad has worked much with electronic instruments. He has composed a number of purely electronic works and used this medium in music for other kinds of art, such as pictures, exhibitions, TV, video, and theatre. His interest has been especially occupied with the integration of electronically and acoustically processed sound in works like *Points to Line* (1997) for euphonium and tape, *Object* (1998) for guitar trio and tape, and *Streif* (2000) for soprano, violin, and tape.

Brustad has composed a number of works for orchestra, such as *Tre Deler* (1986), *Fragments and Shades* (1994), *Prevratim* (1990) for guitar and orchestra, and *Hymn of Creation* (1990) for soprano and orchestra. He has also written for choir, a series of works for different chamber ensembles, and for solo instruments. Brustad has released CDs in his own name and is represented on a number of other recordings.

In 1999 Østfold Chamber Orchestra made a presentation tour with works exclusively by Brustad, among them three premieres. In addition he has been performed by Bergen Philharmonic Orchestra, Trondheim Cathedral Choir, London Guitar Trio, and various solo performers.

Brustad has received a number of scholarships and commissions. He is a member of the Society of Norwegian Composers and NOPA (Norwegian Society of Composers and Lyricists).

Forrest Buchtel (1899–1996)

One of the most prolific writers of school band music, Buchtel studied privately with H. A. VanderCook.

He received his bachelor and master of music education degrees from the VanderCook College of Music and began teaching there in 1931. He also taught in the public schools, including Lane Tech and Amundsen High School.

Stephen Bulla

Stephen Bulla received his degree in arranging and composition from Boston's Berklee College of Music, graduating magna cum laude. His studies helped him develop an interest in the commercial music field, eventually leading to a schedule of full-time composing and recording production.

Presently Bulla has entered his third decade as staff arranger to "The President's Own" United States Marine Band and White House Orchestra. As such he is responsible for the production of music that encompasses many styles and instrumental combinations, most of which are performed for presidential functions and visiting dignitaries.

His musical arrangements were featured on the PBS television series *In Performance at the White House* and have been performed by many artists including Sarah Vaughan, the Manhattan Transfer, Mel Torme, Doc Severinsen, Nell Carter, and Larry Gatlin.

A variety of freelance commercial projects find Bulla in the studio producing new recordings, including the popular *Spiritual to the 'Bone* series of jazz trombone ensemble CDs. In 1990 he was awarded the prestigious ADDY Award for best original music/TV spot, and recently he provided the music score for the *Century of Flight* series on the Discovery Channel.

In 1998 he was honored by the Salvation Army in New York for his extensive contribution to their musical repertoire. This event included a "profile" concert of his compositions, featuring performances by the New York Staff Band.

His commissioned concert works include instrumental compositions that are performed and recorded internationally. The Dutch, British, Swiss, and New Zealand Brass Band Championship organizations have all commissioned test pieces from his pen.

Arthur Butterworth (1923–)

Arthur Butterworth is little known outside his native North of England (since strictly speaking he is a Lancastrian) except in the rather confined world of the brass band for which he has provided effective music that has been widely played. His extensive output of orchestral scores, which includes four symphonies, several concertos, and other large-scale works, ensemble music of great

variety, and some very telling vocal and choral pieces has all been highly praised in its time but little has established itself in the regular repertory.

After leaving the Royal Manchester College of Music, Butterworth began his professional career as a trumpeter with the Scottish National Orchestra (1949–1955) and then with the Hallé (1955–1962). He also taught brass for the former West Riding Education Department for a few years until being appointed lecturer in composition at Huddersfield University Music Department. In 1962 he was appointed associate conductor of the Huddersfield Philharmonic Society and in 1964 became permanent conductor, leaving in 1993.

Gary Buttery

Gary Buttery received his early musical training in the Omaha metropolitan area. He has studied with such noted artists as Roger Bobo, Don Harry, Gene Pokorny, Jack Robinson, and Dan Perantoni. He earned his bachelor and master of music degrees in tuba and in music theory/composition from the University of Northern Colorado. Prior to settling in Connecticut, he performed with the Long Beach Symphony and the San Carlo Opera Company and was on the faculty of Pepperdine University.

Buttery recently retired as principal tubist in the United States Coast Guard Band, the premiere band of the Coast Guard, based in New London, Connecticut. He was also a member of the Atlantic Tuba Quartet; A Different Village, performing international folk music; and Finest Kind, a unique combination of mandolin, tuba, and other "folk" instruments. He also taught at the University of Rhode Island and at Connecticut College, and has performed locally with the Paul Winter Consort and the Morgans. Gary has had numerous new works for tuba written for him, including Roger Kellaway's *Arcades I* for tuba and piano, George Heussenstamm's *Dialogues for Alto Saxophone and Tuba*, Allen Blank's *Divertimento for Tuba and Band*, Richard Penner's *Sharing*, Boston composer Frank Warren's *Seven Duets for Tubassoon*, and Vaclav Nelhybel's *Concerto for Tuba*. Gary has performed throughout the United States as a soloist and clinician, and has the distinction of being the first tuba soloist featured with the NBC Orchestra on Johnny Carson's *Tonight Show*.

Antonio Capuzzi (1755–1818)

Capuzzi was an Italian violinist who composed operas, cantatas, and a great amount of chamber music.

Philip Catelinet

A native of England, Catelinet has been a prolific composer/arranger and a performer/conductor. An active officer in the Salvation Army, his many years of experience include roles as euphonium and tuba soloist, composer, and conductor. While tuba player with the London Symphony Orchestra, he inspired the noted English composer Ralph Vaughn Williams to write the first major concerto for the tuba and orchestra. After coming to the United States, Catelinet was professor of music at Carnegie Mellon University in Pittsburgh for many years.

John Cheetham (1939–)

John E. Cheetham, professor emeritus of music theory and composition at the University of Missouri–Columbia, was born in Taos, New Mexico, in 1939. He received his bachelor's and master's degrees from the University of New Mexico and his doctor of musical arts in composition from the University of Washington.

During his tenure at Missouri, he composed for virtually all media and his works were widely performed in the United States and abroad. Over 25 of his compositions have been published, and recordings of his pieces are available on several labels, including Crystal, Concord, Pro-Arte, Summit, and NPR Classic. In addition, Cheetham has been the recipient of numerous commissions, including from the Kentucky Derby Museum, Texas Tech University, the Atlanta Symphony Brass Quintet, the Central Oklahoma Directors Association, the Springfield (Missouri) Symphony Orchestra, the Summit Brass, and others.

Cheetham is a member of ASCAP and has received ASCAP Special Awards from 1998 through the present. He has also been the recipient of a Centennial Distinguished Alumni Award from the University of New Mexico, and in 1992 won the Abraham Frost Prize in Composition.

Herbert L. Clarke (1867–1945)

Clarke was born in Woburn, Massachusetts, on September 12, 1867. He moved with his family to Toronto in 1880. Since his father was the organist at the Jarvis St. Baptist Church and his three older brothers played with the Regimental Band of the Queen's Own Rifles, it was not surprising that the young Clarke showed an interest in music. He himself said in his autobiography, *How I Became a Cornetist*, that it was growing up "in a musical environment that played a large part in turning me to the musically artistic as a life profession."

In 1893, he joined the Sousa Band as a cornet soloist. After playing at the Chicago Exposition in the same year, he left to play with various other bands, continuing to do so over the next five years. It was during this period that he divorced Lizzie Loudon and married Lillian Bell Hause, with whom he had two more children, Ruby Bell and Herbert L. Clarke, Jr. In 1898 he returned to the Sousa Band, with whom he toured extensively, and later became Sousa's assistant director, conducting the band in many recording sessions. He resigned from the Sousa Band in September of 1917 and returned to Canada to lead the Anglo-Canadian Leather Company Band in Huntsville, Ontario, from 1918 to 1923. Under Clarke's leadership, this band became one of the most celebrated commercial bands in North America.

In 1923, he moved to Long Beach, California, due to his wife's health and conducted the Long Beach Municipal Band until 1943. In April of 1934, he was elected president of the American Bandmasters Association. He died in January 1945 and his ashes were interred at the Congressional Cemetery in Washington, D.C., near the gravesite of John Philip Sousa. His papers and memorabilia are held at the Herbert L. Clarke Library at the University of Illinois at Urbana–Champaign.

Nigel Clarke

Nigel Clarke studied composition at the Royal Academy of Music (where he won the Queen's Commendation for Excellence). He subsequently spent a year in Hong Kong, writing music for their Academy for Performing Arts. Since his return to the UK, Clarke has written original classical pieces for with (among others) the Black Dyke Mills Band and the United States Marine Band. He is currently the head of composition and contemporary music at the London College of Music and Media. Clarke made his film music debut in 1999, working with (as he often does) composer and pianist Michael Csányi-Wills.

Fred L. Clinard, Jr.

Fred L. Clinard, Jr., was born and raised in Nashville, Tennessee, where he graduated from McGavock High School in 1973. He graduated from Tennessee Tech University in 1978 with a BS degree in music education. While at Tech he studied composition with Robert Jager and euphonium with R. Winston Morris.

After college Clinard spent fifteen years as a high school band director in Florida, Tennessee, and Virginia. Currently, Clinard is a financial services professional in the Nashville area and continues to perform, compose, and arrange on a freelance basis.

Dinos Constantinides

Constantinides received diplomas in theory and violin from the Greek Conservatory in Athens,

Greece, and a diploma in violin from the Juilliard School. He received his master's degree in music from Indiana University and his PhD in composition from Michigan State University. He also studied at Brandeis University, Meadowmount School of Music, and the Athens Conservatory.

Constantinides has performed professionally as soloist, chamber musician, section violinist, and concertmaster in many symphony orchestras in the United States and Europe including the Baton Rouge Symphony Orchestra, the Indianapolis Symphony Orchestra, and the State Orchestra of Athens, Greece.

His teaching achievements include a 1994 White House Commission on Presidential Scholars Distinguished Teacher award and a National Foundation for Advancements in the Arts award. He also received several teaching awards from MTNA in both composition and violin.

As a composer, he has received first prizes in the Delius Composition Contest, the L'Ensemble Competition of New York, the National Brooklyn College Chamber Opera Competition, and the First Midwest Chamber Opera Theatre Conference. He has also won 23 consecutive ASCAP Standards Awards in Serious Composition. Other awards include LTMA and Division of the Arts composition commissions, numerous Meet-the-Composer Grants, commissions from ensembles, individuals, and societies, the Daughters of the American Revolution American Medal Award, and the Louisiana governor's and mayor-president's citations for excellence in the arts, as well as a Distinguished Service Award from the American New Music Consortium of New York.

Evan Copley

Dr. Evan Copley is professor of music and chair of the Department of Theory and Composition at the University of Northern Colorado. He has published several theory textbooks, including *Harmony: Baroque to Contemporary,* which are used by music schools throughout the nation. Copley's numerous compositions include symphonic, choral, band, keyboard, and chamber music works. In February 1990, his *Ninth Symphony* was premièred, and in 1986, the Mormon Tabernacle Choir broadcast Copley's motet *In Thee, O God, Do I Put My Trust* on 350 radio stations and forty television stations. His *Third Piano Concerto* was premiered in 1988 by Daniel Graham and the Greeley Philharmonic Orchestra. Also in 1988, Copley was named UNC's Distinguished Scholar of the Year. In the summer of 1991, Copley was named composer-in-residence at the Breckenridge Music Institute. He received his MM and PhD degrees from Michigan State University.

Neal Corwell (1959–)

Dr. Neal Corwell, having previously served as featured soloist with one of the premier service band in Washington, D.C., The United States Army Band "Pershing's Own," from 1981 to 1989, rejoined the military in 2002 and is now once again playing euphonium as a member of the armed services. During the intervening years in the civilian world, he earned his doctorate in music from the University of Maryland and made his living as a freelance musician, appearing overseas and all across the United States as guest euphonium solo artist and composer at numerous events each year. Corwell also was an adjunct faculty member at both Frostburg State University and Shepherd College for several years, teaching low brass and electronic music.

Corwell's longtime interest in composition and electronic music, in combination with his career as a solo artist, has resulted in his production of numerous original works and arrangements for the medium of soloist with pre-recorded accompaniment, and his total output currently includes nearly fifty original works published, ranging in instrumentation from unaccompanied solos to multi-movement orchestral works. Corwell was the composer-in-residence for the Symphony at Deep Creek (McHenry, Maryland) from 1994 to 1999, and was chosen as one of the featured composers for the 1997 Bowling Green (Ohio) International Music and Arts Festival. Other honors include Maryland State Arts Council awards for excellence in both classical music composition and solo instrumental performance in 1999 and 2000. He also won second prize in the 2003 American Music in the United States Armed Forces Composition Competition, an international event sponsored by the National Federation of Music Clubs. Several of his compositions have been included on recent recordings released by the following labels: Mark Records, Crystal Records, RJR Digital, TRYFAN, HRS, and Nicolai Music. To date, Corwell has released three solo Cds: *Distant Images* (1994), *Heart of a Wolf* (2000), and *Out Sitting in His Field* (2004), all of which feature exclusively his own compositions.

Roland Coryn (1938–)

Roland Coryn, born in 1938 in Kortrijk, Belgium, came into contact early with the artistic world. His brother sketched and painted, and his family maintained links with artistic circles. After his musical studies at the Municipal Music Academy in Harelbeke, he pursued further studies at the Royal Conservatory of Ghent. There he earned his higher diploma in viola and chamber music, while continuing to study in the theory department and subsequently receiving his first prize in composition.

As a teacher he held positions at the music academies of Harelbeke, Izegem, and Oostende. In 1979 he was named director in Harelbeke. For many years he held an important function as a teacher of composition at the conservatory in Ghent. On September 1, 1997, he took early retirement in order to devote his full attention to composing.

In the period from 1960 to 1975, Coryn was chiefly active as a performing musician. He played viola in the Belgian Chamber Orchestra, where he came into contact with modern music, and he was a founding member of the Flemish Piano Quartet, which focused on the works of well-known composers and Belgian masters. From 1986 to 1997 he was the leader of the Nieuw Conservatoriumensemble in Ghent, with which he performed mainly contemporary works. This activity proved highly fruitful for his composition class.

As a composer, Coryn has won numerous prizes, including the Tenuto Prize in 1973 (*Quattro Movimenti*), the Jef Van Hoof Prize in 1974 (*Triptiek*), the Koopal Prize in 1986 for his chamber music oeuvre, and the Visser-Neerlandia Prize in 1999 for his complete output.

In 1993 he was elected a member of the Academy of Fine Arts, Letters and Sciences of Belgium.

Vladimir Cosma (1940–)

One of France's and Europe's most distinguished film composers, Vladimir Cosma has scored more than 150 films and TV productions. Though he enjoyed almost immediate success in comedies, he continued experimenting with different styles and genres and this versatility brought him wide international acclaim.

Born on April 13, 1940, in Bucharest, Romania, to the family of a renowned conductor and concert pianist, Cosma studied music from his early years onward, eventually attending the National Conservatory in Bucharest (from which he graduated with two first prizes, for violin and composition). In 1963 he went to Paris to advance his studies at the French Conservatory, where, in addition to his classical background, he developed an interest in jazz, folk music, and film music. Between 1964 and 1967 he toured the world as a concert violinist, visiting the United States, Latin America, and Southeast Asia. A meeting with popular film composer Michel Legrand became the first step toward his future career. Cosma always mentions Legrand's importance, though he also admits the

influence of such composers as Burt Bacharach and Henri Mancini.

Randell Croley (1946–)

Randell Croley was born in 1946 near Knoxville, Tennessee. He received a BM from University of Louisville and later studied with Vincent Persichetti at the Juilliard School of Music.

Barton Cummings

Barton Cummings enjoys a distinguished international musical career. Recognized as an author, composer, conductor, educator, and performing artist, he has pursued these activities successfully for more than forty years.

His consistent and scholarly writing has produced three books, more than 400 articles, scores of reviews, and several editorship positions. His work is constantly cited in articles, books, and dissertations by other authors.

The music of Barton Cummings has been performed throughout the world by such prominent artists and ensembles as Harvey Phillips, Mark Nelson, Mary Ann Craig, Fritz Kaenzig, Dennis Askew, Kenyon Wilson, Susan Bradley, Susan Nigro, Tony Clements, David Deason, Carson Cooman, Janet Polk, Jae Young Heo, San Jose (California) Chamber Orchestra, Bowling Green State University Euphonium-Tuba Ensemble, Colonial Tuba Quartet, Meridian Arts Ensemble Brass Quintet, St. John's Brass Quintet, Prima Toni, Tokyo Bari-Tuba Ensemble, University of Michigan Euphonium-Tuba Ensemble, New Castle Brass Ensemble, Harmonious Brass Choir, University of New Hampshire Concert Choir, University of the Pacific Wind Ensemble, University of Memphis Concert Band, University of North Carolina–Greensboro TubaBand, Georgia Honors Euphonium-Tuba Choir, and the Chicago Symphonic Wind Ensemble.

James Curnow (1943–)

James Curnow was born in Port Huron, Michigan, and raised in Royal Oak, Michigan. He lives in Nicholasville, Kentucky, where he is president, composer, and educational consultant for Curnow Music Press, Inc., of Lexington, Kentucky, publishers of significant music for concert band and brass band. He also serves as composer-in-residence on the faculty of Asbury College in Wilmore, Kentucky, and is editor of all music publications for the Salvation Army in Atlanta, Georgia.

His formal training was received at Wayne State University (Detroit, Michigan) and at Michigan State University (East Lansing, Michigan), where he was a euphonium student of Leonard

Falcone and a conducting student of Dr. Harry Begian. His studies in composition and arranging were with F. Maxwell Wood, James Gibb, Jere Hutchinson, and Irwin Fischer.

Curnow has taught in all areas of instrumental music, both in the public schools (five years), and on the college and university level (26 years). He is a member of several professional organizations, including the American Bandmasters Association, College Band Directors National Association, World Association of Symphonic Bands and Wind Ensembles, and ASCAP. In 1980 he received the National Band Association's Citation of Excellence. In 1985, while a tenured associate professor at the University of Illinois, Champaign-Urbana, Curnow was honored as an outstanding faculty member. Among his most recent honors are inclusion in *Who's Who in America*, *Who's Who in the South and Southwest*, and Composer of the Year (1997) by the Kentucky Music Teachers Association and the National Music Teachers Association. He has received annual ASCAP Standard Awards since 1979.

M. L. Daniels (1931–)

Dr. Daniels retired in 1993 after teaching at Abilene (Texas) Christian University (ACU) for 34 years. He was music department chairman for fifteen years and taught a variety of subjects, including music theory, orchestration, counterpoint, composition, class brass, and class strings. He also served as assistant band director and as orchestra director during a portion of his tenure at ACU. He played trumpet for several season with the Abilene and San Angelo Symphony Orchestras as well.

He has won first place five times in the composition contest sponsored annually by the American String Teachers Association with the National School Orchestra Association, with pieces for both full and string orchestra.

Though his favorite pastime is golf, Daniels regularly judges school bands and orchestras during contest season.

Greg Danner (1958–)

Greg Danner is professor of music theory and composition at Tennessee Technological University. He has received annual ASCAP awards for composition since 1989. Danner was awarded the 2000 Delius Composition Contest vocal category and grand prize for his composition *Time* and the 1999 College Band Directors National Association Composition for Young Band prize for his composition *Walls of Zion*. He is also the recipient of the Louisiana Music Teachers Association Composer Commission Award, and has won

composition contests sponsored by the Taghkanic Chorale and Sigma Alpha Iota music fraternity. He has been commissioned to write works for performance at various music conferences, including the International Brass Festival, New York Brass Conference, International Trumpet Guild, National Flute Association, and College Band Directors National Association.

Danner participated as a resident composer at the Charles Ives Center for American Music and has been an associate in the Kennedy Center for the Performing Arts "Performing Arts Centers and Schools" program. His writings on music and music theory have been published in numerous journals, including *Music Perception, Interface–Journal for New Music Research, Journal of Musicological Research*, and *Journal of Music Theory Pedagogy*.

An active performer, Danner is hornist with the Bryan Symphony Orchestra, the Cumberland Wind Quintet, and the Brass Arts Quintet. He is also active as a studio and freelance musician in the Nashville area.

William Mac Davis

Dr. William Mac Davis is professor of music theory and composition and chair of the Department of Music Theory and Composition at Southwestern Baptist Theological Seminary, where he has taught since 1979. In addition, he is coordinator of instrumental studies and conductor of the Wind Ensemble. In 1993, he founded New-Sound, the seminary's jazz lab band, which he also directs.

A native of Mississippi, Davis holds the bachelor of music and master of music degrees in theory and composition from the University of Mississippi and the doctor of philosophy degree in composition from the University of Utah. He has done post-doctoral study in composition at the Eastman School of Music in Rochester, New York. His composition teachers have included Samuel Adler, Ned Rorem, Vladimir Ussachevsky, Ramiro Cortes, and Raymond Liebau.

His works have been performed throughout the country and in England, Italy, Brazil, China, and Japan. He was a recipient of a composer fellowship for the 1984 Petit Jean Art Song Festival and was featured composer in the 1989 New Music Festival at Sam Houston State University in Huntsville, Texas. Davis received the 1985 Delius Festival Award for Vocal Composition, first prize in the 1980 Ithaca College Choral Composition Contest, and two first prizes and a second prize award in competitions sponsored by the Texas Composers Guild. His *Symphonic Variants on a*

Southern Hymn Tune was selected by the Virginia College Band Directors' Association for its 1995 Symposium of New Band Music and *Rondo Concertante for Euphonium and Orchestra* was recently performed by Southwestern alumnus Don Palmire and The United States Army Orchestra. *Fanfare on a French Carol* was awarded the 1997 Gerald Armstrong Award. He has also received an ASCAP award each year since 1994. His works are published by Theodore Presser, Southern Music Company, Genevox, and Tuba-Euphonium Press. In April of 2001, he conducted the Southwestern Oratorio Chorus and the Fort Worth Chamber Orchestra in the premiere of his work *How Can I Keep from Singing?*

William DeFostis (1953–2003)
William DeFostis was a conductor and composition and theory faculty member, Baylor University (1983–1984), and professor, College of William and Mary (1986–2003).

Joseph DeLuca (1890–1935)
Joseph Orlando (Joe) DeLuca was a renowned euphonium soloist who appeared with many American bands, most notably Sousa's. He began his musical studies at the age of nine in his homeland of Italy. Later he entered a musical conservatory in Perugia, where he studied composition, conducting, and other musical subjects. He obtained his degree from the conservatory at the age of seventeen.

He then became the first trombonist with two opera companies and the conductor of the municipal band in Ripateatina. His reputation as a conductor and soloist spread rapidly and he was in great demand as a soloist with many Italian bands.

After moving to the United States and establishing his reputation here, in 1928 he became the director of bands at the University of Arizona. He held that position until his death, and for several years also served as the director of the Tucson Symphony Orchestra.

Robin Dewhurst
Robin Dewhurst has had many years of experience in the field of media music, writing and arranging music for TV, film, and radio. As a performer he has worked with big bands, small jazz groups, brass bands, and orchestras both on trombone and piano. Currently musical director of the University of Salford Big Band, he also holds the post of head of popular music within the university's music department, is a senior lecturer in music, and is in charge of the department's successful popular music and recording degree program.

His diversity as a composer/arranger has brought him acclaim in a wide range of idioms, and he has received commissions from many named artists (Lisa Stansfield, Paul Young), ensembles (Halle Orchestra, Manchester Camerata, Williams Fairey Brass Band, Andy Prior Orchestra), and media clients (BBC and Independent Radio, Granada, Yorkshire and Channel 4 Television companies). He was awarded the Marty Paitch Arranging Prize for his Big Band arrangement of Prokofiev's *Troika* in the 1990 BBC Radio Big Band Competition.

Dewhurst's master's degree thesis, which examined the works of jazz composer Gil Evans (De Montfort University, 1994), has been well received internationally, and he is regularly invited to give talks on jazz arranging, including guest lectures at the University of York (1996), City of Leeds College of Music (1995/1996), and Orchestre Nationale de Jazz, Paris (1996).

His recent works for brass band are exclusively published by Gramercy Music and are succeeding in establishing his growing reputation as a writer of quality in this field. *Panache* (1995) and *Brasilia* (1996) were commissioned and recorded by the top brass soloists Steven Mead (euphonium) and Brett Baker (trombone), respectively, while other works, including his lyrical reading of *Bess You Is My Woman Now* (1995), arranged for Williams Fairey's *Listen to the Band* recording session, demonstrate his subtle approach to scoring in the context of the full band feature. His work is noted for its keen sense of color and fluency of style and he applies his knowledge of jazz and popular idioms to the potentials of the brass band in new and exciting ways.

Dewhurst is also senior lecturer in popular music at the University of Salford, head of popular music, and course tutor (BAPMR). He has had a long and distinguished career covering recording and high-quality research as well as being a world-respected jazz player.

William Dougherty (1956–)
William P. Dougherty is the Ellis and Nelle Levitt Professor of Music Theory and Composition at Drake University in Des Moines, Iowa. He teaches courses in music theory, composition, and MIDI techniques. His research is directed toward developing a viable semeiotic of music and he has published numerous articles on musical semeiotic, Beethoven, and music and text relationships in the art song. In addition, Dougherty has presented over twenty papers at national and international conferences. He is currently working on a book that details a semeiotic approach

to the settings of songs from Goethe's *Wilhelm Meisters Lehrjahre*. He has twice been awarded National Endowment for the Humanities Summer Fellowships to pursue his research. Also active as a composer, Dougherty has been commissioned to write compositions for the Brass Band of Columbus, the Fine Arts Trio, the Pioneer String Quartet, the Sheboygan Symphony Orchestra, the New Hampshire Music Festival Orchestra, the New England Symphony Orchestra, the New England Wind Ensemble, and several chamber groups and soloists. In 2002, he was commissioned by the Iowa Music Teacher's National Association, and the resulting composition placed second in the MTNA national competition. Dougherty's orchestral and band works are published by MMB Publishers and much of his solo and chamber music is published by Heilman Music. He received his bachelor's degree in music education from Illinois Wesleyan University and his MA and PhD in music theory from Ohio State University. He is currently serving as associate dean for the College of Arts and Sciences.

Domenico Dragonetti (1763–1846)

Dragonetti, an Italian double-bass player, was born in Venice on April 7, 1763. Having become famous as a performer on his instrument, he went to London in 1794, where his playing created a furor. He was the friend of Haydn and of Beethoven, and a well-known character in his day. He died in London on April 16, 1846.

Martin Ellerby

Martin Ellerby is a composer of international standing, whose works have been performed, broadcast, and recorded to critical acclaim across Europe, Asia, and the United States. His catalogue comprises compositions spanning a diverse range of media, including orchestral, choral, concert band, brass band, ballet, instrumental, and chamber, together with a substantial number of commercial orchestrations and arrangements. Ellerby's works are published extensively and recorded on over 75 commercial CDs to date. Key performances have included the BBC Promenade Concerts, Leipzig Gewandhaus, Barbican Centre, Royal Albert Hall, South Bank Centre, and many major international festivals, including Edinburgh, Harrogate, Zurich, and Kuhmo Chamber Music (Finland).

He studied composition with Joseph Horovitz and W. S. Lloyd Webber at the Royal College of Music in London and later privately with Wilfred Josephs.

He has held composer-in-residence posts with the Brass Band Berner Oberland in Switzerland,

the National Youth Brass Band of Great Britain, and the Williams Fairey Band. He is a Liveryman member of the Worshipful Company of Musicians and Freeman of the City of London. He has given lectures at all the principal colleges in the UK as well as many guest seminars at universities in the United States.

Eric Ewazen (1954–)

Eric Ewazen, born in 1954 in Cleveland, Ohio, studied under Samuel Adler, Milton Babbitt, Warren Benson, Gunther Schuller, and Joseph Schwantner at the Eastman School of Music (BM, 1976), Tanglewood, and the Juilliard School (MM, 1978, DMA 1980), where he has been a member of the faculty since 1980. He has been vice president of the League-ISCM, composer-in-residence with the St. Luke's Chamber Ensemble and with the International Trombone Association Convention in 1997, and lecturer for the New York Philharmonic's Musical Encounters Series. He has been a member of the faculty of the Juilliard School since 1980.

A recipient of numerous composition awards and prizes, his works have been commissioned and performed by many chamber ensembles and orchestras in the United States and overseas. His music has been heard at festivals such as Tanglewood, Aspen, Caramoor, and the Music Academy of the West. The soloists in performances of his music include members of the New York Philharmonic, Chicago Symphony, San Francisco Symphony, Los Angeles Philharmonic, Cleveland Orchestra, the Metropolitan Opera Orchestra, the Boston Symphony, and the Philadelphia Orchestra.

Juraj Filas (1955–)

Juraj Filas belongs among representatives of the wave of neo-romanticism that has been appearing in the creation of some young Czech composers since the mid-1970s. He studied singing and composition at the Prague Conservatory and composition at the Prague Academy of Arts and Music. M. Komarek and V. Bednar were his teachers of singing, and J. Z. Bartos and J. Pauer his teachers of composition. Although as singer Filas won three titles of laureates at important statewide contests, his interest in composition has prevailed. He graduated from the Academy in 1981 with the symphonic drama *Palpito* in J. Pauer's class; the latter then guided his postgraduate studies. Since the beginning of the 1980s, Filas has won three titles of laureates at important competitions of composers in Czechoslovakia, his compositions becoming a regular event of the Weeks of New Works end concert life in general. Some of them were relayed by Czechoslovak Radio and Television, recorded on Panton and Supraphon gramophone records, and gradually are finding application abroad (Russia, Austria, Britain, the FRG, and Cuba). Filas coached for some time a number of singers and instrumentalists and the ballet ensembles of the National Theatre and Czechoslovak Television; for five years he was a member of the Kuhn Mixed Choir; and since 1985 he has a teacher at the Academy of Arts and Music in Prague and editor of the Supraphon publishing house. The composer expressed his creative orientation as follows: "It is my dream to come close to such impressive and beautiful music as composed by the giants of the past, especially Verdi, Beethoven, Mahler, but through my own means, to form my own manuscript, i.e. a form through which I might impart a human message, to create musical beauty in my own and topical way. For me it is unthinkable to cast away the tradition, developed for centuries by hundreds of composers as the European musical culture."

Michael Forbes (1973–)

Michael Forbes is currently the assistant professor of tuba and euphonium at Illinois State University (ISU), where he also performs with the ISU Faculty Brass Quintet and conducts the Bloomington-Normal Brass Band, the University Brass Ensemble, and the Normal Euphonium Tuba Society (NETS). He received his doctor of musical arts degree from the University of Maryland, his master of music degree from the University of Wisconsin, and his bachelor of music degree from Pennsylvania State University. Through an exchange program, he also spent a year in Manchester, England, where he studied at the University of Manchester and the Royal Northern College of Music.

Forbes began his career as a tubist with The United States Army Band "Pershing's Own" in Washington, D.C., where he was an active soloist and chamber musician as well as the founder and conductor of The United States Army Brass Tentet. Forbes has also appeared as tubist and soloist with many American orchestras, including the Illinois, Cedar Rapids, Rockford, Alexandria, Aspen, Chautauqua, and Hot Springs Orchestras. He has also served on the faculties of Mary Washington College, Columbia Union College, Frederick Community College, and the Blue Lake Fine Arts Camp. Currently, he is also an associate editor with the *ITEA Journal*.

A regularly commissioned composer and arranger, Forbes's works have been performed by a host of university wind, brass, and tuba/euphonium ensembles as well as by The United States Army Concert and Brass Bands. His works have also been selected for numerous international recordings and competitions (including a works for the International Tuba-Euphonium Conference Quartet Competitions). Editions BIM publishes his original compositions, while his many arrangements for low brass can be found in the catalogs of Music Express, Bernel Music, and the Tuba-Euphonium Press.

Aldo Rafael Forte (1953–)

Aldo Rafael Forte is an internationally renowned composer with many published and recorded works to his credit. Forte is currently composer/ arranger with the United States Air Force Heritage of America Band at Langley Air Force Base in Virginia and adjunct professor of composition at Christopher Newport University in Newport News, Virginia.

Born in Havana, Cuba, in 1953, Forte came to the United States at the age of nine and is now a U.S. citizen. He spent his formative years in Huntsville, Alabama, and was introduced to music at an early age by his father, a professor of mathematics and amateur classical guitarist and guitar maker. Forte credits the encouragement of both of his parents, Dr. Aldo Forte and Maria Forte, with his active pursuit of composition.

Forte has studied composition with Ross Lee Finney, William Presser, and Robert Jager. He holds music degrees from Tennessee Technological University and the University of Southern Mississippi.

Forte has composed a variety of works ranging from chamber pieces to major compositions for band and orchestra. He has received commissions from many musical ensembles. His works have been performed and/or recorded by such diverse groups as the Southwest German Radio Orchestra, the Filharmonie Bohuslav Martinu Orchestra of the Czech Republic, the Alabama Symphony Orchestra, and the North Carolina Symphony Orchestra, and by many bands including those of the University of Georgia, Indiana University of Pennsylvania, the University of North Texas, Kansas State University, the Piedmont Wind Symphony of Winston-Salem, North Carolina, the Mobile Symphonic Pops Band, the University of Alabama, the United States Air Force Heritage of America Band, and "The President's Own" United States Marine Band. Internationally his band works have been performed by the National Dutch Youth Wind Band, the Militarmusik der Voralberg of Bregenz, Austria, the Wind Ensemble of the Queensland Conservatorium in South

Bank, Queensland, Australia, and the University Wind Orchestra of the Western Australia Academy of Performing Arts in Perth. His music has been heard at such places as Carnegie Recital Hall in New York City, the John F. Kennedy Center for the Performing Arts in Washington, D.C., and at numerous music conventions including MEA conventions in Kansas, Maryland, Virginia, North Carolina, Tennessee, Kentucky, and New Mexico, several CBDNA/NBA regional conventions, and at the Mid-West International Band and Orchestra Clinic in Chicago, Illinois. Several All State Bands including those of Texas, Tennessee, New Mexico, Minnesota, and Kentucky have performed his music. Forte is active as a clinician and conductor of his music.

Arthur Frackenpohl (1924–)

Arthur Frackenpohl was born in New Jersey in 1924. He holds degrees from the Eastman School of Music (BA, MA) and McGill University (DM). He also studied composition at Tanglewood in 1948 with Darius Milhaud and with Nadia Boulanger at Fontainebleau in 1950, where he was awarded the first prize in composition.

In 1949 Frackenpohl joined the faculty of the Crane School of Music at the State University of New York (SUNY) at Potsdam. From 1961 until his recent retirement, he served there as professor of music and coordinator of keyboard courses, receiving the SUNY Chancellor's Award for Excellence in Teaching in 1982.

He has been awarded numerous grants and fellowships for composition over the years, including one from the Ford Foundation in 1959–1960 to serve as composer-in-residence for the Hempstead (New York) Public Schools.

Frackenpohl has published over 250 instrumental and choral compositions and arrangements, various recordings, and one book, *Harmonization at the Piano,* for keyboard harmony text.

Gregory Fritze

Gregory Fritze is a prizewinning composer and Fulbright Scholar as well as an active performer, conductor, and educator. He is chair of the composition department at Berklee College of Music, where he has served on the faculty since 1979. He was the conductor for the Berklee Concert Wind Ensemble for fifteen years (1983–1998), an ensemble that specialized in new compositions for winds. He has conducted performances of more than thirty premieres. Always being an advocate for new music, in 1983 Fritze initiated an annual Berklee student composition competition to encourage young composers to write for the band medium, which has yielded more

than a hundred new compositions over the last fifteen years.

He has written over forty compositions for orchestra, band, chamber music, and soloists. His recent composition awards include the 1998 IBLA Grand Prize in Composition by the European International Competition in Ibla, Sicily; a grant from the Massachusetts Council for the Arts in 1997 for his composition for band, *La Tomatina*; Menzione d'Onore (highest award given) of the Mario Bernardo Angelo-Comneno International Music Competition by the Accademia Angelica Costantiniana Arti E Scienze (Rome, Italy) in 1997 for *String Quartet*; eleven awards from the Standard Awards Panel of ASCAP; grants from Meet the Composer; Walt Disney Fellowship; and other composition awards. His *Twenty Characteristic Etudes for Tuba* won first prize in the 1991 Composition Competition sponsored by TUBA. He has been commissioned by many orchestras, concert bands, chamber ensembles, and soloists in the New England area and throughout the world. His compositions include works published by SeeSaw Music, Minuteman Music, TUBA Press, and Musica Nova; they have been performed extensively throughout the world. He is recorded as composer and/or performer on CRI Records, Crystal Records, Mark Records, and others.

Fritze has been a guest lecturer, conductor, and performer at many colleges, universities, and music festivals in the United States, Canada, Japan, and Europe, including Convegno Bandistico Cantonale in Mendrisio, Switzerland; Sapporo (Japan) Music Festival; Musicfest Canada Ottawa; Musicfest Canada Calgary; Musicfest Canada Winnipeg; Musicfest Canada Toronto; Musicfest Canada Vancouver; Massachusetts Instrumental Conductors Association; Rhode Island Music Educators Association; Pennsylvania Music Educators Association; American Band Association; the Mozart Festival (Burlington, Vermont); New York Brass Conference; New England Tuba Festivals; Berklee College of Music High School Jazz Festivals; and others.

In addition to being principal tubist with the Rhode Island Philharmonic Orchestra, he is a member of the Cambridge Symphonic Brass Ensemble and the Colonial Tuba Quartet and performs regularly with various ensembles around New England. Fritze has premiered many works for tuba, including several written especially for him such as the *Concerto for Tuba and Band* by John Bavicchi and the *Concerto for Tuba and Jazz Ensemble* by Ken Pullig. Fritze was born in Allentown, Pennsylvania, in 1954 and received his bachelor's degree in composition from the Boston Conservatory, where he studied composition with John Adams and tuba with Chester Roberts. He received his master's degree in composition from Indiana University in Bloomington, where he studied composition with Thomas Beversdorf, John Eaton, and Fred Fox, and tuba with Harvey Phillips.

James Garrett (1937–1998)

James Allen Garrett received his BSE from Tennessee Tech University in 1959 and his MM from Northwestern University in 1965 and did postgraduate work at Indiana University during 1967–1968, where he studied tuba with Bill Bell and composition with Thomas Beversdorf.

As a composer, Garrett was at the right place at the right time when he was needed the most. During the infancy of the college tuba ensemble, he repeatedly answered the call for compositions and arrangements for his friend Winston Morris and the Tennessee Tech Tuba Ensemble. Garrett had almost thirty compositions and arrangements published for tuba ensemble and many others unpublished. From simple three-part arrangements of folk songs playable by a massed ensemble of 100, to an opera for soloists, choir, and tuba ensemble, Garrett's music not only worked harmonically and technically but is just plain fun. His *Fanfare,* published in 1966, was performed at the recent ITEC in Minneapolis, Minnesota. His compositions have been recorded by the Tennessee Tuba Ensemble, the United States Armed Forces Tuba-Euphonium Ensemble, and the British Tuba Quartet. His arrangements of *Londonderry Air, Wabash Cannonball,* and *Sweet Georgia Brown* have been a staple of tuba-euphonium ensemble repertoire for over 25 years.

One of Garrett's more imaginative projects was the creation of Dr. Pierre Garbage. Compositions by the enigmatic Pierre often contained some sort of musical surprise or use of humor and were written for instruments and voices not normally associated with "traditional serious" music. Pierre's first composition was *Songs in the Fight against Rum (Songs of Might to Cheer the Fight against the Blight of Liquordom).* This is a large work written for two euphoniums, two tubas, tenor solo, barbershop quartet, mixed chorus, female speaker, male speaker, country band, chimes, collection takers, and three clarinets. The craziness of this work is a testament to Jim Garrett's creativity and humor.

Thom Ritter George (1942–)

Thom Ritter George discovered his great interest in music, particularly composition and orchestral conducting, as a boy growing up in Detroit, Michigan. He wrote his first composition when he was ten years old and conducted his first orchestral concert at the age of seventeen. During his high school years, he was a composition student of Harold Laudenslager, a pupil of Paul Hindemith.

George entered the Eastman School of Music in 1960 and studied composition with Thomas Canning, Louis Mennini, Wayne Barlow, John LaMontaine, and Bernard Rogers. George's first published works date from this period of conservatory study and include his *Sonata for Baritone Horn and Piano, Concerto for Bass Trombone and Orchestra, Hymn and Toccata* (band), *Brass Quintet No. 1, Proclamations* (band), and *Concerto for Flute and Orchestra.*

After earning bachelor's (1964) and master's (1968) degrees from the Eastman School, George accepted an appointment as composer/arranger for the United States Navy Band in Washington, D.C. During his military service, he also conducted the Navy Band in performances both in Washington and on tour. He was a frequent performer at the White House during the administration of President Lyndon B. Johnson. George's Washington years marked the creation of his *Western Overture* (band), *Sinfonietta* (orchestra), *Six Canonic Sonatas, Sonata for Clarinet and Piano,* and *Sonata for Flute and Piano.* These last two titles were additions to his series of sonatas written for every orchestra instrument.

As a composer, George has won the Edward B. Benjamin Prize, two Howard Hanson Awards, and the Seventh Sigvald Thompson Award, and has received annual awards from ASCAP since 1965 for his contributions to American music. He has composed more than 350 works, many of which are recorded. His compositions are published by Boosey & Hawkes, G. Schirmer, Southern Music Company, Accura Music, Shawnee Press, and TUBA Press.

David R. Gillingham (1947–)

David Gillingham earned bachelor's and master's degrees in instrumental music education from the University of Wisconsin–Oshkosh and a PhD in music theory/composition from Michigan State University. Gillingham has an international reputation for the works he has written for band and percussion. Many of these works are now considered standards in the repertoire. His commissioning schedule dates well into the first decade of the twenty-first century. His numerous awards include the 1981 DeMoulin Award for *Concerto for Bass Trombone and Wind Ensemble* and the 1990 International Barlow Competition (Brigham Young University) for *Heroes, Lost and Fallen.*

Gillingham's works have been recorded by Klavier, Sony, and Summit and Centaur. His works are regularly performed by nationally recognized ensembles including the Prague Radio Orchestra, Cincinnati Conservatory of Music Wind Ensemble, the University of Georgia Bands, North Texas University Wind Ensemble, Michigan State University Wind Ensemble, Oklahoma State Wind Ensemble, University of Oklahoma Wind Ensemble, Florida State Wind Ensemble, University of Florida (Miami) Wind Ensemble, University of Illinois Symphonic Band, Illinois State Wind Symphony, University of Minnesota Wind Ensemble, Indiana University Wind Ensemble, and the University of Wisconsin Wind Ensemble. Nationally known artists Fred Mills (Canadian Brass), Randall Hawes (Detroit Symphony), and Charles Vernon (Chicago Symphony Orchestra) have performed works by Gillingham. Over sixty of his works for band, choir, percussion, chamber ensembles, and solo instruments are published by C. Alan, Hal Leonard, Southern Music, Music for Percussion, Carl Fischer, MMB, TUBA, I.T.A., and Dorn. Gillingham is a professor of music at Central Michigan University and the recipient of an Excellence in Teaching Award (1990), a Summer Fellowship (1991), a research professorship (1995), and, recently, the President's Research Investment Fund grant for his co-authorship of a proposal to establish an International Center for New Music at Central Michigan University. He is a member of the Society of Composers International and ASCAP and the recipient of the ASCAP Standard Award for Composers of Concert Music from 1996 to 2002.

Vinko Globokar (1934–)

Vinko Globokar was born on July 7, 1934, in a Slovene immigrant family living in Anderny in France. From the age of thirteen to the age of twenty he lived in Ljubljana, where he finished secondary music school and played in the dance orchestra led by one of the giants of Slovene popular music, the composer and conductor Bojan Adamič. In 1955 Globokar received a scholarship and continued his studies at the Paris Conservatoire, where he studied trombone under Professor Andre Lafoss. He graduated in trombone and chamber music and then studied composing and conducting with René Leibowitz.

John Golland (1942–1993)

John Golland was born in Ashton-under-Lyne, UK, on September 14, 1942. Golland was an only child who, after a difficult birth, suffered problems

with his sight until the age of 26, along with other physical disabilities.

At the age of two he was found playing nursery rhymes on his maternal grandmother's piano, and his parents bought their own piano when Golland was aged four, learning with Peggy Mayers outside school. He was educated at St. Mary's Catholic Primary School, Dukinfield, moving to de la Salle College, Salford, on a scholarship at age eleven. At de la Salle he was taught piano by the school music master and began to learn the violin and recorder; he also began to compose and to arrange hymns for the annual speech days. In 1960 he attended teacher training college in Oldham (also de la Salle), beginning his first job as a music teacher at St. Anselm's School, Oldham, in 1964. He also studied part-time at the Royal Manchester College of Music, with Thomas Pitfield (for composition) and Marjorie Clemans (for piano).

In his twenties Golland joined the Stalybridge Band, learning the euphonium; thereafter he regularly wrote and arranged for both brass band and wind band. He conducted the Boarshurst Band and was later the music master of the West Hill Band and Choir (Mossley Brow). In 1970 he became musical director of the Adamson Military Band and turned from full-time school teaching to composition. He later also directed the City of Chester Band, Fodens, James Shepherd Versatile Brass, Dobcross Band, and the W. Harrison Transport Rockingham Band. He also conducted frequently in Switzerland from 1975 onward, and many of his works were written for bands there.

Initially Golland taught in schools full time, but from 1970 concentrated on composition and his work with brass bands. His best-known band works include *Sounds, Atmospheres, Fives and Threes, Rêves d'Enfant*, and *Concertos* for euphonium (two) and flugelhorn. In addition he wrote and arranged incidental music for television (*Dear Ladies*) and for young people, including a children's opera, *The Selfish Giant*. Compositions for other instruments include recorder, orchestra (including three *Sinfoniettas*), and wind quintet. He made over 150 arrangements, ranging from hymn tunes to popular classics. He also wrote regularly for the *British Mouthpiece* about various aspects of the band. In the late 1980s he resumed teaching in the department of Media Studies at Salford College of Technology. Golland died April 14, 1993, after a long illness.

Adam Gorb (1958–)

Adam Gorb was born in 1958 and started composing at the age of ten. At fifteen he wrote a set of piano pieces—*A Pianist's Alphabet*—a selection of which were performed on BBC Radio 3 in 1976. In 1977 he went to Cambridge University to study music, where his teachers included Hugh Wood and Robin Holloway. After graduating in 1980 he divided his time between composition and working as a musician in the theatre. In 1987 he met Paul Patterson and started studying with him privately. He began to devote more time to composition and in 1991 started the advanced composition course at the Royal Academy of Music, gaining a master of music degree in 1992 and graduating in 1993 with the highest honors, including the Principal's Prize.

Compositions include a viola concerto for Martin Outram and the *Docklands Sinfonietta,* given its first performance in 1992; *Metropolis* for wind band, which has won several prizes including the Walter Beeler Memorial Prize in the United States in 1994 and is available on CD; *Prelude, Interlude and Postlude* for piano, which won the Purcell Composition Prize in 1995; *Kol Simcha,* a ballet given over fifty performances by the Rambert dance company; a violin sonata premiered at the Spitalfields Festival in 1996; *Awayday* for wind band, which has had over 100 performances since its premiere in 1996; *Reconciliation* for clarinet and piano, commissioned for the Park Lane Young Artists at the Purcell Room in January 1998; a percussion concerto, given its first performance by Evelyn Glennie and the Royal Northern College of Music Wind Ensemble in 1998; and, most recently, a clarinet concerto for Nicholas Cox and the Royal Liverpool Philharmonic Orchestra and a work for the Royal Northern College Brass Band.

Peter Graham

Peter Graham was born in Lanarkshire, Scotland, where his introduction to music came through brass and piano lessons from his parents. He read music at Edinburgh University, graduating in 1980. During this period he came into contact with Ray Steadman-Allen and Edward Gregson, both of whom encouraged his early efforts at composition. He later undertook post-graduate compositional studies with Edward Gregson at Goldsmiths College, University of London, and holds a PhD in composition.

From 1983 until 1986 he was resident in New York City, where he worked as a freelance composer/arranger and as a publications editor with the S.A. Music Bureau. Since his return to the UK he has worked regularly as an arranger for BBC Television and Radio and has specialized in composition for the British-style brass band. Since the publication of *Dimensions* (1983), he has carved out a niche as an outstanding arranger for brass band and a leading figure among contemporary band composers. His original compositions, which include *The Essence of Time, Montage,* and *On Alderley Edge,* are performed worldwide and have been selected as test pieces for National Championships in Australia, New Zealand, North America, and across Europe.

His music for wind and concert band has been recorded and performed by many of the world's leading ensembles, including the Tokyo Kosei Wind Orchestra and the Royal Norwegian Navy Band. *Harrison's Dream,* commissioned by The United States Air Force Band, won the 2002 ABA/Ostwald Award for composition. Commissioned by BMG/RCA Red Label to arrange and compose an album of xylophone music for virtuoso Evelyn Glennie, the resulting recording was nominated as Best Classical Crossover Album at the 1999 Grammy Awards held in Los Angeles.

He is published principally by Rosehill Music and Boosey & Hawkes, and since 1994 by his Gramercy Music, a company he formed with his wife, Janey, which specializes in the publication of brass, wind, and vocal music. Graham is professor of composition at the University of Salford, Greater Manchester, and has held various posts with some of the UK's finest bands, including a seven-year term as music associate/conductor with the famous Black Dyke Brass Band. He is currently composer-in-residence with Her Majesty's Coldstream Guards Band, the first civilian in the band's history to hold this appointment.

James Grant (1954–)

The music of composer James Grant is known by musicians and audiences for its colorful language, honed craft, and immediacy. In recent years, Grant's music has been performed throughout the United States and in Australia, Azerbaijan, Brazil, Canada, the Czech Republic, England, Finland, Japan, Mexico, and New Zealand by groups ranging from youth orchestras, to community choruses, to professional contemporary chamber ensembles, ballet companies, and orchestras. In addition to receiving first prize in the 1998 Louisville Orchestra competition for new orchestral music, Grant was one of five American composers to win the 2002 Aaron Copland Award.

After completing the DMA degree in composition from Cornell University in 1988, Grant was assistant professor of music at Middlebury College in Vermont. In 1992, Grant left academe to compose and lecture full-time and from 1993 to 1996 served as composer-in-residence to the Fairfax Symphony Orchestra in Fairfax, Virginia. Currently, Grant serves as composer-in-residence to the Bay-Atlantic Symphony in Bridgeton, New Jersey. In May of 2003, his 55-minute work for baritone solo, chorus, and large orchestra based on the prose, poetry, and correspondence of Walt Whitman, *Such Was the War,* was premiered to critical acclaim at the Kennedy Center by the Choral Arts Society of Washington.

Donald Grantham (1947–)

Composer Donald Grantham is the recipient of numerous awards and prizes in composition, including the Prix Lili Boulanger, the Nissim/ ASCAP Orchestral Composition Prize, first prize in the Concordia Chamber Symphony's Awards to American Composers, a Guggenheim Fellowship, three grants from the National Endowment for the Arts, three first prizes in the NBA/William Revelli Competition, two first prizes in the ABA/ Ostwald Competition, and first prize in the National Opera Association's Biennial Composition Competition. His music has been praised for its "elegance, sensitivity, lucidity of thought, clarity of expression and fine lyricism" in a citation awarded by the American Academy and Institute of Arts and Letters. In recent years his works have been performed by the orchestras of Cleveland, Dallas, and Atlanta and the American Composers Orchestra, among many others, and he has fulfilled commissions in media from solo instruments to opera. His music is published by Piquant Press, Peer-Southern, E. C. Schirmer, and Mark Foster, and a number of his works have been commercially recorded. The composer resides in Austin, Texas, and is professor of composition at the University of Texas at Austin. With Kent Kennan he is co-author of *The Technique of Orchestration* (Prentice-Hall).

Lars Graugaard (1957–)

Lars Graugaard, composer and flautist, received a diploma in flute playing from the Royal Danish Academy of Music and is self-taught as a composer. Graugaard started playing improvised music in the late 1970s and became involved in composing a few years later. In the late 1980s he became involved in digital media, and today he has composed more than 130 pieces in all genres with performances in Europe, Asia, Australia, and the Americas, as well as incidental work for stage and cinema. He has recorded several CDs as composer and as flautist for dacapo/Marco Polo, Tutl, Classico, Centaur, EMI, SONY Classical, CBS, and others.

He was composer-in-residence with Odense Symphony Orchestra 1997–1999; artistic director of the ISCM World Music Days 1996, Copenhagen, September 12–17, 1996; member of the executive committee of the International Society for Contemporary Music (Amsterdam) since 1999; and associate professor of Interactive Music at Carl-Nielsen Academy of Music (Denmark) since 1999, where he has developed a three-year course in interactive media for performing musicians.

Edward Gregson (1945–)

Edward Gregson is one of Britain's most versatile composers. His music has been performed, broadcast, and recorded worldwide. He studied composition and piano at the Royal Academy of Music (1963–1967), winning five prizes for composition. Early success was achieved with his *Brass Quintet,* which was broadcast and recorded, as well as being a finalist piece in the 1968 BBC Young Composer's Competition. This was followed by many commissions from, among others, the English Chamber Orchestra and the York Festival. Since then he has written orchestral, chamber, instrumental, and choral music, as well as music for theatre, film, and television.

His concerti for wind instruments are established repertoire in many countries (the *Trumpet Concerto of 1983* has received performances from the Detroit and Louisville Orchestras in the United States, as well as the Rotterdam Philharmonic and BBC Scottish Symphony Orchestras). Other major orchestral works include *Music for Chamber Orchestra* (1968), *Metamorphoses* (1979), *Contrasts* (1983), and *Blazon* (1992). His output also includes two brass quintets, an *Oboe Sonata* (1965), *Piano Sonata* (1983), *Sonata for Four Trombones* (1984), and three choral works: *In the Beginning* (1966), *Missa Brevis Pacem* (1987), and *Make a Joyful Noise* (1988), as well as many works for brass and wind bands. He has recently completed commissions for the Royal Liverpool Philharmonic and Bournemouth Symphony Orchestras, as well as a *Clarinet Concerto* for Michael Collins and the BBC Philharmonic, premiered in Manchester in 1994.

His music for theatre includes commissions for the *York Cycle of Mystery Plays* (1976), *The Plantagenets* (1988), and *Henry IV* Parts I and II (1990), which were both commissioned by the Royal Shakespeare Company for performances in Stratford-upon-Avon and London. In 1988, he was nominated for an Ivor Novello award for his title music for BBC Television's Young Musician of the Year programs, for which he has also regularly acted as a jury member.

Walter Hartley (1927–)

Walter S. Hartley (born February 21, 1927, Washington, D.C.) began composing at age five and became seriously dedicated to it at sixteen. All his college degrees are from the Eastman School of Music of the University of Rochester. He received his PhD in composition there in 1953. Some of his teachers were Burrill Phillips, Thomas Canning, Herbert Elwell, Bernard Rogers, Howard Hanson, and Dante Fiorillo.

At present he is professor emeritus of music and composer-in-residence at State University College, Fredonia, New York. He also taught piano, theory, and composition at the National Music Camp (now Interlochen Arts Camp) at Interlochen, Michigan, from 1956 to 1964.

His list of acknowledged works now numbers over 200, dating from 1949 on, and most of these are published. He is a member of ASCAP, from which he has received an annual award for achievement in serious music since 1962.

His music has been performed by many ensembles, including the National Symphony Orchestra, Oklahoma City Symphony, Eastman-Rochester Orchestra, and the Eastman Wind Ensemble. His *Chamber Symphony* of 1954 was commissioned by the Koussevitsky Foundation, his *Concert Overture* for orchestra received a prize from the National Symphony Orchestra in 1955, and his *Sinfonia No. 3* for brass choir won the 1964 Conn Award. Since then he has received many commissions from college and high school musical organizations. A recently published orchestral work, *Symphony No. 3,* was commissioned by the Greater Buffalo (New York) Youth Orchestra; several band works were commissioned by U.S. service bands. There have been many recordings.

John Hartmann (1830–1897)

John Hartmann, son of a peasant farmer, was born at Auleben, Prussia, on October 24, 1830. He was a composer and bandmaster throughout Europe. Hartmann died in Liverpool in 1897.

William H. Hill (1930–)

William H. Hill was born in 1930 in Paris, Texas. He received his BA from the University of Northern Colorado in 1952. He then continued to study at Northern Colorado, earning a BM degree in 1954 and an MA degree in 1955. While pursuing his studies, he was a member of the Greeley, Colorado, Philharmonic Orchestra and the 529th United States Air Force Band.

In 1955, Hill became woodwind instructor and assistant director of bands at East Texas State University. He was later appointed director of bands. He left East Texas State in 1963 to pursue his doctoral degree at the University of California at Los Angeles. From 1966 to 1969, he taught

saxophone and arranging techniques and conducted several bands at Arizona State University. Hill then went on to teach at California State University from 1972 to 1982. There he was chair of the instrumental music department.

Hill has performed, conducted, and directed clinics in the United States and in England, France, Switzerland, Italy, and Japan. He is the subject of a PhD dissertation by Robert Morsch of the University of Iowa, entitled "William H. Hill: A Man and His Music."

Hill has received many honors, including the Outstanding Alumni Award from the University of Northern Colorado in 1980, ASCAP Serious Music Awards from 1982–1985, and the Phi Mu Alpha Alpheus Award in 1977. He holds memberships in the American Bandmasters Association, the College Band Directors National Association, the American Society of Music Arrangers, the American Federation of Musicians, Music Educator's National Conference, Kappa Kappa Psi, Phi Mu Alpha Symphonia, Phi Delta Kappa, and Phi Beta Mu.

William Himes (1949–)

Himes earned his bachelor and master of music degrees from the University of Michigan. For five years he taught instrumental music in the public schools of Flint, Michigan, where he was also adjunct lecturer in low brass at the University of Michigan–Flint. Himes continues to be in demand as conductor, composer, lecturer, clinician, and euphonium soloist and has appeared throughout the United States, Canada, Australia, New Zealand, Sweden, Denmark, Norway, and the United Kingdom.

Since 1977, Himes has been music director of the Salvation Army's Central Territory, which encompasses the eleven midwestern states. In this capacity he is also conductor of the Chicago Staff Band, an internationally recognized ensemble that he has led on successful tours of Panama, Mexico, Chile, Canada, Singapore, the Philippines, Hong Kong, England, and Australia. The band's 1987 tour of England included performances in the Royal Albert Hall and Buckingham Palace, where Himes was privileged to meet Queen Elizabeth.

Merle Hogg

Merle E. Hogg was born in Lincoln, Kansas, where he attended the public schools. He completed his undergraduate studies at Emporia State University following service in the Navy. After two years teaching public school music, he began graduate study at the University of Iowa, where he earned the MA, MFA, and PhD degrees. During the summer of 1960 he attended the Ecoles d´Art Americaines at Fontainebleau, France, where he studied composition with Nadia Boulanger and trombone with Gabriel Masson and Jean Douay. He was a member of the music faculty at Eastern New Mexico University for nine years and from 1962 to 1992 was a member of the music department faculty at San Diego State University, where he is now professor emeritus and adjunct professor. He is a former member of the San Diego Symphony Orchestra and the San Diego Opera Orchestra.

Joseph Horovitz (1926–)

Joseph Horovitz was born in Vienna in 1926 and emigrated to England in 1938. He studied music at New College, Oxford, while acting as an official lecturer in music appreciation to the forces and giving piano recitals in army camps. After taking his BMus and MA degrees, he studied composition with Gordon Jacob at the Royal College of Music, where he won the Farrar Prize, and for a further year with Nadia Boulanger in Paris.

His first post was as music director of the Bristol Old Vic, where he composed, arranged, and conducted the incidental music for two seasons. The Festival of Britain in 1951 brought him to London as conductor of ballet and concerts at the Festival Amphitheatre. He then held positions as conductor to the Ballet Russes, associate director of the Intimate Opera Company, on the music staff at Glyndebourne, and as guest composer at the Tanglewood Festival. He toured extensively in Great Britain and abroad, conducting major London orchestras as well as on the BBC.

In 1959 he won the Commonwealth Medal for Composition and in 1961 a Leverhulme Research Award to work with Philomusica. He has also won two Ivor Novello Awards. Since 1961 he has taught composition and analysis at the Royal College of Music, where he is now a fellow. From 1969 to 1996 he was an executive council member of the Performing Right Society and president of CISAC's International Council of Composers and Authors of Music from 1981 to 1989. In 1996 he was awarded the Gold Order of Merit of the City of Vienna, and in 2002 the Nino Rota Prize, Italy.

His compositions number sixteen ballets, nine concertos, two one-act operas including *Gentlemen's Island*, and orchestral works including *Fantasia on a Theme of Couperin* (1962) and *Sinfonietta for Light Orchestra* (1971). He has also written several works for brass band, including the *Euphonium Concerto* (1972) and *Concertino Classico* (1985), and also for wind band.

His chamber music includes five string quartets and the often-performed *Sonatina* (1981) for clarinet and piano and the *Music Hall Suite* (1964). His best-known choral compositions are *Horrortorio* (1959), a Hoffnung commission; the award-winning *Captain Noah and His Floating Zoo* (1970); *Summer Sunday* (1975), an ecological cantata; and the oratorio *Samson*.

His activities have extended over a wide range of music, from Son et Lumière productions in England and overseas to scores for theatre, radio, and over seventy TV plays and series.

Hiroshi Hoshina (1936–)

Born in Tokyo in 1936, Hoshina graduated from that city's National University of Fine Arts and Music as a composition major, where his thesis won the Mainichi Music Composition Contest. Aside from his *FuMon* (1987), two additional works have been commissioned for the All Japan Band Contest. In addition, his opera regarding Hiroshima's atomic bomb experience has received worldwide acclaim. Hoshina is a venerable artist of his country; his composition, while traditionally reflective at times, is clearly expressive and visual in contemporary terms. Active as a conductor, clinician, and author, Hoshina is currently professor at Hyogo University of Education.

Alan Hovhaness (1911–2000)

Alan Vaness Chakmakjian was born in the affluent Boston suburb of Somerville, Massachusetts, on March 8, 1911. His father, Haroutiun Vaness Chakmakjian, was an Armenian chemistry professor at Tufts College, and his mother, Madeline Scott, was of Scottish ancestry. Hovhaness's first compositional training was as late as 1932 at Boston's New England Conservatory of Music, under the tutorage of Frederick Converse. By his early twenties (the early 1930s) Hovhaness's music was drawing interest in Boston's music circles. An early musical mentor was Sibelius. The young Hovhaness once attended a Boston concert featuring Sibelius's fourth symphony and commented: "I thought that piece, its great unison melodies, so lonely and original, said everything there was to say . . . and not only about music."

In the mid-1930s Hovhaness wrote music predominantly for small forces. There are several piano works, including one that Rachmaninov played on his concert tours. The 1936 *String Quartet No.1, Op.8* displays a very impressive command of disciplined baroque counterpoint. In particular, the fourth movement treats four contrasting subjects fugally before superimposing all four of them in a virtuosic manner akin to the finale of Mozart's *Jupiter* symphony. With 1937's *Exile Symphony* (now known as *Symphony No.1, Op.17*), the young composer's humanity shone through as he addressed the 1930s persecution of Armenians by the Turks. A significant early success came in 1939 when Leslie Heward, director of music for the BBC in Birmingham, England, conducted three compositions, including the *Exile Symphony*. Heward was very impressed; in a New York interview he considered Hovhaness's music "powerful, virile, and musically very solid; he has guts, sticks to fundamentals . . . he is a genius and will create even greater works."

In 1948 Hovhaness was invited to join the faculty of the Boston Music Conservatory, where he taught for three years while retaining his duties at Boston's Armenian cathedral. His conservatory duties included teaching composition and conducting the student orchestra.

Such regular small successes led to Hovhaness's biggest breakthrough in the mid-1950s. *Symphony No. 2*, entitled *Mysterious Mountain*, was commissioned for Leopold Stokowski's début with the Houston Symphony in October 1955, and brought Hovhaness national exposure and significant mainstream respect. Stokowski introduced *Symphony No. 3* too, a year later at Carnegie Hall.

In 1994, still composing, he remarked, "I don't fear dying because I have so many friends waiting for me on the other side." By 1996 Hovhaness's good health finally began to decline markedly. For the first time in eighty years he was unable to compose. After three years of intensive care, he died in Seattle on June 21, 2000, from a long-term stomach ailment.

Elgar Howarth

Elgar Howarth studied music at Manchester University and the Royal Manchester College of Music, where his first study was composition. His conducting career began in the early 1970s and since then he has appeared regularly with all the leading orchestras of Great Britain, both in the concert hall and in the recording studio. He has appeared at major festivals abroad—mostly in Europe—and toured Japan with the London Sinfonietta, an orchestra he has conducted regularly both in the UK and abroad from the beginning of his career. His operatic achievements cover a wide repertoire and include the world premiere of Ligeti's *Le Grand Macabre* at the Royal Opera in Stockholm, followed by productions of the same work in Hamburg, Paris, and London.

In 1985 he made his debut at Covent Garden with Tippett's *King Priam*, which he later performed with the same company at the Athens Festival. He conducted the world premiere of *Birtwistle's Gawain* at the Royal Opera House, Covent Garden, in May 1991, and the revival in 1994, which has been released by Collins Classics. In 1996 he conducted Henze's *The Prince of Homburg* and Zimmermann's *Die Soldaten*, both at the English National Opera. For his work on these productions he won the 1997 Olivier Award for "Outstanding Achievement in Opera." He retains an interest in composing, especially, as a former trumpet player, for brass instruments. His works are published by Chester Music and Novello and are much recorded, particularly on the Decca label.

Warner Hutchison (1930–)

David Warner Hutchison was born in Denver, Colorado, December 15, 1930. He studied at the Lamont School of Music, University of Denver, Rockmont College, the Sacred Music School at Southwestern Baptist Theological Seminary, and North Texas State University, where he received his PhD in 1971. He studied composition with Roy Harris, Wayne Barlow, Samuel Adler, and Kent Kennan. Dr. Hutchison taught at Houghton College from 1956 to 1958, then at Union University from 1959 to 1966, before coming to New Mexico State University in 1967. He is the recipient of a number of awards and grants including a Ford Foundation and Music Educators National Conference Grant (1967/1968), a MacDowell Colony Fellowship (1973 and 1974), and an ASCAP Standard Award (1972–1984), and was nominated for a Pulitzer Prize in 1971 for *Hornpiece 1 for French Horn and Tape*.

Anthony Iannaccone (1943–)

Anthony Iannaccone studied at the Manhattan School of Music and the Eastman School of Music. His principal teachers were Vittorio Giannini, Aaron Copland, and David Diamond. During the 1960s he supported himself as a part-time teacher (Manhattan School of Music) and orchestral violinist. His catalogue of approximately fifty published works includes three symphonies, as well as smaller works for orchestra, several large works for chorus and orchestra, numerous chamber pieces, a variety of large works for wind ensemble, and several extended a cappella choral compositions.

His music is performed by major orchestras and professional chamber ensembles in the United States and abroad. He is an active conductor of both new music and standard orchestral repertory. In addition to conducting numerous regional and metropolitan orchestras in the United States, he has conducted several European orchestras, including the Bohuslav Martinu Philharmonic, the Bavarian Festival Orchestra, the Janacek Philharmonic, the Moravian Philharmonic, and the Slovak Radio Orchestra. Since 1971, he has taught at Eastern Michigan University, where he conducts the Collegium Musicum in orchestral and choral music of the late eighteenth century.

Brian Israel (1951–1986)
Brian Israel was born in New York City in 1951 and received advanced degrees from Cornell University. His teachers included Karel Husa, Ulysses Kay, Burrill Phillips, Robert Palmer, and Lawrence Widdoes. Israel taught music composition, theory, and history at Syracuse University until his untimely death from leukemia at age 35. During his short career, Israel earned many prizes and commissions for his compositions.

Yasuhide Ito (1960–)
Yasuhide Ito was born in Hamamatsu, Shizuoka Prefecture, on December 7, 1960. He started to take piano lessons in his childhood and began studies of composition in his high school days. His first band composition, *On the March* (1978; published by TRN) was written when he was in his third year of high school. In 1979, he went on to Tokyo University of Fine Arts and Music, majoring in composition, and wrote his graduate work in 1986. Ito's musical talent has been widely recognized since he won prizes at the Shizuoka Music Competition (piano, first prize, 1980), Japan Music Competition (composition, third prize, 1982), the Competition for Saxophone Music (1987), and the Band-masters Academic Society of Japan (the Academy Prize, 1994). In 1987, his *Festal Scenes* saw its U.S. premiere, with Ito himself conducting at the ABA-JBA joint convention, held in Tennessee (*Festal Scenes* is published by TRN).

His work *Gloriosa (Gururiyoza)* for band (1990) has become one of the most frequently played repertories in the world. He has composed 38 band works, among which are *The Symphony* (1990) and *Melodies for Wind Ensemble* (1995), both commissioned by Tokyo Kosei Wind Orchestra. Ito's lectures about Japanese band music at WASBE in 1995 (Hamamatsu) and 1997 (Austria) have had a great influence on the band world. Besides his composition career, Ito is well known as an author and translator. He has written *Kangakki no Meikyoku Meienso (The Masterpieces*

and Great Performances of Wind Instruments) and translated Frank Erickson's *Arranging for the Concert Band*.

Gordon Jacob (1895–1984)
Gordon Jacob, in common with the generation of British composers that includes Vaughan Williams, Ireland, Howells, Bax, and so on, studied with Charles Villiers Stanford; however, any resemblance between his music and that of those composers ends there. Far from the lush, overt romanticism of his elders, his writing is more simple and sparse, inspired partly by baroque and classical models (some of the works under his name are in fact arrangements of baroque music), sometimes angular and dissonant but never inaccessible. He summed up his ethos of composing in this statement: "I think the question of communication is important, because one never wants to write down to an audience, but at the same time I personally feel repelled by the intellectual snobbery of some progressive artists . . . the day that melody is discarded altogether, you may as well pack up music."

Jacob had a special affinity for wind instruments, for which he composed a large body of concerti and chamber music, including the *Trio* for clarinet, viola, and piano, written in 1969. These works demonstrate deep knowledge of instrumental technique, also evident in his authoritative textbooks on composing and orchestral writing.

Robert Jager (1939–)
Robert Jager was born in Binghamton, New York, and is a graduate of the University of Michigan. He served four years in the United States Navy as the staff arranger and composer at the Armed Forces School of Music. Jager is now retired and is professor emeritus at Tennessee Technological University in Cookeville, Tennessee. Jager's credits comprise over 120 published works for band, orchestra, chorus, and various chamber combinations. He has received commissions from some of the finest musical organizations in the world, including the Tokyo Kosei Wind Orchestra; the Republic of China Band Association; the Minot (North Dakota) Symphony Orchestra; the Michigan State University Children's Chorus; the Cumberland Children's Chorus; the universities of Arkansas, Butler, Illinois, Michigan, Michigan State, Nebraska, and Nebraska Wesleyan; Wright State University; the University of Dayton; Purdue; the Tennessee Arts Commission; and all five of the Washington-based military bands: Air Force, Army, Army Field Band, Marines, and

Navy. In addition, he has received grants from Meet the Composer, the Tennessee Arts Commission, and the Margaret Fairbank Jory Copying Assistance Program of the American Music Center.

He has conducted and lectured throughout the United States, Canada, Europe, Japan, and the Republic of China. Additionally, his music has been performed by the National Symphony Orchestra of Washington, D.C., the Nashville (Tennessee) Symphony, the Charlotte (North Carolina) Symphony, the New England Chamber Orchestra, the Oregon Mozart Players, the Bryan Symphony Orchestra of Tennessee, the Minot (North Dakota) Symphony, the Virginia Symphony Orchestra of Norfolk, and the Omsk Philharmonic in Russia.

Jager has received many awards for his compositions, including being the only three-time winner of the American Bandmasters Association Ostwald Award. In addition, he has twice received the Roth Award of the National School Orchestra Association, the Kappa Kappa Psi Distinguished Service to Music Medal in the area of composition, the Friends of Harvey Gaul bicentennial competition, the American School Band Association's Volkwein Award, and, in 2000, his *Dialogues for Two Pianos* won the keyboard category competition in the Delius Competition sponsored by the Delius Association of Florida and Jacksonville University. In 1986, he received a MacDowell Colony Fellowship to compose at the colony in Peterborough, New Hampshire. In 1996, he received the Individual Artist Fellowship in Composition from the Tennessee Arts Commission, and in 1998, was selected to receive Tennessee Tech University's highest faculty award, the Caplenor Faculty Research Award. He is the first faculty member in the art to receive this award.

Axel Jorgensen (1924–)

Axel Borup-Jorgensen grew up in Sweden. He studied piano and instrumentation at the Royal Danish Academy of Music from 1946 to 1950. As an composer he considers himself an autodidact. He has often taken his inspiration from Swedish culture; poetry in particular has been important to him. His style can be characterized as an atonal expressionism, often aphoristic and pointillistic. He is highly esteemed for his originality and uncompromising approach and has received several awards, including the Carl Nielsen Prize and the W.H. PRIZE in connection with the performance of his orchestral work *Marin*. Besides the orchestral works his oeuvre includes about

150 solo and chamber works, where percussion instruments are amply represented.

Tadeusz Kassatti (1948–)

Tadeusz Kassatti, pianist and composer, was born in Cracow, Poland, in 1948. In 1972 he was awarded first prize with distinction at the Cracow Conservatory. He continued his studies at the Geneva Conservatory with Harry Datyner and Luis Hiltbrandt, and in London with Peter Feuchtwanger. He currently teaches at the Conservatoire Populaire de Musique in Geneva.

As a composer he is stylistically eclectic, exploring different fields such as electronic experimental music, theatre and stage productions, and chamber music. Kassatti has produced many recordings and has composed for Swiss and Polish radio.

He is also the author of obligatory pieces played at such international competitions as the International Quintet Competition in Narbonne (France), Philip Jones International Competition in Guebviller (France), and the Tuba-Euphonium International Competition in Budapest (Hungary).

Julius Klengel (1859–1933)

Julius Klengel was the son of a lawyer and a fine amateur musician and was a close friend of Felix Mendelssohn. His family, for many generations, had been professional musicians. Klengel first studied cello with his father and then with Emil Hegar, principal cellist in the Gewandhaus Orchestra and a pupil of Grutzmacher and Davidov.

At fifteen Klengel became a member of the Gewandhaus Orchestra, and at 22 (1881) became principal there. Also in 1881 he was appointed a professor at the Leipzig Conservatory. He remained with the orchestra until 1924. To celebrate his fifty years of service, Furtwangler conducted a jubilee concert with Klengel playing the cello part in a double concerto he had composed for the occasion.

He often concertized in Russia, and gave the first Russian performance of the Haydn *D Major Concerto* in 1887. Klengel was not only a cellist but a fine pianist. It was well known that Klengel could accompany his pupils on the piano, playing everything from memory. He had a vast knowledge of chamber music and all of the idiomatic characteristics of every instrument in the standard repertoire.

Klengel was in close contact with Brahms, Rubenstein, Reger, and other composers of his era, and composed much himself. He wrote four cello concerts, two double cello concertos, and two more for cello and violin. He also wrote a cello sonata, caprices, and the *Hymn for Twelve Cellos*, dedicated to the memory of the conductor Artur Nikisch.

Cay Lennart Larsson (1952–)

Rev. Cay Lennart Larsson, master of theology, philosophy, and music, was born in Stockholm, Sweden, in 1952. He joined the Military Band of Orebro in 1968 and studied music in Orebro, Gothenburg, and New York. He graduated from the Swedish Royal Academy of Music in 1976. Lennart played trombone, bass trumpet, and euphonium in the Orebro Symphony Orchestra and many other local orchestras from 1968 to 1995.

Larsson played jazz in the Black River Band, Orebro Big Band, and Whispering, and was leader of the Candy Stompers and the Ostrich Crash (Strutsen Störtar) and chairman of the Jazz Academy UJÖ.

William P. Latham (1917–2004)

William Peters Latham was born in Shreveport, Louisiana, on January 4, 1917. He was educated in Kentucky, Ohio, and New York, completing degrees in composition and theory at the Cincinnati College of Music in Cincinnati, Ohio. Later, he was awarded a PhD in composition at the Eastman School of Music of the University of Rochester in Rochester, New York (1951). His principal composition teachers were Eugene Goossens and Howard Hanson.

Latham taught theory and composition at the University of Northern Iowa from 1946 to 1965, attaining the rank of professor of music in 1959. In 1965 he joined the faculty of the College of Music at the University of North Texas (UNT) as professor of music and coordinator of composition. He was appointed director of graduate studies in music in 1969. In 1978 he was promoted to the rank of distinguished professor of music, the university's highest rank. Only seven other faculty members of the university had been so honored at that time. He retired from active service at UNT in June 1984, and he was formally designated professor emeritus by the board of regents in November 1984.

Latham composed 118 works; 62 have been published, 56 remain in manuscript, but all have been performed, many throughout the United States, Canada, Europe, and Japan. He received numerous awards and commissions (29). His orchestral works have been performed by the Cincinnati Symphony, the Eastman-Rochester Philharmonic, the Dallas Symphony, the St. Louis Symphony, and Radio Orchestras in Brussels, Belgium, and Hilversum, Holland, under such well-known conductors as Eugene Goossens, Howard Hanson, Thor Johnson, Anshel Brusilow, John Giordano, and Walter Susskind.

Jukka Linkola (1955–)

Composer, conductor, and performing musician Jukka Linkola was born in Helsinki in 1955. From the beginning his most important instrument and a tool of work has been the piano. He studied at the Sibelius Academy and already during his student years he worked as a rehearsal pianist at the Helsinki City Theatre, where he later worked as a conductor in 1975–1990.

Jazz plays an important part in Linkola's production. His octet was in its time one of the most significant groups of Finnish jazz. Linkola has conducted many big bands; for example, UMO (Orchestra of New Music), the big band of EBU, the big band of the Danish Radio, and Bohuslän Big Band. He has taught in projects at, for example, Berklee College of Music, the world-famous music institute in Boston.

Linkola has composed a lot of stage music, operas, and music for plays and films. The opera *Elin* in 1991 was a big stage work. The television opera *Angelika* in 1992 was more like an oratory. *Angelika* was awarded at Paris Opera Screen competition in 1992 and in 1993 it was chosen the best at Cannes Midem Awards. Linkola's third opera is called *Matka (a Journey)* and it was premiered in 1998.

Linkola likes to compose for symphony and chamber orchestras or for big jazz orchestras and he often uses soloists with orchestras. Examples of these works are *Crossings* for tenor saxophone and orchestra in 1983, *Concerto for Trumpet and Orchestra* in 1988, and *Trumpet Concerto II* in 1993. The latest concertos are *Flute Concerto* (1997), *Euphonium Concerto* (1995), *Tuba Concerto* (1995), *Organ Concerto* (2000), and *Horn Concerto* (2000).

In recent years Linkola has composed several choral works; for instance, *Evoe* and *English Series for YL* (Helsinki University male chorus) and *Primitive Music* for Tapiola Choir.

Conducting his own works, Linkola has performed with the Finnish Radio Symphony Orchestra, Helsinki Philharmonic, the Orchestra of the Finnish National Opera, the Opera of Gothenburg, Radio Orchestras of Ljubljana and Prague, and the Orchestra of Aalborg.

Linkola has received several awards for his works. So far he has published about 35 recordings. His whole production, including operas, musicals, orchestra concertos, chamber music, songs, and jazz for various combinations, is immense.

Bent Lorentzen (1935–)

Bent Lorentzen was born in 1935 and studied musicology at the university in Aarhus and at the Royal Danish Academy of Music in Copenhagen. He is a pupil of Knud Jeppesen, Finn Høffding, Vagn Holmboe, and Jörgen Jersild. After his final examination he taught at the Academy of Music in Aarhus for some years. From 1962 to 1971 he taught orchestration and music theory at the Royal Academy of Music in Aarhus. In 1965 Lorentzen attended summer courses in Darmstadt, and in 1967 he worked at the EMS (Electro-acoustic Music Studio) in Stockholm. In 1971 he settled in Copenhagen to make a living for himself as a composer.

Among Bent Lorentzen's works the operas deserve a mention. He has until now composed about a dozen operas, which have been very successful both in Denmark and abroad, particularly in Germany. His work list furthermore contains a series of interesting and often-performed works for orchestra, chamber music, organ music, and choir.

Duncan MacMillan (1956–)

Duncan J. MacMillan, pianist, composer, and teacher, has appeared on civic and collegiate artists series in many states as well as at the Kennedy Center, Washington, D.C. He has also appeared at summer music festivals. In addition to the standard repertoire, he has premiered works by many composers, performs chamber music, and also plays harpsichord.

His compositions have been premiered by symphony and university faculty artists, touring artists, and various chamber music ensembles. His liturgical works have also been premiered in many churches.

MacMillan has held university and college faculty positions teaching piano, music literature, music theory, music history, chamber music, and coaching opera, and has maintained a private piano studio for over 25 years. He now lectures at Eckerd College. His research into the biomechanics of piano technique has included interviewing and collaborating with Barbara Lister-Sink (author of *Freeing the Caged Bird*), attending the Taubman Institute for Piano at Amherst College on faculty research grants, and presenting injury-preventive technique workshops.

He has been affiliated with MTNA chapters in Florida, Oklahoma, Alabama, and Mississippi. He has served as jurist for regional, state, and local piano and young artists competitions throughout the southeastern United States. He was also jurist for the inaugural Michael Hennagin Prize in Composition, an international composers competition.

A native Floridian, MacMillan holds two BA degrees magna cum laude (in psychology and music performance), a certificate in piano and pedagogy, and two master of music degrees (in piano and music theory) from the Florida State University. A member of Phi Beta Kappa, Pi Kappa Lambda, and Phi Mu Alpha, he received his doctor of musical arts degree in piano and literature from the University of Oklahoma after studies on doctoral scholarship at Oxford University. He has been recognized for his accomplishments in *Who's Who in America* and *Who's Who in the South & Southwest*.

Martin Mailman (1932–2000)

Dr. Martin S. Mailman was born on June 30, 1932, in New York City. He served on the College of Music faculty at the University of North Texas in Denton, Texas, for 34 years as the coordinator of composition, regents professor of music, and composer-in-residence. He served for two years in the United States Navy, was a Ford Foundation composer in Jacksonville, Florida, and was the first composer-in-residence at East Carolina University, Greenville, North Carolina.

A composition student of Louis Mennini, Wayne Barlow, Bernard Rogers, and Howard Hanson, he earned his BM, MM, and PhD degrees from the Eastman School of Music, Rochester, New York. He was among the first of contemporary American composers chosen in 1959 to participate in the Young Composers Project sponsored by the Ford Foundation and the National Music Council. Mailman received numerous awards and grants for composition, which include two American Bandmasters Association/Ostwald prizes for composition, the National Band Association/Band Mans Company prize for composition, and the Edward Benjamin Award. He won the 1982 Queen Marie-Jose Prize for composition in Geneva, Switzerland, for his *Concerto for Violin and Orchestra (Variations)*. His works include chamber music, band, choral, and orchestral music, film scores, television music, an opera, and a requiem for chorus, orchestra, and soloists. A frequently sought-after clinician and teacher, Mailman served as guest conductor-composer at more than ninety colleges and universities across the United States and Europe. The impact of his music, teaching, and career is immeasurable, and he is widely regarded as one of America's finest composers.

David Maslanka (1943–)

David Maslanka was born in New Bedford, Massachusetts, in 1943. He attended the Oberlin College Conservatory, where he studied composition with Joseph Wood. He spent a year at the Mozarteum in Salzburg, Austria, and did graduate work in composition at Michigan State University with H. Owen Reed.

Maslanka's works for winds and percussion have become especially well known. They include, among others, *A Child's Garden of Dreams* for Symphonic Wind Ensemble; *Concerto for Piano, Winds and Percussion;* the second, third, and fourth symphonies; *Mass* for soloists, chorus, boys chorus, wind orchestra, and organ; and the two *Wind Quintets.* Percussion works include *Variations of "Lost Love"* and *My Lady White* for solo marimba, and three ensemble works: *Arcadia II: Concerto for Marimba and Percussion Ensemble, Crown of Thorns,* and *Montana Music: Three Dances for Percussion.* In addition, he has written a wide variety of chamber, orchestral, and choral pieces.

Maslanka's compositions are published by Carl Fischer, Inc., Kjos Music Company, Marimba Productions, Inc., the North American Saxophone Alliance, and OU Percussion Press, and have been recorded on Albany, Cambria, CRI, Mark, Novisse, and Klavier labels. He has served on the faculties of the State University of New York at Geneseo, Sarah Lawrence College, New York University, and Kingsborough College of the City University of New York. He now lives in Missoula, Montana. Maslanka is a member of ASCAP.

Lennie Niehaus (1929–)

Lennie Niehaus moved to the West Coast as a child. He worked with Jerry Wald in 1951 and joined Stan Kenton; he served in the U.S. Army from 1952 to 1954, then worked with Kenton again until 1959. With Bud Shank and Art Pepper he was one of the most prominent in the West Coast alto sax school of the period, which seemed to combine the influence of Charlie Parker with the style of Benny Carter. His primary influence was Lee Konitz. He came from a musical family and had a thorough grounding in theory; he knew better than to try to be overelaborate, but could improve on a pop tune with his melodic ideas, and he had nothing to learn about the alto saxophone, his fluency, attack, and swing as good as the best. He retired to commercial work in TV and films (he has often worked with Clint Eastwood), arranging for nightclub acts, and so forth.

Vaclav Nelhybel (1919–1996)

Internationally renowned composer Vaclav Nelhybel was born on September 24, 1919, in Polanka, Czechoslovakia. He studied composition and conducting at the Conservatory of Music in Prague (1938–1942) and musicology at Prague University and the University of Fribourg, Switzerland. After World War II he was affiliated as composer and conductor with Swiss National Radio and became lecturer at the University of Fribourg. In 1950 he became the first musical director of Radio Free Europe in Munich, Germany, a post he held until he immigrated to the United States in 1957. Thereafter, he made his home in America, becoming an American citizen in 1962. After having lived for many years in New York City, he moved to Ridgefield and Newtown, Connecticut, and then, in 1994, to the Scranton area in Pennsylvania. During his long career in the United States he worked as composer, conductor, teacher, and lecturer throughout the world. At the time of his death on March 22, 1996, he was composer-in-residence at the University of Scranton.

A prolific composer, Nelhybel left a rich body of works, among them concertos, operas, chamber music, and numerous compositions for symphony orchestra, symphonic band, chorus, and smaller ensembles. Over 400 of his works were published during his lifetime, and many of his over 200 unpublished compositions are in the process of being published. (Nelhybel's passion for composing was all encompassing and left him little time for "marketing" his works; for this reason, many of his compositions, though commissioned and performed, remained unpublished.) Although Nelhybel wrote the majority of his works for professional performers, he relished composing original, challenging pieces for student musicians and delighted in making music with young players.

Nelhybel was a synthesist and a superb craftsman who amalgamated the musical impulses of his time in his own expression, choosing discriminately from among existing systems and integrating them into his own concepts and methods. The most striking general characteristic of his music is its linear-modal orientation. His concern with the autonomy of melodic line leads to the second and equally important characteristic, that of movement and pulsation, or rhythm and meter. The interplay between these dual aspects of motion and time, and their coordinated organization, results in the vigorous drive so typical of Nelhybel's music. These elements are complemented in many of his works by the tension generated by accumulations of dissonance, the increasing of textural densities, exploding dynamics, and the massing of multi-hued sonic colors. Though frequently dissonant in texture, Nelhybel's music always gravitates toward tonal centers, which makes it so appealing to performers and listeners alike.

Ron Nelson (1929–)

Ron Nelson is a native of Joliet, Illinois. He received his bachelor of music degree in 1952, the master's degree in 1953, and the doctor of music arts degree in 1956 from the Eastman School of Music. He studied in France at the Ecole Normale de Musique and, in 1955, at the Paris Conservatory under a Fulbright grant.

Nelson joined the Brown University faculty the following year as an assistant professor, attaining the rank of associate professor in 1960 and full professor in 1968. He served as chairman of the Department of Music from 1963 to 1973, and in 1991 he was awarded the Acuff Chair of Excellence in the Creative Arts, becoming the first musician to hold the chair.

He has gained wide recognition as a composer of choral, band, and orchestral works. Commissions include the National Symphony Orchestra, Rochester Philharmonic Orchestra, The United States Air Force Band, and numerous colleges and universities. In 1993 his *Passacaglia (Homage on B-A-C-H)* won the "triple crown" of wind band composition competitions by winning the National Band Association prize, the American Bandmasters Association's ABA/Ostwald Band Composition Contest, and the Louis and Virginia Sudler International Wind Band Composition Contest, making Nelson the first composer to win all three competitions within the same period.

Nelson retired from Brown University in 1993 and currently resides in Arizona.

Wolfgang Plagge (1960–)

Wolfgang Plagge was born in Oslo, Norway, of Dutch parents in 1960. At a very early age he showed a genuine interest in classical music, and started playing the piano as well as writing his first compositions at age four. He was ten when he won an international talent competition in English television; one year later he also won the Young Pianists' Competition in Oslo.

In 1972 he made a sensational recital debut in Oslo, with King Olav V present in the auditorium. He went on to win several national and international prizes in the years to follow, among them the Forsberg Legate in 1979 and the Levin Prize in 1987. In 1986 he concluded his six years of study at the Musikhochschule in Hamburg, Germany, with distinction. He pursues an active career as an international pianist and is much in demand as a chamber musician. He has been performing as a soloist with a great number of orchestras in Norway and abroad, and has worked with internationally renowned artists such as Ole Edvard Antonsen, Jens Harald Bratlie, Alexandr Dmitriev, Philippe Entremont, Lutz Herbig, Piotr Janowski, Evgeni Koroliov, Solveig Kringlebotn, Truls Mørk, Robert Oppenheimer, Robert Rønnes, Leif Segerstam, Randi Stene, Roberto Szidon, Lars Anders Tomter, Frøydis Ree Wekre, and many others. He has recorded CDs on the SIMAX, 2L, Crystal, and Norske Gram labels.

Plagge the composer had his first work published at age twelve and has since steadily developed into a mature, original, and prolific creative artist. His works span from liturgic music to symphonic works, and chamber music as well as piano music appears to be a central part. He has a specific interest in winds and has written a number of important works for woodwind and brass in chamber music constellations. Several of his works have already been accepted as standard repertoire: His *First Horn Sonata* has appeared as a mandatory piece in several international wind competitions.

His particular love for and research on medieval music of Northern Europe has been inspirational for a substantial number of works, and still is.

Ever since his student days in Norway and Germany the phenomenon of time has been one of Plagge's main focusing points: Studying the time flow, manipulating our sense of time, and how to utilize time as a forming tool have been central items in his creative process.

Plagge's music is being performed by musicians, ensembles, and orchestras all over the world, and his reputation as a composer is ever growing. In 1996 he was created Composer of the Year with the Trondheim Symphony Orchestra. He received the American ASCAP Award for 2001 and won the Vocal Nord composers contest in 2003. A number of works are recorded on CD; scores can be obtained through 2L e-scores, Musikk-Husets Forlag AS Oslo, or the Norwegian Music Information Center. Plagge is a member of the Norwegian Society of Composers.

Anthony Plog

The music of Anthony Plog has been performed in over thirty countries around the world. He is the recipient of numerous grants and commissions, including the National Endowment for the Arts (for the American Brass Quintet), the Malmo Symphony (Sweden), Nick Norton and the Utah Symphony, the Summit Brass, the GECA Brass Ensemble in France, the Chicago Chamber Musicians, the University of Texas at Austin, and the St. Louis Brass Quintet.

At the beginning of his compositional career Plog wrote almost exclusively for brass, and was published by several of the top brass publishers, including Western International Music and Brass Press. From 1992 to 2001 his exclusive publisher was Editions BIM of Switzerland. He is currently published by Anthony Plog Publications.

In the past ten years Plog has broadened his compositional horizons and now writes in many different mediums. He recently finished a children's opera entitled *How the Trumpet Got Its Toot,* which will be premiered by the Utah Opera in March of 2004. Other new works recently completed are a *Trumpet Sonata,* a *Horn Concerto,* and a comprehensive *Trumpet Method* (to be published in seven volumes by Balquhidder Music).

His brass works have been required pieces on a number of international brass competitions, including the ARD competition in Munich, Germany, and also competitions in Porcia, Italy; Toulon, France; Brno, Czech Republic; and Lieksa, Finland. Most of his brass music has been recorded, with several pieces receiving four or more recordings.

Plog began studying music at the age of ten, and by the age of nineteen he was playing extra trumpet with the Los Angeles Philharmonic under conductors such as Zubin Mehta, James Levine, Michael Tilson Thomas, and Claudio Abbado. His first orchestral position was principal trumpet with the San Antonio Symphony from 1970 to 1973, followed by a two-year stint with the Utah Symphony as associate principal. He left the Utah Symphony in 1976 to pursue a solo and composition career, and while living in Los Angeles from 1976 to 1988 supported himself by playing principal trumpet with the Los Angeles Chamber Orchestra and the Pacific Symphony and by occasionally playing in the film studios (*Star Trek: The Motion Picture, Gremlins, Rocky II* and *III, Altered States,* etc.).

In 1990 he moved to Europe to play solo trumpet with the Malmo Symphony in Sweden, and since 1993 has been a professor at the Staatliche Hochschule fur Musik in Freiburg, Germany. During this time he was co-solo trumpet with the Basel Symphony in Switzerland for three years. He has also toured as co-solo trumpet with the Stockholm Royal Philharmonic (Japan 1992) and the Buenos Aires Symphony (Germany and Holland 1997).

Amilcare Ponchielli (1834–1886)

Amilcare Ponchielli was born in Paderno, Italy, August 31, 1834. He entered the Milan Conservatory in his ninth year and stayed there nine years. While still a student he wrote an operetta, *Il Sindaco Babbeo,* in collaboration with three other students.

When his studies ended, he became an organist in Cremona, and then a bandmaster in Piacenza. During this period he wrote his first opera, *I promessi sposi,* introduced in Cremona in 1856.

Ponchielli became world famous with *La Gioconda,* introduced at La Scala on April 8, 1876. The opera was a triumph at its premiere and it was highly successful when heard throughout Europe. None of the operas Ponchielli wrote after *La Gioconda* were able to repeat either the popular success or the consistently high level of dramatic and musical interest of that work.

In 1881, Ponchielli was appointed maestro di cappella of the Bergamo Cathedral, and from 1883 on he was professor of composition at the Milan Conservatory. In addition to his numerous works for orchestra and opera, he wrote a considerable body of music for military and he is credited with composing the first concerto for euphonium.

Arthur Pryor (1870–1942)

Arthur Willard Pryor was born on September 22, 1870, on the second floor of the Lyceum Theatre, St. Joseph, Missouri. His father was the bandmaster of the town, and the family was living at the theatre. Arthur was the second son born to Samuel D. and Mary (Coker) Pryor. The oldest son, Walter D. Pryor, became a famous cornetist who later was featured on recordings with the great Herbert L. Clarke. The youngest son, Samuel O. Pryor, became known for his skill on the drums and playing in many Kansas City theatre orchestras. Both Walter and Sam Jr. later played in the famous Pryor Band their brother Arthur directed.

Pryor was only 22 when he played his first solo with the Sousa Band during the World Columbian Exposition in Chicago in 1893. According to accounts of the day, he played his own *Thoughts of Love* to a crowd who just stood in awe, then cheered and threw their hats in the air.

That was the first of some 10,000 solos that Pryor estimated he played during the twelve years he was with the Sousa Band.

His great facility at composing grew out of his ability to improvise at the piano. He was able to take a three- or four-note motive and develop it into a theme for a composition. He would also develop a theme from the rhythm and vowel sounds of a person's name. Throughout the years many favorites in the Pryor Band repertoire were Pryor compositions, so much so that at one point he had to make a public statement that he did not also write the popular pieces of John Philip Sousa.

In his promotion of the "healthy growth of our native music, he showed a fondness for the new jazz idiom." He had grown up along the Missouri River and, with his father's show business contacts, had become acquainted with the traveling minstrel shows of the day. St. Joseph is also near Sedalia, Missouri, the birthplace of ragtime. He had developed a good "feel" for jazz, and many of his compositions are in this style. His *Razazza Mazzazza* is called the "king of rags" in the 1906 Victor catalogue. In 1919 he and his band introduced the popular "Swanee" by George Gershwin in a concert in New York City.

However, in all of his musical arrangements he would not add jazz style to a classical composition. While jazz is "legitimate entertainment" ("all right for dancing"), jazz versions of the old masters "have so confused the younger generation that youths put a swing rhythm into music when they think they are playing it straight." Because of this he once called jazz the "parasite of music," lacking originality except in the area of rhythm. He realized the concert band's contribution to American life ("they deserve credit for bringing the people closer to good music") and was saddened to see it supplanted by jazz ensembles as time went by. In the 1920s the Pryor Band moved into the area of radio broadcasting. By the early 1930s he was associated with NBC for broadcasting in New York City. One popular series of concerts he and the band did was called the Cavalcade of America.

Sometimes he would get together the old Pryor Band (as many members as he could find) for an engagement at nearby Asbury Park, scene of his earlier triumphs. It was after a rehearsal for such an engagement, on the night of June 17, 1942, that he suffered a stroke (brain hemorrhage), and died at 5 the next morning. Arthur Jr. conducted the concert, which included his last composition, *We'll Keep Old Glory Flying*, dedicated to the U.S. Armed Forces. He was buried in Glenwood Cemetery near his home. He was an Episcopalian by faith, and he was a charter member of both ASCAP (1914) and the American Bandmasters Association (1929).

Elizabeth Raum (1945–)

Elizabeth Raum is active both as an oboist and as a composer. She earned her bachelor of music in oboe performance from the Eastman School of Music in 1966 and her master of music in composition from the University of Regina, Saskatchewan, Canada, in 1985. She has been awarded an honorary doctorate in humane letters from Mt. St. Vincent University in Halifax, Nova Scotia.

Raum played principal oboe in the Atlantic Symphony Orchestra in Halifax, Nova Scotia, for seven years before coming to Regina in 1975. She now plays principal oboe in the Regina Symphony.

Elizabeth Raum's works have been heard throughout North America, Europe, South America, China, Japan, and Russia, and have been broadcast extensively on the CBC. She has also written for film and video and has won awards for the scores to the documentaries *Saskatchewan River* and *Like Mother, Like Daughter* and the feature length film *Sparkle*. She produced Canada's first classical video with originally written music, entitled *Evolution: A Theme with Variations*, which was premiered at a gala event at the CBC in 1986. Other film collaborations include *Prelude to Parting*, *The Green Man Ballet*, and *Symphony of Youth*, all broadcast on national television.

Raum has been featured in articles in the *New Grove's Dictionary of Music and Musicians*, the *New Grove's Dictionary of Opera*, the *New Grove's Dictionary of Women Composers*, *Opera Canada*, the *Encyclopedia of Music in Canada*, the *TUBA Journal*, *Music Scene*, and *Prairie Sounds*. She has served on juries for the Canada Council, the Saskatchewan Arts Board, the Manitoba Arts Council, the Ontario Arts Council, the CBC, and the Canadian Music Centre.

Alfred Reed (1921–)

Alfred Reed was born on Manhattan Island in New York City on January 25, 1921. His formal music training began at the age of ten, when he studied the trumpet. As a teenager, he played with small hotel combos in the Catskill Mountains. His interests shifted from performing to arranging and composition. In 1938, he started working in the Radio Workshop in New York as a staff composer/arranger and assistant conductor. With the onset of World War II, he enlisted and was assigned to the 529th Army Air Corps Band. During his three and a half years of service, he produced nearly 100 compositions and arrangements for band. After his discharge,

Reed enrolled at the Juilliard School of Music and studied composition with Vittorio Giannini. In 1953, he enrolled at Baylor University, serving as conductor of the symphony orchestra while he earned the bachelor of music degree (1955). A year later, he received his master of music degree. His interest in the development of educational music led him to serve as executive editor of Hansen Publishing from 1955 to 1966. He left that position to become a professor of music at the University of Miami, where he served until his retirement in 1993. He continues to compose and has made numerous appearances as guest conductor in many nations, most notably in Japan.

John Reeman (1946–)

John Reeman was born in 1946 and after following a variety of occupations, including six years as a member of a professional cabaret vocal act, entered Hull University as a mature student to study composition and the flute. He was awarded the annual music prize, an honors degree, and later a master's degree in composition. He currently lives in St. Annes on Sea , UK, with his wife and son, and his time is divided between teaching the flute and composition.

Reeman has written a wide range of works that are regularly performed by both amateur and professional musicians and, although his music encompasses many contemporary techniques, his compositions are characteristically accessible, dramatic, and lyrical.

In 1990 his *Flute Concerto* was one of the final three works in the International Concerto Competition launched to mark the Morley College Centennial, and in 1995 Reeman won the Gregynog Composers' Award of Wales. In 2002 his *Scena for String Quartet* was awarded the first prize in the International Kodaly Institute Competition. Recent performances of his music have been heard at the Dartington Summer School, the Purcell Room, and in various countries including Australia, America, Germany, Japan, and Hungary.

A number of his pieces have been published by companies such as Universal Edition, Novello, Stainer and Bell, Studio Music, Kevin Mayhew, and Spartan Press, and a variety of compositions have been recorded on CDs by Roger Heaton and Stephen Pruslin, the British Tuba Quartet, Tubalaté, and the Opus 20 Ensemble conducted by Scott Stroman.

Goff Richards

Goff Richards was born in Cornwall and after studying at the Royal College of Music and Reading University, embarked on a career as a composer, arranger, and conductor.

His works have been performed by the King's Singers, the Swingle Singers, various BBC Orchestras, Huddersfield Choral Society, London Brass, Evelyn Glennie, Benjamin Luxon, and all leading brass and military bands in England.

He writes extensively for BBC Radio and Television.

BNFL, Brighouse & Rastrick, and the Fodens (Courtois) Band have each produced a CD featuring his music, and a new recording of Goff's ensemble *THE ARCADIANS*, with singers Margaret Richardson and Paul Whelan, has recently been released.

From 1976 to 1989, he lectured in arranging and directed the jazz orchestra at Salford College of Technology. For his contribution to band music throughout the world, in 1990 the college awarded him an Honorary GDBM and the title director big band laureate. Since 1992, he has been directing the jazz orchestra at Chetham's School of Music, Manchester.

As an educational composer he has composed large-scale works for Barnsley Schools (*The River of Time*) and for the East Ayrshire Schools Brass Band and Choir (*A String O'Blethers*), both produced in the year 2000.

As an adjudicator he is widely traveled, having judged various British National Brass Band Area and Finals Contests; the European, Australian, New Zealand, and Dutch Brass Band Championships; SIDDIS Brass, Norway; the National Male Voice Choir Championships of Great Britain; and numerous band contests for BBC Radio and Television.

He has spent three years serving on the BBC's Central Music Advisory Committee and is currently a member of the British Music Writers' Council.

The Cornish Gorsedd made him a Bard in 1976 and he maintains his West Country links as president of the South West Brass Band Association and music advisor to the Cornwall Youth Brass Band

Walter Ross (1936–)

Walter Ross, whose works have been performed in over forty countries, is perhaps best known for his compositions featuring brass and woodwinds. Raised in Nebraska, he became a professional orchestral French horn player by the age of seventeen and went on to gain more performance experience in college as a member of the University of Nebraska symphonic band and as a flute player with a baroque ensemble. Currently he plays bass in the Blue Ridge Chamber Orchestra.

After four years of engineering and astronomy, he switched to music, receiving much of his early compositional training under Robert Beadell. While working on his doctoral degree at Cornell (where he studied under Robert Palmer and Karel Husa), he received an Organization of American States Fellowship to study composition privately under Alberto Ginastera in Argentina.

The influences of his own extensive performance background and his musical training under composers who stressed bright orchestration and rhythmic excitement can be heard in many of Ross's over 100 works. He likes to write music that musicians enjoy performing and audiences enjoy hearing. Many of his recent works are representative of his current interest in neo-modal, pandiatonic composition.

Ross has received a number of awards and prizes and many significant grants and fellowships. His work is widely performed, and many of his compositions have been published and recorded. Currently a resident of Charlottesville, Virginia, he has served as president of the Southeastern Composers League and served as a judge at international composition symposia. He has been a visiting composer at the Aspen Music Festival and a featured composer at several universities and forums and on national and international radio broadcasts, and he is currently a member of the board of the Capital Composers Alliance.

Ole Schmidt (1928–)

Ole Schmidt was born in Copenhagen in 1928. He studied at the city's Royal Conservatoire of Music, where his main courses were in composition, piano, and conducting. After leaving the Conservatoire he continued his conducting studies abroad with Albert Wolff, Nils Grevilius, Rafael Kubelik, and Sergiu Celibidache. Schmidt has held titled positions with the Danish National Radio Symphony Orchestra, Royal Danish Opera, Aarhus Symphony Orchestra, Hamburg Symphoniker, and, in the United States, with the Toledo Symphony Orchestra. He has appeared with several of Europe's foremost orchestras as a guest conductor and worked extensively in Britain with the London Symphony Orchestra, with whom he recorded all the symphonies of Carl Nielsen. Schmidt works with most of the principal Scandinavian orchestras. Elsewhere in recent years he has appeared in Karlsruhe, the Frankfurt Radio Symphony Orchestra, Staatsphilharmonie Rheinland-Pfalz, Saarlandisches Rundfunk Symphonie-Orchester, Hallé Orchestra, Ulster Orchestra, BBC Scottish Symphony Orchestra, and Hong Kong Philharmonic. A devotee of

contemporary music, Schmidt has conducted many premieres and has gradually resumed his own composing activities during his productive years on the podium. His own work ranges across several disciplines and involves pieces for symphony orchestra, symphonic wind band, music for classic silent films, and incidental music for radio and television. He is a recipient of the Carl Nielsen Prize.

Patrick Schulz (1974–)

Patrick Schulz is an adjunct faculty member at Paradise Valley Community College in Phoenix, Arizona, where he teaches courses in music theory and rock music and culture. Originally from Elroy, Wisconsin, Patrick is also finishing a doctorate in music composition at Arizona State University, where he has been a graduate teaching assistant in the theory area and president of the Contemporary Music Society. His compositions have been published by Tuba-Euphonium Press, Encore Music Publishers, and Bernel Music. These works and many others have received numerous performances at international and national conferences and festivals throughout the United States and Canada, including numerous International Tuba-Euphonium Conferences, the Southwest Regional Tuba Conference, three United States Army Band Tuba/Euphonium Conferences, the Southeast Regional Tuba Conference, the C. Buell Lipa Festival, the Fischoff National Chamber Music Competition, the Concert Artists' Guild Chamber Music Competition, and The United States Army Ground Forces Band Tuba/ Euphonium Conference.

Recently, Schulz has been commissioned to write numerous works for a diverse range of performers and ensembles. His *Watercolors* (2002), written for saxophonist David Jenkins, was the winner of the Contemporary Music Society's 2002 Composition Competition and was selected for performance at the 2003 World Saxophone Congress in Minneapolis, Minnesota. *SAROS* (2001), a work that exists for three different instrumental combinations with solo tuba, was commissioned by tubist Curtis Peacock and will soon be recorded by the Helios Saxophone Quartet (with Peacock) on their upcoming CD project. *Concerto for Euphonium and Wind Ensemble* (2000), written for fellow quartet member Demondrae Thurman, has been performed throughout the United States and will be included on Thurman's debut recording along with *Constellation* (1999) for solo trombone or euphonium. Other notable commissions include *RoonSonata* (2003) for euphonium and piano, *Miniatures for Tuba and Piano* (2001), written for Richard Perry (professor of tuba and euphonium at the University of Southern Mississippi), and *Afternoon Song* (1998) for tuba solo and brass quintet.

A Herberger Fellowship recipient and dedicated scholar, Schulz studied composition with the entire composition faculty at Arizona State University (ASU), including Glenn Hackbarth, Jody Rockmaker, Randall Shinn, James DeMars, and Rodney Rogers. While under the supervision of ASU faculty, his chamber work *Shades of Grey* (2003) for saxophone, flute, cello, and piano won first prize in the 2004 Contemporary Music Society's Composition Competition, and his *Lepidoptera* (1999) for flute, clarinet, and piano won second prize in the 2000 Contemporary Music Society's Composition Competition. In addition to recordings released with Sotto Voce, Schulz's works are included on a CD produced by the Contemporary Music Society and *The Way Home* (1999), a recording featuring his works for solo piano performed by the composer.

Schulz received his master's degree in composition from the University of Nebraska–Lincoln and his bachelor's degrees in composition and euphonium performance from the University of Wisconsin–Madison. His compositions are published by Tuba-Euphonium Press, Encore Music Publishers, and TubaQuartet.com. Schulz also plays euphonium with the Sotto Voce Quartet (on the web at www.tubaquartet.com). Sotto Voce has two recordings out with Summit Records (*Consequences* and *Viva Voce! The Quartets of John Stevens*).

Robert Sibbing (1929–)

Robert Sibbing was born in 1929 in Illinois. He earned BM and MA degrees from the University of Iowa and an EdD from the University of Illinois, studying composition with Hunter Johnson, Robert Kelly, Phillip Bezanson, Richard Hervig, Tom Turner, and Phillip Greeley Clapp.

A performer as well as a composer, Sibbing is professor emeritus in saxophone at Western Illinois University and a clarinetist in the Knox-Galesburg Symphony.

Claude T. Smith (1932–1987)

Claude T. Smith was born in Monroe City, Missouri. He received his undergraduate training at Central Methodist College in Fayette, Missouri, and at the University of Kansas. He composed extensively in the areas of instrumental and choral music and his compositions have been performed by leading musical organizations throughout the world. Having over 110 band works, twelve orchestra works, and fifteen choral works, he composed solos for such artists as Doc Severinsen, Dale Underwood, Brian Bowman, Warren Covington, Gary Foster, Rich Matteson, and Steve Seward. Smith taught instrumental music in the public schools of Nebraska and Missouri.

He also served as a member of the faculty of Southwest Missouri State University in Springfield, Missouri, where he taught composition and theory and conducted the university symphony orchestra. Sacred music was also a deep love of Smith's, as he directed a church choir for five years in Cozad, Nebraska, ten years in Chillicothe, Missouri, and nine years in Kansas City, Missouri.

Smith received numerous prestigious commissions including works for The United States Air Force Band, "The President's Own" United States Marine Band, the United States Navy Band, and The United States Army Field Band. His composition *Flight* was adapted as the "official march" of the National Air and Space Museum of the Smithsonian Institute. His orchestra works include compositions for the Kansas City Youth Symphony, the South Bend Young Symphony, the Springfield, Missouri, Symphony and the 1981 Missouri All-State String Orchestra.

Robert W. Smith (1958–)

Robert W. Smith is one of the most popular and prolific composers of concert band and orchestral literature in America today. He has over 500 publications in print with the majority composed and arranged through his long association with Warner Bros. Publications.

Smith's credits include many compositions and productions in all areas of the music field. His original works for winds and percussion have been programmed by countless military, university, high school, and middle school bands throughout the United States, Canada, Europe, Australia, South America, and Asia. His *Symphony #1 (The Divine Comedy)*, *Symphony #2 (The Odyssey)*, and *Africa: Ceremony, Song and Ritual* have received worldwide critical acclaim. His educational compositions, such as *The Tempest, Encanto,* and *The Great Locomotive Chase*, have become standards for developing bands throughout the world. His numerous works for orchestras of all levels are currently some of the most popular repertoire available today. His music has received extensive airplay on major network television. From professional ensembles such as the United States Navy Band and the Atlanta Symphony to school bands and orchestras throughout the world, his music speaks to audiences in any concert setting.

Philip Sparke (1961–)

Philip Sparke was born in London and studied composition, trumpet, and piano at the Royal College of Music, where he gained an ARCM. It was at the college that his interest in bands arose. He played in the college wind orchestra and also formed a brass band among the students, writing several works for both ensembles. At that time, his first published works appeared–*Concert Prelude* (brass band) and *Gaudium* (wind band). A growing interest in his music led to several commissions, his first major one being for the Centennial Brass Band Championships in New Zealand–*The Land of the Long White Cloud.* Further commissions followed from individual bands, various band associations, and the BBC, for whom he three times won the EBU New Music for Band Competition (with *Slipstream, Skyrider,* and *Orient Express*). He has written for brass band championships in New Zealand, Switzerland, Holland, Australia, and the UK and twice for the National Finals at the Albert Hall, and his test pieces are constantly in use wherever brass bands can be found.

A close association with banding in Japan led to a commission *(Celebration)* from and eventual recording of his music with the Tokyo Kosei Wind Orchestra. This opened the door worldwide to his wind band music and led to several commissions, particularly from the United States. In 1996 The United States Air Force Band commissioned and recorded *Dance Movements,* which won the prestigious Sudler Prize in 1997.

His conducting and adjudicating activities have taken him to most European countries, Scandinavia, Australia, New Zealand, Japan, and the United States. He runs his own publishing company, Anglo Music Press, which he formed in May 2000. In September 2000 he was awarded the Iles Medal of the Worshipful Company of Musicians for his services to brass bands.

Jared Spears

Dr. Jared Spears is professor of music emeritus at Arkansas State University (ASU) in Jonesboro, Arkansas. He was born in Chicago, Illinois, and received the BSE degree in music education from Northern Illinois University; the BM and MM in percussion and composition from the Cosmopolitan School of Music; and the DM in composition from Northwestern University. Some of his past teachers include Blyth Own, Alan Stout, and Anthony Donato.

Spears has taught theory, history, composition, percussion, and band on all educational levels, from elementary school through college. Since his retirement from ASU in May of 1999 (after 32 years of teaching), he has maintained a heavy schedule of composing and conducting.

The most outstanding of his awards have been the Faricy Award for Creative Music from Northwestern University School of Music, Award of Merit from the Arkansas Chapter of the National Federation of Music Clubs, Outstanding Educators of America, *International Who's Who in Music* and *Who's Who in the World of Percussion—U.S.A.,* Citations of Excellence from the National Band Association, Sigma Alpha Iota National Arts Associate, and several ASCAP awards. During his tenure at ASU, Spears received the university president's award for the outstanding faculty member, as well as an appointment as a president's fellow.

Jack Stamp (1954–)

Dr. Jack Stamp is professor of music and conductor of bands at Indiana University of Pennsylvania (IUP), where he conducts the wind ensemble and symphony band and teaches courses in undergraduate and graduate conducting. Stamp received his bachelor of science in music education degree from IUP, a master's in percussion performance from East Carolina University, and a doctor of musical arts degree in conducting from Michigan State University, where he studied with Eugene Corporon.

Prior to his appointment at IUP, he served as chairman of the Division of Fine Arts at Campbell University in North Carolina. He also taught for several years in the public schools of North Carolina. In addition to these posts, Stamp served as conductor of the Duke University Wind Symphony (1988–1989) and was musical director of the Triangle British Brass Band, leading them to a national brass band championship in 1989.

Stamp's primary composition teachers have been Robert Washburn and Fisher Tull, though he was strongly influenced by his music theory teachers at IUP and East Carolina. Recent studies include work with noted American composers David Diamond, Joan Tower, and Richard Danielpour.

Denzil Stephens

Denzil Stephens was born in Gurnsey, in the Channel Islands, to musical parents who encouraged him to sing in a youth choir, and started to play a brass instrument from the age of five.

World War II saw Stephens evacuated to England, eventually settling in Halifax, Yorkshire. At the age of fifteen, having won a local talent contest, he was spotted by Black Dyke Mills bandsman Percy Hughes. This then led to a successful audition with Stephens playing solo euphonium with Black Dyke up to his 21st birthday. During this time he won many prizes up and down the country, including the Daily Herald Junior Championships, and was a member of the quartet party that won the All Britain Quartet Championships three years running. The band was also successful at the National Championships under Harry Mortimer and later Alex Mortimer.

Stephens was then called up for National Service, where he eventually joined the Royal Air Force (RAF) Central Band as solo euphonium. Quick accelerated promotion gave him the chance to take the bandsergeant's and bandmasters courses consecutively, passing out in 1956, and having obtained the qualifications of ARCM and LRAM in military and brass bandmastership.

During these three years of study, Harry Mortimer was responsible for Stephens gaining the experience of playing with several London-based orchestras in live concerts, along with a recording of *The Planets* by Gustav Holst with Sir Malcolm Sargaent.

The RAF music service became far more restrained over the years, and Denzil resigned his commission to return to his first love of brass bands. The first major band he trained and conducted was Carton Main Frickley Colliery in 1978, getting them to the finals of the championships and winning the TV Best of Brass in 1979. The soloist prize went to Roger Webster playing the *Nuns Chorus,* in Roger's first year as a principal solo cornet with a championship section band.

He then spent five years with the Cory Band, winning several major contests, including the Pontins Championships three years in succession, BBC Radio Wales Band of the Year three times, and European Champions in 1961. Stephens had many successes with other bands, including Lewis Merthyr, Point of Ayr, and, much more recently, Soudhouse Brass from Plymouth, winning the Exmouth Entertainment Contest overall in September 2003.

Stephens moved from Stafford to Cornwall and eased off from band involvement due to his wife's illness. He was able to compose and arrange music for bands, much of which is published by his own in-house publishing firm Sarnia Music.

John Stevens (1951–)
John Stevens joined the faculty of the University of Wisconsin (UW)–Madison School of Music in 1985, following four years as the tuba/euphonium professor at the University of Miami (Florida) School of Music. Stevens was a freelance performer and composer in New York City for many years. In addition to performing with all the major orchestras in New York, he has toured and recorded with such diverse groups as the Chuck Mangione Orchestra and the American Brass Quintet, and is a former member of the New York Tuba Quartet, Aspen Festival Orchestra, Philharmonic Orchestra of Florida, and the Greater Miami Opera Orchestra. He was also the tuba soloist in the original Broadway production of *Barnum*. Internationally known for his compositions for brass, Stevens has published many works that have become standard repertoire for groups all over the world. His compositions have also been commissioned and/or recorded by many renowned brass soloists and groups. He has combined his talents as a performer and composer in a record album of his own music entitled *Power,* available on Mark Records. Stevens is on the board of directors of TUBA and is also the former director of the UW–Madison School of Music. In addition to his work with the Wisconsin Brass Quintet, he is a frequent soloist, clinician and conductor of brass ensembles, and a member of Symphonia, America's premiere professional tuba/euphonium ensemble.

Roland Szentpali
Roland began playing the euphonium at the age of twelve, moving on to the tuba in the following year and studying with Joseph Baszinka and Gabor Adamik. He is currently a student of Laszlo Szabo at the Franz Liszt Academy in his native city of Budapest, Hungary. Roland is very active as a composer, having written many works for tuba, chamber ensemble, and orchestra in a broad variety of styles. In February of 1994, he performed his own *Concerto for Tuba and Orchestra* in Budapest for live television broadcast. His music has been played and recorded by the Hungarian Radio Orchestra and the Orchestra Hungarian Music Academy Bela Bartok.

David Uber
Dr. David Uber is a leading American composer, whose works for brass, woodwind, and percussion are played extensively around the world. His colorful career in music ranges from award-winning composer to world-class trombonist, college professor to band director. Prominent artists, corporations, and universities have commissioned works by Uber.

Uber was professor of music at the College of New Jersey (formerly known as Trenton State College) for 33 years and was recently awarded the title of emeritus professor of music by that institution. He also served as director of the Princeton University Symphonic Band for ten years. Born in Princeton, Illinois, he has lived in Wyoming, Missouri, Pennsylvania, New York, New Jersey, and Vermont. After his graduation from Carthage College and receiving a scholarship to the Curtis Institute of Music in Philadelphia, Uber served four years in the United States Navy Band and then continued his studies at Columbia University, where he obtained his master of arts and doctor of education degrees. He has been a member of the faculty at the Westminster Choir College in Princeton, New Jersey, and the National Music Camp, Interlochen, Michigan, where he was the director of ensemble music.

Uber has won competitions such as the Fourth Clarinet Choir Competition Contest sponsored by the University of Maryland and Kendor Music, Inc. His award-winning work *Musicale* was published by Kendor. Uber's composition *Odyssey for Symphonic Band* was a prizewinner at Symposium III held at Radford College in Virginia. He has received the prestigious ASCAP Composers Award annually since 1959 and twice received a Merit Award from the College of New Jersey. He won the 1990 TUBA Composition Contest with his book *22 Etudes for Euphonium*. His *Processional for World Peace*, commissioned by the Nobel Peace Prize Forum, received its world premiere in 1992. He has received commissions for original large-scale compositions from Carthage College, the Johnson Wax Company, Dakota State College, Augustana College, Princeton University, the College of New Jersey, the Hillsborough High School Band (New Jersey), the Fairfax City Band (Virginia), and the *Instrumentalist* magazine. Solo works have been commissioned by such famous artists as Harvey Phillips, Don Butterfield, Frank Meredith, John Swallow, Robert Nagel, Dr. Harold Krueger, Wayne Andre, Gerard Schwarz, and Lucas Spiros. He has appeared as adjudicator at Dartmouth College and Castleton State College and as lecturer-clinician with Robert King Music Sales. To date, Uber has published more that 300 works with nineteen major publishers.

Chris Vadala
One of the country's foremost woodwind artists, Chris Vadala is in demand as a jazz/classical performer and educator. He has appeared on more than 100 recordings to date, as well as innumerable jingle sessions and film and TV scores, performing on all the saxophones, flutes, and clarinets. A native of Poughkeepsie, New York, he graduated from the Eastman School of Music, where he earned the honor of the performer's

certificate in saxophone as well as a BM in music education, received an MA in clarinet from Connecticut College, and pursued post-graduate study in woodwinds at Eastman.

Vadala is currently director of jazz studies and saxophone professor at the University of Maryland. Previous academic appointments include teaching studio woodwinds and conducting jazz ensembles at Connecticut College, Montgomery College, Hampton University, Prince George's Community College, and Mount Vernon College, as well as visiting professor of saxophone at the Eastman School of Music, 1995 and 2001.

Vadala's performing career has been highlighted by a long tenure as standout woodwind artist with the internationally recognized Chuck Mangione Quartet, which included performances in all fifty states, Canada, Australia, Japan, the Phillippines, China, Brazil, Mexico, Argentina, Bermuda, Puerto Rico, the Virgin Islands, the Dominican Republic, England, Italy, France, Germany, Austria, the Netherlands, Poland, Belgium, and Switzerland, and performing credits on five gold and two platinum albums, plus two Grammys, one Emmy, and one Golden Globe Award. In addition, he has performed and/or recorded with such greats as Dizzy Gillespie, Quincy Jones, B. B. King, Chick Corea, Ella Fitzgerald, Aretha Franklin, Sarah Vaughn, Natalie Cole, Herbie Hancock, Ray Charles, Henry Mancini, Doc Severinsen, Phil Woods, Joe Lovano, and many others.

Hale A. VanderCook (1864–1949)
Hale A. VanderCook was born in Ann Arbor, Michigan. He was performing in bands by the age of fourteen and became conductor of the J. H. LaPearl Circus Band in 1891. He settled in Chicago and founded VanderCook Cornet School in 1909. The purpose of the school was to train musicians as performers, directors, and teachers. VanderCook composed over seventy marches. Among the most famous are *American Stride, Olevine, Pacific Fleet, Pageant of Columbia,* and *S.S. Theodore Roosevelt.* He published his *Course in Band and Orchestra Directing* in 1916. VanderCook studied cornet with Frank Holton and A. F. Weldon. He published *Modern Method of Cornet Playing in 20 Lessons* in 1922.

Anthony Vazzana
Anthony Vazzana began his formal study of music at age eight. At eleven he received his first scholarship (in piano) at the Emma Willard Conservatory in his native Troy, New York.

Vazzana's formal education includes degrees at the State University of New York, Potsdam, and master's and doctorate at the University of

Southern California. In addition, he did advanced study at Tanglewood and Bennington College in theory and composition.

Among his residencies in composition are three Dorland Mountain Colony and one each at the Bennington College Composers' Conference, MacDowell Colony, Montalvo Arts Center, the Djerassi Foundation, and the Rockefeller Foundation at the Villa Serbelloni in Bellagio, Italy.

He has composed over 100 works, several of which have been performed and broadcast in Europe, Asia, and at new music festivals in the United States with additional performances in South Africa in 1992. A few premieres include *ODISSEA* for orchestra (1988); *METAMOR-PHOSES* for wind orchestra and *DISEGNI II* for piano, cello, and percussion (both in 1989); and *VIAGGI* for trombone octet, *CONCERTO SAPPORO* for euphonium and orchestra, and *LINEA* for solo horn (all three in 1990).

He completed production of and recorded an interview for RAI Radio 3 to accompany the broadcast of *TRINAKIE* for orchestra in Rome, Italy. He has been a frequent guest on radio in live interviews featuring his music. In the United States his works have been broadcast nationally on programs such as on NPR. In Europe his music has been aired over radio in Hilvorshim (Holland), Sudwest Rundfunk (Germany), Radio Copenhagen (Denmark), and Radio Basel (Switzerland) with performances also in the Phillippines and Japan.

Commissions include those by the Duo Contemporain of Holland, the Goldman-Brown Duo, the Southwest Chamber Music Association, the Pasadena Symphony Orchestra, the Davis-Joachim Duo of Canada, and TUBA. Recent commissions include the aforementioned *DISEGNI II,* another for horn and organ premiered at the Musikvereinsaal in Vienna, a concerto for piano and chamber ensemble premiered in New York by the North-South Consonance in 1991, and still another for wind orchestra by the West Texas State University Band. In addition, the ITEA/TUBA-commissioned *CONCERTO SAPPORO* for euphonium and orchestra was performed in August 1990 at the International Conference by soloist Brian Bowman with conductor Keith Brown, and the Sapporo Symphony in Japan. The third panel in his orchestral tryptich, *ORI-ZONTE,* was completed in 1992; the other two panels are *TRINAKIE* and *ODISSEA.*

Carl Vollrath

Carl Vollrath was born in New York City. His parents arrived from Germany and settled in New York in the early 1930s during the rise of Hitler. In 1949 his father decided to retire to Florida and Vollrath joined him there after graduating from high school. He went on to continue his education at Stetson University, where he received a bachelor of music education degree in 1953. After graduating from Stetson, Vollrath joined the West Point Military Academy Band in New York. During that time he also studied at Columbia University and went on to receive his master of music education degree in 1956.

After two years in Miami, Florida, as a music consultant for two public schools, Vollrath decided to further his study of music and entered Florida State University (FSU) to work toward his doctorate in music education. He studied composition with Ernst von Doynanyi and later with John Boda and Carlisle Floyd. His dissertation, the two-act opera *The Quest,* based on the Children's Crusade of 1212, was performed three times by the FSU Opera Workshop. In 1965 he joined the faculty of Troy State University in Troy, Alabama, and remained on the faculty until his retirement. Vollrath's major compositional output includes works for band, six symphonies, and numerous one-movement works.

Himie Voxman (1912–)

Himie Voxman was born in Centerville, Iowa, and attended the University of Iowa (UI) by teaching clarinet to high school students to pay for his college expenses. He obtained his bachelor of science degree with high distinction in chemical engineering in 1933. He then went on to receive his master of arts degree in 1934. He joined the UI faculty in 1939. In 1954, he became director of the School of Music, a position he held for 26 years, until his retirement in 1980. Deservedly so, the Voxman Music Building was named in his honor in 1995. He has published numerous compilations and editions for wind instruments and co-authored four bibliographies of wind instrument literature. In this area of specialization he has served as advisor for over forty doctoral dissertations. He also is a former vice president of the National Association of College Wind and Percussion Instructors, and has held various state and national offices in both the Music Educators National Conference and the MTNA.

William Wiedrich

William Wiedrich is associate professor of conducting at the University of Southern Florida, Tampa, where he conducts the symphony orchestra and wind ensemble. He heads the graduate program in conducting and teaches conducting privately throughout the state of Florida, where he is often engaged as a guest conductor and clinician.

Prior to his appointment at Tampa, Wiedrich held faculty conducting positions at East Carolina University and Michigan State University, and was visiting professor and conductor at the University of Michigan, where he later earned his doctorate. His teachers include Gustav Meier, H. Robert Reynolds, and Larry Rachleff, as well as Gunther Schuller at the Festival at Sandpoint. He also attended the conducting seminar at Tanglewood. He is a member of the board of directors of Quorum, a professional contemporary music ensemble, and is a founding member of Newmusic Tampa, a similar ensemble actively performing in the Tampa Bay area.

A published composer and arranger, Wiedrich is in demand as a clinician and adjudicator throughout the United States. He is active in commissioning works for orchestra, chamber ensemble, and wind ensemble. Groups with whom he has collaborated with have consistently received praise for their sensitive performances.

Christopher Wiggins (1956–)
Christopher Wiggins studied at the Universities of Liverpool, Leeds (Bretton Hall College), London (Goldsmiths College), and Surrey, specializing in composition. He was awarded the Allsop Prize for composition (Liverpool) in 1977 and the Wangford Composers' Prize in 1991. His music has been performed in over thirty countries worldwide and broadcast in five.

His output includes choral, orchestral, chamber (including three string quartets, *Op. 1, Op. 89, and Op. 106*), solo, and educational pieces. A sizeable proportion of his output (over thirty pieces) is for horn/horn ensemble, and these pieces have been extensively performed, particularly in the United States. His music is published in the UK, the United States, and the Netherlands.

Since 1989 Wiggins has enjoyed close links with Estonia and conducted a number of broadcast concerts in Tallinn in the early 1990s. He organized a fund-raising campaign in early 1992 that enabled 35 young musicians and their teachers to visit and work with members of one of the Bedfordshire Youth Orchestras at Easter that year. He was a member of the Luton Symphony Orchestra for over fifteen years, becoming an associate conductor and representing that orchestra on the Luton Arts Council. He was also the first music director of the Luton University Orchestra.

He became a member of the Composers' Guild of Great Britain in the mid-1980s, joining the PRS soon afterward, and served on the executive committee of the Composers' Guild from 1993 until 1996. He is currently a member of the British Academy of Composers & Songwriters, the International Horn Society, ESTA (UK), and the MCPS; a friend of the British Music Information Centre; and an Ordinary Member of Convocation of the University of London.

Philip Wilby (1949–)
Born in Pontefract, UK, in 1949, Philip Wilby was educated at Leeds Grammar School and Keble College, Oxford. Wilby attributes the awakening of his interest in composition to Herbert Howells, whose extracurricular composition classes he attended while a violinist in the National Youth Orchestra of Great Britain. A serious commitment to composition developed during the years at Oxford and, having gained his bachelor of music in composition in 1971, Wilby continued to write music even while working as a professional violinist (first Covent Garden and later with the City of Birmingham Symphony Orchestra). He returned to Yorkshire in 1972 and is principal lecturer in composition at the University of Leeds.

Among his wide-ranging output is a considerable body of wind music, and since 1985 this interest in writing for wind forces has led to a regular residency at the Fresno campus of the University of California, who have commissioned much of Wilby's more recent wind band music. Wilby has also given much time to writing for liturgical purposes and recent works include *St. Paul's Service* (1988), commissioned by St. Paul's Cathedral for John Scott and the Choir of St. Paul's Cathedral, and *The Trinity Service* (1992), commissioned by Norwich Cathedral for the 1992 Norwich Festival of Contemporary Church Music.

In addition to concert music, Wilby has written educational works and incidental music for television. The academic environment at Leeds has also fostered a number of scholarly interests that have led to a remarkable series of reconstructions of Mozart fragments. In 1985 these were the subject of a Yorkshire television documentary featuring the Amadeus String Quartet, and in 1990 they were recorded by the Academy of St. Martin in the Fields for the complete *Philips Mozart Edition*.

Alec Wilder (1907–1980)
Alec Wilder was born Alexander Lafayette Chew Wilder in Rochester, New York, on February 16, 1907. He studied briefly at the Eastman School of Music, but as a composer was largely self-taught. As a young man he moved to New York City

and made the Algonquin Hotel—that remarkable enclave of American literati and artistic intelligentsia—his permanent home, although he traveled widely and often.

It is a relative rarity for a composer to enjoy a close musical kinship with classical musicians, jazz musicians, and popular singers. Wilder was such a composer, endearing himself to a relatively small but very loyal coterie of performers and successfully appealing to their diverse styles and conceptions. He wrote art songs for distinguished sopranos Jan DeGaetani and Eileen Farrell; chamber music for the New York Woodwind and New York Brass Quintets; and large instrumental works for conductors Erich Leinsdorf, Frederick Fennell, Gunther Schuller, Sarah Caldwell, David Zinman, Donald Hunsberger, and Frank Battisti, many of them premiering his works for orchestra or wind ensemble. In the early 1950s, Wilder became increasingly drawn to writing concert music for soloists, chamber ensembles, and orchestras. Up to the end of his life, he produced dozens of compositions for the concert hall, writing in his typically melodious and ingratiating style. His works are fresh, strong, and lyrical, and very much "in the American grain." Many pieces include movements that express a kind of melancholy desolation, an un-self-pitying loneliness, in contrast to the more buoyant and witty surrounding fast movements.

Wilder wrote music because he said it was the only thing that could content his spirit. He declared, "I didn't do well in terms of financial reward or recognition. But that was never the point." Wilder shunned publicity and was uncomfortable with celebrity. If he never was one to get grants, receive commissions, win prizes, it is because he never sought such favors. A deep distrust of institutions, combined with an extraordinary shyness verging on an inferiority complex, prevented him from circulating and operating in the composer's world in the ways generally expected of composers. Nonetheless, his awards eventually—late in life—included an honorary doctorate from the Eastman School of Music, the Peabody Award, an unused Guggenheim Fellowship just before his death, an Avon Foundation grant, the Deems Taylor ASCAP Award, and a National Book Award—all having to do with *American Popular Song: The Great Innovators, 1900–1950* (co-written with James T. Maher), undoubtedly the definitive work on the subject. He included almost everyone who had written a song of quality, but not one word about himself or any of the hundreds—maybe thousands—of pieces he wrote.

Wilder died of lung cancer on Christmas Eve in 1980 in Gainesville, Florida–" just in time to keep from becoming better known," as he might have joked. Wilder hosted the successful NPR 56-show series *American Popular Song* with Loonis McGlohon (his co-writer in later years), which was bringing about a renaissance of popular song. People were beginning to seek interviews with Wilder, and this attention made him nervous. Had he lived, he probably would not have had enough courage to attend either the 1983 ceremony at which he was inducted into the Songwriters' Hall of Fame or the 1991 dedication of the Alec Wilder Reading Room in the Sibley Music Library at the Eastman School of Music.

Luigi Zaninelli

Performers and audiences around the world know the music of Luigi Zaninelli as work that excites the senses and stimulates the mind. Following high school, Gian-Carlo Menotti brought Zaninelli to the Curtis Institute of Music. At age nineteen, the Curtis Institute sent him to Italy to study composition with the legendary Rosario Scalero (the teacher of Samuel Barber and Menotti).

Upon graduation, Zaninelli was appointed to the faculty of the Curtis Institute. In 1958, he began his long relationship with Shawnee Press as composer/arranger/pianist/conductor. In 1964, he returned to Rome to compose film music for RCA Italiana. During that period, Zaninelli became conductor/arranger for Metropolitan Opera soprano Anna Moffo.

During his career, Zaninelli has served as composer-in-residence at the University of Calgary and the Banff School of Fine Arts. Since 1973, he has been the composer-in-residence at the University of Southern Mississippi.

Among his numerous honors are a Steinway Prize, ASCAP awards since 1964, and an Outstanding Achievement Award, Province of Alberta. In 1991, he became the first three-time winner of the Mississippi Institute of Arts and Letters Music Award.

With more than 300 published works to his credit, Zaninelli has been commissioned to compose for all mediums, including opera, ballet, chamber music, orchestra, band, chorus, and solo songs. He also has composed several movie and television scores, including for the PBS documentaries *The Islander, Passover,* and *The Last Confederates.* His one-act opera, *Mr. Sebastian,* was premiered in 1995, followed by the first performance of his first full-length opera, *Snow-White,* in March 1996.

17. Biographical Sketches of Professional Euphoniumists

Bryce Edwards

The following biographies have been compiled through questionnaires sent to professional euphonium players throughout the world. Many were incomplete or in a foreign language and have been reconstructed if possible. The editor does not assume responsibility for incomplete or incorrect information given in each entry. Many of the biographies were found through research in other published sources and made to fit into these guidelines. Some completed questionnaires were received too late for admittance to the listing.

Thank you to the following individuals who gave their time and support developing performer lists and aided in the contacting and researching of many of the performers contained in this chapter: Greg Aitken, Seth Fletcher, Adam Frey, Aaron Marsee, R. Winston Morris, Eric Paull, Harvey Phillips, and Hitomi Yakata-Garcia, as well as all of the international consultants. This editor would also like to thank his wife, Melissa Edwards, for contributions to this chapter and for her loving support. The following information could not have been put together without the help of these hard-working and committed people.

Aitken, Greg
Born: 09/19/1965
Current Positions: Lecturer in euphonium, Queensland Conservatorium of Music, 2001–.
Past Positions: Lecturer in low brass, Queensland University of Technology (1992–2003); lecturer in trombone, University of Southern Queensland (2001–2002); principal bass trombone, Queensland Symphony Orchestra (1989), acting principal trombone (1990).
Contributions: Treasurer and life member Australian Trombone Association; conductor, Brisbane Brass, 1990–.
Education: BMus, Queensland Conservatorium of Music (1984–1987); Licentiate, Trinity College London (1986); Fellowship, Trinity College London (1987); Graduate Diploma of Education, Queensland University of Technology (1997).
Teachers: Michael Barnes, Arthur Walton, Vic Johnson, George Schipke, Arthur Middleton, Paul Terracini, Simone de Haan, Craig Cunningham, Philip Jameson.

Alexander, Ashley
Positions Held: Performed with Tex Beneke, Billy May, and Stan Kenton; member of the Matteson-Phillips Tuba/Jazz Consort; faculty member of Mount San Antonio College, Walnut, California, where he also taught applied music.
Contributions: One of the few jazz euphoniumists.

Alexander, Russell
Dates: 1877–1915
Positions Held: Euphoniumist for the European tour of Barnum and Bailey's Greatest Show on Earth (1897–1902).
Contributions: Composer of the marches *Colossus of Columbia, The Southerner, Olympia Hippodrome, The Exposition Four, The Darlington*.

Araki, Tamao
Current Positions: Principal euphonium, Vivid Brass Tokyo; instructor, Tamagawa University.
Contributions: Third prize, 9th Japan Wind and Percussion Competition (1992); third prize, 12th Japan Wind and Percussion Competition (1995); first prize, 6th Harvey Phillips competition (1988).
Education: BM, Tamagawa University (1989).

Ashworth, Tom
Born: 06/20/1957
Current Positions: Faculty, University of Minnesota, 1990–; featured trombonist, Saint Paul Chamber Orchestra (SPCO); freelance musician.
Past Positions: Lecturer in trombone, Canberra School of Music, Australia (1994–1995); member, Kansas City Symphony Orchestra; teacher of trombone and jazz improvisation, University of Kansas (1987–1990).
Contributions: Host, International Trombone Workshop (1994) and International Tuba-Euphonium Conference (ITEC) (1998); clinician, soloist, and adjudicator throughout the United States, Australia, and Europe; recordings with SPCO, Minnesota Orchestra, Graham Ashton Brass Ensemble, Summit Hill Brass, and Symphonia; recorded a collection of contest solo pieces for Summit Records; recorded music for movies, CDs, and radio/TV jingles.
Education: BM performance, California State University, Fresno (1980); MM performance, University of North Texas (1986).

Teachers: Lawrence Sutherland, Leon Brown, Vern Kagarice, John Kitzman.

Baird, Donald R.
Dates: 1932–1979
Positions Held: Euphonium soloist with The United States Army Band (1956); taught band in the Odessa Public School System at Hood Junior High School (1958–1962); band director at Phillips University (1962–1964); faculty at West Texas State University (1965–1979).
Education: Bachelor's, Phillips University in Enid, Oklahoma (1954); master's, University of Illinois (1957).

Baker, Buddy
Dates: 1932–
Positions: Euphoniumist with the Matteson-Phillips Tuba/Jazz Consort; head of the Brass and Percussion Department at the University of Northern Colorado at Greeley, Colorado.
Education: BM and MM in trombone performance and a performer's certificate from Indiana University.

Ball, Tom
Positions: Freelance musician and music educator, Colorado, 1995–; visiting assistant professor of music at Adams State College (2003–2004); graduate teaching assistant, University of Northern Colorado (2000–2002, 2004–2005), University of Colorado (1996–1998); currently performs and records with several local bands including Conjunto Colores, the Lionel Young Band, Onda, and Jennifer Lane.
Contributions: Has appeared on more than ten CD releases; toured Canada, the Caribbean, and every state in the continental United States; performed with many diverse groups and artists including the Pueblo Symphony, Benny Golson, Rashid Ali, David S. Ware, Ravi Coltrane, George Garzone and the Fringe, Eddie Daniels, Dave and Don Grusin, Nicholas Payton, David Murray, Brian Lynch, Conrad Herwig, Manhattan Transfer, and the Jimmy Dorsey Band; performed at the Blue Note in New York City, Red Rocks Amphitheater, and the Kansas City Jazz and Blues Festival.
Education: BM, trombone performance, Berklee College of Music (1991); MM, trombone performance, University of Colorado (1998); doctor of arts ABD, University of Northern Colorado.

Bandman, David
Current Positions: Euphoniumist/music arranger, The United States Air Force Band Ceremonial Brass (1996–).
Past Positions: Euphoniumist, the United States Air Force Band of the West, Lackland (1988).
Education: BA music, University of North Texas (1983).
Teachers: Vern Kagarice.

Baumgartner, Hans
Born: 07/04/1953
Current Positions: Low brass instructor at various music schools in Berne.
Past Positions: Solo euphonium with Brass Band Posaunenchor Lützelflüh -Grünenmatt, Bibellesebund-Musik Schweiz, Musiklager Allianz Musik Basel, Brass Band Posaunenchor Eschlikon, Brass Band Berner Oberland, Swiss Army Wind Band.
Education: Teaching diploma: Conservatoire Fribourg.
Teachers: Pascal Eicher, Daniel Aegerter, Markus S. Bach, Eric Ball, Albert Benz.

Behrend, Roger
Positions: Soloist, principal euphonium, the United States Navy Band, Washington, D.C.; professor of tuba/euphonium, George Mason University.
Contributions: Founding member, United States Navy Tuba-Euphonium quartet; commissioned and premiered over 25 works for the euphonium; released numerous recordings.
Education: BA, music education, Michigan State University; MM, performance, George Mason University.
Teachers: Leonard Falcone.

Belvin, Cory Daniel
Born: 06/06/1979
Current Positions: Euphonium, The Army Ground Forces Band.
Contributions: Recordings: *Pierre Garbage Festival, For the Kings of Brass, Play That Funky Tuba Right, Boy, Carnegie VI, Euphoniums Unlimited, Music for Saxophone and Symphonic Winds, Tennessee Tech Pride.*
Education: BA, music education, Tennessee Technological University; graduate work at Cincinnati Conservatory of Music.
Teachers: David Wiseman, R. Winston Morris, Tim Northcut.

Bone, Lloyd E. (Jr.)
Born: 12/29/1972
Current Positions: Assistant professor of music, Glenville State College.
Past Positions: Low brass instructor, Music Makers of Cincinnati, 1999–2004; private instructor, 1993–2004; instructor, University of Cincinnati Bearcat Bands, 2002–2004; graduate assistant, University of Cincinnati Conservatory of Music, 2003–2004; Hoffbrau House German Polka Band, Newport, Kentucky, 2003–2004. Band director, music teacher, and Arts Department chair, the Schilling School for Gifted Children, Cincinnati, Ohio (1998–2002); adjunct instructor of low brass, Murray State University, Murray, Kentucky (2001–2003); the Circus Kingdom Circus Band (1993); Mr. Jack Daniel's Original Silver Cornet Band (1996–1997).

Contributions: Various *ITEA Journal* reviews, 1998–current; *ITEA Journal* news editor, 2004–current, and co-editor, *The Euphonium Source Book*. Competitor/participant: 1996 Collegiate All-Star Tuba and Euphonium Ensemble (Chicago), 1997 Verso il Millenio International Euphonium Solo Competition (Riva del Garda, Italy), 1998 International Mock Band Euphonium Excerpt Competition (Minneapolis), and numerous Tennessee Tech. Tuba Ensemble recordings.

Education: Bachelor of music education and English minor, Tennessee Tech. University (1995); master of music, University of Cincinnati College–Conservatory of Music (2001); DMA, University of Cincinnati College–Conservatory of Music (2007).

Teachers: R. Winston Morris, Timothy Northcutt, and Brian Bowman (intermittently).

Bowman, Brian L.

Born: 07/22/1946

Current Positions: Professor of euphonium, University of North Texas, 1999–; member of Summit Brass, 1991–; member of Symphonia.

Past Positions: Teaching: Professor of music, chair—brass performance, Duquesne University (1991–1999); visiting professor of euphonium, University of North Texas (1997–1999); adjunct music faculty, University of Virginia (1990); adjunct professor of euphonium, George Mason University (1983–1991); adjunct music faculty, University of Maryland, College Park, administration and development of DMA program in euphonium (1982–1991); visiting professor of euphonium, Michigan State University (1988); adjunct music faculty, the Catholic University of America (1978–1991); visiting assistant professor of music, Department of Performing Arts, Virginia Polytechnical Institute and State University (1980); visiting professor of music, St. Mary's College of Maryland (1978–1984); teaching fellow, University of Michigan (1969–1970). Professional military band career: Euphonium soloist and section leader of The United States Air Force Band, Washington, D.C. (1976–1991); euphonium soloist and section leader of The United States Armed Forces Bicentennial Band (1974–1976); euphonium soloist and section leader of the United States Navy Band, Washington, D.C. (1970–1974); principal euphonium and soloist with the River City Brass Band (1997–1999).

Contributions: Recorded twenty albums of the Heritage of the March series; principal euphonium and soloist with the River City Brass Band; recorded *Heartland* (1998); ITEA 1st Life Member. Offices held: Euphonium pedagogy editor *TUBA Journal*, euphonium coordinator (1977–1979), vice president (1979–1981), president (1981–1983), past president (1983–1987), chairman–board of directors (1983–1987); currently: member, board of directors member—nominating committee; hosted, planned, and presided over the 1983 ITEA Conference; member of artist board—Summit Brass, board of advisors—Leonard Falcone Competition; former member: National Association of College Wind and Percussion Instructors, International Trombone Association, National Band Association, International Trumpet Guild, National Horn Society, Music Educators National Conference, String Training and Educational Program for African-American Students; board member: North American Brass Band Association; affiliations: KAPPA KAPPA PSI, Pi Kappa Lambda, PHI MU ALPHA; articles published: "You Play a What?," "Brass and Percussion," "Euphonium—Tuba Opportunities in Service Bands," *TUBA Journal*; "The Euphonium—Extinct or Extant!," *Instrumentalist*; euphonium music reviewer—*TUBA Journal* (1975–1976); *Master Class—Euphonium, Accent*; associate editor *TUBA Journal* (1978–1979); "An Interview with Brian Bowman," *Instrumentalist*; "Developing Euphonium Tone," *Instrumentalist*; "The Euphonium in the United States," *Marsy as 14–Revue de Pedagogie Musicale et Choregraphique*; "Playing/Teaching—Help from the Specialists, Euphonium," *Bdguide*; "Euphoniumist Feels the Sting of Neglect and Discrimination," *Wall Street Journal*; "Advice for College Euphonium Applicants," *Instrumentalist*; "Euphonium Technique," *Instrumentalist*; books authored: *Practical Hints for Playing the Baritone (Euphonium), Euphonium Excerpts from the Standard Band and Orchestra Library, DO IT! Play Baritone—Euphonium, Arban Complete Method for Euphonium/Trombone, Instrument and Mouthpiece Design*; design and performance consultant with the Willson Musical Instrument Company; design and testing of the Willson 2900 professional euphonium; developed a line of specialized Brian Bowman euphonium mouthpieces; frequently consulted by euphonium manufactures, including Yamaha, Besson, Hirshbruner, Miraphone, and others in testing and evaluating instruments; honors and awards: only living euphonium soloist listed in *Twentieth Century Brass Soloists* by Michael Meckna; Hokkaido Tuba/Euphonium Association names their annual euphonium solo competition the Brian L. Bowman Solo Competition; received Lifetime Achievement Award from TUBA (1995); selected as Euphonium Player of the Year by the *British Bandsman Magazine* (1989); selected as Outstanding Airman of the Air Force District of Washington (1989); selected as one of the Outstanding Young Men of America (1982).

Education: BMUS performance, University of Michigan (1970); MMUS performance, University of Michigan (1970); DMUS, University of Michigan (1975).

Teachers: Bardell Bowman, Robert L'Heureux, Siguard Swanson, Rex Conner, Robert Lambert, Frank Crisafulli, Wilbur Pursley, Glenn P. Smith, Tyronne Breuneger, John Marcellus, Arnold Jacobs.

Brasch, Harold
Dates: 10/07/1916–11/01/1984
Positions: Principal euphoniumist, the United States Navy Band, Washington, D.C. (1936–1956); freelance clinician and soloist; teacher, International Music Camp, North Dakota (1960–1984); euphoniumist/director/soloist, National Concert Band of America (1975–1984).
Contributions: Arranged many solos for euphonium; first to publicize the euphonium in the United States; first American player to use the "big bore" English model of euphonium; authored many articles; authored *The Euphonium and Four Valve Brasses—An Advanced Tutor.*
Teachers: Herbert L. Clarke.

Breuninger, Tyrone
Current Positions: Affiliate professor of music, Temple University and Rowan University.
Past Positions: Euphonium soloist, Red Hill, Pottstown, and Allentown Bands; trombonist/euphoniumist, Philadelphia Orchestra (1967–1999).

Brown, Joe D.
Born: 06/27/1960
Current Positions: Euphonium instrumentalist and assistant drum major for the United States Navy Band, Washington, D.C., June 1986–.
Past Positions: Euphonium instrumentalist in the United States Naval Academy Band in Annapolis, Maryland, January 1985–June 1986.
Education: BA, music education, Louisiana Tech University; MM performance, University of Northern Colorado.
Teachers: Howard Cohen, Raymond G. Young, Buddy Baker, Brian Bowman.

Burroughs, John S.
Dates: 1916–
Positions: Euphoniumist for the United States Marine Band 1935–1966; charter member of the National Concert Band of America; Polka Band member; the Royal Solomon Islands Police Band.

Call, Glenn
Dates: 1949–
Positions: Principal euphonium with the Continental Band at Fort Monroe, Virginia (1970–1972); instructor of low brass at Nazareth College of Rochester, New York (1975–1976); euphoniumist, the United States Marine Band in Washington, D.C. (1976–?).
Contributions: "Glenn Call Euphoniumist Prize" scholarship given to the first euphonium in the Eastman Wind Ensemble (awarded yearly);

helped organize the first Euphoniumist's Dinner (held in London); published *Euphonia,* "the journal for friends of the euphonium."
Education: Duquesne University, Pittsburgh, Pennsylvania (1967–1969); University of Maryland (1970–1972); Yale College (summer 1972); Southwest Missouri State University, Springfield, Missouri (1972–1975); Eastman School of Music (1975–1976).
Teachers: Walter S. Hoover, Matty Shiner, Art Lehman, Cherry Beauregard.

Campbell, Larry Bruce
Born: 07/20/1940
Current Positions: Professor at Louisiana State University in Baton Rouge 1969–; principal trombonist with the Baton Rouge Symphony 1969–.
Past Positions: Principal trombonist with the San Antonio Symphony (1968–1969); second trombonist with the San Antonio Symphony (1966–1968); principal euphonium with the United States Coast Guard Band in New London, Connecticut (1962–1966); principal euphonium with the Eastman Wind Ensemble (1959–1962).
Contributions: Editor of *New Music* for TUBA (1977–1981); record and CD reviewer for *ITA,* 1973–; *Fantasy for Euphonium* written by Dinos Constaninides for Campbell (1977); *Sounds and Silences* for Trombone Octet written by Liduino Pitombeira for the LSU Trombone Ensemble (2003).
Education: Bachelor of trombone and music education, Eastman School of Music (1962); master of education, Southwest Texas State University, San Marcos, Texas (1968).
Teachers: Emory Remington, Joe Still, Bob Gray, David Glasmire, Gordon Pulis, Rex Conner, Ed Herman.

Chevailler, Jean-Pierre
Born: 1945
Past Positions: Euphonium soloist, Radio Suisse Romande brass ensemble (1968–1977); professor of tenor tuba, Lausanne Conservatoire (1978).
Contributions: Won the Virtuoso Prize of the Lausanne Conservatoire (1980); recorded *Euphonium in Recital* (1980), *The Classic Euphonium* (1989); received the title Euphonium Player of the Year (1983).
Education: Virtuoso diploma, Lausanne Conservatoire (1978).

Childs, David
Born: 1981
Current Positions: Teacher of euphonium, University College of Ripon & York St. John, University of York.
Past Positions: Principal euphonium, National Youth Brass Band of Wales, National Youth Brass Band of Great Britain; principal euphonium,

Brighouse & Rastrick Band; associate, Royal College of Music.

Contributions: Junior International Euphonium Champion (1996); winner, Harry Mortimer Award for Performance (1997); first euphoniumist to win Brass Young Musician of the Year competition.

Education: Bachelor of music, Royal Northern College of Music.

Teachers: Robert Childs.

Childs, Nicholas

Current Positions: Senior tutor in brass band studies at the Royal Northern College of Music; conductor, Black Dyke Brass Band; associate conductor of the National Youth Brass Band of Great Britain; trustee of the Brass Band Heritage Trust.

Contributions: Performs and teaches throughout the United Kingdom, Europe, Australia, the Far East, Canada, and the United States; has appeared with such groups as the BBC Philharmonic, Hallé Orchestra, "The President's Own" United States Marine Band, and the Canadian Brass; featured with nearly every major brass band throughout the world and many wind bands, especially in university settings in the United States, where he has been equally acclaimed for his teaching and clinic work; premiered many new works for brass band; released many recordings as both conductor and soloist.

Childs, Robert

Born: 04/05/1957

Current Positions: Head of brass band studies at Royal Welsh College of Music and Drama Cardiff; musical director of the Buy As You View Cory Band.

Past Positions: Senior lecturer at Royal Northern College of Music, Salford University, Leeds University, Bretton Hall, and University of Hull; principal euphonium with the Black Dyke Mills Band, Brighouse & Rastrick Band, Yorkshire Imperial Band, Grimethorpe Colliery Band.

Contributions: Founder of Doyen Recording Company; columnist in *The British Bandsman;* premiered Howarth *Euphonium Concerto,* Golland *Concerto,* Wilby *Concerto,* Downie *Concerto,* Clarke *Euphonium Concerto;* clinician for Boosey and Hawkes Musical Instruments; toured extensively in the 1980s and 1990s with brother Nicholas as the Childs Brothers; cut many albums as a soloist and as the Childs Brothers.

Education: Master's degree in Advanced Musicology, Leeds University; doctor of musical arts in conducting, Salford University; post-graduate certificate in education, Open University; Associate of the Royal College of Music London; Fellow of the London College of Music.

Teachers: Richard John Childs.

Colburn, Michael J.

Current Positions: Euphoniumist/conductor, "The President's Own" United States Marine Band, 1987–.

Past Positions: Faculty, Keystone Brass Institute (1989, 1992).

Contributions: Clinician; recitalist; recorded *The Golden Age of Brass, Vol. 3.*

Education: BA music performance, Arizona State University (1986); master's conducting, George Mason University (1991).

Teachers: Peter Popiel, Daniel Perantoni, Brian Bowman, David Werden, Arnold Jacobs.

Corwell, Neal

Born: 07/07/1959

Current Positions: The United States Army Band "Pershing's Own," 2002–.

Past Positions: 257th Army Band (2001–2002); euphonium soloist and clinician with The United States Army Band "Pershing's Own" (1981–1989); member of Symphonia; executive member, board of directors for the International Women's Brass Conference; freelance musician in Europe, Asia, and across the United States as guest euphonium artist, clinician, and composer; executive committee member of the ITEA; composer in residence for the Deep Creek Maryland Symphony (1994–1999); adjunct faculty at Frostburg State University and Shepherd College teaching low brass and electronic music; associate editor for the *ITEA Journal.*

Contributions: Founding member of Symphonia; published composer and arranger with specialty in low brass with synthesizer accompaniment; over fifty published original compositions for low brass instruments including numerous solo works with large ensemble accompaniment; solo CDs *Distant Images* (1994), *Heart of a Wolf* (2000), *Out Sitting in His Field* (2003).

Education: BS Frostburg State College (1981); MA George Mason University (1985); DMA University of Maryland (1997).

Teachers: David McCollum, Brian Bowman.

Cottrell, Jeff

Born: 1963

Current Positions: Adjunct tuba/euphonium professor, Hardin Simmons University; performer with Dash Riprock and the Dragons, 1991–; Legend Brass Quintet; Razzamajazz Dixieland band; Johnny D. and the Doo-Wops.

Past Positions: Private lesson instructor.

Contributions: Composer.

Education: BMUS composition, University of North Texas; MMUS performance, University of North Texas; DMUS, University of North Texas.

Teachers: Brian Bowman.

Cox, John

Current Positions: Euphoniumist, The United States Air Force Band Ceremonial Brass (2002–).

Education: James Madison University (1998–2001).
Teachers: Kevin Stees, Roger Behrend.

Craig, Mary Ann
Born: 08/28/1947
Current Positions: Professor of music and director of bands, Montclair State University, Upper Montclair, New Jersey, 1996–.
Past Positions: Professor of music, the College of St. Rose, Albany, New York (1981–1996); instrumental music teacher, Seneca Valley School District, Harmony, Pennsylvania (1970–1972, 1973–1978); lecturer of music, Goulburn College of Advanced Education and Wollongong Conservatorium of Music (1972–1973).
Contributions: ITEA president (2003–2005), vice president (2001–2003), secretary (1997–2001); founder, Colonial Tuba Quartet (1990); founder, Colonial Euphonium and Tuba Institute (1996); recordings: *Out on a Limb* (solo euphonium), *Spectraphonics* (the Colonial Tuba Quartet); commissioned multiple works for euphonium; commissioned multiple works for tuba-euphonium quartet; organized Russia's first tuba-euphonium conference (2003).
Education: Bachelor of music education, Baldwin-Wallace College (1969); master of music education, Indiana University (1970); doctor of music education, Indiana University, Bloomington (1981).
Teachers: Henry Charles Smith III, Keith Brown, Allen Kofsky, Neal Fisher.

Davidson, Bob
Dates: 1939–
Positions: Solo euphonium with Grimethorpe Colliery; solo euphonium with the C.W.S. (Manchester) Band; solo euphonium with Brighouse & Rastrick; solo euphonium with Hammonds Sauce Works Band.

Dayton, Jennifer
Current Positions: Euphoniumist, The United States Air Force Band Ceremonial Brass; member, US Air Force Tuba/Euphonium Quartet; chief librarian, The United States Air Force Band Ceremonial Brass; member of the Capitol Wind Symphony.
Education: BA music education, George Mason University (1995).
Teachers: Roger Behrend, Al Fabrizio.

DeLuca, Joseph
Dates: 1890–1935
Positions: Conductor, Municipal Band of Ripateatina; Creatores Band; Sousa Band (1920–1927); band director at the University of Arizona
Contributions: Great soloist noted for his chordal playing.
Education: Conservatory of Music, Perguia.

Dickman, Marcus Jr.
Born: 09/21/1960
Current Positions: Associate professor, University of North Florida, 1986–; principal euphonium, St. John's River City Brass band; founding member, the Modern Jazz Tuba Project.
Contributions: Winner, 1990 Leonard Falcone Euphonium Competition.
Education: Troy State University (1983); McNeese State University (1985); University of North Texas (1997).
Teachers: Everett Johnson, Frank Jeakle, Ed Bahr, Don Little, Rich Matteson.

Dollard, Joe
Born: 06/03/1961
Current Positions: Euphoniumist, United States Navy Band, Washington, D.C., 1989–, leader, United States Navy Band Brass Quartet, 2000–.
Past Positions: Principal euphonium, Dallas Wind Symphony (1985–1989).
Education: Bachelor of music in jazz studies, North Texas State University (1985).
Teachers: Don Little, Rich Matteson.

Doyle, Arthur
Dates: 1910–
Positions: St. Saviours Band; Melingriffith Band; Munn and Feltons Band; Luton Band; Royal Air Force Central Band; Philharmonia Orchestra of London; B.B.C. Concert Orchestra; London Symphony; London Philharmonic Orchestra; Royal Philharmonic Orchestra of London; City of Birmingham Symphony Orchestra.
Contributions: Founded the Arthur Doyle Concert Band.

Droste, Paul
Positions: Faculty, Ohio State University School of Music (1966–1992); director of marching band (1970–1983).
Contributions: The first DMA degrees in music performance on euphonium; euphonium coordinator of TUBA; founder, Brass Band of Columbus.
Education: BA music education, Ohio State University (1958); MM, Eastman School of Music (1961); DMA music performance, University of Arizona (1971).

Dummer, Lee
Born: 09/20/1953
Current Positions: Professional musician, Twin Cities area.
Past Positions: Professional musician, Twin Cities area.
Contributions: Former editor, *Euphonia* magazine; contributor, *TUBA Journal; Balade* written by John Zdechlik for Dummer; *Sentimentale* written by Jon Smith for Dummer.
Education: Gustavus Adolphus College (1976); Eastman School of Music (1979); Catholic University of America (1979).

Teachers: Mark Lammers, Cherry Beauregard, Arthur Lehman.

Edwards, Bryce A.
Born: 01/30/1978
Current Positions: Freelance musician, 2003–; private lesson instructor, 2003–; clinician, 2003; euphoniumist, Mr. Jack Daniel's Original Silver Cornet Band, 1999–; trombonist, Cumberland County Playhouse, 2004–.
Contributions: Associate editor, *The Euphonium Source Book;* first euphoniumist to win the Derryberry Solo Competition at Tennessee Technological University; first euphoniumist to win the Indiana University Brass Concerto Competition; recordings with the Tennessee Technological Tuba Ensemble: *Pierre Garbage, Kings of Brass;* recorded with *Euphoniums Unlimited;* member, Phi Mu Alpha Sinfonia, Collegiate MENC, and TUBA/ITEA.
Education: BA music education, Tennessee Technological University (2001); MM, euphonium performance, Indiana University, Bloomington (2003).
Teachers: R. Winston Morris, Daniel Perantoni, Atticus Hensley.

Eicher, Pascal
Born: 04/13/1952
Past Positions: Euphonium teacher at the Fribourg Conservatoire (1982–1993); conductor of the Brass Band Bienne (1975–1991); conductor of the Brass Band Fribourg (1995–2001); international adjudicator.
Education: Euphonium diploma Conservatoire Fribourg (1982).
Teachers: Frank Johnson, Len Withington, Lindon Baglyn, John Harrison.

Evéquoz, Jaques
Born: 04/12/1966
Current Positions: Teacher for low brass at Ecole de Musique Vétroz; euphonium soloist of the Rhodania Quartet, 1990–.
Past Positions: Solo euphonium, brass band 13 Etoiles (1983–2001); solo euphonium, National Youth Brass Band of Switzerland (1983–1987); euphonium soloist of the quartet Les Persévérants; award winner of numerous national solo prizes.
Contributions: Dedicated works for euphonium including *Mr. Euphonium* and *Euphonium Fiesta,* by Bertrand Moren.
Education: Euphonium diploma.
Teachers: Géo-Pierre Moren.

Falcone, Leonard
Dates: 1899–1985
Positions: Director of bands at Michigan State University; tuba/euphonium professor at Michigan State University.

Contributions: One of the first euphonium soloists; namesake of the Leonard Falcone Competition.
Education: Michigan State University.

Fisher, Mark
Current Positions: Principal trombonist, Santa Fe Opera; trombonist, Asbury Brass Quintet; freelance musician; principal substitute with Chicago Symphony Orchestra and the Lyric Opera of Chicago; faculty member, Northern Illinois University, Roosevelt University.
Past Positions: Substitute in orchestras of Detroit, Milwaukee, Minnesota, San Francisco.
Contributions: Winner of the TUBA Conference Senior Division Solo Competition (1983); winner of Women's Association of the Minnesota Orchestra Competition (1982).
Education: University of Northern Iowa; New England Conservatory of Music.

Flaten, Tormod
Born: 1975
Positions: Principal euphonium, brass band Eikanger-Bjorsvik Musikklag; euphonium with Norwegian military bands; euphonium with Bergen Philharmonic Orchestra.
Contributions: Norwegian Solo Champion (1996); winner, European Solo Competition in Munich, Germany (1999); winner, International Tuba/Euphonium Festival in Manchester, England (2000).
Education: University of Bergen, Grieg Academy.
Teachers: Kim Lofthouse, Grethe Tonheim.

Fletcher, Seth
Born: 03/01/1980
Current Positions: Euphoniumist, Tintwistle Brass Band, 2003–; euphoniumist, Elision Euphonium Quartet, 2003–.
Past Positions: Low brass teacher, middle Tennessee area (1998–1999, 2001–2003).
Contributions: Soloist with Tintwistle Brass Band, Tennessee Tech Tuba Ensemble, Tennessee Tech Symphony Band, Tennessee Tech Orchestra; recordings with Euphoniums Unlimited (Tennessee Technological University Alumni Euphonium Ensemble), RNCM Wind Orchestra, Tennessee Tech Tuba Ensemble, Tennessee Tech Symphony Band; contributing author, *The Euphonium Source Book.*
Education: MM, Royal Northern College of Music (2004); BM, Tennessee Technological University (2003).
Teachers: Steven Mead, R. Winston Morris, David Thornton.

Franke, Philip
Current Positions: Principal euphoniumist, "The President's Own" United States Marine Band (1981–).
Education: BA music education, University of Illinois.
Teachers: Charles Winking, Dan Perantoni, Robert Gray.

Frey, (Steven) Adam

Born: 03/31/1975

Current Positions: International soloist and teacher; adjunct professor, Emory University; adjunct professor, Georgia State University.

Contributions: Founder of the Euphonium Foundation, Inc., the International Euphonium Institute, Euphonium Enterprises, Inc., Athens Music Publishing; commissioned works and arrangements by Anthony Plog, Duncan MacMillian, Joshua Perry, Thijs Oud; author and reviewer of numerous articles published in *ITEA Journal, Brass Band World, The British Bandsman;* arranger/editor of more than ten euphonium works by Athens Music Publishing; recordings: *Listen to THIS!!* (1998); *Family Portraits* with the Point of Ayr Brass Band (1999), *Collected Dreams* (2003), Metropolitan Wind Symphony (2004).

Education: Bachelor of music performance in euphonium and tuba (magna cum laude), University of Georgia (1997); master's of music (with distinction), Royal Northern College of Music (1999); professional performance diploma (with distinction) Royal Northern College of Music (1999).

Teachers: David M. Randolph, Steven Mead.

Fröscher, Roland

Born: 04/11/1977

Current Positions: Music School Gürbetal, Bern, 2001–; solo euphonium with Brass Band Berneroberland, Switzerland, 2002–; solo euphonium Swiss Army Concert Band.

Education: Teaching diploma at the Hochschule der Künste Bern (2002); soloist diploma at the Hochschule der Künste Bern (2003–).

Teachers: Hans Baumgartner, Thomas Rüedi, Roger Bobo, Bert Joris, Steven Mead, Lance Nagels, Murray Crew, Michel Bequet.

Fukaishi, Sotaro

Born: 12/03/1963

Current Positions: Senzokugakuen College of Music, 1994–; director of Yokohama Euphonium Choir; instructor of Sakuyo College of Music and Senzoku Gakuen College.

Past Positions: Kurashiki Sakuyou Unv (1994–2003).

Contributions: Editor, *Euphonium Popular & Classical Music Best Selection,* Yamaha Music Media Corporation; *Euphonium Fantastic Duet,* Yamaha Music Media Corporation; won the second prize at the ITEC solo competition in Texas; won the third prize at the 3rd Japan Wind and Percussion Competition; won the Yatabe Award; won the third prize at the 2nd International Leonard Falcone Euphonium Competition; performed as a member of the Euphonium Company at ITEC at Kentucky University.

Education: BM, Kunitachi College of Music (1987); diploma course of Tokyo Concervatoire Shobi (1989).

Teachers: Toru Miura.

Gagnaux, Alexandre

Born: 08/08/1966

Current Positions: Member of the Musique de Landwehr de Fribourg, 1986–.

Past Positions: Solo euphonium with Brass Band Fribourg (1983–1989); solo euphonium with Brass Band de Bienne (1990–1992); member of the Jaguar Tuba Quartet (1991–1999).

Contributions: Solo CD *Trilogie* (1997) (première of *Trilogie for Euphonium* by B. Wiggins) Artlab recording; solo CD *Euphonium in Sight* (*Euph. Concerto* with orchestra by V. Cosma).

Teachers: Pierre Oulevey, Denis Renevey, Pascal Eicher.

Good, Rick

Born: 12/21/1961

Current Positions: Associate professor of low brass/associate director of bands, Auburn University, Auburn, Alabama.

Education: BM Ed., Mansfield University of Pennsylvania (1983); MM, Boston University (1984), credits toward degree; MM, Louisiana State University (1993); DMA, Arizona State University (1996).

Teachers: Sam Pilafian, Dan Perantoni, Donald Stanley, Larry Campbell.

Gotcher, Carroll

Born: 12/18/1961

Current Positions: Director of bands, Jackson County Schools, Tennessee; freelance teacher and performer, Euphouria Quartet.

Past Positions: Director of bands, Kingsbury Schools, Memphis, Tennessee.

Contributions: Founder of Euphouria Quartet; commissioned *In Remembrance September 11, 2001,* by Sy Brandon.

Education: BS, Tennessee Technological University (1988); MS, University of Tennessee (1992).

Teachers: R. Winston Morris, W. Sande McMorran, Don Hough.

Griffiths, Morgan

Positions: Principal euphonium, Black Dyke Mills Band; manager, Band Supplies; teacher of euphonium, University of Salford.

Contributions: Youngest principal euphonium, Black Dyke Mills Band; invited to join the Yorkshire Building Society Band; winner, European Championship (five times), All England Masters (once), British Open (twice); named Euphonium Player of the Year (1999).

Teachers: Geoffrey Whitham, John Clough.

Groom, Trevor

Dates: 1934

Positions: Kettering Salvation Army Band; Gus Foorwear Band.

Contributions: Premiered the Horovitz concerto for euphonium at London's Royal Albert Hall.

Teachers: Bert Sullivan.

Ham, Jason

Current Positions: Euphonium, the United States Military Academy Band at West Point, New York (2002–).

Contributions: 2001 winner of the ITEC Solo Euphonium Artist Competition; first-ever euphonium player to appear as a soloist with the People's Liberation Army Band of China; presented the first-ever euphonium recitals in Bulgaria and Macedonia.

Education: Music education and music performance at the University of Georgia.

Teachers: David Randolph, David Zerkel, Kenneth R. Kroesche, Ronald Davis.

Harris, Emily

Born: 02/24/1968

Current Positions: Professor of euphonium, trombone and tuba, Scuola Musicale di Arco, TN, Italy; impressario representing Roger Bobo and Steven Mead.

Past Positions: Professor of low brass, Fiesole Scuola di Musica, FI, Italy; conference coordinator, ITEC, Riva del Garda (1997).

Contributions: Numerous arrangements for brass published by Factotum, Italy.

Education: Royal Conservatory of Music, Toronto, Canada (1986); Mus Bac in trombone performance, University of Toronto (1991); Rotterdams Konservatorium, Netherlands (1995).

Teachers: Cameron Walter, Frank Harmantas, Murray Crewe, Roger Bobo, Steven Mead.

Hatano, Takeshi

Born: 07/13/1970

Current Positions: Nagoya University of Arts, 2003–; Kurashiki Sakuyo University, 2004–.

Education: Kunitachi College of Music (1989–1993); Duquesne University (1993–1995).

Teachers: Toru Miura, Brian Bowman.

Hauser, Joshua

Current Positions: Assistant professor of trombone, Tennessee Technological University; arranger for several genres.

Contributions: Founding member, Bulldog Brass Society; featured solo artist at the 1998 Concourse International de Quintettes de Cuivres; featured with the Filharmonica de Montevideo; performed and recorded with the Louisiana Repertory Jazz Ensemble (*Marching, Ragging, and Mourning: Brass Band Music of New Orleans, 1900–1920*) and Widespread Panic (*'Til The Medicine Takes*); featured soloist and arranger on several jazz and classical compositions on *Shazam!* by the Brass Arts Quintet; featured soloist on his own composition, *EuPhunk*, as a member of Euphoniums Unlimited.

Education: Degrees from: Oberlin College Conservatory, New England Conservatory, and the University of Georgia.

Heidler, Manfred

Born: 05/02/1960

Current Positions: Assistant director of the Germany Air Force Band # 2, Karlsruhe, Germany.

Past Positions: Tenorhorn/baritone soloist and musician of the German Army, Deutsche Bundeswehr.

Education: Tenorhorn and trombone at University of Music at Düsseldorf, Detmolt; conducting at University of Music at Trossingen, Germany; music, science, history, education, psychology at Heinrich-Heine University; PhD, Robert Schumann Music University, Düsseldorf.

Teachers: Franz Lecker, Karl Toubartz, Harry Ries (NL), Horst-Dieter Bolz, Branimir Slokar.

Helseth, Danny

Current Positions: The United States Air Force Concert Band, Bolling AFB, Washington, D.C., 2003–.

Education: Bachelor of music education, Central Washington University (1999); MMus euphonium performance, University of North Texas (2002); PGDip euphonium performance, Royal Northern College of Music (2002).

Teachers: Larry Gookin, Brian Bowman, Steven Mead.

Hensley, Atticus

Born: 11/10/1970

Current Positions: Associate band director, Tullahoma City Schools; full-time private instructor.

Past Positions: Graduate teaching assistant, University of Tennessee at Knoxville; adjunct faculty (music history), Middle Tennessee State University.

Contributions: Commissioned *Sonata for Euphonium and Piano* by Robert Cronin; semi-finalist for the 1999 Leonard Falcone International Euphonium Competition; contributing editor to *The Euphonium Source Book;* founding member of Euphouria Quartet.

Education: Bachelor of arts in music, University of Tennessee at Knoxville (1992); MM, University of Tennessee, Knoxville (1995).

Teachers: George Jones, Sande MacMorran.

Heo, Jae-Young

Positions: Seoul Philharmonic Orchestra (1986); teacher, Seoul National, Yonsei, Chungang Universities and Conservatories.

Contributions: Chairman, Korean Tuba Association (1987–1991).

Education: Chungang University, Seoul, Korea; Cologne College of Music.

Teachers: Hans Gelhar.

Himes, William

Positions: Instrumental music teacher in grades five–twelve; University of Michigan–Flint Campus low brass instructor; bandmaster of Flint Citadel Band of the Salvation Army; territorial music director for the Salvation Army's Central

Territory; bandmaster of the Chicago Staff Band of the Salvation Army.

Education: BA and MA from the University of Michigan.

Teachers: Brian Bowman.

Hokazono, Shoichiro

Born: 1969

Current Positions: Solo euphonium, Central Band of the Japan Air Self Defense Forces; euphonium instructor, Tokyo National University of Fine Arts and Music.

Contributions: Won first prize and grand prize at the 9th Japan Wind and Percussion Competition (1992); won first prize at the Philip Jones International Competition in Guebwiller, France (1997); guest recitalist at ITEC (1995); awarded Euphonium Player of the Year at the Tuba and Euphonium Conference in Great Britain (1997); performed as a special guest in the recital series, "From Bach to Contemporary Music (B to C)" at Tokyo Opera (2000); member of the Saito-Kinen Orchestra conducted by Seiji Ozawa (2002); presented master classes in Japan and the Conservatoire National Superieur de Musique de Paris, France (2002); performed around the world including Europe, the United States, and Asia; recorded four solo CDs as well as appearing in a number of recordings as a guest soloist.

Education: Shobi Conservatory in Tokyo (1994).

Teachers: Toru Miura, Kaoru Tsuyuki, Steven Mead.

Holland, Nancy

Born: 08/14/1954

Current Positions: Special education teacher with Nashville Metro schools.

Contributions: Co-coordinator for Nashville "Tuba-Christmas."

Education: Tennessee Technological University (1976); Delta State University (1977); Tennessee State University (1999).

Teachers: R. Winston Morris, Dennis Royal.

Howard, Noble

Positions: Sousa Band (1928–1930); Ringling Brothers Circus Band (1934–1939); Indianapolis Symphony Orchestra.

Huff, Sharon

Born: 08/08/1959

Current Positions: Associate professor of music at Millikin University, Decatur, Illinois, 2002–; president, International Women's Brass Conference, 2001–.

Past Positions: Music faculty member, Illinois State University, Normal (2001–2002); music faculty member, St. Norbert College, De Pere, Wisconsin (1990–2000); faculty brass quintet, Millikin University (2002); faculty brass quintet, Illinois

State University (2001–2002); Junction quartet (2001–2003).

Contributions: Member of the executive committee and conference coordinator for ITEA (1993–2002); frequent contributor to "New Materials" section of *ITEA Journal;* founder, Junction tuba/euphonium quartet; as member of Junction, commissioned pieces by Todd Fiegel, Alice Gomez, Gail Robertson, Brian Balmages, and Faye-Ellen Silverman; wrote DMA dissertation on Brian Bowman; executive director of the International Women's Brass Conference (1999–2001); advertising coordinator for the 2000 IWBC.

Education: Doctor of musical arts, University of Illinois, Champaign (1994); master of music, University of Illinois, Champaign (1988); bachelor of music education, Illinois State University, Normal (1982).

Teachers: Fritz Kaenzig, Robert Gray, Mickey Moore, Edward Livingston.

Humble, Karl

Dates: 1934–

Positions: Cedar Rapids (Iowa) Municipal Band (1952–1954); The United States Air Force Band in Colorado Springs, Colorado (1957–1962); the United States Marine Band, Washington, D.C.; National Concert Band of America in Washington, D.C.

Education: Coe College in Cedar Rapids; Catholic University in Washington, D.C.; University of Colorado.

Hunter, Angie

Born: 01/06/1962

Current Positions: German Bible Institute, fall 1989–.

Contributions: First winner of the Leonard Falcone International Baritone Competition (1986); founding and current member of the Junction tuba-euphonium quartet 2000–; scheduled guest artist at the Falcone Competition, 2005; at that event—world premiere of a new euphonium work by James Curnow.

Education: Artist's diploma in trombone, Staatliche Hochschule fuer Musik, Trossingen, Germany (1999); MM in euphonium performance, University of Illinois at Urbana-Champaign (1986); BM in euphonium performance, Bowling Green State University, Ohio (1983).

Teachers: Brian Bowman, Fritz Kaenzig, Kenley Inglefield, Abbie Conant, Robert Gray, David Glasmire.

Ito, Akihiko

Born: 07/28/1966

Current Positions: Freelance.

Education: Tokyo National University of Fine Arts and Music, BM degree (1989), MM (1991).

Teachers: Takao Ishikawa, Toru Miura, Kiyoshi Oishi, Steven Mead.

Jackson, James E., III.
Current Positions: Euphoniumist, the United States Coast Guard Band; conductor, Waterford Community Band.
Past Positions: Principal baritone, Lexington Brass Band; soloist, Mid-West International Band and Orchestra Clinic (1997).
Contributions: Founding member, Kentucky Horst Park Four Horsemen Tuba Quartet and the Concord Tuba-Euphonium Quartet; winner, TUBA Tuba-Euphonium Quartet competition (1995); winner, Leonard Falcone International Solo Euphonium Competition (1994).
Education: BA music education, University of Kentucky (1993); MM euphonium performance, George Mason University (1995); candidate, DMA, University of Kentucky.

Jenkins, Mark William
Born: 04/23/1978
Current Positions: Euphoniumist, "The Presidents Own" United States Marine Band, Washington, D.C.
Contributions: Commissioned *Faustbuch* by Elizabeth Raum (2002)
Education: Bachelor's of music performance, University of North Texas (2003); master's of music performance, University of Maryland (2004–).
Teachers: Robert Scann, Brian Bowman, James Kraft.

Jones, William H.
Positions: Principal euphoniumist, The United States Air Force Concert Band (1998–); euphoniumist, River City Band.
Education: BA music performance, Duquesne University.
Teachers: Brian Bowman, Murray Crewe, Roger Hanson, Barry Morrison.

Kellner, Steve
Born: 12/14/1958
Current positions: Euphonium instructor, the Peabody Institute; tuba-euphonium ensemble coach, University of Maryland, College Park; founding member, the Dominion Brass; trombonist, the Chesapeake Orchestra.
Past positions: Principal euphonium, the United States Marine Band (1987–1990, 1996–2004); principal euphonium, The Army Ground Forces Band (1981–1987); principal euphonium, 24th Infantry Division Band (1980–1981); principal euphonium, the Salvation Army Southern Territorial Band (1986–1990).
Contributions: Solos written for Stephen Bulla, *Caprice for Euphonium and Brass Quintet* (1988), Stephen Bulla, *Euphonium Fantasia* (1990), Douglas Court, *Spiritual Fantasy* (2000); founder of the Peabody Institute euphonium studio and tuba and euphonium ensemble; performed as euphonium player with the National Symphony Orchestra, Maryland Symphony, and Washington

Symphonic Brass; twelve national tours with the Marine Band, tour soloist; principal euphonium on numerous Marine Band (more than ten) and Salvation Army brass band recordings; euphonium soloist on two Salvation Army brass band recordings, one with the National Capital Band and one with the Southern Territorial Band.
Education: BM, trombone performance (2005).
Teachers: Robert Schramm, Mark Mordue, Mike Moore, Milt Stevens.

Kilpatrick, Barry
Positions: Professor of trombone and euphonium, State University of New York College (1979–); member of the Concord Brass Quintet; principal trombonist in the Erie Philharmonic Orchestra, principal trombonist, Erie Chamber Orchestra; member, Fredonia Chamber Players; teacher of trombone/euphonium at Interlochen (1985).
Education: BA music, MM performance, University of Wisconsin; DMA, Indiana University.
Teachers: Lewis Van Haney, Dee Stewart, William Richardson, Fred Dart, Allen Chase.

Kimmo, Rantakeisu
Born: 09/01/1966
Current Positions: Military musician in Pohja Military band.
Education: Military Music School, Oulu Conservatoire.
Teachers: Jorma Teeri, Sakari Lamberg, Jukka Myllys.

King, Karl
Dates: 1891–1971
Positions: Ringling Brothers Circus Band; Fort Dodge Municipal Band.
Contributions: Composed many marches and other band music.

Kipfer, Ueli
Born: 12/30/1974
Current Positions: Low brass teacher at the Music School Sumiswald, 1998–; member of the Quintetto Illegale, 2004–; founder and member of the Subito Brass Quartett, 2002–; teacher at the Music Schools of Konservatorium Bern and Oberemmental, 1998–.
Past Positions: Solo euphonium, National Youth Brass Band (1990–1995); solo euphonium, Nobody's Brass (1992–1993); solo euphonium, Brass Band Berneroberland (1997–2002).
Education: Euphonium, Music School Oberemmental (1993); conducting and euphonium, Konservatorium Bern (2000).
Teachers: James Gourlay, Roger Bobo, Steven Mead.

Kranchenfels, Heinrich
Dates: 1917–
Positions: "The President's Own" United States Marine Band (1947–1971); National Concert

Band of America in Washington, D.C.; Board of Advisors, TUBA.

Contributions: Two volumes of *The Art of Euphonium Playing.*

Education: Dolestown High School; Penn State University.

Kroesche, Kenneth R.

Born: 04/12/1963

Current Positions: Associate professor of low brass and coordinator of applied instrumental music, Oakland University, Rochester, Michigan, 2002–; substitute euphonium, Symphonia tuba-euphonium ensemble, 2002–; bass-trombone, Rochester Symphony Orchestra, Rochester, Michigan, 2002–; euphonium, Toledo Symphony Concert Band, Toledo, Ohio, 2003–; principal trombone, Oakland Symphony Orchestra, Rochester, Michigan, 2003–.

Past Positions: Instructor of euphonium, Blue Lake Fine Arts Camp, Twin Lake, Michigan (2003); associate professor of low brass and associate conductor of bands, Western Carolina University, Cullowhee, North Carolina (1995–2002); visiting instructor of euphonium, University of Georgia, Athens (1999); visiting instructor of euphonium, University of Michigan, Ann Arbor (1995–1996); assistant professor of low brass and assistant conductor of bands, Lenoir-Rhyne College, Hickory, North Carolina (1993–1995); instructor of euphonium and tuba (adjunct), University of Michigan–Flint (1991–1993); assistant director of euphonium/tuba ensemble, University of Michigan, Ann Arbor (1991–1993); associate director of bands, William B. Travis High School, Austin, Texas (1986–1989); tenor tuba (euphonium), bass trumpet and substitute trombone, North Carolina Symphony, Raleigh, North Carolina (1994–2002); second trombone, tenor tuba (euphonium), Asheville Symphony Orchestra, Asheville, North Carolina (1997–2002); conductor, music director, and euphonium soloist, Smoky Mountain Brass Band, Cullowhee, North Carolina (1995–1998); second euphonium, Brass Band of Battle Creek, Marshall, Michigan (1991–1993).

Contributions: Founder, American Tuba-Euphonium Quartet; contributing editor of *The Euphonium Source Book;* commissioned and premiered *Introduction and Dance for Euphonium and Brass Band* by Alan Fernie, *Sextet for Euphonium and Woodwind Quintet* by Walter Hartley, *Sonata for Euphonium and Piano* by Stuart Folse, *Reverie No. 3 for Euphonium and Piano* by William Wiedrich.

Education: Bachelor of music, music education, Texas State University, San Marcos, Texas (1986); master of music, performance, University of Michigan, Ann Arbor (1990); doctor of musical arts, performance, University of Michigan, Ann Arbor (1994).

Teachers: Brian Bowman, Charles Hurt, Arnold Jacobs, Fritz Kaenzig, Daniel Perantoni, H. Dennis Smith, J. Lesley Varner, Jerry Young.

Kuo, Yu-Ting

Born: 09/25/1972

Current Positions: Euphonium instructor, Fu-Jen Catholic University, 2001–.

Past Positions: Principal euphonium, National Taiwan Symphony Orchestra Wind Ensemble (1999–2003).

Education: C.N.R. de Rueil-Malmaison, France (1999).

Teacher: Andre Gilbert.

Kurosawa, Hiromi

Born: 02/06/1965

Current Positions: Instructor, Taito-ku; leader and euphonium player of Trailblazers 10 Piece Brass (1999–); euphonium teacher, Souzou Gakuen College (2000–); conducting and euphonium teaching, Fuchu Junior Wind Orchestra (1992–).

Contributions: Invited as guest band to the Great American Brass Band Festival in Kentucky (2000); commissioned a new work by Philip Sparke for ten-piece brass ensemble (2002); commissioned a new work by Goff Richards for ten-piece brass ensemble (2004).

Education: BM, graduated, Kunitachi College of Music (1989).

Teachers: Shinji Ichimura, Toru Miura, Brian Bowman, Steven Mead, Roger Webster.

LaDuke, Lance

Born: 09/11/1967

Current Positions: Principal solo euphonium, River City Brass Band, 2000–; adjunct professor of euphonium, Duquesne University, 2000–; Carnegie Mellon University, 2003–.

Past Positions: The United States Air Force Concert Band, Washington, D.C. (1991–1998).

Education: Michigan State University (1985–1990); University of Akron (1990–1991); George Mason University (1992–1995).

Teachers: Philip Sinder, Tucker Jolly, Brian Bowman.

Lehman, Arthur

Dates: 1917–

Positions: "The President's Own" United States Marine Band (1947–1971); National Concert Band of America in Washington, D.C.; Board of Advisors, TUBA.

Contributions: *The Art of Euphonium Playing* Volumes I and II; many solo commissions and recordings.

Education: Penn State University.

Lineberger, Laura

Born: 06/01/1962

Current Positions: Librarian for The United States Army Band "Pershing's Own."

Past Positions: Euphoniumist for The United States Army Band "Pershing's Own" (1990–2000).

Contributions: First female professional euphoniumist hired for The United States Army Band "Pershing's Own"; board member for the International Women's Brass Conference.

Education: Bachelor's in music education, Ohio State University (1980–1984); master's in music performance, University of Maryland, College Park (1987–1989).

Teachers: Paul Droste, Brian Bowman.

Louder, Earle

Born: 07/30/1932

Current Positions: Retired distinguished professor emeritus, Morehead State University, Morehead, Kentucky; principal and featured euphonium soloist for Keith Brion's New Sousa Band, 1991–; euphoniumist with Symphonia, 1994–; principal and featured euphonium soloist, the Blossom Festival Band of the Cleveland Symphony Orchestra, Blossom Center, Cuyahoga Falls, Ohio, 1976–1999, 2004–; the Blue Lake Festival Band, Blue Lake Fine Arts Camp, Twin Lake, Michigan, 1989–; principal euphonium, Lexington Brass Band, Lexington, Kentucky, 2000–; principal euphonium, Advocate Brass Band, Danville, Kentucky, 1991–; principal euphonium and featured soloist, the New Columbian Brass Band, Danville, Kentucky, 1994–; senior adjudicator for the International Euphonium Solo Competition of the Leonard V. Falcone International Euphonium and Tuba Festival, 1988–.

Past Positions: Principal and featured euphonium soloist and head of the brass department, the United States Navy Band, Washington, D.C. (1956–1968); resident euphonium artist and professor of euphonium, trombone, and tuba, Morehead State University, Morehead, Kentucky (1968–1996); principal euphonium, featured euphonium soloist, and assistant conductor, the Detroit Concert Band, Detroit, Michigan (1976–1994); euphoniumist/conductor, 46th Infantry Division Band, Michigan Army National Guard Headquarters Command, Lansing, Michigan (1952–1956); Philharmonia a Vent, recording wind orchestra, Terre Haute, Indiana (2000–2001).

Contributions: Charter member of TUBA/ITEA (1973); euphonium coordinator for TUBA (1975–1977 and 1999–2001); recipient of the Lifetime Achievement Award from TUBA/ITEA (1998); *Euphonium Music Guide* by Earle L. Louder and David R. Corbin, Jr. (published by the Instrumentalist Publishing Company 1978); music composed for and dedicated to Dr. Earle Louder: *Concerto for Euphonium and Band* by Frederick A. Mueller (1970), *Sonata for Euphonium with Piano* by Christopher Gallaher (1985), *Fanfares, Hymn, and Dance* (3rd Quartet for Euphonium/Tuba Ensemble) by Stephen Bulla (1996); *A Biography of Earle Louder: Euphonium*

Performer and Educator written by Dr. Richard Good (1996).

Education: Bachelor of music education, Michigan State University, East Lansing (1955); one year's work toward a master of music specializing in brass instruments (1956); doctor of music in euphonium performance, Florida State University, Tallahassee (1976).

Teachers: Leonard Falcone, William Cramer, Russell Williams.

Lumpkin, Royce

Born: 02/10/1942

Current Positions: Chair, Department of Music, and professor of music, University of North Carolina, Charlotte, 1998–.

Past Positions: Professor of music, University of North Texas, Denton (1971–1998).

Contributions: Past president of the International Trombone Association; premiered Martin Mailman's *Clastics II* and William Latham's *Eidolons;* principal tenor tuba and bass trumpet, Dallas Symphony Orchestra (1974–1998).

Education: Bachelor of music in music education, University of North Texas (1964); master of music education, University of North Texas (1965); doctor of musical arts, University of Oklahoma (1978).

Teachers: Leon F. Brown, Irvin Wagner.

Maldonado, Luis

Dates: 1957–03/01/1995

Positions: Original member, Brass Band of Battle Creek; assistant professor of low brass, Central Michigan University; faculty member, Interlochen Arts Camp and Blue Lake Fine Arts Camp; member, executive committee of the Leonard Falcone International Euphonium Festival.

Contributions: Authored many articles in the *TUBA Journal;* assisted with the structuring of competitions; performed across the United States and in Japan in solo recitals and as a guest artist with numerous performing organizations including Keith Brion's New Sousa Band and the Detroit Symphony Orchestra; past winner of the Falcone Festival Artist Division Competition and the Japan Euphonium Solo Competition.

Mantia, Simone

Dates: 1873–1951

Positions: Brooklyn Opera Houses; Sousa Band (1896–1904); Pryor's newly formed band; New York Philharmonic Orchestra; Victor Herbert's Orchestra; Metropolitan Opera House Orchestra; Lavalle's Band.

Teachers: Joseph Raffayola.

Marko, Saikko

Born: 02/28/1974

Current Positions: Warrant officer, Savo Military Band, Mikkeli, 1999–; teacher in Mikkeli, 1999–; teacher, Lappeenranta Music School, 2001–.

Education: Military Music School (1991–1995); Päijät-Häme Conservatoire (1998–2002).
Teachers: Juha Salmela, Jukka Myllys.

Marsteller, Loren J.
Born: 07/18/1946
Current Positions: Principal trombone, California Philharmonic Orchestra,1997–; solo baritone, Americus Brass Band (Civil War brass band), 1988–; solo euphonium, Tubadours (Tuba quartet), 1979–; trombone, Brassininity and Premier Brass Quintets, 1997–; euphonium and trombone, Pacific Brass Ensemble, 2002–; baritone, New Custer Band (7th Cavalry), 2001–; principal trombone, Antelope Valley Master Chorale Orchestra, Lancaster, California, 1999–; adjunct professor of trombone and euphonium, California State University, Long Beach, 1988–; Red Lodge Music Festival, Red Lodge, Montana (various years), 1974–.
Past Positions: Euphonium, "The President's Own" United States Marine Band (1968–1971); principal trombone, Calgary Philharmonic Orchestra, Calgary, Alberta, Canada (1972–1974); Sackbut, the Towne Waytes, Vancouver, British Columbia, Canada (1975–1976); principal trombone, Master Symphony Orchestra, Los Angeles (1982–1985); principal trombone, Pageant of the Masters, Laguna Beach, California (1982–1989); solo euphonium, Long Beach Municipal Band (1989–2000); baritone, Ghost Town Militia Band, Knott's Berry Farm, Buena Park, California (1991–1999); solo euphonium, California Wind Orchestra (1987–1996); solo euphonium, Los Angeles Rams' Band (1978–1981); euphonium, (Keith Brion's) New Sousa Band (1991–1994); euphonium, (George Foreman's) New Columbian Brass Band (1995 and 1998); solo trombone, Orquesta de Baja California, Tijuana, Mexico (1993–1999); trombone and euphonium, Tidewater Brass Quintet, St. Mary's City, Maryland (1977–1979). Teacher at University of Calgary, Calgary, Alberta, Canada; University of British Columbia, Vancouver, British Columbia, Canada; Azusa Pacific University, Azusa, California; Biola University, La Mirada, California; California State University, Northridge; Chapman University, Orange, California; Colburn School of Music, Los Angeles; Idyllwild School of Music and the Arts, Idyllwild, California; La Sierra University, Riverside, California; Pepperdine University, Malibu, California; Redlands University, Redlands, California; Whittier College, Whittier, California; Wildwood Music Camp, Big Bear, California.
Contributions: Works commissioned and premiered: *Alter Ego* by George Heussenstamm, for euphonium and tape; *Reincarnation* by Richard Bellis, for trombone and band; *Concerto for Trombone and Band* by Stanley Friedman. Works premiered: *Oration* by Raymond David Burkhart, for solo trombone and brass quintet; *Brass Quintets 7, 8 and 9* by Alec Wilder. Recordings: Loren Marsteller, trombone and euphonium, Americus Brass Band: *Music of the Civil War;* The Dodge City Cowboy Band: *Wild West Music of Buffalo Bill's Cowboy Band, Glory* (Original Motion Picture Soundtrack); Tubadours: *The Mighty Tubadours;* Los Angeles Philharmonic: *Janacek, Sinfonietta, Telarc;* Orquesta de Baja California: *Eugenia Leon interpreta a Cri Cri, BMG de Mexico the Orchestral Music of Meyer Kupferman;* New Custer Brass Band: *Custer's Last Band, Shrine to Music Museum;* Jim Self: *The Big Stretch: Tchaikovsky, Symphony No. 4, Finale.* Motion pictures: *Star Trek III: The Search for Spock, Old Gringo, Dead Again, Geronimo: An American Legend, True Lies, Crimson Tide, Extreme Measures, How the Grinch Stole Christmas, Pearl Harbor.*
Education: Bachelor of music, trombone performance, University of Southern California, Los Angeles (1968); master of music, trombone performance, Catholic University of America, Washington, D.C. (1972).
Teachers: Robert Marsteller, Keith Brown.

Masanori, Fukuda
Born: 12/05/1962
Current Positions: Tokyo Brass Society, 1984–; the Euphonium Company, 1991–; Rustic Bari-Tuba Ensemble, 1982–; Mito the Third High School (music course), 1995–.
Contributions: Solo CDs *Peace and Piece; Brass Band; Brass 8; Brass 6; Funiculi-Funicula Fantasy.*
Education: BMUS, Tamagawa University (1982–1986); MMUS Tamagawa University (1987); conducting, Senzoku Educational Institution College of Music (2001–2003).
Teachers: To-Ru Miura, Kazuyoshi Akiyama, Yoshitomo Kawachi.

Matteson, Rich
Dates: 1929–1993
Positions: North Texas University; clinician for Yamaha Company; co-founder of the Matteson-Phillips Tuba-Jazz Consort.
Contributions: Leading exponent in jazz euphonium and internationally acclaimed euphonium soloist.
Education: Iowa University.

May, Ole June
Dates: 1872–1917
Positions: Great Western Band; the United States Marine Band in Washington, D.C.; Arthur Pryor's Band.
Contributions: Known as "The Man with the Golden Tone."

McGeorge, Ryan
Born: 02/19/1979
Current Positions: "The President's Own" United States Marine Band, 2004–.

Past Positions: Euphonium soloist with the Broadway production *Blast!* (2001–2002).

Education: BM University of North Texas (1997–2004).

Teachers: Brian Bowman, Trisha Baran, Peggy Heinkle-Wolfe, Ross Kallen.

McNally, Robert

Positions: New York Staff Band of the Salvation Army; Territorial Youth Counselor for the U.S. Eastern Territory.

Education: Cincinnati Conservatory of Music.

Mead, Steven

Born: 02/26/1962

Current Positions: Professional euphonium soloist; senior tutor in euphonium, Royal Northern College of Music, Manchester, 1990–; artistic director, British Tuba Euphonium Festivals, 1994–; director, euphonium course, ISEB, Trento, Italy, 1999–; clinician and consultant for Besson Musical Instruments, 1986–; principal euphonium, Brass Band of Battle Creek; founder, euphonium course, Weinberg, Austria, 2001–.

Past Positions: Senior tutor in euphonium, Birmingham Conservatoire (1990–1999); Royal Academy of Music (1990–1995); Royal Scottish Academy, Glasgow (1994–1997); principal euphonium, Desford Colliery, GUS, C.W.S. Glasgow; guest teacher, Music Conservatory, Rotterdam (2001); director and co-director British National Tuba Euphonium Festivals in Birmingham and Manchester (1994–1995, 1997, 1999–2000, 2003); vice president of TUBA (1996–1999); co-artistic director of new USA Brass Band Summer Camp, Avalon (2002–2003).

Contributions: Premiere performances of euphonium works by Philip Sparke, Martin Ellerby, James Curnow, Tadeus Kassatti, Torstein Aagaard-Nilsen, Robert Jager, Vladimir Cosma, Rolf Wihelm, Arthur Butterworth, John Reeman, Thomas Dos, Marco Putz; featured guest at all the major brass band/wind band/low brass festivals, WASBE Festivals, Mid Europe (Schladming), International Tuba Euphonium Festivals, Flicorno D'Oro Festival (Italy); performances with symphony orchestras in the United States, Norway, Finland, Poland, and Germany; performances with wind bands: The United States Army Band, Dutch Marine Band; 36 CDs featured as soloist or guest soloist, including five by the British Tuba Quartet, eleven play-along/feature education euphonium series (all with CD); set up specialist euphonium schools in Nagano (Japan), Holland, Austria, Belgium; given many master classes/workshops in Holland, Germany, Austria, Switzerland, Italy, Spain, Luxembourg, France, Norway, Sweden, Estonia, Russia, Denmark, Finland, the United States, Canada, Japan, Singapore, Belgium, Australia, New Zealand; directed three Dutch tuba festivals and two Belgian festivals; development and design work for

the Besson GS model euphonium and the Besson "Prestige" Euphonium, made by Boosey & Hawkes; designed new range of euphonium/baritone mouthpieces with Denis Wick.

Education: BA (Hons) degree, Bristol University (1983); PGCE, Bath College of Higher Education, Newton Park (1984).

Teachers: Bernhard Roberts, Glyn Bosanko, Trevor Groom, John Iveson, John Fletcher.

Meixner, Brian

Contributions: Recorded solo CD *Genesis;* won first prize at the North American Brass Band Association's Technical Solo Competition (1998); member of the Four Horsemen Tuba Quartet; runner-up at Leonard Falcone International Euphonium Competition (1998).

Education: BA business management, Western Illinois University; BA music education, University of Kentucky.

Teachers: Hugo Magliocco, James Jackson, Skip Gray.

Miles, David

Born: 08/09/1957

Current Positions: Euphoniumist, the United States Navy Band, 1981–.

Contributions: Editor, Tuba-Euphonium Press, 1991–.

Education: BM, Appalachian State University (1978); MM, Morehead State University (1979); DMA, University of Maryland (1991).

Teachers: Brian Bowman, Arthur Lehman, David Fedderly, Earle Louder, Charles Isley, George Kirsten.

Milhiet, Ivan

Born: 01/31/1973

Current Positions: Euphonium teacher at the Conservatoire National Supérieur de Musique de Lyon; teaches several masters classes and seminars; performer with the Orchestre de l'Opéra de Paris, Orchestre Philharmonique de Radio France, Orchestre National de France, Orchestre de Paris.

Contributions: Prize winner at the International Competition of Guebwiller; first prize winner for euphonium and first prize winner for Chamber Music at the Conservatoire National Supérieur de Musique de Paris; sparked interest of contemporary composers Thierry Escaich, Mico Nissim, and Marc Steckar.

Teachers: Fernand Lelong, Robert Childs.

Miller, Dean

Born: 07/14/1978

Current Positions: Euphoniumist, The United States Army Band "Pershing's Own, " 2002–.

Education: BMUS, West Virginia University (1996–2000); University of North Texas (2000–2001).

Teachers: Brian Bowman, H. Keith Jackson, David McCollum.

Miura, Toru

Born: 1948

Current Positions: Solo euphonium with the Tokyo Kosei Wind Orchestra; instructor of euphonium and ensemble at the Kunitachi College of Music, the Sobi Music Academy, the Soai University, and the Toho Gakuen College; board of directors for TUBA and the vice president of the Japan Euphonium-Tuba Association.

Contributions: Performing artist and clinician at the second ITEC (1983), the second IBC (1984), the third ITEC (1986), the fourth ITEC (1990), the fifth ITEC (1992), and the sixth ITEC (1995) and the IBC of the Summit Brass (1996) and the Verso il Millenio (1997); performed as a guest at Eastman W.E. fortieth anniversary concert (1992); performed with Breeze Brass Band; served as euphonium coordinator and vice president for ITEA; solo recordings for SONY include *Invitation to Playing Trombone and Euphonium; Euphonium Method* is published by Doremi Music Company; active as a writer for various professional magazines, including the *Band Journal*, the *Band People*, and the *Pipers*; founded and directs the Tokyo Bari-Tuba Ensemble and the Euphonium Company.

Education: BM, Tokyo National University of Fine Arts and Music (1971); MM, Southern Mississippi University (1973); Eastman School of Music (1973–1974).

Teachers: Kiyoshi Ohishi, Raymond Young.

Morgan, Jason

Born: 03/14/1974

Current Positions: The United States Army Band "Pershing's Own," 1999–.

Education: Central Michigan University (1992–1997); University of New Mexico (1997–1999).

Teachers: Lois Alexander, Luis Maldonado, Mark Cox, Karl Hinterbichler.

Mortimer, Alex

Positions: Luton Red Cross Band; Foden's Motor Works Band; Liverpool Philharmonic Orchestra (1939–1949); C.S.W. Band of Manchester; Black Dykes Band.

Teachers: Fred Mortimer.

Mountain, Wilfred

Positions: Foden's Motor Works Band; Fairey Aviation Band; Manchester C.S.W. Band; Hollywood Tabernacle Salvation Army Band.

Mueller, John

Born: 01/30/1958

Current Positions: Assistant professor of trombone and euphonium, University of Memphis, 2001–; trombonist, Memphis Brass Quintet, 2001–.

Past Positions: Euphonium soloist/section leader, The United States Army Band "Pershing's Own," Washington, D.C. (1980–2001); adjunct faculty, the Catholic University of America, Washington, D.C. (1992–2001).

Contributions: *Euphonic Sounds* recording (1999); *Excursion* by Mike Tomaro, written for Mueller; euphonium coordinator, *TUBA* executive committee (1988–1990) (1990–1992).

Education: BS music education, University of Illinois at Urbana-Champaign (1981); MM trombone performance, the Catholic University of America (1985); DMA trombone performance, the Catholic University of America (1998).

Teachers: Daniel Perantoni, Robert Gray, Milton Stevens, Brian Bowman.

Murchison, Matthew

Born: 05/11/1980

Current Positions: Euphoniumist, River City Brass Band, Pittsburgh, Pennsylvania, 2002–.

Contributions: Co-founder of Mulholland Records and Music; composer, arranger; commissioned works: *Prescott Poem* (2003) by Drew Fennell (for euphonium and piano, brass band, or wind band), *Valtzz!* (1999) by Charles Booker (for euphonium and wind band or piano); solo CD entitled *Everyone but Me;* first euphonium player to win the Pittsburgh Concert Society competition.

Education: Duquesne University (1998–2000); BM, music performance (magna cum laude), University of North Texas (2002).

Teachers: Greg Benson, Denis Winter, Lance LaDuke, Brian Bowman.

Myllys, Jukka

Born: 09/25/1963

Current Positions: Trombonist with the Oulu Symphony, 1996–; conductor of the wind band Viventi, 1999–; euphonium teacher, Sibelius Academy, Helsinki, 2001–; euphonium teacher, Oulu Polytecnics, 2001–.

Past Positions: Karelia Military Band (1984–1989); Pohja Military Band (1989–1996); teacher at Oulu Concervatoire (1990–2002); conductor of the Concervatoire youth wind band (1996–2003).

Contributions: Commissioned solos: *Destination*, Juha T. Koskinen (euphonium and piano), *Blue Gleam of the Arctic Hysteria*, Oliver Kohlenberg (euphonium, piano, percussion), *Euphonium Concerto*, Jukka Linkola (euphonium and symphony orchestra), *Euphonium Concerto*, Harri Ahmas (euphonium and symphony orchestra), *Arion*, Uljas Pulkkis (euphonium and symphony orchestra), *Flibarium*, Leonid Bashmakov (euphonium, flute, English horn, clarinet, piano, and percussion), *Lampi*, Kirmo Lintinen (euphonium and euphonium choir), *Solo VIII*, Kalevi Aho (unaccompanied).

Education: Military Music School, Helsinki (1982); Oulu Conservatoire, Oulu (1992); master of music, Sibelius Academy, Helsinki (1996).

Teachers: Juha Mikander, Lauri Ojala, Tom Bildo.

Nelson, Douglas

Positions: Director, Rochester Echo Singing Association; solo euphonium, Eighth Air Force Band;

teacher, public school system of Durham, New Hampshire; faculty, Keene State College.

Contributions: President, New Hampshire Music Educators Association.

Education: BA music education, MM education, Eastman School of Music, New York; DMA, Hartt School of Music.

Teachers: Donald Knaub, Milan Yancich.

O'Connor, Michael B.

Born: 04/09/1962

Current Positions: Newberry's Victorian Cornet Band, 2002–; University of Delaware (music history), 2001–.

Past Positions: Euphonium, Clyde Beatty-Cole Bros. Circus Band (1986–1992).

Contributions: Founder, Newberry's Victorian Cornet Band (2002); editor, *Historic Brass Society Newsletter,* 2000–.

Education: BS Ed., Tennessee Tech University (1985); MM, Florida State University (1992).

Teachers: R. Winston Morris, Daniel Perantoni, Paul Ebbers.

Oyster, Roger

Born: 12/20/1950

Current Positions: Principal trombone, Kansas City Symphony, 1997–.

Past Positions: Principal trombone, St. Louis Symphony (1988–1995); euphoniumist, the United States Marine Band (1981–1987); euphonium soloist (1985–1987).

Education: BM, University of Michigan, Ann Arbor (1981); MM, Catholic University, Washington, D.C. (1986).

Teachers: Brian Bowman, Abe Torchinsky, Wes Jacobs, Milt Stevens, Jim Olin.

Paull, Eric

Born: 10/16/1971

Current Positions: Adjunct professor of music, Austin Peay State University, 2003–; performer and stage manager, Mr. Jack Daniel's Original Silver Cornet Band, 2001–.

Contributions: Co-editor of *The Euphonium Source Book.*

Education: Louisiana State University (1990–1995); Tennessee Technological University (1995–1997).

Teachers: Daniel Perantoni, R. Winston Morris, Larry Campbell, David Glasmire.

Perfetto, John J.

Positions: Sousa Band (1904–1919); New York World's Fair Band; Patrick Conway Band; Goldman Band.

Perrins, Bernie

Positions: Solothurn Kammerorchester; Hedon Band in England.

Contributions: One of the most wildly traveled euphonium players.

Pierce, Benjamin

Born: 02/28/1977

Current Positions: Instructor of tuba and euphonium, University of Arkansas, 2003–.

Education: BM, Bowling Green State University (1995–1999); MM, University of Michigan (1999–2001); DMA, University of Michigan (2001–2003).

Teachers: Velvet Brown, Fritz Kaenzig.

Portellano, Gerard

Born: 09/23/1970

Current Positions: Teacher in different music schools (Conservatoire National de Région de Bayonne), 2000–.

Past Positions: Freelance euphonium in many French symphonic orchestras: Orchestre National de Lyon, Orchestre National Bordeaux Aquitaine, Orchestre du Capitole de Toulouse, Opéra de Lyon, Orchestre philharmonique de Strasbourg, Orchestre de Paris (1992–2000).

Education: Prix du Conservatoire National Supérieur de Musique de LYON.

Teachers: Mr. Delange, Mr. Celbertson.

Powell, John

Born: 02/28/1968

Current Positions: Founding member, Tubalaté tuba quartet; Silk and Steel euphonium, flute, piano trio, 1990–.

Contributions: 300+ works commissioned for tuba quartet; 25 personal commissioned works and premieres for euphonium, including Chris Wiggins' *Soliloquy No. IX for Solo Euphonium,* Tony Roper's *Sonata,* Stuart Scott's *Episodes and Fanfares,* and Michael Graubart's *Scena II;* first European performance of Ponchielli's *Euphonium Concerto* (1993); euphonium soloist, bandsman, orchestral musician, recording artist, teacher, animateur, band conductor, band trainer, educationalist.

Education: The Royal Northern College of Music, Manchester, UK (1994).

Teachers: Bob Childs, Nick Childs, Steven Mead, Howard Snell, Bob Tucci, Stewart Roebuck.

Powers, Robert J.

Born: 07/22/1958

Current Positions: Euphonium, The United States Army Band "Pershing's Own," 1980–.

Contributions: One of the founding members of The United States Army Band Tuba Euphonium Conference (worked as producer, Armed Forces Tuba Euphonium Ensemble librarian, exhibits coordinator, logistics coordinator, and conference coordinator); commissioned two euphonium solos with band, one euphonium solo with orchestra, and one euphonium solo with brass dectet.

Education: Old Dominion University and Virginia Commonwealth University (1980).

Teachers: Daniel Ramirez, Ron Baedke, Robert Daniel, Brian Bowman.

Raffayola, Joseph
Positions: Patrick Gilmore's Band; Sousa Band (1892–1903)

Robertson, Gail A.
Born: 06/16/1965
Current Positions: Instructor of low brass, Bethune-Cookman College, 2000–; adjunct instructor of tuba and euphonium, University of Central Florida, 2000–; euphoniumist/soloist/stage manager, Keith Brion's New Sousa Band, 1995–; baritone horn, the Brass Band of Battle Creek, 1997, 2001, 2004–; euphoniumist/soloist/arranger, the Brass Band of Central Florida, 1999–; euphoniumist/arranger, Symphonia, 2000–; euphoniumist/arranger, Central Florida Horns and Pipes Brass and Percussion Ensemble, 1993–; euphoniumist, Athena Brass Band, 2003–.
Past Positions: Euphoniumist/arranger/leader, Walt Disney's Tubafours, Hollywood Brass, Wood Chucks Tuba Troop #8822, and Boardwalk Belltones (1989–1999); adjunct instructor of tuba and euphonium, University of Florida (1998–2002); adjunct instructor of euphonium, Seminole and Valencia Community Colleges.
Contributions: Founder of the Orlando "TUBA-MANIA" and Orlando "OCTUBAFEST"; composer of *Suite of Dances* (commissioned by the Band of the U.S. Air Force Reserve); commissioned euphonium solo with piano, *Psychoticism* by Michael Cochran (2003), premiered at the Harvey Phillips "Big Brass Bash"; arranged medley of songs about Harvey Phillips's life called *Celetubration* premiered by Symphonia at Indiana University (summer 2003); arranger of over 100 charts for tuba and euphonium ensemble, marching band, brass ensemble, brass quintet, and British brass band.
Education: BS, University of Central Florida (1987); MM, Indiana University (1989); attended University of Maryland (1989).
Teachers: Roy Pickering, Harvey G. Phillips, Brian L. Bowman.

Rüedi, Thomas
Born: 06/10/1969
Current Positions: Professor for euphonium and chamber music, Hochschule der Künste Bern, Switzerland, 2001–; professor for euphonium and chamber music, Musikhochschule Luzern, Switzerland, 1999–; tenor tuba, Tonhalle Orchestra, Zürich, 2003–; soloist, Synthesis (marimba and euphonium), 2000–.
Past Positions: Solo euphonium with Brass Band Mühledorf (1987–1990); solo euphonium, Sellers Engineering Band (1991–1994); solo euphonium, Swiss Army Brass Band (1996–2003); conductor, Brass Band Bürgermusik Luzern (1995–2002); member of the Tuba Quartett Luzern (1995–2000).
Contributions: Arranger and composer of various works for euphonium and band.

Education: BA LRSM, Sheffield University, UK, 1994.
Teachers: Phillip McCann, Major Peter Parkes, David Moore, Steven Mead.

Sarangoulis, Christopher William
Born: 06/19/1980
Current Positions: Euphonium, The United States Army Field Band, Washington, D.C., 2003–.
Education: BM performance, University of North Texas.
Teachers: Luke Spiros, Brian Bowman.

Saywell, Victor
Positions: Hanwell Band; The Band of H.M. Scots Guards; Kneller Hall; BBC Concert Orchestra.

Schneider, Marco
Born: 02/23/1979
Current Positions: Solo euphonium, Brass Band Bürgermusik, Luzern, 2000–; low brass teacher, Musikschule Michelsamt, Luzern, 2003–.
Education: Teaching diploma, Musikhochschule Luzern (2003); soloist diploma, Musikhochschule Luzern (2004).
Teachers: Hans Duss, Ludwig Wicki, Thomas Rüedi.

Schultz, Karl
Current Positions: Euphoniumist, the United States Naval Academy Band (1996–); euphoniumist, tuba quartet, ceremonial band.
Past Positions: Euphonium soloist, Continental Army Band (1993–1996); member, Dominion Brass Band, Mill Creed Silver Quartette (1993–1996); member Virginia Symphony; member, Tidewater Winds; member, German Band, Busch Gardens Williamsburg (1990–1993).
Contributions: Premiered *Concertino* for euphonium and concert band by David Baines.
Education: BA euphonium performance, Mansfield University (1992).
Teachers: Donald A. Stanley, Stephen P McEuen.

Self, Jimmie E.
Born: 02/28/1952
Current Positions: Adjunct instructor of euphonium and tuba, East Tennessee State University, 1999–; principal trombone, Kingsport Symphony Orchestra, 2002–.
Past Positions: The United States Air Force Band program (1972–1998); principal trombone, Montgomery Symphony, Montgomery, Alabama (1974–1978).
Education: Tennessee Technological University (1970–1972); Troy State University (part-time) (1974–1977); University of New Hampshire (1978–1980); associate degree in applied science (music), Community College of the Air Force; bachelor's degree in music performance (trombone), University of New Hampshire.
Teachers: R. Winston Morris, Steven Norsworthy, Larry Hoepfinger, Ronald Barron.

Shrum, Kenneth E.

Current Positions: Euphoniumist, the United States Naval Academy Band (1986–); various marching/ceremonial bands; member Naval Academy Band Tuba/Euphonium Quartet (1986).

Past Positions: Faculty, Valley Forge Christian College, Pennsylvania.

Contributions: Finalist, Solo Euphonium Competitions, ITEC; member, Phi Mu Alpha Sinfonia, Pi Kappa Lambda, and TUBA.

Education: BA music education, Evangel College (1981); MM trombone performance, University of Missouri (1983); DMA, Arizona State University (1989).

Teachers: Joseph Nigholson, John Leisenring, Dan Perantoni, Gail Wilson.

Smith, Henry

Positions: Philadelphia Orchestra (1955–1967); Rochester Symphony; founder of Philadelphia Brass Ensemble; Minnesota Orchestra.

Contributions: Premiered Alan Hovhaness's *Symphony No. 29 for Baritone and Band.*

Education: BA from the University of Pennsylvania (1952); artist's diploma from the Curtis Institute of Music; Temple University; Indiana University (1968–1971); Saint Olaf College; Luther College.

Spinelli, Eric

Current Positions: Euphoniumist, The United States Air Force Band Liberty Pops, Ceremonial Band, Ceremonial Brass (2001–).

Past Positions: Euphoniumist, Mr. Jack Daniel's Original Silver Cornet Band; Harvey Phillips' Tuba Company; Cincinnati Wind Symphony.

Education: BA music performance/education, Ithaca College (1998); MM performance, University of Cincinnati College Conservatory of Music (2001).

Teachers: Tim Northcut, Glenn Call, David Unland.

Spiros, Lucas

Dates: 1943–

Positions: Barnum and Bailey's Circus Band; Harvard Wind Ensemble; Boston University Wind Ensemble; M.I.T. Brass Ensemble; Band of Nantucket; Ruby Newman Orchestra; Vienna Haffgrav Orchestra; Boston Youth Symphony; Brookline Civic Symphony; 1st Corp Cadet Band of Brookline; American Veterans Band; Boston Police Band; Roma Band; the United States Marine Band of Washington, D.C.

Education: Boston University; the University of New Hampshire; Peabody University; New York University.

Sullivan, Bert

Dates: 1902–

Positions: Melbourne City Band; Harwitch R.M.I. Band; Besses o' th' Barn Band; Munn and Felton Works Band; public school teacher.

Summers, Matthew

Positions: Euphoniumist, "The President's Own" United States Marine Band (1997); euphoniumist, Busch Gardens.

Education: BA euphonium performance, University of Michigan (1998).

Teachers: Stan Dittmer, Fritz Kaenzig.

Swallow, John

Positions: New York Brass Quintet; New England Conservatory of Music.

Contributions: Founding member of the New York Brass Quintet.

Taylor, Robin

Born: 1966

Current Positions: Teacher, Barnsley College.

Past Positions: Principal euphonium, Oxford Concert Brass; euphonium, "G.U.S." Band; principal euphonium, Western Band of the Royal Air Force (1989–1991); principal euphonium, Grimethorpe Colliery Band (1991).

Contributions: Recorded solo CD *Robin Taylor, Euphonium;* won RAF solo competition (two years.); won the Leonard Falcone International Euphonium Competition (1991); best soloist at the British Open Brass Band Championship (1991).

Teachers: David Jenkins, Kim Lofthouse, Trevor Groom.

Thomas, Kelly

Born: 01/10/1975

Current Positions: Professor of tuba/euphonium, University of Arizona, 2001–.

Contributions: Editor of *The Euphonium Source Book.*

Education: Bachelor's music education, Tennessee Technological University (1997); master's music education, Arizona State University (1999); doctorate euphonium performance (ABD), Arizona State University 1999–.

Teachers: R. Winston Morris, J. Samuel Pilafian.

Thompson, Kevin

Born: 11/19/1963

Current Positions: Principal trombone including euphonium and bass trumpet, Malaysian Philharmonic Orchestra, 1998–.

Past Positions: Assistant principal trombone, Cape Town Symphony Orchestra, South Africa (1992–1998); trombone and euphonium, Foothills Brass Quintet, Calgary, Canada (1989–1992).

Contributions: Commissioning and world premiere of Furlong's *Quintet for Euphonium and Strings* (2000); Theobald's *Concerto for Euphonium, Strings, and Percussion* (1998); solo euphonium recording *Euphonic Bach* (1998); solo euphonium recording *Telemann Fantasias* (2004); numerous solo euphonium performances in Canada, the United States, England, South Africa, and Southeast Asia.

Education: University of Victoria, Canada (1984); Canada Council Scholarship for private study, London, England (1984–1985); University of Toronto, Canada (1985–1986).
Teachers: Denis Wick, John Clough, Gordon Sweeney, Eugene Dowling.

Thorton, James
Positions: The United States Marine Band in Washington, D.C.
Contributions: Composer of many band and small ensemble pieces.
Education: Interlochen Music Camp; Dickinson State College; Armed Forces School of Music.
Teachers: Harold Brasch.

Thurman, Demondrae
Born: 06/11/1974
Current Positions: Assistant professor of tuba and euphonium, University of Alabama; euphonium soloist, Sotto Voce Quartet; baritone horn, Brass Band of Battle Creek.
Past Positions: Instructor of low brass, Alabama State University.
Contributions: Instruments (euphoniums and baritones), mouthpieces, repair, etc., and contributing editor of *The Euphonium Source Book.*
Education: DMA trombone performance, University of Alabama, 2003–; MM, University of Wisconsin–Madison (1998); BM, University of Alabama (1996).
Teachers: John Stevens, Mike Dunn, James Jenkins.

Torres, Alberto
Born: 01/13/1968
Current Positions: Principal and solo euphonium, The United States Army Field Band, Washington, D.C. 1999–.
Past Positions: Euphonium soloist, the United States Military Academy Band, West Point, New York (1996–1999); principal and soloist euphonium, the U.S. Continental Army Band, Ft. Monroe, Virginia (1989–1993).
Education: Eastman School of Music (1993–1996).
Teachers: Cherry Beauregard, Mark Kellogg, Henry Howey.

Tropman, Matt
Born: 11/14/1972
Current Positions: Adjunct professor of low brass, Eastern Michigan University; executive director, Brass Band of Battle Creek.
Past Positions: The United States Marine Band (1996–2002).
Contributions: Two solo CDs on Summit Records, *Continuum* and *From the Balcony,* and contributing editor for *The Euphonium Source Book.*
Education: University of Michigan (1995); Arizona State University (1998).
Teachers: Fritz Kaenzig, Luis Maldonado, Sam Pilafian.

Tsuyuki, Kaoru
Current Positions: Instructor of Aichi University of Arts, Toho College of Music; member, euphonium-tuba quartet Shishiza.
Contributions: Third prize, 3rd Japan Wind and Percussion Competition (1986); first prize, 6th Japan Wind and Percussion Competition (1989);
Education: BM, Tokyo National University of Fine Arts and Music (1988); graduated, Conservatoire in Paris (1991).

Tuor, Corsin
Born: 02/11/1963
Current Positions: Low brass teacher, Music School Michelsamt, Luzern; conductor of brass band Bürgermusik Luzern, 2000–.
Past Positions: Solo euphonium with brass band Bürgermusik Luzern; member of the Tuba Quartett Luzern.
Education: Teaching diploma with distinction, Musikhochschule, Luzern, Switzerland (1993).
Teachers: Simon Styles, Ludwig Wicki.

Tuovinen, Tommi
Current Positions: Dragon Military Band, Lappeenranta, Finland.
Past positions: Newlands Military Band, Tammisaari.
Education: Music Conservatory, Iisalmi (1982–1992); Military Music School, Lahti (1995–1996).
Teachers: Seppo Merisalo, Juha Salmela, Marko Saikko.

Ushigami, Ryuji
Born: 02/21/1966
Current Positions: Member, Vivid Brass Tokyo; president, M-Gauge Music School.
Contributions: Second prize, 4th International Leonard Falcone Euphonium Competition (1989); world premiere, *URUWASHIKIMONO NAGAREYUKUNARI* by Jiro Censhu (1990); world premiere, *GINGA HARUKA* by Jiro Censhu; third prize, TubaMania International Competition in Sydney (1999).
Education: BA, Nihon University (1988); diploma course of Tokyo Conservatoire of Shobi (1990).
Teachers: Toru Miura, Teruo Miyagawa, Fumio Goto, Brian Bowman, Steven Mead.

Vevle, Lars
Born: 06/26/1945
Current Positions: The Army Band Western Region, Bergen, Norway, 1966–.
Teachers: Per Brevig, Brian Bowman.

Vinson, Dan
Current Positions: Principal euphonium, the United States Coast Guard Band (1984–); instructor of euphonium, University of Connecticut; instructor of trombone and euphonium, University of

Rhode Island; clinician, Interlochen and Atlanta International Band and Orchestra Clinic.

Contributions: International soloist.

Education: BA music education, University of North Texas (1982); master of science and music education, University of Illinois (1983).

Teachers: Donald Little, Royce Lumpkin, James Curnow, Fritz Kaenzig.

Walford, Joshua
Positions: International Staff Band of the Salvation Army; New York Staff Band of the Salvation Army.

Walker, Mark
Born: 11/07/1969
Current Positions: Professor of low brass, Troy State University, Troy, Alabama.
Past Positions: Euphonium soloist, Busch Gardens, Williamsburg, Virginia; principal euphonium, University of Illinois Symphonic Band and Wind Symphony; assistant director of bands, Temple High School; director of bands, Lamesa High School, Lamesa, Texas.
Education: University of Central Arkansas (1990); Tennessee Tech University (1993); University of Illinois (1993–1995, 2000–2002).
Teachers: Denis Winter, R. Winston Morris, Mark Moore.

Walton, Paul
Born: 02/27/1971
Current Positions: Founder and euphonium player, Tubalaté tuba quartet; principal euphonium, Desford Colliery Band; euphonium tutor, University of Wales, Bangor; associate conductor, BT band, Stockport; freelance euphoniumist/trombonist; euphonium soloist; Besson artiste.
Past Positions: Principal euphonium, Britannia Building Society Band (Fodens); principal euphonium, Continental Airlines Band (NZ); Junior Fellow of the Royal Northern College of Music.
Contributions: Solos written for Paul Walton include *Capriccio for Solo Euphonium* by Frederick Naftel, *Elizabeth Lowry's Wishes* by Philip Henderson; founder of Tubalaté; founder/editor of Breakthrough Music (publishing house specializing in music for low brass); arranger.
Education: Royal Northern College of Music (1995).
Teachers: Nicholas Childs, Robert Childs, Steven Mead, Howard Snell.

Weber, Carlyle G.
Born: 08/26/1953
Current Positions: Low brass adjunct faculty, Indian River Community College; solo and section leader (euphonium), New Gardens Band; solo and section leader (tenor horn), the Music Masters German/Big Band; trombone, Indian River Pops Orchestra; private brass teacher, Treasure Coast Florida area.

Past Positions: Principal euphonium and soloist, The United States Army Field Band, Washington, D.C. (1975–1998) (retired).
Contributions: Writer for *ITEA Journal, Band Director* magazine; co-producer of *USAFB Tuba-Euphonium Instructional Video,* 1997.
Education: BME, Illinois State University (1975); MM, University of Maryland, College Park (1999).
Teachers: Ed Livingston, Arthur Lehman, Milt Stevens.

Werden, David
Born: 04/21/1947
Current Positions: Freelance performer, 1996–; freelance teacher, 1996–; euphonium/tuba in Saints Brass, 1998–; clinician and design consultant for Sterling Musical Instruments (Great Britain) and Custom Music Company (United States), 1990–.
Past Positions: Solo/principal euphonium, the United States Coast Guard Band (1970–1996); principal trombone, Eastern Connecticut Symphony (1972–1974); EE♭ tuba, Classic Brass Band of Connecticut (1988–1989); EE♭ tuba, Sheldon Theater Brass Band (1996); euphonium, Atlantic Tuba Quartet (1976–1996).
Contributions: Founding member, the United States Coast Guard Tuba Quartet; founding member, Atlantic Tuba Quartet; arranger of forty pieces for euphonium, tuba, and other brass and winds; author of the *Blaikley Compensating System, Scoring for Euphonium,* and the *Euphonium Music Guide;* editor of *The Brass Musician* by Arthur Lehman, and *Euphonium Excerpts from the Standard Band and Orchestral Library* by Barbara Payne; co-commissioned *Saxophonium for Euphonium and Saxophone* by George Heussenstamm; commissioned *Euphonium Sketches* by Thomas Briggs.
Education: University of Connecticut (1991–1993); University of Iowa (1965–1970).
Teachers: Robert Whaley, Henry Howie, John Hartman, Arthur Swift, John Hill, Joanna Hersey, Henry Charles Smith.

Whitham, Geoffrey
Dates: 1932–
Positions: Black Dyke Mills Band (1950–1963); Halle Orchestra; Liverpool Orchestra; Birmingham Orchestra; Hammonds Sauce Works Band.

Whittier, Harry
Positions: Patrick Gilmore Band (1988); Reeve's Band.
Contributions: One of the first to use the double-bell euphonium.

Wilkins, Richard
Born: 06/12/1960
Current Positions: Euphonium and training sergeant major, The United States Army Band "Pershing's Own," Washington, D.C.

Education: BMA music education, Lander University (1982).

Teachers: Billy Bolton, Larry Cook, Brian Bowman.

Williamson, R. Mark

Born: 10/07/1960

Current Positions: Partner, law firm of Alston & Bird in Atlanta, Georgia; Fellow of the American College of Trust and Estate Counsel; principal solo Eb horn and utility musician, Georgia Brass Band, Atlanta, Georgia.

Past Positions: The United States Air Force Band, Washington, D.C. (1984–1988); Airmen of Note; member, Acadiana Brass Quintet; assistant conductor of orchestra, Louisiana State University.

Contributions: First quintet-in-residence at Tanglewood, 1982; executive editor of the *Law Review*; named to the Order of the Coif; named in *Best Lawyers in America*; involved with issues affecting musicians, theaters, and other artists, including pro bono representation of low-income artists through Georgia Lawyers for the Arts, of which he is president and board chair.

Education: BM performance, Louisiana State University (1981); master's, University of North Texas (1983); law, Florida State University (1988).

Teachers: Larry Campbell, Leon Brown, Don Little, Milton Stevens.

Wilson, John

Positions: Royal Air Force Central Band, RMS School of Music.

Winter, Denis

Current Positions: Professor of trombone and euphonium, University of Central Arkansas (UCA), 1979–; trombonist, Pinnacle Brass (faculty brass quintet-in-residence at UCA).

Past Positions: The United States Coast Guard Band (1975–1979).

Contributions: Member of Symphonia, 1995–; international performer in Italy and Canada; featured at numerous festivals and conferences throughout the United States, including the Brevard Music Center and the Interlochen Center for the Arts; faculty, Arkansas Governor's School, 1980–; faculty, Blue Lake Fine Arts Camp.

Education: DMA, University of North Texas; MM, New England Conservatory of Music; BM, Ohio University.

Wright, Evan L.

Born: 02/26/1975

Current Positions: Euphonium/trombone, RAAF Central Band, Australia.

Contributions: Founder, Artistic Intelligence (arts research organization).

Education: Bachelor of music, Qld. Conservatorium (1996); MAEMgt, Deakin University (1993).

Teachers: Bill Barker, Arthur Middleton, Phil Davis.

Yamaoka, Jun

Born: 9/27/1965

Current Positions: Freelance euphonium performer; part-time euphonium instructor, jazz improvisation, theory, and arranging instructor, Tokyo Music & Media Arts Shobi, 1997–; Shobi University, 2000–.

Education: Bachelor of music, Kunitachi College of Music (1988); University of North Florida (1989–1991); master of music in jazz studies, University of North Texas (1994).

Teachers: Toru Miura, Norihisa Yamamoto, Don Little, Rich Matteson.

Young, Raymond G.

Positions: Associate director of bands, assistant professor of music education, University of Southern Mississippi (1961); director of bands, supervisor of instrumental music, Trenton, Michigan, Public Schools; member, American Symphonic Band; member and soloist, Detroit Park and Recreation Band (1957–1961).

Contributions: Featured soloist, USA band (1963) and director (1967); member of Kappa Kappa Psi, Phi Mu Alpha, Pi Lambda, MENC, C.B.D.N.A., National Band Association; recorded under the Decca label.

Education: BA, MM, University of Michigan.

Teachers: Dale Harris, Fred Wiest.

Zimmerman, John

Positions: The United States Marine Band in Washington, D.C.

Education: The School of Music, Catholic University.

18. Guide to Trombone/Euphonium Doubling

John Mueller

There are several reasons to play both euphonium and trombone. For one, they are similar in pitch register and mouthpiece size so that initial results come quickly and easily. A young music student may choose to play both trombone and euphonium to fulfill an ensemble need in the school band or for musical curiosity, while an aspiring professional musician may wish to increase employment and performance opportunities. Whatever the motivation, after the initial similarities come important differences that define these two instruments. Ensemble usage, repertoire, tone color, and technique are the chief defining elements. Rudimentary performance on either instrument is often easy, but after that, the level of expertise that one achieves on the second instrument will in large degree depend on one's ability to develop new techniques.

At the professional level, much of the trombone-euphonium doubling that one typically finds is of a limited scope: many of us know "C & E" trombonists who only play trombone on Christmas and Easter, when the demand for brass players is the highest. And on the other side, many professional trombonists play euphonium only on the most common tenor tuba parts in the repertory. But regardless of the situation, success at doubling will be dependent on the ability of the player to recognize the shared techniques and adapt to the new ones. The purpose of this chapter is to offer insights that will allow the potential trombone-euphonium doubler to develop beyond a beginning level to get past merely knowing the slide positions or fingerings, highlight the significant differences in technique, explain the underlying difficulties, and offer practical day-to-day solutions.

Fundamentals

Getting Off to a Good Start

The choice to double on euphonium or trombone is often made by young musicians because of physiological difficulties or personal ambitions.

A short arm reach may necessitate the move to euphonium, or a desire to play in the jazz band or the orchestra is certainly a good reason to take up the trombone. Whatever the reason, it is important that the individual be fundamentally sound in terms of pitch recognition, posture, and basic tone production before taking on the new instrument.

While the timbre of the trombone and euphonium differ, the general sound production and articulation are the same. Before one can expect to double effectively, basic fundamentals must be in place. Good air movement, embouchure formation, tone production, articulation, and awareness of intonation must be established. Existing inadequacies of this sort will complicate the transition to the new instrument.

Certainly one of the most daunting challenges of trombone playing is finding the correct, in-tune slide positions, but tuning is also a problematic issue on euphonium. It is important that the potential doubler develop his or her ear enough to recognize problems with intonation. For some, the trombone's elusive fifth position might pose a major obstacle; but switching from trombone to euphonium will not solve the problem with pitch awareness. All valve instruments require tuning adjustments on most notes because of the set valve-slide lengths and the harmonic series.[1] As a result, pitch has to be corrected via adjustments to the embouchure setting or air speed. The conical bore of the euphonium makes this kind of adjustment easier. This factor will aid a good euphonium player to tune each note, but will add to the inconsistency of the player who does not have a well-trained ear, as notes can more easily slip out of tune.

Good breathing and air speed control are all part of good brass playing. Proper airflow, both inhalation and exhalation, is integral to tone quality, intonation, and articulation. Controlling the air speed and maintaining a stable embouchure are critical to developing range and tone. These aspects will be addressed in more detail later as they pertain to switching between instruments, but the initial foundation is the same. Weak and shallow inhalations must be corrected. Bad posture will affect several aspects of playing, but the biggest hindrance will be to full and relaxed breathing. On either instrument, it is imperative that the instrument comes up to the embouchure rather than the player slouching to the mouthpiece. The airway must be as clear as possible and the lungs be given room to expand to their fullest.

Anyone who has learned to play with excessive tension will also have difficulty with valve/slide technique, articulation, tone quality, and endurance. Tension, no matter where it originates, tends to migrate and affect the entire player. Newness to an instrument often brings about self-consciousness, which can result in nervous tension. Add pre-existing tension to the mix and the result can be very debilitating.

Developing a Sound Concept

Both the trombone and the euphonium have a distinct characteristic sound or timbre. For a novice or advanced doubler, a good sound concept of both instruments is imperative: the correct aural image or sound concept will make learning much quicker as one can associate the correct sound with the appropriate technique, often at the subconscious level. There are several actions that must occur in well-timed succession in order to produce a good brass sound. These include good inhalation/exhalation, well-timed tongue stroke, embouchure setting, and oral cavity shape. Without an aural goal in mind, one can easily get lost in the juggling of simultaneous tasks and never come up with a consistent or correct sound. Listening to recordings and performances of good trombone and euphonium players and playing with them whenever possible are critical.

In developing a proper sound concept, one must consider the musical setting. A brass band euphonium vibrato will not be correct when playing a trombone chorale in a Brahms symphony, nor would a heavy articulation and straight tone be effective for performing German lieder. The best musician is likely to grasp the musical concepts and nuances that will make his or her doubling effective.

Euphonium to Trombone

Tone: *"You sound like a euphonium player on trombone."*

This is a common complaint toward neophyte doublers coming from a euphonium background.

It is commonly known that because the trombone is a "cylindrical" instrument a euphonium player has to deal with more resistance to air stream as it enters the instrument.[2] This increased air resistance often results in one or more problems. The tone will often be "fat" but at the same time airy or unfocused;[3] the pitch will often be low, in spite of pushing in the tuning slide; and detached articulations are often "split" or not cleanly started, especially at louder dynamics. The main culprits in these scenarios are slow air and a soft embouchure setting.

To address the embouchure problem, keep the lower lip and corners of the mouth firm and the chin flat (use a mirror). This is a general formation for all brass instruments.[4] When it comes to the embouchure, the euphonium is often a very forgiving instrument, as its lower air resistance mitigates certain problems. A flaw in the embouchure will sometimes not show itself until the extra resistance of the trombone brings it out. When the embouchure is not working correctly, one will often notice a bunching of the chin, rolling of the lower lip over the bottom teeth, and/or excessive movement of the corners of the mouth.

Slow air speed is a shortcoming often found in conjunction with a soft or weak embouchure. A characteristically good euphonium sound uses a rounder or larger oral cavity, which tends to slow the air. This often translates to more separation between the teeth that can lead to a less firm embouchure setting. Concentrate on speeding up the air stream through the firmed-up embouchure and/or changing the oral cavity (less "OH," more "AH"). If split attacks are frequent, play a series of accented breath articulations ("Ha!" or "HO! ") until the note is clear and focused. This exercise will help to set the balance of air speed and embouchure setting. After breath attacks are consistent, add the tongue stroke to the articulation.

Mouthpiece buzzing and lip slurs are especially effective in working on air and embouchure problems. They should be part of a daily routine prior to the start of doubling. To work on air speed control, practice projecting your air through a well-formed embouchure without the mouthpiece and without buzzing the lips. The lip aperture and air stream should be well defined. Aim the air stream at objects at various distances within the room. Imagine speeding up and projecting the air toward far targets to play high notes, and think of low pitches as being targets closer to you using slower air. Slightly faster air will often help to bring flat notes up to pitch and help to focus the tone, while the slower air aids to lower the pitch and darken the timbre.

If you are playing on a large mouthpiece designed for the euphonium, consider changing to a slightly smaller mouthpiece and/or one that has more of a cup-shaped (rather than a funnel) contour. Also experiment with different back bore and throat combinations. When possible, use one rim size for both instruments; this often helps the transition.

Be judicious with your use of vibrato on trombone. Generally speaking, accepted trombone vibrato is not as wide or as prevalent as euphonium vibrato, especially in orchestral music. Once again, listen to good trombonists in various settings to develop an idea of the sound you want to achieve.

Intonation

Intonation and slide technique are obviously closely related. Because of the trombone's cylindrical design, it is harder to move the pitch using air speed and embouchure. One must be aware of the intonation characteristics of the trombone overtone series in general and the idiosyncrasies of the particular instrument. Know which slide adjustments are required for particular overtones, especially when using alternate positions.

Critical to all tuning is hearing the pitch correctly. Consider using an electronically generated reference pitch so that bad intonation can be recognized aurally rather than visually by watching a tuner. Make sure that you not only employ the arm to move the slide but also keep your wrist positioned to make minor adjustments. A wrist that is stiff or cocked will make small adjustments difficult.

Articulation

We have already seen that embouchure and air difficulties lead to problems with detached articulations. While the tongue stroke should not change significantly, a slightly more pointed tongue may be more effective on trombone.

The legato articulation or legato tonguing is an important skill for the trombonist, but one that many advanced euphonium players never have to develop. It is often describe as a "D" or "L" tongue stroke. The important thing to remember is that the pressure against the roof of the mouth is very light and quick, seeming to dent the air stream rather than stop it. Develop the articulation on a single pitch without moving the slide to establish a consistent air stream and tongue stroke. When the slide is added, the movement

must be late and quick, allowing almost no opportunity for a smear or extended portamento.

Coordinating the slide movement with the articulation can be difficult. Good euphonium valve technique is often developed using tongue-free, legato style in exercises such as the Clarke *Technical Studies*. Approach slide technique in the same free-blowing relaxed manner. Do not be afraid to work on the slide motion in a tongue-free, smear style. After the accurate and relaxed slide motion is achieved, set the tongue stroke separately, before combining with the slide.

Developing Slide Technique

When working on slide technique, it is important to keep the slide arm and wrist relaxed, not only ensuring fluid slide motion but also preventing the onset of tension. Arm tension can affect not only the slide but, if unchecked, can harm air movement, tone, and articulation as it migrates to other body parts. The right elbow should be a comfortable distance away from the rib cage with the wrist firm but flexible. The number of fingers on the hand slide brace will depend on your physiology: the size of your hand, the tracking motion of the slide, your arm, and the comfort of small adjustments using just your wrist. In general, avoid keeping the right palm parallel to the ground. Some trombonists are comfortable with the right palm almost facing the chest (90 degrees from the ground) but most are angled somewhere between parallel and perpendicular to the ground.

To develop a smooth arm motion, practice holding an imaginary trombone and find the arm and wrist angle that feels comfortable as you track a straight slide path. Then adapt it to the instrument. Be patient while developing slide technique, especially if you are already proficient with valves. Impatience with the slide technique development can lead to frustration, which will only add to the potential for excessive tension and inconsistent slide placement.

As mentioned above, it is good to work on particularly difficult exercises or passages without any articulation. Removing the articulation allows more attention to the slide technique as well as to quality of the tone and intonation. Again, using a reference pitch is important for developing the muscle memory that will result in consistent slide placement, which in turn adds confidence and allows you to focus on musical expression.

Related to both slide technique and general posture is the left-hand grip. The left hand must be strong enough to support the instrument with the head in an upright position. As the left hand and arm tire, there can be a tendency to lean forward and to the left. This unbalanced position will affect slide motion, general breathing, and tone as tension creeps into the unbalanced body. To avoid this, limit the length of initial practice sessions and rest your left hand frequently during all sessions. Squeezing a tennis ball or using a similar hand-strengthening device can also help. If your left forefinger is too short to easily reach the hand slide near the mouthpiece shank, consider having a finger ring attached to the slide under the mouthpiece receiver. This will help to balance the instrument and avoid tension and bad posture.

Trombone to Euphonium

Tone: *"You sound like a trombone player on euphonium."*

A typically incorrect sound made by a trombone player on euphonium is characterized by a forced, hard, and brittle quality. The adjustments that a trombone player must make involve adjusting to the weaker resistance to the air stream on euphonium,[5] which will allow the instrument to resonate to its fullest. Reducing the speed of the air through the lips and enlarging the oral cavity (say "OH" instead of "AH") will accomplish this. Conceptualizing a fatter and slower air stream is one method. Think of a column of smoke rising from the bell that fills the room instead of a concentrated beam aimed at the ceiling. Slower air speed is especially critical in the lower register (second partial); too much speed will result in sharp pitch and a tone without resonance and warmth. Listening to examples of good euphonium tone on recordings and in live performances will greatly aid in developing the proper sound concept. The euphonium, when played well, is capable of a very sonorous vocal quality. So be sure to listen to fine vocalists and incorporate those phrasing concept and styles of vibrato into your sound.

Changing to a mouthpiece that is slightly larger and/or has more of a funnel shape (opposed to a cupped bottom) may help. Consider a mouthpiece setup that will allow you to use the same rim on both instruments. Beware of large mouthpieces that quickly open up the mid- and low-register tone at the expense of endurance and intonation in the upper register.

Articulation

A seamless legato sound is a hallmark of good euphonium playing. Trombonists should be sure to blow through legato passages without tonguing. Bumpy and "sticky" lyrical lines typically occur when a trombonist's tongue is unintentionally getting involved. Try buzzing the legato passage on the mouthpiece so that any inadvertent tonguing will be noticeable (and stopped), and then play it on the instrument. Beware of throat tension: should it occur, stop practicing and relax the airway with long full inhalations and exhalations. Trust the valves to create the legato effect without any help from the tongue. Try blowing through the instrument without buzzing while crisply depressing the valves in rhythm.

Developing Valve Technique

One of the overlooked aspects of developing good valve technique and overall good posture on euphonium involves the angle of the lead pipe as comes off the bell to the mouthpiece. On euphoniums in the British design (bell up with vertical piston valves, the bell to the right of the head) this angle affects the position of the right hand as it addresses the valves. If the main body of the instrument is too close to the player, this can cause an awkward and cramped hand position, especially if you have a long upper arm. Be sure to test a new instrument for ergonomics as well as acoustical properties.

Work on scale patterns that are familiar from trombone study and use a metronome. This will allow you to focus on good hand position and valve action without also training the ear to a new pattern. Resist working on new, more advanced valve technique studies until the valve action is comfortable.

The fingers should reach the valves with a natural arch. The pads of the finger should touch the valve buttons. Avoid excessive arching of the fingers and playing on the fingertips close to the nail, which can lead to forearm tension. Conversely, contacting the valve below the first joint will create a longer, slower finger stroke. Work to find a comfortable hand position that works with your overall posture.

For intonation, a four-valve euphonium is certainly more desirable than a three-valve instrument. Most non-compensating euphoniums will have the fourth valve on the right hand, to be played by the fourth or little finger. This can present difficulties, especially when depressing the second and fourth valves. Most compensating euphoniums are designed with the fourth valve near the third-valve slide, to be depressed by the left-hand forefinger. This can create initial coordination problems but is the most desirable for advanced technique.

Posture

As with all brass instruments, it is vital that the instrument comes up to your mouth and not your mouth to the horn. Slouching down to play the euphonium is a chronic problem: many models of euphoniums are configured to a height that is too short to ensure good posture. The bulk and weight of the instrument often leads to the instrument resting on the player's lap. For a person with a short torso, this can be appropriate. However, many players are too tall to use this position and still maintain an erect posture. Do not allow the upper body to slouch and/or crane the neck to meet the mouthpiece. This can result in numerous problems including lack of air support, extra tension, and poor embouchure formation.

To correct this posture issue, either hold the instrument up by supporting it with your left hand (leaving the right hand free to manipulate the valves) or use a lap pillow or other elevating device. Do not rest the euphonium on the right leg. This will create tension, as the torso will have to twist to allow the left arm to reach the instrument. This is especially important if the fourth valve is played by the left hand.

Intonation

Correcting intonation on the euphonium can be quite different from what you are used to on trombone. Getting the instrument to play in tune with itself and tuning to others will involve good pitch awareness and the ability to adjust the pitch with the embouchure, air stream, alternate fingering, and/or a tuning slide adjustment. Using a tuner and/or a reference pitch, practice moving the pitch using just your air speed and embouchure.

The four-valve compensating euphonium will give you the best chance to play in tune, though it may not be appropriate for a very young player. Various devices are available for top-line euphoniums to adjust the main tuning or first-valve slides via a trigger device, thereby avoiding awkward direct reaches to the slide or air stream/embouchure changes.

Be aware that the natural intonation tendencies of the harmonic series are often not as consistent on euphonium as they are on trombone. For instance, the fourth partial, second-valve concert pitch "A" may be very flat when the B♭ and A♭ a half step away are in tune. These anomalies can be consistent throughout a partial or particular to specific fingering of a note.

It is essential to learn where the bad notes are on a particular instrument and know how to adjust them. This is accomplished by anticipating the adjustment before playing the note. Alternate fingerings can be an option, but be aware that a side effect of alternate fingerings can be a significant change in tone quality. You may be dismayed that compared to trombone, the number of viable alternate fingerings on euphonium is limited.

When learning to understand the intonation idiosyncrasies of a particular euphonium, you should use not only a tuner but also an aural reference source, whether an electronic tuner or keyboard or a practice partner. Hearing the correct pitch is essential: there is always the danger, especially with conical instruments, of teaching your ear to accept an out-of-tune fingering. (Remember, the secret of playing any wind instrument in tune is in constantly listening to, and adjusting to, the sounds around you.)

Techniques for Doubling on a Regular Basis

Use the same warm-up/fundamental exercises and etudes where appropriate.

Rather than using two entirely different sets of warm-ups or fundamental exercises, simplify the situation by starting with warm-up routines and scale patterns that are familiar from your primary instrument. By not having to learn new routines, you can focus on the details of tone, intonation, and technique that will lead to successful doubling. Standard warm-ups such as those by Remington and Schlossberg are very appropriate.

When choosing lyrical or technical etudes, those by Bordogni, Fink, Kopprasch, and Blume will serve both euphonium and trombone equally well, especially if they are already familiar to the ear. Choose materials that do not overtax the ear at first; use those with diatonic harmonies and comfortable intervals before moving to more difficult music.

In selection of solo repertoire not all works are equally suited to both instruments, but many are indeed usable on both trombone and euphonium (see suggested repertoire below). Again, do not complicate the technical side of doubling by introducing new music until the fundamentals of the new instrument are solidly in place.

Complementary Aspects of Trombone-Euphonium Doubling

While doubling on trombone and euphonium will require additional time and effort, the end result will justify the commitment. Not only will new skills be acquired but effective doubling can also have very positive cross-over effects for both instruments.

The more frequent use of vibrato and singing style that one gains from euphonium playing can make lyric passages on trombone more effective. This would certainly apply to solo repertoire, but consider the possibilities of adding a more vocal quality to the second trombone solo in Rimsky-Korsakov's *Russian Easter Overture* or similar ensemble solo passage. The ability to play long legato passages on euphonium without interrupting the air stream can translate to a less-intrusive legato technique on trombone when that same full air stream is applied to the legato articulation.

On the other side, the clarity, variety, and precision required of trombone articulations can give a doubler's euphonium playing a more expressive dimension. Quite often the typical repertoire for euphonium does not specify anything but basic detached and tongue-free legato articulations. Trombone playing will of course require the development of legato tonguing technique, but further studies in orchestral and jazz repertoire will reveal a whole new set of articulation requirements that may not otherwise be developed by the euphonium player. The end result of these new articulation skills is more expressive possibilities for euphonium performance, particularly in developing nuance in vocal lieder and jazz.

Trombone and euphonium doubling, when done correctly, makes one more aware and capable of producing varied tone color. Doubling will often expose the performer to new ensemble and repertoire experiences, making one more sensitive to how the sound fits the musical setting. For some euphonium players, playing *senza vibrato* is difficult. The ability of a euphonium to blend with other brasses in non-vibrato passages (e.g., a Gabrieli multiple brass choir canzona) is made easier with some trombone background. Numerous orchestral chorale passages for the trombone section, such as those found in Brahms's symphonies, require fine-tuning, a pure tone, and no vibrato. Developing a pure tone without ever-present vibrato will help to expose intonation problems on euphonium that may otherwise remain masked.

Tone color variation is also a consideration for trombonists. In the second trombone solo in Rimsky-Korsakov's *Russian Easter Overture,* one should emulate the chanting voice of a priest. Euphonium playing can help a trombonist to develop a rounder, darker, less-penetrating sound for this type of playing. Conversely, there are times when the music requires the euphonium to project in more stentorian fashion (Holst's tenor tuba solo in "Mars" from *The Planets,* or the opening of Curnow's *Symphonic Variants for Euphonium and Band*). Being able to apply a trombone-like concept of air speed and crisp articulation is of great value in these and other instances when the euphonium must be heard over a large ensemble.

Within the common tenor tuba/tenor horn repertoire in the symphony orchestra, it is also good to be able to adapt one's sound to the work at hand. A deep, rich, and lyrical euphonium sound is certainly appropriate for the well-known "Bydlo" solo from the Mussorgsky/Ravel version of *Pictures at an Exhibition*. But a more trombone-like approach will help get the penetrating sound required for "Mars" or the tenor horn solo in Mahler's *7th Symphony*.

Enhanced Musical Background

By playing trombone, euphonium players can gain exposure to music and musicians in symphony orchestras, brass quintets, and jazz ensembles that they might not have access to on euphonium. Greater performing opportunities not only enhance one's bank account but also expose individuals to more music and musicians. A euphonium player who only plays in a symphonic band or brass band misses out on experiencing great music and musicians in other genres. Exposure to orchestral music, opera, and jazz will enhance the way one plays in symphonic band or brass band, and in solo situations as well.

Jazz band or combo experience, for instance, would certainly be of help in interpreting solo works like Wilder's *Sonata for Baritone Horn* or Owen's *Variations for Euphonium and Band*. Frequent exposure to opera performances as a member of the opera orchestra will certainly provide help in performing vocal works on euphonium.

"Cross-Training" Materials for Doubling

Listed below are examples of readily available music that are effective on both trombone and euphonium. As stated above, use familiar material to help develop your doubling ability. Beginning method books for trombone and euphonium/baritone are usually very similar and can be used successfully on either instrument. At the intermediate and advanced levels, care must be taken to ensure that the music is technically suitable on both instruments. The list below is merely representative of well-known materials appropriate for cross-training. Many more possibilities exist.

Beginning Methods

Intermediate Method for Trombone & Baritone B.C., R. Skornica; Rubank

Method for Baritone Bks. 1 & 2, W. Beeler; Warner Bros.

Method for Trombone Bks. 1 & 2, W. Beeler; Warner Bros.

Selected Duets, Vol. 1, H. Voxman; Rubank

Intermediate Methods

Advanced Method for Trombone & Baritone B.C., R. Skornica; Rubank

From Treble to Bass Clef, R. Fink; Accura

Scales, G. Pares; Carl Fischer

Selected Duets Vol. II, H. Voxman; Rubank

Studies in Legato, R. Fink; Accura

Advanced Methods

Basic Routines, R. Marsteller; Southern Music

Complete Method (for trombone), T. Arban/Randall-Mantia; Carl Fischer

40 Progressive Studies, H. Tyrell; Boosey & Hawkes

Melodious Etudes, Vol. 1, Bordogni/Rochut; Carl Fischer

Studies in Clefs, V. Blazhevich/Hunsberger; Hal Leonard

Warm-Up Studies, E. Remington/Hunsberger; Accura

Recommended Cross-Training Solo Repertoire

Andante & Allegro, E. Barat; Carl Fischer

Andante & Allegro, T. Ropartz/Shapiro; Carl Fischer

Morceau Symphonique, A. Guilmant; International

Scene de Concert, M. Denmark; Ludwig

Six Sonatas, J. E. Galliard/Fussel-Brown; International

Six Studies in English Folksong; R. Vaughan Williams; Galaxy

Sonata # 6, A. Vivaldi/Ostrander; International

Acknowledgements

The author would like to thank Kenneth Kreitner, PhD, for his editorial assistance and Paige A. Clark, MM, for her background research.

Notes

1. Dan Bachelder and Norman Hunt, *Guide to Teaching Brass,* 6th ed. (New York: McGraw-Hill, 2002), 3–5.

2. Earl Sherburne, "An Analysis of the Blowing Pressure Used for Trombone and Euphonium Tone Production" (PhD diss., University of Minnesota, 1981), 54–55.
3. Bruce Gleason, "Doubling on Euphonium," *Instrumentalist* 45 (1991): 28.
4. Bachelder and Hunt, 23
5. Sherburne, 54–55.

Bibliography

Bachelder, Dan, and Norman Hunt. *Guide to Teaching Brass.* 6th ed. New York: McGraw-Hill, 2002.

Bahr, Edward. "Idiomatic Similarities and Differences of the Trombone and Euphonium in History and Performance." *ITA Journal* 6 (1978): 31–36.

Gleason, Bruce. "Doubling on Euphonium." *Instrumentalist* 45 (1991): 28–35.

McCready, Matthew. "Euphonium Doubling among Orchestral Trombonists." *ITA Journal* 18, No. 1 (1990): 13–15.

Sherburne, Earl. "An Analysis of the Blowing Pressure Used for Trombone and Euphonium Tone Production." Ph.D diss., University of Minnesota, 1981.

Whitener, Scott. *A Complete Guide to Brass.* 2nd ed. Belmont, California: Schirmer-Thomson Learning, 1997.

Suggested Readings

Bowman, Brian. *Practical Hints on Playing the Baritone (Euphonium).* Melville, New York: Belwin-Mills, 1983.

Fink, Reginald. *The Trombonists Handbook.* Athens, Ohio: Accura Music, 1977.

Kagarice, Vern L., et al. *Solos for the Student Trombonist: An Annotated Bibiliography.* Nashville, Tennessee: Brass Press, 1979.

Kleinhammer, Edward. *The Art of Trombone Playing.* Evanston, Illinois: Summy-Birchard Company, 1963.

Knaub, Donald. *Trombone Teaching Techniques.* 2nd ed. Athens, Ohio: Accura Music, 1977.

Wick, Denis. *Trombone Technique.* London: Oxford University Press, 1975.

Winter, Denis. *Euphonium Music Guide.* New London, Connecticut: Whaling Music, 1983.

19. The Euphonium in Jazz

Marcus Dickman

Rich Matteson (1929–1993) was the most noted proponent of the jazz euphonium. He was best known for conducting clinics, directing jazz ensembles, and arranging jazz charts for big band. He studied piano from the ages of three to eighteen. His father was a band director and needed a baritone horn in his school band and had Rich play that instrument.

Matteson grew up in Ada, Minnesota, where touring jazz bands would stop at the local fairgrounds. Rich would frequently listen to the famous bands of the day live and on the radio. He attended Augustana College from 1947–1949. In 1950, he joined the Army and was assigned to an Army band in Colorado Springs, Colorado. There he played tuba in concert band and valve trombone in dance band and began writing and arranging for the dance band. He was discharged in 1952 and traveled with a touring band for a short while.

Influenced by his father, Matteson then attended to the University of Iowa and studied tuba with Bill Gower. At that time there was no such thing as a baritone or euphonium major. He earned a bachelor of music education in 1955 and taught high school music for two years. In 1957 he decided to move to Las Vegas and try to earn a living as a full-time professional musician. He worked for comedian Ish Kabibble in 1957 and joined the highly regarded Bob Scoby Dixieland Band in 1958 playing tuba and an occasional bass trumpet solo. His tuba was an antique BB♭ helicon tuba, which he had purchased from a music store in Rock Island, Illinois. He developed a unique style of tuba playing that imitated the sound and feel of a string bass.

On September 18, 1959, Matteson joined the Dukes of Dixieland, the most popular and well-paid Dixieland band in the nation. They played six or seven nights a week at nightclubs, appeared on television shows, and recorded regularly. One of the people he met was Louis Armstrong, with whom he recorded the album *Satchmo and the Dukes of Dixieland* (1960). This recording session had a great impact on Matteson's career.

When Matteson asked Armstrong how he could play with such emotion (as if an audience was there) during a recording session, Louis replied, "Play for someone you love." Matteson would use Armstrong's advice as one of the cornerstones of his clinics in his later years. Matteson felt that students playing for someone they loved, rather than playing for critics or juries, would put the performers at ease and help them concentrate on the sheer pleasure of music making. Matteson passed away in 1993.

As of today, no player has emerged that has been as successful in promoting the jazz euphonium as Rich Matteson. Nevertheless, euphonium has still not been accepted as a mainstream jazz instrument. For example, it is not even listed in the miscellaneous instrument category in the annual *Downbeat Magazine* reader's poll. There are some world-class performers who double on the instrument, most notably the trombonists John Allred (New York City) and Bill Reichenbach (Los Angeles). Jazz trombone legend Frank Rosolino played *I Thought about You* on an American bell-front euphonium at a recording session in 1972 for the *USAF Serenade in Blue* radio show. Jack Teagarden was a Conn instrument clinician toward the end of his life and performed a few tunes per evening on a Conn baritone that was given to him. Teagarden recorded *Old Man River* on July 1, 1959.

Gus Mancuso and Bernard McKinney were the most active euphonium players in the New York City jazz scene in the late 1950s and early 1960s. McKinney appeared as a sideman with Freddie Hubbard, Slide Hampton, Sun Ra, and others. Gus Mancuso recorded some albums under his own name that have recently been re-issued (see Discography). Betty O'Hara (California) was a multi-instrumentalist who played euphonium part-time. She was known on the west coast and performed at many festivals.

The euphonium has been used in the recording studios sparingly. The limited use has not started any sort of trend for studio trombonists to always bring a euphonium to the session just in case.

Recommended Course of Study

There are many ways to go about becoming more proficient at jazz improvisation. These are recommendations only. Each person should feel free to alter or add anything.

Most brass players in the United States were exposed to jazz by their high school jazz bands. Since euphonium is not utilized in most jazz ensembles, many players have not been exposed to jazz. While many directors will be open to including euphonium in the jazz ensemble, the parts are written for the trombone, which faces forward and has a brighter sound than the euphonium. I recommend learning the slide-playing valve trombone if the director does not like the idea of having a euphonium in the jazz ensemble. Every few years I hear a story about a high school or college student who is discouraged from playing jazz because he or she plays euphonium, but most directors are interested in having ANYONE play in the jazz band.

Since its inception, jazz has been an aural tradition. The best way to internalize jazz style and phrasing is to listen to jazz on a regular basis. You will begin to cultivate your favorite artists and jazz styles. In high school in the late 1970s I began listening to Glenn Miller, Count Basie, Woody Herman, and Tommy Dorsey. My band director also recommended Charlie Parker, Dizzy Gillespie, and others. It was great advice. I did not know much about Stan Kenton until a music professor gave me a copy of *Cuban Fire* in college. Listen to everything about the recording. Listen to each track multiple times and try to catch what the various instruments are doing. Every instrument can contribute original, swinging ideas to the jazz vocabulary.

When learning to improvise jazz on the euphonium, I recommend that you concentrate your listening on trumpet players. One reason is that there are so few jazz euphoniums to emulate. Another is that there are many different substyles to check out. I am not saying not to listen to other instruments but to start out by listening and transcribing trumpet solos. Some notable players to study are Louis Armstrong, Clifford Brown, Miles Davis, Blue Mitchell, Clark Terry,

and others. The tenor sax is another instrument that has a similar range to the euphonium. I recommend Lester Young, Sonny Stitt, Dexter Gordon, John Coltrane, and others. These names are only for beginners who need some place to start. I may have left out your favorite players, but space does not allow me to list everybody.

I recommend the following texts for improvisational study. There are now hundreds of books for learning about jazz improvisation. These are given only as a start.

Listed in title, author, publisher order

Patterns for Jazz, Coker, Gerry, Studio PR
Clarke Technical Studies, Clarke, Herbert L., Fischer
Al Vizzutti Trumpet Method, Vizzutti, Al, Alfred
21 Jazz Trumpet Solos, Sloan, Ken, Aebersold
Effortless Mastery, Werner, Kenny, Aebersold

The Jamey Aebersold jazz play-along series has been a major influence in jazz education for thirty years. The main reason to use the recordings is to make practice less tedious. I recommend volumes 1, 3, 16, and 21 because they work on fundamentals of improvising in all keys. Other volumes are an important means to learn tunes (see www.jazzbooks.com).

Band in a Box (www.pgmusic.com) and MiBAC (www.mibac.com) are very useful tools for practicing jazz improvisation. This computer software sequences a jazz rhythm section when you enter in the chord progression to a tune or exercise. Because of its flexibility you can instantly change the key, tempo, and style of any selection. The quality of the sound depends on how sophisticated your sound module is.

Most colleges and universities offer some sort of improvisation class. If you are not able to enroll, engage a private teacher to help you with jazz improvisation. The aesthetic for learning jazz is different from playing and learning classical music in that the jazz performer needs to be able to accept mistakes in the early stages of development. The only way to learn the right notes is to play a lot of wrong ones!

20. Equipment

Demondrae Thurman

Euphonium Manufacturers and Distributors and Their Products

The lists of euphoniums and baritone horns do not include marching band instruments. Though not represented, marching brass can be purchased at many of the distributors listed in this chapter. Prices of instruments are not included because there are no guarantees that they will be current at the time that this book is published. Contact information for the manufacturers and distributors is listed in appendix A. All of the instruments are upright bells unless otherwise indicated. The inclusion of the word "compensating" and/or the bell size denotes professional instruments. All professional instruments employ the 3 + 1 valve alignment unless otherwise stated. My most heartfelt apologies to any manufacturers or distributors that were inadvertently overlooked. Stay current with new designs and other instrument options by keeping up with publications such as the *ITEA Journal* through the International Tuba and Euphonium Association and the Internet. It is my hope that you will find this chapter helpful.

Manufacturers

Allora
 AA401 Euphonium, 4 valve
 402S Baritone Horn
Amati
 AEP 231 Euphonium, 3 valve
 AEP 241 Euphonium, 4 valve
 AEP 242 Euphonium in C, 4 valve
 AEP 331 Euphonium, 3 valve
 AEP 333 Euphonium, 3 valve
 AEP 341 Euphonium, 4 valve
 ABH 221 Baritone Horn
Bach
 B1103 Euphonium, 3 valve
 B1104 Bell front Euphonium, 3 valve
 B1110 Euphonium, 4 valve
 B1114 Euphonium, ¾ size
Besson
 BE 764 Bell front Euphonium, 3 valve
 BE 762 International Euphonium, 3 valve
 BE 765 International Euphonium, 4 valve
 BE 967 Sovereign Euphonium, 4 valve compensating, 12 inch bell
 BE 968 Sovereign Euphonium, 4 valve compensating, 11 inch bell
 BE 2051 Prestige Euphonium, 4 valve compensating, 11.18 inch bell
 BE 2052 Prestige Euphonium, 4 valve compensating, 12.25 inch bell
 BE 757 Baritone Horn, 3 valve
 BE 955 Baritone Horn, 3 valve compensating
 BE 956 Baritone Horn, 4 valve compensating
Blessing
 B350 Euphonium, 3 valve
B&S
 PT 33 Euphonium, 4 valve
 PT 35 Euphonium, 4 valve
Cerveny
 CEP 531 Oval shaped Euphonium, 4 rotary valve
 CEP 333 Euphonium, 3 rotary valve
 CEP 538 Bell front Euphonium, 4 rotary valve compensating, 11.8 inch bell
 CEP 541 Kaiser Oval Shaped Euphonium, 4 rotary valve compensating, 11.8 inch bell
Conn
 211 Artist Euphonium, 3 valve with front action
 191 Constellation Euphonium, 4 valve
Courtois
 Symphonie 167 RV II MTS Euphonium, 4 valve compensating, 310 mm bell
 Symphonie 267 MTS Euphonium, 4 valve compensating, 310 mm bell
 Symphonie 169 Baritone Horn, 3 valve compensating
 160 Baritone Horn, 3 valve
DEG
 Shafer Model 823 Euphonium, 3 valve
Getzen
 G8230 Baritone, 3 valve
 Model 570 Euphonium, 3 valve
 Model 571 Euphonium, 4 valve
Hirsbrunner
 HBE Standard Euphonium, 4 valve compensating, 11.5 inch bell
 HBE Exclusive Euphonium, 4 valve compensating, 12 inch bell
 HBE Stealth Euphonium, 4 valve compensating, 12 inch bell
Holton
 B601R Bell front Baritone Horn
 B625R Baritone Horn
Jupiter
 464 Bell front Euphonium, 3 valve

466L Convertible Euphonium, 3 valve
468 Euphonium, 3 valve
470 Euphonium, 4valve
474 Euphonium, 3 valve with front action
570L Euphonium, 4 valve
462 Baritone Horn, 3 valve
Kalison Euphonium
Kanstul
    CEU 975 Euphonium, 4 valve compensating,
       12 inch bell
    CEU 980 Convertible Euphonium, 3 valve
    CEU 985 Convertible Euphonium, 3 valve
    CEU 985L Euphonium, 4 valve
King
    625 Diplomat Bell front Euphonium, 3 valve
    627 Diplomat Euphonium, 3 valve
    2266 Artist Bell front euphonium, 4 valve
    2268 Artist Euphonium, 4 valve
    2280 Legend Euphonium, 4 valve
Maestro
    MALWEU Euphonium, 3 valve
    MALWBT Baritone Horn, 3 valve
Meinl Weston
    551 Euphonium, 4 valve compensating, 11.8
       inch bell
    451 Euphonium, 4 valve compensating, 11.8
       inch bell
    51 Euphonium, 4 valve
    50 Euphonium, 3 valve
    49 Baritone Horn, 4 rotary valves
    48 Baritone Horn, 3 rotary valves
Miraphone
    1258 Euphonium, 4 valve compensating, 12
       inch bell
Sterling
    Perantucci Euphonium, 4 valve compensating,
       12 inch bell
VMI
    VO-3171 Euphonium, 4 valve
    VO-3174 Bell front Euphonium, 4 valve
Weril
    H670 Baritone Horn, 3 valve
    H972 Euphonium, 4 valve
    H980 Euphonium, 4 valve
Willson
    2704 Euphonium, 4 valve
    2900 Euphonium, 4 valve compensating, 11.5
       inch bell, European shank
    2950 Euphonium, 4 valve compensating, 12.25
       inch
    2975 Euphonium, front action, 4 valve compen-
       sating, 11.5 inch bell
Winston
    405 LWC Baritone Horn, 3 valve
    415 LWC Euphonium, 3 valve
    420 LWC Euphonium, 3 valve
    525 LWC Euphonium, 4 valve
Yamaha
    YEP 201 Euphonium, 3 valve
    YEP 201M Convertible Euphonium, 3 valve
    YEP 211 Bell front Euphonium, 3 valve
    YEP 321 Euphonium, 4 valve

    YEP 641 Euphonium, 4 valve compensating
    YEP 642 Euphonium, 4 valve compensating
    YEP 842 Euphonium, 4 valve compensating,
       11.8 inch bell
    YBH 301 Baritone Horn, 3 valve
    YBH 621 Baritone Horn, 4 valve compensating

Euphonium Mouthpieces and Accessories

There are very few mouthpieces that are specifically designed for the euphonium. With that in mind, they are given special recognition in this publication. The other mouthpieces are listed by their distributors as trombone mouthpieces. Euphonium mouthpieces have three distinct shanks: small, European, and large. When purchasing a mouthpiece, make sure to specify the correct shank for your instrument. In this publication, mouthpieces with European shanks are denoted, and all other mouthpieces come in small and large shanks unless listed otherwise. The mouthpieces are arranged largest to smallest as it relates to cup and rim size. In the writer's opinion, these mouthpieces will help provide the conical, round sound of the euphonium rather than that of the trombone.

Mouthpieces for Euphonium

Denis Wick. 3, 4 AL, 4.5 AL, (Steve Mead) 2, 3, 3
    M, 3.5, 4, 4 M, 5, B4, B6, B9 (M is for Euro-
    pean shank)
DEG Brian Bowman Model. 1, 2, 3
Doug Elliott LT and XT series. 105–100 rim, J-G
    cup and the #8 shank that relates to the cup let-
    ter Dillon.
Perantucci. PT-2, PT-3, PT-4, AH-1
Schilke (Yamaha). 51D and 52
Warburton. Demondrae model, 3G, 4GD, 4GDE,
    4GS, 4GSE, 5GL (Jones) 5GD, 5GDE, 5G, (E
    is for European shank)

Other Mouthpieces

Bach. (Conn, Benge, Faxx, Greg Black,): 2G,
3G, 4G, 5G, 6.5 AL (2G with Large Bore only)
Greigo. 2, 3, 3.5, 4 (large bore only)
Kelly (plastic). 6.5 AL, 5G, 51 D

Accessories

Hard and Soft Cases, Mutes, Breathing Devices
Hard Cases
DEG Replacement Cases.
Hiscox.
Walt Johnson.

Gig Bags/Soft Cases
Adams.
Altieri Instrument Bags.

Bach.
Bass Bags.
Cronkhite Custom Bags (leather and cordura).
Duralite.
Gewa Bags.
Humes and Berg Tuxedo.
Pro-Tec C-242.
Reunion Blues (leather and cordura) comes in black, brown, or burgundy.
Ritter Band and Orchestra.
Soundwear.
Sterling Deluxe.
Ursula Amrein (leather and cordura).
Woodwind and Brasswind.

Mutes
Denis Wick metal straight mute.
Engemann Aluminum straight mute.
Humes and Berg straight mute.
Humes and Berg Mannie Klein philharmonic straight mute.
NP Griffith Aluminum straight mute.
R&S straight mute.
Tennessee Tech Aluminum straight mute.
TrumCor Straight mute.

Practice Mutes
Denis Wick.
Humes and Berg.
TrumCor Stealth.
Yamaha Silent Brass.

Breathing Devices/Methods
Breath Builder. Ping-pong ball in tube with two hoses.
5 and 6 liter breathing bags.
Portex Inspiron.
The Breathing Gym by Patrick Sheridan and Sam Pilafian.
Voldyne (measures air intake).

Specialized Repair Sources

Many of your basic repairs, such as minor dents and chemical cleaning, can be done at your local music store. The specialists listed here are noted repairmen and can do custom work such as adding valves, venting valves, complete overhauls, and other major repairs.

Jason Bitner
Rayburn Musical Instrument Co., Inc.
263 Huntington Avenue
Boston, MA 02115
617-266-4727
www.rayburnmusic.com

Jim Darby
Capitol Music Center
3834 Harrison Road
Montgomery, AL 36109
334-277-9990

Albert Houde
Baltimore Brass Company
99 Mellor Avenue
Cantonsville, MD 21228
866-882-2230
albert@baltimorebrass.net

Karl Humble, Albuquerque, NM

Rich Ita
Rich Ita's Brass Instrument Workshop
3164 Holly Mill Run
Marietta, GA 30062
888-527-3601
biw@brassinstrumentworkshop.com

Daniel Oberloh
Oberloh Woodwind and Brass Works
18018 First Avenue South
Seattle, WA 98148
206-241-5767
www.oberloh.com

Bob Pallansch, VA
2808 Woodlawn Avenue
Falls Church, VA 22042
703-532-0137
icleide@cox.net

Johnny Paul
Johnny Paul's Music Shop
P.O. Box 1051
Aledo, TX 76008
817-441-9003
jpaul@johnnypaulsmusicshop.com

D. Kevin Powers, Custom Music Company
Custom Music Co.
1930 Hilton Ferndale, MI 48220
800-521-6380
www.custommusiccorp.com

Robb Stewart, CA
14 East Santa Clara Street
Apt. 18
Arcadia, CA 91006
626-447-1904
oldbrass@att.net

Lee Stofer
Lee Stofer Music, Inc.
7881 Runnymede Drive
Jonesboro, GA 30236-2751
703-603-6088
www.tubameister.com

Wayne Tanabes
The Brass Bow
101 North Hickory Avenue
Arlington Heights, IL 60004
847-253-7552
www.thebrassbow.com

Matt Walters
Dillon Music
325 Fulton Street
Woodbridge, NJ 07095
732-634-3399
matt@dillonmusic.com

APPENDIX A: Composers', Publishers', and Manufacturers' Addresses

Joseph Skillen

This list also appears in a constantly updated electronic format on the official Web site of the International Tuba and Euphonium Association (www.iteaonline.org). Should there be further updates or additions to the list, please contact Joseph Skillen at Louisiana State University (jskille@lsu.edu).

A.A. Kalmus Limited, 38 Eldon Way, Paddock Wood, Tonbridge, Kent, England.

AAP, Edition AAP, Aas-Wangsvei 8, N-1613 Fredrikstad. Tel: +47 69 31 09 64. E-mail: frank@nordensten.com.

A M Percussion Publications, PO Box 436, Lancaster, NY, 14086, USA. Tel 1: 716-937-3705, Tel 2: 1-800-317-2882. E-mail: AMPercPub@aol.com. Web site: www.ampercussion.com.

A R Publishing Company, Box 292, Candlewood Isle, CT, 06810, USA.

A & L Musical Enterprises, Inc, 503 Tahoe Street, Natchitoches, LA, 71457-5718, USA. Tel: 318-357-0924. E-mail: ALMEI@aol.com. Web site: http://www.music-usa.org/conners.

AB Carl Gehrmans Musikforlag, Box 6005, SE-102 31 Stockholm, Sweden. Tel: +46 8 610 06 00. Fax: +46 8 610 06 25. E-mail: info@gehrmans.se. Web site: www.sk-gehrmans.se.

Abingdon Press, 201 Eighth Avenue S, PO Box 801, Nashville, TN, 37202-0801, USA. 1-800-251-3320. Fax: 1-800-836-7802. E-mail: aadcock@abingdonpress.com. Web site: www.abingdonpress.com/abingdonpress/default.asp.

Accentuate Music, 4524 14th Street W, Bradenton, FL, 34207-1428, USA.

Accolade Press, 6303 Homestake Pl, Bowie, MD, 20720. Tel: (301) 464-6969. E-mail: bbuck@ccconline.net.

Accura Music, Box 4260, Athens, OH, 45701-4260, USA.

Adams Cases, Pearl Corporation 549 Metroplex Drive, Nashville, TN, 37211-3140, USA. Tel 615-833-4477. Web site: www.pearldrum.com.

Adler Musikverlag, Postfach 9, A-8990 Bad Aussee, Germany, Tel: +43(0)3622/54 588 Fax: +43(0) 3622/55 266 E-mail: atp-records@aon.at. Web site: www.adler-musikverlag.com.

Advance Music, Veronika Gruber GmbH, Maier-ackerstr, 18, D-72108 Rottenburg/N, Germany.

Tel: +49(0) 7472-1832. Fax: +49(0) 7472-24621. E-mail: mail@advancemusic.com. Web site: www.advancemusic.com.

Åkerwall, Martin, Skt, Peders stræde 30 D, 1453 København, Denmark. Tel: +45 33 16 33 40. E-mail: aakerwall@heaven.dk. Web site: www.aakerwall.com.

Albam, Manny, 7 Glengary Road, Croton, NJ, 10520, USA.

Albert. *See* J. Albert & Son Pty, Limited.

Albian Publishing, 6971 Ridgeview Lane W298, Hartland, WI, 53029, USA. Tel: 262-538-1477. E-mail: albianjca@aol.com.

Aldo Bruzzichelll Eds, US Rep: Margun Music, Borgo S, Frediano 8, Florence 1-50124, Italy.

Alessi Music Studio, 15 Anchorage Court, San Rafael, CA, 94903, USA.

Alfred Publishing Company Incorporated, 16380 Roscoe Blvd, PO Box 10003, Van Nuys, CA, 91410, USA. 818-891-5999. Fax: 818-891-2369. E-mail: customerservice@alfred.com. Web site: www.alfred.com.

Allaire Music Publications, 212 2nd Ave, Bradley Beach, NJ, 07720, USA. Tel: 732-988-6188. E-mail: timbroege@aol.com—out of business.

Allans Publishing Limited, US Rep: E. C. Schirmer, Level 1 Building 6 64 Balmain Street, Richmond 3121, Victoria, Australia. Tel: 61 3 8415 8000. Fax: 61 3 8415 8088. E-mail: sales@allanspublishing.com.au. Web site: www.allanspublishing.com.au/default.aspx.

Allen Music Limited, 8168 Benton Way, Arvada, CO, 80003-1810, USA.

Almqvist & Wiksell Publishing Limited, PO Box 7634, S-103 94 Stockholm, Sweden. Tel: +46 8 613 61 00. Fax: +46 8 24 25 43. E-mail: export@city.akademibokhandeln.se. Web site: www.akademibokhandeln.se/akb/awi.html.

Alphonse Leduc Editions Paris, US. *See* Robert King Music Sales, 175 Rue St, Honore, 75040, Paris Cedex 01, France. Tel: +33 (0)1 42 96 89 11. Fax: +33(0)1 42 86 02 83. Web site: www.alphonseleduc.com/english/.

Altieri Instrument Bags, 1 Galapago Street, Denver, CO, 80223, USA. Tel: 303-291-0658. Web site: www.altieribags.com.

Amadeus Verlag, Postfach 473, CH-8405 Winterthur, Switzerland. Tel: +41(0) 52-233-2866. Fax: +41(0) 52-233-5401. E-mail: info@amadeusmusic-ch. Web site: www.amadeusmusic-ch.

Amati USA, Inc, 1124 Globe Ave, PO Box 1429, Mountainside, NJ, 07092, USA. Tel: 908-301-1366.

Amazing Music World. *See* SheetMusicNow.com.

American Composers Alliance, American Composers Edition Incorporated, 73 Spring St, Rm. 505, New York, NY, 10012, USA. Tel: 212-362-8900. Fax: 212-925-6798. E-mail: info@composers.com. Web site: www.composers.com.

American Composers Edition, Incorporated. *See* American Composers Alliance.

American Music Center, 30 West 26th Street, Suite 1001, New York, NY, 10010-2011, USA. Tel: 212-366-5263. Fax: 212-366-5265. E-mail: www.amc.net/contact.html. Web site: www.amc.net.

AMSI, 3706 East 34th Street, Minneapolis, MN, 55406-2702, USA. Fax: (612) 729-4487.

Anderson, Mogens, Peter Rordamsvej 7, 2800 Lyngby, Denmark.

Anderson's Arizona Originals, 524 E. 26th Avenue, Apache Jct, AZ, 85219, USA. Tel: 480-983-2350. Fax: 480-983-2602. E-mail: composer@andersons-originals.com. Web site: www.andersons-originals.com.

Anglo-American Music Publishers (aka: Worldwide Music Publishers), PO Box 161323, Altamonte Springs, FL, 32716-1323 USA. Tel: (407)464-9454. E-mail: wwm32716@yahoo.com. Web site: www.worldwidemusiconline.com.

Anglo Music Press, PO Box 303, Wembley, HA9 8GX, England.

Animando Music Publishers, Tel and Fax: +39 0342 211653. Web site: www.animando.com.

Anton Boehm & Sohn, Postfach 110369—Lange Gasse 26 D—86028 Augsburg 11 Germany.

Anton J. Benjamin, Werderstraße 44—Postfach 2561, D—2000 Hamburg 13 Germany.

Argee Music Press, 720 Terrace Lane, Greencastle, IN, 46135, USA.

Arizona University Music Press, School Of Music, University of Arizona, 355 S. Euclid Ave, Suite 103, Tucson, AZ, 85719, USA. Phone: 520-621-1441. Fax: 520-621-8899. Web site: uapress.arizona.edu/home.htm.

Arpeges, 24 rue Etex, 75018 Paris, France. E-mail: accueil@arpeges.org. Web site: www.arpeges.org.

Ars Nova. *See* Theodore Presser Company.

Ars Polona, Karkowskie Przedmiexcie #7, 00-068 Warszawa, Poland. Tel: +48 (22) 826 12 01. Tel: +48 (22) 826 47 58. Fax: +48 (22) 826 62 40. E-mail: arspolona@arspolona.com.pl. Web site: www.arspolona.com.pl/indexe.htm.

Artia, Foreign Trade Corp Ve Smeckkách 30, Praha 2 Czech Republic.

Arts Lab, AR:Zak, 4, Gusta Green Aston, Birmingham, B4 7ER, England.

Ashley Dealers Incorporated, PO Box 337, Hasbrouck Heights, NJ, 07604, USA.

Assoc Board of the Royal School of Music, US Rep: Theodore Presser Company, 24 Portland Place, London, W1B 1LU, UK. Tel: +44 (0)20 7636 5400. Fax: +44 (0)20 7637 0234. E-mail: abrsm@abrsm.ac.uk. Web site: www.abrsm.ac.uk.

Associated Music Publishers. *See* G. Schirmer, Inc.

Astute Music Ltd, PO Box 17, Winsford, Cheshire, UK. E-mail: info@astute-music.com. Web site: www.astute-music.com.

Athens Music Publishing, 7230 Cloverhurst Court, Cumming, GA, 30041, USA. Fax: 770-754-7881. Web site: www.euphonium.com.

Astoria Verlag, Hospitalstr, 19, D-40597, Düsseldorf, Germany. Tel: (0211) 717996. Fax: (0211) 7184276. E-mail: astoriaverlag@t-online.de.

Atlanta Brass Society Press, 953 Rosedale Road NE, Atlanta, GA, 30306, USA. Tel: 404-875-8822. E-mail: info@atlantabrass.com. Web site: userwww.service.emory.edu/~mmoor02/ABSPress.html.

Atlantic Music Supply Corp, 6124 Selma Avenue, Hollywood, CA, 90029, USA.

Atlantis Publications, 406 E 31st Street, Baltimore, MD, 21218, USA.

Augsburg Fortress Publishers, PO Box 1209, Minneapolis, MN, 55440, USA. Tel: 612-330-3300. Fax: 612-330-3455. E-mail: www.augsburgfortress.org/company/contactus.asp. Web site: www.augsburgfortress.org.

Augsburg Publishing Company. *See* Augsburg Fortress Publishers.

Aulos Music Publishers, PO Box 54, Montgomery, NY, 12549, USA.

Australian Music Centre, Level 4, The Arts Exchange, 18 Hickson Road, The Rocks, Sydney, NSW, Australia. Tel: +61-2-9247 4677. Fax: +61-2-9241 2873. E-mail: info@amcoz.com.au. Web site: www.amcoz.com.au.

Australian Trombone Education Magazine, Queensland Conservatorium of Music, PO Box 3428, South Brisbane Business Center, QLD 4101. Tel: +07 3875 6360. Fax: 07 3875 6282.

Autograph Editions. *See* Philharmusica Corporation.

Avant Music. *See* Western International Music.

Avvakoumov, Valentin, Str, Schotman 9-1-232, St, Petersburg, 193232, Russia.

Award Music Company, Oliveri Dist, Corp, PO Box 591, Oakdale, NY, 11769, USA.

Axelrod Music, 251 Weybosset Street, Providence, RI, 02903, USA. Tel: 401-421-4833. Fax: 401-621-3722.

B&S, Vogtlandische Musikinstrumentenfabrik GmbH, Markneukirchen, Bismarckstrausse 11, 0-9659, Markneukirchen, Germany. Web site: www.ja-musik.de.

B. Schott's Sohne Mainz, US Rep: European American Music, Weihergarten 5, D-55116 Mainz, Tel +49 6131 246-0. Fax +49 6131 246-211.

E-mail and Web site: www.schott-english.com/ nocache/smi_en/#.

Baadsvik Music Shop, Markaplassen 415, 7054 RANHEIM, Norway, Phone: +47 73 57 43 45. Fax: +47 73 57 43 48. E-mail: oystein@baadsvik. com. Web site: www.baadsvik.com.

Bach. *See* Conn-Selmer.

Bales, Kenton, Department of Music, University of Nebraska at Omaha, Omaha, NE, 68182-0245, USA. Tel: 402 554-3359 Tel 2: 402 213-4040. E-mail: kbales@mail.unomaha.edu. Web site: http://music.unomaha.edu/faculty_kbales.html.

Baltimore Horn Club Publication, 7 Chapel Court, Lutherville, MD, 21093, USA. 410-561-9465.

Banks Music Publications, The Old Forge, Sand Hutton, York YO41 I LB London. Tel: (01904) 468472. Fax: (01904) 468679. E-mail: banksramsay@cwcom.net. Web site: www.bank smusicpublications,cwc.net/.

Barenreiter Verlag, PO Box 10 03 29, D-34003 Kassel, Germany. Tel: +49 561 3105-0. Fax: +49 561 3105-176. E-mail: info@barenreiter. com. Web site: www.barenreiter.com.

Barnhouse. *See* C. L. Barnhouse Company.

Baron. *See* M. Baron Company, Incorporated.

Barry Ed, Com e Ind, Av, R, Saenz Pena 1185 80 "N," 1035 Buenos Aires, Argentina. Tel: +54 1 382 3230. Fax: +54 1 383 3946. E-mail: barry@satlink.com.

Bartles, Alfred, 3609A Wilbur Place, Nashville, TN, 37204, USA. Tel: 615-292-9157.

Bartlesville Publishing Company, Box 265, Bartlesville, OK, 74005, USA. 918-333-1502.

Bass Bags. Web site: www.bassbags.co.uk.

Basset Hound Music, 2139 Kress Street, Los Angeles, CA, 90046, USA. Tel: 213-656-6510. E-mail: jimself@BassetHoundMusic.com. Web site: www. jimself.com.

Beasley, Rule, San Monica College, 1815 Pearl, Santa Monica, CA, 90405, USA.

Belaieff. *See* M. P. Belaieff.

Belden, George, 1211 LeLande, Anchorage, AK, 99504, USA. Tel: 907-786-1523. Fax: 907-786-1799. E-mail: beldenanchak@Web sitetv.net.

Belmont Music Publishers, PO Box 231, Pacific Palisades, CA, 90272, USA. Tel: 310-454-1867. Fax: 310-573-1925. E-mail: belmontmusic 90272@yahoo.com. Web site: www.geocities. com/belmontmusic.

Belwin. *See* CPP Belwin Incorporated.

B-flat Music, PO Box 5043, Laytonsville, MD, 20882.

Benedetti, Donald, Trenton State College, Trenton, NJ, 08625, USA.

Benge. *See* Conn-Selmer.

Benjamin. *See* Anton J. Benjamin.

Bennett, Malcolm, "Spennythorne" Cokes Lane, Little Chalfonts, Buckinghamshire, HP8 4UD, United Kingdom.

Benson, Marl Elling, In manuscript form only.

Berben Press. *See* Edizioni Musical Berben.

Berklee Press. *See* Hal Leonard.

Bernel Music LTD. *See* Solid Brass Music Company.

Besson Musical Instruments Ltd, Number One Blackmoor Lane, Croxley Business Park, Watford, Hertfordshire WD18 8GA United Kingdom. Tel: 01923 659700. Web site: www. musicgroup.com.

Bewley Music Incorporated, PO Box 9328, Dayton, OH, 45409, USA. Tel/Fax: 937-253-5812. Web site: www.tubachristmas.com/bewley.html.

Bizet (Editions) Belgium, 13 Rue de la Madeleine, Brussels 1, Belgium.

BKJ Publications, Box 324, Astor Station, Boston, MA, 02123, USA.

Blasmusikverlag Fritz Schultz GmbH, Am Marzengraben 6, W-7800 Freiburg-Tiengen, Germany. Tel: 07664/1431. Fax: 07664/5123.

Blatter, Alfred, 3141 Chestnut Street, Rm#2018, MacAlister Hall, Philadelphia, PA, 19104 Tel: 215-895-2451. E-mail: Alfred,blatter@ drexel.edu.

Blessing, E. K. Blessing Company, 1301 West Beardsley Ave, Elkhart, IN, 46514. Tel: 219-293-0833 or 800-348-7409. Web site: www. ekblessing.com.

Blis Music, 30 Grant Blvd, Brandon, Manitoba, Canada, R7B-2L5.

Bliss, Marilyn, 34-40 79th Street, Apartment 5E, Jackson Heights, NY, 11372, USA.

Blosari Edition Ltd, Blosari Kustannus Edition Ay, PO Box 10, 00251, Helsinki, Finland. Web site: www.blosari.com.

Blumenthaler, Volker. Web site: http://www.volker-blumenthaler.de.

BM, Bjørn Mellemberg. *See* Norsk Musikforlag.

Bocal Music Company, PO Box 3702, Jayhawk Station, Larwrence, KS, 66046. Tel: 785-838-4682. Fax: 785-838-4682. E-mail: ahawkins@ukans. edu. Web site: www.bocalmusic.com.

Boccaccini & Spada Editori Rome, US Rep: Theodore Presser Company, Via Arezzo, 17—00040—Pavona di Albano Laziale—Roma—Italy. Tel: +39(0)6—9310217—9310561 Fax: +39(0) 6—9311903. E-mail: info@boccacciespada. com. Web site: www.boccacciespada.com/.

Boehm. *See* Anton Boehm & Sohn.

Bold Brass Studios, PO Box 77101, Vancouver, BC, V5R 5T4, Canada.

Bonesteel Music Company, PO Box 50862, Denton, TX, 76206, USA.

Booneslick Press, 3802 Frontenac Place, Columbia, MO, 65203, USA. Tel: 573-446-0450. E-mail: cheethamj@missouri.edu. Web site: www. booneslickpress.com.

Boosey & Hawkes, Incorporated, 295 Regent Street, London, W1B 2JH, United Kingdom. Tel: +44 (0) 20 7291 7255. E-mail:www.boosey.

com/pages/shop/help/Contact.asp. Web site: www.boosey.com.

Boptism Music Publishing, Bob Bernotas, 10 Plaza Street East, Apt, 4H, Brooklyn, NY, 11238. Web site: http://store,yahoo.com/boptism-publishing/info.html.

Borik Press.

Bornemann (Editions) Paris, US Rep: Theodore Presser Company, 15 Rue de Tournon, Paris F-75006, France.

Boston Music Company, 215 Stuart Street Boston MA, 02116, USA. Tel 1: 800-863-5150, Tel 2: 617-528-6100. Fax: 617-426-5100. E-mail: info@bostonmusiccompany.com. Web site: www.bostonmusiccompany.com.

Boston Public Library, 700 Boylston St, Boston MA, 02117. Tel: 617-536-5400. E-mail: infor@bpl.org. Web site: www.bpl.org.

Bosworth & Company, Limited, England, US Rep: Brodt Music, 8/9 Frith Street London W1V 5TZ England. Tel: +44 0171 7344961. Fax: +44 0171 7344961. E-mail: bosworthlon@cityscape.co.uk.

Bote and Bock K.G., Hardenbergstraße 9A, D—10623 Berlin, Germany. Tel: +49 30 311003-0. Fax: +49 30 3124281.

Bourne Company, 5 W. 37 Street, New York, NY, 10018, USA. Tel: 212-391-4300. Fax: 212-391-4306. E-mail: bournemusic@worldnet,att.net. Web site: www.bournemusic.com.

Bowdoin College Music Press, Bowdoin College Library, 3000 College Station, Brunswick, ME, 04011-8421. Tel: 207-725-3288. E-mail: scaref@bowdoin.edu. Web site: library.bowdoin.edu/arch/archives/bcmpg.shtml.

Brass Lion, Box 331, Southboro, MA, 01772, USA.

Brass Music Limited. *See* Robert King.

Brass Press, The. *See* Robert King. *Also see* Editions BIM.

Brassquake Press, PO Box 86879, San Diego, CA, 92138, USA. Tel: 619-337-2848.

Brass Wind Publications, 4 St Mary's Road, Manton, Oakham, Leics, LE15 8SU Tel: 01572 737409 and 737210 Fax: 01572 737409 E-mail: brasswnd@glabalnet.co.uk.

Brassworks, 225 Regency Court, Wankesha, WI, 53186, USA.

Brassworks 4 Publishing, 461 Sunrise Pkwy, Farmington, NM, 87401. Tel: 505,860,8122. E-mail: bw4@brassworks4.com. Web site: http://brassworks4.com/.

Breakthrough Music, 5 Turnberry Drive, Wilmslow, Cheshire SK9 2QW, United Kingdom. E-mail: info@breakthroughmusic.co.uk. Web site: www.breakthroughmusic.co.uk.

The Breathing Gym, Focus on Excellence, Inc., 1050 E. Ray Road, Suite A5-149, Chandler, AZ, 85225, USA. Tel: 480-664-9613 or 800-332-2637. Web site: www.breathinggym.com.

Breitkopf & Härtel, Walkmühlstrasse 52, D-65195 Wiesbaden. Tel: +49 611 45008 0. Fax: +49 611 45008 59-61. E-mail: info@breitkopf.com.

Brelmat Music, 241 Kohlers Hill Road, Kutztown, PA, 19530-9181, USA. Tel: 610-756-6324. E-mail: brelmat@gte.net. Web site: www.brelmatmusic.com.

Bristol, Doug, 2106 Halcyon Blvd, Montgomery, AL, 36117, doug@bristolnotes.com.

Brixton Publications, 4311 Braemar Avenue, Lakeland, FL, 33813, USA. Tel/Fax: 863-646-0961. E-mail: sales@BrixtonPublications.com. Web site: www.brixtonpublications.com.

Broadbent and Dunn Ltd, LONDON, Phone: +44 (0)1304 825604. Fax: +44 (0)870 135 3567. E-mail: music@broadbent-dunn.com. Web site: www.broadbent-dunn.com.

Broad River Press, Box 50329, Columbia, SC, 29250, USA.

Brodt Music Company, PO Box 9345, 1409 East Independence Blvd, Charlotte, NC, 28299, USA. Tel 1: 1-800-438-4129, Tel 2: 704-332-2177. Fax: 800-446-0812. E-mail: orders@brodtmusic.com. Web site: www.brodtmusic.com.

Broude Brothers Limited, 141 White Oaks Road, Williamstown, MA, 01267-2257, USA. Tel: 800 225-3197, Tel 2: 413-458-8131. Fax: 413-458-5242. E-mail: broude@sover.net.

Brody, Martin. E-mail: mbrody@wellesley.edu.

Brusick, William R., 165 17th Avenue NE, St, Petersburg, FL, 33704. Tel: 727-821-2494, Tel 2: 727-527-1168. E-mail: sasha17@worldnet.att.net.

BTQ Publications, Meadow View 10, Old Forge Road, Fenny Draton, Warwickshire, CV13 6BD, England.

Bugby, Colin, 32 Irchester Road Rushden, Northamptonshire, NN10 9XE, United Kingdom. Tel: 01933 357838. E-mail: info@colinbugby.co.uk. Web site: http://www.colinbugby.co.uk.

BVD Press, 79 Meetinghouse Lane, Ledyard, CT, 06339, USA. Tel: 860-536-2185. E-mail: bvdpress@snet.net. Web site: http://www.bvdpress.com.

C. F. Peters Corporation, 70-30 80th Street, Glendale NY, 11385. Tel: 718-416-7800. Fax: 718-416-7805. E-mail: sales@cfpeters-ny.com. Web site: www.edition-peters.com/home.html.

C. L. Barnhouse Company, PO Box 680, 205 Cowan Ave, West, Oskaloosa, IA, 52577, USA. Tel: 641-673-8397. Fax: 641-673-4718. E-mail: bbarnhouse@barnhouse.com. Web site: www.walkingfrog.com.

C & E Enterprises, 7341 Amberly Lane, Bldg, 33-410, Delray Beach, FL, 33446, USA. Tel: 561-495-0045.

C & R Publishing Company, Incorporated, PO Box 53513, Fayetteville, NC, 28305, USA.

Camara Music Publishers, 23 LaFond Lane, Orinda, CA, 94563, USA.

Camden House, 668 Mount Hope Avenue, Rochester, NY, 14620-2731. Tel: 585-275-0419. Fax: 585-271 8778. E-mail: boydell@boydellusa.net. Web site: www.camden-house.com.

Camden Music, 19A North Villas, Camden Square, London, England, NW1 9BJ.

Camphouse, Mark D., PO Box 6968, East Main + Adams Streets, Radford Virginia, 24142. Tel: 540-831-5103. Fax: 540-831-6133. E-mail: mcamphou@radford.edu. Web site: www.radford.edu/~mcamphou/.

Canadian Music Centre, 20 St, Joseph Street, Toronto, ON M4Y 1J9. Tel: 416-961-6601. Fax 416-961-7198. E-mail: info@musiccentre,ca. Web site: www.musiccentre,ca/.

Canadian Musical Heritage Society, 120 Walnut Court, Unit 15, Ottawa, ON, Canada, K1R 7W2. Tel: 613-230-3666. Fax: 613-230-6725. E-mail: enquiries@cliffordfordpublications. Web site: www.cmhs,carleton,ca/.

Cantando, Cantando Forlag, PO Box 8019, N-4068 Stavanger, Norway. Tel: +47 51 89 46 01. E-mail: order@cantando.com.

Canzona Publications, Box 10123, Denver, CO, 80210, USA.

Carl Fischer Incorporated, 65 Bleecker St, New York, NY 10012. Tel: 212-777-0900. Fax: 212-477-6996. E-mail: cf-info@carlficher.com. Web site: www.carlfischer.com.

Carlin Music Publishing Company, PO Box 2289, Oakhurst, CA, 93644, USA. 209-683-7613. E-mail: www.carlinamerica.com/contact. Web site: www.carlinamerica.com.

Carp Music, Incorporated. *See* Theodore Presser Company.

Carus-Verlag GmbH, US Rep: Mark Foster, Sales Department, Sielminger Str, 51, D-70771 Lf, -Echterdingen, Tel: +49/ (0) 711-797 330-0. Fax: +49/ (0) 711-797 330-29. E-mail: sales@carus-verlag.com. Web site: www.carus-verlag.com.

Cautius Music, PO Box 32493, Kansas City, MO, 64111.

Cavata Music Publishers. *See* Theodore Presser Company.

Cazes Cuivres, Canada.

CeBeDem, Bruxelles, Brussel.

Cellar Press, 322 Swain Avenue, Bloomington, IN, 47401, USA.

Celluloid Tubas. *See* Fiegel, Todd.

Censhu, Jiro, 1-2-25-301 Terauchi, Toyonaka, Osaka 561-0872, Japan. Tel: 06-6864-2834. Fax: 06-6864-2868. E-mail: jircen@u01,gate01.com.

Cerveny, Amati-Denak, s.r.o. Dukelska 44, 358 25 Kraslice Czech Republic. Web site: www.amati-denak,cz.

Ceskeho hudebniho fondu, 110 00 Praha 1, Parizska 3, Czechoslovakia.

Chamber Brass Library. *See* Mentor Music.

Chamber Music Library, 84 Jefferson St, #2–C, Hoboken, NJ, 07030, USA.

Chandos Music. Web site: www.chandos-records.com.

Chantry Music Press Incorporated. *See* Augsburg Fortress Publishers.

Chappell & Company, LTD. *See* Hal Leonard Publications.

Charles Colin, 315 West 53rd Street, New York, NY, 10019, USA. 212-581-1480. Fax: 212-489-5186. E-mail: info@charlescolin.com. Web site: www.charlescolin.com.

Cherry Classics Music. E-mail: sales@cherry-classics.com. Web site: www.cherry-classics.com.

Cherry Lane Music Company, Incorporated, 6 East 32nd Street, 11th Floor, New York, NY, 10016. Tel: 212,561,3000. E-mail: publishing@cherrylane.com Web site: www.cherrylane.com.

Chester Music Limited, London, 8/9 Frith Street, GB-LONDON W1V 5TZ, England, UK. Tel: +47 0044 20 7434 0066. Fax: +47 0044 20 7287 6329. E-mail: music@musicsales.co.uk. Web site: www.musicsales.co.uk.

Chicken Scratch Press. *See* Windsong Press. Web site: www.windsongpress.com.

Childs, Barney, School of Music, University of Redlands, Redlands, CA, 92373, USA.

Chiron Publications.

Choristers Guild, 2834 W. Kingsley Road, Garland, TX, 75041, USA. Tel: 972-271-1521. Fax: 972-840-3113. E-mail: choristers@choristersguild.org. Web site: www.choristersguild.org.

Cinque Port Music. Web site: www.cinqueportmusic.com.

Cimarron Music Press, 15 Corrina Lane, Salem, CT, 06420. Tel: 860-536-2185. Fax: 860-887-2892. E-mail: sales@cimarronmusic.com. Web site: www.cimarronmusic.com/index,cfm.

Cirone Publications. *See* CPP Belwin, Inc.

Clark Baxley Publications, PO Box 417694, Sacramento, CA, 95481, USA.

Claude Benny Press, c/o Joseph Ott, Department of Music, Emporia State University, Emporia, KS, 66801, USA.

Co-Op Press, Sy Brandon, PO Box 204, Wrightsville, PA, 17368-0204, USA. Tel: 717-252-3385. E-mail: cooppress@suscom.net. Web site: cooppress.hostrack.net/.

Coburn Press. *See* Theodore Presser Company.

Colding-Jorgensen, Henrik, Kildehuset 3, 3,tv, DK-2670 Greve, Denmark. Tel: +45 43 69 32 85. E-mail: mail@hc-j.dk. Web site: www.hc-j.dk/.

Colin. *See* Charles Colin.

Collected Editions Limited, 750 Ralph McGill Blvd NE, Atlanta, GA, 30312, USA. Fax: 404-525-4545.

Columbia Pictures Publications, 15800 N.W. 48th Avenue, Miami, FL, 33014, USA.

Compello, Joseph. *See* Joseph Compello Publications.

Composer's Manuscript Edition, 33 Springfield Gardens, London, Ory, NW9, England.

Composers Library Editions. *See* Theodore Presser Company.

Concordia Publishing House, 3558 South Jefferson Avenue, St, Louis, MO, 63118. Tel: 314-268-1000. Fax: 314-268-1329. E-mail: order@cph.org. Web site: http://www.cph.org/.

Conners Publications Inc, See A & L Musical Enterprises, Inc.

Conn. *See* Conn-Selmer.

Conn-Selmer, Inc, PO Box 310, Elkhart, Indiana, 46515-0310. Tel: 574-522-1675 or 888-348-7426. Web site: www.unitedmusical.com.

Conservatory Publications, 18 Van Wyck, Croton-on-the-Hudson, NY, 10520, USA.

Consort Press, 1755 Monita Drive, Ventura, CA, 93001. Tel: 800-995-7333. Fax: 805-643-9051. E-mail: office@consortpress.com. Web site: www.consortpress.com.

Consortium Musical. *See* Theodore Presser Company.

Constantinides, Dinos, School of Music, Louisiana State University Baton Rouge, LA, 70803-2504. Tel: 225/578-4010. Fax: 225/578-2562. E-mail: cconsta@bellsouth.net. Web site: www.music.lsu.edu/facstaff_frameset.htm.

Cor Publishing Company, 67 Bell Place, Massapequa, NY, 11758, USA.

Courtois, Z. I. de la Boitardiere, B.P., 341-61, rue du Columbier, 37403 Amboise Cedix, France. Tel: 33-47-57-68-68. Web site: www.courtois-paris.com.

CPP Belwin Incorporated, 15800 NW 48 Avenue, Miami, FL, 33014, USA. (305) 620-1500. Fax: (305) 625-3480.

Creation Station, PO Box 301, Marlborough, New Hampshire, 03455-0301, USA. Web site: http://regw9626,members,beeb.net/bpardus.htm.

Criterion Music Corp, 6124 Selma Avenue, Hollywood, CA, 90028, USA. Tel: 323-469-2296. Fax: 323-962-5751.

Crown Music Press, 612 Sedgwick Dr, Libertyville, IL, 60048. Tel: 847-549-7124. Fax: 847-549-7136. E-mail: crownmusicpress@aol.com.

Cumberland Press, 917 8th Avenue S. Nashville, TN, 37203, USA.

Cundy Bettoney. *See* Carl Fischer.

Curnow Music Press, PO Box 142, Wilmore, KY, 40390. Tel: 800-7CU-RNOW. Web site: www.curnowmusicpress.com.

Custom Music Co, 1930 Hilton Ferndale, MI, 48220. Web site: www.custommusiccorp.com.

Czech Music Fund, 118 00 Praha 1, Besední 3, Czechoslovakia. Tel: 257 320 008. Fax: 257 312 834. E-mail: nchf@gts.cz. Web site: www.nchf.cz.

Da Capo Music, 26 Stanway Road, Whitefield, Manchester, United Kingdom, M45 8EG. Tel: 0044 161 766 5950. E-mail: colin@dacapomusic.freeserve.co.uk. Web site: www.dacapomusic.co.uk.

DaCapo Press.

Dako Publishers, 4225 Osage Avenue, Philadelphia, PA, 19104, USA. Tel: 215-386-7247.

Danner, Greg, Tennessee Tech University, Box 5045, Cookeville, TN, 38505, Tel: 931-372-6180. Fax: 931-372-6279. E-mail: gdanner@tntech.edu.

Danish Music Information Center, Gråbrødretorv 16, DK-1154 Copenhagen K, Denmark. Tel: +45 33 11 20 66. Fax: +45 33 32 20 16. E-mail: mic@mic,dk. Web site: www.mic,dk.

Dankwart, Schmidt, Seuerberger Str, 6, D-W-8196, Beuerberg/Achmule, Germany.

Dantallan Incorporated, 11 Pembroke St, Newton, MA, 02458-2122. Tel: 617-244-7230. Fax: 617-244-7230. E-mail: dantinfo@dantalian.com Web site: www.dantalian.com.

David E. Smith Publications, 4826 Shabbona Road, Deckerville, MI, 48427-9988, . Tel: 810/376-9055. Fax: 810/376-8429. E-mail: despub@greatlakes.net. Web site: www.despub.com.

Davis, D. Edward. E-mail: d_edwarddavis@yahoo.com. Web site: www.ickydog.com.

DB Publishing Company, 64 Saint Philip Drive, Clifton, NJ, 07013, USA.

DEG Music Products, Inc, PO Box 968, Lake Geneva, WI, 53147. Tel: 414-248-8314 or 800-558-9416.

De haske muziekuitgave bv, Windas 2, 8441 RC, Heerenveen, Holland, 05139-493, 05139-515.

De Haske. Web site: www.dehaske.com.

DelDresser, Mark Dresser, Professor of Music, UCSD, deldresser@aol.com, www.mark-dresser.com.

Deutscher Verlag fur Musik. *See* Breitkoph & HarTel.

DID Publishing, 123 Steinmann Avenue, Middlebury, CT, 06762, USA.

DiGiovanni, Rocco, 10907 Camarillo Street, North Hollywood, CA, 91602, USA.

Dilia, Vysehradska 288, Nove Mesto, Pargue 2, Czechoslovakia, 2-966-515.

Dillon Music, 325 Fulton St, Woodbridge, NJ, 07095. Tel: 732-634-3399.

Divertimento, Divertimento Music Edition, c/o Magne Murholt, PO Box 757, N-2604 Lillehammer, Norway.

Doblinger Musikverlag, Wein 1, Dorotheergasse 10, A-1011, Wein, Postfach 882. Tel: +43,1, 515,03,0. Fax: +43,1,515,03,51. E-mail: music@doblinger.at. Web site: www.doblinger,at.

Dolmetsch Musical Instruments England, US Rep: Theodore Presser Company.

Domek, Richard, School of Music, University of Kentucky, Lexington, KY, 40506 Tel: 859-257-1966. E-mail: dicty@pop.uky.edu. Web site: www.

uky.edu/FineArts/Music/faculty/richard_domek.htm.

Doms. *See* Johann Doms.

Donemus Publishing House Amsterdam, US Rep: Theodore Presser Company, Paulus Potterstraat 16, NL-1071 CZ Amsterdam NETHERLANDS. Tel: +31 (0)20 3058900. Fax:+31 (0)20 673 35 88 E-mail: info@muziekgroep.nl. Web site: http://www.musiekgroep.nl.

Dorn Publications, Incorporated, PO Box 206, Medfield, MA, 02052 USA. Tel: 508-359-1015. Fax: 508-359-7988. E-mail: dornpub@dornpub.com. Web site: www.dornpub.com.

Dover Publications Incorporated, 31 E. Second Street, Mineola, NY, 11501, USA. Tel: 516-294-7000. Fax: 516-742-5049.

Dramatic Publishing Company, PO Box 129, Woodstock, IL, 60098-0129 Tel: 1-800-448-7469. Fax: 1-800-334-5302. E-mail: CustomerService@dpcplays.com. Web site: www.dramaticpublishing.com/welcome.html.

Dunster Music, 22 Woodcote Avenue, Wallington, Surrey, England.

Dunvagen Music Publishers Incorporated, 632 Broadway, 9th floor, New York, NY, 10012. Tel: 212-979-2080. Fax: 212-473-2842. E-mail: info@dunvagen.com. Web site: www.dunvagen.com.

Duralite Bags, RR #2, Mount Elgin, Ontario, Canada, N0J 1N0. Web site: www.violin.on.ca.

Durand SA Editions Musicales France, US Rep: Theodore Presser Company, 4-6, place de la Bourse, 75002 Paris, FRANCE.

Dutton, Brent, San Diego State University, Music & Dance Room 236, 5500 Campanile Drive, San Diego, CA, 92182. Tel: 619-594-4760. Fax: 619-594-1692. E-mail: dutton@mail.sdsu.edu. Web site: www.music.sdsu.edu.

E. C. Schirmer Music Company, Incorporated, 138 Ipswich Street, Boston, MA, 02215, USA. 617-236-1935. Fax: 617-236-0261 E-mail: office@ecspub.com. Web site: www.ecspub.com.

Earlham Press Limited, London. *See* Theodore Presser Company.

Easton, Ian, c/o Steve Rosse, PO Box R181, Royal Exchange, Sydney 1225, Australia. Tel: 61 41 613 5854. E-mail: steve@tubamania.com.au.

ECS Publishing. *See* EC Schirmer Company.

Ed. Feeling Musique, 15, Rue Guytoin de Moreveau, 75013, Paris, France.

Editio Musica Budapest, Editio Musica Budapest, Vörösmarty tér 1, H-1051 Budapest, Hungary. Tel: +36-1-4833-100. E-mail: musicpubl@emb.hu. Web site: www.emb.hu.

Editio Supraphon, Vodickova 27, 110 00, Praha 1, Czechoslovakia.

Edition Andel Uitgave, Klaprozenlaan 28-30, B-8400 OOSTENDE, Belgium. Tel: +32 59 70 32 22. Fax: + 32 59 70 83 50.

E-mail: andel@skynet,be. Web site: users,skynet, be/andel/.

Edition Elvis, Runeberginkatu 15 A 11, 00100 HELSINKI, Finland. Tel: (09) 407 991. Fax: (09) 440 181. E-mail: elvis@elvissm,pp,fi. Web site: www.musicfinland.com/elvis/EE.html.

Edition Eulenburg. *See* European American Music.

Edition Fazer, Warner/Chappell Music Finland OY, PO Box 169, FIN-02101 Espoo, Finland, Tel +358-9-435 0141. Fax +358-9-455 2162.

Edition Foetisch, 6, rue de Bourg, Lausanne, Switzerland. Fax: 41-21-311-50-11.

Edition Hans Pizka, Pf,1136, D-85541 KIRCHHEIM, Germany. Tel: +49 89 903-9548. Fax: +49 89 903-9414. E-mail: hans@pizka.de. Web site: www.pizka.de.

Edition Helbling, AG, Pfaffikerstr, 6, CH-8604 Volketswil Zurich, Switzerland. Tel: 01 908 1212. Fax: 01 945 6928.

Edition Helios, Kirkeveg 26B, 5690 Tommerup, Denmark.

Edition Ka We, Brederodestraat, 90, 1054 VE Amsterdam, Holland.

Edition Marbot, Mühlenkamp 43, D—2000 Hamburg 60 Germany.

Edition Wilhelm Hansen, U.S. rep: G. Schirmer, Bornholmsgade 1, DK-1266 Copenhagen K, Denmark. Tel: +45 33 11 78 88. Fax: +45 33 14 81 78. E-mail: ewh@ewh.dk. Web site: www.ewh.dk.

Editions 75, 75 rue de la Roquette, 75011, Paris, France. Tel: 01 43 48 90 57. Web site: www.tom,johnson.org.

Editions Aug, Zurfluh, 73 Boulevard Raspail, 75006 Paris, France. Tel: 45,48,68,60. Fax: 42,22,21,15, http://www.zurfluh.com. U.S. agent: Presser.

Editions Billaudot, 14 rue de l'Echiquier, 75010 Paris, France. Tel: 00 33 1 47 70 14 46. Web site: www.billaudot.com.

Editions Bim, PO Box 300, 1674 Vuarmarens, Switzerland. Tel: ++41 (0)21 909 1000. Fax: +41 (0)21 909 1009. E-mail: order@editions-bim.com Web site: www.editions-bim.com.

Editions Choudens, 38, rue Jean-Mermoz, Paris 75008, France. Tel: 01 42 66 62 97. E-mail: editions,choudens@wanadoo,fr.

Editions de L'Oiseau Lyre, B.P. 515, MC-98015 Monaco Cedex. Tel: +(377) 9330 0944. Fax: +(377) 9330 1915 E-mail: oiseaulyre@monaco377.com. Web site: www.oiseaulyre.com/index.html.

Editions du Petit Page, 57, rue Louis Blanc, 75010 Paris. Tel: (+33)1-46-07-79-87. Fax: (+33)1-40-37-52-59. E-mail: commande@petitpage.biz. Web site: http://www.petitpage.biz.

Editions Fertile Plaine, 11 rue de Rosny, 94120, Fontenay sous Bois, France. Tel: (33) 1 48 77 38 12. Fax: (33) 1 48 77 39 85. E-mail: contact@fertileplaine.com Web site: http://www.fertileplaine.com.

Editions Francaises de Musique, 12, rue Magellan, 75008 Paris, France.

Editions Henn, 8, rue de Hesse, CH—1204 Genève, Switzerland.

Editions M. Combre, 14, BD Poissoniere, 75009 Paris, France, 1 48 24 89 24. Fax: 1 42 46 98 82.

Editions Marc Reift, Case postale 308, Route du Golf 122, CH-3963 Crans-Montana Switzerland. Tel: +41 (0) 27 483 12 00. Fax: +41 (0) 27 483 42 43. E-mail: reift@tvs2net.ch. Web site: www.reift,ch.

Editions Max Eschig, 4-6, Place de la Bourse, 75080 PARIS Cedex 2, France. Tel 33 1 44,88,73,73. Fax 33 1 44,88,73,88. E-mail: gerald,hugon,durand-salabert-eschig@bmgintl.com.

Editions Metropolis, Van Ertbornstr, 5, 2018, Antwerpen, Belgium. Tel: 404,902,249.

Editions Musicales Brogneaux, B-1000 Brussels, 73 Avenue Paul Janson, Belgium.

Editions Musicales J. Maurer, Avenue du Verseau 7, B-1200, Brussels, Belgium. Tel: 32 2 770 93 39. Fax: 32 2 770 93 39. E-mail: musicmaurer@hotmail.com.

Editions Musicus, Box 1341, Stamford, CT, 06904, USA.

Editions Ricordi. See Hal Leondard Publishing Corp.

Editions Rideau Rouge, 25 Bd Arago, 75013, Paris, France. Tel: 01 55 43 08 45. Fax: 01 47 57 29 97.

Editions Robert Martin, 106, Grande rue de la Coupée—F, 71850 Charnay Les Macon, France. Tel: 03 85 34 46 81. Fax: 03 85 29 96 16. E-mail: www.edrmartin.com/contact/index.php?sessionID=420717639. Web site: www.edrmartin.com/index.php. (See also: Theodore Presser.).

Editions Salabert, U.S. rep: G. Schirmer & Hal Leonard.

Editions Selmer, 18, rue la Fontaine au Roi, 75011 Paris, France.

Edizioni Curci, Galleria del Corso 4, 20122 Milan, Italy. Tel: +39-02-760361. Fax:+39-02-7601, 4504. E-mail: info@edizionicurci.it. Web site: www.edizionicurci.it.

Edizioni Melodi, Via Quintiliano, 40 Milano, Italy.

Edizioni Musical Berben, Via Redipuglia 65, i-60100 Ancona, Italy. Tel: +39 (71) 20 44 28. Fax: +39 (71) 57 414.

Edizioni Suvini Zerboni, Galleria del Corso, 4, 20122 Milano, Italy. Tel +39,02,770701. Fax +39,02,77070261. E-mail: suvini,zerboni@sugarmusic.com. Web site: www.esz.it.

Edward B. Marks Music Company, c/o Freddy Bienstock Enterprises, 126 East 38th Street, New York, NY, 10016. Tel: 212-779-7977. Fax: 212-779-7920. E-mail: bkalban@carlinamerica.com. Web site: www.ebmarks.com.

Edwin Ashdown Limited, 19 Hanover Street, London W1, England.

Edwin F. Kalmus & Company, Incorporated. See CPP Belwin, Incorporated.

EGI, Eivind Grovens Institutt, Ekebergvn, 59, N-1181 Oslo, Norway. Tel: +47 22 67 91 23.

Egtved ApS (Edition) Denmark. See Wilhelm Hansen Musikverlag.

Eighth Note Publications, 25 Robinson Street, Markham, Ontario, L3P 1N5, Canada. Tel: (905) 471-4450. Fax: (905) 471-5507. E-mail: enp@enpmusic.com. Web site: www.enpmusic.com.

Elite Music Company, 1314 W. Mountain Avenue, Fort Collins, CO, 80521, USA.

Elizabeth Thomi-Berg Verlag, Postfach 12 68, Bahnhofstr, 94 A, D-8032 Grafelfing bei Munchen, Germany. Tel: 089/85 32 79. Fax: 89-854-1857.

Elkan. See Henri Elkan Music Publishing Company, Incorporated.

Elkan-Vogel. See Theodore Presser Company.

Ellin, Ben. See London Tuba Quartet. Web site: www.londontubaquartet.co.uk.

Elliott, Doug. Tel: 301-871-3535. Web site: www.dougelliottmouthpieces.com.

Emberson, Steve, 1387 Ambridge Way, Ottawa, Ontario, K2C 3T3, Canada. Tel: 613-727-3595.

Emerson Edition Limited, Windmill Farm, High Street, Ampleforth, Yorkshire, YO6 4HF, England, 04393 324.

EMI Music Publishing Limited, 138-149 Charing Cross Road, London, WC2H OLD, England.

EMR, See Editions Marc Reift.

Encore Music Publishers, PO Box 786, Troy, MI, 48099-0786, USA. Tel: 1-800-261-5676. Fax: 1-800-261-5676. E-mail: encore@encoremupub.com Web site: www.encoremupub.com.

Engemann Aluminum straight mute.

Engstrom & Sodring Musikforlag A/S, Borgergade 17 DK—1300, Copenhagen Denmark.

Ensemble Publications, PO Box 32, Ithaca, NY, 14851-0032. Tel: 607,592,1778. Fax: 607,273,4655. E-mail: enspub@aol.com. Web site: members.aol.com/EnsPub.

Epstein, Marti. E-mail: mepstein@mail.berklee.edu.

Euphonion Press Publications, PO Box 115, Ellerslie, Maryland, USA. 21529. Tel: 301-724-4286. E-mail: erkitchen@hereintown.net. Web site: euphonionpress,faithWeb site.com.

Euphonium.com, 7230 Cloverhurst Court, Cumming, GA, 30041, 770 241 9119. E-mail: adam@euphonium.com. Web site: www.euphonium.com.

Euphplayer.com publications, T2F Kampung Warisan, Jalan Jelatek, Kuala Lumpur, 54200 Malaysia. E-mail: info@euphplayer.com. Web site: http://www.euphplayer.com.

Euromusic GmbH, Neulerchenfelder Strasse 3-7, A-1160 Vienna, Austria.

European American Music Distributors LLC, 15800 NW 48th Avenue, Miami, FL, 33014. Tel: 305-521-1604. Fax: 305-521-1638. E-mail: eamdc@eamdc.com. Web site: www.eamdc.com.

Ewoton Musikverlag, MitTelfeldstrasse, 4, D-66851, Queidersbach, Germany. Tel: 06371/92300. Fax: 06371/17212. E-mail: vertrieb@ewoton. de. Web site: www.ewoton.de.

Excelsior Music Publishing Company. *See* Theodore Presser Company.

F. E. C. Leuckart Germany. *See* Thomi-Berg, Rheingoldstraße 4, 80639, München. Germany. Tel: 089-17 39 28. Fax: 089-17 60 54.

F M I. Finnish Music Information, Lauttasaarentie 1, FIN-00200 Helsinki, Finland. Tel +358 9 6810 1313. Fax +358 9 682 0770. E-mail: info@mic.teosto.fi. Web site: www.fimic.fi/fimic/fimic.nsf?open.

FTW Publishing, 415 Allyn St, #1, Akron, OH, 44304, USA.

Faber Music Incorporated, Boston, 50 Cross Street, Winchester, MA, 01890, USA. Fax: 617-729-2783.

Faber Music—Britian, 3 Queen Square, London WC1N 3AU, England. Tel: +44 (0) 20 7833 7900. Fax: +44 (0) 20 7833 7939. E-mail: information@fabermusic.com. Web site: www.fabermusic.com.

Facsimile Editions. *See* Carl Fischer Incorporated.

Faimo Edition, Abbotvägen 18, S-74695, SKOK-LOSTER, Sweeden, Tel +46 18 386268.

Faxx Mouthpieces.

Fazer Music Finland, PO Box 126, FIN-00521, Espoo. Tel: +358 9 229 560. Fax: +358 0 455 2162. E-mail: ari,nieminen@warnerchappell.com.

Fema Music Publications, PO Box 395, Naperville, IL, 60566, USA.

Fenette Music, 8, Horse & Dolphin Yard, London, W1V 7LG, England.

Fennica Gehrman, Lonnrotinkatu 20 B, PL 158, 00121 Helsinki, Finland. Tel: (09) 7590 6311. Fax: (09) 7590 6312.

Fentone Publications England, US Rep: Theodore Presser Company, Fleming Road, Corby, Northants, NN17 4SN, ENGLAND. Tel: +44 1536 260981. Fax: +44 1536 401075. E-mail: music@fentone.com. Web site: www.fentone.com.

FEST-MUSIK-HAUS, Box 162, Medina, TX, 78055. Tel: 830-589-2268. E-mail: herbert@festmusik.com. Web site: www.festmusik.com.

Fetter, David, 3413 Oakenshaw Place, Baltimore, MD, 21218, USA. Tel: 410-659-8100. Fax: 410-783-8562. E-mail: davidf@peabody.jhu.edu. Web site: gigue.peabody.jhu.edu/~davidf/.

Fidelio Music Publishing Company, 39 Danbury Avenue, Westport, CT, 06880, USA. Tel: 203-227-5709. Fax: 203-227-5715.

Fiegel, E. Todd, 203 Artemos Drive, Missoula, MT, 59803, USA. Tel: 406-543-0841. E-mail: fiegel@celluloidtubas.com. Web site: www.celluloidtubas.com/html/comp.html.

Finnish Music Information Centre, Lauttasaarentie 1, FI-00200 Helsinki, Finland. Tel +358 9 6810 1313. Fax +358 9 682 0770. E-mail: info@fimic.fi. Web site: www.fimic.fi.

First, Craig. E-mail: cfirst2@comcast.net.

Fischer, Carl. *See* Carl Fischer, Incorporated.

Fleischer Music Collection, Free Library of Philadelphia, Loga Square, Philadelphia, PA, 19103, USA.

Folklore Productions Incorporated, 1671 Appian Way, Santa Monica, CA, 90401, USA. Tel: 213-451-0767. Fax: 213-458-6005.

Foreign Music Distributors (Educational Music Service), 33 Elkay Drive, Chester, NY, 10918, USA. Tel: 845-469-5790. Fax: 845-469-5817. E-mail: sales@emsmusic.com. Web site: www.emsmusic.com.

Forsberg, Charles. E-mail: eggchf@hofstra.edu.

Forte, Aldo, 512 Waters Edge Apt. E, Newport News, VA, 23606, USA. Tel: 757-596-4444. E-mail: aldo@aldoforte.com. Web site: http://www.aldoforte.com.

Foster, Ruben, 5907 South Montgomery Street, Tacoma, WA 98409 Tel: 804-852-9820. E-mail: euphguy3@aol.com.

Frank E. Warren Music Service, 29 S. Main Street, Sharon, MA 02067. Tel: 781-784-0336. Fax: 781-784-0336. E-mail: fewpub@juno.com.

The Franklin Edition, Five Fingers Music, 484 West 43 Street, Suite 21-L, New York, NY, 10036, USA. E-mail: music@thefranklinedition.com Web site: www.thefranklinedition.com/brass.htm.

Frederick Music Publications, 120 N. Charles, McPherson, KS, 67460, USA.

Fredonia Press, 3947 Fredonia Drive, Hollywood, CA, 90068, USA.

Fredrickson, Thomas, School of Music, University of Illinois, 1111 W. Nevada, Urbana, IL, 61801, USA.

Friedrich Hofmeister Musikverlag Büttnerstraße 10 D-04103 Leipzig Germany. Tel: +49-341/9 60 07 50. Fax: +49-341/9 60 30 55. Web site: www.friedrich-hofmeister.de.

Friederich Hofmeister, Ubierstraße 20, 65719 Hofheim am Taunus, Germany. Fax: 06 192 21134.

Friedrich, Kenneth, 1800 E. Stassney, 221, Austin, TX, 78744. E-mail: knuxie35@yahoo.com Web site: www.kfsbrasschamber.homestead.com.

Fritze, Gregory, 1140 Boylston Street, Boston, MA 02215-3695. Tel: 617-266-1400. E-mail: gfritze@berklee.edu. Web site: www.nii.net/~gfritze/questionaire.htm.

Frog Peak Music, PO Box 1052, Lebanon, NH 03755, Tel/Fax: 603-643-9037. Web site: www.frogpeak.org. E-mail: fp@frogpeak.org.

Frost, Frost Music A/S, PO Box 118 Skøyen, N-0212 Oslo, Norway, Tel: +47 23 27 01 86. E-mail: philipkr@online,no.

Frost Noter, A/S P,B, 79 Ankertorget 0133, Oslo, Norway.

Fuentes, David, 1260 Broadway, Flat 2, Somerville, MA, 02144. Tel: 617-776-2042.

Furlong, Greg. E-mail: furlongreg@hotmail.com.

G. Henie USA Incorporated, St, Louis, PO Box 1753 2446 Centerline Ind'l Drive, Maryland Heights, MO, 63043, USA. Fax: 304-991-3807.

G. LeBlanc Company, 7001 Leblanc Blvd, Kenosha, WI, 53141-1415, USA. Tel: 262-658-1644. Fax: 262-658-2824. E-mail: gleblanc@gleblanc. com. Web site: www.gleblanc.com.

G&M Brand Publications, PO Box 367, Aylesbury, Bucks, HP22 4LJ. Tel: 01296 682220 Fax: 01296 681989. E-mail: rsmithco@dircon. co.uk.

G. Ricordi & Company. See Hal Leonard.

G. Ricordi & Company, Limited, London. See Hal Leondard.

G. Schirmer (Australia) Pty, Limited. See Allans Publishing Pty Limited.

G. Schirmer Incorporated, 257 Park Avenue S., New York, NY, 10010, USA. Tel: 212-254-2013. Fax: 212-254-2100. E-mail: schirmer@schirmer.com. Web site: www.schirmer.com.

G. Zanibon, Liberia Musical Zanibon, Piazza Dei Signori 44, 35139 Padova, Italy. Tel: 049 661033.

Galaxy Music Corporation. See E. C. Schirmer.

Galliard Limited, Queen Anne's Road, Great Yarmouth, Norfolk, England.

Garland Publishing, 29 W. 35th Street, New York, New York 10001-2299. Tel: 212-216-7800. Fax: 212-564-7854.

Garrett, James, 5611 Forrester Ridge Road, Lyles, TN, 37098, USA. Deceased.

Gehrmans Musikförlag, See AB Carl Gehrmans Musikforlag.

General Music Publishing Company. See Boston Music Company.

Georg Bauer Musikverlag, 47/49 Luisenstrasse, D-7500 Karlsruhe/Rhein, Germany.

George, Thom Ritter, Department of Music, Idaho State University, PocaTelo, ID, 83209, USA. Tel: 208-282-2260. E-mail: georthom@isu.edu. Web site: www.isu.edu/~georthom/.

Georges Delrieu & Cie, 45, Avenue Jean-Médecin F—06000 Nice France.

Gérard Billaudot Éditeur, 14 rue de l'Echiquier, 75010 Paris, France. Tel: +33 (0)1 47 70 14 46. Fax: +33 (0)1 45 23 22 54. Web site: www. billaudot.com.

Getzen Co, 530 S. Hwy H, Elkhorn, WI, 53121. Tel: 414-723-4221. Web site: www.getzen. com.

Gia Publications, 7404 South Mason Avenue, Chicago, IL, 60638, USA. Tel: 708-496-3800.

Fax: 708 496-3828. E-mail: custserv@giamusic. com. Web site: www.giamusic.com.

Gipps, Ruth, Allfarthings, Hermitage Road, Kenley, Surrey, CR2 5EB, England.

Glorious Sound bvba, De Hulsten 53, B2980 Zoersel, Belgium. Fax: +32 (0)3 605-04-42. E-mail: order@francoisglorieux.com.

Glouchester Press, c/o Heilman Music, Box 1044, Fairmont, WV, 26554, USA. Tel: 304-367-4169. Fax: 304-367-4248. E-mail: tubajohn@mteer. com.

Glover, Jim, 898 Promenade Lawnsberry Drive, Ottawa, Ontario, K1E 1Y1, Canada. Tel: 613-824-4294.

GN,Gudbrandsdalsnoter. See Frost Musi.

Goddard, Mark, Spartan Press Music Publishers Ltd, Strathmashie House, Laggan Bridge, Scottish Highlands PH 20 1BU, UK. Tel: 01528 544770. Fax: 01528 544771. E-mail: Mail@SpartanPress. co.uk. Web site: www.SpartanPress.co.uk.

Godiva Music, 18 Raleigh Road, Coventry, CV2 4AA, England. Tel: 01203 459 409.

Gorb, Adam. E-mail: Adam.gorb@rncm.ac.uk.

Gordon Music Company, PO Box 2250, Canoga Park, CA, 91307, USA. Tel: (805) 647-4776.

Gordon V. Thompson Limited, 85 Scarsdale Road, Don Mills, Ontario, M3B 2R2, Canada.

Gottschalk, Arthur, Shepard School of Music, 1606 Alice Pratt Brown Hall, Rice University, Houston, TX, 77005-1892, USA. Tel: 713-348-2567. E-mail: gottsch@rice.edu. Web site: www. ruf,rice.edu/~musi/facbios/gottschalk.htm.

Gramercy Music, PO Box 41, Cheshire SK8 5HF, United Kingdom. Web site: www.gramercymusic. com.

Grantwood Music Press, c/o James Grant, 7001 Charles Ridge Road, Baltimore, MD, 21204, USA. Tel: 410-825-1390. E-mail: jim@jamesgrantmusic.com. Web site: www. jamesgrantmusic.com.

Graugaard, Lars. Web site: www.graugaard-music, dk.

Great Works Publishing, Incorporated. See Ludwig Music Publishing Company.

Green Bay Music, 26 Dolbear Street, Green Bay, Auckkland 1007, New Zealand. Tel: +64 9 817 3295. Fax: +64 9 849 4642. E-mail: 100243.2322@compuserve.com.

Greg Black Mouthpieces, 623 Eagle Rock Ave, PMB #127, West Orange, NJ, 07052. Tel: 973-736-4997. Web site: www.gregblackmouthpieces. com.

Griego Mouthpieces, W 5460 County Road A, Elkhorn, WI, 53121. Tel: (262) 949-1924. Fax: 262-742-4172. Web site:www.griegomouthpieces. com.

Griffiths Edition, 21 Cefn, Coed Bridgend, Mid Glamorgan, Great Britain, CF31 4PH.

Grosch-Musikverlag, Postfach 1268, Bahnhofstrabe 94A, D-8032 Grafelfing bei Munchen, Germany. Tel: 089 85 32 79. Fax: 089 854 18 57.

Grupo Real Musical, Carretera de Alcorcon a San Martin de Valdeiglesias, KM 9300, 28670 Villaviciosa de Odon, Madrid, Spain. Tel: (34) 1 616 02 08. Fax: (34) 1 616 48 17. Web site: www.realmusical.com.

Gulf Wind Music Press, PO Box 670545, Houston, TX 77267, Tel/Fax: 866-638-5879. Web site: http://home.earthlink.net/~gulfwindmusic. E-mail: gulfwindmusic@earthlink.net.

GunMar Music, Incorporated. *See* Margun/GunMar Music, Incorporated.

Gustav Bosse Verlag, Von der Tann Straße 38—Postfach 417, D—8400 Regensburg 1 Germany.

Gyger, Elliot. E-mail: gyger@fas.harvard.edu.

Haenssler Verlag, PO Box 50, Bismarckstrasse 4, 7303 Neuhausen, Stuttgart, Germany.

Hal Leonard Publishing Corp, PO Box 13819, Milwaukee, WI 53213. Tel: 414-774-3630. Fax: 414-774-3259 E-mail: www.halleonard.com/contact.jsp. Web site: www.halleonard.com.

Hakenberg, Stefan. E-mail: shakenberg@crosssound.com. Web site: www.stefanhakenberg.com.

Hallamshire Music, Bank End, North Somercotes, Louth, Lincs, LN11 7LN, UK. Tel: +44 01507 358141. Fax: +44 01507 358034. Web site: www.hallamshiremusic.co.uk.

Hallwag Verlag, Nordring 4, 3001 Bern, Switzerland. Fax: 41-31-41-41-33.

Hamelle & Cie France. *See* Theodore Presser Company.

Hans Busch Musikforlag, Stubbstigen 3, Lidingo S-181 46, Sweden.

Hansen Music. Web site: www.hansenhousemusic.com.

Hans Schneider, Musikantiquariat U, Musikwiss, verlag, D 8132 Tutzing-Obb, Germany.

Harald Lyche Musikforlag, Postboks 624, Strömsö, N-3003 Drammen. Tel: +00 47 32 24 51 82. Fax: +00 47 32 24 51 89.

Hargail Music Incorporated. *See* CPP Belwin, Incorporated.

Harmonia Uitgave, Nieuw-Loodsdrechtsedijk 105, Postbus 210, 1230 AE Loosdrecht, Nederland. Tel: +31-35-5827595. Fax: +31-35-5827675.

Harold Gore Publishing Company, 314 South Elm, Denton, TX, 76201, USA. Tel: 800-772-5918.

Harvey Phillips Foundation, PO Box 933, Bloomington, IN, 47402, USA. Tel: 812-824-8833. Fax: 812-824-4462. E-mail: philliph@indiana.edu. Web site: www.tubachristmas.com.

Hauser, Joshua. Tel: 931,372,6086. Fax: 931,372,6279. E-mail: jhauser@tntech.edu. Web site: http://iweb.tntech.edu/jhauser/.

Heavy Metal Music, PO Box 954, Mundelein, IL, 60060, USA.

Heilman Music, PO Box 1044, Fairmont, WV, 26554, USA. Tel: 304-366-3758. Fax: 304-367-4248. E-mail: tubajohn@mteer.com.

Heinick, David, Crane School of Music, 44 Pierrepont Avenue, Potsdam, NY, 13676-2294,

USA. Tel: 315-267-2410. E-mail: heiniedg@potsdam.edu.

Heinrichshofen Verlag, Liebigstraße 16 • D 26389 Wilhelmshaven, Germany. Tel: 0 44 21-92 67-0. Fax: 0 44 21-20 20 07. E-mail: info@heinrichshofen.de. Web site: www.heinrichshofen.de.

Helicon Music Corporation. *See* European American Music Distributors Corp.

Henie. *See* G. Henie USA Incorporated.

Henmar Press Incorporated, See C. F. Peters.

Henri Elkan Music Publishing Company, Incorporated, PO Box 965 Planetarium Station, New York, NY 10024. Tel: 212-877-8350. Fax: 212-877-8350. E-mail: helkan@aol.com.

Henry Lemoine et Cie, France. *See* Theodore Presser Company.

Heritage Music Press. *See* Lorenz Corporation.

Hermann Moeck Verlag. *See* European American Music Distributors Corp.

Heugel & Cie Paris. *See* Theodore Presser.

Heussenstamm, George, 5013 Lowell Avenue, La Crescenta, CA, 91214, USA.

Heuwekemeljer (Editions) Netherlands. *See* Theodore Presser Company.

Hewitt, Harry, 345 S. 19th Street, Apt. 3A, Philadelphia, PA, 19103-6637, USA. Tel: 215-985-0963. Fax: 215-985-0736. E-mail: eh1958@tjburke.com.

Hidalgo Music, PO Box 1928 Lyons, CO, 80540, USA. Tel:/Fax: 800 HID-ALGO, Tel/Fax: (303) 823-0152. E-mail: hidalgo@hidalgomusic.com. Web site: www.hidalgomusic.com.

Hildegard Publishing Company. *See* The Theodore Presser Company.

Hip-Bone Music, 119 W. 71st St, #8B, New York, NY 10023. Tel: 1-888-633-2663. E-mail: hipbone@nyc,rr.com. Web site: www.hip-bonemusic.com.

Hinrichsen Edition, Limited. *See* C. F. Peters Corporation.

Hinshaw Music Incorporated, Post Office Box 470, Chapel Hill, NC 27514-0470. Tel: 919-933-1691. Fax: 919-967-3399. E-mail: krolleri@hinshawmusic.com, www.hinshawmusic.com.

Hirsbrunner & Co, AG, Musikinstrumentenfabrik CH-3254, Sumiswald, Switzerland. Tel: 034-71-15-54.

HOA Music Publishers, 756 S. 3rd Street, DeKalb, IL, 60115, USA. 815-756-9730. E-mail: edgrieg@aol.com.

Hofmeister. *See* Friederich Hofmeister.

Holton. *See* Conn-Selmer, Inc.

HoneyRock, 396 Raystown Road, Everett, PA, 15537, USA. Web site: http://www.honeyrock.net/ensm-3.htm.

Hope Publishing Company, 380 S. Main Pl, Carol Stream, IL, 60188, USA. Tel: (630) 665-3200, Tel 2: (800) 323-1049. Fax: (630) 665-2552. E-mail: mailto:hope@hopepublishing.

comhope@hopepublishing.com Web site: www. hopepublishing.com.

Horizon Press, PO Box 483, Newington, VA, 22122, USA.

Hornists' Nest, The, PO Box 253, Buffalo, NY, 14226-0253, USA. Tel: 716-626-9534. E-mail: Lowell,shaw@worldnet.att.net. Web site: home. att.net/~hornistsnest.

Hornseth Music Company, 4318 Hamilton Street #10, Hyattsville, MD, 20781, USA.

Hoyt Editions, 706 W. Halladey, Seattle, WA, 98119, USA. E-mail: HoyEd@aol.com. Web site: www.hoyteditions.com.

Howe, Marvin C., 5105 Bush Road, Interlochen, MI, 49643, USA.

Hiscox Cases Limited, Mill Park Industrial Estate Hawks Green Lane, Cannock, Staffordshire, WS11 7XT, UK. Tel: 44 (0)1543 571420. Web site: www.hiscoxcases.com.

Hug & Company Musikverlage, Musik Hug AG, Stammhaus Limmatquai Postfach 28-30, CH-8022 Zürich, Switzerland. Tel: 01/269 41 41. Fax: 01/269 41 01. E-mail: info, zuerich@musikhug.ch Web site: http://www. musikhug,ch/.

Huhn/Nobile Verlag, Aixhelmer Str, 25, 7000 Stuttgart 75, Germany.

IACS, Postboks 157 Røa, N-0702 Oslo, Norway.

Iceland Music Information Center, Sidumúli 34, 108 Reykjavík, Iceland. Tel: +354 568 3122. Fax: +354 568 3124. E-mail: itm@mic.is. Web site: www.mic.is/english.

Impero Verlag. See Theodore Presser Company.

Imudico Musikforlaget, Mårkærvej 13, DK2630 Tåstrup, Denmark. Tel: 43 71 19 30. Fax: 43 71 19 45. E-mail: kleinert@kleinert.dk Web site: www.kleinert.dk.

Indiana Music Center, 322 Swain, Bloomington, IN, 47401, USA.

Instrumentalist, The, 200 Northfield Road, North-field, IL, 60093, USA. Tel: 1-888-446-6888. Fax: 1-847-446-6263. E-mail: subscriptions@ instrumentalistmagazine.com. Web site: www. instrumentalistmagazine.com.

International Music Company 5 West 37th Street, New York, NY 10018. Tel: 212-391-4200. Fax: 212-391-4306. E-mail: salesmanager@ internationalmusicco.com. Web site: www. internationalmusicco.com.

International Trombone Association Press, 138 Fine Arts Center, University of Missouri-Columbia, Columbia, MO, 65211, USA. Tel: 573-882-0926. Fax: 573-884-7444.

Intrada Music Group, 2220 Mountain Blvd, Suite 220, Oakland, CA 94611. Tel: 510-336-1612. Fax: 510-336-1615. E-mail: intrada@intrada. com. Web site: www.intrada.com.

Ione Press, A division of ECS Publishing Boston Massachusetts.

Iowa State University Press, 2121 State Ave, Ames, IA 50014-8300. Tel: 515-292-0140.

Fax: 515-292-3348. E-mail: director@iowastate press.com. Web site: www.iowastatepress.com.

Israel Brass Woodwind Publications, PO Box 1126, Kfar Sava 44110, Israel. Tel: +972-(0) 9-767-9869. Fax: +972-(0)9-766-2855. E-mail: E-mail@ortav.com Web site: www.ortav.com.

Israel Music Institute, PO Box 8269, IL-61082 Tel Aviv, Israel. Tel: (972)-03-6811010. Fax: (972)-03-6816070. E-mail: musicinst@bezeqint.net. Web site: www.aquanet,co,il/vip/imi/.

Israeli Music Center, 73 Nordau Blvd, Tel Aviv, Israel.

Israeli Music Publications Limited, U.S. agent: Presser, 25 Keren Hayesod, Jerusalem, 94188, Israel.

Italian Book Corporation, 1119 Shore Pkwy, Brooklyn, NY, 11214, USA. Tel: 718-236-5803. Fax: 718-236-5803. E-mail: italbook@worldnet. att.net.

ITEA Journal, Jason Smith, 55 Sunnyside Drive, Athens, OH 45701. Tel: (740) 591-4075. E-mail: smithj10@ohio.edu. Web site: www. iteaonline.org.

Ito, Akihiko, 2108-14, Atsuhara, Fuji-City, Shizuoka, 419-0201, Japan. Tel: +81,0545,71,3786. E-mail: akihiko_ito@mac.com. Web site: http:// sound.jp/euphonium/index.html.

Ito Music. E-mail: library@itomusic.com. Web site: http://www.itomusic.com/index-e.html.

J. Albert & Son Pty, Limited, 9 Rangers Road, Neutral Bay, Sydney, NSW, Australia, 2089. Tel: 61 2 9953 6038. Fax: 61 2 9953 1803. E-mail: contact@albertmusic.com. Web site: www. albertmusic.com.

J. Maurer Editions Musicales. See Editions Musicales J. Maurer.

Jack Spratt Music Company. See Plymouth Music Company, Incorporated.

Jalni Publications. See Boosey & Hawkes & Company.

Jamey Aebersold, PO Box 1244, New Albany, IN 47151-1244, USA. Tel: 1-812-945-4281. Fax: 1-812-949-2006. E-mail: staff@jazzbooks.com. Web site: www.jajazz.com.

Japan Tuba Center, Chitate Kagawa, Shinoro 6-jo 5-chome 5-6, Kita-ku, Sapporo, Japan, 002-8026, Tel/Fax: (81) 11 771 0559. E-mail: order@japantubacenter.com Web site: http:// www.japantubacenter.com.

Jasemusiikki. See Edition Wilhelm Hansen.

Jean White Publications, Library of Congress Call Number M2,3,U6A44.

Jensen Publications. See Hal Leonard Publications.

JML Publications, John Luther, 4713 Contenta Ridge, Santa Fe, New Mexico, 87507, USA. Tel: 505-424-1732. Fax: 505-424-1738 E-mail: jmlwords@msn.com.

Johann Doms, Hubertusallee 24b, D-1000, Berlin 33, Germany.

Johnson Cases, Inc, 15150 Grand Ave Suite #4, Lake Elsinore, CA, 92530. Tel: 951-678-5558. Web site: www. johnsoncases.com.

Jones, Roger, 303 Kenilworth Drive #29, Monroe, LA, 71203, USA.

Josef Weinberger, 12-14 Mortimer Street, London W1T 3JJ. Tel: 44 + (0)20 7580 2827. Fax: 44 + (0)20 7436 9616. E-mail: general.info@jwmail. co.uk. Web site: www.josef-weinberger.com/ weinberger/index.html.

Josef Weinberger Wien GmbH, Music Publishing Group, Neulerchenfelderstraße 3-7, A-1160 Vienna, Austria. Tel: +43 (0)1 403 59 91-0. Fax: +43 (0)1 403 59 91-13. E-mail: musik@ weinberger,co,at. Web site: www.weinberger. co.at.

Josef Weinberger (Germany), Oeder Weg 26, D—60318 Frankfurt am Main. Tel +49 69/ 955 288 30. Fax +49 69/955 288 44. E-mail: mail@josefweinberger.de. Web site: www. josefweinberger.de.

Joseph Boonin. *See* Jerona Music Corporation.

Joseph Compello Publications, 11132 Old Carriage Road, Glen Arm, MD, 21057, USA. Tel: 668-1806.

Joseph Wood Music Company, 148 East Main Street, Norton, MA, 02766, USA.

JTL Publications. *See* EC Schirmer Co.

Jubilate Verlag, Friedhofgasse 8, D-85072 Eichstätt, Germany. Tel: 08421-5332. Fax: 08421-4052. E-mail: info@Jubilate-Verlag.com. Web site: www.jubilate-verlag.com.

Julio Tancredi, 78 Oakwood Avenue, Providence, RI, 02909, USA. Tel: 401-351-1128.

Jupiter Band Instruments, Inc, PO Box 90249, Austin, TX, 78709-0249. Tel: 512-288-7400. Web site: www.jupitermusic.com.

Just Music Scotland, 246 Auldhouse Road, EAST KILBRIDE, G75 9DX, Scotland. Tel: 01355-245674 or International +44 1355 245674. Fax: 01355—231020 or International +44 1355 231020. E-mail: just.music.scotland@zetnet. co.uk.

Kagarice Brass Editions, PO Box 305302, Denton, TX, 76203. Web site: www.kagarice.com/ contact.

Kaland. *See* Norsk Musikksamling.

Kalison, Via Pellegrina Rossi, 96 Milan, Italy. Tel: 02-6453060. Web site: www.kalison.com.

Kallisti Music Press, 810 S. Saint Bernard Street, Philadelphia, PA, 19143, USA. Tel: 215-724-6511. E-mail: kallisti@ix.netcom.com. Web site: pw1.netcom.com/~kallisti/.

Kalmus. *See* A. A. Kalmus Limited.

Kanstul Musical Instruments, 1332 S. Claudina, Anaheim, CA, 92805, USA. Tel: 714-563-1000. Web site: www.kanstul.net.

Karamar Publications, 255 Oser Avenue, Hauppauge, NY, 11788, USA. Fax: 631-273-6349.

Kelly Mouthpieces, 674 South Pioneer Road Fond du Lac, WI, 54935-9190. Web site: www. KellyMouthpieces.com.

Kelly Sebastian Music Publishers, PO Box 13, Hindmarsh, South Australia, 5007.

Kendor Music, Inc, 21 Grove Street, PO Box 278, Delevan, NY 14042-0278, USA. Tel: 716-492-1254. Fax: 716-492-5124. E-mail: customerservice@ kendormusic.com. Web site: www.kendormusic. com.

Keyboard Percussion Publications, 392 Kirby Ave, Elberon, NJ, 07740, USA. Tel: 732-870-8600.

Kibutz Movement League of Composers, 10 Dubnov Street, Tel-Aviv, Isreal.

King. *See* Conn-Selmer.

Kirklee's Music, 609, Bradford Road, Bailiff Bridge, Brighouse, West Yorkshire, HD6 4DN, England. Tel: +44 01484 722855. Fax: +44 01484 723591. E-mail: sales@kirkleesmusic.co.uk. Web site: www.kirkleesmusic.co.uk.

Kistner & Siegel, Adrian-Kiels-Str, 2, 5000 Köln 90, Germany.

KIWI Music Press, Box 1151, Groton, CT, 06340, USA.

Kjos. *See* Neil A. Kjos Music Company.

Kleooubger-Pfaff Music Company, c/o Dr, Paul Dorsam, Music Dept, Box 163, Wm Carey College, Hattiesburg, MS, 39401, USA.

Knox, Charles, (Lux Nova Press) 2103 North Decatur Rd,, #216, Decatur, GA 30033, USA. Tel 1: 888-497-8956, Tel 2: 404-218-2556. E-mail: luxnova@luxnova.com. Web site: www.luxnova. com/comp/cck/.

Ko Ko Enterprises, 1515 Chickees Street, Johnson City, TN, 37601, USA.

Koff Music Company, Box 1442, Studio City, CA, 91604, USA. Tel: 323-656-2264.

KSM Publishing Company, Box 3819, Dallas, TX, 75208, USA.

Kyodo Music. Web site: www.kyodo-music.com.

L'Edition le Grand Orgue, Box 48, Syosset, NY, 11791, USA.

Lackey, Jerry, 18050 Chipstead Drive, South Bend, IN, 46637, USA. Tel: 219-277-1938.

Laissez-Faire Music. *See* TUBA Press.

Lam Larghetto Publishers. E-mail: kino@larghetto. nl, Music distributed by Euphonium.com.

Larrick, Geary, 2337 Jersey Street, Stevens Point, WI, 54481, USA. Tel: 715-341-4367.

Larsen, Libby, 2205 Kenwood Avenue, Minneapolis, MN, 55405, USA. E-mail: info@libbylarsen. com. Web site: www.libbylarsen.com.

Lawson-Gould Music Publishers Incorporated. *See* Warner/Chappell Music Inc.

Lea Pocket Scores. *See* European American Music Distributors Corp.

LeBlanc. *See* G. LeBlanc Company.

Leduc. *See* Alphonse Leduc Editions Paris.

Lema Musikforlag, Vetevagen 24, S 691 48, Karlskoga, Sweden. Tel: 46 586 3 57 17. Fax: 46 586 3 99 20.

Lemirre, Florent, 17 rue Roger Salengro, 59139 Wattignies, France. Tel: 20,95,05,81.

Lemoine. *See* Henry Lemoine et Cie, France.

Les Editions Ouvrieres, 12, Avenue Soeur-Roselie, Paris 13, France.

Leslie Music Supply Canada, 198 Speers Road, Unit 2, Oakville, ON, L6K 2E9, Canada. Tel: 905 844-3109. Fax: 905 844-7637. E-mail: sales@lesliemusicsupply.com. Web site: www. lesliemusicsupply.com.

Les Stallings Music Group, PO Box 1985, Brentwood, TN, 37024-1985, USA.

Lewis Music Press, 124 Newmarket Stornoway, Isle of Lewis, Scotland, HS2 0ED. Tel: +44 (0) 1851 706549. E-mail: sales@lewismusicpress.com Web site: www.lewismusicpress.com.

Liben Music Publishers, 1191 Eversole Road, Cincinnati, OH, 45230-3546, USA. Tel: 513-232-6920. Fax: 1-513-232-1866. E-mail: info@liben. com. Web site: www.liben.com.

Lillenas Publishing Company, 2923 Troost, Kansas City, MO 64109, USA. Tel: 816-931-1900. Fax: 816-412-8390. E-mail and Web site: www. lillenas.com.

Lindenfeld, Harris. *See* Theodore Presser Co.

Lindsay Music England, 23 Hitchin Street, Biggleswade Beds, SG18 8AX, England. Tel: +44 (0)1767 316521. Fax: +44 (0)1767 317221. E-mail: sales@lindsaymusic.co.uk. Web site: www. lindsaymusic.co.uk.

Lino Florenzo, 121 rue Barthelmy Delespaul, 59000, Lille, France.

Lithuanian Music Information and Publishing Centre, Mickeviciaus 29, LT-600, Vilnius, Lithuania. Tel: +370 2 726986. E-mail: center@mipc. vno.osf.lt. Web site: www.nkm.lt/mipc/index2. html.

Litolff Verlag. *See* CF Peters.

London Pro Musica Edition, PO Box 1088, Bradford BD1 3XT, Great Britain. Tel: +44 1274 728 884. Fax: +44 1274 728 882.

London Tuba Quartet. Web site: www. londontubaquartet.co.uk.

Long Island Brass Workshop, PO Box 85, Halesite, NY, 11743, USA.

Lorenz Corporation, Box 802, 501 E. Third Street, Dayton, OH, 45401-0802, USA. Tel: 1-800-444-1144. Fax: 937-223-2042. E-mail: info@lorenz.com. Web site: www.lorenz.com.

Lorge, John, 4450 48th Street, San Diego, CA, 92115, USA.

Loux Music Publishing Company, 2 Hawley Ln, Hannacroix, NY, 12087-0034, USA. Tel: 518 756-2273. Fax: 518 756-2273. E-mail: recordershop@recordershop.com. Web site: www. recordershop.com.

LS Publications, James L. Ellis, 2815 North Florence, El Paso, TX, 79902. Tel: 915-533-7112. E-mail: lspublications@aol.com.

Luck's Music Library Incorporated, 32300 Edward, PO Box 71397, Madison Heights, MI, 48071, USA. Tel: 800-348-8749 Fax: 248-583-1114. E-mail: sales@lucksmusic.com. Web site: www. lucksmusic.com.

Ludwig Doblinger K.G., Dorotheergasse 10, A-1010 Vienna, Austria. Tel: 01/515 03-0. Fax: 01/ 515 03-51. E-mail: music@doblinger.at. Web site: www.doblinger.co.at.

Ludwig Music Publishing Company, 1044 Vivian Drive, Grafton, OH, 44044, USA. Tel: 800-851-1150. E-mail: info@ludwigmusic.com. Web site: www.ludwigmusic.com.

Lunde, Lunde & Co's Forlag,Sinsenvn, 25, N-0572 Oslo, Norway.

Lusitanius Editions, Portugal. Web site: www. lusitanusensemble.net/editions.

Lyceum Music Press. *See* Ensemble Publications.

Lyche,Edition Lyche, Nedre Eikervei 12, N-3045 Drammen, Norway. Tel: +47 32 26 90 02. E-mail: order@lychemusikk,no.

Lyra Music Company, 1841 Broadway Suite 1103, New York, NY, 10023, USA. Tel: 212-246-0724. Fax: 212-246-0781. E-mail: lyrahouse@aol.com. Web site: www.lyramusic.com.

Lyric Brass Publishing, 380 North Colonial Avenue, Westminster, Maryland, 21157, USA. Tel: 410-751-2203. E-mail: publishing@lyricbrass.com. Web site: www.lyricbrass.com/publishing/.

M. Baron Company, Incorporated, Box 149, South Road, Oyster Bay, NY, 11771, USA. Tel: 516-922-1657.

M J Q Music Incorporated, 200 W. 57th Street, New York, NY, 10019, USA.

M. P. Belaieff. *See* CF Peters.

MacMillan, Duncan. E-mail: drmac4@earthlink. net.

Maecenas Music Limited, 5 Bushey Close, Old Barn Lane, Kenley, Surrey CR2 5AU.

Magni Publications. E-mail: info@magnipublications. com. Web site: http://magnipublications.com.

Magnolia Music Press, 6319 Riverbend Blvd, Baton Rouge, LA 70800, USA.

Magnolia Press LTD, The, 344 Angela Court, Lexington, KY, 40515, USA. Tel: 606-272-9867.

Malama Arts Incorporated, PO Box 1761, Honolulu, HI, 96806, USA. Tel: 1-808-329-5828. Fax: 1-808-329-5828. E-mail arts@ilhawaii.net.

Malterer, Edward, Box 763, Morehead State University, Morehead, KY, 40351, USA.

Manas, Adriana I. Figueroa, Darwin 1281, Dorrego, Guaymallen, Mendoza 5519 Argentina. E-mail: adrifg@dynastar.com,ar.

Manduca Music, 861 Washington Ave, Portland, Maine, 04103-2728, USA. Tel 1: 207-773-7012, Tel 2: 1-800-626-3822. Fax: 207-773-6597. E-mail: mark@manducamusic.com. Web site: www.manducamusic.com.

Manhattan Beach Music, 1595 E. 46 Street, Brooklyn, NY, 11234, USA. Tel: 718-338-4137. E-mail: mbmband@aol.com. Web site: members,aol.com/mbmband/.

Manncy Music, 7 Glengray Road, Crofton, NY, 10520, USA.

Manny Gold Music Publisher, 1060 East Ninth Street, Brooklyn, NY, 11230, USA. Tel: 718-258-0374. Fax: 718-258-0236.

Mansarda-Sintra Muziekuitgaven, Noordse Bosje 45D, 1211 BE Hilversum, NL. Tel: (+31) (0) 35-6234211. Fax: (+31) (0) 35-6234230. E-mail: mansarda-sintra@planet,nl. Web site: www.mansarda-sintra.com.

Manuscript Publications, Rt 2, Box 150A, Wrightville, PA, 17368, USA.

Mapa Mundl London. *See* E. C. Schirmer.

Mapleson Music Rental Library, 33 Elkay Drive, Chester, NY, 10918, USA. Tel: 845-469-5790. Fax: 845-469-5817. E-mail: rental@emsmusic.com. Web site: www.emsmusic.com.

Margun Music, Incorporated. *See* Shawnee Press.

Margun/GunMar Music, Incorporated, 167 Dudley Road, Newton Centre, MA, 02159, USA. Tel: 617-332-6398. Fax: 617-969-1079. E-mail: MargunMu@aol.com. Web site: members.aol.com/margunmus.

Mark Foster Music Company. *See* Shawnee Press.

Mark Herman & Ronnie Apter, 5748 W. Brooks Road, Shepherd, MI, 48883-9202, USA. Tel: 517-774-3128. E-mail: ronnie,apter@cmich.edu.

Mark Tezak, Postfach 101360, 5090 Leverkusen 1, Germany,—out of business, See Georg Bauer Musikverlag.

Marks Music. *See* Edward B. Marks Music Company.

Marseg Limited, 18 Farmstead Road, Willowdale, Ontario, ML 2G2, Canada.

Mas, Vicente Navarro, Sergio Carolino, Bairro Da Ota, Do Cidral Lote 25, Vestiaria, 2460-743, Portugal. Tel: 351-96-283-3260. E-mail: sergiofbc@hotmail.com.

Masters Music Publications, Inc. Tel: 561-241-6169. Fax: 561-241-6347. E-mail: info@masters-music.com. Web site: www.masters-music.com.

Max Hieber GmbH, PO Box 330429, 80064 Munich, Germany. Tel: 089-29 00 80-0. Fax: 089-22 97 82. E-mail: info@musikhieber.de. Web site: www.musikhieber.de/index.htm.

MCA Music Corp. *See* Universal Music Publishing.

McCoy Horn Library, PO Box 907, Houston, MN, 55943, USA. Tel: 507,896,4441. Fax: 507,896,4442. E-mail: info@mccoyshornlibrary.com. Web site: www.mccoyshornlibrary.com.

McGinnis & Marx Music Publishers, 236 W. 26 Street No. 11-S, New York, NY, 10001-6736, USA. Tel: 212-243-5233. Fax: 212-675-1630.

McKimm, Barry, See Yarra Yarra Music.

Media Press, Box 250, Elwyn, PA, 19063, USA.

Medici Music Press, 5017 Veach Road, Owensboro, KY, 42303, USA. Tel: 270-684 9233. E-mail: ronalddishinger@yahoo.com. Web site: www.medicimusic.com.

Meechan, Pete, Flat 2, 65 Albany Road, Chorlton, Manchester, M21 0BH, UK. Tel: +44,07811, 019860. E-mail: petemeechan@hotmail.com. Web site: www.petemeechan.com.

Meinl-Weston, Wenzel Meinl GmbH, Musikinstrumentenmanufaktur Seniweg 4, D-82538, Geretsried, Germany. Web site: www.meinl-weston.com.

Mel Bay Publications Inc, PO Box 66, #4 Industrial Drive, Pacific, MO, 63069-0066, USA. Tel: 800-863-5229. Fax: 636-257-5062. E-mail: E-mail@melbay.com. Web site: www.melbay.com.

Menoche, Charles Paul, 237 Old Farm Drive, Newington, CT, 06111, USA. Tel: 860-667-9236. E-mail: menochec@ccsu.edu.

Mentor Music Incorporated, 3301 Carlisle NE, Albuquerque, NM, 87110, USA. Tel 1: 1-800-545-6204, Tel 2: 505-889-9777. Fax: 505-889-9070. E-mail: info@musicmart.com. Web site: www.musicmart.com.

Metropolitan Museum c/o Henry Fischer, RR #1, Box 389, Sherman, CT, 06784, USA.

Mexicanas de Musica SA Ediciones Mexico, Avda Juarez 18 Despacho 206, Mexico, 06050, Mexico, D.F.

Mf Publications, Musikverlag Frank, Schulhausstrasse 22, CH-4528 Zuchwil, Switzerland. Tel: +41 0 32 685 48 80. Fax +41 0 32 685 48 81. E-mail: mf@musikverlag-frank.ch. Web site: www.musikverlag-frank.ch.

MGP, 10 Clifton Terrace, Winchester, Hants, England.

Michigan State University Press, 1405 South Harrison Road, Suite 25 Manly Miles Building, East Lansing, MI, 48823-5245, USA. Tel: 517-355-9543. Fax: 517-432-2611. E-mail: msupress@msu.edu. Web site: msupress.msu.edu.

MIC.NO(MS), Manuscript at Music Information Centre Norway, Tollbugt, 28, N-0157 Oslo, Norway. Tel: +47 22 42 90 90. E-mail: info@mic.no.

Middle Branch Music, PO Box 265, East Randolph, VT, 05401, USA.

Mills Music Library, University of Wisconsin Madison. Web site: www.library.wisc.edu/libraries/Music.

MiraTel, Traunreunter Str, 8, D-84478, Waldkraiburg, Germany, 49-8638-9682-0. Web site: www.miroTel.com.

Miserendino, Joe. Web site: www.joesmusicroom.com.

MMB Music, Incorporated, Contemporary Arts Building, 3526 Washington Avenue, Saint Louis, MO, 63103-1019, USA. Tel 1: 314-531-9635, Tel 2: 800-543-3771. Fax: 314-531-8384. E-mail: info@mmbmusic.com. Web site: www.mmbmusic.com.

MMI Music, PO Box 6141, Brackley, Northants, NN13 6YS, UK. Tel: +44 (0)7751 622780. E-mail: info@mmi-music.co.uk. Web site: www.mmi-music.co.uk.

Modern Editions, PO Box 653, Taylor, Tx, 76574, USA.

Modrana Music Publishers, Ltd, 41 Parklands Way, Poynton, Cheshire, England, SK121AL.

Tel: 01625 875389. Fax: 01625 875389. E-mail: info@modranamusicpromotions.com. Web site: www.modranamusicpromotions.com.

Molenaar Edition BV, PO Box 19, NL-1520 AA, Wormerveer, The Netherlands. Tel: +31—75-628 68 59. Fax: +31—75-621 49 91. E-mail: office@molenaar.com. Web site: www.molenaar.com.

Moore, David Arthur, 1746 South Canton Avenue, Tulsa, OK, 74112, USA. E-mail: davidcomposer@cox.net. Web site: http://members,cox.net/davidcomposer.

Morgens Andresen. E-mail: mogensa@image,dk.

Morning Star Music Publishers, 1727 Larkin Williams Rd, Fenton, MO, 63026. Tel: 800-647-2117. Fax: 636-305-0121. E-mail: morningstar@morningstarmusic.com. Web site: www.morningstarmusic.com.

Moseler Verlag, Hoffmann-v,-F,-Str, 8, 38304 Wolfenbüttel, Germany. Tel: +49—5331—95970. Fax: +49—5331—959720. E-mail: info@moeseler-verlag.de. Web site: www.moeseler-verlag.de.

Mostyn Music, 8 Milvil Court, Milvil Road, Lee-On-Solent, Hampshire, PO13 9LY, UK. Tel: +44,02392,550566. E-mail: enquiries@mostynmusic.com. Web site: http://www.mostynmusic.com.

Mother Lode Music, PO Box 110, Jamestown, CA, 95327, USA. Tel: 209-984-0681. Fax: 209-984-0681.

MS Publications, 1045 Garfield, Oak Park, IL, 60304, USA.

Mueller, Frederick A. Music Department, Morehead State University, Morehead, KY, 40351, USA.

Mu-Hu, Musikk-Husets Forlag A/S, PO Box 822 Sentrum, N-0104 Oslo, Norway. Tel: +47 22 82 59 00. E-mail: oslo@musikk-huset.no.

Muradian, Vazgen, 269 W. 72nd, Street, Apt, 11A, New York, NY, 10023-2713, USA. Tel: 212-724-7452.

Music 70 Music Publishers. *See* Plymouth Music Company, Inc.

Music Arts Company, PO Box 327, Ripon, WI, 54971-0327, USA.

Music Box Dancer Publications Limited, Canada. *See* Theodore Presser Company.

Music Express, PO Box 331, Lambertville, NJ, 08530, USA. Tel: 800-841-1432. Fax: 609-882-3182.

Music for Percussion. *See* Plymouth Music Company, Incorporated.

Music Graphics Press, 121 Washington Street San Diego, CA, 92103, USA. Tel: 619-298-3629.

Music Nove USA, 15 Falcon Road, Sharon, Massachusetts, 02067, USA.

Music in Action. *See* Alfred Publishing Co.

Musica Rara, Le Traversier, Chemin de la Buire, 84170 Monteux, France. Web site: www.musicarara.com.

Music Sales Corp, 257 Park Avenue S., New York, NY, 10010, USA. Tel: 212-254-2100. Fax: 212-254-2013. E-mail: info@musicsales.com. Web site: www.msc-catalog.com.

Music Theatre International, Music Theatre International, 421 West 54th Street, New York, NY, 10019, USA. Tel: 212-541-4684. Fax: 212-397-4684. E-mail: Licensing@MTIshows.com. Web site: www.mtishows.com.

Music Treasure Publications, 620 Fort Washington Ave, No, 1-F, New York, NY, 10040, USA.

Music Bona, Soukenicka 23, Box 45, 110 05 Praha 1, Czech Republic. Fax: +420 224 811 508. E-mail: contact@musicabona.com. Web site: www.musicabona.com.

Musica Budapest (Edition) Hungary. *See* Theodore Presser Company.

Musica Islandica, Rejkjavik, Iceland.

Musical Evergreen, The. *See* Philharmusica Corporation.

Musikk-Huset A/S, Postboks 1459, Vika, Oslo, Norway.

Musicians Publications, 1076 River Road, Trenton, NJ, 08628, USA. Tel: 609-882-8139. Fax: 609-882-3182. E-mail: bhmuspub@aol.com.

Muziekgroep Nederland, Paulus Potterstraat 14, 1071 CZ Amsterdam, The Netherlands. Tel: +31 (0)20-305 89 00. Fax: +31 (0)20-673 35 88. E-mail: info@muziekgroep.nl. Web site: www.muziekgroep.nl.

Musikverlag Elisabeth Thomi-Berg, Postfach 1736, D-82152, Planegg bei Munchen, Germany. Tel: (0 89) 8 59 99 44. Fax: (0 89) 859 33 23. E-mail: info@thomi-berg.de. Web site: www.thomi-berg.de.

Musik Verlage Hans Sikorski, Johnsallee 23, D-20148 Hamburg, Germany. Tel +49 (0)40 41 41 00–0. Fax +49 (0)40 41 41 00—41. E-mail: contact@sikorski.de. Web site: www.sikorski.de.

Musikk-Huset Forlag, Postboks 822, Sentrum, N 0104, Oslo 1, Norway. Tel: (+47) 22 82 59 00. Fax: (+47) 22 42 55 41. E-mail: oslo@musikk-huset,no. Web site: www.musikk-huset.no.

Musikkverkstedet, Rolvseidet, N-1890 Rakkestad, Norway. Tel: +47 69 32 29 50. E-mail: forlag@online.no. Web site: www.musikkverkstedet.no.

Musikverlag Barbara Evans, Sybelstrasse 24, 1000 Berlin 12, Germany. Tel: 030/323/55 98. Fax: 030/323/55 98.

Musikverlag Bruno Uetz, Deutschland: See Uetz Music Publishers.

Musikverlag Frank, See Mf Publications.

Musikverlag Johann Kliment KG, A-1090 Wien, Kolingasse 15, Austria. Tel: 0043/1/317 51 47. Fax: 0043/1/310 08 27. E-mail: office@kliment.at. Web site: www.kliment.at.

Musikverlag Martin Scherbacher, Blumenstetter Str, 6, 72379 Hechingen, Germany. Tel: 0 74 71/4722. Fax: 0 74 71 / 1 26 65. E-mail: www.

scherbacher.de/shop/enter.html. Web site: www. scherbacher.de.

Musikverlag Robert Lienau, Strubbergstrasse 80, 60489 Frankfurt/Main, Germany. E-mail: info@ lienau-frankfurt.de. Web site: www.zimmermann-frankfurt.de.

Musikverlag Rundel GmbH, Untere Gewend-halde 27-29, 88430 Rot an der Rot, Germany. Tel: ++49-8395-94260. Fax: ++49-8395-9426890. E-mail: info@rundel.de. Web site: www.rundel.de/englisch/a-frame.html.

Musikverlag Stafan Reischl, A4181 Oberneukirchen 162,Germany.

Musikverlag Wilhelm Halter, Gablonzerstr, 24, D-76185 Karlsruhe, Germany. Tel +49 (0) 721/567256. Fax +49 (0) 721/562674. E-mail: office@halter.de. Web site: www.halter.de.

Muso's Media, PO Box 188, Kangaroo Flat, Austra-lia, 3555. Tel: +61 (0)3 5447-0873. Fax: +61 (0)3 5447-8178. Web site: www.musosmedia. com,au.

Muziekuitgeverij Saul B. Groen, Ferdinand Bol-straat 6, Amsterdam, Holland.

Nagano, Mitsuhiro, Address: C-102, 2-36-1 Shi-moyugi, Hachioji-Shi, Tokyo, 192-0372 Japan. E-mail: onken@syd.odn.ne.jp. Web site: www2. odn.ne.jp/onken.

Nazarene Publishing House. *See* Lillenas Publishing Company.

Neil A. Kjos Music Company, PO Box 178270, San Diego, CA, 92177-8270, USA. Tel: 858-270-9800. Fax: 858-270-3507. E-mail: E-mail@kjos. com. Web site: www.kjos.com.

Neilsen, Erik. *See* Middle Branch Music.

Neuschel Music. *See* Studio Music.

New Music West, See Theodore Presser Co.

New Valley Music Press of Smith College, Smith College Music Dept, Sage Hall, Northampton, MA, 01063, USA. Tel: 413-585-3150. Fax: 413-585-3180.

New World Enterprises of Montrose Incorporated, 2 Marisa Court, Montrose, NY, 10548, USA. Tel: 914-737-2232. Fax: 914-737-2232.

New York Women Composers Incorporated, 114 Kelburne Avenue, North Tarrytown, NY, 10591, USA. Tel: 914-631-6444. E-mail: nywomencomposers@hotmail.com. Web site: www.ibiblio.org/nywc/.

Nichols Music Company, See Ensemble Publications.

Nick Stamon Press, 4380 Middlesex Drive, San Diego, CA, 92116, USA. Tel: 619-283-1637.

Nicolai Music, c/o Neal Corwell, PO Box 253, Clear Spring, MD, 21722, USA. Tel: 301-842-3307. E-mail: nicolaimusic@erols.com.

NJH Music. Web site: www.bandsman.co.uk/band.htm.

NKF, Norske Komponisters Forlag, c/o Norges Kor-forbund, Tollbugt, 28, N-0157 Oslo, Norway.

Tel: +4722 42 67 20. E-mail: korsenteret@ korforbundet.no.

NMO, Norsk Musikforlag AS, PO Box 1499 Vika, N-0116 Oslo, Norway. Tel: +47 23 00 20 21. E-mail: order@musikforlaget.no.

NMS(Ms), Manuscript with the National Library, Norsk Musikksamling, PO Box 2674, N-0203 Oslo, Norway. Tel: +47 23 27 60 43. E-mail: musikk-nbo@nb,no. Web site: www.nb,no/html/norsk_musikksamling.htm.

Noetzel Edition: See: C. F. Peters.

Noga Music. *See* Ensemble Publications, 00175 POB, 4025 Jerusalem, Israel. E-mail: eanogmus@ netvision.net,il.

Nordic Sounds Ltd, Postboks 726 4004, Stavanger, Norway. Tel: +47 51 52 14 40. Fax: +47 5152 1406 E-mail: post@nordicsounds.com. Web site: www.nordicsounds.com.

Nordiska Muslkforlaget Stockholm. *See* G. Schirmer Incorporated.

Norman Lee Publishing Company. *See* C. L. Barn-house, Company.

Norsk Musikforlag Oslo. *See* MMB Music Incor-porated, PO Box 1499, Vika, N-0116 Oslo. Tel: +47 23 00 20 21. E-mail: order@ musikforlaget.no.

Norsk Musikkinformasjon, Tollbugt, 28, N-0157, Oslo, Norway.

Norsk Notestik. *See* Norsk Musikforlag.

Northcut, Timothy, 5757 Stone Trace Drive, Mason, OH, 45040, USA. Tel: 513-336-0321. E-mail: Timothy,Northcut@uc.edu.

Norwegian Music Center, Tollbugata 28, N-0157 Oslo, Norway. Tel: +47 2242 9090. Fax: +47 2242 9091. E-mail: info@mic.no. Web site: www.mic,no/English.

Noton. *See* Norsk Musikforlag.

Nova Music Limited, England. *See* E. C. Schirmer.

Novello & Company. *See* Theodore Presser Com-pany.

O. Pagani & Brother Incorporated, c/o PD Mus, Headquarters, PO Box 252 Village Sta, New York, NY, 10014, USA. Tel: 212-242-5322.

Obrasso Verlag AG, Baselstrasse 23c, CH-4537, Wiedlisbach, Switzerland. Tel: ++41 (0) 32-637-37-27. Fax: ++41 (0) 32-636-26-44. E-mail: obrasso@bluewin.ch. Web site: www.obrasso.ch.

OH Musik Aps, Jersie Strandvej 5, DK-2680 Solrød Strand, Denmark. Tel: (+45) 56 14 66 44. Fax: (+45) 56 14 66 67. E-mail: oh@ohmusik.dk. Web site: www.ohmusik.dk.

Ohio University ITEA Chapter Composition Series,Jason Smith, 55 Sunnyside Drive, Ath-ens, OH, 45701. Tel: 740-591-4075. E-mail: smithj10@ohio.edu. Web site: oak,cats,ohiou. edu/~smithj10/.

Ohio Valley Tuba Quartet Press, 1870 S. Spring-crest Court, Beavercreek, OH, 45432, USA.

Ongaku No Tomo Sha Corp, Japan. *See* Theodore Presser Company.

ØNMF, Østnorsk Musikkforlag, c/o Hans-Olav Lien, Gullgata 15, N-3513 Hønefoss, Norway. Tel: +47 32 12 63 96.

Opus Music Publishers, 1315 Sherman Place, Evanston, IL, 60201, USA. Tel: 847-475-1544. Fax: 847-475-1544. Web site: www.opusmusic.net/opus.htm.

Ott, Joseph, See Claude Benny Press.

Otto Heinrich Noetzel Verlag, Liebigstraße 16 • D 26389 Wilhelmshaven, Germany,Tel: 0 44 21—92 67-0. Fax: 0 44 21–20 20 07. E-mail: info@heinrichshofen.de. Web site: www.heinrichshofen.de.

Otto Wrede Regina Verlag, Schumannstrasse 35, Postfach 6148, D-65051 Wiesbaden 1, Germany. Tel: (06 11) 52 31 18. Fax: (06 11) 52 07 73.

Ovation, Markaplassen 415, 7054 Ranheim, Norway. Web site: www.baadsvik.com.

Oxford University Press Incorporated, 189 Madison Avenue, New York, NY, 10016, USA. Tel: +1 212 726 6000. Fax: +1 212 726 6440. E-mail: custserv@oup-usa.org.Web site:www.oup-usa.org.

Paganiniana Publications Incorporated, PO Box 427 1 TFH Plaza Third & Union, Neptune City, NJ, 07753, USA. Tel: 908-988-8400. Fax: 908-988-5466.

Panton. See Music Bona.

Paolo Baratto, Rumelbachstr, 39, CH 8153 Rumlang, Switzerland.

Parga Music, 113 Magnolia Lane, Princeton, NJ, 08540, USA. Tel: 609-921-6374.

Parow'sche Musikalien, c/o Kagarice Brass Editions, PO Box 305302, Denton, TX, 76203. Web site: www.kagarice.com/contact.

Pasquina Publishing Company, 5600 Snake Road, Oakland, CA, 94611, USA.

Paterson's Publications. See Peters Edition.

PatrickSheridan.com, #165, 610 N. Alma School Road, Suite #18, Chandler, AZ, 85224-3687, USA. Tel: 602-327-3765. E-mail: patsheridan@earthlink.net. Web site: www.patricksheridan.com.

Patterson, Merlin E., 8810 Bexar Drive, Houston, TX, 77064-7428. Tel: 832-237-2820 E-mail: merlin,patterson@cfisd.net.

Paumanok Press, 974 Hardscrabble Road, Chappaqua, NY, 10514, USA.

Paxman Musical Instruments Ltd, Linton House, 164-80 Union Street, London SE1 0LH, UK. Tel: (0)20 7620 2077. Fax: (0)20 7620 1688. E-mail: info@paxman.co.uk. Web site: www.paxman.co.uk.

Payne, Frank Lynn, PO Box 60806, Oklahoma City, OK, 73146, USA.

Peer International Corporation. See Theodore Presser Company.

Peer Muslkveriag GmbH Hamburg, Postfach 602129, 22231 Hamburg, Germany. Tel: 040/278379-0. Fax: 040/278379-40. E-mail: classicaleur@peermusic.com.

Peer-Southern Organization. See Theodore Presser Company.

Peermusic (UK) LTD. See Theodore Presser Company.

PEL Music Publications, W. 1761 River Oaks Drive, Marinette, WI, 54143, USA. Tel: 715-735-5273. Fax: 715-735-3613. E-mail: paul@pelmusic.com. Web site: www.pelmusic.com.

Pelikan Musikverlag, Zurich, Switzerland.

Peters. See C. F. Peters Corp.

Peters Editions Limited, 10-12 Baches Street, London, N1 6DN, England. Tel: +44 (0)20 7553 4000. Fax: +44 (0)20 7490 4921. E-mail: sales@uk.edition-peters.com. Web site: www.edition-peters.com.

PF Music Company, PO Box 8625, Woodcliff Lake, NJ, 07675, USA.

Philharmonia Music. See Philharmusica Corporation.

Philharmusica Corporation, 250 W. 57th Street, Suites 1527-195, New York, NY, 10107, USA. E-mail: philharmus@aol.com. Web site: http://members,aol.com/philharmus/.

Piccolo Press, Clifford Bevan c/o Piccolo Press, 10 Clifton Terrace, Winchester SO22 5BJ, England. E-mail: clifford,bevan@ntlworld.com. In the United States, c/o Piccolo Press, PO Box 50613, Columbia, SC, 29250, USA. E-mail: piccowinch@aol.com. Web site: www.berliozhistoricalbrass.org/piccolo.htm.

Piedmont Music Company. See Edward B. Marks Music Company.

Pierre Noel, Editeur, 24, boulevard Poissoniere, 75009 Paris, France.

Piston Reed Stick & Bow Publisher, PO Box 107, Convent Station, NJ, 07961-0107, USA.

Pivot Publishing. See Boptism Music Publishing.

Plymouth Music Company, Incorporated, 170 N.E. 33rd Street, Fort Lauderdale, FL, 33334, USA. Tel: 954-563-1844. Fax: 954-563-9006.

Pocono Mountain Music Publishing, 208 Drexel Road, Tobyhanna, PA, USA. Tel: 717-894-4177.

Polskie Wydawnictwo Muzyczne, PWM-Edition, Al, Krasinskiego 11a, 31-111 Krakow, Poland. Tel: 012 220174. Fax: 012 220174. E-mail: internet@pwm.com.pl. Web site: www.pwm.com.pl.

PolyGram International Publishing Incorporated, 1416 N. La Brea Avenue, Los Angeles, CA, 90028-7563, USA. Tel: 818-843-4046. Fax: 818-840-0409.

PP Music. See Manduca Music.

PRB Productions, 963 Peralta Avenue, Albany, CA, 94706-2144, USA. Tel: 510-526-0722. Fax: 510-527-4763. E-mail: PRBPrdns@aol.com. Web site: www.prbpro.com.

Presser: See: Theodore Presser Company.

Prima Musica, 1510 SW 155 Avenue, Weston, FL, 33326, USA. Tel: 877-877-5743. E-mail: info@primamusic.com. Web site: www.primamusic.com.

Prima Vista Musikk, PO Box 24, Pentre, CF417WZ, UK. Tel: +44 01443,433743. Fax: +44 01443, 433743. E-mail: enquiries@primavistamusikk. com. Web site: www.primavistamusikk.com.

Pro Art Publications. *See* Belwin/Warner Brothers.

Progressive Music, Inc, 316 Fifth Avenue, McKeesport, PA, 15132. Tel: 412-672-9623. Fax: 412-672-7633. Web site: www.progressive-musiccompany.com.

Providence Music Press. *See* Hope Publishing Company.

Przedstawicielstwo Wydawnictw Polskich, Krakowskie Przedmiescie 7, Warszawa, Poland.

Puna Music Company. Tel: 201,833,8721. Fax: 201,833,8853. E-mail: jan@punamusic.com. Web site: www.punamusic.com.

Queen City Brass Publications. *See* PP Music.

Quiroga (Ediciones) Madrid. *See* Theodore Presser Company.

RBC Music, PO Box 29128, San Antonio, TX, 78229, USA. Tel: 800-548-0917. Fax: 210-736-2919. E-mail: sales@rbcmusic.com. Web site: www.rbcmusic.com.

R B P Music Publishers, 2615 Waugh Drive, PMB 198, Houston, TX, 77006, USA. E-mail: rbpviola@aol.com. Web site: members.aol.com/rbpviola.

R G O. Orchestral Hire Library, Fuggerstr, 1, POB 27, W-8019 Glonn, Germany. Tel: 8093-44-93. Fax: 8093-23-19.

R. Smith and Company Limited, PO Box 367, Aylesbury, Bucks, HP22 4LW, England. Tel: +44 (0) 1296 682 220. Fax: +44 (0) 1296 681 989. E-mail: sales@rsmith.co.uk. Web site: www. rsmith.co.uk.

Raphael Valerio, Box 16045, Asheville, NC, 28816, USA.

Rakeway Music. *See* Kirklee's Music.

Raum, Elizabeth, 88 Angus Crescent, Regina, Saskatchewan, S4T 6N2, Canada. Tel: 306-525-5585. E-mail: elizraum@sasktel.net. Web site: www.elizabethraum.com.

RBC Publications, PO Box 29128, San Antonio, TX, 78229, USA. Tel: 800-548-0917. Fax: 210-736-2919. E-mail: sales@rbcmusic.com. Web site: www.rbcmusic.com.

Real Musical, See Grupo Real Musical.

Really Good Music, LLC, 121 E. Polk Ave, Eau Claire, WI, 54701, USA. Tel: 715-834-7530. Fax: 715-834-7530. E-mail: contact@reallygoodmusic.com. Web site: www. reallygoodmusic.com.

Rebu Music Publications, Box 504, RD 1, Wallingford, VT, 05773, USA. Tel: 802-446-2630.

Rebus Music, 10 E. 16th Street, No, 5, New York, NY, 10003, USA.

Red Frog Music, Boswinde 43, 1852 XG Heiloo, The Netherlands. Tel: (072) 505 28 68. Fax: (072) 505 28 68. E-mail: info@redfrogmusic,nl. Web site: redfrogmusic.nl.

Regina Verlag. *See* Otto Wrede Regina Verlag.

Regus Publisher, 10 Birchwood Lane, White Bear Lake, MN, 55110, USA. Tel: 612-426-4867.

Reimers (Edition) Stockholm, US Rep: Theodore Presser Company, Box 17051, S-161, 17 Bromma, Stockholm, Sweden. Tel: (08) 704 02 80. Fax: (08) 80 42 28. E-mail: info@editionreimers.se. Web site: www.editionreimers.se.

Reunion Blues, 397 Cortland Avenue #212 San Francisco, CA, 94110. Web site: www. reunionblues.com.

Richard Schauer Music Publishing London. *See* Theodore Presser Company.

Ricordi. *See* G. Ricordi & Company.

Ritter Bags, PO Box 84, NE 46 4, WY, England. Tel: 44 1434 609 394. Web site: www.ritter-bags.com.

Rivera Editores, Valencia, Spain, Sergio Carolino, Bairro Da Ota, Do Cidral Lote 25, Vestiaria, 2460-743, Portugal. Tel: 351-96-283-3260. E-mail: sergiofbc@hotmail.com.

Robbins Music, c/o Columbia Pictures Publications.

Robert Fairfax Birch Publications. *See* Theodore Presser Company.

Robert King Music Sales, Incorporated, 140 Main Street, North Easton, MA, 02356-1499, USA. Fax: 508-238-2571. E-mail: commerce@rkingmusic. com. Web site: www.rkingmusic.com.

Robert Martin Editions France, US Rep: Theodore Presser Company, 106 Grande Rue de la Coupée, 71850 Charnay-lès-Macon, France. Tel: 03 85 34 46 81. Fax: 03 85 29 96 16. Web site: www.edrmartin.com.

Roberton Publications England, US Rep: Theodore Presser Company, The Windmill Wendover, Aylesbury Bucks, HP22 6JJ, England. Tel: 01296 623107. Fax: 01296 696536.

Roder Bernd, Presse ud Verlagsservice Baumweg 6, 5206 Neunkirchen-Seelscheid, Germany.

Rodgers & Hammerstein Concert Library, 229 West 28th Street, 11th floor, New York, NY, 10001, USA. Tel: 212-268-9300. Fax: 212-268-1245. E-mail: editor@rnh.com. Web site: www. rnh.com.

Roger Dean Publishing Company. *See* Lorenz Corporation.

Roger Rhodes Music Limited, 352 West 56th St #4-D, New York, NY, 10019-4249, USA. Tel: 212-245-5045. E-mail: roger@rogerrhodesmusic.net. Web site: www.rogerrhodesmusic.com.

Rojker, Kjell, Kogevej 8 B, Frejerslev, 4690 Haslev, Denmark.

Rondo-Independent Music Dist of Scandinavia, PO Box 49, Solod Strand, Denmark.

Rosehill Music Publishing Company, Limited. *See* Winwood Music.

Rottler, Werner, Schmledberg 19, 8011 Buch am Buchsberg, Germany.

Roundtree Music, PO Box 2254, Reston, VA 20195-2254, USA.

Royal Danish Brass Pub. *See* Oh Musik aps.

Rozen, Jay. E-mail: jay_rozen@hotmail.com.

Rubank, Incorporated. *See* Hal Leonard.

Rufer Verlag, Postfach 11 43, Hauptstrab e 23 u, 27, D-6946 Gorxheimertal, Germany. Tel: 0 362 01 29 47-0. Fax: 0 62 01 29 47-20.

Russell, Armand, University of Hawaii, Music, 2411 Dole Street, Honolulu, HI, 96822, USA. E-mail: armrussell@earthlink.net.

Ryker Associates, Inc, ryker@gol.com.

Saga Music Press, 12550 9th Avenue NW, Seattle, WA, 98177, USA.

The Salvation Army USA Eastern Territory, 440 West Nyack Road, West Nyack, NY, 10994-1739, USA. Web site: http://www.salvationarmy-usaeast.org/music/index,shtm.

Salvationist Publishing and Supplies, 1 Tiverton Street, London SE1 6NT. Tel: 020 7367 6580 Fax: 020 7367 6589. E-mail: Mail_Order@sp-s.co.uk. Web site: www.bandstand.demon.co.uk/sp&s.htm.

Sam Fox Music Sales. *See* Plymoth Music Company, Inc.

Sam Fox Publishing Company. *See* Theodore Presser Co.

Samfundet til udgivelse af Dansk Musik, Gråbrø-drestræde 18,1, 1156 Copenhagen K, Denmark. Tel: +45 33 13 54 45. Fax: +45 33 93 30 44. E-mail: sales@samfundet,dk. Web site: www. samfundet,dk.

Sampson, David, 166 West Hanover Avenue, Mor-ristown, New Jersey, 07960, USA.

Sanjo Music Company, Box 7000-104, Palos Verdes, CA, 90274, USA. Tel: 310-541-8213.

Santorella Publications Ltd, 13 Pleasant Avenue, Danvers, MA, 01923. Tel: 877-600-0049. E-mail: tony@santopub.com. Web site: www. santorellapublication.com/contactus.htm.

Sarnia Music, 12 The Meadows, St Dennis, Cornwall, P126 8DR Web site: www.sarnia-music.com.

Saruya, Toshiro. E-mail: t-s-333@fd,catv,ne,jp.

Sassetti, Bernardo, Sergio Carolino, Bairro Da Ota, Do Cidral Lote 25, Vestiaria, 2460-743, Portugal Tel: 351-96-283-3260 E-mail: sergiofbc@hotmail.com.

SB Music. E-mail: scjb@sb-music.co.uk. Web site: www.sb-music.co.uk.

Schaffner Publishing Company, 224 Penn Avenue, Westmont, NJ, 08108-1839, USA. Tel: 609-854-3760. Fax: 609-854-5584.

Scherzando Editions Musicales, 14, rue Auguste Orts, Brussels, Belgium.

Schilke Music Products, Inc, 4520 James Place, Melrose Park, IL, 60160. Tel: 708-343-8858. Web site: www.schilkemusic.com.

Schirmer. *See* E. C. Schirmer Music Company, Incorporated.

Schirmer. *See* G. Schirmer.

Schmitt Publications, Schmitt Music Centers, 2400 Freeway Boulevard, Brooklyn Center, MN,

55430-1799, USA. Tel: 800-767-3434. Fax: 763-566-9932. E-mail: info@schmittmusic.com. Web site: www.schmittmusic.com.

Schola Cantorum, 76, rue des Saints-Peres, 75007 Paris, France.

Schott. *See* B. Schott's Sohne Mainz.

Schott & Company, Limited, London, US Rep: European American Music, 48 Great Marlbor-ough Street, London, W1V 2BN, England. Tel: (+44) 171 494 1487. Fax: (+44) 171 437 0263. E-mail: promotions@schott-music.com. Web site: www.schott-english.com.

Schott Freres, 30, rue Saint Jean, Brussels, Belgium. Tel: (02) 5123980. Fax: (02) 514845.

Schulz, Patrick, W9340 Delanay Road, Elroy, WI, 53929. Tel: 608-462-5045. E-mail: pschulz93@ yahoo.com.

Scottish Music Information Centre, 1 Bowmont Gardens, Glasgow, G12 9LR, Scotland. Tel: +44 (0) 141 334 6393. Fax: +44 (0) 141 337 1161. E-mail: info@smic.org.uk. Web site: www.smic. org.uk.

Sekretariat for ny Kompositionsmusik. *See* SNYK.

Seesaw Music Corporation Publishers, 2067 Broad-way, New York, NY, 10023, USA. Tel: 212-874-1200.

Sengstack Group Limited, 180 Alexander Street, Princeton, NJ, 08540, USA. Tel: 609-497-3900. Fax: 609-924-1618.

Serans, X. Carlos, Sergio Carolino, Bairro Da Ota, Do Cidral Lote 25, Vestiaria, 2460-743, Portugal. Tel: 351-96-283-3260. E-mail: sergiofbc@hotmail.com.

Shawnee Press Incorporated, Delaware Water Gap, PA, 18327-1099, USA. Tel 1: 800-962-8584, Tel 2: 717-476-0550. Fax: 717-476-5247.

SheetMusicNow.com. *See* Sheet Music Now A/S.

Sheet Music Now A/S, Roarsvej 2, 1,t,v, 2000 Frederiksberg, Copenhagen, Denmark. Tel: +45 3833 2823. Fax: +45 3833 2831. E-mail: info@sheetmusicnow.com. Web site: www. sheetmusicnow.com.

Sheridan, Patrick. *See* PatrickSheridan.com.

Simton Musikproduktion und Verlang, Berweg 2, 8170 Bad Tolz, Germany.

Sloan, Gerald, 1735 E Overcrest St, Fayetteville, AR, 72703, USA. Tel: 479-443-4587.

Sloway Music Editions. Web site: www.slowaymusic. com.

Smith, Jason R., 2 Honeysuckle Way, Granite Falls, NC, 28630, USA. Tel: 513-784-9655.

Smith Publications/Sonic Art Editions, 2617 Gwynndale Avenue, Baltimore, MD, 21207, USA. Tel: 410-298-6509. Fax: 410-944-5113. E-mail: sylvias@smith-publications.com. Web site: www.smith-publications.com.

Snoek's Muziekhandel, Pannekoekstraat 62A, 3011 LJ Rotterdam, Holland,Tel: 010-4137874.

Snow, David, 21 Bishop Street, New Haven, CT, 06511, USA. E-mail: dsnow@erols.com.

SNYK—Danish Secretariat for Contemporary Music, Gråbrødredtorv 16,2 tv, 1152 København K. Tel 33 93 00 24. E-mail: snyk@snyk.dk. Web site: www.snyk.dk.

Societe d'Editions Musicales Internationales Paris, US Rep: Peer-Southern Organization, 5 Rue Lincoln, Paris, F-75008, France.

Sohgaku-Sha, Sohgaku-Sha, Tohky Bldg, 3F; Kami-Ochiai, Shinjuky-ku, Tokyo 161, Japan.

Solid Brass Music Company, 71 Mt, Ranier Drive, San Rafael, CA, 94903, USA. Tel 1: 415-479-1337, Tel 2: 800-873-9798. Fax: 415-472-0603. E-mail: dick@sldbrass.com. Web site: www.sldbrass.com.

Sonante Publications, PO Box 74, Station F, Toronto, Ontario, M4Y 2L4, Canada.

Sonic Arts, Incorporated, Room 302, 3-3-14 Azabudai, Minato-ku pref 106, Japan.

SOS Music Services, 1817 29th Avenue E, Tuscaloosa, AL, 35405, USA.

Sound Ideas Publications, PO Box 7612, Colorado Springs, CO, 80933, USA.

Soundspells Productions, 86 Livingston Street, Rhinebeck, NY, 12572, USA. Tel: 914-876-6295. Fax: 914-876-6295. Web site: www.jamesarts.com/soundspells.htm.

Soundwear, Schallershofer Str,110 91056, Erlangen, Germany. Tel: 44 0049 9131 75190. Web site: www.soundwear.com.

Southern Music Company, PO Box 329, 1100 Broadway, San Antonio, TX, 78292, USA. Tel 1: 210-226-8167, Tel 2: 800-284-5443. Fax: 210-223-4537. E-mail: info@southernmusic.com. Web site: www.southernmusic.com.

Southern Music Publishing Company, Limited, London, US: Peer-Southern Organization, 8 Denmark Street, London, WC2 BLT, England.

Southern Music Publishing Company, (also see: Theodore Presser Company), 1740 Broadway, New York, NY, 10019, USA.

SP & S. *See* Salvationist Publishing & Supplies.

Spaeth/Schmid Blechbläsernoten Lise-Meitner-Str,9 72202 Nagold Germany Tel: 0049/7452/818454. Fax: 0049/7452/818456. E-mail: info@spaeth-schmid.de. Web site: www.spaeth-schmid.de.

Spartan Press Music Publishers Ltd, Strathmashie House, Laggan Bridge, Scottish Highlands PH 20 1BU, UK. Tel: 01528 544770. Fax: 01528 544771. E-mail: Mail@SpartanPress.co.uk. Web site: www.SpartanPress.co.uk.

Spears, Jared, Box 2259, State University, AR, 72467, USA.

Spectrum Music Publishers, PO Box 5187, Greensboro, NC, 27435, USA.

Stadt- und Universitätsbibliothek, Bockenheimer Landstrasse 134-138, 60325 Frankfurt am Main 1, Germany. Tel: (069) 21239-230. Fax: (069) 21239-062. Web site: www.stub.uni-frankfurt.de.

Stainer & Bell Limited, London, U.S. agent: E. C. Schirmer Music Company, PO Box 110 Victoria House, 23 Gruneisen Road, London, N3 1DZ, England. Tel: +44 (0)20 8343 3303. Fax: + 44 (0)20 8343 3024. E-mail: post@stainer.co.uk. Web site: www.stainer.co.uk.

Stansfeld Music Company, 9709 Roosevelt Way NE, Seattle, WA, 98115, USA.

Stauffer Press, Box 101082, Birmingham, AL, 35210, USA. Tel: 205-951-3881.

Stegmann, Richard, 87 Wurzburg, Waldkugelweg 5a, Germany.

Stephen Shoop Music Publications, 507 S.W. Main Street, Ennis, TX, 75119, USA. Tel: 972-875-9754. E-mail: tuba@hyperusa.com.

Step Two Musikverlag, Neulerchenfelder Strasse 3-7, A-1160 Vienna, Austria.

Sterling. *See* Custom Music.

Sterling Deluxe Bags. *See* Custom Music.

Stevens, John D., 1606 Baker Avenue, Madison, WI, 53705, USA. Tel: 608-233-6199.

STIM. *See* Swedish Music Information Center.

Stockhausen-Verlag, c/o Ione H. Stephens, 2832 Maple Lane, Fairfax, VA, 22031, USA. Tel: 703-560-3039.

Stockhausen-Verlag, Kettenberg 15, 51515, Kürten, Germany. Web site: www.stockhausen.org/stockhausen_verlag.html.

Stril, c/o Tom Brevik, Edvardsensgt, 19, N-5035 Bergen-Sandviken, Norway,. Tel: +47 55 32 42 54.

Stroud, Richard, 131 Huntoon, Eureka, CA, 95501, USA.

Studio Music Company, 77-79 Dudden Hill Lane, London, NW10 1BD, England. Tel: 020-8830-0110. Fax: 020-8451-6470. Web site: www.studio-music.co.uk.

Summy-Birchard Publishing Company, 15800 N.W. 48th Avenue, Miami, FL, 33014, USA. Tel: 305-620-1500. Fax: 305-621-1094.

Svarda, William, 4532 Creek View Drive, Middletown, OH, 45042, USA.

Svensk Musik—Swedish Music Information Center, Box 27327, S-102 54 Stocholm, Sweden, Telefon +46 08 783 88 00.

Swand Publications, 120 North Longcross Road, Linthicum Heights, MD, 21090, USA.

Sweden Music AB, Mariehallsvagen 35, PO Box 20504, S -161 02 Bromma, Sweden. Tel: 46 8 14 30 20. Fax: 46 8 21 53 33.

Swedish Music Information Center—STIM, Sandhamnsgatan 79, Box 27327, S-102 54 Stockholm, Sweden. Tel: +46 8 783 88 00. Fax: +46 8 783 95 10. E-mail: swedmic@stim.se. Web site: www.mic.stim.se.

Swiss Music Edition, Tossertobelstrasse 12, CH-8400 Winterthur, Switzerland. Tel: +41 52 213 55 27/29. Fax: +41 52 213 09 95. E-mail: info@edition-swiss-music.ch. Web site: www.edition-swiss-music.ch.

Symphony Land, 24 Rue Utrillo, 93370 Montfer-meil, France.

SZK Music, 52 Briarwood St, Carindale, Q, Austra-lia, 4152. E-mail: tuba@tubacentral.com. Web site: www.tubacentral.com.

Szkutko, John, SZK Music, 52 Briarwood St, Carindale, Q, Australia, 4152. Web site: www. tubacentral.com/szkmusic.

T.A.P, Music. *See* TAP Music Sales.

TAP Music Sales, 1992 Hunter Avenue, Newton, IA, 50208, USA. Tel: 641-792-0352. E-mail: tapmusic@tapmusic.com. Web site: www. tapmusic.com.

T.I.S. Publications, PO Box 669, Bloomington, IN, 47402, USA.

T R N Music Publishers, Inc, PO Box 197-2700 Airport Road, Alto, NM, 88312, USA. Tel 1: 866-623-2472, Tel 2: 505-336-2688. Fax: 505-336-2687. E-mail: sales@trnmusic.com. Web site: www.trnmusic.com.

Taan-Band Music, P,b, 48-5931, Manger, Norway. Tel: +47 5634 7102. Fax: +47 5634 7103. E-mail: aagaardnilsen@online.no. Web site: home.online.no/~tonilsen/.

Taiga Press, PO Box 81382, Fairbanks, AK, 99708, USA. Tel: 907-455-6235. Fax: 907-455-4815. E-mail: jla@alaska.net.

Tanglewind Music, 65 Carless Avenue, Harborne, Birmingham, B17 9BN, England. Tel: +44 (0)121 426 3711. Fax: +44 (0)121 428 3074 Web site: www.tanglewindmusic.com.

Taunus Verlag Musikverlag H,-L, Grahl, Im Staffel 106, 60389 Frankfurt am Main, Germany. Tel: 069-471588.

Taurus Press, 17 The Common, Troston, Bury St, Edmunds, Suffolk, England.

Tempo Music Publications, 501 East Third Street, PO Box 802, Dayton, OH, 45401-0802. Tel: 800,444,1144. Fax: 937,223,2042. E-mail: info@lorenz.com. Web site: www.lorenz.com.

Tennessee Tech Mutes, Tech Tuba Mutes, TTU-ITEA Box 5045, TTU, Cookeville, TN, 38505. Web site: http://orgs.tntech.edu/tuba/.

Tenuto Publications. *See* Theodore Presser Com-pany.

Tezak. *See* Mark Tezak.

Themes & Variations, 39 Danbury Avenue, West-port, CT, 06880, USA. Tel: 203-227-5709. Fax: 203-227-5715. E-mail 1: jwwaxman@aol.com, E-mail 2: tnv@tnv.net. Web site: www.tnv.net.

Theobald, Jim. E-mail: jimthoeb@earthlink.net.

Theodore Presser Company, 588 North Gulph Road, King of Prussia, PA, 19406, USA. Tel: 610-525-3636. Fax: 610-527-7841. E-mail: presser@presser.com. Web site: www.presser.com.

Thornes Music, 18 Sundorne Crescent, Sun-dorne, Shrewsbury, Shropshire, England, SY1 4JE Phone: 44 (0)1743 231150, E:mail: rogerthorne@thornesmusic.freeserve.co.uk.

Thompson Edition, 231 Plantation Road, Rock Hill, SC, 29732-9441, USA. Tel: 803-366-4446.

Fax: 360-234-5601. E-mail: sales@thompsonedition.com. Web site: www.thompsonedition.com.

Thore Ehrling Musik AB, Box 21133, 10031 Stock-holm, Sweden. Tel: +46 8 30 50 25. Fax: +46 8 30 98 12.

Tierra del Mar Music, 3348 S. Calle Del Albano, Green Valley, AZ, 85614, USA. Tel: 520-625-9005. E-mail: oboegreg@tierradelmar.org. Web site: tierradelmar.org.

Tierolff Muziekcentrale, PO Box 18, Markt 90-92, 4700 AA Roosendaal, Holland. Tel: ++31 (0) 165 541255. Fax: ++31 (0) 165 558339. E-mail: musicinfo@tierloff,nl. Web site: www.tierloff.nl.

Tillander Enterprises, 260 West End Avenue Suite 7A, New York, NY, 10023, USA. Tel: 212-874-4892.

Tinoco, Luis. E-mail: sergiofbc@hotmail.com.

Tokyo Bari Tuba Ensemble, c/o Toru Miura, 2-112, Shih Tamagawa Hgim, 1048-1 Nakanoshima, Kama-Ku, Kamasaki City, Kanagawa Prefecture, 214, Japan.

Tonika. *See* Norsk Musikforlag.

Tonos Musikverlag, Holzhofallee 15, D-64295, Darmstadt, Germany. Tel: +49 06151 39040. Fax: +49 06151 3904 90. E-mail: mail@tonos-online.de. Web site: www.tonos-online.de.

Touch of Brass Music Corporation, c/o Ward Music LTD, 412 W. Hastings Street, Vancouver, BC, V6B 1L3, Canada. Tel: 604-682-5288.

Toyama, Yuzo, c/o Kaijimoto Concert Management Company, Limited, attn: Junichi Isogai 8-6-25, Chuo-ku, Tokuo 104, Japan.

Transatlantiques (Editions Musicales) Paris, US Rep: Theodore Presser Company, 151 avenue Jean—Jaures, F—75019 Paris, France, Paris, F-75018, France.

Transcontinental Music Publications, 633 Third Ave-nue, 6th floor, New York, NY, 10017-6778, USA. Tel 1: 800-455-5223, Tel 2: 212-650-4101. Fax: 212-650-4109. E-mail: tmp@uahc.org. Web site: www.etranscon.com.

Trigram Music, Incorporated. *See* Wimbledon Music Incorporated/Trigram Music Inc.

Trio Music Edition. *See* Hal Leonard.

TRIO Musik Edition, Martin Lamprecht, Gewer-bestrasse 2, D-84562 Mettenheim-Hart, Tel ++ 49 8631 16 41 60. Fax ++49 8631 16 41 62. E-mail: info@trio-musik.de.

Triple Letter Brand, PO Box 396, Tenafly, NJ, 07670, USA.

Tritone Press. *See* Theodore Presser Company.

Tromba Publications, 2253 Bellaire Street, Denver, CO, 80207, USA. Tel: 303-322-8608. Fax: 303-322-8608. E-mail: gendsley@ecentral.com. Web site: www.dmamusic.org/tromba.

Trumcor Mutes, 8176 San Benito Way, Dallas, TX, 75218. Tel: 214-321-0606. Web site: www.trumcor.com.

Tuba Classics, PO Box 186, Kelly, WY, 83011,USA. Tel: 307-734-6868.

The Tuba Exchange, 1825 Chapel Hill Road Durham, NC 27707. Web site: www.tubaexchange.com.

Tuba-Euphonium Press, 3811 Ridge Road, Annandale, VA, 22003, USA. Fax: 703-916-0711. E-mail: dmiles@erols.com. Web site: www. tubaeuphoniumpress.com.

TUBA Journal, Jason Smith, 55 Sunnyside Drive, Athens, OH, 45701, USA. Tel: 740-591-4075. E-mail: smithj10@ohio.edu.

TUBA Press. *See* Tuba Euphonium Press.

Tubalaté. Web site: www.dws.ndirect.co.uk/tubalate. htm.

TubaMania International, PO Box R 181 Royal Exchange, Sydney, NSW 1225, Australia. Tel: +61 41 613 5854. E-mail: Steve@tubamania. com.au.

TubaMania Press, c/o Steve Rosse. E-mail: steve@ tubamania.com.au.

TUBA Press. *See* Tuba Euphonium Press.

Tuba/Euphonium Music Publications, Out Of Business.

TubaQuartet.com, c/o Michael Forbes 1103 N. Fell Ave, Bloomington, IL, 61701, USA.

Uber, David, 283 Mountain View Road, Wallingford, VT, 05773-9321.

Uetz Music Publishers, Voigtei 39, D-38820, Halbertstadt, Germany. Tel: ++49-3941-570040. Fax: ++49-3941-570041. Web site: www.uetz.de/ music.

Uitgave Molenaar, Postbus 19, N,V, Wormerveer, 1520AA, Holland.

Unicorn Music Company. *See* Boston Music Company.

UNITUBA Press, Out of Business.

Universal Edition. *See* European American Music.

Universal Songs BV, US Rep: Theodore Presser Company, Oude Enghweg 24 Postbus 305, Hilversum, 1200 AH, Netherlands.

Universe Publishers. *See* Theodore Presser Company, PO Box 1900, Orem, UT, 84059, USA.

Universe Publishing. *See* Universe Publishers.

University Microfilm, 300 N. Zeeb Road, Ann Arbor, MI, 48106-1346, USA. Tel 1: 800-521-0600, Tel 2: 734-761-4700. E-mail: info@il.proquest. com. Web site: www.umi.com.

University of Massachusetts Press, Box 429, Amherst, MA, 01004, USA. Tel (Orders): 413-545-2219, Tel (Editorial): 413-545-2217. Fax (Orders): 800-488-1144. Fax (Main): 413-545-1226. E-mail: info@umpress.umass.edu. Web site: www. umass.edu/umpress/.

University of Miami Press. *See* Sam Fox Music Sales.

University of York Music Press, Department of Music, University of York, Heslington, York Y010 5DD, United Kingdom. Tel: 01904 432434. E-mail: uymp@york.ac.uk. Web site: www.uymp.co.uk.

Ursula Amrein, Im Gleisdreieck 31, D-23566 Lübeck, Germany. Tel: 49-(0)451-622972. Web site: www.music-amrein.com.

Vanderbeek & Imrie Ltd, 15 Marvig, Lochs, Isle of Lewis, Scotland, PA86 9QP. Tel: 01851 880216.

Vaughan, Rodger D., 226 W. Borromeo, Placentia, CA, 92670, USA.

Veanova, Marcus Thranesgt, 18, 2821 Gjøvik, Norway. Tel: +47 61 18 08 19. E-mail: ketilvea@lycos.com.

Veb Friedrich Hofmeister—Leipzig, Karlstrasse 10, 0-7010 Leipzig, Germany. Tel: 0341/20 99 08. Fax: 0341/29/51/14.

Velvet Music Edition. Tel: 814-867-3017. Fax: 814-867-3017. E-mail: velvet@lazerlink.com. Web site: www.velvetbrown.net.

Verda Stelo Music, PO Box 67, Ashburn, VA, 20146-0067. E-mail: info@davidgaines.org. Web sites: www.cafepress.com/verdastelo or www. davidgaines.org.

Verlag Merseburger, Postfach 10 38 80, 34038 Kassel, Berlin, Germany. Tel: (0561) 78 98 09-0. Fax: (0561) 78 98 09-16. E-mail: info@merseburger. de. Web site: www.merseburger.de.

Verlag Neue Musik, Grabbeallee 15, D-13156, Berlin, Germany. Tel: +49-30-61 6981-0. Fax: +49-30-61 6981-21. E-mail: vnm@verlag-neue-musik.de. Web site: www.verlag-neue-musik.de.

Verlag Von Paul Zschocher, Hamburg, Germany.

Viola World Publications, 2 Inlander Road, Saratoga Springs, NY, 12866, USA. Tel: 518-583-7177. Fax: 518-583-7177. E-mail: violaworld@aol. com. Web site: www.viola.com/violaworld.

Virgo Music Publishers, 9018 Walden Road, Silver Spring, MD, 20901, USA. Tel: 301-588-0836. Fax: 301-588-0836.

Virgo Music Publishers, Virgo House, 47 Cole Bank Road, Hall Green, Birmingham, B94 6DT, England. Tel: +44 (0) 121-778-5569. Fax: +44 (0) 121-778-5569, E-mail: virog@printed-music. com.

Visible Music, 276 Massachusetts Avenue No, 411, Arlington, MA, 02174, USA. Tel: 617-641-4741.

Vivace Press, NW 310 Wawawai Road, Pullman, WA, 99163-2959, USA. Tel: 800-543-5429. Fax: 509-334-3551. E-mail: yordy@vivacepress. com. Web site: www.vivacepress.com.

VMI. *See* B&S.

VNM, Vest-Norsk Musikkforlag, PO Box 59, N-5321 Kleppestø, Norway. Fax: +47 56 14 38 00.

Vydavatelstvi Chf-Praha, 150 00 Praha 5-Smichov, Radlicka 99, Czechoslovakia. Tel: 53 41 37-8. Fax: 54 86 27.

W. W. Norton and Company, Incorporated, 500 Fifth Avenue, New York, NY, 10110, USA. Tel 1: 800-233-4830, Tel 2: 212-354-5500. Fax 1: 800-458-6515. Fax 2: 212-869-0856.

Wakefield, Anthony. Web site: www.sibelius-music.com/cgibin/user_page,pl?url=anthony wakefield.

Walker, Gwyneth, Brainstorm Road, Braintree, VT, 05060-9209, USA. Tel: 212-656-1367. Fax: 212-656-1367. E-mail: walkermuse@aol.com. Web site: www.gwynethwalker.com.

Wallan Music Company, 170 NE 33rd Street, Fort Lauderdale, FL, 33334, USA.

Wandle Music Limited, 26 Chiltern Street, London, W1M 1PH, England.

Warburton Music Products, PO Box 1209, Geneva, FL, 32732. Tel: 407-366-1991 or 800-638-1950. Web site: www.warburton-usa.com.

Warner Brothers Music, 265 Secaucus Road, Secaucus, NJ, 07094-2037, USA.

Warner Chappel Music Scandinavia AB, Vendevagen 85B, S-182 15 Danderyd, Sweden. Tel: 011-46-8-755-1210. Fax: 011-46-8-755-1596. Web site: www.warnerchappell.se/wcmse/home2,jsp.

Warner Chappell Musikverlag GmbH, Diefenbachgasse 35, A-1150 Vienna, Austria. Tel: 011-43-1-894-1920. Fax: 011-43-1-894-1615.

Warner/Chappell Music Incorporated, 9000 Sunset Boulevard, Penthouse, Los Angeles, CA, 90069, USA. Tel: 310-273-3323. Fax: 310-271-4843.

Warren, Frank. *See* Frank E. Warren Music Service.

Warwick Music Limited, 1 Broomfield Road, Earlsdon, Coventry, England CV5 6JW. Tel: +44 (0)24 7671 2081. Fax: +44 (0)24 7671 2550. E-mail: sales@warwickmusic.com. Web site: www.warwickmusic.com.

Watts, Charles, 1503 Sherrill Boulevard, Murfreesboro, TN, 37130, USA.

Wehr's Music House, 3533 Baxter Drive, Winter Park, FL, 32792, USA. Web site: www.wehrsmusic-house.com.

Weinberger. *See* Josef Weinberger.

Weintraub Music Company. *See* G. Schirmer.

Welcher, Dan, See Theodore Presser Company.

Wenström-Lekare, Lennart, Ynglävagen 20, 182 62 Djursholm, Sweden.

Weril Coporation, PO Box 392 Lake Geneva, WI 53147. Tel: 262-248-8896 or 888-888-4446. Web site: www.weril.com.

Werle, Floyd, 5504 Aldrich Lane, Springfield, VA, 22151, USA. Tel: 703-941-5276.

Wessner, John, 822 E. Joppa Road, Baltimore, MD, 21204, USA.

West Wind Music, 3072 S. Laredo Cir, Aurora, CO, 80013-1806, USA.

Western International Music, 3707 65th Avenue, Greeley, CO, 80634-9626, USA. Tel: 970-330-6901. Fax: 970-330-7738. E-mail: wimbo@wiminc.com. Web site: www.wiminc.com.

Westleaf Editions, RD #2, Box 2770, Cox Brook Road, Northfield, VT, 05663, USA. Tel: 802-485-8019. Fax: 802-495-3972. E-mail: bathory@maltedmedia.com. Web site: members,aol.com/kalvos/westleaf.htm.

Whaling Music Publishers, See Cimarron Music & Productions.

White, Ian, 13 Tugela Road, West Croydon, Surrey, CR202HB, United Kingdom. E-mail: drianwhite@hotmail.com.

White, Joseph Pollard, Department of Music, Christopher Newport University, Newport News, Virginia. Tel: 757-594-8789. E-mail: joseph.white@cnu.edu.

White, Winton, CNFJ N46, PSC 473 Box 12, EPO, AP, 96349-0051. E-mail: Winton,C,White@biola.edu.

Wick, Denis. Web site: www.deniswick.com.

Wilfredo Cardoso, Esmeraldo 1075, Buenos Aires 1007, Argentina.

Wilhelm Hansen Musikforlag, Bornholmsgade 1, DK-1266 Copenhagen K, Denmark. Tel: +45 33 11 78 88. Fax: +45 33 14 81 78. E-mail: ewh@ewh,dk. Web site: www.ewh.dk/index_en.asp.

Wilhelm Zimmermann, Musikverlag Zimmermann, Strubbergstraße 80, 60489, Frankfurt am Main, Germany. Tel: 069/97 82 86-72. Fax: 069/97 82 86-79. E-mail: info@zimmermann-frankfurt.de. Web site: www.zimmermann-frankfurt.de/v1.shtml.

William A. Pfund, 35629 County Road #41, Eaton, CO, 80615, USA. Tel: 970-454-2642.

William Elkin Music Services, Station Road Industrial Estate, Norwich, Norfolk, NR13 6NS, England. Tel: +44(0)1603 721302. Fax: +44(0)1603 721801. E-mail: info@elkinmusic.co.uk. Web site: www.elkinmusic.co.uk.

William Grant Still Music, 1109 S. Univ. Plaza Way, Suite #109, Flagstaff, AZ, 86001-6317, USA. Tel: 928-526-9355. Fax: 928-526-0321. E-mail: wgsmusic@bigplanet.com. Web site: www.williamgrantstill.com.

Williams Music Publishing Company, 300 Fallen Leaf lane, Roswell, GA, 30075, USA. Tel: 404-518-8861. E-mail: wmp@mindspring.com.

Willis Music Company, 7380 Industrial Road, Florence, KY, 41042, USA. Tel 1: 800-354-9799, Tel 2: 606-283-2050. Fax: 606-283-1784. E-mail: willis@willis-music.com. Web site: www.willismusic.com.

Willson Band Instruments Co, CH-8890, Flums, Switzerland. Tel: 081-733-14-78. Web site: www.swissprofi.ch.

Wilson, Curtis, Texas Christian University, School of Music, PO Box 297500, Ft, Worth, Texas, 76129, USA. Tel: 817-257-6625. E-mail: c.wilson3@tcu.edu.

Wilson, Kenyon, 1739 Bentridge Drive, Kennesaw, GA, 30144, USA. Tel: 404-694-1156. E-mail: kwilson@fulbrightweb.org.

Wimbledon Music Incorporated/Trigram Music Inc, 1801 Century Park East (Suite 2400), Los Angeles, CA, 90067-2326, USA. Tel: 310-556-9683. Fax: 310-277-1278. E-mail: webmaster@wimbtri.com. Web site: www.wimbtri.com.

Wind Music Incorporated, 153 Highland Parkway, Rochester, NY, 14620, USA.

WindSong Press, PO Box 146, Gurnee, IL, 60031, USA. Tel: 847 223-4586. Fax: 847 223-4580. E-mail info@WindSongPress.com. Web site: www.windsongpress.com.

Wingert-Jones Music, Incorporated, 11225 Colorado, Kansas City, MO, 64137-2502, USA. Tel: 1-800-625-3254. Fax: 1-816-765-3232. E-mail: wjmusic@wjmusic.com. Web site: www.wjmusic.com.

Winston, E. M. Winston Co, 3323 Merritt Ave, Bronx, NY 10475. Tel: 718-231-4870 or 800-456-1841. Web site: www.emwinston.com.

Winteregg, Steven L., 419 Westview Place, Englewood, OH, 45322, USA. Tel: 936-836-8593. E-mail: Swint@erinet.com. Web site: ww,amc.net/member/Steven_Winteregg/home.html.

Winwood Music Publishers, Unit 7, Fieldside Farm, Quainton Bucks, HP22 4DQ England. Tel: 00 44 (0)1296 655777. Fax: 00 44 (0)1296 655778. E-mail: sales@winwoodmusic.com.

Wiscasset Music Publishing Company, Box 380810, Cambridge, MA, 02138-0810, USA. Tel: 617-492-5720. Fax: 617-492-4031.

Wolfgang G. Haas-Musikverlag Köln, 90 07 48, D-51117 Köln, Germany. Tel: ++49 (0) 2203-98 88 3-0. Fax: 02203/98883-50. E-mail: info@hass-koeln.de. Web site: www.haas-koeln.de.

Woodbrass Music SA, Rte de Fribourg 30, CH-1724 Praroman-Le Mouret. Tel: +41 26 413 40 13. Fax: +41 26 413 45 55. E-mail: office@woodbrass-music,ch. Web site: www.woodbrass-music,ch.

Woodson, Thomas (Bear) C., 3636 N. Campbell Ave, Apt, 3119, Tucson, AZ, 85719-1545, USA.

Tel: 520-881-2558. E-mail: bearwoodson@cox.net or CorEnFa@E-mail,msn.com.

Woodsum Music, Limited, RFD 2 Box 244, Harrison, MA, 04040, USA. Tel: 207-583-4875.

Woodwind and Brasswind, 4004 Technology Dr, South Bend, IN, 46628. Tel: 574-251-3500 or 800-348-5003. Web site: www.wwbw.com.

World Library Publications, 3815 N Willow Road, PO Box 2701, Schiller Park, IL, 60176, USA. Tel: 1-800-566-6150. Fax: 1-888-957-3291 International Tel: 1-847-233-2752, International Fax: 1-847-671-5715. E-mail: wlpcs@jspaluch.com. Web site: www.wlpmusic.com.

Wright and Round, The Cornet Office, PO Box 157, Glos, GLI ILW, UK. Tel: +44 (0)1452 523438. Fax: +44 (0)1452 385631. Web site: www.wrightandround.com. E-mail: inquire@wrightandround.com.

Wright & Round Limited. *See* Solid Brass Music Company.

Wspolczesna Muzyka Polska.

Yamaha Band and Orchestral Division, 3445 East Paris Ave, S.E., PO Box 899, Grand Rapids, MI, 49512-0899, USA. Tel: 616-940-4900. Web site: www.yamaha.com.

Yamaha Kyohan Company Limited, Koshin Building 3F, 6-12-13 Ginza Chuo-ku, Tokyo pref, 104, Japan.

Yamaha Music Foundation, 3-24-22, Shimo-Meguro, Meguro-ku, Tokyo 153-8666, Japan. Tel: 03-5773-0808. Fax: 03-5773-0857. Web site: www.yamaha-mf,or,jp/conte.html.

Yarra Yarra Music, PO Box 30, Warrandyte 3113 Victoria, Australia. Tel: +61 3 9844 1194. E-mail: barrymckimm@hotmail.com.

Ybarra Music, PO Box 665, Lemon Grove, CA, 91946, USA. Tel: 619 462-6538. Fax: 619 462-6565. E-mail: vbraun8368@aol.com.

Zanibon. *See* G. Zanibon.

Zdechlik, John P., 3860 Van Dyke, White Bear Lake, MN, 55110, USA. Tel: 651,426,4575.

Zen-On Music Company Ltd, 2-13-3 Kamiochiai, Shinjuku-ku, Tokyo, 161-0034. Web site: www.zen-on,co,jp.

Zonn, Paul Martin, 122 Bay View Drive, Hendersonville, TN, 37075, USA. Tel: 615 264-6392. Fax: 615 264-6395. E-mail: wzonn@paulmartinzonn.com. Web site: www.paulmartinzonn.com.

Zurfluh. *See* Editions Aug, Zurfluh.

APPENDIX B: Recording the Euphonium

Neal Corwell

The author of this appendix, in addition to several years of teaching electronic music and recording techniques at the college level, has recorded and produced numerous recording projects during the last twenty years, most of which involved the euphonium.

The perfect recording, like the perfect performance, is an elusive goal. Making matters more difficult is the fact that there is no consensus, even among the most accomplished and experienced recording engineers, as to the best method of capturing the true sound of an instrument. There are several reasons why experts differ in their opinions and methods, not the least of which is that assessment of the final product is almost entirely a subjective matter. Also significant is that a multitude of acoustic variables may affect the recording process. I do not profess to have all the answers for those in search of the perfect euphonium recording, but in this appendix I will endeavor to provide general guidelines and practical advice that may assist you in the creation of a quality recording that matches your hopes and expectations.

Project Planning

When planning a recording project, there are many factors to take into consideration such as time and budget constraints, and available facilities and equipment. Also to be taken into consideration is the intended use of the final recording. In other words, are you putting together an entire solo CD intended for public release and sale, are you preparing an audition recording for submission to an audition or contest, or do you just wish to record a recital for the benefit of friends and family who are unable to attend the live performance? These various projects require varying levels of planning, time, and commitment.

Of the three examples given, the CD project will require the most time and effort. You cannot afford to take any aspect of such a recording for granted because the final product is likely to be closely scrutinized and critiqued by many listeners, and you will have to live with the results for a long time. There are several different paths that may be taken to complete such a daunting task. One would be to rent studio time and pay recording engineers to record and edit your project. This can, of course, be very expensive. In addition to the heavy financial burden, you may also feel rushed for time and pressured to accept a final product with which you are not entirely satisfied.

Your expenses can be reduced if you have free or low-cost access to a recording space such as a church sanctuary or school auditorium. If you are further able to borrow quality recording equipment for use in this recording space, you will save even more money. However, be aware that setting up equipment for recording and monitoring (listening to playback) in a space not designed for recording may be a time-consuming task. Also, because the project may require days, weeks, or even months to complete, you may have to frequently tear down the equipment to make room for other events taking place in the same space.

Another option would be a home studio setup. This is likely to be the least expensive option, and will offer you the most scheduling flexibility. The performer will be more likely to feel relaxed and unhurried, and there will also be plenty of time for experimenting with alternative microphone placements and other aspects of the recording process. One can repeat the cycle of recording, followed by listening and evaluation, at leisure until satisfactory results are achieved. The opportunity to experiment unhurriedly, coupled with today's relatively low costs for renting or purchasing professional-level recording equipment, makes home recording a viable option for creating a quality CD project. There are, however, some disadvantages, perhaps the most notable being that the average home doesn't include a large performance space with good acoustic properties. Some shortcomings in this area may be overcome by altering the acoustics of a room through various means to include the strategic placement of sound-absorbent materials or sound diffusion panels (a topic that will be discussed in more detail later). The decision to record in a small space with its inherent lack of natural quality reverberation makes it more likely you will be dependent on digital effects and equalization to enhance the original recorded signal. Such enhancement, if done poorly, can detract from the final product, so care must be taken with this aspect of the project.

If your recording project is the preparation of an audition tape (for convenience we'll use the word "tape" although today the most likely audio format will be CD), you will follow much the same procedures as for an entire CD project. However, the process is not as involved and will not require as much time. For one thing, you will not need to record as much music, and your choice of repertoire may be decided for you by an audition or contest selection committee. Also, because the goal is to provide an accurate representation of your playing, and the final tape will only be heard by the audition or selection committee, it doesn't have to meet the standards of near technical perfection that we expect of a CD for public release. Obviously you will wish to create a quality recording, but a few minor imperfections such as a noise in the hall, a recording space that is too dry, or even slight note glitches here and there are acceptable. With today's DAWs (digital audio workstations) it is possible to cut and paste notes, adjust pitch, and edit other parameters of the original recording to digitally create a note-by-note "perfect" performance, but a recording created in this manner is not truly representative of your playing. As a matter of fact, many calls for submission tapes now specify that they are to be "unedited," and as one who has often served on audition panels, I can testify that I am suspicious of submissions that sound overproduced. I feel the performer is trying to hide something and is not being totally honest. Even if not specifically requested, I advise you on ethical grounds not to submit a tape that has been improved by significant editing. Submitting such a tape would not only be dishonest, it would also prove to be a waste of time for both you and the panel of jurors if you were summoned to an audition or invited to the finals of a contest based on such a false representation. In addition, you could be taking away an opportunity from someone more deserving, someone who is a more advanced player but submitted an honest unedited recording.

Making a live recording of a performance, though not necessarily a simple or easy task, is not likely to require as much of a commitment of time and resources as the types of projects already mentioned. This is particularly true if the final product is intended only as a courtesy memento for the soloist, something to share with friends and family and other interested parties who were unable to attend the live performance. Such an audience is not likely to be overly critical of the technical features of the recording. A minimum of time is required because there are no retakes in this situation. The recording begins with the first note of the music and ends as the final applause dies away. Some setup time will be needed, but often this is minimal because recital halls frequently have a pre-existing or installed microphone-to-recorder configuration in place, perhaps even with the optimum sound level adjustment already pre-determined. If this is the situation, the recording technician merely powers up the equipment and hits the "record" button. If a performance is successful, a live recording will serve well as source material for an audition tape because it is unedited and therefore an accurate representation of one's playing. The soloist need only select the best-performed movements or compositions for inclusion on such a tape. If the entire recital was truly outstanding in every sense, meaning that a wonderful overall performance was recorded with quality equipment configured in a well-conceived recording setup in a hall with good acoustics, one could even use a live recording as a marketable CD project. Creating a CD in such a fashion would truly be an exemplary model of optimum efficiency as far as use of time and financial resources.

Recording Method Options

There are different ways of approaching the task of recording the euphonium. The path you choose will depend on the performance space, the equipment available, the number of performers involved, the amount of time you have to devote to the project, and personal preferences. I'll now present some options to help you choose the method that best suits your needs.

A large performance space usually works well for a rich and resonant instrument such as the euphonium. If such a space is available, and it is acoustically desirable, meaning it has a pleasant reverberation time that enhances the sound of the instrument without causing it to sound muddled, you may wish to use a simple recording configuration whereby the signal from the microphones is sent through a mixer directly to a two-track (stereo) recorder. A setup of such simplicity is an option only when a good room or hall is available. Sometimes, even in a good room, several microphones are needed to fully capture the sound of the instrument and room successfully. This is not a problem as long as your audio mixer has as many inputs as you have microphones. The mixer will combine all incoming signals into the two tracks (left and right channels) being sent to the two-track master recorder.

If the acoustics of the room are undesirable and/or very "dry" (lacking in much reverberation time), you will want to place the microphone(s) close to the performer and enhance the input of the microphones with artificial reverberation created by an effects module. This enhancement of the original signal can be done in "real time" (live) during the recording session via the mixer, but it is best to record the sound "dry" (in this usage the word means "without effects added") and wait to add effects until a later time (once effects are added, the signal is said to be "wet"). If you decide to follow this route, it is in your best interest to purchase, rent, or borrow a high-quality effects module, because a good initial recording can easily by marred by the addition of poor-quality effects.

If the microphone configuration is rather elaborate and/or you feel enhancement of the audio signal is needed, it would be to your advantage to use a multi-track recorder. Because it can record signals from different inputs onto separate channels, a multi-track gives you the opportunity, during the recording session, of postponing many decisions about precisely how the final product will sound until a later, more convenient time. During the recording session, you need only record the various inputs onto separate available tracks. Then, during the subsequent "mixing" session (in which all the recorded tracks are combined via the mixer into a stereo signal to be recorded by a two-track master recorder), you may experiment with combining and enhancing the recorded tracks in numerous ways to include varied volume levels, equalization settings, effects, and pan settings (placements to left, right, or center within the stereo field) until the ideal balance between all these factors is achieved. The mixing session ideally takes place after performers, technicians, and producers have had a chance to rest. The mixing session is usually held in a superior listening environment with high-quality monitor speakers. It is therefore much easier to make good decisions during the mixing session than it is while in the midst of a recording session on a remote recording site, when the pressure is on to record the live performer within a given time frame, and where sometimes the only way to monitor the recorded signal is with headphones.

If you have access to a multi-track recorder, you have another recording option open to you, the option of "overdubbing." Because a multi-track machine has several available tracks (often sixteen, 24, 32, or even more), and any of those individual tracks may be set in either the playback or record mode at any given time, you may record one track (or several tracks) while listening to another track or group of tracks. This process is called overdubbing because you are recording or "dubbing" one track "over" another. If you are recording a euphonium solo with piano accompaniment, for example, you could record the piano first and then add the solo later. If recording a piece with multiple euphoniums, one player could perform all the parts. While recording a single solo line, the multiple tracks may be taken advantage of by recording multiple takes of a passage onto separate tracks. After listening and choosing the best-performed portions of the passage, you may then assemble them by recording them onto another available track (a process called track "bouncing"). This destination track, comprised of all the best takes, is called a "composite" track. A piano accompaniment may be assembled in the same manner.

Planning and patience are required to record using the overdubbing method. Before you may even begin recording the actual euphonium or accompaniment parts, a reference track must be created. The performer will listen to the reference track through headphones while performing his or her part. The reference track may be a simple metronome click (called a "click track") indicating the tempo of the piece, or it may be more elaborate, containing an entire percussion part, verbal cues, or even another performance of the piece as performed by a synthesizer or ensemble. What is needed on the reference track will be determined by the nature of the composition. You will also need to determine in advance the most advantageous order in which parts should be recorded. To use the piano and euphonium combination as an example, it will usually be easier to record the piano first. However, there may be instances where the soloist freely leads the way through a passage or composition and the piano merely follows along, perhaps intermittently adding underlying chords. In such a circumstance, it will be easier to record the solo first.

The choice of overdubbing as a method of recording an ensemble composition offers both advantages and disadvantages. The possibility of having one individual perform several ensemble parts provides the opportunity of recording a large ensemble piece in a small space with a minimum number of mikes, and with a "virtual" ensemble of equally talented performers, minus the scheduling issues associated with assembling a group of people. However, rhythmic synchronization can be a challenge when overdubbing. In most situations, a click track, which can be created to follow tempo changes and various beat subdivisions, works well, but sometimes the use of such a track is not appropriate. This is particularly true of free sections, such as cadenzas, that have no regular rhythmic pulse. My solution, while recording the cadenza within my composition *Ritual*, for euphonium/tuba duo, was to act as conductor for the tubist (Velvet Brown) as we recorded her part. Because her part was recorded in keeping with the pace and note durations I felt appropriate, it was not difficult for me to later add the euphonium part in perfect rhythmic synchronization with the tuba. Although my part was added over a year later, in the final recording it sounds as though she and I are in the same room. An additional solution for synchronizing problematic entrances and other intricate spots is to record a spoken vocal track of verbal cues to guide the performer decisively through challenging passages.

Intonation can be problematic when overdubbing because pitch problems inadvertently recorded on the first tracks will have a negative impact on subsequent recorded tracks, forcing undesirable adjustments of pitch unless the source of the problem is re-recorded. Keeping a tuner handy is one obvious way to avoid intonation problems, but often it is also helpful to record, as both a rhythmic and pitch reference, a version of an ensemble piece onto a single track, in addition to, and separate from, the click track. Instead of looking at a tuner, the performer can make subtle pitch adjustments "by ear" as one does naturally when playing within an ensemble. When preparing to record multiple-part ensemble pieces using only one or two players, I usually first record a complete synthesizer performance of the piece with the aid of a sequencer. The synthesizer version is typically not musically appealing, but it is accurate pitch-wise and therefore an excellent reference for listening to in headphones while adding the acoustic parts.

Bypassing the overdubbing method in favor of recording a group of performers simultaneously has numerous advantages. The individual members of a high-quality ensemble can easily perform together in rhythmic synchronization and with good intonation, without the need for a pre-recorded reference track. They also, with good communication and cooperation, will be able to quickly resolve issues of articulation and style conformity. Yet another positive factor is that an ensemble may require less actual recording time for a project. For example, in theory it only requires four minutes of recording time for an eight-part ensemble to perform a complete take of a composition of four minutes in duration. However, for one individual to record the eight separate parts of the same composition would require at least 32 minutes (eight times four minutes equals=32 minutes) plus the time required to create the reference track(s). It is also true, however, that a single performer within an ensemble can easily ruin for the entire group what was otherwise a perfect take, possibly necessitating numerous takes of a single passage. Another factor to consider is that when all members of an ensemble are recorded simultaneously, depending upon the miking method used, it will probably be difficult to alter and adjust the ensemble balance after the recording session is complete. In contrast, the overdubbing method offers complete flexibility down to the final mixing session with regard to ensemble balance and stereo placement of individuals within the ensemble. Clearly the availability of consistent performers is a key factor in determining what method to use when recording an ensemble composition.

When recording a solo with a pre-existing recorded accompaniment, overdubbing the solo while listening to the accompaniment through headphones is the simplest, and probably the most logical, recording method. A stereo accompaniment may easily be transferred to two tracks of a multi-track recorder with virtually no audio degradation, and if it is available in a digital storage medium, such as CD or DAT, it can be cloned to a digital multi-track recorder without ever leaving the digital realm. The nature of works within this performance genre is such that, by design, the composer/arranger has pre-recorded a musical performance that, in addition to complementing the solo part, serves as a reference track for the live performer. Therefore, no click track or other type of reference track is needed. Despite the advantages of overdubbing, there may be circumstances where one may wish to forgo this procedure in favor of recording both soloist and pre-recorded accompaniment together in the same performance space. This is a desirable option when a high-quality hall is available because both accompaniment and soloist may take advantage of the favorable acoustics of the room. When using this method, the pre-recorded audio goes through several processes before being re-recorded. It must first be converted into an analog signal, amplified, passed through speakers, re-recorded by micro-phones, processed through a pre-amp and mixer, and then finally converted back into digital audio. Because there are so many steps added to the audio-electrical chain, there is an increased risk of degrading the audio quality of the original recorded accompaniment. This procedure also increases the difficulty of editing the performance because a solo part by itself is much easier to edit than a solo part that has already been combined with accompaniment onto a single audio track. Another disadvantage of combining the solo and accompaniment in the same performance space at the beginning of the recording process is that it makes it more difficult, after the initial recording session, to adjust balance between accompaniment and soloist.

Microphone Selection and Placement

No one disputes the fact that microphones are a vital link in the recording process. There are, however, many divergent views on the subject of microphone selection and placement. This difference of opinion is not surprising when the wide array of choices available to today's record-ing engineers is taken into consideration. Over the years I have accumulated a wealth of data and advice, much of it conflicting, concerning this topic. Having sifted through all this informa-tion, and done some experimentation on my own, the best I can do is share with you my personal conclusions about what equipment and methods work best for capturing the true sound of the euphonium.

Whether using a single microphone near the instrument, or a matched pair of microphones for stereo recording from farther away in a large hall, my preference when recording the euphonium is for small-diaphragm condenser microphones. More specifically, my microphone of choice is the Schoepps MK4 capsule with a CMC6 body. A less-expensive option, which I've also found to work well, is the Shure SM81. Condenser micro-phones of the small-diaphragm variety generally have the "flattest" response of any microphone type. In other words, they are less likely to "color" the sound by emphasizing or de-emphasizing cer-tain frequencies. Condenser microphones with a diaphragm size of larger than ¾ of an inch are classified as large-diaphragm condensers. A high-quality large-diaphragm condenser will also do a good job of recording most instruments, but there usually will be some coloration of the sound. This is regarded as a positive characteris-tic in many situations, especially when recording

vocals, hence the dominance of this microphone type in today's recording studios. All condenser microphones, regardless of size, work well at both short and long distances, making them quite ver-satile. Another characteristic shared by all con-densers is that they all require a power source to operate. Some only require batteries, but most use "phantom power," which is typically supplied from the mixer via the microphone cable. If using a mixer that does not supply phantom power, a dedicated phantom power supply unit may be inserted between the microphone and mixer.

Some engineers recommend a "ribbon" micro-phone for recording brass instruments. The basis for their choice is that this microphone type "warms" the sound and also can withstand high volume levels without distorting. However, since the euphonium is an inherently warm-sounding instrument, and because most euphoniumists do not tend to play excessively loud, I've not found ribbon microphones to be particularly useful. "Dynamic" microphones are another common microphone type. They are relatively inexpensive, durable, and do not require a power source, but they are not as sensitive or accurate as condenser or ribbon microphones. I therefore never use them for studio recording. Dynamic microphones are, however, quite suitable for live performance amplification, and they are my preferred micro-phone in situations calling for real-time process-ing of live sound through a digital effects unit.

Once a microphone has been selected, deci-sions must be made, and experiments conducted, regarding microphone placement. In order to place microphones effectively, one must have a basic understanding of "polar patterns," which are patterns descriptive of the sensitivity of a micro-phone with regard to direction. For example, a microphone with a cardioid polar pattern (so-called because when charted two-dimensionally the pattern resembles the shape of a heart) is not as sensitive to sounds emanating from behind the microphone as it is to sounds directly in front of it. Such microphones are said to be "directional" because they favor sound sources toward which they are pointed. The designation of "super-cardioid" simply means that a micro-phone has exaggerated directional characteristics. An "omni" microphone, in contrast, is equally sensitive in all directions. The two microphones I have specifically mentioned (the Schoepps and the Shure) are directional cardioid microphones, as are most microphones used in live and record-ing situations. The fact that they do not indis-criminately respond to all sounds equally is advantageous because they can be focused on the instrument you wish to record, while at the same time minimizing the microphone pickup of undesirable extraneous noises coming from a different direction.

The space between sound source and microphone is called the "working distance," and placement choices in this regard can encompass anywhere between two extremes. The microphone may be placed very near the performer or spatially separated from the instrument by a large distance. "Close-miking" is the term used to describe placement near the performer. This technique minimizes the effect of the performance space, because the microphone picks up very little signal from the room itself. I've developed a preference for using a single microphone at a close working distance for my solo recording projects. One reason for my choice is that my favorite solo recordings are those that include all the sounds associated with live performance: the subtle clicking of the valves, the performer's breaths, and so on. These sounds make the performance more real and exciting to me, and as a performer, this is also the way I am accustomed to hearing the euphonium. For this realism to be captured, the microphone must be placed nearby, hence my preference for this approach. Interestingly enough, there are many people who do not wish to hear any of these so-called "extraneous" performance sounds. They therefore dislike close-miked recordings for precisely the same reason that I prefer them. Another basic reason for the choice of close-miking technique for my projects is that most of my recording has been done in a home-based studio where space is limited. I do not have a large reverberant performance hall, or even a large high-ceilinged space, at my disposal. Therefore, there is simply not enough room to physically place the microphone at a large distance from the instrument. Also, there is little motivation for trying to capture the "sound of the room," because my current recording space, a small acoustically "dry" cubicle lined with sound-absorbent materials, has very little reverberant sound available for capture.

This brings up the very practical subject of what to do if you do not have access to a desirable recording space. If, for example, circumstances dictate that you record in an average-sized room as may be found in the typical home, close-miking will be helpful, but this technique alone will not eliminate all problems. My first recordings were done in a rectangular drywall-lined room. The sound reflective properties of the low ceiling and nearby parallel walls had a negative impact because sound waves bounced quickly off of these hard surfaces, arriving at the microphone only slightly later, and not much softer, than the original sound waves emanating directly from the bell of the euphonium. These strong early reflections, said to be "out-of-phase" with the original signal, have a negative impact because they cancel out or accentuate certain frequencies. This phenomenon may manifest itself in a "hollow" sounding recording. The solution was to decrease the strength of these early reflected sound waves. This was done by attaching sound-absorbent foam wedges to the ceiling above the microphone and placing other absorbent materials, such as pillows or a mattress, in front of the nearest walls. I also placed a towel over the nearby metal music stand to minimize its reflective properties. You may also wish to place sound-absorbent materials over windows. This serves a dual purpose, as it reduces sound reflection and also prevents nuisance sounds, such as traffic noise, from leaking into the recording space. If unwanted noise does intrude into the recording space, it may be dramatically reduced or eliminated by pointing the head of the microphone away from the offending sound source. This works because a directional microphone is designed to reject sounds coming from the rear. Remember, microphones do not process sound in the same way as do human ears, so noise that seems quite audible to us might go undetected by a microphone.

When close-miking, it is important not to place the microphone too near the sound source. For one thing, placing the microphone too closely will produce an unwanted boost in the low frequencies, called "proximity effect." Also, because the euphonium is a lower-registered instrument with a sound rich in harmonics, a little distance gives the sound waves more time to fully develop. For this development to take place, the performer may need to be seated in order to create enough acoustic space between the bell of the instrument, the microphone, and the ceiling. I usually place the microphone two to three feet above the bell, and three to four feet in front or behind the performer (although when miking an individual within an ensemble I may need to shorten these distances). Placement of the microphone in front of the performer is the most typical choice, but placing it behind can help reduce the volume of undesirable performance-related noises coming from the embouchure of the performer or the instrument itself. I prefer to aim the "axis" of the microphone (an imaginary line drawn straight out from the center of the microphone's diaphragm) toward a point slightly above the farthest rim of the euphonium bell. This reduces the microphone pickup of the undesirable high-pitched sibilant sounds that naturally emanate from the bell. Because they reach the microphone "off-axis" (from an angle), they are reduced in volume level. You should never place the microphone on the bell side of the instrument with the axis pointed down directly into the center of the bell, because this position will strongly emphasize these undesirable sibilant frequencies.

When recording in a large space with good acoustics, the placement of a pair of microphones for stereo recording some distance away from the performer, at least ten or twelve feet away, is usually a good choice. This setup takes advantage of the natural reverberant characteristics of the performance space. As the microphones are moved farther from the performer, the amount of direct sound from the instrument being recorded will decrease and more of the room itself will be heard. In other words, as you move toward the back of a hall, you increase the amount of the hall's reverberation picked up by the microphones. The optimum distance for microphone placement will depend on the room's characteristics and your personal preference for mixture of direct and reverberant sound. Two microphones are used in stereo recording to approximate the way we hear with our two ears, and the angle relationship and distance between these two microphones can be varied in several ways. Probably the most common microphone placement for stereo recording is one in which the two microphone heads, spaced about eight inches apart, are pointed away from one another, with each directed toward one side by approximately a 45-degree angle: the microphone on the left pointing to the left, and the other to the right. This is called "ORTF" placement. Another frequently used setup, called "X-Y" or "near-coincident" miking, calls for pointing the two microphones inward toward one another at approximately the same angle with the microphone heads nearly touching. In this case, the microphone on the right is pointing toward the left, and vice versa. A third choice entails separating the microphones by several feet and pointing them straight toward the front of the hall, parallel to one another. All three of these placement approaches may potentially yield good results. So-called "stereo" microphones actually consist of two matched microphones mounted together in one casing. In most stereo microphones, the components are fixed and the angle and distance between the two microphone diaphragms cannot be altered. This is clearly a disadvantage when compared to the other choice of two separate but identical microphones. However, in some of the more expensive stereo microphones, the angle relationship between the two microphones, and even the polar pick-up patterns of the individual microphones, may be altered, sometimes by remote control.

The use of a large recording space does not dictate the use of stereo miking from a distance. If a room has undesirable acoustical properties you would like to minimize, or if you prefer the sound of an instrument from the perspective of a microphone placed nearby, close-miking is still an option. You may also wish to close-mike the euphonium in stereo, most likely using a "near-coincident" placement of the stereo pair. Yet another option is to add a third microphone on the individual, an omni, behind the close-in stereo pair. When recording an ensemble, a distant stereo setup usually works well, and is certainly the simplest choice from a technical standpoint. However, close-miking is often employed because it allows individual members of the ensemble to be isolated from one another, permitting independent control of timbre, balance, and panning. You may also choose to combine two divergent microphone placement approaches by placing, in addition to individual microphones, a stereo pair at some distance in the hall to capture the sound of the ensemble as a whole. In addition to blending these varied input sources, one may wish to add yet another stereo pair to the mix, this pair facing the back of the hall, in order to focus exclusively on the reverberant sound emanating from the performance space.

When close-miking individuals within an ensemble, it is important to avoid phasing problems. Many microphones in close proximity to one another can easily interfere with one another in a negative fashion. When a single instrument is recorded simultaneously from different microphones, these similar but slightly different "out-of-phase" signals can potentially cancel out each other at certain frequencies. The resultant volume changes can usually be detected by toggling between the mono and stereo buttons on the mixer's monitor output selection switch. If the two signals exhibit a marked difference in volume you need to make adjustments to the microphone setup by placing the individuals and their microphones more distant from one another. A good rule of thumb is that microphones should be three times the distance from one another as they are from their sound source. In other words, if the microphones are all placed two feet from their assigned instruments, they should ideally be six feet from one another. If this amount of space is not available, the sound rejection characteristics of directional microphones should be taken advantage of by redirecting them to reduce the pickup of adjacent instruments.

With so many options available, it can be difficult to decide what microphones to use and what placement works best. Ultimately you must trust your ears when making final decisions in this regard. When searching for the optimum placement of a distant stereo microphone, I suggest having a trusted assistant walk the space while you perform and choose a spot he or she thinks sounds good. This will serve as a good starting point in the search for the best microphone location. When close-miking, you should compare different microphone configurations by making several test recordings of a pre-determined musical passage or series of passages. This test piece should feature excerpts that are loud and soft, high and low, and sustained and detached. If you have access to a multi-track recorder and multiple microphones, you have the advantage of being able to directly compare tracks recorded simultaneously from different perspectives. A generous amount of time should be allotted for this test phase at the beginning of your first recording session. Time spent thus is time well spent. It would be foolish to rush through this important decision-making step in the process, because once you've begun recording in earnest, you cannot make changes without discarding previously recorded takes. Once the optimum setup for your

situation is found, it is important that you document every aspect of the project because you may need to re-create the configuration at some point in the future. Write down all settings and parameters of the mixer and other devices involved in the audio chain, and make a note of every aspect of microphone placement. Photographs of the microphone setup, taken from various angles, are also a valuable documentation tool.

Conclusion

The goal of this article has been to provide a maximum of practical advice and information, with a minimum of unexplained technical jargon. If you wish to learn more about the subjects discussed, please do not hesitate to seek out other sources. However, in addition to consulting other reference materials, I advise you to also pursue the alternative educational approach of "learning by doing." Experimentation will lead to a deeper understanding of all aspects of the recording process, and will help you to come to your own conclusions about what methods work best for recording the euphonium. There are many texts available, and many electronic gizmos at your disposal, but when it comes down to making important decisions concerning a music recording project, I believe that a musician must first and foremost trust his or her own ears and musical instincts.

APPENDIX C: Continuing Symposia, Competitions, Events, Festivals, and Summer Study

Lisa M. Hocking and Matthew J. Tropman

Notes on this appendix:

Events in this appendix are listed alphabetically. Information is organized in the following manner:

NAME

LOCATION

SUMMARY INFORMATION (dates, eligibility)

COSTS (including tuition, accompanist fees, accommodation)

PRIZES (in any)

CONTACT INFORMATION (address, phone, E-mail, website)

Detailed information for many events may change annually. Some rotate location, eligibility, and dates. Tuition and other fees also may vary. Information provided is current at time of publication. Please refer to contact information provided.

Events included in this appendix have been selected based on the following criteria:

Euphonium-specific focus

International scope

Substantial cash or other awards such as performance opportunities

Many smaller regional events that include or accept euphonium participants, but are not specifically oriented toward euphonium, have been omitted. The following resources may be of help in locating such events and/or finding the most current information on events included in the appendix:

www.chamber-music.org/

Official website of Chamber Music America. Includes a categorized listing of national and international music events. Subscription required. Printed copy available for $135.

www.ITEAonline.org

Official website of the International Tuba Euphonium Association (ITEA). Contains information about upcoming events such as the International Tuba Euphonium Conference (ITEC). Updated regularly.

Access All Areas
Tempe, AZ

Held for multiple one-week sessions annually in June. Check website for details

For euphonium and tuba players of any age. Intensive training on fundamentals and solo and orchestral repertoire. Ten participants per session accepted based on taped audition

Cost: $950. Travel and accommodation not included

www.patricksheridan.com

www.PerformanceSuccess.org

ARTS—Arts Recognition and Talent Search
Miami, FL

Annual; dates vary

For high school seniors or seventeen- to eighteen-year-old performers

U.S. citizens or permanent residents; jazz portion open to international participants

Entrance Fee: $25/$35 depending on application date

Prizes: $100–$300

Deadlines: June 1st (early registration); October 1st (regular registration)

www.nfaa.org

nfaa@nfaa.org

305-377-1140

NFAA/ARTS

800 Brickell Ave., Suite 500

Miami, FL 33131

Artists International's Annual New York Debut Award Auditions
New York, NY

Annual; check contact info. for updated information

No age limit; open to all instrumentalists and singers except those having already given a New York debut recital

Entrance Fee: $75

Prizes: Solo recital in Merkin, Alice Tully, or Carnegie Hall. Fully sponsored

Deadlines: check contact information

521 5th Avenue, Suite 1700

New York, NY 10017

212-292-4257

Astral Anni Baker Prize
Philadelphia, PA
Biennial; rotating instruments/voice
Check website for eligibility ages, which may vary
    depending on year
Entrance Fee: $50
Prizes: $15,000; four additional study grants of
    $2,500 each
Deadline: may vary
230 S. Broad St., 3rd Floor
Philadelphia, PA 19102
215-735-6999

Bar Harbor Brass Week
College of the Atlantic, Bar Harbor, Maine
Held annually, one week during summer months
High school, college, and pre-professional brass
    musicians are eligible
Check contact information for fees and schedule
Bar Harbor Brass Week
9 Evergreen Lane
Haddonfield, NJ 08033
www.barharborbrass.org

Blue Lake Fine Arts Camp
Twin Lake, MI
Summer camp program for band instrumen-
    talists in elementary, intermediate, and high
    school. Two-week sessions rotate annually
    from roughly late June to early August; contact
    camp for detailed information about upcoming
    sessions
Cost: The basic fee per two week session is
    $910. The fee includes instruction, room, and
    meals. Campers are admitted free to all camp
    events. Because there are additional fees for
    some majors and electives, students planning to
    enroll in such programs should add this to their
    tuition cost on the application. See website for
    online application and complete details
Prizes: Some camp sessions may include a stu-
    dent solo competition. Winner performs with
    the Blue Lake Festival Orchestra broadcast on
    local radio
Blue Lake Fine Arts Camp
300 East Crystal Lake Rd.
Twin Lake, MI 49457
Phone: 800-221-3796
Fax: 231-893-5120
www.BlueLake.org

Brevard Music Center
Brevard, NC
Wide variety of music and arts educational pro-
    gramming available from late June to early
    August each summer. Specific dates vary from
    year to year. The Instrumental Studies program

offers experience in standard repertory for stu-
    dents of band and orchestral instruments aged
    14 and older including a Young Artist Division
    and an Advanced Artist Division.
Cost: $4,100 for the 2005 summer session. Fee
    may vary from year to year. The single fee
    includes: tuition; room and board for six and
    a half to eight weeks, depending on program;
    private lesson fee; practice room fee; on-campus
    health services; admission to all Festival events
    (more than 80 events in the full session). Schol-
    arship opportunities available.
Deadline: March 1 for year attending
P.O. Box 312
349 Andante Lane
Brevard, NC 28712
Student Admissions 828-862-2140
Main office 828-862-2100
Fax 828-884-2036
www.brevardmusic.org

CRS National Festival for the Performing Arts
    Competition
Broomall, PA
Held annually; for soloists and chamber music,
    no age limit
Entrance Fee: $50
Prizes: recording and National appearance oppor-
    tunities; artist representation
Deadline: June 15th; check website for updated
    information
724 Winchester Road
Broomall, PA 19008
610-544-5920
www.erols.com/crsnews

Carmel Chamber Music Competition
Carmel, CA
For chamber ensembles comprising three to six
    players, average age under 26
Entrance Fee: $15 per musician
Prizes: $3,000
Deadlines: check website for updated infor-
    mation
P.O. Box 221458
Carmel, CA 93922
831-625-2212
www.chambermusicmontereybay.org

Carmel Music Society Competition
Carmel, CA
Held annually, rotating instrumental/vocal/
    piano. For CA residents or full-time students
    in CA. Also accepts non-residents born in CA.
    Check website for current information.

Entrance Fee: $25

Prizes: Grand prize:$2,000 award plus $2,000 in performance opportunities; Second prize: $1,500 Third prize $1,000. Five (5) $300 prizes also awarded

Deadline: may vary annually. Check contact information.

P.O. Box 1144
Carmel, CA 93921
831-625-9938
www.carmelmusic.org

Concert Artists Guild International Competition
New York, NY

Held annually, Deadline may vary annually. Check contact information

Cost: $75 application fee

Prizes: $5,000; Recital at Weill Recital Hall, Carnegie; Management contract; Commissioning opportunities; numerous performance prizes

850 Seventh Ave., Suite 1205
New York, NY
212-333-5200
www.concertartists.org

Deutches Tuba Forum
Hammelburg, Germany

For tuba, euphonium and bariton players; study and interaction with International euphonium/ tuba artists; different artists featured at each festival

Usually held every other year; Check contact information

Cost: ??
www.tubaforum.de

East and West Artist International Auditions
New York, NY

Held annually; instrumentalists, small ensembles (up to five members), vocalists. Competitors must be 18 or over

Entrance Fee: $37 each member (chamber groups), $87 for soloists

Prizes: Sponsored performance at Weill Recital Hall at Carnegie Hall

Deadline: check contact information

310 Riverside Drive, Suite 313
New York, NY 10025
212-222-2433
ewartists@hotmail.com

Fischoff Chamber Music Competition
South Bend, IN

Held annually; participants enter either senior or junior division

Senior Division: participants must be 39 years of age or younger at the time of competition. Average age cannot exceed thirty

Junior Division: participants must be eighteen years of age or younger at the time of competition; with the exception of current high-school students

Entrance Fee: $30 per musician

Prizes (Senior Division): Grand Prize $5,000 plus concert tour; First Prize $3,000 cash; Second Prize $2,000; Third Prize $1,000

Prizes (Junior Division): First Prize $2,000; Second Prize $1,500; Third Prize $1,000

Additional award of $500

Deadline: Deadline may vary annually. Check contact information

P.O. Box 1303
South Bend IN 46624
219-237-4871
www.fischoff.org

Fredericton International Tuba Fest
Fredericton, New Brunswick, Canada

Held annually; two days of workshops, ensembles and clinics

Cost: Registration: adults $50 CDN, students $15 CDN

Fredericton International Tuba Fest—2005
UNB Centre for Musical Arts
PO Box 4400
Fredericton NB E3B 5A3, Canada
Phone/Fax 506 453-4697
rriding@unb.ca
www.unb.ca/FineArts/Music/Centre/ TubaFest/

Friday Woodmere Music Club Young Artists Competition
North Bellmore, NY

Held biennially; participants must be instrumentalists thirteen to eighteen years old

Entrance Fee: $25

Prizes: First $700; Second $350; Third $150

Deadline: Deadline may vary annually. Check contact information

976 Newbridge Road
North Bellmore, NY 11710
516-221-4680

German Brass Academy
Krefeld, Germany

Held annually for musicians in quartets, quintets, or soloists

Cost: Passive Participants 100 €; Active Participants 200 €; Quintet members 250 €; Quartet members 320 €

German Brass Academy

C/o Musikschule Krefeld
Uerdinger Strasse 420
D-47800 Krefeld
Germany
+49-2152-590011
www.germanbrassacademy.com

Haddonfield Symphony Young Instrumentalists
  Solo Competition
Haddonfield, NJ
Held annually; rotates between piano, strings,
  and woodwind/brass/marimba. For musicians
  sixteen to 25 years old. Must be a resident or
  attending school in New Jersey or the follow-
  ing states: Maine, New Hampshire, Vermont,
  Massachusetts, Connecticut, Rhode Island,
  New York, Pennsylvania, Delaware, Maryland,
  District of Columbia
Entrance Fee: $50
Prizes: First $2,000 plus concert with Haddonfield
  Symphony; Second $500
Deadline: Deadline may vary annually. Check
  contact information.
P.O. 212
20 Washington Ave.
Haddonfield, NJ 08033
856-429-1880
www.haddonfield-symphony.org

Harvey Phillips Northwest Big Brass Bash
Two-day festival open to all tuba/euphonium
  players; location changes annually; see website
  for details
Events include guest artist recital/masterclass, and
  large ensemble rehearsal/performance. Tuition
  charged for participants but all concerts are free
  and open to the public
www.hpnwbbb.org

Interlochen Center for the Arts
Interlochen, MI
Offering a wide variety of camp and other educa-
  tional opportunities. Also home to a perform-
  ing arts high school
Summer Camp sessions are available to all instru-
  mental musicians and singers
Two-, three-, four-, and six-week sessions are
  available
Application deadline: February 15 (Dec/Jan
  applications encouraged)
Acceptance notification no later than April 15
Junior, intermediate, and high school summer
  sessions run from late June to early August
Note: Specific dates change from year to year. See
  website for detailed information

Cost: Broad tuition range depending on the
  specific camp/course of study selected. Numer-
  ous scholarships and works study opportunities
  available
Interlochen Center for the Arts
Admissions Office
PO Box 199 (US Mail)
4000 Hwy. M-137 (FedEx, UPS, Airborne Ex)
Interlochen, MI 49643
Phone: 231-276-7472
Fax: 231-276-7464
www.Interlochen.org

International Competition for Brass Instrument
  Ensembles
Passau, Germany
Dates: October 2004, Deadline: June 1, 2004
Eligibility: Amateur, professional ensembles of
  any number
Cost: Amateur: 120 €; Professional: 170 €
Prizes: Amateur: First 1,500 €; Second 1,000
  €; Third 500 €. Professional: First 4,000 €;
  Second 2,000 €; Third 1,000 €
Statische Musikschule Passau
Blechblaeserwettbewerb
Landrichterstr. 42
93034 Passau
+0049 851 966 850
www.blechblaeser-wettbewerb.de

International Music Contest-Chamber Music
Caltanissetta, Italy
Eligibility: Section A-Instrumental duet with or
  without piano, Section C-Three or more instru-
  ments with or without piano. Age must not
  exceed 37, or average age of 35 for ensembles.
Cost: 52 €
Prizes: Section A: First 3,615 €; Second 2,582
  €; Third 1,550 €. Section C: First 5,165 €;
  Second 3,615 €; Third 2,582 €
www.musicamera.caltanissetta.it

International Tuba-Euphonium Conference
For tuba and euphonium players of all levels.
  Membership in the International Tuba-Euphonium Society encouraged but not required.
Rotates on an every-other-year basis between a single International conference or several Regional
  conferences. Check contact information.
Cost: varies depending upon ITEA membership
  status; individual hosts may also set different fees.
Prizes: Most ITEA conferences offer a variety of
  competitions with cash or equipment prizes.
  Competitions are organized and held at the
  discretion of the conference host, and usually

include student and artist level competitions on euphonium and tuba in areas such as solo performance, band and orchestral excerpts, chamber music and street music.
www.ITEAonline.org

International Women's Brass Conference and Competitions
Conference and competitions held tri-annually, dates and locations vary.
See website for detailed information.
www.iwbc-online.org

Japan Wind and Percussion Competition
Tokyo, Japan
Held annually; dates and instruments vary, refer to website for detailed information. 2004 competition included euphonium, tuba, bassoon, and clarinet.
Cost: 30,000 ¥ (approx. $300) entrance fee
Deadline: September 15 of competition year
Prizes: 1st: 700,000 ¥; 2nd: 400,000 ¥; 3rd: 200,000 ¥; 4th and 5th: 50,000 ¥
Japan Musical Education and Culture Promotion Society
4-15-9 Hongo, Bunkyo-ku, Tokyo 113-0033 Japan
Phone: 81 3 3814 2977
www.jmecps.or.jp/e-wp.htm

Jeju Brass Competition
Jeju, South Korea
Eligibility: Soloists, or brass quintets with musicians born on or after Jan 1, 1973
Cost: $100 entry fee
Prizes: Solo: First $5,000; Second $3,000; Third $2,000. Quintet: First $10,000, Second $7,000, Third $5,000. Special Prize: $1,500
Jeju Folk Tourism Town
837-20, 1-do 2-dong
Jeju City, Jeju Do, Korea 690-832
+82-64-750 7583
www.chejusbf.or.kr

Jennings Butterfield Young Artist Competition (Symphony of the West Valley)
Sun City, AZ
Held annually; rotates between piano, vocal, winds/brass/percussion, and strings. For post High School, 28 or under on January 30 of competition year. Contestants must be residents of AZ, CA, CO, NV, NM or UT.
Entrance Fee: Fee may vary annually. Check contact information.
Prizes: First $2,000 and performs on a subscription concert in the year of competition victory; Second $1,000, Third $500

Deadline: may vary annually. Check contact information.
P.O. Box 1417
Sun City AZ 85372
623-972-4484

Kingsville International Young Performers Competition
Kingsville, TX
Held Annually.
Pre-college and college div.; must be under 26.
Entrance Fee; $30
Prizes: Pre College: First $1,000, Second $500, Third $200
College: First $1,000, Second $500; Third $200 plus various performance opportunities and other cash awards.
Deadline: Deadline may vary annually. Check contact information.
P.O. Box 2873
Kingsville, TX 78363
361-592-2374
www.kingsvillemusic.com

Ladies Musical Club Annual Solo Competition
Seattle, WA
Annual competition for piano, voice, strings, and wind players; ages twenty to 35, residents or music students in following states: Washington, Alaska, Oregon, Idaho, Montana
Cost: $35 application fee
Prizes: $2,000 awarded to four winners; winners featured in concerts and workshops across Washington State
Cobb Building
1305 4th Avenue, Suite 500
Seattle, WA 98101
206-622-6882

Leonard Falcone International Euphonium and Tuba Festival
Blue Lake Fine Arts Camp, Twin Lake, MI
Held annually in August
Cost: Artist level, $55; Student level, $40; to receive written comments, $25
Deadlines: March 15; late deadline March 31 of competition year
Prizes: Artist level, up to $2250; Student level, up to $1000
Tom Broka
5200 Parkway Ct.
Bay City, MI 48706
(989) 684-0462
tbroka@hotmail.com
www.ferris.edu/SpecialEvents/falcone

Lieksa Brass Week and Euphonium Competition
Lieksa, Finland
Brass week held annually in summer, dates vary.
    Competition instruments rotate annually; inau-
    gural euphonium competition held in 2004
Cost: 70 € (approx. $100) entrance fee
Prizes: 1st: 5,000 €; 2nd: 3,000 €; 3rd: 2,000 €
Lieksan Vaskiviikko
Koski-Jaakonkatu 4
FIN -81700 Lieksa
Phone: +358-13-689 4147
Fax: +358-13-689 4915
brass.week@lieksa.fi
www.lieksabrass.com

Music Teachers National Association Student
    Competitions
Held annually; dates and locations vary, see web-
    site for details.
Divisional and national competitions
Eligibility: Three levels of competition: Junior
    (age eleven to fourteen), Senior (age fifteen to
    eighteen), Young Artist (age nineteen to 26).
    Chamber music competition, three to six play-
    ers (average age eighteen to 26).
Cost: Junior: $70 entry fee; $100 for others
Prizes: Up to $3,000 depending on competition
www.mtna.org/competitions.htm

New York Brass Conference
Held annually, varying locations in New York
N.Y. Brass Conference
315 W. 53 St., NY, NY 10019
(212) 581-1480
nybc@charlescolin.com
www.charlescolin.com/nybc

Olga Koussevitzky Young Artist Awards Com-
    petition
New York, NY
Held annually; rotating between strings, winds,
    piano and voice. Competitors must be between
    the ages of eighteen and 26 as of April 1st of
    year entering.
Entrance Fee: $50
Prizes: First, second and third prizes totaling
    $3,500. Various performance opportunities.
    Deadline may vary annually. Check contact
    information
125 Riverside Drive No.12A
New York, NY 10024
212-873-6851

Osaka International Chamber Music Competi-
    tion and Festa
Osaka, Japan

Festa portion of competition is open to any instru-
    ment combination of two to six performers.
Entry Fee: 20,000 ¥
Prizes: First 2,000,000 ¥; Second 1,000,000 ¥;
    Third 600,000 ¥
www.jmcf.or.jp

Potomac Festivals International Euphonium and
    Tuba Competition
George Mason University, Potomac Music Acad-
    emy, Fairfax, VA
Held annually; inaugural competition held in
    2004
Cost: Artist level, $60; Young artist, $40; Student
    level, $25; Quartet, $75
Accompanist Fee: $40
Prizes: Range from $25 to $600 for soloists;
    first place artist level performs with one of the
    premiere U.S. military bands; up to $400 for
    quartet competition.
Eligibility: Artist level: any age, but not perform-
    ing professional; Young Artist: no older than
    18, cannot be enrolled college student; Stu-
    dent level: age fourteen or younger. Quartets
    must be two euphoniums and two tubas.
International   Euphonium   and   Tuba
    Competition
Department of Music
George Mason University
4400 University Drive, MS 3E3
Fairfax, VA 22030
www.gmu.edu/departments/music/summer

Rafael Mendez Brass Institute
University of Colorado, Boulder, CO
Held annually in summer for high school, college,
    amateur, young professional brass players
Cost: $375 tuition, plus room/board; pre-formed
    ensembles receive 20% discount
Rafael Mendez Brass Institute
College of Music, UCB 301
Boulder, CO 80309
www.colorado.edu/music/Mendez

Sauerland-Herbst Brass Festival
Hochsauerland district, Germany
Held in fall of 2004; in-depth schedule and infor-
    mation found on website
0291/941270
Hochsauerlandkreis
Fachdienst Kultur/Musikschule
Steinstrasse 27, 59872 Meschede
www.sauerland-herbst.de

The International Euphonium Institute
Emory University, Atlanta, GA

Held annually, summer

Cost: Full tuition: $450; Course auditor: $250; One-day tuition: $100

Scholarship opportunities available, see website for details.

Housing cost: $350–$415, including meals; $105, meals only

IEI, c/o Mr. Adam Frey, IEI Director

7230 Cloverhurst Court

Cumming, GA 30041

www.euphonium.com/IEI2005Homepage.htm

Tuba & Euphonium Workshop

Florida State University, Tallahassee, FL

Held annually in summer for high school students.

Cost: Tuition: $200; Housing/Food: $72

850-644-9934

www.music.fsu.edu/pr/summer-camps_workshops.htm

U.S. Army Band Tuba-Euphonium Conference

Ft. Meyer, VA

Held annually in January; free and open to the public; featuring various International Tuba/Euphonium artists; see website for details

www.army.mil/armyband/events/tuba

William C. Byrd Young Artist Competition

Flint, MI

Held annually, rotation between winds (2005), voice, piano and strings

Deadlines: Application: Jan. 17, 2005; Auditions: March 5, 2005

Cost: Entry fee $25, optional accompanist fee $75

Prizes: First $2,500 with contract to appear with Flint Symphony, $2,500 award after appearing with orchestra; Second $2,500; Additional $1,000 Finalist prize

www.byrdartists.com

APPENDIX D: The Freelance Euphoniumist

Bryce Edwards

The freelance euphoniumist can find work in opportunities such as part-time small ensembles, performance in jazz, playing as an extra with an orchestra, the recording industry, and teaching. Most euphoniumists find it difficult not to include other instruments in their performance and teaching abilities.

Part-Time Small Ensembles

There are several different genres in which a euphoniumist can become involved in a performance medium. Religious organizations, brass bands, and community organizations are examples of these genres.

Many contemporary religious organizations will employ euphonium players as part of extended worship sessions (revivals, religious holidays, etc.) with euphonium parts. However, these occasions are few and far between. Churches will employ euphoniumists in place of trombonists in regular situations (Sunday services, meetings, etc.) if needed, since finding a brass player is their only concern. Use this opportunity to ask about performing solos during the church services to further your future playing opportunities.

There are numerous brass bands in North America, and while most are unable to provide a salary high enough to live on, many provide money in some amount for performing at special occasions. These performing ensembles are also willing to pay soloists and clinicians to come in and work with their ensembles.

Community bands are also a way to perform and get paid. As in brass bands, the pay is usually not high enough to be the only source of income, but this is an excellent opportunity to get acquainted with area band directors and musicians. These connections can lead to work with schools as a clinician, soloist, and private lesson teacher.

Jazz

Fortunately for instrumentalists, jazz is not an area with strict codes and traditions on instrumentation. Any instrument is welcome to the field of improvisation. To become a euphoniumist in jazz, all that is needed is experience. Working with a rhythm section and a higher brass or reed player is an excellent way to "hone" one's skills. Once one has established a jazz group, begin booking at local clubs and other shows. Perform as frequently as possible with a good group.

Playing as an Extra with an Orchestra

The best way for a euphoniumist to receive the chance to perform with an orchestra is to become acquainted with the trombone section and the tubist. By taking some lessons with these personnel, you can not only better your playing but also demonstrate your ability to the individual. Demonstrating to the section your ability and willingness to collaborate will increase your chances of being called to perform the euphonium part. If you get the chance to audition for a group on trombone or bass trumpet, mention euphonium as your primary instrument and you might get on the "sub list" as a trombonist, bass trumpeter, or euphoniumist. Otherwise, most orchestras will substitute a tuba or trombone player without a second thought. Plan ahead and note future performance dates featuring a piece that could use a euphonium, such as:

Barber	*Third Essay for Orchestra*
	Symphony No. 2
Bartok	*Kossuth*
Bax	*Overture to Picaresque Comedy*
	Symphony No. 2 in E Minor and C Minor
Birtwhistle	*Gowain*
Ginastera	*Chorale 150*
Gottschalk	*Symphony "A Night in the Tropics"*
Harris	*Symphony No. 1*
	Symphony No. 2
	Symphony No. 3
	Symphony No. 5

	Symphony No. 7
	Symphony No. 9
	Ode to Friendship
	Give Me the Splendid
	Silent Sun
	When Johnny Comes
	Marching Home
Holst	*The Planets*
Janacek	*Sinfonietta*
	Capriccio
	Totenhaus Suite
	Violin Concerto
Kay	*Stars and Stripes (after Sousa)*
	Western Symphony
Mahler	*Symphony No. 7*
Meyerbeer	*Le Prophete*
Mussorgsky	*Pictures at an Exhibition*
Respighi	*Pini di Roma*
Schuman, W.	*Credendum*
Shostakovich,	*L'age d'or*
	The Bolt
	The Tale of the Priest and His Blockhead Servant
Strauss	*Don Quixote*
	Ein Heldenleben
Strauss, Sr. Johann	*Radetzky March*
Traditional	*The Saucy Arethusa*
Turnage	*Three Screaming Popes*
Yardumain	*Passacaglia, Recitative and Fugue*
	Symphony No. 2

Recording

The demand for euphoniumists in the recording studio is minimal. Most recording ensembles do not contain a euphonium since it is not included in the standard orchestral instrumentation. However, occasionally the instrument is needed. In this case, your only opportunity to get the job is through networking or auditioning as a trombonist, as mentioned earlier. Unfortunately in most cases, a trombonist will be used out of convenience because it is cheaper for the recording industry to pay a doubling fee to one member than to hire another musician.

Teaching

Teaching is almost unavoidable by any euphonium artist trying to make a living. Since there are only a few purely euphonium teaching positions available at the college/university level, professors are required to include either trombone, tuba, or both in their studios. The situation for private lesson teachers is often the same.

In order to begin teaching privately, contact all local middle, junior, and high school band directors. The lesson teacher must be willing to (1) potentially teach all brass instruments; (2) travel as needed; (3) work with directors to teach during the school day or have the facilities available for use after school hours; and (4) conduct sectionals of brass instruments. Persistence is the key to making any of this happen.

A private lessons teacher can increase his or her ability to teach exclusively euphonium by maintaining an awareness of local/regional contests and honor groups. If students are well prepared and dominate the upper standings, their lesson teacher has a better chance of acquiring more students who wish to become part of that teacher's studio.

Small Ensembles

Starting a euphonium/tuba quartet can also be a means to make money and perform some quality literature. The tuba quartet scene is exploding with new literature and there is always a need for small ensemble performers. Theme parks, weddings, clubs, receptions, festivals, and many more places and events are awaiting your participation. Just the novelty of such an interesting combination of instruments can help with bookings. Arranging your own literature is a great way to improve music skills as well as provide your ensemble with great music for performance. Having a repertoire list that includes all genres (pop, rock, classical, etc.) is another great way to captivate the listener.

Conclusion

Most of the professional euphoniumists out there have to make their own professions. There are only a few who can do just euphonium performance for a living. If one wants to survive playing the euphonium for money, one must diversify one's playing abilities and other skills to include many different settings (orchestra, band, small ensemble, solo, jazz, etc.), include the trombone (if not other instruments) in one's list of performable instruments, and be aggressive in one's bookings.

Contributors

Co-Editors

Lloyd E. Bone Jr. is currently in his second year as visiting assistant professor of music at Glenville State College in Glenville, West Virginia, and news editor for the *ITEA Journal*. Bone has also taught at the University of Cincinnati College—Conservatory of Music, Murray State University in Murray, Kentucky, and the Schilling School for Gifted Children in Cincinnati, Ohio. He has performed at competitions and has toured with such groups as Mr. Jack Daniel's Original Silver Cornet Band and the Circus Kingdom Band. Bone earned his bachelor of music education degree at Tennessee Technological University and his master's of music from the University of Cincinnati College—Conservatory of Music.

Eric Paull is an adjunct professor of music at Austin Peay State University and an active professional musician who frequently tours with Mr. Jack Daniel's Original Silver Cornet Band. He has been involved in numerous musical projects that range from the recording studio to radio and broadcast television. Paull received his degrees from Louisiana State University and Tennessee Technological University and has studied with Larry Campbell, Winston Morris, and Daniel Perantoni.

Assistant Editors

Brian L. Bowman enjoys a distinguished career as a soloist, clinician, recording artist, educator, and administrator. Currently professor of music (euphonium) in the College of Music at the University of North Texas, Bowman has also served on the music faculty of eight other universities. He is the author of *Practical Hints for Playing the Euphonium/Baritone Horn* and frequently publishes articles in professional journals. His edition of the *Arban Complete Method* is the only complete bass clef edition of this famous brass method. In 1989, Bowman was awarded the *British Magazine's* Euphonium Player of the Year and in 1995 he was given the Lifetime Achievement Award from TUBA.

Neal Corwell was featured euphonium soloist during the 1980s with The United States Army Band "Pershing's Own," in Washington, D.C., and in 2002 he rejoined that prestigious military organization. Corwell has served on the executive committee of ITEA and as a board member of IWBC, and he is a founding member of Symphonia. He has completed several solo CDs and is in demand internationally as a guest soloist, clinician, and composer.

Adam Frey earned a bachelor of music magna cum laude with high honors in euphonium and tuba performance at the University of Georgia and a master of music with distinction and a professional performance diploma with distinction from the Royal Northern College of Music in Manchester, England. He teaches as an adjunct professor at Georgia State University and as an artist affiliate at Emory University, serves as artistic director of the International Euphonium Institute, and runs the euphonium specialist publishing company Euphonium.com. Frey has performed with various ensembles and has an extensive and diverse recording catalog.

Contributors

Marc Dickman is associate professor of music at the University of North Florida. He was hired by Rich Matteson in 1986. Dickman earned degrees from Troy State University, McNeese State University, and the University of North Texas.

Bryce Edwards is currently euphoniumist with Mr. Jack Daniel's Original Silver Cornet Band and trombonist with the Cumberland County Playhouse in Crossville, Tennessee. In his free time, Edwards teaches privately in and around Putnam County, Tennessee. He holds a bachelor of science degree in music education from Tennessee Technological University and a master's of music in euphonium performance from Indiana University. His teachers include Winston Morris, Daniel Perantoni, and Atticus Hensley.

Seth D. Fletcher is currently a graduate teaching assistant at the University of North Carolina–Greensboro, where he teaches music theory and aural techniques. He recently studied with euphonium virtuoso Steven Mead at the Royal Northern College of Music (RNCM) in Manchester, England; played solo euphonium with the RNCM Brass Band and Symphonic Wind Band; and performed and recorded with the RNCM Wind Ensemble, in addition to moonlighting with the Tintwistle Brass Band. He holds a bachelor's degree in music education from Tennessee Technological University and has been awarded numerous scholarships and awards, including being named a Fulbright Finalist in 2003–2004.

Carroll Gotcher earned degrees from Tennessee Technological University and the University of Tennessee at Knoxville. He is a high school band director in Jackson County (Gainesboro), Tennessee, and a private low-brass teacher around the middle Tennessee area. He performs extensively with the euphonium quartet Euphouria and with the Nashville Wind Ensemble. He is also a busy freelance trombone and euphonium player with local and regional big bands and jazz combos.

Atticus Hensley is a graduate of the University of Tennessee, Knoxville, where he received an undergraduate degree in applied music and a master's degree in euphonium performance. While at the University of Tennessee, he was a two-time winner of the UT Concerto competition and a Presser Scholar. Since graduating in 1995, he has performed as a soloist and as a member of the Euphouria Quartet and was a semi-finalist in the 1999 Leonard Falcone International Euphonium Competition. Hensley taught as a graduate assistant at the University of Tennessee and has been an adjunct faculty member at Middle Tennessee State University. Currently, he teaches sixth-grade band and is the applied brass specialist in Tullahoma, Tennessee.

Lisa M. Hocking is a 2005 graduate of the University of Michigan, where she earned her bachelor of music degree in euphonium performance, with teacher certification. She studied euphonium with Professor Fritz Kaenzig. Hocking has enjoyed performing with the nineteenth-century–style Dodworth Saxhorn Band of Ann Arbor, Michigan, as well as the Ozark Mountains British Brass Band of Springdale, Arkansas. Currently, Hocking is completing her master of music degree in euphonium performance at the University of Arkansas, where she studies with Benjamin Pierce.

Sharon Huff holds a bachelor of music education degree from Illinois State University and the master of music and doctorate of musical arts from the University of Illinois. She is currently a faculty member at Millikin University, where she teaches brass methods, conducting, applied tuba, and applied euphonium; supervises student teachers; and coaches several brass ensembles.

Huff previously taught at Illinois State University in Normal and St. Norbert College near Green Bay, Wisconsin. She is president of the International Women's Brass Conference and served on the executive board as Conferences Coordinator for the ITEA from 1993 to 2002.

Kenneth R. Kroesche is associate professor of trombone, euphonium, and tuba at Oakland University in Rochester, Michigan. He has served in a similar role at Western Carolina University and has held teaching positions at Lenoir-Rhyne College, University of Michigan–Flint, and the Schools of Music of the Universities of Michigan and Georgia. He holds a master's and doctorate in performance from the University of Michigan, in addition to a bachelor of music education degree from Texas State University in San Marcos, Texas. He performs extensively as a euphonium soloist.

John Mueller has been assistant professor of trombone at the University of Memphis since August 2001. Previously, Mueller was a member of The United States Army Band in Washington, D.C., for 21 years. He is active as a soloist, clinician, and adjudicator on both trombone and euphonium. He has performed extensively at colleges, universities, and music camps across the United States, as well as in Europe, Japan, and Australia. Mueller holds a bachelor's degree in music education from the University of Illinois, Champaign-Urbana, and a master's and doctorate in trombone performance from the Catholic University of America.

Michael B. O'Connor is a musicologist and performer on historic euphoniums. He holds a master's degree in euphonium performance from the Florida State University, where he is completing a doctorate in historical musicology. O'Connor earned a bachelor's in music education from Tennessee Technological University, where he played principal euphonium in the Tennessee Tech Tuba Ensemble. He has served as a musicologist at the University of Delaware, the College of New Jersey, and Towson University. Currently, he directs and plays euphonium for Newberry's Victorian Cornet Band, a group that performs band music from the late nineteenth century on period instruments.

Joseph Skillen is on the faculty at Louisiana State University, where he teaches applied tuba and euphonium, coaches chamber music, performs with the faculty brass quintet, teaches graduate courses in literature and pedagogy, and guides research projects. Skillen has been principal tubist in several American orchestras and has performed with touring ensembles and presented solo performances throughout the world. Skillen has recorded on the Vestige, Bernel, Mark Masters, and Mark Custom labels. His debut solo CD with pianist Jan Grimes, *Blue Plate Special,* was released in January 2002. He holds degrees from Tennessee Technological University, Pennsylvania State University, and Michigan State University.

Kelly Thomas was appointed tuba/euphonium instructor and director of pep bands at the University of Arizona in 2001. Thomas holds a bachelor of music degree in music education from Tennessee Technological University and a master of music degree in music education from Arizona State University, where he is currently completing a doctor of musical arts degree. Thomas has appeared as a soloist as well as a member of the Tennessee Tech Tuba Ensemble. He is a founding member and tubist for the Original Wildcat Jass Band, a traditional touring New Orleans and Chicago jazz band. He has also worked with numerous high schools as a brass instructor and clinician.

Demondrae Thurman studied euphonium, trombone, and conducting at the University of Alabama and the University of Wisconsin–Madison. Thurman can be heard as a soloist and as a member of the Sotto Voce Quartet on the Summit Records label. He has been extremely active as a soloist and clinician, has been a guest artist at several conferences, and has premiered numerous works for solo euphonium. He is also an active chamber musician. Currently, Thurman teaches at the University of Alabama, where he is assistant professor of tuba and euphonium. He has also taught at Alabama State University, the University of Montevallo, and Troy State University.

Matthew J. Tropman, former solo euphonium with "The President's Own" United States Marine Band in Washington, D.C., now serves as adjunct professor in low brass at Eastern Michigan University. He has released two CDs on Summit Records, has been featured in solo performances at various venues, and has performed with the Detroit Symphony, the Harrisburg Symphony, and the National Repertory Orchestra. He is an active clinician and recitalist, having performed and taught throughout the United States as well as for engagements in Spain, Finland, Germany, Great Britain, and Canada. He has given master classes and served as guest faculty at numerous institutions including the Eastman School and the Peabody Conservatory.

Mark J. Walker serves as assistant director of bands and assistant professor of music at Troy University. He is also the executive director of the Middle School Southeastern United States Band Clinic and Honor Bands, is on the board of the Southeastern United States Band Clinic, and is the director of the "Sound of the South" Summer Music Camp and Director's Clinic. As an author, his articles have appeared in state and national music education publications. Walker earned his bachelor's degree in music education at Tennessee Technological University and his master's and doctorate degrees from the University of Illinois at Urbana-Champaign. As a performer, Walker can be heard on the compact disc *Euphoniums Unlimited* on the Mark Records label.

Advisor

R. Winston Morris is professor of music and instructor of tuba and euphonium at Tennessee Technological University, where he has been on the faculty since 1967. He is regarded as the leading authority on the literature for the tuba, was one of the founding fathers of TUBA, and is acknowledged worldwide as the major authority on the development of the tuba ensemble. He was the senior editor for *The Tuba Source Book* and *Guide to the Tuba Repertoire: The New Tuba Source Book,* and is conductor of Symphonia and Euphoniums Unlimited and founder and co-producer of the Modern Jazz Tuba Project. As a performer on the tuba, Morris has toured extensively and is very active as a soloist and presenter of tuba clinics and master classes.

INDEX

Aagaard-Nilsen, Torstein, 116, 139, 151, 191, 195, 196, 268, 294, 318, 319, 443
Aarflot, Hogne, 294
Aaron, Henry, 175
Abbey Brass, 300
Abilene Christian University, 455
Abraham, Gerald, 435
Achilles, Darin Lyn, 418
Ackermann, H., 254
Ackford, 116
Acuff, Bill, 329
Adam, 285
Adam, Adolphe, 19, 76, 91, 309
Adam, Claus, 447
Adams, B., 335
Adams, Dan, 218
Adams, Pepper, 308
Adams, Peter H., 435
Adams, Stephen, 19, 78, 280, 303, 304, 308
Adkins, Hector Ernest, 438, 441
Adler, Guido, 435
Adler, Samuel, 152, 188, 268, 280, 318, 336, 411, 412, 438, 444, 455, 457, 466
Adnams, Gordon A., 173
Adolphe, 290
Aebersold, Jamey, 516
Aebersold, Rolf, 325
Aegerter, Daniel, 486
Agrell, Jeffrey, 315
Ahbez, Eden, 327
Ahmas, Harri, 139
Aho, Eric, 276, 292
Aho, Kalevi, 196, 444
Ahrendt, Karl, 447
Ahrens, Christian, 433
Ahrens, Jay, 197
Air Combat Command Heritage of America Band, 326
Aitken, Greg, 485
Akiyama, Kazuyoshi, 498
Alary, G., 85, 258, 259
Albaniz, Issac, 19, 82, 187
Albertasaurus Tuba Quartet, 276, 309, 321
Albian, Franco, 19, 20, 75, 77, 91, 92, 160, 257, 259
Albiez, Cédric, 96, 121, 131, 276
Albinoni, Tomaso, 20, 74, 81, 85, 166, 181, 238, 260
Albrechtsberger, Johann Georg, 20, 76, 80, 85
Alchemy, 276, 300, 333
Alcock, 171
Aldbourne Band, 301
Alder, Jim, 171
Alder Valley Aldershot Brass, 282, 326
Alen, Hugo, 313
Alessi, Joseph, 243, 263, 265
Alexander, Ashley, 276, 307, 429, 485
Alexander, L., 23, 292, 424
Alexander, Lois, 27, 500
Alexander, Louis, 25
Alexander, Russell, 485
Alfén, Hugo, 286, 294, 330
Alford, Harold, 252, 271
All Star Brass, 317
Allen, J. Lathrop, 4
Allen, Marshall, 308
Allison, Gordon, 276
Allred, John, 276, 306, 515
All-Star Band, 336
Altenburg, Johann Ernst, 219
Alven, Hugo, 78

Amano, Masamichi, 92
Ameller, Andre, 75, 78, 79, 82, 87
American Brass Band Journal, 325
American Serenade Band, 289, 302
Americus Brass Band, 498
Ammer, Christine, 434
Amoosm, K., 116
Amos, K., 282
Amsden, Arthur, 236
Ananda, Leah, 308
Anders, V. Andy, 427
Anderson, A. O., 438
Anderson, Eugene D., 152, 160, 190, 243, 274, 276, 424, 445
Anderson, Leroy, 171, 316
Anderson, Mark, 171, 179, 188
Anderson, Paul G., 432, 438
Anderson, Scott, 203
Anderson, Tommy Joe, 196
Andersson, Mikael, 39
Andersson, Ulf, 305
Andraud, Albert J., 228, 231, 260
Andresen, Morgens, 92, 116, 140, 310, 435, 440, 445
Andrews, George W., 436
Andrews, Len, 321, 335
Andrews, Paul, 276, 302
Anfilov, Gleb, 431
Angell, Martin, 140
Angell, Michael, 184
Angst, Adolf, 92
Antens, Ron, 292, 293
Anthony, G. W., 189
Anthony, Phil, 277, 293
Anthony, Yvonne, 20, 75, 78, 79
Antrobus, Michael, 288
Apel, Willie, 434
Apostol, Alexei, 11
Appalachian State University, 499
Apperson, Ron, 421
Appleton, Walter, 132, 230, 277
Aquino, 276
Araki, Tamao, 162, 228, 231, 277, 333, 485
Arban, Jean-Baptiste, 20, 77, 83, 116, 190, 202, 208, 211, 215, 227, 235, 243, 244, 248, 250, 263, 265, 271, 277–279, 281, 284–290, 294, 296–300, 302, 303, 305, 309–311, 315–317, 319, 320, 334, 445, 513
Arcadelt, Jacob, 20, 77, 78, 272, 283, 445
Arcadio, Bernard, 324, 325
Archer, Stephen, 122, 277
Archimede, Alexander, 244
Ares, Rob, 320
Arizona State University, 409, 412, 445, 476, 477, 489, 492, 503, 504
Arkansas State University, 478
Arlen, Harold, 289, 319, 327, 329
Armed Forces School of Music, 504
Armeespiel, Schweizer, 322
Armitage, Dennis, 20, 75, 78, 152, 160, 162, 164, 168, 169, 171, 188, 216, 218, 219, 221, 238
Armstrong, Louis, 515, 516
Arndt, Felix, 171
Arne, Thomas A., 20, 75
Arnold, Denis, 434
Arnold, J., 234
Arnold, Malcolm, 234, 252
Arnold, Marucs, 298, 327, 328
Arnsted, Jørgen Voigt, 422
Aronson, Lee, 152
Arthur Pryor's Band, 498
Artiga, Angeles López, 21, 81
Arwood, Jeffrey, 332, 426

Asbury Brass Quintet, 294, 491
Asbury College, 454
Ashbridge, David, 216
Ashcroft, Norman, 303, 334
Ashmore, Derek, 129, 287
Ashworth, Tom, 277, 325, 326, 485
Askew, Dennis Weston, 426
Askill, John, 431
Athena Brass Band, 502
Atlanta Symphony Brass Quintet, 452
Atlanta Temple Band of the Salvation Army, 299
Atlantic Tuba Quartet, 276, 277, 334, 335, 451
Attaignant, 180
Aubain, Jean Emmanuel, 82, 87
Auber, D., 254
Aubuchon, David L., 152
Auburn University, 492
Aud, Jean, 181, 190
Audoire, Norman, 116, 298, 300, 333
Augustana College, 515
Ausfahl, Jeff, 152
Ausfahl, Richard Joseph, 152
Austin Peay State University, 501
Ayers, Jesse, 272
Ayres, Richard, 171
Azzara, Christopher D., 246

Baader-Nobs, Heidi, 92
Babb, Michael, 116
Babbit, Milton, 457
Bach, Anna Magdalena, 116
Bach, C. P. E., 21
Bach, Jan, 21, 76, 92, 140, 268, 294, 318, 410, 411, 412, 426, 445
Bach, Johann Cristoph, 78, 85
Bach, Johann Sebastian, 21, 22, 23, 41, 75–82, 85, 87, 91, 92, 98, 105, 116, 139, 152, 153, 160–162, 165–169, 171, 172, 177, 181, 184, 189, 193, 196–199, 207, 209, 216, 218, 219, 223, 228, 234, 236, 238, 239, 244, 258, 259, 262, 268, 272–274, 276, 277, 279, 280, 282–286, 289, 293–296, 299, 300, 303, 307, 310, 314, 324, 325, 326, 328–332
Bach, Markus S., 486
Bach, Vincent, 228, 281, 329, 421, 433, 446
Bach, W. F., 23, 78
Bacharach, A. L., 436
Bachelder, Daniel F., 20, 23, 25, 44, 50, 77, 161, 170, 197, 261, 513
Backus, John, 431
Bacon, Thomas, 62, 313
Badarak, Mary Lynn, 153
Baedke, Ron, 501
Baer, Doug, 156
Baetens, Charles, 254
Bagley, E. E., 252
Baglin, Lyndon, 104, 122, 129, 132, 133, 135, 227, 232, 277, 278, 296, 431
Baglyn, Lindon, 491
Bahnert, Heinz, 431, 433, 441
Bahr, Ed, 490
Bahr, Edward R., 156, 405, 410, 421, 422, 423, 490, 513
Bailey, Richard, 239
Bailey, Wayne, 405–407
Baines, Anthony, 239, 406, 436
Bainum, 252, 253
Baird, Donald R., 427, 486
Bakaleinikov, Vladimir, 291, 434
Baker, 136
Baker, Brett, 84

CPSIA information can be obtained at www.ICGtesting.com
Printed in the USA
BVOW09*0902250816

460047BV00042B/76/P